W9-BQZ-993

CHURCHILL
BY HIMSELF

To Barbara, Ian and Mary;

In memory of the
pioneer recorders of Churchill's wisdom:
Sir Colin Coote,
F. B. Czarnomski,
Kay Halle;

And in memory of
the *true* person of the twentieth century:
The Rt. Hon. Sir Winston Leonard Spencer Churchill
KG OM CH TD FRS

"One who never turned his back
but marched breast forward,
Never doubted clouds would break,
Never dreamed, though right were worsted,
Wrong would triumph,
Held we fall to rise,
Are baffled to fight better,
Sleep to wake."

– Lady Diana Cooper, 1965

CHURCHILL
BY HIMSELF

THE DEFINITIVE COLLECTION
OF QUOTATIONS

FOREWORD BY LADY SOAMES

INTRODUCTION BY SIR MARTIN GILBERT

EDITED BY RICHARD M. LANGWORTH

PUBLICAFFAIRS
NEW YORK

Published in the UK in 2008 by Ebury Press, an imprint of Ebury Publishing
A Random House Group Company

Published in the United States in 2008 by PublicAffairs™,
a member of the Perseus Books Group.

Library of Congress Control Number: 2008934239
ISBN: 978-1-58648-638-9

First Edition

10 9 8 7 6 5 4 3 2 1

CONTENTS

PREFACE

THE REAL
CHURCHILL

" 'Why study Churchill?' I am often asked. 'Surely he has nothing to say to us today?' Yet in my own work, as I open file after file of Churchill's archive, from his entry into Government in 1905 to his retirement in 1955 (a fifty-year span!), I am continually surprised by the truth of his assertions, the modernity of his thought, the originality of his mind, the constructiveness of his proposals, his humanity, and, most remarkable of all, his foresight. "

– Sir Martin Gilbert CBE [1]

Churchill by Himself has a simple mission: to offer readers the most complete, attributed, annotated and cross-referenced collection of Winston Churchill quotations, ripostes, aphorisms, sayings and reflections ever published. In the words of Thomas Jefferson, it contains everything Churchill said about life, liberty and the pursuit of happiness.

"Everything" is probably an exaggeration. Most of this book's 350,000 words are Churchill's; yet they represent about 0.2 per cent of his 15 million published words – books, articles, speeches, letters and papers. Doubtless I have overlooked deserving quotations; but I do believe that the kernel of his wit, wisdom and timeless relevance is captured here.

Churchill's words, and 35 million more words about him, written or said by colleagues, biographers and friends, are the digital database that informs this book (see Acknowledgements). Optical scans of this immense literature produced a database that tracks quotations to their source. Each of the 4,120 entries is backed by verifiable sources; no item is included unless it can be attributed. The same technology also made it possible to cite numerous "red herrings" – quotes wrongly attributed to Churchill – in Appendix I.

Why do we need another Churchill quote book? Because, despite some fine early efforts, no previous book offered a comprehensive, accurate portrayal of his timelessness, prescience, wit and wisdom.

The Internet, so helpful in many ways, is of limited assistance, bedizened as it is with corruptions, or words Churchill never said. Some he quoted from someone else; some are urban myths that have never been reliably attributed. For example, though he famously remarked that democracy is "the worst form of Government, except for all those other forms that have been tried from time to time", he did not originate that line – and never claimed that he did. (Actually, he had many wiser observations about democracy, all of which are in this book.)

---

1 "Churchill for Today," *Finest Hour* 73, Fourth quarter 1991, 11.

The Quality of Words

Like the Bible, Winston Churchill is quoted by philosophers, thinkers and politicians of every persuasion, because after fifty years of prominence on the political scene – unmatched by any other political figure – he was around long enough to say something they approve of (or can bend to their liking). But the reason Churchill is such an appealing source of quotations, I think, is the robust quality of his words.

Backed by a photographic memory of the great writers he read as a youth, and with his own impressive vocabulary, Churchill honed his prose in the most challenging venue of all: the House of Commons. Michael Dobbs, who writes historical novels so grounded in accuracy as to make them seem like fact, noted the crucial nature of Commons experience:

> Those who make it to their feet in the Chamber place themselves in the hands of hazard, for no sooner do they start speaking than they discover that the green carpet they are standing on has turned to sand. Sometimes they are able to make an impression in the parliamentary sands that will endure, some mark that will linger after them for their children and grandchildren to admire. More often, however, the footprints are washed away with the evening tide. And sometimes politicians discover they've stepped into quicksand that is just about to swallow them whole.[2]

It is impossible to overstate the influence of that famous assembly which Churchill saw as his natural home. A third of the quotations herein – by far the largest from any single source – are from House of Commons debate, and true, Churchill did step into quicksand on occasion. Yet he left a mark that lingers still.

Churchill himself said modestly that if he found the right words "... you must remember that I have always earned my living by my pen and by my tongue".[3] His written canon is as voluminous as his speeches: he wrote over forty titles in over sixty volumes and thousands of articles. His countless letters are captured in the companion volumes of the official biography or collections such as Lady Soames's *Speaking for Themselves: The Personal Letters of Winston and Clementine Churchill.*

I might not be going too far to suggest that Britain survived to preserve world liberty in 1940 because it was led by a professional writer. At a time when there was little else to fight with, Churchill "mobilised the English language", as Edward R. Murrow said, "and sent it into battle".

Anyone who questions the value of reading the "great books" should consider Churchill. What he did not originate himself usually came from his capacious memory of the classics, from the Bible to Shakespeare. In April 1941, at a grim time in World War II, with Britain still alone and no sign of American or Russian intervention, he offered his countrymen the words of Clough, knowing, in that more literate age, that they instantly recognised them:

For while the tired waves, vainly breaking,
  Seem here no painful inch to gain,
Far back, through creeks and inlets making,
  Comes silent, flooding in, the main.
And not by eastern windows only,
  When daylight comes, comes in the light;
In front the sun climbs slow, how slowly!
  But westward, look, the land is bright.[4]

---

2 Dobbs, Michael, *Whispers of Betrayal.* London: HarperCollins, 2000.
3 Westminster Hall, London, 30 November 1954.
4 Last two stanzas of "Say Not the Struggle Nought Availeth" by English poet Arthur Hugh Clough (1819–61).

That was a moment – and there were many more, on subjects great and small, large and petty. To the Queen, whom he adored, he wrote in 1955:

Our Island no longer holds the same authority of power that it did in the days of Queen Victoria. A vast world towers up around it and after all our victories we could not claim the rank we hold were it not for the respect for our character and good sense and the general admiration not untinged by envy for our institutions and way of life. All this has already grown stronger and more solidly founded during the opening years of the present Reign, and I regard it as the most direct mark of God's favour we have ever received in my long life that the whole structure of our new formed Commonwealth has been linked and illuminated by a sparkling presence at its summit.[5]

"And if you will allow the remark in parenthesis, ladies and gentlemen," asked Professor David Dilks after quoting the above, "do you not sometimes long for someone at the summit of our public life who can think and write at that level?"[6]

Churchill is also frequently cited from private conversation which, his daughter Lady Soames reflected, was not very different from his "speech form". Why, aside from his fame, did so many people record his remarks? Broadcaster Collin Brooks believed it was because Churchill was the "supreme example" of a rare breed – individuals who both talk much, and talk well, even though they do not always deal with profound subjects:

His renown as a talker is not helped, but harmed, by the specimens of his quick, sometimes malicious, wit which fly around the clubs and penetrate into the gossip features of newspapers....

Never was a talker so variously gifted, so ardently listened-to, so little of a prig; never was a man so wedded to precision and verbal nicety so little of a pedant....Sir Winston Churchill would have been equally welcomed by Falstaff in Eastcheap, Ben Jonson at the Mermaid, or Burke and Johnson at the Mitre, that is, in any coterie where the talk is masculine, the wit and humour spontaneous, the erudition unparaded, and where gusto is the prime quality.[7]

Consistency and Judgement

Once a felicitous phrase had occurred to him, Churchill never hesitated to reuse it, result-ing in a remarkable consistency over half a century. For example, I frequently tripped over the words "curious fact" employed to describe a particular characteristic of the British people, and entered it in my search engine. I found that Churchill used "curious fact" ten times, each time to illustrate things that seemed odd or noteworthy, from Gurth and Wamba's discussions of the origin of Norman beef (in his 1933 retelling of *Ivanhoe*), to Parliament's preference to discuss television rather than foreign affairs in 1953. Each instance of "curious fact" is in this book. The array tells us much about his thought.

Labouring in the vineyard of his words, I was impressed by his judgement which – contrary to his critics from the World War I Dardanelles episode onward – was remarkably apposite and usually valid. Ted Sorensen, adviser and speechwriter to President Kennedy, emphasised the importance of judgement over organisation, structure, procedures and machinery: "These are all important, yes, but nothing compared to judgment." Two

---

5 WSC to the Queen, from Sicily, 18 April 1955, OB VIII, 1127–8.
6 Dilks, David, "The Queen and Mr. Churchill," *Finest Hour* 135, Summer 2007; from remarks to the Royal Society of St. George, 6 February 2007.
7 Brooks, Collin, in Eade, 240, 248.

professors of business, after years studying leadership in every sector of American life, came "to the inescapable conclusion that judgment regularly trumps experience.... Leadership is, at its marrow, the chronicle of judgment calls."[8]

But Churchill frequently tempered his initial judgements by reconsidering, and if necessary modifying them. "He always had second and third thoughts," wrote William Manchester, "and they usually improved as he went along. It was part of his pattern of response to any political issue that while his early reactions were often emotional, and even unworthy of him, they were usually succeeded by reason and generosity."[9]

His skill as a communicator and qualities as a sage aside, without World War II Churchill could have been an historical footnote. Yet we would have still had the literature that won a Nobel Prize; five thick volumes' worth of oratory before 1940; reflections about life and living, tyranny and liberty; a memorable wit; a joyous humanity. Who is to say we might still not have this book?

The Loaded Pause

Finest Hour senior editor James Lancaster, who significantly assisted in preparing this book (see Acknowledgements), reminds me of a Churchill oratorical technique that is hard to convey in print, the calculated use of interruptions with some remarks by an observer of the post-war Parliamentary scene:

> Planning his speech, Winston thinks of everything. He even, one suspects, looks ahead to see where he is likely to be interrupted. Then, if the interruptions come, he is, more often than not, ready for them with a telling reply. He certainly did this in his Budget speeches as Chancellor. Those speeches were so framed that his announcements of tax changes came in reply to interruptions. He would "talk round" the point until some Opposition M.P. shouted impatiently, "What about it?" and then – back would come the announcement with a bang....
>
> "Where does the family start?" asked Winston rhetorically. He answered his own question – "It starts with a young man falling in love with a girl!" Eagerly his opponents seized the chance to laugh. But he was in no whit disconcerted. It seemed that this was precisely what he had decided in advance that they would do, for he beamed at them and chortled – "Well, no suitable alternative has yet been found!" The passage was remembered for that joke.[10]

Rationale of the Work

The only Churchill entry in the first edition of the *Oxford Dictionary of Quotations*, published May 1941, was "terminological inexactitude" (Chapter 2). But a month earlier, Churchill had responded to Roosevelt's February quote of Longfellow (Chapter 1, "Give Us the Tools") by broadcasting Clough's lines above, and *ODQ* editor Bernard Darwin noted this in his introduction: "We were if possible more sure than ever that Mr. Churchill was the man for our money." Today the *ODQ* has forty-one Churchill entries: commendable, but hardly sufficient.

The last pre-World War II edition of *Bartlett's Familiar Quotations* (WSC: "...an

---

8 Bennis, Warren and Tichy, Noel, "Judgment Trumps Experience," *New York Times*, 29 November 2007.
9 Manchester I, 843–4.
10 Cawthorne, Graham, "The Fabulous Parliamentarian" in *Mr. Speaker, Sir* (London: Hume Press, 1952), 24–6.

admirable work, and I studied it intently."[11]) contained no Churchill quotations at all. The current edition has sixty-nine. One must admire the editorial economy which produced such a refined collection. It is hoped that this book has done a little better.

As editor I have tried to avoid notes suggesting the relevance of Churchill's words to contemporary affairs. What is in our minds today may not be so compelling a decade hence. Although I have identified people, places and things for the reader, I have tried not to explain or rationalise Churchill's thought. He needs no interpreter to focus his relevance, amid so many problems similar but not identical to his own.

For example, the messianic intensity with which the Labour left opposed Britain's atomic bomb testing in the Fifties is remindful of a similar fervour against accepting any measures of national defence that are in the least debatable among certain modern politicians. But this may not be an issue years from now, if peace should have ever come to the world. In any case, Churchill's words will remain. They speak for themselves.

Not all quotations are singular, nor is it my thesis that our man is the only source of noble sentiments. He had, however, a unique eloquence, and the vast river of archives that he left in his public and private papers makes it possible to discover more worthy quotations than in the papers of most leaders.

It may be said that I have put the best possible spin on his words through my explanatory notes. But Churchill lived life large. If his mistakes, like his achievements, were on a grand scale, I believe the latter outweighed the former. There is no "revisionist" here.

This book really is "Churchill by Himself". As he remarked in his 1946 "Iron Curtain" speech at Fulton, "There is nothing here but what you see." The quotations are strictly his own. I made a studied effort to avoid quoting him out of context. It may be said that some of his remarks are just common sense; my reply is: how often do we encounter a politician who delivers so much of that?

Order of Presentation

The usual order is alphabetical by subject, then chronological by date (as in Chapter 1, The Immortal Words). But some chapters require reordering for optimum readability. For example, quotations on America (Chapter 8) are subdivided first into the Anglo-American "Special Relationship" (a Churchill theme throughout his life), and then by general remarks about America and Americans.

Other chapters, such as those on the two World Wars, the Between Wars period and the Nuclear Age (16 to 19) are subdivided first by year (so as to keep pace with events as they happened), and second as "general observations" alphabetically by subject. In this way the reader can follow the events of World War II, say, without being disrupted by a strictly alphabetical presentation.

References

For the sake of brevity, I have not reproduced the full title of each reference, but provided (in this Preface and throughout) "key words" which are identified in the Bibliography.

For example, "OB" refers to the Official Biography, *Winston S. Churchill*. "OB, CV5/3" refers to the Official Biography, *Companion Volume V, Part 3: Documents: The Coming of War 1936–1939*. "Crisis IV" refers to volume IV, *The Aftermath*, in *The World Crisis*, Churchill's memoir of World War I. "Marsh" refers to Eddie Marsh's *A Number of People*; "Nicolson II" refers to volume II of Harold Nicolson's diaries. Works of prolific authors,

---

11 MEL, 130.

such as Martin Gilbert, are usually identified by two words: "Gilbert, Search" refers to Sir Martin's superb account of his own work: *In Search of Churchill*. All these references are exhaustively cited in the Bibliography.

Any quotation *without* a specific reference is from Churchill's speeches in the House of Commons, where the reference should be assumed to be the Parliamentary Debates (Hansard) or *Winston S. Churchill: His Complete Speeches 1897–1963* ("CS I" through "CS VIII"). Quotations originating anywhere else are always attributed, either to the *Complete Speeches* or to individual Churchill speech volumes (see Bibliography).

In a few cases – such as "Stairway to a Dark Gulf" (Chapter 1), also quoted in "Wars of Great Powers" (Chapter 30) – a Commons speech is *not* from Hansard or the *Complete Speeches* but from one of his published speech volumes. In this case it is from *Arms and the Covenant* ("Covenant"). But this fine peroration was not reproduced in Hansard and, therefore, is not in the *Complete Speeches*. It is possible that Churchill, an indefatigable reviser, added these words to his book. In the few cases where his books differ from Hansard, I have reproduced the published word.

Dating

The date cited is the earliest date attributable to the quotation. It is sometimes possible precisely to date a World War II quotation, even though it came from Churchill's post-war memoirs, because a date is attached to it; if not, the date supplied is the date of first publication of the volume or article.

For example, Churchill's pithy note on the wartime policy of "safety first" (Chapter 12, War...Risks) is dated 3 November 1940 because it is so dated in *Their Finest Hour*, even though that book was not published until 1949. But his observation that "no one can guarantee success in war" (Chapter 12, War...Victory) is dated 1949 because it carries no specific *earlier date* in the same volume.

Locations

Venues and locations, other than London, Chartwell and Downing Street, are supplied if available. Quotations from radio broadcasts are identified as such, and sources noted. If an entry appeared in both an article and a book, the title is that used in the book.

False Quotes

An amusing piece of bad advice often recounted by quotations editors is: "If in doubt, attribute any well-known and apposite saying to Churchill, Shakespeare, the American Declaration of Independence, Chairman Mao, or the Bible. It adds the weight of authority and, with a bit of luck, no one will notice." Oh yes they will!

Sir Martin Gilbert adds: "The dilemma of establishing authenticity is ever-present with Churchill, around whom everyone naturally wishes to attach their favourite story." Many old chestnuts "give Churchill as their source to make them more interesting. Did Churchill ever say to Nancy Astor, 'If I were your husband, I would drink it?' after she had said, 'If I were your wife I would put poison in your coffee'? I have no idea, though several old-timers suggested to me that the original of Winston in this tale was in fact F.E. [Smith] (a much heavier drinker than Churchill, and a notorious acerbic wit)."[12]

As everyone knows, the Internet is a veritable electronic Hyde Park Corner of words

---

12 Gilbert, Search, 232.

and opinions. To rely on it for proof of a Churchill quotation is perilous. It is full of supposed quotations he either never said, or repeated from some prior speaker. The test of any quotation, on the Internet or elsewhere, is whether it is accompanied by attribution. If not, it may be pure invention – or words put in Churchill's mouth.

Take for example WSC's famous line to Roosevelt, emerging naked from his bath: "The Prime Minister of Great Britain has nothing to hide from the President of the United States."[13] Can it be believed? As nothing very momentous hinges on the issue, and given the imprudence of imputing untruth to WSC's bodyguard Walter Thompson (who first quoted it), and with considerable attribution, I concluded that it can.

Harry Hopkins, FDR's adviser, repeated his version of this remark (using "conceal" instead of "hide") often enough to raise at least a presumption in favour of its veracity. As against such considerations is the testimony of Churchill himself. Robert Sherwood once screwed up the courage to ask him point blank whether the story was true or false. WSC said it was "nonsense", that he "never received the President without at least a bath towel wrapped around him".

As to the declaration itself, Churchill added: "I could not possibly have made such a statement as that. The President himself would have been well aware that it was not strictly true." Yet Churchill also told the King that he was "the only man in the world to have received the head of a nation naked". (Chapter 33, Ripostes…Naked encounter.)

Truth, however, is elusive, and what is most important in this unportentous incident is that whatever the actual facts, the reported words are consistent with Winston Churchill's personality. More significantly, they are consistent with the extraordinary lack of ceremony that characterised the relationship of Churchill and Roosevelt: the collegial way they worked together, despite many disagreements.

Churchill in Retrospect

As editor of *Finest Hour* for a quarter century, I have come to regard our man as unique. Speaking recently with Lady Soames on one of her father's prescient observations, I was struck when she remarked, entirely spontaneously, and I thought a little wistfully: "He was one of a kind, wasn't he?" Indeed he was.

Let the late Grace Hamblin, a secretary from 1932, summarise Winston Churchill in words congruent to those of Martin Gilbert at the beginning of this preface:

At the end I went down with the family to the funeral, near his beloved birthplace, Blenheim, and to me that quiet, humble service in the country churchyard was much more moving than had been the tremendous pomp and glory of the state ceremony in London….[and] I pondered on what had made this dynamic but gentle character so beloved and respected—and such a wonderful person to work for.

I think one found first of all that there was courage. He had no fear of anything, moral or physical. There was sincerity, truth and integrity, for he couldn't knowingly deceive a cabinet minister or a bricklayer or a secretary. There was forgiveness, warmth, affection, loyalty and, perhaps most important of all in the demanding life we all lived, there was humour, which he had in abundance.…

One of those many, many letters Lady Churchill received came from a member of your community here in America, and it has always been in my mind:

"That he died is unimportant, for we must all pass away. That he lived is momentous to the destiny of decent men. He is not gone. He lives wherever men are free."[14]

---

13 Thompson, Assignment, 248; Lowenheim, 8; Pilpel, 142.
14 Hamblin, Grace, "Chartwell Memories," International Churchill Conference, Dallas, 1987; reprinted after her death in *Finest Hour* 117, Winter 2002–03.

ACKNOWLEDGEMENTS

The Digital Resource

In 1997 Karl-Georg Schon, a Churchillian and university student in Germany, offered to send me digital scans of "a few books by and about Sir Winston". He had access to the then relatively new optical scanning equipment, and to a fine Churchill library. I was pleased with the thought of having some books I could search with a computer "find" command.

To my surprise Mr. Schon presented me with a large box of now obsolete zip disks, which contained not only all of Churchill's published works but hundreds of others: a hundred biographies and specialised studies of Churchill; sixty memoirs by his colleagues or contemporaries; thirty on the Churchill family; fifty on history and politics closely related to or involving Churchill.

Particularly helpful were scans of the sixteen Companion or Document Volumes to the official biography published to date, whose indexes include only surnames. Sir Martin Gilbert, who compiled most of those volumes, was delighted to have a set of these for his own use.

Since then I have received key additional scanning assistance from Wayne Brent, president of a Culver City, California scanning company, Zuma Corporation, and Zuma's capable technical wizard, Alfred Alvarez. They furnished me with scans of the eight-volume, 10,000-page *Winston S. Churchill: His Complete Speeches 1897–1963*; the unique *Collected Essays of Sir Winston Churchill*; and the entire contents of *Finest Hour*, which I have edited since 1982.

Churchill's published works number thirteen million words, over five million in the posthumous *Complete Speeches*. Adding at least two million more in the Companion Volumes of the Official Biography, even allowing for some speeches published twice, Churchill easily produced over fifteen million published words. The literature about him amounts to over thirty-five million words, to which Sir Martin alone has contributed ten million.

For years I was unable easily to access these scanned documents since most were contained in 100-page rich text format (.rtf) files. The 1,600,000-word, six-volume *Second World War*, for example, alone was scanned in thirty-seven separate files. To search just these files for Churchill's comments about de Gaulle, say, took hours, with file after file coming up empty. Not until the advent of the Macintosh G-4 computer was I able to access them on my hard drive, and still the sheer quantity of individual files made searching a process of hit and miss.

Enter my son Ian, a software engineer, who was able to post my digital treasure trove on a private website, coupled to a search engine that could find any word or phrase (the vast majority from Churchill's own works) in seconds.

Ian's creation made it possible to find not only every Churchill word or phrase published, but to compare the ways he used them or edited them in different contexts or volumes. I now can wade through a canon of fifty million words in no more time than it takes to search for cooking recipes on Google.

My digital tool offered amusing opportunities to display mysterious powers. For a scholarly discussion of *The Gathering Storm*, Churchill's first volume of World War II memoirs, I pronounced solemnly that he used the phrase "there is no doubt" thirteen times – in many cases when there *really was* considerable doubt! "I am impressed that Mr. Langworth read *The Gathering Storm* so closely and kept such impressive records," said the professor leading the discussion. I sheepishly admitted that finding this datum had consumed all of thirty seconds.

Throughout this exercise my sole interest has been to verify the words of Winston Churchill – and only Winston Churchill. I have made an effort to avoid quoting the words of others, and to credit those who first published each quotation. I only regret that I have lost track of Karl-Georg Schon. I owe him a copy.

Selecting the Entries

The finest reference system in the world is no use if you don't know what to search for. The selections here, researched through my database, are based on my readings, writings and editing over twenty-five years in *Finest Hour*, "the Journal of Winston Churchill", published by the Churchill Centre and Churchill Museum at the Cabinet War Rooms (www.winstonchurchill.org); and from communications with people who write to the Centre.

My selection of material was abetted by editing 120 issues of *Finest Hour* and my task of answering for the Churchill Centre questions we constantly receive – up to six or eight a day, perhaps 1,500 a year – from people worldwide, from government officials to media, scholars to schoolchildren – who constantly ask if Churchill said "X" and on what occasion. (Or, more commonly, "What did he say about Y?")

A frequent request is: "Please tell me everything Churchill said about the Russians, and can I have it by the end of the week?" (We answer these by saying we do not write essays, and referring the questioner to the search engine at winstonchurchill.org).

But verification of quotes is the chief reason people inquire. Sometimes a remark they send us is wrong, or something he never said at all – the basis of my Red Herrings (Appendix I) of false attributions. We try to reply helpfully to all questioners, often relying on my digital file, sometimes on the expert specialists who contribute to *Finest Hour*. For ten or twelve years, I have carefully recorded all these answers, which form a major part of this book's manuscript.

Among the many books cited in the bibliography are three pioneer Churchill quotations works which deserve special note: Sir Colin Coote's *Maxims and Reflections of the Rt. Hon. Sir Winston Churchill* (1947), later revised and extended as *Sir Winston Churchill: A Self-Portrait* (1954); F. B. Czarnomski's *The Wisdom of Winston Churchill* (1956); and Kay Halle's *Irrepressible Churchill* (1966).

Sir Colin, one-time editor of the *Daily Telegraph*, was a Churchill friend and colleague who first had the idea to capture Sir Winston's notable remarks. Professor F. B. Czarnomski compiled a comprehensive work, dated and attributed, mainly from Parliamentary sources. Kay Halle, who almost married Randolph Churchill, was a friend of his family for thirty years. I had the pleasure of corresponding with her for many years, and was even able to find the copy of *Lord Randolph Churchill*, bearing her bookplate, which Randolph had given her but which strayed from her library.

Each of these was an honest reporter, anxious not to embroider or invent passages, or to edit and "improve" what Churchill said. All tried hard to provide good organisation, dates and attribution. All three are sadly gone now. Their work abides, and is cherished.

Grateful Thanks

To the aforementioned Karl-George Schon, Wayne Brent and Alfredo Alvarez, who scanned the material; and to Ian Langworth, whose programming ability made it possible rapidly to search it, my debt is enormous. Plainly this book would not exist without them.

Equal thanks go to my wife Barbara, who has been such a support throughout this project, as in our life together. Her editorial acumen and judgement, her efforts to ferret out answers to difficult questions, were indispensable. Her patience with the Internet (much greater than mine) is almost as great as her patience with me. To borrow a phrase Sir Winston used with respect to Lady Churchill: "Here firm, though all be drifting."

Along with Barbara, Gail Greenly, the only secretary I have ever had, laboured long and hard manually to enter innumerable quotations into the database, and their efforts are deeply appreciated.

Lady Soames and Sir Martin Gilbert, who provide the foreword and introduction, dear friends both over the years, have constantly encouraged me, as reviewers and critics, by their intimate knowledge of what I call "The Saga". I appreciate also Nonie Chapman for faithfully printing reams of email manuscript for Lady Soames's perusal.

Two senior editors of *Finest Hour*, Paul Courtenay and James Lancaster, gamely waded through drafts, offering numerous corrections and improvements, and providing dozens of important entries I had overlooked. At the eleventh hour, we realised that I had neglected to check the database against the actual printed word – that profound inaccuracies existed, and that every entry had to be reviewed. Mr Lancaster checked Chapters 10, 12, 16, 18, 20, 28 and 29. *Finest Hour* deputy editor David Turrell, coming in cold, skilfully and succinctly checked Chapters 21–3, 26–7, 30–31 and 34. My wife Barbara and I checked the rest. This marathon consumed three weeks of toil but vastly improved what I had drafted. My gratitude to them all is immeasurable.

Winston S. Churchill, owner of his grandfather's literary copyrights, reviewed the advance drafts and kindly encouraged me from the beginning of the project.

Churchill Centre administrators Daniel N. Myers, Mary Dwyer and Karen Linebarger aided my work by forwarding and commenting on the many requests they receive for quote verification – *and* spared me repetition by recording my answers, which they spun out themselves the next time the same question arose. Several Churchill Centre trustees, directors and honorary members have helped and inspired entries, including Randy Barber, David Boler, Laurence Geller, Christopher Matthews, Marcus Frost, General Colin L. Powell, Ambassador Paul H. Robinson, Suzanne Sigman and David Turrell. Phil Reed, director of the Churchill Museum and Cabinet War Rooms and executive vice-president of the Churchill Centre, has been warmly supportive.

Thanks also to Ralph Keyes, editor-author, *The Quote Verifier*, for a pleasant joint quest for attributions to Churchill entries in his book; equally for helping me get into my bones the essence and language of a good book of quotations. Fred Shapiro, editor of *The Yale Book of Quotations*, was also a source of sound judgement and advice on several important entries.

I can never sufficiently thank Gordon Wise, my agent at Curtis Brown, Ltd., for finding the best publisher possible in Ebury Press, and for his consistent good advice throughout. His assistant, Shaheeda Sabir, never failed to answer or solve numerous problems and perplexities; their counterpart at Curtis Brown in New York, Nathan Bransford, placed the work with the American publishers.

With Gordon's predecessor, Anthea Morton-Saner, I first proposed this book over a bottle of Australian Chardonnay one night in London, being careful to open the bottle first. Anthea not only liked the idea, but came up with the title, and I owe her a case of Pol Roger for her friendship and inspiration.

The editors at Ebury Press, Andrew Goodfellow and Charlotte Cole; and Clive Priddle at Perseus Books and Public Affairs in New York, deserve an advance thanks, for as I write this, most of my work is done and theirs is just beginning. Their skills and acumen are up to the task.

Many others – some gone now, God bless them – deserve credit for their help, inspiration, research or material over the years. In alphabetical order they include but are not limited to Professor Paul Addison; Senator Harry F. Byrd, Jr.; Professor Antoine Capet; Minnie S. Churchill; Peregrine S. Churchill; The Hon. Clark Clifford; Ronald I. Cohen; Sir John Colville; Professor David Dilks; Michael Dobbs; Ronald Golding; Grace Hamblin; Glenn Horowitz; Ralph Keyes; Professor Warren Kimball; Sir Fitzroy Maclean; Sir Anthony Montague Browne; Professor James W. Muller; Edmund Murray; Elizabeth Nel; Oscar Nemon; Christian Pol-Roger; Professor David Reynolds; Andrew Roberts; The Hon. Celia Sandys; Christopher, Lord Soames; Professor David Stafford; Haakon Waage; Mark Weber; and Lady Young, daughter of Oscar Nemon. Lastly I thank the irreplaceable character who left us such grand words to sort through: Sir Winston himself. Where we all would be without him? Where indeed.

I am most anxious to hear from readers who wish to offer comments or corrections, at the email address below. Any errata will be published and regularly updated on the Churchill Centre website at http://xrl.us/j2uc8.

Richard M. Langworth
"High Tide"
Eleuthera, Bahamas
cbh-rml@sneakemail.com

FOREWORD

by Lady Soames LG DBE

This handsome *tome* – for it requires a sturdier noun than *book* to describe this noble volume – will equally serve the needs and interests of true and knowledgeable "Churchillians", and newcomers to what Richard Langworth himself calls *The Saga*.

Richard (born 1941) came upon Winston Churchill almost accidentally – watching the State Funeral on television (in his own words): "…It dawned on me that this was a person I ought to know more about." He has set about that task ever since.

There is no risk of contradiction in saying that – between them – Sir Martin Gilbert (WSC's official biographer) and Richard Langworth cover factually and in depth the life (and the context in which that life was lived) of Winston Churchill.

Richard has created an archival store-house of facts covering every aspect of Churchill's life. In this task he has been significantly helped by his son Ian, who is an IT "guru". The fruits of their labours he now offers to all those whose interest has been awakened in an easily accessible form. We owe them a debt of gratitude.

Mary Soames

INTRODUCTION

by *Sir Martin Gilbert CBE*

Richard Langworth puts all those interested in Winston Churchill in his debt. This book is a marvellous compendium of Churchill's written and spoken words, a true encyclopaedia of wit and wisdom, by far the most comprehensive yet published, and an essential companion for writers, teachers and students alike, as well as for anyone in any walk of life who wants to gain a real sense of Churchill in his own words: of who Churchill was and what he stood for.

It has been my good fortune to have known Richard for almost as long as I have been working in the Churchill vineyard. Few people have such a wide knowledge of Churchill's published words and of the context in which he wrote or spoke them. This knowledge – without which this book could not have been written – is based on a vast array of works written by Churchill himself.

Churchill's published works included several substantial histories and collections of speeches: in all more than fifty volumes of his own writings and words. From his first published book, *The Story of the Malakand Field Force* in 1898, to his last major work, the four-volume *A History of the English Speaking Peoples*, published between 1956 and 1958, Churchill was neither a stranger to expressing thoughts in words, or shy in doing so. Richard Langworth has supplemented these sources with material in the Hansard record of Parliamentary debates, in the collected Churchill speeches edited by Robert Rhodes James, from many autobiographies and biographies, from those who have sent quotations in to him, and from the Official Churchill Biography, the first two volumes of which were written by Churchill's son Randolph, and the following six volumes by myself. Also made full use of here are the comprehensive "companion" volumes of documents that are an integral part of the Official Biography.

As the helpful chapter categories show, there is no area of life and thought about which Winston Churchill did not have something to say. Among the thirty-four categories are Maxims, Churchillisms, Anecdotes and Stories, Germany, Russia and America, the World Scene, the Cold War and the Nuclear Age, Political Theory and Practice, Education, and War. From terse phrases to sustained thought pieces, there is a remarkable diversity and wisdom to be found in this book.

The reader who works through the scheme that Richard Langworth has devised will come to have a true picture of Churchill's mind, his ideas and his ideals. Starting with The Immortal Words – a section that should be recited aloud by all those who love the use of words to convey powerful sentiments – we are taken on a journey as dramatic and as unexpected as those of Columbus, Magellan, Cortes or Cook. Read aloud, as Randolph Churchill so relished doing when he was writing about his father, whether or not learned by heart, these first pages, like many of those that follow, can stir the blood, warm the soul, amuse and enlighten.

This is a long book, and rightly so. Many rewards will accrue to those who read it in its entirety. It can be read in small segments, set aside, and taken up again, read in moments of leisure and at times of reflection. Churchill was consistent in his thought, and diverse in his expression. He could take ordinary episodes of history or politics and enliven them with wit and insight.

Richard has ensured that every aspect of Churchill's long, controversial and creative career, and every facet of Churchill's versatile, unusual and wide-ranging mind is here for the reader to follow, absorb and enjoy. They can follow Churchill's own advice, quoted here, about the books in his library: "Peer into them. Let them fall open where they will. Read on from the first sentence that arrests the eye. Then turn to another. Make a voyage of discovery, taking soundings of uncharted seas."

This magisterial volume invites just such a voyage. There are few books of which it can truly be said that it is unputdownable. This book is one of them. It combines in grand measure two unique factors. One is the reading, knowledge and enthusiasm of a modern Churchillian, who is also a Commander of the Order of the British Empire for making Churchill's work better known in the United States and internationally, Richard Langworth. The second factor is the words of a master wordsmith and exponent of large causes, who was at the centre of British political life for more than half a century, and who bestrode the international stage in both war and peace, Sir Winston Churchill.

Martin Gilbert
Honorary Fellow
Merton College, Oxford

CHURCHILL
BY HIMSELF

1

THE
IMMORTAL
WORDS

*"Withhold no sacrifice, grudge no toil, seek no sordid gain,
fear no foe. All will be well."*[15]

"In all our long history we have never seen a greater day than this."
With Attlee on Victory in Europe Day, 8 April 1945.

I t is appropriate to begin with these famous quotations which together made Winston Churchill a household name a lifetime ago. To the greatest words of 1940 I have added several from earlier and later times which deserve inclusion, either for their lyrical beauty and emotional impact or their stark relevance to modern times.

Churchill was not always original. The late Colin Coote, who collected the first book of Churchillian expressions more than half a century ago,[16] observed that "Nobody soaked in

15 WSC speaking at Château Laurier, Ottawa, 14 January 1952. Stemming, 219.
16 Coote, *Maxims and Reflections of the Rt. Hon. Winston S. Churchill CH MP.* London: Eyre & Spottiswoode, 1947, 11.

history ever is [original], because, consciously or unconsciously, in any situation they remember that it has happened before, and what were the reactions on noble spirits."

Coote added, for example, that "blood, toil, tears, and sweat" was "a direct echo of Garibaldi's address to his followers after the defence of the Roman Republic had collapsed and he was about to start on his march across Italy". Or again, when in his first speech as Prime Minister, Mr. Churchill defined his policy as "to make war", he was echoing Clemenceau's "Je fais la guerre"; and the famous passage in a later speech about fighting "on the beaches, in the hills, in the streets" recalls the same leader's fierce declamation in 1918: "I shall fight in front of Paris, within Paris, behind Paris."[17]

But nothing, as Sir Winston said, surpasses 1940. Denounced by some as purple prose, those words rallied a nation when there was little with which to fight. Ronald Golding, one of Churchill's Scotland Yard bodyguards in 1946, was an RAF squadron leader when he first heard the famous voice, crackling over the ether on a primitive wireless. "After those speeches," he said, "we *wanted* the Germans to come."

Far away in his barracks, a young soldier named Caspar Weinberger heard the same words on American radio. "I don't know about the others," said the man who would become U.S. Secretary of Defense, "but I was certainly moved more completely than I had been by any speech since."[18]

Perhaps these words sound like purple prose today, but I can recount many occasions when people who had heard them over crackling, surreptitious radio broadcasts in occupied Europe, would grasp the arm of Lady Soames to say how much her father's words had meant, in those times, in that hour.

These quotations are ranged in chronological order and identified by their most famous phrase. Space precludes providing more than the highest of the high spots, but more are available in an admirable collection, *Never Give In!: The Best of Winston Churchill's Speeches*, selected and edited by Sir Winston's grandson; in Churchill's own war speech volumes; and in the massive *Complete Speeches*, edited by Sir Robert Rhodes James.

Are You Quite Sure?

They sound so very cautious and correct, these deadly words. Soft, quiet voices purring, courteous, grave, exactly-measured phrases in large peaceful rooms. But with less warning cannons had opened fire and nations had been struck down by this same Germany. So now the Admiralty wireless whispers through the ether to the tall masts of ships, and captains pace their decks absorbed in thought. It is nothing. It is less than nothing. It is too foolish, too fantastic to be thought of in the twentieth century. Or is it fire and murder leaping out of the darkness at our throats, torpedoes ripping the bellies of half-awakened ships, a sunrise on a vanished naval supremacy, and an island well-guarded hitherto, at last defenceless? No, it is nothing. No one would do such things. Civilisation has climbed above such perils. The interdependence of nations in trade and traffic, the sense of public law, the Hague Convention, Liberal principles, the Labour Party, high finance, Christian charity, common sense have rendered such nightmares impossible. Are you quite sure? It would be a pity to be wrong. Such a mistake could only be made once—once for all.

1911. (CRISIS I, 48–9.)

General Colin Powell asked me to attribute this favourite quotation in 1992. In one of his finest passages about war, WSC is describing the Agadir Crisis of 1911, when, amid quiet, diplomatic messages, Germany and France rattled sabres following the arrival of a German naval vessel at the port of Agadir in French Morocco.

---

17 Ibid., 11.
18 Address to the International Churchill Conference, Parker House, Boston, 2 November 1985.

Armistice Day 1918

It was a few minutes before the eleventh hour of the eleventh day of the eleventh month. I stood at the window of my room looking up Northumberland Avenue towards Trafalgar Square, waiting for Big Ben to tell that the War was over....And then suddenly the first stroke of the chime. I looked again at the broad street beneath me. It was deserted. From the portals of one of the large hotels absorbed by Government Departments darted the slight figure of a girl clerk, distractedly gesticulating while another stroke of Big Ben resounded. Then from all sides men and women came scurrying into the street. Streams of people poured out of all the buildings. The bells of London began to clash....Flags appeared as if by magic. Streams of men and women flowed from the Embankment. They mingled with torrents pouring down the Strand on their way to acclaim the King....

The curtain falls upon the long front in France and Flanders. The soothing hands of Time and Nature, the swift repair of peaceful industry, have already almost effaced the crater fields and the battle lines which in a broad belt from the Vosges to the sea lately blackened the smiling fields of France....Is this the end? Is it to be merely a chapter in a cruel and senseless story? Will a new generation in their turn be immolated to square the black accounts of Teuton and Gaul? Will our children bleed and gasp again in devastated lands? Or will there spring from the very fires of conflict that reconciliation of the three giant combatants, which would unite their genius and secure to each in safety and freedom a share in rebuilding the glory of Europe?

1927. (CRISIS III PART 2, 541–4.)

The Locust Years

The Minister for the Coordination of Defence has argued as usual against a Ministry of Supply....The First Lord of the Admiralty in his speech the other night went even farther. He said, "We are always reviewing the position." Everything, he assured us, is entirely fluid. I am sure that that is true. Anyone can see what the position is. The Government simply cannot make up their minds, or they cannot get the Prime Minister to make up his mind. So they go on in strange paradox, decided only to be undecided, resolved to be irresolute, adamant for drift, solid for fluidity, all-powerful to be impotent. So we go on preparing more months and years—precious, perhaps vital, to the greatness of Britain—for the locusts to eat.

1936, 12 NOVEMBER.

Stairway to a Dark Gulf

I have watched this famous island descending incontinently, fecklessly, the stairway which leads to a dark gulf. It is a fine broad stairway at the beginning, but after a bit, the carpet ends. A little further on there are only flagstones, and a little further on still, these break beneath your feet....if mortal catastrophe should overtake the British Nation and the British Empire, historians a thousand years hence will still be baffled by the mystery of our affairs. They will never understand how it was that a victorious nation, with everything in hand, suffered themselves to be brought low, and to cast away all that they had gained by measureless sacrifice and absolute victory—gone with the wind!

Now the victors are the vanquished, and those who threw down their arms in the field and sued for an armistice are striding on to world mastery. That is the position—that is the terrible transformation that has taken place bit by bit. I rejoice to hear from the Prime Minister that a further supreme effort is to be made to place us in a position of security. Now is the time at last to rouse the nation. Perhaps it is the last time it can be roused with a chance of preventing war, or with a chance of coming through to victory should our efforts to prevent war fail. We should lay aside every hindrance and endeavour by uniting the whole force and spirit of our people to raise again a great British nation standing up before all the world; for such a nation, rising in its ancient vigour, can even at this hour save civilization.

1938, 24 MARCH. (COVENANT, 465–6.)

This fine peroration, on the last page of Arms and the Covenant, *was not reproduced in Hansard and, therefore, the Rhodes James Complete Speeches. It is quite possible that Churchill added these words in his book; but in every case where his books differ from Hansard, I have preferred the published word.*

Munich: Defeat without a War

I will begin by saying what everybody would like to ignore or forget but which must nevertheless be stated, namely that we have sustained a total and unmitigated defeat, and that France has suffered even more than we have. The utmost my Rt. Hon. Friend the Prime Minister [Neville Chamberlain] has been able to secure by his immense exertions, by all the great efforts and mobilization which took place in this country, and by all the anguish and strain through which we have passed in this country, the utmost he has been able to gain for Czechoslovakia in the matters which were in dispute has been that the German dictator, instead of snatching the victuals from the table, has been content to have them served to him course by course....

And do not suppose that this is the end. This is only the beginning of the reckoning. This is only the first sip, the first foretaste of a bitter cup which will be proffered to us year by year unless, by a supreme recovery of moral health and martial vigour, we arise again and take our stand for freedom as in the olden time.

1938, 5 OCTOBER.

Let Us to the Task

Come then: let us to the task, to the battle, to the toil—each to our part, each to our station. Fill the armies, rule the air, pour out the munitions, strangle the U-boats, sweep the mines, plough the land, build the ships, guard the streets, succour the wounded, uplift the downcast and honour the brave. Let us go forward together in all parts of the Empire, in all parts of the Island. There is not a week, nor a day, nor an hour to lose.

1940, 27 JANUARY. FREE TRADE HALL, MANCHESTER. (CS VI, 6186.)

Blood, Toil, Tears and Sweat

I would say to the House, as I said to those who have joined this Government: "I have nothing to offer but blood, toil, tears, and sweat."

We have before us an ordeal of the most grievous kind. We have before us many, many long months of struggle and of suffering. You ask, what is our policy? I will say: It is to wage war, by sea, land and air, with all our might and with all the strength that God can give us: to wage war against a monstrous tyranny, never surpassed in the dark, lamentable catalogue of human crime. That is our policy. You ask, What is our aim? I can answer in one word: Victory— victory at all costs, victory in spite of all terror, victory, however long and hard the road may be; for without victory, there is no survival.

1940, 13 MAY.

First speech as Prime Minister. The famous words had a lengthy gestation. Churchill first deployed "blood and sweat" in London to Ladysmith via Pretoria (1900); he used "their sweat, their tears, their blood" referring to the Russians fighting the Central Powers in World War I in The Eastern Front *(1931). "Blood, sweat and tears" came together in his 1939 article, "Can Franco Restore Unity and Strength to Spain" (*Daily Telegraph*, reprinted in* Step by Step *("Hope in Spain"). See Appendix III.*

Be Ye Men of Valour

This is one of the most awe-striking periods in the long history of France and Britain. It is also beyond doubt the most sublime. Side by side, unaided except by their kith and kin in the great Dominions and by the wide Empires which rest beneath their shield—side by side, the British and French peoples have advanced to rescue not only Europe but mankind from the foulest and most soul-destroying tyranny which has ever darkened and stained the pages of history. Behind them...gather a group of shattered States and bludgeoned races...upon all of whom the long night of barbarism will descend, unbroken even by a star of hope, unless we conquer, as conquer we must; as conquer we shall.

Today is Trinity Sunday. Centuries ago words were written to be a call and a spur to the faithful servants of Truth and Justice: "Arm yourselves, and be ye men of valour, and be in readiness for the conflict; for it is better for us to perish in battle than to look upon the outrage of our nation and our altar. As the Will of God is in Heaven, even so let it be."

1940, 19 MAY. BROADCAST, LONDON. (BLOOD, 334.)

WSC beautifully paraphrased this from the biblical Book of Maccabees, not in all Bibles but present in the versions he knew and loved.

In the King James Apocrypha, 1 Maccabees chapter III, he read:

58 And Judas said, Arm yourselves, and be valiant men, and see that ye be in readiness against the morning, that ye may fight with these nations that are assembled together against us to destroy us and our sanctuary.

59 For it is better for us to die in battle, than to behold the calamities of our people and our sanctuary.

60 Nevertheless, as the will of God is in heaven, so let him do.

Never Surrender

...we shall not flag or fail. We shall go on to the end, we shall fight in France, we shall fight on the seas and oceans, we shall fight with growing confidence and growing strength in the air, we shall defend our island, whatever the cost may be, we shall fight on the beaches, we shall fight on the landing grounds, we shall fight in the fields and in the streets, we shall fight in the hills; we shall never surrender, and even if, which I do not for a moment believe, this island or a large part of it were subjugated and starving, then our Empire beyond the seas, armed and guarded by the British Fleet, would carry on the struggle, until, in God's good time, the new world, with all its power and might, steps forth to the rescue and the liberation of the old.

1940, 4 JUNE.

Their Finest Hour

What General Weygand called the Battle of France is over. I expect that the battle of Britain is about to begin. Upon this battle depends the survival of Christian civilisation. Upon it depends our own British life, and the long continuity of our institutions and our Empire. The whole fury and might of the enemy must very soon be turned on us. Hitler knows that he will have to break us in this island or lose the war. If we can stand up to him, all Europe may be free and the life of the world may move forward into broad, sunlit uplands. But if we fail, then the whole world, including the United States, including all that we have known and cared for, will sink into the abyss of a new Dark Age made more sinister, and perhaps more protracted, by the lights of perverted science. Let us therefore brace ourselves to our duties, and so bear ourselves that, if the British Empire and its Commonwealth last for a thousand years, men will still say, "This was their finest hour."

1940, 18 JUNE.

War of the Unknown Warriors

And now it has come to us to stand alone in the breach, and face the worst that the tyrant's might and enmity can do. Bearing ourselves humbly before God, but conscious that we serve an unfolding purpose, we are ready to defend our native land against the invasion by which it is threatened. We are fighting *by* ourselves alone; but we are not fighting *for* ourselves alone. Here in this strong City of Refuge which enshrines the title-deeds of human progress and is of deep consequence to Christian civilisation; here, girt about by the seas and oceans where the Navy reigns; shielded from above by the prowess and devotion of our airmen—we await undismayed the impending assault. Perhaps it will come tonight. Perhaps it will come next week. Perhaps it will never come. We must show ourselves equally capable of meeting a sudden violent shock or, what is perhaps a harder test, a prolonged vigil. But be the ordeal sharp or long, or both, we shall seek no terms, we shall tolerate no parley; we may show mercy—we shall ask for none....

This is no War of chieftains or of princes, of dynasties or national ambition; it is a War of peoples and of causes. There are vast numbers not only in this island but in every land, who will render faithful service in this War, but whose names will never be known, whose deeds will never be recorded. This is a War of the Unknown Warriors; but let all strive without failing in faith or in duty, and the dark curse of Hitler will be lifted from our age.

1940, 14 JULY. BROADCAST, LONDON.
(BLOOD, 391–4.)

The Few

The gratitude of every home in our Island, in our Empire, and indeed throughout the world, except in the abodes of the guilty, goes out to the British airmen who, undaunted by odds, unwearied in their constant challenge and mortal danger, are turning the tide of the world war by their prowess and by their devotion. Never in the field of human conflict was so much owed by so many to so few. All hearts go out to the fighter pilots, whose brilliant actions we see with our own eyes day after day; but we must never forget that all the time, night after night, month after month, our bomber squadrons travel far into Germany, find their targets in the darkness by the highest navigational skill, aim their attacks, often under the heaviest fire, often with serious loss, with deliberate careful discrimination, and inflict shattering blows upon the whole of the technical and war-making structure of the Nazi power. On no part of the Royal Air Force does the weight of the war fall more heavily than on the daylight bombers who will play an invaluable part in the case of invasion and whose unflinching zeal it has been necessary in the meanwhile on numerous occasions to restrain.

1940, 20 AUGUST.

Vive la France

Frenchmen! For more than thirty years in peace and war I have marched with you, and I am marching still along the same road. Tonight I speak to you at your firesides, wherever you may be, or whatever your fortunes are. I repeat the prayer around the *louis d'or, "Dieu protège la France"*....Here in London, which Herr Hitler says he will reduce to ashes, and which his aeroplanes are now bombarding, our people are bearing up unflinchingly. Our Air Force has more than held its own. We are waiting for the long-promised invasion. So are the fishes.... Frenchmen: re-arm your spirits before it is too late. Remember how Napoleon said before one of his battles: "These same Prussians who are so boastful today were three to one at Jena, and six to one at Montmirail."

Never will I believe that the soul of France is dead. Never will I believe that her place amongst the greatest nations of the world has been lost for ever!....Remember we shall never stop, never weary, and never give in...We seek to beat the life and soul out of Hitler and Hitlerism. That alone, that all the time, that to the end....

Goodnight then: sleep to gather strength for the morning. For the morning will come.

Brightly will it shine on the brave and true, kindly upon all who suffer for the cause, glorious upon the tombs of heroes. Thus will shine the dawn. *Vive la France!* Long live also the forward march of the common people in all the lands towards their just and true inheritance, and towards the broader and fuller age.

1940, 21 OCTOBER. BROADCAST TO FRANCE, LONDON. (BLOOD, 463–5); (BATTLE, 295–7); CHRISTIAN POL-ROGER TO THE EDITOR.

According to Churchill's speech volume Into Battle, *this speech was broadcast in both English and French, the latter version beginning: "*Français! Pendant plus de trente ans, en temps de paix comme en temps de guerre, j'ai marché avec vous et je marche encore avec vous aujourd'hui, sur la Même route.*" In his postwar recording, as now reproduced on BBC audio CDs, Churchill after "*Français*" said: "*C'est moi, Churchill, qui vous parle.*"*

This tremendous message, in the midst of France's agony and during the London Blitz, stirred loyal French hearts and, in the words of many patriots, inspired the Resistance. The Prussians were routed by an outnumbered Napoleon at the Battles of Jena on 14 October 1806 and Montmirail on 11 February 1814.

Give Us the Tools

The other day, President Roosevelt gave his opponent in the late Presidential Election [Mr. Wendell Willkie] a letter of introduction to me, and in it he wrote out a verse, in his own handwriting, from Longfellow, which he said, "applies to you people as it does to us". Here is the verse:

Sail on, O Ship of State!
Sail on, O Union, strong and great!
Humanity with all its fears,
With all the hopes of future years,
Is hanging breathless on thy fate!

What is the answer that I shall give, in your name, to this great man, the thrice-chosen head of a nation of a hundred and thirty millions? Here is the answer which I will give to President Roosevelt: Put your confidence in us. Give us your faith and your blessing, and, under Providence, all will be well. We shall not fail or falter; we shall not weaken or tire. Neither the sudden shock of battle, nor the long-drawn trials of vigilance and exertion will wear us down. Give us the tools, and we will finish the job.

1941, 9 FEBRUARY. BROADCAST, LONDON.
(CS VI, 6351.)

The stanza is from Longfellow's long poem, "The Building of the Ship" (1849).

"Westward Look, the Land is Bright!"

Last time I spoke to you I quoted the lines of Longfellow which President Roosevelt had written out for me in his own hand. I have some other lines which are less well known but which seem apt and appropriate to our fortunes tonight, and I believe they will be so judged wherever the English language is spoken or the flag of freedom flies:

For while the tired waves, vainly breaking,
Seem here no painful inch to gain,
Far back, through creeks and inlets making,
Comes silent, flooding in, the main.
And not by eastern windows only,
When daylight comes, comes in the light;
In front the sun climbs slow, how slowly!
But westward, look, the land is bright.

1941, 27 APRIL. BROADCAST, LONDON.
(UNRELENTING, 100.)

The verses comprise the last two stanzas of "Say Not the Struggle Nought Availeth", by Arthur Hugh Clough (1819–61). To quote Professor David Dilks,

...if you will allow the remark in parentheses, ladies and gentlemen, do you not sometimes long for someone at the summit of our public life who can think and write at that level?

Britain Alone

And now the old lion with her lion cubs at her side stands alone against hunters who are armed with deadly weapons and impelled by desperate and destructive rage. Is the tragedy to repeat itself once more? Ah no! This is not the end of the tale. The stars in their courses proclaim the deliverance of mankind. Not so easily shall the onward progress of the peoples be barred. Not so easily shall the lights of freedom die.

But time is short! Every month that passes adds to the length and to the perils of the journey that will have to be made. United we stand. Divided we fall. Divided, the dark age returns. United, we can save and guide the world.

1941, 16 JUNE. BROADCAST, LONDON.
(UNRELENTING, 167–8.)

Radio broadcast to America after receiving the Honorary Degree of Doctor of Laws of the University of Rochester.

Deliverance is Sure

Do not despair, brave Norwegians: your land shall be cleansed not only from the invader but from the filthy quislings who are his tools. Be sure of yourselves, Czechs: your independence shall be restored. Poles, the heroism of your people standing up to cruel oppressors, the courage of your soldiers, sailors and airmen, shall not be forgotten: your country shall live again and resume its rightful part in the new organization of Europe. Lift up your heads, gallant Frenchmen: not all the infamies of Darlan and of Laval shall stand between you and the restoration of your birthright. Tough, stout-hearted Dutch, Belgians, Luxemburgers, tormented, mishandled, shamefully cast-away peoples of Yugoslavia, glorious Greece, now subjected to the crowning insult of the rule of the Italian jackanapes: yield not an inch! Keep your souls clean from all contact with the Nazis; make them feel even in their fleeting hour of brutish triumph that they are the moral outcasts of mankind. Help is coming; mighty forces are arming in your behalf. Have faith. Have hope. Deliverance is sure.

1941, 24 AUGUST. (UNRELENTING, 236–7.)

Masters of Our Fate

The mood of Britain is wisely and rightly averse from every form of shallow or premature exultation. This is no time for boasts or glowing prophecies, but there is this—a year ago our position looked forlorn and well nigh desperate to all eyes but our own. Today we may say aloud before an awe-struck world, "We are still masters of our fate. We still are captain of our souls."

1941, 9 SEPTEMBER.

America and Britain Together

I am a child of the House of Commons. I was brought up in my father's house to believe in democracy. "Trust the people"—that was his message. I used to see him cheered at meetings and in the streets by crowds of working men way back in those aristocratic Victorian days when, as Disraeli said, the world was for the few, and for the very few. Therefore I have been in full harmony all my life with the tides which have flowed on both sides of the Atlantic against privilege and monopoly, and I have steered confidently towards the Gettysburg ideal of "government of the people by the people for the people"....

Prodigious hammer-strokes have been needed to bring us together again, or if you will allow me to use other language, I will say that he must indeed have a blind soul who cannot see that some great purpose and design is being worked out here below, of which we have the honour to be the faithful servants. It is not given to us to peer into the mysteries of the future. Still, I avow my hope and faith, sure and inviolate, that in the days to come the British and American peoples will for their own safety and for the good of all walk together side by side in majesty, in justice, and in peace.

1941, 26 DECEMBER. UNITED STATES CONGRESS, WASHINGTON.

For the source of the final words see Chapter 20, People...Cockran.

Some Chicken

We have not journeyed all this way across the centuries, across the oceans, across the mountains, across the prairies, because we are made of sugar candy.

Look at the Londoners, the Cockneys; look at what they have stood up to. Grim and gay with their cry, "We can take it," and their wartime mood of "What is good enough for anybody is good enough for us." We have not asked that the rules of the game should be modified. We shall never descend to the German and Japanese level, but if anybody likes to play rough, we can play rough too. Hitler and his Nazi gang have sown the wind; let them reap the whirlwind....

The French Government had at their own suggestion solemnly bound themselves with us not to make a separate peace....But their generals misled them. When I warned them that Britain would fight on alone, whatever they did, their Generals told their Prime Minister and his divided Cabinet, "In three weeks England will have her neck wrung like a chicken." Some chicken; some neck.

1941, 30 DECEMBER. CANADIAN PARLIAMENT, OTTAWA. (UNRELENTING, 365–7.)

End of the Beginning

The Germans have been outmatched and outfought with the very kind of weapons with which they had beaten down so many small peoples, and also large unprepared peoples. They have been beaten by the very technical apparatus on which they counted to gain them the domination of the world. Especially is this true of the air and of the tanks and of the artillery, which has come back into its own on the battlefield. The Germans have received back again that measure of fire and steel which they have so often meted out to others.

Now this is not the end. It is not even the beginning of the end. But it is, perhaps, the end of the beginning.

1942, 10 NOVEMBER. MANSION HOUSE, LONDON. (END, 266.)

Following victory in the Battle of Alamein.

English-Speaking Peoples

Twice in my lifetime the long arm of destiny has reached across the oceans and involved the entire life and manhood of the United States in a deadly struggle. There was no use in saying "We don't want it; we won't have it; our forebears left Europe to avoid these quarrels; we have founded a new world which has no contact with the old." There was no use in that. The long arm reaches out remorselessly, and every one's existence, environment, and outlook undergo a swift and irresistible change....

But to the youth of America, as to the youth of all the Britains, I say "You cannot stop." There is no halting-place at this point. We have now reached a stage in the journey where there can be no pause. We must go on. It must be world anarchy or world order. Throughout all this ordeal and struggle which is characteristic of our age, you will find in the British Commonwealth and Empire good comrades to whom you are united by other ties besides those of State policy and public need. To a large extent, they are the ties of blood and history. Naturally I, a child of both worlds, am conscious of these.

Law, language, literature—these are considerable factors. Common conceptions of what is right and decent, a marked regard for fair play, especially to the weak and poor, a stern sentiment of impartial justice, and above all the love of personal freedom, or as Kipling put it: "Leave to live by no man's leave underneath the law"—these are common conceptions on both sides of the ocean among the English-speaking peoples.

1943, 6 SEPTEMBER. HARVARD UNIVERSITY, CAMBRIDGE, MASSACHUSETTS. (ONWARDS, 182–3.)

Although transcripts read "youth of Britain", recordings made at the time show that WSC used the more poetic "all the Britains", pronouncing the last word as "Bri-tanes".

The Tests of Freedom

The question arises, "What is freedom?" There are one or two quite simple, practical tests by which it can be known in the modern world in peace conditions—namely: Is there the right to free expression of opinion and of opposition and criticism of the Government of the day? Have the people the right to turn out a Government of which they disapprove, and are constitutional means provided by which they can make their will apparent? Are their courts of justice free from violence by the Executive and from threats of mob violence, and free from all association with particular political Parties? Will these courts administer open and well-established laws which are associated in the human mind with the broad principles of decency and justice? Will there be fair play for poor as well as for rich, for private persons as well as Government officials? Will the rights of the individual, subject to his duties to the State, be maintained and asserted and exalted? Is the ordinary peasant or workman, who is earning a living by daily toil and striving to bring up a family free from the fear that some grim police organization under the control of a single party, like the

Gestapo, started by the Nazi and Fascist parties, will tap him on the shoulder and pack him off without fair or open trial to bondage or ill-treatment? These simple practical tests are some of the title-deeds on which a new Italy could be founded.

1944, 28 AUGUST. (DAWN, 170.)

When asked how he would judge whether the new Italian government was a true democracy. (In the original, each query formed a paragraph.)

Victory in Europe

This is your victory! It is the victory of the cause of freedom in every land. In all our long history we have never seen a greater day than this. Everyone, man or woman, has done their best. Everyone has tried. Neither the long years, nor the dangers nor the fierce attacks of the enemy, have in any way weakened the independent resolve of the British nation. God bless you all.

1945, 8 MAY. MINISTRY OF HEALTH, LONDON. (VICTORY, 129.)

"Home is the Sailor"

I have great hopes of this Parliament, and I shall do my utmost to make its work fruitful. It may heal the wounds of war, and turn to good account the new conceptions and powers which we have gathered amid the storm. I do not underrate the difficult and intricate complications of the task which lies before us; I know too much about it to cherish vain illusions; but the morrow of such a victory as we have gained is a splendid moment both in our small lives and in our great history. It is a time not only of rejoicing but even more of resolve. When we look back on all the perils through which we have passed and at the mighty foes we have laid low and all the dark and deadly designs we have frustrated, why should we fear for our future? We have come safely through the worst.

"Home is the sailor, home from the sea,
And the hunter home from the hill."

1945, 16 AUGUST. (VICTORY, 238–9.)

This was Churchill's final review of the war and his first major speech as Leader of the Opposition.

Iron Curtain

From Stettin in the Baltic to Trieste in the Adriatic, an Iron Curtain has descended across the Continent. Behind that line lie all the capitals of the ancient states of central and eastern Europe. Warsaw, Berlin, Prague, Vienna, Budapest, Belgrade, Bucharest and Sofia, all these famous cities and the populations around them lie in what I must call the Soviet sphere, and all are subject in one form or another, not only to Soviet influence, but to a very high and, in many cases, increasing measure of control from Moscow. Athens alone—Greece with its immortal glories—is free to decide its future at an election under British, American and French observation....

On the other hand I repulse the idea that a new war is inevitable; still more that it is imminent....If we adhere faithfully to the Charter of the United Nations and walk forward in sedate and sober strength seeking no one's land or treasure, seeking to lay no arbitrary control upon the thoughts of men; if all British moral and material forces and convictions are joined with your own in fraternal association, the high-roads of the future will be clear, not only for us but for all, not only for our time, but for a century to come.

1946, 5 MARCH. WESTMINSTER COLLEGE, FULTON, MISSOURI. (SINEWS, 105.)

Hope for the Future

If the human race wishes to have a prolonged and indefinite period of material prosperity, they have only got to behave in a peaceful and helpful way towards one another, and science will do for them all that they wish and more than they can dream....Nothing is final. Change is unceasing and it is likely that mankind has a lot more to learn before it comes to its journey's end....We might even find ourselves in a few years moving along a smooth causeway of peace and plenty instead of roaming around on the rim of Hell. For myself I am an optimist—it does not seem to be much use being anything else—and I cannot believe that the human race will not find its way through the problems that confront it, although they are separated by a measureless gulf from any they have known before....Thus we may by patience, courage, and in orderly progression reach the shelter of a calmer and kindlier age.

1954, 9 NOVEMBER. GUILDHALL, LONDON. (ALLIANCE, 193–5.)

National Geographic's *Churchill issue (August, 1965) stitched some of these inspiring remarks together with words from a 1952 speech in Canada: "Withhold no sacrifice, grudge no toil, seek no sordid gain, fear no foe. All will be well."*

2

MAXIMS

"When we have degenerated, as we must eventually degenerate,
when we have lost our intrinsic superiority...our morals will be
gone, but our Maxims will remain."[19]

"Nothing...is so exhilarating as to be shot at without result."
In a British tommy's helmet during World War II.

Over a long life, Churchill offered so much advice that compiling a list of his maxims is a formidable task. To reduce the vast number of remarks that might qualify for this section, I have favoured brevity, maxims *originated* by Churchill, and, to the greatest extent possible, remarks about a single subject. Lengthier expressions will be found in Chapter 3 (Churchillisms); interesting expressions he derived from others are in Chapter 4 (Writer and Speaker). Retorts and comebacks, which sometimes take the form of maxims, are in Chapter 33 (Ripostes). Maxims attributed to WSC but originated by others are in Appendix I.

Winston Churchill's love of English, mastery of the language, and his long Parliamentary experience combined to produce maxims on human life and conduct that are singularly fascinating and continually relevant. He had deep beliefs. He stuck to them, never tempering his remarks for momentary political advantage, often indeed saying quite the opposite of what a pollster might have advised him to say.

---

19 WSC, Savrola, 124.

Abundance

There never will be enough for everything while the world goes on. The more that is given the more there will be needed.

1926, JUNE.

WSC added: "That is what makes life so interesting."

Acquisition

...how much harder it is to build up and acquire, than to squander and cast away.

1933. (RIVER ABR. ED., XI.)

Churchill was referring to India, whose further devolution he opposed, ultimately in vain. He preceded this remark with:

It is my hope that the story which these pages contain may be some help and encouragement to those young men and women who have still confidence in the destiny of Britain in the Orient.

Action

...there is great hope provided action is taken worthy of the opportunity.

1952. (WW2 V, 35.)

Adversity

...the threat of adversity is a necessary factor in stimulating self-reliance.

1925, 28 APRIL.

Age

A woman is as old as she looks; a man is as old as he feels; and a boy is as old as he is treated.

1942, 14 JANUARY, WHITE HOUSE, WASHINGTON. (WARD, 166.)

WSC's comment at dinner, related by FDR's companion, Daisy Suckley, in her diaries.

Allies

...when one looks at the disadvantages attaching to alliances, one must not forget how superior are the advantages.

1943, 21 SEPTEMBER.

There is only one thing worse than fighting with allies, and that is fighting without them.

1945, 1 APRIL, CHEQUERS. (BRYANT, TRIUMPH, 349.)

Quoted in Alanbrooke's Diaries. Clementine Churchill suggests a similar remark was made earlier, writing to WSC on 23 November 1943:

So don't allow yourself to be made angry. I often think of your saying, that the only worse thing than Allies is not having Allies!

Anti-Semitism

...anti-Semitism may be a good starter, but it is a bad sticker.

1932, 30 AUGUST, MUNICH. (OB V, 448.)

WSC to Hitler's friend, Ernst "Putzi" Hanfstaengel, who tried in vain to arrange a meeting between WSC and Hitler. In the election of 31 July 1932, the Nazi Party had won 230 seats, against 133 for the Social Democrats and 78 for the Communists. Much later in speeches, Churchill altered the phrase to "...bad stayer". See also Chapter 17, Between the Wars.

Anticipation

...in life's steeplechase one must always jump the fences when they come.

1930. (MEL, 218.)

Anxieties

We have a lot of anxieties, and one cancels out another very often.

1943, 22 SEPTEMBER.

Architecture

We shape our buildings, and afterwards our buildings shape us.

1943, 28 OCTOBER.

A German air raid destroyed the Commons chamber on 10 May 1941. The old House was rebuilt in 1950 in its old form, remaining insufficient to seat all its members. Churchill was against "giving each member a desk to sit at and a lid to bang" because, he explained, the House would be mostly empty most of the time; whereas, at critical votes and moments, it would fill beyond capacity, with members spilling out into the aisles, creating a suitable "sense of crowd and urgency".

Armaments

Nobody keeps armaments going for fun. They keep them going for fear.

1945, 23 NOVEMBER.

Bombing

Learn to get used to it. Eels get used to skinning.

1940, June. (Secret, 10.)

A wry remark added to a speech in secret session. See also Chapter 22, Politics: The Home Front...Cartoons for the first use of this line.

Breaking vs. mending

It is easier to break crockery than to mend it.

1948, 21 April, Conservative Women's Council, Albert Hall, London. (Unite, 297.)

Bribery

It was very much better to bribe a person than kill him, and very much better to be bribed than to be killed.

1953, 30 April.

Budget

An announcement of a prospective surplus is always a milestone in a budget....

1925, 28 April.

Bulldog

The nose of the bulldog has been slanted backwards so that he can breathe without letting go.

1914, 11 September, London Opera House. (OB III, 76.)

On 28 August 1914, in a naval action in the Heligoland Bight, the Royal Navy sank three German cruisers and damaged three others without a loss. Churchill used this phrase referring to the Navy in his first public speech after the outbreak of World War I. The Manchester Guardian *recorded:*

At the moment of delivery, with extraordinary appositeness, it was particularly vivid, as the speaker was able by some histrionic gift to suggest quite the bulldog as he spoke.

Capitalism and Socialism

The inherent vice of capitalism is the unequal sharing of blessings. The inherent virtue of Socialism is the equal sharing of miseries.

1945, 22 October.

Caution

Where every step is fraught with grave consequences and with real peril to the cause, deliberate and measured action is not merely prudent, but decent....

1910, 22 February.

Certainty

As the man whose mother-in-law had died in Brazil replied, when asked how the remains should be disposed of, "Embalm, cremate and bury. Take no risks!"

1938, 28 April. ("Britain's Deficiencies in Aircraft Manufacture," *Daily Telegraph*; Step, 226.)

Change

There is nothing wrong in change, if it is in the right direction. To improve is to change, so to be perfect is to have changed often.

1925, 23 June. (Ephesian, 3rd ed., 1936, 288.)

Exchange in the House of Commons with Philip Snowden when Churchill defended his first budget.

I expect you will find that change is the best kind of rest.

1939, 17 December. (WW2 I, 413.)

Change of mind

To change your mind is one thing; to turn on those who have followed your previous advice is another.

1922, 31 August. (OB, CV4/3, 1972.)

WSC to Lord Sydenham, who said he had changed his mind and now opposed a Jewish National Home in Palestine, and that the Balfour Declaration in favour thereof was achieved by underhand methods.

Chartwell

A day away from Chartwell is a day wasted.

Passim. (Grace Hamblin, 1987 Churchill Conference, Dallas.)

A frequent tribute to his home in Kent. Longtime secretary Grace Hamblin recalled:

...as we got to the precinct, he'd cast everything aside. All the papers would go flying and the car rug on the floor; the dog would be pushed aside, the secretary pushed aside, everything pushed aside, ready to

leap out. And he'd say, "Ah, Chartwell".
Personally I'd always felt the same and
wanted to say, "Yes, ah, Chartwell."

Chivalrous gallantry

Chivalrous gallantry is not among the peculiar
characteristics of excited democracy.

1899. (SAVROLA, 102.)

Companions

How much easier it is to join bad companions
than to shake them off!

1943, 31 AUGUST. BROADCAST, LONDON.
(ONWARDS, 177.)

Conferences

Hope flies on wings, and international conferences plod afterwards along dusty roads.

1925: 7 JANUARY, PARIS. (OB, CV5/1, 334.)

Remarks at a conference of Finance Ministers.

Confidence

It is one thing to feel confident and it is
another to impart that confidence to people
who do not like your plan, and who feel the
same confidence in their knowledge as you do
in yours.

1925, 10 JUNE.

Conscience

The only guide to a man is his conscience, the
only shield to his memory is the rectitude and
sincerity of his actions.

1940, 12 NOVEMBER.

From his tribute to Neville Chamberlain.
Churchill added,

> It is very imprudent to walk through life
> without this shield, because we are so
> often mocked by the failure of our hopes;
> but with this shield, however the fates
> may play, we march always in the ranks
> of honour.

For more of this quotation see Chapter 20,
People ... Chamberlain, Neville.

Conscience and muddle cannot be reconciled; conscience apart from truth is mere
stupidity...

1948, 15 JULY.

Contrast

The glory of light cannot exist without its
shadows.

1931, MARCH. ("A SECOND CHOICE,"
STRAND MAGAZINE; THOUGHTS, 10.)

Corporate opinion

All human processes expressing corporate
opinion are vitiated by imperfections.

1928, 14 JUNE.

Churchill believed emphatically in the
supremacy of Parliament and the rule of
the majority; but he also recognised that the
majority's opinion was not infallible.

Courage

Courage is not only common, but cosmopolitan.

1898. (MALAKAND, 207.)

A friend of Lady Randolph also credited WSC
with: "In sport, in courage, and in the sight of
heaven, all men meet on equal terms"; but this
is nowhere to be found in WSC's canon.

Men and kings must be judged in the testing
moments of their lives. Courage is rightly
esteemed the first of human qualities because,
as has been said, it is the quality which guarantees all others.

1931, JULY. ("ALFONSO THE UNLUCKY,"
STRAND MAGAZINE; GC, 137.)

"As has been said" likely refers to Samuel
Johnson's "...Sir, you know courage is reck-
oned the greatest of all virtues; because,
unless a man has that virtue, he has no secu-
rity for preserving any other." Included here
because Churchill improves on Johnson.

Criticism

Criticism in the body politic is like pain in the
human body. It is not pleasant, but where
would the body be without it?

1940, 27 JANUARY.

This maxim was preceded by:

> We do not resent the well-meant criticism
> of any man who wishes to win the war. We
> do not shrink from any fair criticism, and
> that is the most dangerous of all. On the

contrary, we take it earnestly to heart and seek to profit by it.

Criticism is easy; achievement is more difficult.

1941, 22 January.

Danger

Dangers which are warded off and difficulties which are overcome before they reach a crisis are utterly unrecognised. Eaten bread is soon forgotten.

1919, 29 October.

When danger is far off we may think of our weakness; when it is near we must not forget our strength.

1939, 28 June.

Dealing in guineas

Those who dealt in guineas were not usually of the impoverished class.

1903, 26 June.

The guinea coin, first struck in 1664 from gold obtained from Guinea, was originally valued at 30 shillings. From 1717 it was 21 shillings or one pound, one shilling, and commonly used by the upper classes, or in adverts pitched towards them.

Death

Wait and see how you feel when the tide is running the other way. It does not seem so easy to die when death is near.

1899, 24 November, Pretoria.
(Ladysmith, 107; Boer, 49.)

WSC to a Boer soldier who said he would fight for ever.

Death in politics

In war you can only be killed once, but in politics many times.

(Ca. 1904.)

Tentatively included as likely, but not proven. Many references cite this remark but without attribution. Halle references a 1902 newspaper interview, but provides no title or date. Manchester footnotes a non-existent entry in the official biography document volumes when WSC supposedly said this to a reporter in

spring 1904, just before he quit the Conservatives for the Liberals.

Deeds and consequences

The advantage and significance of deeds is that they bring consequences.

1949, 14 October, Conservative Conference, Earl's Court, London. (Balance, 107.)

Defeat

For defeat there is only one answer … victory.

1941, 10 June.

Preceding this he said:

> *Defeat is bitter. There is no use in trying to explain defeat. People do not like defeat and they do not like the explanations, however elaborate or plausible, which are given of them.*

Defeat in youth

…one must never be discouraged by defeats in one's youth, but continue to learn throughout one's whole life.

1948, 12 May, University of Oslo. (Unite, 326.)

Democracy

Democracy is more vindictive than Cabinets.

1901, 13 May. (MBA, 23.)

See also Chapter 30, Predictions…Wars of Peoples.

Denial

Some people will deny anything, but there are some denials that do not alter the facts.

1910, 31 March.

Despair

It is a crime to despair. We must learn to draw from misfortune the means of future strength.

1938, 4 October. ("France After Munich," Daily Telegraph; Step, 275.)

Destiny

The veils of the future are lifted one by one, and mortals must act from day to day.

1940, 21 April. (WW2 I, 500.)

Only one link in the chain of destiny can be handled at a time.

1945, 18 February.

Churchill preceded this by comparing 1945 to 1940:

If a man is coming across the sea to kill you, you do everything in your power to make sure he dies before finishing his journey. That may be difficult, it may be painful, but at least it is simple. Now we are entering a world of imponderables, and at every stage occasions for self-questioning arise.

It is always wise to look ahead, but difficult to look farther than you can see.

1952, 23 JULY.

See also "Retrospect" herein, and, for a red herring, Appendix I...Looking backward.

Difficulties

Difficulties must not affright us. If some stand out, all the more must the others be banded together.

**1936, 20 JULY. ("HOW TO STOP WAR,"
EVENING STANDARD; STEP, 27.)**

WSC would be bewildered by the modern habit of substituting the "issues" for "difficulties". He knew exactly what difficulties were, and he stood no nonsense from them.

Don't argue the matter. The difficulties will argue for themselves.

1941, 30 MAY, LONDON. (WW2 V, 66.)

Prime Minister to Chief of Combined Operations: Churchill's first directive on what became the Mulberry Harbours used in the Normandy invasion of 1944: "They must float up and down with the tide..." See Chapter 18, World War II...1945/D-Day Mulberry Harbours.

Difficulties mastered are opportunities won.

**1943, 21 MARCH. BROADCAST, LONDON.
(ONWARDS, 38.)**

Face to face, difficulties which appear really insuperable at a distance are very often removed altogether from our path.

1944, 27 OCTOBER.

Diplomacy

The reason for having diplomatic relations is not to confer a compliment, but to secure a convenience.

1949, 17 NOVEMBER.

Disinterested man

Rare and precious is the truly disinterested man.

1899. (RIVER I, 26.)

Doing nothing

Things do not get better by being let alone. Unless they are adjusted, they explode with a shattering detonation.

1927. (CRISIS III PART 1, 239.)

Contrary advice to Volume I of the same book; WSC is oversimplifying.

Doing our best

...how little we should worry about anything except doing our best.

1951. (WW2 IV, 494.)

Doing without

So we have had to dispense with the indispensable.

1922, 11 JULY.

Dual control

Dual control is two persons attempting to control one thing. The reverse process is one person attempting to control two things.

1920, 11 MARCH.

Empires of the mind

The empires of the future are the empires of the mind.

**1943, 5 SEPTEMBER, HARVARD UNIVERSITY,
CAMBRIDGE, MASSACHUSETTS. (ONWARDS, 185.)**

Having outlined in glowing terms the possibilities of Basic English (see Chapter 4, Writer and Speaker), he exhorted listeners with this phrase.

Energy

...energy of mind does not depend on energy of body....energy should be exercised and not exhausted.

**1944, 1 JANUARY, MARRAKESH. (WW2 V, 393;
OB VII, 632.)**

Engineers

We need a lot of engineers in the modern world, but we do not want a world of modern engineers.

**1948, 12 MAY, UNIVERSITY OF OSLO.
(EUROPE, 327.)**

WSC preceded this remark:

Gradually, as I have passed through life, I have developed a strong feeling that a university training should not be too practical in its aims. Young people study at universities to achieve knowledge, and not to learn a trade. We must all learn how to support ourselves, but we must also learn how to live.

Evil

It is an important thing to diagnose the evil, but unless the malady be recognised it is idle to attempt to seek the remedy.

1926, 21 JUNE.

Evils can be created much quicker than they can be cured.

1951, 2 OCTOBER, LIVERPOOL. (STEMMING, 123.)

Facts

You must look at facts, because they look at you.

1925, 7 MAY.

Facts are better than dreams.

1948. (WW2 I, 527.)

On taking office as Prime Minister, 10 May 1940. See also Chapter 31, Personal Matters... Premiership.

United wishes and goodwill cannot overcome brute facts.

1951. (WW2 IV, 290.)

Facts plus

Sir, it is not only the facts that count.

1948, 8 MARCH. (EUROPE, 268.)

Churchill was protesting the diminution of the Royal Navy by the Labour Government, arguing that the sad facts were the result of an even sadder policy.

Failure

Even [man's] greatest neglects or failures may bring him good. Even his greatest achievements may work him ill.

1936. (MARLBOROUGH III, 136.)

Fate

What a slender thread the greatest of things can hang by.

1940, 10 AUGUST, CHEQUERS. (GILBERT, LIFE, 670.)

WSC was contemplating the Battle of Britain.

Finance

In finance, everything that is agreeable is unsound and everything that is sound is disagreeable.

1926, 15 MARCH, WALDORF HOTEL, LONDON. (CS IV, 3871.)

Foresight

Plant a garden in which you can sit when digging days are done.

1921, DECEMBER. ("PAINTING AS A PASTIME," STRAND MAGAZINE; THOUGHTS, 229.)

When you are leaving for an unknown destination it is a good plan to attach a restaurant car at the tail of the train.

1922, 11 OCTOBER. (BEAVERBROOK, DECLINE, 221.)

WSC's reply when asked why Sir Philip Sassoon, Parliamentary Private Secretary to David Lloyd George, had been so lucky in his jobs. It was the eve of the general election in which Lloyd George's coalition government was defeated.

How little can we foresee the consequences either of wise or unwise action, of virtue or of malice!

1948. (WW2 I, 157.)

WSC added,

Without this measureless and perpetual uncertainty, the drama of human life would be destroyed.

Fortune, fickle

Sometimes when [Fortune] scowls most spitefully, she is preparing her most dazzling gifts.

1931, 30 AUGUST. ("B-P [BADEN-POWELL]," SUNDAY PICTORIAL; GC, 235.)

Free Market

If you destroy a free market you create a black market.

1949, 3 FEBRUARY.

He added: "If you have 10,000 regulations you destroy all respect for the law."

Friendship

One always measures friendships by how they show up in bad weather.

1948, 10 JULY, WOODFORD, ESSEX. (UNITE, 368.)

See also Chapter 20, People...Beaverbrook.

Fright and death

...it is much better to be frightened now than to be killed hereafter.

1934, 28 NOVEMBER.

Future

The future is unknowable, but the past should give us hope.

1958. (HESP IV, 387.)

Germans

A Hun alive is a war in prospect.

1940, 13 OCTOBER, CHEQUERS. (OB VI, 841.)

Give us the tools

Give us the tools, and we will finish the job.

1941, 9 FEBRUARY. BROADCAST, LONDON. (CS VI, 6351.)

Addressing the USA and Roosevelt, referring to the Lend-Lease Act. For the surrounding remarks, see Chapter 1, Immortal Words.

Great causes

Strength is granted to us all when we are needed to serve great causes.

1946, 15 MARCH, WALDORF-ASTORIA, NEW YORK. (SINEWS, 120.)

We must always be ready to make sacrifices for the great causes; only in that way shall we live to keep our souls alive.

1948, 12 MAY, HOTEL BRISTOL, OSLO. (UNITE, 330.)

Those who serve supreme causes must not consider what they can get but what they can give.

1950, 11 AUGUST. COUNCIL OF EUROPE, STRASBOURG. (BALANCE, 351.)

Great men

One mark of a great man is the power of making lasting impressions upon people he meets.

1930, FEBRUARY. ("[JOSEPH] CHAMBERLAIN," PALL MALL; GC, 35.)

Often in the casual remarks of great men one learns their true mind in an intimate way.

1936. (MARLBOROUGH III, 212.)

Harsh laws

Harsh laws are at times better than no laws at all.

1906, 28 FEBRUARY.

Hatred

Hatred plays the same part in government as acids in chemistry.

1929. (CRISIS IV, 304.)

Help vs. harm

Help each other when you can, but never harm.

1938, 22 NOVEMBER. (WW2 I, 259.)

WSC to Alfred Duff Cooper, later Viscount Norwich.

High ground

Do not quit the heights.

1943, 25 NOVEMBER. (WW2 V, 636.)

Hindsight

After things are over it is easy to choose the fine mental and moral positions which one should adopt.

1950. (WW2 III, 207.)

History

Persevere towards those objectives which are lighted for us by all the wisdom and inspiration of the past.

1948, 7 MAY. CONGRESS OF EUROPE, THE HAGUE. (EUROPE, 315.)

Study history, study history. In history lie all the secrets of statecraft.

1953, 27 MAY. (OB VIII, 835.)

Reported following WSC's Coronation luncheon remarks at Westminster Hall: WSC to James Humes, later a presidential speechwriter and author of books on Churchill, then an American schoolboy at Stowe on an English-Speaking Union Scholarship.

Honours

Honours should go where death and danger go...

1916, 24 JULY.

Hopes and realities

Nourish your hopes, but do not overlook realities.

1935, 31 MAY.

Hot topics

When you have to hold a hot coffee-pot, it is better not to break the handle off ...

1944, 22 FEBRUARY.

Humanities

No technical knowledge can outweigh knowledge of the humanities.

1948, 12 MAY, UNIVERSITY OF OSLO. (EUROPE, 327.)

Hypocrisy

Few people practise what they preach...

1929, AUGUST. ("BERNARD SHAW," PALL MALL; GC, 30.)

Idealism

The human race cannot make progress without idealism...

1942, 12 APRIL. (WW2 IV, 194.)

Ideas

Ideas acquire a momentum of their own.

1927, JULY. ("CONSISTENCY IN POLITICS," PALL MALL; THOUGHTS, 26.)

I think that no idea is so outlandish that it should not be considered with a searching, but at the same time, I hope, with a steady eye.

1940, 23 MAY.

This maxim explains much of Churchill's approach to his chiefs of staff, who were often frustrated by the impracticability of some of his military proposals.

Ifs

We live in a world of "ifs."

1899. (RIVER I, 235.)

Imagination

...imagination without deep and full knowledge is a snare...

1950. (WW2 III, 516.)

Imperialism and economics

...imperialism and economics clash as often as honesty and self-interest.

1898. (MALAKAND, 150.)

Impulse

Almost the chief mystery of life is what makes one do things.

1931, FEBRUARY. ("PERSONAL CONTACTS," STRAND MAGAZINE; THOUGHTS, 31.)

Innovation

We must beware of needless innovation, especially when guided by logic.

1942, 17 DECEMBER.

Invitations

It is a very fine thing to refuse an invitation, but it is a good thing to wait till you get it first.

1911, 22 FEBRUARY.

Jaw to jaw

Meeting jaw to jaw is better than war.

1954, 26 JUNE. CONGRESSIONAL LUNCHEON, WASHINGTON. (OB VIII, 1004.)

Commonly misquoted as "Jaw, jaw is better than war, war," an expression coined four years later by Harold Macmillan, on a visit to Australia.

Joy

Soberness and restraint do not necessarily prevent the joyous expression of the human heart.

1945, 1 MAY.

Joys and sorrows

Let us treasure our joys but not bewail our sorrows.

1931, MARCH. ("A SECOND CHOICE," STRAND MAGAZINE; THOUGHTS, 10.)

Judgement

We shall not be judged by the criticisms of our opponents but by the consequences of our acts.

1926, 22 APRIL.

Jurisprudence

The first maxim of English jurisprudence is that complainers should come into Court with clean hands.

1914, 28 APRIL.

Justice

Justice moves slowly and remorselessly upon its path, but it reaches its goal eventually.

1929, 23 JULY.

One ought to be just before one is generous.
1947, 6 DECEMBER, BELLE VUE, MANCHESTER.
(EUROPE, 216.)

KBO
We must just KBO.
1941, 11 DECEMBER. (OB VI, 1273.)

WSC to private secretary John Peck. Churchill's familiar maxim, usually delivered to colleagues and family, and abbreviated in polite company. It stood for "Keep Buggering On".

King vs. ace
The king cannot fall unworthily if he falls to the sword of the ace.
1912. (BONHAM CARTER, 211.)

WSC to Edward Marsh as he lost a king in a trick.

Languages
The recognition of their language is precious to a small people.
1906, 31 JULY.

From a speech in favour of ratifying the Transvaal Constitution, recognising the Boer language, which he considered magnanimous to the Boer inhabitants.

Libraries
Nothing makes a man more reverent than a library.
1921, DECEMBER. ("PAINTING AS A PASTIME," STRAND MAGAZINE; THOUGHTS, 218.)

Life
Usually youth is for freedom and reform, maturity for judicious compromise, and old age for stability and repose.
1927, JULY. ("CONSISTENCY IN POLITICS," PALL MALL; THOUGHTS, 26.)

Life is a whole, and good and ill must be accepted together.
1931, MARCH. ("A SECOND CHOICE," STRAND MAGAZINE; THOUGHTS, 10.)

…live dangerously; take things as they come; dread naught, all will be well.
1932, 5 JANUARY. ("MY NEW YORK MISADVENTURE," DAILY MAIL; ESSAYS IV, 88.)

The journey has been enjoyable and well worth the taking – once.
1965, JANUARY. (LORD SOAMES TO THE EDITOR.)

Said to his son-in-law, Christopher Soames, on his deathbed.

Line of least resistance
It always looks so easy to solve problems by taking the line of least resistance.
1946, 24 MAY. (SINEWS, 150.)

Luck
…you never can tell whether bad luck may not after all turn out to be good luck.
1930. (MEL, 116.)

Magnanimity
As we have triumphed, so we may be merciful; as we are strong, so we can afford to be generous.
1906, 21 MARCH.

An example of WSC's consistency: forty years later it was "In victory, magnanimity." See World War II in this chapter.

…you don't want to knock a man down except to pick him up in a better frame of mind.
1949, 25 MARCH, RITZ-CARLTON HOTEL, NEW YORK. (BALANCE, 35.)

Mankind
Man is spirit.
1955, 3 APRIL, 10 DOWNING STREET. (OB VIII, 1123.)

Final words to his non-Cabinet ministers upon WSC's retirement as Prime Minister, according to Lord De L'Isle and Dudley as quoted by Martin Gilbert.

Mankind, productive capacity
The productive capacity of the human race is greater this afternoon than it ever was before.
1947, 4 OCTOBER, BRIGHTON. (EUROPE, 158.)

Mankind, unchanged
The power of man has grown in every sphere except over himself.
1953, 10 DECEMBER, TOWN HALL, STOCKHOLM. (CS VIII, 8515.)

Lady Churchill read this acceptance speech of the Nobel Prize for Literature, at which she represented her husband. Churchill was in Bermuda conferring with President Eisenhower and French Premier Laniel.

Martyrdom

They could not have martyrdom without the accessories of the faggot and the stake, and if a man made his protest he ought to be prepared to pay the price.

1904, 19 JULY.

Lord Dundonald had commanded the Canadian militia, which he had criticised, and had then been recalled.

Milk into babies

There is no finer investment for any community than putting milk into babies.

1943, 21 MARCH. BROADCAST, LONDON. (ONWARDS, 40.)

WSC recycled and improved this maxim from a remark he made at the City Carlton Club on 28 June 1939:

> *There is no more far-seeing investment for a nation than to put milk, food, and education into young children.*

Mind as rifle

Don't turn your mind into an ammunition wagon, but turn it into a rifle to fire off other people's ammunition.

1900. (EPHESIAN, 73.)

Churchill's advice to his cousin Shane Leslie at Eton, before WSC left for his American/Canadian lecture tour.

Mistakes and luck

Men may make mistakes, and learn from their mistakes. Men may have bad luck, and their luck may change.

1942, 2 JULY.

Moral force

Moral force is, unhappily, no substitute for armed force, but it is a very great reinforcement…

1937, 21 DECEMBER.

Myths

At times of crisis, myths have their historical importance.

CA. 1933. (DILKS, "THE GREATNESS OF BILL DEAKIN," *FINEST HOUR* 131, SUMMER 2006.)

WSC to Bill Deakin, his literary assistant on WSC's History of the English Speaking Peoples. *Churchill had insisted on including the story (generally regarded as myth) that King Alfred served as a kitchen-boy to a Saxon housewife, who upbraided him for not rescuing her cakes, which were burning in her oven while the King was distracted by preparing his weapons for a crucial battle with the Danes. (HESP I: 114.)*

National borrowing

When you borrow money from another country for the sacred purpose of national rehabilitation, it is wrong to squander it upon indulgences.

1947, 4 AUGUST. CONSERVATIVE RALLY, BLENHEIM PALACE. (EUROPE, 109.)

National collapse

When a country collapses, the chaos reproduces itself in every microcosm.

1941, JULY. (HASSALL, 631.)

Eddie Marsh: "Winston was in great form… talking of the difficulties among the Free French."

National conscience

A nation without a conscience is a nation without a soul. A nation without a soul is a nation that cannot live.

1951, 16 SEPTEMBER. RAF BENEVOLENT FUND BROADCAST, LONDON. (STEMMING, 117.)

National defence

It is no use examining national defence in the abstract…

1934, 30 JULY.

WSC added:

> *…and talking in vague and general terms about hypothetical dangers and combinations which cannot be expressed.*

To urge the preparation of defence is not to assert the imminence of war. On the contrary, if war were imminent, preparations for defence would be too late.

1934, 28 NOVEMBER.

Natural processes

It is sometimes wise to allow natural processes to work, and crimes and follies to be paid in coin from their own mint.

1938, 22 FEBRUARY.

Churchill, speaking after the resignation of Anthony Eden as Chamberlain's Foreign Minister, was referring to the possibility that Italy might have withdrawn disillusioned from Libya and Ethiopia.

Nature

Nature will not be admired by proxy.

1898. (MALAKAND, 118.)

WSC gave this as the reason for not describing the night-time beauty of the North-West Frontier of India.

Necessity

It is no use saying, "We are doing our best." You have got to succeed in doing what is necessary.

1916, 7 MARCH. (CS III, 2409.)

Negotiations

Quit murdering and start arguing.

1920, 2 OCTOBER, WAR OFFICE.
(OB, CV4/2, 1217.)

WSC to his cousin Shane Leslie, who asked what advice Churchill would give to Sinn Fein in Ireland.

News-making

It is better to be making the news than taking it; to be an actor rather than a critic.

1898. (MALAKAND, 97.)

Old and new

Do not let spacious plans for a new world divert your energies from saving what is left of the old.

1941, 6 JANUARY. (WW2 III, 638.)

Prime Minister to Minister of Public Works and Buildings.

Opportunity

...everyone has his day, and some days last longer than others.

1952, 29 JANUARY.

Parliament

The object of Parliament is to substitute argument for fisticuffs.

1951, 6 JUNE.

Peace-keeping hypocrisy

I would rather have a peace-keeping hypocrisy than straightforward, brazen vice, taking the form of unlimited war.

1937, 14 APRIL.

Perfection

Nothing is perfect on the human stage...

1948, 16 NOVEMBER.

...perfect solutions to our difficulties are not to be looked for in an imperfect world....

1951, 17 NOVEMBER, SHEFFIELD.

The maxim "Nothing avails but perfection" may be spelt shorter: "Paralysis."

1942, 6 DECEMBER. (WW2 IV, 808.)

Perseverance

We must go on and on like the gun-horses, till we drop.

1940S. (NEL, 37.)

WSC to a wartime secretary, Elizabeth Nel: "...he stopped once to ask if I were tired, and when I told him I was not, he said [this]."

When one crest line is abandoned it is necessary to return to the next. Halting at a "half-way house" mid-way in the valley is fatal.

1906, JANUARY.

It is like going up a mountain. Each successive peak appears in turn the summit, and yet there is always another pinnacle beyond.

1906, 31 JULY.

On writing the new Transvaal constitution.

Continue to pester, nag, and bite.

1941, 26 MARCH. (WW2 III, 142.)

WSC to Sir Ronald Campbell, British Ambassador to Belgrade, urging him to continue attempting to convince Yugoslavia to stand with Greece against the Germans.

We must learn to be equally good at what is short and sharp and what is long and tough.

1941, 29 OCTOBER, HARROW SCHOOL.
(UNRELENTING, 286.)

...never give in, never, never, never, never—in nothing, great or small, large or petty—never give in except to convictions of honour and good sense.

1941, 29 OCTOBER, HARROW SCHOOL.
(UNRELENTING, 287.)

WSC added: "Never yield to force; never yield to the apparently overwhelming might of the enemy." It is sometimes said that Churchill once gave a three-word speech: "Never give in." The speech containing these words, about twenty minutes, was given to the boys at his old school, Harrow, during the first of many visits in his later years.

Personal relations

There is all the difference in the world between a man who knocks you down and a man who leaves you alone.

1944, 24 MAY.

Personnel

You should never harness a thoroughbred to a dung-cart.

1941, 17 FEBRUARY. (KENNEDY, BUSINESS, 80.)

Churchill's first Minister of Information, Alfred Duff Cooper, resigned because he insisted on having the sole power to decide on the release of information. This remark was made to Duff's successor, Brendan Bracken, in Duff's presence; the latter took it cheerfully. See Chapter 20, People...Duff Cooper.

Pleasure

...when one is trying to give pleasure it is always well to do it in the best possible way.

1951, 6 NOVEMBER.

Political action

In politics when you are in doubt what to do, do nothing ... when you are in doubt what to say, say what you really think.

1905, 26 JULY, NORTH-WEST MANCHESTER.
(CS I, 413.)

Politicians

Politicians rise by toils and struggles. They expect to fall; they hope to rise again.

1931, JULY. ("ALFONSO THE UNLUCKY,"
STRAND MAGAZINE; GC, 131.)

Politics

It is a fine game to play the game of politics and it is well worth a good hand before really plunging.

1895, 16 AUGUST, ALDERSHOT. (OB, CV1/1, 583.)

WSC to his mother.

Power and mercy, weakness and strife

The finest combination in the world is power and mercy. The worst combination in the world is weakness and strife.

1919, 3 MARCH.

Power and pomp

But on the whole it is wise in human affairs, and in the government of men, to separate pomp from power.

1952, 14 JANUARY, CHÂTEAU LAURIER, OTTAWA.
(STEMMING, 218.)

For more of this quotation see Chapter 7, British Government...Monarchy.

Power and responsibility

Where there is great power there is great responsibility...where there is no power there can, I think, be no responsibility.

1906, 28 FEBRUARY.

Power to give

It is certainly more agreeable to have the power to give than to receive.

1949, 28 APRIL.

Principles

It is always more easy to discover and proclaim general principles than to apply them.

1936, 31 MARCH, LONDON. (WW2 I, 164.)

Private address to the Conservative Members Committee on Foreign Affairs, dated "the end of March".

People who are not prepared to do unpopular things and to defy clamour are not fit to be Ministers in times of stress.

1943, 29 NOVEMBER, CAIRO. (WW2 V, 637.)

Churchill was commenting favourably on the Cabinet's decision to support the Home Secretary, Herbert Morrison, in releasing the Mosleys from prison. Sir Oswald and Lady Mosley had been imprisoned at the outset of the war for suspected fascist leanings.

In critical and baffling situations it is always best to recur to first principles and simple action.

1951, 17 MARCH. PARTY POLITICAL BROADCAST, LONDON. (STEMMING, 34.)

Procrastination

I have always heard that procrastination was the thief of time, but in this case procrastination seemed to me to have been particularly profitable.

1906, 2 AUGUST.

Referring to a rise in Ceylon fishery rights by the government, which had procrastinated long enough for a record catch in 1905.

Prophets

A hopeful disposition is not the sole qualification to be a prophet.

1927, 30 APRIL.

Quarrels

The worst quarrels only arise when both sides are equally in the right and in the wrong.

1936, 10 AUGUST. ("THE SPANISH TRAGEDY," EVENING STANDARD, LONDON; STEP, 38.)

Radical Imperialists

I have always noticed that whenever a radical takes to Imperialism he catches it in a very acute form.

1901, 13 MAY.

Sir Charles Dilke (1843–1911), a Liberal Imperialist, had come out in favour of an increase in Army estimates.

Recrimination

...the use of recriminating about the past [is] to enforce effective action at the present.

1936, 29 MAY.

Four years later, by then in charge, Churchill took a different approach; see next entries.

We are not in a position to say tonight, "The past is the past." We cannot say, "The past is the past," without surrendering the future.

1938, 14 MARCH.

...if we open a quarrel between the past and the present we shall find that we have lost the future.

1940, 18 JUNE.

WSC repeated this remark on 28 November 1945 at a meeting of the Conservative Party Central Council. A similar comment is in Chapter 18, World War II...Need for Unity.

Redress of grievances

...the redress of the grievances of the vanquished should precede the disarmament of the victors.

1935, NOVEMBER. ("THE TRUTH ABOUT HITLER," STRAND MAGAZINE; GC, 167.)

Repetition

In the problems which the Almighty sets his humble servants things hardly ever happen the same way twice over...

1948. (WW2 I, 374.)

For contradictory advice see War wounds herein and Chapter 31, Personal Matters...Déjà vu.

Resources

The sledge is bare of babies, and though the pack may crunch the driver's bones, the winter will not be ended.

1914, 2 FEBRUARY. (OB, CV2/3, 1861.)

From a letter to Prime Minister H. H. Asquith:

...I do not love this naval expenditure and am grieved to be found in the position of taskmaster. But I am myself the slave of facts and forces which are uncontrollable unless naval efficiency is frankly abandoned. The result of all this pressure and controversy leaves me anxious chiefly lest the necessary services have been cut too low.

Retrospect

We cannot undo the past, but we are bound to pass it in review in order to draw from it such lessons as may be applicable to the future....

1936, 16 APRIL.

The longer you can look back, the farther you can look forward.

1944, 2 MARCH. ROYAL COLLEGE OF PHYSICIANS, LONDON. (DAWN, 24.)

Often misquoted (see Appendix I). Churchill continued:

This is not a philosophical or political argument—any oculist will tell you this is true. The wider the span, the longer the continuity, the greater is the sense of duty in individual men and women, each contributing their brief life's work to the preservation and progress of the land in which they live, the society of which they are members, and the world of which they are the servants.

Right and consistent

...it is better to be both right and consistent. But if you have to choose—you must choose to be right.

1952, 11 OCTOBER. (STEMMING, 344.)

Speech to the Conservative Party Conference.

Right and hard

Things are not always right because they are hard, but if they are right one must not mind if they are also hard.

1948, 9 OCTOBER, LLANDUDNO, WALES. (EUROPE, 419.)

Right and honest

It is a fine thing to be honest, but it is very important for a Prime Minister to be right.

1923, 16 NOVEMBER. FREE TRADE HALL, MANCHESTER. (CS IV, 3399.)

Churchill preceded this by a reference to the Prime Minister: "Mr. Baldwin is a very honest man; he tells us so himself." Less than a year later, to everyone's surprise including Churchill's, "Honest Stan" appointed WSC Chancellor of the Exchequer.

Right and irresponsible

Perhaps it is better to be irresponsible and right than to be responsible and wrong.

1950, 26 AUGUST. PARTY POLITICAL BROADCAST, LONDON. (BALANCE, 355.)

Prime Minister Attlee had called WSC irresponsible for suggesting that Germany contribute to the defence of Western Europe. WSC added that he was "thankful not to be responsible for what has happened to our country and its Empire during the last five years".

Right and wrong

Except in so far as force is concerned, there is no equality between right and wrong.

1945, 26 MAY. (WW2 VI, 504.)

WSC to President Truman, who ventured to suggest that he should meet privately with Stalin before he saw WSC; Churchill had had enough of that with Roosevelt.

The true guide of life is to do what is right.

1951, 15 OCTOBER, HUDDERSFIELD. (STEMMING, 147.)

Risk

You must put your head into the lion's mouth if the performance is to be a success.

1900, 19 FEBRUARY. CINGOLO NECK, SOUTH AFRICA. (LADYSMITH, 388–9; BOER, 175.)

Safety

To try to be safe everywhere is to be strong nowhere.

1951. (WW2 IV, 14.)

WSC to Australian Prime Minister John Curtin, who replied,

Just as you foresaw events in Europe, so we felt that we saw the trend of the Pacific situation more clearly than was realised in London.

WSC responded:

It was their duty to study their own position with concentrated attention. We had to try to think for all.

Satisfaction

How often in life must one be content with what one can get!

1943, 26 DECEMBER. (WW2 V, 385.)

Secrets

…it is wonderful how well men can keep secrets they have not been told…

1900, 31 MARCH. NEAR PIETERS, NATAL, SOUTH AFRICA. (HAMILTON'S, 4; BOER, 226.)

On failing to learn of an intended plan of campaign from senior officers.

Settlements

The best evidence of the fairness of any settlement is the fact that it fully satisfies neither party.

1926, 27 JANUARY. TREASURY, LONDON. (CS IV, 3824.)

Churchill was speaking on the signing of an agreement settling the Italian war debt to Britain.

It is a sort of British idea that when you reach agreement you take the rough with the smooth.

1948, 16 FEBRUARY.

Shot at without result

Nothing in life is so exhilarating as to be shot at without result.

1898. (MALAKAND, 117.)

Famously quoted by a well-read Churchillian, President Ronald Reagan, after surviving an assassin's bullet in 1981.

Simplicity

Out of intense complexities, intense simplicities emerge.

1927. (CRISIS III PART 1, 140.)

Life, which is so complicated and difficult in great matters, nearly always presents itself in simple terms.

1941, 27 MARCH.

All the greatest things are simple, and many can be expressed in a single word: Freedom; Justice; Honour; Duty; Mercy; Hope.

1947, 14 MAY. UNITED EUROPE MEETING, ALBERT HALL, LONDON. (EUROPE, 77.)

Sink or swim

It is not enough to float. We have to swim…

1952, 11 JUNE. PRESS ASSOCIATION, SAVOY HOTEL, LONDON. (STEMMING, 300.)

WSC was remarking that the challenges of peace were at least as great as in the late war.

Slothfulness

Let not the slothful chortle.

1940s.

Lord Mountbatten to the Edmonton Churchill Society, 1966.

Social reform

All social reform…which is not founded upon a stable medium of internal exchange becomes a swindle and a fraud.

1947, 4 OCTOBER, BRIGHTON. (EUROPE, 158.)

Solvency and security

Solvency is valueless without security, and security is impossible to achieve without solvency.

1953, 5 MARCH.

Speechmaking

It is pretty tough to reshape human society in an after-dinner speech.

1941, MARCH. (BEN MOSHE, 282.)

Response to the draft of a long after-dinner speech which Halifax, the British Ambassador in Washington, was planning to give in March, 1941.

Spite

Nothing should be done for spite's sake.

1944, 26 MAY. (WW2 V, 628.)

Success

Success always demands a greater effort.

1940, 13 DECEMBER. (WW2 II, 541.)

WSC to Robert Menzies, Prime Minister of Australia.

Sufficiency

Enough is as good as a feast.

1918, 25 APRIL.

Churchill, then Minister of Munitions, was explaining that shell output could have been even larger than it was, although it was "enough".

Temptations

Would you be strong morally or physically? You must resist temptations.

1898. (SAVROLA, 114.)

Theory and practice

Concede the theory and you have no trouble in practice.

1945, 19 MARCH. (DIARIES OF CABINET SECRETARY SIR NORMAN BROOK, *NEW YORK TIMES*, 22 JANUARY 2006.)

On allowing women to become Members of Parliament.

Thought

Thought arising from factual experience may be a bridle or a spur.

1952. (WW2 V, 514.)

Thought or Action

After all, a man's Life must be nailed to a cross of either Thought or Action.

1930. (MEL, 127.)

Thoughts in words

One can usually put one's thoughts better in one's own words.

1940, 19 JULY. (WW2 II, 21.)

Thrift

It is a great mistake to suppose that thrift is caused only by fear; it springs from hope as well as from fear; where there is no hope, be sure there will be no thrift.

1908, 10 OCTOBER, DUNDEE. (PEOPLE'S, 146.)

Tidiness and symmetry

Tidiness is a virtue, symmetry is often a constituent of beauty...

1945, 22 OCTOBER.

Time

Time and money are largely interchangeable terms.

1926, 19 JULY.

No one should waste a day.

1948, 30 APRIL, ALBERT HALL, LONDON. (UNITE, 308.)

Tributes

...a favourable verdict is always to be valued, even if it comes from an unjust judge or a nobbled umpire.

1931, 29 APRIL.

During the 1931 Budget debate, Lloyd George and the Liberals had praised Churchill's previous administration of the Exchequer (1924–29).

Trust

In stormy weather one must trust to the man at the helm...

1900, 13 APRIL. BETHANY, SOUTH AFRICA. (HAMILTON'S, 24; BOER, 235.)

Truth

This truth is incontrovertible. Panic may resent it, ignorance may deride it, malice may distort it, but there it is.

1916, 17 MAY.

In wartime, Truth is so precious that she should always be attended by a bodyguard of lies.

1943, 30 NOVEMBER, TEHERAN. (WW2 V, 338.)

WSC uttered this famous line when Stalin approved of issuing fake invasion plans. Thus "Operation Bodyguard" became the name for deception plans for "Overlord", the 1944 invasion of France. M. Hirsh Goldberg in The Book of Lies *(1990) claimed that Stalin had initiated the "bodyguard" remark from an old Russian proverb, and Churchill was just quoting it back to him. Soviet records reveal WSC saying: "Sometimes truth has to be safeguarded with the aid of untruth," but do not mention a Russian proverb.*

Truth and honour

Let no one swerve off the high road of truth and honour.

1945, 14 FEBRUARY, ATHENS. (VICTORY, 42.)

Speech before 50,000 Greeks on the country's future.

Truth and mendacity

...if truth is many-sided, mendacity is many-tongued....

1940, 8 MAY. (OB, CV6 /1, 1247.)

WSC was defending the government in the failing Norwegian campaign.

Truths and causes

The dominant forces in human history have come from the perception of great truths and the faithful pursuance of great causes.

1950, 28 MARCH.

Tyranny

Always be on guard against tyranny, whatever shape it may assume.

1945, 15 NOVEMBER. BRUSSELS UNIVERSITY.
(SINEWS, 38.)

Unexpected

The element of the unexpected and the unforeseeable...saves us from falling into the mechanical thraldom of the logicians.

1946, 7 MAY. LONDON. (SINEWS, 123.)

Speech on receiving the Freedom of Westminster.

Unteachable mankind

Unteachable from infancy to tomb—There is the first and main characteristic of mankind.

1928, 21 MAY, EXCHEQUER. (OB, CV5/1, 1291.)

Letter to Lord Beaverbrook after reading Beaverbrook's Politicians and the War. *Previous to this statement Churchill had written:*

Think of all these people—decent, educated, the story of the past laid out before them—What to avoid—what to do etc.—patriotic, loyal, clean—trying their utmost—What a ghastly muddle they made of it!

At the end of his letter WSC added: "No more War." In Virginia in 1946 WSC told the state General Assembly: "It has been said that the dominant lesson of history is that mankind is unteachable." The operative word, and his use of it in 1928 and

1929 (see Chapter 11, Nations of the World...Canada/1929), leads me to believe WSC himself was the first sayer.

Vanquished enemies

If you want your horse to pull your wagon, you have to give him some hay.

1945, 5 FEBRUARY, YALTA. (GILBERT, LIFE, 818.)

Churchill was arguing against demanding extreme reparations by Germany, like those which followed World War I.

Vengeance

Nothing is more costly, nothing is more sterile, than vengeance.

1946, 5 JUNE.

Vengeance is the most costly and dissipating of luxuries.

1948, 10 DECEMBER.

Victory's problems

The problems of victory are more agreeable than those of defeat, but they are no less difficult.

1942, 11 NOVEMBER. (END, 290.)

Virtue vs. wickedness

Virtuous motives, trammelled by inertia and timidity, are no match for armed and resolute wickedness.

1948. (WW2 I, 149.)

He added:

A sincere love of peace is no excuse for muddling hundreds of millions of humble folk into total war.

Virtuous circle

[Tax relief] will substitute a virtuous circle for the vicious circle.

1928, 24 APRIL. BROADCAST, LONDON.
(CS IV, 4400.)

Speaking of rate reductions for coal, coke and patent fuel, mining timber, iron stone, iron ore and manganese ore, and limestone for blast furnaces and steel works.

War and democracy

We have had nothing else but wars since democracy took charge.

1947. (OB VIII, 369.)

This remark (see Chapter 5, Anecdotes and Stories...The Dream) displays a certain misgiving over democracy, manifested throughout Churchill's life. He thought, for example, that a meeting among kings and heads of state might have prevented World War I; that a plenary session between the Big Three might have quelled the Cold War – regardless of what democratic bodies did.

War and peace

...those who can win a war well can rarely make a good peace, and those who could make a good peace would never have won the war.

1930. (MEL, 346.)

WSC added: "It would perhaps be pressing the argument too far to suggest that I could do both." A remarkable precedent to his feelings fifteen years later, when he was dismissed by his country after winning the war to come.

War wounds

Nobody is ever wounded twice on the same day.

1899, SOUTH AFRICA. (TAYLOR, 173.)

Churchill said this to the engineer of the armoured train when ambushed by the Boers near Chieveley. He later recommended the engineer, who stayed calm and eventually drove the locomotive away, for the Albert Medal.

Weakness and treason

Weakness is not treason, though it may be equally disastrous.

1948. (WW2 I, 154.)

Wealth and commonwealth

To hunt wealth is not to capture commonwealth.

1934, 29 DECEMBER. ("ROOSEVELT FROM AFAR," COLLIERS; GC REV. ED., 241.)

Wealth and poverty

The production of new wealth must precede commonwealth, otherwise there will only be common poverty.

1945, 16 AUGUST.

You may try to destroy wealth, and find that all you have done is to increase poverty.

1947, 12 MARCH.

Wicked and dictators

The wicked are not always clever, nor are dictators always right.

1950. (WW2 III, 329.)

Win or lose

If we win, nobody will care. If we lose, there will be nobody *to* care.

1941, 25 JUNE.

Wisdom

All wisdom is not new wisdom.

1938, 5 OCTOBER.

Churchill used the maxim several times in his speeches from 1938 to 1947; this is the first appearance.

It would be great reform in politics if wisdom could be made to spread as easily and as rapidly as folly.

1947, 10 SEPTEMBER.

Women

It is hard, if not impossible, to snub a beautiful woman; they remain beautiful and the rebuke recoils.

1900. (SAVROLA, 57.)

Work

It is no use doing what you like; you have got to like what you do.

1925, DECEMBER. ("HOBBIES," PALL MALL; THOUGHTS, 217.)

Many things are learnt by those who live their whole lives with their main work...

1928, AUGUST. ("HERBERT HENRY ASQUITH," PALL MALL; GC, 86.)

World War II: 1940

But nothing surpasses 1940.

1949. (WW2 II, 555.)

For the full context of this maxim, see Chapter 6, Britain and Empire ... achievement.

World War II: Moral

In war, Resolution. In defeat, Defiance. In victory, Magnanimity. In peace, Goodwill.

1930. (MEL, 346.)

Churchill first published this moral in his 1930 autobiography, stating that he had offered it for a war memorial in France, but that it was not accepted. He did not forget, and deployed it as the moral for his WW2 memoirs. The first phrase was originally "In war, Fury".

Wrongdoing

…it is always very difficult to know, when you embark on the path of wrongdoing, exactly where to stop.

1911, 22 FEBRUARY.

Youth

…Youth, Youth, Youth; efficient youth marching forward from service in the field…

1944, 29 NOVEMBER. (DAWN, 260.)

Misquoted by Harold Nicolson in his diary as "Youth, youth, youth and renovation, energy, boundless energy."

3

CHURCHILLISMS

*"I had picked up a wide vocabulary and had a liking for words
and for the feel of words fitting and falling into their places like
pennies in a slot."* [20]

"Most sensible suit I ever had. Did you know that I designed it myself?"
At Chartwell, ca. 1950.

Churchill's love of English was nowhere more agreeably expressed than in words and expressions he created – or old lines to which he gave new life. All those herein are ones he invented, including Battle of the Bulge, Minimum Standard and Naval Holiday. Expressions he did not invent but made famous, such as "Iron Curtain", are in the next chapter.

Remarkable for a man of his abilities, Churchill had no university training and was weak, though not illiterate, in Latin. He derived his vocabulary from voracious reading, from the adventure stories of George Alfred Henty and Robert Louis Stevenson, to Gibbon's and Macaulay's histories, to the learned works of Plato, Darwin and Malthus. With a potent memory he absorbed *Bartlett's Familiar Quotations*, the Parliamentary Debates, whole tracts of Shakespeare and Macaulay.[21] The King James Bible, Darrell Holley wrote, was Churchill's "primary source of interesting illustrations, descriptive images, and stirring phrases … For him it is the *magnum opus* of Western civilization…"[22]

---

20 WSC, MEL, 124.
21 For more details on his self-education, see the introduction to Chapter 24.
22 Holley, 7.

Old words, he said, were the best of all, and he indulged in them: correctitude, palimpsest, parlementaire, guttersnipe, purblind. If a word didn't exist to suit him, he would invent one: paintatious, improvose, Namsosed, bottlescape. When Churchill wished to "destrigulate" (deadhead) the rhododendrons, his meaning was clear to friends, though the word is unknown to lexicographers. WSC would also create new words out of common ones: "re-rat" for deserting your party the second time, "fearthought" for futile worrying. His French was much better than he let on, and he was not above inventing French words too, as in his threat to de Gaulle: "*je vous liquiderai*".

Churchill's curiosity about words produced his best creations. If a worthy individual received a peerage, why not give the unworthy a "disappearage"? There were the words "inchoate" and "abyss" – so why not "choate" and "byss"? City names often end in "-opolis"; so a cotton town could be nicknamed "Cottonopolis". If there were generalis-simos in the Army, why not admiralissimos in the Navy? Socialists strive for utopias, but produce only "queuetopias". The prefix "un-" was of special interest, as in "unsordid" for America's Lend-Lease bill during World War II, or "undisinflation" when he mocked a colleague's jargon. We can imagine what he would think about Politically Correct fad-words, such as "issues" instead of "difficulties". Difficulties are fine, he said; they argue "perfectly well for themselves" (previous chapter).

His usage was whimsical as well as inventive, as for example when he named his hen coop "Chickenham Palace"; or when he compared people to llamas, eagles, bulldogs, pugs and bees; or used their names to describe their functions: his chauffeur Bullock drove "the bullock cart". Playing on names was a hobby: "Can'tellopolus" for Greek Prime Minister Kanellopoulos, "Prince Palsy" for Paul of Yugoslavia. Thanks to Churchill, the name of Norway's fascist ruler, Quisling, entered dictionaries as a synonym for traitor. It is not proven that Churchill called John Foster Dulles "dull, duller, Dulles" (see Appendix I), but it would have been just like him.

He was fond of alliteration, speaking of the age of "gape and gloat", of "dull, drilled, docile" German soldiery. He liked to turn common expressions on their heads: "mouth to hand" and "preach what we practise". Or he would tweak a common phrase to suit his purpose: Japan's goal was to "make hell while the sun shines". Venereal disease was "Pox Britannica". There was a prison called Wormwood Scrubs, and the Labour Party would "reduce us to one vast Wormwood Scrubbery". Wishing for songs like those of World War I during World War II, he wryly contemplated "Stop the Home Fires Burning".

Then there are those novel word-combinations that nobody else ever seemed to think of – anticipatory plagiarism (for an idea expressed by someone before him), terminological inex-actitude, drizzle of empires, canting bus driver, wincing marquis, epileptic corpse – and that wonderful line from Hoe Farm in June 1915: "The garden gleams with summer jewelry."

Of the 367 Churchill citations in the second (current) edition of the *Oxford English Dictionary*, quite a few are Churchill's contributions to English lexicography: parlemen-taire, revirement, roulement, quislings, sangared, triphibian. Although the etymology of the first three is French, they are all now English words.

Admiralissimo

Yamamoto, the Japanese Admiralissimo, was preparing to challenge American power in the Central Pacific by seizing Midway Island...

1951. (WW2 IV, 220.)

"Generalissimo" is in most dictionaries, but not "Admiralissmo"; the Oxford English Dictionary *credits it to Churchill.*

Afterlight

Judged in afterlight these views can hardly be contested.

1923. (CRISIS I, 493.)

Churchill also used "afterlight" in Marlborough, Great Contemporaries *and* The Second World War.

All for Al

Al for All, and All for Al.

1928, 10 AUGUST. (SOAMES, SPEAKING, 327.)

Alfred E. Smith (1873–1944), four-term Governor of New York, Democratic presidential candidate, 1928. Churchill offered this slogan to his friend Bernard Baruch for Smith's campaign. WSC privately favoured the Democrat in every US Presidential election from 1912.

All sound and all nonsense

The Socialists have spared no expense in producing a policy for the next election. There is a great deal in it that is sound sense, as well as a lot more that is all sound and all nonsense.

1959, 20 MARCH, WOODFORD, ESSEX.
(ALLIANCE, 312.)

American Eagle and Bulldog

For Mark Clark and Bedell Smith, the latter of whom arrived early in September as Chief of Staff to Eisenhower, I coined the titles "the American Eagle" and "the American Bulldog". You have to look at their photographs to see why.

1951. (WW2 IV, 472.)

Amiable malice

[Mr. Lloyd George], forgetting himself for a moment, and, perhaps, with a certain vein of amiable malice which came to the top at the moment, said that there was a vulgar and ill-informed agitation and stunt on this subject, and so on.

1927, 13 APRIL.

Anti-complacency opinion

All the disadvantages are not on one side, and certainly they are not all on our side. I think that conforms to the standards of anti-complacency opinion in this country.

1943, 11 FEBRUARY.

Anticipatory plagiarism

Mr. Lowe seems to have been walking over my footsteps before I had trodden them, because he said, trying to explain what had occurred to the satisfaction of a very strict House in those days: "And so each year will take money from its successor, and this process may go on till the end of time, although how it will be settled when the world comes to an end I am at loss to know." It was unconscious anticipatory plagiarism.

1927, 19 MAY.

A droll way to admit someone had an idea before you. Robert Lowe, First Viscount Sherbrooke (1811–92), Liberal MP (1852–80), Gladstone's Chancellor of the Exchequer, 1868–73. WSC admired him, and undoubtedly his 1870 remark:

The Chancellor of the Exchequer is a man whose duties make him more or less of a taxing machine. He is entrusted with a certain amount of misery which it is his duty to distribute as fairly as he can.

Battle of the Bulge

Evidently this battle will be known as the Battle of the Bulge.

1940, 16 MAY, PARIS. (ISMAY, 127.)

Churchill's use of this phrase preceded by more than four years Hitler's attempted breakout, in the selfsame Ardennes Forest where the Germans broke through in 1940. WSC made this remark to French General Gamelin, slapping him "heartily on the shoulder (the General winced)", according General Ismay. Churchill did not recall the French term for "bulge" (saillant) and satisfied himself with "boolge".

Bees of Hell

At the Ministry of Munitions we were the bees of Hell, and we stored our hives with the pure essence of slaughter. It astonishes me to read in these after years the diabolical schemes for killing men on a vast scale by machinery or chemistry to which we passionately devoted ourselves.

1927. (CRISIS III PART 2, 481–2.)

Blood, toil, tears and sweat

I have nothing to offer but blood, toil, tears and sweat.

1940, 13 MAY.

See Appendix II for the long trail of origins of this phrase and variations thereof, which Churchill was evolving as early as 1900 and can be traced as far back as Cicero and Livy ("sweat and blood"), the poet John Donne in 1611 ("...thy Teares, or Sweat, or Bloud".) See also Keyes, 15–16, 28.

Blood, toil, tears and sweat (addendum)

I stand by my original programme, blood, toil, tears and sweat...to which I added five months later, "many shortcomings, mistakes and disappointments".

1942, 27 JANUARY.

Bloodthirsty guttersnipe

So now this bloodthirsty guttersnipe must launch his mechanized armies upon new fields of slaughter, pillage and devastation.

1941, 22 JUNE. BROADCAST, LONDON.
(UNRELENTING, 171.)

A reference to Hitler, made famous when he invaded the Soviet Union in June 1941.

Boneless Wonder

I remember when I was a child, being taken to the celebrated Barnum's circus, which contained an exhibition of freaks and monstrosities, but the exhibit...which I most desired to see was the one described as "The Boneless Wonder." My parents judged that that spectacle would be too revolting and demoralising for my youthful eyes, and I have waited 50 years to see the Boneless Wonder sitting on the Treasury Bench.

1931, 28 JANUARY.

Said of Prime Minister Ramsay MacDonald (see also Chapter 20, People).

Bottlescape

This is my bottlescape.

PASSIM.

The word was invented as a title for his famous still life of bottles. See Chapter 25, Painting...Still life for Churchill's command to the children looking for bottles for the painting.

British Restaurants

I hope the term "Communal Feeding Centres" is not going to be adopted. It is an odious expression, suggestive of Communism and the workhouse. I suggest you call them "British Restaurants." Everybody associates the word "restaurant" with a good meal, and they may as well have the name if they cannot get anything else.

1941, 21 MARCH. (WW2 III, 663.)

WSC to Minister of Food.

Bullock cart

I think I'll have the Bullock cart.

1950S. (HAMBLIN, CHURCHILL PROCEEDINGS 1987.)

Secretary Grace Hamblin explained that this referred to a large Humber, furnished by the government pool, that usually took Churchill back and forth to London, driven by a chauffeur whose name was Bullock.

"Byss"

I had a feeling once about Mathematics, that I saw it all—Depth beyond depth was revealed to me—the Byss and the Abyss.

1930. (MEL, 41.)

For more of this quotation see Chapter 24, Education...Mathematics. For a related invention, see "Choate" below.

Camel and gnats

I have heard of people aiming at a gnat and swallowing a camel, but I have never before heard of people who, having already swallowed a camel, come forward and plead that their gullets are not sufficiently expansive to accommodate a gnat.

1910, 12 APRIL.

WSC was moving a modest amendment to a major bill. The phrase may not originate with WSC ("I have heard..."), but he liked it well enough to repeat it at least twice...

The three programmes of 1912, 1913 and 1914 comprised the greatest additions in power and cost ever made to the Royal Navy.... the supreme ships of the Navy, on which our life depended, were fed by oil and could only be fed by oil. The decision to drive the smaller craft by oil followed naturally upon this. The camel once swallowed, the gnats went down easily enough.

1923. (CRISIS I, 131.)

Now that I have shown Hon. Members the camel they have already swallowed, I hope they will address themselves with renewed sense of proportion to this somewhat inconsiderable gnat.

1941, 27 FEBRUARY.

This "camel" was relieving newly appointed ministers from the requirement to run for office in a by-election. The "gnat" was defining "office of profit" to mean profit to the State, not the office-holder.

Can'tellopolus

Kanellopoulos, Can'tellopolus, Kantellopolous ....All right. I'll see him!

1942, AUGUST, CAIRO. (EDEN, A., 339.)

Panagiotis Kanellopoulos (1902–86), Greek Prime Minister, 1945 and 1967. Churchill often invented his own words for various Greek politicians. Sir Alexander Cadogan, Undersecretary of State for Foreign Affairs, heard these mutterings from Churchill's bathroom, between the splashings and gurgles. For another Greek twist see Chapter 33, Ripostes...Feet of Clay.

Canting bus driver

Never let me see that-that-that canting bus-driver again.

1941. ("CHURCHILL THE CONVERSATIONALIST," COLLIN BROOKS IN EADE, 246.)

WSC wrote this (in red ink) of Frank Pick, head of the London Passenger Transport Board, to Minister of Information Duff Cooper after hearing that Pick had been relieved of his post. See Chapter 20, People...Pick.

Capacious harangue

After listening to his [Mr. William Graham's] capacious harangue and its immaculate delivery, one would never have thought that the speaker was the representative of an Administration which, having reduced this country almost to beggary, had fled from their posts in terror of the consequences which were approaching them.

1931, 15 SEPTEMBER.

William Graham (1887–1932) was a Scottish Labour MP, then President of the Board of Trade.

Chattering little cad

Personally, I think Lloyd George a vulgar, chattering little cad...

1901, 23 DECEMBER. (OB, CVI/2, 104.)

WSC to J. Moore Bayley (1858–1911), a solicitor and Conservative politician and an admirer of WSC's father, Lord Randolph Churchill. Churchill's attitude was soon to change as he became, first Lloyd George's fellow Liberal, then his disciple, then his co-campaigner against privilege and for the Welfare State, and finally a Cabinet minister in Lloyd George's governments.

Cheeked, abused and girded

Britain has always floated upon her Navy. Her great Indian Empire has gone down one drain, and now the Admiralty proclaims that the British Home Fleet has gone down another. Can you wonder, with these weapons, that you are cheeked by Chile, abused by the Argentine and girded at by Guatemala?

1948, 8 MARCH. (EUROPE, 268.)

A fine example of alliteration, as WSC protested the diminution of the Royal Navy by the post-war Labour Government.

Chew barbed wire

Are there not other alternatives than sending our armies to chew barbed wire in Flanders?

1914, 29 DECEMBER. (GILBERT, JEWS, 25.)

WSC to Asquith, advocating an alternative to trench warfare.

Chickenham Palace Gardens

It's called Chickenham Palace. [And, pointing to a "noisome and messy little piece of bare ground":] And that is Chickenham Palace Gardens.

1949. (GILBERT, SEARCH, 313.)

From Sir Archibald Sinclair's account to Lord Beaverbrook, after a visit to Chartwell:

> *He took me around the farms, showed me shorthorns and Jerseys and then a brick hen house he had built himself: Chickenham Palace ... What kind of hens? I asked. "Oh, I don't bother about the details," growled Winston.*

Choate

How could the peoples know?....What choate and integral conviction could they form?

1929. (CRISIS IV, 127–8; ROWSE, 400.)

A. L. Rowse wrote:

Eddie [Marsh] brought down an infuriated mob of grammarians upon Winston's head by passing the word "choate" which the latter deemed to exist: "inchoate" existed, what more natural than to suppose therefore that there must be a word "choate"?....[Eddie] thought it a useful addition to the language.

Chumbolly

The Chumbolly must do his duty and help you with your milk, you are to tell him so from me. At his age greediness and even swinishness at table are virtues.

1911, 2 JUNE. (OB, CV 2/2, 1087.)

WSC to Clementine ("my precious pussy cat") shortly after the birth of his son Randolph, to whom they gave this evocative nickname. Other nicknames for children were evocative but not as unique: "mule" (Sarah) and "cream-gold kitten" (Marigold).

Clatter and buzz, gape and gloat

A man or woman earnestly seeking a grown-up life…will make the best of all the pupils in this age of clatter and buzz, of gape and gloat.

1953, 11 MARCH. PAUL ADDISON TO THE EDITOR, QUOTING THE LETTER IN PREM 11/35, PUBLIC RECORDS OFFICE.

WSC to Florence Horsbrugh, Minister for Education 1951–54. The Trades Union Congress received Churchill's permission to reproduce the letter, which appeared in their 1953 Annual Report, pp. 173–4.

Collective ideologists

…collective ideologists (those professional intellectuals who revel in decimals and polysyllables).

1953, 10 OCTOBER. CONSERVATIVE PARTY CONFERENCE, MARGATE. (ALLIANCE, 61.)

Correctitude

…while observing every form of official correctitude he sought ruthlessly "the way out."

1931, NOVEMBER ("THE U-BOAT WAR," DAILY TELEGRAPH; THOUGHTS, 90.)

A favourite nineteenth-century word, "correctitude" appears a dozen times in his writings: a combination of "correct" and "rectitude".

Cottonopolis

[We are] dependent absolutely for the maintenance of that marvellous structure of Lancashire industry, which is the wonder of the world and which has located Cottonopolis here in this unexpected spot; dependent absolutely upon the free imports of food and raw material.

1909, 6 DECEMBER, FREE TRADE HALL, MANCHESTER. (CS II, 1380; CRISIS V, 246.)

This is the first of two instances of "Cottonopolis". In The Aftermath, *Churchill used it to describe Lodz in central Europe.*

Destrigulate

1938, MARCH. (HASSALL, 612.)

Eddie Marsh, Churchill's private secretary, used the term "destrigulating the rhododendrons" (deadheading stalks, snatching out the shrivelled blossoms) – a word he said had been coined by Churchill. "Could one ever be said to destrigulate redundant epithets?" someone asked him. "Certainly not," Eddie replied, "the word is strictly horticultural."

Disappearage

No, but perhaps a disappearage…

1953, 14 AUGUST. (COLVILLE, FRINGES, 675.)

To his son-in-law Christopher Soames, who suggested that Sir Harry Mackeson, a Conservative MP, should be relieved as Secretary for Overseas Trade, but did not deserve a peerage.

Dismal Desmonds

Again and again the Chancellor [Sir Stafford Cripps] was warned from this side of the House and by financial authorities outside that he was living in a fool's paradise. But all these warnings were in vain. I think he made some remark about "Dismal Desmonds." Was that his phrase or did one of his colleagues achieve this alliterative gem?

1949, 28 SEPTEMBER.

"Dismal Desmond" was a pre-World War II toy dog, pink with droopy ears. A stylist as fond of alliteration as Churchill inevitably focused on the term.

Drinkable address

44 Avenue de Champagne is the world's most drinkable address.

1947, EPERNAY, FRANCE.

Declared to Odette Pol-Roger concerning the address of his favourite producer of bubbly, Pol Roger Champagne. Christian Pol-Roger to the editor.

Drizzle of empires

A drizzle of empires, falling through the air.

1918, 30 OCTOBER. (HASSALL, 456.)

Churchill to Eddie Marsh, after the surrender of Turkey on 29 October 1918: "It was yesterday that Turkey gave in," Marsh wrote, "and it will be Austria tomorrow."

Dull, drilled, docile

I see also the dull, drilled, docile, brutish masses of the Hun soldiery plodding on like a swarm of crawling locusts.

1941, 22 JUNE. BROADCAST, LONDON.
(UNRELENTING, 172.)

Superb alliteration was a memorable part of this famous speech on the German invasion of Russia.

Earl Marshal/Air Marshal

What a relief to be confronted by an Earl Marshal instead of an Air Marshal.

1940, DECEMBER. (COLVILLE, CHURCHILLIANS, 77.)

Remark to the Duke of Norfolk, referring to the constant confrontations Churchill was being forced to bear between his friend Max Beaverbrook, Minister of Aircraft Production, and the air marshals of the RAF. See also Chapter 20, People...Beaverbrook.

Earthly palimpsest

The trenches criss-cross one another; the monuments of dead commanders and shot-torn regiments are of different years. An earthly palimpsest of tragedy!

1929, 16 DECEMBER. ("WHAT I SAW AND HEARD IN AMERICA," DAILY TELEGRAPH; ESSAYS IV, 47.)

Not a new word, but an obscure and lovely one. A palimpsest is a manuscript written over a partially obscured older manuscript in such a way that the original writing can still be read under the newer writing. Used here to describe American Civil War battlefields, it was revived in 1947, when WSC used it to denounce the Labour Government. See Chapter 4, Writer and Speaker...expressions.

Epileptic corpse

He is no better than an epileptic corpse.

1936. (HALLE, IRREPRESSIBLE, 131.)

Berating Baldwin for failing to tell the truth about German rearmament.

Fearthought

Fearthought is futile worrying over what cannot be averted or will probably never happen.

1937, 15 OCTOBER. ("WAR IS NOT IMMINENT," EVENING STANDARD; STEP, 164.)

Female llama

A female llama who has been surprised in her bath.

1959, 6 DECEMBER. (MORAN, 313.)

Moran wrote:

Was it true, [Lady Limerick] asked, that he had likened de Gaulle to a female llama who had been surprised in her bath? Winston pouted, smiled and shook his head. But his way of disavowing the remark convinced me that he was in fact responsible for this indiscretion, though on reflection he might not care to have it attributed to him.

Freaks of fortune

I am afraid I cannot give any explanation of the freaks of fortune in the world.

1910, 20 APRIL.

Ghostly but glittering

The battlefields were wonderful...and I was able to re-people them with ghostly but glittering armies. A surprise was their great size. Ramillies, Oudenarde and Blenheim all seemed to me bigger than Austerlitz or Gettysburg, and far bigger than Waterloo.

1932, 19 SEPTEMBER, SALZBURG. (OB, CV5/2, 475.)

To historian Keith Feiling, during WSC's visit to Marlborough's battlefields. Again alliteration produces the perfect image.

Glittering pall

Over the landscape, brilliant with sunshine, snow had spread a glittering pall.

1906. (LRC, 820.)

Glittering scum

Cultured people are merely the glittering scum which floats upon the deep river of production.

1929, 26 AUGUST, CALGARY, ALBERTA. (GILBERT, LIFE, 493.)

Churchill's retort to his son Randolph, who remarked after visiting the oilfields of Alberta that oil magnates were too uncultured to know how to spend their money properly.

Gospeller

Like Henry VIII, he decapitated Papists and burned hot Gospellers on the same day for their respective divergences in opposite directions from his central, personal and artificial compromise.

1923. (CRISIS I, 29.)

Gradgrind and Dryasdust

We reject, however, with scorn all those learned and laboured myths that Moses was but a legendary figure...We remain unmoved by the tomes of Professor Gradgrind and Dr. Dryasdust.

1931, 8 NOVEMBER. ("MOSES," *SUNDAY CHRONICLE*; THOUGHTS, 214.)

"Gradgrind" is a severe schoolmaster in Dickens's Hard Times. *"Dryasdust" comes from both Scott (1771–1832) and Carlyle (1795–1881), whose introductory chapter to Oliver Cromwell's* Letters and Speeches *is entitled, "Anti-Dryasdust". In a 1933 letter to*

WSC, Alfred Duff Cooper compared Churchill's life of Marlborough *favourably to works of "the Dryasdust cold-blooded historian".*

Great state of affairs

Come in, come in, but tell me of no great affairs of State. There are none. There is only a great state of affairs.

1951. (CAWTHORNE, 41.)

Improvose and dore

[Churchill to his naval aide:] I sent him a signal—"Improvise and dare"....He improvose and dore.

1943, 24 NOVEMBER. (PAWLE, 266.)

An example of playing with English: WSC made words where lexicographers fear to tread. General Sir Henry Maitland ("Jumbo") Wilson, Commander-in-Chief Middle East, had defended with few troops the Greek island of Leros.

Irishism

As I said the other night in the small hours of the morning... [Laughter]. That is an Irishism; I mean the other *day* in the small hours of the morning.

1925, 12 DECEMBER.

Je vous liquiderai

Si vous m'obstaclerez, je vous liquiderai!

1943, 5 JULY. (KERSAUDY, 248; NICOLSON II, 303.)

While "liquider" is a normal French word, there is no verb "obstacler"; WSC again makes a verb out of a noun. This is de Gaulle's version (Kersaudy); Harold Nicolson quoted it in proper French but I believe de Gaulle's is more authentic. Churchill's words were even more mangled recently by The Times Literary Supplement: *"Et, marquez mes mots, mon ami – si vous me double-crosserez, je vous liquiderai."*

Klop

When I say "Klop," Miss Shearburn, that is what I want.
[At other times:] Gimme klop!

PASSIM. ("SECRETARY TO CHURCHILL," MARY T. G. THOMPSON, IN EADE, 158; GILBERT, SEARCH, 300.)

WSC had an aversion to staples and paper clips, and preferred his documents to be "klopped" and joined by a "treasury tag". When an earlier secretary, Kathleen Hill, was first asked for "klop", she proudly produced the 15-volume Der Fall des Hauses Stuart *by the German historian Onno Klopp (1822–1903). "Christ almighty!" WSC roared.*

Lay an egg

I've been living on the Second World War. Now I shall live on this history [of the English Speaking Peoples]. I shall lay an egg a year— a volume every twelve months should not mean much work.

1953, 19 AUGUST. MORAN, 486.

"Now in my business, 'laying an egg' has a rather different connotation." (Actor Robert Hardy in an address to the Churchill Centre, San Francisco, 1991.)

Lion-hearted limpets

It is hard on any country when no one is looking after it. Mr. Attlee combines a limited outlook with strong qualities of resistance. He now resumes the direction and leadership of that cluster of lion-hearted limpets…who are united by their desire to hold on to office at all costs to their own reputations and their country's fortunes, and to put off by every means in their power to the last possible moment any contact with our democratic electorate.

1951, 27 APRIL. PRIMROSE LEAGUE, ALBERT HALL, LONDON. (CS VIII, 8196.)

Prime Minister Attlee had returned to Parliament from a brief hospitalisation.

Lush disorganisation

Pray remember that the British people are no longer in a mood to tolerate such lush disorganisation.

1943. (CAWTHORNE, 69.)

Magic of averages

There is exhilaration in the study of insurance questions because there is a sense of elaborating new and increased powers which have been devoted to the service of mankind. It is not only a question of order in the face of confusion. It is not only a question of collective strength of the nation to render effective the thrift and the exertions of the individual,

but we bring in the magic of averages to the aid of the million.

1911, 25 MAY. (CS II, 1819.)

First occurrence of a phrase Churchill used on at least eight different occasions with respect to national insurance, between 1911 and 1948. He also referred to "the doctrine of averages" in a letter to his mother (6 April 1897), remarking on not being killed in the Malakand expedition.

Make hell while the sun shines

…it may be that the Japanese, whose game is what I may call "to make hell while the sun shines," are more likely to occupy themselves in…seizing island bases for defensive purposes…

1942, 27 JANUARY.

Microphone and murder

These men [Mussolini and Hitler] of the microphone and murder…

1936, NOVEMBER. (YOUNG, 124.).

Churchill at his alliterative best, as reported by Frank Owen, later editor of the London Evening Standard *(1938–41). Sent to Owen's boss, Lord Beaverbrook, it was forwarded to Churchill in jest – partly. Owen had also reported:*

> *…we had a strenuous defence from Winston of Liberal Democracy (with the working classes in their appropriate place).*

Minimum Standard

Dimly across gulfs of ignorance I see the outline of a policy which I call the Minimum Standard. It is national rather than departmental. I am doubtful of my power to give it concrete expression. If I did, I expect before long I should find myself in collision with some of my best friends like for instance John Morley, who at the end of a lifetime of study and thought has come to the conclusion that nothing can be done.

1908, 14 MARCH, COLONIAL OFFICE. (OB, CV2/2, 755.)

WSC to H. H. Asquith, referring to unemployment insurance, which, in the later Liberal Government under Asquith, he would have a role in creating.

Mock-turtle soup

This contest is between "the turtle soup of Tory Imperialism and the mock-turtle soup of Liberal Imperialism."

1900. (BROAD, 31.)

Churchill speaking at the Oldham election in 1900, his second attempt at the seat which, this time, he won.

Mouth to hand

I lived in fact from mouth to hand.

1948. (WW2 I, 62.)

Churchill loved to turn common expressions on their ends. See also: Preach what we practise.

Munitionless retreat

The devoted onset of the Russian armies which saved Paris in 1914; the mastered agony of the munitionless retreat....has [Nicholas II] no share in these?

1927. (CRISIS III PART 1, 224.)

Mush, Slush and Gush

The cause of disarmament will not be attained by Mush, Slush and Gush. It will be advanced steadily by the harassing expense of fleets and armies, and by the growth of confidence in a long peace.

1932, 26 MAY. ("SOME PLAIN SPEAKING ABOUT GENEVA," DAILY MAIL; ESSAYS I, 299.)

Namsosed

We shall need skis for that [landing again on the coast of Norway] and we don't want to go and get Namsosed again. We've had enough of that.

1940, 9 AUGUST. CHEQUERS. (OB, CV6/2, 639, 745, 764.)

WSC refers to the outcome of operations where the enemy have control over the air, such as Namsos, Norway, north of Trondheim, where the British were thrown back in April 1940. On 30 August, WSC said airborne radar would prevent "being Namsosed again"; on 3 September he thought "The Army will be able to land at many points without the risk of being Namsosed."

Naval holiday

Before the war I proposed to [head of the German Navy] von Tirpitz a naval holiday. If this had been accepted, it would enormously have eased the European tension, and possibly have averted the catastrophe.

1937, 17 SEPTEMBER. ("FRIENDSHIP WITH GERMANY," EVENING STANDARD; STEP, 155.)

WSC meant a temporary stoppage in German and British new battleship construction; proposed in 1911, it was rejected by the Germans.

Nettle and the dock

In looking at the views of these two Hon. Members I have always marvelled at the economy of nature which had contrived to grow from a single stock the nettle and the dock.

1905, 24 JULY.

Edgar Vincent, First Viscount D'Abernon (1857–1941), Conservative MP 1899–1906, was a diplomat. His brother, Sir Charles Edward Howard Vincent (1849–1908), Conservative MP 1885–1908, was a soldier.

Nickel lining

And now the British housewife, as she stands in the queue to buy her bread ration, will fumble in her pocket in vain for a silver sixpence. Under the Socialist Government nickel will have to be good enough for her. In future we shall be able to say: "Every cloud has a nickel lining."

1946, 5 OCTOBER, BLACKPOOL.

On the Labour Government's decision to mint sixpence coins made of nickel.

Non-undisincentive

We should call it a non-undisincentive.

1950, 22 JUNE.

Stafford Cripps, then Chancellor of the Exchequer, had called the purchase tax a "disincentive". When a Tory MP said he thought the tax was not a fiscal weapon, WSC interjected his own description of it.

Non-undisinflation

The word "disinflation" has been coined in order to avoid the unpopular term "deflation"....I suppose that presently when "disinflation" also wins its bad name, the Chancellor [Sir Stafford Cripps] will call it "non-undisinflation" and will start again.

1949, 27 OCTOBER.

Obsolesce into obsoleteness

If it was not passed, the docks, which already have become obsolescent will have to be allowed to obsolesce into obsoleteness.

1908, 12 NOVEMBER. (CS II, 1127.)

Churchill wanted government control over London's dock facilities.

Old turnip

Well, the light is at last out of that old turnip.

1937. (HALLE, IRREPRESSIBLE, 134.)

Referring to Stanley Baldwin, who appeared in the House of Commons Smoking Room after having resigned as Prime Minister.

Order of the Boot

How can I accept the Order of the Garter, when the people of England have just given me the Order of the Boot?

1945, SEPTEMBER. (FISHMAN, 296; CHARMLEY, 647.)

WSC declining the Garter from King George VI following the 1945 election. Remarkably, this famous remark has a doubtful pedigree, occurring only twice in the scanned litera-ture: Jack Fishman's often inaccurate My Darling Clementine *and John Charmley's much better researched* Churchill: The End of Glory. *Neither cites attribution. Fishman incorrectly states that the King had offered Churchill the Order of the Bath...in which case Churchill would have had a "cold water" quip...*

Paintatious

This is a most paintatious place!

PASSIM. (SOAMES, CLEMENTINE, 204.)

Used throughout his years as a painter (1915–58). In Clementine Churchill, *Mary Soames writes of a holiday in 1921:*

> *...he continually felt drawn to "painta-tious" (his own adjective) places, where the sun might be expected to shine brightly and continuously.*

Parlementaire

At dawn on the 21st General Klopper sent out a parlementaire with an offer to capitulate, and at 7.45 a.m. German officers came to his head-quarters and accepted his surrender.

1951. (WW2 IV, 376.)

On the British surrender of Tobruk in June 1942. The word, like "revirement" following, found its way into the Oxford *English* Dictionary *thanks to Churchill. It means some-one who comes to parley or discuss a truce.*

Pelf

It is a g[rea]t chance to put my whole case in an agreeable form to an attentive audience. And the pelf will make us feel v[er]y comfort-able. Therefore when darkness falls, behold me in my burry, writing, dictating & sifting papers like the Editor of a ha'penny paper.

1921, 29 DECEMBER, CANNES. (OB, CV4/3, 1707.)

WSC to his wife, on the writing of The World Crisis 1916–1918:

> *LG [Lloyd George] read two of my chap-ters in the train & was well content with the references to himself.*

While the word "pelf", a Middle English term taken from the French "pelfre" for "spoils", is not Churchill's, it displays the depth of his self-education. The nearest definition to what he meant here is "filthy lucre", thus the verb "to pilfer".

Pink pansies

They are no more than a set of pink pansies.

1945, 19 DECEMBER. (NICOLSON 1907–63, 330.)

WSC to Malcolm Bullock on younger members of the Tory Party. Harold Nicolson commented:

> *His sense of the combative renders him insensitive to the gentle gradations of the human mind.*

Pox Britannica

Pox Britannica!

1907. (DALTON, "WINSTON: A MEMOIR," NEW STATESMAN, 1965.)

On his African journey, Churchill was informed by a Colonial governor of the alarming spread of venereal disease among the natives.

Preach what we practise

Let us preach what we practise—let us practise what we preach.

> 1945, 5 MARCH. WESTMINSTER COLLEGE, FULTON, MISSOURI. (SINEWS, 97.)

Prince Palsy

Our intervention in Greece caused the revolution in Yugoslavia which drove out Prince "Palsy", and delayed the German invasion of Russia by six weeks.

> 1941, 26 MARCH. (BOOTHBY, 61.)

Prince Paul of Yugoslavia (1893–1976) was regent of Yugoslavia for King Peter II from 1934 until he signed a pact with Nazi Germany in March 1941. Resulting protests caused him to flee, a pro-British government took over, but Yugoslavia was soon attacked by Hitler.

Pumpkin and Pippin

Have you spoken to Pumpkin? [Fitzroy Maclean: "Pumpkin, Prime Minister? I'm afraid I don't understand what you mean."]

Why that great big general of mine. And what have you done with Pippin?....Good God, they haven't got the code! Shall we scramble?

> 1944, SPRING. (MACLEAN, *CHURCHILL PROCEEDINGS*, 1987.)

Fitzroy Maclean with WSC on radio telephone. "Pumpkin" was the portly General Maitland Wilson; "Pippin" was WSC's son Randolph, who was fighting with Maclean and the Yugoslav partisans. Invited to use the scrambler, Fitzroy replied that he thought he was scrambled. Later Maclean

> *caught a pretty American WAC sergeant playing their conversation back to herself, rocking with laughter: "And an English accent too," she said.*

Purblind worldlings

...there are thoughtless dilettanti or purblind worldlings who sometimes ask us: "What is it that Britain and France are fighting for?" To this I answer: "If we left off fighting you would soon find out."

> 1940, 30 MARCH. BROADCAST, LONDON. (BLOOD, 290.)

Queuetopia

Why should queues become a permanent, continuous feature of our life? Here you see clearly what is in their minds. The Socialist dream is no longer Utopia but Queuetopia. And if they have the power this part of their dream will certainly come true.

> 1950, 28 JANUARY, WOODFORD COUNTY HIGH SCHOOL FOR GIRLS. (CS VIII, 7912.)

Quislings

Indomitable patriots take different paths; quislings and collaborationists of all kinds abound; guerrilla leaders, each with their personal followers, quarrel and fight.

> 1944, 22 FEBRUARY.

Vidkun Quisling (1887–1945), Norwegian army officer and fascist politician, Minister-President of occupied Norway 1942–45, executed for treason at the end of the war. He actually held a CBE (1929, revoked 1940) for his earlier aid to British interests in Russia. Churchill is associated with the use of his name as a synonym for traitor.

Re-rat

Anyone can rat, but it takes a certain amount of ingenuity to re-rat.

> 1941, 26 JANUARY, CHEQUERS. (COLVILLE, FRINGES I, 410; HALLE, IRREPRESSIBLE, 53.)

Possibly this familiar form of his expression is manufactured, since I have tracked no attribution. But "re-rat" has been mentioned too often by sound sources to doubt that Churchill coined it. The most reliable reference is Sir John Colville's diary, which paraphrases WSC: "They had said you could rat but you couldn't re-rat."

Reign on the hearts

I also remembered that wise French saying, *"On ne règne sur les âmes que par le calme."*

> 1951. (WW2 IV, 54.)

A closer English expression is "be calm to control the souls of men".

Revirement

If on a general *revirement* of Naval Policy the Cabinet decide to reduce the quota, it would be indispensable that a new exponent should be chosen.

1913, 18 DECEMBER. ADMIRALTY. (CRISIS I, 173–4.)

WSC to H. H. Asquith. "Revirement" is French for a shift of opinion. In another letter to Sir Edward Grey a week later, WSC quoted his remarks to Asquith. In a 1919 letter he referred to a revirement *of French policy towards the Russian Bolsheviks.*

Roulement

Could not the British when the crisis of the battle was over start a "roulement" of tired British divisions to quiet parts of the French front?

1927. (CRISIS III PART 2, 436.)

Roulement, the French word for rotation, was introduced in English by, and is in the Oxford English Dictionary *because of, Churchill, who also used it twice in his World War II memoirs years later.*

Sangared

Both infantry and guns are strongly sangared among the rocks and stones of the kopjes, and they are provided with seven days' supplies of food at the very least.

1900, 25 JULY, CAPE TOWN, SOUTH AFRICA. (CORRESPONDENT, 340.)

"Sangar" (earlier "sungar") is widely used by the British Army in India (also in 2003 in Iraq and Afghanistan) to mean a stone parapet which gives protection in rocky terrain where it is impossible to dig. It is adapted from the Hindi word "sunga". WSC turned the noun into a verb, which I am not sure reflects his usual respect for the English language.

Siren Suit

Most sensible suit I ever had. Did you know that I designed it myself? You notice I have one extra large breast pocket. That's to hold my cigars.

1940s–1950s. (REYNOLDS, Q., 148; NEL, 32; MURRAY, 238.)

"Siren Suit" was WSC's term for what some staff called his "rompers". Originally of workaday fabrics, they grew increasingly luxurious as WSC warmed to them, and he would sometimes appear on smart occasions in a Siren Suit made of blue velvet. Bodyguard

Edmund Murray wrote that it was

> *usually worn if a comfortable day with friends around the house was contemplated, while a grey lounge suit normally indicated that visitors, rather than close friends, were expected.*

Slatternly

Whatever one may think about democratic government, it is just as well to have practical experience of its rough and slatternly foundations.

1929, OCTOBER. ("LORD ROSEBERY," PALL MALL, GC, 6.)

A mid-seventeenth-century word meaning "slovenly".

Sofari

Sofari sogoodi!

1907, NOVEMBER, AFRICA. (HASSALL, 138.)

A phrase of WSC's during his African journey of late 1907. Randolph Churchill wrote:

> *After twenty days safari which carried Churchill and his party from Lake Victoria to Gondokoro, some 900 miles south of Khartoum, "sofari so goody" Churchill was wont to say at the end of each day of the march.*

Safari is Swahili for "journey".

Soft underbelly

The soft underbelly of the Axis.

1942, 11 NOVEMBER. (MARK CLARK TO THE EDMONTON CHURCHILL SOCIETY, 1 JUNE 1970.)

WSC deployed this phrase in arguing for attacking Germany through Italy and the Mediterranean. General Mark Clark, who had some of that responsibility, remarked that he found it "one tough gut".

Some chicken – some neck

When I warned them [the French Government] that Britain would fight on alone whatever they did, their generals told their Prime Minister and his divided Cabinet, "In three weeks England will have her neck wrung like a chicken." Some chicken; some neck.

1941, 30 DECEMBER. CANADIAN PARLIAMENT, OTTAWA. (UNRELENTING, 367.)

Spurlos versenkt

I have searched the benches opposite with my eyes, but I cannot see any sign of the burly and engaging form of the Rt. Hon. Gentleman. He has departed "spurlos versenkt," as the German expression says—sunk without leaving a trace behind.

1946, 31 MAY. (CS VII, 7337.)

Referring to the resignation of Mr. Ben Smith, the Minister of Food in the post-war Labour Government.

Squalid caucus boss and butcher

I always hate to compare Napoleon with Hitler, as it seems an insult to the great Emperor and warrior to connect him in any way with a squalid caucus boss and butcher.

1943, 28 SEPTEMBER.

For the complete quotation see Chapter 20, People...Hitler.

Squalid nuisance

Unless The Rt Hon. Gentleman changes his policy and methods...he will be as great a curse to this country in time of peace as he was a squalid nuisance in time of war.

1945, 6 DECEMBER.

A dripping sarcasm about his political nemesis, Aneurin Bevan.

"Stop the Home Fires Burning"

I must write to Novello and tell him to produce a good war song—but this time it will have to be "Stop the Home Fires Burning".

1940, CHEQUERS. (HALLE, IRREPRESSIBLE, 172.)

WSC to Sir John Slessor, musing on the relative dearth of WW2 songs compared to WW1. According to Kay Halle, they actually could see the distant horizon towards London aglow with fires from the bombings. Ivor Novello composed "Keep the Home Fires Burning" during World War I.

Stricken field

The Emir [Ahmed Fedil] had faithfully discharged his duty, and he was hurrying to his master's assistance with a strong and well-disciplined force of not less than 8,000

men when, while yet sixty miles from the city, he received the news of "the stricken field."

1899. (RIVER II, 255–6.)

First occurrence of a favourite phrase. WSC may have read it in Scott or Macaulay, but it is more likely that he remembered it from a poem by John McCrae (later famous for "In Flanders Field"). In "The Unconquered Dead" (1895), first stanza, McCrae had written:

> *Not we the conquered! Not to us the blame*
> *Of them that flee, of them that basely*
>   *yield;*
> *Nor ours the shout of victory, the fame*
> *Of them that vanquish in a stricken field.*

Churchill used "stricken field" in reference to the Battle of Majuba (Boer, 275); to his father in the House of Commons in 1901 (see Tattered Flag herein); to the Dervish empire (MAJ, 117); to Foch (Blood, 166); and to Charles II (HESP II, 298).

Summer jewelry

...the garden gleams with summer jewelry. We live vy simply—but with all the essentials of life well understood & well provided for— hot baths, cold champagne, new peas, & old brandy.

1915, 19 JUNE. (OB, CV3/2, 1042.)

WSC to his brother Jack. He was on holiday at Hoe Farm, Godalming, Surrey, where he brooded over his dismissal from the Admiralty, and learned to paint. Like many of his generation who wrote letters in longhand, WSC used contractions "vy, wh, yr" for "very, which, your".

Suñer or later

[Lady Churchill: "I hope this was not wrong diplomatically."]

Well, we will know Suñer or later!

1954. (JOHN SPENCER CHURCHILL IN HALLE, IRREPRESSIBLE, 328.)

Lady Churchill reported a request from the Spanish Foreign Minister (pronounced "Soon-yaire"), thought to have been pro-Nazi, who had asked her to help place his niece in an English convent.

Tattered flag

Wise words, Sir, stand the test of time, and I am very glad the House has allowed me, after an interval of fifteen years, to raise the tattered flag I found lying on a stricken field.

1901, 12 May.

Churchill's second speech in the House of Commons was a bravura performance. The "tattered flag" was his father Lord Randolph's call, fifteen years earlier, for more economy in the budget. See "Stricken field" herein. Thirty-nine years later to the day, in his first speech as Prime Minister, WSC would raise another tattered flag on a very stricken field.

Terminological inexactitude

The conditions of the Transvaal Ordinance under which Chinese labour is now being carried on do not, in my opinion, constitute a state of slavery. A labour contract…may not be a healthy or proper contract, but it cannot in the opinion of His Majesty's Government be classified as slavery in the extreme acceptance of the word without some risk of terminological inexactitude.

1906, 22 February. (OB II, 167.)

Randolph Churchill wrote:

This celebrated example of polysyllabic humour was always to be misunderstood and to be regarded as a nice substitute for "lie", which it plainly was not intended to be.

Toil, blood, death, squalor

War, today is bare—bare of profit and stripped of all its glamour. The old pomp and circumstance are gone. War now is nothing but toil, blood, death, squalor, and lying propaganda.

1932, 10 March. Radio interview, New York. (Gilbert, Wilderness, 45.)

See Appendix II for the development of Churchill's "Blood, toil, tears and sweat".

Triphibian

He [Lord Louis Mountbatten] is what…I will venture to call "a complete triphibian."

1943, 31 August. Broadcast, London. (Onwards, 179.)

"Triphibious" (capable of living or operating on land, water and air) entered the Oxford English Dictionary in 1986. Its first appearance was by Leslie Hore-Belisha in The Times of 4 November 1941, who wrote of "amphibious – or rather triphibious – raids" on the enemy coast. Churchill is usually credited with the noun triphibian, though its first appearance seems to be in the Baltimore Sun of 26 October 1935: one Constantine Vlachos saw his invention collapse during a demonstration: "The device…called a triphibian, has never been seen off the ground," his wife said.

Ungrateful volcano

We are paying eight millions a year for the privilege of living on an ungrateful volcano out of which we are in no circumstances to get anything worth having.

1922, 1 September. (OB, CV4/3, 1974.)

Unsent letter to Lloyd George, referring to Iraq.

Unregulated unthinkability

It is only a little while ago that I heard ministers say, and read diplomatic documents which said, that rearmament was unthinkable —"Whatever happens, we cannot have that. Rearmament is unthinkable." Now all our hope is to regulate the unthinkable. Regulated unthinkability—that is the proposal now; and very soon it will be a question of making up our minds to unregulated unthinkability.

1934, 14 March.

Unsordid

[President Roosevelt] devised the extraordinary measure of assistance called Lend-Lease, which will stand forth as the most unselfish and unsordid financial act of any country in all history.

1945, 17 April.

This word to describe Lend-Lease was first coined by Churchill on 10 November 1941; see Chapter 8, America…Lend-Lease. Often incorrectly believed to have been said about the post-war Marshall Plan.

Wincing marquis

Lord Lansdowne has explained, to the amusement of the nation, that he claimed no right on behalf of the House of Lords to mince the Budget. All, he tells us, he has asked for, so far as he is concerned, is the right to wince when swallowing it. Well, that is a much more modest claim. It is for the Conservative Party to judge, whether it is a very heroic claim for one of their leaders to make. If they are satisfied with the wincing Marquis, we have no reason to protest.

1909, 26 JULY. ST. ANDREW'S HALL, NORWICH. (CS II, 1294.)

Winstonian

It is very kind of you to write me such a long letter. It will be carefully preserved among the Winstonian archives.

1905, 9 MAY. MOUNT STREET, LONDON. (OB, CV2/1, 391.)

When no word was available, WSC at an early age began to coin his own. About a year later, when someone asked about the politics of his private secretary, Eddie Marsh, WSC replied, "I hope he's a fully qualified Winstonian." As the years passed, of course, his contemporaries used it to describe Churchill's friends and causes – not always in the positive sense.

Woomany

You will let me come up for a week to see you and Woomany I am sure.

1888, 12 JANUARY. (OB, CV 1/1, 152.)

Winston's name for his beloved nanny, Elizabeth Everest (see Chapter 20, People), a word that seemed to combine thoughts like "woman and home", which she forever represented to him.

Wop (explosion)

The *wop!* of the distant explosion came back, like the echo of the report.

1899. (RIVER I, 423.)

Wormwood Scrubbery

The Socialist ideal is to reduce us to one vast Wormwood Scrubbery.

1946, 12 MARCH.

Churchill went on to explain that at Wormwood Scrubs prison in West London:

there is only one official to every four prisoners, whereas up to the present we have the advantage of only one official to look after every eight wage-earners or producers.

Wounded canary

I am not going to tumble around my cage like a wounded canary. You knocked me off my perch. You have now got to put me back on my perch. Otherwise I won't sing.

1944, 2 APRIL. (NICOLSON II, 358.)

On a clause in the Education Bill which threatened the Government with losing a vote of confidence. "Everybody was ruffled and annoyed," wrote Harold Nicolson. "The only person who really enjoyed it was Winston himself. He grinned all over."

Wuthering Height

Thank God we have seen the last of that Wuthering Height!

CIRCA 1940. ("CHURCHILL THE CONVERSATIONALIST," COLLIN BROOKS IN EADE, 246.)

Said of a "tall lugubrious colleague" according to Collin Brooks, editor of the Sunday Dispatch *1936–38. Most sources agree that it was in reference to Sir John Reith, who as BBC director had kept Churchill off the air during the Wilderness Years, but who was later made Minister of Transport and then Works in the wartime coalition. Wuthering Heights, Emily Brontë's only novel, was published in 1847.*

4

WRITER AND SPEAKER

"...if I found the right words you must remember that I have always earned my living by my pen and by my tongue."[23]

"...don't try to be subtle or clever. Use a pile driver."
Campaigning in North West Manchester, 24 April 1908.

Churchill's skills as a wordsmith and orator are so pervasive that it is difficult to isolate quotations which define his literary style. The following display his love of language and the principles that made him a great communicator.

Languages were important to Churchill in different ways. Included here are his advice about English: his views on book and speech composition, dating, dictation, style and usage.[24] Other languages were different. Unlike modern newscasters and some politicians, he saw no reason to patronise foreigners by overemphasising their pronunciation. In fact, he tried very hard to Anglicise words that did not appeal to him. He frowned on name changes – like Iran for Persia or Ankara for Angora – and studiously pronounced the Uruguayan

---

23 WSC's remarks on his eightieth birthday celebrations at Westminster Hall, London, 30 November 1954. Churchill, Winston S., *The Unwritten Alliance*. London: Cassell, 1961, 202.
24 Churchill also championed "Basic English", but not for himself. See this subject in Chapter 24, Education.

capital as *Monty-viddy-oh*. Perhaps he didn't notice when China went from Peiping to Peking to Beijing, but we have a fair idea what he would think about it.

Churchill crisply dismissed faddish expressions and jargon, and looked diffidently upon the newspapers, and those who wrote for them – although he wrote himself, very profitably, over the years. Towards individual journalists he was magnanimous. "Do not be afraid to criticise, young man," he once told an overawed editor, "I am a professional journalist."

Oddities that fit well here include the very first words he spoke in Parliament, a passage which Colin Coote called "musical English", his comments on Shakespeare, books of quotations (speak of the devil), and the Nobel Prize for Literature – which he won not for *The Second World War*, as is commonly believed, but for his mastery of historical and biographical description, and for his speeches defending human freedom.

In the "Ps" are "The Collected Poems of Winston Churchill": as far as I know, the sum of his poetry. At the end of this chapter is an assortment of favourite and despised words and expressions – not those he coined himself (see previous chapter) but those that caught his attention, and should perhaps catch ours. Reading Churchill has a side benefit professionals will appreciate: it makes you a better writer.

Authors

The fortunate people in the world—the only really fortunate people in the world, in my mind—are those whose work is also their pleasure. The class is not a large one, not nearly so large as it is often represented to be; and authors are perhaps one of the most important elements in its composition. They enjoy in this respect at least a real harmony of life. To my mind, to be able to make your work your pleasure is the one class distinction in the world worth striving for...

1908, 17 FEBRUARY. AUTHOR'S CLUB, LONDON. (CS I, 903.)

Authors' opinions

There will not be wanting those, who will remind me, that in this matter [frontier policy] my opinion is not supported by age or experience. To such I shall reply, that if what is written is false or foolish, neither age nor experience should fortify it; and if it is true, it needs no such support. The propositions of Euclid would be no less indisputable were they propounded by an infant or an idiot.

1899. (MALAKAND, SILVER LIBRARY ED., 303–4.)

Book composition

I write a book the way they built the Canadian Pacific Railway. First I lay the track from coast to coast, and then I put in all the stations.

CIRCA 1946. (GRAEBNER, 69.)

Chronology is not a rigid rule and there are many occasions when a departure from it is a good thing. Nevertheless, I think it true to say that chronology is the secret of narrative.

1949, 15 JUNE. (OB VIII, 742.)

WSC to Conseulo Balsan, who was writing her memoirs, published in 1953 as The Glitter and the Gold. *WSC's approach is scrupulously followed by his official biographer, Sir Martin Gilbert.*

Book design

You see how easily it opens, it is not necessary to break the back of the book to keep it open. I made them take away a quarter of an inch from the outer margins of the two pages, and then add the half inch gained to the inner margin. Look at it, Charles. It lies open like an angel's wings.

1956, 29 FEBRUARY. (MORAN, 736.)

Commenting on the page design of the English edition of his History of the English Speaking Peoples, *a distinctly tall and elegant set of volumes. Traditional books tend to have a small inner and large outer margins, but a large gutter is easier for the reader. A book printer says: "There are no technical constraints; it is a simple question of page set-up."*

Book titles:

A Roving Commission

Scribners have telegraphed "All heartily

favour Roving Commission with some sub-title cable whether Butterworth approves." I think it will be difficult to beat "A Roving Commission," with the subtitle "Memories [or] Memoirs of my Youth." Pray let me know what you think about this as soon as possible.

1930, 9 AUGUST. (OB, CV5/2, 174.)

WSC to English publisher Thornton Butterworth. In his youth, WSC had read the novels of G. H. Henty, including Henty's A Roving Commission. *WSC liked it, used it for the first chapter of* Ian Hamilton's March, *then thirty years later as the subtitle of* My Early Life. *Charles Scribner preferred it for the early American editions. After the war, with WSC world famous, Scribner restored* My Early Life. *Incidentally, the term was used in speeches by both Churchill (1909) and Harold Nicolson (1919).*

Amid These Storms
What about "Amid These Storms"? I like it better than any I have thought of...

1932, 31 MAY. (OB, CV V/2, 437.)

WSC to Charles Scribner, proposing the American title for Thoughts and Adventures. *Scribner had proposed* Thoughts and Reflections *and* Through Stormy Years, *to avoid "two subjects connected by 'and'". Churchill's alternative was editorially superior.*

Arms and the Covenant
We have provisionally decided on the title as "War in Masquerade" from Dryden's Absalom and Achitophel— "and peace itself is war in masquerade."

It is possible that we may later think of a better title, and I suppose it would always be possible to change it, even if the initial blurb has gone out. But for my part I am fully satisfied with it as it stands. The cover should then read:
WAR IN MASQUERADE by Winston S. Churchill (compiled by Randolph S. Churchill).

1938, 27 APRIL. (OB, CV5/3, 1008.)

WSC to publisher George Harrap. The title was changed to The Locust Years *(7 May), and before publication (24 June) to* Arms and the Covenant. *For how someone else accidentally supplied Churchill's American title* While England Slept, *see Appendix I.*

Book writing

To sit at one's table on a sunny morning, with four clear hours of uninterruptible security, plenty of nice white paper, and a Squeezer pen [laughter]—that is true happiness.

1908, 17 FEBRUARY. AUTHOR'S CLUB, LONDON.
(CS I, 903.)

A "Squeezer pen" refers to the then relatively new fountain pen, which was refilled by dipping the nib in ink and squeezing a bladder.

It was great fun writing a book....It built an impalpable crystal sphere around one of interests and ideas. In a sense one felt like a goldfish in a bowl; but in this case the goldfish made his own bowl. This came along everywhere with me. It never got knocked about in travelling, and there was never a moment when agreeable occupation was lacking. Either the glass had to be polished, or the structure extended or contracted, or the walls required strengthening.

1930. (MEL, 226.)

Writing a long and substantial book is like having a friend and companion at your side, to whom you can always turn for comfort and amusement, and whose society becomes more attractive as a new and widening field of interest is lighted in the mind.

1948. (WW2 I, 157.)

Referring to his History of the English Speaking Peoples *which, though nearly complete in 1939, was delayed by the war and began publication in 1956.*

Writing a book is an adventure. To begin with it is a toy, then an amusement. Then it becomes a mistress, and then it becomes a master, and then it becomes a tyrant and, in the last stage, just as you are about to be reconciled to your servitude, you kill the monster and fling him to the public.

1949, 2 NOVEMBER. GROSVENOR HOUSE, LONDON.
(CHURCHILL ARCHIVES CENTRE.)

Several published versions of this quotation are incorrect or incomplete (some eliminate "fling him to the public"). The words above are from the original speaking notes for Churchill's address after receiving The Times *Literary Award. [Churchill Archives Centre Cambridge,*

CHUR 5/28A.] (I have made one correction, which WSC no doubt made when he spoke: the draft notes read "became a mistress", which is certainly ungrammatical.)

Certainly I have been fully qualified so far as the writing of books about wars is concerned; in fact, already in 1900, which is a long time ago, I could boast to have written as many books as Moses, and I have not stopped writing them since, except when momentarily interrupted by war, in all the intervening period.

1950, 4 JULY. ROYAL UNITED SERVICES INSTITUTION, LONDON. (BALANCE, 304.)

The "five books of Moses" were Genesis, Exodus, Leviticus, Numbers and Deuteronomy, the first five chapters of the Old Testament, although many Biblical scholars dispute that he wrote them.

Books

"What shall I do with my books?" was the question; and the answer, "Read them," sobered the questioner. But if you cannot read them, at any rate handle them and, as it were, fondle them. Peer into them. Let them fall open where they will. Read on from the first sentence that arrests the eye. Then turn to another. Make a voyage of discovery, taking soundings of uncharted seas. Set them back on your shelves with your own hands. Arrange them to your own plan, so that if you do not know what is in them, you at least know where they are. If they cannot be your friends, let them at any rate be your acquaintances.

1921, DECEMBER. ("PAINTING AS A PASTIME," STRAND MAGAZINE; THOUGHTS, 219.)

Books, in all their variety, offer the human intellect the means whereby civilisation may be carried triumphantly forward.

1937, 8 NOVEMBER. STATEMENT FOR THE NATIONAL BOOK FAIR. (OB, CV5/3, 833.)

Shorter versions of this quotation abound, but are inaccurate.

Brevity

Pray inform me on one sheet of paper…

1940S. (EDEN, G. AND GRETTON, PASSIM.)

Churchill's preference for brief reports dates at least as far back as World War I:

As he records in The World Crisis, *he called in 1914 for a "report on one sheet of paper" showing all the anti-aircraft guns available, afloat and ashore. – Guy Eden.*

Above all, complacency was impossible with the thought that a "Pray-inform-me-on-one-sheet-of-paper-why…" might descend at any moment. – Admiral Gretton.

Clarity and cogency can be reconciled with a greater brevity…it is slothful not to compress your thoughts.

1940S. (ISMAY, 169.)

It is sheer laziness not compressing thought into a reasonable space.

1941, 11 JANUARY. (WW2 III, 639.)

Prime Minister to Foreign Secretary.

Is it really necessary to describe the *Tirpitz* as the *Admiral von Tirpitz* in every signal?

This must cause a considerable waste of time for signal men, cipher staff and typists. Surely *Tirpitz* is good enough for the beast.

1942, 27 JANUARY. (WW2 IV, 752.)

Prime Minister to First Lord of the Admiralty. Alfred von Tirpitz (1849–1930) was the father of the modern German navy in World War I.

This Treasury paper, by its very length, defends itself against the risk of being read.

1956, 24 JUNE, MARSHALLS MANOR, SUSSEX. (MORAN, 746.)

Cabinet secretary Norman Brook to Lord Moran. Brook added: "At most Cabinets he coined at least one remarkable phrase."

Chartwell factory

Do come and see my factory. This is my factory. This is my secretary.…And to think I once commanded the fleet.

1930S. (HAMBLIN, CHURCHILL PROCEEDINGS 1987.)

Given his extraordinary literary output in the 1930s, Churchill rightly referred to Chartwell as his "factory". His remark was recalled with a smile by his long-time secretary, Grace Hamblin, who knew he said this to tease her.

On another occasion WSC said, "She's quite uneducated," but, seeing her distress he added, "...but she arranges flowers beautifully."

Classical literature
...even as a schoolboy I questioned the aptness of the Classics for the prime structure of our education. So they told me how Mr. Gladstone read Homer for fun, which I thought served him right...

1930. (MEL, 37.)

I began to see that writing, especially narrative, was not only an affair of sentences, but of paragraphs. Indeed I thought the paragraph no less important than the sentence. Macaulay is a master of paragraphing. Just as the sentence contains one idea in all its fullness, so the paragraph should embrace a distinct episode; and as sentences should follow one another in harmonious sequence, so the paragraphs must fit on to one another like the automatic couplings of railway carriages.

1930. (MEL, 225–6.)

Date style
It is not the fourteenth September. If anything it is the one thousand nine hundred and fifty-third September. You should express it either as "the 14th of September" or as "September 14."

1953, NOVEMBER. (MONTAGUE BROWNE, 156.)

WSC's eyes fell on a pile of letters awaiting signature, dated in the form (for example), "14th September 1953". Anthony Montague Browne "meekly acquiesced".

Dictation
Oh dear, she's very young. I mustn't frighten her!....Don't worry if you don't get it all—I always remember what I've said.

1930S. (HAMBLIN, *CHURCHILL PROCEEDINGS* 1987.)

The first part of this quotation is WSC to his wife when a nineteen-year-old secretary reported for work; the second part is his remark to the secretary on her first dictation.

Drafts
Your task, my boy, is to make Cosmos out of Chaos.

1947, 14 MAY. (OB VIII, 331.)

WSC to literary assistant Denis Kelly, after introducing Kelly to the messy Chartwell muniment room, which Kelly had to organise for the drafting of WSC's war memoirs.

The fact that I did not use it in no way detracts from the help you gave me. It gave me a rope with which to crawl ashore till I could walk on my own feet up the beach.

1950. (OB VIII, 528.)

Thanks for a speech brief to George Christ, Parliamentary Liaison Officer, Conservative Central Office, and editor of the party newsletter, who helped WSC with his speeches. Although Christ pronounced his name to rhyme with "wrist", when Churchill needed his help he liked to exclaim: "Send for Christ!"

Early authors
I have always been very much struck by the advantage enjoyed by people who lived at an earlier period of the world than one's own. They had the first opportunity of saying the right thing. Over and over again it had happened to me to think of something which I thought was worth saying, only to find that it had been already exploited, and very often spoiled, before I had an opportunity of saying it.

1927, 19 MAY.

See also Churchillisms...anticipatory plagiarism.

English
And what a noble medium the English language is. It is not possible to write a page without experiencing positive pleasure at the richness and variety, the flexibility and the profoundness of our mother-tongue.

1908, 17 FEBRUARY. AUTHOR'S CLUB, LONDON.
(CS I, 905.)

English literature is a glorious inheritance which is open to all—there are no barriers, no coupons, and no restrictions. In the English language and in its great writers there are great riches and treasures, of which, of course, the Bible and Shakespeare stand alone on the highest platform.

1949, 2 NOVEMBER. GROSVENOR HOUSE, LONDON.
(CS VII, 7883.)

We have history, law, philosophy and literature; we have sentiment and common interest; we have a language which even the Scottish Nationalists will not mind me referring to as English.

1954, 8 AUGUST. ENGLISH-SPEAKING UNION DINNER, LONDON. (ALLIANCE, 154.)

English vs. American terminology

There have also been lost to the enemy 6,200 guns, 2,550 tanks and 70,000 trucks, which is the American name for lorries, and which, I understand, has been adopted by the combined staffs in North-West Africa in exchange for the use of the word petrol in place of gasolene.

1943, 19 MAY. CONGRESS, WASHINGTON. (ONWARDS, 100.)

Such a tit-for-tat exchange of expressions was greatly to WSC's liking.

Fact and truth

Words, which are on proper occasions the most powerful engines lose their weight and power and value when they are not backed by fact or winged by truth, when they are obviously the expression of a strong feeling, and are not related in any way to the actual facts of the situation.

1926, 22 APRIL.

Facts vs. feelings

It is a deplorable thing that, when persons are engaged in acute political controversy, they sometimes allow their language to be rather the means of giving relief to their feelings than an actual description of the facts. That is, no doubt, a very melancholy fact for us to reflect upon, but it has gone on in the past in English politics and it may sometimes recur in the future—I tremble to think that something of this nature may even at this moment be going on in this very city.

1908, 23 MARCH.

Facts vs. rumour

History cannot proceed by silences. The chronicler of ill-recorded times has none the less to tell his tale. If facts are lacking, rumour must serve. Failing affidavits, he must build with gossip.

1933. (MARLBOROUGH I, 300.)

See also Maxims...myths.

Foreign names

I refuse to call it El Alamein. Like those asses who talk about Le Havre. *Havre* [to rhyme with carver] the place is to any decent man. Now this third battle must be called "The Battle of Egypt." Harold, see to that at once. Tell your people henceforward to call it The Battle of Egypt.

1942, 6 NOVEMBER. (NICOLSON 1907–63, 269.)

In the event, Churchill did use "Alamein" but refused to countenance "El".

In all correspondence, it would be more convenient to use the word "Persia" instead of "Iran," as otherwise dangerous mistakes may easily occur through the similarity of Iran and Iraq....Formal correspondence with the Persian Government should of course be conducted in the form they like.

CIRCA 1942. (WW2 III, 426.)

I do not consider that names that have been familiar for generations in England should be altered to study the whims of foreigners living in those parts. Where the name has no particular significance the local custom should be followed. However, Constantinople should never be abandoned, though for stupid people Istanbul may be written in brackets after it. As for Angora, long familiar with us through the Angora cats, I will resist to the utmost of my power its degradation to Ankara.

...bad luck...always pursues people who change the names of their cities. Fortune is rightly malignant to those who break with the traditions and customs of the past. As long as I have a word to say in the matter Ankara is banned, unless in brackets afterwards. If we do not make a stand we shall in a few weeks be asked to call Leghorn Livorno, and the BBC will be pronouncing Paris "Paree." Foreign names were made for Englishmen, not Englishmen for foreign names. I date this minute from St. George's Day.

1945, 23 APRIL. (WW2 VI, 642–3.)

WSC to the Foreign Office.

It is for me a high honour to receive today the Charlemagne Prize in this famous German and European city of Aachen, which some call Aix-la-Chapelle.

1956, 10 MAY, AACHEN. (ALLIANCE, 289.)

Speech on receiving the Charlemagne Prize in Germany's westernmost city, bordering the Low Countries. He was recalling its name under the Napoleonic First Empire.

Foreign pronunciation

...I must say, even from the point of view of the ordinary uses of English, that it is not customary to quote a term in a foreign language, a capital town, a geographical place, when there exists a perfectly well-known English equivalent. It is usual to say "Paris"—not "Paree."

1938, 5 MAY.

The news which has come from *Monty-viddy-oh* has been received with thankfulness....The pocket battleship Graf *Speee*...has met her doom.

1939, 18 DECEMBER.

After the scuttling of the Graf Spee off Montevideo, Uruguay, on 15 December.

Jack, when you cross Europe you land at Marsay, spend a night in Lee-on and another in Par-ee, and, crossing by Callay, eventually reach Londres. I land at Marsales, spend a night in Lions, and another in Paris, and come home to LONDON!

CIRCA 1940. ("CHURCHILL THE CONVERSATIONALIST," COLLIN BROOKS IN EADE, 247.)

WSC to his friend Jack Seely, later Lord Mottistone.

Don't be so BBC—the place is WALLS-HAVEN!

CIRCA 1940. (PAWLE, 68.)

When Captain Pim, who ran WSC's map room, pronounced Walshaven as "Varls-harvern".

I always thought it was a most unfortunate and most tiresome thing when both Persia and Mesopotamia changed their names at about the same time to two names which were so much alike—Iran and Iraq. I have endeavoured myself in the domestic sphere to avoid such risks [in naming Ministers].

1941, 7 MAY.

Sebastapol's good enough for me, young man.

1945, 13 FEBRUARY, YALTA. (HALLE, IRREPRESSIBLE, 160.)

After the Yalta conference he was told by a Russian-speaking RAF officer that arrangements had been made to fly him home via "Sevastapol".

History

[I am] horribly entangled with the Ancient Britons, the Romans, the Angles, Saxons and Jutes, all of whom I thought I had escaped for ever when I left school!

1938, 20 AUGUST. (OB, CV5/3, 1123.)

WSC to Lord Halifax.

History with its flickering lamp stumbles along the trail of the past, trying to reconstruct its scenes, to revive its echoes, and kindle with pale gleams the passion of former days.

1940, 12 NOVEMBER.

As history unfolds itself, by strange and unpredictable paths, we have little control over the future and no control at all over the past.

1952, 16 JANUARY. SOCIETY OF CINCINNATI, WASHINGTON. (CS VIII, 8323.)

Interpreters

Interpreters of the world unite! You have nothing to lose but your audiences.

1945, 8 FEBRUARY, YALTA. (OB VII, 1195.)

Churchill's Marxian second to a toast by Stalin to their interpreters, which, according to Air Marshal Portal, "went with a bang".

Jargon

Let us have an end of such phrases as these: "It is also of importance to bear in mind the following considerations..." or "Consideration should be given to the possibility of carrying into effect..." Most of these woolly phrases are mere padding, which can be left out altogether or replaced by a single word. Let us not shrink from using the short expressive phrases, even if it is conversational.

1940, 9 AUGUST. (OB, CV6/2, 636.)

Memorandum to "my colleagues and their staffs".

In this Debate we have had the usual jargon about "the infrastructure of a supra-national authority." The original authorship is obscure; but it may well be that these words "infra" and "supra" have been introduced into our current political parlance by the band of intellectual highbrows who are naturally anxious to impress British labour with the fact that they learned Latin at Winchester. Although we may not relish the words, no one will wish to deny the old-school-tie contingent their modest indulgence in class self-consciousness.

1950, 27 June.

A sideswipe at Labour's Hugh Gaitskell, who went to Winchester, while addressing the Schuman Plan for a European coal and steel community, predecessor to the EU.

This grimace is a good example of how official jargon can be used to destroy any kind of human contact or even thought itself.

1951. (WW2 IV, 516.)

Soviet Foreign Minister Molotov wrote a 1942 memo that WSC deprecated on literary as well as practical grounds:

[We] will be in a position to draw the necessary conclusions as to the real state of affairs, particularly in regard to certain irregularities in the actions of the respective British naval authorities.

Language

The greatest tie of all is language....Words are the only things that last for ever. The most tremendous monuments or prodigies of engineering crumble under the hand of Time. The Pyramids moulder, the bridges rust, the canals fill up, grass covers the railway track; but words spoken two or three thousand years ago remain with us now, not as mere relics of the past, but with all their pristine vital force.

1938, 15 May. ("The Union of the English-Speaking Peoples," *News of the World*; Essays IV, 438.)

Language, foreign

To have a second language at your disposal, even if you only know it enough to read it with pleasure, is a sensible advantage....to secure the enormous boon of a second literature. Choose well, choose wisely, and choose one.

1925, December. ("Hobbies," *Pall Mall*; Thoughts, 219–20.)

Language, political

We all remember how Queen Elizabeth dealt with poetry and blank verse—"Marry, this is something. This is rhyme! But this"—the blank verse—"is neither rhyme nor reason."

1948, 15 July.

On a complicated clause in the bill for suspension of the death penalty offered by the Labour Government.

Language, strong

I have no objection to a proper use of strong language, but a certain amount of art and a certain amount of selective power is needed, if the effect is to be produced.

1925, 9 December.

Latin

The foreigners and the Scotch have joined together to introduce a pronunciation of Latin which divorces it finally from the English tongue....They have distorted one of my most serviceable and impressive quotations into the ridiculous booby "Wainy, Weedy, Weeky." Punishment should be reserved for those who have spread this evil.

1930. (MEL, 37.)

Since Churchill rarely used "Scotch" for "Scots", we may assume that he did so here on purpose.

I must now warn the House that I am going to make an unusual departure. I am going to make a Latin quotation. It is one which I hope will not offend the detachment of the old school tie and will not baffle or be taken as a slight upon the new spelling brigade. Perhaps I ought to say the "new spelling squad" because it is an easier word. The quotation is "Arma virumque cano," which, for the benefit of our Winchester friends, I may translate as "Arms and the men I sing." That generally describes my theme.

[Mr. Hugh Gaitskell (Lab.): "Should it not be 'man,' the singular instead of the plural?"]

Little did I expect that I should receive assistance on a classical matter from such a quarter. I am using the word "man" in a collective form which, I think, puts me right in grammar. Let me now come to arms, about which I believe there is no classical dispute.

1953, 5 MARCH.

Maiden speech

[Lloyd George] had a moderately phrased amendment [but] soon became animated and even violent. I constructed in succession sentence after sentence to hook on with after he should sit down....Then Mr. Bowles whispered "You might say 'instead of making his violent speech without moving his moderate amendment, he had better have moved his moderate amendment without making his violent speech.'" Manna in the wilderness was not more welcome!....I was up before I knew it, and reciting Tommy Bowles's rescuing sentence. It won a general cheer....Everyone was very kind. The usual restoratives were applied, and I sat in a comfortable coma till I was strong enough to go home.

1930. (MEL, 378–80.)

It is difficult to avoid the conclusion that the moderation of the Amendment was the moderation of the Hon. Member's political friends and leaders, and that the bitterness of his speech is all his own.

1901, 18 FEBRUARY.

Churchill's first words in Parliament, which Thomas Bowles MP had suggested to him as a follow-on to Lloyd George, above. They are often misquoted, including by Churchill himself in My Early Life:

...instead of making his violent speech without moving his moderate amendment, he had better have moved his moderate amendment without making his violent speech.

Mein Kampf *as the Koran*

All was there—the programme of German resurrection, the technique of party propaganda; the plan for combating Marxism; the concept of a National-Socialist State; the rightful position of Germany at the summit of the world. Here was the new Koran of faith

and war: turgid, verbose, shapeless, but pregnant with its message.

1948. (WW2 I, 43.)

"Musical English"

His open, gay, responsive nature, his witty, ironical, but never unchivalrous tongue, his pleasing presence, his compulsive smile, made him much courted by his friends, of whom he had many and of whom I was one. Young for the Cabinet, heir to splendid possessions, happy in all that surrounded him, he seemed to have captivated Fortune with the rest.

1923. (CRISIS I, 233; COOTE, 88.)

Reference is to Auberon Herbert, Eighth Baron Lucas and 11th Baron Dingwall (1876–1916), Minister of Agriculture when presumed killed flying over German lines. The quotation is included for what Colin Coote called

Sir Winston's talent for writing musical English. Note how the adjective "responsive" is echoed later by the unusual adjective "compulsive".

Newspapers (Media)

Fancy cutting down those beautiful trees we saw this afternoon to make pulp for those bloody newspapers, and calling it civilisation.

1929, 11 AUGUST, QUEBEC. (OB V, 341.)

Comment to his son Randolph after they had driven through Canadian woodlands.

These gentlemen of the press were listening carefully to every word you said—all eagerly anxious for a tiny morsel of cheese which they could publish. And you go and give them a whole ruddy Stilton!

1941. ("CHURCHILL AND CENSORSHIP," REAR ADMIRAL G. P. THOMSON IN EADE, 147–8.)

Rebuke to a General who had spoken too openly about an upcoming attack on Benghazi in North Africa.

A few critical or scathing speeches, a stream of articles in the newspapers, showing how badly the war is managed and how incompetent are those who bear the responsibility—these obtain the fullest publicity; but the marvellous services of seamanship and devotion, and the organization behind them, which prove at every stage and step the soundness of our national life; the inconquerable, the inexhaustible adaptiveness and ingenuity of the British mind, the iron, unyielding, unwearying tenacity of the British character, by which we live, by which alone we can be saved, and by which we shall certainly be saved—and save the world—these, though fully realized by our foes abroad, are sometimes overlooked by our friends at home.

1941, 25 JUNE.

The newspapers, with their alluring headlines, do not do justice to the proportion of current events. Everyone is busy, or is oppressed by the constant cares and difficulties of daily life. Headlines flicker each day before them. Any disorder or confusion in any part of the world, every kind of argument, trouble, dispute, friction or riot all flicker across the scene. People go tired to bed, at the end of their long, bleak, worrying days, or else they cast care aside, and live for the moment.

1946, 12 DECEMBER.

The Press Association plays an important part in our national life by presenting from minute to minute the news about all kinds of things happening all over the world.

1952, 11 JUNE. PRESS ASSOCIATION LUNCHEON, LONDON. (STEMMING, 298.)

Nobel Prize for Literature

I notice that the first Englishman to receive the Nobel Prize was Rudyard Kipling and that another equally rewarded was Mr. Bernard Shaw. I certainly cannot attempt to compete with either of those. I knew them both quite well and my thought was much more in accord with Mr. Rudyard Kipling than with Mr. Bernard Shaw. On the other hand, Mr. Rudyard Kipling never thought much of me, whereas Mr. Bernard Shaw expressed himself in most flattering terms.

1953, 15 OCTOBER.

Official statement to the press. Churchill was the first statesman and seventh Briton to be awarded the Nobel Prize for Literature.

The roll on which my name has been inscribed represents much that is outstanding in the world's literature of the 20th century....I am

proud, but also I must admit, awestruck at your decision to include me. I do hope you are right. I feel we are both running a considerable risk and that I do not deserve it. But I shall have no misgivings if you have none.

1953, 10 DECEMBER, STOCKHOLM. (CS VIII, 8515.)

The speech including these comments was read in Stockholm by Lady Churchill; WSC was in Bermuda meeting with Eisenhower and French Premier Laniel.

Novel

I have consistently urged my friends to abstain from reading it [*Savrola*].

1930. (MEL, 169.)

Churchill was always diffident about his 1899 novel. Scholars have since cited it as an important glimpse of his personal aspirations, self-image and developing philosophy.

Emerson said, "Never read any book that is not a year old." I can at least give reassurance on this point, since *Savrola* first appeared in print in *Macmillan's Magazine* in 1897 [1899] when I was twenty-three.

The preface to the first edition in 1900 [1899] submitted the book "with considerable trepidation to the judgement or the clemency of the public." The intervening fifty-five years have somewhat dulled though certainly not changed my sentiments on this point.

1956, 20 JANUARY. (SAVROLA, 1956 ED., [IX].)

WSC was wrong on the dates; Savrola *was serialised by* Macmillan's Magazine *from May to December 1899. This delayed the English edition until 1900, but the American edition was published in November 1899.*

Oratory

Of all the talents bestowed upon men, none is so precious as the gift of oratory. He who enjoys it wields a power more durable than that of a great king. He is an independent force in the world. Abandoned by his party, betrayed by his friends, stripped of his offices, whoever can command this power is still formidable.

1897. (OB, CV1/2, 816.)

From his unpublished essay, "The Scaffolding of Rhetoric".

From what I have seen I know that there are few more fascinating experiences than to watch a great mass of people under the wand of the magician. There is no gift—so rare or so precious as the gift of oratory so difficult to define or impossible to acquire.

1896, 5 NOVEMBER. (OB, CV1/2, 700.)

WSC to his American mentor, Bourke Cockran.

There is nothing that gives greater pleasure to a speaker than seeing his great points go home. It is like the bullet that strikes the body of the victim.

1927, 28 APRIL.

One must not yield too easily to the weaknesses of audiences. There they were; what could they do? They had asked for it, and they must have it.

1930. (MEL, 219.)

Reflecting on his maiden political speech, to the Primrose League at Claverton Manor, now the American Museum, Bath, 1897.

You are perfectly right! Not born in the very least—just hard, hard work.

1942, 6 NOVEMBER. (NICOLSON II, 259.)

Churchill was thanking Harold Nicolson for an article on his oratory. Nicolson said he hoped he had been right in saying that WSC was not a born orator.

Oratory – composition

Amid the smoke he saw a peroration, which would cut deep into the hearts of a crowd; a high thought and a fine simile expressed in that correct diction which is comprehensible even to the most illiterate, and appeals to the most simple....His ideas began to take the form of words to group themselves into sentences; he murmured to himself; the rhythm of his own language swayed him; instinctively he alliterated. Ideas succeeded one another, as a stream flows swiftly by and the light changes on its waters. He seized a piece of paper and began hurriedly to pencil notes. That was a point; could not tautology accentuate it? He scribbled down a rough sentence, scratched it out, polished it, and wrote it in again. The sound would please their ears, the sense improve and stimulate their minds. What a game it was! His brain contained the cards he had to play, the world the stakes he played for.

1899. (SAVROLA, 63.)

WSC is describing the hero of his novel, patterned after himself; but this is also his consistent method of composing a speech.

And so the struggle will continue, continue? until victory—has been achieved....no, no— And so we will fight on until the day has come!

1940. (MENZIES, 79.)

Menzies was explaining that Churchill would mutter in a low voice his "first draft" of a sentence, while the stenographer, with her silent typewriter, would record nothing. Then WSC would arrive at the final version and speak up, as she took it down.

I wasn't talking to you, Norman, I was addressing the House of Commons.

UNDATED. (THOMPSON, R. W., 247.)

WSC to his valet, Norman MacGowan, who rushed into WSC's bathroom after hearing ominous mutterings.

Oratory – style

Though he [Savrola] spoke very quietly and slowly, his words reached the furthest ends of the hall. He showed, or perhaps he feigned, some nervousness at first, and here and there in his sentences he paused as if searching for a word....Loud cheers rose from all parts of the hall. His voice was even and not loud, but his words conveyed an impression of dauntless resolution.

1900. (SAVROLA, 97–8.)

Churchill gives as good a description of his own oratorical style as we could hope to have.

If you have an important point to make, don't try to be subtle or clever. Use a pile driver. Hit the point once. Then come back and hit it again. Then hit it a third time.

1919. (PARAPHRASED FROM DONALDSON, 78.)

Advice to the Prince of Wales, later Edward VIII.

Improvised be damned! I thought of it this morning in my bath and I wish now I hadn't wasted it on this crowd.

1932. (MANCHESTER I, 32.)

At a Conservative Party conference Churchill asked,

It is for this you propose to fling away the ancient heritage bequeathed to us by the architects of our magnitude and renown?

Harold Nicolson asked if he had improvised this final phrase extemporaneously.

Oratory – World War II

I was very glad that Mr Attlee described my speeches in the war as expressing the will not only of Parliament but of the whole nation. Their will was resolute and remorseless, and as it proved, unconquerable. It fell to me to express it, and if I found the right words you must remember that I have always earned my living by my pen and by my tongue. It was a nation and race dwelling all round the globe that had the lion heart. I had the luck to be called upon to give the roar. I also hope that I sometimes suggested to the lion the right places to use his claws.

1954, 30 NOVEMBER. WESTMINSTER HALL, LONDON.
(ALLIANCE, 202–3.)

Speech on his eightieth birthday. The first sentence is misquoted by Moran (655) as, "I have never accepted what many people said – namely that I inspired the nation."

Poetry

Malta to Yalta

No more let us falter!
From Malta to Yalta!
Let nobody alter!

1945, 1 JANUARY. (WW2 VI, 295.)

WSC to Roosevelt. Churchill added:

I elaborated this for private use: "No more let us alter or falter or palter. From Malta to Yalta, and Yalta to Malta." Perhaps it was as well I did not cable it.

Page Proofs

Strait away,
without delay,
I want the page proofs day by day.
On January 4,
I leave this shore,
nor will you catch me any more!

1926, 12 DECEMBER. (GILBERT, LIFE, 479.)

Churchill to Harold Bourne, manager of the publishers Thornton Butterworth, who recalled

how cross Churchill could get if the proof chapters were not in order, but how, after every storm, there seemed to be "an additional glint in his humorous eyes".

Puggy-wug

Oh, what is the matter with poor Puggy-wug?
Pet him and kiss him and give him a hug.
Run and fetch him a suitable drug,
Wrap him up tenderly all in a rug,
That is the way to cure Puggy-wug.

1930S. (CHURCHILL, S., 28.)

WSC's youngest daughter Mary had a pug who became ill. "My father was greatly upset at our distress," wrote her sister Sarah, "and although he really thought that poetry, though enjoyable, was a minor sort of thing – prose being much more important – he composed this ditty for Mary and me...which we all chanted while Puggy was ill."

The Influenza

Oh how shall I its deeds recount
Or measure the untold amount
  Of ills that it has done?
From China's bright celestial land
E'en to Arabia's thirsty sand
  It journeyed with the sun.

O'er miles of bleak Siberia's plains
Where Russian exiles toil in chains
  It moved with noiseless tread;
And as it slowly glided by
There followed it across the sky
  The spirits of the dead.

The Ural peaks by it were scaled
And every bar and barrier failed
    To turn it from its way;
Slowly and surely on it came,
Heralded by its awful fame,
    Increasing day by day.

On Moscow's fair and famous town
Where fell the first Napoleon's crown
    It made a direful swoop;
The rich, the poor, the high, the low
Alike the various symptoms know,
    Alike before it droop.

Nor adverse winds, nor floods of rain
Might stay the thrice-accursed bane;
    And with unsparing hand,
Impartial, cruel and severe
It travelled on allied with fear
    And smote the fatherland.

Fair Alsace and forlorn Lorraine,
The cause of bitterness and pain
    In many a Gallic breast,
Receive the vile, insatiate scourge,
And from their towns with it emerge
    And never stay nor rest.

And now Europa groans aloud,
And 'neath the heavy thunder-cloud
    Hushed is both song and dance;
The germs of illness wend their way
To westward each succeeding day
    And enter merry France.

Fair land of Gaul, thy patriots brave
Who fear not death and scorn the grave
    Cannot this foe oppose,
Whose loathsome hand and cruel sting,
Whose poisonous breath and blighted
    wing
Full well thy cities know.

In Calais port the illness stays,
As did the French in former days,
    To threaten Freedom's isle;
But now no Nelson could o'erthrow
This cruel, unconquerable foe,
    Nor save us from its guile.

Yet Father Neptune strove right well
To moderate this plague of Hell,
    And thwart it in its course;
And though it passed the streak of brine
And penetrated this thin line,
    It came with broken force.

For though it ravaged far and wide
Both village, town and countryside,
    Its power to kill was o'er;
And with the favouring winds of Spring
(Blest is the time of which I sing)
    It left our native shore.

God shield our Empire from the might
Of war or famine, plague or blight
    And all the power of Hell,
And keep it ever in the hands
Of those who fought 'gainst other lands,
    Who fought and conquered well.

1890, HARROW. (CHAPLIN, 55–7.)

Churchill's longest poem, included for its literary qualities.

Political Correctness

I hope you have all mastered the official Socialist jargon which our masters, as they call themselves, wish us to learn. You must not use the word "poor"; they are described as the "lower income group." When it comes to a question of freezing a workman's wages the Chancellor of the Exchequer speaks of "arresting increases in personal income." The idea is that formerly income taxpayers used to be the well-to-do, and that therefore it will be popular and safe to hit at them. Sir Stafford Cripps does not like to mention the word "wages," but that is what he means. There is a lovely one about houses and homes. They are in future to be called "accommodation units." I don't know how we are to sing our old song "Home Sweet Home." "Accommodation Unit, Sweet Accommodation Unit, there's no place like our Accommodation Unit." I hope to live to see the British democracy spit all this rubbish from their lips.

1950, 8 FEBRUARY, CARDIFF. (BALANCE, 181.)

P.C. of course wasn't known in his day; but the practice was already getting established.

The Socialist Party are very mealy-mouthed today, and the Chancellor of the Exchequer [Sir Stafford Cripps] is very delicate in his language. One must not say "deflation," but only "disinflation." In a similar manner, one must not say "devaluation," but only "revaluation," and finally, there is the farce of saying that there must be no increase in personal incomes when what is meant is no increase in wages. However, the Chancellor felt that a certain broad prejudice attaches to the word "income" and that consequently no one would mind saying that incomes shall not increase—but wages, no. However, it is wages that he means, I am sure that the British electors will not be taken in by such humbug. I suppose that presently when "disinflation" also wins its bad name, the Chancellor will call it "non-disinflation" and will start again....

1949, 27 OCTOBER.

Earlier in 1949, the Labour Government had devalued ("revalued") the pound from $4 to $2.80.

Pot-boilers

Why will people keep referring to that bloody pot-boiler?

1961. (MONTAGUE BROWNE, 305; HAMBLIN, CHURCHILL PROCEEDINGS 1987.)

Remark when his private secretary sent a copy of Thoughts and Adventures, *containing his essay "Moses", to David Ben-Gurion. Secretary Grace Hamblin reported:*

"potboilers", as he called them [were] articles for magazines or the national newspapers on topical subjects....very exciting because they were done in one evening, quickly put out and sent off usually the next day. He got his money very quickly, which he liked too. We all liked doing potboilers.

Punctuation

Eddie: You are very free with your commas. I always reduce them to a minimum: and use "and" or an "or" as a substitute not as an addition. Let us argue it out.

[Eddie Marsh: "I look on myself as a bitter enemy of *superfluous commas*, and I think I could make a good case for any I have put in—but I won't do it any more!"]

Eddie: No do continue. I am adopting provisionally. But I want to argue with you.

1922, 31 AUGUST. (HASSALL, 498.)

In the art of drafting [Income Tax Law] there seems to be a complete disdain of the full stop, and even the humble colon is an object to be avoided.

1927, 19 APRIL.

Quotations

It is a good thing for an uneducated man to read books of quotations....The quotations when engraved upon the memory give you good thoughts.

1930. (MEL, 130.)

I am reminded of the professor who, in his declining hours, was asked by his devoted pupils for his final counsel. He replied, "Verify your quotations."

1951. (WW2 IV, 616.)

Reading

Young people, I believe, should be careful in their reading, as old people in eating their food. They should not eat too much. They should chew it well.

1934, 21 APRIL. ("HAVE YOU A HOBBY?," ANSWERS; ESSAYS IV, 288.)

Shakespeare

My Lord Hamlet, may I use your lavatory?

1950S. (HALLE, IRREPRESSIBLE, 96.)

WSC to Richard Burton in Burton's dressing room, after Churchill had sat in a front row, speaking the lines of Hamlet *with him. "I could not shake him off," Burton said to Jack Paar. "I tried going fast, I tried going slow; we did cuts. Every time there was a cut an explosion occurred. He knew the play absolutely backwards; he knows perhaps a dozen of Shakespeare's plays intimately."*

Shakespeare, whose magic finger touches in succession most of the peaks of English history and lights them with the sunrise so that all can see them standing out above the mountainous disorder, has brought Hubert to our ken.

1956. (HESP I, 262.)

Churchill describing Hubert de Burgh (1165–1243), Justiciar of England during the reigns of John and Henry III.

Speech transcript editing

[Loud and prolonged applause.]

1902. (HALLE, IRREPRESSIBLE, 49.)

The editor of the Morning Post *showed Churchill a proof of one of his speeches before it went to press. WSC substituted this bracketed description for "[cheers]."*

Style

I affected a combination of the styles of [Thomas] Macaulay and [Edward] Gibbon, the staccato antitheses of the former and the rolling sentences and genitival endings of the latter; and I stuck in a bit of my own from time to time.

1930. (MEL, 225.)

On the writing of The River War, *1899. Thomas Babbington Macaulay (1800–59) was a poet, historian and Whig politician whose negative writings on the First Duke of Marlborough Churchill sought to correct in his own biography of the Duke. Edward Gibbon (1737–94), historian and MP, wrote* The Decline and Fall of the Roman Empire.

Short words are best and the old words when short are best of all.

1949, 2 NOVEMBER. *THE TIMES* LITERARY AWARD PRESENTATION, LONDON. (CS VII, 7885.)

Personally, I like short words and vulgar fractions.

1953, 10 OCTOBER, MARGATE. (ALLIANCE, 61.)

Churchill had been using the phrase "vulgar fractions" since his autobiography. See Education…mathematics.

Traditional wording

I recollect well at the end of the last war, more than a quarter of a century ago, that the House…did not feel inclined for debate or business, but desired to offer thanks to Almighty God, to the Great Power which seems to shape and design the fortunes of nations and the destiny of man; and I therefore beg, Sir, with your permission to move:

"That this House do now attend at the Church of St. Margaret, Westminster, to give humble and reverent thanks to Almighty God for our deliverance from the threat of German domination."

This is the identical Motion which was moved in former times.

1945, 8 MAY. (VICTORY, 128.)

One of Churchill's most endearing traits was his ability to cast back into history for just the right words. After all, in 1945 there was nothing to improve on this motion made in 1918.

Usage

I picked up a wide vocabulary and had a liking for words and for the feel of words fitting and falling into their places like pennies in the slot.

1930. (MEL, 123.)

…you distinguish in several cases between enemy aircraft "out of action" or "destroyed". Is there any real difference between the two, or is it simply to avoid tautology? If so, this is not in accordance with the best authorities on English. Sense should not be sacrificed to sound.

1940, 27 MAY. (WW2 II, 560.)

Prime Minister to Secretary of State for Air.

What is the meaning of the expression "Failed to silence machine-gun posts"? It seems an odd description of an action. Evidently what happened was only a skirmish. Surely the way to silence machine-gun posts is to bring up some guns and shell them.

1942, 5 MAY. (WW2 IV, 755.)

WSC to Chief Imperial General Staff.

We "invade" all countries with whom we are at war. 2. We "enter" all subjugated Allied lands we wish to "liberate." 3. With regard to a country like Italy, with whose Government we have signed an armistice, we "invaded" in the first instance, but, in view of the Italian cooperation, we must consider all further advances by us in Italy to be in the nature of "liberation."

1944, 25 FEBRUARY. (WW2 V, 608.)

Prime Minister to Foreign Secretary.

War correspondents

"All the danger of war and one-half percent the glory": such is our motto, and that is the reason why we expect large salaries.

1900, 22 APRIL. DEWETSDORP, SOUTH AFRICA. (HAMILTON'S, 58; BOER, 250.)

Churchill was slightly misquoting the fictional character Jorrocks, in Robert Smith Surtees's novel Handley Cross, on fox hunting: "...the image of war without its guilt and only five-and-twenty percent of its danger."

[War correspondents] have been allowed to roam all over the battlefield, taking their chance of getting killed, and sending home their very full messages whenever they can reach a telegraph office. This is what the Press have always asked for, and it is what they got. These war correspondents, moving about amid the troops and sharing their perils, have also shared their hopes and have been inspired by their buoyant spirit. They have sympathised with the fighting men whose deeds they have been recording, and they have, no doubt, been extremely anxious not to write anything which would spread discouragement or add to their burdens.

1942, 2 JULY.

Word-pictures

The room, in the grey light with its half-empty glasses and full ashtrays, looked like a woman, no longer young, surprised by an unsympathetic dawn in the meretricious paints and pomps of the previous night.

1900. (SAVROLA, 117–18.)

A thrifty piece of description, offered with the economy of words for which Churchill was renowned.

Words and Expressions: Favourites

All cats are grey
In the night all cats are grey.

1942, 1 SEPTEMBER. (WW2 IV, 479; MARLBOROUGH I, 187.)

WSC to Roosevelt, on telling US from British troops in the landings in North Africa, but not original. The aphorism dates very far back in English, Spanish, German and Latin texts. Churchill probably remembered his version

from Cervantes, Don Quixote, *Part 2, Ch. 33 (1605). John Heywood's* Proverbs, *Part 1, Ch. 5 (1546) records: "When all candles be out, all cats be grey." Churchill first used the expression in* Marlborough.

At your throat or at your feet
The Hun is always either at your throat or at your feet.

1943, 19 MAY, CONGRESS, WASHINGTON. (ONWARDS, 100.)

Often credited to Churchill, who preceded this with, "The German Army has once again proved the truth of the saying..." For the surrounding remarks, see Germany...1943.

Battledore and shuttlecock
If you have at the one end this vast organization and at the other end the veto of the House of Lords, able to dismiss by a contemptuous gesture any Government, why, they will play battledore and shuttlecock with your liberties.

1910, 10 JANUARY, BIRMINGHAM. (MARSH, 173.)

Not original, but an example of WSC's memory: Battledore and Shuttlecock *was a racquet game that evolved into Badminton in the mid-1800s. (Eddie Marsh, who referred to the words as "battlecock and shuttledore", remarked of this oration, "I saw one eyelid bat.")*

Bona fides
What does bona fides mean? I know it is Latin but there are enough public school men opposite who ought to be able to translate it. In my belief, it means good faith, common honesty, decent Parliamentary behaviour.

1951, 21 JUNE.

Breadth of a comma
I am glad that we have found a common ground to stand on, though it be only the breadth of a comma.

1910, 7 JULY.

Buggins' turn
The departmental view is no doubt opposed to long tenures and the doctrine of "Buggins' turn" is very powerful.

1944, 19 MARCH. (WW2 V, 616.)

Deployed by WSC on four occasions, "Buggins' Turn" means promoting by seniority rather than merit. The Oxford English Dictionary *credits Admiral Lord Fisher with using it first in 1901.*

Crushed

The word you want is "crushed."

1957. DENIS KELLY TO THE EDITOR.

Working on the abridgement to Churchill's war memoirs, which would appear in 1959, literary assistant Denis Kelly received this message from WSC, who had crossed out Kelly's draft:

Germany was outmatched, outfought, surrounded by superior forces, isolated and occupied.

Curate's egg

However we may regard Sir Stafford Cripps's record there is no doubt he has shouldered the main weight of the Government's task. He has a brain, which, at any rate, is something to begin with. He has also a conscience which, like the curate's egg, is good in parts.

1948, 21 APRIL. ROYAL ALBERT HALL, LONDON. (EUROPE, 301.)

The curate's egg stemmed from an 1895 Punch *cartoon. Served a bad egg, the young curate told his host the bishop: "Oh no, my Lord, I assure you, parts of it are excellent."*

English

I am all for "British," but it is a pity that "English" should be a word never mentioned—or hardly ever.

1949, 11 OCTOBER. (COOTE, 213.)

See also Britain, Empire and Commonwealth.... England.

Find out

Well, find out!

PASSIM. (GRACE HAMBLIN, *CHURCHILL PROCEEDINGS* 1987.)

His secretary reports this well-worn expression:

He'd say, "Do you know where Lord Beaverbrook is this weekend?" "No, I'm afraid I don't." "Well, find out!" So one got into the habit of saying, "No, I'm afraid I don't but I'll find out." Which was a much better answer.

Fish and chips

It would not, I feel, be a good arrangement to have a separate Department for every industry of national importance. These two industries [Agriculture and Fisheries] have been long associated departmentally and, after all, there are many ancient links between fish and chips.

1954, 17 JUNE.

Churchill was responding to a suggestion to separate the Ministry of Agriculture from the Ministry of Fisheries.

Gathering Storm

The Gathering Storm.

1948. (REYNOLDS D., 85.)

Erroneously said to have been inspired by H. G. Wells, or copied from a chapter title in Wells's The War of the Worlds, *this title for Churchill's first volume of World War II memoirs was suggested by his agent, Emery Reves. (Perhaps Reves read Wells – or* The Federalist, *where the phrase appeared in 1788.) Churchill had suggested* Towards Catastrophe; *his publishers thought it too negative. Reves also suggested* Gathering Clouds *and* The Brooding Storm. *On 31 January 1948, Churchill was given a sheet of paper with two titles:* Towards Catastrophe *and* The Gathering Storm. *He put a line through the first.*

Goddams

You know, it wasn't our fault. The English were just working for the Burgundians. Probably you will find in [this manuscript] that the French called us "Goddams." It is still a term we use a good deal. It is a fine thing to keep these old conservative practices.

1952, PALAIS BOURBON, PARIS. (*THE TIMES*; HALLE, IRREPRESSIBLE, 310.)

Churchill was examining the manuscript of Joan of Arc's trial.

Infanticide

"Infanticide" is a better word.

1948, 15 JULY.

Sir Hartley Shawcross, speaking on the Criminal Justice Bill, had referred to "child-killing".

Iron Curtain

An iron curtain is drawn down upon their front. We do not know what is going on behind. There seems little doubt that the whole of the region Lubeck-Trieste-Corfu will soon be completely in their hands. [Following American withdrawal] a broad band of many hundreds of miles of Russian-occupied territory will isolate us from Poland....it would be open to the Russians in a very short time to advance if they chose, to the waters of the North Sea and the Atlantic.

1945, 12 MAY. (OB VIII, 7.)

WSC to President Truman. Churchill's first use of a term which he made famous nine months later at Fulton, Missouri. Although Churchill is most famous for coining this phrase, he was not its originator. Its first appearance was in 1918, when the Russian émigré philosopher Vasily Rozanov, in Apocalypse of Our Time, *wrote of "an iron curtain descending on Russian history". Next, Ethel Snowden's* Through Bolshevik Russia *(1920) described Russia as being behind an "Iron Curtain". It resurfaced with Goebbels in* Das Reich *(25 February 1945); and at Fulton in 1946 (below). See also Nuclear Age.*

From Stettin in the Baltic to Trieste in the Adriatic, an iron curtain has descended across the Continent. Behind that line lie all the capitals of the ancient states of central and eastern Europe. Warsaw, Berlin, Prague, Vienna, Budapest, Belgrade, Bucharest and Sofia, all these famous cities and the populations around them lie in what I must call the Soviet sphere, and all are subject in one form or another, not only to Soviet influence but to a very high and in many cases increasing measure of control from Moscow.

1946, 5 MARCH. WESTMINSTER COLLEGE, FULTON, MISSOURI. (SINEWS 100; OB VIII, 7.)

Labour

Labour! It is a great word. It moves the world, it comprises the millions, it combines many men in many lands in the sympathy of a common burden.

1906, 11 OCTOBER. ST. ANDREW'S HALL, GLASGOW.

Leave the past to history

In case at any forthcoming General Election there may be an attempt to revive these former controversies, we are taking steps to have little booklets prepared recording the utterances at different moments, of all the principal figures involved in those baffling times. For my part, I consider that it will be found much better by all Parties to leave the past to history, especially as I propose to write that history myself.

1948, 23 JANUARY.

Man vs. Woman

...just the ordinary man who keeps a wife and family, who goes off to fight for his country when it is in trouble, goes to the poll at the appropriate time, and puts his cross on ballot paper showing the candidate he wishes to be elected to Parliament...he is the foundation of democracy. And it is also essential to this foundation that this man...

[Dr. Edith Summerskill (Lab., Fulham, West): "And woman."]

I beg pardon. There is always the stock answer that man *embraces* woman, unless the contrary appears in the context.

1944, 8 DECEMBER. (CS VII, 7051.)

Alas this brilliant riposte lacks the fun in print that it must have had when delivered. Dr. Summerskill considered Churchill's usage sexist; it was not, but she received the answer she probably expected.

Masse de Manœuvre

Où est la masse de manœuvre?

1940, 16 MAY, PARIS. (WW2 II, 42.)

Not invented by Churchill, but a military term testifying to his command of French. Stated to French army commander General Gamelin ("Where are your reserves?"). Gamelin replied "Aucune" ("There are none"). General Spears, WSC's representative to the French command, added that Churchill *"simply could not grasp it at first, it sounded so incredible, but, when it did penetrate, was like a cold hand placed on his heart"*.

Melting the iceberg
The Government stock is very low. They are like a great iceberg which has drifted into warm seas and whose base is being swiftly melted away, so that it must topple over.

1935, 2 MARCH. (OB, CV5/2, 1097.)

Palimpsest of jargon and officialese
It was one of those rigmaroles and grimaces produced by the modern bureaucracy into whose hands we have fallen—a kind of vague palimpsest of jargon and officialese with no breadth, no theme, and, above all, no facts.

1947, 31 MARCH. (EUROPE, 53.)

See this chapter...jargon and Churchillisms... earthly palimpsest.

Parricide
It was a state of things that no one had ever contemplated...The statutes of ancient Rome contained no provision for the punishment of parricide, but when the first offender appeared it was found that satisfactory arrangements could be made to deal with him.

1915, 15 FEBRUARY.

Churchill was referring to the new menace of the submarine, adding:

> But it must not be supposed because the attack is extraordinary that a good defence and a good reply cannot be made.

Phantasmagoria
We turned aside not indeed to the uplands of the Delectable Mountains, but into a strange corridor of things like anagrams and acrostics called Sines, Cosines and Tangents. Apparently they were very important, especially when multiplied by each other, or by themselves!....I have never met any of these creatures since....they passed away like the phantasmagoria of a fevered dream.

1930. (MEL, 40.)

Although a longer rendition of this remark is in Personal...mathematics, the word

"phantasmagoria" deserves special attention. It is not a Churchill invention, but the need to consult the Oxford English Dictionary *("a shifting series of real or imaginary figures as in a dream") evidences Churchill's depth of vocabulary.*

Piebald
I well appreciate the necessity of preserving the piebald complexion of my pony.

1941, FEBRUARY. (ROBERTS, EMINENT, 203.)

WSC understood the need to maintain balance in his precarious wartime coalition. When the extreme socialist Wilfred Paling (see Ripostes...Dirty dogs and palings) replaced the deceased Lord Tryon as Parliamentary Secretary at the Ministry of Pensions, Churchill appointed the Duke of Norfolk to the junior Agriculture position vacated by Lord Moyne, who had moved to the Colonial Office.

Piles and water
The Venetian Republic would have perished in a moment if the waters of the Mediterranean had ever broken down the supports on which the city was raised above them; and the life of Egypt was bound up with the inundation of the Nile. And the Venetians were always thinking about their piles, and the Egyptians were always thinking about their water.

1908, 8 APRIL, DARWEN, LANCASHIRE. (MARSH, 172–3.)

In reference to outside dangers to Britain. Eddie Marsh, who recorded this, added: "It was a tribute to his power over an audience that nobody appeared to give any untoward application to these words."

Plungeon
In fact, however, though he omitted to post a guard on the plungeon beyond his right flank, he had not fallen far short of ordinary military routine....Contrary to most accounts, the rebels knew about the Bussex Rhine, and Grey and his horsemen, improvidently leaving Godfrey behind, rode forward, looking for the plungeon.

1933. (MARLBOROUGH I, 188.)

Plungeon, meaning a ford in a river, was used only twice by Churchill, both times on this page of his Marlborough biography. The Bussex Rhine was an impassable ditch protecting Bridgwater, Somerset, in the Battle of Sedgemoor, a failed rebellion against James II in 1685.

Protectionist bottle

Protection is like dram drinking—it produces a transient exhilaration that is succeeded by other less satisfactory symptoms, and in the cheerless grey of the morning no remedy can be found for the fumes of the previous night's debauch except another pull at the Protectionist bottle.

1910, 10 JANUARY, BIRMINGHAM. (CS II, 1455.)

Snafu

Yes, it should have been; indeed it was our intention to do it. It is only as the result of what in the United States is known as a "snafu"—which word I have added to my vocabulary—that you were not consulted about it.

1952, 1 JULY.

A Member asked why Britain wasn't consulted about Korean bombing operations. "Snafu" means "situation normal: all fouled up". (Sometimes another f-word is substituted.)

Stand firm

Neither is the expression "Stay Put" really applicable to the districts where fighting is going on. First of all, it is American slang; secondly, it does not express the fact. The people have not been "put" anywhere. What is the matter with "Stand Fast" or "Stand Firm"? Of the two I prefer the latter. This is an English expression and it says exactly what is meant...

1941, 3 OCTOBER. (WW2 III, 660.)

Temple of Peace

We must make sure that its [the United Nations'] work is fruitful, that it is a reality and not a sham, that it is a force for action, and not merely a frothing of words, that it is a true temple of peace in which the shields of many nations can some day be hung up, and not merely a cockpit in a Tower of Babel....I spoke earlier of the Temple of Peace.

Workmen from all countries must build that temple.

1946, 5 MARCH. WESTMINSTER COLLEGE, FULTON, MISSOURI. (SINEWS, 95, 98.)

Totalisator

...the question is whether there is any moral distinction between a gang of bookmakers shouting in a ring and a totalisator electrically working and ticking off the odds from moment to moment. I cannot see any moral distinction between the two.

1928, 16 MARCH.

A totalisator is a device showing the number and amount of bets staked on a race, used to facilitate the division of winnings among those backing the winner.

Trade not aid

I am very much in favour of "trade not aid" and of our earning our living by all our toil and effort.

1953, 9 JUNE.

"Trade Not Aid" was the phrase of R. A. Butler, who wanted freer entry of British goods in the American market, rather than gifts or loans.

Trepanning bombs

I am told that there is good evidence to show that the system of dealing with time-bombs by trepanning is proving very successful....Will you please let me have a report on the extent to which trepanning is being used.

1940, 14 SEPTEMBER. (WW2 II, 319.)

WSC to Secretary of State for War. "Trepanning" was an ancient practice of opening the skull to operate on the brain, or to remove a core from a cylindrical object. Apparently WSC was the first to apply the word to defusing bombs. Earlier, in 1934, Churchill had entitled Chapter 14 of Marlborough, vol. 2, "Trepanning an Army".

Troubled like Martha

The Operations Division, hitherto troubled like Martha over many things, had not been able to think far enough ahead. In May a small planning section was instituted, charged with the study of policy and preparation of plans; and this was later in the year expanded into a separate Division.

1927. (CRISIS III PART 2, 363.)

See Luke 10:38–42, King James version:

38. Now it came to pass, as they went, that he entered into a certain village: and a certain woman named Martha received him into her house.
39. And she had a sister called Mary, which also sat at Jesus' feet, and heard his word.
40. But Martha was cumbered about much serving, and came to him, and said, Lord, dost thou not care that my sister hath left me to serve alone? bid her therefore that she help me.
41. And Jesus answered and said unto her, Martha, Martha, thou art careful and troubled about many things:
42. But one thing is needful: and Mary hath chosen that good part, which shall not be taken away from her.

United Nations
The title of "United Nations" was substituted by the President for that of "Associated Powers"....I showed my friend the lines from Byron's *Childe Harold*:

Here, where the sword United Nations drew,
Our countrymen were warring on that day!
And this is much—and all—which will not
pass away.

1942, 1 JANUARY. (WW2 III, 605.)

The President has chosen the title "United Nations"....This is much better than "Alliance," which places him in constitutional difficulties, or "Associated Powers," which is flat.

1942, 3 JANUARY. (WW2 III, 607.)

Unum necessarium
But Bromley clinched matters by saying bluntly that unless [Robert] Walpole were got out of the way it would not be possible for the Government to carry through their business. His knowledge was too great, his attacks too damaging. His exclusion was, he said, the *unum necessarium*.

1938. (MARLBOROUGH IV, 434–5.)

The Latin means "the one term and condition." Bromley was the Commons Speaker.

Words and Expressions: Disfavoured

Accidentally ignored
I must point out that the expression "accidentally ignored" is a contradiction in terms.

1952, 1 JULY.

Adumbrated
A few days later, and without any new facts being presented, or indeed existing, a far larger set of proposals was adumbrated. That is not a word I like.

1951, 15 FEBRUARY.

Baloney
I should prefer to have an agreed definition of the meaning of "baloney" before I attempted to deal with such a topic.

1953, 24 FEBRUARY.

Churchill was responding to an MP who described his economic planning as "baloney".

Envisage
Mr. Speaker, let us envisage—an unpleasant and overworked word.

1953, 5 MARCH.

Grand Remonstrance
...my father set out to examine me [on history]. The period was Charles I. He asked me about the Grand Remonstrance; what did I know about that? I said that in the end the Parliament beat the King and cut his head off. This seemed to me the grandest remonstrance imaginable.

1930. (MEL, 125.)

Hackneyed tag
I think with as much reason you might also call the Ten Commandments a hackneyed tag.

1901, 13 MAY.

The Chief Secretary for Ireland had applied "hackneyed tag" to arms expenditures in Ireland.

Infrastructure

As to this new word [infrastructure] with which he [Mr. Shinwell, Minister of Defence] has dignified our language, but which perhaps was imposed upon him internationally. I can only say that we must have full opportunity to consider it and to consult the dictionary.

1950, 20 APRIL.

Maximum, The

Now the Secretary of State for War [Mr. Hore-Belisha], I will not say incorrigible, but impenitent, tells us the new Bren gun is being produced at a maximum. What does that mean? What is the maximum? The wit of man, of a man in a fix, could not devise a more vague and misleading phrase.

1938, 17 NOVEMBER.

Outwith

I must thank the Hon. Gentleman for making me acquainted with the word "outwith," with which I had not previously had the pleasure of making acquaintance. For the benefit of English Members I may say that it is translated "outside the scope of." I thought it was a misprint at first.

1944, 5 DECEMBER.

Pluto-Democracies

From that moment the German Government ceased to define its foreign policy as anti-Bolshevism, and turned its abuse upon the "pluto-democracies."

1948. (WW2 I, 287.)

WSC is describing the warming of Russo-German relations in May 1939, with the dismissal of the Jewish Litvinov as Soviet Foreign Minister. The first citation to "Pluto-Democracy" in the Oxford English Dictionary *is 1895.*

Prefabricated

...we must have a better word than "prefabricated" [for houses]. Why not "ready-made"?

1944, 2 APRIL. (WW2 V, 618.)

WSC to Minister of Works.

Quantify

I was shocked to hear [Sir Stafford Cripps use the word "quantify"]. I hope he never uses it again....Another expression that is very common today is, "in short supply." Why can't you say "scarce"? Then there is "broken down." All that means is "sifting," or if you wish to be more erudite, you say "analyse."

1940S. (CAWTHORNE, 76.)

Churchill was a powerful advocate of compactness and the avoidance of flowery substitutes for ordinary words. One can only imagine what he would say about the modern practice of making verbs out of nouns: "We will effort that today." (Yet he was not reluctant to make verbs out of French nouns – see previous chapter!)

Screened

That is a curious phrase [screened] which has crept in. "Sifted" would have been a more natural word..."Screened" is a modern vulgarism.

1947, 7 MAY.

Unilateral

If the bride or bridegroom fails to turn up at church, the result is not what, to use an overworked word, is called a "unilateral" wedding. The absolute essence of the matter is that both parties should be there.

1946, 12 DECEMBER.

5
ANECDOTES
AND STORIES

"...at times of crisis, myths have their historical importance...the
source of inspiration to those dim distant figures, the Counts of the
Saxon shore, striving to defend the island." [25]

"There I sat with the great Russian bear on one side of me, with paws
outstretched...the poor little English donkey..."

Winston Churchill was no fountain of stories, like US Presidents Truman and Reagan, but when he told one, it was often memorable. Like Aesop, he deployed anecdotes to make a point, often an important one, as in his famous "Disarmament Fable", where he used animals much as Orwell did later, to demonstrate the fallacy of the disarmament movement and the nature of man.

His most revealing composition was his bittersweet short story "The Dream", conjured up as a "private article" in 1947 and not published until after his death, about the return of his father, still aged only forty, while Churchill himself is now seventy-four. When Lady Thatcher was presented with a limited edition of "The Dream" by the

---

25 WSC, quoted by F. W. Deakin, Foundation Suisse Winston Churchill, April 1970.

Churchill Centre in 1993, she wrote that she stayed up all night reading it: "I was totally fascinated by the imagination of the story, and how much it reveals of Winston the man and the son."

Humour is never far from the surface of Churchill's screed, and there is lots here, with some irony – imagining himself as the "donkey" at Teheran, or how St. George and the Dragon would "negotiate" in the age of appeasement. Anecdotes like "Birth of Britain" move us still; his determination to preserve noble myths, as of King Alfred and the burning of the cakes, say different things to different readers about Churchill the historian.

Bear, Buffalo and Donkey

I realised at Teheran for the first time what a small nation we are. There I sat with the great Russian bear on one side of me, with paws outstretched, and on the other side the great American buffalo, and between the two sat the poor little English donkey who was the only one, the only one of the three, who knew the right way home.

1944, 1 AUGUST. (PELLING, 546; WHEELER-BENNETT, 96.)

WSC to Violet Bonham Carter, eight months after the Teheran conference. See also WW2...1943/Teheran.

Birth of Britain

Our story centres in an island, not widely sundered from the Continent, and so tilted that its mountains lie all to the west and north, while south and east is a gently undulating landscape of wooded valleys, open downs, and slow rivers. It is very accessible to the invader, whether he comes in peace or war, as pirate or merchant, conqueror or missionary....A province of the Roman Empire, cut off and left to sink or swim in the great convulsion of the Dark Ages; reunited to Christendom, and almost torn away from it once more by the heathen Dane; victorious, united, but exhausted, yielding, almost without resistance, to the Norman Conqueror; submerged, it might seem, within the august framework of Catholic feudalism, was yet capable of reappearing with an individuality of its own. Neither its civilisation nor speech is quite Latin nor quite Germanic. It possesses a body of custom which, whatever its ultimate sources may be...is being welded into one Common Law. This is England in the thir-teenth century, the century of Magna Carta, and of the first Parliament.

1956. (HESP I, VIII–IX.)

Disarmament Fable

Once upon a time all the animals in the Zoo decided that they would disarm, and they arranged to have a conference to arrange the matter. So the Rhinoceros said when he opened the proceedings that the use of teeth was barbarous and horrible and ought to be strictly prohibited by general consent. Horns, which were mainly defensive weapons, would, of course, have to be allowed. The Buffalo, the Stag, the Porcupine, and even the little Hedgehog all said they would vote with the Rhino, but the Lion and the Tiger took a different view. They defended teeth and even claws, which they described as honourable weapons of immemorial antiquity. The Panther, the Leopard, the Puma, and the whole tribe of small cats all supported the Lion and the Tiger. Then the Bear spoke. He proposed that both teeth and horns should be banned and never used again for fighting by any animal. It would be quite enough if animals were allowed to give each other a good hug when they quarrelled. No one could object to that. It was so fraternal, and that would be a great step towards peace. However, all the other animals were very offended with the Bear, and the Turkey fell into a perfect panic.

The discussion got so hot and angry, and all those animals began thinking so much about horns and teeth and hugging when they argued about the peaceful intentions that had brought them together that they began to look at one another in a very nasty way. Luckily the keepers were able to calm them down and persuade them to go back quietly to their cages, and they began to feel quite friendly with one another again.

1928, 25 OCTOBER. ALDERSBROOK ROAD, WEST ESSEX (THEN PART OF HIS CONSTITUENCY). (COVENANT, 17.)

Ignorance

When I hear people talking in an airy way of throwing modern armies ashore here and there as if they were bales of goods to be dumped on a beach and forgotten, I really marvel at the lack of knowledge which still prevails of the conditions of modern war....[critics also remind me of] the sailor who jumped into a dock to rescue a small boy from drowning. About a week later this sailor was accosted by a woman who asked, "Are you the man who picked my son out of the water the other night?" The sailor replied modestly, "That is true, ma'am." "Ah," said the woman, "you are the man I am looking for. Where is his cap?"

1943, 21 SEPTEMBER. (ONWARDS, 201–2.)

King Alfred

The story of Alfred is made known to us in some detail in the pages of Asser, a monk of St. David's, who became Bishop of Sherborne. The Bishop dwells naturally upon the religious and moral qualities of his hero; but we must also remember that, in spite of ill-health, he was renowned as a hunter, and that his father had taken him to Rome as a boy, so that he had a lively comprehension of the great world...Alfred, though also devout, laid the emphasis upon policy and arms....He lived as Robin Hood did in Sherwood Forest long afterwards. This is the moment when those gleaming toys of history were fashioned for the children of every age. We see the warrior-king disguised as a minstrel harping in the Danish camps. We see him acting as a kitchen-boy to a Saxon housewife.

1956. (HESP I, 104, 114.)

Churchill did not *say, "Anecdotes are the gleaming toys of House of Commons history," as is sometimes stated.*

...at times of crisis, myths have their historical importance: the cakes symbolise a myth of British resistance in their sternest hour against the foreign invader, and were the source of inspiration to those dim distant figures, the Counts of the Saxon shore, striving to defend the island.

1956. (DEAKIN, OP.CIT., FOOTNOTE PAGE 69.)

WSC, when asked why he was including Bishop Asser's myth in his History of the English Speaking Peoples.

Medical Quandary

A man called Thomson went to a surgeon and asked him to castrate him. The surgeon demurred, but when the man persisted and argued he eventually agreed, and took him into hospital. The morning after the operation Thomson woke up in great discomfort. He noticed that the man in the next bed was in pain and was groaning. He leant towards him over the side of the bed. "What did they do to you," he called. The man replied: "I've been circumcised." "Good Lord," Thomson exclaimed, "that's the word I couldn't remember when the surgeon asked me what I wanted done."

1944, 21 SEPTEMBER. (MORAN, 198.)

An anecdote delivered from WSC's bath, in between many "splashings and gurglings", as Moran remembered it.

Nature of Man

I read somewhere that when the ancient Athenians, on one occasion, overpowered a tribe in the Peloponnesus which had wrought them great injury by base, treacherous means, and when they had the hostile army herded on a beach naked for slaughter, they forgave them and set them free, and they said: "This was not because they were men; it was done because of the nature of Man."

1945, 18 JANUARY.

Norman from Saxon

One summer evening...Gurth the Swineherd and Wamba the Jester [were] fresh from their famous colloquy on the curious fact that oxen, pigs and sheep, which were Saxons while they lived and had to be tended, were, when the time came to cook them, transformed in death into Norman beef, pork and mutton, and thus qualified to figure on noble boards.

1933, 12 MARCH. ("IVANHOE," RETOLD IN NEWS OF THE WORLD.)

Objections

I remember it was the fashion in the army when a court-martial was being held and the prisoner was brought in, that he should be asked if he objected to being tried by the president or to any of those officers who composed the court martial. On one occasion a prisoner was so insubordinate as to answer, "I object to the whole bloody lot of you."

1927, 9 FEBRUARY.

The word "bloody", not permitted in Parliamentary discourse in 1927, is represented by a long dash in Hansard.

Optimists and Pessimists

We remember the sardonic war-time joke about the optimist and the pessimist. The optimist was the man who did not mind what happened so long as it did not happen to him. The pessimist was the man who lived with the optimist.

1938, 1 DECEMBER. ("HOW STAND BRITAIN AND FRANCE SINCE MUNICH?," *DAILY TELEGRAPH*; STEP, 293.)

Powder to the Bear

I have often tried to set down the strategic truths I have comprehended in the form of simple anecdotes, and they rank this way in my mind. One of them is the celebrated tale of the man who gave the powder to the bear. He mixed the powder with the greatest care, making sure that not only the ingredients but the proportions were absolutely correct. He rolled it up in a large paper spill, and was about to blow it down the bear's throat. *But the bear blew first.*

1951. (WW2 IV, 279.)

Exactly what the powder was, WSC left to his listeners. But, since he said this in the context of his warning to General Auchinleck that the Germans might attack first in Africa, he certainly meant it in the context of helpful advice.

Spanish Prisoner

I believe we have been all these months in the position of the Spanish prisoner who languished for twenty years in a dungeon until one morning the idea struck him to push the door, which had been open all the time.

1915, 6 OCTOBER. (OB, CV3/2, 1204.)

WSC to Arthur Balfour, his successor at the Admiralty, arguing for a renewal of the naval attack on the Dardanelles. This was a favourite story. WSC used it in The World Crisis, *retold it in the 1930s during debate on the India Act, and again in a 1947 article, "The Highroad of the Future".*

St. George and the Dragon

[Nowadays] St. George would arrive in Cappadocia accompanied not by a horse, but by a secretariat. He would be armed not with a lance, but with several flexible formulas. He would, of course, be welcomed by the local branch of the League of Nations Union. He would propose a conference with the dragon—a Round Table Conference, no doubt—that would be more convenient for the dragon's tail. He would make a trade agreement with the dragon. He would lend the dragon a lot of money of the Cappadocian taxpayers. The maiden's release would be referred to Geneva, the dragon reserving all his rights meanwhile. Finally, St. George would be photographed with the dragon (inset—the maiden).

1933, 24 APRIL. ROYAL SOCIETY OF ST. GEORGE, LONDON. (COVENANT, 91–2.)

WSC was mocking what he saw as the "easy mark" Britain was becoming in international negotiations such as the Round Table Conference on India.

Stag and Hounds

Last night the Hon. Member for Bilston [Mr. Will Nally] drew an affecting picture of my personal position; the noble stag was dying, the curs were at his throat: his own friends behind him were hogs....the hounds, as the Hon. Member for Bilston put it, do not worry me.... I must say that the maiden glance of the Hon. Member for Bilston at the House of Commons should impress us somewhat with the unfavourable impression we produce upon him. Here are hogs, there are hounds. I trust that the longer experience of this Chamber will make him realize that both these branches of the animal kingdom have their virtues.

1945, 6 DECEMBER.

The Dream

One foggy afternoon in November 1947 I was painting in my studio at the cottage down the hill at Chartwell. Someone had sent me a portrait of my father....The canvas had been badly torn, and though I am very shy of painting human faces I thought I would try to make a copy of it....

I was just trying to give the twirl to his moustache when I suddenly felt an odd sensation. I turned round with my palette in my hand, and there, sitting in my red leather upright armchair, was my father. He looked just as I had seen him in his prime....

"What year is it? [he said]. I don't remember anything after ninety-four. I was very confused that year....So more than fifty years have passed. A lot must have happened."

"It has indeed, Papa."

"Tell me about it." [Winston recounts the sad history of 1895–1947.]

"Winston, you have told me a terrible tale. I would never have believed that such things could happen. I am glad I did not live to see them. As I listened to you unfolding these fearful facts you seemed to know a great deal about them. I never expected that you would

develop so far and so fully. Of course you are too old now to think about such things, but when I hear you talk I really wonder you didn't go into politics. You might have done a lot to help. You might even have made a name for yourself."

He gave me a benignant smile. He then took the match to light his cigarette and struck it. There was a tiny flash. He vanished. The chair was empty. The illusion had passed. I rubbed my brush again in my paint, and turned to finish the moustache. But so vivid had my fancy been that I felt too tired to go on. Also my cigar had gone out, and the ash had fallen among all the paints.

1947. ("THE DREAM," OB VIII, 364–5, 372.)

There is room here only for the very beginning and end of "The Dream". It is part of the artistry of this imaginary, wistfully beautiful story that Winston's father, briefly brought back to life aged about forty, is never allowed to know what his seventy-four-year-old son has accomplished.

Other quotations from "The Dream" are in Government...Monarchy, socialism, and women; Maxims...War and democracy; Nations...Ireland, and South Africa; Personal... His father's son; Predictions...World War III; Reflections...War and democracy; and Russia... Postwar dangers. The full text is in the Official Biography and individual editions now out of print. (See www.bookfinder.com.)

6

BRITAIN, EMPIRE AND COMMONWEALTH[26]

"I am a bit sceptical about universal suffrage for the Hottentots even if refined by proportional representation. The British and American Democracies were slowly and painfully forged and even they are not perfect yet."[27]

"And over all this...is the golden circle of the Crown."
Prime Minister's farewell to HM the Queen, 4 April 1955.

Churchill believed that Parliamentary government under a sovereign who reigned but did not rule was the most perfect form of democracy. He preferred the unwritten British constitution to the written American one, however much he admired the latter's wording, and wondered privately if the US system of recurrent elections wasn't a detriment to waging war (see America...Constitution).

---

26 This chapter includes British Colonies of Churchill's day that are now independent, such as Uganda. Major nations and dominions where Britain once held some degree of authority – Australia, Canada, Egypt, Iraq, Ireland, New Zealand and Palestine – are in Chapter 11.

27 WSC to President Eisenhower, 8 August 1954. Boyle, Eisenhower, 167.

The British people, he thought, were activated more by sentiment than material goals. The working man had "a deep-seated and natural love of fair-play", evident when Britain went to war in 1914 and 1939. In war as the danger grows, the British become "progressively less nervous". They are always willing to be told the worst – as long as the teller seeks no sordid gain.

Churchill considered the union of past and present, Crown and Parliament, Empire and Commonwealth a "golden circle" unique in the world. Although he saw and sought to mend the rents in British society – particularly as a young Liberal crusading for old-age pensions, prison reform and a "Minimum Standard" – he regarded his country with all its faults the prime example of civilisation.

He is well known for his devotion to the Empire, and for his famous declaration that he had not become the King's first minister to preside over its liquidation. But he saw the end coming quite early (see Empire and Commonwealth...Decline) and towards the end he was resigned to it, not without a proud nostalgia.

To those who came after him goes the credit, or the blame, for what the Commonwealth is today. But when Churchill spoke of "opening up the jungles" and "mitigating poverty", he meant exactly what he said about the Empire's record.

By 1820, as Mark Steyn has written, medical progress in an insignificant country off the coast of Europe created a decisive demographic. Suddenly, thanks to a precipitous decline in infant mortality, a tiny island had the surplus manpower to settle an empire.

And, Steyn added, the little island provided the administrative and business climate in the West Indies, India, Canada, Australia, New Zealand and the Pacific. (And Africa, though sadly, it largely didn't take there.) Fortunately for the world, this demographic transformation occurred in a country which even then had a long-established system of law, property rights and personal freedom. Imagine what the planet would look like today if the first country to conquer infant mortality had been, say, Japan, Russia or Germany.

Churchill believed firmly that the Empire had been a boon to the native peoples within it, and mourned its decline with a nostalgia born of certitude that the Empire was a "beneficent" force. "I am sure it would be an evil day for the very large populations of East Africa and of Uganda," he said in 1908, "if they were handed over from the careful, the disinterested control of British officials to the mere self-interest of some small local community."[28]

It is legitimate to consider whether Churchill's great clarion calls of British pride, sentiment and instinct, as he saw it, still apply in the less homogeneous nation that is Britain today. "But what is the purpose which has brought us all together?" he asked. "It is the conviction that the life of Britain, her glories and message to the world, can only be achieved by national unity, and national unity can only be preserved upon a cause which is larger than the nation itself."[29] Does this still apply to all Britons, all races and religions, who strive as he said of King George VI, "to fear God and nothing else in the world may hope to do"?[30] The reader may judge.

Yes, he was an old-fashioned Victorian who yearned for Britain's "Antonine Age". But if British hearts reading these words are not imbued however temporarily with a renewed love of country, they are stony hearts indeed.

---

28 National Liberal Club, 17 January 1908, reporting on his observations of British East Africa. CS I, 860.
29 House of Commons, 9 May 1938.
30 Broadcast, London, 7 February 1952, following the death of George VI. Stemming, 238.

Achievements of Britain

Little Englander as I suppose I shall be called, I have seen enough in peace and war of its frontiers and dominion to know that it could not stand for a year on a purely material foundation. The life and strength of our authority springs from moral and not from physical forces. Liberty and justice, English honesty, and English tolerance have raised the character of our homely island life above the standard of neighbouring nations...

1903, 11 NOVEMBER. BIRMINGHAM TOWN HALL. (FFT, 43.)

In this island we have today achieved in a high degree the blessings of civilization. There is freedom; there is law; there is love of country...there is a widening prosperity. There are unmeasured opportunities of correcting abuses and making further progress.

1938, 2 JULY, BRISTOL. (BLOOD, 53.)

If we in this small island have gradually grown to a considerable estate, and have been able to give our wage-earners some relief from the harder forms of economic pressure, and to build up a decent, tolerant, compassionate, flexible, and infinitely varied society, it is because in all the great crises of our history, the interest of Britain has marched with the progress and freedom of mankind.

1939, 20 APRIL. CANADA CLUB, LONDON. (BLOOD, 152–3.)

With all our shortcomings, conditions in this country were a model to Europe and to many parts of the United States.

1943, 17 APRIL. (WW2 IV, 847.)

If it be true, as has been said, that every country gets the form of government it deserves, we may certainly flatter ourselves. The wisdom of our ancestors has led us to an envied and enviable situation. We have the strongest Parliament in the world. We have the oldest, the most famous, the most honoured, the most secure, and the most serviceable, monarchy in the world. King and Parliament both rest safely and solidly upon the will of the people expressed by free and fair election on the basis of universal suffrage.

1945, 15 MAY.

There has never been a community in the world like ours. Here in this small island we maintain forty-six millions of people, who played a greater part per head in winning the world war than any other people, and who, before the war, had developed a standard of living and social services above that of any country in Europe and in many respects above that of the United States. These forty-six millions differ from every other community that has ever existed in the world by the fact that they are perched upon the completely artificial foundation of not providing even one half of their food, and being dependent for the purchase of the bulk of their food and raw materials on persuading foreign customers to accept the wares and the services they offer. Vast, intricate, delicate, innumerable, are the methods of acquiring external wealth which the British nation has developed in recent generations, and the population has grown step by step upon the livelihood produced.

1945, 28 NOVEMBER. FRIENDS HOUSE, LONDON. (SINEWS, 52.)

Ambiguity, blessings of

In England the political opinion of men and parties grows like a tree shading its trunk with its branches, shaped or twisted by the winds, rooted according to its strains, stunted by drought or maimed by storm....In our affairs as in those of Nature there are always frayed edges, borderlands, compromises, anomalies. Few lines are drawn that are not smudged. Across the ocean it is all crisp and sharp.

1931, FEBRUARY. ("PERSONAL CONTACTS," STRAND MAGAZINE; THOUGHTS, 33.)

Britain, like any other country, is always changing but, like nature never draws a line without smudging it. We have not the sharp logic of Continental countries.

1947, 16 MAY, AYR, SCOTLAND. (EUROPE, 99–100.)

This brief comment captures many Churchillian themes. See Churchillisms...Minimum standard and the following entry.

The English never draw a line without blurring it.

1948, 16 NOVEMBER.

Classes

There have always been men of power and position, who have sacrificed and exerted themselves in the popular cause; and that is why there is so little class-hatred here, in spite of all the squalor and misery which we see around us.

1908, 14 MAY. KINNAIRD HALL, DUNDEE. (LIBERALISM, 201.)

Our aristocracy has largely passed from life into history; but our millionaires—the financiers, the successful pugilists and the film stars who constitute our modern galaxy and enjoy the same kind of privileges as did the outstanding figures of the 17th and 18th centuries—are all expected to lead model lives.

1933. (MARLBOROUGH I, 39.)

We have had a leisured class. It has vanished. Now we must think of the leisured masses.

1953, 27 JULY. (MORAN, 475.)

Climate

...the British people have always been superior to the British climate. They have shown themselves capable of rising above it, and certainly they have derived from it many of those strong enduring principles and ways of life which make their existence in our island home different from any other community in the world.

1948, 10 JULY, WOODFORD, ESSEX. (EUROPE, 368.)

Constitution

The central principle of civilization is the subordination of the ruling authority to the settled customs of the people and to their will as expressed through the Constitution.

1938 2 JULY, BRISTOL. (BLOOD, 53.)

Criticisms, Churchill's

...I see little glory in an Empire which can rule the waves and is unable to flush its sewers.

1901, 23 DECEMBER. (OB, CV2/1, 104.)

Churchill on the subject of the British labourer who, Churchill maintained, was weaker, smaller, and less healthy than his American counterpart. This was a portent of Churchill's radical period of the early 1900s. (In 1908, WSC's private secretary Charles Masterman wryly remarked: "Winston is full of the poor, whom he has just discovered.")

I do not think that there is any great country in the world where there are so many strong forces of virtue and vitality as there are in our own country. But there is scarcely any country in the world where there is so little organisation.

1909, 26 JULY. NORWICH. (LIBERALISM, 280.)

The British Lion, so fierce and valiant in bygone days, so dauntless and unconquerable through all the agony of Armageddon, can now be chased by rabbits from the fields and forest of his former glory. It is not that our strength is seriously impaired. We are suffering from a disease of the will. We are the victims of a nervous collapse, of a morbid state of mind.

1931, 5 MARCH, LIVERPOOL. (INDIA, 84–5.)

WSC was referring to Parliamentary urgings for passage of the India Bill, which would move India closer to full independence.

Historians have noticed, all down the centuries, one peculiarity of the English people which has cost them dear. We have always thrown away after a victory the greater part of the advantages we gained in the struggle. The worst difficulties from which we suffer do not come from without. They come from within. They do not come from the cottages of the wage-earners. They come from a peculiar type of brainy people always found in our country, who, if they add something to its culture, take much from its strength.

Our difficulties come from the mood of unwarrantable self-abasement into which we have been cast by a powerful section of our own intellectuals. They come from the acceptance of defeatist doctrines by a large proportion of our politicians....

Nothing can save England if she will not save herself. If we lose faith in ourselves, in our capacity to guide and govern, if we lose our will to live, then indeed our story is told.

1933, 24 APRIL. ROYAL SOCIETY OF ST. GEORGE, LONDON. (COVENANT, 92–3.)

Can we produce that complete unity and that impulse in time to achieve decisive military victory with the least possible prolongation of the world's misery or must we fall into jabber, babel and discord while victory is still unattained? It seems to me to be the supreme question alike of the hour and the age. This is no new problem in the history of mankind.

Very often have great combinations almost attained success and then at the last moment cast it away. Very often have the triumphs and sacrifices of armies come to naught at the conference table. Very often the eagles have been squalled down by the parrots. Very often, in particular, the people of this island, indomitable in adversity, have tasted the hard-won cup of success only to cast it away.

1945, 18 JANUARY.

Defence of

I hope that if evil days should come upon our own country, and the last army which a collapsing Empire could interpose between London and the invader were dissolving in rout and ruin, that there would be some—even in these modern days—who would not care to accustom themselves to a new order of things and tamely survive the disaster.

1899. (RIVER II, 162.)

A remarkable example of the consistency of Churchill's thought, it was this attitude that distinguished him from virtually every other potential leader when Britain was faced with rout and ruin in 1940.

Our country should suggest to the mind of a potential paratrooper the back of a hedgehog rather than the paunch of a rabbit.

1951, 6 DECEMBER

Destiny of Britain

Undoubtedly, this new twentieth century is not in many ways so favourable to us as the nineteenth century. A new world is growing up around us, far larger than anything previously seen, and filled with giant states and competitors.

1928, 24 JULY.

It may well be that the most glorious chapters of our history are yet to be written. Indeed, the very problems and dangers that encompass us and our country ought to make Englishmen and women of this generation glad to be here at such a time. We ought to rejoice at the responsibilities with which destiny has honoured us, and be proud that we are guardians of our country in an age when her life is at stake.

1933, 24 APRIL. ROYAL SOCIETY OF ST. GEORGE, LONDON. (COVENANT, 93.)

We rise or we fall together. Indeed, if we survive today it is because even in bygone times our ancestors so managed that in the main the special interests of Britain conformed to the general interests of the world.

1935, 24 OCTOBER.

We have sung of "the wonderful giants of old" but can any one doubt that this generation is as good and as noble as any the nation has ever produced, and that its men and women can stand against all tests? Can any one doubt that this generation is in every way capable of carrying on the traditions of the nation and handing down its love of justice and liberty and its message undiminished and unimpaired?

1940, 18 DECEMBER, HARROW SCHOOL. (UNRELENTING, 20.)

I have an invincible confidence in the genius of Britain. I believe in the instinctive wisdom of our well-tried democracy. I am sure they will speak now in ringing tones, and that their decision will vindicate the hopes of our friends in every land and will enable us to march in the vanguard of the United Nations in majestic enjoyment of our fame and power.

1945, 30 JUNE. ELECTION BROADCAST, LONDON. (VICTORY, 211.)

If ever there was a moment, when after all our victories and service to the cause of human freedom every patriotic man and woman ought to be thinking about the country and taking a long view, that moment is *now*.

1950, 4 FEBRUARY. TOWN HALL, LEEDS. (BALANCE, 179.)

...it is barely ten years since we upheld on our strong, unyielding shoulders the symbols, the honour and even perhaps the life of the free world...It does indeed seem hard that the traditions and triumphs of a thousand years should be challenged by the ebb and flow of markets and commercial and financial transactions in the vast swaying world....In all history there has never been a community so large, so complex, so sure of its way of life, poised at such a dizzy eminence and on so precarious a foundation.

1952, 11 JUNE. PRESS ASSOCIATION LUNCHEON, LONDON. (STEMMING, 299.)

England

I am a great admirer of the Scots. I am quite friendly with the Welsh, especially one of them [Lloyd George]. I must confess to some sentiment about Old Ireland, in spite of the ugly mask she tries to wear. But this is not their night. On this one night in the whole year we are allowed to use a forgotten, almost a forbidden word. We are allowed to mention the name of our own country, to speak of ourselves as "Englishmen," and we may even raise the slogan "St. George for Merrie England"....

There are a few things I will venture to mention about England. They are spoken in no invidious sense. Here it would hardly occur to anyone that the banks would close their doors against their depositors. Here no one questions the fairness of the courts of law and justice. Here no one thinks of persecuting a man on account of his religion or his race. Here everyone, except the criminals, looks on the policeman as a friend and servant of the public. Here we provide for poverty and misfortune with more compassion, in spite of all our burdens, than any other country. Here we can assert the rights of the citizen against the State, or criticize the Government of the day, without failing in our duty to the Crown or in our loyalty to the King....

1933, 24 APRIL. ROYAL SOCIETY OF ST. GEORGE, LONDON. (COVENANT, 91–2.)

Englishmen and Arabs

The Arab was an African reproduction of the Englishman; the Englishman a superior and civilised developement [sic] of the Arab.

1899. (RIVER I, 25.)

The older spelling of "development" prevails throughout the first edition of The River War.

Experience

We are at once more experienced and more truly united than any people in the world.

1933, 24 APRIL. ROYAL SOCIETY OF ST. GEORGE, LONDON. (COVENANT, 93; ALLIANCE, 39.)

On St. George's Day (actually the 23rd), twenty years later WSC used the same words to the Honourable Artillery Company: "I didn't get shouted down when I said it twenty years ago tonight."

Foreign policy of

Putting the preservation of peace in the first place, what is the next great object that we must have in view? It is to secure our national freedom of choice to remain outside a European war, if one should break out. That I put as the more direct and more practical issue, subordinate to, but not less important than, the preservation of peace....We cannot afford to confide the safety of our country to the passions or the panic of any foreign nation which may be facing some desperate crisis. We must be independent. We must be free. We must preserve our full latitude and discretion of choice. In the past we have always had this freedom and independence.

1934, 8 MARCH.

We must ask ourselves whether we wish to be dependent on France for our domestic safety. We must ask ourselves whether we can accept the protection of a foreign country for any long period of time without losing that freedom to place our own interpretation upon our Continental obligations which, it seems to me, is absolutely vital to the sound conduct of our affairs. We have these obligations, but we still have the right to judge according to our sense of justice and the circumstances of the time.

1934, 30 JULY.

Nearly three decades before Churchill had said,

We do not mind even if we become dependent on foreign nations, because we know that by that very fact we make foreign nations dependent upon us.

But then he was referring to trade, not military protection.

British policy for four hundred years has been to oppose the strongest power in Europe by weaving together a combination of other countries strong enough to face the bully. Sometimes it is Spain, sometimes the French monarchy, sometimes the French Empire, sometimes Germany. I have no doubt who it is now. But if France set up to claim the overlordship of Europe, I should equally endeavour to oppose them. It is thus through the centuries we have kept our liberties and maintained our life and power.

1936, 6 MAY. (OB, CV5/3, 143.)

We are an old nation. It is nearly a thousand years since we were conquered. We have built up our state and way of life slowly and gradually, across the centuries. Therefore we can afford to make exertions for peace which would not be easy in a race less sure of itself and of its duty.

1939, 28 JUNE. CARLTON CLUB, LONDON.
(BLOOD, 177–8.)

Geography

Our island is surrounded by the sea. It always has been, and although the House may not realize it, the sea was in early times a great disadvantage because an invader could come across the sea and no one knew where he would land; very often he did not know himself.

1933, 14 MARCH.

Golden circle

In the British Empire we not only look out across the seas towards each other, but backwards to our own history, to Magna Carta, to Habeas Corpus, to the Petition of Right, to Trial by Jury, to the English Common Law and to Parliamentary democracy. These are the milestones and monuments that mark the path along which the British race has marched to leadership and freedom. And over all this, uniting each Dominion with the other and uniting us all with our majestic past, is the golden circle of the Crown. What is within the circle? Not only the glory of an ancient unconquered people, but the hope, the sure hope, of a broadening life for hundreds of millions of men.

1939, 20 APRIL. CANADA CLUB, LONDON.
(CS VI, 6107.)

Churchill uses "golden circle of the Crown" in at least six speeches, meaning various things at various times, but always including Crown and Parliament, Commonwealth and Empire.

It is the golden circle of the Crown which alone embraces the loyalties of so many States and races all over the world. It is the symbol which gathers together and expresses those deep emotions and stirrings of the human heart which make men travel far to fight and die together, and cheerfully abandon material possessions and enjoyments for the sake of abstract ideas.

1945, 15 MAY.

As I look upon the future of our country in the changing scene of human destiny I feel the existence of three great circles among the free nations and democracies. I almost wish I had a blackboard. I would make a picture for you. I don't suppose it would get hung in the Royal Academy, but it would illustrate the point I am anxious for you to hold in your minds. The first circle for us is naturally the British Commonwealth and Empire, with all that that comprises. Then there is also the English-speaking world in which we, Canada, and the other British Dominions and the United States play so important a part. And finally there is United Europe. These three majestic circles are co-existent and if they are linked together there is no force or combination which could overthrow them or even challenge them.

1948, 9 OCTOBER, LLANDUDNO, WALES.
(EUROPE, 417.)

Our cause is sacred: peace and freedom. The way for us in Britain to serve this cause is plain. There are linked together the three circles I have often described. First, the British Empire, and Commonwealth of Nations growing in moral and physical strength. Secondly, the irrevocable association of the English-speaking world, around the great republic of the United States. Thirdly, the safety and revival of Europe in her ancient fame and long-sought unity. In all these circles we in this hard-pressed but unvanquished island have a vital part to play and if we can bear the weight we may win the crown of honour.

1952, 3 MAY. POLITICAL BROADCAST, LONDON.
(STEMMING, 286.)

Humbug

I had no idea in those days of the enormous and unquestionably helpful part that humbug plays in the social life of great peoples.

1930. (MEL, 70.)

In the 1890s, WSC had helped tear down barricades thrown up at the Empire Theatre, Leicester Square, to shield passers-by from "vice". By 1930 he wondered if those barriers did not have a purpose after all.

Independence

...we have our own dream and our own task. We are with Europe, but not of it. We are linked, but not comprised. We are interested and associated, but not absorbed. And should European statesmen address us in the words which were used of old, "Wouldest thou be spoken for to the king, or the captain of the host?," we should reply, with the Shunammite woman: "I dwell among mine own people."

1938, 9 May. ("The United States of Europe," News of the World; Essays II, 185.)

In the Bible, the Shunammite acted out of kindness and not for personal gain. From II Kings 4:

8. *And it fell on a day, that Elisha passed to Shunem, where was a great woman; [she had wealth or position in the community] and she constrained him to eat bread....*

13. *And he [Elisha] said unto him, [his servant Gehazi]: Say now unto her, Behold, thou hast been careful for us with all this care; what is to be done for thee? wouldest thou be spoken for to the king, or to the captain of the host? And she answered, I dwell among mine own people.*

...of all races in the world our people would be the last to consent to be governed by a bureaucracy. Freedom is their life-blood.

1943, 21 March. World broadcast, London. (Onwards, 41.)

In my country the people can do as they like, although it often happens that they don't like what they have done.

1946, 1 February. Press conference, Havana, Cuba. (Gilbert, Life, 864.)

When his daughter Sarah voiced her intentions to marry the Austrian music hall performer Vic Oliver he told her, "Do what you like, but like what you do."

I care above all for the brotherhood of the English-speaking world, but there could be no true brotherhood without independence founded as it can only be on solvency.

We do not want to live upon others and be kept by them, but faithfully and resolutely to earn our own living, without fear or favour, by the sweat of our brow, by the skill of our craftsmanship and the use of our brains.

1953, 10 October, Margate. (Alliance, 59.)

Industry

This is no country of vast spaces and simple forms of mass production. We have important and substantial basic industries. We have an agriculture which out of self-preservation we are expanding to the utmost. But it is by many thousands of small individual enterprises and activities that the margin by which alone we can maintain ourselves has been procured.

1945, 28 November. Friends House, London. (Sinews, 52.)

The foundation of this island's commerce was cheap and abundant coal. Upon this the brains, inventiveness, good business management and enterprise of our people enabled our population to double itself in a century. Now here, living, breathing, toiling, suffering, what is to happen if the foundation fails?

1947, 6 December, Belle Vue, Manchester. (Europe, 217.)

The commercial and industrial greatness of this island at the beginning of my lifetime was unrivalled in the world. All its businesses and firms and small employers, and careful obliging shopkeepers were the result of much wisdom and many virtues. All this was not built up as Socialist speakers would have you believe by sharks and rogues exploiting the masses. There was more in it than that....We can never keep our population even at its present standards without foreign help, unless all these forces are working at their utmost compass underneath well-known laws, vigilantly strengthened wherever necessary to correct abuses.

1950, 4 February, Leeds. (Balance, 178.)

We certainly could never earn our living by world trade or even exist in this island without full recognition of all forms of exceptional individual contribution, whether by genius, contrivance, skill, industry or thrift.

1951, 9 October, Woodford, Essex. (Stemming, 139.)

Influence

British influence is healthy and kindly, and makes for the general happiness and welfare of mankind.

1901, 13 May.

Churchill added, addressing the demand for a larger army:

And we shall make a fatal bargain if we allow the moral force which this country has so long exerted to become diminished, or perhaps even destroyed, for the sake of the costly, trumpery, dangerous military playthings, on which the Secretary of State for War has set his heart.

See also People...Brodrick.

London

...when after the enemy wearied of his attack upon the capital and turned to other parts of the country, many of us in our hearts felt anxiety lest the weight of attack concentrated in those smaller organisms should prove more effective than when directed on London, which is so vast and strong that she is like a prehistoric monster into whose armoured hide showers of arrows can be shot in vain.

1941, 14 July. County Hall, London. (Unrelenting, 185.)

...London will never be conquered, and will never fail, and...her renown, triumphing over every ordeal, will long shine among men.

1944, 6 July.

London, like a great rhinoceros, a great hippopotamus, saying: "Let them do their worst. London can take it." London could take anything. My heart goes out to the Cockneys. Any visitors we may happen to have here today—and many great nations are represented here, by all those who have borne arms with us in the struggle—they echo what I say when I say "GOOD OLD LONDON!"

1945, 9 May. Ministry of Health, London.

For more of this quotation see World War II...1945/May.

Personally I must confess that there was one quite old ruin which seemed to me to deserve at least as much attention as those which owed their destruction to Hitler. I am very glad that...we rescued the Temple of Mithras from the progress of modern civilisation, whether in its destruction or reconstructive form. I must congratulate you on having got a magnificent new roof over your heads and amid all the problems of housing for the people not to have left Gog and Magog out in the cold.

1954, 9 November. Lord Mayor's Banquet, Guildhall, London. (Alliance, 192.)

Gog and Magog (named for nations of the earth deceived by Satan, Revelations XX:7–9) were a pair of 1708 nine-foot statues destroyed in the Blitz; during the rebuilding of the House of Commons they were replaced by replicas.

National goals and aspirations

We are not going to measure the strength of great countries only by their material resources. We think that the supremacy and the predominance of our country depends upon the maintenance of the vigour and health of its population, just as its true glory will always be found in the happiness of its cottage homes.

1909, 4 May.

...if we wish to detach ourselves and lead a life of independence from European entanglements, we have to be strong enough to defend our neutrality.

1933, 14 March.

It must always be assumed, of course, that Great Britain will stand by her obligations. Probably she will be better than her legal word...

1933, 23 March.

We must do our duty, but we must do it only in conjunction with other nations and in accordance with obligations which others recognize as well. We are not strong enough—I say it advisedly—to be the law-giver and spokesman of the world.

1935, 11 July.

To be easily reconciled to the idea of race extinction is to be morbid. It is contrary to the life spirit of the world and neglectful of the purposes of the Creator or of the creative force. I am on the side of those who wish to see the British race and Empire last as long as possible, and guide the world away from harm and evil through long sunshine centuries.

1938, 25 SEPTEMBER. ("THE EFFECT OF MODERN AMUSEMENTS ON LIFE AND CHARACTER," NEWS OF THE WORLD; ESSAYS IV, 473.)

We must confront our perils and trials with that national unity which cannot be broken, and a national force which is inexhaustible. We must confront them with resilience and ingenuity which are fearless, and above all with the inflexible will-power to endure and yet to dare for which our island race has long been renowned. Thus, and thus alone, can we be worthy champions of that grand alliance of nearly thirty States and nations which without our resistance would never have come into being, but which now has only to march on together until tyranny is trampled down.

1942, 26 MARCH. CONSERVATIVE CENTRAL COUNCIL, CAXTON HALL, LONDON. (END, 108.)

Under our ancient monarchy, that bulwark of British liberties, that barrier against dictatorships of all kinds, we intend to move forward in a great family, preserving the comradeships of the war, free for ever from the class prejudice and other forms of snobbery from which in modern times we have suffered less than most other nations, and from which we are now shaking ourselves entirely free. Britain is a fertile mother, and natural genius springs from the whole people.

1943, 21 MARCH. BROADCAST, LONDON. (ONWARDS, 42.)

We seek no profit, we covet no territory or aggrandisement. We expect no reward and we will accept no compromise. It is on that footing that we wish to be judged, first in our own consciences and afterwards by posterity.

1943, 30 JUNE, GUILDHALL, LONDON. (ONWARDS, 124.)

Freedom will be erected on unshakable foundations, and at her side will be Right and Justice; and I am sure of this, that when the victory is gained we shall show a poise and temper as admirable as that which we displayed in the days of our mortal danger, that we shall not be led astray by false guides either into apathy and weakness or into brutality, but that the name of our dear country, our island home, will, by our conduct, by our clairvoyance, by our self-restraint, by our inflexible tenacity of purpose, long stand in honour among the nations of world.

1943, 29 SEPTEMBER. ROYAL ALBERT HALL, LONDON. (ONWARDS, 224–5.)

We are resolved to make this Island solvent, able to earn its living and pay its way....we have no assurance that anyone else is going to keep the British Lion as a pet.

1951, 22 DECEMBER. BROADCAST, LONDON. (STEMMING, 214.)

Churchill was departing for Washington, where he hoped to secure an American loan. He used the identical sentence in a speech at Woodford on 6 January 1959.

National life

Here in this country we know that no dark designs are harboured by our Government against the peace or well-being of any country. There may be mistakes, there may be muddles; but no dark designs are harboured by any British Prime Minister or Foreign Secretary. He could not live under the conditions of British Cabinet Government if it were otherwise. But foreign countries do not always attribute to us this innocence.

1933, 13 APRIL.

The new England, or the new Britain, for we have our Welsh and Scottish friends represented [a voice: "And Northern Ireland"] —and Northern Ireland which we never forget—the new Britain and the old Britain have always dwelt side by side in our land, and it is by the union and inter-play of the new impulses and the great traditions both working together…that we have contrived to build up over generations that basis of life with its rights and tolerances, its individual freedom, its collective associations, and, above all, its infinite power of self-improvement and national progress, that decent way of life which the broad masses of our people share and for which they now show themselves prepared to fight, and if need be to die.

1942, 26 MARCH, CAXTON HALL, LONDON. (END, 104.)

People, British

...the English are essentially a warlike, though not a military, people; that is to say they are always ready to fight, though not always prepared to do so.

1897, 15 OCTOBER. NOWSHERA, INDIAN FRONTIER. (WAR CORRESPONDENT, 78.)

...a blunderbuss is a traditional weapon with which the British householder defends himself from those who seek to plunder him.

1901, 13 MAY.

The whole foundation of our political system is the equality of rights and the equal importance and value of the political rights enjoyed by persons in every class.

1911, 30 MAY.

...the British public, and the great nation which inherits this somewhat foggy island, are less likely to be grateful for benefits received than they are for evils averted.

1927, 13 APRIL.

There is no doubt that there is more betting done in England than in any other equal community in the world, and there is no doubt that it is done in more disagreeable and irritating conditions, more unsatisfactory conditions, than in any other country in the world.

1928, 16 MARCH.

"Tell the truth to the British people." They are a tough people, a robust people. They may be a bit offended at the moment, but if you have told them exactly what is going on, you have insured yourself against complaints and reproaches which are very unpleasant when they come home on the morrow of some disillusion.

1932, 23 NOVEMBER.

The British people are good all through. You can test them as you would put a bucket into the sea, and always find it salt. The genius of our people springs from every class and from every part of the land. You cannot tell where you will not find a wonder. The hero, the fighter, the poet, the master of science, the organiser, the artist, the engineer, the administrator or the jurist—he may spring into fame. Equal opportunity for all, under free institutions and equal laws—there is the banner for which we will do battle against

all rubber-stamp bureaucracies or dictatorships.

1945, 13 JUNE. ELECTION BROADCAST, LONDON. (VICTORY, 197.)

Golding, look at this: Improper advances.... below zero...76 years old...Makes you proud to be an Englishman!

1946. RONALD GOLDING TO THE EDITOR.

According to Ronald Golding, a Scotland Yard detective seconded to Churchill in 1946, Churchill read a news article that an elderly gentleman was arrested on a very cold evening in Hyde Park "for making improper advances to a young lady".

The British race is not actuated mainly by the hope of material gain. Otherwise we should long ago have sunk in the ocean of the past. It is stirred on almost all occasions by sentiment and instinct, rather than by programmes or worldly calculation.

1946, 5 OCTOBER, BLACKPOOL. (SINEWS, 215.)

The British working man, especially the radical element, has a deep-seated and natural love of fair play...

1947, 16 MAY, AYR, SCOTLAND. (EUROPE, 97.)

In a long and varied life I have constantly watched and tried to measure the moods and inspirations of the British people. There is no foe they will not face. There is no hardship they cannot endure. Whether the test be sharp and short or long and wearisome, they can take it. What they do not forgive is false promises and vain boastings.

1947, 4 OCTOBER, BRIGHTON. (EUROPE, 154.)

... the British nation from time to time gives way to waves of crusading sentiment. More than any other country in the world, it is at rare intervals ready to fight for a cause or a theme, just because it is convinced in its heart and soul that it will not get any material advantage out of the conflict.

1948. (WW2 I, 143.)

See also War...Advantage in.

There is a deep fund of common sense in the English race and they have all sorts of ways, as has been shown in the past, of resisting and limiting the imposition of State autocracy.

1950, 13 FEBRUARY. USHER HALL, EDINBURGH.
(BALANCE, 198.)

My faith is unbroken in the strength, genius, and inexhaustible resourcefulness of the British race.

1952, 4 FEBRUARY, WALTHAMSTOW. (COOTE, 213.)

People in war

The British people have taken for themselves this motto—"Business carried on as usual during alterations on the map of Europe."

1914, 9 NOVEMBER. GUILDHALL, LONDON.
(CS III, 2340.)

No demand is too novel or too sudden to be met. No need is too unexpected to be supplied. No strain is too prolonged for the patience of our people. No suffering nor peril daunts their hearts. Instead of quarrelling, giving way as we do from time to time to moods of pessimism and of irritation, we ought to be thankful that if such trials and dangers were destined for our country we are here to share them, and to see them slowly and surely overcome.

1918, 25 APRIL. MINISTRY OF MUNITIONS, LONDON.
(CS III, 2610.)

When the British people make up their minds to go to war they expect to receive terrible injuries. That is why we tried to remain at peace as long as possible.

1940, 5 SEPTEMBER.

I go about the country whenever I can escape for a few hours or for a day from my duty at headquarters, and I see the damage done by the enemy attacks; but I also see side by side with the devastation and amid the ruins quiet, confident, bright and smiling eyes, beaming with a consciousness of being associated with a cause far higher and wider than any human or personal issue. I see the spirit of an unconquerable people. I see a spirit bred in freedom, nursed in a tradition which has come down to us through the centuries, and which will surely at this moment, this turning-point in the history of the world, enable us to bear our part in such a way that none of our race who come after

us will have any reason to cast reproach upon their sires.

1941, 12 APRIL, BRISTOL. (UNRELENTING, 87.)

They [the British] are the only people who like to be told how bad things are, who like to be told the worst...

1941, 10 JUNE.

War is a hard school, but the British, once compelled to go there, are attentive pupils.

1944, 2 AUGUST.

The British people do not, as is sometimes thought, go to war for calculation, but for sentiment.

1945, 2 APRIL. (WW2 VI, 431.)

WSC to Marshal Stalin; one of their last communications.

It is a curious fact about the British Islanders, who hate drill and have not been invaded for nearly a thousand years, that as danger comes nearer and grows they become progressively less nervous; when it is imminent they are fierce; when it is mortal they are fearless. These habits have led them into some very narrow escapes.

1948. (WW2 I, 310.)

Regrets

I have anxiously asked the question, "What are power politics?" I know some of our friends across the water so well that I am sure I can always speak frankly without causing offence. Is having a navy twice as big as any other navy in the world power politics? Is having the largest air force in the world with bases in every part of the world power politics? Is having all the gold in the world power politics? If so, we are certainly not guilty of these offences, I am sorry to say. They are luxuries that have passed away from us.

1945, 18 JANUARY.

My first impression on looking round the scene at home in November as Minister of Defence was a sense of extreme nakedness such as I have never felt before in peace or war—almost as though I was living in a nudist colony.

1952, 5 MARCH.

"Rule Britannia"

Going back a long time...to 27 March 1936 [Mr. Baldwin] said, according to the *Daily Herald*..."We shall have to give up certain of our toys—one is 'Britannia rules the Waves.'"....As has been often pointed out, it is "Britannia rule the Waves"—an invocation, not a declaration of fact. But if the idea "Rule Britannia" was a toy, it is certainly one for which many good men from time to time have been ready to die.

1951, 19 APRIL.

"Rule Britannia" by James Thomson (1700–48) was put to music by Thomas Augustine Arne (circa 1740) and is sung as an unofficial national anthem.

On the first night when I visited the wardroom the officers were singing songs. At the end they sang the chorus of "Rule, Britannia." I asked them what were the words. Nobody knew them. So I recited some of Thomson's noble lines myself...

1954. (WW2 VI, 23.)

Churchill was recalling his visit to a British motor torpedo boat on 17 July 1944. The words he supplied were:

The nations, not so blest as thee,
Must in their turn to tyrants fall:
While thou shalt flourish great and free,
The dread and envy of them all.
The Muses, still with freedom found,
Shall to thy happy coasts repair:
Blest isle! with matchless beauty crowned,
And manly hearts to guard the fair.

Scotland

Now that I shall be commanding a Scottish battalion, I should like you to send me a copy in one volume of Burns. I will soothe and cheer their spirits by quotations from it. I shall have to be careful not to drop into a mimicry of their accent! You know I am a great admirer of that race. A wife, a constituency, and now a regiment attest the sincerity of my choice!

1916, 3 JANUARY, BELGIUM. (OB, CV3/2, 1354.)

WSC to his wife.

I have myself some ties with Scotland which are to me of great significance—ties precious and lasting. First of all, I decided to be born on St. Andrew's Day—and it was to Scotland I went to find my wife, who is deeply grieved not to be here today through temporary indisposition. I commanded a Scottish battalion of the famous 21st Regiment for five months in the line in France in the last war. I sat for fifteen years as the representative of "Bonnie Dundee," and I might be sitting for it still if the matter had rested entirely with me.

1942, 12 OCTOBER. USHER HALL, EDINBURGH. (END, 237.)

My faith in the free peoples of the British Isles and in Northern Ireland is strong. I do not believe that we are at the end of all our glories, and it is in the struggle to prevent such a catastrophe that all the sanity, wisdom and steadfast tenacity of the Scottish race must be engaged.

1951, 18 MAY, GLASGOW. (STEMMING, 87.)

Sense of humour

It is always, I think, true to say that one of the main foundations of the British sense of humour is understatement...

1950, 27 JULY.

Trade

Why should sixty millions' worth of manufactured goods be sent into the United Kingdom, unloaded there, warehoused there, made up into fresh cargoes, loaded into ships again, and distributed at a profit all over the world? Other harbours are as wide and deep as ours; other climates are quite as genial—other skies are just as blue. Why should the world's shipping labour in the chops of the Bristol Channel, or crowd up the dreary reaches of the Mersey? It is because our harbours are more nearly as nature made them; because the perverted ingenuity of man has not been occupied in obstructing them with fiscal stake nets and tariff mud bars. That is why they come.

1904, 19 FEBRUARY. FREE TRADE HALL, MANCHESTER. (FFT, 56–7.)

Reprinted in 1905 pamphlet entitled, "Why I am a Free Trader".

At present we stand on very firm ground in respect of food....The harvests of the world are at our disposal, and, by a system which averages climatic risks, we secure not only a low but a fairly stable price....With that marvellous operation by which the crowded population of this island is fed, we cannot take the responsibility of interfering.

1905, 8 MARCH.

Tradition

It is this union of past and present, of tradition and progress, this golden chain, never yet broken, because no undue strain is placed upon it, that has constituted the peculiar merit and sovereign quality of English national life.

1931, FEBRUARY. ("PERSONAL CONTACTS," STRAND MAGAZINE; THOUGHTS, 32.)

In moving steadily and steadfastly from a class to a national foundation in the politics and economies of our society and civilisation, we must not forget the glories of the past, nor how many battles we have fought for the rights of the individual and for human freedom.

1943, 21 MARCH. BROADCAST, LONDON. (ONWARDS, 40–41.)

Mr. Attlee [said], "How can we clear up in six years the mess of centuries?" The mess of centuries! This is what the Prime Minister considers Britain and her Empire represented when in 1945 she emerged honoured and respected from one end of the world to the other by friend and foe alike after her most glorious victory for freedom. "The mess of centuries"—that is all we were.

The remark is instructive because it reveals with painful clarity the Socialist point of view and sense of proportion. Nothing happened that was any good until they came into office. We may leave out the great struggles and achievements of the past—Magna Carta, the Bill of Rights, Parliamentary institutions, Constitutional Monarchy, the building of our Empire—all these were part of "the mess of centuries." Coming to more modern times, Gladstone and Disraeli must have been pygmies. Adam Smith, John Stuart Mill...and in our lifetime Balfour, Asquith and Morley, all these no doubt were "small fry." But at last a giant and a Titan appeared to clear up "the mess of centuries." Alas, he cries, he has had only six years to do it in....Now the Titan wants another term of office.

1951, 12 OCTOBER. WOODFORD, ESSEX. (STEMMING, 142.)

Unity

But what is the purpose which has brought us all together? It is the conviction that the life of Britain, her glories and message to the world, can only be achieved by national unity, and national unity can only be preserved upon a cause which is larger than the nation itself.

1938, 9 MAY.

The House will observe in the Royal Proclamation the importance and significance assigned to the word "Realm." There was a time—and not so long ago—when the word "Dominion" was greatly esteemed. But now, almost instinctively and certainly spontaneously, the many States, nations and races included in the British Commonwealth and Empire, have found in the word "Realm" the expression of their sense of unity, combined in most cases with a positive allegiance to the Crown or a proud and respectful association with it.

1952, 11 FEBRUARY.

Although we often deal in Parliament with differences between us, we must not forget the deep foundations underlying the whole of our British national life. Whenever danger from abroad or extraordinary stress or difficulty at home comes to the front you will always find the united strength and brains of the nation available for its solution and for warding off the peril.

1953, 27 OCTOBER, DOWNING STREET. (COOTE, 113.)

Victorian Britain

How these Victorians busied themselves and contended about minor things! What long, brilliant, impassioned letters they wrote each other about refined personal and political issues of which the modern Juggernaut progression takes no account! They never had to face, as we have done, and still do, the possibility of national ruin. Their main foundations were never shaken. They dwelt in an age of British splendour and unchallenged leadership. The art of government was exercised within a limited sphere. World-revolution, mortal defeat, national subjugation, chaotic degeneration, or even national bankruptcy, had not laid steel claws upon their sedate, serene, complacent life.

1929, OCTOBER. ("THE EARL OF ROSEBERY," PALL MALL; GC, 10.)

This was the British Antonine Age. Those who were its children could not understand why it had not begun earlier or why it should ever stop. The French Revolution had subsided into tranquillity; the Napoleonic Wars had ended at Waterloo; the British Navy basked in the steady light of Trafalgar, and all the navies of the world together could not rival its sedate strength.

1929, NOVEMBER. ("JOHN MORLEY," *PALL MALL*; GC, 57.)

I was a child of the Victorian era, when the strength of our country seemed firmly set, when its position in trade and on the seas was unrivalled, and when the realization of the greatness of our Empire and of our duty to preserve it was ever growing stronger. In those days the dominant forces in Great Britain were very sure of themselves and of their doctrines. They thought that they could teach the world the art of government, and the science of economics....Very different is the aspect of these anxious and dubious times.

1933. (MEL, 9–10.)

Vulnerability of Britain

What is the destiny of our country to be? Nothing is settled for or against us....We stand at the crossways. If we stand on in the old happy-go-lucky way, the richer classes ever growing in wealth and in number, and ever declining in responsibility, the very poor remaining plunged or plunging even deeper into helpless, hopeless misery—then I think there is nothing before us but savage strife between class and class...nothing but that dual degeneration which comes from the simultaneous waste of extreme wealth and of extreme want.

1909, 4 SEPTEMBER, LEICESTER. (CS II, 1317.)

Alone among the great modern states, we can neither defend the soil upon which we live nor subsist upon its produce.

1914, 17 MARCH.

It may be hard for our island people, with their long immunity, to realize this ugly, unpleasant alteration in our position. We are an undefeated people. Nearly a thousand years have passed since we were subjugated by external force. All our outlook for several generations has been influenced by a sense of invincible, inexpugnable security at home. That security is no longer absolute or certain, and we must address

our minds courageously, seriously, to the new conditions under which we have now to dwell, and under which Continental nations have always dwelt.

1937, 4 MARCH.

We have more to lose by war than any human organisation that has ever existed. The peculiar structure and distribution of the British Empire or Commonwealth of Nations is such that our safety has increasingly been found in reconciling and identifying British interest with the larger interests of the world.

1930, 15 FEBRUARY. ("THE UNITED STATES OF EUROPE," *SATURDAY EVENING POST*.)

If the French woke up tomorrow morning and found that all the rest of the world had sunk under the sea, and that they were alone, they could make a pretty good living for themselves from their fertile soil. But if Britain woke up tomorrow morning and found nothing but salt water on the rest of the globe, about one-third of our people would disappear.

1950, 4 FEBRUARY. TOWN HALL, LEEDS. (BALANCE, 179.)

Wales

Môr o gân yw Cymru i gyd. [All Wales is a sea of song.]

1951, 6 NOVEMBER.

WSC had appointed Welshman David Llewellyn as an under-secretary to the Home Office charged with Welsh affairs, announcing, "His name is quite well known throughout the Principality." A Welsh MP shouted: "Pronounce it." "I will," said Churchill – "Llewellyn." Then he stunned the House with this phrase, which he had heard at an Eisteddfod (Welsh festival) thirty years before.

Wars of Britain

...in all the great struggles in which we have been engaged, we have survived and emerged victorious not only because of the prowess of great commanders or because of famous battles gained by land and sea, but also because the true interests of Britain have coincided with those of so many other States and nations, and that we have been able to march in a great company along the high road of progress and freedom for all.

1939, 13 APRIL.

We were always, being a peaceful nation, backward in preparation. But we always won. In all the long wars I have seen in my life, we have always won; and in the last of them our glory and our virtue have been admired by friend and foe.

1947, 28 OCTOBER.

Weekend

I want to draw the attention of the House to the "timing" of the Italian stroke. [The invasion of Albania, on Good Friday, 7 April 1939.] The British habit of the week-end and the great regard which the British pay to holidays which coincide with the festivals of the Church, is studied abroad. You can see it on many occasions, and that moment is the dangerous moment. I do not suggest that, for this particular stroke in Albania, Good Friday was selected out of any desire to insult that day, but undoubtedly it was also the first day after Parliament had dispersed and consequently no immediate question could be raised.

1939, 13 APRIL.

As James Lancaster notes, tyrants frequently took advantage of the weekend. On Fridays, Hitler marched into Austria (1938) and Czechoslovakia (1939). On Saturdays, Germany declared war on Russia (1914) and occupied the Rhineland (1936). On Sundays, Germany invaded France (1914, 1940), Norway (1940) and Russia (1941), and Japan attacked Pearl Harbor (1941).

World War II and Britain

It may be true...that this country will at the outset of this coming and to my mind almost inevitable war be exposed to dire peril and fierce ordeals. It may be true that steel and fire will rain down upon us day and night scattering death and destruction far and wide. It may be true that our sea-communications will be imperilled and our food-supplies placed in jeopardy. Yet these trials and disasters, I ask you to believe me, Mr. Lippmann, will but serve to steel the resolution of the British people, and to enhance our will for victory.

1939, 14 JUNE. (NICOLSON I, 403.)

WSC to American columnist Walter Lippmann at a dinner with Kenneth Clark (Director of

the National Gallery) and the Julian Huxleys. Julian, brother of Aldous, was a biologist, author and internationalist, later the first director of UNESCO at the United Nations.

As we move through these tremendous times, with their swift success and formidable or glittering events, we must not overlook, or consider as matters of mere routine, those unceasing daily and nightly efforts of millions of men and women which constitute the foundation of our capacity to wage this righteous war wherever it may carry us, all over the world.

1943, 14 MAY. BROADCAST, LONDON.
(ONWARDS, 87.)

Upon Britain fell the proud but awful responsibility of keeping the Flag of Freedom flying in the Old World till the forces of the New World could arrive. But now the tornado has passed away. The thunder of the cannons has ceased, the terror from the skies is over, the oppressors are cast out and broken, and we find ourselves breathless but still alive exhausted but free. The future stands before us to make or mar.

1945, 16 NOVEMBER, BRUSSELS. (SINEWS, 42.)

We fought alone against tyranny for a whole year, not purely from national motives. It is true that our lives depended upon our doing so, but we fought the better because we felt with conviction that it was not only our own cause but a world cause for which the Union Flag was kept flying in 1940 and 1941. The soldier who laid down his life, the mother who wept for her son, and the wife who lost her husband, got inspiration and comfort and felt a sense of being linked with the universal and the eternal by the fact that we fought for what was precious not only for ourselves but for mankind.

1950, 27 JUNE.

Empire and Commonwealth

Achievements

The British Empire is held together by moral not by material forces. It has grown up in liberty and silence. It is not preserved by restriction and vulgar brag. The greatest triumphs of our race have been won not for

Britain only, but for mankind. When we suppressed the slave trade we were fighting in the cause of humanity....Look where you will, you will see at every stage on the long and dangerous path on which we have moved, from the condition of a small poor island people to the enjoyment and responsibility of world-wide dominion, it has been written in letters of shining gold; "The victory of Britain means the welfare of the world."

1904, 19 FEBRUARY. FREE TRADE HALL, MANCHESTER. (FFT, 72–3.)

It is a sober fact that the British Empire produces within its limits every commodity which luxury can imagine or industry require.

1905, 8 MARCH.

We have our faults, and our social system has its faults, but we hope that with God's help, we shall be able to prove for all time, or at any rate, for a long time, that a State or Commonwealth of Nations, founded on long-enjoyed freedom and steadily-evolved democracy, possesses amid the sharpest shocks the faculty of survival in a high and honourable, and indeed, in a glorious degree.

1941, 18 MARCH, LONDON. (UNRELENTING, 62.)

In a world of confusion and ruin, the old flag flies.

1944, 21 APRIL.

Aden and Somaliland

...the moment that Aden is transferred to the Colonial Office it will be possible to amalgamate the administration of Aden and Somaliland. Somaliland and Aden are really the most happy marriage that could be made. They are really necessary to one another.

1921, 17 JULY.

Administration

Governments who have seized upon power by violence and by usurpation have often resorted to terrorism...but the august and venerable structure of the British Empire, where lawful authority descends from hand to hand and generation after generation, does not need such aid. Such ideas are absolutely foreign to the British way of doing things.

1920, 8 JULY.

African Empire

...the chronic bloodshed which stains the West African seasons is odious and disquieting. Moreover the whole enterprise is liable to be represented by persons unacquainted with Imperial technology as the murdering of natives and the stealing of lands.

1906, JANUARY. (HYAM, 208.)

Churchill's paternalistic view of the civilising role of the Empire in Africa is represented by this remark (on West African places where the Empire was not involved), and the following remark on British possessions in East Africa.

All forms of cruelty to natives are to be reprobated, but there is one form of cruelty which is especially odious; it is when it takes the form of the exploitation of natives for the purpose of gain.

1906, 28 FEBRUARY.

Under the Treaty of Vereeniging we undertook that no franchise should be extended to natives before the grant of self-government. I am not going to plunge into the argument as to what the word "native" means, in its legal or technical character, because in regard to such a treaty, upon which we are relying for such grave issues, we must be bound very largely by the interpretation which the other party places upon it; and it is undoubted that the Boers would regard it as a breach of that treaty if the franchise were in the first instance extended to any persons who are not white men. We may regret that decision. We may regret that there is no willingness in the Transvaal and Orange River Colony to make arrangements which have been found not altogether harmful in Cape Colony. But we are bound by this treaty. Meanwhile we make certain reservations. Any legislation which imposes disabilities on natives which are not imposed on Europeans will be reserved to the Secretary of State, and the Governor will not give his assent before receiving the Secretary of State's decision.

1906, 31 JULY. (LIBERALISM, 147.)

Quoted at length here because some words (from "it is undoubted" to "not white") are often cited to show that Churchill was a racist. WSC had many faults, but if you intend to cite one, always quote the full remark.

But the real argument I would urge upon the Liberal party, as a cause for our not relaxing our efforts to develop these countries is the interest of the native races who dwell there....I was pleasantly impressed with the manner in which a great number of our civil and military officers whom I met construed their duty towards the native populations among whom they lived. I found them resolved to protect these populations against the mere exploiter and the speculator, and those who merely wished to use them for some financial advantage. [Cheers.] I am sure it would be an evil day for the very large populations of East Africa and of Uganda if they were handed over from the careful, the disinterested control of British officials to the mere self-interest of some small local community.

1908, 18 JANUARY. NATIONAL LIBERAL CLUB, LONDON. (CS I, 861.)

A correspondent once told me that the British Empire to which Churchill was so devoted was nothing more than the prime example of an "opportunistic land grab". I begged to differ.

I have some knowledge of the native populations in these regions and certainly we are to regard them as the greatest trust that is confided to us, because they are the most helpless of the population, and it is for us to see that they are better, and not worse, from one responsible charge of the country.

1921, 14 JULY.

While it could be argued that Churchill's approach to Africa was a variation of Kipling's "White Man's Burden", it can also be stated that his interest in the betterment of the native population was more genuine than that of most of his contemporaries.

Characteristics

There were two kinds of Imperialism. There was the Imperialism of the camp, about which some of them who were leaving the Protectionist Party knew something, and there was the Imperialism of the caucus, about which they had known something during the last few months. They ought to distinguish between the amateur Imperialists who gave their lives on the field, and the professional Imperialists who got their living by practising

it in politics; they ought to distinguish between the sentiment which united us to our colonies, and the bastard Imperialism which was ground out by a Party machine and was convenient for placing a particular set of gentlemen in power.

1904, 16 MAY. (BONHAM CARTER, 119–20.)

...the British Empire existed on the principles of a family and not on those of a syndicate.

1907, 7 MAY. IMPERIAL CONFERENCE, DOWNING STREET. (LIBERALISM, 168.)

The British Empire must be a house of many mansions, in which there shall be room for each and all to develop to the fullest his personal or national contribution to the common united welfare and to the strength of the indivisible whole.

1911, 11 MARCH. TROCADERO RESTAURANT, LONDON. (CS II, 1720.)

From John 14:2, one of Churchill's favourite Biblical allusions. See Commonwealth of Nations below.

What the British Empire exhibits more than anything else is the result of freedom of growth.

1922, 2 MARCH

We have fully informed and consulted all the self-governing Dominions, these great communities far beyond the oceans who have been built up on our laws and on our civilization, and who are absolutely free to choose their course, but are absolutely devoted to the ancient Motherland, and who feel themselves inspired by the same emotions which lead me to stake our all upon duty and honour.

1940, 18 JUNE.

Alone among the nations of the world we have found the means to combine Empire and liberty. Alone among the peoples we have reconciled democracy and tradition; for long generations, nay, over several centuries, no mortal clash or religious or political gulf has opened in our midst. Alone we have found the way to carry forward the glories of the past through all the storms, domestic and foreign, that have surged about, and thus to bring the labours of our forebears as a splendid inheritance for modern progressive democracy to enjoy.

1940, 9 OCTOBER. CAXTON HALL, LONDON. (BLOOD, 458–9.)

Among the various forces that hold the British Empire together is…"enlightened self-interest." That has a valuable and important part to play, but I am sure he would not make the mistake of placing it in front of those deeper and more mysterious influences which cause human beings to do the most incalculable, improvident, and, from the narrow point of view, profitless things. It is our union in freedom and for the sake of our way of living which is the great fact, reinforced by tradition and sentiment, and it does not depend upon anything that could ever be written down…

1944, 21 APRIL.

The maxim of Lord Beaconsfield, Imperium et Libertas, is still our guide. This truth has already been proved abundantly since those words were spoken. Without freedom there is no foundation of Empire; without Empire there is no safeguard for our freedom.

1945, 15 MARCH. CENTRAL HALL, WESTMINSTER. (VICTORY, 75.)

Commonwealth of Nations

For some years the tendency of Socialist and Left-Wing forces has been to gird at the word "Empire" and espouse the word "Commonwealth," because Oliver Cromwell cut off King Charles's head and all that. Also, I suppose, because the word "Commonwealth" seems to have in it some association with, or suggestion of, the abolition of private property and the communal ownership of all forms of wealth. This mood is encouraged by the race of degenerate intellectuals of whom our island has produced during several generations an unfailing succession—these very high intellectual persons who, when they wake up every morning have looked around upon the British inheritance, whatever it was, to see what they could find to demolish, to undermine, or cast away.…

One must notice in the Gracious Speech, and in other utterances on which Ministers have lately advised the King, the calculated omission of three words which have hitherto claimed many loyalties and much agreement…"Empire"…"Dominion"… "British."…Indeed, I wonder myself that the word "Commonwealth" should satisfy the requirements of Socialist statesmanship.…

That, at any rate, would achieve what appears to be the ideal of the Socialist Government in respect of the British Empire, of committing nobody to anything at any time in any way.

1948, 28 OCTOBER.

The "Gracious Speech" or "Speech from the Throne", delivered by the monarch, sets out the programme of the government, but does not necessarily endorse it.

It is the duty of us all…to try our best to make this new expression of the unity of the world-wide association of States and nations a practical and lasting success, and that is the course which we on this side of the House intend to steer.

1949, 28 APRIL.

Not since the days of the Roman Empire has a single nation carried so great a responsibility for the lives of men and women born outside her shores as Great Britain does today. Within her forty or so dependent territories dwell eighty million people for whose welfare and enlightenment Britain is, to a greater or less degree, answerable.

There has been no lack of critics, at home and abroad, to belittle Britain's colonial achievement and to impugn her motives. But…look where you will, you will find that the British have ended wars, put a stop to savage customs, opened churches, schools and hospitals, built railways, roads and harbours, and developed the natural resources of the countries so as to mitigate the almost universal, desperate poverty. They have given freely in money and materials and in the services of a devoted band of Civil Servants; yet no tax is imposed upon any of the colonial peoples that is not spent by their own governments on projects for their own good.

I write "their own governments" advisedly, for however much diverse conditions may necessitate different approaches, the British have for long had one goal in view for their overseas territories: their ultimate development into nations freely associated within the Commonwealth framework. The present state of the Commonwealth is the proof of the sincerity of this policy.

1960. (INGRAMS, VII.)

In 1960 Her Majesty's Stationery Office published eight books on British possessions in Africa and the Americas, asking Churchill to write the foreword, identical in each. The result represents some of WSC's final words on the Empire-Commonwealth.

Decline of Empire

The policy of ceding British protected territory and British protected subjects in order to get round some diplomatic difficulty, or to assuage the disputes of foreign countries, or even to pay our own way from year to year in the modern world, is a very dangerous one for this country to open. When we are considering our vast, innumerable possessions and the reduced state of our means of defence, and at the same time the obvious hunger which is exhibited in so many quarters on the continent of Europe, it seems to me that any steps that might tend to direct appetites upon ourselves should be viewed with the utmost caution and scrutinized with the greatest strictness by Parliament.

1935, 11 July.

On a proposal to cede a portion of British Somaliland to Italy.

If the British Empire is fated to pass from life into history, we must hope it will not be by the slow process of dispersion and decay, but in some supreme exertion for freedom, for right and for truth.

1939, 20 April. Canada Club, London.
(Blood, 153–4.)

We mean to hold our own. I have not become the King's First Minister in order to preside over the liquidation of the British Empire. For that task, if ever it were prescribed, someone else would have to be found....

1942, 9 November. Mansion House, London.
(End, 268.)

There were, when I was young, some statesmen whose names are honoured, who spoke of the Colonies as burdens, and of the Dominions as fruit which would fall from the tree when ripe. I did not live myself in days when those speeches were made, but I remember well times of great anxiety about the Empire at the end of the last century.

1944, 21 April.

On the morrow of our victory and of our services, without which human freedom would not have survived, we are divesting ourselves of the mighty and wonderful empire which had been built up in India by two hundred years of effort and sacrifice, and the number of the King's subjects is being reduced to barely a quarter of what it has been for generations. Yet at this very moment and in the presence of this unparalleled act of voluntary abdication, we are still ceaselessly abused by the Soviet wireless and by certain unfriendly elements in the United States for being a land-grabbing Imperialist power seeking expansion and aggrandisement. While Soviet Russia is expanding or seeking to expand in every direction, and has already brought many extra scores of millions of people directly or indirectly under the despotic control of the Kremlin and the rigours of Communist discipline, we, who sought nothing from this war but to do our duty and are in fact reducing ourselves to a fraction of our former size and population, are successfully held up to world censure.

1946, 5 October, Blackpool. (Sinews, 210.)

I read with great interest all that you have written me about what is called Colonialism....In this I must admit I am a laggard. I am a bit sceptical about universal suffrage for the Hottentots even if refined by proportional representation. The British and American Democracies were slowly and painfully forged and even they are not perfect yet. I shall certainly have to choose another topic for my swan song: I think I will stick to the old one, "The Unity of the English-speaking peoples." With that all will work out well.

1954, 8 August. (Boyle, Eisenhower, 167.)

Eisenhower had suggested that Churchill make a speech in support of colonial self-government.

I could have defended the British Empire against anyone, except the British people.

Circa 1955. Sir Anthony Montague Browne to
the editor.

Empire goals and aspirations

Let us then seek to impress year after year upon the British Empire an inclusive and not an exclusive character. We who sit on this side

93

of the House, who look forward to larger brotherhoods and more exact standards of social justice, value and cherish the British Empire because it represents, more than any other singular organisation has ever represented, the peaceful co-operation of all sorts of men in all sorts of countries, and because we think it is, in that respect at least, a model of what we hope the whole world will some day become.

1907, 15 JULY.

Cologne Cathedral took 600 years to build....So let it be with the British Commonwealth. Let us build wisely, let us build surely, let us build faithfully, let us build, not for the moment but for future years, seeking to establish here below what we hope to find above—a house of many mansions, where there shall be room for all.

1908, 14 MAY. KINNAIRD HALL, DUNDEE.
(LIBERALISM, 202.)

Churchill's first use of a Biblical allusion (John 14:2) which he invoked on many key occasions: writing to Roosevelt; predicting the liberation of Europe, and at the Fulton "Iron Curtain" speech in 1946. Other appearances are in Religion...Biblical shorthand and Nuclear Age...Treaties.

The shores of History are strewn with the wrecks of Empires. They perished because they were found unworthy. We would court— and deserve—the same fate if, in the coming years, we so denied our destiny and our duty. The problem of the empty lands is one which we cannot evade. Our answer must be Population and Development.

1938, 22 MAY. ("PEOPLING THE WIDE, OPEN SPACES OF EMPIRE," *NEWS OF THE WORLD*, ESSAYS IV, 444.)

Gibraltar

For certain purposes it may be convenient to reckon Gibraltar in home waters, but there is no intention of assuming that for strategical purposes its distance from home can be ignored.

1913, 22 JANUARY.

I am sure we shall gain nothing by offering to "discuss" Gibraltar at the end of the war. Spaniards will know that, if we win, discussion would not be fruitful; and if we lose, they would not be necessary. I do not believe mere verbiage of this kind will affect the Spanish decision. It only shows weakness and lack of confidence in our victory, which will encourage them the more.

1940, 21 JUNE. (OB VI, 584–5.)

WSC to Halifax, quashing a proposed offer to Spain to "discuss" Gibraltar "after the war" in the hopes of averting a Spanish declaration of war. John Colville later reflected that this "was the sort of typical nonsense that Winston was very good at stopping".

The establishment of the apes on Gibraltar should be twenty-four and every effort should be made to reach this number as soon as possible and maintain it thereafter.

1944, 1 SEPTEMBER. (WW2 VI, 607.)

WSC to Colonial Secretary. Legend has it that if the apes ever leave Gibraltar Britain's rule there will end. From Churchill's time the ape colony has thrived magnificently.

Justice

We cannot imprison him or deport him without flat violation of every solid principle of British justice....If we are to employ medieval processes, at least let us show medieval courage and thoroughness. Think of the expense that would be saved. A dose of laudanum, costing at the outside five shillings, is all that is required. There would be no cost of maintenance, no charges for transportation, no legal difficulties, no need to apply to the Portuguese, no fear of the habeas corpus. Without the smallest money or expense the peace of the Protectorate would be secured, and a "dangerous character" obnoxious to the Government, removed.

1907. (HYAM, 492.)

WSC on the suggested deportation of a troublesome, detained African chief: a quotation that can easily be cropped out of context. I have no doubt that the famous impish expression was on Churchill's face when he recommended the use of laudanum.

Maintaining the Empire

We have got all we want in territory, but our claim to be left in undisputed enjoyment of vast and splendid possessions, largely acquired by war and largely maintained by force, is one which often seems less reasonable to others than to us.

1914, 17 MARCH.

For someone often described as an unrepentant imperialist, Churchill had a remarkable capacity for looking upon cherished institutions from the outside as well as the inside.

Over a long period of years the peace and order of the British Empire was, in fact, maintained by about seventy-five battalions abroad and seventy-five at home, with the due proportion of the other arms. Is it not a wonder, and is it not an admirable fact, that the Imperial authority should have been maintained over these vast expanses comprising more than one-fifth, I believe, of the entire population of the world by less than a quarter of a million of white soldiers? To find a parallel you have to go back to the greatest period of the Roman Empire, to the age of the Antonines; to find a parallel for so great and so wide a peace being sustained upon so slender an armed force you have to go back to the Antonines, and even then the parallel is greatly in favour of the British example.

1920, 23 FEBRUARY.

Malta

For now nearly two years Malta has stood against the enemy. What a thorn it has been in their side! What toll it has taken of their convoys! Can we wonder that a most strenuous effort has been made by Germany and Italy to rid themselves of this fierce aggressive foe. For the last six weeks over 450 German first-line strength in aircraft, and perhaps 200 Italian, have been venting their fury on Malta. An unending intermittent bombardment has fallen upon the harbour and city, and sometimes as many as 300 aircraft have attacked in a single day. The terrific ordeal has been borne with exemplary fortitude by the garrison and people. Very heavy losses have been inflicted upon the enemy's air strength.

1942, 23 APRIL.

Politics of Empire

Every one will agree, from whatever part of the King's dominions he comes, or to whatever Party he belongs, that colonial affairs suffer very much when brought into the arena of British Party politics.

1907, 7 MAY. IMPERIAL CONFERENCE, LONDON.
(LIBERALISM, 166.)

Somaliland

See Aden.

Uganda

Uganda is defended by its insects.

1908. EDITOR'S OBSERVATION.

An inscription by WSC on a copy of his travel book, My African Journey.

The Nile springs out of the Victoria Nyanza, a vast body of water nearly as wide as the Thames at Westminster Bridge, and this imposing river rushes down a stairway of rock from fifteen to twenty feet deep, in smooth, swirling slopes of green water. It would be perfectly easy to harness the whole river and let the Nile begin its long and beneficent journey to the sea by leaping through a turbine. It is possible that nowhere else in the world could so enormous a mass of water be held up by so little masonry.

1908. (MAJ, 74–5.)

WSC was at Jinja in 1907, observing what was then called Ripon Falls, a watercourse submerged when building the nearby Owen Falls Dam (now the Nalubaale Power Station). In 1954 the Queen inaugurated the Owen Falls Scheme at the adjacent spot and sent a message to Churchill:"Your vision has become reality" (OB II, 235).

Fancy mistaking a hippopotamus—almost the largest surviving mammal in the world—for a water lily. Yet nothing is more easy.

1908. (MAJ, 103.)

Unity of Empire

Some foreigners mock at the British Empire because there are no parchment bonds or hard steel shackles which compel its united action. But there are other forces, far more subtle and far more compulsive, to which the whole fabric spontaneously responds. These deep tides are flowing now. They sweep away in their flow differences of class and Party. They override the vast ocean spaces which separate the Dominions of the King. The electric telegraph is an old story; the wireless broadcast is a new one; but we rely on a process far more widespread and equally instantaneous. There are certain things which could happen, which it would not be necessary for us to argue about. No Constitutional issues would arise. Everyone, in the loneliest ranch, or in the most self-centred legislature, would see Duty staring him in the face, and all hearts would have the same conviction. And not only the same conviction, but the same resolve to action.

1939, 20 APRIL.

Looking at the British Empire, say, thirty years ago, in 1914, on the eve of the First Great War, all foreign opinion, especially German opinion, was convinced that this vast structure of Empire, created and coming into full life in Victorian times, had reached a condition of ricketyness and looseness when a single violent shock would bring it clattering down and lay it low for ever. [But when war was declared] the whole of the peoples of the British Empire, of every race and every clime, had already sprung to arms.

What is this miracle, for it is nothing less, that called men from the uttermost ends of the earth, some riding twenty days before they could reach their recruiting centres, some armies having to sail 14,000 miles across the seas before they reached the battlefield? What is this force, this miracle which makes governments, as proud and sovereign as any that have ever existed, immediately cast aside all their fears, and immediately set themselves to aid a good cause and beat the common foe?....It is our union in freedom and for the sake of our way of living which is the great fact, reinforced by tradition and sentiment, and it does not depend upon anything that could ever be written down in any account kept in some large volume.

1944, 21 APRIL.

Virgin Islands

[In a defence discussion a Cabinet minister asked, "So where are the British Virgin Islands, anyway?"]

A hell of a long way from the Isle of Man, I hope!

CIRCA 1953. SIR ANTHONY MONTAGUE BROWNE TO THE EDITOR.

7

BRITISH
GOVERNMENT

*"The time-honoured ceremonial and procedure in which Crown
and Parliament have played their part today carry with them to
anxious minds the balm of confidence and serenity....
we feel the inspiration of old days, we feel the splendour of
our political and moral inheritance."* [31]

"It is probably easier to form a Cabinet...in the heat of battle."
The War Cabinet, 16 October 1941. *Seated:* Anderson, Churchill, Attlee, Eden.
Standing: Greenwood, Bevin, Beaverbrook, Wood.

This chapter covers Churchill's thoughts on government institutions – but not political theory and practice, or domestic and international politics. The difference is a rather fine line, so students of Churchill the politician should refer also to Chapters 21–3. Included among "institutions" are the intangible as well as the tangible. Elections, checks and balances, division of powers, civilian control of the military, and the Sovereign's Address are as much institutions of British government as the Houses of Parliament, Home Office or Exchequer. Political activities or their result – such as amendments, centralisation and political cause and effect – are found in Chapter 21, Political Theory and Practice. While this chapter includes general remarks on the role of parties, specific political movements, such as Socialism, Fascism, Democracy and conditions

---

31 WSC, House of Commons, 21 November 1940

achieved by political means, including Churchill's definitions of civilisation, are in Chapter 21.

We all know how highly Churchill held British Parliamentary democracy, but not everyone has read his precise thoughts on how it works, or should work – from the size and layout of the House of Commons, to the roles and duties of Ambassadors, Ministers, Governments and Opposition. He distinguished carefully between the responsibilities of a Member of Parliament and a Minister; he had sensible thoughts about the role of a constitutional monarch. As a young man he had read Parliamentary debates for the past fifty years, and was familiar with the language, demeanour and courtesies of the House from his first day as a Member: a member of the Privy Council was "Rt. Hon.", one of his own party "Hon. Friend", an MP who had served in the forces was "Hon. and Gallant", a legal scholar was "Hon. and Learned". Rarely if ever did he forget the protocol of the place he considered his "natural home".

Ambassadors

The zeal and efficiency of a diplomatic representative is measured by the quality and not by the quantity of the information he supplies.

1941, 17 FEBRUARY. (WW2 III, 653.)

All the great Ambassadors who have exercised influence have remained long at their posts....The natural term of an Ambassador's mission should be six years unless he is guilty of incompetence or divergence from the Government's policy, when of course he cannot be recalled too soon.

1944, 19 MARCH. (WW2 V, 616.)

WSC to Foreign Secretary Anthony Eden, approving the move of Sir Noel Charles from Rio to Italy.

Ambassadors are not sent as compliments but as necessities for ordinary daily use. The more difficult relations are with any country in question, the more necessary it is to have the very highest form of representation on the spot.

1948, 10 DECEMBER.

Bureaucracy

In the conduct of vast, nation-wide administration there must be division of functions, and there must be proper responsibility assigned to the departmental chiefs....For good or ill, in all sensible organisation you must leave the execution of policies already prescribed to the responsible ministers and departments. If they cannot do it, no one can. It is to them that complaints should be addressed.

1941, 29 JULY.

Nothing makes departments so unpopular as these acts of petty bureaucratic folly which come to light from time to time, and are, I fear, only typical of a vast amount of silly wrongdoing by small officials or committees.

1944, 27 MAY. (WW2 V, 629.)

Prime Minister to Minister of Fuel and Power.

Cabinet

The Cabinet is the creature of the House of Commons. It springs from the House of Commons and dwells in the House of Commons. It is checked and corrected by the House of Commons, and by the shrug of the shoulder of the Private Members of the House the Cabinet can be scattered.

1911, 16 FEBRUARY.

It is probably easier to form a Cabinet, especially a Coalition Cabinet, in the heat of battle than in quiet times. The sense of duty dominates all else, and personal claims recede.

1949. (WW2 II, 8.)

Chancellor of the Exchequer

There seemed to be something about the air of 11 Downing Street peculiarly exhilarating, something which not only gave to the occupant of that building clear views on financial questions, but which very often imparted to him the courage of a martyr and the most unalterable convictions. It was all the more remarkable that the atmosphere should have the effect when they reflected upon the obscurity which prevailed at the residence of the Prime Minister next door....

1904, 16 MAY.

Number 11 is the official residence of Britain's Chancellor of the Exchequer.

It would be grossly unconstitutional to suggest that any Chancellor of the Exchequer had the power to veto proposals of expenditure. He has not that power, and he has never had that power.

1926, 28 APRIL.

Checks and balances

I do feel most strongly that there ought to be in the machinery of the state something which corresponds to the governor of an engine, which does to some extent regulate the speed of the machinery.

1909, 17 FEBRUARY.

Civil servants

...a State official or employee has only to keep his office hours punctually and do his best and if anything goes wrong he can send in the bill to the Chancellor of the Exchequer. He truly is what is called "disinterested," in the sense that he suffers no penalty for error.

1951, 2 OCTOBER, LIVERPOOL. (STEMMING, 124.)

Civilian control of military

There is general agreement on this side of the House with what [Mr. Herbert Morrison] calls the traditional view that the constitutional and civil authorities should control the actions of the military commanders.

1951, 11 APRIL.

Constitution

Why, the British Constitution is mainly British common sense.

1908, 14 MAY. KINNAIRD HALL, DUNDEE.
(LIBERALISM, 201.)

There is a saying in England, "Experience bought is better is better than taught." We have bought the experience. I do not complain at all of the workings of our constitutional democratic system. If the majority of the people of Britain, on the morrow of our survival and victory, felt as they did, it was right that they should have their way.

1946, 5 OCTOBER, BLACKPOOL. (SINEWS, 204.)

WSC was referring to his ousting as Prime Minister in July 1945.

Debate

In my opinion, based upon the experience of the most famous men whose names have adorned the records of the House, no national emergency short, let us say, of the actual invasion of this country itself, ought in any way to restrict or prevent the entire freedom of Parliamentary discussion.

1901, 18 FEBRUARY.

Well, I am in favour of government by talking. I am strongly in favour of it as opposed to government by terror [cheers] or government by corruption—or government by bayonet—or government by superstition or government by claptrap. [Cheers.]

1923, 13 NOVEMBER. COAL TRADE BENEVOLENT ASSOCIATION DINNER, GUILDHALL, LONDON.
(CS IV, 3395.)

...some people's idea of it [debate] is that they are free to say what they like, but if anyone says anything back, that is an outrage.

1943, 13 OCTOBER.

I have made myself the spokesman for the greatest possible freedom of debate even if it should lead to sharp encounters and hard words.

1948, 13 MAY. NORWEGIAN PARLIAMENT, OSLO.
(EUROPE, 335.)

Disagreement is much more easy to express, and often much more exciting to the reader, than agreement. The highest common factor of public opinion is not a fertile ground for lively epigrams and sharp antithesis. The expression of broad and simple principles likely to command the assent and not to excite the dissent of vast communities must necessarily be in guarded terms. I should not myself fear even the accusation of platitude in such a statement if it only sought the greatest good of the greatest number.

1954, 12 JULY.

Division of powers

...a natural and healthy emulation between the two Chambers may be conducive to their ultimate efficiency and improvement.

1948, 15 JULY.

The wisdom of our ancestors for more than 300 years has sought the division of power in the Constitution. Crown, Lords and Commons have been checks and restraints upon one another. The limitation of the power of the Monarchy was the cause for which, as Liberals used to say, "Hampden died in the field and Sidney on the scaffold." The concentration of all power over the daily lives of ordinary men and women in what is called "the State", exercised by what is virtually single-chamber government, is a reactionary step contrary to the whole trend of British history and to the message we have given to the world.

1951, 15 OCTOBER, HUDDERSFIELD.
(STEMMING, 150.)

John Hampden (c. 1595–1643) was killed fighting with Cromwell and the Roundheads against Charles I in the Civil War. Algernon Sidney (1622–43, grandson of John Hampden) was a republican executed for treason against Charles II in the post-Cromwell Restoration. Churchill in 1951 would expect every schoolchild to know this.

Both here and across the ocean, over the generations and the centuries, the idea of the division of powers has lain deep at the root of our development. We do not want to live in a system dominated either by one man or one theme. Like nature, we follow in theme the paths of variety and change and our faith that in the mercy of God things will get better and better if we all try our best.

1953, 27 MAY, ST. STEPHEN'S HALL, WESTMINSTER.

Elections

The principle of "one vote, one value" is in itself an orthodox and unimpeachable principle of democracy. It is a logical, numerical principle. If the attempt be made to discriminate between man and man because one has more children and lives in the country, it would be arguable that we should discriminate because another man has more brains or more money, or lives in the town, or for any other of the many reasons that differentiate one human being from another. The only safe principle, I think, is that for electoral purposes all men are equal, and that voting power, as far as possible, should be evenly distributed among them.

1906, 5 APRIL.

At the bottom of all the tributes paid to democracy is the little man, walking into the little booth, with a little pencil, making a little cross on a little bit of paper—no amount of rhetoric or voluminous discussion can possibly diminish the overwhelming importance of that point.

1944, 31 OCTOBER.

It is odious to us that Governments should seek to maintain their rule otherwise than by free, unfettered elections by the mass of the people. Governments derive their just powers from the consent of the governed, says the Constitution of the United States. This must not evaporate in swindles and lies propped up by servitude and murder.

1945, 16 AUGUST.

I have the strong view that voting should be compulsory, as it is in Australia and in Holland, and that there should be a small fine for people who do not choose to exercise their civic duty.

1948, 23 JUNE.

Parliamentary democracy can only express itself by regular and not infrequent appeals to the electorate, but no one has ever suggested that prolonged electioneering is capable of settling our problems at home, or warding off our dangers from abroad. One can hardly imagine anything more unfortunate in Britain than that we should find ourselves at the present juncture split in half on domestic politics, with both parties gathering and arranging their forces for another trial of strength. That this should continue for many months without remedy can only be disastrous to our prosperity, and may well endanger both our life and even our survival as a great power.

1950, 15 JULY. SALTRAM PARK, PLYMOUTH.
(BALANCE, 325.)

As the United States system of mandated four-year elections and extended primary elections reaches unprecedented lengths, the wisdom of this advice is ever more relevant.

...elections exist for the sake of the House of Commons and not the House of Commons for the sake of elections.

1953. (HALLE, IRREPRESSIBLE, 322–3.)

Kay Halle noted that Churchill believed even a government with a small majority should run its course:

> Annual elections might turn the House into a "vote-catching machine looking for a springboard" ... he thought of the House as a wide-angle lens with a wide embrace of many fields.

I have fought more elections than anyone here, or indeed anyone alive in the country—Parliamentary elections—and on the whole they are great fun. But there ought to be interludes of tolerance, hard work and study of social problems between them. Having rows between politicians might be good from time to time, but it is not a good habit of political life.

1953, 3 NOVEMBER.

Finance

The control of finance by the representative Assembly is the keystone of all that constitutional fabric upon which and within which all of us here have dwelt safely and peacefully throughout our lives....Take finance away from the House of Commons, take the complete control of financial business away from the representative Assembly, and our whole system of government, be it good, bad, or indifferent, will crumble to pieces like a house of cards.

1909, 8 OCTOBER. NATIONAL LIBERAL CLUB, LONDON. (CS II, 1325.)

Finance and taxation

The whole procedure of our Parliament arises primarily from the consideration of finance, and finance is the peg on which nearly all our discussions are hung, and from which many of them arise. That is the historic origin of a great portion of the House of Commons procedure, and there is no more deeply rooted maxim than the maxim of "grievances before supply."

1907, 7 MAY. IMPERIAL CONFERENCE, LONDON. (LIBERALISM, 169.)

It is...a political impossibility to allow two Chambers, constituted as the House of Lords and the House of Commons are constituted, to have simultaneous control of finance.

1910, 21 MARCH.

Control over taxation and the revenues of the state has always been the foundation on which Parliamentary Government has rested, and indeed there is no other foundation upon which it can rest. Once the state acquires sources of revenue independent of Parliament, then the power of Parliament to curb and check maladministration is seriously diminished.

1950, 18 MAY. USHER HALL, EDINBURGH. (BALANCE, 278.)

Governments

There are two supreme obligations which rest upon a British government. They are of equal importance. One is to strive to prevent a war, and the other is to be ready if war should come.

1939, 28 JUNE. CARLTON CLUB, LONDON. (BLOOD, 178.)

If democracy and Parliamentary institutions are to triumph in this war, it is absolutely necessary that Governments resting upon them shall be able to act and dare, that the servants of the Crown shall not be harassed by nagging and snarling, that enemy propaganda shall not be fed needlessly out of our own hands and our reputation disparaged and undermined throughout the world.

1942, 2 JULY.

...because a government cannot at every moment give an explanation of what it is doing and what is going on, it would be, and it will be, a great mistake to assume that nothing is being done.

1942, 11 NOVEMBER.

Compassion, charity and generosity are noble virtues, but the Government should be just before they are generous.

1947, 12 MARCH.

Governments, reports to the Commons

It is the interest and privilege of the House to receive full statements on public affairs from the Executive. No band of Members has any right to stand between the House and this great advantage. In time of war it is more important than in time of peace.

1942, 19 DECEMBER. (WW2 IV, 814.)

Governments, wartime powers of

The power of the Executive to cast a man into prison without formulating any charge known to the law, and particularly to deny him judgement by his peers for an indefinite period, is in the highest degree odious, and is the foundation of all totalitarian Governments, whether Nazi or Communist....Nothing can be more abhorrent to democracy than to imprison a person or keep him in prison because he is unpopular. This is really the test of civilisation.

1943, 121 NOVEMBER. (WW2 V, APPENDIX F, 635.)

Prime Minister to Home Secretary, anent the release of the Oswald Mosleys, who had been arrested at the outset of WW2 as security risks. This statement has application today in the debate over the extension of such laws in undeclared wars. Sir Oswald Mosley (1896–1980) was the founder of the British Union of Fascists in 1932.

House of Commons

If I had to choose between the interests of the dignity of the House of Commons and its freedom I would pronounce for its freedom. It could not enjoy real dignity unless its debates were free.

1905, 15 MARCH.

Five or ten years' experience as a Member of this House is as fine an all-round education in public affairs as any man can obtain.

1941, 27 FEBRUARY.

The House of Commons...is the citadel of British liberty; it is the foundation of our laws; its traditions and privileges are as lively today as when it broke the arbitrary power of the Crown and substituted that Constitutional Monarchy under which we have enjoyed so many blessings....I do not know how else this country can be governed than by the House of Commons playing its part in all its broad freedom in British public life.

1943, 28 OCTOBER.

The House of Commons is a living and deathless entity which survived unflinchingly the tests and hazards of war. It preserved our constitutional liberties under our ancient monarchy in a manner which has given a sense of stability, not only in this island but as an example to nations in many lands...an institution which all the world recognises as one of the great features of the modern civilised world.

1948, 26 MAY.

WSC was speaking at the laying of the foundation-stone of the new House of Commons, a faithful replica of the original which had been destroyed by German bombs in 1941.

It is not necessarily a humiliation to a Government to defer to the House of Commons' feelings and to genuine sense established in debates, provided that it does not sacrifice any moral principle or inflict injury or injustice on the public.

1952, 11 OCTOBER, SCARBOROUGH.
(CS VIII, 8413–14.)

House of Commons chamber

There are two main characteristics of the House of Commons....The first is that its shape should be oblong and not semi-circular. Here is a very potent factor in our political life. The semi-circular assembly, which appeals to political theorists, enables every individual or every group to move round the centre, adopting various shades of pink according as the weather changes....The second characteristic...is that it should not be big enough to contain all its Members at once without overcrowding...If the House is big enough to contain all its Members, nine-tenths of all debates will be conducted in the depressing atmosphere of an almost empty or half-empty Chamber. The essence of good House of Commons speaking is the conversational style, the facility for quick, informal interruptions and exchanges. Harangues from a rostrum would be a bad substitute for the conversational style [which] requires a fairly small space, and there should be on great occasions a sense of crowd and urgency. There should be a sense of the importance of much that is said, and a sense that great matters are being decided, there and then, by the House.

1943, 28 OCTOBER.

WSC's rebuilding recommendations were followed precisely; the chamber remains too small for all its Members to this day, albeit wired for television and the internet.

The [party] system is much favoured by the oblong form of Chamber. It is easy for an individual to move through those insensible gradations from Left to Right, but the act of crossing the floor is one which requires serious consideration. I am well informed on this matter, for I have accomplished that difficult process not only once but twice.

Logic is a poor guide compared with custom. Logic, which has created in so many countries semi-circular assemblies with buildings that give to every Member, not only a seat to sit in, but often a desk to write at, with a lid to bang, has proved fatal to Parliamentary Government as we know it here in its home and in the land of its birth.

1943, 28 OCTOBER.

It excites world wonder in the Parliamentary countries that we should build a Chamber, starting afresh, which can only seat two-thirds of its Members. It is difficult to explain this to those who do not know our ways. They cannot easily be made to understand why we consider that the intensity, passion, intimacy, informality and spontaneity of our Debates constitute the personality of the House of Commons and endow it at once with its focus and its strength.

1950, 24 OCTOBER.

WSC took a dim view of chambers like the US Congress; see Political Theory and Practice... Assembly chambers.

House of Commons debate

The House of Commons is the great leveller. To win its heart may not require the highest attainments or the noblest enthusiasms, but it pricks every bubble, it shatters every sham. The way to get on there is not to be a great orator, who has at his command those glowing periods which the populace can never resist. Indeed, the most successful demagogues have often proved the most abject failures when they rose to address Mr. Speaker. The only short cut to the ear of the House is sober common sense, a businesslike way of saying the right thing at the right moment, and a resolute avoidance of claptrap or gush.

1905, APRIL. (INTERVIEW BY "VIVIAN," *PALL MALL*.)

The essence and foundation of House of Commons debating is formal conversation. The set speech, the harangues addressed to constituents, or to the wider public out of doors, has never succeeded much in our small, wisely built chamber.

1930, DECEMBER. ("CLEMENCEAU – THE MAN AND THE TIGER," *STRAND MAGAZINE*; GC, 198.)

If the House is not able to discuss matters which the country is discussing, which fill all the newspapers, which everyone is anxious and preoccupied about, it loses its contact; it is no longer marching step by step with all the thought that is in progress in the country.

1945, 24 AUGUST.

Interruptions which have no purpose but to continue the argument are not a fair use of the right of interruption.

1948, 15 JULY. (EUROPE, 387.)

House of Commons night sittings

Many objections could be urged against all-night sittings, but the ancestors of present Members had not been afraid to subject themselves to considerable strain and exertion in the interests of public and free discussion.

1905, 15 MARCH.

House of Commons power

The House of Commons is not an absolute power, its power is not unchecked. There never was a more sensitive body in the whole history of the world. I can understand it being criticized for being too sensitive sometimes. There are 670 members in touch with many constituencies, differing one from another in character and complexion, sitting here month after month in touch with their constituencies, in touch with public opinion, in touch with the criticism of the Press, in touch with each other, in touch with reason, in touch with reality.

1911, 22 FEBRUARY.

It may sound rather a vain thing for a Member of Parliament to say, but it seems to me that this House is a recognized addition to the defences of Great Britain, that we are safer when the House is sitting, and that the power and will of this House count very much, and, properly commanded, will reinforce the power of His Majesty's Government.

1939, 2 AUGUST.

Here in this country the House of Commons is master all the time of the life of the Administration. Against its decisions there is only one appeal, the appeal to the nation, an appeal it is very difficult to make under the conditions of a war like this, with a register like this, with air raids and invasion always hanging over us.

1942, 29 JANUARY.

House of Commons representation

In regard to the representation of the House of Commons, there are two principles which have come into general acceptance. The first is: "One man, one vote"—there was an old joke about "man embracing woman except where the contrary appears in the text"...and the second is "one vote, one value." The first has been almost entirely achieved....with regard to "one vote, one value," nothing like so much progress has been made.

1948, 16 FEBRUARY.

House of Commons in war

The House is absolutely master. If its confidence is not extended to the Government, if it does not believe that the war is being well managed, if it thinks it can make arrangements which would lead to the war being better managed, it is the duty and the right of the House to express its opinion, as it can do in a proper and a constitutional manner.

1942, 17 FEBRUARY.

...the duty of the House of Commons is to sustain the Government or to change the Government. If it cannot change it, it should sustain it. There is no working middle course in war-time.

1942, 2 JULY.

House of Lords

They [the Conservatives] will not have to defend an ideal Second Chamber; they will not be able to confine themselves to airy generalities about a bicameral system and its advantages; they will have to defend this Second Chamber as it is—one-sided, hereditary, unpurged, unrepresentative, irresponsible, absentee.

....I will retort the question of the Leader of the Opposition by another question. Has the House of Lords ever been right?....in the

main the lines of difference are increasingly becoming the lines of cleavage between the rich and the poor. Let that reflection be with us in the struggle which we are now undertaking, and in which we shall without pause press forward, confident of this, that if we persevere, we shall wrest from the hands of privilege and wealth the evil, ugly and sinister weapon of the Peers' veto, which they have used so ill so long.

1907, 29 JUNE.

This speech marks the beginning of the controversy between the Liberal Government and the House of Lords, which resulted in the Parliament Act, limiting the power of the Lords to reject Bills passed by the Commons.

Two great political Parties divide all England between them in their conflicts. Now it is discovered that one of these Parties possesses an unfair weapon....with which it can harass, vex, impede, affront, humiliate, and finally destroy the most serious labours of the other. When it is realized that the Party which possesses this prodigious and unfair advantage is in the main the Party of the rich against the poor, of the classes and their dependents against the masses, of the lucky, the wealthy, the happy, and the strong, against the left-out and the shut-out millions of the weak and poor, you will see how serious the constitutional situation has become.

1909, 30 JANUARY, NOTTINGHAM.
(LIBERALISM, 228.)

WSC's radical period was never better displayed than in this speech.

It is not perhaps surprising in a country so fond of tradition, so proud of continuity as ourselves, that a feudal assembly of titled persons, with so long a history and so many famous names, should have survived to exert an influence upon public affairs at the present time. We see how often in England the old forms are reverently preserved after the forces by which they are sustained, and the uses to which they were put, and the dangers against which they were designed, have passed away.... Year by year it would have faded more completely into the past to which it belongs until, like Jack-in-the-Green or

Punch-and-Judy, only a picturesque and fitfully lingering memory would have remained.

1909, 26 JULY, NORWICH. (LIBERALISM, 283.)

A remarkable but quite temporary reversal of Churchill on the British traditions he almost always defended; but the House of Lords controversy was serious, and WSC was a serious advocate of reform.

[The Conservative Peers] have got rather roughly mauled in the process [of the Lords debate]. Do not let us be too hard on them. It is poor sport almost like teasing goldfish.... These ornamental creatures blunder on every hook they see, and there is no sport whatever in trying to catch them. It would be barbarous to leave them gasping on the bank of public ridicule upon which they have landed themselves. Let us put them back gently, tenderly into their fountains and if a few bright gold scales have been rubbed off in what the Prime Minister calls the variegated handling they have received, they will soon get over it.

1909, 4 SEPTEMBER, LEICESTER. (OB II, 326–7.)

That this body...should claim the right to make and unmake Governments is a spectacle which a year ago no one would have believed could happen; and which fifty years ago no peer would have dared to suggest: and which two hundred years ago....would have been settled by charges of cavalry and the steady advance of iron-clad pikemen.

1909, 29 DECEMBER, BOARD OF TRADE.
(PEOPLE'S, 46.)

Lord Curzon quotes a great French agnostic and adopts his phrase: "All civilisations are the work of aristocracies." It would be much more true to say that the upkeep of aristocracy has been the hard work of all civilisations.

1910, 10 JANUARY, BIRMINGHAM. (CS II, 1453;
JAMES LANCASTER TO THE EDITOR.)

The French "agnostic" quoted by Curzon was Joseph Ernest Renan (1823–92), a philosopher and prolific writer whose books include the six-volume Origins of Christianity, *a two-volume* History of Israel *and the work by which he is best known,* The Life of Jesus.

The idea that [the foundation of the State is] dependent upon the existence of a second Chamber, of any second Chamber, let alone of this comical anachronism... is surely the most melancholy and humiliating drivel that ever issued from a political party in a period of marked intellectual degradation.

1910, 31 MARCH

If you have a motor-car...you have to have a brake. There ought to be a brake. A brake, in its essence, is one-sided; it prevents an accident through going too fast. It was not intended to prevent accidents through going too slow. For that you must look elsewhere....you must look to the engine and of course to the petrol supply. For that there is the renewed impulse. To prevent your going too slow you must look to the renewed impulse of the people's will; but it is by the force of the engine, occasionally regulated by the brake, that the steady progress of the nation and of society is maintained.

1947, 11 NOVEMBER.

Response to a complaint that the Lords had an undue bias in favour of the status quo. WSC's change of view since 1909–10 was palpable.

The attitude and function of a Second Chamber in any land is essentially one of safeguarding and delaying violent or subversive measures which may endanger the long-gathered heritage of the whole people, without the gravity and significance of the issues involved being fairly and intelligibly placed before them.

1948, 28 OCTOBER.

...I hold strongly that the elected representatives of the people, and the House of Lords, in its relation established by the Parliament Act, should both share in the shaping of legislation.

1952, 11 OCTOBER, SCARBOROUGH.
(STEMMING, 343.)

Judiciary

There is scarcely anything more important in the government of men than the exact—I will even say the pedantic—observance of the regular form by which the guilt or innocence of accused persons is determined.

1908. (MAJ, 28.)

I think it is desirable that persons concerned with the administration of justice should carefully acquaint themselves with the nature and character of any punishment which they may be authorised to order.

1910, 24 FEBRUARY.

We are reminded how in a state of savagery every man is armed and is a law unto himself, but that civilisation means that courts are established, that men lay aside arms and carry their causes to the tribunal. This presupposes a tribunal to which men, when they are in doubt or anxiety, may freely have recourse. It presupposes a tribunal which is not incapable of giving a verdict.

1935, 2 MAY.

The judge has not only to do justice between man and man. He also—and this is one of his most important functions considered incomprehensible in some large parts of the world—has to do justice between the citizens and the State.

1954, 23 MARCH.

…judges have to maintain, and do in fact maintain, though free from criticism, a far more vigorous standard than was required from any class I knew in this Realm. What would be thought of a Lord Chief Justice if he won the Derby? [Laughter.] Yet I could cite a solid precedent where such an act had been perpetrated by a Prime Minister who, on the whole, had got away with it all right. [Laughter.]

1954, 23 MARCH.

Churchill was referring to Lord Rosebery, (Prime Minister 1894–1895), whose horses, Ladas and Sir Visto, won the Derby in 1895 and 1896. Having established his own stable of race horses after the war, WSC knew the sport thoroughly. The Aga Khan recalled hearing Churchill "reciting the names of the last fifty Derby winners and their breeding, an extraordinary exhibition of memory" (Aga Khan, "Churchill the Sportsman" in Marchant, 144–5).

The independence of the judiciary from the executive is the prime defence against the tyranny and retrogression of totalitarian government.

1954, 7 APRIL. (ALLIANCE, 137.)

Accepting in absentia a Doctorate of Law from New York University.

Majority rule

Under our representative institutions it is occasionally necessary to defer to the opinions of other people.

1909, 16 JULY.

Parliament does not rest on unanimity; democratic assemblies do not act on unanimity. They act by majorities.

1945, 21 SEPTEMBER.

Members of Parliament

We believe Members of Parliament are representatives, and not delegates.

1911, 22 FEBRUARY.

In by-gone days…Hon. Members led troops and squadrons of the Fleet and performed all kinds of functions of government at the same time as they conducted their work here. Some of the things that they did would not entirely commend themselves to our present tighter standards of decorum but, none the less…this House should be a House of active, living personalities, engaged to the hilt in the national struggle.…

1940, 21 NOVEMBER.

In the palmy days of Queen Victoria, great respect was paid to the position of a Member of Parliament. His status and authority were everywhere considered. He was much looked up to. Then came an interlude. As the franchise became more democratic, it grew to be the fashion in certain social circles to speak with contempt about Members of Parliament as a class and as a type. They were represented as mere spouters and chatterboxes, the putters of awkward questions and the raisers of small points of procedure. Kipling wrote his poem: "Pagett, M.P., was a liar, and a fluent liar therewith."

1941, 27 FEBRUARY.

"Pagett, M.P." is a poem in Kipling's Departmental Ditties and Other Verses (1886). The first stanza:

Pagett, M.P., was a liar, and a fluent liar therewith –

He spoke of the heat of India as the
"Asian Solar Myth";
Came on a four months' visit, to "study
the East," in November,
And I got him to sign an agreement
vowing to stay till September.

For another phrase which was pulled out
of "Pagett, M.P.", see Chapter 31, Personal
Matters...Rudeness.

...service in the House of Commons ranks with the highest service in the State. Any Member of Parliament or Peer of Parliament has a right to decide at his discretion whether he will fulfil that service or give some other form. Members of either House are free, if at any time they consider their political duties require it, and reasonable notice is given, to withdraw from the Armed Forces or any other form of service in order to attend Parliament.

I could not possibly agree to any smirching of this principle.

1941, 10 DECEMBER. (WW2 III, 755.)

It would be a great pity if the whole of this great armoury, which dignifies very much the position of a Private Member in the House and emphasises his rights and dignities as against the purely delegate conception, which is a very dangerous one, were to be lost.

1945, 16 AUGUST.

Churchill was protesting about what he saw as
Labour's attempt to stifle the Opposition.

Members of Parliament, University Members

I have frequently disagreed very much with some of the statements made by University Members. Of course it may be that the trend of things is to put the most gifted intellectuals in this country more solidly upon the Conservative side. That, no doubt, is an explanation of the Rt. Hon. Gentleman's [Attlee's] change of position.

1953, 20 OCTOBER.

Prime Minister Attlee had abolished the seats
previously provided for British Universities in
Parliament; by 1953 he was urging Churchill
to re-establish them.

Ministers

The position of a minister is one of considerable difficulty. He often has to defend rather an awkward case. When favourable facts are wanting he has to depend upon the nimbleness of his wits, and when these fail him he has to fall back upon the loyalty of his supporters.

1906, 5 APRIL.

In small matters prestige counts. In small matters, taunts are very provoking and jeers wound, but in larger matters, in great matters affecting the whole life and prosperity of the country, it would be shameful if ministers who were charged with responsibility allowed their judgements to be influenced by fear of the taunts to which they might be subjected.

1925, 6 AUGUST.

I am a Parliamentarian myself, I have always been one. I think that a Minister is entitled to disregard expert advice. What he is not entitled to do is to pretend he is acting upon it, when, in fact, he is acting contrary to it.

1947, 7 MAY.

Ministers vs. MPs

There is a gulf fixed between private conduct and that of persons in an official, and above all, in a Ministerial position. The abuse or misuse for personal gain of the special powers and privileges which attach to office under the State is rightly deemed most culpable, and, quite apart from any question of prosecution under the law, is decisive in respect of Ministers.

1949, 3 FEBRUARY.

There is, of course, a difference between what a private Member of Parliament may say, even if his words carry far, and what a Minister can do.

1949, 12 MAY.

Ministry of Munitions

Once the whole organisation was in motion, it never required change. Instead of struggling through the jungle on foot I rode comfortably on an elephant, whose trunk could pick up a pin or uproot a tree with equal ease, and from whose back a wide scene lay open.

1927. (CRISIS III PART 2, 300.)

Upon becoming Minister of Munitions in 1917,
WSC reorganised his staff of 12,000 into a
dozen groups under a council of businessmen.

Monarchy

There is an old constitutional doctrine that the King can do no wrong, and if the King does what is thought to be wrong it is his bad advisers who are blamed; but to apply that doctrine to the controversial head of a political government would be an altogether undue extension of the principle.

1936, 6 APRIL.

In these few words, WSC establishes the importance of separating the role of head of state from head of government.

When our beloved Sovereign and the Queen come from their battered palace to a building which is not without evidence of the strokes of war, when the Sovereign comes to open Parliament in person and all his faithful Commons to the discharge of their duties, at every step, in every measure, in every formality, and in every resolution that we pass, we touch customs and traditions which go back far beyond the great Parliamentary conflicts of the seventeenth century; we feel the inspiration of old days, we feel the splendour of our political and moral inheritance.

1940, 21 NOVEMBER.

Being a strong monarchist, I am in principle in favour of constitutional monarchies as a barrier against dictatorships, and for many other reasons. It would be a mistake for Great Britain to try to force her systems on other countries, and this would only create prejudice and opposition.

1941, 15 MARCH. (WW2 III, 663.)

In our island, by trial and error and by perseverance across the centuries, we have found out a very good plan. Here it is: The Queen can do no wrong. Bad advisers can be changed as often as the people like to use their rights for that purpose. A great battle is won: crowds cheer the Queen. What goes wrong is carted away with the politicians responsible. What goes right is laid on the altar of our united Commonwealth and Empire....It is natural for Parliament to talk and for the Crown to shine.

1953, 27 MAY. CORONATION LUNCHEON, ST. STEPHEN'S HALL, WESTMINSTER. (ALLIANCE, 26.)

Monarchy, coronation

I, whose youth was passed in the august, unchallenged and tranquil glories of the Victorian Era, may well feel a thrill in invoking, once more, the prayer and the Anthem, "God Save the Queen!"

1952, 7 FEBRUARY. BROADCAST, LONDON. (STEMMING, 240.)

WSC was broadcasting on the death of George VI, but at the same time turning to the new Elizabethan era that now lay ahead.

The arrangements for the Procession are in the hands of the Coronation Committee and I expect that they will recommend that only military formations should be included. [Hon. Members: "Why?"] You must think of the spectators.

1952, 18 NOVEMBER.

As the great scroll of history unfolds, many complicated incidents occur which it is difficult to introduce effectively into the pattern of the likes and dislikes of the epoch in which we live.

1953, 15 APRIL. (COOTE, SELF-PORTRAIT, 295.)

WSC was asked why Britain should refer to 1066 to determine the style and titles of its new Queen.

Monarchy vs. republic

These are the days when in other countries ignorant people are often disposed to imagine that progress consists in converting oneself from a monarchy into a republic. In this country we have known the blessings of limited monarchy. Great traditional and constitutional chains of events have come to make an arrangement, to make a situation, unwritten, which enables our affairs to proceed on what I believe is a superior level of smoothness and democratic progress.

1944, 18 MAY. LUNCHEON IN HONOUR OF JOHN CURTIN, PRIME MINISTER OF AUSTRALIA. (DAWN, 80.)

Monarchy vs. Socialism

The Socialists are quite in favour of the Monarchy, and make generous provisions for it....Of course they have a few rebels, but the old Republicanism of Dilke and Labby is dead as mutton. The Labour men and the trade unions look upon the Monarchy not only as a national but a nationalised institution. They even go to the parties at Buckingham Palace. Those who have very extreme principles wear sweaters.

1947. ("THE DREAM," OB VIII, 367.)

C.W. Dilke (1769–1864) and Henry Du Pre Labouchere ("Labby", 1831–1912) were Liberal critics of the monarchy and advocates of a republic. For the background of this article, see Anecdotes and Stories...The Dream.

Opposition

The responsibilities of the Opposition are limited to aiding the Government in the measures which we agree are for national safety and also to criticising and correcting ... any errors and shortcomings which may be apparent, but the Opposition are not responsible for proposing integrated and complicated measures of policy. Sometimes [they] do but it is not [their] obligation.

1950, 12 SEPTEMBER.

Well, I have been a leader of an Opposition too. In a free country one is always allowed to have an Opposition....In England we even pay the Leader of the Opposition a salary of £2000 a year to make sure that the Government is kept up to the mark. I have no doubt that Mr. Attlee...will devote himself to his constitutional task with the zeal which, under totalitarian systems, might well lead him to Siberia or worse.

1952, 14 JANUARY. STATE DINNER, OTTAWA. (STEMMING, 216.)

Parliament

The congestion of Parliament is a disease, but the futility of Parliament is a mortal disease.

1911, 16 FEBRUARY.

Parliament can compel people to obey or to submit, but it cannot compel them to agree.

1926, 27 SEPTEMBER.

It must be remembered that the function of Parliament is not only to pass good laws, but to stop bad laws.

1944, 4 APRIL.

If you want to reduce the power of Parliament, let it sit every day in the year, one-fifth part filled, and then you will find it will be the laughing-stock of the nation...

1944, 29 NOVEMBER.

...it is not Parliament that should rule; it is the people who should rule through Parliament.

1947, 11 NOVEMBER.

It is quite true that nothing can bind a Parliament. Every Parliament is entirely free to behave like a gentleman or like a cad; every Parliament is entirely free to behave honestly or like a crook. Such are the sovereign rights of this august assembly.

1948, 16 FEBRUARY.

Parliament length

It is only the continuance of the war and the extraordinary conditions which it imposes and forces upon us all that justifies us in remaining together as a Parliament. I certainly could not take the responsibility of making far-reaching controversial changes which I am not convinced are directly needed for the war effort, without a Parliament refreshed by contact with the electorate.

1943, 13 OCTOBER.

"Contact with the electorate" was a favourite phrase. WSC considered frequent contact essential, and realised that the extended length of the wartime Parliament was caused only by the protracted conflict.

Parliament vs. private persons

Mr. Speaker, I think that great Parties should endeavour to avoid conflicts with private persons....[It] is never worth while for a great Party to pursue a private person, and least of all when that private person happens also to be a political opponent.

1906, 21 MARCH.

Churchill was referring to Lord Milner, British colonial administrator in South Africa, who had been censured by Parliament. See People...Milner.

Parliamentary inquiries

...the Minister for the Coordination of Defence came forward with a plan. It was the kind of plan which is always popular, always acceptable, and always most effective in allaying agitation and staving off Parliamentary questions. His plan was to have an inquiry. There would be an inquiry over which he himself would preside. Of course, once that has been announced, obviously all other questions whenever they are raised can be answered most effectively by saying, "Hush! The inquiry is still proceeding; the case is sub judice. We must not interrupt these most searching toils and studies which are being undertaken. We must wait with patience until the whole matter can be presented." That inquiry is still proceeding.

1936, 20 JULY.

Parliamentary press

The important function that the Press Gallery has to discharge is to give a fair and truthful representation of what has passed in the House of Commons. In my lifetime, I have seen the reporting of the debates in Parliament sink a great deal as a factor in our public life. Far less space is given to it in the newspapers, but apart from that, the debates are not read with as great attention as they used to be, by a far smaller audience, 50 years ago, when I first cast my eyes on this scene of strife and turmoil.

1952, 28 OCTOBER.

Parliamentary privilege

Privilege means parliamentary privilege. It is a privilege which protects Parliament, its Members, its officers, its witnesses, counsels, people who appear before it or its committees, and also petitioners....It does not protect or refer to the electors or the general public.

1951, 21 MARCH.

"Breaches of privilege", if the Speaker rules that there is a prima facie case for investigation, are usually referred to an all-party Committee of Privileges.

Parties

Much might be said for and against the two-Party system. But no one can doubt that it adds to the stability and cohesion of the State. The alternation of Parties in power, like the rotation of crops, has beneficial results. Each of the two Parties has services to render in the development of the national life; and the succession of new and different points of view is a real benefit to the country.

1907, 25 JUNE.

...party government is an outstanding feature of our political systems of all branches of the English speaking race all over the world. I know of no equal force which assures the stability of democratic institutions.

1910, 31 MARCH.

...these are the qualifications of a good Party man—you must know how to put your Party before yourself, and you must know the occasions when to put nation before Party.

1943, 22 SEPTEMBER.

[Mr. Attlee, then Prime Minister] the other day accused me of being party minded. Everyone would naturally be shocked if a party leader were party minded! But we are all party minded in the baffling and unhappy period between election decisions.

1950, 19 SEPTEMBER.

Party conflict and party government should not be disparaged. It is in time of peace, and when national safety is not threatened, one of those conditions of a free Parliamentary democracy for which no permanent substitute is known.

1954. (WW2 VI, 509.)

Party manifesto

I do not admit as democratic constitutional doctrine that anything that is stuck into a party manifesto thereupon becomes a mandated right if the electors vote for the party who draw up the manifesto. [Interruption.] ...why not add the word "etc." in the list of planks in the party platform? We could then be told: Do you not see these letters, "etc."... Does that not give us the right and impose upon us the obligation to do anything we please?

1951, 7 FEBRUARY.

Popular will

We welcome any country where the people own the Government, and not the Government the people.

1948, 7 MAY. THE HAGUE, NETHERLANDS. (EUROPE, 313.)

Similarly a few days later from the balcony of Oslo City Hall, Churchill said,

...in our island, we are a crowned democracy. The monarch is the servant of the people. We are a country, and you are a

country, where the people own the government, and not the government the people.

...I have served forty-five of the last forty-
eight years in the House of Commons, which
we pride ourselves is the cradle of parlia-
mentarianism and a pattern for all nations.
  In our parliamentary system we can be
assured that the will of the people will
always find open and free expression. With
us, the government is the servant of the
people and not its master.

1948, 12 MAY. STORTING (NORWEGIAN
PARLIAMENT), OSLO. (EUROPE, 334.)

Prime Minister

The dignity of a Prime Minister, like a lady's
virtue, is not susceptible of partial diminution.

1905, 24 JULY.

I am your servant, and you have the right to
dismiss me when you please. What you have
no right to do is to ask me to bear responsibilities without the power of effective
action, to bear the responsibilities of Prime
Minister but clamped on each side by strong
men...

1942, 1 JULY.

I reminded my two great comrades [Roosevelt
and Stalin] on more than one occasion that I
was the only one of our trinity who could at
any moment be dismissed from power by the
vote of a House of Commons freely elected on
universal franchise, or could be controlled
from day to day by the opinion of a War
Cabinet representing all parties in the State....
They could order; I had to convince and
persuade. I was glad that this should be so. The
process was laborious, but I had no reason to
complain of the way it worked.

1952. (WW2 V, 340–41.)

*Referring to the Teheran Conference, where
WSC was hosting his birthday party, 30
November 1943.*

Question time

When the word "we" is used in answer to
Questions it means His Majesty's Government.

1906, 25 JUNE.

Someone had accused Prime Minister

*Campbell-Bannerman of using the "Royal
we" during Question Time (see next entry).*

Question time is one of the most lively and
vital features of Parliamentary life.

1942, 19 DECEMBER. (WW2 IV, 814.)

*WSC to Foreign Secretary and Majority Whip.
Question Time is that period in the
Parliamentary week when Members are
allowed to ask questions of the Prime Minister,
provided that they confine themselves to questions and do not attempt to make a speech – a
distinction that often poses difficult judgements upon the Speaker.*

Secret session

It would be better to do what has been
promised, that is, have a discussion without
the enemy listening. I know a good deal about
all this business. I have very good advisers
who check, I can assure Hon. Members, what
I say, so that I do not inadvertently let out
something detrimental, but Hon. Members
have not the same opportunity. A perfectly
well-meaning speech might be resented by the
troops when it got around and make them say:
"Well, they have said this in the House of
Commons." We must be careful, and therefore
I should not recommend a public debate.

1944, 6 JULY.

Sovereign's Address

The Debate on the Address is the traditional
Parliamentary opportunity for reviewing the
whole political situation, and it is the one great
opportunity of the year upon which grievances
can be discussed.

1929, 3 JULY.

*The Sovereign's Address, also called the
"Gracious Speech" or "Speech from the
Throne", is given by the monarch. It sets out
the programme of the government, but does
not necessarily endorse it, and a "Debate on
the Address" duly follows.*

I am very glad that the closing session of this
long ten years' Parliament should show all
due respect for the traditional and ceremonial
occasions which ignorant, unthinking people,
who have not meditated upon these matters or

studied the true movement of events and of forces in the human breast might easily regard as meaningless punctilio. Here in the Speech from the Throne and in the Debate on the Address may be seen all the workings of the British Constitution, or all the principal workings. The Sovereign, advised by his Ministers, delivers the Gracious Speech. The House then proceeds to express their thanks, but have a perfect right to move Amendments saying that they regret that this or that has been put into or left out of the Gracious Speech, and if they carry such an Amendment, the Government of the day is defeated on a major point of confidence, and it is not easy to conceive a situation in which they could continue to retain their office.

1944, 29 NOVEMBER.

Speaker of the House of Commons

In these hard party fights under democratic conditions, as in football matches and the like, there are moments when the umpire gets a very rough time.

1951, 15 NOVEMBER.

The Speaker, an office dating to the fourteenth century, is the presiding officer of the House of Commons, responsible for maintaining order, and able to issue punishment for infractions. Traditionally the Speaker renounces all party affiliation, does not take part in debate, and does not vote except to break ties – and only then according to conventions that preserve his or her non-party status.

...the Speaker represents and embodies the spirit of the House of Commons and that spirit, which has transported itself to so many lands and climates and to countries far outside our sphere, is one of the gleaming and enduring glories of the British and in a special way, if I may say so, of the English message to the world.

1951, 15 NOVEMBER.

Trial by jury

The ancient Anglo-Saxon foundation of all our system of criminal justice is trial by jury....We regard it as a fundamental safeguard of our democratic liberties and life, and a principle which has been woven into the whole history of our judicial system, that the supreme question, "Guilty or Not Guilty?" shall be decided by ordinary folk.

1948, 15 JULY.

Vote counting

In several Continental countries, when it was known that the ballot-boxes would be in charge of the British Government for three weeks, astonishment was expressed that there could be any doubt about the result. However, in our country these matters are treated exactly as if they were a cricket match or other sporting event. Long may it so continue.

1954. (WW2 VI, 519.)

Vote of Confidence

The Government ask for a Vote of Confidence, but I hope they will not make the mistake of thinking that it is a testimonial, or a bouquet, or that it arises from long-pent-up spontaneous feelings of enthusiasm which can no longer be held in check.

1936, 6 APRIL.

Defeat of a Motion of Confidence requires one of two actions: resignation of the government or a request for dissolution and a general election.

...I ask the House for a Vote of Confidence. I hope that those, if such there be, who sincerely in their hearts believe that we are not doing our best and that they could do much better, I hope that they will carry their opinion to its logical and ultimate conclusion in the Lobby. Here I must point out, only for the benefit of foreign countries, that they would run no risk in doing so. They are answerable only to their consciences and to their constituents. It is a free Parliament in a free country....I am proud of this. It is one of the things for which we are fighting.

1941, 7 MAY.

It is because things have gone badly and worse is to come that I demand a Vote of Confidence.

1942, 27 JANUARY.

Let every man act now in accordance with what he thinks is his duty in harmony with his heart and conscience.

1942, 29 JANUARY.

War Office

I have always cherished the hope that the removal of the War Office from the dilapidated rabbit warren which they occupy in a street whose very name is Pall Mall would inaugurate a new and brighter era of Administration. Nothing in their present methods favours that hope, and when I was walking by Whitehall the other day I noticed—and it seemed full of gloomy presage of the future—that the New War Office building is to be put up on the site previously occupied by the Asylums Board and offices of the Lunacy Commissioners.

1903, 19 JANUARY, OLDHAM. (MBA, 66.)

...I am going to do something that has never been done before, and I hope the House will not be shocked at the breach of precedent. I am going to make public a word of praise for the War Office. In all the forty years I have served in this House I have heard that Department steadily abused before, during, and after our various wars. And if my memory serves me aright I have frequently taken part in the well-merited criticism which was their lot.

1944, 2 AUGUST.

Women in Parliament

I didn't like the idea of their entering Parliament but it turned out better than I feared....

Concede the theory and you have no trouble in practice....You can use women in AA [antiaircraft] batteries: why not in foreign Service....Anything in law to prevent a woman becoming a judge?

1945, 19 MARCH. (DIARIES OF CABINET SECRETARY SIR NORMAN BROOK, NEW YORK TIMES, 22 JANUARY 2006.)

See People...Astor for Churchill's private remark to the first woman Member of Parliament.

Even the women have votes....They are a strong prop to the Tories....It did not turn out as badly as I thought...Some of them have even been Ministers. There are not many of them. They have found their level....it has made politicians more mealy-mouthed than in your day. And public meetings are much less fun. You can't say the things you used to.

1947. (THE DREAM, OB VIII, 368.)

Lady Thatcher, reading the Churchill Centre's edition of WSC's imaginary conversation with his father, was not at all taken aback, telling the editor that she found the story enthralling: "How much it reveals of Winston the man and the son." For the background of this piece, see Anecdotes and Stories...The Dream.

8

AMERICA

"What an extraordinary people the Americans are!...This is a very great country, my dear Jack."[32]

"I have steered confidently towards the Gettysburg ideal..."
American Thanksgiving Day, Albert Hall, 23 November 1944.

If there was ever an "Anglo-American Special Relationship", surely its inventor was Winston Spencer Churchill. Imbued by love for his mother and a fascination with her homeland, the young Winston read widely in US history, politics and literature. He was a student of the 1861–65 American Civil War, whose brother-against-brother hubris appealed to his romantic nature and photographic memory – as Roosevelt learned when, passing through Frederick, Maryland in May 1943, Churchill recited without pause Whittier's long and moving (though somewhat inaccurate) poem, "Barbara Frietchie".

Churchill's love affair with what he routinely referred to as "The Great Republic" began with his first visit to the United States in 1895. There he was welcomed by his mother's friend Bourke Cockran: at forty-one a Democrat Member of Congress and a maverick politician like Churchill would become. Cockran had fought Grover Cleveland for the 1892 presidential nomination. In 1896, preferring principle to politics, he would temporarily leave the Democrats to support the Republican William McKinley. This was a brave desertion in those days of strict party loyalty, which Winston himself would emulate when he quit the Tories for the Liberals in 1904.

---

32 Churchill to his brother Jack, 10 and 15 November 1895, OB 1, 268.

During visits to America between the wars, Churchill became impressed with the vast-ness, energy and potential of his "mother's land"; he wrote witty articles on his travels, with titles like "What I Saw and Heard in America" and "Land of Corn and Lobsters", concluding that the country's potential was unmatched in the world.

Temperamentally and philosophically, Churchill was more at home with the Democrats of his day than the Republicans; though he considered Democrat Woodrow Wilson a naïve dreamer, he was more disappointed in the Republican-led Congress, which had denied Wilson's bid to bring the United States into the League of Nations. As World War II loomed, Churchill found a natural ally in Franklin Roosevelt, whose New Deal he had faintly criticised in a pre-war essay,[33] but whose clear-sightedness regarding Hitler was more appealing to Churchill than the imaginings of his own British colleagues.

In 1933, long before he and Roosevelt became friends, Churchill entertained the President's son James at Chartwell, saying: "I wish to be Prime Minister and in close and daily communication with the President of the United States." Churchill then sketched a pound and dollar sign intertwined. "Pray bear this to your father from me," he told James Roosevelt. "Tell him this must be the currency of the future...the sterling dollar."[34]

Buoyed by his meeting with FDR in August 1941, where they jointly issued the Atlantic Charter communiqué, Churchill engaged Roosevelt in history's most remarkable relationship between two heads of government. It waned later, as Roosevelt sought understanding with the Russians at the expense of what he considered Churchill's outmoded ideas of empire. Yet their mutual respect survived. After visiting Roosevelt's grave in Hyde Park Churchill turned away, eyes brimming, and someone heard him sigh softly, "Lord, how I loved that man."[35]

In 1946, out of power but not audiences, Churchill was back in America to deliver the watershed "Iron Curtain" speech, at President Truman's invitation, in Fulton, Missouri. It heralded the advent of the Cold War. Returning to Downing Street in 1951, the threat of the nuclear age now fully apparent, he worked ceaselessly for an Anglo-American rapproche-ment with the Soviets. But he was frustrated by Eisenhower, who compared post-Stalinist Russia to a woman of the streets. She might have a new dress, the President said, but "there was the same whore underneath it".[36]

It is a remarkable fact – as I often inform disbelieving Republicans – that we must go back to Theodore Roosevelt to find a Republican presidential candidate whom Churchill preferred, meaning 1908, since "TR" ran as an independent in 1912. Churchill considered Harding a foolish isolationist, Coolidge short-sighted, Hoover ineffectual. He was devoted to their Democrat successors, Roosevelt and Truman, and quietly supported Democrat Adlai Stevenson in 1952 and 1956. Though he despised Joseph Kennedy, America's defeatist Ambassador to Britain in the early part of World War II, he admired his son, who as President proclaimed Churchill an honorary American citizen in 1963.

Churchill did like Eisenhower, his wartime comrade. Out of office when the Suez Crisis threatened to wreck the "special relationship" in 1956, Churchill wrote sadly to the President: "I do believe, with unfaltering conviction, that the theme of the Anglo-American alliance is more important today than at any time since the war."[37]

---

33 Churchill, Winston S., "While the World Watches," *Colliers*, 29 December 1934, 24–5, 49. Republished as "Roosevelt from Afar," in Churchill's *Great Contemporaries*, revised and extended edition, London: Thornton Butterworth, 1938. Interestingly deleted from wartime editions of *Great Contemporaries*, but reinserted in post-war editions.
34 Halle, Kay, *Irrepressible Churchill*. Cleveland and New York: World, 1966, 7–8.
35 Pilpel, Robert, *Churchill in America 1895–1961*. New York: Harcourt, Brace, Jovanovich, 1976, 225.
36 Colville, John, *Fringes of Power: Downing Street Diaries 1939–1945*. New York: Norton, 1985, 348.
37 Macmillan, Harold, *Riding the Storm 1956–1959*. New York: Harper & Row, 1971, 175.

Churchill was not an uncritical lover. Though his best-known public criticism about America was "toilet paper too thin, newspapers too fat!",[38] he had harsh words in private for certain American institutions and leaders. Politically he was convinced of the superiority of the British system, with its unwritten constitution, and the British tendency to see things in shades of grey, not black and white.

But Churchill never lost faith in America's destiny or capacity for good. His greatest disappointment in old age, one of his closest colleagues and I agreed, was that the "special relationship" never really blossomed as he had wished.[39] Surely he would be cheered by recent Anglo-American collaborations over the Falklands, Afghan and Iraq wars. As leaders on both sides of the Atlantic never cease to remind us, Churchill's thoughts and ideas are with us yet. Whether we pay heed will vary – as it always has – with the situation.

Robert Pilpel, author of *Churchill in America*, believes WSC's American love affair began the day he first arrived in New York: "We can never know for certain how a person would have developed if one or another aspect of his life had been different. But what is clear with regard to Churchill – as his letters at the time and his writings in later years attest – is that a life which before 1895 seemed destined to yield a narrow range of skimpy achievements became from 1895 onwards a life of glorious epitomes and stunning vindications.

"Credit Bourke Cockran, New York's overflowing hospitality, the railroad journey to Tampa and back, or the rampant vitality of a nation outgrowing itself day by day. Credit whatever you will, but do not doubt that Winston's exposure to his mother's homeland struck a spark in his spirit. And it was this spark that illuminated the long and arduous road that would take him through triumphs and tragedies to his rendezvous with greatness."[40]

So as to trace the development of Churchill's thought on America, quotations are arranged alphabetically and then chronologically. The Special Relationship, the most enduring theme of Churchill's political philosophy, has the largest section, in which I have not tried to break down the subject matter, feeling it more important to let his words on that subject fall in the order they did originally.

The Anglo-American "Special Relationship"

England and America are divided by a great ocean of salt water, but united by an eternal bathtub of soap and water.

> **1900, 8 DECEMBER. PRESS CLUB, NEW YORK.**
> **(PILPEL, 36.)**

Remarked repeatedly on his first American lecture tour, 1900–01.

I have always thought that it ought to be the main end of English statecraft over a long period of years to cultivate good relations with the United States.

> **1903, 22 JUNE.**

Churchill's first expression of a lifelong conviction came much earlier than one might think.

Deep in the hearts of the people of these islands...lay the desire to be truly reconciled before all men and all history with their kindred across the Atlantic Ocean, to blot out the reproaches and redeem the blunders of a bygone age, to dwell once more in spirit with them, to stand once more in a battle at their side, to create once more a union of hearts, to write once more a history in common. That was our heart's desire....One feels in the presence of a Great Design of which we can

38 Halle, Kay, *Irrepressible Churchill.* Cleveland: World, 1966, 240. Response at a White House press conference after the 1944 Quebec conference, when asked what he thought of the United States.
39 Sir Anthony Montague Browne, conversation with the editor, 1983.
40 Pilpel, Robert, " 'What an Extraordinary People': What Churchill Owed the Great Republic," *Finest Hour* 125, Winter 2004–05, 37.

only see a small portion, but which is developing and unfolding swiftly, and of which we are the necessary instruments.

1918, 4 JULY. LIBERTY DAY MEETING, LONDON. (CS III, 2615.)

From a speech entitled, "The Third Great Title Deed of Anglo-American Liberties".

We must keep in step with them. They are our kinsmen from across the ocean. They are our sons returned from a long estrangement.

1918, 3 AUGUST. (OB, CV4/1, 366.)

Unsent draft letter written during a bout of wartime anti-Americanism. By "long estrangement", Churchill could have been reflecting on the century that had passed since the War of 1812.

I felt a strong feeling of sentiment when I saw in the Newspapers yesterday afternoon that the Coldstream Guards and the United States Marines were standing side by side. It looked to me as if once again the great unconquerable forces of progressive and scientific civilization were recognizing all they had in common and all they would have to face in common. [Cheers.]

1927, 25 MARCH. GREAT EASTERN HOTEL, LONDON. (CS I, 4155.)

Frankly I think we are all in the same boat....We have slipped off the ledge of the precipice and are at bottom. The only thing now is not to kick each other while we are there. No action can well be taken by any one country alone. But will it not be sufficient if two or three countries take the step of revaluating commodities to the 1927 level?....I firmly believe that if the United States and Great Britain, though their agents, the Federal Reserve and the Bank of England, would agree that credits shall be expanded and commodities revaluated to the 1927 or possibly the 1928 level, we can restore to human society the benefits which it has lost by the hideous processes of deflation....

My confidence in the British Empire is as great as is my confidence in the United States. We still have the everlasting fundamentals to deal in and to consider. In the words of one of your own statesmen: "The earth is a generous mother. She will produce food for all her children if they will but cultivate her soil in justice and in peace."

1932, 2 FEBRUARY. UNION LEAGUE, CHICAGO. (*CHICAGO TRIBUNE*, 3 FEBRUARY 1932.)

Routinely repeated in roughly the same words at each stop on his 1932 lecture tour of America. For the statesman quoted at the end of this passage, see People...Cockran.

...if the United States were willing to come into the European scene as a prime factor, if they were willing to guarantee to those countries who take their advice that they would not suffer for it, then an incomparably wider and happier prospect would open to the whole world. If they were willing not only to sign, but to ratify, treaties of that kind, it would be an enormous advantage. It is quite safe for the British Empire to go as far in any guarantee in Europe as the United States is willing to go, and hardly any difficulty in the world could not be solved by the faithful cooperation of the English-speaking peoples. But that is not going to happen tomorrow.

1932, 23 NOVEMBER.

I wish to be Prime Minister and in close and daily communication by telephone with the President of the United States. There is nothing we could not do if we were together.

1933, 8 OCTOBER, CHARTWELL. (OB, CV5/3, 734.)

Following the election of President Roosevelt, Churchill felt drawn, from afar, to this man of courage and vision, grappling with economic chaos. One weekend at Chartwell, Roosevelt's son James was among the guests. After dinner Churchill asked each guest in turn to express his or her "fondest wish". When his own turn came, WSC answered without a moment's hesitation.

It is this power of words—words written in the past; words spoken at this moment; words printed in the newspapers; words sent speeding through the ether in a Transatlantic broadcast; the flashing interchange of thought—that is our principal agency of union.

1938, 15 MAY. ("THE UNION OF THE ENGLISH-SPEAKING PEOPLES," *NEWS OF THE WORLD*; ESSAYS IV, 438.)

It is no exaggeration to say that the future of the whole world and the hopes of a broadening civilization founded upon Christian ethics depend upon the relation between the British Empire or Commonwealth of Nations and the USA. The identity of purpose and persistence of resolve prevailing throughout the English-speaking world will, more than any other single fact, determine the way of life which will be open to the generations and perhaps to the centuries which follow our own.

1941, 9 JANUARY. PILGRIMS SOCIETY LUNCHEON, LONDON. (CS VI, 6326.)

The British Empire and the United States will have to be somewhat mixed up together in some of their affairs for mutual and general advantage. For my own part, looking out for the future, I do not view the process with any misgivings. I could not stop it if I wished; no one can stop it. Like the Mississippi, it just keeps rolling along. Let it roll! Let it roll on full flood, inexorable, irresistible, benignant, to broader lands and better days.

1941, 20 AUGUST. (OB VI, 743.)

Report to the House after his Argentia Bay, Newfoundland meeting with Roosevelt, which formulated the Atlantic Charter. The "rolling along" is from the famous and daring Broadway musical Show Boat, *whose signature song was "Ol' Man River". John Colville reports that WSC sang the tune all the way back to Downing Street in the car after his BBC broadcast of the speech.*

When I looked upon that densely-packed congregation of fighting men of the same language, of the same faith, of the same fundamental laws and the same ideals, and now to a large extent of the same interests, and certainly in different degrees facing the same dangers, it swept across me that here was the only hope, but also the sure hope, of saving the world from measureless degradation.

And so we came back across the ocean waves, uplifted in spirit, fortified in resolve. Some American destroyers which were carrying mails to the United States marines in Iceland happened to be going the same way too, so we made a goodly company at sea together.

1941, 24 AUGUST. BROADCAST, LONDON. (UNRELENTING, 239.)

Oh! That is the way we talked to her while we were wooing her; now that she is in the harem, we talk to her quite differently!

1941, 9 DECEMBER. (BRYANT, TIDE, 231.)

WSC's reply to a colleague who urged a cautious approach to America following Pearl Harbor.

Prodigious hammer-strokes have been needed to bring us together again, or if you will allow me to use other language, I will say that he must indeed have a blind soul who cannot see that some great purpose and design is being worked out here below, of which we have the honour to be the faithful servants. It is not given to us to peer into the mysteries of the future. Still, I avow my hope and faith, sure and inviolate, that in the days to come the British and American peoples will for their own safety and for the good of all walk together side by side in majesty, in justice, and in peace.

1941, 26 DECEMBER. CONGRESS, WASHINGTON. (UNRELENTING, 361.)

Churchill's first of three speeches to Congress.

The other day I crossed the Atlantic again to see President Roosevelt. This time we met not only as friends, but as comrades, standing side by side and shoulder to shoulder, in a battle for dear life and dearer honour in the common cause and against a common foe. When I survey and compute the power of the United States and its vast resources and feel that they are now in with us, with the British Commonwealth of Nations all together, however long it lasts, till death or victory, I cannot believe there is any other fact in the whole world which can compare with that. That is what I have dreamed of, aimed at and worked for, and now it has come to pass.

1942, 15 FEBRUARY. BROADCAST, LONDON. (END, 66.)

The experience of a long life and the promptings of my blood have wrought in me conviction that there is nothing more important for the future of the world than the fraternal association of our two peoples in righteous work both in war and peace.

1943, 19 MAY. CONGRESS, WASHINGTON. (ONWARDS, 92.)

Churchill's second speech to Congress.

Upon the fraternal association and intimate alignment of policy of the United States and the British Commonwealth and Empire depends, more than on any other factor, the immediate future of the world....If they fall apart and wander astray from the commanding beacon light of their destiny, there is no end or measure to the miseries and confusion which await modern civilization.

1943, 30 JUNE. GUILDHALL, LONDON.
(ONWARDS, 126.)

Great Britain and the United States all one? Yes, I am all for that, and you mean me to run for President?

1943, AUGUST. PRESS CONFERENCE, QUEBEC.
(HALLE, AMERICA AND BRITAIN, 33; GRAEBNER, 106.)

But after the war, Churchill told his Life *editor, Walter Graebner: "I could never run for President of the United States"; see Presidency herein.*

...to the youth of America, as to the youth of all the Britains, I say, "You cannot stop." There is no halting-place at this point. We have now reached a stage in the journey where there can be no pause. We must go on. It must be world anarchy or world order. Throughout all this ordeal and struggle which is characteristic of our age, you will find in the British Commonwealth and Empire good comrades to whom you are united by other ties besides those of State policy and public need. To a large extent, they are the ties of blood and history. Naturally I, a child of both worlds, am conscious of these....

This gift of a common tongue is a priceless inheritance, and it may well some day become the foundation of a common citizenship. I like to think of British and Americans moving about freely over each other's wide estates with hardly a sense of being foreigners to one another. But I do not see why we should not try to spread our common language even more widely throughout the globe and, without seeking selfish advantage over any, possess ourselves of this invaluable amenity and birthright.

If we are together nothing is impossible. If we are divided all will fail. I therefore preach continually the doctrine of the fraternal association of our two peoples, not for any

purpose of gaining invidious material advantages for either of them, not for territorial aggrandizement or the vain pomp of earthly domination, but for the sake of service to mankind and for the honour that comes to those who faithfully serve great causes.

1943, 6 SEPTEMBER. HARVARD UNIVERSITY,
CAMBRIDGE, MASSACHUSETTS. (ONWARDS, 182–6.)

...the United States have an immense interest in the prosperity of Great Britain and of the British Empire, and their own prosperity could not survive for many years in the midst of a ruined world or in the presence of a ruined and broken Britain. It is in the working of these practical forces that we must put our trust for the future, and I am sure that it is along such paths, and through such influences, that a happy outcome will eventually be reached. United, these two countries can, without the slightest injury to other nations or to themselves, almost double each other's power and safety.

1945, 6 DECEMBER.

Neither the sure prevention of war, nor the continuous rise of world organisation will be gained without what I have called the fraternal association of the English-speaking peoples. This means a special relationship between the British Commonwealth and Empire and the United States. This is no time for generalities, and I will venture to be precise. Fraternal association requires not only the growing friendship and mutual understanding between our two vast but kindred systems of society, but the continuance of the intimate relationship between our military advisers, leading to common study of potential dangers, the similarity of weapons and manuals of instructions, and to the interchange of officers and cadets at technical colleges. It should carry with it the continuance of the present facilities for mutual security by the joint use of all Naval and Air Force bases in the possession of either country all over the world.

1946, 5 MARCH. WESTMINSTER COLLEGE, FULTON,
MISSOURI. (SINEWS, 98.)

Churchill went on to explain why this concept was no threat to any other country:

...there are the special relations between the United States and the South American Republics. We British have our twenty years Treaty of Collaboration and Mutual

Assistance with Soviet Russia....The British have an alliance with Portugal unbroken since 1384....None of these clash with the general interest of a world agreement, or a world organisation; on the contrary they help it....Special associations between members of the United Nations which have no aggressive point against any other country, which harbour no design incompatible with the Charter of the United Nations, far from being harmful, are beneficial and, as I believe, indispensable.

In these last years of my life there is a message of which I conceive myself to be a bearer. It is a very simple message which can be well understood by the people of both our countries. It is that we should stand together. We should stand together in malice to none, in greed for nothing, but in defence of those causes which we hold dear not only for our own benefit, but because we believe they mean the honour and the happiness of long generations of men....

I read the other day that an English nobleman, whose name is new to me, has stated that England would have to become the forty-ninth state of the American Union. I read yesterday that an able American editor had written that the United States ought not to be asked to re-enter the British Empire. It seems to me, and I dare say it seems to you, that the path of wisdom lies somewhere between these scarecrow extremes.

1946, 8 MARCH. GENERAL ASSEMBLY OF VIRGINIA, RICHMOND. (SINEWS, 109–10.)

...none who took part in it will forget the spectacle presented that sunlit morning on the crowded quarterdeck—the symbolism of the Union Jack and the Stars and Stripes draped side by side on the pulpit; the American and British chaplains sharing in the reading of the prayers; the highest naval, military, and air officers of Britain and the United States grouped in one body behind the President and me; the close-packed ranks of British and American sailors, completely intermingled, sharing the same books and joining fervently together in the prayers and hymns familiar to both.

I chose the hymns myself "For Those in

Peril on the Sea" and "Onward, Christian Soldiers." We ended with "O God, Our Help in Ages Past"....It was a great hour to live. Nearly half those who sang were soon to die.

1950. (WW2 III, 384.)

A moment of high drama in Churchill's memoirs was this description of divine services on HMS Prince of Wales *with Roosevelt in August, 1941. His final sentence refers to the sinking of* Prince of Wales, *along with HMS* Repulse, *with heavy loss of life, off Singapore on 10 December 1941.*

The drawing together in fraternal association of the British and American peoples, and of all the peoples of the English-speaking world, may well be regarded as the best of the few good things that have happened to us and to the world in this century of tragedy and storm.

1950, 4 JULY. DORCHESTER HOTEL, LONDON. (BALANCE, 309.)

It is not a matter of whether there is a war with China or not, but whether there is a rift between Britain and the United States or not. That is the thought that haunts me...on every ground, national, European, and international, we should allow no minor matters—even if we feel keenly about them—to stand in the way of the fullest, closest, intimacy, accord and association with the United States.

1951, 10 MAY.

I have never accepted a position of subservience to the United States. They have welcomed me as the champion of the British point of view. They are a fair-minded people.

1951, 10 OCTOBER, WOODFORD, ESSEX. (STEMMING, 122.)

I remind you that many of the most famous English statesmen have taken the side of the colonists. I have been refreshing my memory during the morning by reading the elder Pitt, and I quote: "If I were an American, as I am an Englishman, and foreign troops were landed in my country, I would never lay down my arms—never, never, never." These are the kind of words which roll along the centuries and play their part in wiping out the bitterness of former quarrels and in effacing the tragedies that have occurred, so that we remember battles only to celebrate the military virtues of those who took part on both sides.

1952, 16 JANUARY. SOCIETY OF CINCINNATI, WASHINGTON. (CS VIII, 8323.)

The General Society of Cincinnati, founded 1783, originally comprised US and French officers who had served at least three years in the American Revolutionary War. Present-day members must be descended from such officers. For WSC's descent, see American Revolution herein.

For centuries England has held the seas against every tyrant, wresting command of them from Spain and then from France, protecting our hemisphere from penetration by European systems in the days of U.S. weakness. [Now the United States] in the plenitude of her power, bearing as we did the awful burden of atomic command and responsibility for the final word of peace or war, surely we could make room for Britain to play her historic role upon that western sea whose floor is white with the bones of Englishmen.

1952, 17 JANUARY, WASHINGTON. (ACHESON, 602.)

WSC to the fifth and final plenary meeting of the 1952 Washington conference, with reference to the Atlantic Command. Reprised by US Secretary of State Acheson, who recalled this as "one of Mr. Churchill's greatest speeches".

I am honoured indeed by these experiences which I believe are unique for one who is not an American citizen. It is also of great value to me, on again becoming the head of His Majesty's Government, to come over here and take counsel with many trusted friends and comrades of former anxious days....I have not come here to ask you for money to make life more comfortable or easier for us in Britain. Our standards of life are our own business and we can only keep our self-respect and independence by looking after them ourselves.

1952, 17 JANUARY. CONGRESS, WASHINGTON. (STEMMING, 220.)

Churchill's third of three speeches to Congress. After "money" Churchill is sometimes said to have added "...for myself..." and brought the house down. But this does not appear in any text, and must remain unproven.

I can only hope that the American people will not suppose that the House of Commons is unfriendly to them or that we are simply naggers and fault finders.

1952, 1 JULY.

Let us stick to our heroes John Bull and Uncle Sam.

1953, 9 NOVEMBER. MANSION HOUSE, LONDON. (ALLIANCE, 82.)

The British and American Democracies were slowly and painfully forged and even they are not perfect yet.

1954, 8 AUGUST. (BOYLE, EISENHOWER, 167.)

WSC to President Eisenhower.

Never be separated from the Americans.

1955, 5 APRIL, DOWNING STREET. (OB VIII, 1123.)

Final words to his non-Cabinet ministers, according to Viscount De L'Isle.

There is not much left for me to do in this world and I have neither the wish nor the strength to involve myself in the present political stress and turmoil. But I do believe, with unfaltering conviction, that the theme of the Anglo-American alliance is more important today than at any time since the war.

1956, 22 NOVEMBER. (MACMILLAN, STORM, 175.)

Churchill to Eisenhower concerning the Suez Crisis.

I am, as you know, half American by blood, and the story of my association with that mighty and benevolent nation goes back nearly ninety years to the day of my Father's marriage. In this century of storm and tragedy I contemplate with high satisfaction the constant factor of the interwoven and upward progress of our peoples. Our comradeship and our brotherhood in war were unexampled. We stood together, and because of that fact the free world now stands. Nor has our partnership any exclusive nature: the Atlantic community is a dream that can well be fulfilled to the detriment of none and to the enduring benefit and honour of the great democracies.

1963, 9 APRIL. (CS VIII, 8709.)

WSC's letter of thanks to President Kennedy for Honorary American Citizenship, read at the citizenship ceremony by his son Randolph.

America and the Americans

American eagle

The eagle should permit the small birds to sing and care not wherefore they sang.

1945, 4 FEBRUARY, YALTA. (OB VII, 1176.)

Why not put the eagle's neck on a swivel so that it could turn to the right or left as the occasion presented itself?

1946, 4 MARCH. EN ROUTE FULTON, MISSOURI. (HALLE, AMERICA AND BRITAIN, 17.)

Presidential aide Clark Clifford recollection. Truman explained that he had revised the President's Seal so that the eagle, instead of facing the quiver of arrows, faced the olive branch of peace.

There are no people in the world who are so slow to develop hostile feelings against a foreign country as the Americans, and there are no people who, once estranged, are more difficult to win back. The American eagle sits on his perch, a large, strong bird with formidable beak and claws. There he sits motionless, and M. Gromyko is sent day after day to prod him with a sharp pointed stick— now his neck, now under his wings, now his tail feathers. All the time the eagle keeps quite still. But it would be a great mistake to suppose that nothing is going on inside the breast of the eagle.

1946, 5 JUNE.

Andrei Andreyevich Gromyko (1909–89), Soviet politician and diplomat. Entering the Soviet foreign department after Stalin's purges in 1939, he became Ambassador to the US in 1943, and to the United Nations in 1946. He was the Ambassador in London (1952–53), Foreign Minister (1957–85) and Chairman of the Presidium of the Supreme Soviet (1985–88). WSC was referring to Gromyko's tactics at the UN organising conference in San Francisco, April–June 1945.

American Embassy

The only territorial claim I am prepared to make on behalf of the British Commonwealth and Empire is—the return to my country by the United States of Grosvenor Square!

1945, JANUARY, YALTA. (CAWTHORNE, 37.)

American forebears

The great Burke has truly said, "People will not look forward to posterity who never look backward to their ancestors," and I feel it most agreeable to recall to you that the Jeromes were rooted for many generations in American soil, and fought in Washington's armies for the independence of the American Colonies and the foundation of the United States. I expect I was on both sides then. And I must say I feel on both sides of the Atlantic Ocean now.

1941, 16 JUNE. BROADCAST, LONDON. (UNRELENTING, 165–6.)

Broadcast to the USA after receiving an honorary degree from the University of Rochester (New York). Churchill's mother was the former Jennie Jerome. In this same address Churchill tells of his mother being born in Rochester. The Jerome family certainly lived in Rochester, but the fact is that Jennie was born in Brooklyn.

By the way, I cannot help reflecting that if my father had been American and my mother British instead of the other way round, I might have got here on my own. In that case, this would not have been the first time you would have heard my voice. In that case I should not have needed any invitation, but if I had, it is hardly likely it would have been unanimous. So perhaps things are better as they are.

1941, 26 DECEMBER. CONGRESS, WASHINGTON. (UNRELENTING, 353–4.)

This remark, at the outset of Churchill's first of three speeches to a joint session of the US Congress, brought down the house. Suddenly, stolid isolationists, who had long suspected (correctly) WSC's intentions to drag America into the war, were on their feet applauding. The fact that Japan had attacked Pearl Harbor just three weeks earlier had turned the tide in Churchill's favour.

American Revolution

I regard this as a most memorable day in my crowded life, and you have conferred on me an honour which I deeply value.... I was on both sides in the war between us and we.

1952, 16 JANUARY, WASHINGTON. (CS VIII, 8323.)

WSC was descended from an officer (Lt. Reuben Murray) who fought in Washington's

Army, making him eligible for membership in the Society of Cincinnati. He was elected to the Society in 1947, and installed in 1952.

Army

The impression made upon the hard-pressed French by this seemingly inexhaustible flood of gleaming youth in its first maturity of health and vigour was prodigious. None were under twenty, and few were over thirty. As crammed in their lorries they clattered along the roads, singing the songs of a new world at the tops of their voices, burning to reach the bloody field, the French Headquarters were thrilled with the impulse of new life....Half trained, half organised, with only their courage, their numbers and their magnificent youth behind their weapons, they were to buy their experience at a bitter price. But this they were quite ready to do.

1927. (CRISIS III PART 2, 454.)

It is the wish and also the desire of General Eisenhower that the battle for Normandy should be viewed as a whole....But this should certainly not prevent the British House of Commons from expressing its unstinted admiration for the splendid and spectacular victories gained by the United States troops under General Bradley, both at Cherbourg and in the southward march, now become almost a gallop down the peninsula. The Germans have certainly had remarkable opportunities of revising the mocking and insulting estimate which they put upon the military value of the American army at the time they declared war upon the great Republic.

1944, 2 AUGUST.

Now is the time to say firmly U.S. soldier eats five times what ours does: U.S. civilians eating as never before: we will never be behindhand with them in sacrifices: but let them cut down themselves before presuming to address us.

1945, 12 MARCH. (DIARIES OF CABINET SECRETARY SIR NORMAN BROOK, *NEW YORK TIMES*, 22 JANUARY 2006.)

There was no greater exhibition of power in history than that of the American army fighting the battle of the Ardennes with its left hand and advancing from island to island towards Japan with its right.

1945, 6 APRIL. (COLVILLE, FRINGES II, 227.)

There have been many occasions when a powerful state has wished to raise great armies, and with money and time and discipline and loyalty that can be accomplished. Nevertheless the rate at which the small American Army of only a few hundred thousand men, not long before the war, created the mighty force of millions of soldiers, is a wonder in military history.

1946, 9 MARCH. PENTAGON, WASHINGTON. (SINEWS, 112.)

At the end I said to Ismay (to whom I am indebted for this account), "What do you think of it?" He replied, "To put these troops against German troops would be murder." Whereupon I said, "You're wrong. They are wonderful material and will learn very quickly." To my American hosts however I consistently pressed my view that it takes two years or more to make a soldier. Certainly two years later the troops we saw in Carolina bore themselves like veterans.

1951. (WW2 IV, 347.)

WSC and his chief of staff had reviewed raw American troops training in South Carolina, June 1942.

Atlanta, Georgia

What lovely country surrounds the city of Atlanta! Its rich red soils, the cotton-quilted hills and uplands, the rushing, turgid rivers, are all alive with tragic memories of the Civil War.

1933, 5 AUGUST. ("LAND OF CORN AND LOBSTERS," COLLIER'S; ESSAYS IV, 266.)

Audiences

At intervals during the last forty years I have addressed scores of great American audiences in almost every part of the Union. I have learnt to admire the courtesy of these audiences; their sense of fair play; their sovereign sense of humour, never minding the joke that is turned against themselves; their earnest, voracious desire to come to the root of the matter, and to be well and truly informed on Old World affairs.

1941, 16 JUNE. BROADCAST, LONDON. (UNRELENTING, 166.)

Boston, Massachusetts

I am told that a Boston lunch party is greatly to be preferred to a Boston Tea Party.

1949, 1 APRIL, BOSTON. (REYNOLDS D., 201.)

California

...a more beautiful region I have hardly ever seen. The long strip of hilly or undulating country, rising often into mountain ranges, presents, through fifteen degrees of latitude, a smiling and varied fertility. Forests, vineyards, orange groves, olives, and every other form of cultivation which the natives desire, crowns or clothes the sunbathed peaks and valleys. The Pacific laps the long-drawn shores, and assures at all seasons of the year an equable and temperate climate....a spacious, delectable land, where we may work or play on every day in the year.

1929, 23 DECEMBER. ("NATURE'S PANORAMA IN CALIFORNIA," *DAILY TELEGRAPH*; ESSAYS IV, 49.)

Capitalism in

Mr. Herbert Morrison, in a momentary lapse into candour, told us at Liverpool...that without American aid we should be facing one or two millions unemployed....We may indeed ask ourselves how it is that capitalism and free enterprise enable the United States not only to support its vast and varied life and needs, but also to supply these enormous sums to lighten the burden of others in distress.

1948, 21 APRIL.

When I see the present Socialist Government denouncing capitalism in all its forms, mocking with derision and contempt the tremendous free enterprise capitalist system on which the mighty production of the United States is founded, I cannot help feeling that as a nation we are not acting honourably or even honestly.

1948, 10 JULY, WOODFORD, ESSEX. (EUROPE, 374.)

Characteristics of Americans

What an extraordinary people the Americans are! Their hospitality is a revelation to me and they make you feel at home and at ease in a way that I have never before experienced.

1895, 10 NOVEMBER, NEW YORK. (OB I, CV1/1, 597.)

WSC to his mother after arriving for the first time in America.

This is a very great country my dear Jack. Not pretty or romantic but great and utilitarian. There seems to be no such thing as reverence or tradition. Everything is eminently practical and things are judged from a matter of fact standpoint.

1895, 15 NOVEMBER, NEW YORK. (OB I, 268.)

WSC to his brother Jack.

No people respond more spontaneously to fair play. If you treat Americans well they always want to treat you better.

1943, 29 MAY, WASHINGTON. (WW2 IV, 730.)

WSC to Clement Attlee.

In years of peace, the peoples of the British Commonwealth and those of the United States are easy-going folk, wishing to lead a free life, with active politics and plentiful opportunities of innocent diversion and of national self-improvement. They do not covet anything from others, perhaps because they have enough themselves; and they have often failed to keep a good look-out upon their own safety. They have many martial qualities, but they certainly do not like drill. Nevertheless, when they are attacked and assailed and forced in defence of life and liberty to make war, and to subject all their habits of life to war conditions and to war discipline, they are not incapable...of making the necessary transformation....Such nations do not become exhausted by war. On the contrary, they get stronger as it goes on.

1943, 8 JUNE.

The Americans can always be trusted to do the right thing, once all other possibilities have been exhausted.

CIRCA 1944.

Unattributed and included tentatively. Certainly he would never have said it publicly; he was much too careful about slips like that. It cannot be found in any memoirs of his colleagues. I have let it stand as a likely remark, for he certainly had those sentiments from time to time in World War II. (See for example the last entry under this heading.)

When American military men approach some serious situation they are wont to write at the head of their directive the words "over-all strategic concept". There is wisdom in this, as it leads to clarity of thought….Our American military colleagues, after having proclaimed their "over-all strategic concept" and computed available resources, always proceed to the next step—namely, the method.

1946, 5 MARCH. WESTMINSTER COLLEGE, FULTON, MISSOURI. (SINEWS, 94–5.)

Churchill went on to explain why this concept was no threat to any other country:

There are already the special United States relations with Canada which I have just mentioned, and there are the special relations between the United States and the South American Republics. We British have our twenty years Treaty of Collaboration and Mutual Assistance with Soviet Russia. I agree with Mr. Bevin, the Foreign Secretary of Great Britain, that it might well be a fifty years Treaty so far as we are concerned. We aim at nothing but mutual assistance and collaboration.

Nor should it be supposed as you would imagine, to read some of the Left-Wing newspapers, that all Americans are multi-millionaires of Wall Street. If they were all multi-millionaires that would be no reason for condemning a system which has produced such material results.

1948, 21 APRIL. ROYAL ALBERT HALL, LONDON. (EUROPE, 300.)

Silly people, and there were many, not only in enemy countries, might discount the force of the United States. Some said they were soft, others that they would never be united. They would fool around at a distance. They would never come to grips. They would never stand bloodletting. Their democracy and system of recurrent elections would paralyse their war effort. They would be just a vague blur on the horizon to friend or foe. Now we should see the weakness of this numerous but remote, wealthy, and talkative people. But I had studied the American Civil War, fought out to the last desperate inch.

1950. (WW2 III, 540.)

Churchill was recalling his feelings after hearing that the Japanese had attacked Pearl

Harbor and his following telephone conversation with President Roosevelt, who had told him, "We're all in the same boat now."

Their national psychology is such that the bigger the Idea the more wholeheartedly and obstinately do they throw themselves into making it a success. It is an admirable characteristic, providing the Idea is good.

1952. (WW2 V, 494.)

Chattanooga, Tennessee

And who would miss Chattanooga, lying in its cup between the Blue Ridge and Lookout Mountain? The scenery itself is exhilarating, but to it all is added the intense significance of history. All these rugged heights and peaks have their meaning in military topography: a short drive to the battlefield of Chickamauga, kept like a beautiful park, with many of the field batteries standing in the very positions where they fought, is enough to reward the visitor.

1933, 5 AUGUST. ("LAND OF CORN AND LOBSTERS," COLLIER'S; ESSAYS IV, 266.)

Chicago, Illinois

There is a splendour in Chicago and a life-thrust that is all its own.

1933, 5 AUGUST. ("LAND OF CORN AND LOBSTERS," COLLIER'S; ESSAYS IV, 266.)

Christmas

I spend this anniversary and festival far from my country, far from my family, yet I cannot truthfully say that I feel far from home. Whether it be the ties of blood on my mother's side, or the friendships I have developed here over many years of active life, or the commanding sentiment of comradeship in the common cause of great peoples who speak the same language, who kneel at the same altars, and, to a very large extent, pursue the same ideals, I cannot feel myself a stranger here in the centre and at the summit of United States. I feel a sense of unity and fraternal association which, added to the kindliness of your welcome, convinces me that I have a right to sit at your fireside and share your Christmas joys….

Let the children have their night of fun and laughter. Let the gifts of Father Christmas delight their play. Let us grown-ups share to the full in their unstinted pleasures before we turn again to the stern task and the formidable years that lie before us, resolved that, by our sacrifice and daring, these same children shall not be robbed of their inheritance or denied their right to live in a free and decent world. And so, in God's mercy, a happy Christmas to you all.

1941, 24 DECEMBER. WHITE HOUSE, WASHINGTON. (UNRELENTING, 350.)

Cincinnati, Ohio

Cincinnati, I thought, was the most beautiful of the inland cities of the Union. From the tower of its unsurpassed hotel the city spreads far and wide its pageant of crimson, purple and gold, laced by silver streams that are great rivers.

1933, 5 AUGUST. ("LAND OF CORN AND LOBSTERS," COLLIERS; ESSAYS IV, 266.)

Cincinnati architectural historian Sue Ann Painter, who brought this remark to my attention, found in her research that the hotel Churchill mentioned was the Netherland Plaza, still a Cincinnati landmark; WSC's visit was verified by the hotel's archives.

Civil War

Mr. Punch was against the South, and we had a picture of a fierce young woman, Miss Carolina, about to whip a naked slave, a sort of Uncle Tom, with a scourge which, not being yet myself removed out of the zone of such possibilities, I regarded as undoubtedly severe. I was all for the slave.

1931, JUNE. ("CARTOONS AND CARTOONISTS," STRAND MAGAZINE; THOUGHTS, 13.)

I was driving the other day not far from the field of Gettysburg, which I know well, like most of your battlefields. It was the decisive battle of the American Civil War. No one after Gettysburg doubted which way the dread balance of war would incline, yet far more blood was shed after the Union victory at Gettysburg than in all the fighting which went before.

1943, 19 MAY. CONGRESS, WASHINGTON. (ONWARDS, 102.)

The Battle of Gettysburg was at an end. Twenty-three thousand Federals and over twenty thousand Confederates had been smitten by lead or steel....Lee confronted his foe on the morrow and offered to fight again. But

no one knew better that it was decisive. With every personal resource he gathered up his army. An immense wagon train of wounded were jolted, springless, over sixteen miles of crumpled road. "Carry me back to old Virginia." "For God's sake kill me"....For a week the Confederates stood at bay behind entrenchments with their backs to an unfordable river...[On 14 July] Lee, after a cruel night march, was safe on the other side of the river. He carried with him his wounded and his prisoners. He had lost only two guns, and the war.

1958. (HESP IV, 240–41.)

It was typical of Churchill's searching historical imagination that in 1930 he wrote a remarkable "what if" essay, "If Lee Had Not Won the Battle of Gettysburg", postulating that all the terrible things that happened in World War I were avoided by Lee's victory.

Constitution

The rigid Constitution of the United States, the gigantic scale and strength of its party machinery, the fixed terms for which public officers and representatives are chosen, invest the President with a greater measure of autocratic power than was possessed before the war by the Head of any great State. The vast size of the country, the diverse types, interests and environments of its enormous population, the safety-valve function of the legislatures of fifty Sovereign States, make the focusing of national public opinion difficult, and confer upon the Federal Government exceptional independence of it except at fixed election times. Few modern Governments need to concern themselves so little with the opinion of the party they have beaten at the polls; none secures to its supreme executive officer, at once the Sovereign and the Party Leader, such direct personal authority.

1927. (CRISIS III PART 1, 228.)

"Fifty states" was an error, although a prescient one. Former Virginia Senator Harry Byrd, Jr., speaking to a Churchill Centre conference in 1991, recalled a visit to Churchill in London in 1952, before the US elections. WSC treated him to a lecture on American constitutional practices that, Byrd said, was better than anything he had ever had in college.

...the magnitude and the character of the electoral processes of the United States make it increasingly difficult, if not indeed already impossible, for any life-long politician to become a successful candidate for the Presidency. The choice of the party managers tends more and more to fall upon eminent citizens of high personal character and civic virtue who have not mingled profoundly in politics or administration, and who in consequence are free from the animosities and the errors which such combative and anxious experiences involve.

1927. (CRISIS III PART 1, 228.)

Among the 1932–2008 US presidents, Bush II, Clinton, Reagan, Carter, Kennedy, Eisenhower, Truman and Roosevelt all meet Churchill's definition of non-lifelong politicians without national experience. Of course, presidents are chosen differently nowadays – but only Bush I and Nixon are exceptions. Johnson and Ford merely inherited the job.

There is no-one to replace him [Roosevelt].... On the other hand, the Constitution says there must be an election, and even now when it is twenty months away all thoughts are turned to the question of who is to hold the power. We should certainly not allow such a state of affairs in our country, but a written Constitution makes slaves of its subjects and is in this case totally unfitted to the waging of war.

1943, 28 MAY, GIBRALTAR. (SOAMES, SPEAKING, 482–3.)

WSC to his wife shortly after his 1943 visit to America and second speech to Congress.

The whole history of this country shows a British instinct—and I think I may say, a genius—for the division of power. The American constitution, with its checks and counter checks, combined with its frequent appeals to the people, embodied much of the ancient wisdom of this island.

1947, 11 NOVEMBER.

The British race have always abhorred arbitrary and absolute government in every form. The great men who founded the American constitution expressed this same separation of authority in the strongest and most durable form. Not only did they divide executive, legislative and judicial functions, but also by instituting a federal system they preserved immense and sovereign rights to local communities and by all these means they have maintained—often at some inconvenience—a system of law and liberty under which they thrived and reached the physical and, at this moment, the moral leadership of the world.

1950, 28 JANUARY, WOODFORD, ESSEX. (BALANCE, 168; STEMMING, 150.)

WSC repeated these lines almost word for word in Huddersfield on 15 October 1951. Although he often retreaded a favourite phrase, this is one of the few cases where he repeated an entire paragraph.

We must be very careful nowadays—I perhaps all the more, because of my American forebears—in what we say about the American constitution. I will therefore content myself with the observation that no constitution was written in better English.

1953, 27 MARCH, ST. STEPHEN'S HALL, LONDON. (ALLIANCE, 26.)

A clever remark acknowledged Churchill's belief that the unwritten British constitution was a superior instrument to the American. WSC often despaired of America's recurrent elections, which kept bad politicians in office and good ones challenged to stand again when they least needed the distraction: a subject that continues to trouble thoughtful Americans today. This is also redolent of his philosophy that "the British never draw a line without blurring it". See next entry.

Contrasts with Britain

In England the political opinion of men and parties grows like a tree shading its trunk with its branches, shaped or twisted by the winds, rooted according to its strains, stunted by drought or maimed by storm. In America opinions are taken from the standard textbooks and platforms are made by machinery according to the exigencies of party without concern for individuals. We produce few of their clear-cut political types or clear-cut party programmes. In our affairs as in those of Nature there are always frayed edges, borderlands, compromises, anomalies. Few lines are drawn that are not smudged. Across the ocean it is all crisp and sharp.

1931, FEBRUARY. ("PERSONAL CONTACTS," *STRAND MAGAZINE*; THOUGHTS, 32.)

You may be larger and we may be the older. You may be the stronger, sometimes we may be the wiser.

1949, 25 MARCH, NEW YORK. (BALANCE, 39.)

In the military as in the commercial or production spheres the American mind runs naturally to broad, sweeping, logical conclusions on the largest scale. It is on these that they build their practical thought and action. They feel that once the foundation has been planned on true and comprehensive lines all other stages will follow naturally and almost inevitably. The British mind does not work quite in this way. We do not think that logic and clear-cut principles are necessarily the sole keys to what ought to be done in swiftly changing and indefinable situations....There is room for much argument about both views. The difference is one of emphasis, but it is deep-seated.

1950. (WW2 III, 596–7.)

Criticism of America

It is not open to the cool bystander...to set himself up as an impartial judge of events which would never have occurred had he outstretched a helping hand in time.

1929. (CRISIS IV, 131.)

The United States had remained neutral from 1914 to 1917, yet had become a sharp critic of Europe after World War I.

I want no criticism of America at my table. The Americans criticise themselves more than enough.

1950S, DOWNING STREET. (NEMON, 51B.)

Currency

I paid my fare across Brooklyn Bridge with a paper dollar, I should think the most disreputable "coin" the world has ever seen. I wondered how to reconcile the magnificent system of communication with the abominable currency....I have found what may be a solution. The communication of New York is

due to private enterprise while the state is responsible for the currency...

1895, 12 NOVEMBER, NEW YORK. (OB, CV1/1, 598.)

WSC to his Aunt Leonie.

Pray bear this [the "Sterling Dollar"] to your father from me. Tell him this must be the currency of the future.

1933, 8 OCTOBER. (HALLE, IRREPRESSIBLE, 7–8.)

When James Roosevelt visited Chartwell, WSC drew an intertwined pound and dollar sign which he referred to as the "Sterling Dollar". What if, James replied, his father wished to call it the "Dollar Sterling"? WSC replied with a smile, "It is all the same."

Declaration of Independence

The Declaration of Independence is not only an American document. It follows on Magna Charta and the Bill of Rights as the third great title-deed on which the liberties of the English-speaking people are founded. By it we lost an Empire, but by it we also preserved an Empire.

1918, 4 JULY. LIBERTY DAY MEETING, LONDON. (CS III, 2615.)

Depression

I do not think America is going to smash. On the contrary I believe that they will quite soon begin to recover. As a country descends the ladder of values many grievances arise, bankruptcies and so forth. But one must never forget that at the same time all sorts of correctives are being applied, and adjustments being made by millions of people and thousands of firms. If the whole world except the United States sank under the ocean that community could get its living. They carved it out of the prairie and the forests. They are going to have a strong national resurgence in the near future. Therefore I wish to buy sound low priced stocks. I cannot afford any others.

1932, 21 JUNE. (OB, CV5/2, 442.)

WSC to H. C. Vickers, of Vickers, da Costa and Co., stockbrokers.

Destiny of America

Will the United States throw their weight into the scales of peace and law and freedom while time remains, or will they remain spectators until the disaster has occurred; and then, with infinite cost and labour, build up what need not have been cast down? This is the riddle of a Sphinx who under the mask of loquacity, affability, sentimentality, hard business, machine-made politics, wrong-feeling, right-feeling, vigour and weakness, efficiency and muddle, still preserves the power to pronounce a solemn and formidable word.

1938, 4 AUGUST. ("THE UNITED STATES AND EUROPE," *DAILY TELEGRAPH*; STEP, 254.)

Twice in my lifetime the long arm of destiny has reached across the oceans and involved the entire life and manhood of the United States in a deadly struggle. There was no use in saying "We don't want it; we won't have it; our forebears left Europe to avoid these quarrels; we have founded a new world which has no contact with the old." There was no use in that. The long arm reaches out remorselessly, and every one's existence, environment, and outlook undergo a swift and irresistible change.

1943, 6 SEPTEMBER. HARVARD UNIVERSITY, CAMBRIDGE, MASSACHUSETTS. (ONWARDS, 181.)

Destroyers for bases

There will be no delay in bringing the American destroyers into active service; in fact, British crews are already meeting them at the various ports where they are being delivered. You might call it the long arm of coincidence. I really do not think that there is any more to be said about the whole business at the present time. This is not the appropriate occasion for rhetoric. Perhaps I may, however, very respectfully offer this counsel to the House: When you have got a thing where you want it, it is a good thing to leave it where it is.

1940, 5 SEPTEMBER.

Referring to the loan of fifty obsolete American destroyers for vitally needed convoy duty in the Royal Navy, in exchange for American bases on British colonies in the West Indies and Atlantic.

Discovery of

I am afraid the Americans do not come into this volume, because it was only in "fourteen

hundred and ninety-two Columbus over the ocean flew."

1956, 16 APRIL. (OB VIII, 1193.)

WSC to Eisenhower; he was always mindful that the Vikings had been to America before Columbus.

Elections

I ventured to warn the Government before this happened, in May or June of last year, of the extreme unwisdom of making the Debt Settlement an issue at the American elections. The consequences of Lausanne have been to force all the candidates for Congress and the Senate, on both sides of politics, to give specific pledges and to make definite declarations upon this subject. We all know what happens at elections.

1932, 23 NOVEMBER.

Churchill's permanent vexation over war debts in the 1920s and pre-Hitler 1930s was the unwelcome triangle trade in which America made loans to Germany, which used the loans to pay war reparations to Britain, which in turn was repaying its own war loans to the United States. The 1932 Lausanne conference ended World War I reparations.

Faults

Toilet paper too thin, newspapers too fat!

1944, SEPTEMBER. PRESS CONFERENCE, WASHINGTON. (HALLE, IRREPRESSIBLE, 240.)

Churchill's response when a young lady asked if he had any complaints about the United States.

Food

Americans of every class live on lighter foods than their analogues in England. Fruit, vegetables and cereals play a much larger part in their bills of fare than with us, and they eat chicken much more often than meat—by which of course I mean beef and mutton.

1933, 5 AUGUST. ("LAND OF CORN AND LOBSTERS," *COLLIER'S*; ESSAYS IV, 262.)

For further comments on American cuisine see Tastes...coffee, seafood, dessert.

Geography

Here, in the broad United States, with a respectable ocean on either side of us, we can look out upon the world in all its wonder and in all its woe.

1943, 6 SEPTEMBER. HARVARD UNIVERSITY, CAMBRIDGE, MASSACHUSETTS. (ONWARDS, 181.)

Twice the United States has had to send several millions of its young men across the Atlantic to find the war; but now war can find any nation, wherever it may dwell, between dusk and dawn.

1946, 5 MARCH. WESTMINSTER COLLEGE, FULTON, MISSOURI. (SINEWS, 101–2.)

Isolationism

On the one hand, one hundred million strong, stood the young American democracy. On the other cowered furtively, but at the same time obstinately, and even truculently, the old European diplomacy. Here young, healthy, hearty, ardent millions, advancing so hopefully to reform mankind. There, shrinking from the lime-lights, cameras and cinemas, huddled the crafty, cunning, intriguing, high-collared, gold-laced diplomatists. Tableau! Curtain! Slow music! Sobs: and afterwards chocolates!

1929. (CRISIS IV, 138.)

Churchill held it a tragedy that American idealism clashed with European Realpolitik at the Versailles Conference following the end of World War I. Had the two sides been reconciled, and worked together in the post-war period through the League of Nations, he was certain that the horrors of a second world conflict would have been avoided.

...will you wait until British freedom and independence have succumbed, and then take up the cause when it is three-quarters ruined, yourselves alone? I hear that they are saying in the United States that because England and France have failed to do their duty therefore the American people can wash their hands of the whole business. This may be the passing mood of many people, but there is no sense in it.

1938, 16 OCTOBER. BROADCAST, LONDON. (BLOOD, 87–8.)

Had the United States taken, before the First World War or between the wars, the same interest and made the same exertions...to preserve peace and uphold freedom which I thank God she is doing now, there might never have been a First War and there would certainly never have been a Second. With their mighty aid, I have a sure hope there will not be a third.

1953, 10 OCTOBER. (ALLIANCE, 66.)

Journalism

...the essence of American journalism is vulgarity divested of truth. Their best papers write for a class of snotty housemaids and footmen and even the nicest people here have so much vitiated their taste as to appreciate the style.

1895, 15 NOVEMBER, NEW YORK. (OB, CV1/1, 600.)

WSC to his brother Jack, commenting on American press attacks on his friend the Congressman Bourke Cockran.

Lend-Lease

The President and Congress of the United States, having newly fortified themselves by contact with their electors, have solemnly pledged their aid to Britain in this war because they deem our cause just, and because they know their own interests and safety would be endangered if we were destroyed. They are taxing themselves heavily. They have passed great legislation. They have turned a large part of their gigantic industry to making munitions which we need. They have even given us or lent us valuable weapons of their own.

1941, 27 APRIL. BROADCAST, LONDON. (UNRELENTING, 99.)

The March 1941 Lend-Lease Act ultimately provided $50 billion in supplies and materiel to Britain, Russia, France and China through 1945. Britain, which received 60 per cent of the aid, leased bases to the US in Newfoundland, Bermuda and the West Indies.

The end of our financial resources was in sight....Then came the majestic policy of the President and Congress of the United States in passing the Lend and Lease Bill, under which in two successive enactments about £3,000,000,000 sterling were dedicated to the cause of world freedom without—mark this, for it is unique—the setting up of any account in money. Never again let us hear the taunt that money is the ruling thought or power in the hearts of the American democracy. The Lend and Lease Bill must be regarded without question as the most unsordid act in the whole of recorded history.

1941, 10 November. Mansion House, London. (Unrelenting, 298.)

See also Churchillisms...unsordid. Often incorrectly believed to have been said about the post-war Marshall Plan.

Marines

...the United States Marines were undaunted. In spite of ceaseless air attack they held and improved their position, while a supply service by sea was improvised and the captured airfield was brought into use. From this moment fighters and dive-bombers manned by the Marines worked from Guadalcanal itself and gave instant relief....The climax of the battle on land now came. For ten days from October 19, 1942, the Marines in close jungle fighting held all their positions and beat the Japanese to a standstill.

1952. (WW2 V, 17.)

On the recapture of Guadalcanal in October 1942.

Marshall Plan

How are we keeping going from day to day? Let me tell you. We are living on the last remaining assets and overseas investments accumulated under the capitalistic system— that is what we are living on: we are living on them in the hope that we may bridge the gap before the new American grant-in-aid under the Marshall Plan comes in. Our last reserves will then be nearly gone, and even with the American help there will be a heavy deficit to be met each year on all our overseas purchases.

1948, 14 February.

The European Recovery Program, enacted in July 1947 and often designated for Secretary of State George Marshall, ultimately provided $13 billion in economic and technical assistance to Western Europe, Greece and Turkey. The Soviet Union rejected the plan and labelled it "dollar imperialism".

Miami, Florida

I am very glad therefore to have an opportunity of expressing my thanks to Miami Beach, to Miami and to Florida and to all this shining coast for so easy and agreeable a wayside halt on the road we all have to travel.

1946, 26 February, Miami. (Sinews, 89.)

Military leadership

To create great Armies is one thing; to lead them and to handle them is another. It remains to me a mystery as yet unexplained how the very small staffs which the United States kept during the years of peace were able to not only build up the armies and Air Force units, but also to find the leaders and vast staffs capable of handling enormous masses and of moving faster and farther than masses have ever been moved in war before.

1951. (WW2 IV, 348.)

Monroe Doctrine

For at least two generations we were, as the American writer Walter Lippmann has reminded us, a guardian, and almost a guarantor, of the Monroe Doctrine upon which, as Canning's eye foresaw, the free development of South America was founded. We and the civilized world owe many blessings to the United States, but we have also in later generations made our contribution to their security and splendour.

1946, 7 May. Guildhall, London. (Sinews, 125.)

Moral sentiment

...it is customary to use all the many valid, solid arguments about American interests and American safety, which depend upon the destruction of Hitler and his foul gang and even fouler doctrines. But in the long run— believe me, for I know—the action of the United States will be dictated, not by methodical calculations of profit and loss, but by moral sentiment, and by that gleaming flash of resolve which lifts the hearts of men and nations, and springs from the spiritual foundations of human life itself.

1941, 27 April. Broadcast, London. (Unrelenting, 94.)

Churchill ended this broadcast with the ringing quotation, "Westward, look, the land is bright!" See "Immortal words".

Naval equality

Peace-loving, kind-hearted, pussy-footed people have been so busy disarming the English-Speaking Peoples that they have developed a new naval power in the Far East. Why should the English-Speaking Peoples not build new ships for their fleets? We know that those fleets will never be used against one another. They are far more likely to be needed against a common enemy. If the United States wishes to build a new ship I would say, "Build it and God bless you."

1932, 2 FEBRUARY. UNION LEAGUE, CHICAGO. (*CHICAGO TRIBUNE*, 3 FEBRUARY 1932.)

New York, New York

Nothing of course can equal the world-famous silhouette of New York from the sea. It is a spectacle the magnificence of which is perhaps unsurpassed in the whole world and, though each building taken separately may have its failings, the entire mass of these vast structures is potent with grandeur and beauty.

1933, 5 AUGUST. ("LAND OF CORN AND LOBSTERS," *COLLIER'S*; ESSAYS IV, 266.)

Niagara Falls, New York

I saw them before you were born. I came here first in 1900. [Reporter: "Do they look the same?"] Well, the principle seems the same. The water still keeps falling over.

1943, NIAGARA FALLS. (OB VII, 469.)

Party politics

A new Party will arise like perhaps the Republican Party of the United States of America—rich, materialist, and secular—whose opinion will turn on tariffs, and who will cause the lobbies to be crowded with the touts of protected industries.

1903, 28 MAY.

Warning against the possibility of a "tariff lobby" in the House of Commons.

We sedulously avoid all special associations with one party or the other in the United States. Republicans and Democrats are the same to us. Our sympathies are with the American nation and with those whom it chooses by the process of democratic election to guide its vast affairs.

1948, 12 APRIL. PILGRIMS DINNER FOR MRS. ROOSEVELT, SAVOY, LONDON. (EUROPE, 290.)

I am not going to choose between Republicans and Democrats. I want the lot!

1954, 28 JUNE. PRESS CONFERENCE, WASHINGTON. (PILPEL, 262.)

Pearl Harbor

Lastly, if you will forgive me for saying it, to me the best tidings of all is that the United States, united as never before, have drawn the sword for freedom and cast away the scabbard.

1941, 26 DECEMBER. CONGRESS, WASHINGTON. (UNRELENTING, 358.)

No American will think it wrong of me if I proclaim that to have the United States at our side was to me the greatest joy....So we had won after all! Yes, after Dunkirk; after the fall of France; after the horrible episode of Oran; after the threat of invasion...we had won the war. England would live; Britain would live; the Commonwealth of Nations and the Empire would live....I thought of a remark which Edward Grey had made to me more than thirty years before—that the United States is like "a gigantic boiler. Once the fire is lighted under it there is no limit to the power it can generate." Being saturated and satiated with emotion and sensation, I went to bed and slept the sleep of the saved and thankful.

1950. (WW2 III, 539–40.)

Recalling the night of 7 December 1941, after hearing that the Japanese had attacked Pearl Harbor, and his telephone conversation with President Roosevelt, who had told him, "We're all in the same boat now."

Pioneers

The Americans took but little when they emigrated from Europe except what they stood up in and what they had in their souls. They came through, they tamed the wilderness, they became what old John Bright called "A refuge for the oppressed from every land and clime." They have become today the greatest state and power in the world, speaking our own language, cherishing our common law, and pursuing, like our great Dominions, in broad principle, the same ideals.

1947, 28 OCTOBER.

Sidney Silverman, MP, declared that the Americans were "shabby moneylenders".

WSC replied, "That is no service to our country nor is it true," and continued as above.

Presidency

I could never run for President of the United States. All that handshaking of people I didn't give a damn about would kill me. Ten minutes here. Ten minutes there...Not for me.

CIRCA 1949. (GRAEBNER, 106.)

Prohibition

I do not think we are likely to learn much from the liquor legislation of the United States.

1927, 11 APRIL.

There is what is called the doctrine of the unclean thing. That is a doctrine which has become dominant in regard to liquor legislation in the United States of America. That doctrine is that the State must in no way touch the unclean thing; that it should prohibit it by law, and in no circumstances should derive any advantage from it. That is a very important and a very respectable kind of doctrine, but we have no reason to suppose that it has worked much better than the view which has prevailed up to the present time in this Island in regard to liquor, which is, that you should tax it but, that you should regulate this form of luxury consumption and should not hesitate to take profit to the State if in so doing you are also able to diminish the evil.

1928, 16 MARCH.

It is possible that the dry, bracing electrical atmosphere of North America makes the use of alcohol less necessary and more potent than the moist, humid climate of Britain...I must confess that on one occasion I was taken to a "speakeasy". I went, of course, in my capacity as a Social Investigator.

1932, 14 AUGUST. ("PROHIBITION," *THE SUNDAY CHRONICLE*; ESSAYS IV, 108, 111.)

It was explained to me that nothing in the laws of the United States forbids the convivial consumption in a private house of any stores of liquor which happened to be in the host's private cellars before Prohibition became effective in 1920. Many people must have had very large and well-stocked cellars in those distant days, and these supplies have lasted

extremely well. Indeed one might almost believe that, like the widow's cruse, they miraculously replenish themselves.

1933, 5 AUGUST. ("LAND OF CORN AND LOBSTERS," *COLLIER'S*; ESSAYS IV, 263.)

A cruse is an earthenware pot, and Churchill's allusion was from the Biblical story of the widow's cruse that was constantly replenished. From I Kings XVII 12–16, viz...

12 *And she said, As the Lord thy God liveth, I have not a cake, but an handful of meal in a barrel, and a little oil in a cruse...*

14 *For thus saith the Lord God of Israel, the barrel of meal shall not waste, neither shall the cruse of oil fail, until the day that the Lord sendeth rain upon the earth.*

16 *And the barrel of meal wasted not, neither did the cruse of oil fail, according to the word of the Lord, which he spake by Elijah.*

Quality of goods

...the American engines were sooner delivered and £1,000 cheaper. They broke down rarely....The fact that they were considerably faster soon won them a good reputation on the railway, and the soldier who travelled to the front was as anxious to avoid his country's locomotives as to preserve its honour. "They were," said one of the subalterns, "the products of a higher class of labour than that employed in England"....There is no pleasure in recording these facts. They have not, unfortunately, even the merit of being new.

1899. (RIVER I, 298–9.)

On American vs. British locomotives in the Sudan.

Race relations

In countries where there is only one race broad and lofty views are taken of the colour question. Similarly, States which have no overseas colonies or possessions are capable of rising to moods of great elevation and detachment about the affairs of those who have.

1951. (WW2 IV, 185.)

Ironically, this telling remark was turned on its head two decades later, when a then-nearly all-white Europe criticised America's fraught race relations.

Responsibility of America

Yet supposing (as I do not for one moment suppose) that Mr. Kennedy were correct in his tragic utterance, then I for one would willingly lay down my life in combat, rather than, in fear of defeat, surrender to the menaces of these most sinister men. It will then be for you, for the Americans, to preserve and to maintain the great heritage of the English-speaking peoples. It will be for you to think imperially, which means to think always of something higher and more vast than one's own national interests. Nor should I die happy in the great struggle which I see before me, were I not convinced that if we in this dear island succumb to the ferocity and might of our enemies, over there in your distant and immune continent the torch of liberty will burn untarnished and (I trust and hope) undismayed.

1939, 14 JUNE. (NICOLSON I, 403.)

WSC to American columnist Walter Lippmann at a dinner with Kenneth Clark, Director of the National Gallery and the Julian Huxleys. (Julian, brother of Aldous, was a biologist, author and internationalist.) Lippmann had said that the American Ambassador, Joseph Kennedy, had informed him that war was inevitable and that Britain would be beaten.

The price of greatness is responsibility. If the people of the United States had continued in a mediocre station, struggling with the wilderness, absorbed in their own affairs, and a factor of no consequence in the movement of the world, they might have remained forgotten and undisturbed beyond their protecting oceans: but one cannot rise to be in many ways the leading community in the civilized world without being involved in its problems, without being convulsed by its agonies and inspired by its causes.

1943, 6 SEPTEMBER. HARVARD UNIVERSITY, CAMBRIDGE, MASSACHUSETTS. (ONWARDS, 182.)

The United States stands at this time at the pinnacle of world power. It is a solemn moment for the American Democracy. For with primacy in power is also joined an awe-inspiring accountability to the future. If you look around you, you must feel not only the sense of duty done but also you must feel anxiety lest you fall below the level of achievement.

1946, 5 MARCH. WESTMINSTER COLLEGE, FULTON, MISSOURI. (SINEWS, 94.)

Churchill inherited from his father, and passed on to his son, a well-worn admonition: "We must never fall below the level of events."

Rochester, New York

To me, Rochester makes a personal appeal. Here it was that my grandfather and his brother, having married two sisters, built two small, old-fashioned houses in what was then the best quarter of the town, and linked them by a bridge. Here they founded the newspaper which is still the leading daily.

1933, 5 AUGUST. ("LAND OF CORN AND LOBSTERS," COLLIER'S; ESSAYS IV, 266.)

Churchill's mother is sometimes incorrectly said to have been born in Rochester (it was Brooklyn). WSC did not repeat the error here.

San Francisco, California

San Francisco, earthquake-defying, makes a fine counterpart as it gazes on the Pacific. Nothing could be more different from San Francisco than Los Angeles, the one towering up under its cloud canopy, its buildings crowded together on the narrow promontory; the other spreading its garden villas over an enormous expanse, a system of rural townships basking in the sunlight.

1933, 5 AUGUST. ("LAND OF CORN AND LOBSTERS," COLLIER'S; ESSAYS IV, 266.)

Statue, Washington

It gives me the greatest pleasure that the statue should stand on both American and British soil, and I feel that it will rest happily and securely on both feet.

1964. SIR ANTHONY MONTAGUE BROWNE TO THE EDITOR.

The statue, by William McVey, at the British Embassy on Constitution Avenue in Washington, was erected in 1966, and so located that Churchill's left foot is on British soil (grounds of the Embassy), and his right on American soil, outside the Embassy grounds.

Territorial ambitions

It is true that American thought is at least disinterested in matters which seem to relate to territorial acquisitions, but when wolves are about the shepherd must guard his flock, even if he does not himself care for mutton.

1954. (WW2 VI, 399.)

Touring America

I should like to spend a fortnight in California, and have a few days besides to veer and haul upon. I do not want to have too close an itinerary. One must have time to feel a country and nibble some of the grass. Suppose therefore I had reached the Grand Canyon by September 21, would it not be well to go to Salt Lake City, Denver, Chicago; arriving at Chicago October 1? I promised Mr. Ford to see his Works at Detroit (Query—should I see them from Toronto on the way out). It looks only a night's journey. Now say October 3 leave the Great Lakes for the Atlantic shore. An important question arises—Ought I not to go through Pittsburgh to Washington straight away, and pay my respects to the President, say about October 7, or should I go first to New York and strike South? Anyhow after Washington I want to go to Richmond and to see the battle field of Gettysburg.

1929, 7 JULY. (OB, CV5/2, 16.)

WSC to Bernard Baruch, requesting advice on his 1929 tour of North America, which very nicely lays out his appreciation for particular regions of the country.

Virginia

The people of Virginia and, above all, the people of Richmond, have proved in the past that they have strong nerves and that they can face not only facts but fate with fortitude and pride.

1946, 8 MARCH. GENERAL ASSEMBLY OF VIRGINIA, RICHMOND. (SINEWS, 107.)

War effort, American

When I think of the measureless output of ships, munitions and supplies of all kinds with which the United States has equipped herself and has sustained all the fighting allies in generous measure, and of the mighty war she is conducting, with troops of our Australian and New Zealand Dominions, over the spaces of the Pacific Ocean, this House may indeed salute our sister nation as being at the highest pinnacle of her power and fame.

1944, 28 SEPTEMBER.

War sentiment

Yes, it is nearly always so with nations—but not with the Americans. They are moving into the war by sentiment. I could make out a very strong case to show why it would pay America to keep out.

1941, 16 FEBRUARY, DITCHLEY PARK. (KENNEDY, BUSINESS, 79.)

Churchill in a conversation in French with Polish General Sikorski and the Polish Ambassador. It was suggested that the Turks would enter the war when they concluded it was in their national interest.

West Point

I was not twenty at the time of the Cuban War, and only a Second Lieutenant, but I was taken to an inspection at West Point and treated as if I had been a General.

1954, 8 APRIL. (MORAN, 576.)

Churchill was in fact twenty at that time, but not yet twenty-one.

Worth of America

The United States has shown itself more worthy of trust and honour than any government of men or associations of nations that has ever reached pre-eminence by their action on the morrow of the common victory won by all.

1949, 25 MARCH, NEW YORK. (BALANCE, 32.)

9

GERMANY

*"Since 1911 much more than a quarter of a century had passed,
and still mortal peril threatened us at the hands of the same
nation.....Once again we must fight for life and honour against
all the might and fury of the valiant, disciplined, and ruthless
German race. Once again! So be it."*[41]

"I saw the Emperor today....This army is a terrible engine."
WSC greets the Kaiser (mounted), German Army manoeuvres,
15 September 1909.

Churchill's view of Germany was a combination of admiration, concern, reproach and magnanimity, and sometimes all four at once. He recognised the talents and gifts of the German race, but deplored their penchant for "blood-lust", traits which he said "combine in the most deadly manner the qualities of the warrior and the slave".

At the same time he admitted that "my hate had died with their surrender", and in both World Wars Churchill was in the vanguard of those relative few arguing for lenient treatment of the defeated enemy.

In 1919 he wanted to send shiploads of food to the German ports Britain had tried to blockade in the late war. In 1945 he wrote sadly to his wife of the forty-mile-long columns fleeing before the Soviet advance, and he literally walked out of the conference at which

---

41 Churchill, Winston S., *The Second World War*, vol. I, *The Gathering Storm*. London: Cassell, 1948, 321.

Stalin proposed shooting 50,000 Nazi officials. After the war, he was the first prominent statesman to argue for Franco-German rapprochement: "There can be no revival of Europe without a spiritually great France and a spiritually great Germany." This would win him the trust and friendship of men such as Adenauer, who hoped to build the new Federal Republic on the ashes of a totalitarian past.

As a personal matter Churchill preferred visiting France to visiting Germany, which he only saw in detail as an author exploring Marlborough's battlefields. He spoke French but not German, and had many more French than German friends. Nevertheless, magnanimity was always part of his German formulae.

Related quotations are in Chapters 20 and 23; in the former, see entries for Adenauer, Berchtold, Bismarck, Hanfstaengl, Hess, Himmler, Hindenberg, Hitler, Kaiser Wilhelm II, Ribbentrop, Rommel and Spee.

Character of

Ah! foolish-diligent Germans, working so hard, thinking so deeply...poring over long calculations, fuming in newly-found prosperity, discounted amid the splendour of mundane success, how many bulwarks to your peace and glory did you not, with our own hands, successively tear down!

1923. (CRISIS I, 41.)

An immense responsibility rests upon the German people for this subservience to the barbaric idea of autocracy. This is the gravamen [of the charge] against them in history—that, in spite of all their brains and courage, they worship Power, and let themselves be led by the nose.

1930, NOVEMBER. ("THE TRUTH ABOUT THE EX-KAISER," STRAND MAGAZINE; GC, 23.)

Churchill stated this truth over three years before Hitler came to power.

...the most formidable people in the world, and now the most dangerous, a people who inculcate a form of blood-lust in their children, and lay down the doctrine that every frontier must be the starting out point for invasion.

1933, 14 NOVEMBER, DEVONSHIRE. (CS V, 5301–2.)

[The Germans] combine in the most deadly manner the qualities of the warrior and the slave. They do not value freedom themselves, and the spectacle of it in others is hateful to them. Whenever they become strong they seek their prey, and they will follow with an iron discipline anyone who will lead them to it....Nazi tyranny and Prussian militarism are the two main elements in German life which must be absolutely destroyed. They must be absolutely rooted out if Europe and the world are to be spared a third and still more frightful conflict.

1943, 21 NOVEMBER.

[Cabinet Minister: "The trouble with the Germans is that they are like a lot of sheep; they will follow anybody."]

Oh, it is far worse than that, they are *carnivorous* sheep!

1943. LORD MOUNTBATTEN TO THE EDMONTON CHURCHILL SOCIETY, 1966.

Concessions to

...I do not think that we need break our hearts in deploring the treatment that Germany is receiving now. Germany is not satisfied; but no concession which has been made has produced any very marked appearance of gratitude. Once it has been conceded it has seemed less valuable than when it was demanded.

1933, 13 APRIL.

Delusions

In the German view, which Herr Hitler shares, a peaceful Germany and Austria were fallen upon in 1914 by a gang of wicked designing nations, headed by Belgium and Serbia, and would have defended herself successfully if only she had not been stabbed in the back by the Jews. Against such opinions it is vain to argue.

1939, 28 APRIL.

The grammar error "herself" as recorded in the transcript.

Democracy in

So far as it remains in the power of this island people to influence the course of events, we must strive over a period of years to redeem and to reincorporate the German and the Japanese peoples in a world system of free and civilized democracy. The idea of keeping scores of millions of people hanging about in a sub-human state between earth and hell, until they are worn down to a slave condition or embrace Communism, or die off from hunger, will only, if it is pursued, breed at least a moral pestilence and probably an actual war.

1946, 5 JUNE.

My hope is that free, liberal civilization and democratic Parliamentary processes will win the soul of Germany for Europe, and that the great underlying harmonies of the European family will predominate over the feuds that have hitherto rent our famous parent Continent and brought upon it miseries and humiliations beyond the power of statistics to measure or language to describe.

1948, 28 OCTOBER.

I hope we continue to use our influence and resources, such as they are, to make the German people or the states and principalities of Germany able to govern themselves and earn good livelihood as soon as possible. I am hoping that the states of Germany—Bavaria, Saxony, Würtemberg, Hanover and others— may regain much of their old individuality, and rights. I am sure that it is along that road that both France and Britain will find it easiest to advance....

1948, 10 DECEMBER.

Encirclement claims

[Count Metternich] said people were trying to ring Germany round and put her in a net....I said, how could she be netted when she had an alliance with two other first-class Powers, Austria-Hungary and Italy? *We* had often stood quite alone for years at a time without getting flustered.

1923. (CRISIS I, 54.)

"Plus ça change, plus c'est la même chose." Said to WSC in 1911 by Count Metternich, German Ambassador to Britain, these words were often repeated in the 1930s by Hitler.

What, then, is this talk about encirclement? It is all nonsense. There is nothing that we ask for ourselves under collective security that we will not willingly concede, nay earnestly proffer, to Germany. Let her join the club, and make her great contribution and share its amenities and immunities.

1936, 5 NOVEMBER.

Fate of Germany

No one can say how far Herr Hitler's empire will extend before this war is over, but I have no doubt that it will pass away as swiftly as, and perhaps more swiftly than, did Napoleon's empire, although, of course, without any of its glitter or its glory.

1940, 5 SEPTEMBER.

These gangs of bandits have sought to darken the light of the world; have sought to stand between the common people of all the lands and their march forward into their inheritance. They shall themselves be cast into the pit of death and shame, and only when the earth has been cleansed and purged of their crimes and their villainy shall we turn from the task which they have forced upon us...

1941, 30 DECEMBER. CANADIAN PARLIAMENT, OTTAWA. (UNRELENTING, 365.)

I am convinced that the British, American, and Russian peoples, who have suffered measureless waste, peril and bloodshed twice in a quarter of a century through the Teutonic urge of domination, will this time take steps to put it beyond the power of Prussia or of all Germany to come at them again with pent-up vengeance and long-nurtured plans.

1943, 21 SEPTEMBER.

Fear of Churchill

The Germans believe I am one of their most formidable enemies. They will not stop short of assassination.

1940, 20 AUGUST, LONDON. (THOMPSON, SHADOW, 15.)

WSC to his bodyguard, Detective Thompson.

Friendship with

When we are asked whether we will grasp the proffered hand of German friendship, I think we should answer "Yes," but at the same time one wants to know what happens after that. Often when these conversations begin they go nicely for a certain time, and then it appears that what the Germans want is that peace and good-will should be translated forthwith into tangible and solid immediate benefits to themselves. Very often it is suggested that we should promise to do something, or, what is perhaps even more difficult, stand by and see something or other done that may not be desirable. When the conversations reach that point, they become halting and embarrassed.

1937, 21 DECEMBER.

Iron Cross

At the start of the last war the Iron Cross was a highly prized decoration, but by 1918 it had been granted so freely that it was little valued except, I believe, by Herr Hitler who, it is alleged, gave it to himself some time later. After the Armistice, the Germans, who are a most adaptive people, manufactured large numbers of Iron Crosses for sale to the French troops as souvenirs. In the present war they have already some fifteen new medals and twenty-nine new distinctive badges. They have not yet reached the stage of manufacturing them for sale to the Allies.

1944, 22 MARCH

Menace of

I dread the day when the means of threatening the heart of the British Empire should pass into the hands of the present rulers of Germany. I think we should be in a position which would be odious to every man who values freedom of action and independence, and also in a position of the utmost peril for our crowded, peaceful, population engaged in their daily toil. I dread that day, but it is not, perhaps, far distant.

1934, 8 MARCH.

Beware. Germany is a country fertile in military surprises. The great Napoleon, in the years after Jena, was completely taken by surprise by the strength of the German army which fought the War of Liberation. Although he had officers all over the place, the German army which fought in the campaign of Leipzig was three or four times as strong as he expected.

1934, 28 NOVEMBER

At Jena, in what was then Prussia, on 14 October 1806, superior numbers of Prussians under Friederich Wilhelm III were routed by Napoleon.

Field-Marshal Goering—who is one of the few Germans who has been having a pretty good time for the last few years—says that we have been spared so far because Nazi Germany is so humane. They cannot bear to do anything to hurt anybody. All they ask for is the right to live and to be let alone to conquer and kill the weak. Their humanity forbids them to apply severities to the strong.

1939, 12 NOVEMBER. BROADCAST, LONDON (CV5/1, 359.)

You must never underrate the power of the German machine. It is the most terrible machine that has been created. After the last war they kept the brains of the German army together. They kept their Great Staff together. Although their weapons were taken away, this tremendous association of people who think about nothing but war, studying war, ruthless scientific war, was held together, thousands of them, and they were able to train and build up an army which, as you saw, in a few weeks shattered to pieces the once famous army of France, and which has marched into country after country and laid it low, and laid low every form of opposition, and only now in the vast spaces of Russia is confronted with this immense and valiant race which has stood against them…

1942, 31 OCTOBER. WESTMINSTER HALL, LONDON. (END, 258–9.)

Mercantile advantage

[Russia] can not only make us mobilise 100,000 soldiers on the Indian Frontier to the further detriment of this unfortunate country's finance but also can do sufficient harm to our carrying trade and indirectly to our industries to give the filthy Germans a chance of finally gaining the commercial supremacy of the world. But I fear my views would be unpopular in a jingo age.

1898, 22 MAY, BANGALORE, INDIA. (OB, CV1/2, 938.)

WSC to his mother, approving of the British government's reluctance to antagonise Russia. Included with some trepidation, lest we see "filthy Germans" taken out of context to represent his general view – which it does not.

Absolved from all the burden of reparations, with a moratorium upon all commercial debts, with her factories equipped to the very last point of science by British and American money, freed from internal debt, mortgages, fixed charges, debentures and so forth by the original flight from the mark, Germany only awaits trade revival to gain an immense mercantile ascendancy throughout the world.

1932, 11 JULY.

National passions of

When we read about Germany, when we watch with surprise and distress the tumultuous insurgence of ferocity and war spirit, the pitiless ill-treatment of minorities, the denial of the moral protection of civilized society to large numbers of individuals solely on the ground of race—when we see that occurring in one of the most gifted, learned, scientific, and formidable nations in the world, one cannot help feeling glad that the fierce passions that are raging in Germany have not found, as yet, any other outlet but upon Germans.

1933, 23 MARCH.

Hitler had become German Chancellor on 30 January 1933.

Nazi Party

Germany is ruled by a handful of autocrats who are the absolute masters of that gifted nation. They are men who have neither the long interests of a dynasty to consider, nor those very important restraints which a democratic Parliament and constitutional system impose upon any executive government. Nor have they the restraint of public opinion, which public opinion, indeed, they control by every means which modern apparatus renders possible.

1934, 8 MARCH.

...there is more danger in this new kind of [party] dictatorship than there would be in a military dictatorship, because you have men who, to relieve themselves from that peril which confronts them at home, might plunge into a foreign adventure of catastrophic character to the whole world.

1934, 13 JULY.

Churchill was commenting on the nature of the Hitler dictatorship, having declared that "Germany is arming...particularly in the air."

Like the Communists, the Nazis tolerate no opinion but their own. Like the Communists, they feed on hatred. Like the Communists, they must seek, from time to time, and always at shorter intervals, a new target, a new prize, a new victim. The dictator in all his pride, is held in the grip of his Party machine. He can go forward; he cannot go back. He must blood his hounds and show them sport, or else, like Actaeon of old, be devoured by them. All-strong without, he is all-weak within.

1938, 16 OCTOBER. BROADCAST, LONDON.
(BLOOD, 86.)

Actaeon, hero of Thebes in Greek mythology, was turned into a stag by Artemis, the hunt goddess, and was devoured by his own dogs.

The character of Hitler's Nazi Party was such as to destroy almost all independent elements in the German people. The struggle was fought to the bitter end. The mass of the people were forced to drain the cup of defeat to the dregs. A headless Germany has fallen into the hands of the conquerors.

1945, 16 AUGUST.

Nazi transformation

What a transformation has taken place in the last two or three years! Two or three years ago it was considered sentimental, intellectual, liberally minded, to speak words of encouragement and compassion, and even to speak patronizingly of the German people, and to seek opportunities of making gestures to raise them up to more and greater equality with other countries. Now we see them with their grievances unredressed, with all their ambitions unsatisfied, continuing from strength to strength, and the whole world waits from week to week to hear what are the words which will fall from the heads of the German nation. It is a woeful transformation which has taken place.

1935, 31 MAY.

New Order

What is this New Order which they seek to fasten first upon Europe and if possible—for their ambitions are boundless—upon all the continents of the globe? It is the rule of the

Herrenvolk—the master race—who are to put an end to democracy, to parliaments, to the fundamental freedoms and decencies of ordinary men and women, to the historic rights of nations; and give them in exchange the iron rule of Prussia, the universal goose-step, and a strict, efficient discipline enforced upon the working-classes by the political police, with the German concentration camps and firing parties, now so busy in a dozen lands, always handy in the background. There is the New Order.

1941, 24 AUGUST. BROADCAST, LONDON.
(UNRELENTING, 236.)

Nuremberg trials

The Nuremberg trials are over, and the guilty leaders of the Nazi regime have been hanged by the conquerors. We are told that thousands yet remain to be tried, and that vast categories of Germans are classed as potentially guilty because of their association with the Nazi regime. After all, in a country which is handled as Germany was, the ordinary people have very little choice about what to do. I think some consideration should always be given to ordinary people.

1946, 12 NOVEMBER.

Occupation of Europe

A river of blood has flowed and is flowing between the German race and the peoples of nearly all Europe. It is not the hot blood of battle, where good blows are given and returned. It is the cold blood of the execution yard and the scaffold, which leaves a stain indelible for generations and for centuries.

1941, 10 NOVEMBER. MANSION HOUSE, LONDON.
(UNRELENTING, 295.)

Certainly we see the Germans hated as no race has ever been hated in human history, or with such good reason. We see them sprawled over a dozen once free and happy countries, with their talons making festering wounds, the scars of which will never be effaced. Nazi tyranny and Prussian militarism, those two loathsome dominations, may well foresee and dread their approaching doom.

1943, 31 AUGUST. BROADCAST, LONDON.
(ONWARDS, 179.)

People

I bear no grudge; I have no prejudice against the German people. I have many German friends, and I have a lively admiration for their splendid qualities of intellect and valour and for their achievements in science and art. The re-entry into the European circle of a Germany at peace within itself, with a heart devoid of hate, would be the most precious benefit for which we could strive, and supreme advantage which alone could liberate Europe from its peril and its fear, and I believe that the British and French democracies would go a long way in extending the hand of friendship to realize such a hope.

1935, 24 OCTOBER.

There is no difficulty at all in having cordial relations between the peoples. Our hearts go out to them. But they have no power. But never will you have friendship with the present German Government. You must have diplomatic and correct relations, but there can never be friendship between the British democracy and the Nazi power, that power which spurns Christian ethics, which cheers its onward course by a barbarous paganism, which vaunts the spirit of aggression and conquest, which derives strength and perverted pleasure from persecution, and uses, as we have seen, with pitiless brutality the threat of murderous force. That power cannot ever be the trusted friend of the British democracy.

1938, 5 OCTOBER.

...the German people, industrious, faithful, valiant, but alas! lacking in the proper spirit of civic independence, liberated from their present nightmare, would take their honoured place in the vanguard of human society.

1938, 16 OCTOBER. BROADCAST, LONDON.
(BLOOD, 88.)

When I got out of the car and walked about among them, except for one old man who shook his head disapprovingly, they all began to cheer. My hate had died with their surrender and I was much moved by their demonstrations, and also by their haggard looks and threadbare clothes.

1952. (WW2 VI, 545.)

On recalling his tour of shattered Berlin with President Truman on 16 July 1945.

Politics

...politics in Germany are not what they are over here. There you do not leave Office to go into Opposition. You do not leave the Front Bench to sit below the Gangway. You may well leave your high office at a quarter of an hour's notice to drive to the police station, and you may be conducted thereafter, very rapidly, to an even harder ordeal.

1934, 13 JULY.

Propaganda

There is an extraordinary volume of German propaganda in this country, of misstatements made on the highest authority—which everyone knows could be easily disproved—but which obtain currency, and which, because they are not contradicted, are accepted as part of the regular facts on which the public rely. Ministers and Members who are in agreement with the policy of the Government must exert themselves to explain these matters to an anxious, but loyal and courageous public.

1936, 26 MARCH.

Refugees

I am free to confess to you that my heart is saddened by the tales of masses of German women and children flying along the roads everywhere in 40-mile long columns to the West before the advancing Armies. I am clearly convinced that they deserve it; but that does not remove it from one's gaze.

1945, 1 FEBRUARY, MALTA. (SOAMES, SPEAKING, 512.)

WSC to his wife. Churchill's sympathy was at once directed to innocents, even among a despised enemy. As he said later of Germany, "my hate died with their surrender".

I am particularly concerned, at this moment, with the reports reaching us of the conditions under which the expulsion and exodus of Germans from the new Poland are being carried out. Between eight and nine million persons dwelt in those regions before the war. The Polish Government say that there are still 1,500,000 of these....But enormous numbers are utterly unaccounted for. Where are they gone, and what has been their fate? The same conditions may reproduce themselves in a modified form in the expulsion of great numbers of Sudeten and other Germans from Czechoslovakia. Sparse and guarded accounts of what has happened and is happening have filtered through, but it is not impossible that tragedy on a prodigious scale is unfolding itself behind the iron curtain which at the moment divides Europe in twain.

1945, 16 AUGUST.

Revenge

The enormous contingents of German youth growing to military manhood year by year are inspired by the fiercest sentiments, and the soul of Germany smoulders with dreams of a War of Liberation or Revenge....Germany is a far stronger entity than France, and cannot be kept in permanent subjugation.

1924, SEPTEMBER. ("SHALL WE ALL COMMIT SUICIDE?," PALL MALL; THOUGHTS, 178.)

Socialism

In spite of the great numbers of the Socialist Party in Germany, in spite of the high ability of its leaders, it has hardly any influence whatever upon the course of public affairs. It has to submit to food taxes and to conscription; and I observe that Herr Bebel, the distinguished leader of that Party...admitted with great candour, that there was no other country in Europe so effectively organised as Germany to put down anything in the nature of a violent Socialist movement.

1906, 11 OCTOBER. ST. ANDREW'S HALL, GLASGOW. (LIBERALISM, 161.)

Vulnerability of

Certainly a continental country like Germany, with large foreign armies on its frontiers, would be most unwise to run the risk of exposing itself to intensive bombing attacks from this island upon its military centres, its munition establishments, and its lines of communication, at a time when it was engaged or liable to be engaged by the armies of another first-class Power.

1934, 28 NOVEMBER.

Women in the military

It is very remarkable that the most virile and militaristic nation at the present time—the Germans—have set their faces like flint against using women as fighters. They hold to the broad human principle that the woman's place is in the home and that the male protects her. Their arrangements are perfected to give the women plenty to do in making war-stores and munitions.

1938, FEBRUARY. ("WOMEN IN WAR," STRAND MAGAZINE; ESSAYS I, 386.)

WSC was more liberal on the role of British women. See "women" entries in Chapter 22.

World War II bombing

The civil population of Germany have, however, an easy way to escape from these severities. All they have to do is to leave the cities where the munitions work is being carried on—abandon their work, and go out into the fields, and watch their home fires burning from a distance. In this way they may find time for meditation and repentance; there they may remember the millions of Russian women and children they have driven out to perish in the snows, and the mass executions of peasantry and prisoners-of-war which in varying scales they are inflicting upon so many of the ancient and famous peoples of Europe. There they may remember that it is the villainous Hitlerite regime which is responsible for dragging Germany through misery and slaughter to ultimate ruin, and learn that the tyrant's overthrow is the first step to world liberation.

1942, 10 MAY. BROADCAST, LONDON. (END, 129; HARMON, "ARE WE BEASTS?," PASSIM.)

A quotation you don't hear every day, amid the cacophony stating (incorrectly) that Churchill ordered (and exulted in) the bombing of Dresden, which had actually been requested by the Russians while WSC was en route to Yalta. There was a grim logic to his recommendations.

Are we beasts? Are we taking this too far?

1943, 29 JUNE, CHEQUERS. (OB VII, 437: LADY SOAMES TO THE EDITOR.)

WSC said this after sitting bolt upright during a film showing the bombing of German towns from the air. This was a typical reaction of a man whose humanity was never lacking. "He would have done anything to win the war," his daughter said, "and I daresay he had to do some pretty rough things. But they didn't unman him."

World War II defeat

Now we are reaching a period when the Germans will be conquered completely, and Europe will be entirely liberated from their thrall. The brutal hosts which marched so enthusiastically upon us, their eyes alive with greed and the passion of war and the earnest desire for mastery over others, have reached a time when they will be added to those long, melancholy, and humiliating streams of prisoners who, having done the worst to the world, have no hope but in its mercy.

1945, 21 APRIL, BRISTOL UNIVERSITY. (VICTORY, 116.)

In the forefront of any survey of the world stands Germany, a vanquished nation. "Stands," I said—no, prostrate, shattered. Seventy or eighty millions of men and women of an ancient, capable and terribly efficient race are in a ruined famished condition in the heart of Europe.

1946, 12 NOVEMBER.

World War II in North Africa

The proud German Army has by its sudden collapse, sudden crumbling and breaking up, unexpected to all of us, the proud German Army has once again proved the truth of the saying, "The Hun is always either at your throat or your feet;" and that is a point which may have its bearing upon the future. But for us, arrived at this milestone in the war: we can say "One Continent redeemed."

1943, 19 MAY. CONGRESS, WASHINGTON. (ONWARDS, 100.)

10

RUSSIA

"Trying to maintain good relations with a Communist is like wooing a crocodile. You do not know whether to tickle it under the chin or to beat it over the head. When it opens its mouth you cannot tell whether it is trying to smile or preparing to eat you up!" [42]

"Is there still a Tsar?"..."Yes, but he is not a Romanoff."
WSC with Roosevelt and Stalin at Teheran, November 1943.

Churchill never warmed to Russia. When he was a subaltern, it posed a threat to British India. In World War I, trying to succour the Czar by forcing the Dardanelles, he was drummed out of the Admiralty; and he was no sooner gone than the Czar was, too. The Germans smuggled Lenin into Russia like a "culture of typhoid", and when after Hitler's invasion he declared allegiance to Russia, Stalin was already demanding to know when he would launch the Second Front.

Yalta ended with Churchill thinking – or hoping – he could trust Stalin, only to be frustrated, and denounced by the Kremlin as a warmonger when he warned of the Iron Curtain at Fulton in 1946. After Russia acquired the atomic bomb, Churchill spent his waning years in office trying desperately to reach an understanding that would avoid World War III. Neither Stalin's successors nor Eisenhower reciprocated – until a few weeks after he retired, when they promptly got together with Churchill's successor in the first Big Three summit since 1945.

It is valid to conclude that Churchill looked upon the Russians as creatures of

---

42 WSC, Downing Street, 24 January 1944.

opportunity, and formed British policy likewise. He liked and admired individual Russians, such as Litvinov and Savinkov; and he felt a twinge of pity for Nicholas II. But the word he most often used for Russians in general was "crocodiles".

Churchill instinctively feared the Communist ideology that held Russia in thrall from 1917. As Minister of War in 1919 he supported sending Allied troops to aid the White Russians, who were ultimately routed. Later he said he hoped never to have to choose between the Communist and Nazi ideologies; and he predicted the demise of both. Knowing him as we do from these pages, it is not hard to visualise him rejoicing at the demise of the Soviet Union, and hoping for a happy future in that tormented land.

See Chapter 20 for comments on Czar Nicholas II, Lenin, Litvinov, Molotov, Savinkov, Stalin and Trotsky.

Contemplating Russia

If Russia is to be saved, as I pray she may be saved, she must be saved by Russians. It must be by Russian manhood and Russian courage and Russian virtue that the rescue and regeneration of this once mighty nation and famous branch of the European family can alone be achieved. Russia must be saved by Russian exertions, and it must be from the heart of the Russian people and with their strong arm that the conflict against Bolshevism in Russia must be mainly waged.

1919, 19 FEBRUARY. MANSION HOUSE, LONDON.
(GILBERT, LIFE, 410–11.)

Was there ever a more awful spectacle in the whole history of the world than is unfolded by the agony of Russia? This vast country, this mighty branch of the human family, not only produced enough food for itself, but, before the War, it was one of the great granaries of the world, from which food was exported to every country. It is now reduced to famine of the most terrible kind, not because there is no food—there is plenty of food—but because the theories of Lenin and Trotsky have fatally and, it may be finally, ruptured the means of intercourse between man and man, between workman and peasant, between town and country...[The Communists] have driven man from the civilisation of the twentieth century into a condition of barbarism worse than the Stone Age, and left him the most awful and pitiable spectacle in human experience, devoured by vermin, racked by pestilence, and deprived of hope.

1920, 3 JANUARY. VICTORIA HALL, SUNDERLAND.
(CS III, 2919–20.)

In Russia we have a vast, dumb people dwelling under the discipline of a conscripted army in war-time; a people suffering in years of peace the rigours and privations of the worst campaigns; a people ruled by terror, fanaticisms, and the Secret Police. Here we have a state whose subjects are so happy that they have to be forbidden to quit its bounds under the direst penalties; whose diplomatists and agents sent on foreign missions have often to leave their wives and children at home as hostages to ensure their eventual return.

1929, AUGUST. ("GEORGE BERNARD SHAW,"
PALL MALL; GC, 33.)

Intentions of

I cannot forecast to you the action of Russia. It is a riddle wrapped in a mystery inside an enigma: but perhaps there is a key. That key is Russian national interest. It cannot be in accordance with the interest or the safety of Russia that Germany should plant itself upon the shores of the Black Sea, or that it should overrun the Balkan States and subjugate the Slavonic peoples of South-Eastern Europe. That would be contrary to the historic life-interests of Russia.

1939, 1 OCTOBER. BROADCAST, LONDON.
(BLOOD, 205–6.)

I do not believe that Soviet Russia desires war. What they desire is the fruits of war and the indefinite expansion of their power and doctrines.

1946, 5 MARCH. WESTMINSTER COLLEGE, FULTON,
MISSOURI. (SINEWS, 103.)

Leadership

Everybody has always underrated the Russians. They keep their own secrets alike from foe and friends.

1942, 23 APRIL.

We are in the presence of the collective mind, whose springs of action we cannot define. There are thirteen or fourteen very able men in the Kremlin who hold all Russia and more than a third of Europe in their control. Many stresses and pressures, internal as well as external, are working upon them, as upon all human beings. I cannot presume to forecast what decisions they will take, or to observe what decisions they may have already taken; still less can I attempt to foresee the time factor in their affairs.

1946, 23 OCTOBER.

After Stalin had reacted angrily to his "Iron Curtain" speech the previous March, Churchill began referring to a plural Soviet leadership rather than to Stalin, possibly because, in the back of his mind, he still could not accept that he should not have trusted Stalin's promises in 1945.

While [in 1942] going through the streets of Moscow, which seemed very empty, I lowered the window for a little more air, and to my surprise felt that the glass was over two inches thick. This surpassed all records in my experience.

1951. (WW2 IV, 428–9.)

Menace of

It would be a measureless disaster if Russian barbarism overlaid the culture and independence of the ancient States of Europe.

1942, 21 OCTOBER. (WW2 IV, 504.)

What will lie between the white snows of Russia and the white cliffs of Dover?

1945, 23 FEBRUARY, CHEQUERS. (OB VII, 1232.)

WSC was musing about what would happen when the Allies had destroyed Germany.

People

No one has been a more consistent opponent of Communism than I have for the last twenty-five years. I will unsay no word that I have spoken about it. But all this fades away before the spectacle which is now unfolding. The past with its crimes, its follies and its tragedies, flashes away. I see the Russian soldiers standing on the threshold of their native land, guarding the fields which their fathers have tilled from time immemorial. I see them guarding their homes where mothers and wives pray—ah yes, for there are times when all pray—for the safety of their loved ones, the return of the breadwinner, of their champion, of their protector. I see the ten thousand villages of Russia, where the means of existence was wrung so hardly from the soil, but where there are still primordial human joys, where maidens laugh and children play. I see advancing upon all this in hideous onslaught the Nazi war machine, with its clanking, heel-clicking, dandified Prussian officers, its crafty expert agents fresh from the cowing and tying-down of a dozen countries. I see also the dull, drilled, docile, brutish masses of the Hun soldiery plodding on like a swarm of crawling locusts. I see the German bombers and fighters in the sky, still smarting from many a British whipping, delighted to find what they believe is an easier and a safer prey.

1941, 22 JUNE. BROADCAST, LONDON. (UNRELENTING, 172.)

I record as they come back to me these memories, and the strong impression I sustained at the moment of millions of men and women being blotted out or displaced for ever. A generation would no doubt come to whom their miseries were unknown but it would be sure of having more to eat and bless Stalin's name. I did not repeat Burke's dictum, "If I cannot have reform without injustice, I will not have reform." With the World War going on all round us it seemed vain to moralise aloud.

1951. (WW2 IV, 448.)

Sad testimony to the possibility that, optimist though he was, Churchill knew what he was dealing with in the Soviet Union.

Policy towards Russia

[We could send part of the British Fleet to the Baltic] to ensure superiority over Germany in that sea. It would stay there permanently, based on a Russian port of which we should obtain the use under this plan.

1936, 19 APRIL. (OB V, 723.)

Quoted in a note by Maurice Hankey to Sir Thomas Inskip describing WSC's "fantastic plan". At the suggestion of Permanent Under-Secretary for Foreign Affairs Sir Robert

Vansittart, WSC maintained a close relationship with Soviet Ambassador Ivan Maisky, who had friendly inclinations towards Britain. As early as the mid-1930s, WSC advocated a Russo-Franco-British common front against Hitler. This, he thought, trumped whatever he thought of Communism, because Soviet ambitions were thus far confined to Soviet borders, while Hitler's threat was global, or at least pan-European.

What can we do to help Russia? There is nothing that we would not do. If the sacrifice of thousands of British lives would turn the scale, our fellow-countrymen would not flinch.

1942, 23 APRIL.

Never forget that Bolsheviks are crocodiles.... I cannot feel the slightest trust or confidence in them. Force and facts are their only realities.

CIRCA 1942. CLASSIFIED LETTERS RELEASED BY THE PUBLIC RECORD OFFICE, LONDON, 2002.

I feel also that their word is their bond. I know of no Government which stands to its obligations, even in its own despite, more solidly than the Russian Soviet Government. I decline absolutely to embark here on a discussion about Russian good faith.

1945, 27 FEBRUARY.

Interesting, given the quotation above. Churchill was quickly to be disabused of this notion. For his contemporary belief that he could trust Stalin, see People...Stalin.

From what I have seen of our Russian friends and Allies during the war, I am convinced that there is nothing they admire so much as strength, and there is nothing for which they have less respect than weakness, especially military weakness. For that reason the old doctrine of a balance of power is unsound. We cannot afford, if we can help it, to work on narrow margins, offering temptations to a trial of strength.

1946, 5 MARCH. WESTMINSTER COLLEGE, FULTON, MISSOURI. (SINEWS, 103.)

I tell you—it's no use arguing with a Communist. It's no good trying to convert a Communist or persuade him. You can only deal with them on the following basis...by having superior force on your side on the matter in question—and they must also be convinced that you will use—you will not hesitate to use—those forces, if necessary, in the most ruthless manner...that you are not restrained by any moral consideration if the case arose from using that force with complete material ruthlessness. And that is the greatest chance of peace, the surest road to peace.

1949, 25 MARCH. RITZ-CARLTON HOTEL, NEW YORK. (BALANCE, 37.)

I had always thought it was a wrong thing, capable of breeding disastrous quarrels, that a mighty land-mass like the Russian Empire, with its population of nearly two hundred millions, should be denied during the winter months all effective access to the broad waters.

1952. (WW2 V, 336.)

Revolution

Russia was to be the first to fall, and in her fall to open upon herself a tide of ruin in which perhaps a score of millions of human beings have been engulfed. The consequences of these events abide with us today. They will darken the world for our children's children.

1923. (CRISIS II, 511.)

All sorts of Russians made the revolution. No sort of Russian reaped its profit.

1931. (CRISIS V, 350.)

Bolshevism is a great evil, but it has arisen out of great social evils.

1919, 29 MAY.

The Bolsheviks robbed Russia at one stroke of two most precious things, peace and victory—the victory that was within her grasp and the peace which was her dearest desire. Both were swept away from her. The victory was turned into defeat. As for the peace, her life ever since has been one long struggle of agonizing war.

1919, 5 NOVEMBER.

Just when the worst was over, when victory was in sight, when the fruits of measureless sacrifice were at hand, the old Russia had been dragged down, and in her place there ruled "the nameless beast" so long foretold in Russian legend. Thus the Russian people were deprived of Victory, Honour, Freedom, Peace and Bread. Thus there was to be no Russia in the Councils of the Allies, only an abyss which still continues in human affairs.

1929. (CRISIS IV, 71.)

Meanwhile, the German hammer broke down the front and Lenin blew up the rear.... broke, all collapsed, all liquefied in universal babble and cannonade, and out of the anarchy emerged the one coherent, frightful entity and fact—the Bolshevik punch....The Supreme Committee—sub-human or super-human which you will—crocodiles with master minds, entered upon their responsibilities upon November 8.

1929. (CRISIS IV, 79–80.)

Soviet system

...in Russia a man is called a reactionary if he objects to having his property stolen, and his wife and children murdered.

1919, 5 NOVEMBER.

There is not one single social or economic principle or concept in the philosophy of the Russian Bolshevik which has not been realised, carried into action, and enshrined in immutable laws a million years ago by the White Ant.

1927, JULY. ("MASS EFFECTS IN MODERN LIFE," PALL MALL; THOUGHTS, 185.)

But the dull, squalid figures of the Russian Bolsheviks are not redeemed in interest even by the magnitude of their crimes. All form and emphasis is lost in a vast process of Asiatic liquefaction.

1929, DECEMBER. ("LEON TROTSKY, ALIAS BRONSTEIN," PALL MALL; GC, 128.)

The Soviet government have a different philosophy, namely, Communism, and use to the full the methods of police government, which they are applying in every State which has fallen a victim to their liberating arms....Except in so far as force is concerned, there is no equality between right and wrong.

1945, 26 MAY. (WW2 VI, 504.)

WSC to President Truman, responding to the President's suggestion that he should meet Stalin somewhere in Europe before he saw Churchill.

[His father's ghost: "Is there still a Tsar?"]
Yes, but he is not a Romanoff. It's another family. He is much more powerful, and much more despotic.

1947. (*THE DREAM*, OB VIII, 371.)

For the background of this article, see Anecdotes and Stories ... The Dream.

I have had the opportunity several times of seeing in conditions of grave business some of these commissars who form the oligarchy in the Kremlin and their chiefs, and I can tell you that these men are apt to form designs and to carry them out, and that when confronted with farces and shams they very often retaliate by strong and real measures.

1951, 15 FEBRUARY.

Strangling at birth

...I think the day will come when it will be recognized without doubt, not only on one side of the House, but throughout the civilized world, that the strangling of Bolshevism at its birth would have been an untold blessing to the human race.

[Mr. Seymour Cocks (Lab.): "If that had happened we should have lost the 1939–45 war."]
No, it would have prevented that war.

1949, 26 JANUARY.

World War I aftermath

One might as well legalise sodomy as recognize the Bolsheviks.

1919, 24 JANUARY, PARIS. (GILBERT, LIFE, 408.)

Churchill had a disagreement with Lloyd George, who had suggested inviting the Bolshevik leaders to confer with the victorious Allies at Prinkipo, Turkey.

[The White Russians] are now engaged in fighting against the foul baboonery of Bolshevism.

1919, 19 FEBRUARY. MANSION HOUSE, LONDON. (OB IV, 257.)

After having defeated all the tigers and lions I don't like to be beaten by baboons.

1919, 8 APRIL, PARIS. (OB, CV4/1, 609.)

The inherent vice of Bolshevism appears to rot simultaneously, every part of the social structure of Russia, including even the military tyranny on which alone the Soviet power now depends.

1919, 29 MAY.

Since the Armistice my policy would have been "Peace with the German people, war on the Bolshevik tyranny." Willingly or unavoidably, you have followed something very near the reverse.

1920, 24 MARCH. (CRISIS IV, 377.)

Churchill to Prime Minister Lloyd George.

Were they [Britain, France and America] at war with Soviet Russia? Certainly not; but they shot Soviet Russians at sight. They stood as invaders on Russian soil. They armed the enemies of the Soviet Government....But war—shocking! Interference—shame! It was, they repeated, a matter of indifference to them how Russians settled their own internal affairs. They were impartial—Bang!

1929. (CRISIS IV, 235.)

Britain, France and the United States intervened unsuccessfully on the side of the White Russians and against the Bolsheviks during the Russian Civil War, 1920–22. Churchill supported the effort, while ridiculing the Allies' attempt at "plausible deniability".

They also proposed to send a detachment of the Young Men's Christian Association to offer moral guidance to the Russian people.

1929. (CRISIS IV, 95.)

Churchill was ridiculing the token American commitment to the White Russians fighting Lenin.

World War I Alliance

Some general formula such as "safeguarding the permanent fruits of the Revolution" might be devised which would render common action possible having regard to the cruel and increasing pressure of the Germans....Let us never forget that Lenin and Trotsky are fighting with ropes round their necks. They will leave office for the grave. Show them any real chance of consolidating their power, of getting some kind of protection against the vengeance of a counter-revolution, and they would be non-human not to embrace it....In the main, the intellect of Russia, including the Bolsheviks, must, whatever happens in the long run, be hostile to Prussian militarism and therefore

drawn towards the Allied parliamentary democracies.

1918, APRIL. (GILBERT, LIFE, 389–90.)

In two remarkable Cabinet memos, Churchill suggested an Allied representative persuade Lenin to re-enter the war against Germany, in exchange for the Allies guaranteeing Lenin's revolution. This was however a momentary impulse. See also People...Roosevelt, Theodore.

World War II invasion by Germany

At four o'clock this morning Hitler attacked and invaded Russia. All his usual formalities of perfidy were observed with scrupulous technique....Hitler is a monster of wickedness, insatiable in his lust for blood and plunder. Not content with having all Europe under his heel or else terrorized into various forms of abject submission, he must now carry his work of butchery and desolation among the vast multitudes of Russia and of Asia....I see advancing...in hideous onslaught the Nazi war-machine, with its clanking, heel-clicking, dandified officers, its crafty expert agents fresh from the cowing and tying-down of a dozen countries.

1941, 22 JUNE. BROADCAST, LONDON. (UNRELENTING, 170–72.)

Executions in cold blood are being perpetrated by the German police-troops upon the Russian patriots who defend their native soil. Since the Mongol invasions of Europe in the sixteenth century, there has never been methodical, merciless butchery on such a scale, or approaching such a scale. We are in the presence of a crime without a name.

1941, 24 AUGUST. BROADCAST, LONDON. (CS VI, 6475.)

World War II war effort

When I look at all that Russia is doing and the vast achievements of the Soviet armies, I should feel myself below the level of events if I were not sure in my heart and conscience that everything in human power is being done, and will be done, to bring British and American forces into action against the enemy with the utmost speed and energy, and on the largest scale.

1943, 11 FEBRUARY.

...it is the Russian armies who have done the main work in tearing the guts out of the German army. In the air and on the oceans we could maintain our place, but there was no force in the world which could have been called into being, except after several more years, that would have been able to maul and break the German army unless it had been subjected to the terrible slaughter and manhandling that has befallen it through the strength of the Russian Soviet armies.

1944, 2 August.

I have always believed and I still believe that it is the Red Army that has torn the guts out of the filthy Nazis.

October, 1944, Moscow. (Thompson, Shadow, 146.)

WSC responding to a toast by Stalin.

11
NATIONS

"The world on the verge of its catastrophe was very brilliant.
Nations and Empires crowned with princes and potentates rose
majestically on every side, lapped in the accumulated treasures of the
long peace. All were fitted and fastened – it seemed securely – into
an immense cantilever." [43]

"We welcome any country where the people own the Government..."
The Hague, Netherlands, 7 May 1948.

The canon is replete with references to hundreds of nations; those represented here are ones that particularly involved Churchill. Comparative word counts should not be taken as an indication of his esteem, but his degree of involvement: he had far more to do with Irish affairs than Canadian, for example.

Included here are Burma, Egypt, India, Iraq, Ireland and Palestine, over which Britain once wielded suzerainty; and the "Great Dominions" of Australia, Canada, New Zealand and South Africa. British colonies of Churchill's day that have since become independent, such as Uganda, will be found in Chapter 6.

Generally he admired small states that stood up for their rights – Greece, Yugoslavia, Denmark and Norway all contributed heroics despite cruel occupation. And he despised countries which allowed themselves to be subjugated without a struggle. Of Belgium's sudden withdrawal in 1940 he was censorious; historians have since said he was much too hard on King Leopold.

---

43 Churchill's thoughts on the eve of war in 1914. Crisis I, 188.

Churchill never altered his view that Britain's record in India was admirable, and had set the stage for the democracy that country became. He engineered an Irish Treaty that kept the peace there for nearly fifty years, and though he resented Irish Premier de Valera's refusal of Irish ports during World War II, he nursed a sentiment for "old Ireland" that was sincere throughout his life.

As to the countries with which he contended, his record of prescience was mixed, albeit better than most. He had Hitler's number from the start. He was soon on to Mussolini, but voiced admiration for Il Duce in earlier days when Italy was still a former wartime ally. He considered Japan a minor threat almost up to the loss of Singapore, which he once considered an impregnable barrier to a Japanese attack on Australia. He should never have trusted Stalin. But hindsight is cheap, and far too easily indulged. Here is the record, as he said the words; the words speak for themselves.

Abyssinia (Ethiopia)

No one can keep up the pretence that Abyssinia is a fit, worthy and equal member of a league of civilized nations. The wisdom of the British policy was shown in our opposing her admission to the League....I share the feeling common throughout the country of sympathy for the primitive feudal people of Abyssinia who are fighting for their hearths and homes and for the ancient freedom of their mountains against a scientific invader. The native independence of Abyssinia cannot be made a matter for compromise or barter.

1935, 24 OCTOBER.

It was a satisfaction for me to see for the first time in the flesh Haile Selassie, that historical figure who pleaded the cause of his country amid the storms of the League of Nations, who was the first victim of Mussolini's lust for power and conquest, and who was also the first to be restored to his ancient throne by the heavy exertions of our British and Indian armies in the far-off days of 1940 and 1941.

1945, 27 FEBRUARY.

Haile Selassie (1892–1975), "The Lion of Judah", Emperor of Ethiopia, 1930–34.

Albania

What has happened to the negotiations with Albania by which we were to have some satisfaction given to us for the murder of forty British naval men and the grievous injury to many more, by a state we have helped and nourished to the best of our ability? That is not

a matter which can be ignored or forgotten, because it occurred in time of peace, and cannot be, as it were swept into the vast, confused catalogue of human injuries and wrong deeds which were done on both sides in the course of the great war.

1948, 23 JANUARY.

Six months later WSC renewed his inquiry, saying,

> Not the slightest satisfaction has been obtained for the outrage of ingratitude and treachery. I could give you many other instances which prove how British rights and British lives are being disregarded by minor foreign states to a degree never known before in the history of our country.

Argentina

We all feel deep regret and also anxiety, as friends of Argentina, that in this testing time for nations she has not seen fit to take her place with no reserve or qualification upon the side of freedom, and has chosen to dally with the evil, and not only with the evil, but with the losing side. I trust that my remarks will be noted, because this is a very serious war.

1944, 2 AUGUST.

Under Juan Peron, Argentina was maintaining a neutral posture very late in World War II.

Armenia

As for Turkish atrocities: marching till they dropped dead the greater part of the garrison at Kut; massacring uncounted thousands of helpless Armenians, men, women, and children together, whole districts blotted out in one administrative holocaust—these were beyond human redress.

1929. (CRISIS IV, 157.)

Australia

The armies [in Gallipoli] are like men fighting on a high and narrow scaffold above the surface of the earth...to step back means not merely defeat, but destruction. That is why I have always in speaking of this dwelt upon the immense importance of every yard of ground, of every furlong that is gained by the heroic courage of our soldiers and of our superb Australian fellow citizens.

1915, 17 SEPTEMBER, ENFIELD LOCK.
(CS III, 2387.)

The fighting line of the British, Australian and Canadian Armies is holding nearly forty of the finest divisions of the German Army on its front. The Australians are in contact with the enemy. What we have above all things is the feeling that behind the fighting line there is a resolute, intense, sagacious, driving power, which by every means, social, political, military, naval, will be carrying our cause forward to victory.

1916, 23 JUNE. RITZ HOTEL, LONDON.
(CS III, 2458.)

Dinner for Australian Prime Minister W. M. Hughes.

We are doing our utmost in the Mother Country to meet living perils and onslaughts. We have sunk all party differences and have imposed universal compulsory service, not only upon men, but women. We have suffered the agonising loss of two of our finest ships which we sent to sustain the Far Eastern War. We are organising from reduced forces the utmost further naval aid....We have successfully disengaged Tobruk, after previously relieving all your men who so gallantly held it for so long. I hope therefore you will be considerate in the judgment which you pass upon those to whom Australian lives and fortunes are so dear.

1942, 14 JANUARY. (WW2 IV, 10–11.)

WSC to Prime Minister Curtin, who replied, "We make no apologies for our effort, or even for what you argue we are not doing." Churchill fired back. See Maxims...safety.

A young nation, like Australia, dwelling in a continent growing ample food for itself and for export, may try experiments in Socialism without the risk of fatal injury, but the fifty million gathered together in this small island are in a very different position.

1950, 21 JANUARY. PARTY BROADCAST, LONDON.
(BALANCE, 157.)

The heart of the country, over a million square miles, has attracted delvers after metals and ranchers of cattle, but it remains largely uninhabited. The silence of the bush and the loneliness of the desert are only disturbed by the passing of some transcontinental express, the whirr of a boomerang, or the drone of a pilotless missile.

1958. (HESP IV, 122.)

Austria

The public mind has been concentrated upon the moral and sentimental aspects of the Nazi conquests of Austria—a small country brutally struck down, its Government scattered to the winds, the oppression of the Nazi party doctrine imposed upon a Catholic population, and upon the working classes of Austria and of Vienna, the hard ill-usage of persecution which indeed will ensue—which is probably in progress at the moment—of those who, this time last week, were exercising their undoubted political rights, discharging their duties faithfully to their own country.

1938, 14 MARCH.

The control of Vienna enables the economic fortunes of all the States of the Danubian Basin to be manipulated, exploited, and controlled so as to favour German designs, and for the benefit of German finance, trade and arms.

1938, 24 MARCH.

Hitler had engineered the Anschluss, an act of union between Nazi Germany and Austria; and German troops had marched into the Austrian capital on 12 March.

Thus, by every device, from the stick to the carrot, the emaciated Austrian donkey is made to pull the Nazi barrow up an ever-steepening hill.

1938, 6 JULY. ("THE RAPE OF AUSTRIA," *DAILY TELEGRAPH*; STEP, 249.)

Baltic States

These small States have stood. They are intact today. They have maintained their existence precariously. Quivering and shaking, but still standing, they have held back not only the Bolshevik armies but the more devastating Bolshevik propaganda which, applied to people in the depths of misery, just recovering from the convulsions of the War, without any of the resources of a civilised State, offers every temptation to internal disorder and anarchy.

1919, 29 JULY. (CS III, 2831.)

See also Latvia, Lithuania and Estonia.

During the winter of 1918 and the early summer of 1919…it is not surprising that the independence of Estonia, Latvia and Lithuania existed for the time being only in the aspirations of their inhabitants and the sympathies of the allied and associated Powers.

1929. (CRISIS IV, 100.)

We have never recognised the 1941 frontiers of Russia except *de facto*. They were acquired by acts of aggression in shameful collusion with Hitler. The transfer of the peoples of the Baltic states to Soviet Russia against their will would be contrary to all the principles for which we are fighting this war and would dishonour our cause.

1942, 8 JANUARY. (WW2 III, 615.)

WSC to Anthony Eden, who had urged him to take up with Roosevelt "immediate recognition" of the 1941 Soviet borders on the basis of "stark realism". Churchill's reply was resolute; the pressure of events made him relent in March 1942, only to revert to his original position after the war.

Hitler had cast them away like pawns in his deal with the Soviets before the outbreak of war in 1939. There had been a severe Russian and Communist purge. All the dominant personalities and elements had been liquidated in one way or another. The life of these strong peoples was henceforward underground. Presently, as we shall see, Hitler came back with a Nazi counter-purge. Finally, in the general victory the Soviets had control again. Thus the deadly comb ran back and forth, and back again, through Estonia, Latvia, and

Lithuania. There was no doubt however where the right lay. The Baltic States should be sovereign independent peoples.

1950. (WW2 III, 615.)

Belgium

The House will be aware that the King of the Belgians yesterday sent a plenipotentiary to the German Command asking for a suspension of arms on the Belgian front.…The Belgian Government has dissociated itself from the action of the King and declaring itself to be the only legal Government of Belgium, has formally announced its resolve to continue the war at the side of the Allies.…

Whatever our feelings may be upon the facts so far as they are known to us, we must remember that the sense of brotherhood between the many peoples who have fallen into the power of the aggressor and those who still confront him will play its part in better days than those through which we are passing.

1940, 28 MAY.

…at the last moment when Belgium was already invaded, King Leopold called upon us to come to his aid, and even at the last moment we came. He and his brave, efficient army, nearly half a million strong, guarded our left flank, thus kept open our only line of retreat to the sea. Suddenly, without prior consultation, with the least possible notice, without the advice of his ministers and upon his own personal act, he sent a plenipotentiary to the German command, surrendered his army, and exposed our whole flank and means of retreat.

1940, 4 JUNE.

King Leopold III bravely prolonged Belgian resistance to the Germans long enough to help the Dunkirk evacuation proceed, and did in fact notify George VI that he would have to surrender. Confronted over his statement in 1949, Churchill declared that he was reporting the situation as he knew it at the time; but his remarks were not in keeping with his usual magnanimity.

Burma

A palace intrigue [in 1878] secured the throne to Prince Theebaw [sic], and the new reign was inaugurated by an indiscriminate massacre of the late King's other sons, with their mothers, wives, and children. Eight cart-loads of butchered princes of the blood were cast, according to custom, into the river. The less honourable sepulchre of a capacious pit within the gaol was accorded to their dependents.

1906. (LRC, 420.)

Thibaw Min (1859–1916) was the last king of Burma, which was annexed to the British Empire by Lord Randolph Churchill on 1 January 1886. WSC was comparing Burma's condition before the annexation with conditions afterwards.

U Aung San went over to the Japanese and raised what we might call a quisling army to come in at the tail of the Japanese and help conquer the country for Japan. Great cruelties were perpetrated by his army. They were not very effective in fighting, but in the infliction of vengeance upon the loyal Burmese—the Burmese who were patriotically fighting with British and Indian troops to defend the soil of Burma from the Japanese conquerors—great cruelties were perpetrated on those men, because they had helped us to resist the Japanese.

1947, 5 NOVEMBER.

General Aung San (1915–47) brought about Burma's independence in 1942 by cooperating with the Japanese. Britain won Burma back and then granted it independence in 1948. Aung San was the father of Nobel peace laureate Aung San Suu Kyi, ironically placed under house arrest by the military government in 1990. See Churchillisms…Quisling.

Canada

I have had a most successful meeting at Winnipeg. Fancy 20 years ago there were only a few mud huts—tents…and last night a magnificent audience of men in evening dress & ladies half out of it, filled a fine opera house and we took $1,150 at the doors.

1901, 22 JANUARY. WINNIPEG, MANITOBA. (OB, CV1/2, 1231.)

Letter to his mother during his Canadian lecture tour.

The French Canadians derived greater pleasure from singing "God Save the King" than from singing "Rule Britannia."

1904, 19 JULY.

The difficulties are to appreciate the immense size of this country which goes on for thousands of miles of good fertile land, well watered, well wooded, unlimited in possibilities. How silly for people to live crowded up in particular parts of the Empire when there is so much larger and better a life open here for millions. Half the effort of the war would have solved all these problems. However, the world is known to be unteachable.

1929, 12 AUGUST. ON A TRAIN EN ROUTE TO QUEBEC. (OB, CV5/2, 45–6.)

WSC to his wife.

So let us go ahead together. You drive your furrows in this great land and make it fertile, make cities of power and science, make the resources at your disposal draw forward the chariot of development.

1919, 22 AUGUST, REGINA, SASKATCHEWAN. (DILKS, 90.)

I have been wonderfully received in Canada. Never in my whole life have I been welcomed with so much genuine interest and admiration as throughout this vast country…

Darling I am greatly attracted to this country. Immense developments are going forward. There are fortunes to be made in many directions. The tide is flowing strongly. I have made up my mind that if Neville Chamberlain is made leader of the Conservative Party or anyone else of that kind, I clear out of politics and see if I cannot make you and the kittens a little more comfortable before I die. Only one goal still attracts me, and if that were barred I should quit the dreary field for pastures new. As Daniel Peggotty says, "There's mighty lands beyond the seas." However the time to take decision is not yet.

1929, 27 AUGUST. BANFF SPRINGS HOTEL, ALBERTA. (OB, CV5/2, 61–2.)

The nearest Churchill came to becoming a Canadian rancher! Daniel Peggotty was the Yarmouth fisherman, brother of David Copperfield's nurse, in Dickens's David Copperfield (1850). The goal that still attracted him was the Premiership.

Canada is the linchpin of the English-speaking world. Canada, with those relations of friendly affectionate intimacy with the United States on the one hand and with her unswerving fidelity to the British Commonwealth and the Motherland on the other, is the link which...spanning the oceans, brings the continents into their true relation and will prevent in future generations any growth of division between the proud and the happy nations of Europe and the great countries which have come into existence in the New World.

1941, 4 SEPTEMBER. MANSION HOUSE, LONDON. (UNRELENTING, 244.)

Canada is a potent magnet, drawing together those in the new world and in the old whose fortunes are now united in a deadly struggle for life and honour against the common foe. The contribution of Canada to the Imperial war effort, in troops, in ships, in aircraft, in food and in finance, has been magnificent.

1941, 30 DECEMBER. CANADIAN PARLIAMENT, OTTAWA. (UNRELENTING, 363.)

A very odd thing that when I woke up very early this morning, I thought what a pity I haven't got one of those lovely Canadian hats....people often think I am hot-headed. It fits beautifully, and is large enough to allow for any swelling which may take place.

1941, 31 DECEMBER. PRESS CONFERENCE, OTTAWA. (DILKS, 220.)

Churchill had been presented with a British Columbia seal wedge cap.

Canada has become in the course of this war an important seafaring nation, building many scores of warships and merchant ships, some of them thousands of miles from salt water, and sending them forth manned by hardy Canadian seamen to guard the Atlantic convoys and our vital life-line across the ocean. The munition industries of Canada have played a most important part in our war economy. Last, but not least, Canada has relieved Great Britain of what would otherwise have been a debt for these munitions of no less than $2,000,000,000.

1943, 31 AUGUST. BROADCAST, LONDON. (ONWARDS, 174–5.)

There are no limits to the majestic future which lies before the mighty expanse of Canada with its virile, aspiring, cultured and generous-hearted people. Canada is the vital link in the English-speaking world and joins across the Atlantic Ocean the vast American democracy of the United States with our famous old island and the fifty millions who keep the flag flying here.

1951, 19 NOVEMBER. GUILDHALL, LONDON. (STEMMING, 193.)

...Churchill knew that the Canadian Army Corps was the only really formidable force he had in Britain during the period when Hitler might easily have decided to throw his effort on to an invasion.

This year will see the Eighty-fifth Anniversary of Canada's Confederation. A magnificent future awaits Canada if only we can all get through the present hideous world muddle. When I first came here after the Boer War these mighty lands had but five million inhabitants. Now there are fourteen. When my grandchildren come here there may well be 30 million. Upon the whole surface of the globe there is no more spacious and splendid domain open to the activity and genius of free men, with one hand clasping in enduring friendship the United States, and the other spread across the ocean both to Britain and to France. You have a sacred mission to discharge. That you will be worthy of it I do not doubt. God bless you all.

1952, 14 JANUARY. CHÂTEAU LAURIER, OTTAWA. (STEMMING, 219.)

Speaking at the 2007 International Churchill Conference in Vancouver, British Consul Martin Cronin said:

In the summer of 1940 British land forces, having evacuated from Dunkirk, were unready to face invasion, and the First Canadian Division was a vitally important part of our defences.

I have had a lovely welcome from the people of Ottawa this time and it is a great comfort and stimulant to me to feel their warm, spontaneous spirit carrying with it approval of much that I have done in a very long life....

I have often regretted that as on this occasion, time and pressure have prevented me going further afield throughout your vast domain. But I have been all over Canada in my time and I have the most vivid pictures in my mind of many places from Halifax to Kicking Horse Valley and further on to Vancouver, where I caught a lovely salmon, a beautiful salmon, in the harbour in about twenty minutes. In fact I think one of the only important places that I have never visited in Canada is Fort Churchill which was named after my ancestor John Churchill, the First Duke of Marlborough, who succeeded the Duke of York, afterwards James II, as Governor of the Hudson Bay Company....All that part of the world is growing in importance, both commercial and strategic. Nowadays, in fact, a wonderful thing about your country is that there is hardly any part of it where something new and very valuable may not spring to life any day either on the surface of the soil or underneath it.

1954, 30 JUNE. BROADCAST, OTTAWA.
(DILKS, 426.)

China

I have never been one of those who attach too much importance to those stories we are told from South Africa, about Chinese coolies petitioning for the continuance of flogging and struggling to get back to South Africa after being repatriated. They seem to me to be statements which are only credible on the assumption that the Chinese are an even more peculiar people than we believe them to be....the Chinese have a very peculiar code of ethics, which makes them regard it as a more dishonourable thing not to pay a gambling debt than to commit murder.

1906, 8 JUNE.

China, as the years pass, is being eaten by Japan like an artichoke, leaf by leaf....If the Chinese now suffer the cruel malice and oppression of their enemies, it is the fault of the base and perverted conception of pacifism their rulers have ingrained for two or three thousand years in their people.

1937, 3 SEPTEMBER. ("THE WOUNDED DRAGON,"
EVENING STANDARD; STEP, 151, 153.)

I was very much astonished when I came over here after Pearl Harbor to find the estimate of values which seemed to prevail in high American quarters, even in the highest, about China. Some of them thought that China would make as great a contribution to victory in the war as the whole British Empire together. Well, that astonished me very much. Nothing that I picked up afterwards led me to think that my astonishment was ill-founded....I think on the whole you will not find a large profit item entered on that side of the ledger, but that doesn't alter our regard for the Chinese people.

1949, 25 MARCH. RITZ-CARLTON HOTEL, NEW
YORK. (BALANCE, 34.)

Ought we to recognise them [Communist China] or not? Recognising a person is not necessarily an act of approval. I will not be personal, or give instance. One has to recognise lots of things and People in this world of sin and woe that one does not like. The reason for having diplomatic relations is not to confer a compliment, but to secure a convenience.

1949, 17 NOVEMBER.

WSC referred to this early support of British recognition (and did make it personal) about a year later. See People ... Bevan.

But I am by no means sure that China will remain for generations in the Communist grip. The Chinese said of themselves several thousand years ago: "China is a sea that salts all the waters that flow into it." There is another Chinese saying about their country which dates only from the fourth century: "The tail of China is large and will not be wagged." I like that one. The British democracy approves the principle of movable party heads and unwaggable national tails.

1952, 17 JANUARY. CONGRESS, WASHINGTON.
(STEMMING, 223.)

From his third and final speech to a Joint Session of Congress.

It would be silly to waste bombs in the vague inchoate mass of China, and wrong to kill thousands of people for no purpose.

1952, 19 MARCH. CABINET DEFENCE COMMITTEE,
LONDON. (OB VIII, 716.)

Cuba

The most remarkable fact seems to be that two armies will shoot at each other for hours and no one will get hit. I believe that statisticians say that in a battle it takes 2,000 bullets to kill a man. When the calculations are arranged I think it will be found that in the Cuban war it took 2,000 bullets to miss each individual combatant.

1895, 15 DECEMBER, NEW YORK. (OB, CV1/1, 620.)

Interview on his observations of the Cuban revolution for the New York World.

Here was a place where real things were going on. Here was a scene of vital action. Here was a place where anything might happen. Here was a place where something would certainly happen. Here I might leave my bones.

1930. (MEL, 91.)

Churchill recalling his 1895 impressions of Cuba in his autobiography.

Your minute about raising certain legations to the status of embassies. I must say I think Cuba has as good a claim as some of the other places—*la perla de las Antilles*. Great offence will be given if all the others have it and this large, rich, beautiful island, the home of the cigar, is denied.

1944, 5 FEBRUARY. (WW2 V, 607.)

WSC to Foreign Secretary Anthony Eden.

Czechoslovakia

To English ears, the name of Czechoslovakia sounds outlandish. No doubt they are only a small democratic State, no doubt they have an army only two or three times as large as ours, no doubt they have a munitions supply only three times as great as that of Italy, but still they are a virile people; they have their treaty rights, they have a line of fortresses, and they have a strongly manifested will to live freely.

1938, 14 MARCH.

Here was the model democratic State of Central Europe, a country where minorities were treated better than anywhere else. It has been deserted, destroyed and devoured. It is now being digested.

1938, 16 OCTOBER. BROADCAST TO THE USA, LONDON. (BLOOD, 84.)

The German invaders pursue with every method of cultural, social and economic oppression their intention of destroying the Czech nation. Students are shot by scores and tormented in concentration camps by thousands. All the Czech Universities have closed... [their libraries] pillaged or destroyed. The works of their national writers have been removed from the public libraries. More than two thousand periodicals and newspapers have been suppressed. Prominent writers, artists and professors have been herded into the concentration camps. The public administration and judicature have been reduced to chaos. The Czech lands have been plundered....A hundred thousand Czech workmen have been led off into slavery to be toiled to death in Germany. Eight millions of Czechs—a nation famous and recognizable as a distinct community for many centuries past in Europe—writhes in agony under the German and Nazi tyranny.

1940, 27 JANUARY. FREE TRADE HALL, MANCHESTER. (BLOOD, 264.)

Be of good cheer. The hour of your deliverance will come. The soul of freedom is deathless; it cannot and will not perish.

1940, 30 SEPTEMBER. BROADCAST TO THE CZECHS, LONDON. (OB VI, 819.)

Denmark

We are also at this moment occupying the Faroe Islands, which belong to Denmark and which are a strategic point of high importance, and whose people showed every disposition to receive us with warm regard. We shall shield the Faroe Islands from all the severities of war and establish ourselves there conveniently by sea and air until the moment comes when they will be handed back to the Crown and people of Denmark, liberated from the foul thraldom in which they have been plunged by the German aggression.

1940, 11 APRIL.

Here I may mention a debt which Britain owes to the ancient Danes. We did not regard it as such at the time. The Danish sailors from the "long ships" who fought ashore as soldiers brought with them into England a new principle represented by a class, the peasant-yeoman-proprietor...The centuries did not destroy their original firmness of character nor their deep attachment to the soil. All through English history this strain continued to play its part, and to this day the peculiar esteem in which law and freedom are held by the English-speaking peoples in every quarter of the globe may be shrewdly and justly referred to a Viking source.

1950, 10 October. Copenhagen University.
(Balance, 386.)

Egypt

...it is beyond dispute that the Egyptian is not a fighting animal....He may be cruel. He is never fierce. Yet he is not without courage—a courage which bears pain and hardship in patience, which confronts ill-fortune with indifference, and which looks on death with apathetic composure. It is the courage of down-trodden peoples, and one which stronger breeds may often envy, though they can scarcely be expected to admire.

1899. (River I, 152–3.)

[If the Nile were dammed at Aswan] the profits of the people and Government of Egypt would be more than doubled. The wealth and happiness of the amiable peasants of the Delta would grow; their contentment would react on the prosperity of other countries. All the world would gain advantage from those extra eight metres of masonry.

The Temple of Philae intervenes. The raising of the waterlevel would submerge it. I will not assail the small but beautiful ruin. Let us believe that the god to whom it was raised was once worthy of human reverence, and would willingly accept as a nobler memorial the life-giving lake beneath which his temple would be buried. If it were not so, then indeed it would be time for a rational and utilitarian generation to tear the monument of such a monster to pieces, so that no stone remained upon the other, and thus prevent for ever the sacrifice of 1,485 million cubic metres of water—the most cruel, most wicked, and most senseless sacrifice ever offered on the altar of a false religion.

1899. (River II, 18–19.)

Britain began damming at Aswan, on the first catatract of the Nile, in 1899–1902 and raised the dam twice through 1933. But Churchill's Nile god was assuaged when the Temple was moved to higher ground by the United Nations Educational, Scientific and Cultural Organization (UNESCO) between 1960 and 1980.

He [Lord Cromer] presented me to the Khedive the other morning. I was much amused by observing the relations between the British Agent and the *de jure* Ruler of Egypt. The Khedive's attitude reminded me of a school-boy who is brought to see another school-boy in the presence of the headmaster. But he seemed to me to be an amiable young man who tries to take an intelligent interest in the affairs of his kingdom, which, since they have passed entirely beyond his control, is, to say the least of it, very praiseworthy.

1899, 3 April, Cairo. (OB I, 441.)

WSC to his mother. Khedives (lords) ruled Egypt and Sudan from 1805 to 1914. WSC met the Khedive Abbas II, who sided with the Turks in World War II and was deposed by the British, who declared Egypt a protectorate.

...I could not bear his leaving without seeing the Sphinx....We motored there...Roosevelt and I gazed at her for some minutes in silence. She told us nothing and maintained her inscrutable smile. There was no use waiting longer.

1952. (WW2 V, 371.)

With Roosevelt in Egypt, December 1943, following the Teheran conference.

Estonia

The Estonians, to some extent supplied with British arms, have made a very stout fight and have really shown the weakness of the Bolshevists for quite small forces have been driven back, the Estonians being stout-hearted and having fought well.

1919, 25 March. (CS III, 2724.)

Finland

Only Finland—superb, nay sublime—in the jaws of peril—Finland shows what free men can do. The service rendered by Finland to mankind is magnificent. They have exposed for all the world to see, the military incapacity of the Red Army and of the Red Air Force. Many illusions about Soviet Russia have been dispelled in these few fierce weeks of fighting in the Arctic Circle.

1940, 20 January. Broadcast, London.
(Blood, 251.)

France

We all know that the French are pacific. They are quite as pacific as we are...But the French seem much nearer to the danger than we are. There is no strip of salt water to guard their land and their liberties. We must remember that they are the only other great European country that has not reverted to despotism or dictatorship in one form or another.

1935, 24 OCTOBER.

For good or for ill the French people have been effectively masters in their own house, and have built as they chose upon the ruins of the old régime. They have done what they like. Their difficulty is to like what they have done.

1936, 18 SEPTEMBER. ("A TESTING TIME FOR FRANCE," *EVENING STANDARD*; STEP, 52.)

A familiar refrain oft heard by WSC's family was "do what you like, but like what you do". Here he effectively turns it on its head.

Many...are apt to regard the French as a vain, volatile, fanciful, hysterical nation. As a matter of fact they are one of the most grim, sober, unsentimental, calculating and tenacious races in the world....The British are good at paying taxes, but detest drill. The French do not mind drill, but avoid taxes. Both nations can still fight, if they are convinced there is no other way of surviving; but in such a case France would have a small surplus and Britain a small army.

1937, 25 JUNE. ("VIVE LA FRANCE!," *EVENING STANDARD*; STEP, 131–2.)

The House will feel sorrow at the fate of the great French nation and people to whom we have been joined so long in war and peace, and whom we have regarded as trustees with ourselves for the progress of a liberal culture and tolerant civilization of Europe.

1940, 25 JUNE.

...the French were now fighting with all their vigour for the first time since the war broke out.

1940, 3 JULY. (COLVILLE, FRINGES I, 215.)

In July 1940, a British squadron destroyed the leading ships of the French fleet at their ports in North Africa when the French refused to either surrender them or sail them to neutral ports. See also World War II...1940.

Faith is given to us, to help and comfort us when we stand in awe before the unfurling scroll of human destiny. And I proclaim my faith that some of us will live to see a fourteenth of July when a liberated France will once again stand forward as the champion of the freedom and the rights of man. When the day dawns, as dawn it will, the soul of France will turn with comprehension and kindness to those Frenchmen and Frenchwomen, wherever they may be, who in the darkest hour did not despair of the Republic.

1940, 14 JULY.

Bastille Day, 14 July, is the French national holiday.

Our old comradeship with France is not dead. In General de Gaulle and his gallant band, that comradeship takes an effective form. These free Frenchmen have been condemned to death by Vichy, but the day will come, as surely as the sun will rise tomorrow, when their names will be held in honour, and their names will be graven in stone in the streets and villages of a France restored in a liberated Europe to its full freedom and its ancient fame.

1940, 20 AUGUST.

Frenchmen! For more than thirty years in peace and war I have marched with you. I am marching still along the same road. Tonight I speak to you at your firesides, wherever you may be, or whatever your fortunes are. I repeat the prayer upon the *louis d'or, "Dieu protège la France."* Here at home in England, under the fire of the Boche, we do not forget the ties and links that unite us to France...Here in London, which Herr Hitler says he will reduce to ashes...our Air Force has more than held its own. We are waiting for the long-promised invasion. So are the fishes.

1940, 21 OCTOBER. BROADCAST TO FRANCE, LONDON. (BLOOD, 463; CS VI, 6297.)

The Almighty in His infinite wisdom did not see fit to create Frenchmen in the image of Englishmen....In a State like France which has experienced so many convulsions— Monarchy, Convention, Directory, Consulate, Empire, Monarchy, Empire and finally Republic—there has grown up a principle founded on the "droit administratif" which undoubtedly governs the action of many French officers and officials in times of revolution and change. It is a highly legalistic habit of mind and it arises from a subconscious sense of national self-preservation against the dangers of sheer anarchy.

1942, 10 DECEMBER.

For forty years I have been a consistent friend of France and her brave army; all my life I have been grateful for the contribution France has made to the culture and glory of Europe, and above all for the sense of personal liberty and the rights of man which has radiated from the soul of France. But these are not matters of sentiment or personal feeling. It is one of the main interests of Great Britain that a friendly France should regain and hold her place among the major powers of Europe and the world. Show me a moment when I swerved from this conception, and you will show me a moment when I have been wrong.

1944, 2 AUGUST.

I am going to give you a warning: be on your guard, because I am going to speak, or try to speak, in French, a formidable undertaking and one which will put great demands on your friendship for Great Britain.

1944, 12 NOVEMBER. HOTEL DE VILLE, PARIS. (DAWN, 246.)

Acknowledging the welcome of the Paris Liberation Committee.

I rejoice in the undoubted growing recovery of France; but I want to warn you that the kind of political whirligig under which France lives, which is such great fun for the politicians and for all the little ardent parties into which they are divided, would be fatal to Britain. We cannot afford to have a period of French politics in Westminster.

1950, 4 FEBRUARY. LEEDS. (BALANCE, 179.)

The Frogs are getting all they can for nothing, and we are getting nothing for all we can.

1954, 31 MAY, DOWNING STREET. (SOAMES, SPEAKING, 581.)

WSC was referring to a Geneva conference following the collapse of France's position in Indo-China.

Ghana

[The Nkrumah regime] has imprisoned hundreds of Opposition members without trial and is thoroughly authoritarian in tendency. I have little doubt that Nkrumah would use the Queen's visit to bolster up his own position. No doubt Nkrumah would be much affronted if the visit were now cancelled and Ghana might leave the Commonwealth. I am not sure that that would be a great loss. Nkrumah's vilification of this country and his increasing association with our enemies does not encourage one to think that his country could ever be more than an opportunist member of the Commonwealth family. Is it too late for the Queen's plans to be changed?

1961, 19 OCTOBER, LONDON. (OB VIII, 1330–31.)

WSC to Prime Minister Harold Macmillan: the only example I have found of his intervention in international affairs after the 1956 Suez Crisis. Churchill was now close to eighty-seven; yet he felt strongly enough about Ghana's first Prime Minister, Kwame Nkrumah, to urge that the Queen's visit to Ghana be postponed. This could not be done, and took place without incident from 9 to 20 November.

Greece

Without the slightest provocation, with no pretence at parley, Signor Mussolini has invaded Greece, or tried to do so, and his aircraft have murdered an increasing number of Greek civilians, women and children in Salonika and many other open Greek towns. The Greek King, his Government and the Greek people have resolved to fight for life and honour, lest the world should be too easily led in chains.

1940, 5 NOVEMBER.

In October, Mussolini had invaded Greece, whose defenders forced the Italians to retreat – the first Allied land victory of World War II. This caused Hitler to send troops to assist Italy, probably postponing his invasion of Russia in 1941.

...there is one small heroic country to whom our thoughts today go out in new sympathy and admiration. To the valiant Greek people and armies—now defending their native soil from the latest Italian outrage, to them we send from the heart of old London our faithful promise that, amid all our burdens and anxieties, we will do our best to aid them in their struggle, and that we will never cease to strike at the foul aggressors in ever-increasing strength from this time forth until the crimes and treacheries which hang around the neck of Mussolini and disgrace the Italian name have been brought to condign and exemplary justice.

1940, 9 November. Mansion House, London.
(Blood, 488.)

Hitler has told us that it was a crime in such circumstances on our part to go to the aid of the Greeks. I do not wish to enter into argument with experts.

1941, 7 May.

I think it would be most unfair and wrong, and very silly, in the midst of a defence which has so far been crowned with remarkable success, to select the loss of the Crete salient as an excuse and pretext for branding with failure or belittling with taunt the great campaign for the defence of the Middle East, which has so far prospered beyond all expectations, and is now entering upon an even more intense and critical phase.

1941, 10 June.

Whether Greece is a monarchy or a republic is a matter for Greeks and Greeks alone to decide. All we wish you is good, and good for all.

1944, 26 December, Athens. (Dawn, 309.)

At a conference of all parties and interests brought together after British forces had forestalled a power seizure by the communist E.L.A.S. Churchill was subsequently accused of trying to instal a government favourable to Britain.

The bitter misunderstandings which have arisen in the United States and in degenerate circles at home are only a foretaste of the furies which will be loosed about every stage of the peace settlement. I am sure in Greece I found one of the best opportunities for wise action that this war has tossed to me from its dark waves.

1945, 1 February. En route to Malta.
(OB VII, 1167.)

WSC to his wife. In December 1944 he had brokered a ceasefire between communist and royalist forces, incurring the wrath of the US

State Department; but his action probably saved Greece from going communist. This validated Churchill's much-criticised 1944 meeting with Stalin, in which they agreed on "spheres of influence". Stalin, as promised, stayed out of Greece – temporarily. Soviet efforts to communise Greece with Tito as surrogate began again after the war, but were forestalled by the Truman Doctrine.

Let right prevail. Let party hatreds die. Let there be unity; let there be resolute comradeship; Greece for ever! Greece for all!

1945, 14 February, Athens. (WW2 VI, 348.)

The Greeks rival the Jews in being the most politically-minded race in the world....No two cities have counted more with mankind than Athens and Jerusalem. Their messages in religion, philosophy, and art have been the main guiding lights of modern faith and culture....Personally I have always been on the side of both...

1952. (WW2 V, 470–71.)

Iceland

We, and later the Americans, have undertaken to keep war away from this country. But you will all realize that if we had not come others would. We will do all in our power to make sure that our presence here shall cause as little trouble as possible in the lives of the Icelanders. But at the moment your country is an important base for the protection of the rights of the nations. When the present struggle is over, we, and the Americans, will ensure that Iceland shall receive absolute freedom. We come to you as one cultured nation to another, and it is our aim that your culture in the past may be joined to your progress in the future as a free people.

1940, August, Reykjavik. (Unrelenting, 229–30.)

Forestalling a possible German occupation, British and later American troops garrisoned Iceland commencing in May 1940. Iceland voted for independence in July 1944 and the occupation was ended in 1946.

India

The Sikh is the guardian of the marches. He was originally invented to combat the Pathan.

1898. (Malakand, 193.)

Sikhs, mainly from Punjab, were traditionally a highly respected component of British forces. Pathans were the inhabitants of the North-West Frontier Province of British India.

By one who stands on some lofty pass or commanding point in Dir, Swat or Bajaur, range after range is seen as the long surges of an Atlantic swell, and in the distance some glittering snow peak suggests a white-crested roller, higher than the rest.

1898. (MALAKAND, 1.)

...we wonder whether the traveller shall some day inspect, with unconcerned composure, the few scraps of stone and iron which may indicate the British occupation of India....Yet, perhaps, if that unborn critic of remote posterity would remember that "in the days of the old British" the rice crop had been more abundant, the number of acres under cultivation greater, the population larger, and the death rate lower, than at any time in the history of India—we should not be without a monument more glorious than the pyramids.

1898. (MALAKAND, 95–6.)

...on what does our rule in India depend? It is not on terror, it is not on physical force, it is not on the superior knowledge of our Government. I say that 30,000 civilians and 70,000 soldiers would be utterly insufficient to preserve our rule in India for a month if it were not known that our motives were pure and lofty, and that we sought the welfare of the Indian people. British justice is the foundation-stone of British dominion. Destroy that, and the whole stately and stupendous edifice which the glories and sacrifices of ten generations have upreared will come clattering to the ground.

1904, 19 FEBRUARY. FREE TRADE HALL, MANCHESTER. (FFT, 71.)

[Lord Irwin's] attitude towards India has throughout been an apology. He has not shown sufficient confidence in the indispensable work which our country has done, and is doing, for India, or in British resolution that it shall not be interrupted or destroyed. That is the sole foundation upon which the peaceful and successful administration of India can be based....you will ask me what, then, are we to

make of our promises of Dominion status and responsible government. Surely we cannot break our word! There I agree. The formal, plighted word of the King-Emperor is inviolable. It does not follow, however, that every Socialist jack-in-office can commit this great country by his perorations....But except as an ultimate visionary goal, Dominion status like that of Canada or Australia is not going to happen in India in any period which we can even remotely foresee.

1931, 30 JANUARY, MANCHESTER. (INDIA, 75, 79–80.)

Lord Irwin later became Lord Halifax, who as Foreign Secretary posed as many frustrations to Churchill as he did when Viceroy of India.

It makes me sick when I hear the Secretary of State saying of India, "She will do this," and "she will do that." India is an abstraction....India is no more a political personality than Europe. India is a geographical term. It is no more a united nation than the Equator.

1931, 26 MARCH. CONSTITUTIONAL CLUB, LONDON. (CS V, 5011.)

There is confusion over the date. The above is most likely to be correct (preceding or following the Albert Hall speech, per the Complete Speeches*). By this time, Gandhi had stopped his civil disobedience campaign and was in negotiations with Viceroy, Lord Irwin (later Halifax).*

...the departure of the British from India, which Mr. Gandhi advocates, and which Mr. Nehru demands, would be followed first by a struggle in the North and thereafter by a reconquest of the South by the North and of the Hindus by the Moslems. This danger has not escaped the crafty foresight of the Brahmins....now that there is spread throughout India the belief that we are a broken, bankrupt, played-out power, and that our rule is going to pass away and be transferred in the name of the majority to the Brahmin sect, all sorts of greedy appetites have been excited and many itching fingers are stretching and scratching at the vast pillage of a derelict Empire.

1931, 18 MARCH. ROYAL ALBERT HALL, LONDON. (INDIA, 128, 130.)

If the Viceroys and Governments of India in the past had given half as much attention to dealing with the social conditions of the masses of the Indian people as they have to busying themselves with negotiating with unrepresentative leaders of the political classes for constitutional changes—if they had addressed themselves to the moral and material problems which are at the root of Indian life, I think it would have been much better for the working folk of Burnley and Bombay, of Oldham and Ahmadabad.

1931, 9 JULY.

You know the weight which I attach to everything you say to me, but I did not feel I could take responsibility for the defence of India if everything had again to be thrown in the melting pot....Anything like a serious difference between you and me would break my heart, and would surely deeply injure both our countries at the height of this terrible struggle.

1942, 12 APRIL. CHEQUERS. (LOWENHEIM, 204.)

WSC to Roosevelt, after FDR had expressed regret that negotiations with the Indian Congress had broken down. If his Cabinet had not supported him, WSC wrote (WW2 IV, 195):

I would not have hesitated to lay down my personal burden, which at times seemed more than a man could bear.

See also Ripostes ... Indians.

I hate Indians. They are a beastly people with a beastly religion.

1942, 9 SEPTEMBER. (AMERY DIARIES II, 833; CHURCHILL PROCEEDINGS 1994–95.)

William F. Buckley, Jr. said of this remark:

I don't doubt that the famous gleam came to his eyes when he said this, with mischievous glee – an offence, in modern convention, of genocidal magnitude.

Churchill was reacting to a declaration by the Indian Congress Party that only passive resistance should be offered to any Japanese invaders. This remark is often quoted to suggest WSC's racism – which is denied by his friendships with such Indians as Birla and Nehru, and his final words to Gandhi. See People...Gandhi.

All the great countries in this war count their armies by millions, but the Indian Army has a peculiar characteristic not found in the armies of Britain or the United States or Russia or France or in the armies of our foes, in that it is entirely composed of volunteers. No one has been conscripted or compelled. The same thing is broadly true throughout our great Colonial Empire.

1943, 30 JUNE. GUILDHALL, LONDON.
(ONWARDS, 125.)

Once again, India and her vast population have reposed serenely among the tumults and hurricanes of the world behind the Imperial shield. The fact should sometimes be noted that under British rule in the last eighty years incomparably fewer people have perished by steel or firearms in India than in any similar area or community on the globe.

1944, 28 SEPTEMBER.

India is a continent as large as and more populous than Europe, and not less deeply divided by racial and religious differences than Europe. India has no more unity than Europe, except that superficial unity which has been created by our rule and guidance in the last 150 years.

1946, 7 MAY.

We declare ourselves ready to abandon the mighty Empire and Continent of India with all the work we have done in the last 200 years, territory over which we possess unimpeachable sovereignty. The Government are, apparently, ready to leave the 400 million Indians to fall into all the horrors of sanguinary civil war—civil war compared to which anything that could happen in Palestine would be microscopic; wars of elephants compared with wars of mice.

1946, 1 AUGUST.

...there [are] choices...before the British Parliament. The first is to proceed with ruthless logic to quit India regardless of what may happen there....The second is to assert the principle...that the King needs no unwilling subjects and that the British Commonwealth of Nations contemplates no compulsory partnership...that those who wish to make their own lives in their own way may do so, and the gods be with them....We must not allow

British troops or British officers in the Indian Army to become the agencies and instruments of enforcing caste Hindu domination upon the 90 million Muslims and the 60 million Untouchables; nor must the prestige or authority of the British power in India, even in its sunset, be used in partisanship on either side of these profound and awful cleavages.

1946, 12 DECEMBER.

...the Socialist Government on gaining power threw themselves into the task of destroying our long-built-up and splendid structure in the East with zeal and gusto, and they certainly have brought widespread ruin, misery and bloodshed upon the Indian masses, to an extent no man can measure, by the methods with which they have handled the problem.

1947, 4 OCTOBER, BRIGHTON. (EUROPE, 148.)

While it is easy to view Churchill as an unreconstructed imperialist on the matter of India, his own words testify that his views were more enlightened, and tempered by concern for the masses.

What about the deaths of half a million people in India? Enjoying democratic freedom!

1947, 5 NOVEMBER. (GILBERT, LIFE, 877.)

Reply to a plea to give Burma "the same democratic freedom that we enjoy ourselves". Churchill had predicted that prematurely leaving India, before border questions were settled, would cause a bloodbath, which had already begun at this time. The ultimate death toll was between one and two million.

Our Imperial mission in India is at an end—we must recognise that. Some day justice will be done by world opinion to our record there, but the chapter is closed....We must look forward. It is our duty, whatever part we have taken in the past, to hope and pray for the well-being and happiness of all the peoples of India....we must wish them all well and do what we can to help them on their road. Sorrow may lie in our hearts but bitterness and malice must be purged from them, and in our future more remote relations with India we must rise above all prejudice and partiality and not allow our vision to be clouded by memories of glories that are gone for ever.

1948, 28 OCTOBER.

The human race cannot make progress without idealism, but idealism at other people's expense, and without regard to the ruin and slaughter which fall upon millions of humble homes, cannot be considered as its highest or noblest form. The President's mind was back in the American War of Independence, and he thought of the Indian problem in terms of the thirteen colonies fighting George III...I, on the other hand, was responsible for preserving the peace and safety of the Indian continent....

1951. (WW2 IV, 194.)

I have worked very hard with Nehru. I told him he should be the light of Asia, to show all those millions how they can shine out, instead of accepting the darkness of Communism.

1955, 18 FEBRUARY. (OB VIII, 1095.)

WSC to Eden's private secretary Evelyn Shuckburgh. In the long run, Churchill's advice proved correct.

Iran (Persia)

It is a very melancholy thing to contemplate the possibility of an ancient capital of a monarchy like that of Persia being engulfed in the tides of barbarism, and a culture which, though primitive in many respects, is nevertheless ancient, being swamped and beaten down under the heel of a Bolshevik invasion; but there must be some limit to the responsibilities of Britain.

1920, 15 DECEMBER.

Iraq (Mesopotamia)

There is something very sinister to my mind in this Mesopotamian entanglement...[We seem] compelled to go on pouring armies and treasure into these thankless deserts. We have not got a single friend in the press upon the subject, and there is no point of which they make more effective use to injure the Government. Week after week and month after month for a long time to come we shall have a continuance of this miserable, wasteful, sporadic warfare, marked from time to time certainly by minor disasters and cuttings off of troops and agents, and very possibly attended by some very grave occurrence.

1920, 31 AUGUST, WAR OFFICE. (OB, CV4/2, 1199.)

Unsent letter, WSC to Prime Minister David Lloyd George.

Whatever your policy might be, it would certainly be in the highest degree imprudent to let it be thought that this country, having accepted the [British] mandate, having entered into territory of that kind, having incurred, accepted, and shouldered responsibilities towards every class inhabiting it, was in a moment of irritation or weakness going to cast down those responsibilities, to leave its obligations wholly undischarged, and to scuttle from the country regardless of what might occur.

1920, 15 DECEMBER.

I am deeply concerned about Iraq. The task you have given me is becoming really impossible. Our forces are reduced now to very slender proportions...I do not see what political strength there is to face a disaster of any kind, and certainly I cannot believe that in any circumstances any large reinforcements would be sent from here or from India. There is scarcely a single newspaper—Tory, Liberal or Labour—which is not consistently hostile to our remaining in this country. The enormous reductions which have been effected have brought no goodwill, and any alternative Government that might be formed here— Labour, Die-hard or Wee Free—would gain popularity by ordering instant evacuation. Moreover in my own heart I do not see what we are getting out of it. Owing to the difficulties with America, no progress has been made in developing the oil. Altogether I am getting to the end of my resources.

1922, 1 SEPTEMBER, COLONIAL OFFICE. (OB, CV4/3, 1973–74.)

Over eighty years later this secret message from Churchill to Prime Minister Lloyd George was quoted frequently, but in 1922 the situation was quite different. Britain was quarrelling with Turkey ("The Turkish menace has got worse") and oil was not a factor except as a way of Iraq meeting her own expenses – America was the main oil producer, and Britain's supply was assured via Iran.

I consider that Marshal of the Royal Air Force Lord Trenchard is the founder of the Royal Air Force. He it was who proposed to me, when I was Air Minister in 1919, that Mesopotamia should be held by air power, thus releasing a number of army divisions, which cost us

£40,000,000 a year to maintain in that Country. This proved, in a manner patent to all intelligent minds, the part which the air would play not only in war but in peace.

1943, 1 APRIL.

Ireland

And in this desperate situation the Dublin Fusiliers arrived! Trumpeters sounded the charge and the enemy were swept from the field.

1901, 12 JANUARY, CHICAGO. (PILPEL, 54–5.)

On Churchill's 1900–01 North American lecture tour, he often faced audiences of Irish-Americans, who naturally took the Boer side over Britain's war in South Africa. In this lecture, Churchill blunted his critics with this remark. Their jeering stopped, and they suddenly burst into applause.

The discontent that prevailed between England and Ireland arose not so much from differences of religion and race as from the belief that the English connection was not a profitable nor paying one. If Ireland were more prosperous she would be more loyal, and if more loyal more free.

1904, 8 MAY.

...there never was a time when there was a great number of moderate sensible people who were prepared to give consideration to the Irish question without passion, to see what a rotten system of government prevailed in that country, and to approach one of the most difficult, as it was one of the most attractive, questions which could occupy the minds of English politicians.

1905, 20 FEBRUARY.

The Times is speechless and takes three columns to express its speechlessness; *The Spectator*, that staid old weekly, has wobbled back to where it never should have wobbled from; the Ulster Unionists declare that the Government has forfeited all the confidence that they never had in it, and thousands of people who never under any circumstances voted Liberal before are saying that under no circumstances will they ever vote Liberal again.

1908, 14 MAY, DUNDEE. (LIBERALISM 193.)

Churchill jocularly referred to an "awful thing" that had happened: the Liberal Party had declared in favour of Home Rule in Ireland.

I strongly urge that this question shall not be settled by the shouting of ordinary Party cries of bigotry and intolerance, but that a fair effort should be made by Parliament to do justice to it, in the light of the conditions of the age in which we are living, and not upon the principles of moving and stirring events which happened centuries ago.

1911, 15 FEBRUARY.

It would be a great disaster to Ireland if the Protestant population in the North stood aloof from a National Parliament....

I defy respectfully, and I dialectically defy you, by the utmost exercise of your imagination, to conjure up or picture even any set of circumstances in which the ruin of England would not mean the ruin of Ireland also....Never before has so little been asked, never before have so many people asked for it.

1912, 30 APRIL.

An interesting juxtaposition with his later and more famous remark about the RAF during the Battle of Britain in 1940: "Never was so much owed, by so many, to so few." Though Home Rule did not come until after World War I, Churchill hewed to the belief that Ireland should be united. Though union was not possible when he helped write the Irish Free State bill, he continued to hope that reason and fair play would ultimately see Ulster united with the south. As with the Arabs and Jews in Palestine, he was an incurable optimist.

How is it that the great English Parties are shaken to their foundations and even shattered, almost every generation, by contact with Irish affairs?....Ireland is not a daughter State. She is a parent nation.....If Irish unity can be achieved, it can only be because the Government of the Irish Free State will have convinced Ulster of its loyal association with the British Empire and will have offered Ulster conditions of security and partnership in every way satisfactory to her.

1921, 15 DECEMBER.

I remember on the eve of the Great War...we discussed the boundaries of Fermanagh and Tyrone. Both of the great political parties were at each other's throats. The air was full of talk of civil war....Then came the Great War....Every institution, almost, in the world was strained. Great Empires have been overturned. The whole map of Europe has been changed. The position of countries has been violently altered. The modes of thought of men, the whole outlook on affairs, the grouping of parties, all have encountered violent and tremendous changes in the deluge of the world, but as the deluge subsides and the waters fall short, we see the dreary steeples of Fermanagh and Tyrone emerging once again. The integrity of their quarrel is one of the few institutions that has been unaltered in the cataclysm which has swept the world.

1922, 16 FEBRUARY.

WSC introducing the Irish Free State Bill to Parliament.

Let us now see what is the interest of Southern Ireland in this matter. What is their heart's desire more than anything else? [Hon. Members: "A republic."] Not at all; that is a delusion, and my Hon. Friends are absolutely at sea when they say so. A Republic is an idea most foreign to the Irish mind, associated with the butcheries of Cromwell in their minds and foreign to all the native genius of the Irish race, which is essentially monarchical. [Major C. Lowther: "Why have they an Irish Republican army if it is so foreign to them?"] Because they have been fighting for position against this country.

1922, 16 FEBRUARY.

...in Ireland almost everything happens when you do not expect it, and anything which any large number of people expect never happens.

1922, 12 APRIL.

Let us on our part be very careful that we do all we have to do in scrupulous and meticulous good faith....Let us not be led by impatience, by prejudice, by vexation, by anxiety, into courses which would lay us open to charges of fickleness or levity in dealing with those issues so long lasting as the relations between the two islands.

1922, 31 MAY.

"Love of Ireland" are the words which Sir John Lavery has inscribed on his picture of the dead Irish leader [Michael Collins]. They are deserved; but with them there might at the end be written also "To England Honour and Good Will." A great Act of Faith had been performed on both sides of the Channel, and by that Act we dearly hoped that the curse of the centuries would at last be laid.

1924, JANUARY. ("THE IRISH TREATY," *PALL MALL;* THOUGHTS, 162.)

See also People...Collins.

I cherish the hope that some day all Ireland will be loyal, and because it is loyal be united within itself and united to the British Empire.

1926, 2 MARCH, BELFAST.

Churchill remembered and alluded to this speech, quoting himself closely, at a Lord Mayor's banquet at Mansion House in 1955, where he accepted the Freedom of Belfast.

They [Sir James Craig and Michael Collins] both glowered magnificently, but after a short, commonplace talk I slipped away upon some excuse and left them together. What these two Irishmen, separated by such gulfs of religion, sentiment, and conduct, said to each other I cannot tell. But it took a long time, and as I did not wish to disturb them, mutton chops etc. were tactfully introduced about one o'clock. At four o'clock the Private Secretary reported signs of movement on the All-Ireland front and I ventured to look in. They announced to me complete agreement reduced to writing. They wanted to help each other in every way...

1929. (CRISIS IV, 317.)

In January 1922, Churchill had invited the Ulster Prime Minister, Sir James Craig, to meet Michael Collins on neutral ground, his own room at the Colonial Office, to discuss the Irish Treaty.

My nurse, Mrs. Everest, was nervous about the Fenians. I gathered these were wicked people and there was no end to what they would do if they had their way. On one occasion when I was out riding on my donkey, we thought we saw a long dark procession of Fenians approaching. I am sure now it must

have been the Rifle Brigade out for a route march. But we were all very much alarmed, particularly the donkey, who expressed his anxiety by kicking. I was thrown off and had concussion of the brain. This was my first introduction to Irish politics!

1930. (MEL, 16.)

The Fenians were an Irish secret revolutionary organisation favouring independence from England by force.

I must confess to some sentiment about old Ireland, in spite of the ugly mask she tries to wear.

1933, 24 APRIL. ROYAL SOCIETY OF ST. GEORGE, LONDON. (COVENANT, 91.)

The dark forces in Ireland renew themselves from year to year. When some are conciliated, others present themselves. They are very powerful in Ireland now. No one has ever been brought to justice in Ireland since the Treaty for murdering an Englishman. There is a whole organisation of secret men bound together on the old principle that England's danger is Ireland's opportunity....Southern Ireland is not a Dominion; it has never accepted that position. It is a State based upon a Treaty, which Treaty has been completely demolished. Southern Ireland, therefore, becomes a State which is an undefined and unclassified anomaly. No one knows what its juridical and international rights and status are.

1938, 5 MAY.

The fact that we cannot use the South and West Coasts of Ireland to refuel our flotillas and aircraft and thus protect the trade by which Ireland as well as Great Britain lives, is a most heavy and grievous burden and one which should never have been placed on our shoulders, broad though they be.

1940, 5 NOVEMBER.

[At the onset of World War I] Irishmen, whose names I always bear in my memory with regard, John Redmond and his brother, and others of the old Irish Parliamentary Party, which fought us for so many years in this House, pleading the cause of Ireland, with great eloquence and Parliamentary renown; there they were, making these speeches of absolute support and unity with this country until everybody said everywhere "The brightest spot in the world is Ireland." It may be that a grand opportunity was lost then. We must keep our eyes open. I always keep mine open on the Irish question.

1944, 21 APRIL.

Owing to the action of Mr. de Valera, so much at variance with the temper and instinct of thousands of Southern Irishmen who hastened to the battlefront to prove their ancient valour, the approaches which the Southern Irish ports and airfields could so easily have guarded were closed by the hostile aircraft and U-boats. This was indeed a deadly moment in our life, and if it had not been for the loyalty and friendship of Northern Ireland we should have been forced to come to close quarters with Mr. de Valera or perish for ever from the earth. However...we left the de Valera government to frolic with the Germans and later with the Japanese representatives to their heart's content.

1945, 13 MAY.

In the case of the Irish ports, in the spring of 1938, absolutely wrong political data, in my opinion, were put before the Chiefs of Staff—another set of Chiefs of Staff—and they gave advice which nearly brought us to our ruin. [Laughter]. I have heard all this mocking laughter before in the time of a former Government. I remember being once alone in the House, protesting against the cession of the Southern Irish ports. I remember the looks of incredulity, the mockery, derision and laughter I had to encounter on every side, when I said that Mr. de Valera might declare Ireland neutral.

1946, 24 MAY.

No one knows what they are. They are neither in nor out of the Empire. But they are much more friendly to us than they used to be. They have built up a cultured Roman Catholic system in the South. There has been no anarchy or confusion. The bitter past is fading.

1947. ("THE DREAM," OB VIII, 368.)

"It's a long way to Tipperary," but a visit there is sometimes irresistible.

1948. (WW2 I, 215.)

Israel

...the coming into being of a Jewish State in Palestine is an event in world history to be viewed in the perspective, not of a generation or a century, but in the perspective of a thousand, two thousand or even three thousand years.

1949, 26 JANUARY.

See also Palestine.

Remember, I was for a free and independent Israel all through the dark years when many of my most distinguished countrymen took a different view. So do not imagine for a moment that I have the slightest idea of deserting you now in your hour of glory.

1949, 29 MARCH, NEW YORK. (HALLE, IRREPRESSIBLE, 90; PILPEL, 235.)

A Jewish audience had asked Churchill what he thought about the rapidly concluding war between Israel and Arab neighbours, which resulted in armistices with Egypt (24 February 1949), Lebanon (23 March) and Jordan (3 April).

The Greeks rival the Jews in being the most politically-minded race in the world. ....No two cities have counted more with mankind than Athens and Jerusalem.

1952. (WW2 V, 470–71.)

For more of this quotation see Greece.

But you ought to let the Jews have Jerusalem; it is they who made it famous.

1955, 18 FEBRUARY. (OB VIII, 1095.)

WSC to Eden's private secretary Evelyn Shuckburgh.

Italy

If I had been an Italian I am sure I should have been entirely with you from the beginning to the end of your victorious struggle against the bestial appetites and passions of Leninism....Your movement has rendered a service to the whole world. The greatest fear that ever tormented every Democratic or Socialist leader was that of being outbid or surpassed by some other leader more extreme than himself. It has been said that a continual movement to the Left, a kind of fatal landslide towards the abyss, has been the character of all revolutions. Italy has shown that there is a way to combat subversive forces.

1927, 20 JANUARY. PRESS STATEMENT, ROME. (CS IV, 4126–7.)

The first words of this passage have often been extracted from the rest to suggest that Churchill approved of Fascism. As the context shows, what he approved of was Italy not falling to Bolshevism, which he then feared more than anything. The remark is redolent of his usual courtliness to foreign hosts. As the years passed and circumstances changed, his view of Fascism darkened.

...a cloud has come over the old friendship between Great Britain and Italy, a cloud which may very easily not pass away, although undoubtedly it is everyone's desire that it should. It is an old friendship, and we must not forget, what is a little-known fact, that at the time Italy entered into the Triple Alliance in the last century she stipulated particularly that in no circumstances should her obligations under the Alliance bring her into armed conflict with Great Britain.

1935, 11 JULY.

What ought to be our policy towards Italy? At any rate, we can see what it ought not to be. It ought not to be a policy of nagging. Very serious antagonism existed between Great Britain, doing her part as a member of the League of Nations, and Italy over the conquest of Abyssinia. In that antagonism we have not prevailed. We have been humiliated, but we have not been dishonoured. However we may have been guided, we are not regarded there as knaves or cowards.

1936, 5 NOVEMBER.

Behind this fine façade there was every sign that the Italian dictator, at any rate, was in a very difficult position: the industrious, amiable Italian people long overstrained; everything in the country eaten up in order to augment the magnificence of the state; taxes enormous; finances broken; officials abounding; all kinds of indispensable raw materials practically unpurchasable across the exchange; Abyssinia a curse, a corpse bound on the back of the killer; Libya and Spain, perhaps 400,000 men overseas, all to be

maintained by a continuous drain on the hard-driven ground-down people of Italy.

1938, 22 FEBRUARY.

Down the ages above all other calls comes the cry that the joint heirs of Latin and Christian civilisation must not be ranged against one another in mortal strife.

1940, 16 MAY. (WW2 II, 107.)

WSC to Mussolini, a failed attempt to keep Italy out of the war.

People who go to Italy to look at ruins won't have to go as far as Naples and Pompeii in future.

1940, 10 JUNE. (OB, CV6/2, 279.)

From the diaries of John Colville, who wrote:

He was in a very bad temper, snapped almost everybody's head off, wrote angry minutes to the First Sea Lord, and refused to pay any attention to messages given him orally.

We are also told that the Italian navy is to come out and gain sea superiority in these waters. If they seriously intend it, I shall only say that we shall be delighted to offer Signor Mussolini a free and safe-guarded passage through the Straits of Gibraltar in order that he may play the part to which he aspires. There is a general curiosity in the British fleet to find out whether the Italians are up to the level they were at in the last war or whether they have fallen off at all.

1940, 18 JUNE.

Tonight I speak to the Italian people....We have never been your foes till now....How has all this come about, and what is it all for? Italians, I will tell you the truth. It is because one man, and one man alone, has ranged the Italian people in deadly struggle against the British Empire, and has deprived Italy of the sympathy and intimacy of the United States of America. That he is a great man I do not deny, but that after eighteen years of unbridled power he has led your country to the horrid verge of ruin, can be denied by none....one man has arrayed the trustees and inheritors of ancient Rome upon the side of the ferocious, pagan barbarians. There lies the tragedy of Italian history, and there stands the criminal who has wrought the deed of folly and of shame.

1940, 23 DECEMBER. BROADCAST TO ITALY, LONDON. (CS VI, 6322.)

I have never known a case of a great athlete being a great general—no prize-fighter has ever been a good general. The only exception might be in the Italian Army, where a general might find it useful to be a good runner.

1941, 16 FEBRUARY, DITCHLEY PARK. (KENNEDY, 79.)

WSC speaking in French, to Polish General Sikorski and the Polish Ambassador.

One man, and one man alone, has brought [the Italians] to this pass. There was no need for them to go to war; no one was going to attack them. We tried our best to induce them to remain neutral, to enjoy peace and prosperity and exceptional profits in a world of storm. But Mussolini could not resist the temptation of stabbing prostrate France, and what he thought was helpless Britain, in the back. Mad dreams of imperial glory, the lust of conquest and of booty, the arrogance of long-unbridled tyranny, led him to his fatal, shameful act. In vain I warned him; he would not hearken.

1942, 29 NOVEMBER. BROADCAST, LONDON. (END, 299.)

The hyena in his nature broke all bounds of decency and even commonsense....One man and the régime he has created have brought these measureless calamities upon the hard-working, gifted and once happy Italian people, with whom, until the days of Mussolini, the English-speaking world had so many sympathies and never a quarrel. How long must this endure?

1942, 29 NOVEMBER. WORLD BROADCAST, LONDON. (END, 299.)

No one wishes to take the native soil of Italy from the Italians, who will have their place in Europe after the war. The trouble is that they allow themselves to be held in bondage by intriguers, with the result that they are now in a terrible plight. I think they would be well advised to throw themselves upon the justice of those whom they have so grossly attacked....Of this you may be sure: we shall continue to operate on the Italian donkey at both ends, with the carrot and with a stick.

1943, 25 MAY. PRESS CONFERENCE, WASHINGTON, D.C. (ONWARDS, 104.)

The Italian surrender was a windfall, but it had nothing to do with the date fixed for harvesting the orchard. The truth is that the Armistice announcement was delayed to fit in with the attack, and not the attack delayed to fit in with the announcement.

1943, 21 SEPTEMBER.

The fate of Italy is indeed terrible, and I personally find it very difficult to nourish animosity against the Italian people. The overwhelming mass of the nation rejoiced in the idea of being delivered from the subtle tyranny of the Fascists, and they wished, when Mussolini was overthrown to take their place as speedily as possible by the side of the British and American armies who, it was expected, would quickly rid the country of the Germans.

1944, 24 MAY.

The process of waiting was by no means unprofitable. Italy was courted by both sides, and gained much consideration for her interests, many profitable contracts, and time to improve her armaments....Once Hitler was embroiled with Russia this happy state might have been almost indefinitely prolonged, with ever-growing benefits, and Mussolini might have stood forth in the peace or in the closing year of the war as the wisest statesman the sunny peninsula and its industrious and prolific people had known.

WW2 II, 106.

A crisp review of the disastrous mistake Mussolini made by plunging Italy into the war in June 1940.

Japan

Japan is at the other end of the world. She cannot menace our vital security in any way. She has no reason whatever to come into collision with us. She has every reason to avoid such a collision. The only sufficient cause which could draw us into a war with Japan would be if she invaded Australia. Does anybody imagine she is going to do so?....It is an absolute absurdity. Even if America stood inactive Japan would be ruined. She would never attempt it.

1924, 15 DECEMBER. (OB, CV5/1, 306.)

WSC to Prime Minister Stanley Baldwin. This remark is sometimes used to suggest WSC's naïveté about Japan. When it was written, Japan was a recent, honoured ally in World War I.

As long as the British Navy is undefeated, and as long as we hold Singapore, no invasion of Australia or New Zealand by Japan is possible....Can one suppose that Japan, enjoying herself in the mastery of the Yellow Sea, would send afloat a conquering and colonising expedition to Australia? It is ludicrous. More than one hundred thousand men would be needed to make any impression upon Australian manhood.

1939, 27 MARCH. (OB, CV5/3, 1415–16.)

Secret memorandum on Sea Power sent by WSC to Neville Chamberlain. Note the qualifier, "as long as we hold Singapore...".

I do not believe that Japan, deeply entangled in China, nay, bleeding at every pore in China, her strength ebbing away in a wrongful and impossible task, and with the whole weight of Russia upon her in the north of China, will wish to make war upon the British Empire until she sees how matters go in Europe.

1939, 28 JUNE. CITY CARLTON CLUB, LONDON.
(BLOOD, 181.)

Japan waited two years to see how matters went in Europe – and made the wrong choice.

For five long years the Japanese military factions, seeking to emulate the style of Hitler and Mussolini, taking all their posturing as if it were a new European revelation, have been invading and harrying the five hundred million inhabitants of China. Japanese armies have been wandering about that vast land in futile excursions, carrying with their carnage, ruin and corruption, and calling it the "Chinese Incident."

1941, 14 AUGUST. BROADCAST, LONDON.
(UNRELENTING, 234–5.)

I must admit that, having voted for the Japanese alliance nearly forty years ago, in 1902, and having always done my very best to promote good relations with the island Empire of Japan, and always having been a sentimental well-wisher to the Japanese and an admirer of their many gifts and qualities, I should view with keen sorrow the opening of a conflict

between Japan and the English-speaking world. [But] should the United States become involved in war with Japan, the British declaration will follow within the hour.

1941, 10 NOVEMBER. MANSION HOUSE, LONDON.
(UNRELENTING, 297.)

"Sir...In view of these wanton acts of unprovoked aggression, committed in flagrant violation of international law...His Majesty's Ambassador at Tokyo has been instructed to inform the Imperial Japanese Government in the name of His Majesty's Government in the United Kingdom that a state of war exists between our two countries.

I have the honour to be, with high consideration, Sir, Your obedient servant, Winston S. Churchill."

Some people did not like this ceremonial style. But after all when you have to kill a man it costs nothing to be polite.

1941, 8 DECEMBER, LONDON. (WW2 III, 542–3.)

Mamoru Shigemitsu (1887–1957), Ambassador to the Soviet Union (1936–38) and to Britain (1938–41) was not killed after all. As Japan's Minister of Foreign Affairs at the end of World War II, he signed the instrument of surrender on USS Missouri *on 2 September 1945. Convicted of war crimes, he was sentenced to seven years' imprisonment, but was paroled in 1950 and again served as Foreign Minister in 1954–56.*

It may be that these societies, dazzled and dizzy with their own schemes of aggression and the prospect of early victories, have forced their country against its better judgment into war. They have certainly embarked upon a very considerable undertaking. [Laughter]....it becomes still more difficult to reconcile Japanese action with prudence or even with sanity. What kind of a people do they think we are? Is it possible they do not realize that we shall never cease to persevere against them until they have been taught a lesson which they and the world will never forget?

1941, 26 DECEMBER. CONGRESS, WASHINGTON.
(UNRELENTING, 359–60.)

Churchill's first speech to Congress. When he asked "What kind of a people do they think we are," he brought the House to its feet, with even previous isolationist senators and representatives cheering.

No one must underrate any more the gravity and efficiency of the Japanese war machine. Whether in the air or upon the sea, or man to man on land, they have already proved themselves to be formidable, deadly, and, I am sorry to say, barbarous antagonists.

1942, 15 FEBRUARY. BROADCAST, LONDON. (END, 69.)

Following the Japanese conquest of Singapore.

It was most fortunate that, led away by their dark conspiracies and schemes, dizzy and dazzled from poring over plans, they sprang out upon a peaceful nation with whom they were at that time in peaceful parley, and were led away and tottered over the edge and, for the sake of sinking half a dozen ships of war and beating up a naval port, brought out against them the implacable energies and the measureless power of the 130 million educated people who live in the United States. We have much to be thankful for.

1942, 31 OCTOBER. WESTMINSTER CENTRAL HALL, LONDON. (END, 257.)

What fools the Japanese ruling caste were to bring against themselves the mighty, latent war-energies of the great Republic, all for the sake of carrying out a base and squalid ambuscade!

1944, 26 MARCH. BROADCAST, LONDON. (DAWN, 42.)

Japan, with all her treachery and greed, remains unsubdued. The injury she has inflicted... and her detestable cruelties call for justice and retribution.

1945, 8 MAY. BROADCAST, LONDON. (VICTORY, 126.)

So far as it remains in the power of this island people to influence the course of events, we must strive over a period of years to redeem and to reincorporate the German and the Japanese peoples in a world system of free and civilized democracy. The idea of keeping scores of millions of people hanging about in a sub-human state between earth and hell, until they are worn down to a slave condition or embrace Communism, or die off from hunger, will only, if it is pursued, breed at least a moral pestilence and probably an actual war.

1946, 5 JUNE.

Jordan

I have no hostility for the Arabs. I think I made most of the settlements over fourteen years ago governing the Palestine situation. The Emir Abdullah is in Transjordania, where I put him one Sunday afternoon at Jerusalem.

1936, 24 MARCH.

Latvia

I would advise the following reply to the Prime Minister of Latvia:—I assure Your Excellency that the freedom, safety and well-being of Latvia and of the other Baltic States is a matter of earnest concern to His Majesty's Government in conjunction with the other Great Powers. The influence of His Majesty's Government will be consistently used to secure each of these States full and free development under an autonomous constitution in accordance with the wishes of their people.

1919, 22 SEPTEMBER. (OB, CV4/2, 866.)

WSC to David Lloyd George.

The President of Latvia was deported to Russia, and Mr. Vyshinsky arrived to nominate a Provisional Government to manage new elections....On August 3–6 [1940] the pretence of pro-Soviet friendly and democratic Governments was swept away, and the Kremlin annexed the Baltic States to the Soviet Union.

1949. (WW2 II, 120–21.)

The President of Latvia, Karlis Ulmanis (1877–1942) died in Siberia. His great-nephew, Guntis, was President of newly independent Latvia from 1993 to 1999.

Lithuania

...the small port and district of Memel, situated on the other side of the river Niemen, was the only means by which Lithuania could obtain that outlet to the sea without which it could not exist as an independent State. It was hoped that the Lithuanians would voluntarily join themselves once more to Poland. This they refused, and could not be compelled. Thus eventually Memel, a German town of about 30,000 inhabitants, surrounded by rural districts largely Lithuanian-speaking, was eventually assigned to Lithuania, under elaborate securities for local autonomy.

1929. (CRISIS IV, 210.)

On June 14 [1940], the day Paris fell, Moscow had sent an ultimatum to Lithuania accusing her and the other Baltic States of military conspiracy against the USSR and demanding radical changes of government and military concessions. On June 15 Red Army troops invaded the country, and the President, Smetona, fled into East Prussia....On August 3–6 the pretence of pro-Soviet friendly and democratic Governments was swept away, and the Kremlin annexed the Baltic States to the Soviet Union.

1949. (WW2 II, 120–21.)

Morocco

What a wonderful country, this Morocco. This sunlight, this wonderful air, these flowers. We English have always needed a place like this to come to for sunshine.

1943, JANUARY, CASABLANCA. (HALLE, IRREPRESSIBLE, 211.)

[Marrakesh is] the Paris of the Sahara, where all the caravans had come from Central Africa for centuries to be heavily taxed *en route* by the tribes in the mountains and afterwards swindled in the Marrakesh markets, receiving the return, which they greatly valued, of the gay life of the city, including fortune-tellers, snake-charmers, masses of food and drink, and on the whole the largest and most elaborately organised brothels in the African continent. All these institutions were of long and ancient repute.

1943, 24 JANUARY, CASABLANCA. (WW2 IV, 622.)

WSC to President Roosevelt. They duly travelled to the city where a famous photo was taken of WSC gazing admiringly as the President looked out over the Atlas.

Everybody liked shoving their paws into the dish and remembered with pleasure that fingers were made before forks. The Glaoui is as old as I am but quite lively. He pretends to know neither French nor English, but I believe he understands everything that is said, at least in French....[The dancers, men and women] were dressed up in quilts and blankets—they looked like bundles of cotton waste....The music brays and squawks and tom-toms, and the singing, which was maintained throughout, was a masterly compendium of discords...

1950, 25 DECEMBER, MARRAKESH. (SOAMES, SPEAKING, 558.)

Churchill was visiting El Hadji Thami El Glaoui, the Pasha of Marrakesh and hereditary Sultan of the Atlas. Despite his well-known love for Marrakesh, his impressions of its ruler and his entertainments were anything but politically correct.

Go and put on something warm. They say of the breeze off the Atlas that it is too gentle to blow out a candle, but strong enough to snuff out the life of a man.

1955. (MONTAGUE BROWNE, 250.)

Netherlands

Only yesterday, while the sailors from a British submarine were carrying ashore on stretchers eight emaciated Dutchmen whom they had rescued from six days' exposure in an open boat, Dutch aviators in Holland, in the name of strict and impartial neutrality, were shooting down a British aircraft which had lost its way. I do not reproach the Dutch, our valiant allies of bygone centuries; my heart goes out to them in their peril and distress, dwelling as they do in the cage with the tiger. But when we are asked to take as a matter of course interpretations of neutrality which give all the advantages to the aggressor and indict all the disadvantages upon the defenders of freedom, I recall a saying of the late Lord Balfour: "This is a singularly ill-contrived world, but not so ill-contrived as that."

1940, 30 MARCH.

New Zealand

You can be sure that as your duty will not fail, so your success will be achieved.

1943, 4 FEBRUARY. NEW ZEALAND DIVISION, TRIPOLI. (ONWARDS, 12.)

Norway

We have the most profound sympathy with the Norwegian people. We have understood the terrible dilemma in which they have been placed. Their sentiments, like those of every other small country, were with the Allies. They writhed in helpless anger while scores of their ships were wantonly sunk and many hundreds of their sailors cruelly drowned. They realize fully that their future independence and freedom are bound up with the victory of the Allies. But the feeling of powerlessness in the ruthless grip of Nazi wrath made them hope against hope until the last moment that at least their soil and their cities would not be polluted by the trampling of German marching columns or their liberties and their livelihood stolen away by foreign tyrants. But this hope has been in vain. Another violent outrage has been perpetrated by Nazi Germany against a small and friendly power, and the Norwegian Government and people are today in arms to defend their hearths and homes.

1940, 11 APRIL.

Although Hitler has treacherously received a large part of Norway it is perhaps forgotten that, like our own people the Norwegians live largely by the sea. The French and the British mercantile marine can now rely upon the invaluable support and co-operation of the Norwegian merchant fleet, the fourth largest in the world, and on the services of seamen whose skill and daring are well known.

1940, 8 MAY.

Although little mentioned in accounts of the war, the contribution of the large Norwegian and Danish merchant fleets to the war effort is something every Norwegian and Dane is aware and proud of. What rewards are to be given to these heroic men?

1943, 14 APRIL. (HAAKON WAAGE TO THE EDITOR.)

Message to Lord Selborne about the Norwegians who destroyed a year's production of German heavy-water (necessary to the Nazi atom bomb project) at Vermork. Haakon Waage writes:

Though very short, this message is laden with drama given the issue at stake, when almost nobody knew the full picture. It tells a lot about Churchill who, in his busy schedule, could find time to attend to rewarding these patriots.

Your Majesty, you have said in the course of your gracious speech that we, at that time, after the fall of France, that we were all alone. Well, I am very glad to be able to say that at that time we had the Norwegian Merchant Navy, and that great enormous fleet of tankers, of other vessels too—but above all of tankers—carrying from all parts of the world

that vital essence of war-making capacity. We did not feel entirely alone because we had that invaluable help from Norway, given at great cost for many. Many a good ship was sunk, and I remember how your Prime Minister of those days said, "We feel as if they are our own children."...the help which came from Norway was a very important factor in the victory over the U-boats [when] our existence depended on the lifeline across the Atlantic....It was this lifeline which we had to maintain, and the addition of many millions of tons of merchant shipping, manned by hardy and courageous men from Norway, played a very definite part in our existence.

1948, 11 MAY. ROYAL PALACE, OSLO.
(EUROPE, 323.)

...if I must add one word of criticism to the Vikings [it is] that they were entirely lacking in any conception of neutrality.

1948, 12 MAY. UNIVERSITY OF OSLO.
(EUROPE, 327.)

Two days later at an Oslo banquet Churchill mentioned the United States "which the Vikings discovered long before Christopher Columbus".

You were fallen upon in a shameful manner, in a treacherous manner. You did your utmost all through, and when you could do no more in Norway than maintain a sullen and inflexible defiance of your conquerors, still your ships went across the seas and carried the necessary supplies in the teeth of the U-boats, which was one of the great contributory factors in the final ultimate victory.

1948, 13 MAY. OSLO CITY HALL. (CAPPELLENS.)

Palestine

...it is manifestly right that the Jews, who are scattered all over the world, should have a national centre and a National Home, where some of them may be reunited. And where else could that be but in this land of Palestine, with which for more than 3,000 years they have been intimately and profoundly associated?

1921, 28 MARCH, JERUSALEM. (OB IV, 565.)

To a Palestinian Arab delegation in Jerusalem.

I said last year that our policy was one of moderation, endeavouring to persuade one side to concede and the other to forbear, endeavouring to keep a certain modicum of military force available in order to prevent violent collisions between the two sides.

1922, 9 MARCH.

It is hard enough, in all conscience, to make a new Zion, but if over the portals of the new Jerusalem you are going to inscribe the legend "No Israelite need apply," I hope the House will permit me in future to confine my attention exclusively to Irish matters.

1922, 4 JULY.

A canny reference to the well-known sign in Boston shop windows, "Help wanted. No Irish need apply." See also Israel.

Too much current was put on the cables and the cables have fused. That may be a reason for mending the cables and reducing the current. It is surely no reason for declaring that electricity is a fluid too dangerous for civilisation to handle.

1937, 23 JULY. ("PALESTINE PARTITION," *EVENING STANDARD*; STEP, 140.)

WSC was referring to the immigration of 40,000 Jews to Palestine, which many people thought was excessive.

I accuse His Majesty's Government of having been, for more than three years, incapable of forming a coherent opinion upon the affairs of Palestine....Do not let it be forgotten that people are dying there, that they are being executed and meeting grisly deaths from day to day and week to week, while here all that can be done is to have from time to time Debates and pay each other compliments, and, above all, run no risks of taking any decision.

1938, 24 NOVEMBER.

So far from being persecuted, the Arabs have crowded into the country and multiplied till their population has increased more than even all world Jewry could lift up the Jewish population. Now we are asked to decree that all this is to stop and all this is to come to an end. We are now asked to submit—and this is what rankles most with me—to an agitation

which is fed with foreign money and ceaselessly inflamed by Nazi and by Fascist propaganda.

1939, 23 MAY. (CS VI, 6137.)

The 1939 Palestine White Paper, drafted by the Colonial Office, was known among Jews as the Black Paper. It laid an immigration limit of 75,000 Jews during the next five years. Churchill opposed it and, when he became Prime Minister, ignored it.

I'm committed to creation of a Jewish national Home in Palestine. Let us go on with that; and at the end of war we shall have plenty of force with which to compel the Arabs to acquiesce in our designs. Don't shirk our duties because of difficulties.

1943, 2 JULY. (DIARIES OF CABINET SECRETARY SIR NORMAN BROOK, *NEW YORK TIMES*, 22 JANUARY 2006.)

The Rt. Hon. and Learned Gentleman, the President of the Board of Trade [Sir Stafford Cripps] spoke of the past twenty-five years as being the most unkind or unhappy Palestine has known. I imagine that it would hardly be possible to state the opposite of the truth more compendiously....

The idea that the Jewish problem could be solved or even helped by a vast dumping of the Jews of Europe into Palestine is really too silly to consume our time in the House this afternoon.

1946, 1 AUGUST.

To abandon India, with all the dire consequences that would follow therefrom, but to have a war with the Jews in order to give Palestine to the Arabs, amid the execration of the world, appears to carry incongruity of thought and polity to levels which have rarely been attained in human history.

1946, 12 NOVEMBER.

Scuttle, everywhere, is the order of the day— Egypt, India, Burma. One thing at all costs we must preserve: the right to get ourselves world-mocked and world-hated over Palestine, at a cost of £82 million.

1947, 12 MARCH.

...the whole question of the Middle East might have been settled...on the morrow of victory, and...an Arab Confederation...and one Jewish State might have been set up, which would have given peace and unity throughout the whole vast scene.

1948, 10 DECEMBER.

Poland

Poland has saved herself by her exertions and will I trust save Europe by her example.

1920, 29 AUGUST. (OB IV, 427.)

Sir Martin Gilbert described this remark as "echoing Pitt at the Guildhall in 1805", referring to England after the Battle of Trafalgar. Macaulay's biography of Pitt quotes the great statesman: "Let us hope that England, having saved herself by her energy, may save Europe by her example." However, Churchill's words are more often quoted by historians.

I rejoice that Poland has been reconstituted....The Polish Corridor is inhabited almost entirely by Poles, and it was Polish territory before the Partition of 1772. This is a matter which in quiet times, with increasing goodwill, Europe should have set itself—and might well some day set itself—to solve.

1933, 13 APRIL.

The Corridor, devised at Versailles, gave Poland access to the sea, slicing between German East Prussia and the rest of Germany. It included part of Polish Pomerania along the Vistula River, but excluded the Free City of Danzig.

Poland is not a ghost: Poland is a reincarnation. I think it is a wonderful thing that Polish unity should have re-emerged from long hideous eclipse and bondage.

1933, 13 APRIL. (COVENANT, 78.)

The British and French ambassadors visited the [Polish] Foreign Minister, Colonel Beck, or sought to visit him, in order to ask for some mitigation in the harsh measures being pursued against Czechoslovakia about Teschen. The door was shut in their faces.

1938, 5 OCTOBER.

Churchill forever blamed Poland for complicity in Hitler's designs by its rapaciousness for Czech territory following the Munich agreement, causing him considerable trouble with exiled Poles during and after the war.

Danzig is not only a city. It has become a symbol. An act of violence against the Polish Republic, whether it arises from without or from within, will raise an issue of world importance....An attack upon Poland at the present time would be a decisive and irrevocable event. It is of the highest importance that the Nazi party in Germany should not mislead themselves upon the temper of the British and French democracies.

1939, 28 JUNE. CARLTON CLUB, LONDON. (BLOOD, 180–81.)

...Poland has been again overrun by two of the great powers which held her in bondage for 150 years, but were unable to quench the spirit of the Polish nation. The heroic defence of Warsaw shows that the soul of Poland is indestructible, and that she will rise again like a rock, which may for a spell be submerged by a tidal wave, but which remains a rock.

1939, 1 OCTOBER. BROADCAST, LONDON. (BLOOD, 205.)

Germany had massacred Poland, and Russia, then Germany's ally, had rushed in to seize about 30 per cent of Poland.

In German-occupied Poland the most hideous form of terrorism prevails....At one place three hundred were lined up against the wall; at another a group of drunken German officers are said to have shot seventy hostages in prison; at another a hundred and thirty-six Polish students, some of whom were only twelve or thirteen years old, were butchered. Torture has been used. Press gangs seize men and women in the streets and drive them off in droves to forced labour in Germany.

1940, 27 JANUARY. FREE TRADE HALL, MANCHESTER. (BLOOD, 264–5.)

This war against the mechanized barbarians, who, slave-hearted themselves, are fitted only to carry their curse to others—this war will be long and hard. But the end is sure; the end will reward all toil, all disappointments, all suffering in those who faithfully serve the cause of European and world freedom. A day will dawn, perhaps sooner than we have now a right to hope, when the insane attempt to found a Prussian domination on racial hatred, on the armoured vehicle, on the secret police, on the alien overseer, and on still more filthy Quislings, will pass like a monstrous dream.

1941, 3 MAY. BROADCAST TO POLAND, LONDON. (UNRELENTING, 104.)

See Churchillisms...Quisling. Churchill possibly chose 3 May for this broadcast because it is the Polish National Holiday: the day when Parliament adopted the Constitution in 1791.

We strove long, too long, for peace, and suffered thereby; but from the moment when we gave our guarantee that we would not stand by idly and see Poland trampled down by Nazi violence, we have never looked back, never flagged, never doubted, never flinched. We were sure of our duty, and we have discharged it, and will discharge it, without swerving or slackening, to the end.

1943, 30 JUNE. GUILDHALL, LONDON. (ONWARDS, 124.)

I took occasion to raise personally with Marshal Stalin the question of the future of Poland. I pointed out that it was in fulfilment of our guarantee to Poland that Great Britain declared war upon Nazi Germany; that we had never weakened in our resolve, even in the period when we were all alone; and that the fate of the Polish nation holds a prime place in the thoughts and policies of His Majesty's Government and of the British Parliament. It was with great pleasure that I heard from Marshal Stalin that he, too, was resolved upon the creation and maintenance of a strong integral independent Poland as one of the leading powers in Europe. He has several times repeated these declarations in public, and I am convinced that they represent the settled policy of the Soviet Union.

1944, 22 FEBRUARY.

The Russian armies now stand before the gates of Warsaw. They bring the liberation of Poland in their hands. They offer freedom, sovereignty and independence to the Poles. They ask that there should be a Poland friendly to Russia. This seems to me very reasonable, considering the injuries which Russia has suffered through the Germans marching across Poland to attack her.

1944, 2 AUGUST.

Churchill was to be disappointed in his hopes. While Warsaw rose in rebellion, the Red Army rested across the Vistula; only when the Germans had put down all Polish national resistance did it march in, defying the entreaties of Churchill and Roosevelt.

I welcome this opportunity of paying tribute to the heroism and tenacity of the Polish Home Army and the population of Warsaw, who, after five years of oppression, have yet fought for nearly two months to contribute all in their power to the expulsion of the Germans from the capital of Poland.

1944, 26 SEPTEMBER.

...it is our persevering and constant aim that the Polish people, after their sufferings and vicissitudes, shall find in Europe an abiding home and resting-place, which, though it may not entirely coincide or correspond with the pre-war frontiers of Poland, will nevertheless be adequate for the needs of the Polish nation and not inferior in character and quality, taking the picture as a whole, to what they previously possessed.

1944, 27 OCTOBER.

I am absolutely convinced that it is in the profound future interest of the Polish nation that they should reach agreement with the Soviet Government about their disputed frontiers in the east before the march of the Russian armies through the main part of Poland takes place.

1944, 15 DECEMBER.

It would be a great pity to stuff the Polish goose so full of German food that it died of indigestion.

1945, 7 FEBRUARY, YALTA. (OB VII, 1189.)

WSC to Stalin in reference to compensating Poland for losses of territory to the east by shifting her borders west into what had been German territory.

Most solemn declarations have been made by Marshal Stalin and the Soviet Union that the sovereign independence of Poland is to be maintained, and this decision is now joined-in both by Great Britain and the United States....His Majesty's Government will never forget the debt they owe to the Polish troops who have served them so valiantly, and to all those who have fought under our command. I earnestly hope it may be possible to offer the citizenship and freedom of the British Empire, if they so desire.

1945, 27 FEBRUARY.

I must put on record my own opinion that the provisional western frontier agreed upon for Poland, running from Stettin on the Baltic, along the Oder and its tributary, the Western Neisse, comprising as it does one quarter of the arable land of all Germany, is not a good augury for the future map of Europe....I think a mistake has been made, in which the Provisional Government of Poland have been an ardent partner, by going far beyond what necessity or equity required....There are few virtues that the Poles do not possess—and there are few mistakes they have ever avoided.

1945, 16 AUGUST.

I have been censured for wrongly championing the Russian claims to the Curzon Line. So far as the Curzon Line is concerned, I hold strongly that this was a rightful Russian frontier, and that a free Poland should receive compensation at the expense of Germany both in the Baltic and in the West, going even to the line of the Oder and the Eastern Neisse. If I and my colleagues erred in these decisions we must be judged in relation to the circumstances of the awful conflict in which we were engaged....

Poland is denied all free expression of her national will. Her worst appetites of expansion are encouraged. At the same time, she is held in strict control by a Soviet-dominated government who do not dare have a free election under the observation of representatives of the three or four Great Powers. The fate of Poland seems to be an unending tragedy, and we, who went to war, all ill-prepared, on her behalf, watch with sorrow the strange outcome of our endeavours.

1946, 5 JUNE.

Churchill had accepted the Curzon Line as Poland's eastern border at Yalta, incurring the wrath of the Polish government in exile in London, whose leaders were later lured to Moscow and arrested. Post-war Poland thus lost traditional territory to Russia, while being compensated by portions of German Silesia. She also lost her independence.

Serbia

This hardy warlike stock, "the Prussians of the Balkans," whose teeth were whetted in centuries of unrecorded ferocious struggles with the Sultan's troops, respected nothing that stood in their way....fearing naught and enduring all, they pursued their immense design through the terrors and miseries of Armageddon, and have, in fact, achieved their purpose at its close.

1931. (CRISIS V, 20.)

The Serbs' "purpose" was the unification of Yugoslavia. The term "Prussians of the Balkans" was applied widely to the Bulgarians before Churchill borrowed it for the Serbs. It seems to have originated in 1903, when the Russian Chancellor, Prince Lobanov, applied it angrily to the Bulgarians in their quest for independence.

South Africa

...the truth is that the bribery market in the Transvaal has been spoiled by the millionaires. I could not afford with my slender resources to insult them [the sentries] heavily enough.

1899, 22 DECEMBER. (LADYSMITH, 181; BOER, 81.)

On his failure to bribe the sentries to help him escape from the Boer prison camp in Pretoria.

The individual Boer, mounted in suitable country, is worth three to five regular soldiers....There is plenty of room here for a quarter of a million men....more irregular corps are wanted. Are the gentlemen of England fox hunting? Why not a Leicestershire Light Horse?

1899. MORNING POST, LONDON. (MARTIN, 44.)

Hamilton thanked him. "This is a bad day for us."

"What can you expect," was the answer characteristic of the Boer—the privileged of God—"from fighting on a Sunday?"

1900, 10 AUGUST. (HAMILTON'S, 120; BOER, 278.)

In the worst British defeat of the First Boer War, at Majuba Hill in Natal, on 27 February 1881, 280 out of 405 British soldiers were captured or wounded. The rout gave voice to the cry in the Second (1899–1902) Boer War of "Avenge Majuba."

No people in the world received so much verbal sympathy and so little practical support as the Boers. If I were a Boer fighting in the field—and if I were a Boer I hope I should be fighting in the field—I would not allow myself to be taken in by any message of sympathy, not even if it were signed by a hundred Hon. Members.

The Boer is a curious combination of the squire and the peasant, and under the rough coat of the farmer there are very often to be found the instincts of the squire....

1901, 18 FEBRUARY.

From WSC's maiden speech in the House of Commons. This astonishing statement during the Anglo-Boer war caused a colleague to remark, "that's the way to throw away votes"; but it was indicative of WSC's lifelong appreciation for the qualities of honourable opponents.

The recuperative power of the Transvaal, daubed and smeared all over with gold, is enormous.

1901, 17 JULY.

It must be self-evident to every one who had studied the South Africa question that the loyal cooperation of the Boers in the settlement of South Africa would be such a dazzling bribe, such an enormous advantage, that it would be inconceivable that any government acquainted with the conditions should refuse to make any considerable sacrifices to secure so desirable an end.

1902, 21 JANUARY.

Here lies the answer to historians who say that Churchill failed to insist on racial equality in the aftermath of the South African war.

Was it not rather a sad thing that Johannesburg, the great spring of wealth, where all the gold rose to the surface of the ground and where they ought to be able to pay the best wages and offer the most attractive conditions, should be in the mind of the South African native a place of melancholy tribulation and hard work?

1904, 5 MAY.

For an unrepentant Victorian, Churchill certainly had advanced ideas on the plight of natives in South Africa. See also World Politics...Racism.

In this land of bewildering paradox [South Africa] good produces evil and evil produces good. The gold mines, so long needed to repair the annual deficits, have proved to be the greatest of curses, overwhelming the land from end to end with blood and fire, leaving an evil legacy of debt and animosity behind.

1906, 28 FEBRUARY.

If we were able by some good fortune to make a settlement in the Transvaal between the two races which would be lasting, which would give the Boers direct partnership in the British Empire so that both races might work and live together and wrangle together in the rough-and-tumble of representative institutions, then I say we should have achieved a work which would linger in the minds of the people of South Africa....

1906, 8 JUNE.

As typical example as can be found of Churchill's lifelong moral, "In victory, magnanimity." His philosophy of reconciliation between British settlers and the defeated Boers had much to do with the end of strife in that divided land.

With all our majority we can only make it the gift of a Party; they [the Conservative Party] can make it the gift of England.

1906, 31 JULY. (LIBERALISM, 148.)

On approving the Transvaal Constitution.

...the Government [should] take steps to improve the lot of the Chinese labourer. It would in future prevent fines, collective punishments and criminal penalties being imposed for noncriminal offences...."undercut cruelty" by subsidizing repatriation....The spectacle of the Chinaman wandering over the veldt, his hand against every man and every man's hand against him, with half the world between him and his home in China, is as degrading, hideous, and pathetic as any this civilised and Christian nation has made itself responsible for in modern years.

1906, 15 AUGUST.

No responsible statesman, and no British Cabinet, so far as I know, ever contemplated any other solution of the South African problem but that of full self government....If our policy should end in mocking disaster, then the resulting evil would not be confined to South Africa....if the near future should unfold to our eyes a tranquil, prosperous, consolidated Afrikander nation under the protecting aegis of the British Crown, then the good also will not be confined to South Africa; then the cause of the poor and the weak all over the world will have been sustained; and everywhere small peoples will get more room to breathe, and everywhere great empires will be encouraged by our example to step forward—and it only needs a step—into the sunshine of a more gentle and more generous age....

1906, 17 DECEMBER.

The Boers were the most humane people where white men were concerned. Kaffirs were a different story, but to the Boer mind the destruction of a white man's life, even in war, was a lamentable and shocking event. They were the most good-hearted enemy I have ever fought against in the four continents in which it has been my fortune to see active service.

1930. (MEL, 272.)

England should never have [conquered the Boers]. To strike down two independent republics must have lowered our whole position in the world. It must have stirred up all sorts of things. I am sure the Boers made a good fight. When I was there I saw lots of them. Men of the wild, with rifles, on horseback. It must have taken a lot of soldiers.

1947. ("THE DREAM," OB VIII, 369.)

WSC's father's ghost in his short story, The Dream, asks what happened in the Boer War. Churchill replies, "We conquered the Transvaal and the Orange Free State." He then supplies his father's response, above.

Spain

The Spaniards have long memories, and I was not surprised when, in the Great War, they showed themselves extremely frigid towards a combination which included the descendants of the Napoleonic invaders, the United States who had stripped them of the last vestiges of their Colonial Empire, and Great Britain...who still held Gibraltar.

1931, APRIL. ("ARTHUR JAMES BALFOUR," *STRAND MAGAZINE*; GC, 162.)

The Spaniards, to whom democratic institutions carry with them the hope of some great new advance and amelioration, regarded Alfonso as an obstacle to their progress. The British and French democracies...regarded the king as a sportsman; the Spaniards knew him as a ruler.

1931, JULY. ("ALFONSO XIII," *STRAND MAGAZINE*; GC, 137.)

It is not a question of opposing Nazism or Communism, but of opposing tyranny in whatever form it presents itself; and, as I do not find in either of these two Spanish factions which are at war any satisfactory guarantee that the ideals which I care about would be preserved, I am not able to throw myself in this headlong fashion into the risk of having to fire cannon immediately on the one side or the other of this trouble. I have found it easier to maintain this feeling of detachment from both sides because, before we gave any help to either side we ought to know what the victory of that side would mean to those beaten.

When millions of people are lacerated and inflamed against each other by reciprocal injuries, some element of outside aid and even of outside pressure is indispensable.

1937, 14 APRIL.

Churchill is often criticised for failing to support the Republicans in the Spanish Civil War. His view was that both sides were equally despicable, but moreover, Spain was a distraction from Germany.

Some people think that our foreign policy towards Spain is best expressed by drawing comical or even rude caricatures of General Franco; but I think there is more in it than that.

1944, 24 MAY.

"Constructive engagement" probably sums up WSC's policy towards Franco, who had the art of landing on his feet.

None of us likes the Franco regime, and, personally, I like it as little as I like the present British administration, but, between not liking a government and trying to stir up a civil war in a country, there is a very wide interval. It is said that every nation gets the government it deserves. Obviously, this does not apply in the case of Great Britain.

1946, 5 JUNE.

Sudan

We are left sad and sorrowful in the dark, until the stars light up and remind us that there is always something beyond.

1899. (RIVER I, 6.)

Describing the pitch-black African night.

Where everything is hot and burning, the caustic plants appear superfluous.

1899. (IBID.)

Describing the vegetation in the Sudanese desert. In the 1902 abridged edition this is revised to be a rhetorical question: "Why should there be caustic plants where everything is hot and burning?"

At once slovenly and uxorious, [the Sudanese soldier] detested his drills and loved his wives with equal earnestness.

1899. (RIVER I, 156.)

The numerous graves of Greek traders—a study of whose epitaphs may conveniently refresh a classical education—protest that the climate [near Suakin] is pestilential.

1899. (RIVER I, 190.)

From the growing workshops at Wady Halfa the continued clatter and clang of hammers and the black smoke of manufacture rose to the African sky. The malodorous incense of civilisation was offered to the startled gods of Egypt.

1899. (RIVER I, 290.)

WSC's doubt about industry in unspoilt places often bubbled to the surface. In the Canadian wilderness in 1929 he remarked,

> *Fancy cutting down those beautiful trees we saw this afternoon to make pulp for those bloody newspapers, and calling it civilisation.*

See Chapter 4...Newspapers (Media).

"Mad fanaticism" is the depreciating comment of [the Dervish's] conquerors. I hold this to be a cruel injustice. Nor can he be a very brave man who will not credit them with a nobler motive, and believe that they died to clear their honour from the stain of defeat. Why should we regard as madness in the savage what would be sublime in civilized man?

1899. (RIVER II, 162.)

Africa always claims its forfeits; and so the four white men who had started together from Mombassa returned but three to Cairo. A military internment involves the union of two of the most impressive rituals in the world. The day after the Battle of Omdurman it fell to my lot to bury those soldiers of the 21st Lancers, who had died of their wounds during the night. Now after nine years, in very different circumstances, from the other end of Africa, I had come back to this grim place where so much blood has been shed, and again I found myself standing at an open grave, while the yellow glare of the departed sun still lingered over the desert, and the sound of funeral volleys broke its silence.

1908, KHARTOUM. (MAJ, 124.)

Remarking on the death from cholera of his servant, George Scrivings, during his expedition to Africa, in the same place where so many had died nine years before in the conquest of Khartoum.

Turkey

Hitherto, Turkey has maintained a solid barrier against aggression from any quarter, and by so doing, even in the darkest days, has rendered us invaluable service in preventing the spreading of the war through Turkey into Persia and Iraq, and in preventing menace to the oil fields of Abadan, which are of vital consequence to the whole eastern war.

1943, 11 FEBRUARY.

The hopes we cherished of Turkey boldly entering the war in February or March, or at least according us the necessary bases for air action—those hopes faded. After giving £20,000,000 worth of British and American arms to Turkey in 1943 alone, we have suspended the process and ceased to exhort Turkey to range herself with the victorious United Powers, with whom she has frequently declared that her sympathies lie, and with whom, I think, there is no doubt that her sympathies do lie. The Turks at the end of last year and the beginning of this year magnified their dangers. Their military men took the gloomiest view of Russian prospects in south Russia and in the Crimea.

1944, 24 MAY.

I have the authority of the Turkish Government to announce here today in the House of Commons that on the basis of the Anglo-Turkish Alliance, Turkey has broken off all relations with Germany. This act infuses new life into the Alliance. No one can tell whether Germany or Bulgaria will attack Turkey. If so, we shall make common cause with her and shall take the German menace as well as we can in our stride. Turkish cities may receive the kind of bombardment we have never shrunk from here. Herr von Papen may be sent back to Germany to meet the blood bath he so narrowly escaped at Hitler's hands in 1934. I take no responsibility for that.

1944, 2 AUGUST.

This was the culmination – late but satisfying – of Churchill's efforts to bring Turkey into the war on the side of the Allies. German Ambassador to Turkey Franz von Papen was not executed but received the Knight's Cross. Acquitted at Nuremberg, he lived until 1969.

Turkey became conscious of unexpected military weakness after the war had started in earnest on account of the influence—the decisive influence—of new weapons with which she was quite unprovided, and which we were not in a position to supply. As these weapons exercise a decisive effect on the modern battlefield, the Turks felt that they could no longer confide their safety to their renowned infantry and to the artillery of the last war.

1945, 27 FEBRUARY.

Yugoslavia

Early this morning the Yugoslav nation found its soul. A revolution has taken place in Belgrade and the Ministers who but yesterday signed away the honour and freedom of the country are reported to be under arrest. This patriotic movement arises from the wrath of a valiant and warlike race at the betrayal of their country by the weakness of their rulers and the foul intrigues of the Axis Powers.

1941, 27 MARCH, LONDON. (UNRELENTING, 69.)

The valiant, steadfast people, whose history for centuries has been to struggle for life, and who owe their survival to their mountains and to their fighting qualities, made every endeavour to placate the Nazi monster...[they] refused even to enter into effective Staff conversations with Greece or with Turkey or with us, but hugged the delusion that they could preserve their independence by patching up some sort of pact or compromise with Hitler. Once again we saw the odious German poisoning technique employed. In this case, however, it was to the Government rather than to the nation that the doses and the inoculation were administered....A boa constrictor, who had already covered his prey with his foul saliva and then had it suddenly wrested from his coils, would be in an amiable mood compared with Hitler, Goering, Ribbentrop and the rest of the Nazi gang when they experienced this bitter disappointment....A ferocious howl of hatred from the supreme miscreant [Hitler] was the signal for the actual invasion.

1941, 9 APRIL.

The whole tradition of military Europe has been in favour of *les noces de guerre* [war marriages], and nothing could be more natural and nothing could be more becoming than that a young king should marry a highly suitable princess on the eve of his departure for the war....The King and the Princess are strongly in favour of it, and in my view in this tangle they are the only ones whose opinions should weigh with us. The Foreign Office should discard 18th century politics and take a simple and straightforward view....We might be back in the refinements of Louis XIV instead of the lusty squalor of the 20th century....My advice to the King...will be to go to the nearest Registry office and take a chance. So what?

1943, 11 JULY. (WW2 V, 571–2.)

Prime Minister to Foreign Secretary. Peter II (1923–70) succeeded to the throne in 1934 but the country was ruled by a regent, Prince Paul. He married Princess Alexandra of Greece and Denmark in 1944 and was deposed by Tito's Communist assembly the following year.

Do you intend to make your home in Yugoslavia after the war?

[Sir Fitzroy Maclean: "No."]

Neither do I. That being so, don't you think we had better leave it to the Yugoslavs to work out their own form of government? What concerns us most now is who is doing the most damage to the Germans.

1943, DECEMBER. (MACLEAN, CHURCHILL PROCEEDINGS, 1987.)

WSC to Fitzroy Maclean (see People), who had reminded him that Tito's partisans, whom Churchill was supporting, were Communist-led.

In the autumn of 1941, Marshal Tito's Partisans began a wild and furious war for existence against the Germans. They wrested weapons from the Germans' hands, they grew rapidly in numbers; no reprisals, however bloody, whether upon hostages or the villages, deterred them. For them, it was death or freedom. Soon they began to inflict heavy injury upon the Germans and became masters of wide regions. Led with great skill, organised on the guerrilla principle, they were at once elusive and deadly.

1944, 22 FEBRUARY.

I am the earliest outside supporter of Marshal Tito. It is more than a year since in this House I extolled his guerrilla virtues to the world. Some of my best friends and the Honourable and Gallant Member for Preston [Randolph Churchill] are there with him or his Forces now. I earnestly hope he may prove to be the saviour and the reunifier of his country, as he is undoubtedly at this time its undisputed master.

1945, 18 JANUARY.

See also Chapter 18, World War II...1944.

Yugoslavia since Hitler's invasion and conquest in April 1941 had been the scene of fearful events....In the mountains there began again the fierce guerrilla with which the Serbs had resisted the Turks for centuries....This confronted the Germans with a problem which could not be solved by the mass executions of notables or persons of substance. They found themselves confronted by desperate men who had to be hunted down in their lairs. No reprisals, however bloody, upon hostages or villages deterred them...

1952. (WW2 V, 408–9.)

12

WAR

*"Much as war attracts me & fascinates my mind with its
tremendous situations – I feel more deeply every year – & can
measure the feeling here in the midst of arms – what vile &
wicked folly & barbarism it all is."*[44]

"War is very cruel. It goes on for so long." Gen. Sikorski,
Churchill and Gen. de Gaulle in Britain, January 1941.

hurchill sadly concluded that "the story of the human race is war", and, at least
before the advent of apocalyptic nuclear weapons, regarded wars as recurring
phenomena. Because he always urged fighting with "might and main" he is regarded
incorrectly as a warrior-statesman, and some authors have truncated his quotations without
the context to make him fit their vision of him. Although Churchill always fought fiercely
once war had begun, his overriding cause was peace.

His precepts in war were simple: take the initiative, accept risk, prefer action to inaction, and never give in until victory is won. Yet he was convinced that victory must be
followed by magnanimity. He respected gallant foes, from the Boers in South Africa to
Rommel in North Africa. He consistently urged the lenient treatment of prostrate
enemies, from the Transvaal rebels of the early 1900s to the Germans in 1945. In 1918,
at the end of the first German war, he made himself unpopular with his colleagues by

---

44 WSC was writing to his wife from Germany, where he was observing German army manoeuvres,
15 September 1909. Randolph S. Churchill, *Winston S. Churchill, Companion Volume II, Part 2*.
London: Heinemann, 1967, 912.

urging that ships laden with food be sent to blockaded Hamburg, to succour the former enemy.

Churchill sought to avoid war by diplomacy and negotiation, and succeeded, in the case of Ireland in 1922, by helping to negotiate a treaty that kept the peace for fifty years. Around the same time he found himself in the Middle East, trying (vainly as it turned out) to settle boundaries and nationalities that would bring peace and progress to the lands of the former Ottoman Empire. A quarter century later he was hoping (vainly again) that the arrangements reached at Yalta and Potsdam would bring peace and liberty to Eastern Europe. And in the nuclear age he worked unceasingly for what he called an "accommodation" or "settlement" with the Soviets. The last great goal of his life was peace itself – still elusive in his last years, and the cause of much regret on his part.

From Queen Victoria's little wars to World War II and all the lesser engagements that have followed, many things never change. But in an age where wars are fought but not declared – when declaring war is no longer fashionable – Churchill has much to tell us about the element of chance, the inevitability of mistakes, and the certainty of disappointments before victory is won.

I have arranged this chapter by subject with entries in chronological order.

Aphorisms and Reflections

Ah, horrible war, amazing medley of the glorious and the squalid, the pitiful and the sublime, if modern men of light and leading saw your face closer, simple folk would see it hardly ever.

1900, 22 JANUARY. (LADYSMITH, 292; BOER, 131.)

War never pays its dividends in cash on the money it costs.

1901, 17 JULY.

If ever a single nation were able to back the strongest fleet with an overwhelming army, the whole world would be in jeopardy, and a catastrophe would swiftly occur.

1912, 18 MARCH.

An explanation of Churchill's aim for Britain: supreme on the seas, but with a relatively small army.

The story of the human race is War. Except for brief and precarious interludes there has never been peace in the world; and before history began murderous strife was universal and unending. But the modern developments surely require severe and active attention.

1929. (CRISIS IV, 451.)

War, which used to be cruel and magnificent, has now become cruel and squalid.

1930. (MEL, 79.)

Nothing but genius, the daemon in man, can answer the riddles of war, and genius, though it may be armed, cannot be acquired, either by reading or by experience. In default of genius nations have to make war as best they can and, since that quality is much rarer than the largest and purest diamonds, most wars are mainly tales of muddle. But when from time to time it flashes upon the scene, order and design with a sense almost of infallibility draw out from hazard and confusion.

1934. (MARLBOROUGH II, 93.)

War is very cruel. It goes on for so long.

1937, 14 APRIL.

There is only one thing certain about war, that it is full of disappointments and also full of mistakes.

1941, 27 APRIL. BROADCAST, LONDON. (UNRELENTING, 96.)

...if you will not fight for the right when you can easily win without bloodshed; if you will not fight when your victory will be sure and not too costly; you may come to the moment when you will have to fight with all the odds against you and only a precarious chance of survival. There may even be a worse case. You may have to fight when there is no hope of victory, because it is better to perish than live as slaves.

1948. (WW2 I, 272.)

On the British guarantee to Poland, spring 1939.

...no one can guarantee success in war, but only deserve it.

1949. (WW2 II, 484.)

War is mainly a catalogue of blunders.

1950. (WW2 III, 316.)

Churchill was referring to the Soviet failure to form a Balkan front against Hitler, adding,

it may be doubted whether any mistake in history has equalled that of which Stalin and the Communist chiefs were guilty...

Advent of war

Wars come very suddenly. I have lived through a period when one looked forward, as we do now, with anxiety and uncertainty to what would happen in the future. Suddenly something did happen—tremendous, swift, overpowering, irresistible.

1934, 7 FEBRUARY.

Wars do not always wait until all the combatants are ready. Sometimes they come before any are ready, sometimes when one nation thinks itself less unready than another, or when one nation thinks it is likely to become not stronger, but weaker, as time passes.

1936, 10 MARCH.

Allies

The manoeuvre which brings an ally into the field is as serviceable as that which wins a great battle.

1923. (CRISIS II, 21.)

To hear some people talk, however, one would think that the way to win the war is to make sure that every Power contributing armed forces and branches of these armed forces is represented on all the councils and organisations which have to be set up, and that everybody is fully consulted before anything is done. That is in fact the most sure way to lose a war.

1942, 27 JANUARY.

In working with Allies it sometimes happens that they develop opinions of their own.

1942, 10 DECEMBER. (SECRET, 79.)

When you have half a dozen theatres of war in various parts of the globe, there are bound to be divergences of view....These divergences

are of emphasis and priority rather than of principle. They can only be removed by the prolonged association of consenting and instructed minds.

1943, 11 FEBRUARY.

Amphibious operations

They have to fit together like a jewelled bracelet.

1940, MAY. (ISMAY, 120.)

Comment on Britain's abortive amphibious landings which tried to eject the Germans from Norway in April–May 1940.

All large amphibious operations, especially if they require the cooperation of two or more countries, require long months of organisation, with refinements and complexities hitherto unknown in war. Bold impulses, impatient desires, and sudden flashes of military instinct cannot hasten the course of events.

1943, 30 JUNE. GUILDHALL, LONDON. (ONWARDS, 132.)

Above all, the initial lodgment must be strong.

1952. (WW2 V, 76.)

Surprise, violence, and speed are the essence of all amphibious landings.

1952. (WW2 V, 126.)

This and the foregoing were contemporary comments before the 1944 invasion of Europe.

Boer War

The Second Boer War (1899–1902) was a hard-fought conflict between the British Empire and two independent South African republics, the Transvaal and Orange Free State. It ended with their absorption into the Empire, but not without generous provisions and a constitution which Churchill helped to promulgate. See also Nations...South Africa.

Keep cool men! This will be interesting for my paper!

1899, 15 NOVEMBER. CHIEVELEY, SOUTH AFRICA. (MACCALLUM SCOTT, 43.)

In the famous ambush of his armoured train, Churchill organised the escape of many British troops while himself being captured and interned as a prisoner of war in Pretoria.

...nothing was so thrilling as this: to wait and struggle among these clanging, rending iron boxes, with the repeated explosions of the shells and the artillery, the noise of the projectiles striking the cars, the hiss as they passed in the air, the grunting and puffing of the engine—poor, tortured thing, hammered by at least a dozen shells, any one of which, by penetrating the boiler, might have made an end of all—the expectation of destruction as a matter of course, the realization of powerlessness, and the alternations of hope and despair—all this for seventy minutes by the clock with only four inches of twisted iron work to make the difference between danger, captivity, and shame on the one hand—safety, freedom, and triumph on the other.

1899, 20 NOVEMBER, PRETORIA. (LADYSMITH, 89–90; BOER, 40–41.)

Sir,—I have the honour to inform you that as I do not consider that your Government have any right to detain me as a military prisoner, I have decided to escape from your custody. I have every confidence in the arrangements I have made with my friends outside, and I do not therefore expect to have another opportunity of seeing you. I therefore take this occasion to observe that I consider your treatment of prisoners is correct and humane, and that I see no grounds for complaint. When I return to the British lines I will make a public statement to this effect. I have also to thank you personally for your civility to me, and to express the hope that we may meet again at Pretoria before very long, and under different circumstances. Regretting that I am unable to bid you a more ceremonious or a personal farewell,

I have the honour, to be, Sir,
Your most obedient servant,
Winston Churchill.

1899, 10 DECEMBER, PRETORIA. (LADYSMITH, 176–7; BOER, 78–9.)

WSC to M. de Souza, Secretary of War, South African Republic, before he escaped from Boer clutches in Pretoria.

I entered a small grove of trees which grew on the side of a deep ravine. Here I resolved to wait till dusk. I had one consolation: no one in the world knew where I was—I did not know

myself....My sole companion was a gigantic vulture, who manifested an extravagant interest in my condition, and made hideous and ominous gurglings from time to time.

1899, 22 DECEMBER. LOURENÇO MARQUES (NOW MAPUTO, MOZAMBIQUE). (LADYSMITH, 195–6; BOER, 87.)

This comment is dated as above, when it was originally written and cabled to The Morning Post *for its original appearance.*

I remember that it poured with rain, and there was very little to look at in the gloom, but, nevertheless, it was not possible to stand unmoved and watch the ceaseless living stream—miles of stern-looking men marching in fours so quickly that they often had to run to keep up, of artillery, ammunition columns, supply columns, baggage, slaughter cattle, thirty great pontoons, white-hooded, red-crossed ambulance waggons, all the accessories of an army hurrying forward under the cover of night—and before them a guiding star, the red gleam of war.

1900, 22 JANUARY. VENTER'S SPRUIT, SOUTH AFRICA. (LADYSMITH, 277; BOER, 125.)

On the Battle of Trichardt's Drift, in which British forces tried but failed to cross the Tugela River and relieve besieged Ladysmith.

I have often noticed that when political controversy becomes excited, persons of choleric dispositions and limited intelligences are apt to become rude...if I am a traitor, at any rate I was fighting the Boers in South Africa when Colonel Kenyon Slaney was slandering them at home....I had the honour of serving in the field for our country while this gallant, fire-eating Colonel was content to kill Kruger with his mouth in the comfortable security of England.

1901. (MACCALLUM SCOTT, 240.)

The alliteration of "Kenyon Slaney" and "slandering them at home" is amusing. Col. Kenyon Slaney had called WSC a traitor for arguing in favour of lenient treatment of the Boers after their defeat. Stephanus J. P. Kruger (1825–1904), known as "Oom Paul", was President of Transvaal, 1883–1900, and the Boer leader in the war.

Bombing policy

In a war between two States with equal air forces it would not pay—I put it no higher; leave out morality, humanity and the public law of Europe—it would not pay, from the military self-preservation standpoint of any Power engaged in an equal fight to waste its strength upon non-combatants and open towns.

1933, 14 MARCH.

My dear Sir, this is a military and not a civilian war. You and others may desire to kill women and children. We desire (and have succeeded in our desire) to destroy German military objectives. I quite appreciate your point. But my motto is "Business before Pleasure."

1940, 17 OCTOBER. (NICOLSON II, 121–2.)

Reply to a correspondent, Robert Cary MP, who said the public demanded all-out bombing of Germany.

Causes of war

The only test by which human beings can judge war responsibility is Aggression; and the supreme proof of Aggression is Invasion.

1929. (CRISIS IV, 439.)

...there is no greater danger than equal forces. If you wish to bring about war, you bring about such an equipoise that both sides think they have a chance of winning. If you want to stop war, you gather such an aggregation of force on the side of peace that the aggressor, whoever he may be, will not dare to challenge.

1934, 13 JULY.

Great wars come when both sides believe they are more or less equal, when each thinks it has a good chance of victory.

1947, 14 OCTOBER. AL SMITH MEMORIAL SPEECH, LONDON. (EUROPE, 165.)

Chance as a factor

War is a game with a good deal of chance in it, and, from the little I have seen of it, I should say that nothing in war ever goes right except occasionally by accident.

1901, 12 MARCH.

In war...chance casts aside all veils and disguises, and presents herself nakedly from moment to moment....You may walk to the right or to the left of a particular tree, and it makes the difference whether you rise to command an Army Corps, or are sent home crippled and paralysed for life.

1926, APRIL. ("WITH THE GRENADIERS," COSMOPOLITAN; THOUGHTS 71.)

In January 1916 Churchill took command of a Scottish battalion which had suffered greatly in the battles of 1915. For nearly four weeks he trained them behind the lines, and then, for three months, he commanded them in the front line. On several occasions he was nearly killed by shellfire.

Very few set-piece battles that have to be prepared over a long period of time work out in the way they are planned and imagined beforehand. The unexpected intervenes at every stage. The will-power of the enemy impinges itself upon the prescribed or hoped-for course of events. Victory is traditionally elusive. Accidents happen. Mistakes are made. Sometimes right things turn out wrong, and quite often wrong things turn out right. War is very difficult, especially to those who are taking part in it or conducting it.

1941, 11 DECEMBER.

Chemical warfare

It is sheer affectation to lacerate a man with the poisonous fragment of a bursting shell and to boggle at making his eyes water by means of lachrymatory gas. I am strongly in favour of using poisoned gas against uncivilised tribes. The moral effect should be so good that the loss of life should be reduced to a minimum. It is not necessary to use only the most deadly gasses: gasses can be used which cause great inconvenience and would spread a lively terror and yet would leave no serious permanent effects on most of those affected.

1919, 12 MAY. (OB, CV4/1, 649.)

Departmental minute at the War Office. The second sentence is often quoted without the rest, to suggest that WSC was recommending the use of poison gas rather than tear gas on "uncivilised tribes".

Nothing could be more repugnant to our feelings than the use of poison gas, but there is no logic at all behind the argument that it is quite proper in war to lay a man low with high-explosive shell, fragments of which inflict poisonous and festering wounds, and altogether immoral to give him a burn with corrosive gas or make him cough and sneeze or otherwise suffer through his respiratory organs....

The attitude of the British Government has always been to abhor the employment of poison gas. As I understand it, our only procedure is to keep alive such means of studying this subject as shall not put us at a hopeless disadvantage if, by any chance, it were used against us by other people.

1932, 13 MAY.

Civilian control

Modern war is total, and it is necessary for its conduct that the technical and professional authorities should be sustained and if necessary directed by the Heads of Government, who have the knowledge which enables them to comprehend not only the military but the political and economic forces at work, and who have the power to focus them all upon the goal.

1943, 19 MAY. CONGRESS, WASHINGTON. (ONWARDS, 97.)

See also Political Theory and Practice... Civilian control of the military.

Commitment and Perseverance

How hard to build. How easy to evacuate. How hard to capture. How easy to do nothing. How hard to achieve anything. War is action, energy & hazard. These sheep only want to browse among the daisies.

1916, 22 FEBRUARY, FLANDERS. (SOAMES, SPEAKING, 179.)

WSC to his wife, referring to the British wartime coalition government, which had excluded him, and specifically to Arthur Balfour, who had replaced him as First Lord of the Admiralty in 1915.

It is no doubt easy for people to say—as they can unanswerably say— "There is no room for compromise in war. You must make up your mind one way or the other. It is no use falling

between two stools. For good or for ill, right or wrong, in war you must know what you want and what you mean and hurl your whole life and strength into it and accept all hazards inseparable from it."

1920, 25 APRIL. ("THE REAL KITCHENER," *ILLUSTRATED SUNDAY HERALD*, ESSAYS 3, 28.)

WSC favoured the old expression "falling between two stools", which he later deployed in the rearmament debate (30 July 1934), to Hitler's invasion of Russia (WW2 III, 84), and to the post-war rearmament of Germany (15 February 1951).

Conduct of war

Almost the first of the great principles of war is to seize the initiative, to rivet the attention of the enemy on your action, and to confront him with a series of novel and unexpected situations which leave him no time to pursue a policy of his own.

1917, 21 FEBRUARY.

There is no principle in war better established than that everything should be massed for the battle.

1929. (CRISIS II, 429.)

WSC was discussing the Dardanelles campaign, in which commanders had flatly ignored this principle. See also Writer and Speaker... Words/Masse de Manoeuvre.

People must be taught not to despise the small shelter. Dispersal is the sovereign remedy against heavy casualties.

1940, 8 OCTOBER.

I never "worry" about action, but only about inaction.

1940S. PASSIM. (OB, CV6/2, XVI.)

...anyone who supposes that there will not be mistakes in war is very foolish. I draw a distinction between mistakes. There is the mistake which comes through daring, what I call a mistake towards the enemy, in which you must always sustain your commanders, by sea, land or air. There are mistakes from the "safety-first" principle, mistakes of turning away from the enemy; and they require a far more acid consideration.

1941, 7 MAY.

There are times when so many things happen, and happen so quickly...You may fail to connect it with what you are advocating at the particular moment. Throughout a long and variegated Parliamentary life this consideration has led me to keep a watchful eye on that danger myself. You never can tell. There are also people who talk and bear themselves as if they had prepared for this war with great armaments and long, careful preparation. But that is not true. In two and a half years of fighting we have only just managed to keep our heads above water.

1942, 27 JANUARY.

One of my fundamental ideas has always been the importance of keeping as many options as possible open to serve the main purpose, especially in time of war.

1942, 8 MARCH. (WW2 IV, 173.)

In our wars the episodes are largely adverse, but the final results have hitherto been satisfactory. Away we dash over the currents that may swirl around us, but the tide bears us forward on its broad, resistless flood. In the last war the way was uphill almost to the end. We met with continual disappointments, and with disasters far more bloody than anything we have experienced so far in this one. But in the end all the oppositions fell together, and all our foes submitted themselves to our will.

1942, 9 NOVEMBER. MANSION HOUSE, LONDON. (END, 265.)

...batteries should be able to do the bulk of the work themselves if materials are provided. Where outside assistance is required priority should be given to the most exposed positions.

1944, 28 FEBRUARY. (WW2 V, 609.)

Anything can be done once or for a short time, but custom, repetition, prolongation, is [are] always to be avoided when possible in war.

1944, 10 JUNE, NORMANDY. (WW2 VI, 11.)

I have thought that it is sometimes unwise of generals to try to foresee with meticulous exactness just what will happen after a battle has been fought. A battle hangs like a curtain across the future. Once that curtain is raised or rent we can all see how the scenery is arranged, what actors are left upon the scene, and how they appear to be related to one another.

1944, 31 OCTOBER.

This idea of not irritating the enemy did not commend itself to me....Good, decent, civilised people, it appeared, must never themselves strike till after they have been struck dead....There were still months of pretended war. On the one side endless discussions about trivial points, no decisions taken, or if taken rescinded, and the rule "don't be unkind to the enemy; you will only make him angry". On the other, doom preparing—a vast machine grinding forward ready to break upon us!

1948. (WW2 I, 454.)

WSC was criticising the reluctance of the Anglo-French allies to take offensive action against Germany (such as mining the Rhine) in the opening months of the war, for fear it might produce retaliation.

...in the main, war consists of the same tunes, played through the ages, though sometimes only on a reed flute or a bagpipe and sometimes through a full modern orchestra.

1950, 4 JULY. ROYAL UNITED SERVICES INSTITUTE, LONDON. (BALANCE, 306–7.)

...On these vast matters on which so many lives depend there is always a great deal of guesswork. So much is unknown and immeasurable. Who can tell how weak the enemy may be behind his flaming fronts and brazen mask? At what moment will his will-power break? At what moment will he be beaten down?

1952. (WW2 V, 370–71.)

Death in battle

Looking at these shapeless forms, coffined in a regulation blanket, the pride of race, the pomp of empire, the glory of war appeared but the faint and unsubstantial fabric of a dream; and I could not help realising with Burke: "What shadows we are and what shadows we pursue."

1897, INDIA. (MALAKAND, 206.)

...soldiers must die, but by their death they nourish the nation which gave them birth.

1943, 14 JULY. BROADCAST TO POLISH FORCES, LONDON. (ONWARDS, 136.)

On the death of General Sikorski in an air crash on 5 July 1943.

Declaring war

In the strong stream of war the swimmer is swirled helplessly about hither and thither by the waves, and he can by no means tell where he will come to land, or, indeed, that he may not be overwhelmed in the flood.

1899, 20 NOVEMBER, PRETORIA. (LADYSMITH, 76; BOER, 35.)

Never, never, never believe any war will be smooth and easy, or that anyone who embarks on that strange voyage can measure the tides and hurricanes he will encounter. The Statesman who yields to war fever must realise that once the signal is given, he is no longer the master of policy but the slave of unforeseeable and uncontrollable events. Antiquated War Offices, weak, incompetent or arrogant Commanders, untrustworthy allies, hostile neutrals, malignant Fortune, ugly surprises, awful miscalculations—all take their seat at the Council Board on the morrow of a declaration of war. Always remember, however sure you are that you can easily win, that there would not be a war if the other man did not think he also had a chance.

1930. (MEL, 246.)

Defeat

The penalties of defeat are frightful. After the blinding flash of catastrophe, the stunning blow, the gaping wounds, there comes an onset of the diseases of defeat. The central principle of a nation's life is broken, and all healthy, normal control vanishes, there are few societies that can withstand the conditions of subjugation. Indomitable patriots take different paths; quislings and collaborationists of all kinds abound; guerrilla leaders, each with their personal followers, quarrel and fight.

1944, 22 FEBRUARY.

See Churchillisms...Quisling.

Defence

Two things stop the offensive movements of armies: (a) Bullets and fragments of shell which destroy the motive power of men, and (b) The confusion of the conflict.

1916, 9 NOVEMBER. (CRISIS III PART 2, 303.)

From WSC's paper, "The greater application of mechanical power to the prosecution of an offensive on land".

...if one side fights and the other does not, the war is apt to become somewhat unequal.

1940, 25 MAY. (OB, CV6/2, 139.)

Democracy in wartime

When a peaceful democracy is suddenly made to fight for its life, there must be a lot of trouble and hardship in the process of turning over from peace to war.

1939, 1 OCTOBER. BROADCAST, LONDON. (BLOOD, 207.)

Peaceful Parliamentary countries, which aim at freedom for the individual and abundance for the mass, start with a heavy handicap against a dictatorship whose sole theme has been war, the preparation for war, and the grinding up of everything and everybody into its military machine.

1939, 12 NOVEMBER.

During the last 250 years the British Parliament has fought several great and long European wars with unwearied zeal and tenacity, and carried them all to a conclusion. In this war they are fighting not only for themselves, but for Parliamentary institutions wherever they have been set up all over the globe.

1940, 27 JANUARY. FREE TRADE HALL, MANCHESTER. (BLOOD, 262.)

Immense surrenders of their hard-won liberties have been voluntarily made by the British people in order in time of war to serve the better the cause of freedom and fair play, to which, keeping nothing back, they have devoted all that they have and all that they are. Parliament stands custodian of these surrendered liberties, and its most sacred duty will be to restore them in their fullness when victory has crowned our exertions and our perseverance.

1940, 21 NOVEMBER.

It has been aptly remarked that Ministers, and indeed all other public men when they make speeches at the present time, have always to bear in mind three audiences, one our own fellow countrymen, secondly, our friends abroad, and thirdly, the enemy. This naturally makes the task of public speaking very difficult.

1941, 12 NOVEMBER.

The duty of a democracy in wartime is not to conceal but to confuse, "not the silence of the oyster serene in its grotto, but the smudge and blur of the cuttlefish."

1943, QUEBEC. (DILKS, 239.)

There is, I gather, in some quarters the feeling that the way to win the war is to knock the Government about, keep them up to the collar, and harry them from every side; and I find that hard to bear with Christian patience.

1944, 22 FEBRUARY.

Deterrence

It is really for consideration whether, having gone so far, the bolder course might not be the safer. All attempts to bridge a twelve-foot stream by an eight-foot plank are doomed to failure, and the plank is lost. It is a concession, no doubt, to bring forward a nine-foot plank, but again that may be lost. The great point in view is to achieve the object, and to produce the effect of an adequate deterrent.

1938, 24 MARCH.

For more of this famous speech see Chapter 1...Stairway to a Dark Gulf.

A country like ours, possessed of immense territory and wealth, whose defence has been neglected, cannot avoid war by dilating upon its horrors, or even by a continuous display of pacific qualities, or by ignoring the fate of the victims of aggression elsewhere. War will be avoided, in present circumstances, only by the accumulation of deterrents against the aggressor.

1938, 24 MARCH.

If one does not prepare before a war, one has to prepare after, and be very thankful if time is given. But all this disparity of proportion will rectify itself in the passage of time. All comes even at the end of the day, and all will come out yet more even when all the days are ended.

1941, 2 DECEMBER.

Enemy

The sun no longer seemed hot or the hours long. After all, they were there. We had not toiled up on a fruitless errand. The fatigues of the march, the heat, the insects, the discomforts—all were forgotten. We were "in touch"; and that is a glorious thing to be, since it makes all the features of life wear a bright and vivid flush of excitement, which the pleasures of the chase, of art, of intellect, or love can never excel and rarely equal.

1899. (RIVER II, 72–3.)

On making contact with the Dervish Army before the Battle of Omdurman, Sudan, 1898.

Let 'em have it. Remember this. Never maltreat the enemy by halves.

1940. 23 SEPTEMBER. (OB VI, 803.)

WSC after giving an order for 100 heavy bombers to attack Berlin.

I once had a horse that got badly rubbed in a ship coming over from Ireland. The inside of one hind leg was quite raw. It would have kicked a man's brains out if he had tried to doctor it. The vet put a twitch on its nose, and then he could rub the leg with disinfectant or do anything he liked, while the horse stood trembling. That illustrates the initiative. I told them that story at the time of Gallipoli. Once you grab the enemy by the nose, he will be able to think of nothing else.

1941, 17 FEBRUARY, DITCHLEY PARK. (KENNEDY, 79.)

Churchill's formulation is far more elegant than, but closely remindful of, President Lyndon Johnson's famous aside, "If you've got 'em by the balls their hearts and minds will follow."

In war and policy one should always try to put oneself in the position of what Bismarck called "the Other Man." The more fully and sympathetically a Minister can do this the better are his chances of being right.

1950. (WW2 III, 516.)

European war

A European war cannot be anything but a cruel, heartrending struggle, which, if we are ever to enjoy the bitter fruits of victory, must demand, perhaps for several years, the whole manhood of the nation, the entire suspension of peaceful industries, and the concentrating to one end of every vital energy in the community.

1901, 13 MAY. (MBA, 22–3.)

Misdated 12 May in Mr. Brodrick's Army. Churchill was one of the first to realise that transformation among the modern states of

Europe meant that a European war would be far more hazardous to populations than the "Little Wars" of the Victorian era, fought by small professional armies and without the participation of vast populations. His warnings were borne out in 1914.

The first indispensable condition of democratic progress must be the maintenance of European peace. War is fatal to liberalism. Liberalism is the world-wide antagonist of war.

1906, 11 OCTOBER. ST. ANDREW'S HALL, GLASGOW.
(LIBERALISM, 158.)

Home front

It is not the enemy in front that I fear, but the division which too often makes itself manifest in progressive ranks—it is that division, that dispersion of forces, that internecine struggle in the moments of great emergency, in the moments when the issue hangs in the balance—it is that which, I fear, may weaken our efforts and may perhaps deprive us of success otherwise within our grasp.

1908, 4 MAY. KINNAIRD HALL, DUNDEE.
(LIBERALISM, 195.)

This nation at war is an army; it must be looked upon as an army; it must be organised like an army; it must be directed like an army; and it ought to be rationed and provided and supplied like an army.

1916, 16 NOVEMBER.

In that supreme emergency we shall not hesitate to take every step, even the most drastic, to call forth from our people the last ounce and the last inch of effort of which they are capable. The interests of property, the hours of labour, are nothing compared with the struggle for life and honour, for right and freedom, to which we have vowed ourselves.

1940, 19 MAY. BROADCAST, LONDON. (BLOOD, 333.)

The strain of protracted war is hard and severe upon the men at the executive summit of great countries, however lightly care may seem to sit upon them. They have need of all the help and comfort their fellow countrymen can give them.

1943, 30 JUNE. GUILDHALL, LONDON.
(ONWARDS, 123.)

Intelligence

My Rt. Hon. Friend the Member for Devonport [Mr. Leslie Hore-Belisha] and some others have spoken of the importance in war of full and accurate intelligence of the movements and intentions of the enemy. That is one of those glimpses of the obvious and of the obsolete with which his powerful speech abounded.

1941, 7 MAY.

I do not admit the assumption that the enemy knows all that is attributed to him.

1941, 1 JUNE. (WW2 III, 686–7.)

Legality and justice

There can be no justice if in a mortal struggle the aggressor tramples down every sentiment of humanity, and if those who resist him remain entangled in the tatters of violated legal conventions.

1940, 30 MARCH. BROADCAST, LONDON.
(BLOOD, 288–9.)

Limited war

We hope there will be no other wars, but even if there are wars in the future, we need not assume that they will be world wars involving all the Powers of the world, with no outside Powers to impose a restraint upon the passions of the belligerents or to judge of the merits of their cause.

1932, 13 MAY.

Machinery of war

Machines save life, machine-power is a substitute for man-power, brains will save blood, manoeuvre is a great diluting agent to slaughter and can be made to reduce the quantity of slaughter required to effect any particular object. Generally it is not considered in the simple use of force but in the adroit augmentation and application of force. A great manoeuvre of war, the kind of manoeuvres for which the great generals of the past were rendered famous, bear the same relation to the ordinary application of force as the pulley or lever in its ordinary application of power.

1917, 5 MARCH.

Magnanimity

I read your newspapers and the reports of recent meetings industriously and all reveal the same spirit. "Give them a lesson they will never forget." "Make an example." "Condign punishment." "Our turn now." These are the phrases or ideas which recur. It is the spirit of revenge. It is wrong, first of all because it is morally wicked; and secondly because it is practically foolish. Revenge may be sweet, but it is also most expensive...While we continue to prosecute the war with tireless energy and remorselessly beat down all who resist—to the last man if necessary—we must also make it easy for the enemy to accept defeat. We must tempt as well as compel.

1900, 29 MARCH. NATAL, SOUTH AFRICA. (OB, CV1/2, 1162.)

Letter to the Natal Witness *urging a lenient post-war settlement with the Boers.*

I have always urged fighting wars and other contentions with might and main till overwhelming victory, and then offering the hand of friendship to the vanquished. Thus, I have always been against the Pacifists during the quarrel, and against the Jingoes at its close... Lord Birkenhead mentioned to me a Latin quotation which seems to embody this idea extremely well. *"Parcere subjectis et debellare superbos,"* which he translated finely, "Spare the conquered and war down the proud." I seem to have come very near achieving this thought by my own untutored reflections. The Romans have often forestalled many of my best ideas, and I must concede to them the patent rights in this maxim.

1930. (MEL, 346.)

WSC favoured a policy of conciliation towards the Boers after their defeat in South Africa. For another appearance of this Latin quotation see Leadership...Magnanimity.

Matériel

Every morning in the remote nothingness there appeared a black speck growing larger and clearer, until with a whistle and a welcome clatter, amid the aching silence of ages, the "material" train arrived, carrying its own water and 2,500 yards of rails, sleepers, and accessories. At noon came another speck, developing in a similar manner into a supply train, also carrying its own water, food and water for the half-battalion of the escort and the 2,000 artificers and platelayers, and the letters,

newspapers, sausages, jam, whiskey, soda, and cigarettes which enable the Briton to conquer the world without discomfort.

1899. (RIVER I, 291.)

Victory is the beautiful, bright-coloured flower. Transport is the stem without which it could never have blossomed. Yet even the military student, in his zeal to master the fascinating combinations of the actual conflict, often forgets the far more intricate complications of supply.

1899. (RIVER I, 276.)

It is true that as against a civilized foe, it is most undesirable that the Dum-Dum bullet should be used, and I believe that in the early days of the South African War a good deal of inconvenience was caused by the fact that the ammunition had to be changed.

1906, 19 JULY.

Dum-Dum bullets, designed to expand on impact, appeared in the early 1890s at the Dum Dum arsenal near Calcutta, India.

It would not make any difference whether the enemy declared oil to be contraband or not. His declaration would remain a dead-letter unless or until he was able to make it effective by force. Unless he were able to stop on the seas oil ships attracted to this country by high prices, his calling oil contraband would make absolutely no difference to us or to it. The oil would come just the same and it would burn just as well.

1914, 17 JUNE.

There is no such thing as a maximum. The more heavy guns, the more ammunition, and the more long-range guns you have behind your trench lines, the more you save the lives of our own soldiers and accelerate the conclusion of the war.

1916, 24 JULY.

The union under one authority of design and supply is the foundation of production on a great scale, and this is specially true when the character of the production is constantly varying and developing. The interests of design and supply are naturally at variance, design seeking a swift and immediate road to perfection, and supply succeeding only through standardized output.

1918, 25 APRIL.

My Rt. Hon. Friend [Foreign Secretary Sir John Simon] said that he wished to make it more difficult for the invader, and for that reason, I gather, heavy guns, tanks and poison gas are to be relegated to the evil category of offensive weapons. The invasion of France by Germany in 1914, however, reached its climax without the employment of any of these weapons at all. The heavy gun is to be described as an offensive weapon. It is all right in a fortress; there it is virtuous and pacific in its character; but bring it out into the field—and, of course, if it were needed it would be brought out into the field—and it immediately becomes naughty, peccant, militaristic, and has to be placed under the ban of civilization.

1932, 13 MAY.

In these sombre fields in the first year you have to sow, and in the second year you harrow; the third year is your harvest. In the first year you make your machine tools and designs. In the second year you make your plants and lay them out. You marshal and secure your labour, skilled and unskilled. In the third year come deliveries. No doubt all those processes overlap and you get, over three years, a yield rising very sharply in the latter period; but broadly speaking, the effective result comes only in the third year.

1936, 21 MAY.

Churchill spoke from experience, having been Minister of Munitions for the last two years of WWI.

Medals

The object of giving medals, stars and ribbons is to give pride and pleasure to those who have deserved them. At the same time a distinction is something which everybody does not possess. If all have it, it is of less value. There must, therefore, be heartburnings and disappointments on the border line. A medal glitters, but it also casts a shadow. The task of drawing up regulations for such awards is one which does not admit of a perfect solution....All that is possible is to give the greatest satisfaction to the greatest number and to hurt the feelings of the fewest.

1944, 22 MARCH.

Military branches

No satisfactory line of division can really be drawn between the Navy and the Air, between the Air and the Army, and between the Navy and the Army. Every attempt to draw such a line has failed.

1922, 21 MARCH.

Military commanders

I like commanders on land and sea and in the air to feel they have behind them a strong Government...They will not run risks unless they feel that they need not look over their shoulders or worry about what is happening at home, unless they feel they can concentrate their gaze upon the enemy.

1942, 2 JULY.

You may take the most gallant sailor, the most intrepid airman, or the most audacious soldier, put them at a table together—what do you get? The sum of their fears.

1943, 16 NOVEMBER. (MACMILLAN, BLAST, 352.)

Churchill's reply when someone remarked that the Chiefs of Staff system was a good one. He began by saying "Not at all. It leads to weak and faltering decisions – or rather indecisions."

"It would seem," as I wrote, "that the sum of all American fears is to be multiplied by the sum of all British fears, faithfully contributed by each Service."

1951. (WW2 IV, 584.)

On differences of opinion between the American and British military leaders on how to exploit the victory in North Africa in 1942.

Misfortunes of war

In war misfortunes may come from faults or errors in the High Command. They may also come from the enemy being far too strong, or fighting far too well.

1942, 23 APRIL.

One set of adverse circumstances may counterbalance and even cancel out another.

1951. (WW2 IV, 457.)

Negotiations

Many things in life are settled by the two-stage method. For instance, a man is not prevented from saying, "Will you marry me, darling?" because he has not got the marriage contract, drawn up by the family solicitors, in his pocket.

1943, 31 JULY. (WW2 V, 59.)

WSC to Anthony Eden, suggesting that the Italians might surrender more rapidly if they were sent "an envoy" than the "legal verbiage of the Instrument of Surrender".

There is nothing improper in belligerents meeting to discuss their affairs even while actual battles are going on. All history abounds in precedents.

1954, 25 FEBRUARY.

Operation names

Operations in which large numbers of men may lose their lives ought not to be described by code-words which imply a boastful and over-confident sentiment, such as "Triumphant," or, conversely, which are calculated to invest the plan with an air of despondency, such as "Woebetide," "Massacre," "Jumble," "Trouble," "Fidget," "Flimsy," "Pathetic," and "Jaundice." They ought not to be names of a frivolous character, such as "Bunnyhug," "Billingsgate," "Aperitif," and "Ballyhoo." They should not be ordinary words often used in other connections, such as "Flood," "Smooth," "Sudden," "Supreme," "Fullforce," and "Fullspeed." Names of living people— Ministers or Commanders—should be avoided; e.g. "Bracken."

2. After all, the world is wide, and intelligent thought will readily supply an unlimited number of well-sounding names which do not suggest the character of the operation or disparage it in any way and do not enable some widow or mother to say that her son was killed in an operation called "Bunnyhug" or "Ballyhoo."

3. Proper names are good in this field. The heroes of antiquity, figures from Greek and Roman mythology, the constellations and stars, famous racehorses, names of British or American war heroes, could be used, provided they fall within the rules above.

1943, 8 AUGUST. (WW2 V, 583.)

Prime Minister to Lord Ismay. In the modern world, this wise advice has been utterly forgotten.

Operations

It often happens in war that an operation which is successful on a small scale becomes vicious if it is multiplied by three, four, or five times.

1940, 8 MAY.

Military operations must be judged by the success which attends them rather than by the sentiments which inspired them, though these, too, may play their part in the verdict of history and in the survival of races.

1941, 7 MAY.

An operation of war cannot be thought out like building a bridge; certainty is not demanded, and genius, improvisation, and energy of mind must have their parts.

1951. (WW2 IV, 831.)

Policy

I have noticed [a tendency in war] to hush everything up, to make everything look as fair as possible, to tell what is called the official truth, to present a version of the truth which contains about seventy-five per cent of the actual article. So long as a force gets a victory somehow, all the ugly facts are smoothed and varnished over, rotten reputations are propped up, and officers known as incapable are allowed to hang on and linger in their commands in the hope that at the end of the war they may be shunted into private life without a scandal.

1901, 12 MARCH.

By a sober and modest conduct, by a skilful diplomacy, we can in part disarm and in part divide the elements of potential danger. But two things have to be considered: First, that our diplomacy depends in great part for its effectiveness upon our naval position; and that our naval strength is the one great balancing force which we can contribute to our own safety and to the peace of the world. Secondly, we are not a young people with a blank record and a scanty inheritance. We have won for ourselves, in times when other powerful nations were paralysed by barbarism or internal war, an exceptional share of the wealth and traffic of the world.

1914, 17 MARCH.

[Any defeatism] should be stamped out...with all the vigour of public opinion.

1918, 8 OCTOBER, GLASGOW. (OB IV, 153.)

Even taking the lowest view of human nature, nations in war do not usually do things which give them no special advantage, and which grievously complicate their own position.

1934, 8 March.

It is quite certain that the British Empire will never fight a war contrary to the Covenant of the League of Nations. Any attempt to embark upon a war of aggrandisement or pride or ambition would break the British Empire into fragments, and any Government that was even suspected of such a motive would be chased from power long before its machinations could become effective.

1935, 24 October.

It is nearly always right to pursue a beaten foe with all one's strength, and even to run serious risks in doing so; but, of course, there comes a time when the pursuers outstrip the utmost limits of their own supplies, and where the enemy, falling back on his own depots, is able once again to form a front.

1944, London. (Dawn, 237.)

The British and Americans do not war with races or governments as such. Tyranny, external or internal, is our foe whatever trappings and disguises it wears, whatever language it speaks, or perverts.

1953, 4 July. Dorchester Hotel, London. (Balance, 310.)

Prisoners of war

I'm not a bit soft, but I can't stand for killing in mass. You need not accept a man's surrender, but if you do you mustn't kill him. The Russians would blot out their prisoners-of-war without a moment's hesitation.

1944, 9 October, Moscow. (Moran, 208.)

What is a prisoner of war? He is a man who has tried to kill you and, having failed to kill you, asks you not to kill him. Long before the Christian revelation, the world had found out by practice that mercy towards a beaten enemy was well worth while and that it was much easier to gain control over wide areas by taking prisoners than by making everyone fight to the death against you.

1952, 1 July.

This statement, made in mature hindsight after World War II, is closer to Churchill's true beliefs about the policy of "unconditional surrender" which he was obliged to defend after Roosevelt enunciated it in 1943. See World War II...Unconditional surrender.

Resistance

One thing is absolutely certain, namely, that victory will never be found by taking the line of least resistance.

1940, 15 January. (WW2 I, 438.)

It is not only a question of the time that is gained by fighting strongly, even if at a disadvantage, for important points. There is also this vitally important principle of stubborn resistance to the will of the enemy.

1941, 10 June.

Responsibility

Any clever person can make plans for winning a war if he has no responsibility for carrying them out.

1951. (WW2 IV, 499.)

Risk-taking

"Safety first" is the road to ruin in war, even if you had the safety, which you have not.

1940, 3 November. (WW2 II, 477.)

...you will not have any means of abridging this war, or, indeed, of emerging from it safely, unless risks are run. Risks do imply that when forfeit is exacted, as it may be when a great ship is sunk or some bold attack repulsed with heavy slaughter, the House must stand by the Government and the military commanders.

1940, 19 December.

The Admirals, Generals and Air Marshals chant their stately hymn of "Safety First." The Shinwells, Wintertons and Hore-Belishas do their best to keep us up to the mark. In the midst of this I have to restrain my natural pugnacity by sitting on my own head. How bloody!

1941, 30 October. (OB VI, 1227.)

You have to run risks. There are no certainties in war. There is a precipice on either side of you—a precipice of caution and a precipice of over-daring.

1943, 21 September.

Science and medicine in warfare

It was a curious fact that while soldiers and sailors for scientific war might be produced more rapidly than in former times, the great weapon took a longer time to produce.

1903, 14 MAY.

On the time necessary to create and maintain a modern navy.

Science and invention are sweeping all before them. The same science applies to all three Services alike, and its application must play a large part in all your plans and outlook. Nothing like this was known in the 19th century, and in those days the segregation of the Services seemed comparatively simple. The Navy, to quote Lord Fisher, was a dismal mystery surrounded by seasickness, and had nothing in common, except good conduct, with the barrack square and the red-coated Army of those days. The Air Force did not exist.

1934, 21 MARCH.

Fanned by the fierce winds of war, medicine, science and surgical art have advanced unceasingly, hand in hand. There has certainly been no lack of subjects for treatment. The medical profession at least cannot complain of unemployment through lack of raw material.

1947, 10 SEPTEMBER. GUILDHALL, LONDON.
(EUROPE, 137.)

Speech to the International Congress of Physicians.

Secrecy

It would not be a good thing for me to go into details of this. It might suggest ideas to other people which they have not thought of, and they would not be likely to give us any of their ideas in exchange.

1940, 18 JUNE.

...we have also a number of interesting variants of very great ingenuity, which I cannot tell the House about today, because we do not know whether the enemy have had an opportunity of testing them and tasting them. It is only when I know they know that the secrets can be unfolded. One has to be very careful, because people object very much indeed if anything is revealed which seems to take away

any chance that our troops may enjoy in this country and with our Allies.

1944, 2 AUGUST.

I sympathize very much, as an old former journalist and war correspondent, with the many able representatives of the Press who waited here from day to day, but I know they understood. All these matters have to be secret, and there cannot be any detailed information given here from day to day, or even at the end of the proceedings. The enemy will learn soon enough, in due course, all that we have decided here. I think we said this last year, now I come to think of it—almost these very words. Well, they have learned. What was then secret is now public. What was then concealed is now apparent. What was then in egg is now afoot. What was then a tender sprout has become a gigantic forest tree. What was then a design has become a blow, a mortal blow to the greatest of the military powers which have ranged themselves up against civilization and the progress of the world.

1944, 16 SEPTEMBER, QUEBEC. (DAWN, 172.)

Strategy

...good strategy even in failure often produces compensations.

1936. (MARLBOROUGH III, 242.)

Surrender

Military defeat or miscalculation can be redeemed. The fortunes of war are fickle and changing. But an act of shame would deprive us of the respect which we now enjoy throughout the world, and this would sap the vitals of our strength.

1941, 27 APRIL. BROADCAST, LONDON.
(UNRELENTING, 94.)

Commenting on the grim military situation in Greece, where Britain had vainly striven to aid that invaded country.

If one has to submit it is wasteful not to do so with the best grace possible.

1943, 10 OCTOBER. (WW2 V, 193.)

...the term "unconditional surrender" does not mean that the German people will be enslaved or destroyed. It means, however, that the Allies will not be bound to them at the moment of surrender by any pact or obligation. There will be, for instance, no question of the Atlantic Charter applying to Germany as a matter of right and barring territorial transferences or adjustments in enemy countries. No such arguments will be admitted by us as were used by Germany after the last war, saying that they surrendered in consequence of President Wilson's fourteen points. Unconditional surrender means that the victors have a free hand. It does not mean that they are entitled to behave in a barbarous manner, nor that they wish to blot out Germany from among the nations of Europe. If we are bound, we are bound by our own consciences to civilization. We are not to be bound to the Germans as the result of a bargain struck.

1944, 22 FEBRUARY.

Churchill was forced into defending the policy of Unconditional Surrender first enunciated by Roosevelt at the Casablanca Conference in 1943. WSC feared that the denial of any possibility of terms might cause more Germans to fight to the bitter end, extending the war. See Victory.

Tactics

In war, if you are not able to beat your enemy at his own game, it is nearly always better to adopt some striking variant, and not to be content merely with doing the same thing as your enemy is doing, only not doing it quite so well or on quite so large a scale.

1916, 17 MAY.

Ten-Years Rule

Now, I think there was a great deal to be said for the ten-years rule in 1919 and in 1924. As a matter of fact, the time has passed—the ten years have expired without the world being disturbed by a major war. As a means of giving a rough-and-ready guide to Departments the ten-years rule in those days was valuable, but, of course, it had to be revised each year. Every year you had to see whether it was ten, nine or eight years, or whether you had to abandon the principle altogether. There is nothing, I think, that anyone who supported that principle in those years after the War has any reason to regret.

1936, 10 MARCH.

The Ten-Years Rule, used in military planning, was based on the assumption that there would be no major war for the next decade; it was abandoned in the late 1930s.

Victorian wars

This kind of war was full of fascinating thrills. It was not like the Great War. Nobody expected to be killed. Here and there in every regiment or battalion, half a dozen, a score, at the worst thirty or forty, would pay the forfeit; but to the great mass of those who took part in the little wars of Britain in those vanished light-hearted days, this was only a sporting element in a splendid game. Most of us were fated to see a war where the hazards were reversed, where death was the general expectation and severe wounds were counted as lucky escapes, where whole brigades were shorn away under the steel flail of artillery and machine-guns, where the survivors of one tornado knew that they would certainly be consumed in the next or the next after that.

1930. (MEL, 195.)

Victory

Once you are so unfortunate as to be drawn into a war, no price is too great to pay for an early and victorious peace.

1901, 13 MAY.

There are transactions in the government of states on which people may hold strong opinions, but which it may be much wiser, in the tolerance of overwhelming victory, deliberately to consign to silence and oblivion.

1906, 21 MARCH.

An early manifestation of Churchill's consistent admonition: "In victory, magnanimity."

The utility of war even to the victor may in most cases be an illusion. Certainly all wars of every kind will be destitute of any positive advantage to the British Empire, but war itself, if ever it comes, will not be an illusion—even a single bullet will be found real enough.

1912, 18 MARCH.

There are two maxims which should always be acted upon in the hour of victory....The first is Do not be carried away by success into demanding more than is right or prudent. The second is Do not disband your army until you have got your terms.

1919, 3 MARCH.

The second of these maxims was invoked by Churchill a quarter century later, when he urged Truman not to withdraw American forces from Germany until an acceptable arrangement had been worked out with the Soviets.

War dead

There is really no limitation to the number of different ways in which the desire to show reverence and affection to the memory of the fallen, and to preserve that memory, have manifested themselves. But the great mass of those who fell could not indulge in expensive monuments, and the thing that is deeply ingrained in soldierly breasts is that all should be treated alike, general and private, prince and peasant, all who lie there in common honour, and that the wealthy should forgo in this matter that which their wealth would enable them to obtain.

1919, 17 DECEMBER.

Remember we have a missing generation, we must never forget that—the flower of the past, lost in the great battles of the last war. There ought to be another generation in between these young men and us older figures who are soon, haply, to pass from the scene. There ought to be another generation of men, with their flashing lights and leading figures. We must do all we can to try to fill the gap, and, as I say, there is no safer thing to do than to run risks in youth.

1944, 29 NOVEMBER.

War debts

All the greatest economists, John Stuart Mill at their head, have always spoken of the evils of borrowing for the purposes of war, and have pointed out that as far as possible posterity should be relieved and the cost of what is consumed in the war be met at the time. That is a counsel of perfection, but nobody has ever come nearer to it than the late Chancellor of the Exchequer [Sir Kingsley Wood].

1943, 22 SEPTEMBER.

War industries

There is no doubt that this method of the widely distributed manufacture of components ought to be as much a part of the life of an industrial country in this present unhappy modern age as the practice of archery on the village green was in medieval England. It is the simplest and most primary method by which the freedom of a country can be assured, and it is the very heart of modern national defence.

1936, 10 MARCH.

There is also a certain increase in short absenteeism. Not only in the mining trade, but throughout the industries of the country, there are small ailments which I must say, I think are not entirely dissociated from the dietary changes to which we have subjected ourselves and the régime under which we live.

1943, 13 OCTOBER.

The first year yields nothing; the second very little; the third a lot; and the fourth a flood.

1948. (WW2 I, 263.)

War profiteers

We hear a lot about the conscription of wealth. I prefer the salutary principle of taking the profit out of war. If we should be involved, unhappily, in a war, let us make sure, by elaborate and carefully considered legislation beforehand, that no one is going to come out of it with private gain while others are dying for their country.

1938, 17 NOVEMBER.

Waste

...there is bound to be both extravagance and waste in time of war. In our country, accustomed to strict Parliamentary supervision, this waste arises very rarely from fraud or corruption. It arises sometimes from inefficiency, and is capable of correction. It arises most of all, I think, from excessive zeal in preparing against dangers which often change, and sometimes fade as soon as they are faced; and still more from the well-intentioned desire of every branch and section to reach 100 per cent standard of safety, which, of course, is never attainable in war.

1940, 27 FEBRUARY.

Women in war

Women are already playing a great part in this war, but they must play a still greater part. The technical apparatus of modern warfare gives extraordinary opportunities to women. These opportunities must be fully used, and here again the movement must be towards the harder forms of service and nearer to the fighting line.

1941, 2 DECEMBER.

This war effort could not have been achieved if the women had not marched forward in millions and undertaken all kinds of tasks and work for which any other generation but our own…would have considered them unfitted; work in the fields, heavy work in the foundries and in the shops, very refined work on radio and precision instruments, work in the hospitals, responsible clerical work of all kinds, work throughout the munitions factories, work in the mixed batteries…. Nothing has been grudged, and the bounds of women's activities have been definitely, vastly, and permanently enlarged.

1943, 29 SEPTEMBER. ROYAL ALBERT HALL, LONDON. (ONWARDS, 223.)

13
CHURCHILL
AND THE AIR

"We remembered that it was upon the advice of the Air Ministry that Mr. Baldwin had made the speech which produced so great an impression in 1933 when he said that there was really no defence. 'The bomber will always get through.' We had therefore no confidence in any Air Ministry departmental committee...." [45]

"For good luck before I started I put your locket on."
WSC and Clementine with a flying machine at Hendon, 1914.

Churchill was a pilot trainee until a series of near-misses caused him to give it up at the urgent request of his wife. As a young MP, he was a leading proponent of the Air Service as a major branch of the military. As Sir Martin Gilbert has noted, Churchill in 1909 was already urging his colleagues in the British government "to make contact with the Wright Brothers in the United States, in order to be at the cutting edge of the science of aviation". [46]

---

45 Churchill, Winston S., *The Second World War*, vol. I, *The Gathering Storm*. London: Cassell, 1948, 116.
46 Gilbert, Sir Martin, "Churchill and Bombing Policy." Fifth Churchill Lecture, Churchill Centre, Washington, D.C., October 2005; an expanded version of this lecture appeared in the Centre's journal *Finest Hour* 136, Winter 2007–08.

As First Lord of the Admiralty, Churchill established the Royal Naval Air Service, which played important roles both in attacking enemy ground formations near Dunkirk and in attacks on German naval shipping. Before war ended he was already urging Anglo-French cooperation in the design and manufacture of long-distance bombers, which he felt would be much more effective than the ponderous, slow-moving Zeppelins that had threatened London.

As Secretary of State for Air from 1919 to 1921, Churchill argued for adequate funding for the fledgling Royal Air Force, which atrophied in the euphoria following the peace of Versailles. He had no compunction against the use of bombing to serve a greater good: during his ministry he authorised bombing Sinn Fein terrorists in Ireland, insurgents in Iraq, and Arabs who attacked the Jewish town of Petakh Tikvah in Palestine.[47]

During the 1930s, when his lonely voice warned against the rise of Nazi Germany, the military aspect that most concerned Churchill was the air. Repeatedly he harangued the governments of those years, to bolster and expand the Royal Air Force, particularly its fighter squadrons. (See also Chapter 17.) Belatedly and insufficiently equipped as it was, the RAF prevented a German invasion in 1940.

Churchill's pronouncements on air bombardment date from before World War I, when very few of his contemporaries were thinking so far ahead as he. But most of the quotations here are from the Thirties, when the question of air defence was paramount. Unlike Prime Minister Stanley Baldwin, who was resigned to the likelihood of devastating bomber attacks should war ever occur, Churchill argued for defence as well as offence, and came close to advocating what we later knew as radar and surface-to-air missiles. Typically, he felt the frustration of those who saw only reasons for doing nothing. "There is no use gaping vacuously on the problems of the air," he said in 1933. He was for solutions: "guns which fire upwards" (1914), and other methods "to enable the earth to control the air" (1935).

Airmen

All hearts go out to the fighter pilots, whose brilliant actions we see with our own eyes day after day; but we must never forget that all the time, night after night, month after month, our bomber squadrons travel far into Germany, find their targets in the darkness by the highest navigational skill, aim their attacks, often under the heaviest fire, often with serious loss, with deliberate careful discrimination, and inflict shattering blows upon the whole of the technical and war-making structure of the Nazi power. On no part of the Royal Air Force does the weight of the war fall more heavily than on the daylight bombers, who will play an invaluable part in the case of invasion and whose unflinching zeal it has been necessary in the meanwhile on numerous occasions to restrain.

1940, 20 AUGUST.

For more of this speech paying tribute to "The Few", see Chapter 1.

The devotion and gallantry of the attacks on Rotterdam and other objectives are beyond all praise. The charge of the Light Brigade at Balaclava is eclipsed in brightness by these almost daily deeds of fame.

1941, 30 AUGUST. (WW2 III, 730.)

In a daylight raid on German shipping in Rotterdam, seven out of seventeen British bombers had been lost.

Bombing considerations

The Hon. Gentleman opposite made our flesh creep the other night by suggesting the dropping of bombs from airships on the House of Commons. If that event should happen, I am confident that the Members of this House

---

47 Gilbert, op. cit.

would gladly embrace the opportunity of sharing the perils which the soldiers and the sailors have to meet.

1913, 26 MARCH.

In World War II the House of Commons was indeed bombed: on 10 May 1941, the first anniversary of Churchill's becoming Prime Minister.

No responsible officer at the War Office or at the Admiralty whom I ever met before the war anticipated that Zeppelins would be used to drop bombs indiscriminately on undefended towns and the countryside. This was not because of any extravagant belief in human virtue in general, or in German virtue in particular, but because it is reasonable to assume that your enemy will be governed by good sense and by a lively regard for his own interests.

1916, 17 MAY.

This is the moment to attack the enemy, to carry the war into his own country, to make him feel in his own towns and in his own person something of the havoc he has wrought in France and Belgium....While the new heavy French machines, of which you were speaking to me will strike by night at all the nearer objectives, the British, who alone at the moment have the experience, apparatus and plans already made to bomb not only by night but in broad daylight far into Germany, must be assured of the means to carry out their role.

1918, 18 AUGUST. HOTEL RITZ, PARIS.
(OB CV4/1, 377.)

WSC to Louis Loucheur, French Air Minister. The bombers Churchill put in hand made vital raids on German military targets in October 1918, hastening the end of the war.

...no one can doubt that a week or ten days' intensive bombing attack upon London would be a very serious matter indeed. One could hardly expect that less than 30,000 or 40,000 people would be killed or maimed...The most dangerous form of air attack is the attack by incendiary bombs.

1934, 28 NOVEMBER.

Happily, WSC exaggerated the actual effects of the coming Blitz, which were grim enough: during the six years of World War II, when 51,509 were killed in London bombings.

Civil aviation

Civil aviation must fly by itself; the Government cannot possibly hold it up in the air.

1920, 11 MARCH.

I think you may say that civil aviation bears the same relation to the fighting force as the mercantile marine has for so many generations borne to the Royal Navy.

1934, 28 NOVEMBER.

Defence considerations

If war breaks out tomorrow foreign airships, no doubt, might do a certain amount of mischief and damage before they got smashed up, which would not be very long, but it is foolish to suppose that in their present stage of development they could produce results which would decisively influence the course of events.

1913, 26 MARCH.

Passive defence against such an attack is perfectly hopeless and endless. You would have to roof in the world to be quite sure. Something may be done, and something has been done by the provision of guns which fire upwards, and by searchlights which train throughout the entire arc, but the only real security upon which sound military principles will rely is that you should be master of your own air.

1914, 17 MARCH.

There is the same kind of helplessness and hopelessness about dealing with this air problem as there is about dealing with the unemployment problem, or the currency question, or the question of economy. All the evils are vividly portrayed, and the most admirable sentiments are expressed, but as for a practical course of action, solid footholds on which we can tread step by step, there is in this great sphere, as in other spheres of government activity, a gap, a hiatus, a sense that there is no message from the lips of the prophet. There is no use gaping vacuously on the problems of the air. Still less is there any use in indulging in pretence in any form.

1933, 14 MARCH.

...there seem to me to be four lines of protection by which we can secure the best chance, and a good chance, of immunity for our people from the perils of air war—a peaceful foreign policy; the convention regulating air warfare;

the parity in air to invest that convention with validity and, arising out of that parity, a sound system of home defence in addition to all these other arrangements if they all fail.

1934, 8 MARCH.

The flying peril is not a peril from which one can fly. It is necessary to face it where we stand. We cannot possibly retreat. We cannot move London. We cannot move the vast population which is dependent on the estuary of the Thames. We cannot move the naval bases which are established along our southern coasts with the great hereditary naval populations living around them....

Certainly nothing is more necessary, not only to this country but to all peace-loving and peace-interested Powers in the world and to world civilization, than that the good old earth should acquire some means or methods of destroying sky marauders.

1934, 28 NOVEMBER.

...defensive measures against aeroplane attacks...is a matter in which all countries, in my opinion, have a similar interest—all peaceful countries. It is a question not of one country against another, but of the ground against the air, and unless the dwellers upon the earth can manage to secure the air above their heads, it is almost impossible to forecast the misfortunes and fears which this invention, of which the world has proved itself so utterly unworthy, may bring upon them.

1935, 19 MARCH.

[I am] concerned with the methods which can be invented, adopted or discovered to enable the earth to control the air, to enable defence from the ground to exercise control—domination—upon aeroplanes high above its surface....Merely to fire at an aeroplane in the air is like trying to shoot a flying duck with a pea-rifle. What must be aimed at is not the hitting of the aeroplane, but the creation of conditions in the air around the aeroplane which are extremely noxious if not destructive to it....

It is only in the twentieth century that this hateful conception of inducing nations to surrender by terrorizing the helpless civil population and by massacring the women and children has gained acceptance and countenance

amongst men. If it continues, one can clearly see that the conquest of the air may mean the subjugation of mankind and the destruction of our civilization...[we] more than any other nation would gain by such a discovery.

1935, 7 JUNE.

Gliders

Gliders are a wonderful means of training pilots, giving them air sense.

1934, 30 JULY.

Invention and production

There is a danger of these proposals [for experiments with a Wright aeroplane] being considered too amateurish. The problem of the use of aeroplanes is a most important one, and we should place ourselves in communication with Mr Wright himself, and avail ourselves of his knowledge.

1909, 25 FEBRUARY. (OB, CV2/3, 1874.)

Rendered in the first person and in present tense from the report of the Committee of Imperial Defence Sub-Committee on Aerial Navigation.

Why should we fear the air? We have as good technical knowledge as any country. There is no reason to suppose that we cannot make machines as good as any country. We have—though it may be thought conceited to say so—a particular vein of talent in air piloting which is in advance of that possessed by other countries....That being so, I ask the Government to consider profoundly and urgently the whole position of our air defence.

1933, 14 MARCH.

My right Hon. Friend [Sir Thomas Inskip, Minister for the Coordination of Defence]...said that, if we had begun to expand our air force three years ago, or words to that effect, we should be worse off than we are now—we should be cumbered with a mass of inferior machines. This is an altogether new defence for the miscalculation which the Government have admitted in respect of the relative strength of the British and German air forces...[This] was not an accident: this was some deep design, a truly Machiavellian stroke of policy, which enabled us to pretend that a miscalculation had been made while all the time we were holding back in order to steal a march on other countries by the production of great numbers of machines of the latest type. That is a most remarkable defence.

1936, 20 JULY.

We have learned to fly. What prodigious changes are involved in that new accomplishment! Man has parted company with his trusty friend the horse and has sailed into the azure with the eagles, eagles being represented by the infernal [loud laughter]—er, I mean internal—combustion engine, ah, *engine*. Where, then, are those broad oceans, those vast staring deserts? They are shrinking beneath our very eyes. Even elderly Parliamentarians like myself are forced to acquire a high degree of mobility.

1943, 6 SEPTEMBER. HARVARD UNIVERSITY, CAMBRIDGE, MASSACHUSETTS. (ONWARDS, 182.)

"Ah, engine" is in the recorded speech.

When in 1940 the chief responsibility fell upon me and our national survival depended upon victory in the air, I had the advantage of a layman's insight into the problems of air warfare resulting from four long years of study and thought based upon the fullest official and technical information. Although I have never tried to be learned in technical matters, this mental field was well lit for me.

1948. (WW2 I, 124.)

Offence

In an aerial war the greatest form of defence will undoubtedly be offence.

1922, 21 MARCH.

...there is a sensible improvement in our means of dealing with German raids upon this Island, and a very great measure of security has been given to this country in day-time—and we are glad that the days are lengthening. But now the moonlight periods are also looked forward to by the Royal Air Force as an opportunity for inflicting severe deterrent losses upon the raiders, as well as for striking hard at the enemy in his own territory. The fact that our technical advisers welcome the light—daylight, moonlight, starlight—and that we do not rely for our protection on darkness, clouds and mists, as would have been the case some

time ago, is pregnant with hope and meaning.

1941, 9 APRIL.

Broadly speaking, our agreed programme is a crescendo of activity on the Continent, starting with an ever increasing air offensive both by night and day and more frequent and large-scale raids, in which United States troops will take part.

1942, 17 APRIL. (WW2 IV, 287.)

Hitler made a contract with the demon of the air, but the contract ran out before the job was done, and the demon has taken on an engagement with the rival firm. How truly it has been said that nations and people very often fall by the very means which they have used and built their hopes upon, for their rising-up!

1942, 20 JUNE.

Royal Air Force

These squadrons are formed very much in the way in which we are assured the human race was originally formed. A rib is taken from one body and starts out on an independent existence of its own.

1937, 27 JANUARY.

There never has been, I suppose, in all the world, in all the history of war, such an opportunity for youth. The Knights of the Round Table, the Crusaders, all fall back into the past—not only distant but prosaic; these young men, going forth every morn to guard their native land and all that we stand for, holding in their hands these instruments of colossal and shattering power, of whom it may be said that "Every morn brought forth a noble chance, And every chance brought forth a noble knight," deserve our gratitude, as do all of the brave men who, in so many ways and on so many occasions, are ready, and continue ready, to give life and all for their native land.

1940, 4 JUNE.

The quotation (two lines in the original) is from Tennyson's "Morte d'Arthur".

The three great days of 15th August, 15th September and 27th September [1940] have proved to all the world that here at home over our own island we have the mastery of the air. That is a tremendous fact. It marks the laying down of the office [Chief of the Air Staff] which he has held with so much distinction for the last three years by Sir Cyril Newall, and it enables us to record our admiration to him for the services he has rendered. It also marks the assumption of new and immense responsibilities by Sir Charles Portal, an officer who, I have heard from every source and every side, commands the enthusiastic support and confidence of the Royal Air Force.

1940, 8 OCTOBER.

Excluding Dominion and Allied squadrons working with the Royal Air Force, the British islanders have lost 38,300 pilots and air crews killed and 10,400 missing, and over 10,000 aircraft since the beginning of the war and they have made nearly 900,000 sorties into the North European theatre.

1944, 22 FEBRUARY.

Strength of air forces

It is also said, "What do we want all this service aviation for? Instead of this let us go in for some splendid new development of civil aviation"....I do not say for a moment that those are not good objects in themselves if only we had the money for them, but when it comes to cutting in upon necessities in order to provide what, after all, at their best are conveniences, surely we should be committing a very great folly....A day would come when powerful nations, beginning to recover from the War, and to gather their power together again, would become the cause of rumours in this country. There would be rumours that in the heart of Germany or Russia there were great aerial developments of a very serious character, or of a character which might easily have a military complexion.

1920, 1 MARCH. (CS III, 3075–7.)

Given that Churchill is frequently accused of having engineered the disarmament in the 1920s which he deplored in the 1930s, this remark is an interesting counterpoint.

Not to have an adequate air force in the present state of the world is to compromise the foundations of national freedom and independence.

1933, 14 MARCH.

Air Estimates introduced in the Commons had placed strong emphasis on combating locusts and carrying supplies to flood-stricken parts of Britain.

I cannot conceive how...we can delay in establishing the principle of having an air force at least as strong as that of any Power that can get at us. I think that is a perfectly reasonable thing to do. It would only begin to put us back to the position in which we were brought up. We have lived under the shield of the navy. To have an Air Force as strong as the air force of France or Germany, whichever is the stronger, ought to be the decision which Parliament should take, and which the National Government should proclaim.

1934, 7 FEBRUARY.

...if Germany continues this expansion and if we continue to carry out our scheme, then some time in 1936 Germany will be definitely and substantially stronger in the air than Great Britain.

1934, 30 JULY.

It is absolutely certain that we have lost air parity already both in the number of machines and in their quality. It is certain that at the end of this year we shall be far worse off relatively than we are now. Our home defence force will be for a long period ahead a rapidly diminishing fraction of the German air force.

1935, 2 MAY.

Air armaments are not expressed merely by the air squadrons in existence or the aeroplanes which have been made; they cannot be considered apart from the capacity to manufacture. If, for instance, there were two countries which each had 1,000 first-line aeroplanes, but one of which had the power to manufacture at the rate of 100 a month and the other at the rate of 1,000 a month, it is perfectly clear that air parity would not exist between those two countries very long.

1935, 31 MAY.

The air power of any country cannot be measured by the number of aeroplanes, nor by any of the particular definitions which are given. It must be measured by the number of aeroplanes which can be placed in the air simultaneously and maintained in action month after month. It is dependent not only on the number of organised squadrons, but upon the expansive power of industrial plant.

1936, 10 MARCH.

The sole method that is open is for us to regain our old island independence by acquiring that supremacy in the air which we were promised, that security in our air defences which we were assured we had, and thus to make ourselves an island once again. That, in all this grim outlook, shines out as the overwhelming fact. An effort at rearmament, the like of which has not been seen, ought to be made forthwith, and all the resources of this country and all its united strength should be bent to that task.

1938, 5 OCTOBER.

Threat from the air

This cursed, hellish invention and development of war from the air has revolutionized our position. We are not the same kind of country we used to be when we were an island, only 20 years ago. That is the thing that is borne in upon me more than anything else. It is not merely a question of what we like and what we do not like, of ambitions and desires, of rights and interests, but it is a question of safety and independence. That is what is involved now as never before.

1934, 7 FEBRUARY.

I agree with what I imagine were his feelings when he [Stanley Baldwin] wished that neither aeroplanes nor submarines had ever been invented. I am sure they have both been deeply detrimental to the special interests and security of this island; and I agree also with his general theme that the air power may either end war or end civilization.

1933, 14 MARCH.

In November 1932 Baldwin had stated

I think it is well for the man in the street to realise that there is no power on earth which can protect him from being bombed. Whatever people may tell him, the bomber will always get through. ....The only defence is in offence, which means that you have to kill more women and children more quickly than the enemy if you want to save yourselves.

Churchill believed in air defence as well as offence.

When one considers the enormous range of foreign aeroplanes and the speeds at which they travel—200, 230 and 240 miles an hour—it is evident that every part of this small island is...almost equally within range of attack.

1934, 28 NOVEMBER.

You came into big things as an accident of naval power when you are an island. The world had confidence in you. You became the workshop of the world. You populated the island beyond its capacity. Through an accident of air power you will probably cease to exist.

1935. OB V, 838.

Wing-Commander Tor Anderson (who delivered much information to Churchill on air strength in the 1930s) to Martin Gilbert:

You would give Churchill a new idea, he would say nothing. Two hours later, while feeding the goldfish he would come out with the flaw in what you said...He said [this] to me once speaking of Britain, and, as it were, to Britain.

From being the least vulnerable of all nations we have, through developments in the air, become the most vulnerable.

1935, 19 MARCH.

It may be that great ordeals are coming to us in this Island from the air. We shall do our best to give a good account of ourselves; and we must always remember that the command of the seas will enable us to bring the immense resources of Canada and the New World into play as a decisive ultimate air factor, a factor beyond the reach of what we have to give and take over here.

1939, 1 OCTOBER.

It seems quite clear that no invasion on a scale beyond the capacity of our land forces to crush speedily is likely to take place from the air until our Air Force has been definitely overpowered. In the meantime, there may be raids by parachute troops and attempted descents of airborne soldiers.

1940, 18 JUNE.

14

CHURCHILL
AND THE ARMY

"Ascetics and recluses have in their endeavours to look beyond the grave suffered worse things. Nor will the soldier in the pursuit of fame and the enjoyment of the pleasures of war, be exposed to greater discomforts than Diogenes in his tub, or the Trappists in their monastery." [48]

"Why don't we go across and have a look at the other side?"
Crossing the Rhine into Germany, 25 March 1945.

Although Churchill twice headed the Navy and was a consistent supporter of the Air Force, his own training and fighting experiences were with the Army. He read widely on military strategy and tactics, both as a cadet at Sandhurst and later. He knew the subject thoroughly: sufficient indeed to drive generals such as Alanbrooke to apoplexy as he challenged, prodded and criticised them, while never in the end taking a decision against the concerted opinion of his chiefs of staff. Professor Paul Addison said he was "authoritative...but not authoritarian". And he was a very good listener.

---

48 Churchill, Winston S., *The Story of the Malakand Field Force*. London: Longmans, Green, Silver Library edition, 1899, 253.

Churchill's view of a soldier's life began with the romance of Queen Victoria's little wars: his breathtaking description of his first sight of the Dervish Army at Omdurman is perhaps so bedizened with colourful prose because he had known in advance that this splendid foe would soon be cut to ribbons by British firepower. But later, when he experienced trench warfare and observed the horrible waste of human life on the Western Front of World War I, he realised "what vile and wicked folly" it all was. He hoped there would be, as he wrote to Lord Beaverbrook, "no more war".

Quotations here involve officers and men, with Army technical apparatus such as tanks, with cavalry and infantry. His praise of the "Desert Army" of World War II knew no bounds; his description of the cavalry has all the verve of a Victorian novel; his appreciation of the sacrifice and devotion of the troops is consistent throughout his canon. Having trained for, fought in and reported five wars himself, he was well qualified to lead his country when the greatest war in history threatened her life.

Aphorisms and Reflections

The army was not an inanimate substance, it was a living thing. Regiments were not like houses; they could not be pulled down and altered structurally to suit the convenience of the occupier and the caprice of the owner. They were more like plants: they grew slowly if they were to grow strong; they were easily affected by conditions of temperature and soil; and if they were blighted or transplanted they were apt to wither, and then they could only be revived by copious floods of public money.

1904, 8 AUGUST.

...when an army has been brought into the field in the best condition, in the largest possible numbers, in a spirit of the highest enthusiasm, at the most favourable season, and on the best possible ground—then, I think, when our army has been brought into that situation, we can afford to await the supreme arbitrament with a cool and serene composure; and this mood of composure and of calmness may ripen into a kind of joyous and warlike heartiness, if we can also feel that the cause for which we are fighting is broadly and grandly a true and righteous cause.

1909, 9 OCTOBER. NATIONAL LIBERAL CLUB, LONDON. (LIBERALISM, 309.)

The object of the army is to produce war power. Everything else that takes place leading to the lining up of men in battle is the preliminary steps [sic] by which the final result is achieved.

1916, 23 MAY.

In making an army, three elements are necessary, men, weapons and money. There must also be time.

1948, 1 DECEMBER

Army, American

I must pay my tribute to the United States Army, not only in their valiant and ruthless battle-worthy qualities, but also in the skill of their commanders and the excellence of their supply arrangements. When one remembers that the United States four or five years ago was a peace-loving Power, without any great body of troops or munitions, and with only a very small regular army to draw their commanders from, the American achievement is truly amazing. After the intense training they have received for nearly three years, or more than three years in some cases, their divisions are now composed of regular professional soldiers whose military quality is out of all comparison with hurriedly-raised war-time levies.

1944, 28 SEPTEMBER.

Army, British

...standing armies, which abound on the European continent, are not indigenous to the British soil; they do not flourish in our climate, they are not suited to our national character, and though with artificial care and at a huge and disproportionate cost we may cultivate and preserve them, they will after all only be poor, stunted, sickly plants of foreign origin.

1901, 13 MAY.

England, through the character of her people—who did not mind fighting, but detested drill—necessarily had very largely to depend, and her insular position made it possible for her to do, in great crises, on an army of emergency.

1903, 24 FEBRUARY.

It was an extraordinary thing that, although they had only a small army, it was not well-armed, and although it was such an expensive army, it was practically without quick-firing guns.

1903, 16 JULY.

Army, British Eighth (World War II)

This noble Desert Army, which has never doubted its power to beat the enemy, and whose pride had suffered cruelly from retreats and disasters which they could not understand, regained in a week its ardour and self-confidence. Historians may explain Tobruk. The Eighth Army has done better: it has avenged it.

1942, 11 NOVEMBER.

...when history is written and all the facts are known, your feats will gleam and glow, and will be a source of song and story long after we who are gathered here have passed away.

1943, 3 FEBRUARY, TRIPOLI. (ONWARDS, 11.)

Here is one more example, if there need be, of Churchill's magnificent use of short, simple words and compact sentences.

The Desert Army is the product of three years of trial and error and the continued perfecting of transport, communications, supplies and signals, and the rapid moving forward of airfields and the like.

1943, 11 FEBRUARY.

Army, Dervish

The dawn is growing fast. Veil after veil is lifted from the landscape. What is this shimmering in the distant plain? Nay—it is lighter now—what are these dark markings beneath the shimmer? *They are there!* These enormous black smears are thousands of men; the shimmering is the glinting of their weapons....A glorious sunrise is taking place behind us; but we are admiring something else. It is already light enough to use field-glasses. The dark masses are changing their values. They are already becoming lighter

than the plain; they are fawn-coloured. Now they are a kind of white, while the plain is dun. In front of us is a vast array four or five miles long. It fills the horizon till it is blocked out on our right by the serrated silhouette of Surgham Peak. This is an hour to live.

1930. (MEL, 198.)

Churchill's mesmerising account of his first sight of the Dervish Army at Omdurman, 1898.

Artillery

Now I must say something about the artillery. I've had very little help from our Chairman because he was mostly on the bow and arrow; after that we got to the musketoon and the tripod, and there there was the period when our artillery really came boldly out on the battlefield.

1953, 23 APRIL. ST. GEORGE'S DAY DINNER, HONOURABLE ARTILLERY COMPANY. (ALLIANCE, 36.)

The Chairman was apparently Alanbrooke, though he is not identified in the texts. The double "there" is as stated.

Cavalry

It was true that the lance was not so noticeable in time of war as in time of peace, but even then the lance-pole, showing up above hedgerows and kopjes, was a sure tell-tale of the movement of mounted men. I hope the Government would go boldly forward and throw away "ironmongery" altogether. Modern war was fought with firearms, and if cavalry were to play a great role on the battlefield in the future they would have to use modern weapons, and not the sharp sticks and long irons with which the wars of savagery and medieval chivalry were conducted.

1904, 14 APRIL. (CZARNOMSKI, 196.)

...cavalry manoeuvre in column and fight in line....even divisions of cavalry could be made to present a front in an incredibly short time as the preliminary to that greatest of all cavalry events—the Charge. It is a shame that War should have flung all this aside in its greedy, base, opportunist march, and should turn instead to chemists in spectacles, and chauffeurs pulling levers of airplanes or machine guns.

1930. (MEL, 78.)

In one respect a cavalry charge is very like ordinary life. So long as you are all right, firmly in your saddle, your horse in hand, and well armed, lots of enemies will give you a wide berth. But as soon as you have lost a stirrup, have a rein cut, have dropped your weapon, are wounded, or your horse is wounded, then is the moment when from all quarters enemies rush upon you....

Suddenly in the midst of the troop up sprung a Dervish. How he got there I do not know. He must have leaped out of some scrub or hole. All the troopers turned upon him thrusting with their lances: but he darted to and fro causing for the moment a frantic commotion. Wounded several times, he staggered towards me raising his spear. I shot him at less than a yard. He fell on the sand, and lay there dead. How easy to kill a man!

1930. (MEL, 206–8.)

Combined chiefs (World War II)

I would turn aside for a moment to emphasize how perfect is the cooperation between the commanders of the British and American Armies. Nothing like it has ever been seen before among allies. No doubt language is a great help, but there is more in it than that. In all previous alliances the staffs have worked with opposite numbers in each department and liaison officers, but in Africa General Eisenhower built up a uniform staff, in which every place was filled with whoever was thought to be the best man, and they all ordered each other about according to their rank, without the slightest regard to what country they belonged to....I cannot doubt that it will be found most serviceable, and unique also in all the history of alliances.

1944, 22 FEBRUARY.

Continuity of policy

Nothing was more important than continuity in the policy of the army. It was not a limited liability company which could be recast or reconstructed in accordance with the state of the money market; and if subjected to frequent and violent changes very grave and grievous consequences might ensue, which it might take years to repair.

1905, 23 FEBRUARY.

Corps strength

...one [corps] is quite enough to begin to fight savages, and three are not enough even to begin to fight Europeans....If we are hated, they will not make us loved...If we are in danger, they will not make us safe. They are enough to irritate; they are not enough to overawe. They cannot make us invulnerable, but they may very likely make us venturesome.

1901, 12 MAY.

Churchill's second speech in the House was the first of his speeches on Army reform over the next two years, a battle he finally won.

...while the Fourth Army Corps has got its General, the General has not yet got his Army Corps—though I observe from the papers that he is to take up his command on the first of April. As for the two remaining Army Corps, they are still in the air, organised apparently on the Marconi system....I do not hesitate to say that there are numerous cases of officers, particularly popular officers, being appointed to commands which either do not exist or only partially exist, and I characterise these methods as wasteful and uncandid, and as throwing gold dust in the eyes of the public.

1903, 13 FEBRUARY, WALLSEND. (MBA, 76–8.)

...in spite of every calumny and lie uttered or printed, the truth comes to the top, and it is known alike by peoples and by rulers that on the whole British influence is healthy and kindly, and makes for the general happiness and welfare of mankind. And we shall make a fatal bargain if we allow the moral force which this country has so long exerted to become diminished, or perhaps even destroyed for the sake of the costly, trumpery, dangerous military playthings on which the Secretary of State for War has set his heart.

1901, 13 MAY.

From an important speech in which Winston took up his father's old cause of economy and opposed War Secretary St. John Brodrick's proposal for three Army corps.

Discipline

The bond of discipline is subtle and sensitive. It may be as tense as steel or as brittle as glass. The main element of discipline in the British

Service is a sense of justice and a sense of willing association among great bodies of men with the general policy of their country.

1919, 3 March.

Enlistment

The vital foundation of any army was the period of enlistment.

1905, 23 February.

Equipment

We are now in the third year of openly avowed rearmament. Why is it, if all is going well, there are so many deficiencies? Why, for instance, are the Guards drilling with flags instead of machine guns? Why is it that our small Territorial Army is in a rudimentary condition? Is that all according to schedule? Why should it be, when you consider how small are our forces? Why should it be impossible to equip the Territorial Army simultaneously with the Regular Army?

1938, 25 May.

The equipment of our army at the outbreak of war was of the most meagre and deficient character, and the deficiencies made themselves most marked—and still make themselves most marked—in the very type of weapons for which there is the greatest possible demand.

1941, 10 June.

Fitness for command

I am doubtful whether the fact that a man has gained the Victoria Cross for bravery as a young officer fits him to command an army twenty or thirty years later. I have noticed more than one serious misfortune which arose from such assumptions.

1930. (MEL, 319.)

General staff

Those gilded and gorgeous functionaries with brass hats and ornamental duties who multiplied so luxuriously on the plains of Aldershot and Salisbury.

1905, 1 March. (Gilbert, Life, 170.)

Churchill was criticising the new Secretary of State for War, Hugh Arnold-Foster, for high expenditure on the General Staff.

I have been told that in the British Army there are fewer bayonets and fewer sabres per general than in any other army in the world, except the Venezuelan army.

1903, 23 February. (MBA, 92.)

Generals

One of the most remarkable features of the British army for a great number of years had been its number of generals.

1903, 24 February.

…the best generals are those who arrive at the results of planning without being tied to plans.

1930. (MEL, 227.)

Housing

It is quite impossible to maintain a permanent service in healthy discipline without that reasonable degree of comfort which can only be afforded by permanent habitation.

1919, 15 December.

Infantry

When I was a soldier, infantry used to walk and cavalry used to ride. But now the infantry require motor-cars, and even the tanks have to have horse boxes to take them to battle.

1943. (Ismay, 270.)

Regretting the elaborate mechanised equipment required by modern armies.

Military units

…there is no organisation in the world so complete as the organisation by which a military unit is maintained.

1916, 16 August.

Militia and Yeomanry

[Secretary of State for War St. John Brodrick] introduced into the House of Commons a Bill called the Militia and Yeomanry Bill, one part of which proposed to make a reserve for the Militia out of men who had served in the Regular Army, and the other part of which proposed to make a reserve for the Regular Army out of men who had served in the Yeomanry. That is a plan which rather reminds one of people who are said to make a living by taking in each other's washing.

1903, 19 January. Oldham. (MBA, 62–3.)

Officers

Many congratulations on becoming an officer and a gentleman. Don't let the double promotion go to your head.

1895. (MACLEAN, *CHURCHILL PROCEEDINGS*, 1987.)

WSC to Charles Maclean, father of Sir Fitzroy Maclean (see People); Charles, like WSC, was commissioned in 1895. Sir Fitzroy Maclean of Dunconnel KT (1911–96) was a diplomat, writer and politician, a swashbuckler and favourite of WSC, whom he served in the war as special representative to Tito and the Yugoslav partisans.

You do not rise by the regulations, but in spite of them. Therefore in all matters of active service the subaltern must never take "No" for an answer. He should go to the front at all costs.

1900. (HAMILTON'S, 123; BOER, 279.)

Churchill certainly profited by his own advice.

Live well but do not flaunt it. Laugh a little, and teach your men to laugh—great good humour under fire— war is a game that is played with a smile. If you can't smile, grin. If you can't grin, keep out of the way till you can.

1916, 27 JANUARY. PLOEGSTEERT, BELGIUM. (OB III, 651.)

Letter to his wife recounting his homily to his men before entering the trenches for the first time.

...I shall always urge that the tendency in the future should be to prolong the courses of instruction at the colleges rather than to abridge them, and to equip our young officers with that special technical professional knowledge which soldiers have the right to expect from those who can give them orders, if necessary, to go to their deaths. It is quite clear that class or wealth or favour will not be allowed in the modern world to afford dividing lines.

1946, 9 MARCH. PENTAGON, WASHINGTON. (SINEWS, 114.)

Reform

...what is army reform? I take it to be one of two things. Either it means the same efficiency at a reduced cost, or increased efficiency for the same cost. Perhaps it might mean greatly increased efficiency for a slightly increased cost. But the one thing it certainly does not mean is a larger number of regular soldiers.

1901, 13 MAY.

Soldier life

It will be said that the troopers, getting flurried, would shoot each other. That is very likely. A certain loss of life is inseparable from war, and it makes little difference whether a man is shot by his own side or cut down by the other. But even the rawest recruit in the moment of extreme agitation has a distinct preference for shooting his enemies rather than his friends.

1899. (RIVER I, 141.)

The wise man on the field of honour will be distinguished by his appetite, which at once proclaims his care for the future, his disdain for the past, and his composure in the present.

1899. (RIVER II, 169.)

Be calm! Nobody is ever wounded twice in the same day.

1899, 15 NOVEMBER. CHIEVELEY, SOUTH AFRICA. (TAYLOR, 173.)

WSC's advice to the engineer during the ambush of his armoured train.

The healthy, open-air life, the vivid incidents, the excitement, not only of realisation, but of anticipation, the generous and cheery friendships, the chances of distinction which are open to all, invest life with keener interests and rarer pleasures. The uncertainty and importance of the present, reduce the past and future to comparative insignificance, and clear the mind of minor worries. And when all is over, memories remain which few men do not hold precious. As to the hardships, these though severe may be endured.

1899. (MALAKAND, 1899 ED., 252–3.)

...the bullet is brutally indiscriminating, and before it the brain of a hero or the quarters of a horse stand exactly the same chance to the vertical square inch.

1900. (LADYSMITH, 137; BOER, 61.)

A man had been found leaning forward on his rifle, dead. A broken pair of field glasses, shattered by the same shell that had killed their owner, bore the name "M'Corquodale." The name and the face flew together in my mind. It was the last joined subaltern of Thorneycroft's Mounted Infantry—joined in the evening, shot at dawn.

Poor gallant young Englishman! He had soon "got his job." The great sacrifice had been required of the Queen's latest recruit.

1900, 25 JANUARY. VENTER'S SPRUIT, SOUTH AFRICA. (LADYSMITH, 338; BOER, 151.)

H. S. M'Corquodale had a nodding acquaintance with Churchill when both were boys at Harrow School. The day before the Battle of Spion Kop WSC heard his name called and "saw M'Corquodale's cheery face"; his old schoolmate had just joined the mounted infantry that evening.

There is no more delicious moment in the day than this, when we light the fire and, while the kettle boils, watch the dark shadows of the hills take form, perspective, and finally colour, knowing that there is another whole day begun, bright with chance and interest, and free from all cares. All cares—for who can be worried about the little matters of humdrum life when he may be dead before the night? Such a one was with us yesterday—see, there is a spare mug for coffee in the mess—but now gone for ever.

1900, 4 FEBRUARY. SPEARMAN'S HILL, SOUTH AFRICA. (LADYSMITH, 339–40; BOER, 152.)

Here life itself, life at its best and healthiest, awaits the caprice of the bullet. Let us see the development of the day. All else may stand over, perhaps for ever. Existence is never so sweet as when it is at hazard.

1900, 4 FEBRUARY. SPEARMAN'S HILL, SOUTH AFRICA. (LADYSMITH, 340; BOER, 152.)

As in the shades of a November evening I, for the first time, led a platoon of Grenadiers across the sopping fields...the conviction came into my mind with absolute assurance that the simple soldiers and their regimental officers, armed with their cause, would by their virtues in the end retrieve the mistakes and ignorances of Staffs and Cabinets, of Admirals, Generals, and politicians—

including, no doubt, many of my own. But, alas, at what a needless cost!

1923. (CRISIS II, 500.)

Battalion Headquarters when in the line was strictly "dry." Nothing but strong the tea with the condensed milk, a very unpleasant beverage...The Companies' messes in the trenches were...allowed more latitude. As I have always believed in the moderate and regular use of alcohol, especially under conditions of winter war, I gladly moved my handful of belongings from Ebenezer Farm to a Company in the line.

1927, FEBRUARY. ("WITH THE GRENADIERS," *NASH'S PALL MALL*; THOUGHTS, 70.)

Colonel Byng and I shared a blanket. When he turned over I was in the cold. When I turned over I pulled the blanket off him and he objected. He was the Colonel. It was not a good arrangement. I was glad when morning came.

1930. (MEL, 332.)

Julian Hedworth George Byng (1862–1935), known as "Bungo", here described in 1899, later commanded the Canadian Corps and British Third Army in World War I. He became the First Viscount Byng of Vimy and was Governor General of Canada, 1921–26.

I was soon awakened by firing....A bullet ripped through the thatch of our hut, another wounded an orderly just outside. I should have been glad to get out of my hammock and lie on the ground. However, as no one else made a move, I thought it more becoming to stay where I was. I fortified myself by dwelling on the fact that the Spanish officer whose hammock was slung between me and the enemy's fire was a man of substantial physique; indeed one might almost have called him fat ... I have never been prejudiced against fat men....Gradually I dropped asleep.

1930. (MEL, 99.)

WSC recounting his experiences as a soldier-correspondent for the Daily Graphic *in Cuba, 1895.*

War is a game to be played with a smiling face, but do you think there is laughter in my heart? We travel in style and round us there is great luxury and seeming security, but I never forget the man at the front, the bitter struggles, and the fact that men are dying...

1943, 26 NOVEMBER. (CHURCHILL, SARAH, 63.)

WSC to his daughter Sarah, often quoted out of context, using only the first eleven words.

Tanks

It would be quite easy in a short time to fit up a number of steam tractors with small armoured shelters, in which men and machine guns could be placed, which would be bullet-proof. Used at night they would not be affected by artillery fire to any extent. The caterpillar system would enable trenches to be crossed quite easily, and the weight of the machine would destroy all wire entanglements.

1915, 5 JANUARY, ADMIRALTY.
(OB, CV3/1, 377–8.)

WSC to Prime Minister H. H. Asquith; his letter marked the first step in the development of the tank.

As we could not go round the trenches, it was evidently necessary to go over them.

1923. (CRISIS II, 71.)

Churchill was always seeking ways to circumvent the awful slaughter of trench warfare. His impetus had much to do with the evolution of the tank in WWI.

In the last war, tanks were built to go three or four miles an hour and to stand up to rifle or machine-gun bullets. In the interval the process of mechanical science had advanced so much that it became possible to make a tank which could do 15, 20, or 25 miles an hour and stand up to cannon fire. That was a great revolution, by which Hitler has profited. That is a simple fact which was perfectly well known to the military and technical services three or four years before the war. It did not spring from German brains. It sprang from British brains, and from brains like those of General de Gaulle in France, and it has been exploited and turned to our grievous injury by the uninventive but highly competent and imitative Germans.

1941, 7 MAY.

This tank, the A.22, was ordered off the drawing board, and large numbers went into production very quickly. As might be expected, it had many defects and teething troubles, and when these became apparent the tank was appropriately rechristened the "Churchill." These defects have now been largely overcome.

1942, 2 JULY.

How do you make a tank? People design it, they argue about it, they plan it and make it, and then you take the tank and test and re-test it. When you have got it absolutely settled then, and only then, you go into production. But we have never been able to indulge in the luxury of that precise and leisurely process. We have had to take it straight off the drawing-board and go into full production, and take the chance of the many errors which the construction will show coming out after hundreds and thousands of them have been made.

1942, 2 JULY.

The idea of having a spear-point or battering ram of heavy armoured vehicles to break the enemy's front and make a hole through which the lighter vehicles can be pushed has a very high military significance. A certain number of such vehicles should be attached to armies, and possibly even corps, in each theatre. The wart-hog must play his part as well as the gazelle....What has happened to the amphibious tank? Surely a float or galosh can be made to take a tank of the larger size across the Channel under good conditions once a beach landing has been secured.

1943, 23 APRIL. (WW2 IV, 850.)

Prime Minister to Cabinet Secretary Sir Edward Bridges and Brigadier Ian Jacob for Defence Committee (Supply).

Territorials (Reserves)

When I think how these young men who join the Territorials come forward, almost alone in the population, and take on a liability to serve anywhere in any part of the world...I marvel at their patriotism. It is a marvel, it is also a glory, but a glory we have no right to profit by unless we can secure proper and efficient equipment for them.

1936, 12 NOVEMBER.

Trench railways

The foundation of a good trench line is a system of light railways far more extensive and elaborate than anything we have at the present time. It is only by means of light railways that all the enormous varieties and quantities of trench stores necessary for the making of a solid line and keeping them in repair can be conveyed to the Front, such as pumping machinery, steel dugouts, revetting material; and all that variety of trench stores can only be brought in sufficient quantities to the front by a very elaborate and extensive network of railways and light railways.

1916, 24 JULY.

Volunteers

A national army is quite different from an army of volunteers, who were produced largely by the pressure in the economic market. I am all for volunteers who come from some uplifting of the human soul, some spirit arising in the human breast.

1947, 6 MAY. (CZARNOMSKI, 388.)

15

NAVAL
PERSON

*"We may now picture this great Fleet, with its flotillas and cruisers,
steaming slowly out of Portland Harbour, squadron by squadron,
scores of gigantic castles of steel wending their way across the misty,
shining sea, like giants bowed in anxious thought. We may picture
them again as darkness fell, eighteen miles of warships running at
high speed and in absolute blackness through the narrow Straits,
bearing with them into the broad waters of the North the safeguard
of considerable affairs.... The king's ships were at sea."*[49]

"It was a great hour to live. Nearly half those who sang were soon to die."
Farewell to Roosevelt and USS *Augusta*, August 1941.

C hurchill, who began his famous correspondence with Roosevelt signing letters "Naval Person", shared the President's affinity for the sea. But Roosevelt had risen only to Assistant Secretary of the Navy; Churchill had run it, becoming First Lord of

---

49 On 28 July 1914, on his own initiative, Churchill as First Lord of the Admiralty sent the Fleet to its war station in Scapa Flow. From *The World Crisis*, vol. I, *1911–1914*. London: Thornton Butterworth, 1923, 212–13.

the Admiralty in 1911, supervising the conversion from coal to oil and the development of fast, powerful dreadnought battleships, and fighting the early World War at sea.

Working with the fiery, brilliant but unpredictable Admiral "Jacky" Fisher, Churchill had secured Britain's vital command of the North Sea, bottling up the German High Seas Fleet. And then, with Fisher's support, he had sponsored and promoted the Dardanelles expedition to open a second front in the Great War, by sailing a fleet to Constantinople and forcing Turkey out of the war.

Alas when the expedition met with initial reverses (see Chapter 16), the mercurial Fisher reversed himself and abruptly resigned. A government crisis ensued and Churchill was relieved in May 1915.

"The Dardanelles haunted him for the rest of his life," Clementine Churchill later recalled to Sir Martin Gilbert. "He always believed in it. When he left the Admiralty he thought he was finished....I thought he would never get over the Dardanelles; I thought he would die of grief."[50]

Fate, however, saw Churchill back at the Admiralty he had "quitted in pain and sorrow" almost exactly a quarter century later, to confront again the same Germany that had nearly won the last war. He applied all of his old vigour, with the same willingness to take risks, occasional rashness and distrust of conventional opinion. When Britain was forced to abandon Norway to the Nazis, in spring 1940, some said Churchill was facing another Dardanelles; but faced with national extinction, the country couldn't be without him. Almost twenty-five years to the day he had quit the Admiralty in 1915, Churchill found himself Prime Minister.

Quotations here present Churchill's broad naval philosophy. Specific naval actions and policies will also be found in the chapters on the two World Wars. It will be noticed that many occur in March or April – the time when the annual Naval Estimates were presented to Parliament.

Aphorisms and Reflections

...when we consider our naval strength we are not thinking of our commerce, but of our freedom. We are not thinking of our trade, but our lives.

1912, 18 MARCH.

...if we assert our claim, as we intend to do, to the supreme position on the seas, it is also our duty so to conduct ourselves that other nations will feel that that great power and that great responsibility which are a necessity to us shall be used in such a manner as to be a menace to none, and a trust held for all.

1912, 20 MARCH.

None of these Powers need, like us, navies to defend their actual independence or safety. They build them so as to play a part in the world's affairs. It is sport to them. It is life and death to us.

1914, 17 MARCH.

WSC was speaking of the great powers and smaller states building navies in the years before World War I.

...the Navy has a dual function. In war it is our means of safety; in peace it sustains the prestige, repute and influence of this small island; and it is a major factor in the cohesion of the British Empire and Commonwealth. The tasks which the Navy has performed in peacetime are hardly less magnificent than those they have achieved in war. From Trafalgar onwards, for more than 100 years Britannia ruled the waves. There was a great measure of peace, the freedom of the seas was maintained, the slave trade was extirpated, the Monroe Doctrine of the United States found its sanction in British naval power—and that has been pretty well recognized on the other side of the Atlantic—and in those happy days the cost was about £10 million a year.

1948, 8 MARCH.

50 Gilbert, Martin, *Winston S. Churchill*, vol. III, *The Challenge of War 1914–1916*. London: Heinemann, 1971, 473.

Aces and kings

I am horrified to learn that the Admiralty propose to scrap the five 15-inch battleships of the Royal Sovereign class....The House would hardly gather from the euphemistic phrase the Parliamentary Secretary employed— "replacement" —that these two ships are to be destroyed....In other days I used to say that when the ace is out the king is the best card.

1939, 16 MARCH.

Admirals

It is dangerous to meddle with Admirals when they say they can't do things. They have always got the weather or fuel or something to argue about.

1941, DECEMBER. (WW2 III, 591–2.)

WSC to US Navy Secretary Knox, who had told him,

We ordered our fleet to fight a battle with the Japanese to relieve Wake Island, and now within a few hours of steaming the Admiral has decided to turn back. What would you do with your Admiral in a case like this?

Admiralty

I don't want tea—I don't want anything— anything in the world. Your father has just offered me the Admiralty....the fading light of evening disclosed in the far distance the silhouettes of two battleships steaming slowly out of the Firth of Forth. They seemed invested with a new significance to me....Look at the people I have had to deal with so far [as Home Secretary]—judges and convicts! This is a big thing—the biggest thing that has ever come my way—the chance I should have chosen before all others. I shall pour into it everything I've got.

1911, 30 SEPTEMBER. DIRLETON, EAST LOTHIAN, SCOTLAND. (BONHAM CARTER, 249.)

WSC to Violet Bonham Carter, who wrote:

His whole life was invested with a new significance. He was tasting fulfilment. Never, before or since, have I seen him more completely and profoundly happy. It seemed like Journey's End. It was in fact the beginning of a journey which did not

end for him till 1945. I was struck by...first, the sense of dedication to a task which Fate had designed him to fulfil, and secondly his unquestioning confidence in his power to fulfil it. These attitudes remained constant throughout his life.

You cannot deal with offices in the abstract. You must think of offices in connection with the men who fill them, and I do not think that it is very likely that during my tenure of office I shall ever be called upon to proceed in isolation, without the support of the principal members of the Board of Admiralty.

1912, 20 MARCH.

There is a great deal of difference between being responsible for giving an order, on which the loss of several valuable ships might swiftly follow, and merely expressing an opinion, however well-informed, however sincere, however courageous, without such responsibility.

1940, 8 MAY.

In a speech about the British withdrawal from Norway.

Armed merchantmen

I have never doubted that it is a melancholy fact in the present state of European civilization and at this period that we should have to go back to putting weapons of war on peaceful trading vessels.

1913, 17 JULY.

Battleships

We always believed before the war [World War I] that battleships could never be laid down without our knowledge. The Germans were entitled to build 10,000-ton ships according to the Treaty, but they, by a concealment which the Admiralty were utterly unable to penetrate, converted these into 26,000-ton ships. Let us be careful when we see all these extremely awkward incidents occurring.

1935, 22 JULY.

Convoys

We have had hardly any losses at sea in our heavily escorted troop convoys. Out of about 3,000,000 soldiers who have been moved under the protection of the British Navy about the world, to and fro across the seas and oceans, about 1,348 have been killed or drowned, including missing. It is about 2,200 to one against your being drowned if you travel in British troop convoys in this present war.

1943, 11 FEBRUARY.

Decoys

I know what's wrong with those ships. There are no seagulls round them. That would be noticed immediately by enemy planes. I must arrange to have food thrown from these ships so that seagulls will hover round the dummies.

1941. (SHADOW 26.)

Churchill to his bodyguard Walter Thompson, as they viewed a fleet comprising dummy warships, erected to convince German reconnaissance aircraft that Britain had more vessels than it really did.

Destroyers

The destroyer has two functions. Its first function is to destroy the enemy's torpedo craft by gunfire in its own waters. Its second function is the attack by the torpedo on the heavy ships of the enemy.

1914, 17 MARCH.

Churchill has been inaccurately credited with inventing the term "destroyer" (for light vessels built to protect battleships from torpedo boats). The Encyclopaedia Britannica traces the term to the 1890s, long before WSC arrived at the Admiralty. See also Nomenclature.

Empire solidarity

There is no more valuable principle of Imperial federation than this principle, which I am bringing forward tonight, of inter-Dominion action. The homely old tale of the bundle of sticks, each of which could be snapped separately, but which bound together were unbreakable, is the last word in the naval strategy of the British Empire.

1913, 26 MARCH.

Finance

If [I] might presume to lay down any principle at all, [I] should say that the first and main principle which should animate British statecraft in the

realm of Imperial defence was the promotion of the steady transfer of expenditure from military to marine….[Expenditure should be] something like two to one on the side of the Navy.

1902, 6 MARCH.

The foundation of naval policy is finance.

1912, 18 MARCH.

Every capital ship sanctioned by Parliament affects the finance of three years. There are therefore, in each year, ships which are begun, ships which are finished, and ships which are under construction throughout the whole twelve months.

1913, 26 MARCH.

If I had proposed to take £12,000,000 from the Navy, all the Liberal Party would have been bound to rise up and say: "Hosannah! Let us, if you will, have a second- or third-class Navy, but, whatever happens, we must have first-class roads."

1927, 28 APRIL.

A set of short-term half-wits in time of peace may brush away old vessels with all kinds of penny wise, pound foolish arguments and, if they have the political power, I have no doubt that they will find many experts to testify that these vessels are useless, especially if the experts have a hope that they are going to get new ones built in their place….but, when war comes, that is not what you feel.

1948, 8 MARCH.

First Sea Lord

The First Sea Lord moves the fleet. No one else moves it.

1917, 5 MARCH.

The First Sea Lord is the professional head of the navy, subject to the directions of the civilian First Lord of the Admiralty.

Fleet Commanders

…command of a battle fleet is far more intimate and personal than any functions discharged by generals on land.

1916, 7 MARCH.

Fleet strength

The spectacle which the naval armaments of Christendom afford at the present time will no doubt excite the curiosity and the wonder of future generations.

1912, 18 MARCH.

...in times of peace we measure the relative naval construction of two navies by percentages, and that is perhaps as good a way as any other. In naval war, and especially in modern naval war, another system of calculation becomes dominant. Battles are not decided by ratios or percentages. They yield definite and absolute results, and the strength of conflicting navies ought to be measured, and is measured, not as in peace by comparison, but by subtraction.

1912, 18 MARCH.

In the sphere of naval competition everything is relative. The strength of one navy is its strength compared to another....Margins of naval strength which are sufficient, when the times come to compel a victory, are insufficient to maintain peace.

1913, 26 MARCH.

[The 1922 Washington Naval Treaty] is a declaration that the British Empire accepts the position of a second Power at sea....If the idea of a hostile United States is not ruled out, this Treaty is impossible; if it is ruled out, it is quite unnecessary....You call it a Treaty of Disarmament. Do not delude yourselves with that. Nothing is going to happen under this Treaty which will give any satisfaction to the Germans in respect of the Clauses of the Treaty of Versailles....A setback has been caused by these Conferences through the well meant attempts of nations not themselves in danger to regulate and cut down defences of those that are.

1930, 2 JUNE.

The Washington Naval Treaty set tonnage limitations on capital ships and aircraft carriers between the signatories: Japan, 60 per cent of US/UK; France and Italy, 33 per cent of US/UK in capital ships, 44 per cent in aircraft carriers. The Treaty was modified in 1930 but in 1934 Japan gave notice that it would terminate the agreement.

Then there was the Naval Treaty of London, which I am glad to think the Conservative Party voted against. It is cramping and fettering our naval development, not merely the

scale but the actual form and shape of our naval expenditure, in a manner which is certainly detrimental.

1933, 23 MARCH.

The 1930 treaty, between the UK, USA, Japan, France and Italy, regulated submarine warfare and limits on shipbuilding.

For the navy, at any rate, we should regain freedom of design. We should get rid of this London Treaty which has crippled us in building the kind of ships we want, and has stopped the United States from building a great battleship which she probably needed and to which we should have not had the slightest reason to object.

1934, 7 FEBRUARY.

Invasion defence

...in order that our naval defence shall be fully effective, there must be sufficient military force in this country to make it necessary for an invader to come in such large numbers that he will offer a target to the Navy, and certainly would be intercepted if he embarked.

1914, 17 MARCH.

Magnetic mines

A strident effort has been made by German propaganda to persuade the world that we have laid these magnetic mines ourselves in the fairways of our own harbours in order, apparently, to starve ourselves out. When this inanity expired amid general derision, the alternative claim was made that the sinking of the neutrals by mine was another triumph of German science and seamanship, and should convince all nations that the German mastery of the seas was complete.

1939, 6 DECEMBER.

The magnetic mine, and all the other mines with which the narrow waters, the approaches to this Island, are strewn, do not present us with any problem which we deem insoluble. It must be remembered that in the last war we suffered very grievous losses from mines, and that at the climax more than six hundred British vessels were engaged solely upon the task of minesweeping. We must remember that. We must always be expecting some bad things from Germany, but I will venture to say that it is with growing confidence that we await the further developments or variants of their attack.

1940, 20 JANUARY. BROADCAST, LONDON. (BLOOD, 250.)

I feel entitled to say that we see our way to mastering this magnetic mine and other variants of the same idea. How this has been achieved is a detective story written in a language of its own. Magnetism is a very exact science, and its complications and refinements can all be explored and measured. To be modest, we do not feel at all outdone in science in this country by the Nazis.

1940, 27 FEBRUARY.

Mediterranean

To gain and hold command of the Mediterranean in case of war is a high duty of the Fleet. Once that is achieved all European land forces on the shores of North Africa will be decisively affected. Those that have command of the Mediterranean behind them can be reinforced to any extent and supplied to any extent. Those that have no such command will be like cut flowers in a vase.

1939, 16 MARCH.

NATO command

I am sure that no one knows so much about dealing with U-boats…as the British Admiralty, not because we are cleverer or braver than others, but because, in two wars, our existence has depended upon overcoming these perils. When you live for years on end with mortal danger at your throat, you learn in a hard school.

1951, 19 APRIL.

It had been proposed that an American Admiral be supreme commander in the North Atlantic.

Naval invention

The usefulness of a naval invention ceases when it is enjoyed by everyone else.

1913, 26 MARCH.

Naval power

…steam and the telegraph have enormously increased, as compared with sailing days, the thoroughness and efficiency of superior sea power.

1915, 15 FEBRUARY.

Naval science

The navy is passing through a period not merely of expansion, but of swift and ceaseless development. It is, in fact, a vast scientific business of ever-growing range and complexity, stimulated and governed by inventions and improvements in almost every sphere of applied mechanics, forced without cessation to enter upon new paths of research and of the application of the results of research, and fanned to the highest point of activity by the rapid advance in every direction of rival Powers.

1913, 26 MARCH.

Churchill, together with the important aid of Admiral Fisher, had transformed the Royal Navy, switching its chief motive power from coal to oil, and building the dreadnought class of fast capital ships.

Navy, American

…it would have been better for us to have said to the United States, "Build whatever you will; your navy is absolutely ruled out of our calculations, except as a potential friend."

1932, 13 MAY.

I have always thought that the union of these two great forces [the British and American navies], not for purposes of aggression or narrow selfish interest, but in an honourable cause, constitutes what I may call the sheet-anchor of human freedom and progress.

1939, 19 MAY. CORN EXCHANGE, CAMBRIDGE. (BLOOD, 167.)

Who said a Wasp couldn't sting twice?

1942, 9 MAY. (WW2 IV, 273.)

The American aircraft carrier USS Wasp *made two trips to Malta, laden with Spitfires for the island's defence.* Wasp *was sunk by Japanese torpedoes on 15 September 1942.*

Navy, French

Orders were instantly given to stop them at Casablanca, or if that failed, to prevent them entering Dakar. If we could not cork them in, we could, at least, we hoped, have corked them out.…

1940, 8 OCTOBER.

The Royal Navy had prevented three French destroyers carrying Vichy partisans from entering Dakar Harbour. *See Nations...France, and operations against the French fleet in World War II...1940.*

Navy, German

The purposes of British naval power are essentially defensive. We have no thoughts, and we have never had any thoughts of aggression, and we attribute no such thoughts to other great Powers. There is, however, this difference between the British naval power and the naval power of the great and friendly Empire—and I trust it may long remain the great and friendly Empire—of Germany. The British Navy is to us a necessity and, from some points of view, the German Navy is to them more in the nature of a luxury. Our naval power involves British existence. It is existence to us; it is expansion to them. We cannot menace the peace of a single Continental hamlet, no matter how great and supreme our Navy may become. But, on the other hand, the whole fortunes of our race and Empire, the whole treasure accumulated during so many centuries of sacrifice and achievement, would perish and be swept utterly away if our naval supremacy were to be impaired. It is the British Navy which makes Great Britain a great power. But Germany was a great power, respected and honoured all over the world, before she had a single ship...

1912, 9 FEBRUARY, GLASGOW. (OB II, 563.)

Considered by WSC's son and biographer "perhaps his most important speech as First Lord", this declaration had an unintended effect in Germany, where WSC's remarks were interpreted to mean he thought their fleet was superfluous ("luxus flotte"). Thus Germany was further encouraged to continue the naval arms race.

Let us suppose that some distinguished and powerful person who has played a great part in life dies, and his posts, offices, appointments and possessions are distributed, and then he suddenly comes back from the dead. A great deal of inconvenience would be caused. That is what has happened in the resuscitation of German naval power.

1935, 11 JULY.

Nomenclature

I agree with the First Sea Lord about the needlessness of repeating the word "vessel," and his wish to simplify all titles to one word.

I should like the word "destroyer" to cover ships formerly described as "fast escort vessels"....I do not like the word "whaler," which is an entire misnomer, as they are not going to catch whales....What is, in fact, the distinction between an "escorter," a "patroller" and a "whaler" as now specified? It seems most important to arrive at simple conclusions quickly on this subject....

1940, 25 FEBRUARY. (WW2 I, 599.)

WSC to Controller of the Navy and others. "Fast escort vessels" became known as "Hunt class destroyers", "whalers" as "corvettes" and later, "frigates". Escort vessels became "sloops", which sailors will recognise as another misnomer. See also Destroyer.

Obsolescence

It is wrong and wasteful to build a single ship for the Navy before it is wanted. Up to the moment when the contract for a battleship has been definitely signed, the vessel is the heir to all the expanding naval science of the world, but from the day when the design has been finally fixed, she becomes obsolescent, and she has become a wasting security.

1912, 18 MARCH.

A certain inconsistency is evident here. Nearly a quarter century later, Churchill would deride Sir Thomas Inskip, Minister for Coordination of Defence, for saying that if Britain had built more fighter aircraft sooner, as he had recommended, they would sooner be obsolete. But of course the situation was different.

Every year the great nations of Christendom not only make obsolete the fleets of their rivals, but they make obsolete their own fleets. They do that without adding in the least either to their actual security or relative strength.

1913, 26 MARCH.

Similar thoughts encouraged Churchill to urge the Germans to join with Britain in proclaiming a moratorium on ship production, hoping to stop the naval arms race that preceded World War I. See Churchillisms...Naval Holiday.

Refitting

This particular episode of the repair and refitting of the Valiant is exactly like using 1,000 skilled men to dig a hole in the ground, and then, when they have dug it, using them again to fill it up. Why, even in the convict prisons, the idea of useless labour has been rightly condemned and abolished.

1948, 8 MARCH.

Royal Naval College

Hello, Dickie, enjoying your supper? Any complaints?

[Dickie, later Lord Mountbatten: "Well, yes sir. We only get two sardines for supper on Sunday, we would sooner have three."]

Admiral, make a note. These young gentlemen want three sardines for supper on Sunday, not two!

1913, MAY. RNC, DEVONPORT.
(LORD MOUNTBATTEN TO THE EDMONTON
CHURCHILL SOCIETY, 1966.)

Mountbatten added:

I was a great hero. All my companions thought I was wonderful and brave...We never got three sardines for supper. That convinced me that Mr. Churchill was unreliable! (See "Two-Power standard" below.)

Don't you know that you are laying impious hands on the Ark of the Covenant? Don't you know that this naval system has existed since Nelson?

1941. (MENZIES, 74.)

Robert Menzies had expressed disappointment with the management of the Royal Naval College.

Royal Navy

It is the Navy which alone can secure the food and commerce on which the crowded population of England depends....Do not overlook what naval supremacy means. It does not mean merely the command of the Channel, or of the Mediterranean, or of the Atlantic or of the Persian Gulf—it means something much wider than that—it means the power to send our ships wherever the waters roll, to fly our flag on every sea, to land our troops on any shore.

1903, 13 FEBRUARY, WALLSEND. (MBA, 80.)

There was one advantage we possessed over other countries in Europe, which enabled us to have a Navy far greater and better than they could have, no matter how great were the sacrifices they made, and that was, while all these Powers had to depend upon a great army and to consider enormous land preparations for the defence of their frontiers, we, in this Island, were able to concentrate the whole of our energies and strength upon the fleet.

1903, 14 MAY.

The Royal Navy, especially after the toning-up which it has received, is unsurpassed in the world and is still the main bulwark of our security; and even at this eleventh hour, if the right measures are taken and if the right spirit prevails in the British nation and the British Empire, we may surround ourselves with other bulwarks equally sure, which will protect us against whatever storms may blow.

1936, 10 MARCH.

Sailors

It would ill become this House to vote year after year unexampled millions for the grim machinery of modern naval war, and then to grudge the officers and men of the fleet—without whose devotion these prodigious engines would only be worthless metal—the rewards which are their due, and which are necessary for their comfort and their contentment.

1912, 22 JULY.

Wonderful exertions have been made by our Navy and Air Force; by the hundreds of minesweeping vessels which with their marvellous appliances keep our ports clear in spite of all the enemy can do; by the men who build and repair our immense fleets of merchant ships; by the men who load and unload them; and, need I say, by the officers and men of the Merchant Navy who go out in all weathers and in the teeth of all dangers to fight for the life of their native land and for a cause they comprehend and serve.

1941, 27 APRIL. BROADCAST, LONDON.
(UNRELENTING, 98.)

Sea engagements

Indeed, the more we force ourselves to picture the hideous course of a modern naval engagement, the more one is inclined to believe that it will resemble the contest between Mamilius and Herminius at the battle of Lake Regillus, or the still more homely conflict of the Kilkenny cats. That is a very satisfactory reflection for the stronger naval power.

1912, 18 March.

The battle, possibly mythical, was described in Macaulay's Lays of Ancient Rome *which fascinated WSC as a boy. It was a Roman victory, led by Mamilius over Herminius and the Etruscans, possibly between 509 and 493 BC. The* Oxford English Dictionary *describes a "Kilkenny cat" as "one of a pair of cats fabled to have fought until only their tails remained". Hence the phrase describes "combatants who fight until they annihilate each other".*

A vessel which has no weapon of any kind to fire is afraid of a vessel which has perhaps only a rifle if it is faster.

1913, 17 July.

If you want to make a true picture in your mind of a battle between great modern ironclad ships you must not think of it as if it were two men in armour striking at each other with heavy swords. It is more like a battle between two egg-shells striking each other with hammers.

1914, 17 March.

In old wars the capture or destruction of ships was nearly always accompanied by an act of surrender which was a proper and very necessary subject of investigation by court-martial. But mines and submarines, especially submarines, create conditions entirely novel, presenting to naval officers problems of incomparable hazard and difficulty. In these circumstances a court-martial would frequently be inappropriate in our judgment, and often even harmful.

1915, 15 February.

Submarines

There are a few points on which I am not convinced. Of these the greatest is the question of the use of submarines to sink merchant vessels. I do not believe this would ever be done by a civilised Power.

1914, 1 January. (Crisis II, 280.)

WSC to Lord Fisher. They were soon disabused of this notion.

Of course, there never was a German submarine in Scapa....in November 1918, after the mutiny of the German fleet, a German submarine manned entirely by officers seeking to save their honour, perished in a final desperate effort. Thus none ever penetrated the lair of the Grand Fleet.

1923. (Crisis I, 381.)

WSC's judgement was premature. On 14 October 1939 the German U-47, commanded by a daring captain named Gunter Prien, penetrated the anchorage in Scapa Flow, Orkney and torpedoed the battleship HMS Royal Oak. The passages were then blocked with granite boulders known as the "Churchill barriers".

If the number of submarines remains few and constant... there is a very fair prospect of the proportion of losses not increasing in anything like the same ratio as the proportion of shipping. One knows that if you want a big bag of pheasants you beat them out of the cover in twos and threes, whereas if it is intended to shoot the cover over again the whole lot should be driven out as quickly as possible in the largest numbers. If rabbits run across a ride past a limited number of guns, their best chance is to run unexpectedly and all at once.

1917, March. (Crisis III Part 2, 366.)

Torpedoes

The torpedo, compared with the gun, is a weapon of much more limited application. The number of torpedoes which can be constructed in a given time is itself subject to certain limits. Any trained artillerist or naval gunner can hit with a gun, but to make a submerged attack with a torpedo requires a much bigger degree of skill and training.

1917, 21 February.

Two-Power standard

...a very important naval and strategic truth which I have several times endeavoured to impress upon the House [is] the difficulty under which the strongest naval power always lies of being ready to meet at its average moment the attack of the next strongest naval power at its selected moment.

1913, 26 March.

Formerly we have followed the two-Power standard—that is to say, 10 percent, over the two next strongest Powers. Now that standard has become quite meaningless. The two next strongest Powers, if you take the whole world, would be Germany and the United States, and if you left out the United States, as common sense would dictate, the two next strongest Powers would be Germany and France, which is not a very helpful or reasonable standard to adopt. As a matter of fact, in 1914–15 we shall be conforming to both these tests, absurd and unreasonable though they be.

1914, 17 MARCH.

Refer to note under Royal Naval College. Lord Mountbatten, in a notable speech to the Edmonton Churchill Society, in 1966 (see http://xrl.us/bbpod):

I took advantage of my relationship with the head of the Navy, my father [WSC's First Sea Lord at the oubreak of war, Prince Louis of Battenberg] to ask him what his job was. He said: "My boy, my job is to keep the fleets of the Royal Navy at operational strength and at immediate readiness to be certain of defeating the next greatest powers in the world in battle." I said: "That's quite a job." "Yes," said my father, "but what makes it easy is I have a splendid minister in Mr. Winston Churchill who gives me all his support." So I made a mental note: Mr. Churchill perhaps, after all, reliable.

[Through the early 1900s] all British naval arrangements had proceeded on the basis of the two-Power standard, namely, an adequate superiority over the next two strongest Powers, in those days France and Russia. The possible addition of a third European Fleet more powerful than either of these two would profoundly affect the life of Britain. If Germany was going to create a Navy avowedly measured against our own, we could not afford to remain "in splendid isolation" from the European systems.

1923. (CRISIS I, 21.)

Vulnerability on the seas

There is a difference between military and naval anxiety, which the House will appreciate. A division of soldiers cannot be annihilated by a Cavalry patrol. But at any moment a great ship, equal in war power…to a division or an army, may be destroyed without a single opportunity of its fighting strength being realised, or a man on board having a chance to strike a blow in self-defence.

1914, 27 NOVEMBER.

16

WORLD WAR I

"So now the Admiralty wireless whispers through the ether to the tall masts of ships, and captains pace their decks absorbed in thought.... No, it is nothing. No one would do such things. Civilisation has climbed above such perils. The interdependence of nations in trade and traffic, the sense of public law, the Hague Convention, Liberal principles, the Labour Party, high finance, Christian charity, common sense have rendered such nightmares impossible. Are you quite sure? It would be a pity to be wrong. Such a mistake could only be made once – once for all."[51]

"A strange light began...to fall and grow upon the map of Europe."
Medals ceremony with General Pershing, July 1919.

Although Churchill called World War II the "Unnecessary War", he had no such view of the war that preceded it. And although he had tried repeatedly to assuage the rivalries and enmities that caused it – such as his proposals for a "Naval Holiday" in Anglo-German warship construction, or a peace conference between the European heads of state – he, unlike some of his Cabinet colleagues, considered World War I almost inevitable.

True to his nature, Churchill plunged into it heart and soul, and fought it out to the bitter end. As he was being cast aside by Asquith in 1915, following the Dardanelles débâcle and Lord

---

51 Crisis I, 48–9. For more of this remarkable quotation see Chapter 1.

Fisher's resignation from the Admiralty, Clementine Churchill sent the Prime Minister a wise and prescient evaluation: "Winston may in your eyes & in those with whom he has to work have faults but he has the supreme quality which I venture to say very few of your present or future Cabinet possess – the power, the imagination, the deadliness, to fight Germany."[52]

The Dardanelles, which broke him for a time, figures large in this chapter; but there are many other subjects of key importance to Churchill's view of history: France's stopping the Germans on the Marne, which he had predicted to within a couple of days;[53] the frightful slaughter of Tannenberg, Verdun and Passchendaele; Germany's flaws and the fall of the Kaiser; the errors of Versailles and the reparations and war debts it imposed; thoughtful contemplations over whether this was really "the war to end wars" or, as Foch suggested, only "an Armistice for twenty years".[54] His thoughts on Armistice Day (1918...Victory) are among the finest words in English on the sad futility of the war that did not after all end wars....

I write "Churchill's view" with design and emphasis, because this is of course his own version of events: "a contribution to history", as he sometimes put it, not history itself. Certainly he shares the blame for the failed expedition to the Dardanelles, although historians have since revealed the many hands responsible.

Certainly he was often unpopular with his colleagues for repeatedly championing his causes. His confidence in himself was at many points his undoing; and yet, when one looks around at the War Cabinets of those days, it is hard to find characters of equal mettle, as determined as he was to bring the war to a victorious conclusion.

Churchill himself never doubted his abilities, though for a time he despaired of being allowed to exercise them. From Flanders in 1916 he contemplated what his death would mean: "...no more tangles to unravel, no more anxieties to face, no more hatreds & injustices to encounter: joy of all my foes, relief of that old rogue [Asquith], a good ending to a chequered life, a final gift – unvalued – to an ungrateful country – an impoverishment of the war-making power of Britain wh[ich] no one w[oul]d ever know or measure or mourn".[55]

In many ways his death in 1916 would have meant exactly that. What it would have meant in the war to follow is left happily to the imagination.

To track the war in rough chronological order, I have sorted the quotations which relate to specific events by year (1914–19), and then in order of publication. This does not provide a perfectly accurate chronology, but seemed the best way to allow the reader to follow events without disrupting my rule that all quotations must be dated by the time they were uttered or published.

1914

Advent of the war

At the beginning of this War megalomania was the only form of sanity.

1915, 15 NOVEMBER.

Events also got on to certain lines and no one could get off them again. Germany clanked obstinately, recklessly, awkwardly, towards the crater, and dragged us all in with her.

1923. (CRISIS I, 13–14.)

Liberal politics, the People's Budget, Free Trade, Peace, Retrenchment and Reform—all the war cries of our election struggles began to seem unreal in the presence of this new preoccupation. Only Ireland held her place among the grim realities which came one after another into view. No doubt other Ministers had similar mental experiences.

1923. (CRISIS I, 52.)

The Cabinet on Friday afternoon [24 July 1914] sat long revolving the Irish problem....

---

52 Soames, Clementine, 123.
53 See Chapter 30, Churchill clairvoyant...World War I.
54 WW2 I, 7.
55 OB, CV3/2, 1467.

The discussion turned principally upon the boundaries of Fermanagh and Tyrone....the Cabinet was about to separate, when the quiet grave tones of Sir Edward Grey's voice were heard reading a document which had just been brought to him from the Foreign Office. It was the Austrian note to Serbia....This note was clearly an ultimatum; but it was an ultimatum such as had never been penned in modern times. As the reading proceeded it seemed absolutely impossible that any State in the world could accept it, or that any acceptance, however abject, would satisfy the aggressor. The parishes of Fermanagh and Tyrone faded back into the mists and squalls of Ireland, and a strange light began immediately, but by perceptible gradations, to fall and grow upon the map of Europe.

1923. (CRISIS I, 192–3.)

Like many others, I often summon up in my memory the impression of those July days. The world on the verge of its catastrophe was very brilliant. Nations and Empires crowned with princes and potentates rose majestically on every side, lapped in the accumulated treasures of the long peace. All were fitted and fastened—it seemed securely—into an immense cantilever. The two mighty European systems faced each other glittering and clanking in their panoply, but with a tranquil gaze....The old world in its sunset was fair to see.

But there was a strange temper in the air. Unsatisfied by material prosperity the nations turned restlessly towards strife internal or external. National passions, unduly exalted in the decline of religion, burned beneath the surface of nearly every land with fierce, if shrouded, fires.

1923. (CRISIS I, 188.)

I wondered whether armies and fleets could remain mobilized for a space without fighting and then demobilize.

I had hardly achieved this thought when another Foreign Office box came in. I opened it and read "Germany has declared war on Russia." There was no more to be said. I walked across the Horse Guards Parade and entered 10, Downing Street....I said that I intended instantly to mobilize the Fleet notwithstanding the Cabinet decision, and

that I would take full personal responsibility to the Cabinet the next morning. The Prime Minister, who felt himself bound to the Cabinet, said not a single word, but I was clear from his look that he was quite content.

1923. (CRISIS I, 216–17.)

Churchill sent the fleet to its war stations on Saturday 1 August. After Churchill's fall from office in 1915 his old nemesis Lord Kitchener came to cheer him by saying, "Well, there is one thing at any rate they cannot take from you. The fleet was ready." See Chapter 17, People...Kitchener.

The terrible "Ifs" accumulate. If my first thoughts on July 27 of sending the *New Zealand* to the Mediterranean had materialized; if we could have opened fire on the *Goeben* during the afternoon of August 4; if we had been less solicitous for Italian neutrality; if Sir Berkeley Milne had sent the *Indomitable* to coal at Malta instead of Biserta; if the Admiralty had sent him direct instructions when on the night of the 5th they learned where the *Goeben* was; if Rear-Admiral Troubridge in the small hours of August 7 had not changed his mind; if the *Dublin* and her two destroyers had intercepted the enemy during the night of the 6th–7th—the story of the *Goeben* would have ended here.

1923. (CRISIS I, 255.)

On the escape to Turkey of the German battle-cruiser SMS Goeben *following a chase across the eastern Mediterranean at the outbreak of the war in August 1914.* Goeben *became the Turkish battleship* Yavuz *and, remarkably, remained the flagship of the Turkish fleet until 1950. She was not scrapped until 1973.*

There was a man [Princip] who fired the shots that killed the Archduke and his wife at Sarajevo. There was the man [Kaiser Wilhelm] who, deliberately, accepting the risk of a world war, told the Austrian emperor that Germany would give him a free hand against Serbia and urged him to use it. There was the man [Berchtold] who framed and launched the ultimatum to Serbia.

1931. (CRISIS V, 82.)

Churchill ascribed to these men the touching off the war, but not its causes, which were far more profound. See also People...Kaiser Wilhelm and Berchtold.

Let me remind the House of the sort of thing that happened in 1914. There was absolutely no quarrel between Germany and France. One July afternoon the German ambassador drove down to the Quai d'Orsay and said to M. Viviani, the French Prime Minister, "We have been forced to mobilize against Russia, and war will be declared. What is to be the position of France?" The French Prime Minister made the answer, which his Cabinet had agreed upon, that France would act in accordance with what she considered to be her own interests. The ambassador said, "You have an alliance with Russia, have you not?" "Quite so," said the French Prime Minister. And that was the process by which, in a few minutes, the area of the struggle, already serious in the east, was enormously widened and multiplied by the throwing in of the two great nations of the west.

1934, 7 FEBRUARY.

I remember coming out of the Cabinet meeting on an August afternoon in 1914, when war was certain, and the Fleet was already mobilized, with this feeling: "How are we to explain it all to Canada, Australia, South Africa and New Zealand; nay, how are we to explain it all to our own people in the short time left?" But, when we came out from the fierce controversy of the Cabinet room into the open air, the whole of the peoples of the British Empire, of every race and every clime, had already sprung to arms. Our old enemies, recent enemies, Generals Botha and Smuts, were already saddling their horses to rally their commandos to the attack on Germany...

1944, 21 APRIL.

Antwerp's defence

It is remarkable that Lord Esher should be so much astray....We must conclude that an uncontrollable fondness for fiction forbade him to forsake it for fact. Such constancy is a defect in an historian.

1922, 30 JANUARY. (OB IV, 757.)

Responding to Lord Esher, editor and historian, who had criticised Churchill's defence of

Antwerp in 1914. WSC, who arrived on scene to direct the Belgians, prolonged the defence long enough to safeguard the Channel ports.

Marne victory

We can see more clearly across the mists of Time how Hannibal conquered at Cannae, than why Joffre won at the Marne.

1929. (CRISIS IV, 444.)

Though evenly matched, the Franco-British armies decisively routed the German army at the Marne in September 1914. Gen. Joseph Joffre was the French commander-in-chief. Hannibal defeated a superior Roman force in 216 BC.

Tannenberg defeat

The Battle of Tannenberg inaugurated the memorable partnership of Hindenburg and Ludendorff....It stands among the renowned associations of Great Captains in history.

1931. (CRISIS V, 206.)

Hindenburg and Ludendorff, in this colossal battle, almost completely destroyed the Russian Second Army. WSC invented for it a joint monogram, "HL", no doubt having in mind the alliance of Marlborough and Eugene.

1915

Coalition Government (Asquith)

I wanted us to go to the Tories when we were strong....not in misfortune to be made an honest woman of.

1915, JUNE. (BONHAM CARTER, 427–8.)

When Churchill expressed regret over the formation of a coalition under her father, Liberal Prime Minister H. H. Asquith, Violet Bonham Carter asked him if, after all, a coalition wasn't desirable.

Dardanelles and Gallipoli

With the armies bogged down in useless trench warfare, Churchill looked for a way round the impasse and his eye lit upon a proposal to send a fleet of surplus warships through the Dardanelles into the Sea of Marmora. The perhaps optimistic idea was that warships appearing off Constantinople would cow Turkey into surrendering, allowing Britain and France to succour the hard-pressed Russians. The project, which admirals deemed possible with "ships alone", stalled in March 1915 when Turkish mines caused the Anglo-French fleet to withdraw from the entrance to the narrow waterway. In late April troops were then sent, belatedly and with inadequate leadership and preparations, to secure the Gallipoli Peninsula in European Turkey; they failed with great loss of life, and all forces were withdrawn by late 1915. Churchill, the most ardent champion of the project, received most of the blame. When in May his First Sea Lord, Admiral Fisher, resigned in protest over the Dardanelles (despite initial enthusiasm), Asquith formed a Coalition government with the Conservatives. Their price was Churchill's resignation from the Admiralty. It was the nadir of his career. By the end of 1915 he had left to fight in Flanders, vowing never again to undertake a cardinal operation of war without plenary authority to see it through.

Shall we by decisive action, in hopes of shortening the conflict, marshal and draw in the small nations in the North and in the South who now stand outside it? Or shall we plod steadily forward at what lies immediately in our front? Shall our armies toil only in the mud of Flanders, or shall we break new ground? Shall our fleets remain contented with the grand and solid results they have won, or shall they ward off future perils by a new inexhaustible audacity.

1914, DECEMBER. (CRISIS I, 504–5.)

I think we had better hear what others have to say about the Turkish plans before taking a decided line. I w[oul]d not grudge 100,000 men because of the great political effects in the Balkan Peninsula but Germany is the foe, & it is bad war to seek cheaper victories & easier antagonists.

1915, 4 JANUARY. (OB III, 236.)

WSC to First Sea Lord (Fisher): as solid a proof as there is that Churchill was not the instigator of the Dardanelles/Gallipoli operation. In fact, he was still entertaining doubts when operations began on 19 February 1915.

The Dardanelles delay through weather from the 19th to the 24th inclusive was v[er]y vexatious to me, & hard to bear. But now they have moved forward again, and so far everything shows the soundness of the plan. The capacity to run risks is at famine prices. All play for safety.

1915, 26 FEBRUARY, ADMIRALTY. (OB, CV3/1, 580.)

WSC to his brother Jack.

There is more blood than paint upon these hands. All those thousands of men killed. We thought it would be a little job, and so it might have been if it had been begun in the right way.

1915, JULY. HOE FARM, GODALMING, SURREY. (MORGAN, 615.)

Ted Morgan writes: "...the ageing poet Wilfrid Blunt, still elegantly Byronic, had visited Hoe Farm [Churchill's holiday retreat after being dismissed from the Admiralty over the Dardanelles] and found Winston bitter over his political fortunes. Blunt thought he would have gone mad save for Clemmie."

...I will not have it said that this was a civilian plan, foisted by a political amateur upon reluctant officers and experts...

All through this year I have offered the same counsel to the Government—undertake no operation in the West which is more costly to us in life than to the enemy; in the East, take Constantinople; take it by ships if you can; take it by soldiers if you must; take it whichever plan, military or naval, commends itself to your military experts, but take it, and take it soon, and take it while time remains....But it seems to me that if there were any operations in the history of the world which, having been begun, it was worth while to carry through with the utmost vigour and fury, with a consistent flow of reinforcements, and an utter disregard of life, it was the operation so daringly and brilliantly begun by Sir Ian Hamilton in the immortal landing of the 25th April....

1915, 15 NOVEMBER.

The expedition was nearing its end now, but Churchill never changed his mind.

After weighing and sifting all the expert evidence with the personal knowledge I had of all the officers concerned, I recommended it to the Prime Minister and the War Council in the presence of my principal naval advisers, believing, as did everyone there, that I carried them with me, and I pressed it with all the resources at my disposal. I recommended it to the War Council and to the French Government, not as a certainty, but as a legitimate war gamble, with stakes that we could afford to lose for a prize of inestimable value—a prize which, in the opinion of the highest experts there was a fair reasonable chance of our winning, a prize which at that time could be won by no other means. On that basis clearly understood it was accepted by all concerned.

1915, 15 November.

A fifth of the resources, the effort, the loyalty, the resolution, the perseverance vainly employed in the battle of the Somme to gain a few shattered villages and a few square miles of devastated ground, would in the Gallipoli Peninsula, used in time, have united the Balkans on our side, joined hands with Russia, and cut Turkey out of the war.

1917, 5 March. (OB IV, 10.)

Churchill's testimony to the Dardanelles Commission.

It will always be incredible to future ages that every man in this country did not rally to an enterprise which carried with it such immense possibilities, and which required such limited resources to carry it into effect. It will always be incredible that for the sake of a dozen old ships and half a dozen extra divisions, more or less, and a few hundred thousand rounds of high explosive shells, we failed to gain a prize specially adapted to our Oriental interests and other amphibious power, and which, by cutting Turkey out of the War, and uniting in one federation the States of the Balkan Peninsula, would have brought us within measurable distance of lasting success.... Your Commission may condemn the men who tried to force the Dardanelles, but your children will keep their condemnation for all who did not rally to their aid.

1917, 20 March.

Churchill in Parliament on the Dardanelles Commission.

Not to persevere—that was the crime.

1923. (Crisis II, 169.)

[My only consolation for the failure of the Dardanelles] was that God wished things to be prolonged in order to sicken mankind of war, and that therefore He had interfered with a project that would have brought the war to a speedier conclusion.

1929, Atlantic Voyage. (Gilbert, Search, 227.)

WSC to Leopold Amery (Amery diaries).

Hypnotised states

Some of these small states are hypnotized by German military pomp and precision. They see the glitter, they see the episode; but what they do not see or realize is the capacity of the ancient and mighty nations against whom Germany is warring to endure adversity, to put up with disappointment and mismanagement, to recreate and renew their strength, to toil on with boundless obstinacy through boundless suffering to the achievement of the greatest cause for which men have fought.

1915, 15 November.

From Churchill's farewell speech to the House before leaving for the Western Front. The States he referred to were Balkan nations such as Bulgaria, which had become convinced that victory lay with the Central Powers.

Ultimate victory

There is no reason to be discouraged about the progress of the War. We are passing through a bad time now, and it will probably be worse before it is better, but that it will be better if we only endure and persevere, I have no doubt whatever....It is not necessary for us, in order to win the War, to push the German lines back over all the territory they have absorbed, or to pierce them. While the German lines extend far beyond their frontiers, while their flag flies over conquered capitals and subjugated provinces, while all the appearances of military success attend their arms, Germany may be defeated more fatally in the second or third year of the war than if the Allied Armies had entered Berlin in the first.

1915, 15 November.

1916

Coalition Government (Lloyd George)

It is now the fashion to speak of the Lloyd George War Cabinet as if it gave universal satisfaction and conducted the war with unerring judgment and unbroken success. On the contrary, complaints were loud and clamant. Immense disasters, such as the slaughter of Passchendaele, the disaster at Caporetto in 1917, the destruction of the Fifth Army after March 21st, 1918—all these and others befell that rightly famous Administration. It made numerous mistakes. No one was more surprised than its members when the end of the war came suddenly in 1918, and there have even been criticisms about the character of the Peace which was signed and celebrated in 1919.

1942, 24 FEBRUARY.

Lice

War is declared, gentlemen, on the lice.

1916. (COWLES, 210.)

Churchill's first words to the Sixth Royal Scots Fusiliers, when he took command of the battalion in France. One of his officers, Andrew Dewar Gibb, added:

> *With these words was inaugurated such a discourse on* pulex Europaeus, *its origin, growth and nature, its habitat and its importance as a factor in wars ancient and modern, as left one agape with wonder at the force of its author.*

Out of power

God for a month of power & a good shorthand writer.

1916, 3 JANUARY, FLANDERS. (OB, CV3/2, 1354.)

WSC in a letter to his wife from the trenches.

Slaughter on the Western Front

This war proceeds along its terrible path by the slaughter of infantry...I say to myself every day. What is going on while we sit here, while we go away to dinner or home to bed? Nearly 1,000—Englishmen, Britishers, men of our race are knocked into bundles of bloody rags every twenty-four hours, and carried away to hasty graves or to field ambulances.

1916, 23 MAY.

WSC's horror at the senseless slaughter on the Western Front made him a strong partisan of the Dardanelles campaign; he was no less appalled by the trenches after Gallipoli had been abandoned.

Before the war it had seemed incredible that such terrors and slaughters, even if they began, could last more than a few months. After the first two years it was difficult to believe that they would ever end.

1927. (CRISIS III PART 2, 509.)

How many have gone? How many more to go? The Admiralty is fast asleep and lethargy & inertia are the order of the day. However everybody seems delighted—so there is nothing to be said. No plans, no enterprise, no struggle to aid the general cause. Just sit still on the spacious throne and snooze.

1916, SEPTEMBER. (GILBERT, LIFE, 367.)

WSC to his brother-in-law, Bill Hozier.

Verdun

From the moment when he received the news of the total evacuation of the Gallipoli Peninsula, the opportunity of General von Falkenhayn, Chief of the German General Staff, was to pronounce the word *ROUMANIA*. He pronounced instead the word *VERDUN*.

1927. (CRISIS III PART 1, 82.)

The Battle of Verdun (February–December 1916) cost over a quarter million lives. It resulted in a German repulse and German General Falkenhayn's replacement by Paul von Hindenburg. WSC criticised Falkenhayn's decision to attack the French fortress of Verdun instead of Romania, with its rich prizes of oil fields and granaries.

1917

America enters the war

[There are] only two ways of winning the war, and they both begin with A. One is aeroplanes and the other is America....Everything else is swept away.

1917, 4 SEPTEMBER, MUNITIONS COUNCIL. (GILBERT, LIFE, 378.)

Churchill was later misquoted as expressing regret, in the 1930s, that America entered the war, only to desert her allies in the making of a permanent peace. This comment during the war itself is remarkably consistent with his views of the need to bring America into World War II two decades later.

There is no need to exaggerate the material assistance given by the United States to the Allies. All that could be sent was given as fast and as freely as possible, whether in manhood, in ships or in money. But the war ended long before the material power of the United States could be brought to bear as a decisive or even as a principal factor...

But if the physical power of the United States was not in fact applied in any serious degree to the beating down of Germany; if for instance only a few score thousand Germans fell by American hands; the moral consequence of the United States joining the Allies was indeed the deciding cause in the conflict...

Suddenly a nation of one hundred and twenty millions unfurls her standard on what is already the stronger side; suddenly the most numerous democracy in the world, long posing as a judge, is hurled, nay, hurls itself into the conflict. The loss of Russia was forgotten in this new reinforcement. Defeatist movements were strangled on the one side and on the other inflamed.

1927. (CRISIS III PART 1, 226–7.)

Churchill's words do not suggest the conclusion by revisionist writers or false quotations (see Appendix I ... America and World War I). Quite the contrary, as this and the following entry suggest.

American historians will perhaps be somewhat lengthy in explaining to posterity exactly why the United States entered the Great War on April 6, 1917, and why they did not enter at any earlier moment. American ships had been sunk before by German submarines; as many American lives were lost in the *Lusitania* as in

all the five American ships whose sinking immediately preceded the declaration of war. As for the general cause of the Allies, if it was good in 1917 was it not equally good in 1914? There were plenty of reasons of high policy for staying out in 1917 after waiting so long.

It was natural that the Allies, burning with indignation against Germany, breathless and bleeding in the struggle, face to face with mortal dangers, should stand amazed at the cool, critical, detached attitude of the great Power across the Atlantic.

1927. (CRISIS III PART 1, 227.)

Passchendaele

Nearly 800,000 of our British men have shed their blood or lost their lives here during 3½ years of unceasing conflict. Many of our friends & my contemporaries all perished here. Death seems as commonplace & as little alarming as the undertaker. Quite a natural ordinary event, which may happen to anyone at any moment, as it happened to all these scores of thousands who lie together in this vast cemetery, ennobled and rendered for ever glorious by their brave memory.

1918, 23 FEBRUARY, FRANCE. (OB, CV4/1, 252.)

WSC to his wife after visiting the battlefield, the Third Battle of Ypres, which the Allies won after suffering half a million casualties, and the Germans a quarter million.

In six weeks at the farthest point we had advanced four miles. Soon the rain descended, and the vast crater fields became a sea of choking fetid mud in which men, animals and tanks floundered and perished hopelessly....But the German losses were always on a far smaller scale. They always had far fewer troops in the cauldron. They always took nearly two lives for one and sold every inch of ground with extortion....

The full severity of a Flanders winter gripped the ghastly battlefield. Ceaselessly the Menin gate of Ypres disgorged its streams of manhood. Fast as the cannons fired, the ammunition behind them flowed in faster. Even in October the British Staff were planning and launching offensives and were confident of reaching the goal of decisive results. It was not until the end of November that final failure was accepted. "*Boche* is bad and *Boue* [Mud] is bad," said Foch, then little more than an observer of events, "but *Boche* and *Boue* together ... Ah!" He held up warning hands....

[General Robertson wrote to Haig on 27 September 1917:] "My own views are known to you. They have always been 'defensive' in all theatres but the West. But the difficulty is to *prove* the wisdom of this now that Russia is out. I confess I stick to it more because I see nothing better, and because my instinct prompts me to stick to it, than because of any good argument by which I can support it." These are terrible words when used to sustain the sacrifices of nearly four hundred thousand men.

1927. (CRISIS III, PART 2, 337–9.)

1918

Engagement

We sit in calm, airy, silent rooms opening upon sunlit and embowered lawns, not a sound except of summer and of husbandry disturbs the peace; but seven million men, any ten thousand of whom could have annihilated the ancient armies, are in ceaseless battle from the Alps to the Ocean.

1929, JULY. ("MARSHAL FOCH," PALL MALL; GC, 118.)

German collapse

The mighty framework of German Imperial Power...shivered suddenly into a thousand individually disintegrating fragments....The faithful armies were beaten at the front and demoralised from the rear. The proud, efficient Navy mutinied. Revolution exploded in the most disciplined and docile of States. The Supreme War Lord [Kaiser Wilhelm] fled.

1927. (CRISIS III PART 2, 540.)

Haig's armies

His [Sir Douglas Haig's] armies bore the lion's share in the victorious advance, as they had already borne the brunt of the German assault....And ever his shot-pierced divisions, five times decimated within the year, strode forward with discipline, with devotion and with gathering momentum.

1927. (CRISIS III PART 2, 516.)

Kaiser's fate

It was evident however that the lawyers would have to have their say....This also opened up a vista both lengthy and obscure.

1929. (CRISIS IV, 43.)

On the demand for hanging Kaiser Wilhelm II in 1918. See also People...Kaiser Wilhelm.

Upon the brow from which the diadem of empire had been smitten, he [Mr. Lloyd George] would have set a crown of martyrdom; and Death, with an all-effacing gesture, would have re-founded the dynasty of the Hohenzollerns upon a victim's tomb.

1930, NOVEMBER. ("THE EX-KAISER," STRAND MAGAZINE; GC, 24.)

The 1918 election slogan "Hang the Kaiser", tacitly asserted by Lloyd George, was thwarted when Holland refused to give up the exiled Kaiser Wilhelm; so we shall never know if his martyrdom might have revived the Hohenzollern Empire, or only further encouraged the Nazis.

Modernisation

...the progress during the War has already been extraordinary, and when the military victory has been gained by our Fleets and Armies, and the industries of Britain are liberated from their present trammels, when they return from war to peace, they will return vivified, renovated, purged, re-equipped, re-organized and modernized to an extent which would not be conceivable in peaceful times and which could not have been achieved by the patient and sagacious labours of an entire generation in tranquillity.

1918, 25 APRIL.

Munitions shortages

I remember at the Ministry of Munitions being told that we were running short of...bauxite and steel, and so forth; but we went on, and, in the end the only thing we ran short of was Huns. One fine morning we went down to our offices...and found they had all surrendered.

1941, 27 MARCH.

Spoken at a London luncheon for US Ambassador John Winant, London.

Offensive rushes

...every offensive lost its force as it proceeded. It was like throwing a bucket of water over the floor. It first rushed forward, then soaked forward, and finally stopped altogether until another bucket could be brought.

1918, 24 MARCH. (CRISIS III PART 2, 423.)

Churchill had returned to London from an inspection of the battlefield after the German breakout in March 1918. At Downing Street, Lloyd George asked him how it would be possible to hold any positions on the battlefront now that carefully fortified lines had been taken.

Victory

I cannot but think we have much to be thankful for, and more still to hope for in the future.

1918, 9 DECEMBER. (CRISIS IV, 48.)
WSC TO DAVID LLOYD GEORGE.

It was a few minutes before the eleventh hour of the eleventh day of the eleventh month. I stood at the window of my room looking up Northumberland Avenue towards Trafalgar Square, waiting for Big Ben to tell that the War was over....Victory had come after all the hazards and heart-breaks in an absolute and unlimited form. All the Kings and Emperors with whom we had warred were in flight or exile. All their Armies and Fleets were destroyed or subdued. In this Britain had borne a notable part, and done her best from first to last....

The minutes passed. I was conscious of reaction rather than elation. The material purposes on which one's work had been centred, every process of thought on which one had lived, crumbled into nothing. The whole vast business of supply, the growing outputs, the careful hoards, the secret future plans—but yesterday the whole duty of life—all at a stroke vanished like a nightmare dream, leaving a void behind....What was to happen to our three million Munition workers? What would they make now? How would the roaring factories be converted? How in fact are swords beaten into plough-shares?....

And then suddenly the first stroke of the chime. I looked again at the broad street beneath me. It was deserted. From the portals of one of the large hotels absorbed by Government Departments darted the slight figure of a girl clerk, distractedly gesticulating while another stroke of Big Ben resounded. Then from all sides men and women came scurrying into the street. Streams of people poured out of all the buildings. The bells of London began to clash. Northumberland Avenue was now crowded with people in hundreds, nay, thousands....Flags appeared as if by magic. Streams of men and women flowed from the Embankment. They mingled with torrents pouring down the Strand on their way to acclaim the King....

Is this the end? Is it to be merely a chapter in a cruel and senseless story? Will a new generation in their turn be immolated to square the black accounts of Teuton and Gaul? Will our children bleed and gasp again in devastated lands? Or will there spring from the very fires of conflict that reconciliation of the three giant combatants, which would unite their genius and secure to each in safety and freedom a share in rebuilding the glory of Europe?

1927. (CRISIS III PART 2, 541–4.)

The choice is in our own hands. Like the Israelites of old, blessing and cursing is set before us. Today we can have the greatest failures or the greatest triumph, as we choose. There is enough for all. The earth is a generous mother. Never did science offer such fairy gifts to man. Never did their knowledge and organisation stand so high. Repair the waste. Rebuild the ruins. Heal the wounds. Crown the victors. Comfort the broken and broken-hearted. There is the battle we have now to fight. There is the victory we have now to win. Let us go forward together.

1918, 26 NOVEMBER. DUNDEE. (CS III, 2645.)

This is the first known occurrence of the famous peroration, "Let us go forward together," which he repeatedly used in World War II. It also closely prefigures the 1940 charge, "...plough the land, build the ships, guard the streets, succour the wounded, uplift the downcast and honour the brave." (See Chapter 1.)

During the first four years of the last war the Allies experienced nothing but disaster and disappointment. That was our constant fear: one blow after another, terrible losses, frightful dangers. Everything miscarried. And yet at the end of those four years the morale of the Allies was higher than that of the Germans, who had moved from one aggressive triumph to another, and who stood everywhere triumphant invaders of the lands into which they had broken....During that war we repeatedly asked ourselves the question: How are we going to win? and no one was able to answer it with much precision, until at the end, quite suddenly, quite unexpectedly, our terrible foe collapsed before us, and we were so glutted with victory that in our folly we threw it away.

1940, 18 June.

1919

Aftermath

The greater part of Europe and the greater part of Asia are plunged in varying degrees of disorder and anarchy. Vast areas in both these Continents, inhabited by immense and once thriving populations, are convulsed by hunger, bankruptcy and revolution. The victorious Allies, on whom there rests the responsibility for enabling the world to get to work again, are themselves exhausted in a very serious degree; and all these elements of difficulty and uncertainty vitiate, or threaten to vitiate, our calculations. At every point must be added the enormous tangle of winding up the war effort, and adjusting with as little waste as possible the complications of war-time finance.

1919, 3 March.

When all was over, Torture and Cannibalism were the only two expedients that civilized, scientific, Christian States had been able to deny themselves: and these were of doubtful utility.

1923. (Crisis I, 11.)

...when the war of the Giants was over, the war of the Pygmies began. All sorts of races who counted for nothing, or stood aside from, or were protected in, the dire struggle of the world, hurried up with their pretensions while the great combatants lay gasping. Then came a period which it was easy to predict, when the victors forgot, and the vanquished remembered....

The disease of Defeat was Bolshevism.... The disease of Victory was different. It was an incapacity to make Peace.

1937, 11 November. ("Armistice – Or Peace?," Evening Standard; Step, 172–3.)

After the First World War, when I went to the War Office, I put away all the medium and heavy artillery that had been made and everybody completely forgot about it. It cost hardly anything to keep and then it came out and was of great use and value when we had to make provision for the defence of this county against the possibilities of invasion in 1940 and 1941.

1948, 1 December.

British war debt

It imposed upon Great Britain, much impoverished by the war, in which...she had fought from the first day to the last, the payment of thirty-five millions sterling a year for sixty-two years. The basis of this agreement...a severe and improvident condition for both borrower and lender. [President Calvin Coolidge remarked, "They hired the money, didn't they?"] This laconic statement was true, but not exhaustive.

1948. (WW2 I, 19–20.)

Churchill's vexation over World War I debts was that America made loans to Germany, which used the loans to pay war reparations to Britain, which in turn was repaying its own war loans to the United States.

German reparations

We and America took under the Peace Treaty three great liners from Germany. The Germans surrendered them at a valuation and then borrowed the money to build two very much better ones. They immediately captured the Blue Riband of the Atlantic, and they have it still. Now the loans with which the Germans built these ships are subject to a moratorium, while we are unable to go on with our new Cunarder because of our financial crisis. That is typical of what I mean when I say that Germany has not nearly so much reason to complain as some people suppose....I have always held the view that these war debts and reparations have been a great curse.

1932, 11 July.

Germany has paid since the War an indemnity of about one thousand millions sterling, but she has borrowed in the same time about two thousand millions sterling with which to pay that indemnity and to equip her factories.

1932, 23 NOVEMBER.

Versailles Treaty

...it is by the territorial settlements in Europe that the Treaties of 1919 and 1920 will finally be judged. Here we are in contact with those deep and lasting facts which cast races of men into moulds and fix their place and status in the world. Here we stir the embers of the past and light the beacons of the future. Old flags are raised anew; the passions of vanished generations awake; beneath the shell-torn soil of the twentieth century the bones of long dead warriors and victims are exposed, and the wail of lost causes sounds in the wind.

1929. (CRISIS IV, 202.)

The draft Treaty presented to the Germans prescribed the absolute cession of Upper Silesia, after the Ruhr the richest iron and coal district in the German Empire, to the Poles. This was the greatest blot upon the draft Treaty with Germany.

1929. (CRISIS IV, 210–11.)

In applying this principle of nationalism to the defeated States after the war it was inevitable that mistakes and some injustices should occur. There are places where the populations are inextricably intermingled. There are some countries where an island of one race is surrounded by an area inhabited by another. There were all kinds of anomalies, and it would have defied the wit of man to make an absolutely perfect solution.

1933, 13 APRIL.

Mr. Lloyd George seems to suppose that he is entitled to some special claim to interpret the Treaty of Versailles and other treaties which ended the War. It is quite true that he had a great deal to do with the making of that Treaty, but once a treaty is signed it becomes an international instrument which everyone can judge, and I personally prefer the measured opinion of the jurists upon whom the Foreign Office relies.

1933, 7 NOVEMBER.

Personally, having lived through all these European disturbances and studied carefully their causes, I am of opinion that if the Allies at the peace table at Versailles had not imagined that the sweeping away of long-established dynasties was a form of progress, and if they had allowed a Hohenzollern, a Wittelsbach, and a Habsburg to return to their thrones, there would have been no Hitler.

1945, 26 APRIL. (WW2 VI, 643.)

WSC to Sir Hughe Knatchbull-Hugessen, then British Ambassador in Brussels.

World War I: General Observations

British contribution

More than 80 per cent. of the British casualties of the Great War were English. More than 80 per cent. of the taxation is paid by the English taxpayers. We are entitled to mention these facts, and to draw authority and courage from them.

1933, 24 APRIL. ROYAL SOCIETY OF ST. GEORGE, LONDON. (COVENANT, 92.)

Casualties

During the whole war the Germans never lost in any phase of the fighting more than the French whom they fought and frequently inflicted double casualties upon them....In all the British offensives, the British casualties were never less than 3 to 2 and often nearly double the corresponding German losses.

1927. (CRISIS III PART 1, 53–4.)

The importance Churchill attached to this statement is shown by his underlining these words in his original text. Colin Coote noted that WSC disproved any claimed benefits of a "war of attrition" by giving the relative casualties. "It is, however, not irrelevant that the Germans could stand their lesser casualties less than the Allies could stand greater."

Causes of the war

The war had been fought to make sure that the smallest state should have the power to assert its lawful rights against even the greatest, and this will probably be for several generations an enduring fact.

1929. (CRISIS IV, 159.)

Germany's flaw

It was the fatal weakness of the German Empire that its military leaders, who knew every detail of their profession and nothing outside it, considered themselves, and became, arbiters of the whole policy of the state. In France throughout the War, even in its darkest and most convulsive hours, the civil government, quivering to its foundations, was nevertheless supreme....

1930, 14 JULY. ("LUDENDORFF'S 'ALL – OR NOTHING,'" DAILY TELEGRAPH; THOUGHTS, 108–9.)

Germany's navy

Defeat to Germany at sea means nothing but loss of the ships sunk or damaged in battle. Behind the German "Dreadnoughts" stand four and a half million soldiers and a narrow sea-front bristling with fortresses and batteries. Nothing we could do, after a naval victory, could affect the safety or freedom of a single German hamlet.

1914, 17 MARCH.

Medicine and science

We have now entered on an exceptionally intricate phase of highly scientific warfare in which the relative progress of the two sides cannot be accurately measured from day to day.

1918, 25 APRIL.

Healing and surgery....returned them again and again to the shambles. Nothing was wasted that could contribute to the process of waste.

1929. (CRISIS IV, 453.)

WSC was commenting on continued fighting after World War I.

Nature of the war

We cannot go on treating the war as if it were an emergency which can be met by make-shifts. It is, until it is ended, the one vast, all-embracing industry of the nation, and it is until it is ended the sole aim and purpose of all our lives.

1916, 22 AUGUST.

But nothing daunted the valiant heart of man. Son of the Stone Age, vanquisher of nature with all her trials and monsters, he met the awful and self-inflicted agony with new reserves of fortitude....The vials of wrath were full: but so were the reservoirs of power.

1923. (CRISIS I, 11.)

Prolongation

It would be an unmeasured crime to prolong this war for one unnecessary day. It would be an unmeasured and an immeasurable blunder to make peace before the vital objects are achieved.

1917, 3 OCTOBER. ALDWYCH CLUB, LONDON. (CS III, 2575.)

See also World War II...Prolongation.

Tank tactics

None should be used until all can be used at once. They should be disposed secretly along the whole attacking front two or three hundred yards apart. Ten or fifteen minutes before the assault these engines should move forward....Nothing but a direct hit from a field gun will stop them....*If artillery is used to cut wire, the direction and imminence of the attack is proclaimed days beforehand.*

1915, 3 DECEMBER. (CRISIS II, 87.)

From Churchill's paper, "Variants of the Offensive", written two years before tanks were successfully used, at Cambrai, and twenty-five years before the Germans put this concept into deadly practice. See other tank entries in Chapters 12 and 14.

17

BETWEEN
THE WARS
1919-1939

"How often in the history of nations has the golden opportunity been allowed to slip away! How often have rulers and Governments been forced to make in foul weather the very journey which they have refused to make prosperously in fair weather!"[56]

"I lived mainly at Chartwell, where I had much to amuse me."
With daughter Mary at Chartwell, Westerham, Kent, 1925.

By "appeasement", Churchill in *The Second World War* was referring to the handling of Nazi Germany, but over the course of a long career he held many attitudes towards appeasement, and his approach varied, even in the same 1930s that saw him so outspoken about Hitler.

---

56 WSC, House of Commons, 17 December 1906: a remarkably apt reflection on the years to come.

The Italian invasion of Abyssinia in October 1935, for example, provided Churchill with an opportunity for positive appeasement. At the Stresa Conference earlier that year, Britain, France and Italy had agreed to maintain the independence of Austria. With that goal in mind, Churchill was reluctant to support sanctions imposed by the League of Nations on Italy after Mussolini's African incursions. The sanctions certainly worsened Anglo-Italian relations, thrusting Il Duce further towards Hitler, eventually to the point where he uttered no protest over Hitler's absorption of Austria in 1938.

Churchill's early approaches to Mussolini had been cautious, even admiring. His critics believed this betrayed WSC's fascist tendencies, quoting his early description of Mussolini as "the greatest law-giver among living men". Professor Paul Addison quotes a 1933 remark by Sir Samuel Hoare, the Secretary of State for India, to Lord Willingdon, the Viceroy of India: "I believe that at the back of his mind he thinks that he will not only smash the Government but that England is going Fascist and that he, or someone like him, will eventually be able to rule India as Mussolini governs north Africa."[57] But this was a misinterpretation.

Churchill *did* hold firm beliefs, as Sir Martin Gilbert writes: "No aggression, he warned, from wherever it came, could be condoned. All aggressive action must be judged, not from the standpoint of Right and Left, but of 'right or wrong'....his support for a Middle Way between Fascism and Communism was gaining ground. It was for this standpoint that Churchill looked on the Spanish Civil War. 'I refuse to become the partisan of either side,' he declared. As to Communism and Nazism, he added: 'I hope not to be called upon to survive in the world under a Government of either of these dispensations'."[58]

Churchill's abhorrence of tyrannical regimes was tempered by *realpolitik*, an ability to recognise and to oppose the greater danger. Had Germany after Versailles evolved into a peaceful democratic state, with no designs on other countries, 1935 may have found Churchill condemning Italy, and choosing sides in Spain the following year. But almost uniquely among prominent leaders, he always focused on the most essential.

The quotations arranged here, almost all from House of Commons debates, are mainly from the 1930s. Together they provide a remarkable window on WSC's campaign to warn the nation of Hitler's intentions: a period many including this writer regard as his true finest hour.

As in the previous chapter, date-sensitive quotations are grouped in chronological order by year; more general quotations follow, alphabetically by subject. Because of its culminating nature, the 1938 Munich pact and Churchill's long speech following it are excerpted at length.

The chronological entries are grouped under the same three headings Churchill used in his book of 1928–38 speeches, *Arms and the Covenant*: Germany Disarmed; Germany Arming; Germany Armed.

---

57 Addison, Home Front, 314.
58 Gilbert, Political Philosophy, 98.

Germany Disarmed

1922–32

The century thus far...

What a disappointment the 20th century has been....

We have seen in ev[ery] country a dissolution,
a weakening of those bonds,
a challenge to those principles,
a decay of faith
an abridgement of hope
on wh[ich] structure & ultimate
existence
of civilised society depends.
We have seen in ev[ery] part of the globe
one g[rea]t country after another
wh[ich] had erected an orderly, a peaceful
a prosperous structure of civilised society,
relapsing in hideous succession
into bankruptcy, barbarism or anarchy.
Can you doubt, my faithful friends
as you survey this sombre panorama,
that mankind is passing through a period
marked
not only by an enormous destruction
& abridgement of human species,
not only by a vast impoverishment
& reduction in means of existence
but also that destructive tendencies
have not yet run their course?
And only intense, concerted & prolonged
efforts
among all nations
can avert further & perhaps even greater
calamities.

1922, 11 NOVEMBER. ARMISTICE DAY, DUNDEE.
(OB IV, 915.)

These are Churchill's verbatim notes, in his favoured "speech form", which picked out his lines in their proper cadence. The text above is therefore somewhat different than in published versions of his speech.

France and Germany

France with her dwindling but well-armed population sees the solid German block of seventy millions producing far more than twice her number of military males each year, towering up grim and grisly....When you have been three times invaded in a hundred years by Germany and have only escaped destruction the last time because nearly all the other nations of the world came to your aid, which they certainly do not mean to do again, you cannot help feeling anxious about this ponderous mass of Teutonic humanity piling up beyond the frontier.

1931, 31 MARCH. (OB V, 408.)

Text submitted to the Hearst newspaper New York American, *and published on 5 April with the title, "Austro-German Union Would Aid World Peace says Winston Churchill". Through World War I, France had been invaded by Germany in 1815, 1870 and 1914.*

I would say to those who would like to see Germany and France on an equal footing in armaments. "Do you wish for war?" For my part, I earnestly hope that no such approximation will take place during my lifetime or that of my children....

I come now to the proposals of qualitative disarmament about which [the Foreign Secretary] was so very insistent. He told us that it was difficult to divide weapons into offensive and defensive categories. It certainly is, because almost every conceivable weapon may be used either in defence or offence....Take the tank. The Germans, having invaded France, entrenched themselves; and in a couple of years they shot down 1,500,000 French and British soldiers who were trying to free the soil of France. The tank was invented to overcome the fire of machine guns with which the Germans were maintaining themselves in France, and it did save a lot of life in the process of eventually clearing the soil of the invader. Now, apparently, the machine gun, which was the German weapon for holding on to thirteen provinces of France, is to be the virtuous, defensive machine gun, and the tank, which was the means by which these lives were saved, is to be placed under the censure and obloquy of all just and righteous men.

1932, 13 MAY.

On 10 April 1932 in the final round of the German Presidential election, Field Marshal von Hindenburg received 19,300,000 votes, Adolf Hitler 13,400,000.

Now the demand is that Germany should be allowed to rearm. Do not delude yourselves. Do not let His Majesty's Government believe—I am sure they do not believe—that all that Germany is asking for is equal status....All these bands of sturdy Teutonic youths, marching through the streets and roads of Germany, with the light of desire in their eyes to suffer for their Fatherland, are not looking for status. They are looking for weapons, and, when they have the weapons, believe me they will then ask for the return of lost territories and lost colonies....

I cannot recall any time when the gap between the kind of words which statesmen used and what was actually happening in many countries was as great as it is now. The habit of saying smooth things and uttering pious platitudes and sentiments to gain applause, without relation to the underlying facts, is more pronounced now than it has ever been in my experience....

I say quite frankly, though I may shock the House, that I would rather see another ten or twenty years of one-sided armed peace than see a war between equally well-matched Powers or combinations of Powers—and that may be the choice.

1932, 23 NOVEMBER.

In the Reichstag elections on 1 September, the National Socialists had polled 37.3 per cent. In another election on 6 November, they polled 33.1 per cent. On 2 December, Hindenburg appointed General von Schleicher German Chancellor.

Maintaining peace

Under Augustus Caesar the peace of the world was maintained by 800,000 armed men. But today twenty million trained reserves are required to guard the jigsaw frontiers of twenty jealous, impoverished and truculent nations of the continent of Europe. This cannot continue indefinitely without leading from the conflicts of countries to conflicts of continents.

1932, 2 FEBRUARY. UNION LEAGUE, CHICAGO.
(*CHICAGO TRIBUNE*, 3 FEBRUARY 1932.)

Two weeks after Churchill's speech, Japan proclaimed the puppet state of Manchukuo in Manchuria, China.

1933

Four-Power Pact

The Pact or Agreement so incontinently accepted has to be amended, has to be modified to fit the views of the small nations in the League. It has to be modified again to meet special claims. It has to be modified again to meet the requirements of France, and it very soon reaches the point where it loses the adherence of Germany. It is no good, saying it is merely "much ado about nothing". That is not so. Harm has been done, disturbance has been created, suspicion has been spread, and English influence has lost a measure of its virtue and added a measure to its responsibility....

Nothing in life is eternal, of course, but as surely as Germany acquires full military equality with her neighbours while her own grievances are still unredressed and while she is in the temper which we have unhappily seen, so surely should we see ourselves within a measurable distance of the renewal of general European war.

1933, 13 APRIL.

In July 1933 Italy, Germany, Britain and France, in a watered-down treaty, reaffirmed their adherence to the League of Nations covenant, Locarno Treaties and Kellogg-Briand Pact. Mussolini had hoped this would reduce the power of small states in the League of Nations. The agreement did encourage the German-Polish Non-Aggression Pact of 1934. Hitler would soon laugh at both treaties.

France

As long as France is strong and Germany is but inadequately armed there is no chance of France being attacked with success, and therefore no obligation will arise under Locarno for us to go to the aid of France. I am sure, on the other hand, that France, which is the most pacific nation in Europe at the present time, as she is, fortunately, the most efficiently armed, would never attempt any violation of the Treaty or commit an overt act against Germany...

1933, 23 MARCH.

A week earlier on 16 March, the German Reichstag had passed an Enabling Bill giving Hitler full dictatorial powers.

Misrepresentations

He [Mr. Lloyd George] represented that Germany might have a few thousand more rifles than was allowed by the Treaty, a few more Boy Scouts, and then he pictured the enormous armies of Czechoslovakia and Poland and France, with their thousands of cannon, and so forth. If I could believe that picture I should feel much comforted, but I cannot. I find it difficult to believe it in view of the obvious fear which holds all the nations who are neighbours of Germany and the obvious lack of fear which appears in the behaviour of the German Government and a large proportion of the German people....

[Mr. Lansbury] said just now that he and the Socialist Party would never consent to the rearming of Germany....but is [he] quite sure that the Germans will come and ask him for his consent before they rearm? Does he not think they might omit that formality and go ahead without even taking a card vote of the Trades Union Congress?

1933, 7 NOVEMBER.

George Lansbury (1859–1940), Labour MP 1910–12, 1922–40, was at this time Leader of the Labour Party. Three weeks before Churchill's remark, Germany had left the disarmament conference in Geneva and resigned from the League of Nations. By now Hitler had eliminated all non-Nazi elements in the German government: in the November Reichstag election, only Nazi candidates were allowed and they obtained 95 per cent of the vote.

National spirit

I think of Germany, with its splendid clear-eyed youth marching forward on all the roads of the Reich singing their ancient songs, demanding to be conscripted into an army; eagerly seeking the most terrible weapons of war; burning to suffer and die for their fatherland. I think of Italy, with her ardent Fascisti, her renowned Chief, and stern sense of national duty. I think of France, anxious, peace-loving, pacifist to the core, but armed to the teeth and determined to survive as a great nation in the world.

1933, 17 FEBRUARY, OXFORD. (OB V, 456.)

Speech at the Anti-Socialist and Anti-Communist Union. Two weeks earlier, von Schleicher had resigned as German Chancellor and Adolf Hitler had taken his place, heading a coalition government.

Platitudes and humbug

We ought not to deal in humbug. There are good people in this country who care about disarmament. In many ways I think they are wrong, but I do not see why they should be tricked. I think they should have the plain truth told them, and if they disagree they have their constitutional remedy....

You talk of secret diplomacy, but let me tell you that there is a worse kind of secret diplomacy, and it is the diplomacy which spreads out hope and soothing-syrup for the good, while all the time winks are exchanged between the people who know actually what is going on....

I hope and trust that the French will look after their own safety, and that we shall be permitted to live our life in our island without being again drawn into the perils of the Continent of Europe.

1933, 14 MARCH.

Two weeks before this speech the Reichstag was set afire, and on 5 March, Reichstag elections returned the National Socialists with 44 per cent and 17 million votes.

The Way Ahead

We all desire to see peace and goodwill established among the nations, old scores forgotten, old wounds healed, the peoples of Christendom united to rebuild their portion of the world, to solve the problem of their toiling masses, to give a higher standard of life to the harassed populations....Our first supreme object is not to go to war. To that end we must do our best to prevent others from going to war. But we must be very careful that, in so doing, we do not increase the risk to ourselves of being involved in a war if, unfortunately, our well-meant efforts fail to prevent a quarrel between other Powers.

1933, 23 MARCH.

Germany Arming

1934

Disarmament sidetracks

I was taken to task the other day for saying that the Lord Privy Seal [Mr. Eden] in his mission to the three capitals in Europe had failed. I have listened to his very agreeably delivered speech, so excellent in its phrasing and so well meant in its sentiments, and I am bound to say that the farthest I can go in altering my statement that his mission had failed is to say that up to the present, at any rate, it has not succeeded....False ideas have been spread about the country that disarmament means peace....

The Romans had a maxim: "Shorten your weapons and lengthen your frontiers." But our maxim seems to be: "Diminish your weapons and increase your obligations." Aye, and "diminish the weapons of your friends."

1934, 14 MARCH.

On the rejection of a MacDonald Plan for equilibrium in armaments between the great powers.

Eight years ago we were told that disarmament had been discussed at Geneva. For two and a half years the actual conference has been proceeding. The Leader of the Liberal Opposition [Sir Herbert Samuel] has, therefore, had a good run for his experiment. His hope has been abounding. It has preserved him at every stage from seeing the facts.

1934, 30 JULY.

German intentions

A new situation has been created, largely in the last few years...by rubbing this sore of the Disarmament Conference until it has become a cancer, and also by the sudden uprush of Naz-ism in Germany, with the tremendous covert armaments which are proceeding there today.

...I cannot see in the present administration of Germany any assurance that they would be more nice-minded in dealing with a vital and supreme situation than was the Imperial Government of Germany...[We may] be confronted on some occasion with a visit from an ambassador, and may have to give an answer in a very few hours; and if that answer is not satisfactory, within the next few hours the crash of bombs exploding in London and cataracts of masonry and fire and smoke will warn us of any inadequacy which has been permitted in our aerial defences....

1934, 7 FEBRUARY.

In an agreement with Poland on 26 January, Hitler had renounced for ten years all claims to the Polish Corridor. On 31 January a British white paper made further proposals for disarmament.

What is the great new fact which has broke in upon us during the last eighteen months? Germany is rearming. That is the great new fact which rivets the attention of every country in Europe, indeed in the world, and which throws almost all other issues into the background....What was the use of going to a division? You might walk a majority round and round the Lobbies for a year, and not alter the facts by which we are confronted.

1934, 28 NOVEMBER.

During a debate on the rate of Germany's rearmament effort.

International blackmail

Never in our history have we been in a position where we could be liable to be blackmailed, or forced to surrender our possessions, or take some action which the wisdom of the country or its conscience would not allow.

1934, 28 NOVEMBER.

Pacifism

I do not suppose there has ever been such a pacifist-minded Government. There is the Prime Minister [Ramsay MacDonald] who in the war proved in the most extreme manner and with very great courage his convictions and the sacrifices he would make for what he believed was the cause of pacifism. The Lord President of the Council [Stanley Baldwin] is chiefly associated in the public mind with the repetition of the prayer, "Give peace in our time."

1934, 30 JULY.

Notice the attribution of "peace in our time". The words would become a famous irony in 1938.

Preponderance of force

When you have peace you will have disarmament. But there has been during these years a steady deterioration in the relations between different countries and a rapid increase in armaments that has gone on in spite of the endless flow of oratory, of well-meaning sentiments, of perorations, and of banquets. Europe will be secure when nations no longer feel themselves in danger as many of them do now. Then the pressure and the burden of armaments will fall away automatically, as they ought to have done in a long peace, and it might be quite easy to seal a movement of that character by some general agreement....

I could not see how better you can prevent war than by confronting an aggressor with the prospect of such a vast concentration of force, moral and material, that even the most reckless, even the most infuriated leader, would not attempt to challenge those great forces.

[Twenty years ago] we had a supreme fleet; nobody could get at us in this island; and we had powerful friends on the continent of Europe, who were likely to be involved in any quarrel before we were. But today, with our aviation in its present condition, we are in a far worse position....

1934, 13 JULY.

On 8 July French Foreign Minister Barthou supported by British Foreign Minister Sir John Simon proposed an "Eastern Locarno" pact between Russia, Poland, Czechoslovakia, Germany and the Baltic States.

1935

Abyssinia invaded

I do not believe that Signor Mussolini would have embarked upon his Abyssinian venture but for the profound preoccupation of France in German rearmament, and, I must add, but for the real or supposed military and naval weakness of Great Britain. It was the fear of a re-armed Germany that led France to settle her differences with Italy at the beginning of this year, and very likely when these matters were being settled what is called a free hand in Abyssinia was thrown in. We may regret it, but we must first see and consider the forces

operative upon France before we presume to utter reproaches.

1935, 4 OCTOBER.

Anglo-German Naval Treaty

We have, however unintentionally, nullified and stultified the League of Nations' condemnation of treaty-breaking in respect of armaments, in which we were ourselves concerned, in which, indeed, we took a leading part. We have, it seems to me, revealed, again quite unintentionally, a very considerable measure of indifference to the interests of other Powers, particularly Powers in the Baltic, who were encouraged by our example to join with us in the League of Nations in condemning treaty-breaking. In the name of what is called practical realism we have seemed to depart...from the principle of collective security in a very notable fashion.

1935, 11 JULY.

The Anglo-German Naval Agreement of July 1935, signed without French approval, set the size of the German navy at 35 per cent of the tonnage of the Royal Navy, much larger than allowed by the Versailles Treaty. The treaty ultimately failed because the Germans regarded it as an Anglo-German alliance against France and Russia, the British only as a step towards disarmament.

Under the [1935] Anglo-German Agreement no provision was made, as some of us suggested, that old ships should be counted at a lower tonnage than new ships in estimating the tonnage of German naval construction. If we keep the Royal Sovereigns, Germany would be entitled under the Treaty to build two additional battleships in the four-year period in question, and they have asked us to state in advance, as they have a right to ask, what we propose to do. We have promised to scrap or sink the first two Royal Sovereigns, and I presume that there is no hope now of rescuing the others from that imprudent decision.

1939, 16 MARCH.

Franco-Soviet talks

Stalin and Molotov were of course anxious to know above all else what was to be the strength of the French Army on the Western

Front: how many divisions? what period of service? After this field had been explored, Laval said: "Can't you do something to encourage religion and the Catholics in Russia? It would help me so much with the Pope [Pius XII]." "Oho!" said Stalin. "The Pope! How many divisions has *he* got?" Laval's answer was not reported to me; but he might certainly have mentioned a number of legions not always visible on parade.

1948. (WW2 I, 105–6.)

In May 1935 French Premier Pierre Laval travelled to Moscow to discuss the Franco-Soviet mutual assistance pact signed in Paris on 2 May. Vyacheslav Mikhailovich Molotov was President of the Communist Party, 1930–41, and Minister of Foreign Affairs, 1939–56.

German air strength

Although the House listened to me with close attention, I felt a sensation of despair. To be so entirely convinced and vindicated in a matter of life and death to one's country, and not to be able to make Parliament and the nation heed the warning, or bow to the proof by taking action, was an experience most painful.

1935, 19 March. (WW2 I, 96.)

We are entering upon a period of danger and difficulty. And how do we stand in this long period of danger? There is no doubt that the Germans are superior to us in the air at the present time, and it is my belief that by the end of this year, unless their rate of construction and development is arrested by some agreement, they will be possibly three, and even four, times our strength.

1935, 22 May.

German armaments

Here, again, mystery shrouds all German preparations. At various points facts emerge which enable a general view to be taken. Enormous sums of money are being spent on German aviation and upon other armaments. I wish we could get at the figures which are being spent upon armaments. I believe that they would stagger us with the terrible tale they would tell of the immense panoply which that nation of nearly 70 millions of people is assuming, or has already assumed.

1935, 19 March.

The arms production has the first claim on the entire industry of Germany. The materials required for the production of armaments are the first charge on the German exchange. The whole of their industry is woven into an immediate readiness for war. You have a state of preparedness in German industry which was not attained by our industry until after the late War had gone on probably for two years.

1935, 31 May.

Germany is already well on her way to become, and must become incomparably, the most heavily armed nation in the world and the nation most completely ready for war. There is the dominant factor; there is the factor which dwarfs all others, affecting the movements of… politics and diplomacy in every country throughout Europe; and it is a melancholy reflection that in the last hours of this Parliament we have been the helpless, perhaps even the supine, spectators of this vast transformation to the acute distress of Europe, and to our own grievous disadvantage.…There is even a theory that the Germans are re-arming only out of national self-respect and that they do not mean to hurt anyone at all. Whatever you believe, whatever you think…[I submit] that we cannot have any anxieties comparable to the anxiety caused by German re-armament.

1935, 24 October.

Others were distracted by the "dwarf" matters: on 4 October Italy invaded Abyssinia, and the League Assembly voted sanctions against Italy six days later. Churchill refused to be distracted by what he saw as a side issue.

Recently he [Hitler] has offered many words of reassurance, eagerly lapped up by those who have been so tragically wrong about Germany in the past. Only time can show, but, meanwhile, the great wheels revolve; the rifles, the cannon, the tanks, the shot and shell, the air-bombs, the poison-gas cylinders, the aeroplanes, the submarines, and now the beginnings of a fleet, flow in ever-broadening streams from the already largely war-mobilised arsenals and factories of Germany.

1935, November. ("Hitler and His Choice," *Strand Magazine*; GC 172.)

In a Commons speech six months later Churchill repeated:

I confess that I have been occupied with this idea of the great wheels revolving and the great hammers descending day and night in Germany, making the whole ...population into one disciplined war machine.

In Colliers *in 1937 he again wrote: "While the great wheels revolve in the German Fatherland ... "*

Policy and armaments

It used to be said that armaments depend on policy. It is not always true, but I think that at this juncture it is true to say that policy depends, to a large extent, upon armaments. It is true to say that we have reached a position where the choice of policy is dictated by considerations of defence.

1935, 2 MAY.

1936

Abdication of responsibility

I have been staggered by the failure of the House of Commons to react effectively against those dangers. That, I am bound to say, I never expected. I never would have believed that we should have been allowed to go on getting into this plight, month by month and year by year, and that even the Government's own confessions of error would have produced no concentration of Parliamentary opinion and force capable of lifting our efforts to the level of emergency. I say that unless the House resolves to find out the truth for itself it will have committed an act of abdication of duty without parallel in its long history.

1936, 12 NOVEMBER.

Two days earlier Sir Thomas Inskip, Minister for the Coordination of Defence, had said:

The years have passed in the atmosphere of the ten-years rule and the Disarmament Conference. [No one could] organise supply on the basis of any design which has not yet been thoroughly tested and proved. ....you cannot recover the years that the locusts have eaten. ....[Mr. Churchill is] largely pushing at an open door.

Two days after Churchill's remarks, in the 1935 General Election, the Government was returned with a majority of 247.

Baldwin's failure

Some few weeks ago Sir Austen Chamberlain made a most serious speech of criticism, and even of censure, addressed to the Prime Minister [Baldwin] in his own presence. It astonished me that the Prime Minister did not rise at once and say whatever occurred to him to say....

There ought to be the cut-and-thrust of debate, and I am surprised that the Rt. Hon. Gentleman, if not at that moment, at any rate at the earliest opportunity, did not take up the points of argument which were addressed to him. If issues of this kind are pushed aside...there is bound to be a weakening in the ties which unite the House to the Government and which preserve the vitality of our Parliamentary institutions.

1936, 6 APRIL.

Owing to past neglect, in the face of the plainest warnings, we have now entered upon a period of danger greater than has befallen Britain since the U-boat campaign was crushed; perhaps, indeed, it is a more grievous period than that, because at that time at least we were possessed of the means of securing ourselves and of defeating that campaign. Now we have no such assurance.

1936, 12 NOVEMBER.

I have never heard such a squalid confession from a public man as Baldwin offered us yesterday.

1936, 13 NOVEMBER. (OB V, 799.)

Churchill to Sir Archibald Boyd-Carpenter (a Harrow chum). Prime Minister Baldwin had replied to Churchill thus:

Supposing I had gone to the country and said that Germany was rearming and that we must rearm, does anybody think that this pacific democracy would have rallied to that cry at that moment? I cannot think of anything that would have made the loss of the election from my point of view more certain.

After suggesting he had no such intention, Baldwin finally resigned on 28 May 1937.

When I first went into Parliament, now nearly forty years ago...the most insulting charge which could be made against a Minister...short of actual malfeasance, was that he had endangered the safety of the country...for electioneering considerations. Yet such are the surprising qualities of Mr. Baldwin that what all had been taught to shun has now been elevated into a canon of political virtue.

1936, 11 DECEMBER. ("THE PLEDGE OF FRANCE," *EVENING STANDARD*; STEP, 77.)

British Government's failures

The gravamen of the criticism which lies against Government is that they did not realize effectively, or at any rate that they did not act in accordance with, the marked deterioration in world affairs which occurred in 1932 and 1933. They continued to adhere to a policy which was adapted to one set of circumstances after an entirely different set of circumstances had supervened. They persisted in spite of all that we could say to the contrary. I suppose they resented the warnings which were given although the warnings which I gave the House were sober warnings, specific warnings, and friendly warnings.

1936, 10 MARCH.

When we think of the great power and influence which this country exercises we cannot look back with much pleasure on our foreign policy in the past five years. They certainly have been very disastrous years.

1936, 26 MARCH.

Cast aside

This was not the first time—or indeed the last—that I have received a blessing in what was at the time a very effective disguise.

1948. (WW2 I, 157.)

Churchill, who was not asked to join the Government after Baldwin handily won the 1935 election, wrote:

Mr. Baldwin knew no more than I how great was the service he was doing me in preventing me from becoming involved in all the Cabinet compromises and shortcomings of the next three years...

For Churchill's other "effectively disguised" blessing see Chapter 33, Ripostes...Election 1945.

Confident aggressors

The world seems to be divided between the confident nations who behave harshly, and the nations who have lost confidence in themselves and behave fatuously.

1936, 8 JANUARY, MARRAKESH. (OB, CV5/3, 10.)

WSC to his wife. Anthony Eden had become Foreign Secretary on 23 December, which WSC regarded as a hopeful sign.

False security

Broadly speaking, since the arrival of Herr Hitler in power three years ago the Germans have spent about £1,500,000,000 sterling upon warlike preparations directly or indirectly. The money has been raised by internal borrowing, and the revenues of Germany are already mortgaged two or three, or possibly four, years ahead. These figures are stupendous. Nothing like them has ever been seen in time of peace....

It is a general impression that we are overhauling Germany now...and that every month our relative position will improve. That is a delusion. It is contrary to the truth this year, and probably for many months next year....Germany will be outstripping us more and more even if our new programmes are accepted, and we shall be worse off at the end of this year than we are now, in spite of all our exertions....

1936, 10 MARCH.

We are going away on our holidays. Jaded ministers, anxious but impotent Members of Parliament, a public whose opinion is more bewildered and more expressionless than anything I can recall in my life—all will seek the illusion of rest and peace.

1936, 20 JULY.

Minister for the Coordination of Defence

It would seem, on the face of it, rather odd to invite the coordinator after the coordination is, according to the Government White Paper, already perfect and complete; to appoint the man who is to concert the plan after it has already been made, and embodied in the detailed Estimates for the current year.

1936, 10 MARCH.

A Government White Paper had proposed a Ministry for the Coordination of Defence to be headed by the entirely unsuited Sir Thomas Inskip. Since Churchill was hoping for a Cabinet appointment, his criticisms were relatively mild. His friend Professor Lindemann called Inskip's appointment "the most cynical thing that has been done since Caligula appointed his horse as consul" (OB V, 716).

We know now that these machine tools which we are about to order should have been ordered then, but were overlooked…A hideous hiatus of eight months must elapse before it can manifest itself, and after that it takes another eight months to make a gun. So that an enormous vista of anxiety lies before us, what I may call this valley of the shadow that we are going to move through for a long time—month after month of deep anxiety, when efforts will be made increasingly every month, every week, when anxiety will grow in the nation, when my Rt. Hon. Friend will be exerting himself night and day. I have no doubt. God speed him in it, but, all the same…he will be paying the penalty of these previous neglects.

1936, 29 May.

He [Sir Thomas Inskip, Minister for Coordination of Defence] has an office so absurdly constructed that the very conditions of his commission reveal a confusion of mind and a lack of comprehension in those who have defined it. He has allowed himself to become the innocent victim of responsibilities so strangely, so inharmoniously, so perversely grouped, endowed with powers so cribbed and restricted, that no one, not even Napoleon himself, would be able to discharge them with satisfaction.

1936, 20 July.

Inskip then stated that, had Britain begun building more aeroplanes two or three years ago as WSC had urged, they would have been "out of date" by 1936. Churchill suggested that by the same argument, they should put off building aeroplanes now.

Ministry of Supply

A friend of mine the other day saw a number of persons engaged in peculiar evolutions, genuflections and gestures….He wondered whether it was some novel form of gymnastics, or a new religion…or whether they were a party of lunatics out for an airing….they were a Searchlight Company of London Territorials, who were doing their exercises as well as they could without having the searchlights.

1936, 12 November.

Munitions

I heard the other day the following remark: "You would surely not deprive the Secretary of State for War of the responsibility for his own munitions supply?" That is exactly what I would do. Curiously enough, those words sound like an echo from the past. They were the very words which I heard Lord Kitchener use in the early months of 1915. "I could never give up," he said, "responsibility for the ammunition of the army." But he had to. He had to be made to, and unless he had been made to and been willing to give it up—afterwards he was thankful—his soldiers could never have been supplied with all that they needed. This is one of the lessons which we all had to learn with blood and tears. Have we really got to learn them all over again now?

1936, 21 May.

Period of calm

When you are drifting down the stream of Niagara, it may easily happen that from time to time you run into a reach of quite smooth water, or that a bend in the river or a change in the wind may make the roar of the falls seem far more distant; but your hazard and your preoccupation are in no way affected thereby.

1936, 6 April.

Prospects

Five years ago all felt safe, five years ago all were looking forward to peace, to a period in which mankind would rejoice in the treasures which science can spread to all classes if conditions of peace and justice prevail. Five years ago to talk of war would have been regarded not only as a folly and a crime, but almost as a sign of lunacy. Look at the difference in our position now!

1936, 26 March.

Rhineland

What is the real problem, the real peril? It is not reoccupation of the Rhineland, but this enormous process of the rearmament of Germany....This Rhineland business is but a step, is but a stage, is but an incident in this process. There is fear in every country, all round. Even here, in this country, with some protection from distance, there is fear....What is the fear and what is the question which arises from that fear? It is, "How are we going to stop this war which seems to be moving towards us in so many ways?"

1936, 26 MARCH.

On 7 March Hitler reoccupied the Rhineland, denounced the Versailles and Locarno treaties, but stated that the reoccupation was "purely symbolic". Churchill remained relatively silent on the Rhineland; he was hoping for office in the Government and restricted his advice to the French minister Flandin, whom he implored to take a firm stand on the situation.

Germany is now fortifying the Rhine zone, or is about to fortify it....The creation of a line of forts opposite to the French frontier will enable the German troops to be economized on that line, and will enable the main forces to swing around through Belgium and Holland. That is for us a danger of the most serious kind. Suppose we broke with France. Suppose the efforts to divide the last surviving free democracies of the Western world were successful and they were sundered, and suppose that France, isolated, could do no more than defend her own frontier behind Belgium and Holland by prolonging her fortress line, those small countries might very speedily pass under German domination, and the large colonial empires which they possess would no doubt be transferred at the same time. These are matters that ought not to escape our attention.

1936, 6 APRIL.

I advised M. Flandin to demand an interview with Mr. Baldwin before he left. This took place at Downing Street. The Prime Minister received M. Flandin with the utmost courtesy. Mr. Baldwin explained that although he knew little of foreign affairs he was able to interpret accurately the feelings of the British people. And they wanted peace. M. Flandin says that

he rejoined that the only way to ensure this was to stop Hitlerite aggression while such action was still possible. France had no wish to drag Great Britain into war; she asked for no practical aid, and she would herself undertake what would be a simple police operation, as, according to French information, the German troops in the Rhineland had orders to withdraw if opposed in a forcible manner. Flandin asserts that he said that all that France asked of her Ally was a free hand. This is certainly not true. How could Britain have restrained France from action to which, under the Locarno Treaty, she was legally entitled? The British Prime Minister repeated that his country could not accept the risk of war.

1948. (WW2 I, 153–4.)

Pierre Flandin (1889–1958) was French Foreign Minister when Hitler occupied the Rhineland. He had been French Prime Minister in 1934–35.

Tank development ignored

The tank was a British invention. This idea, which has revolutionized the conditions of modern war, was a British idea forced on the War Office by outsiders. Let me say they would have just as hard work today to force a new idea on it. I speak from what I know. During the war we had almost a monopoly, let alone the leadership, in tank warfare, and for several years afterwards we held the foremost place. To England all eyes were turned. All that has gone now. Nothing has been done in "the years that the locust hath eaten" to equip the Tank Corps with new machines.

1936, 12 NOVEMBER.

Time running out

The days of saving money on armaments have gone by. They may well return in happier conditions, but in this grim year of 1936, and still more in its ominous successor, our aim, our task, is not to reduce armaments. It is something even more intense, even more vital—namely, to prevent war, if war can be staved off. Horrible war, blasting in its devastation the prosperity of the world, can only be prevented by the marshalling of preponderant forces, sustained by world opinion, as a deterrent to any aggressor who breaks the peace.

There is no greater mistake than to suppose that platitudes, smooth words, timid policies, offer today a path to safety. Only by a firm adherence to righteous principles sustained by all the necessary "instrumentalities," to use a famous American expression, can the dangers which close so steadily upon us and upon the peace of Europe be warded off and overcome....

1936, 5 NOVEMBER.

A government report had stated that capital ships could not be constructed so as to be immune from air attack; yet to cease building them would lead to grave risk of disaster.

Germany Armed

1937

Air parity lost

We have been most solemnly promised parity. We have not got parity. Would the Rt. Hon. Gentleman [Inskip] rise in his place and say he could contend that we have parity at the present time with this Power which is in striking distance of our shores in first-line strength? I say we have not got the parity which we were promised. We have not nearly got it, we have not nearly approached it. Nor shall we get it during the whole of 1937, and I doubt whether we shall have it, or anything approaching it, during 1938. I feel bound to make these statements.

1937, 27 JANUARY.

Sir Thomas Inskip had declared that of 124 squadrons projected for home defence, 100 would be formed by the end of March, but 22 of them would be on a one-squadron basis. He added that he hoped the remainder might be formed, though not necessarily at full complement, by July. See also entries from this period in the chapter on Air and Air Power.

Arms race

When the perils are distant, it is right to dwell upon defects and deficiencies, so that they may be made good in time; but when they come much nearer, it is perhaps natural, and also prudent and healthy, to dwell, in public at any rate, upon resources rather than upon defects, and to take a fair stock of our strength no less than of the hazards of our position.

When a whole continent is arming feverishly, when mighty nations are laying aside every form of ease and comfort, when scores of millions of men and weapons are being prepared for war, when whole populations are being led forward or driven forward under conditions of exceptional overstrain, when the finances of the proudest dictators are in the most desperate condition, can you be sure that all your programmes so tardily adopted will, in fact, be executed in time?....

1937, 4 MARCH.

Naval and Air Estimates had been presented with increases of approximately one-third. Inskip, Chamberlain and Hoare were telling various audiences that it cost millions of pounds to rebuild the country's defences, and hoping it would never again let them "fall into disrepair", as Inskip put it.

Drift to catastrophe

We seem to be moving, drifting, steadily, against our will, against the will of every race and every people and every class, towards some hideous catastrophe. Everybody wishes to stop it, but they do not know how.

1937, 14 APRIL.

Ribbentrop meeting

Well, I suppose they asked me to show him [Ribbentrop] that, if they couldn't bite themselves, they kept a dog who could bark and might bite.

1937, 12 MAY. (BROAD, WINSTON CHURCHILL, 211.)

The Cabinet had asked Churchill to join them for lunch with Joachim von Ribbentrop (1893–1946, German Ambassador to Britain, 1936–38). The quote is Churchill's reply to Josiah Wedgwood, who had been surprised that Churchill had been invited. For Churchill's remarks see People...Ribbentrop.

1938

Alarm bell

One healthy growl from those benches three years ago—and how different today would be the whole layout of our armaments production! Alas, that service was not forthcoming. We have drifted on in general good-natured acquiescence for three whole years—not for three whole years of ignorance or unawareness, but for three whole years with the facts glaring us full in the face....

Is not this the moment when all should hear the deep, repeated strokes of the alarm bell, and when all should resolve that it shall be a call to action, and not the knell of our race and fame?

1938, 17 NOVEMBER.

From a long, post-Munich speech, "The Case for a Ministry of Supply". Ominously for the future, on 28 October fresh pogroms occurred in Germany and all Polish Jews were expelled from the Reich.

Austrian Anschluss

The gravity of the event of the 11th of March cannot be exaggerated. Europe is confronted with a programme of aggression, nicely calculated and timed, unfolding stage by stage, and there is only one choice open, not only to us, but to other countries who are unfortunately concerned—either to submit, like Austria, or else to take effective measures while time remains to ward off the danger and, if it cannot be warded off, to cope with it.

1938, 14 MARCH.

After assuring Austria of her independence the year before, Hitler summoned Austrian Chancellor Schussnig to Berchtesgaden in February and demanded that the Nazi Seyss-Inquart be appointed Austrian Minister of the Interior and Security. In London, The Times stated that "no one but a fanatic" would believe this meant that German Nazism could take root in Austria. Hitler proclaimed the German Anschluss or union with Austria on 13 March.

British supply failures

If Germany is able to produce in these three years equipment and armament of every kind for its Air Force and for sixty or seventy divisions of the Regular Army, how is it that we have been unable to furnish our humble, modest military forces with what is necessary? If you had given the contract to Selfridge or to the Army and Navy Stores, I believe that you would have had the stuff to-day.

1938, 25 MAY.

Selfridge founded the famous department store, Selfridge's.

Czechoslovakia threatened

I listened with the utmost attention to all that the Prime Minister said about our relations to Czechoslovakia, and it seems to me that he has gone a long way in making a commitment. First, I was very glad to hear him reaffirm his adherence and that of the Government to the obligations of the Covenant of the League. Under the Covenant of the League...we are obliged not to be neutral, in the sense of being indifferent, if Czechoslovakia is the victim of unprovoked aggression....

If we do not stand up to the dictators now, we shall only prepare the day when we shall have to stand up to them under far more adverse conditions.

1938, 24 MARCH.

The Covenant [of the League of Nations] does not prescribe that we should go to war for Czechoslovakia, or any other country, but only that we should not be neutral in the sense of being indifferent as between an aggressor and the victim of aggression.

1938, 9 MAY, MANCHESTER. (BLOOD, 24–5.)

Having absorbed Austria and reoccupied the Rhineland, Hitler was now massing troops along the Czech border; Czechoslovakian forces were mobilized on 20–21 May. Two weeks later, Sudeten Nazis led by Herr Henlein published a list of demands for unification with the Reich; the Czech Government pronounced these "unacceptable" and proposed instead a plan for "cantonal self-government" and other generous concessions. Hitler rejected them.

Eden's resignation

From midnight till dawn I lay in my bed consumed by emotions of sorrow and fear. There seemed one strong young figure standing up against long, dismal, drawling tides of drift and surrender, of wrong measurements and feeble impulses. My conduct of affairs would have been different from his in various ways, but he seemed to me at this moment to embody the life-hope of the British nation, the grand old British race that had done so much for men, and had yet some more to give. Now he was gone. I watched the daylight slowly creep in through the windows, and saw before me in mental gaze the vision of Death.

1948. (WW2 I, 201.)

Eden resigned as Chamberlain's foreign minister on 20 February 1938. This is one of the few published admissions of WSC's doubts about Britain's ability to survive.

French army

The peace of Europe rests today upon the French army. That army at the present time is the finest in Europe, but with every month that passes its strength is being outmatched by the ceaseless development of the new formations into which the vastly superior manhood of Germany is being cast. Almost any foreign policy is better than duality or continual chops and changes.

1938, 22 FEBRUARY.

Kristallnacht

The question which we have to vote upon, in my opinion, is little less than this: Are we going to make a supreme additional effort to remain a great Power, or are we going to slide away into what seem to be easier, softer, less strenuous, less harassing courses, with all the tremendous renunciations which that decision implies? Is not this the moment when all should hear the deep, repeated strokes of the alarm bell, and when all should resolve that it shall be a call to action, and not the knell of our race and fame?

1938, 17 NOVEMBER.

Churchill was speaking a week after Kristallnacht, "the night of broken glass", the ransacking of 8,000 Jewish shops and 1,688 synagogues, with 267 set on fire. Over 30,000 Jews were sent to concentration camps. One revisionist writer labelled Kristallnacht "the most outrageous event in Nazi Germany between Munich and the march into Prague" – a period of only four months which nicely eliminates the Rhineland, Austria and the Sudetenland from consideration...

Ministry of Supply

The Secretary of State for War [Mr. Hore Belisha], acclaiming his achievement of being in advance of schedule, almost invites us to place a chaplet of wild olives upon his brow. I assert that the Air Ministry and the War Office are absolutely incompetent to produce the great flow of weapons now required from British industry. I assert, secondly, that British industry is entirely capable of producing an overwhelming response both in respect of the air and of military materiel of all kinds both in quality and in quantity.

1938, 25 MAY.

Labour's Hugh Dalton demanded an inquiry into the state of Britain's air defences and supported the creation of a Ministry of Supply. Neville Chamberlain rejected both.

Take the astounding admission that modern guns available for the defence of London would have been doubled in number but for the bankruptcy of a small firm charged with an essential part. I beg the Prime Minister to face the force of that admission. He is a busy man of high competence himself. Is it not shocking that such a thing should have happened?....My right hon. Friend the Air Minister [Sir Kingsley Wood] has not been long enough in the office to grow a guilty conscience....

1938, 17 NOVEMBER.

The Government proposed to make the Air and War Ministries responsible for their own supply, instead of a Ministry of Supply which Churchill advocated. The proposed alternative, he said, "cannot deliver the goods in time but...can offer any amount of concerted explanation of why they have not been delivered".

Munich: Choosing between War and Shame

I think we shall have to choose in the next few weeks between war and shame, and I have very little doubt what the decision will be.

1938, 13 AUGUST. (OB, CV5/3 1117.)

WSC to Lloyd George.

...we seem to be very near the bleak choice between War and Shame. My feeling is that we shall choose Shame, and then have War thrown in a little later on even more adverse terms than at present.

1938, 11 SEPTEMBER, CHARTWELL. (CV5/3,1155; MANCHESTER II, 334, 364.)

WSC to Lord Moyne, responding to an invitation to Antigua. William Manchester wrote:

In almost any gathering, it would have been indiscreet to remark... "Churchill says the Government had to choose between war and shame. They chose shame. They will get war, too."

With Hitler threatening war over the Sudetenland and the Czechs mobilising, Chamberlain flew to meet Hitler at Berchtesgaden on 15 September, Godesberg on the 26th and Munich on the 30th. The final meeting was attended by Mussolini and French Premier Daladier but not the Czechs, who were refused admittance. They were told they must give up the Sudetenland and the fortress line that alone defended Czechoslovakia from Germany. Returning from Munich on 1 October, Chamberlain announced that he had achieved "peace in our time".

Munich Eve

Now is time at last to rouse the nation. Perhaps it is the last time it can be roused with a chance of preventing a war, or with a chance of coming through to victory should our efforts to prevent war fail. We should lay aside every hindrance and endeavour by uniting the whole force and spirit of our people to raise again a great British nation standing up before all the world; for such a nation, rising in its ancient vigour, can even at this hour save civilization.

1938, 24 MARCH.

My hope is, therefore, that these perils will pass. If they pass, the road will be open to many good solutions for the mutual benefit of all. The road will also be open to a large expansion in the daily life of the great masses of the people of every race. We might indeed see a movement forward which would raise the human race to new levels of security and well-being, such as have not been attained in any former age. But whatever may happen, foreign countries should

know—and the Government is right to let them know—that Great Britain and the British Empire must not be deemed incapable of playing their part and doing their duty as they have done on other great occasions which have not yet been forgotten by history.

1938, 27 AUGUST, THEYDON BOIS, ESSEX. (BLOOD, 59.)

At Nuremberg on 12 September, Hitler promised that the "oppression" of Sudeten Germans in Czechoslovakia would be ended.

Munich Pact

It is the hour, not for despair, but for courage and rebuilding; and that is the spirit which should rule our minds.

1938, 4 OCTOBER. ("FRANCE AFTER MUNICH," DAILY TELEGRAPH; STEP, 275.)

I will begin by saying what everybody would like to ignore or forget but which must nevertheless be stated, namely that we have sustained a total and unmitigated defeat, and that France has suffered even more than we have....The utmost my Rt. Hon. Friend the Prime Minister [Neville Chamberlain] has been able to secure by all his immense exertions, by all the great efforts and mobilization which took place in this country, and by all the anguish and strain through which we have passed in this country, the utmost he has been able to gain for Czechoslovakia in the matters which were in dispute has been that the German dictator, instead of snatching the victuals from the table, has been content to have them served to him course by course.

We really must not waste time, after all this long debate, upon the difference between the positions reached at Berchtesgaden, at Godesberg and at Munich. They can be very simply epitomised, if the House will permit me to vary the metaphor: £1 was demanded at the pistol's point. When it was given, £2 were demanded at the pistol's point. Finally, the dictator consented to take £1 17s. 6d. and the rest in promises of goodwill for the future....

I am not quite clear why there was so much danger of Great Britain or France being involved in a war with Germany at this juncture if, in fact, they were ready all along to sacrifice Czechoslovakia. The terms which the Prime Minister brought back with him...could easily have been agreed, I believe, through the ordinary diplomatic channels at any time during the summer....

All is over. Silent, mournful, abandoned, broken, Czechoslovakia recedes into the darkness. She has suffered in every respect by her association with the western democracies and with the League of Nations, of which she has always been an obedient servant. She has suffered in particular from her association with France, under whose guidance and policy she has been actuated for so long....

We are in the presence of a disaster of the first magnitude which has befallen Great Britain and France. Do not let us blind ourselves to that. It must now be accepted that all the countries of central and eastern Europe will make the best terms they can with the triumphant Nazi power. The system of alliances in central Europe upon which France has relied for her safety has been swept away, and I can see no means by which it can be reconstituted....

Many people, no doubt, honestly believe that they are only giving away the interests of Czechoslovakia, whereas I fear we shall find that we have deeply compromised, and perhaps fatally endangered, the safety and even the independence of Great Britain and France. This is not merely a question of giving up the German colonies, as I am sure we shall be asked to do. Nor is it a question only of losing influence in Europe. It goes far deeper than that. You have to consider the character of the Nazi movement and the rule which it implies.

...what I find unendurable is the sense of our country falling into the power, into the orbit and influence of Nazi Germany, and of our existence becoming dependent upon their good will or pleasure....

I do not grudge our loyal, brave people, who were ready to do their duty no matter what the cost, who never flinched under the strain of last week—I do not grudge them the natural, spontaneous outburst of joy and relief when they learned that the hard ordeal would no longer be required of them at the moment; but they should know the truth. They should know that there has been gross neglect and deficiency in our defences; they should know that we have sustained a defeat without a war, the consequences of which will travel far with

us along our road; they should know that we have passed an awful milestone in our history, when the whole equilibrium of Europe has been deranged, and that the terrible words have for the time being been pronounced against the western democracies: "Thou art weighed in the balance and found wanting."

1938, 5 OCTOBER.

Alfred Duff Cooper resigned as First Lord of the Admiralty on 2 October, as the House of Commons began a three-day debate on Czechoslovakia. Churchill cried when he heard of this. Czech President Beneš resigned on the 5th as Churchill was rising to speak these words; a week later Beneš left for exile. Germany completed her occupation of part of Czechoslovakia, exceeding in many cases the agreed boundaries; the Gestapo arrived with its customary programme of arrests and deportations.

Munich postscript

Alexander the Great remarked that the people of Asia were slaves because they had not learned to pronounce the word "No." Let that not be the epitaph of the English-speaking peoples, or of Parliamentary democracy, or of France, or of the many surviving liberal States of Europe.

1938, 16 OCTOBER. BROADCAST, LONDON. (BLOOD, 88.)

I shall be asked, "Have you no confidence in His Majesty's Government?" Sir, I say "Yes" and "No." I have great confidence that these Hon. and Rt. Hon. Friends of mine will administer faithfully and well the Constitution of this country, that they will guard its finances in a thrifty manner, that they will hunt out corruption wherever it may be found, that they will preserve the peace and order of our streets and the impartiality of our courts and keep a general hold upon Conservative principles. [Laughter.] In all these matters I have a sincere and abiding confidence in them. But if you ask whether I have confidence in their execution of Defence programmes, even in their statements as to the degree to which those Defence programmes have at any moment advanced then I must beg the House not to press me too far. [Renewed laughter.]

1938, 17 NOVEMBER.

Sir Hugh Seely (Lib.) moved an amendment to the Address calling for a Ministry of Supply, on which Churchill spoke favourably. The amendment was defeated, Chamberlain taking up WSC's last words:

...if I were asked whether judgment is the first of my right hon. Friend's many admirable qualities I should have to ask the House of Commons not to press me too far.

Churchill replied on 9 December; see below.

The Prime Minister said in the House of Commons the other day that where I failed, for all my brilliant gifts etc, was in the faculty of judgment. I would gladly submit my judgments about foreign affairs and National defence during the last five years to comparison with his own....In February [he] said that the tension in Europe had greatly relaxed; a few weeks later Nazi Germany seized Austria. I predicted that he would repeat this statement as soon as the shock of the rape of Austria passed away. He did so in the very same words at the end of July. By the middle of August Germany was mobilising for those bogus manoeuvres which, after bringing us all to the verge of a world war, ended in the complete destruction and absorption of the republic of Czechoslovakia. At the Lord Mayor's Banquet in November at the Guildhall, he told us that Europe was settling down into a more peaceful state. The words were hardly out of his mouth before the Nazi atrocities upon the Jewish population resounded throughout the civilised world.

> 1938, 9 DECEMBER, CHINGFORD, ESSEX.
> (OB, CV5/3, 1302.)

WSC's reply to Chamberlain; see note above.

Munitions

We are told that "All is ready for a Minister of Munitions on the outbreak of war." Lord Zetland tells us that all that happens is that he or some other noble personage has to press a button. I hope that it is not a button like the last gaiter button which was talked of before the war of 1870. He has only to press this button and a Ministry of Munitions will leap into being fully armed like Minerva from the head

of the Minister for the Coordination of Defence. Do not let the House believe that, I beg of it.

> 1938, 25 MAY.

Napoleon was told, when declaring war against Prussia, that his army was "ready to the last gaiter button".

Prospects

Two years ago it was safe, three years ago it was easy, and four years ago a mere dispatch might have rectified the position. But where shall we be a year hence? Where shall we be in 1940?

> 1938, 24 MARCH.

Roosevelt's hand rejected

That Mr. Chamberlain...should have possessed the self-sufficiency to wave away the proffered hand stretched out across the Atlantic leaves one, even at this late date, breathless with amazement.

> 1948. (WW2 I, 199.)

In January 1938, Roosevelt had proposed inviting representatives of the European nations to Washington for a conference in order to try to resolve disagreements.

1939

Baltic strategy

The German navy in the next few years will not be able to form a line of battle for a general engagement. One would expect that cruisers and submarines would be sent out to attack commerce, but I think you may take it as absolutely certain that the prime object of the German navy will be to preserve command of the Baltic...not only because of the supplies she can obtain from the Scandinavian countries, and the influence she can exert over them, but because the loss of naval command in the Baltic would lay the whole of the Baltic shores of Germany open to attack or possible invasions from other Baltic powers, of which the largest and most important is, of course, the Soviet Union.

> 1939, 16 MARCH.

On 21 March the Lithuanian Foreign Minister, invited to Berlin, surrendered the Baltic port of Memel to Germany. On the 31st, Britain guaranteed Poland against aggression, extending this guarantee to Greece and Rumania two weeks later.

Conscription

...when we aspire to lead all Europe back from the verge of the abyss on to the uplands of law and peace, we must ourselves set the highest example. We must keep nothing back. How can we bear to continue to lead our comfortable, easy life here at home, unwilling even to pronounce the word "compulsion," unwilling even to take the necessary measure by which the armies that we have promised can alone be recruited and equipped? How can we continue—let me say it with particular frankness and sincerity—with less than the full force of the nation incorporated in the governing instrument?

1939, 13 APRIL.

Czechoslovakia absorbed

Many people at the time of the September crisis thought they were only giving away the interests of Czechoslovakia, but with every month that passes you will see that they were also giving away the interests of Britain, and the interests of peace and justice.

1939, 14 MARCH, WALTHAM ABBEY. (BLOOD, 119.)

On 15 March Hitler marched into Prague and the rump Czech Republic was extinguished. A German protectorate of Bohemia and Moravia was proclaimed in its place.

They [Hitler and Mussolini] cannot pursue their course of aggression without bringing about a general war of measureless devastation. To submit to their encroachments would be to condemn a large portion of mankind to their rule; to resist them, either in peace or war, will be dangerous, painful and hard. There is no use at this stage in concealing these blunt facts from anyone. No one should go forward in this business without realizing plainly both what the cost may be, and what are the issues at stake....

The Government which allowed Czechoslovakia to be broken and disarmed was suddenly surprised and horrified that Herr Hitler should march into Prague and actually subjugate the Czech people. This damnable outrage opened the eyes of the blind, made the deaf hear, and even in some cases the dumb spoke....

1939, 19 MAY. CORN EXCHANGE, CAMBRIDGE.
(BLOOD, 166.)

Chamberlain had denounced Hitler's perfidy over Czechoslovakia the day before in Birmingham, and two days later finally announced creation of a Ministry of Supply.

Eve of war

When Herr Goebbels' Nazi propaganda blares and blethers upon the ether that Britain and France have lost the capacity to make war if it is forced upon them, we do not get angry because we know it is not true. We know that our sufferings will be very hard and we are determined not to be guilty of bringing about a crash, the consequences of which no man can measure. We know also that we could only throw ourselves into such a struggle if our consciences were clear.

If I support the Government today, it is not because I have changed my views. It is because the Government have in principle and even in detail adopted the policy I have urged. I only hope they have not adopted it too late to prevent war.

1939, 28 JUNE. CARLTON CLUB, LONDON.
(BLOOD, 77–8.)

There is a hush hanging over Europe, nay, over all the world....What kind of a hush is it? Alas! it is the hush of suspense, and in many lands it is the hush of fear. Listen! No, listen carefully; I think I hear something—yes, there it was quite clear. Don't you hear it? It is the tramp of armies crunching the gravel of the parade-grounds, splashing through rain-soaked fields, the tramp of two million German soldiers and more than a million Italians—going on manoeuvres—yes, only on manoeuvres...just like last year. After all, the Dictators must train their soldiers. They could scarcely do less in common prudence, when the Danes, the Dutch, the Swiss, the Albanians—and of course the Jews—may leap out upon them at any moment and rob them of their living-space...

1939, 8 AUGUST. BROADCAST TO AMERICA, LONDON.
(BLOOD, 196–7.)

On 1 September, without a declaration of war, Hitler invaded Poland. World War II had begun.

Guarantee to Poland

[Britain's position] is similar to what happened last year, but with the important difference that this year no means of retreat are open to us. We had no Treaty obligations to Czechoslovakia. We had never guaranteed their security. But now we have given an absolute guarantee to Poland that if she is the object of unprovoked aggression, we in company with our French allies will be forced to declare war upon Germany. There is the brute fact which stares us in the face.

1939, 28 June. Carlton Club, London.
(Blood, 175.)

Chamberlain announced reports of large-scale military measures in and around Danzig and the Polish Corridor in 3 July. At the end of the month, when the Opposition proposed that Parliament, after rising for summer recess on 4 August, should reconvene again two weeks later, he declined to do so.

History, which, we are told, is mainly the record of the crimes, follies and miseries of mankind, may be scoured and ransacked to find a parallel to this sudden and complete reversal of five or six years' policy of easy-going placatory appeasement, and its transformation almost overnight into a readiness to accept an obviously imminent war on far worse conditions and on the greatest scale....But now at last was the end of British and French submission. Here was decision at last, taken at the worst possible moment and on the least satisfactory ground, which must surely lead to the slaughter of tens of millions of people.

1948. (WW2 I, 271–2.)

Churchill maintained, with some justice, that guaranteeing the integrity of Poland in 1939 was far harder than it would have been to guarantee Czechoslovakia in 1938, and that war in 1938 would have offered better odds than in 1939.

Judgement compared

I personally accept what the Prime Minister [Neville Chamberlain] says, and when he makes solemn public declarations I believe that he will do his best to carry them out. I trust his good faith in every respect, but that does not really dispose of the whole issue. It might be that his good faith was in no way in question, either about the rising of the House or other matters at all, but there might be a difference of judgement. I use the word "judgement" with some temerity, because my Rt. Hon. Friend twitted me some time ago about that notorious defect which I have in my composition. I have not looked up all his own declarations in any captious spirit, and I will not pursue that this afternoon, but it is quite clear that the judgement which the Prime Minister might form upon the facts as they unfolded would be a legitimate and natural topic upon which differences of opinion would arise between us.

1939, 2 August.

See the earlier debate about their comparative judgements: 1938...Munich postscript.

Poland and Russia

But it must be vividly impressed upon the Government of Poland that the accession of Soviet Russia in good earnest to the peace bloc of nations may be decisive in preventing war, and will in any case be necessary for ultimate success. One understands readily the Polish policy of balancing between the German and the Russian neighbour, but from the moment when the Nazi malignity is plain, a definite association between Poland and Russia becomes indispensable.

1939, 4 May. ("The Russian Counterpoise," Daily Telegraph; Step, 344.)

Chamberlain having now guaranteed Poland, which he could not protect, WSC argued for approaches to the Soviets, either by Poland or his own country, in the face of Hitler's Germany. Chamberlain ignored him.

1940

Eve of disaster

Each one [of the neutral nations] hopes that if he feeds the crocodile enough, the crocodile will eat him last. All of them hope that the storm will pass before their turn comes to be devoured. But I fear—I fear greatly— the storm will not pass.

1940, 20 JANUARY.

Holland, Luxembourg and Belgium, which had steadfastly proclaimed their strict neutrality, were invaded on 10 May 1940. Luxembourg was overrun in hours; the Dutch surrendered on the 14th, the Belgians, after a heroic defence, on the 28th.

Between the Wars: General Reflections

Air defence

The danger which might confront us…would expose us not only to hideous suffering, but even to mortal peril, by which I mean peril of actual conquest and subjugation. It is just as well to confront those facts while time remains to take proper measures to cope with them. I may say that all these possibilities are perfectly well known abroad, and no doubt every one of them has been made the subject of technical study.

1934, 28 NOVEMBER.

For the first time for centuries we are not fully equipped to repel or to retaliate for an invasion. That to an island people is astonishing. Panic indeed! The position is the other way round. We are the incredulous, indifferent children of centuries of security behind the shield of the Royal Navy, not yet able to wake up to the woefully transformed conditions of the modern world.

1935, 22 MAY.

Prime Minister Baldwin had admitted on this date that he was "completely wrong… completely misled" on the matter of German aircraft.

Appeasement reflections

…this great country nosing from door to door like a cow that has lost its calf, mooing dolefully now in Berlin and now in Rome—when all the time the tiger and the alligator wait for its undoing.

1938, 1 MARCH. (NICOLSON I, 328.)

Harold Nicolson to Vita Sackville-West: "Winston was enormously witty." (An account

of a luncheon of the Focus Group, anti-appeasement MPs and others brought together by Churchill.)

The word "appeasement" is not popular, but appeasement has its place in all policy. Make sure you put it in the right place. Appease the weak, defy the strong. It is a terrible thing for a famous nation like Britain to do it the wrong way round.

1950. (OB VIII, 529.)

Appeasement in itself may be good or bad according to the circumstances. Appeasement from weakness and fear is alike futile and fatal. Appeasement from strength is magnanimous and noble and might be the surest and perhaps the only path to world peace. When nations or individuals get strong they are often truculent and bullying, but when they are weak they become better mannered. But this is the reverse of what is healthy and wise.

1950, 14 DECEMBER.

Six months earlier at Plymouth, WSC had said:

To work from weakness and fear is ruin. To work from wisdom and power may be salvation.

Arms and ideas

…arms—the instrumentalities, as President Wilson called them—are not sufficient by themselves. We must add to them the power of ideas.

1938, 16 OCTOBER. BROADCAST TO THE UNITED STATES, LONDON. (BLOOD, 88.)

Churchill was always careful to fashion his speeches to Americans in terms they related to, referencing even American Presidents he disliked, and the American Revolution, which he looked upon with a certain amount of regret.

Choice for Europe

Europe is approaching a climax. I believe that climax will be reached in the lifetime of the present Parliament. Either there will be a melting of hearts and a joining of hands between great nations which will set out upon realizing the glorious age of prosperity and freedom which is now within the grasp of the millions of toiling people, or there will be an explosion and a catastrophe the course of which no imagination can measure, and beyond which no human eye can see.

1936, 23 APRIL.

...we are told that we must not involve ourselves in a quarrel about ideologies. If this means that we are not to back Communism against Naz-ism or vice versa, we all agree. Both doctrines are equally obnoxious to the principles of freedom. Certainly we should not back one against the other. But surely we must have an opinion between Right and Wrong? Surely we must have an opinion between Aggressor and Victim?

1938, 9 MAY. FREE TRADE HALL, MANCHESTER.
(BLOOD, 25.)

Some believe Churchill ignored the threat of Soviet Russia in his single-minded worry over Nazi Germany. In fact, it was a manifestation of his priorities: the USSR posed no significant aggressive threat to the world of the 1930s.

Collective security

If there were, over a prolonged period of time, some general cause of anxiety, which all nations, or many nations, felt, then possibly forces might come together for that purpose which, after that danger had happily been tided over, might still subsist permanently in amity.

1934, 13 JULY.

With the death of von Hindenburg on 2 August, Hitler appointed himself "leader and chancellor" of Germany. In a plebiscite, 38.4 million voted for Hitler and 7 million abstained or voted against him.

It seems undoubted that there is an effective policy open to us at the present time by which we may preserve both our safety and our freedom. Never must we despair, never must we give in, but we must face facts and draw true conclusions from them. The policy of detachment or isolation, about which we have heard so much and which in many ways is so attractive, is no longer open. If we were to turn our backs upon Europe, thereby alienating every friend, we should by disinteresting ourselves

in their fate invite them to disinterest themselves in ours.

1935, 2 MAY.

[We could send] part of the British Fleet to the Baltic to ensure superiority over Germany in that sea. It would stay there permanently, based on a Russian port of which we should obtain the use under this plan.

1936, 20 APRIL. (OB V, 723.)

Quoted in a note by Maurice Hankey to Sir Thomas Inskip. For the background to this astonishing proposal, and WSC's search for a Soviet alliance in the mid-1930s, see Chapter 10, Russia...Policy towards.

Upon the rock of the Covenant many nations great and small, are drawing constantly and swiftly together. In spite of the disappointments of the past, in spite of many misgivings, difficulties and ridiculings, that process is continuing, and these nations are welding themselves into what will some day be a formidable yet benignant alliance, pledged to resist wrong-doing and the violence of an aggressor.

1937, 4 MARCH.

Worry has been defined by some nerve-specialists as a "spasm of the imagination." The mind, it is said, seizes hold of something and simply cannot let it go. Reason, argument, threats, are useless. The grip becomes all the more convulsive. But if you could introduce some new theme, in this case the practical effect of a common purpose and of cooperation for a common end, then indeed it might be that these clenched fists would relax into open hands, that the reign of peace and freedom might begin, and that science, instead of being a shameful prisoner in the galleys of slaughter, might pour her wealth abounding into the cottage homes of every land.

1937, 14 APRIL.

If a number of states were assembled around Great Britain and France in a solemn treaty for mutual defence against aggression; if they had their forces marshaled in what you may call a Grand Alliance; if they had their staff arrangements concerted: if all this rested, as it can honourably rest, upon the Covenant of the League of Nations, in pursuance of all the purposes and ideals of the League of Nations: if that were sustained, as it would be, by the moral sense of the world; and if it were done in the year 1938 and, believe me, it may be the last chance there will be for doing it then I say that you might even now arrest this approaching war.

1938, 14 MARCH.

Dependence

All history has proved the peril of being dependent upon a foreign State for home defence instead of upon one's own right arm. This is not a Party question, not a question between pacifists and militarists, but one of the essential independence of character of our island life and its preservation from intrusion or distortion of any kind.

1934, 8 MARCH.

Dictators

Dictators ride to and fro upon tigers from which they dare not dismount. And the tigers are getting hungry.

1937, 11 NOVEMBER. ("ARMISTICE – OR PEACE?," EVENING STANDARD; STEP, 174.)

Fear and submission

Short of being actually conquered, there is no evil worse than submitting to wrong and violence for fear of war. Once you take the position of not being able in any circumstances to defend your rights against the aggression of some particular set of people, there is no end to the demands that will be made or to the humiliations that must be accepted.

1927, 22 JANUARY, EZE, FRANCE. (OB, CV5/1, 917–18.)

WSC to Stanley Baldwin who, as Prime Minister in the 1930s, did not heed his advice.

French pacifism

The reasons why France does not present herself in her full strength at the present time are not to be found among the working masses, who are also the soldiers of France, but in certain strata of the middle-class and the well-to-do. Something of this kind can also be seen in Great Britain.

1938, 1 DECEMBER. ("FRANCE AND ENGLAND," DAILY TELEGRAPH; STEP, 294.)

Geography of bombing

The frontiers of Germany are very much nearer to London than the seacoasts of this island are to Berlin, and whereas practically the whole of the German bombing air force can reach London with an effective load, very few, if any, of our aeroplanes can reach Berlin with any appreciable load of bombs. That must be considered as one of the factors in judging between the two countries.

1935, 19 MARCH.

Method and plan

...it is no use espousing a cause without having also a method and a plan by which that cause may be made to win. I would not affront you with generalities. There must be the vision. There must be a plan, and there must be action following upon it. We express our immediate plan and policy in a single sentence: "Arm, and stand by the Covenant." In this alone lies the assurance of safety, the defence of freedom, and the hope of peace....

Ought we not to produce in defence of Right, champions as bold, missionaries as eager, and if need be, swords as sharp as are at the disposal of the leaders of totalitarian states?

1938, 9 MAY. FREE TRADE HALL, MANCHESTER. (BLOOD, 20–21, 26.)

Three days later Lord Halifax, now British Foreign Secretary, raised the question of recognising the Italian conquest of Abyssinia by the League of Nations.

Mutual assured destruction

When all is said and done as regards defensive methods...pending some new discovery, the only direct measure of defence upon a great scale is the certainty of being able to inflict simultaneously upon the enemy as great damage as he can inflict upon ourselves. Do not let us under-value the efficacy of this procedure. It may well prove in practice—I admit you cannot prove it in theory—capable of giving complete immunity.

1934, 28 NOVEMBER.

Nazified Europe

We cannot afford to see Nazidom in its present phase of cruelty and intolerance, with all its hatreds and all its gleaming weapons, paramount in Europe.

1935, 24 OCTOBER.

Preparedness

Mark you, in time of peace, in peace politics, in ordinary matters of domestic affairs and class struggles, things blow over, but in these great matters of defence, and still more in the field of actual hostilities, the clouds do not roll by. If the necessary measures are not taken, they turn into thunderbolts and fall on your heads....

It is not only the supreme question of self-preservation that is involved in the realization of these dangers, but also the human and the world cause of the preservation of free Governments and of western civilization against the ever advancing forces of authority and despotism.

1935, 31 MAY

Will there be time to put our defences in order? We live in contact with the unknown, but we are not defenceless now. Will there be time to make these necessary efforts, or will the awful words "too late" be recorded? I will never despair that we can make ourselves secure. The Royal Navy, especially after the toning up which it has received, is unsurpassed in the world, and is still the main bulwark of our security; and even at this eleventh hour, if the right measures are taken and if the right spirit prevails in the British nation and the British Empire, we may surround ourselves with other bulwarks equally sure, which will protect us against whatever storms may blow.

1936, 10 MARCH.

We are told that we must not interfere with the normal course of trade, that we must not alarm the easygoing voter and the public. How thin and paltry these arguments will sound if we are caught a year or two hence, fat, opulent, free-spoken—and defenceless.

1936, 21 MAY.

The more you are prepared and the better you are known to be prepared, the greater is the chance of staving off war and of saving Europe from the catastrophe which menaces it.

1938, 25 MAY.

Shadow factories

We ought to begin the reorganisation of our civil factories so that they can be turned over rapidly to war purposes. All over Europe that is being done, and to an...amazing extent. They are incomparably more efficient than anything that existed in the days of Prussian Imperialism before the war. Every factory in those countries is prepared to turn over to the production of some material for the deplorable and melancholy business of slaughter. What have we done? There is not an hour to lose. Those things cannot be done in a moment. The process should be started, and the very maximum of money that can be usefully spent should be spent from today on...

1934, 7 FEBRUARY.

Shadow factories are defence plants, built in anticipation of war to supply military equipment.

You ought now—I said this two years ago, but it is still true today—to have every factory in the country planned out, not only on paper, but with the necessary jigs, gauges and appliances handy, hung up on the spot, so that they could turn over at once in time of war to some form of war production.

1938, 25 MAY.

Ten-Years Rule

I remember in the days of the late Conservative Administration...that we thought it right to take as a rule of guidance that there would be no major war within ten years in which we should be engaged. Of course, such a rule can only be a very crude guidance to the military and naval chiefs who have to make their plans, and it had to be reconsidered prospectively at the beginning of each year. I believe that it was right in all the circumstances.

1934, 7 FEBRUARY.

The Ten-Years Rule had been abandoned by the mid-Thirties, or at least no longer talked of.

Versailles Treaty

What, then, has become of the Carthaginian peace of which we used to hear so much? That has gone. Some of it may have been written down in the Versailles Treaty, but its clauses have never been put into operation. There has been no Carthaginian peace. Neither has there been any bleeding of Germany white by the conquerors. The exact opposite has taken place. The loans which Britain and the United States particularly, and also other countries, have poured into the lap of Germany since the firing stopped, far exceed the sum of reparations which she had paid; indeed, they have been nearly double. If the plight of Germany is hard—and the plight of every country is hard at the present time—it is not because there has been any drain of her life's blood or of valuable commodities from Germany to the victors. On the contrary, the tide has flowed the other way. It is Germany that has received an infusion of blood from the nations with whom she went to war and by whom she was decisively defeated.

1932, 11 JULY.

Prime Minister Ramsay MacDonald had returned this day from the Lausanne Peace Conference, at which Britain, Germany and France agreed to suspend reparations imposed on defeated countries by the Versailles Treaty of 1919.

I have heard, as every one has of late years, a great deal of condemnation of the treaties of peace, of the Treaties of Versailles and of Trianon. I believe that that denunciation has been very much exaggerated, and in its effect harmful....Europe today corresponds to its ethnological groupings as it has never corresponded before. You may think that nationalism has been excessively manifested in modern times. That may well be so. It may well be that it has a dangerous side, but we must not fail to recognize that it is the strongest force now at work....It should be the first rule of British foreign policy to emphasize respect for these great Treaties, and to make those nations whose national existence depends upon and arises from the Treaties, feel that no challenge is levelled at their security.

1933, 13 APRIL.

Churchill rejected the argument of extreme elements in Germany who claimed that they were being hemmed in or deprived of living space; thus the second part of this statement.

Vulnerability of London

With our enormous Metropolis here, the greatest target in the world, a kind of tremendous, fat, valuable cow tied up to attract the beast of prey, we are in a position in which we have never been before, and in which no other country in the world is at the present time.

1934, 30 JULY.

Retrospectives on the 1930s

A thousand years hence it will be incredible to historians that the victorious Allies delivered themselves over to the vengeance of the foe they had overcome.

1938, 10 JANUARY, FRANCE. (SOAMES, SPEAKING, 433.)

WSC to his wife: two months later Churchill would voice the identical sentiments in the House of Commons. See Immortal Words...Dark gulf.

When I think of the fair hopes of a long peace which still lay before Europe at the beginning of 1933...I cannot believe that a parallel exists in the whole course of history. So far as this country is concerned the responsibility must rest with those who have had the undisputed control of our political affairs. They neither prevented Germany from rearming, nor did they rearm ourselves in time. They quarrelled with Italy without saving Ethiopia. They exploited and discredited the vast institution of the League of Nations and they neglected to make alliances and combinations which might have repaired previous errors, and thus they left us in the hour of trial without adequate national defence or effective international security.

1938, 5 OCTOBER.

...we were so glutted with victory that in our folly we threw it away.

1940, 18 JUNE. (BLOOD, 367.)

...I saw it all coming and cried aloud to my own fellow-countrymen and to the world, but no one paid any attention. Up till the year 1933 or even 1935, Germany might have been saved from the awful fate which has overtaken her, and we might all have been spared the miseries Hitler let loose upon mankind. There never was a war in all history easier to prevent by timely action than the one which has just desolated such great areas of the globe. It could have been prevented in my belief without the firing of a single shot, and Germany might be powerful, prosperous and honoured today; but no one would listen and one by one we were all sucked into the awful whirlpool.

1946, 5 MARCH. WESTMINSTER COLLEGE, FULTON, MISSOURI. (SINEWS, 103–4.)

Delight in smooth-sounding platitudes, refusal to face unpleasant facts, desire for popularity and electoral success irrespective of the vital interests of the State, genuine love of peace and pathetic belief that love can be its sole foundation, obvious lack of intellectual vigour in both leaders of the British Coalition Government, marked ignorance of Europe and aversion from its problems in Mr. Baldwin, the strong and violent pacifism which at this time dominated the Labour-Socialist Party, the utter devotion of the Liberals to sentiment apart from reality, the failure and worse than failure of Mr. Lloyd George, the erstwhile great wartime leader, to address himself to the continuity of his work, the whole supported by overwhelming majorities in both Houses of Parliament: all these constituted a picture of British fatuity and fecklessness which, though devoid of guile, was not devoid of guilt, and, though free from wickedness or evil design, played a definite part in the unleashing upon the world of horrors and miseries which, even so far as they have unfolded, are already beyond comparison in human experience.

1948. (WW2 I, 69–70.)

It would be wrong in judging the policy of the British Government not to remember the passionate desire for peace which animated the uninformed, misinformed, majority of the British people, and seemed to threaten with political extinction any party or politician who dared to take any other line. This, of course, is no excuse for political leaders who fall short of their duty. It is much better for parties or politicians to be turned out of office than to imperil the life of the nation....Those who scared the timid MacDonald-Baldwin Government from their path should at least keep silent.

1948. (WW2 I, 88.)

A statement of principle that was rare then, and rarer today. WSC refers to the October 1933 East Fulham by-election where a Socialist pacifist beat the Conservative, convincing Mr. Baldwin not to press rearmament. See also People...Baldwin and MacDonald.

We cannot doubt the sincerity of the Leaders of the Socialist and Liberal parties. They were completely wrong and mistaken, and they bear their share of the burden before history. It is indeed astonishing that the Socialist Party should have endeavoured in after years to claim superior foresight...

1948. (WW2 I, 91.)

Even broadly read students of Churchill must go a long way to find a more comprehensive indictment of his party, his colleagues, and all other parties. Yet even in these heavy criticisms we find traces of magnanimity.

18
WORLD WAR II

"In the Second World War every bond between man and man was to perish. Crimes were committed by the Germans under the Hitlerite domination to which they allowed themselves to be subjected, which find no equal in scale and wickedness with any that have darkened the human record....Deliberate extermination of whole populations was contemplated and pursued by both Germany and Russia in the Eastern war. The hideous process of bombarding open cities from the air, once started by the Germans, was repaid twenty-fold by the ever-mounting power of the Allies, and found its culmination in the use of the atomic bombs which obliterated Hiroshima and Nagasaki." [59]

"...I saw it all coming and cried aloud to my own fellow-countrymen and to the world, but no one paid any attention."

orld War II was different from and worse than past conflicts, as Churchill wrote, but one of the differences for which we must be grateful is that Britain was led by a professional writer. Churchill claimed of his war memoirs: "This is not history

– this is my case," and he set out that case from his and Britain's standpoint. In his speeches during the war and his memoirs afterwards, he often ignored unpleasant facts, or put his own spin on them. Yet few writers were so magnanimous, refusing for example to criticise his predecessors for the sake of unity and the national effort.

More than at any other time in his career, Churchill's words conveyed, as Robert Pilpel wrote, a sense of "warm communion...[a] sensation of fraternal intimacy, of being taken into confidence as a fellow member of the English-speaking tribe. Then there was the wonderful Britishness of expression: the robust roast-beef-and-pewter phrases, rolling cadences, portentous Latinate locutions – alien yet eerily familiar, the echo of a racial memory."[60]

Manfred Weidhorn compares Churchill's account with a great novel: "Such is the eerie sense of *déjà vu* and *ubi sunt*....The collapse of the venerable and once mighty France and Churchill's agony are beautifully rendered by the sensuous detail of the old gentlemen industriously carrying French archives on wheelbarrows to bonfires...Near the end of the work appears one of the greatest scenes of all. On the way to the Potsdam conference, Churchill flies to Berlin and its 'chaos of ruins'. Taken to Hitler's chancellery, he walks through its shattered halls for 'quite a long time'...The great duel is over; the victor stands on the site from which so much evil originated....'We were given the best first-hand accounts available at that time of what had happened in these final scenes.'"[61]

Amid the pathos, humour bubbles incessantly to the surface, Pilpel writes, "as though Puck had escaped from *A Midsummer Night's Dream* and infiltrated *Paradise Lost*".[62] Churchill "simply refuses to overlook the light side", Weidhorn adds. "Such a tone, markedly different from the histrionics of the other side, may well be a secret of survival. As Shaw said, he who laughs lasts."[63]

Even when annoyed, the humour remains, as when Churchill responds to an invasion exercise which assumes the Germans land five divisions on the British coast, saying he should be glad "if the same officers work out a scheme for our landing an exactly similar force on the French coast..." (See Invasion of Britain.) When he regretfully sacks General Auchinleck, he does so following a meeting "in a wire-netted cube, full of flies and important military personages". (See 1942...North Africa: Auchinleck's dismissal.)

Churchill's speeches and memoirs of World War II comprise a prose epic, not without flaws or bias, but indispensable for anyone who seeks understanding of the events that made us what we are today. Yet Churchill composed nearly 2.5 million words about the war, and only one-tenth of 1 per cent are presented here. The process of selecting his most poignant and pregnant words required many omissions and much editing. Readers interested in more should acquire his six volumes of *The Second World War*, which are readily available in inexpensive form.

In order to follow the events of the war I have provided date-specific entries chronologically as events occurred. After these, his more general remarks are arranged alphabetically by subject.

Six of these subjects received Churchill's attention repeatedly: the Blitz, the possibility of invasion, war prospects, strategy and goals, summaries of the war situation, and the U-boat peril. These are sorted according to the date most applicable. (A post-war comment, let us say in 1949, about one of these topics in a specific year, for example

---

60 Pilpel, ix.
61 Weidhorn, 104, 170.
62 Pilpel, ix.
63 Weidhorn, 169.

1942, is sorted with the 1942 entries, though as usual it carries the date it was first uttered or published.)

For Churchill's personal reactions to climacterics[64] of the war (return to the Admiralty, 1939; becoming Prime Minister, 1940) see Chapter 31.

1939

Theme of The Gathering Storm

HOW THE ENGLISH-SPEAKING PEOPLES THROUGH THEIR UNWISDOM, CARELESSNESS AND GOOD NATURE ALLOWED THE WICKED TO REARM.

1948. (WW2 I, IX.)

Churchill's themes of his six volumes of war memoirs approximately apply to the chronological breakdown here (but not exactly: the theme above really applies to 1919–39). Since he regarded the breaks and punctuation as vital to his words, they are inserted verbatim.

Advent of the war

Holiday time, ladies and gentlemen! Holiday time, my friends across the Atlantic!...

Let me look back—let me see. How did we spend our summer holidays twenty-five years ago? Why, those were the very days when the German advance guards were breaking into Belgium and trampling down its people on their march towards Paris! Those were the days when Prussian militarism was—to quote its own phrase—"hacking its way through the small, weak, neighbour country" whose neutrality and independence they had sworn not merely to respect but to defend.

1939, 8 AUGUST. BROADCAST TO AMERICA, LONDON. (BLOOD, 195.)

Outside, the storms of war may blow and the lands may be lashed with the fury of its gales, but in our own hearts this Sunday morning there is peace. Our hands may be active, but our consciences are at rest....

This is not a question of fighting for Danzig or fighting for Poland. We are fighting to save the whole world from the pestilence of Nazi tyranny and in defence of all that is most sacred to man. This is no war for domination or

imperial aggrandisement or material gain; no war to shut any country out of its sunlight and means of progress. It is a war, viewed in its inherent quality, to establish, on impregnable rocks, the rights of the individual, and it is a war to establish and revive the stature of man.

1939, 3 SEPTEMBER.

"Such was Churchill's stature," Sir Martin Gilbert wrote, "that, although out of office for more than ten years, he was asked to speak next" (after the Prime Minister and Arthur Greenwood for the Labour Party) upon Britain's declaration of war on Germany.

The Prime Minister's broadcast informed us that we were already at war, and he had scarcely ceased speaking when a strange, prolonged, wailing noise, afterwards to become familiar, broke upon the ear. My wife came into the room braced by the crisis.... We gave the Government a good mark for this evident sign of preparation, and...made our way to the shelter assigned to us, armed with a bottle of brandy and other appropriate medical comforts.

1948. (WW2 I, 319.)

I felt a serenity of mind and was conscious of a kind of uplifted detachment from human and personal affairs. The glory of Old England, peace-loving and ill-prepared as she was, but instant and fearless at the call of honour, thrilled my being and seemed to lift our fate to those spheres far removed from earthly facts and physical sensation.

1948. (WW2 I, 320.)

Since 1911 much more than a quarter of a century had passed, and still mortal peril threatened us at the hands of the same nation. Once again defence of the rights of a weak State, outraged and invaded by unprovoked aggression, forced us to draw the sword. Once again we must fight for life and honour against all the might and fury of the valiant,

---

64 "Climacteric", an unusual word (its first appearance in the *Oxford English Dictionary* was in 1601) was frequently used by WSC to describe critical moments or periods.

disciplined, and ruthless German race. Once again! So be it.

1948. (WW2 I, 321.)

No doubt at the beginning we shall have to suffer, because of having too long wished to lead a peaceful life. Our reluctance to fight was mocked at as cowardice. Our desire to see an unarmed world was proclaimed as the proof of our decay. Now we have begun. Now we are going on. Now, with the help of God, and with the conviction that we are the defenders of civilization and freedom, we are going to persevere to the end.

1939, 1 OCTOBER. BROADCAST, LONDON.
(BLOOD, 209.)

1940

Theme of Their Finest Hour

HOW THE BRITISH PEOPLE
HELD THE FORT
ALONE
TILL THOSE WHO HITHERTO HAD
BEEN HALF BLIND WERE
HALF READY.

1949. (WW2 II, xi.)

German navy

It is true that the *Deutschland* escaped the clutches of our cruisers by the skin of her teeth, but the *Spee* still sticks up in the harbour of Montevideo as a grisly monument and as a measure of the fate in store for any Nazi warship which dabbles in piracy on the broad waters.

1940, 20 JANUARY. BROADCAST, LONDON.
(BLOOD, 250.)

Devoted to the Anglicising of foreign words, Churchill inevitably pronounced the name of the German Graf Spee *as "speeee" and Uruguay's capital as "Monty-vid-ee-oh".*

Dare and endure

This is no time for ease and comfort. It is the time to dare and endure.

1940, 27 JANUARY, MANCHESTER. (BLOOD, 259.)

Sinking of the Graf Spee

The warrior heroes of the past may look down, as Nelson's monument looks down upon us

now, without any feeling that the island race has lost its daring or that the examples they set in bygone centuries have faded as the generations have succeeded one another. It was not for nothing that Admiral Harwood, as he instantly and at full speed attacked an enemy which might have sunk any one of his ships by a single successful salvo from its far heavier guns, flew Nelson's immortal signal of which neither the new occasion, nor the conduct of all ranks and ratings, nor the final result were found unworthy.

1940, 23 FEBRUARY. GUILDHALL, LONDON.
(BLOOD, 270.)

Sir Henry Harwood (1888–1950) commanded the squadron of HMS Achilles, Ajax *and* Exeter, *which sank the German battleship* Graf Spee *off the River Plate, Uruguay, in December 1940. Nelson's signal, flown at Trafalgar, was, "England expects that every man will do his duty."*

Western Front

...more than a million German soldiers, including all their active divisions and armoured divisions, are drawn up ready to attack, at a few hours' notice, all along the frontiers of Luxembourg, of Belgium and of Holland. At any moment these neutral countries may be subjected to an avalanche of steel and fire; and the decision rests in the hands of a haunted, morbid being, who, to their eternal shame, the German peoples in their bewilderment have worshipped as a god.

1940, 30 MARCH. BROADCAST, LONDON.
(BLOOD, 291.)

On 18 March Hitler and Mussolini met at the Brenner Pass. On the 20th French Premier Daladier resigned and was replaced by Paul Reynaud.

Why we fight

Although the fate of Poland stares them in the face, there are thoughtless dilettanti or purblind wordlings who sometimes ask us: "What is it that Britain and France are fighting for?" To this I answer: "If we left off fighting you would soon find out."

1940, 30 MARCH. BROADCAST, LONDON.
(BLOOD, 290.)

Denmark and Norway

We have probably arrived now at the first main crunch of the war. But we certainly find no reason in the fact of what has just happened, and still less in our own hearts, to deter us from entering upon any further trials that may lie before us. While we will not prophesy or boast about battles still to be fought, we feel ourselves ready to encounter the utmost malice of the enemy and to devote all our life strength to achieve the victory in what is a world cause.

1940, 11 APRIL.

Germany invaded Denmark and Norway on 9 April, ostensibly to prevent Franco-British occupation of those lands.

May Day 1940

If I were the first of May, I should be ashamed of myself.

1940, 1 MAY. (OB VI, 279.)

WSC to John Colville, as a sudden squall descended on Horse Guards Parade. Amidst worries of a German invasion of Holland and Belgium, the War Cabinet had authorised landings south of Narvik, ultimately futile, to counteract the German invasion of Norway. (Colville, then an ardent Chamberlainite, wrote in his diary, "Personally, I think he ought to be ashamed of himself.")

First speech as Prime Minister

You ask, what is our aim? I can answer in one word: Victory—victory at all costs, victory in spite of all terror, victory, however long and hard the road may be; for without victory, there is no survival.

1940, 13 MAY.

For a fuller excerpt see Chapter 1.

Doubts

God alone knows how great it is. All I hope is that it is not too late. I am very much afraid it is. We can only do our best.

1940, 10 MAY. (THOMPSON, SHADOW, 37.)

Churchill to Detective Thompson, a rare moment of stark candour after Thompson observed that the task facing the Prime Minister was a great one.

France invaded

...an apocalyptic vision of the war...[I see myself] in the heart of Canada, directing, over an England razed to the ground by high explosive bombs and over France whose ruins were already cold, the air war of the New World against the Old dominated by Germany.

1940, 15 MAY, PARIS. (LANGER AND GLEASON, 453; KERSHAW, 26.)

Included with some doubt, from the notes of Paul Baudouin, Secretary of the French Cabinet and a determined defeatist. Baudouin undoubtedly cited this to highlight what he saw as WSC's delusions; yet it is not hard to imagine WSC expressing such a last-resort declaration to the French.

...the German eruption swept like a sharp scythe around the right and rear of the Armies of the north [and] cut off all communications between us and the main French armies.... Behind this armoured and mechanized onslaught came a number of German divisions in lorries, and behind them again there plodded comparatively slowly the dull brute mass of the ordinary German army and German people, always so ready to be led to the trampling down in other lands of liberties and comforts which they have never known in their own.

1940, 4 JUNE.

Outside in the garden of the Quai d'Orsay clouds of smoke arose from large bonfires, and I saw from the window venerable officials pushing wheel-barrows of archives on to them. Already therefore the evacuation of Paris was being prepared.

1949, PARIS. (WW2 II, 42.)

Few save Churchill could find the words to describe the hubris on 16 June; see also Manfred Weidhorn's comment in the introduction to this chapter.

Options

If we could get out of this jam by giving up Malta and Gibraltar and some African colonies I would jump at it. But the only safe way is to convince Hitler that he cannot beat us.

1940, 26 MAY, DOWNING STREET. (CABINET MINUTES CAB 65/13, CONFIDENTIAL ANNEXES.)

Rendered here in the first person from War Cabinet Minutes. The first sentence is often cited; the second rarely. Halifax had proposed asking Mussolini to "mediate" negotiations; Churchill, then hardly secure in office, acknowledged the proposal but discounted the possibility. Mussolini meanwhile was rejecting Roosevelt's similar request (Kershaw, 31).

Future generations may deem it noteworthy that the supreme question of whether we should fight on alone never found a place upon the War Cabinet agenda. It was taken for granted and as a matter of course by these men of all parties in the State, and we were much too busy to waste time upon such unreal, academic issues.

1949. (WW2 II, 157.)

Often cited as a "counterfactual" by critics, this statement is in fact true. Differences of opinion over whether to consider terms did not alter the War Cabinet's opinion that, if faced with surrender or fighting on, they would fight on. See following entry; also Chapter 29, Leadership...Courage.

Dunkirk

We must be very careful not to assign to this deliverance the attributes of a victory. Wars are not won by evacuations....

...our thankfulness at the escape of our army and so many men, whose loved ones have passed an agonising week, must not blind us to the fact that what has happened in France and Belgium is a colossal military disaster....

I have, myself, full confidence that if all do their duty, if nothing is neglected and if the best arrangements are made, as they are being made, we shall prove ourselves once again able to defend our island home, to ride out the storm of war, and to outlive the menace of tyranny, if necessary for years, if necessary alone.

1940, 4 JUNE.

I shall never understand why the German Army did not finish the British Army at Dunkirk.

1944, SEPTEMBER. EN ROUTE TO THE CONTINENT.
(WINSTON S. CHURCHILL IN *FINEST HOUR* 136,
AUTUMN 2006, 51.)

WSC to André de Staerke, a Belgian diplomat and friend, while flying over Dunkirk. De Staerke suggested they ask a German general (possibly von Runstedt), imprisoned in Brussels. De Staerke added:

The question was put on the PM's behalf to the German commander, whose reply spoke volumes for the different mentality of the Germans than the British: "I had no orders!"

Fall of France

The news from France is very bad and I grieve for the gallant French people who have fallen into this terrible misfortune. Nothing will alter our feelings towards them or our faith that the genius of France will rise again. What has happened in France makes no difference to our actions and purpose. We have become the sole champions now in arms to defend the world cause. We shall do our best to be worthy of this high honour. We shall defend our island home, and with the British Empire we shall fight on unconquerable until the curse of Hitler is lifted from the brows of mankind. We are sure that in the end all will come right.

1940, 17 JUNE. BROADCAST, LONDON. (BLOOD, 353.)

I am not reciting these facts for the purpose of recrimination. That I judge to be utterly futile and even harmful. We cannot afford it....We have to think of the future and not of the past.

1940, 18 JUNE.

Blackout in London

Darkness had almost fallen on the blacked-out streets. I saw everywhere long queues of people, among them hundreds of young girls in their silk stockings and high-heeled shoes, who had worked hard all day and were waiting for bus after bus, which came by already overcrowded, in the hope of reaching their homes for the night. When at that moment the doleful wail of the siren betokened the approach of the German bombers, I confess to you that my heart bled for London and the Londoners.

1941, 14 JULY. COUNTY HALL, LONDON.
(UNRELENTING, 184.)

Attack on the French fleet

The transference of these ships to Hitler would have endangered the security of both Great Britain and the United States. We therefore had no choice but to act as we did, and to act forthwith.…When you have a friend and comrade at whose side you have faced tremendous struggle and your friend is smitten down by a stunning blow, it may be necessary to make sure that the weapon that has fallen from his hands shall not be added to the resources of your common enemy. But you need not bear malice because of your friend's cries of delirium and gestures of agony. You must not add to his pain; you must work for his recovery. The association of interest between Britain and France remains. The cause remains. Duty inescapable remains.

1940, 14 JULY. BROADCAST, LONDON.
(BLOOD, 389–90.)

WSC on a BBC broadcast, on authorising the destruction of the main ships of the French battle fleet at Oran, Algeria. Later Churchill wrote: "…no act was ever more necessary for the life of Britain and for all that depended upon it.…"

Here was this Britain which so many had counted down and out, which strangers had supposed to be quivering on the brink of surrender to the mighty power arrayed against her, striking ruthlessly at her dearest friends of yesterday and securing for a while to herself the undisputed command of the sea. It was made plain that the British War Cabinet feared nothing and would stop at nothing.

1949. (WW2 II, 211.)

Battle of Britain

We are really doing our very best. There are no doubt many mistakes and shortcomings. A lot of things are done none too well. Some things that ought to be done have not yet been done…[But Britain's effort has] justly commanded the wonder and admiration of every friendly nation in the world.

1940, 17 SEPTEMBER. (SECRET, 21.)

On [15 September] the Luftwaffe, after two heavy attacks on the 14th, made its greatest concentrated effort in a resumed daylight attack on London. It was one of the decisive battles of the war, and, like the Battle of Waterloo, it was

on a Sunday. I was at Chequers.…I drove over to Uxbridge and arrived at the Group Headquarters.…One after another signals came in, "40 plus," "60 plus"; there was even an "80 plus".…Presently the red bulbs showed that the majority of our squadrons were engaged.…I became conscious of the anxiety of the Commander, who now stood still behind his subordinate's chair. Hitherto I had watched in silence. I now asked: "What other reserves have we?" "There are none," said Air Vice-Marshal Park. In an account which he wrote about it afterwards he said that at this I "looked grave." Well I might. What losses should we not suffer if our refuelling planes were caught on the ground by further raids of "40 plus" or "50 plus"! The odds were great; our margins small; the stakes infinite.

1949. (WW2 II, 293–6.)

Space prevents all but a small fraction of this chilling extract from Churchill's visit to No. 11 Fighter Group HQ at Uxbridge, north London. The full account may be read in Their Finest Hour, *Chapter XVI, "The Battle of Britain".*

Message to the forces

It is a message of good cheer to our fighting Forces on the seas, in the air, and in our waiting Armies in all their posts and stations, that we send them from this capital city. They know that they have behind them a people who will not flinch or weary of the struggle—hard and protracted though it will be; but that we shall rather draw from the heart of suffering itself the means of inspiration and survival, and of a victory won not only for ourselves but for all; a victory won not only for our own time, but for the long and better days that are to come.

1940, 11 SEPTEMBER. BROADCAST, LONDON.
(BLOOD, 432.)

Need for unity

I say, let pre-war feuds die; let personal quarrels be forgotten, and let us keep our hatreds for the common enemy. Let Party interest be ignored, let all our energies be harnessed, let the whole ability and forces of the nation be hurled into the struggle, and let all the strong horses be pulling on the collar. At no time in the last war were we in greater peril than we are now, and I urge the House strongly to deal with these matters not in a precipitate vote, ill debated and on a widely discursive field, but in grave time and due time in accordance with the dignity of Parliament.

1940, 8 MAY.

Although I feel the broadening swell of victory and liberation bearing us and all the tortured peoples onwards safely to the final goal, I must confess to feeling the weight of the war upon me even more than in the tremendous summer days of 1940. There are so many fronts which are open, so many vulnerable points to defend, so many inevitable misfortunes, so many shrill voices raised to take advantage, now that we can breathe more freely, of all the ruins and twists of war. Therefore, I feel entitled to come to the House of Commons, whose servant I am, and ask them not to press me to act against my own conscience and better judgment and make scapegoats in order to improve my own position, not to press me to do things which may be clamoured for at the moment but which will not help in our war effort, but, on the contrary, to give me their encouragement and to give me their aid.

1942, 27 JANUARY.

Home Guard

...in that terrible summer, when we stood alone, and as the world thought, forlorn, against the all-powerful aggressor with his vast armies and masses of equipment, Mr. Anthony Eden, as Secretary of State for War, called upon the Local Defence Volunteers to rally round the searchlight positions. Shotguns, sporting rifles, and staves, were all they could find for weapons; it was not until July that we ferried safely across the Atlantic the 1,000,000 rifles and 1,000 field guns, with ammunition proportionable, which were given to us by the Government and people of the United States by an act of precious and timely succour.

1943, 14 MAY. BROADCAST, FROM AMERICA.
(ONWARDS, 87–8.)

North Africa campaign

On December 12 a "catastrophic telegram" came from Graziani. He contemplated retiring as far as Tripoli....He was indignant that he should have been forced into so hazardous an advance upon Egypt by Rommel's undue influence on Mussolini. He complained that he had been forced into a struggle between "a flea and an elephant." Apparently the flea had devoured a large portion of the elephant.

1949. (WW2 II, 547.)

The advance of Gen. Rodolfo Graziani towards Cairo was halted by Gen. Richard O'Connor's Western Desert Force, with the loss of five Italian divisions.

1941

Theme of The Grand Alliance
HOW THE BRITISH FOUGHT ON
WITH HARDSHIP THEIR GARMENT
UNTIL SOVIET RUSSIA AND
THE UNITED STATES
WERE DRAWN
INTO THE GREAT CONFLICT.

1950. (WW2 III, ix.)

War stride

Far be it from me to paint a rosy picture of the future....But I should be failing in my duty if, on the other side, I were not to convey the true impression, that this great nation is getting into its war stride.

1941, 22 JANUARY.

Allies

So I derive confidence that the will-power of the British nation, expressing itself through a stern, steadfast, unyielding House of Commons, once again will perform its liberating function and humbly exercise and execute a high purpose among men; and I say this with the more confidence because we are no longer a small Island lost in the Northern mists, but around us gather in proud array all the free nations of the British Empire, and this time from across the Atlantic Ocean the mighty Republic of the United States proclaims itself on our side, or at our side, or, at any rate, near our side.

1941, 7 MAY.

The last was a case of very accurate thinking; the United States was "near" Britain's side, but nowhere near going to war.

Desert warfare

Here, the fortunes of war are subject to violent oscillation, and mere numbers do not count. On the contrary, the movement in the desert of large numbers would, if things went wrong, lead only to disaster on a larger scale. That is what happened to the Italians.

1941, 7 MAY.

Russia invaded

I have only one single purpose—the destruction of Hitler—and my life is much simplified thereby. If Hitler invaded Hell I would at least make a favourable reference to the Devil in the House of Commons.

1941, 21 JUNE, CHEQUERS. (COLVILLE,
FRINGES I, 480.)

Hitler had invaded Russia. Churchill was speaking to his Private Secretary, Jock Colville. Reconstructed in the first person from Sir John Colville's diaries, which recorded the remark in the third person.

The Russian armies and all the peoples of the Russian Republic have rallied to the defence of their hearths and homes. For the first time Nazi blood has flowed in a fearful torrent...The aggressor is surprised, startled, staggered. For the first time in his experience mass murder has become unprofitable. He retaliates by the most frightful cruelties....And this is but the beginning. Famine and pestilence have yet to follow in the bloody ruts of Hitler's tanks. We are in the presence of a crime without a name.

1941, 24 AUGUST. BROADCAST, LONDON.
(UNRELENTING, 234.)

Well aware of the power of words, WSC tended to say "Russia" or "Russian Republic" when he approved of what they were doing, and "Soviet Russia" or "the Bolsheviks" when he did not.

Minister of Production

I have not been told who is to be this superman who, without holding the office of Prime Minister, is to exercise an overriding control and initiative over the three Departments of Supply and the three Ministers of Supply. Where is the super-personality who, as one of the members of the War Cabinet, will dominate the vast entrenched, established, embattled organisation of the Admiralty to whose successful exertions we owe our lives? Where is the War Cabinet Minister who is going to teach the present Minister of Aircraft Production how to make aircraft quicker and better than they are being made now? Who is the War Cabinet Minister who is going to interfere with Lord Beaverbrook's control and discharge of the functions of Minister of Supply duly and constitutionally conferred upon him? When you have decided on the man, let me know his name, because I should be very glad to serve under him, provided that I were satisfied that he possessed all the Napoleonic and Christian qualities attributed to him.

1941, 29 JULY.

On a stillborn proposal for a Minister of Production.

Anniversary of World War I

Harry [Hopkins] returned dead-beat from Russia, but is lively again now. We shall get him in fine trim on the voyage. We are just off. It is twenty-seven years ago to-day that Huns began their last war. We must make a good job of it this time. Twice ought to be enough. Look forward so much to our meeting. Kindest regards.

1941, 4–5 AUGUST. HMS PRINCE OF WALES.
(WW2 III, 381.)

WSC to Roosevelt, as he left Britain for their Atlantic meeting at Placentia Bay, Newfoundland, with FDR's adviser Harry Hopkins.

Atlantic Charter

I thought you would like me to tell you something about the voyage which I made across the ocean to meet our great friend, the President of the United States. Exactly where we met is a secret, but I don't think I shall be indiscreet if I go so far as to say that it was "somewhere in the Atlantic"....

We had the idea, when we met there—the President and I—that without attempting to draw up final and formal peace aims, or war aims, it was necessary to give all peoples, and especially the oppressed and conquered peoples, a simple, rough and ready wartime statement of the goal towards which the

British Commonwealth and the United States mean to make their way...

There are, however, two distinct and marked differences in this joint declaration from the attitude adopted by the Allies during the latter part of the last war; and no one should overlook them. The United States and Great Britain do not now assume that there will never be any more war again. On the contrary, we intend to take ample precautions to prevent its renewal in any period we can foresee by effectively disarming the guilty nations while remaining suitably protected ourselves.

The second difference is this: that instead of trying to ruin German trade by all kinds of additional trade barriers and hindrances as was the mood of 1917, we have definitely adopted the view that it is not in the interests of the world and of our two countries that any large nation should be unprosperous or shut out from the means of making a decent living for itself and its people by its industry and enterprise. These are far-reaching changes of principle upon which all countries should ponder.

1941, 24 AUGUST. BROADCAST, LONDON.
(UNRELENTING, 231.)

Churchill made far more of the Atlantic Meeting than Roosevelt, who was by no means ready or able to declare war. But the mutual goals he describes remained consistent.

I don't know what will happen if England is fighting alone when 1942 comes.

1941, AUGUST. (SHERWOOD I, 374.)

WSC to Roosevelt confidant Harry Hopkins. Sherwood writes:

He pointed out...that the British had lost 50,000 tons of shipping in the past two days. He said that Hitler was keeping clear of the 26th Meridian, which constituted Roosevelt's frontier of the Western Hemisphere...so there was little prospect of an "incident" serious enough to bring the United States into the war. He asked Hopkins if he felt inclined to express any hope for the future. If Hopkins replied directly to this, I can find no copy of it in his papers. But he made the following note which he attached to the Churchill message: "I talked to the President about this cablegram and the only thing we can

make out of it is that Churchill is pretty depressed and takes it out on us in this fashion." This was quite so.

Gold reserves

How much gold have we actually got left in this island or under our control in South Africa? Don't be alarmed: I am not going to ask you for anything.

1941, 28 AUGUST. (WW2 III, 728.)

Prime Minister to Chancellor of the Exchequer.

North Africa campaign

The Army of the Nile has asked and it was given. They sought and they have found. They knocked and it has been opened unto them.

1941, 9 FEBRUARY.

Sterner days

Do not let us speak of darker days; let us rather speak of sterner days. These are not dark days; these are great days—the greatest days our country has ever lived; and we must all thank God that we have been allowed, each of us according to our stations, to play a part in making these days memorable in the history of our race.

1941, 29 OCTOBER, HARROW SCHOOL.
(UNRELENTING, 288.)

When WSC visited his old school in 1940, Harrow added a verse for him to the school song "Stet Fortuna Domus", in which, for 1941, he obtained permission to change the word "darker" to "sterner":

Nor less we praise in sterner days
  The leader of our nation,
And CHURCHILL'S name shall win acclaim
  From each new generation.
While in this fight to guard the Right
  Our country you defend, Sir.
Here grim and gay we mean to stay,
  And stick it to the end, Sir.

In 1941, Harrow altered the last four lines to reflect the new war situation:

For you have the power in danger's hour,
  Our freedom to defend, Sir!
Though long the fight, we know the right
  Will triumph in the end, Sir!

Hitler's predictions

It is a month ago that I remarked upon the long silence of Herr Hitler, a remark which apparently provoked him to make a speech in which he told the German people that Moscow would fall in a few days. That shows, as everyone I am sure will agree, how much wiser he would have been to go on keeping his mouth shut.

1941, 12 NOVEMBER.

Pearl Harbor

In two or three minutes Mr. Roosevelt came through. "Mr. President, what's this about Japan?" "It's quite true," he replied. "They have attacked us at Pearl Harbor. We are all in the same boat now." I put Winant on to the line and some interchanges took place, the Ambassador at first saying, "Good," "Good"—and then, apparently graver, "Ah!" I got on again and said, "This certainly simplifies things. God be with you," or words to that effect.

1941, 7 DECEMBER, CHEQUERS. (WW2 III, 538.)

Churchill, dining with US Ambassador John Winant and FDR's emissary Averell Harriman, had been given the news of the Japanese attack by his butler Sawyers. He immediately put in a call to the President.

Just these gangs and cliques of wicked men and their military or party organizations have been able to bring these hideous evils upon mankind. It would indeed bring shame upon our generation if we did not teach them a lesson which will not be forgotten in the records of a thousand years.

1941, 11 DECEMBER.

...Governments and peoples do not always take rational decisions. Sometimes they take mad decisions, or one set of people get control who compel all others to obey and aid them in folly....However sincerely we try to put ourselves in another person's position, we cannot allow for processes of the human mind and imagination to which reason offers no key.

Madness is however an affliction which in war carries with it the advantage of SURPRISE.

1950. (WW2 III, 536.)

For personal evaluations of the Japanese attack see America...Pearl Harbor.

Christmas message

Let the children have their night of fun and laughter. Let the gifts of Father Christmas delight their play. Let us grown-ups share to the full in their unstinted pleasures before we turn again to the stern task and the formidable years that lie before us, resolved that, by our sacrifice and daring, these same children shall not be robbed of their inheritance or denied their right to live in a free and decent world.

And so, in God's mercy, a happy Christmas to you all.

1941, 24 DECEMBER. BROADCAST, WHITE HOUSE, WASHINGTON. (UNRELENTING, 341.)

1942

Theme of The Hinge of Fate

HOW THE POWER OF THE
GRAND ALLIANCE
BECAME PREPONDERANT.

1951. (WW2 IV, xi.)

Germany First

In our conferences in January 1942, between the President and myself, and between our high expert advisers, it was evident that, while the defeat of Japan would not mean the defeat of Germany, the defeat of Germany would infallibly mean the ruin of Japan.

1943, 19 MAY. CONGRESS, WASHINGTON. (ONWARDS, 93.)

Japan

But there is no question of regarding the war in the Pacific as a secondary operation. The only limitation applied to its vigorous prosecution will be the shipping available at any given time.

1942, 27 JANUARY.

Fall of Singapore

There must at this stage be no thought of saving the troops or sparing the population. The battle must be fought to the bitter end at all costs.

1942, 10 FEBRUARY. (WW2 IV, 87.)

WSC to Gen. Wavell, C-in-C Far East.

It may well be that we shall never have a formal pronouncement by a competent court upon the worst disaster and largest capitulation in British history.

1951. (WW2 IV, 81.)

Attlee considered but rejected a Royal Commission on the Singapore débâcle in 1946.

But now when it was certain that all was lost at Singapore I was sure it would be wrong to enforce needless slaughter, and without hope of victory to inflict the horrors of street fighting on the vast city, with its teeming, helpless, and now panic-stricken population. I told General Brooke where I stood, and found that he also felt that we should put no more pressure from home upon General Wavell, and should authorise him to take the inevitable decision, for which, by this telegram, we should share the responsibility:

PRIME MINISTER TO GENERAL WAVELL, 14 FEBRUARY 1942

You are of course the sole judge of the moment when no further result can be gained at Singapore.

1951. (WW2 IV, 92.)

Malta

Malta is the first instance of an air force being maintained against odds often of ten to one from a few airfields, all under constant bombardment....It may be that presently the German air forces attacking Malta will have to move eastward to sustain the impending offensive against Southern Russia. If so, we shall have topped the ridge.

1942, 23 APRIL. (SECRET, 67–8.)

Battleships Scharnhorst and Gneisenau

I have read this document to the House because I am anxious that Members should realise that our affairs are not conducted entirely by simpletons and dunderheads as the comic papers try to depict, and in particular that the Admiralty which I regard as an incomparable machine for British protection in spite of all the misfortunes and accidents that have happened, deserves a very broad measure of confidence and gratitude.

1942, 23 APRIL. (SECRET, 53–4.)

On an Admiralty note admitting that the deadly German battleships, at Brest, might successfully sail home through the Channel – which they did. Scharnhorst *was sunk in the*

Battle of the North Cape, 26 December 1943. Gneisenau *survived and ended her life as a blockship in Gotenhafen in 1945.*

Tobruk falls

I am the most miserable Englishman in America—since Burgoyne.

1942, 21 JUNE, WASHINGTON. (HALLE, IRREPRESSIBLE, 200.)

Churchill had been informed of the surrender to Rommel, on 20 June, of the British garrison at Tobruk – one of the worst British defeats of WW2. General John Burgoyne (1722–92) surrendered to the Americans at the Battle of Saratoga on 17 October 1777, during the American Revolution.

Some people assume too readily that, because a Government keeps cool and has steady nerves under reverses, its members do not feel the public misfortunes as keenly as do independent critics. On the contrary, I doubt whether anyone feels greater sorrow or pain than those who are responsible for the general conduct of our affairs.

1942, 2 JULY.

Defeat is one thing; disgrace is another.

1951. (WW2 IV, 344.)

Churchill was with Roosevelt and Hopkins. He wrote:

Nothing could exceed the sympathy and chivalry of my two friends. There were no reproaches; not an unkind word was spoken. *"What can we do to help?" said Roosevelt.*

Middle East and Mediterranean defeats

We are at this moment in the presence of a recession of our hopes and prospects in the Middle East and in the Mediterranean unequalled since the fall of France. If there are any would-be profiteers of disaster who feel able to paint the picture in darker colours, they are certainly at liberty to do so.

1942, 2 JULY.

The Germans under Rommel had regained the initiative in North Africa, and nowhere in the Mediterranean could Britain point to a victory.

Vote of Confidence

I have not made any arrogant, confident, boasting predictions at all. On the contrary, I have stuck hard to my "blood, toil, tears and sweat," to which I have added muddle and mismanagement, and that, to some extent I must admit, is what you have got out of it.

1942, 2 JULY.

On 1 July 1942, Sir John Wardlaw-Milne (Cons., Kidderminster) moved:

That this House, while paying tribute to the heroism and endurance of the Armed Forces of the Crown in circumstances of exceptional difficulty, has no confidence in the central direction of the war.

This is a serious charge, tabled very rarely in the House. Churchill's Government defeated the motion, 475 to 25.

I sent my encouragement [to General Auchinleck in North Africa] on the morrow of the Vote of Censure debate, which had been an accompaniment to the cannonade.

1942, 4 JULY. (WW2 IV, 385.)

North Africa: Auchinleck's dismissal

On August 5 I visited the Alamein positions....Thence we proceeded along the front to his headquarters behind the Ruweisat Ridge, where we were given breakfast in a wire-netted cube, full of flies and important military personages.

(WW2 IV, 414.)

It was a terrible thing to have to do. He took it like a gentleman. But it was a terrible thing. It is difficult to remove a bad General at the height of a campaign: it is atrocious to remove a good General. We must use Auchinleck again. We cannot afford to lose such a man from the fighting line.

1942, 6 NOVEMBER. (NICOLSON II, 259.)

On his removal of the able General Claude Auchinleck from the North African command. Auchinleck's dual role ultimately fell to Alexander (C-in-C Middle East) and his subordinate Montgomery (Commander 8th Army).

Cave-building in Egypt

But I had my table of facts and figures and remained dissatisfied. The scale was far too small. The original fault lay with the Pharaohs for not having built more and larger Pyramids. Other responsibilities were more difficult to assign.

1951. (WW2 IV, 468.)

Lamenting delay in building the Tura caves, near Cairo (with stones from the Pyramids), which were needed for military repair work.

North Africa: Alexander's assignment

1. Your prime and main duty will be to take or destroy at the earliest opportunity the German-Italian Army commanded by Field Marshal Rommel, together with all its supplies and establishments in Egypt and Libya.

2. You will discharge or cause to be discharged such other duties as pertain to your Command without prejudice to the task described in paragraph 1, which must be considered paramount in His Majesty's interests.

1942, 10 AUGUST. (END, 282.)

Prime Minister to General the Hon. Sir Harold Alexander, Commander-in-Chief, Middle East. Six months later, February 1943, Field Marshal Sir Harold Alexander replied. See 1943/February...North Africa: Alexander's reply.

North Africa: campaign

This desert warfare has to be seen to be believed. Large armies, with their innumerable transport and tiny habitations, are dispersed and scattered as if from a pepper-pot over the vast indeterminate slopes and plains of the desert, broken here and there only by a sandy crease or tuck in the ground or an outcrop of rock. The ground in most places, especially on all commanding eminences, is rock with only an inch or two of sand on the top, and no cover can be obtained for guns or troops except by blasting.

1942, 8 SEPTEMBER.

North Africa: victory at Alamein

I have never promised anything but blood, tears, toil and sweat. Now, however, we have a new experience. We have victory—a remarkable and definite victory. The bright gleam has caught the helmets of our soldiers, and warmed and cheered all our hearts....

When I read of the coastal road crammed with fleeing German vehicles under the blasting attacks of the Royal Air Force, I could not but remember those roads of France and Flanders, crowded, not with fighting men, but with helpless refugees—women and children—fleeing with their pitiful barrows and household goods, upon whom such merciless havoc was wreaked. I have, I trust, a humane disposition, but I must say I could not help feeling that what was happening, however grievous, was only justice grimly reclaiming her rights.

1942, 10 NOVEMBER. LORD MAYOR'S DAY LUNCHEON, MANSION HOUSE, LONDON. (END, 265–7.)

Following the first Battle of Alamein in July, for which Auchinleck deserves credit, the German-Italian advance towards Egypt was stopped. The second battle, under Montgomery (23 October to 2 November), ended Germany's hope to gain control of Suez, Egypt or the Middle Eastern oil fields. See also Chapter 1...End of the Beginning.

It marked in fact the turning of "the Hinge of Fate." It may almost be said, "Before Alamein we never had a victory. After Alamein we never had a defeat."

1951. (WW2 IV, 541.)

Vichy France occupied

I never had the slightest doubt myself that Hitler would break the Armistice, overrun all France and try to capture the French fleet at Toulon; such developments were to be welcomed by the United Nations, because they entailed the extinction for all practical purposes of the sorry farce and fraud of the Vichy Government. This was a necessary prelude to that reunion of France without which French resurrection is impossible....[Now] all Frenchmen are equally under the German yoke, and will learn to hate it with equal intensity.

1942, 29 NOVEMBER. BROADCAST, LONDON. (END, 300.)

On 11 November 1942, Hitler occupied the portion of France he had ostensibly left independent. He hoped also to capture the French

fleet at Toulon, but French naval authorities were able to scuttle the ships while delaying the Germans with negotiations.

1943

Casablanca Conference

The dominating aim which we set before ourselves at the Conference at Casablanca was to engage the enemy's forces on land, on sea, and in the air on the largest possible scale and at the earliest possible moment....We have to make the enemy burn and bleed in every way that is physically and reasonably possible, in the same way as he is being made to burn and bleed along the vast Russian front from the White Sea to the Black Sea.

1943, 11 FEBRUARY.

Sardinia

I absolutely refuse to be fobbed off with a sardine.

1943, JANUARY. (ISMAY, 287.)

WSC on the proposal that the Allies take Sardinia before Sicily.

Eighth Army

In the words of the old hymn, you have "nightly pitched your moving tents a day's march nearer home."

1943, 3 FEBRUARY, TRIPOLI. (ONWARDS, 10.)

Speech to troops of the Eighth Army. The quotation is from a hymn by Scottish poet James Montgomery (1771–1854):

Here in the body pent,
Absent from Him I roam,
Yet nightly pitch my moving tent
A day's march nearer home.

North Africa: Alexander's reply

[General Alexander to Prime Minister, February 1943: "Sir: The Orders you gave me on August [10], 1942, have been fulfilled. His Majesty's enemies, together with their impedimenta, have been completely eliminated from Egypt, Cyrenaica, Libya, and Tripolitania. I now await your further instructions."]

Well, obviously, we shall have to think of something else.

1943, 8 FEBRUARY. (ONWARDS, 25.)

Unwarranted promises

... I feel I can truthfully say that I only wish to do my duty by the whole mass of the nation and of the British Empire as long as I am thought to be of any use for that. Therefore I tell you round your firesides tonight that I am resolved not to give or to make all kinds of promises and tell all kinds of fairy tales to you who have trusted me and gone with me so far, and marched through the valley of the shadow, till we have reached the upland regions on which we now stand with firmly planted feet.

1943, 21 MARCH. BROADCAST, LONDON. (ONWARDS, 34–5.)

Stalingrad and Tunisia

We cannot doubt that Stalingrad and Tunisia are the greatest military disasters that have ever befallen Germany in all the wars she has made, and they are many. There is no doubt from the statements of captured generals that Hitler expected his Tunisian army to hold out at least until August, and that this was the view and intention of the German High Command. The suddenness of the collapse of these great numbers of brave and skilful fighting men, with every form of excellent equipment, must be regarded as a significant and in a sense characteristic of the German psychology which was shown after Jena and also at the very end of the last war.

1943, 8 JUNE.

At Jena on 14 October 1806, superior numbers of Prussians under Friedrich Wilhelm III were routed by Napoleon. It was one of WSC's favourite allusions.

Tunisia losses

The British losses in Tunisia have been severe. The English Army, since they crossed the frontier from Tripolitania, have sustained about 11,500 casualties, and the First Army about 23,500 casualties, in all 35,000 killed, missing, and wounded during the campaign in the two British Armies....

The total number of prisoners who have passed through the cages of all the allies now amounts to over 248,000 men, an increase of 24,000 on the previously published total, and there must certainly have been 50,000 of the enemy killed, making a total loss of about 300,000 men to the enemy in Tunisia alone.

1943, 8 JUNE. (ONWARDS 116.)

First Quebec Conference

Everything here has gone off well. We have secured a settlement of a number of hitherto intractable questions e.g., the South-East Asia Command, "Tube Alloys," and French Committee recognition. On this last we all had an awful time with Hull, who has at last gone off in a pretty sulky mood....Stalin has of course studiously ignored our offer to make a further long and hazardous journey in order to bring about a tripartite meeting. In spite of all this I do not think his manifestations of ill temper and bad manners are preparatory to a separate peace with Germany, as the hatreds between the two races have now become a sanitary cordon in themselves.

1943, 25 AUGUST, QUEBEC. (WW2 V, 83–4.)

Prime Minister to Deputy Prime Minister and War Cabinet. "Tube Alloys" was the atomic bomb project. Many of the attempted accommodations with Stalin were based on the possibility that he might make a separate peace with Germany – feared more in Washington than in London. This conference chiefly set out plans for Operation Overlord, the invasion of France in 1944.

Combined chiefs of staff

The only hope is the intimacy and friendship which has been established between us and between our High Staffs. If that were broken I should despair of the immediate future....I need scarcely say the British Chiefs of Staff fully share these views. I must add that I am more anxious about the campaign of 1944 than about any other in which I have been involved.

1943, 27 OCTOBER. (WW2 V, 280.)

WSC to Roosevelt prior to the Teheran Conference.

Russian successes

That monstrous juggernaut engine of German might and tyranny has been beaten and broken, outfought and outmanoeuvred by Russian valour, generalship and science, and it has been beaten to an extent which may well prove mortal.

1943, 9 NOVEMBER. MANSION HOUSE, LONDON. (ONWARDS, 264.)

Teheran Conference

We are the trustees for the peace of the world. If we fail there will be perhaps a hundred years of chaos. If we are strong we can carry out our trusteeship....I do not want to enforce any system on other nations. I ask for freedom and for the right of all nations to develop as they like. We three must remain friends in order to ensure happy homes in all countries.

1943, 28 NOVEMBER, TEHERAN. (WW2 V, 318–19.)

WSC to Roosevelt and Stalin.

I realised at Teheran for the first time what a small nation we are. There I sat with the great Russian bear on one side of me, with paws outstretched, and on the other side the great American buffalo and between the two sat the poor little English donkey who was the only one, the only one of the three, who knew the right way home.

UNDATED, CA. 1943–44. (PELLING, 546; WHEELER-BENNETT, 96.)

WSC to Violet Bonham Carter.

The cross-Channel invasion was fixed for May, subject naturally to tides and the moon. It was to be aided by a renewed major Russian offensive....The frontiers of the new Poland had been broadly outlined both in the east and in the west. The Curzon Line, subject to inter-pretation in the east, and the line of the Oder, in the west, seemed to afford a true and lasting home for the Polish nation after all its suffer-ings....But vast and disastrous changes have fallen upon us in the realm of fact. The Polish frontiers exist only in name, and Poland lies quivering in the Russian-Communist grip. Germany has indeed been partitioned, but only by a hideous division into zones of military occupation. About this tragedy it can only be said IT CANNOT LAST.

1952. (WW2 V, 358–60.)

Churchill was aware of how little Britain counted among the Big Three, and of

Roosevelt's confidence that he (and only he) could work with Marshal Stalin. See also 1945 for the Yalta and Potsdam conferences.

1944

Theme of Closing the Ring

HOW
NAZI GERMANY WAS ISOLATED
AND
ASSAILED ON ALL SIDES.

1951. (WW2 V, xi.)

Anzio

Am very glad that you are pegging out claims rather than digging in beach-heads.

1944, 21 JANUARY. (WW2 V, 426.)

WSC to General Alexander, who had reported landing over 36,000 men at Anzio, Italy.

...I had hoped that we were hurling a wild cat on to the shore, but all we got was a stranded whale.

1944, 31 JANUARY. (WW2 V, 432.)

Later WSC referred to "Suvla Bay all over again": the British landing north of the Gallipoli bridgehead in summer 1915, where British generals, instead of advancing, had dug in, giving the Turks time to bring up adequate reinforcements. WSC also told the Chiefs of Staff:

> We hoped to land a wild cat that would tear out the bowels of the Boche. Instead we have stranded a vast whale with its tail flopping about in the water.

Misquoted in Manchester (Last Lion II) *and Colville* (The Churchillians).

Unity

My hope is that the generous instincts of unity will not depart from us...[so that we] become the prey of the little folk who exist in every country and who frolic alongside the Juggernaut car of war to see what fun or notoriety they can extract from the proceed-ings.

1944, 22 FEBRUARY.

D-Day

It is rather remarkable that a secret of this character, which had to be entrusted from the beginning, to scores, very soon to hundreds, and ultimately to thousands of people, never leaked out either in these islands or the wide expanses of the United States....

The great episode seemed to every one to be the crossing of the Channel, with its stormy waters, swift currents, and eighteen-foot rise and fall of the tide, and above all the changes of weather...That was the element, this possible change in the weather, which certainly hung like a vulture poised in the sky over the thoughts of the most sanguine.

1944, 2 AUGUST.

WSC had used the hanging vulture analogy ever since his escape from the Boers in 1899, when a "gigantic vulture" hovered over him and "made hideous and ominous gurglings..." (Ladysmith, 196).

The speed with which the mighty British and American armies in France were built up is almost incredible. In the first twenty-four hours a quarter of a million men were landed, in the teeth of fortified and violent opposition....Enormous masses of armour of the highest quality and character gave them extraordinary offensive power and mobility.

1944, 28 SEPTEMBER.

D-Day: Mulberry Harbours

They *must* float up and down with the tide. The anchor problem must be mastered. The ships must have a side-flap cut in them, and a drawbridge long enough to overreach the moorings of the piers. Let me have the best solution worked out. Don't argue the matter. The difficulties will argue for themselves.

1941, 30 MAY. (WW2 V, 66.)

Prime Minister to Chief of Combined Operations: Churchill's first directive on what became the floating Mulberry Harbours used in the Normandy invasion of 1944. Note the date – but WSC's idea really began in a 1917 minute to Lloyd George, proposing floating harbours to attack the Friesian Islands of Borkum and Sylt.

In view of the many accounts which are extant and multiplying of my supposed aversion from any kind of large-scale opposed-landing, such as took place in Normandy in 1944, it may be convenient if I make it clear that from the very beginning I provided a great deal of the impulse and authority for creating the immense apparatus and armada for the landing of armour on beaches, without which it is now universally recognised that all such major operations would have been impossible.

1949. (WW2 II, 224.)

Churchill alone had been demanding plans for re-establishing a front on the continent as early as 1940; his reluctance to invade prematurely was based on his recollection of the Gallipoli landings in World War I, as expressed poignantly to General Marshall: "I see the sea filled with corpses."

Defending the Government

If the worst came to the worst I might have a shot at it myself.

1944, 9 MARCH. (DAWN, 54.)

When asked by journalists if he would select a member of the Government to speak on its behalf.

Italian campaign stalled

But all this bites much deeper when you see and feel it on the spot. Here was this splendid army, equivalent to twenty-five divisions, of which a quarter were American, reduced till it was just not strong enough to produce decisive results against the immense power of the defensive. A very little more, half what had been taken from us, and we could have broken into the valley of the Po, with all the gleaming possibilities and prizes which lay open towards Vienna.

1954. (WW2 VI, 96.)

WSC regretted not exploiting Allied gains in Italy.

Pius XII and the war

The one [topic] that bulked the largest at this audience [with Pope Pius XII], as it had done with his predecessor eighteen years before, was the danger of Communism. I have always had the greatest dislike of it; and should I ever have the honour of another audience with the Supreme Pontiff I should not hesitate to recur to the subject.

1954. (WW2 VI, 103.)

Tito: a close encounter

I saw before me five yards away [Tito's] two formidable guardians....I have a very large oblong gold cigar case which belonged to Lord Birkenhead and was given to me by his family after his death. This was in my right-hand pocket. I grasped it firmly and marched toward them. Arrived within two yards I drew it from my pocket as if it were a pistol. Luckily they grinned with delight and we made friends. But I do not recommend such proce-dure in similar cases.

1944, 12 AUGUST, NAPLES. (SIR FITZROY MACLEAN
TO THE EDITOR.)

Sir Fitzroy recalled:

For a split second I saw their trigger fingers tighten and I only had time to hope that whatever was about to happen would take me with it. ...As we sat down to dinner I took out a large khaki handkerchief and wiped the sweat from my face.

Finland and Romania

The armistice terms agreed upon for Finland and Romania bear, naturally, the imprint of the Soviet will—and here I must draw attention to the restraint which has characterized the Soviet treatment of these two countries, both of which marched blithely behind Hitler in his attempted destruction of Russia, and both of which added their quota of injuries to the immense volume of suffering which the Russian people have endured, survived, and have triumphantly surmounted.

1944, 28 SEPTEMBER.

Not redolent of WSC's usual magnanimity. Finland had after all fought for life and liberty when ruthlessly invaded by Stalin as Hitler was seizing western Europe. In 1940, Churchill had called Finland "sublime in the jaws of peril". See Nations...Finland.

Hitler's follies

He has lost, or will lose when the tally is complete, nearly a million men in France and the Low Countries. Other large armies may well be cut off in the Baltic States, in Finland, and in Norway. Less than a year ago, when the relative weakness of Germany was already becoming apparent, he was ordering further aggressive action in the Aegean, and the reoccupation of the islands which the Italians had surrendered, or wished to surrender. He has scattered and squandered a very large army in the Balkan Peninsula, whose escape will be very difficult; twenty-seven divisions, many of them battered, are fighting General Alexander in Northern Italy. Many of these will not be able to recross the Alps to defend the German Fatherland. Such a vast frittering-away and dispersal of forces has never been seen, and is, of course, a prime cause of the impending ruin of Germany.

1944, 28 SEPTEMBER.

Jewish Brigade

I know there are vast numbers of Jews serving with our Forces and the American Forces throughout all the Armies, but it seems to me indeed appropriate that a special Jewish unit, a special unit of that race which has suffered inde-scribable torments from the Nazis, should be represented as a distinct formation amongst the forces gathered for their formal overthrow....

1944, 28 SEPTEMBER.

Second Quebec Conference

It is a year since we met here. Well, no one can say that the conference last year was simply of an idle and agreeable character. Out of it came decisions which are now engraved upon the monuments of history. Out of it came arrange-ments by which our vast armies were hurled across the sea, forced their way on shore in the teeth of the enemy's fire and fortifications, broke up his armed strength, and liberated, almost as if by enchantment, the dear and beautiful land of France, so long held under the corroding heel of the Hun.

1944, 16 SEPTEMBER, QUEBEC. (DILKS, 343.)

Our confidence in the Chiefs of Staff—British confidence and the confidence of the War Cabinet—has steadily grown. In consequence of the fact that there have been no changes, the men who met together at Quebec knew each other well, were united in bonds of compre-hension and friendship...

1944, 28 SEPTEMBER.

Second Quebec: Morgenthau Plan

I'm all for disarming Germany, but we ought not to prevent her living decently...You cannot indict a whole nation. At any rate, what is to be done should be done quickly. Kill the criminals, but don't carry on the business for years.

1944, 13 SEPTEMBER. CITADEL, QUEBEC. (MORAN, 190.)

The proposal of US Treasury Secretary Morgenthau, to deprive Germany of all industry and turn her into a pastoral country, was ultimately opposed by Churchill, though he wavered a few times when importuned by his anti-German scientific adviser, Professor Lindemann.

Disunity among allies

There are all sorts of matters which are extremely important upon which we might expend a great deal of energy and pugnacity, but at present we must do our best to keep our pugnacity for export purposes.

1944, 6 OCTOBER.

...as the sense of mortal peril has passed from our side to that of our cruel foes, they gain the stimulus of despair, and we tend to lose the bond of combined self-preservation, or are in danger of losing it.

1945, 18 JANUARY.

Salvaging Greece

Anthony and I are going out to see what we can do to square this Greek entanglement. Basis of action: the King does not go back until a plebiscite in his favour has been taken. For the rest, we cannot abandon those who have taken up arms in our cause, and must if necessary fight it out with them. It must always be understood that we seek nothing from Greece, in territory or advantages. We have given much, and will give more if it is in our power. I count on you to help us in this time of unusual difficulty.

1944, 26 DECEMBER. (WW2 VI, 273.)

WSC to President Roosevelt, who was critical of Britain's effort to broker a compromise regency that, at the time, probably saved Greece from a communist takeover.

1945

Theme of Triumph and Tragedy

HOW THE GREAT DEMOCRACIES
TRIUMPHED,
AND SO WERE ABLE TO RESUME
THE FOLLIES
WHICH HAD SO NEARLY
COST THEM THEIR
LIFE.

1954. (WW2 VI, xi.)

Onslaught on the Reich

The Allies are resolved that Germany shall be totally disarmed, that Nazism and militarism in Germany shall be destroyed, that war criminals shall be justly and swiftly punished, that all German industry capable of military production shall be eliminated or controlled, and that Germany shall make compensation in kind to the utmost of her ability for damage done to Allied nations.

1945, 27 FEBRUARY.

Yalta Conference

If we had spent ten years on research we could not have found a worse place in the world.

1945, JANUARY. (OB VII, 1159.)

WSC to Harry Hopkins. With Stalin unwilling to leave Russia, the Big Three gathered at the war-ravaged Crimean city of Yalta, where decent amenities were few, though the Russians tried to import luxuries. At their first meeting, hordes of flies attacked the legs of the seated dignitaries.

A small lion was walking between a huge Russian bear and a great American elephant, but perhaps it will prove to be the lion who knew the way.

1945, 24 FEBRUARY, CHEQUERS. (OB VII, 1233.)

WSC to John Colville, Czech President Beneš and Foreign Secretary Masaryk. Churchill had had similar thoughts at the previous conference, with the animals slightly changed; see Teheran.

It was a disaster—because the President is a dying man.

1945, 28 FEBRUARY. (SIR JOHN COLVILLE
TO THE EDITOR.)

WSC to John Colville upon returning from Yalta. Roosevelt, as the only head of state present, was forced in his weakened state and ill health to preside at all the meetings, and Churchill believed this allowed Stalin to push through his demands with insufficient opposition from FDR.

I am not prepared to say that everything discussed at Yalta could be made the subject of a verbatim report.

1945, 7 JUNE. (DURING QUESTION TIME.)

The Agreement which was made at Yalta, to which I was a party, was extremely favourable to Soviet Russia, but it was made at a time when no one could say that the German war might not extend all through the summer and autumn of 1945, and when the Japanese war was expected to last for a further eighteen months from the end of the German war.

1946, 5 MARCH. WESTMINSTER COLLEGE, FULTON, MISSOURI. (SINEWS, 102.)

Crossing the Rhine

I am jealous. You succeeded where I failed. Tomorrow nothing shall stop me. Sleep soundly; you might have slept more soundly still.

1945, 24 MARCH, GERMANY. (COLVILLE, FOOTPRINTS, 187.)

Churchill on Operation Plunder, the crossing of the Rhine, which Eisenhower, Montgomery and Brooke would not let him attend personally. WSC's private secretary Colville took it upon himself to venture across, and returned with a blood-stained tunic. Monty gave Colville's party a dressing down, but Churchill stood up for them, and said this to Colville as they turned in that evening.

Hitler's gift

HITLER, PERSONALLY.

1945, 25 MARCH, FRANCE. (TAYLOR, 388.)

WSC wrote this greeting on a 240 mm shell during his visit to the Rhine. The shell was fired in the direction of Berlin.

Linking with the Russians

I deem it highly important that we should shake hands with the Russians as far to the east as possible.

1945, 2 APRIL. (WW2 VI, 409.)

WSC to Gen. Eisenhower, who proceeded in accord with instructions, and did not strike out for Vienna, Prague and Berlin as Churchill wished.

Presidential transition

We can now see the deadly hiatus which existed between the fading of President Roosevelt's strength and the growth of President Truman's grip of the vast world problem. In this melancholy void one President could not act and the other could not know.

1954. (WW2 VI, 399.)

For quotations on Roosevelt at his death, see Chapter 20.

V-E Day

For five years you've brought me bad news, sometimes worse than others. Now you've redeemed yourself.

1945, 7 MAY, DOWNING STREET. (OB VII, 1336.)

WSC to Captain Pim, who ran his "map room", and brought him the news of Germany's surrender as he awoke on 7 May. General Jodl signed the instrument of surrender at 2:41 a.m. at Eisenhower's headquarters in Germany.

I recollect well at the end of the last war, more than quarter of a century ago, that the House...did not feel inclined for debate or business, but desired to offer thanks to Almighty God, to the Great Power which seems to shape and design the fortunes of nations and the destiny of man; and I therefore beg, Sir, with your permission to move "That this House do now attend at the church of St. Margaret, Westminster, to give humble and reverent thanks to Almighty God for our deliverance from the threat of German domination." This is the identical motion which was moved in former times.

1945, 8 MAY.

My dear friends, I hope you have had two happy days. Happy days are what we have worked for, but happy days are not easily worked for. By discipline, by morale, by industry, by good laws, by fair institutions—by those ways we have won through to happy days for millions and millions of people. You have been attacked by a monstrous enemy—but you never flinched or wavered. London, like a great rhinoceros, a great hippopotamus, saying: "Let them do their worst. London can take it." London could take anything. My heart goes out to the Cockneys. Any visitors we may happen to have here today—and many great nations are represented here, by all those who have borne arms with us in the struggle—they echo what I say when I say "GOOD OLD LONDON!"….God bless you all. May you long remain as citizens of a great and splendid city. May you long remain as the heart of the British Empire.

1945, 9 MAY. BALCONY OF MINISTRY OF HEALTH, LONDON. (VICTORY, 129–30.)

The second of two speeches Churchill gave following victory over Germany. The first will be found in Chapter 1.

I told you hard things at the beginning of these last five years; you did not shrink, and I should be unworthy of your confidence and generosity if I did not still cry: Forward, unflinching, unswerving, indomitable, till the whole task is done and the whole world is safe and clean.

1945, 13 MAY. WORLD BROADCAST, LONDON. (VICTORY, 138.)

Potsdam Conference

[Berlin] was nothing but a chaos of ruins…Then we entered the Chancellery, and for quite a long time walked through its shattered galleries and halls. Our Russian guides then took us to Hitler's air-raid shelter. I went down to the bottom and saw the room in which he and his mistress had committed suicide, and when we came up again they showed us the place where his body had been burned. We were given the best first-hand accounts available at that time of what had happened in these final scenes.

1954. (WW2 VI, 545–6.)

I take no responsibility beyond what is here set forth for any of the conclusions reached at Potsdam….I intended, if I were returned by the electorate, as was generally expected, to come to grips with the Soviet Government on this catalogue of decisions. For instance, neither I nor Mr. Eden would ever have agreed to the Western Neisse being the [Polish]

frontier line. The line of the Oder and the Eastern Neisse had already been recognised as the Polish compensation for retiring to the Curzon Line, but the overrunning by the Russian armies of the territory up to and even beyond the Western Neisse was never and would never have been agreed to by any Government of which I was the head. Here was no point of principle only, but rather an enormous matter of fact affecting about three additional millions of displaced people.

1954. (WW2 VI, 581.)

Resignation

It only remains for me to express to the British people, for whom I have acted in these perilous years, my profound gratitude for the unflinching, unswerving support which they have given me during my task, and for the many expressions of kindness which they have shown towards their servant.

1945, 26 JULY. STATEMENT FROM 10 DOWNING STREET. (VICTORY, 213.)

There was more than a little hint of irony in this message, for his party had been rejected in the election by an overwhelming majority, though he himself had been handily returned. For other comments on the 1945 election see Personal, Politics – domestic, and Ripostes.

Atomic bomb

The decision to use the atomic bomb was taken by President Truman and myself at Potsdam, and we approved the military plans to unchain the dread, pent-up forces….There are voices which assert that the bomb should never have been used at all. I cannot associate myself with such ideas. Six years of total war have convinced most people that had the Germans or Japanese discovered this new weapon, they would have used it upon us to our complete destruction with the utmost alacrity. I am surprised that very worthy people, but people who in most cases had no intention of proceeding to the Japanese front themselves, should adopt the position that rather than throw this bomb, we should have sacrificed a million American, and a quarter of a million British lives in the desperate battles and massacres of an invasion of Japan.

1945, 16 AUGUST.

V-J Day

Once again the British Commonwealth and Empire emerges safe, undiminished, and united from a mortal struggle. Monstrous tyrannies which menaced our life have been beaten to the ground in ruin, and a brighter radiance illumines the Imperial Crown than any which our annals record. The light is brighter because it comes not only from the fierce but fading glare of military achievement...but because there mingle with it in mellow splendour the hopes, joys, and blessings of almost all mankind. This is the true glory, and long will it gleam upon our forward path.

1945, 15 AUGUST.

World War II: General Observations

Allies

We know that other hearts in millions and scores of millions beat with ours; that other voices proclaim the cause for which we strive; other strong hands wield the hammers and shape the weapons we need; other clear and gleaming eyes are fixed in hard conviction upon the tyrannies that must and shall be destroyed.

1941, 18 MARCH. LUNCHEON, LONDON.
(UNRELENTING, 62.)

We are sea animals, and the United States are to a large extent ocean animals. The Russians are land animals. Happily, we are all three air animals. It is difficult to explain fully all the different characteristics of the war effort of various countries but I am sure that we made their leaders feel confidence in our loyal and sincere resolve to come to their aid as quickly as possible and in the most effective manner, without regard to the losses or sacrifices involved so long as the contribution was towards victory.

1942, 8 SEPTEMBER.

Atrocities

One of the most extraordinary things that I have ever known in my experience is the way in which German illegalities, atrocities and brutalities are coming to be accepted as if they were part of the ordinary day-to-day conditions of war. Why, Sir, the neutral Press makes more fuss when I make a speech telling them what is their duty than they have done when hundreds of their ships have been sunk and many thousands of their sailors have been drowned or murdered, for that is the right word, on the open sea....It is not at all odd that His Majesty's Government are getting rather tired of it. I am getting rather tired of it myself.

1940, 27 FEBRUARY.

All over Europe, races and States [are] under the dark, cruel yoke of Hitler and his Nazi gang. Every week his firing parties are busy in a dozen lands. Monday he shoots Dutchmen; Tuesday, Norwegians; Wednesday, French and Belgians stand against the wall; Thursday it is the Czechs who must suffer. And now there are the Serbs and the Greeks to fill his repulsive bill of executions. But always, all the days, there are the Poles. The atrocities committed by Hitler upon the Poles, the ravaging of their country, the scattering of their homes, the affronts to their religion, the enslavement of their man-power, exceed in severity and in scale the villainies perpetrated by Hitler in any other conquered land.

1941, 3 MAY. BROADCAST, LONDON.
(UNRELENTING, 103.)

Since the Mongol invasions of Europe in the sixteenth century, there has never been methodical, merciless butchery on such a scale, or approaching such a scale.

1941, 24 AUGUST. BROADCAST, LONDON.
(UNRELENTING, 234.)

Beer

A serious appeal was made to me by General Alexander for more beer for the troops in Italy. The Americans are said to have four bottles a week, and the British rarely get one. You should make an immediate effort, and come to me for support in case other departments are involved. Let me have a plan, with time schedule, for this beer.

1944, 23 OCTOBER. (WW2 VI, 609.)

Prime Minister to Secretary of State for War.

Blitz over Britain

...we would rather see London laid in ruins and ashes than that it should be tamely and abjectly enslaved.

1940, 14 JULY.

Statisticians may amuse themselves by calculating that after making allowance for the working of the law of diminishing returns, through the same house being struck twice and three times over, it would take ten years, at the present rate, for half the houses of London to be demolished. After that, of course, progress would be much slower....

In all my life, I have never been treated with so much kindness as by the people who have suffered most. One would think one had brought some great benefit to them, instead of the blood and tears, the toil and sweat, which is all I have ever promised.

1940, 8 OCTOBER.

When we got back into the car, a harsher mood swept over this haggard crowd. "Give it 'em back," they cried, and, "Let *them* have it too." I undertook forthwith to see that their wishes were carried out; and this promise was certainly kept.

1949. PECKHAM, LONDON. (WW2 II, 308.)

The next target was Birmingham, and three successive raids from the 19th to the 22nd of November [1940] inflicted much destruction and loss of life....When I visited the city...It was the dinner hour and a very pretty girl ran up to the car and threw a box of cigars into it....She said, "I won the prize this week for the highest output." This gift must have cost her two or three pounds. I was very glad (in my official capacity) to give her a kiss.

1949. (WW2 II, 333.)

...I have seen many painful scenes of havoc, and of fine buildings and acres of cottage homes blasted into rubble-heaps of ruin. But it is just in those very places where the malice of the savage enemy has done its worst, and where the ordeal of the men, women and children has been most severe, that I found their morale most high and splendid....Old men, little children, the crippled veterans of former wars, aged women, the ordinary hard-pressed citizen or subject of the King, as he likes to call himself, the sturdy workmen who swing the hammers or load the ships, skilful craftsmen, the members of every kind of A.R.P. [Air Raid Precautions] service, are proud to feel that they stand in the line together with our fighting men, when one of the greatest of causes is

being fought out, as fought out it will be, to the end. This is indeed the grand heroic period of our history, and the light of glory shines on all.

1941, 27 APRIL. BROADCAST, LONDON.
(UNRELENTING, 91–3.)

...if tonight the people of London were asked to cast their vote whether a convention should be entered into to stop the bombing of all cities...the people of London with one voice would say to Hitler: "You have committed every crime under the sun. Where you have been the least resisted there you have been the most brutal....We will have no truce or parley with you, or the grisly gang who work your wicked will. You do your worst—and we will do our best." Perhaps it may be our turn soon; perhaps it may be our turn now.

1941, 14 JULY. LONDON COUNTY HALL.
(UNRELENTING, 186.)

Given after a review of Civil Defence forces in Hyde Park.

Against giving such limelight to this incident...Flaunting weakest feature...What notice taken of all who died in air attack? Moreover we said earlier "no panic": this makes it clear there was panic....

1943, 4 MARCH. (DIARIES OF CABINET SECRETARY
SIR NORMAN BROOK, *THE NEW YORK TIMES*, 22
JANUARY 2006.)

On the night of 3 March 1943, over 170 civilians were killed in Bethnal Green tube station during a Luftwaffe raid. Churchill opposed a public inquiry on morale grounds.

The speeches of the German leaders, from Hitler downwards, contain mysterious allusions to new methods and new weapons which will presently be tried against us. It would, of course, be natural for the enemy to spread such rumours in order to encourage his own people, but there is probably more in it than that.

1943, 21 SEPTEMBER.

Indeed there was: the V1 and V2 rocket-bombs were dropped on parts of south-eastern England in 1944–45. Though relatively few had been mobilised before Allied invaders captured and neutralised their launching site, the V-wapons caused the deaths of 8,938 civilians and 2,917 servicemen, over 25,000 people were seriously injured, and 107,000 homes were destroyed.

...there is no doubt that the Germans are preparing on the French shore new means of assault on this country, either by pilotless aircraft, or possibly rockets, or both, on a considerable scale. We have long been watching this with the utmost vigilance. We are striking at all evidence of these preparations on occasions when the weather is suitable for such action and to the maximum extent possible without detracting from the strategic offensive against Germany.

1944, 22 FEBRUARY.

To the blood-curdling threats which German propaganda has been making in order to keep up the spirit of their people and of their satellites, there have been added the most absurd claims about the results of the first use of the secret weapon....Considering the modest weight and small penetration-power of these bombs, the damage they have inflicted by blast effect has been extensive. It cannot at all be compared with the terrific destruction by fire and high explosives with which we have been assaulting Berlin, Hamburg, Cologne, and scores of other German cities and other war-manufacturing points in Germany.

1944, 6 JUNE.

About 10,000 V1 flying bombs or "doodle-bugs", a kind of early forebear of the cruise missile, were fired at England from June 1944 through March 1945.

The House will, I think, be favourably surprised to learn that the total number of flying bombs launched from the enemy's stations have killed almost exactly one person per bomb....Is this attack going to get worse or is it going to be beat like the magnetic mine, or beat like the attempted destruction of Britain by the aeroplane, or beat as the U-boat campaign was beat? Will new developments, on the other hand, of a far more formidable character, come upon us? Will the rocket bomb come? Will improved explosives come? Will greater ranges, faster speeds, and larger war-heads come upon us? I can give no guarantee that any of these evils will be entirely prevented before the time comes, as come it

will, when the soil from which these attacks are launched has been finally liberated from the enemy's grip.

1944, 6 JULY.

The danger of flying bombs was soon eliminated as the onrushing Allies overwhelmed their launching sites in Western Europe.

Bomb squads

One squad [comprised] the Earl of Suffolk, his lady private secretary, and his rather aged chauffeur. They called themselves "the Holy Trinity." Their prowess and continued existence got around among all who knew. Thirty-four unexploded bombs did they tackle with urbane and smiling efficiency. But the thirty-fifth claimed its forfeit. Up went the Earl of Suffolk in his Holy Trinity. But we may be sure that..."all the trumpets sounded for them on the other side."

1948. (WW2 II, 320.)

Causes of the war

This war would never have come unless, under American and modernising pressure, we had driven the Hapsburgs out of Austria and Hungary and the Hohenzollerns out of Germany. By making these vacuums we gave the opening for the Hitlerite monster to crawl out of its sewer on to the vacant thrones. No doubt these views are very unfashionable....

1941, 8 APRIL. (WW2 IV, 640.)

WSC to the Foreign Office.

After the end of the World War of 1914 there was a deep conviction and almost universal hope that peace would reign in the world....The phrase "the war to end war," was on every lip, and measures had been taken to turn it into reality....Instead, a gaping void was opened in the national life of the German people...and into that void after a pause there strode a maniac of ferocious genius, the repository and expression of the most virulent hatreds that have ever corroded the human breast—Corporal Hitler.

1948. (WW2 I, 3–9.)

These exact words, with the ellipses (no doubt arranged by WSC himself) are the first one hears as Churchill reads excerpts of his war memoirs on phonograph (now CD) recordings of his memoirs and speeches. The words rang in the editor's ears, put me on to The Gathering Storm, and the rest, as they say, is history.

Civil Defence

In this war, so terrible in many aspects and yet so inspiring, men and women who have never thought about fighting or being involved in fighting before have been proud to emulate the courage of the bravest regiments of His Majesty's armies, and proud to find that, under the fire of the enemy, they could comport themselves with discipline and with composure. It is that quality, universally spread among our people, which gives us the foundation from which we shall prosecute to the end this righteous war for the freedom and future of mankind.

1941, 14 JULY. HYDE PARK, LONDON.
(UNRELENTING, 179.)

Coal miners

…some day, when children ask, "What did you do to win this inheritance for us, and to make our name so respected among men?" one will say: "I was a fighter pilot"; another will say: "I was in the Submarine Service"; another: "I marched with the Eighth Army"; a fourth will say: "None of you could have lived without the convoys and the Merchant Seamen"; and you in your turn will say, with equal pride and with equal right: "We cut the coal."

1942, 31 OCTOBER. WESTMINSTER CENTRAL HALL.
(END, 261.)

Speech to a conference of coal-owners and miners. Churchill used a similar formulation on various occasions. His detective, Walter Thompson, remembered him addressing Eighth Army troops, saying,

After this War is over, it will be sufficient for you to say when you are asked "What did you do?" to reply, "I marched with the Eighth Army."

Code-breakers

[They were] the geese who laid the golden eggs and never cackled.

1940s, PASSIM. (OB VI, 612.)

Referring to the code-breakers at Bletchley Park, Buckinghamshire, who broke the German "Enigma" codes, providing WSC with critical intelligence. The decrypts, originally called "Boniface", later became "CX", a standard two-letter symbol for a British secret agent in enemy territory. But Churchill continued to refer to "Boniface". He also called the decrypts his "hens".

Command authority

[In 1946] General Marshall told me at Malta how astonished he was that we British had not suggested any transfer of the command from Eisenhower to a British commander, although we had such an enormous superiority of divisions engaged in the fighting for Tunis. This idea never crossed my mind. It was contrary to the whole basis on which the President and I had worked.

1951. (WW2 IV, 619.)

I did not suffer from any desire to be relieved of my responsibilities. All I wanted was compliance with my wishes after reasonable discussion.

1951. (WW2 IV, 78.)

Commandos

We think of the Commandos, as they came to be called—a Boer word become ever-glorious in the annals of Britain and her Empire—and of their gleaming deeds under every sky and clime. We think of the Airborne Forces and Special Air Service men who hurled themselves unflinching into the void—when we recall all this, we may feel sure that nothing of which we have any knowledge or record has ever been done by mortal men which surpasses the splendour and daring of their feats of arms.

1948, 21 MAY. COMMANDO MEMORIAL,
WESTMINSTER ABBEY. (EUROPE UNITE, 337.)

A little-known but inspiring speech in tribute to the Commandos, Airborne Forces and Submarine Service.

Commandos and submariners

In this ancient Abbey, so deeply wrought into the record, the life and the message of the British race and nation—here where every inch of space is devoted to the monuments of the past and to the inspiration of the future—there will remain this cloister now consecrated to those who gave their lives in what they hoped would be a final war against the grosser forms of tyranny. These symbolic images of heroes, set up by their fellow-countrymen in honour and remembrance, will proclaim, as long as faithful testimony endures, the sacrifices of youth resolutely made at the call of duty and for the love of our island home and all it stands for among men.

> 1948, 21 May. Commando Memorial, Westminster Abbey. (Europe Unite, 336–7.)

Critics

...there is a kind of criticism which is a little irritating. It is like a bystander who when he sees a team of horses dragging a heavy wagon painfully up a hill cuts a switch from the fence...and belabours them lustily....My Rt. Hon. Friend [David Lloyd George] spoke of the great importance of my being surrounded by people who would stand up to me and say, "No, No, No." Why, good gracious, has he no idea how strong the negative principle is in the constitution and working of the British warmaking machine? The difficulty is not, I assure him, to have more brakes put on the wheels; the difficulty is to get more impetus and speed behind it. At one moment we are asked to emulate the Germans in their audacity and vigour, and the next moment the Prime Minister is to be assisted by being surrounded by a number of "No-men" to resist me at every point and prevent me from making anything in the nature of a speedy, rapid and, above all, positive constructive decision.

> 1941, 7 May.

Earlier in this speech Churchill had stuck the Pétain label on his old mentor; it haunted Lloyd George for the duration.

A handful of Members can fill a couple of days' debate with disparaging charges against our war effort, and every ardent or disaffected section of the Press can take it up, and the whole can cry a dismal cacophonous chorus of stinking fish all round the world.

> 1941, 29 July.

...I appeal to all patriotic men on both sides of the Atlantic Ocean to stamp their feet on mischief-makers and sowers of tares wherever they may be found, and let the great machines roll into battle under the best possible conditions for their success.

> 1943, 11 February.

Duty, honour, country

This selection of quotes seems happily to fit the motto of the US Military Academy.

I know of nothing more remarkable in our long history than the willingness to encounter the unknown, and to face and endure whatever might be coming to us, which was shown in September by the whole mass of the people of this island in the discharge of what they felt sure was their duty. There never was a war which seemed so likely to carry its terrors at once into every home, and there never was a war to which the whole people entered with the same united conviction that, God helping, they could do no other.

> 1940. 27 January. Free Trade Hall, Manchester. (Blood, 257.)

...I take up my task with buoyancy and hope. I feel sure that our cause will not be suffered to fail among men. At this time I feel entitled to claim the aid of all, and I say, "Come, then, let us go forward together with our united strength."

> 1940, 13 May.

The whole of the warring nations are engaged, not only soldiers, but the entire population, men, women, and children. The fronts are everywhere. The trenches are dug in the towns and streets. Every village is fortified. Every road is barred. The front line runs through the factories....There seems to be every reason to believe that this new kind of war is well suited to the genius and the resources of the British nation and the British Empire and that, once we get properly equipped and properly started, a war of this kind will be more favourable to us than the sombre mass slaughters of the Somme and Passchendaele.

> 1940, 20 August.

I have thought in this difficult period, when so much fighting and so many critical and complicated manoeuvres are going on, that it is above all things important that our policy and conduct should be upon the highest level, and that honour should be our guide.

> 1941, 27 April. Broadcast, London. (Unrelenting, 93.)

A wonderful story is unfolding before our eyes. How it will end we are not allowed to know. But on both sides of the Atlantic we all feel, I repeat, all, that we are a part of it, that our future and that of many generations is at stake....We may be proud, and even rejoice amid our tribulations, that we have been born at this cardinal time for so great an age and so splendid an opportunity of service here below.

1941, 16 JUNE. BROADCAST, LONDON. (UNRELENTING, 167.)

All the world, even our best friends, thought that our end had come. Accordingly, we prepared ourselves to conquer or perish. We were united in that solemn, majestic hour; we were all equally resolved at least to go down fighting. We cast calculations to the winds; no wavering voice was heard; we hurled defiance at our foes; we faced our duty, and, by the mercy of God, we were preserved. It fell to me in those days to express the sentiments and resolves of the British nation in that supreme crisis of its life. That was to me an honour far beyond any dream or ambitions I had ever nursed, and it is one that cannot be taken away.

1942, 10 MAY. BROADCAST, LONDON. (END, 124.)

Let us rise to the full level of our duty and of our opportunity, and let us thank God for the spiritual rewards He has granted for all forms of valiant and faithful service.

1943, 6 SEPTEMBER.

"Not in vain" may be the pride of those who have survived and the epitaph of those who fell.

1944, 28 SEPTEMBER.

We have our mistakes, our weaknesses and failings, but in the fight which this island race has made, had it not been the toughest of the tough; if the spirit of freedom which burns in the British breast had not been a pure, dazzling, inextinguishable flame, we might not yet have been near the end of this war.

1945, 21 APRIL. BRISTOL UNIVERSITY. (VICTORY, 116.)

Enemy

Anyone who can kill a Hun or even an Italian has rendered a good service.

1941, 28 APRIL. (GILBERT, LIFE, 697.)

Not an offhand remark, this was written in a directive for the Defence of Egypt.

Those who fight the Germans fight a stubborn and resourceful foe, a foe in every way worthy of the doom prepared for him.

1941, 11 DECEMBER.

It may well be that those guilty races who trumpeted the glories of war at the beginning will be extolling the virtues of peace before the end. It would certainly seem right, however, that those who fix, on their own terms, the moment for beginning wars should not be the same men who fix, on their own terms, the moment for ending them. These observations are of a general character, but not without their particular application.

1943, 8 JUNE.

Food and matériel

Many of the most valuable foods are essential to the manufacture of vital war material. Fats are used to make explosives. Potatoes make the alcohol for motor spirit. The plastic materials now so largely used in the construction of aircraft are made of milk. If the Germans use these commodities to help them to bomb our women and children, rather than to feed the populations who produce them, we may be sure that imported foods would go the same way, directly or indirectly, or be employed to relieve the enemy of the responsibilities he has so wantonly assumed.

1940, 20 AUGUST.

Gambler's desperation

We have to reckon with a gambler's desperation. We have to reckon with a criminal who by a mere gesture has decreed the death of three or four million Russian and German soldiers. We stand here still as the champions. If we fail, all fails, and if we fall, all will fall together.

1941, 29 JULY.

German General Staff

The German General Staff system, which we failed to liquidate after the last war, represents an order comprising many thousands of highly trained officers and a school of doctrine of long, unbroken continuity. It possesses great skill, both in the handling of troops in action and in their rapid movement from place to place. The recent fighting in Italy should leave no doubt on these points.

1944, 22 FEBRUARY.

German satellites

We must not add needlessly to the weight of our task or the burden that our soldiers bear. Satellite States, suborned or overawed, may perhaps, if they can help to shorten the war, be allowed to work their passage home.

1943, 21 SEPTEMBER.

Harold Nicolson wrote:

"The satellite States", he continued, "suborned and overawed..." and then he raised his arm as if about to deliver the most terrific thunderbolt from his rich armoury of rhetoric, but he dropped his arm suddenly and took off his spectacles, "...may perhaps be allowed to work their passage home", he concluded, grinning. It is in this that one finds his mastery of the House. It is the combination of great flights of oratory with sudden swoops into the intimate and conversational. Of all his devices it is the one that never fails. (Nicolson II, 321).

Health

...the task of preserving the health and well-being of this enormous community in the Thames Valley, exceeding eight million souls, living under artificial conditions of civilisation, and supplying them with food and all other necessities and of making provision for those whose homes have been destroyed or who have had to be evacuated—all this and much else have, as the House will realise, cast a strain upon the machinery of government which calls for ceaseless exertion by all authorities concerned.

1940, 17 SEPTEMBER.

Holocaust

None has suffered more cruelly than the Jew the unspeakable evils wrought on the bodies and spirits of men by Hitler and his vile regime. The Jew bore the brunt of the Nazis' first onslaught upon the citadels of freedom and human dignity. He has borne and continued to bear a burden that might have seemed to be beyond endurance. He has not allowed it to break his spirit; he has never lost the will to resist. Assuredly in the day of victory the Jew's sufferings and his part in the struggle will not be forgotten. Once again, at the appointed time, he will see vindicated those principles of righteousness which it was the glory of his fathers to proclaim to the world.

1941, 14 NOVEMBER. (UNRELENTING, 310–11.)

Message to the Jewish Chronicle on its centenary.

Is there any reason to raise this matter with the Cabinet? Get anything out of the air force you can—and invoke me if necessary.

1944, 7 JULY. (SIR MARTIN GILBERT, CHURCHILL CENTRE HOLOCAUST LECTURE, WASHINGTON, 1993.)

Churchill's minute to Eden on a report requesting bombing the railroad lines to Auschwitz, an altogether unique reaction, according to his biographer Sir Martin Gilbert.

There is no doubt that this is probably the greatest and most horrible crime ever committed in the whole history of the world, and it has been done by scientific machinery by nominally civilised men in the name of a great State and one of the leading races of Europe. It is quite clear that all concerned in this crime who may fall into our hands, including the people who only obeyed orders by carrying out the butcheries, should be put to death after their association with the murders has been proved.

1944, 11 JULY. (OB VII, 847.)

After the invading Allies began discovering the German death camps.

I must say that I had no idea, when the war came to an end, of the horrible massacres which had occurred; the millions and millions that have been slaughtered. That dawned on us gradually after the struggle was over.

1946, 1 AUGUST.

As his biographer Sir Martin Gilbert has shown, Churchill had only limited awareness of the extent of the Holocaust during the war; his reactions to the news were in keeping with his character.

Initial advantages

When peaceful nations like the British and the Americans, very careless in peacetime about their defences, care-free, unsuspecting nations...are set upon by highly-organised, heavily-armed conspirators, planning and calculating in secret for years on end, exalting war as the highest form of human effort, glorifying slaughter and aggression, prepared and trained to the last point science and discipline can carry them, is it not natural that the peaceful, unprepared, improvident peoples should suffer terribly and that the wicked, scheming aggressors should have their reign of savage exaltation?

1942, 12 OCTOBER. USHER HALL, EDINBURGH. (END, 240.)

Invasion of Britain

We are told that Herr Hitler has a plan for invading the British Isles. This has often been thought of before. When Napoleon lay at Boulogne for a year with his flat-bottomed boats and his Grand Army, he was told by someone: "There are bitter weeds in England." There are certainly a great many more of them since the British Expeditionary Force returned.

1940, 4 JUNE.

[In the three months after Dunkirk] our people worked to the utmost limit of their moral, mental and physical strength. Men fell exhausted at their lathes, and workmen and working women did not take their clothes off for a week at a time. Meals, rest and relaxation all faded from their minds, and they just carried on to the last ounce of their strength.

1941, 29 JULY.

There is such a thing as sheer exhaustion, both of the spirit and the animal. I thought of Wellington's mood in the afternoon of the Battle of Waterloo: "Would God that night or Blücher would come." This time we did not want Blücher.

1948. (WW2 II, 404.)

Arthur Wellesley, First Duke of Wellington (1769–1852) was the victor over Napoleon at Waterloo, 1815. Wellington's ally at Waterloo was the Prussian Field Marshal Gebhard Leberecht von Blücher.

The shipping available and now assembled is sufficient to carry in one voyage nearly half a million men. We should, of course, expect to drown a great many on the way over, and to destroy a large proportion of their vessels. But when you reflect upon the many points from which they could start, and upon the fact that even the most likely sector of invasion, i.e., the sector in which enemy fighter support is available for their bombers and dive-bombers, extending from the Wash to the Isle of Wight, is nearly as long as the whole front in France from the Alps to the sea, and also upon the dangers of fog or artificial fog, one must expect many lodgements or attempted lodgements to be made on our Island simultaneously.

1940, 17 SEPTEMBER. (SECRET, 23.)

On this date in Berlin, Hitler postponed Operation Sea Lion indefinitely.

...the plain fact that an invasion, planned on so vast a scale, has not been attempted in spite of the very great need of the enemy to destroy us in our citadel...that fact constitutes in itself one of the historic victories of the British Isles and is a monumental milestone on our onward march.

1940, 5 NOVEMBER.

I presume the details of this remarkable feat have been worked out by the staff concerned. Let me see them. For instance, how many ships and transports carried these five divisions? How many armoured vehicles did they comprise? How many motor lorries, how many guns, how much ammunition, how many men, how many tons of stores, how far did they advance in the first forty-eight hours, how many men and vehicles were assumed to have landed in the first twelve hours, what percentage of loss were they debited with? What happened to the transports and store-ships while the first forty-eight hours of fighting was going on? Had they completed emptying their cargoes, or were they still lying inshore off the beaches? What naval escort did they have? Was the landing at this point protected by superior enemy daylight fighter formations? How many fighter aeroplanes did the enemy have to employ, if so, to cover the landing-places?...

I should be very glad if the same officers would work out a scheme for our landing an exactly similar force on the French coast at the same extreme range of our fighter protection, and assuming that the Germans have naval superiority in the Channel.

1941, 30 March. (WW2 III, 668.)

WSC to Chiefs of Staff Committee challenging the assumptions of the invasion exercise Victor, in which five German divisions were assumed to have landed on the Norfolk coast despite heavy opposition, fought their way ashore and were in action within forty-eight hours. WSC's riposte is as good an argument as there is for his constant questioning of his generals, although he never overruled them.

Look at the mistake that Hitler made in not trying invasion in 1940....We had not, at that time, fifty tanks; we had a couple of hundred field-guns, some of them brought out of museums...Think what [the Germans] would do to us if they got here. Think what they would do to us, we who have barred their way to the loot of the whole world, we whom they hate the most because they dread and envy us the most.

1942. 31 October. Westminster Central Hall, London. (End, 257.)

We have come to the conclusion that this particular method of warning [ringing the church bells] was redundant and not well adapted to the present conditions of war. For myself, I cannot help feeling that anything like a serious invasion would be bound to leak out.

1943, 22 April.

...when imagining the horrors of a Hun invasion, there rose that last consoling thought which rises naturally in unconquerable races and unenslavable men resolved to go down fighting—"you can always take one with you."

1943, 14 May. Broadcast, Washington. (Onwards, 88.)

Manpower

Man-power—and when I say that I intend of course woman-power—is at a pitch of intensity at the present time in this country which was never reached before, not even in the last war, and certainly not in this. I believe our man-power is not only fully extended, but applied on the whole to the best advantage.

I have a feeling that the community in this Island is running at a very high level, with a good rhythm, and that if we can only keep our momentum—we cannot increase our pace—that very fact will enable us to outclass our enemies and possibly even our friends.

1943, 13 October.

Mechanisation

I am, of course, aware that a mechanised army makes an enormous additional drain....I have thought nevertheless for some time that the Army and Air Force—the Navy not so much—have a great need to comb their tails in order to magnify their teeth.

1941, 22 January.

Music

I think we should have to retain a certain amount of power in the selection of the music. Very spirited renderings of "Deutschland Über Alles" would hardly be permissible.

1941, 15 March.

Nationalisation

We must also be careful that a pretext is not made of war needs to introduce far-reaching social or political changes by a side wind.... The argument proceeds not on moral grounds but on whether in fact we could make a better business of the whole thing for ourselves, a more fertile business for the nation as a whole, by nationalisation than by relying on private enterprise and competition.

1943, 13 October.

Although Churchill was uneasy about it, wartime government controls did become a pretext for the Labour Party's nationalisation reforms after they won control of the government following the 1945 general election.

Neutral countries

We have the greatest sympathy for these forlorn countries, and we understand their dangers and their point of view; but it would not be right, or in the general interest, that their weakness should feed the aggressor's strength and fill to overflowing the cup of human woe. There can be no justice if in a mortal struggle the aggressor tramples down every sentiment of humanity, and if those who resist him remain entangled in the tatters of violated legal conventions.

1940, 30 MARCH.

See also Chapter 11, Belgium, Norway, etc.

Occupied nations

A fearful game of chess proceeds from check to mate by which the unhappy players seem to be inexorably bound...the fact that the British Empire stands invincible, and that Nazidom is still being resisted, will kindle again the spark of hope in the breasts of hundreds of millions of down-trodden or despairing men and women throughout Europe, and far beyond its bounds, and from these sparks there will presently come cleansing and devouring flame.

1940, 20 AUGUST.

These ringing words were uttered when nearly all of Western Europe was Nazified, and Britain under assault from the air.

Wickedness, enormous, panoplied, embattled, seemingly triumphant, casts its shadow over Europe and Asia. Laws, customs and traditions are broken up. Justice is cast from her seat. The rights of the weak are trampled down. The grand freedoms of which the President of the United States has spoken so movingly are spurned and chained. The whole stature of man, his genius, his initiative and his nobility, is ground down under systems of mechanical barbarism and of organised and scheduled terror.

1941, 16 JUNE. BROADCAST, LONDON.
(UNRELENTING, 167.)

Do not despair... yield not an inch! Keep your souls clean from all contact with the Nazis; make them feel even in their fleeting hour of brutish triumph that they are the moral outcasts of mankind. Help is coming; mighty forces are arming in your behalf. Have faith. Have hope. Deliverance is sure.

1941, 24 AUGUST. WORLD BROADCAST, LONDON.
(UNRELENTING, 236–7.)

The complete peroration should be read in Chapter 1...Deliverance is Sure.

...when we remind ourselves of the frightful tyrannies and cruelties with which the German armies, their gauleiters and subordinate tormentors, are now afflicting almost all Europe; when we read every week of the mass executions of Poles, Norwegians, Dutchmen, Czechoslovaks, Frenchmen, Yugoslavs and Greeks; when we see these ancient and honoured countries, of whose deeds and traditions Europe is the heir, writhing under this merciless alien yoke, and when we see their patriots striking back with every week a fiercer and more furious desperation, we may feel sure that we bear the sword of justice, and we resolve to use that sword with the utmost severity to the full and to the end.

1943, 30 JUNE. GUILDHALL, LONDON.
(ONWARDS, 130–31.)

Post-war planning

I must say a word about the function of the Minister charged with the study of post-war problems and reconstruction. It is not his task to make a new world, comprising a new Heaven, a new earth, and no doubt a new hell (as I am sure that would be necessary in any balanced system).

1941, 22 JANUARY.

I regard it as a definite part of the duty and responsibility of this National Government to have its plans perfected in a vast and practical scheme to make sure that in the years immediately following the war food, work and homes are found for all. No airy visions, no party doctrines, no party prejudices, no political appetites, no vested interests, must stand in the way of the simple duty of providing beforehand for food, work, and homes.

1943, 9 NOVEMBER. MANSION HOUSE, LONDON.
(ONWARDS, 267.)

...the world must be made safe for at least fifty years. If it was only for fifteen to twenty years then we should have betrayed our soldiers.

1952, TEHERAN. (WW2 V, 318.)

Prolongation of the war

Having, at the end of my life, acquired some influence on affairs, I wish to make it clear that I would not needlessly prolong this war by a single day; and my hope is that if and when British people are called by victory to share in the august responsibilities of shaping the future, we shall show the same poise and temper as we did in the hour of mortal peril.

1943, 21 SEPTEMBER.

See also World War I...prolongation.

Prospects

The Prime Minister frequently appraised possibilities for the immediate future, among which these are the most significant.

Directions have been given by the Government to prepare for a war of at least three years. That does not mean that victory may not be gained in a shorter time. How soon it will be gained depends upon how long Herr Hitler and his group of wicked men, whose hands are stained with blood and soiled with corruption, can keep their grip upon the docile, unhappy German people. It was for Hitler to say when the war would begin; but it is not for him or for his successors to say when it will end.

1939, 1 OCTOBER.

See also Personal...Déjà vu.

If we are conquered, all will be enslaved, and the United States will be left single-handed to guard the rights of man. If we are not destroyed, all these countries will be rescued and restored to life and freedom.

1939, 12 NOVEMBER.

Certainly it is true that we are facing numerical odds; but that is no new thing in our history. Very few wars have been won by mere numbers alone. Quality, will-power, geographical advantages, natural and financial resources, the command of the sea, and, above all, a cause which rouses the spontaneous surgings of the human spirit in millions of hearts—these have proved to be the decisive factors in the human story.

1940, 20 JANUARY. BROADCAST, LONDON.
(BLOOD, 253.)

If members of the present Administration were finished and others came in to parley amid the ruins, you must not be blind to the fact that the sole remaining bargaining counter with Germany would be the Fleet, and, if this country was left by the United States to its fate, no one would have the right to blame those then responsible if they made the best terms they could for the surviving inhabitants. Excuse me, Mr. President, putting this nightmare bluntly. Evidently I could not answer for my successors, who in utter despair and helplessness might well have to accommodate themselves to the German will.

1940, 20 MAY, DOWNING STREET. (OB, CV6/2, 93; CHURCHILL PAPERS 20/14.)

A stark appraisal of reality should Britain go down in the coming battle.

The war is bound to become a bloody one for us now, but I hope our people will stand up to bombing, and the Huns aren't liking what we are giving them. But what a tragedy that our victory in the last war should have been snatched from us by a lot of softies!

1940, 15 JUNE, CHEQUERS. (COLVILLE, FOOTPRINTS, 87.)

Long, dark months of trials and tribulations lie before us. Not only great dangers, but many more misfortunes, many shortcomings, many mistakes, many disappointments will surely be our lot. Death and sorrow will be the companions of our journey; hardship our garment; constancy and valour our only shield. We must be united, we must be undaunted, we must be inflexible. Our qualities and deeds must burn and glow through the gloom of Europe until they become the veritable beacon of its salvation.

1940, 8 OCTOBER.

I ask you to witness, Mr. Speaker, that I have never promised anything or offered anything but blood, tears, toil, and sweat, to which I will now add our fair share of mistakes, shortcomings and disappointments....When I look back on the perils which have been overcome, upon the great mountain waves through which the gallant ship has driven, when I remember all that has gone wrong, and remember also all that has gone right, I feel sure we have no need to fear the tempest. Let it roar, and let it rage. We shall come through.

1941, 7 MAY.

In the past we have had a light which flickered, in the present we have a light which flames, and in the future there will be a light which shines over all the land and sea.

1941. 8 DECEMBER.

There never has been a moment, there never could have been a moment, when Great Britain or the British Empire, single-handed, could fight Germany and Italy, could wage the Battle of Britain, the Battle of the Atlantic, and the battle of the Middle East—and at the same time stand thoroughly prepared in Burma, the Malay peninsula, and generally in the Far East, against the impact of a vast military Empire like Japan, with more than seventy mobile divisions, the third Navy in the world, a great air force, and the thrust of eighty or ninety millions of hardy, warlike Asiatics.

1942, 27 JANUARY. (END, 27.)

We have reached a period in the War when it would be premature to say that we have topped the ridge, but now we see the ridge ahead.

1942. 16 MAY. TOWN HALL, LEEDS. (END, 137.)

You ask me how I view the future. I view it with hope, and, I trust, with undiminished firmness of spirit. Great operations impend which are in full accordance with your own conceptions and on which we are all agreed. We must have the fibre and fortitude to endure the delays and await the outcome.

1942, 22 SEPTEMBER. (WW2 IV, 501.)

WSC to Sir Stafford Cripps.

There is danger in wishful thinking that victory will come by internal collapse of the Axis. Victory depends on force of arms. I stand pat on a knock-out, but any windfalls in the way of internal collapse will be fully accepted.

1943, 25 MAY. PRESS CONFERENCE, WASHINGTON. (ONWARDS, 104.)

...our chickens are not yet hatched, though one can hear them pecking at their shells.

1943, 7 SEPTEMBER. (DILKS, 298.)

Do not let us add to our difficulties by any lack of clarity of thinking or any restive wavering in resolve. Upon the whole, with all our faults and the infirmities of which we are rightly conscious, this Island is a model to the world in its unity and its perseverance towards the goal.

1943, 13 OCTOBER.

Unless some happy event occurs on which we have no right to count, and the hand of Providence is stretched forth in some crowning mercy, 1944 will see the greatest sacrifice of life by British and American armies, and battles far larger and more costly than Waterloo or Gettysburg will be fought. Sorrow will come to many homes in the United Kingdom and throughout the great Republic. British and American manhood—true brothers in arms—will attack and grapple with the deadly foe.

1943, 9 NOVEMBER. MANSION HOUSE, LONDON. (ONWARDS, 267.)

A key to Churchill's leadership was that he never tried to minimise the costs of war.

...any attempt to estimate the date when the war with Germany can be officially declared over could be no more than a guess. A political convulsion in Germany might bring it to a speedy end at any time, but against that must be set the iron control of German life in all its forms, including the army, which has been established by Hitler's storm troops and secret police. This exceeds anything previously known among men.

1944, 31 OCTOBER.

We have sacrificed everything in this war. We shall emerge from it, for the time being, more stricken and impoverished than any other victorious country.

1945, 18 JANUARY.

Rationing

The hen has been part and parcel of the country cottager's life since history began. Townsfolk can eke out their rations by a bought meal.

1942, 16 JULY. (WW2 IV, 781.)

Prime Minister to Minister of Food.

It is absolutely contrary to logic and good sense that a person may not give away or exchange his rations with some one who at the moment he feels has a greater need. It strikes at neighbourliness and friendship.

1942, 21 NOVEMBER. (WW2 IV, 806.)

WSC to Minister of Food.

Retrospectives on the War

I have the feeling that after the second Thirty Years' War, for that is what it is, through which we have just passed, mankind needs and seeks a period of rest. After all, how little it is that the millions of homes in Europe represented here to-day are asking. What is it that all these wage-earners, skilled artisans, soldiers, and tillers of the soil require, deserve, and may be led to demand? Is it not a fair chance to make a home, to reap the fruits of their toil, to cherish their wives, to bring up their children in a decent manner and to dwell in peace and safety, without fear or bullying or monstrous burdens or exploitations, however this may be imposed upon them? That is their heart's desire. That is what we mean to win for them.

1948, 7 MAY. THE HAGUE, NETHERLANDS.
(EUROPE, 315.)

I have often wondered however what would have happened if two hundred thousand German storm troops had actually established themselves ashore. The massacre would have been on both sides grim and great. There would have been neither mercy nor quarter. They would have used Terror, and we were prepared to go all lengths. I intended to use the slogan "You can always take one with you"...But none of these emotions was put to the proof. Far out on the grey waters of the North Sea and the Channel coursed and patrolled the faithful, eager flotillas peering through the night. High in the air soared the fighter pilots, or waited serene at a moment's notice around their excellent machines. This was a time when it was equally good to live or die.

1949. (WW2 II, 246.)

Rota the lion

A gentleman, Mr. Thomson, kindly presented me with a lion...."Rota" was the lion's name...He was a male lion of fine quality and in eight years became the father of many children. The assistant secretary who had been with me in the airplane came with some papers. He was a charming man, highly competent, but physically on the small side. Indulging in chaff, I now showed him a magnificent photograph of Rota with his mouth open, saying, "If there are any

shortcomings in your work I shall send you to him. Meat is very short now." He took a serious view of this remark. He repeated to the office that I was in a delirium.

1951. (WW2 IV, 651–2.)

Second Front

We have been preparing under "Bolero" for 1,100,000 men, and this is the first intimation we have had that this target is to be abandoned. We had no knowledge that you had decided to abandon for ever "Round-up," and all our preparations were proceeding on a broad front under "Bolero."

It seems to me that it would be a most grievous decision to abandon "Round-up." "Torch" is no substitute for "Round-up" and only engages thirteen divisions as against the forty-eight contemplated for "Round-up." All my talks with Stalin, in Averell's presence, were on the basis of a postponed "Round-up," but never was it suggested that we should attempt no Second Front in Europe in 1943, or even 1944.

1942, 24 NOVEMBER. (WW2 IV, 584.)

WSC to Roosevelt, underscoring his commitment to the invasion of France ("Round-up", later "Overlord"), with Anglo-American troops built up in England ("Bolero"). Churchill added, "The President lost no time in correcting this misunderstanding..." ("Torch" was the invasion of North Africa.)

I see the Channel being full of corpses of defeated allies.

1943, 11 JULY, LONDON. (LAMB, 225)

Churchill to US Secretary of War Stimson.

Personally, I always think of the Third Front as well as the Second Front. I have always thought that the Western democracies should be like a boxer who fights with two hands and not one. I believe that the great flanking movement into North Africa, made under the authority of President Roosevelt and of His Majesty's Government, for whom I am a principal agent, will be regarded in the after time as quite a good thing to do in all the circumstances.

1943, 31 AUGUST. BROADCAST, LONDON.
(ONWARDS, 177.)

War was war but not folly, and it would be folly to invite a disaster which would help nobody.

1951. (WW2 IV, 431.)

Recalling his meeting Stalin in August 1942, to explain why there was as yet no Second Front.

The Channel tides have a play of more than twenty feet, with corresponding scours along the beaches. The weather is always uncertain, and winds and gales may whip up in a few hours irresistible forces against frail human structures. The fools or knaves who had chalked "Second Front Now" on our walls for the past two years had not had their minds burdened by such problems. I had long pondered upon them.

1952. (WW2 V, 67.)

Sirens

There is really no good sense in having these prolonged banshee howlings from sirens two or three times a day over wide areas, simply because hostile aircraft are flying to or from some target which no one can possibly know or even guess. All our precaution regulations have hitherto been based on this siren call, and I must say that one must admire the ingenuity of those who devised it as a means of spreading alarm. Indeed, most people now see how very wise Ulysses was when he stopped the ears of his sailors from all siren songs and had himself tied up firmly to the mast of duty.

1940, 5 SEPTEMBER.

The final "all clear" sounded on VE-Day, 8 May 1945, but London's lights did not come on again until mid-July.

Strategy and winning the war

One of the ways to bring this war to a speedy end is to convince the enemy, not by words but by deeds, that we have both the will and the means not only to go on indefinitely but to strike heavy and unexpected blows. The road to victory may not be so long as we expect. But we have no right to count upon this. Be it long or short, rough or smooth, we mean to reach our journey's end.

1940, 20 AUGUST.

I am often asked to say how we are going to win the war. I remember being asked that last time very frequently, and not being able to give a very precise or conclusive answer. We kept on doing our best...and then one day we saw those who had forced the struggle upon the world cast down their arms in the open field and immediately proceed to beg for sympathy, mercy, and considerable financial support.

1941, 7 NOVEMBER. GUILDHALL, LONDON.
(UNRELENTING, 290.)

To hear some people talk...the way to win the war is to make sure that every Power contributing armed forces and every branch of these armed forces is represented on all the councils and organisations...that everybody is fully consulted before anything is done. That is...the most sure way to lose a war. You have to be aware of the well-known danger of having "more harness than horse"...

1942, 27 JANUARY.

...it is in the dragging-out of the war at enormous expense, until the democracies are tired or bored or split, that the main hopes of Germany and Japan must now reside. We must destroy this hope, as we have destroyed so many others, and for that purpose we must beware of every topic however attractive and every tendency however natural which turns our minds and energies from this supreme objective of the general victory of the United Nations.

1943, 1 MAY. CONGRESS, WASHINGTON.
(ONWARDS, 656.)

At the present stage of the war in Europe our overall strategic concept should be the engagement of the enemy on the largest scale with the greatest violence and continuity. In this way only shall we bring about an early collapse. Here is the prime test.

1944, 28 JUNE. (WW2 VI, APPENDIX D, 656.)

Note by the Prime Minister on the invasion of the south of France (which he considered a waste of resources) and European theatre operations. In "overall strategic concept", Churchill was using what he fancied (and often noted) was American jargon.

To shorten this war, to bring it to an end, to bring soldiers home, to give them a roof over their heads, to re-establish the free life of our country, to enable the wheels of commerce to revolve, to get the nations out of their terrible frenzy of hate, to build up something like a human world and a humane world—it is that that makes it so indispensable for us to struggle to shorten, be it even by a day, the course of this terrible war.

1944, 28 September.

Harsh as it may seem to say, a terrible thing to say in dealing with our own precious flesh and blood, it is our interest and the American interest that the whole Western front, and the air everywhere at all possible flying times, should be in continuous action against the enemy, burning and bleeding his strength away at every opportunity and on all occasions, if we are to bring this horror to an end.

1945, 18 January.

During the last three months an element of baffling dualism has complicated every problem of policy and administration. We had to plan for peace and war at the same time. Immense armies were being demobilized; another powerful army was being prepared and dispatched to the other side of the globe. All the personal stresses among millions of men eager to return to civil life, and hundreds of thousands of men who would have to be sent to new and severe campaigns in the Far East, presented themselves with growing tension. This dualism affected also every aspect of our economic and financial life. How to set people free to use their activities in reviving the life of Britain, and at the same time to meet the stern demands of the war against Japan, constituted one of the most perplexing and distressing puzzles that in a long life-time of experience I have ever faced.

1945, 16 August.

WSC is suggesting that the country is of two minds: pursue the peace that had broken out in Europe, or pursue the war against Japan. On this day the choice no longer needed to be made.

Submariners

We think of the forty British submarines, more than half our total submarine losses, sunk amid the Mediterranean minefields alone, of the heroic deaths of the submarine commanders and crews who vanished for ever in the North Sea or in the Atlantic Approaches to our nearly-strangled island.

1948, 21 May. Commando Memorial, Westminster Abbey. (Europe Unite, 337–8.)

Another example of precise semantics. The Germans went to sea in "U-boats", the British in "submarines". WSC never mixed the terms.

Summaries of the war situation

The most important of Churchill's frequent commentaries were made in Parliament and usually thereafter on the wireless.

In the last war [1914–18] millions of men fought by hurling enormous masses of steel at one another. "Men and shells" was the cry, and prodigious slaughter was the consequence. In this war nothing of this kind has yet appeared. It is a conflict of strategy, of organisation, of technical apparatus, of science, mechanics, and morale....one may say that throughout all Europe for one man killed or wounded in the first year perhaps five were killed or wounded in 1914–1915.

1940, 20 August.

With a gasp of astonishment and relief the smaller neutrals and the subjugated states saw that the stars still shone in the sky. Hope, and within it passion, burned anew in the hearts of hundreds of millions of men. The good cause would triumph. Right would not be trampled down. The flag of Freedom, which in this fateful hour was the Union [Jack], would still fly in all the winds that blew.

1949. (WW2 II, 556.)

WSC occasionally wrote "Union Jack", but technically it is a jack only when flown on the bow of a ship.

We may, I am sure, rate this tremendous year [1940] as the most splendid, as it was the most deadly, year in our long English and British story...nothing surpasses 1940. By the end of that year this small and ancient Island, with its devoted Commonwealth, Dominions, and attachments under every sky, had proved itself capable of bearing the whole impact and weight of world destiny....But I and my faithful colleagues who brooded with accurate information at the summit of the scene had no lack of cares. The shadow of the U-boat blockade already cast its chill upon us. All our plans depended upon the defeat of this menace. The Battle of France was lost. The Battle of Britain was won. The Battle of the Atlantic had now to be fought.

1949. (WW2 II, 555.)

Thus far then have we travelled along the terrible road we chose at the call of duty. The mood of Britain is wisely and rightly averse from every form of shallow or premature exultation. This is no time for boasts or glowing prophecies, but there is this—a year ago our position looked forlorn and well nigh desperate to all eyes but our own. Today we may say aloud before an awestruck world, "We are still masters of our fate. We are still captain of our souls."

1941, 9 SEPTEMBER.

We did not make this war, we did not seek it. We did all we could to avoid it. We did too much to avoid it. We went so far at times in trying to avoid it as to be almost destroyed by it when it broke upon us. But the dangerous corner has been turned, and...there is a place for everyone, man and woman, old and young, hale and halt; service in a thousand forms is open. There is no room now for the dilettante, the weakling, for the shirker, or the sluggard.

1941, 30 DECEMBER. CANADIAN PARLIAMENT,
OTTAWA. (UNRELENTING, 364–6.)

We toil through a mighty maze, but I can assure you it is not without plan.

1945, 18 JANUARY. (VICTORY, 5.)

No mood of boastfulness, of vain glory, of over-confidence must cloud our minds; but I think we have a right which history will endorse to feel that we had the honour to play a part in saving the freedom and the future of the world.

1942, 29 NOVEMBER. BROADCAST, LONDON.
(END, 296.)

...instead of one peak period fading out or dovetailing into the other, there is an overlap, or double peak period, in the two wars which we are waging together on opposite sides of the globe.

1945, 27 FEBRUARY.

...for us in Britain and the British Empire, who had alone been in the struggle from the first day to the last and staked our existence on the result, there was a meaning beyond what even our most powerful and most valiant Allies could feel. Weary and worn, impoverished but undaunted and now triumphant, we had a moment that was sublime. We gave thanks to God for the noblest of all His blessings, the sense that we had done our duty.

1954. (WW2 VI, 477.)

Tanks vs. infantry

In the last war we devised the tank to clear a way for the infantry, who were otherwise held up by the intensity of machine-gun fire. On this occasion it was the infantry who would have to clear the way for the tanks, to break through the crust and liberate the superior armour.

1942, 11 NOVEMBER.

U-boat peril

German U-boats, Churchill said, were "the only thing that ever frightened me". The greatest threat to Britain's survival that Germany, unable to invade the island, offered, they threatened to strangle the British Isles by cutting off their sustenance. After fearful tolls, they were overcome by Anglo-American naval supremacy, the convoy system, and airborne patrols.

Such is the U-boat war—hard, widespread and bitter, a war of groping and drowning, a war of ambuscade and stratagem, a war of science and seamanship.

1939, 26 SEPTEMBER.

...the Royal Navy has immediately attacked the U-boats, and is hunting them night and day—I will not say without mercy, because God forbid we should ever part company with that, but at any rate with zeal and not altogether without relish.

1939, 1 OCTOBER. BROADCAST, LONDON.
(BLOOD, 206.)

We are exposed to a form of attack justly considered abominable, but we are making successful headway against it. I must warn the House that continual losses must be expected. No immunity can be guaranteed at any time.

There will not be in this war any period when the seas will be completely safe; but neither will there be, I believe, any period when the full necessary traffic of the Allies cannot be carried on.

1939, 8 NOVEMBER.

When I see statements, as I have done lately, that the Germans during 1940 will have as many as 400 U-boats in commission...I wonder if they are producing the U-boat captains and crews by a similar method.

1939, 6 DECEMBER.

There are two people who sink U-boats in this war, Talbot. You sink them in the Atlantic and I sink them in the House of Commons. The trouble is that you are sinking them at exactly half the rate I am.

CIRCA 1941. (*SUNDAY TIMES*, 13 JULY 1980.)

Captain Talbot (whom WSC later sacked) was Director of Anti-Submarine Warfare.

I went through, as a minister, some of the worst periods of the U-boat attack in the last war. I have studied the conditions long and carefully, and have thought often about them in the intervening years. Nothing that happened then, nothing that we imagined in the interval, however alarming it seemed at the time, was comparable to the dangers and difficulties which now beset us. I repeat that every high authority I know of, if asked in cold blood a year ago how we should get through, would have found it impossible to give a favourable answer. I have no doubt that the able experts who advise Hitler told him that our doom was certain.

1941, 25 JUNE. (SECRET, 28.)

The first of all our dangers is the U-boat peril. That is a very great danger. Our food, our means of making war, our life, all depend upon the passage of ships across the sea. The whole power of the United States to manifest itself in this war depends upon the power to move ships across the sea....what a terrible waste it is to think of all these great ships that are sunk...

1942, 31 OCTOBER. WESTMINSTER CENTRAL HALL, LONDON. (END, 258.)

The only thing that ever really frightened me during the war was the U-boat peril....I was even more anxious about this battle than I had been about the glorious air fight called the Battle of Britain.

1949. (WW2 II, 529.)

Unconditional surrender

The displacement of Ribbentrop by von Papen [as German Foreign Minister] would be a milestone of importance, and would probably lead to further disintegration in the Nazi machine. There is no need for us to discourage this process by continually uttering the slogan "Unconditional Surrender." As long as we do not have to commit ourselves to dealing with any particular new figure or new Government our advantage is clear. We certainly do not want, if we can help it, to get them all fused together in a solid desperate block for whom there is no hope. I am sure you will agree with me that a gradual break-up in Germany must mean a weakening of their resistance, and consequently the saving of hundreds of thousands of British and American lives.

1943, 14 AUGUST. (WW2 V, 584.)

WSC to Eden. At Casablanca in January 1943, Roosevelt proclaimed that the Allies demanded "Unconditional Surrender" from Germany. Although Churchill immediately seconded him, he feared the policy might stiffen German resistance. Franz von Papen (1879–1969) was German Chancellor briefly in 1932 and abetted Hitler's appointment in 1933. Indicted at Nuremberg, he was acquitted because "political immorality" was considered outside the court's jurisdiction.

I am not of opinion that a demand for unconditional surrender will prolong the war. Anyhow, the war will be prolonged until unconditional surrender has been obtained.

1945, 16 JANUARY.

A contrary view to the above, but by then victory was much closer.

We are no extirpators of nations, or butchers of peoples. We make no bargain with you. We accord you nothing as a right. Abandon your resistance unconditionally. We remain bound by our customs and our nature.

1945, 18 JANUARY. (VICTORY, 24.)

War aims

When the war is over there will be a short lull during which we will have the opportunity to establish a few basic principles, of justice, of respect for the rights and property of other nations, and indeed of respect for private property so long as its owner was honest and its scope moderate....But all this talk about war aims is absurd at the present time: the Cabinet Committee to examine the question had produced a vague paper, four fifths of which was from the Sermon on the Mount and the remainder an Election Address.

1941, 26 JANUARY, CHEQUERS. (COLVILLE, FRINGES I, 411.)

...I have always been a bit shy of defining war aims, but if these great communities, now struggling not only for their own lives but for the freedom and progress of the world, emerge victorious, there will be an electric atmosphere in the world which may render possible an advance towards a greater and broader social unity and justice than could otherwise have been achieved in peace-time in a score of years. We are no theorists or doctrinaires. Trade unionists are practical men aiming at practical results. I might say that our aim will be to build a society in which there will be wealth and culture, but where wealth shall not prey on commonwealth, nor culture degenerate into class and pride.

1941, 27 MARCH. TRADES UNION LUNCHEON, LONDON. (UNRELENTING, 72.)

Illustrative of biographer Martin Gilbert's one-sentence summary of Churchill:

> He was a great humanitarian who was himself distressed that the accidents of history gave him his greatest power at a time when everything had to be focused on defending the country from destruction, rather than achieving his goals of a fairer society.

I have, as the House knows, hitherto consistently deprecated the formulation of peace aims or war aims—however you put it—by His Majesty's Government, at this stage. I deprecate it at this time, when the end of the war is not in sight, when the conflict sways to and fro with alternating fortunes, and when conditions and associations at the end of the war are unforeseeable.

1941, 9 SEPTEMBER.

...we are all of us defending something which is, I won't say dearer, but greater than a country, namely, a cause. That cause is the cause of freedom and of justice; that cause is the cause of the weak against the strong; it is the cause of law against violence, of mercy and tolerance against brutality and iron-bound tyranny. That is the cause that we are fighting for.

1942, 5 DECEMBER. TOWN HALL, BRADFORD. (END, 307.)

...in the casting-down of this monstrous Nazi engine of tyranny, cruelty, greed and aggression—in the casting of it down shattered in pieces, something will have been achieved by the whole human race which will affect in a decisive manner its future destinies, and which will even in our own time be marked by very sensible improvement in the conditions under which the great masses of the people live.

1943, 29 SEPTEMBER. ROYAL ALBERT HALL, LONDON. (ONWARDS, 224.)

War crimes

Agree the trial will be a farce. Indictment: facilities for counsel. All sorts of complications ensue as soon as you admit a fair trial. I would take no responsibility for a trial—even though U.S. wants to do it. Execute the principal criminals as outlaws—if no Ally wants them.

1945, 12 APRIL. (DIARIES OF CABINET SECRETARY SIR NORMAN BROOK, *THE NEW YORK TIMES*, 22 JANUARY 2006.)

WSC never lost his sense of alternate scenarios, as the following quotation indicates.

It shows that if you get into a war, it is supremely important to win it. You and I would be in a pretty pickle if we had lost.

1946. (ISMAY, 157.)

WSC to General Ismay, referring to published results of the Nuremberg trials of Nazi war criminals.

19

NUCLEAR
AGE AND
COLD WAR

"We knew the world would not be the same. A few people laughed...A few people cried...Most people were silent. I remembered the line from the Hindu scripture the Bhagavad Gita..... 'Now I am become death, the destroyer of worlds.' I suppose we all thought that, one way or another."

– *J. Robert Oppenheimer* [65]

"The bomb brought peace, but men alone can keep that peace."
Premier again after the October 1951 General Election.

Time magazine named Churchill "Man of the Half-Century" in 1950, and since nobody else had appeared to challenge him in the fifty years since, there was some expectation that he would remain on top for 2000. But in late 1999, a *Time* that Henry Luce would

---

65 Oppenheimer, Robert, scientific director of the Manhattan Project, Los Alamos 1945. Referenced in *www.atomicarchive.com*. The full quotation from the *Bhagavad Gita* is in chapter 11, verse 32: "The Supreme Lord said: I am death, the mighty destroyer of the world, out to destroy. Even without your participation all the warriors standing arrayed in the opposing armies shall cease to exist."

not have recognised proclaimed Albert Einstein "Person of the Century". In response, *Finest Hour* offered two factoids: 1) Winston Churchill wrote "Shall We All Commit Suicide?", the first entry below, warning of a future nuclear holocaust, fifteen years before Einstein sent his famous letter to President Roosevelt, warning of the same possibility; 2) It was Albert Einstein who suggested that the world was far more likely to come to grief from bad politics than bad physics. And somewhere along the line in 1940, Winston Churchill had saved civilisation.

Notwithstanding that *Time*'s citation is designed to sell magazines, and that Churchill was proclaimed the leading figure of the past century by just about every other authority, *Time*'s lurch was a disappointment. Churchill is forever seen by light thinkers as a man of war, who had his moment in 1940 and faded away. Few recall his lonely campaign for a "final settlement" with the Soviets in the 1950s, as the H-bomb appeared and the terror of imminent extinction flickered.

What he said as the Nuclear Age unfolded speaks for itself. We all have our views on the validity of his quest. Whether the Soviet Union post-Stalin was a changed country or, as Eisenhower believed, the same whore in a new dress, will forever be debated by historians. But there is no doubt that Churchill recognised the apocalyptic nature of the hydrogen bomb early – even earlier than he recognised the dangers of Hitler. And his efforts to reach at least a peaceful stand-off were principled and noble.

As with previous chapters in this section, I have arranged the obviously time-sensitive quotations first in chronological order as applicable, and the general observations later.

1924–44

Future prospects

Mankind has never been in this position before. Without having improved appreciably in virtue or enjoying wiser guidance, it has got into its hands for the first time the tools by which it can unfailingly accomplish its own extermination....Death stands at attention, obedient, expectant, ready to serve, ready to shear away the peoples *en masse*; ready, if called on, to pulverize, without hope of repair, what is left of civilization. He awaits only the word of command. He awaits it from a frail, bewildered being, long his victim, now—for one occasion only—his Master...

May there not be methods of using explosive energy incomparably more intense than anything heretofore discovered? Might not a bomb no bigger than an orange be found to possess a secret power to destroy a whole block of buildings—nay, to concentrate the force of a thousand tons of cordite and blast a township at a stroke? Could not explosives even of the existing type be guided automatically in flying machines by wireless or other rays, without a human pilot, in ceaseless procession upon a hostile city, arsenal, camp or dockyard?

1924, SEPTEMBER. ("SHALL WE ALL COMMIT SUICIDE?," *PALL MALL*; THOUGHTS, 177–8.)

First published in volume form (with "All" deleted from the title) by Eilert Printing Co., New York, 1924. Republished with original title in Thoughts and Adventures.

If the hydrogen atoms in a pound of water could be prevailed upon to combine together and form helium, they would suffice to drive a thousand-horsepower engine for a whole year. If the electrons, those tiny planets of the atomic systems, were induced to combine with the nuclei in the hydrogen the horsepower liberated would be 120 times greater still. There is no question among scientists that this gigantic source of energy exists. What is lacking is the match to set the bonfire alight, or it may be the detonator to cause the dynamite to explode. The scientists are looking for this.

1931, DECEMBER. ("FIFTY YEARS HENCE," *STRAND MAGAZINE*; THOUGHTS, 198.)

Churchill quoted from this article in his last major speech to the House of Commons, on 1 March 1955.

Another great war, especially an ideological war, fought as it would be not only on frontiers but in the heart of every land with weapons far more destructive than men have yet wielded, would spell the doom, perhaps for many centuries, of such civilization as we have been able to erect since history began to be written....We can only try our best, and if we cannot solve the problem we can at least make sure that it is faced in all its sombre magnitude while time remains.

1944, 15 DECEMBER.

1945–49

Atomic bomb

This revelation of the secrets of nature, long mercifully withheld from man, should arouse the most solemn reflections in the mind and conscience of every human being capable of comprehension. We must indeed pray that these awful agencies will be made to conduce to peace among the nations, and that instead of wreaking measureless havoc upon the entire globe, may become a perennial fountain of world prosperity.

1945, 6 AUGUST. (VICTORY, 224.)

Statement released by Attlee, but drafted by Churchill before the change of government, released following the dropping of the first atomic bomb on Hiroshima.

On 17th July there came to us at Potsdam the eagerly-awaited news of the trial of the atomic bomb in the [New] Mexican desert. Success beyond all dreams crowded this sombre, magnificent venture of our American allies. The detailed reports...could leave no doubt in the minds of the very few who were informed, that we were in the presence of a new factor in human affairs, and possessed of powers which were irresistible.

1945, 16 AUGUST.

From Churchill's final review of the war and his first major speech as Leader of the Opposition in the House of Commons.

What was gunpowder? Trivial. What was electricity? Meaningless. This atomic bomb is the Second Coming in Wrath.

1945, 22 JULY, POTSDAM. (STIMSON DIARY; MEE, 164.)

WSC's response to US General Groves's report on the successful atom bomb test in New Mexico. "Now I know what happened to

Truman," Churchill allegedly went on. "When he got to the meeting after reading the report, he was a changed man. He told the Russians just where they got on and off and generally bossed the whole meeting."

Anglo-American cooperation

If the population of the English-speaking Commonwealths be added to that of the United States with all that such cooperation implies in the air, sea, all over the globe and in science and in industry, and in moral force, there will be no quivering, precarious balance of power to offer its temptation to ambition or adventure. On the contrary, there will be an overwhelming assurance of security.

1946, 5 MARCH. WESTMINSTER COLLEGE, FULTON, MISSOURI. (SINEWS, 104.)

The problems of the aftermath, the moral and physical exhaustion of the victorious nations, the miserable fate of the conquered, the vast confusion of Europe and Asia, combine to make a sum total of difficulty, which, even if the Allies had preserved their wartime comradeship, would have taxed their resources to the full. Even if we in this island had remained united, as we were in the years of peril, we should have found much to baffle our judgment, and many tasks that were beyond our strength....If two countries who are great friends agree on something which is right, they are "ganging up," so they must not do it. We should brush aside these terms of prejudice.

1946, 5 JUNE.

Treaties and collaboration

We British have our twenty years Treaty of Collaboration and Mutual Assistance with Soviet Russia....it might well be a fifty years Treaty so far as we are concerned. We aim at nothing but mutual assistance and collaboration....."In my father's house are many mansions." Special associations between members of the United Nations which have no aggressive point against any other country, which harbour no design incompatible with the Charter of the United Nations, far from being harmful, are beneficial and, as I believe, indispensable.

1946, 5 MARCH. WESTMINSTER COLLEGE, FULTON, MISSOURI. (SINEWS, 99.)

The quoted phrase is one of Churchill's favourites, from John 14:2, used in his speeches as early as 1908. See Chapter 6.... Commonwealth of many mansions; and Appendix IV.

Post-war prospects

We have had nothing else but wars since democracy took charge...[In the last two,] thirty million men were killed in battle. In the last one seven million were murdered in cold blood, mainly by the Germans. They made human slaughter-pens like the Chicago stockyards. Europe is a ruin. Many of her cities have been blown to pieces by bombs. Ten capitals in Eastern Europe are in Russian hands. They are Communists now, you know—Karl Marx and all that. It may well be that an even worse war is drawing near. A war of the East against the West. A war of liberal civilisation against the Mongol hordes. Far gone are the days of Queen Victoria and a settled world order. But, having gone through so much, we do not despair.

1947. (*THE DREAM*, OB VIII, 371.)

The sad final peroration by Winston to his father's ghost, in WSC's short story.

Skeletons with gleaming eyes and poisoned javelins glare at each other across the ashes and rubble heaps of what was once the august Roman Empire....[shouldn't there be a place for] Europe, the Mother Continent and fountain source not only of the woes, but of most of the glories of modern civilisation?

1947, 4 JANUARY. ("THE HIGHROAD OF THE FUTURE," *COLLIERS*; ESSAYS II, 460–63.)

Contracting world

Take all these improvements in locomotion; what do they do but make the world grow smaller, making the heritage of man a far more restricted sphere? It is very convenient of course to flash about, but after all the life of man does not depend upon the external conditions to which he is subjected, provided of course that they are compatible with the maintenance of his existence.

1948, 18 NOVEMBER. UNIVERSITY OF LONDON. (EUROPE, 468.)

The advantages of the nineteenth century, the literary age, have been largely put away by this terrible twentieth century with all its confusion and exhaustion of mankind.

1948: AS ABOVE. (EUROPE, 468; BALANCE, 388.)

This speech is one of the few where Churchill repeated some sentences word for word in a subsequent speech: when he received an honorary doctorate from the University of Copenhagen, 10 October 1950. See also Churchill at Large...Humanity.

North Atlantic Treaty Organization

We give our thanks to the United States for the splendid part they are playing in the world....The sacrifices are very great. In addition to the enormous sums sent to Europe under Marshall aid, the Atlantic Pact entails further subsidies for military supplies...all this has to be raised by taxation from the annual production of the hard-working American people, who are not all Wall Street millionaires....[Nothing like it] has ever been seen in all history. We acknowledge it with gratitude, and we must continue to play our part...

1949, 12 MAY.

On an act of Parliament approving the NATO pact.

1950–56

1951 General Election

A Bevan-coloured Government or even a Bevan-tinted Government or tainted (to change the metaphor excusably) might well lead to our still being left in the front-line of danger without our fair share of influence upon the course of events.

1951, 9 OCTOBER, WOODFORD, ESSEX. (STEMMING, 139.)

Churchill was commenting on the apparent split between the Bevan Socialists and more moderate members of the Labour Party, and the likely effect if the Bevanites won control of the party. See Chapter 20...Bevan.

...the *Daily Mirror* coined a phrase...which is being used by the Socialist Party...."Whose finger," they asked, "do you want on the trigger,

Attlee's or Churchill's?" I am sure we do not want any fingers upon any trigger. Least of all do we want a fumbling finger....it will not be a British finger that will pull the trigger of a Third World War....Although we should certainly be involved in a struggle between the Soviet Empire and the free world, the control and decision and the timing of that horrible event would not rest with us.

1951, 6 OCTOBER. LOUGHTON COUNTY HIGH SCHOOL, ESSEX. (STEMMING, 130.)

1952 British atomic bomb test

The report of a recent special survey showing that there is very little animal or bird life on Monte Bello Islands was one of the factors in the choice of the site for the test of the United Kingdom atomic weapon. I should add, however, that an expedition which went to the islands fifty years ago reported that giant rats, wild cats, and wallabies were seen, and these may have caused the Hon. Member some anxiety. However the officer who explored the islands recently says that he found only some lizards, two sea eagles and what looked like a canary sitting on a perch.

[Lt. Col. Lipton (Lab.) asked which governments had been invited to send observers to British atom bomb tests.] It was after full consideration of all those points that I gave my somewhat comprehensive or rather exclusively comprehensive answer, "None, sir."

1952, 21 MAY

Reply to a question by Emrys Hughes (Lab.) over the destruction of wildlife from British nuclear tests. The canary line may have referred to Hughes's Hon. Friend, Sidney Silverman, often pilloried by Churchill as a bird on a perch. (See Chapter 33...Silverman's perch.)

1953 Bermuda Conference

EXCELLENT JOURNEY. ALL WELL. GOAT SPLENDID. LOVE W.

1953, 2 DECEMBER. HAMILTON, BERMUDA. (SOAMES, SPEAKING, 576.)

WSC's telegram to his wife upon arriving in Hamilton for the Three-Power conference with Eisenhower and Laniel. Reference is to the goat mascot of the Royal Welch Fusiliers, who were on parade as Churchill's plane landed.

When I meet [Stalin's successor] Malenkov we can build for peace....Ike...doesn't think any good can come from talks with the Russians. But it will pay him to come along with us. I shall do what I can to persuade him. I might stay longer here [Bermuda] than I meant, at any rate if I could persuade Ike to stay too.

1953, 3 DECEMBER, HAMILTON, BERMUDA. (MORAN, 536.)

In the event Eisenhower refused at Bermuda to consider any "meeting at the summit", as Churchill called it and proposed, with the new leaders of the Soviet Union.

[Dulles says] nothing but evil can come out of meeting with Malenkov. Dulles is a terrible handicap. Ten years ago I could have dealt with him. Even as it is I have not been defeated by this bastard. I have been humiliated by my own decay.

1953, 7 DECEMBER. HAMILTON, BERMUDA. (MORAN, 540.)

With WSC arguing for a summit with the new Soviet leaders and Eisenhower remarking that the USSR was still the same old whore in a new dress, the Bermuda Conference moved the world no closer to the lasting peace Churchill sought. For more on this remark see People...Dulles.

We are to gang up against them without any reference to the "Locarno" idea. The statement about Europe ends with the challenge about a united Germany in EDC [European Defence Community] or NATO, for which Russia is to give up the Eastern Zone. Many people would think that we are deliberately riding for a fall. Perhaps we are...We cannot accept as justified or permanent the present division of Europe.

1953, 7 DECEMBER. HAMILTON, BERMUDA. (LARRES, 316; BRITISH NATIONAL ARCHIVES, PREM 11/418. M 330/53.)

WSC to Eden regarding the final communiqué of the Bermuda Conference.

1956 Suez Crisis

It serves Anthony [Eden] right. He has inherited what he let me in for.

1956, 8 AUGUST. (MORAN, 748.)

There is not much left for me to do in this world and I have neither the wish nor the strength to involve myself in the present political stress and turmoil. But I do believe, with unfaltering conviction, that the theme of the Anglo-American alliance is more important today than at any time since the war.

1956, 22 NOVEMBER. (MACMILLAN, STORM, 175.)

WSC private letter to Eisenhower; his last foray into Anglo-American relations.

[The Suez operation was] the most ill-conceived and ill-executed imaginable....I would never have dared; and if I had dared, I would certainly never have dared stop.

1956, 29 NOVEMBER. (COLVILLE, FRINGES II, 392.)

WSC to John Colville, who asked him if he had been Prime Minister, would he have launched the invasion of Suez.

Nuclear Age: General Observations

Breathing space

The human race is going through tormenting convulsions, and there is a profound longing for some breathing space, for some pause in the frenzy.

1951, 8 OCTOBER. BROADCAST, LONDON. (STEMMING, 136.)

...the world also needs patience. It needs a period of calm rather than vehement attempts to produce clear-cut solutions. There have been many periods when prompt and violent action might have averted calamities. This is not one of them. Even if we entered on a phase only of easement for five or ten years that might lead to something still better when it ended.

1953, 10 OCTOBER, MARGATE. (ALLIANCE, 64.)

WSC would soon take his quest for "easement" of the Cold War to Bermuda, only to find it rejected by Eisenhower and Dulles.

Cold War

It is part of the established technique of the "cold war" the Soviets have begun against us all, that in any country which has fallen into their power, people of character and men of heart and personality outstanding in any walk of life, from the manual worker to the university professor, shall be what is called in their savage jargon "liquidated".

1948, 9 OCTOBER. LLANDUDNO, WALES. (EUROPE, 412.)

Are we winning the cold war?....Well this can't be decided, I think, by looking at Europe alone. We must first look to the East. The worst event, I'm sure Mr Luce will agree with me in this—I'm sure the worst event since the fighting stopped has been the subjugation of a large part of China by Communism. There's your most formidable event.

1949, 25 MARCH. RITZ-CARLTON HOTEL, NEW YORK. (BALANCE, 34.)

What is called the Cold War—which is not a legal term—continues. What we are faced with is not a violent jerk but a prolonged pull.

1953, 3 MARCH.

Churchill did not, as is sometimes alleged, invent the phrase "Cold War". The best attribution is to Herbert Bayard Swope, who occasionally wrote speeches for Bernard Baruch. It is also mistakenly attributed to columnist Walter Lippmann, from his 1947 book, The Cold War.

Defence

...we must satisfy ourselves that every possible effort has been used so to organise our [defence] forces as to procure a true economy with its twin sister, efficiency. To say such things is to utter platitudes. To do them is to render public service.

1951, 6 DECEMBER

Deterrence

The bomb brought peace, but men alone can keep that peace, and henceforward they will keep it under penalties which threaten the survival not only of civilization but of humanity itself.

1945, 16 AUGUST.

The argument is now put forward that we must never use the atomic bomb until, or unless, it has been used against us first. In other words, you must never fire until you have been shot dead. That seems to me undoubtedly a silly thing to say and a still more imprudent position to adopt. Moreover, such a resolve would certainly bring war near.

1950, 14 DECEMBER.

It is my belief that by accumulating deterrents of all kinds against aggression we shall, in fact, ward off the fearful catastrophe, the fears of which darken the life and mar the progress of all the peoples of the globe.

1952, 17 JANUARY. CONGRESS, WASHINGTON. (STEMMING, 226–7.)

When I was a schoolboy, I was not good at arithmetic, but I have since heard it said that certain mathematical quantities when they pass through infinity, change their signs from plus to minus—or the other way round....This rule may have a novel application, and that when the advance of destructive weapons enables everyone to kill everybody else, nobody will want to kill anyone at all.

1953, 3 NOVEMBER.

Divided world

The Bolshevisation of the Balkans proceeds apace and all the Cabinets of Central, Eastern and Southern Europe are in Soviet control, excepting only Athens. This brand I snatched from the burning on Christmas Day.

1945, 24 SEPTEMBER, ANTIBES. (OB VIII, 154.)

WSC to his wife. See also World War II... Greece.

It is better to have a world united than a world divided; but it is also better to have a world divided than a world destroyed. Nor does it follow that even in a world divided there should not be equilibrium from which a further advance to unity might be attempted as the years pass by. Anything is better than this ceaseless degeneration of the heart of Europe. Europe will die of that.

1946, 5 JUNE.

Churchill viewed the post-war wreckage of Europe with fear for the future. His prescription to end it began with the reconciliation of France and Germany; see quotations under those headings.

...the world was divided into peoples that owned the governments and governments that owned the peoples.

1949, 31 MARCH. MASSACHUSETTS INSTITUTE OF TECHNOLOGY, BOSTON. (BALANCE, 42.)

We live in a period, happily unique in human history, when the whole world is divided intellectually and to a large extent geographically between the creeds of Communist discipline and individual freedom, and when at the same time, this mental and psychological division is accompanied by the possession by both sides of the obliterating weapons of the nuclear age.

1955, 1 MARCH.

Hydrogen bomb

...the hydrogen bomb carries us into dimensions which have never confronted practical human thought and have been confined to the realms of fancy and imagination.

1954, 5 APRIL.

...when Mr. Sterling Cole, the Chairman of the United States Congressional Committee, gave out a year ago—February 17, 1954—the first comprehensive review of the hydrogen bomb, the entire foundation of human affairs was revolutionized, and mankind placed in a situation both measureless and laden with doom.

1955, 1 MARCH.

Mankind's choice

Science, which now offers us a Golden Age with one hand, offers at the same time with the other hand the doom of all that we have built up inch by inch since the Stone Age. My faith is in the high progressive destiny of man. I do not believe we are to be flung back into abysmal darkness by those fearsome discoveries which human genius has made. Let us make sure that they are servants, but not our masters.

1951, 23 OCTOBER, PLYMOUTH. (STEMMING, 173.)

What is the scene which unfolds before us tonight? It is certainly not what we had hoped to find after all our enemies had surrendered unconditionally and the great world instrument of the United Nations had been set up to make sure that the wars were ended. It is certainly not that. Peace does not sit untroubled in her vineyard. The harvests of new and boundless wealth which science stands ready to pour into the hands of all peoples, and of none perhaps more than the people of Canada, must be used for exertions to ward off from us the dangers and unimaginable horrors of another world war....We have surmounted all the perils and endured all the agonies of the past. We shall provide against and thus prevail over the dangers and problems of the future. Withhold no sacrifice, grudge no toil, seek no sordid gain, fear no foe. All will be well. We have, I believe, within us the life-strength and guiding light by which the tormented world around us may find the harbour of safety, after a storm-beaten voyage.

1952, 14 JANUARY. CHÂTEAU LAURIER, OTTAWA. (STEMMING THE TIDE, 216–19.)

There is no doubt that if the human race are to have their dearest wish and be free from the dread of mass destruction, they could have, as an alternative, what many of them might prefer, namely, the swiftest expansion of material well-being that has ever been within their reach, or even within their dreams.

1953, 3 NOVEMBER. (ALLIANCE, 78.)

National Geographic's Churchill issue (August 1965) stitched these inspiring remarks together with those from a 1954 London speech about how to achieve "a prolonged and indefinite period of material prosperity".

Which way shall we turn to save our lives and the future of the world? It does not matter so much to old people; they are going soon anyway; but I find it poignant to look at youth in all its activity and ardour and, most of all, to watch little children playing their merry games, and wonder what would lie before them if God wearied of mankind.

1955, 1 MARCH. (ALLIANCE, 226.)

From WSC's last major speech in the House of Commons.

Mutual assured destruction

Pending some new discovery, the only direct measure of defence upon a great scale is the certainty of being able to inflict simultaneously upon the enemy as great damage as he can inflict upon ourselves.

1934, 28 NOVEMBER.

Although this first quotation on a doctrine later to be known as "Mutual Assured Destruction" came before the nuclear age, Churchill himself had warned of the dangers of the atomic bomb ten years earlier; see first entry in this chapter.

Moralists may find it a melancholy thought that peace can find no nobler foundations than mutual terror.

1950, 28 MARCH.

...a third World War is unlikely to happen [because] both sides know that it would begin with horrors of a kind and on a scale never dreamed of before by human beings.

1952, 14 OCTOBER. SAVOY HOTEL, LONDON. (STEMMING, 351.)

Then it may well be that we shall by a process of sublime irony have reached a stage in this story where safety will be the sturdy child of terror, and survival the twin brother of annihilation....The [nuclear] deterrent does not cover the case of lunatics or dictators in the mood of Hitler when he found himself in his final dug-out. That is a blank....

Major war of the future will differ, therefore, from anything we have known in the past, in this one significant respect, that each side, at the outset, will suffer what it dreads the most, the loss of everything that it has ever known of....

1955, 1 MARCH.

Nuclear proliferation

I may say that I am in entire agreement with the President that the secrets of the atomic bomb should so far as possible not be imparted at the present time to any other country in the world. This is in no design or wish for arbitrary power, but for the common safety of the world.

1945, 16 AUGUST.

It would nevertheless be wrong and imprudent to entrust the secret knowledge or experience of the atomic bomb, which the United States, Great Britain and Canada now share, to the world organization, while it is still in its infancy. It would be criminal madness to cast it adrift in this still agitated and non-united world. No one in any country has slept less well in their beds because this knowledge, and the method and the raw materials to apply it, are at present largely retained in American hands. I do not believe we should all have slept so soundly had the positions been reversed and if some Communist or Neo-Fascist State monopolized for the time being these dread agencies....

The dark ages may return—the Stone Age may return on the gleaming wings of science, and what might now shower immeasurable material blessings upon mankind, may even bring about its total destruction. Beware I say; Time may be short.

1946, 5 March. Westminster College, Fulton, Missouri. (Sinews, 96–9.)

In these present days we dwell strangely and precariously under the shield and protection of the atomic bomb. The atomic bomb is still only in the hands of a State and nation which we know will never use it except in the cause of right and freedom. But it may well be that in a few years this awful agency of destruction will be widespread and the catastrophe following from its use by several warring nations will not only bring to an end all that we call civilization but may possibly disintegrate the globe itself.

1946, 19 September, Zürich University. (Sinews, 201.)

Peace through strength

Peace will not be preserved by pious sentiments expressed in terms of platitudes or by official grimaces and diplomatic correctitude, however desirable this may be from time to time. It will not be preserved by casting aside in dangerous years the panoply of warlike strength. There must be earnest thought. There must also be faithful perseverance and foresight. Greatheart must have his sword and armour to guard the pilgrims on their way. Above all, among the English-speaking peoples, there must be the union of hearts based upon conviction and common ideals. That is what I offer. That is what I seek.

1946, 8 March. General Assembly of Virginia, Richmond. (Sinews, 110.)

From a twenty-minute speech in Richmond shortly after the Fulton "Iron Curtain" speech. Virginians commemorated it sixty years later.

I do not hold that we should rearm in order to fight. I hold that we should rearm in order to parley.

1951, 8 October. Broadcast, London. (CS VIII, 8257.)

Seventeen days later on 25 October, Churchill returned to power as Prime Minister.

Penalties of war

The penalties have grown to an extent undreamed of; and at the same time, many of the old incentives which were the cause of the beginning of so many wars, or features in their beginning, have lost their significance. The desire for glory, booty, territory, dynastic or national aggrandizement; hopes of a speedy and splendid victory with all its excitement—and they are all temptations from which even those who only fight for righteous causes are not always exempt—are now superseded by a preliminary stage of measureless agony from which neither side could at present protect itself.

1952, 5 March.

Preserving the peace

Scarred and armed with experience, we intend to take better measures this time than could ever previously have been conceived in order to prevent a renewal, in the lifetime of our children or our grandchildren at least, of the horrible destruction of human values which has marked the last and the present world wars.

1944, 24 May.

Retrospectives and final thoughts

Tyranny presents itself in various forms but it is always the same, whatever slogans it utters, whatever name it calls itself by, whatever liveries it wears. It is always the same and makes a demand on all free men to risk and do all in their power to withstand it.

1948, 9 May, Amsterdam. (Europe, 319.)

The outstanding feature of the twentieth century has been the enormous expansion in the numbers who are given the opportunity to share in the larger and more varied life which in previous periods was reserved for the few and for the very few....

[But] little did we guess that what has been called The Century of the Common Man would witness as its outstanding feature more common men killing each other with greater facilities than any other five centuries put together in the history of the world.

1949, 31 MARCH. MASSACHUSETTS INSTITUTE OF TECHNOLOGY, BOSTON. (BALANCE, 40–42.)

After the First War, when the victors had disarmed the Germans and their allies, no powerful organized army remained upon the scene except the French Army. After this war the armed might of Russia has emerged steadily.... The second difference, which arose out of the realization of the first, was that the United States, instead of retiring into isolation, instead of demanding full and prompt repayment of debts and disinteresting herself in Europe...has made the great counterpoise upon which the freedom and the future of our civilization depends.

1950, 30 NOVEMBER.

Churchill had just been named "Man of the Half-Century" by Time *magazine (see introduction).*

20
PEOPLE

*"These essays on Great Men of our age...[have] brought them back
to me, and made me feel how much has changed in our political life.
Perhaps this is but the illusion which comes upon us all as we grow
older. Each succeeding generation will sing with conviction the
Harrow song, 'There were wonderful giants of old.' Certainly we
must all hope this may prove to be so."*[66]

"Everyone can help in some way or other." Clementine, WSC,
Gertrude Bell, T. E. Lawrence, WSC's bodyguard Inspector Thompson,
at the Pyramids, 1921.

Awell-known American polemicist recently sent me research questions involving his
new book – one of those iconoclastic best-sellers about why it was wrong to fight
World War II, why Churchill, however heroic, bankrupted Britain, lost the Empire,
and produced a half century of Cold War.

The Churchill Centre is an equal-opportunity researcher so I provided the references he
asked for. In the process we talked about Churchill and people. "Gratitude was not the
Great Man's long suit," my critical friend declared. "Churchill suggested that poor Robert
Boothby, who went to the wall for him, be put on a bomb disposal unit."

"What's the source?" I asked. One can always take isolated remarks made in heat or in
haste or spontaneously, in unguarded private moments, and read all sorts of distortions into

---

66 WSC, GC, 1.

them. The relevant Boothby quotations (and this is not exactly what Churchill said) are assembled herein for the reader's judgement. Reading them, I think most readers will conclude that Churchill's standards of integrity were such that he reacted violently towards anyone who fell short – even his friends.

The idea that Churchill cared nothing for other people, so frequently inferred by his critics, resounds oddly to students of his words. I don't suggest that a spontaneous outburst is no clue to his thoughts. But in reviewing what Churchill said about people, what we mainly find in the end is understanding and magnanimity.

As I worked on this chapter (the largest in the book) I was struck by how often Churchill's final view of someone ended on a generous note – even towards those he had severely criticised. Indeed I found only two people about whom Churchill was ultimately censorious. (No, they are not Hitler and Mussolini.)

Churchill knew or wrote about an amazing array of characters: Presidents from McKinley to Eisenhower, historical figures from Caesar to Napoleon, magnificoes, potentates, heroes, villains, dictators and democrats. Reading his appraisals, one is hard-pressed to find shafts of pure hatred. About "guttersnipes" like Hitler he was vituperative; yet even here there were traces of a stubborn willingness to try to find something worthwhile, somewhere.

When the German radio announced that Hitler had died "fighting with his last breath against Bolshevism", Churchill murmured: "Well, I must say I think he was perfectly right to die like that." Years later WSC's former private secretary Sir John Colville told me, "I had the impression that somehow he grudgingly approved."[67] Churchill did not know when he said this that Hitler had committed ignominious suicide. And Churchill too had expected to die "fighting with his last breath", had the Germans invaded and hewn their way to Downing Street.

The people who attracted Churchill's attention would require volumes, and he himself compiled one: his highly readable *Great Contemporaries*. Yet many of those he admired – like Bracken, Beaverbrook and Birkenhead, his wife's "three terrible Bs" – rarely received his public encomiums. Privately, it was another story. And for a remarkable number of political adversaries, there remained a measure of affection or respect that was characteristic of Churchill – an aspect of politics that has almost vanished today.

Christopher Matthews, a Churchill Centre Trustee, recalls an amazing sight. It was 1981, after President Reagan had been shot and nearly killed. The first outsider allowed into the President's hospital room was Matthews's then-boss, Speaker of the House Thomas P. "Tip" O'Neill. A doctor entering the room was astonished to find O'Neill on his knees praying, holding the unconscious President's hand – this partisan Democrat who had opposed Reagan, and would again. It scarcely surprises one to know that Reagan and O'Neill were ardent admirers of Winston Churchill.[68]

One of my own favourite quotations along these lines is from 1960, when Sir Winston learned of the death of his great Labour nemesis, Aneurin Bevan. To the astonishment of listeners, WSC launched into an impromptu valedictory – about the man he had once called the "Minister of Disease". Then, suddenly, halfway through and in mid-sentence, Churchill paused and inquired, *sotto voce*: "Are you sure he's dead?"

---

67 Sir John Colville, conversation with the editor, 1985.
68 Christopher Matthews's remarks after receiving the Churchill Centre's Emery Reves Award for journalistic achievement, Willard Hotel, Washington, DC, 25 October 2007.

Adenauer, Dr. Konrad

Dr. Adenauer may well be deemed the wisest German statesman since the days of Bismarck. I have greatly admired the perseverance, courage, composure and skill with which he has faced the complex, changing, uncertain and unpredictable situations....

1953, 11 May.

Konrad Hermann Joseph Adenauer (1876–1967), German statesman, first Chancellor of the German Federal Republic (1959–63).

Alexander, Albert ("A. V.")

The former First Lord has now become Minister of Defence. I would like to take the occasion of offering him my hearty congratulations and of saying that we look forward with confidence to his discharge of these duties. The Rt. Hon. Gentleman has a very special ability and experience, and I, personally, have always felt the warmest regard for him on account of the very rough times we went through together during the war.

1946, 12 November.

Albert Victor Alexander (1885–1965), Labour MP, thrice First Lord of the Admiralty, once during WWII; Minister of Defence in the postwar Labour Government.

Alexander, Field Marshal Sir Harold

...I personally feel comfort in having at the Cabinet table one whose eye in military matters I have learned to trust and whose judgment of values and of difficult events has so often shone in courage and in wisdom.

1952, 1 July.

Harold Rupert Leofric George Alexander, Field Marshal the Hon. Sir Harold Alexander, later Earl Alexander of Tunis (1891–1969), Commander 15th Army Group in WWII, later the last British Governor General of Canada. Churchill is also reported to have said of him, "He is no glory-hopper."

Amery, Leopold

[Harrow] school possessed the biggest swimming-bath I had ever seen....Naturally it was a good joke to come up behind some naked friend, or even enemy, and push him in....I saw a boy standing in a meditative posture wrapped in a towel on the very brink. He was no bigger than I was, so I thought him fair game. Coming stealthily behind, I pushed him in...."You're in for it," they said. "Do you know what you have done? It's Amery—he's in the Sixth Form. He is Head of his House..." I determined to apologise immediately. I approached the potentate in lively trepidation. "I am very sorry," I said. "I mistook you for a Fourth Form boy. You are so small." He did not seem at all placated by this; so I added in a most brilliant recovery, "My father, who is a great man, is also small." At this he laughed, and...signified that the incident was closed.

I have been fortunate to see a good deal more of him, in times when three years' difference in age is not so important as it is at school.

1930. (MEL, 31–2.)

Leopold Charles Maurice Stennett Amery (1873–1955), Conservative MP, 1911–45, one of WSC's few allies in the 1930s. Famous for his speech quoting Cromwell, which hastened the departure of Neville Chamberlain in May 1940: "...In the name of God, go!" Secretary of State for India in WSC's wartime coalition government.

Asquith, Herbert Henry ("H. H.")

...if, as was inevitable in the rough and tumble of life, he was forced to submit and bow to the opinions of others, to the force of events, to the passions of the hour, it was often with barely concealed repugnance and disdain. If one is to select his greatest characteristic, this massive finality stands forth, for good or ill, above and beyond all others.

1928, August. ("Herbert Henry Asquith," Pall Mall; GC, 89.)

H. H. Asquith, First Earl of Oxford and Asquith (1852–1928) was the last Liberal Prime Minister (1908–16). He and Churchill had their ups and downs; WSC believed Asquith "fed him to the wolves" over the Dardanelles crisis in 1915, but was in the end magnanimous.

For the rest he basked in the sunshine and read Greek. He fashioned with deep thought impeccable verses in complicated metre, and recast in terser form classical inscriptions which displeased him. I could not help much in this.

1928, AUGUST. (IBID., *PALL MALL*; GC, 87, 90.)

Asquith was Churchill's guest on two Mediterranean cruises aboard the Admiralty yacht Enchantress *in 1912 and 1913. Colin Coote wrote:*

The scion of Balliol proved to have a mind which "opened and shut smoothly and exactly like the breech of a gun", and Sir Winston rather found that the bigger the gun the greater the bore (Coote, 64).

At forty, with a massive legal record behind him, he was Home Secretary. At fifty he was Prime Minister. He made his way by his distinction in the House of Commons debate, clear-cut, lucid argument, expressed in happy terms with many a glint of humour and flash of repartee, brevity as well as clarity—these were his weapons in those days of lengthy, sonorous harangues. He was no ebullient orator pouring forth his sentimental or passionate appeal. But few there were who could face him in the tense debating of issues, large or small....He was determined to broaden the road and break down the remaining barriers so as to enable ever larger numbers of ordinary people to win their place in an expanding society and have a fair share of the show.

1950, 6 DECEMBER.

Asquith, Raymond

The War, which found the measure of so many, never got to the bottom of him, and when the Grenadiers strode into the crash and thunder of the Somme, he went to his fate cool, poised, resolute, matter-of-fact, debonair. And well we know that his father, then bearing the supreme burden of the State, would proudly have marched at his side.

1928, AUGUST. ("HERBERT HENRY ASQUITH," *PALL MALL*; GC, 84.)

Raymond Asquith (1878–1916), eldest son of Prime Minister Asquith, who died at the Somme.

Astor, Nancy

Lady Astor, like Bernard Shaw, enjoys the best of all worlds....She denounces the vice of gambling in unmeasured terms, and is closely associated with an almost unrivalled racing stable. She accepts Communist hospitality and flattery, and remains the Conservative Member for Plymouth....The Russians have always been fond of circuses and travelling shows....here was the World's most famous intellectual Clown and Pantaloon in one, and the charming Columbine of the capitalist pantomime.

1929, AUGUST. ("BERNARD SHAW," *PALL MALL*; GC, 32.)

Nancy Witcher Astor, Viscountess Astor CH (1879–1964), the first woman to take a seat in Parliament, was MP for Plymouth Sutton, 1919–45. (Sinn Fein's Countess Markievicz was elected for Dublin in 1918, but did not take her seat.) This remark was made after Astor's visit to Russia, together with George Bernard Shaw. See also Shaw, and Astor entries in Ripostes and Appendix I.

I heard the Noble Lady the Member for the Sutton Division of Plymouth express her dislike of any contact with Bolshevik Russia. Where was this dislike when she paid a visit to Soviet Russia with Mr. Bernard Shaw? The Noble Lady was treated with great consideration. But the point which the House should notice—it is a very serious point, and I hope I shall be able to put it without any offence—is that the time when she went to Russia and gave all her applause and credit to Russia, was a time when the influence of Russia was deeply detrimental to the interests of this country.

1939, 13 APRIL.

I feel you have come into my bathroom and I have only a sponge with which to defend myself

1919, 12 JANUARY. (NICOLSON, 1939–45, 451.)

Letter from Harold Nicolson to his son, Nigel. Nancy Astor, making one of her last speeches in Commons in 1945, told the House that when she first entered the Commons (1 December 1919), Churchill was very cold to her and she had asked him why, then quoting his reply.

Atatürk (Mustapha Kemal)

...the only Dictator with the aureole of martial achievement.

1937, 11 NOVEMBER. ("ARMISTICE OR PEACE?," EVENING STANDARD; STEP, 174.)

Mustapha Kemal (1881–1938), army officer, leader of the "Young Turks", founder of the Turkish Republic, President of Turkey 1923–38. Bestowed with the surname "Atatürk" ("father of the Turks") by the Turkish National Assembly in 1934.

The tears which men and women of all classes shed upon his bier were a fitting tribute to the life work of a man at once the hero, the champion, and the father of modern Turkey. During his long dictatorship a policy of admirable restraint and goodwill created, for the first time in history, most friendly relations with Greece.

1938, 15 DECEMBER. ("NEW LIGHTS IN EASTERN EUROPE," EVENING STANDARD; STEP, 297.)

Churchill's grief was genuine; he had long admired the great Turk who had adopted Churchillian principles of "summits" and compromise with ancient foes.

Attlee, Clement

Get up, get up, Lord Privy Seal! This is no time for levity.

1935. (TAYLOR, 366.)

Clement Richard Attlee (1883–1967), Labour MP, Deputy Prime Minister in the wartime coalition, Labour Prime Minister 1945–51. At this time, as Lord Privy Seal, Attlee had fallen over his seat in the Commons chamber.

Yes! Like the grub that feeds on the Royal Jelly and thinks it's a Queen Bee.

1946. (SIR JOHN FOSTER MP; HALLE, IRREPRESSIBLE, 271–2.)

When told that Prime Minister Attlee was performing well as Prime Minister.

He has much to be modest about.

1946, MARCH. ON TRAIN BOUND FOR FULTON, MISSOURI.

According to the late Truman aide Clark Clifford, who accompanied WSC and Truman

to Fulton for Churchill's famous "Iron Curtain" speech, this remark was preceded by President Truman: "Clement Attlee came to see me the other day. He struck me as a very modest man." Other variations of this quotation are inaccurate.

He is too wise [to go to Moscow]. He dare not absent himself from his Cabinet at home. He knows full well that when the mouse is away the cats will play.

1946, 29 DECEMBER. (NICOLSON III, 82.)

Nicolson reporting a recollection of Jack Churchill, WSC's brother, when someone asked WSC why Attlee, the new Prime Minister, did not go out to Moscow to see Stalin.

Mr. Attlee combines a limited outlook with strong qualities of resistance.

1951, 27 APRIL, ROYAL ALBERT HALL, LONDON. (STEMMING, 65.)

His real struggle is less with the Tories than with his own Left Wing followers. His choice is therefore a hard one. The best he can do is to be a piebald.

1955, 16 MAY, WOODFORD. (UNWRITTEN, 253.)

Auchinleck, General Sir Claude

Although the battle is not yet finished, I have no hesitation in saying that, for good or ill, it is General Auchinleck's battle. Watching these affairs, as it is my duty to do, from day to day, and often from hour to hour, and seeing the seamy side of the reports as they come in, I have felt my confidence in General Auchinleck grow continually, and although everything is hazardous in war, I believe we have found in him, as we have also found in General Wavell, a military figure of the first order.

1941, 11 DECEMBER.

Field Marshal Sir Claude John Eyre Auchinleck (1884-1981), known as "The Auk", British WWII Army general, Commander-in-Chief Middle East (1941–42). In the event, however, Churchill replaced Auchinleck for insufficient progress against the Germans in North Africa. See also Auchinleck's dismissal, World War II...1942, August.

Baden-Powell, Lord

He was a man of character, vision and enthusiasm, and he passed these qualities on to the movement which has played, and is playing, an important part in moulding the character of our race. Sturdiness, neighbourliness, practical competence, love of country, and above all, in these times, indomitable resolve, daring, and enterprise in the face of the enemy, these are the hallmarks of a Scout …"Be Prepared" to stand up faithfully for Right and Truth however the winds may blow.

1942, 16 JULY, BOY SCOUTS ASSOCIATION, LONDON. (END, 191.)

Robert Stephenson Smyth Baden-Powell, First Baron Baden-Powell (1857–1941), known as "B-P", founder of the Boy Scouts.

Baldwin, Stanley

[Mr. Baldwin] is still quite a distinguished painter in our academy. If I were to criticise him at all I would say his work lacked a little in colour, and was also a little lacking in the precise definition of objects in the foreground. He too has changed not only his style but also his subjects.…Making a fair criticism, I must admit there is something very reposeful about the half-tones of Mr. Baldwin's studies.

1932, 30 APRIL, ROYAL ACADEMY BANQUET, BURLINGTON HOUSE, LONDON. (CS, 5154.)

Stanley Baldwin, First Earl Baldwin of Bewdley (1867–1947), Conservative MP and three times Prime Minister (1923–24, 1924–29, 1935–37). Churchill held him chiefly responsible for Britain's failure to rearm sufficiently in the 1930s.

In those days the Lord President was wiser than he is now; he used frequently to take my advice.

1935, 22 MAY.

Comparing 1920, when Baldwin was a junior minister, with 1935 when he was Lord President of the Council.

Occasionally he stumbled over the truth, but hastily picked himself up and hurried on as if nothing had happened.

1936. (HALLE, IRREPRESSIBLE, 133.)

Not verified except as "Ear-Witness" by Kay Halle, whose reliability leads to its being included here.

It has been my fortune to have ups and downs in my political relations with him, the downs on the whole predominating perhaps, but at any rate we have always preserved agreeable personal relations, which, so far as I am concerned, are greatly valued.

1936, 12 NOVEMBER.

I have never heard such a squalid confession from a public man as Baldwin offered us yesterday.

1936, 13 NOVEMBER. (OB, CV5/3, 405.)

WSC to Sir Archibald Boyd-Carpenter. Prime Minister Baldwin had just made an amazing statement:

Supposing I had gone to the country and said that Germany was rearming and that we must rearm, does anybody think that this pacific democracy would have rallied to that cry at that moment? I cannot think of anything that would have made the loss of the election from my point of view more certain.

A countrified businessman who seemed to have reached the Cabinet by accident..

1941. (HALLE, IRREPRESSIBLE, 181.)

I wish Stanley Baldwin no ill, but it would have been much better if he had never lived.

1946, JANUARY. (GILBERT, SEARCH, 106.)

Martin Gilbert writes:

In my long search for Churchill, few letters have struck a clearer note than this one. Churchill was almost always magnanimous…But he saw Baldwin as responsible for the "locust years" when Britain, if differently led, could have easily rearmed, and kept well ahead of the German military and air expansion.

No, not dead. But the candle in that great turnip has gone out.

1950, 17 AUGUST. (NICOLSON III, 193.)

Balfour, Arthur

I have sometimes doubted whether the Rt. Hon. Gentleman's policy has been so disingenuous, so haphazard, so dictated by circumstances beyond his control, as I would gladly believe, whether in fact it is merely a serious and honest, but a somewhat undignified, attempt to keep the Cabinet together rather than a tactical deployment to commit a great Party to a new policy against which its instinct revolts and distrusts—a policy which in the mind of the wisest and oldest counsellors in its ranks would lead to ruin and failure…

1903, 14 AUGUST.

Arthur James Balfour, First Earl of Balfour (1848–1930), Prime Minister 1902–05. He succeeded Churchill as First Lord of the Admiralty in May 1915.

The Rt. Hon. Gentleman's leadership of the House had been much praised in the newspapers whose editors he had ennobled and promoted.

1904, 2 AUGUST.

Balfour was then Prime Minister; Churchill had deserted Balfour's party, the Conservatives, three months earlier.

The Rt. Hon. Gentleman, the First Lord of the Treasury, had never changed his Party; but he had often changed his opinions.

1905, 15 MARCH.

Churchill was referring to the fact that he, in contrast to the Prime Minister, Arthur Balfour, had never changed his opinions, even when they required him to change parties.

Office at any price was his motto, at the sacrifice of any friend or colleague, at the sacrifice of any principle, by the adoption of any manoeuvre, however miserable or contemptible.

1905, 5 APRIL.

That old grey tabby is going to abolish the Naval Division.

1916, 18 FEBRUARY. (FLANDERS; SOAMES, SPEAKING, 179.)

WSC to his wife. Balfour, who replaced Churchill as First Lord of the Admiralty in 1915, was set to eliminate the Royal Naval Division Churchill had set up.

With the highest subtlety and ingenuity he devised a succession of formulas designed to enable people who differed profoundly to persuade themselves they were in agreement.

When it came to the resignation of Ministers, he was careful to shed Free Trade and Protectionist blood as far as possible in equal quantities. Like Henry VIII, he decapitated Papists and burned hot Gospellers on the same day for their respective divergencies in opposite directions from his central, personal and artificial compromise.

1923. (CRISIS I, 28–9.)

…I saw a furious scene in the House of Commons when an Irish member, rushing across the floor in a frenzy, shook his fist for a couple of minutes within a few inches of his face. We young fellows behind were all ready to spring to his aid upon a physical foe; but Arthur Balfour, Leader of the House, regarded the frantic figure with no more and no less than the interest of a biologist examining through a microscope the contortions of a rare and provoked insect.…He possessed and practised the art of always appearing interested in any subject that was raised, or in any person with whom he was talking.…

He would very soon have put Socrates in his place, if that old fellow had played any of his dialectical tricks on him. When I go to Heaven, I shall try to arrange a chat between these two on some topic, not too recondite for me to follow.…He passed from one Cabinet to the other, from the Prime Minister [H. H. Asquith] who was his champion to the Prime Minister [Lloyd George] who had been his most severe critic, like a powerful graceful cat walking delicately and unsoiled across a rather muddy street.…

I saw with grief the approaching departure, and—for all human purposes—extinction, of a being high-uplifted above the common run. As I observed him regarding with calm, firm and cheerful gaze the approach of Death, I felt how foolish the Stoics were to make such a fuss about an event so natural and so indispensable to mankind. But I felt also the tragedy which robs the world of all the wisdom and treasure gathered in a great man's life and experience and hands the lamp to some impetuous and untutored stripling, or lets it fall shivered into fragments upon the ground.

1931, APRIL. ("ARTHUR JAMES BALFOUR," *STRAND MAGAZINE*; GC, 151–63.)

The first scene was in 1905; Balfour was Prime Minister, 1902–05.

Baruch, Bernard

Mr. Bernard Baruch…was the head of the War Industries Board during the two years I was Minister of Munitions. We made friends over a long period of official cables on grave business, and have preserved these relations through the now lengthening years of peace.

1931, 4 JANUARY. (*DAILY MAIL*; ESSAYS IV, 91.)

Bernard Mannes Baruch (1870–1965), financier and presidential adviser, chairman of the War Industries Board in WWI, where he met Churchill. One of WSC's oldest and dearest friends, he helped recoup many of Churchill's losses in the 1929 Stock Market Crash. He continued to advise WSC during his last quest for peace in the 1950s.

Beatty, Admiral Sir David

In Sir David Beatty we have a Commander-in-Chief who, by his gifts and also by his exceptional training, not only possesses the regular qualifications which admirals of distinction possess, but who has, perhaps in a greater degree than almost any of the principal officers of the fleet, what may be called the "war mind."

1917, 21 FEBRUARY.

Admiral of the Fleet David Beatty, First Earl Beatty (1871–1936), was Churchill's favourite WWI Admiral, aggressive and showy; he commanded HMS Lion *during the Battle of Jutland in 1916, where he lost two battle-cruisers but gained prestige. Churchill first met Beatty when the latter tossed him a bottle of champagne in the Sudan in 1898. See Chapter 32…Champagne.*

He did not think of *matériel* as an end in itself but only as a means. He thought of war problems in their unity by land, sea and air. His mind had been rendered quick and supple by the situations of polo and the hunting-field, and enriched by varied experiences against the enemy on Nile gunboats, and ashore….I was increasingly struck with the shrewd and profound sagacity of his comments expressed in language singularly free from technical jargon.

1923. (CRISIS I, 88.)

Beaverbrook, Lord

Some people take drugs; I take Max.

1941 CA. (SIR JOHN COLVILLE TO THE EDITOR.)

William Maxwell Aitken, First Baron Beaverbrook (1879–1964), Anglo-Canadian press owner and politician, WSC's first Minister of Aircraft Production. One of Churchill's oldest and dearest friends, though they did not always see eye to eye. Their relationship spanned half a century.

Max is a good friend in foul weather. Then, when things are going well, he will have a bloody row with you over nothing.

1944, 22 SEPTEMBER. (MORAN, 199.)

Often misquoted as "Max is a foul weather friend," which is not attributable.

People who did not know the services he had rendered during his tenure of office or his force, driving power, and judgment as I did often wondered why his influence with me stood so high. They overlooked our long association in the events of the First World War and its aftermath….We belonged to an older political generation. Often we had been on different sides in the crises and quarrels of those former days; sometimes we had even been fiercely opposed; yet on the whole a relationship had been maintained which was a part of the continuity of my public life, and this was cemented by warm personal friendship.

1950. (WW2 IV, 66–7.)

Beneš, Edvard

He was a master of administration and diplomacy. He knew how to endure with patience and fortitude long periods of adverse fortune. Where he failed—and it cost him and his country much—was in not taking violent decisions at the supreme moment. He was too experienced a diplomatist, too astute a year-to-year politician, to realise the moment and to stake all on victory or death. Had he told his cannons to fire at Munich time the Second World War would have begun under conditions far less favourable to Hitler, who needed many months to make his army and his armour.

1952. (WW2 V, 400.)

Edvard Beneš (1884–1948) Czech leader and patriot, second President of Czechoslovakia. Churchill tended to pronounce his name as "Beans".

Berchtold, Count von

He meant, at all costs, by hook or by crook, to declare war on Serbia. In the whole world that was the only thing that counted with him. That was what Germany had urged. That he must have; and that he got. But he got much more too.

1931. (CRISIS V, 102.)

Count Leopold von Berchtold (1863–1942). Austria-Hungary's Foreign Minister at the outbreak of the First World War.

Beresford, Lord Charles

He is one of those orators of whom it was well said, "Before they get up, they do not know what they are going to say; when they are speaking, they do not know what they are saying; and when they sit down, they do not know what they have said."

1912, 20 DECEMBER.

Charles William de la Poer Beresford, First Baron Beresford (1846–1919), British Admiral and MP.

Bevan, Aneurin

I should think it was hardly possible to state the opposite of the truth with more precision. I back up those who seek to establish democracy and civilization. The Hon. Member must learn to take as well as to give. There is no one more free with interruptions, taunts, and jibes than he is. I saw him—I heard him, not saw him—almost assailing some of the venerable figures on the bench immediately below him. He need not get so angry because the House laughs at him; he ought to be pleased when they only laugh at him.

1944, 8 DECEMBER.

Aneurin ("Nye") Bevan (1897–1960), Welsh Labour MP, founder of the National Health Service. Bevan had interrupted WSC's speech on the Belgian capitulation by asking: "Is it not a fact that the military authorities in Belgium are satisfied that the Belgian Prime Minister unwarrantedly asked for the intervention of British troops?" See also Chapter 33...Dead birds.

The Rt. Hon. Gentleman threatened us the other night with the disclosure of certain scandals if we asked questions about figures—"putrefying corpses," he called them—for which his predecessors....were responsible....We cannot have a Minister of Health living among a lot of putrefying corpses.

1945, 6 DECEMBER.

There is however a poetic justice in the fact that the most mischievous political mouth in wartime has also become, in peace, the most remarkable administrative failure.

1946, 5 OCTOBER, BLACKPOOL. (SINEWS, 207.)

One would have thought that a man who had been only a burden to our war effort in the years of storm and the sort of thing we had to carry along on our shoulders—and who had received high office in the days of victory would have tried to turn over a new leaf and redeem his past....

We speak of the Minister of Health, but ought we not rather to say Minister of Disease, for is not morbid hatred a form of mental disease, and indeed a highly infectious form? Indeed, I can think of no better step to signalise the inauguration of the National Health Service than that a person who so obviously needs psychiatrical attention should be among the first of its patients.

...the odium of the words used by Mr. Bevan will lie upon the Socialist Government as a whole. We will not easily forget that we have been described as "lower than vermin" and in common with the 10 millions who voted Tory at the last election, and the 13 or 14 millions who are going to vote Tory at the next election, we will take whatever lawful and constitutional steps are possible to free ourselves from further ill-usage by highly-paid Ministers of the Crown.

1948, 10 JULY, WOODFORD GREEN, ESSEX. (UNITE, 370.)

I was giving the Rt. Hon. Gentleman an honourable mention for having, it appears by accident, perhaps not from the best motives, happened to be right.

1951, 6 DECEMBER.

I was, I think, the first in this House to suggest, in November 1949, recognition of the Chinese Communists....I thought it would be a good thing to have diplomatic representation. But if you recognise anyone it does not necessarily mean that you like him. We all, for instance, recognise the Rt. Hon. Gentleman, the Member for Ebbw Vale [Mr. Bevan].

1952, 1 JULY.

According to several sources, Churchill added an aside: "I recognise him as a fact!" For similar sentiments see "China...Recognising".

A great man, the founder of the National Health Service, a tremendous advocate for Socialism and his party...er, are you sure he's dead?

1960. (SIR JOHN COLVILLE TO THE EDITOR.)

When Churchill was informed of Nye Bevan's death.

Bevin, Ernest

It is incredible what follies Bevin has committed. No one but he could have managed to quarrel at the same time with Germans and French, with Russians and Americans, with Arabs and Jews.

1950, APRIL, CHARTWELL. (SOAMES, SPEAKING, 556.)

WSC to his wife. Ernest Bevin (1881–1951), Labour MP, Minister of Labour in the wartime coalition, Foreign Secretary in the post-war Labour Government. Churchill was always careful to accent the "vin" in his name to distinguish him from Nye Bevan. Ordinarily Churchill was an admirer of the Labour Foreign Minister, who served in his wartime coalition; this was quite a departure from the norm. See following entries.

...he takes his place among the great Foreign Secretaries of our country, [and,] in his steadfast resistance to Communist aggression, in his strengthening of our ties with the United States and in his share of building up the Atlantic Pact, he has rendered services to Britain and to the cause of peace which will long be remembered.

1951, 17 MARCH. BROADCAST, LONDON. (STEMMING, 29.)

Birkenhead, Lord

Just at the time when we feel that our public men are lacking in the power to dominate events, he has been taken. This was the occasion, and these were the very years, for the full fruition of his service to our country.

1930, 30 OCTOBER. (OB, CV5/2, 215.)

Frederick Edwin Smith, First Earl of Birkenhead (1872-1930), known as "F.E.", Conservative MP and lawyer, brilliant orator (many of his remarks have since been attached to Churchill), and WSC's best friend. These are WSC's remarks at the Other Club (which he and F.E. had founded in 1911) following Birkenhead's untimely death at the age of fifty-eight.

He had all the canine virtues in a remarkable degree—courage, fidelity, vigilance, love of the chase...

F.E. was the only one of my contemporaries from conversation with whom I have derived the same pleasure and profit as I got from Balfour, Morley, Asquith, Rosebery and Lloyd George. One did feel after a talk with these men that things were simpler and easier, and that Britain would be strong enough to come through all her troubles. He has gone, and gone when sorely needed. His record remains. It is not in every aspect a model for all to copy. Whose is? He seemed to have a double dose of human nature. He burned all his candles at both ends. His physique and constitution seemed to be capable of supporting indefinitely every form of mental and physical exertion. When they broke the end was swift. Between the setting of the sun and night there was only the briefest twilight. It was better so. Prolonged ill-health and deprivation of all the activities upon which his life was built would have pressed very hard upon him....

Some men when they die after busy, toilsome, successful lives leave a great stock of scrip and securities, of acres or factories or the goodwill of large undertakings. F.E. banked his treasure in the hearts of his friends, and they will cherish his memory till their time is come.

1936, 1 MARCH. ("BIRKENHEAD," NEWS OF THE WORLD; GC, 109, 116.)

Bismarck, Otto von

The great Bismarck—for there were once great men in Germany—is said to have observed towards the close of his life that the most potent factor in human society at the end of the nineteenth century was the fact that the British and American peoples spoke the same language.

1943, 6 SEPTEMBER. HARVARD UNIVERSITY.
(ONWARDS, 184.)

Otto Eduard Leopold, Prince Bismarck (1815–98), Prussian statesman, unifier of Germany.

Bonar Law, Andrew

The raw and rowdy Under-Secretary, whom the nakedness of the land, and the jealousies of his betters, have promoted to the leadership of the Tory Party...

1915. (THOMPSON, YANKEE, 180.)

Drafted but not used. Andrew Bonar Law (1858–1923), Conservative MP, Prime Minister 1922–23.

How is our ambitious invalid? What about our gilded tradesman?

1922. (CHISHOLM-DAVIE, 190.)

Prime Minister Andrew Bonar Law was ill.

You dance like a will-o'-the-wisp so nimbly from one unstable foothold to another that my plodding paces can scarcely follow you....The words which you now tell me you employed, and which purport to be a paraphrase, if not an actual quotation, are separated by a small degree of inaccuracy and misrepresentation from the inaccuracy and misrepresentation of the condensed report.

CIRCA 1922. (BEAVERBROOK, POLITICIANS
1914–1916, 32–3.)

Beaverbrook wrote:

Bonar Law always underrated Churchill's character – by which I mean the power of holding resolutely to those things in politics which one believes to be true. Both had entered the House of Commons at the same time, but they had never been intimate. Bonar Law got office before Churchill, but the latter would never

regard him as an equal, and always treated him in a patronising way up to the outbreak of war [WWI].

Bonham Carter, Lady Violet

In Lady Violet Bonham Carter we have not only a Liberal of unimpeachable loyalty to the Party, but one of the finest speakers in the country. Her speech against Socialism which was so widely read two months ago recalled the style of old and famous days.

1950, 28 JANUARY, WOODFORD GREEN, ESSEX.
(BALANCE, 162.)

Helen Violet Bonham Carter, Baroness Asquith of Yarnbury (1887–1969), daughter of Prime Minister H. H. Asquith and a lifelong friend of WSC.

Boothby, Robert

...[He] has been one of my personal friends, often a supporter at lonely and difficult moments, and I have always entertained a warm personal regard for him. If it is painful to us, it is also a loss to all. It is a loss to His Majesty's Government, who lose a highly competent and industrious Minister, one of the few of that generation who has attained advancement and who has discharged his tasks with admitted and recognised distinction.

1941, 28 JANUARY. (CS, 6341.)

Robert John Graham Boothby, Baron Boothby (1900–86), Conservative MP 1923–58, Parliamentary private secretary to Churchill, 1926–29. One of the few young Tories who supported WSC over disarmament, Boothby left the government when a select committee accused him of using his office in the Ministry of Food for financial gain. Churchill's public sympathy was not matched by his private feelings; see next entry.

[He should] join a bomb disposal squad as the best way of rehabilitating himself in the eyes of his fellow men. After all, the bombs might not go off.

1941, 31 JANUARY. (OLSON, 351; STUART, 90.)

Author Lynne Olson states that WSC never criticised "social equals" such as Birkenhead, Beaverbrook and the Duke of Westminster. But their peccadilloes were not committed as public officials. Churchill's standards of honesty were such that he reacted violently towards officials who fell short, including "social equals".

Bossom, Alfred

Bossom, Bossom, that's an odd name! Neither one thing nor the other.

UNDATED. (LORD MOUNTBATTEN TO THE EDMONTON CHURCHILL SOCIETY, 1966.)

WSC inquired the name of a speaker, and was told it was architect Alfred Bossom, Baron Bossom (1881–1965), a popular Conservative known for his lavish receptions.

Botha, Louis

As a matter of principle General Botha would be the last person to avail himself of the influence of a Member of Parliament in order to obtain for himself special terms which other Boers did not get.

1905, 26 MARCH. (CZARNOMSKI, 49.)

Louis Botha (1862–1919), South Africa soldier-statesman; first Prime Minister of Transvaal, 1907; first Prime Minister of the Union of South Africa, 1910–19. In his autobiography Churchill stated that he had been "a veritable saviour" of his country.

Bracken, Brendan

Mr. Bracken is a Member of Parliament of distinguished standing and exceptional ability. He has sometimes been almost my sole supporter in the years when I have been striving to get this country properly defended, especially from the air. He has suffered, as I have done, every form of official hostility. Had he joined the ranks of the time-servers and careerists who were assuring the public that our air force was larger than that of Germany, I have no doubt that he would long ago have attained high office.

1940, 2 JUNE. (LYSAGHT, 177.)

Brendan Bracken, First Viscount Bracken (1901–58), newspaper owner and editor, Irish-born Conservative MP 1929–51. An outspoken Churchill partisan, he nicknamed Baldwin "the iron-monger" and Chamberlain "the coroner". Minister of Information 1941–45. One of WSC's closest associates.

Tell me one thing only, Pat. How did he die?…Poor, dear Brendan.

1958, AUGUST, CAP D'AIL, FRANCE. (BOYLE, 349.)

WSC to a mutual friend after Bracken's death.

Brodrick, St. John

…if the capacity of a War Minister may be measured in any way by the amount of money he can obtain from his colleagues for military purposes, the Rt. Hon. Gentleman will most certainly go down to history as the greatest War Minister this country has ever had.

1901, 13 MAY.

William St. John Fremantle Brodrick, First Earl of Midleton (1856–1942), Conservative MP 1860–1907. Secretary of State for War 1901–03.

I had ever noticed that the Rt. Hon. Gentleman always made a very good speech when he was in a very difficult position: the more there was to be said against the cause he was defending, the better the speech he made.

1903, 24 FEBRUARY. (CZARNOMSKI, 57.)

Brooke, Rupert

Rupert Brooke is dead. A telegram from the Admiral at Lemnos tells us that this life has closed at the moment when it seemed to have reached its springtime. A voice had become audible, a note had been struck, more true, more thrilling, more able to do justice to the nobility of our youth in arms engaged in this present war, than any other—more able to express their thoughts of self-surrender, and with a power to carry comfort to those who watch them so intently from afar. The voice has been swiftly stilled. Only the echoes and the memory remain; but they will linger.

1915, 26 APRIL. ("RUPERT BROOKE," *THE TIMES*; ESSAYS III, 18.)

Rupert Chawner Brooke (1887–1915) a poet famous for his World War I sonnets, notably "The Soldier". Irish poet William Butler Yeats described him as "the handsomest young man in England".

Bryan, William Jennings

What Bryan has done is like an inebriate regulating a chronometer with a crowbar.

1896, 31 AUGUST. (OB, CV1 PART 1, 678.)

Churchill to Bourke Cockran (q.v.) William Jennings Bryan (1860–25), American politician, three-time Democratic nominee for President. Churchill, who viewed Bryan as a demagogue, was commenting on Bryan's proposal to inflate the currency through free silver.

Hugh Richard Heathcote Cecil, First Baron Quickswood (1869–1956), Conservative MP 1895–1906 and 1910–37, known as "Linky". The son of Prime Minister Lord Salisbury, he was an early ally of Winston and eponymous leader of the young Tory rebels known as the "Hughligans". Best Man at WSC's wedding.

Buller, General Sir Redvers

Buller was a characteristic British personality. He looked stolid. He said little, and what he said was obscure...Certainly he was a man of a considerable scale. He plodded on from blunder to blunder and from one disaster to another, without losing either the regard of his country or the trust of his troops, to whose feeding as well as his own he paid serious attention.

1930. (MEL, 248.)

General Sir Redvers Henry Buller (1839–1908), British general active in the Boer War.

Butler, R. A.

He is always patting himself on the back, a kind of exercise that no doubt contributes to his excellent condition.

1954, 1 DECEMBER.

Richard Austen Butler, Baron Butler of Saffron Walden (1902–82), Conservative MP, known as "Rab", Chancellor of the Exchequer 1951–55 and mooted, but twice passed over, for the Premiership.

Caesar, Julius

Julius Caesar gained far more by his clemency than by his prowess.

1952, 1 JULY. (CZARNOMSKI, 203.)

Gaius Julius Caesar (circa 100–44 BC), Roman military political leader and emperor, builder of the Roman Empire.

Cecil, Lord Hugh

Here for the first time, and I am afraid almost for the last, I met a real Tory, a being out of the seventeenth century, but equipped with every modern convenience and aptitude.

1931, FEBRUARY. ("PERSONAL CONTACTS," STRAND MAGAZINE; THOUGHTS, 35.)

Chamberlain, Austen

There was brilliancy in decay; the human body preyed on itself and gained feverish energy in the process of exhaustion. When expenditure increased waste increased. He did not make that as a special charge against this Government. It was true of all Governments.

1904, 16 MAY.

Sir Joseph Austen Chamberlain (1863–1937), son of Joseph Chamberlain and half-brother of Neville, Conservative MP 1902–37.

...he donned an orchid regardless of expense and screwed on an eyeglass regardless of discomfort.

1907, 18 MAY, EDINBURGH. (MORGAN, 191.)

Churchill was describing Chamberlain at the Colonial Conference in spring 1907; Austen affected an eyeglass in imitation of his famous father, Joseph Chamberlain. Like his father, Austen was a keen protectionist, which was anathema to WSC.

Eden's appointment [as Foreign Secretary] does not inspire me with confidence. I expect the greatness of his office will find him out. Austen would have been far better; and I wonder why he was overlooked. Poor man, he always plays the game and never wins it.

1935, 26 DECEMBER, RABAT, MOROCCO.
(OB, CV5 PART 2, 1363.)

WSC to his wife. But see also Chapter 18, 1938...Eden's resignation.

Chamberlain, Joseph

Mr. Chamberlain loves the working man, he loves to see him work!

1905, APRIL. (TAYLOR, 225, QUOTING HERBERT VIVIAN IN PALL MALL.)

Joseph Chamberlain (1836–1914), the great Conservative statesman, an early mentor to *young Churchill, split with WSC over Free Trade (he favoured protective tariffs); he was leader of Liberal Unionists in Parliament and the father of Austen and Neville Chamberlain.*

Sorry I am that he is out of the battle, not only on personal but on public grounds. His fiercest opponents would welcome his re-entry into the political arena, if only for the fact that we should then have a man to deal with and someone whose statement of the case for his side would be clear and bold, whose speeches would be worth reading and worth answering, instead of the melancholy marionettes whom the wire-pullers of the Tariff Reform League are accustomed to exhibit on provincial platforms.

1909, 29 JANUARY, NOTTINGHAM. (CS, 1105.)

He loved the roar of the multitude, and with my father could always say "I have never feared the English democracy." The blood mantled in his cheek, and his eye as it caught mine twinkled with pure enjoyment. I must explain that in those days we had a real political democracy led by a hierarchy of statesmen, and not a fluid mass distracted by newspapers.

1930. (MEL, 372.)

I have many vivid memories of the famous "Joe." He was always very good to me....At the time when I looked out of my regimental cradle and was thrilled by politics, Mr. Chamberlain was incomparably the most live, sparkling, insurgent, compulsive figure in British affairs.

**1930, FEBRUARY. ("CHAMBERLAIN,"
PALL MALL; GC, 43.)**

Chamberlain, Neville

When we have the Prime Minister here, what is the good of worrying about the Foreign Secretary? What is the point in crying out for the moon when you have the sun, when you have the bright orb of day in whose refulgent beams all the lesser luminaries hide their radiance?

1938, FEBRUARY. (BROAD, 255.)

Arthur Neville Chamberlain (1869–1940), Prime Minister 1937–40. WSC was remarking on the appointment of Lord Halifax as Foreign Secretary. A number of MPs had protested at the appointment because Halifax was in the House of Lords. Churchill's dripping sarcasm

towards Chamberlain ("the bright orb of day in whose refulgent beams...") was as cutting as it was amusing.

Has [N.C.] ever heard of Saint Anthony the Hermit? Saint Anthony the Hermit was much condemned by the Fathers of the Church because he refused to do right when the Devil told him to. My Rt. Hon. Friend should free himself from this irrational inhibition, for we are only at the beginning of our anxieties.

1938, 25 MAY.

Speaking on the advent of Chamberlain's ministry on 1 June 1937, Churchill had said,

> I cannot go so far as to call it a paternal interest, because, speaking candidly, it is not quite the sort of Government I should have bred myself. If it is not paternal, at any rate I think I may call it an avuncular interest.

A good word stayed in his mind...

Chamberlain is a Birmingham town councillor who looks at our national affairs through the wrong end of a municipal drainpipe.

CIRCA 1938. (KING, MALICE, 112.)

According to Cecil King's Memoirs, Churchill said this to Byron, Commons lobby correspondent of the Daily Mirror.

In the depths of that dusty soul there is nothing but abject surrender.

CIRCA 1938. (RHODES JAMES, 338.)

It doesn't matter where you put it [the podium], as long as he has the sun in his eyes and the wind in his teeth.

**1939. DRUMLANRAIG, SCOTLAND.
(GILBERT, SEARCH, 23.)**

Churchill to his long-time friend Molly, Duchess of Buccleuch, who informed him that Chamberlain was coming to address the local Conservatives. Her actual quote was "shun in hish eyesh...."

The fierce and bitter controversies which hung around him in recent times were hushed by the news of his illness and are silenced by his death. In paying a tribute of respect and of regard to an eminent man who has been taken from us, no one is obliged to alter the opinions which he has formed or expressed upon issues which have become a part of history; but at the Lychgate we may all pass our own conduct and our own judgments under a searching review....

History with its flickering lamp stumbles along the trail of the past, trying to reconstruct its scenes, to revive its echoes, and kindle with pale gleams the passion of former days. What is the worth of all this? The only guide to a man is his conscience; the only shield to his memory is the rectitude and sincerity of his actions...

It fell to Neville Chamberlain in one of the supreme crises of the world to be contradicted by events, to be disappointed in his hopes, and to be deceived and cheated by a wicked man. But what were these hopes in which he was frustrated? What was that faith that was abused? They were surely among the most noble and benevolent instincts of the human heart—the love of peace, the toil for peace, the strife for peace, the pursuit of peace, even at great peril, and certainly to the utter disdain of popularity or clamour. Whatever else history may or may not say about these terrible, tremendous years, we can be sure that Neville Chamberlain acted with perfect sincerity according to his lights and strove to the utmost of his capacity and authority, which were powerful, to save the world from the awful, devastating struggle in which we are now engaged....

When, contrary to all his hopes, beliefs and exertions, the war came upon him, and when, as he himself said, all that he had worked for was shattered, there was no man more resolved to pursue the unsought quarrel to the death. The same qualities which made him one of the last to enter the war, made him one of the last who would quit it before the full victory of a righteous cause was won....

He was, like his father and his brother Austen before him, a famous Member of the House of Commons, and we here assembled this morning, Members of all parties, without a single exception, feel that we do ourselves and our country honour in saluting the memory of one whom Disraeli would have called an "English worthy."

1940, 12 NOVEMBER.

Because of its beautiful magnanimity, I have quoted these remarks at length from WSC's tribute following the death of Chamberlain. The phrase "English worthy" was beloved of Churchill, who first used it in his 1906 biography of his father, attributing it to Benjamin Disraeli.

Well, of course I could have done it the other way round.

1940, 11 NOVEMBER. (GILBERT, LIFE, 683.)

After secretary Kathleen Hill had complimented WSC on his tribute to Neville Chamberlain in the House of Commons. Kathleen Hill to Sir Martin Gilbert, 1982.

...that was not an insuperable task, since I admired many of Neville's great qualities. But I pray to God in his infinite mercy that I shall not have to deliver a similar oration on Baldwin. That indeed would be difficult to do.

1940, 22 NOVEMBER. (NICOLSON II, 129.)

After being complimented on his tribute to Chamberlain. Churchill was far more censorious towards Baldwin. See People...Baldwin.

[He] was alert, business-like, opinionated and self-confident in a very high degree. Unlike Baldwin, he conceived himself able to comprehend the whole field of Europe, and indeed the world. Instead of a vague but none the less deep-seated intuition, we had now a narrow, sharp-edged efficiency within the limits of the policy in which he believed....His all-pervading hope was to go down to history as the great Peacemaker, and for this he was prepared to strive continually in the teeth of facts, and face great risks for himself and his country....I should have found it easier to work with Baldwin, as I knew him, than with Chamberlain; but neither of them had any wish to work with me except in the last resort.

1948. (WW2 I, 173–4.)

Chaplin, Charlie

He is a marvellous comedian—bolshy in politics and delightful in conversation.

1929, 29 SEPTEMBER, BARSTOW, CALIFORNIA.

(OB, CV5/2, 97.)

WSC to his wife. Sir Charles Spencer Chaplin (1889–1977), English comedy actor and Hollywood film star. Although it was a common expression that he may have used in conversation, this is the only instance of "bolshy" (from "Bolshevik") in the canon.

It is Mr Chaplin's dream to play tragic roles as well as comic ones. The man whose glorious fooling made Shoulder Arms a favourite with war-weary veterans of the trenches wants to re-interpret Napoleon to the world. There are other characters, as far removed from those in which he won pre-eminence, which he desires to portray.

Those who smile at these ambitions have not appreciated Chaplin's genius at its true worth. No mere clown, however brilliant, could ever have captured so completely the affections of the great public. He owes his unrivalled position as a star to the fact that he is a great actor, who can tug at our heartstrings as surely as he compels our laughter. There are moments, in some of his films, of an almost unbearable poignancy.

1935, 26 OCTOBER. ("EVERYBODY'S LANGUAGE," COLLIER'S; ESSAYS III, 249.)

Churchill, Lady Randolph

I wish you could have seen her as she lay at rest—after all the sunshine and storm of life was over. Very beautiful and splendid she looked. Since the morning with its pangs, thirty years had fallen from her brow.

She recalled to me the countenance I had admired as a child when she was in her heyday and the old brilliant world of the eighties and nineties seemed to come back.

1921, 1 JULY. (OB, CV4 PART 3, 1532.)

WSC's mother (1854–1921) was the former Jennie Jerome; she married Lord Randolph Churchill in early 1874. WSC to Anne, Lady Islington, on the death of his mother.

My mother made the same brilliant impression upon my childhood's eye. She shone for me like the Evening Star. I loved her dearly—but at a distance. [In advancing my career she] cooperated energetically from her end. In my interest she left no wire unpulled, no stone unturned, no cutlet uncooked.

1930. (MEL, 19, 167.)

Churchill, Lord Randolph

Like Disraeli, he had to fight every mile in all his marches.

1906. (LRC, XII.)

In his speeches he revealed a range of thought, an authority of manner, and a wealth of knowledge, which neither friends nor foes attempted to dispute.

1906. (LRC, 145.)

WSC's father (1849–95) was Leader of the House of Commons and rose to be Chancellor of the Exchequer, but resigned over a trivial matter at the end of 1886 and did not rise again. He died aged only forty-six, most likely of a brain tumour.

My father died on January 24 [1895] in the early morning. Summoned from a neighbouring house where I was sleeping, I ran in the darkness across Grosvenor Square, then lapped in snow. His end was quite painless. Indeed he had long been in stupor. All my dreams of comradeship with him, of entering Parliament at his side and in his support, were ended. There remained for me only to pursue his aims and vindicate his memory.

1930. (MEL, 76.)

Although I had talked with him so seldom and never for a moment on equal terms, I conceived an intense admiration and affection for him and, after his early death, for his memory. I read industriously almost every word he had ever spoken and learnt by heart large portions of his speeches. I took my politics almost unquestioningly from him. He seemed to me to have possessed in the days of his prime the key alike to popular oratory and political action. Although Lord Randolph Churchill lived and died a loyal Tory, he was in fact during the whole of his political life, and especially during its finest phase after he had left office for ever, a liberal-minded man. He saw no reason why the old glories of Church and State, or King and Country, should not be reconciled with modern democracy; or why the masses of working people should not become the chief defenders of those ancient institutions by which their liberties and progress had been achieved.

1931, FEBRUARY. ("PERSONAL CONTACTS," STRAND MAGAZINE; THOUGHTS, 31–2.)

But for a year I looked at life round a corner. They made a joke about it in those days at the Carlton Club. "I hear Randolph's son met with a serious accident." "Yes? Playing a game of 'Follow my Leader.'" "Well, Randolph is not likely to come to grief in that way!"

1930. (MEL, 44–5.)

In 1888, after he had fallen from a tree at Bournemouth and ruptured his kidney, his father, Lord Randolph Churchill, brought a surgeon to Winston's side.

I remember [that my father said] a man who can't take a knockdown blow isn't worth a damn.

1949, 25 MARCH, NEW YORK. (BALANCE, 33.)

Churchill, Sir Winston (the first)

...a curious fact is that in his administration of his duties he got into the bad books of the Duke of York [over a grant] which the Duke of York had been given of the Irish estates of the regicides. The Duke's rascally agents, "the worst under-instruments he could well light on," as the Lord-Lieutenant Ormonde described them, made claim after claim on the basis of this grant, and effectively prevented the commissioners from dealing with the cases of the poor and deserving. One summer's morning Sir Winston Churchill lost his temper with the Duke's agents, calling them "a pack of knaves and cheats that daily betrayed their master."

1933. (MARLBOROUGH I, 47–8.)

One of the several "curious facts" in Churchill's canon, this one is an interesting precursor to the second Sir Winston's own early radical ideas towards the poor and deserving. The first Sir Winston Churchill (1620–88), author of Divi Britannici *[being a Remark upon the Lives of all the Kings of this Isle], was the father of the First Duke of Marlborough. The Duke of York was the future King James II and VII, younger brother and successor of Charles II.*

Churchill, Winston (American novelist)

Mr. Winston Churchill presents his compliments to Mr. Winston Churchill, and begs to draw his attention to a matter which concerns them both....He has no doubt that Mr. Winston Churchill will recognise from this letter—if indeed by no other means—that there is grave danger of his works being mistaken for those of Mr. Winston Churchill. He feels sure that Mr. Winston Churchill desires this as little as he does himself. In future to avoid mistakes as far as possible, Mr. Winston Churchill has decided to sign all published articles, stories, or other work "Winston Spencer Churchill" and not "Winston Churchill" as formerly....He takes this occasion of complimenting Mr. Winston Churchill upon the style and success of his works, which are always brought to his notice whether in magazine or book form, and he trusts that Mr. Winston Churchill has derived equal pleasure from any work of his that may have attracted his attention.

1899, 7 JUNE, LONDON. (MEL, 231–2.)

Winston Churchill the novelist (1871–1947) replied:

Mr. Winston Churchill is extremely grateful to Mr. Winston Churchill for bringing forward a subject which has given Mr. Winston Churchill much anxiety. Mr. Winston Churchill appreciates the courtesy of Mr. Winston Churchill in adopting the name of "Winston Spencer Churchill" in his books, articles, etc. Mr. Winston Churchill makes haste to add that, had he possessed any other names, he would certainly have adopted one of them....Mr. Winston Churchill will take the liberty of sending Mr. Winston Churchill copies of the two novels he has written. He has a high admiration for the works of Mr. Winston Spencer Churchill and is looking forward with pleasure to reading Savrola.

The two Churchills met in Boston during English Winston's lecture tour in 1901, where the American threw a dinner for him. Great camaraderie prevailed and both agreed there would be no more confusion, but the English Churchill got the bill! American Winston published numerous popular novels including Richard Carvel, The Crisis, The Inside of the Cup, A Modern Chronicle, A Far Country, The Crossing, Coniston, The Title-Mart, The Celebrity, Mr. Crewe's Career, *and a single non-fiction work,* A Traveller in Wartime. Winston Spencer Churchill published only one novel, Savrola.

Why don't you go into politics? I mean to be Prime Minister of England: it would be a great lark if you were President of the United States at the same time.

1900, 17 DECEMBER, BOSTON. (OB I, 353.)

WSC to WC. Related to Randolph Churchill by Mrs. John Churchill, daughter-in-law of the American novelist, who did win election to the New Hampshire Legislature (1903, 1905) but rose no higher, being defeated in a run for Governor on the Bull Moose ticket in 1912. He did live long enough to see the other Winston as Prime Minister.

When a year later I visited Boston, Mr. Winston Churchill was the first to welcome me. He entertained me at a very gay banquet of young men, and we made each other complimentary speeches. Some confusion, however, persisted; all my mails were sent to his address and the bill for the dinner came in to me. I need not say that both these errors were speedily redressed.

1930. (MEL, 233.)

Clemenceau, Georges

The truth is that Clemenceau embodied and expressed France. As much as any single human being, miraculously magnified, can ever be a nation, he was France. Fancy paints nations in symbolic animals—the British Lion, the American Eagle, the Russian double-headed ditto, the Gallic Cock. But the Old Tiger, with his quaint, stylish cap, his white moustache and burning eye, would make a truer mascot for France than any barnyard fowl.

1930, DECEMBER. ("CLEMENCEAU – THE MAN AND THE TIGER," STRAND MAGAZINE; GC, 192.)

Georges Clemenceau (1841–1929), known as "The Tiger" from his aggressive politics in the French Chamber, French Prime Minister, 1906–09, 1917–20. Churchill heard Clemenceau declare,

No more pacifist campaigns, no more German intrigues, neither treason nor half treason – war, nothing but war.

This recollection is from 20 November 1917 in Paris.

The Clemenceau of the Peace was a great statesman. He was confronted with enormous difficulties. He made for France the best bargain that the Allies, who were also the world, would tolerate. France was disappointed; Foch was disappointed, and also offended by personal frictions. Clemenceau, unrepentant to the end, continued to bay at the Church. The Presidency passed to an amiable nonentity [Paul Deschanel], who soon tumbled out of a railway carriage.

1930, DECEMBER. (OP. CIT., 198–9.)

Clemenceau might be said to have been a French Churchill; like WSC, he was dismissed from the affairs of his country after saving it from disaster.

Cockran, Bourke

I must record the strong impression which this remarkable man made upon my untutored mind [WSC was then twenty-one]. I have never seen his like, or in some respects his equal. With his enormous head, gleaming eyes and flexible countenance, he looked uncommonly like the portraits of Charles James Fox. It was not my fortune to hear any of his orations, but his conversation, in point, in pitch, in rotundity, in antithesis, and in comprehension, exceeded anything I have ever heard.

1931, FEBRUARY. ("PERSONAL CONTACTS," STRAND MAGAZINE; THOUGHTS, 32.)

William Bourke Cockran (1854–1923), born in Ireland, emigrated 1871, New York congressman 1887–1921. His influence on young Winston between 1895 and 1905 replaced and probably surpassed that of WSC's father. (McMenamin and Zoller, passim.)

Cockran by that "frequent recurrence to first principles" which the American Constitution enjoins had evolved a complete scheme of political thought which enabled him to present a sincere and effective front in every direction according to changing circumstances. He was pacifist, individualist, democrat, capitalist, and a "Gold-bug." Above all he was a Free-Trader and repeatedly declared that this was the underlying doctrine by which all the others were united. Thus he was equally opposed to socialists, inflationists and protectionists, and he resisted them on all occasions. In consequence there was in his life no lack of fighting. Nor would there have been had he lived longer.

1931, FEBRUARY. ("PERSONAL CONTACTS," STRAND MAGAZINE; THOUGHTS, 33.)

In this passage Churchill could have been describing himself, except that Cockran died in his early sixties. This certainly shows the degree of Cockran's influence over WSC's political philosophy.

Bourke Cockran…taught me to use every note of the human voice as if playing an organ. He could play on every emotion and hold thousands of people riveted in great political rallies when he spoke.

1955. (GILBERT, SEARCH, 279.)

WSC to Adlai Stevenson, quoted in 1965 by Anita Leslie. Martin Gilbert adds:

WSC [had quoted to Stevenson] many long passages from Cockran's speeches. Adlai Stevenson told the assembled guests that he hoped he had managed to impress on them two things: "Churchill's astounding memory, and the fact that he was always eager to attribute any of his own development or prowess or talent to America". The next evening, while walking in a London street, Stevenson had a heart attack and died.

Collins, Michael

…though I must admit that deep in my heart there was a certain gulf between us—we never to the best of my belief lost the basis of a common understanding.

Michael Collins acted up to his word in his relations with the British Government. The strains and stresses upon him at times were unimaginable. Threatened always with death from those whose methods he knew only too well, reproached by darkly sworn confederates with treason and perjury, the object of a dozen murder conspiracies, harassed to the depth of his nature by the poignant choices which thrust themselves upon him, swayed by

his own impulsive temperament, nevertheless he held strictly to his engagements with the Ministers of a Government he had so long hated but at last learned to trust. He was determined that the Irish name should not be dishonoured by the breach of the Treaty made in all good faith and goodwill.

1924, JANUARY. ("THE IRISH TREATY," PALL MALL; THOUGHTS, 162.)

Michael John ("Mick") Collins (1890–1922), Minister for Finance in the Irish Republic, IRA Director of Intelligence, commander in chief of the national army. He was part of the delegation that negotiated the Anglo-Irish Treaty in 1921, largely because of which he was assassinated in 1922. See also Chapter 33…Dead or Alive.

Coolidge, Calvin

I rest myself on President Coolidge's remarks that the less America takes from France the more that would leave for us.

1925, 2 JANUARY. (OB CV5 PART 1, 329.)

WSC to Sir Otto Niemeyer. John Calvin Coolidge, Jr. (1874–1933), 30th President of the United States (1923–29).

The basis of [the reparations agreement] was considered, not only in this Island, but by many disinterested financial authorities in America, to be a severe and improvident condition for both borrower and lender. "They hired the money, didn't they?" said President Coolidge. This laconic statement was true, but not exhaustive….

1948. (WW2 I, 20.)

Cripps, Stafford

He is a lunatic in a country of lunatics, and it would be a pity to move him.

1940, DECEMBER. (COLVILLE, FRINGES I, 368.)

The Hon. Sir Richard Stafford Cripps (1889–1952), Labour MP, Chancellor of the Exchequer in the post-war Labour Government. In the wartime coalition he was Ambassador to Russia, Minister of Aircraft Production and the leader of a conciliatory mission to India. Colville had suggested that Cripps "was being wasted in Russia".

It is perhaps as well that I was not accompanied by my colleague, the Minister of Aircraft Production...for there is a man who habitually takes his meal off a handful of peas, and, when he gets a handful of beans, counts that his Christmas feast!

1943, 19 MAY, WASHINGTON. ("CHURCHILL THE CONVERSATIONALIST," COLIN BROOKS IN EADE, 247.)

Sir Stafford Cripps is under the profound delusion that he can build up an immense, profitable export trade while keeping everything at the minimum here at home. Look what he is doing to the motor car industry. It is astonishing so clever a lawyer should not have got his case up better. He is a great advocate of "Strength through Misery." He tried this theme on the public when he entered the Government in February, 1942. I did not like it. I preferred "Strength through Victory," and that is what we got. And that is what we have got to get now.

1945, 28 NOVEMBER.

Neither of his colleagues can compare with him in that acuteness and energy of mind with which he devotes himself to so many topics injurious to the strength and welfare of the State.

1946, 12 DECEMBER.

Sir Stafford Cripps is an able and upright man, tortured and obsessed by his Socialist tenets.

1947, 16 MAY, AYR. (UNITE, 96.)

Stafford Cripps was a man of force and fire. His intellectual and moral passions were so strong that they not only inspired but not seldom dominated his actions. They were strengthened and also governed by the working of a powerful, lucid intelligence and by a deep and lively Christian faith. He strode through life with a remarkable indifference to material satisfaction or worldly advantages.

1952, 23 APRIL.

As almost always with Churchill, his final tribute to a political foe was warm and generous.

Cromwell, Oliver

The central point in my memory [of Dublin] is a tall white stone tower which we reached after a considerable drive. I was told it had been blown up by Oliver Cromwell. I understood definitely that he had blown up all sorts of things and was therefore a very great man.

1930. (MEL, 16.)

Oliver Cromwell (1599–1658) was Lord Protector of Republican England from 1653 until his death.

Crossman, R. H. S.

The Hon. Member is never lucky in the coincidence of his facts with the truth.

1954, 14 JULY. (CZARNOMSKI, 89.)

Richard Howard Stafford Crossman (1907–74), Labour MP and editor of the New Statesman.

Curzon, George

He was at twenty-one notorious as "The Coming Man."

The word "notorious" is used advisedly, for with all this early glitter there mingled an innocent but none the less serious tarnish. His facility carried him with a bound into prolixity; his ceremonious diction wore the aspect of pomposity; his wide knowledge was accused of superficiality....[Curzon's] reverses were supported after the initial shocks with goodwill and dignity. But undoubtedly they invested the long and strenuous career with ultimate disappointment. The morning had been golden; the noontide was bronze; and the evening lead. But all were solid, and each was polished till it shone after its fashion.

1929, JANUARY. ("GEORGE CURZON," PALL MALL; GC, 174, 184.)

The Hon. George Nathaniel Curzon, First Marquess Curzon of Kedleston KG GCSI GCIE PC (1859–1925), Viceroy of India and Conservative Foreign Secretary.

Czar Nicholas II

He had made many mistakes, what ruler had not?....At the summit where all problems are reduced to Yea or Nay, where events transcend the faculties of men and where all is inscrutable, he had to give the answers. His was the function of the compass-needle. War or no war? Advance or retreat? Right or left? Democratize or hold firm? Quit or persevere?

These were the battlefields of Nicholas II. Why should he reap no honour from them?....He is about to be struck down. A dark hand, gloved at first in folly, now intervenes. Exit Czar. Deliver him and all he loved to wounds and death. Belittle his efforts, asperse his conduct, insult his memory; but pause then to tell us who else was found capable.

1927. (CRISIS III PART 1, 224–5.)

Nicholas Alexsandrovich Romanov (1868–1918), last Emperor of Russia, abdicated 1917, killed with his entire family by the Bolsheviks in 1918. Churchill's magnanimity here blends with his dogged faith in monarchies far more absolute than his own. Yet, as he said, what replaced the fallen empires of World War I were things far worse.

Dalton, Hugh

The Hon. Gentleman is trying to win distinction by rudeness.

1926, 10 MAY.

Edward Hugh John Neale Dalton, Baron Dalton (1887–1962), Labour MP, 1922–51, Chancellor of the Exchequer, 1945–47. During the General Strike, Dalton had criticised Churchill's British Gazette for not publishing an appeal for a peaceful settlement. His father was a major figure in the Church of England; Queen Victoria referred to Hugh as "Canon Dalton's horrid little boy".

Dr. Dalton, the practitioner who never cured anyone, in his "rake's progress" at the Exchequer, spent in his Budgets for three years over £10,000,000,000.

1948, 14 FEBRUARY. BROADCAST, LONDON. (UNITE, 242.)

Darlan, François

I hold no brief for Admiral Darlan. Like myself he is the object of the animosities of Herr Hitler and of Monsieur Laval. Otherwise I have nothing in common with him....The Government and to a large extent the people of the United States do not feel the same about Darlan as we do. He has not betrayed them. He has not broken any treaty with them. He has not vilified them. He has not maltreated any of their citizens. They do not think much of him, but they do not hate him and despise him as

we do over here. Many of them think more of the lives of their own soldiers than they do about the past records of French political figures.

1942, 10 DECEMBER. (SECRET, 79–80.)

François Darlan (1881–1942), French Naval officer, Admiral of the Fleet in Vichy France, professed support for the Allies but tended to play both sides against the middle.

de Gaulle, Charles

L'homme du destin.

1940, 13 JUNE, TOURS. (OB VI, 535.)

Charles André Joseph Marie de Gaulle (1890–1970), French general, Free French leader in WWII, President of the Fifth Republic (1958–69). WSC said this ("Man of destiny") to de Gaulle while visiting the expiring French government, which had fled from Paris.

I am no more enamoured of him than you are but I would rather have him on the committee than strutting about as a combination Joan of Arc and Clemenceau.

1943, 10 JANUARY, CASABLANCA. (HALLE, IRREPRESSIBLE, 212.)

Roosevelt said he did not know what to do about de Gaulle.

Look here! I am the leader of a strong, unbeaten nation. Yet every morning when I wake my first thought is how can I please President Roosevelt, and my second thought is how can I conciliate Marshal Stalin. Your situation is very different. Why then should your first waking thought be how you can snap your fingers at the British and Americans?

1943, JANUARY, CASABLANCA. (OB VII, 646.)

Comic relief has been afforded by the attempt to bring de Gaulle to the altar where Giraud has been waiting impatiently for several days! [De Gaulle] thinks he is Clemenceau (having dropped Joan of Arc for the time being), and wishes Giraud to be Foch, i.e., dismissible at Prime Minister Clemenceau's pleasure! Many of these Frenchmen hate each other far more than they do the Germans, and all I have met care more for power and place than for the liberation of their country. When a country undergoes so frightful a catastrophe as France, every other evil swarms down upon her like carrion crows.

1943, 24 JANUARY, CASABLANCA. (SOAMES, SPEAKING, 475.)

Roosevelt and Churchill were trying to bring the two French generals together, to unite in a single Free French opposition to Vichy. See also People...Giraud.

I brought him up from a pup, but I never got him properly trained to the house!

1943, MAY. (OTTAWA; BIRKENHEAD, HALIFAX, 537.)

Greatest living barrier to reunion and restoration of France: insensate ambition.

1943, JUNE. (DIARIES OF CABINET SECRETARY SIR NORMAN BROOK, *NEW YORK TIMES*, 22 JANUARY 2006.)

...I have had many differences with General de Gaulle, but I have never forgotten, and can never forget, that he stood forth as the first eminent Frenchman to face the common foe in what seemed to be the hour of ruin of his country, and possibly of ours; and it is only fair and becoming that he should stand first and foremost in the days when France shall again be raised, and raise herself, to her rightful place among the great Powers of Europe and of the world.

1944, 2 AUGUST.

I preserved the impression, in contact with this very tall, phlegmatic man: "Here is the Constable of France." He returned that afternoon [16 June 1940] in a British aeroplane, which I had placed at his disposal, to Bordeaux. But not for long.... [On the 17th he] drove to the airfield with his friend Spears to see him off. They shook hands and said good-bye, and as the plane began to move de Gaulle stepped in and slammed the door. The machine soared off into the air, while the French police and officials gaped. De Gaulle carried with him, in this small aeroplane, the honour of France.

1949. (WW2 II, 189, 192.)

I understood and admired, while I resented his arrogant demeanour. Here he was—a refugee, an exile from his country under sentence of death, in a position entirely dependent upon the goodwill of the British government, and

also now of the United States. The Germans had conquered his country. He had no real foothold anywhere. Never mind; he defied all. Always, even when he was behaving worst, he seemed to express the personality of France— a great nation, with all its pride, authority and ambition.

1950. (WW2 IV, 611.)

de Valera, Eamon

Mr. de Valera, oblivious to the claims of conquered peoples, has also given his croak in this sense. No sooner had he clambered from the arena into the Imperial box, than he hastened to turn his thumb down upon the first prostrate gladiator he saw.

1938, 4 FEBRUARY. ("THE DUSK OF THE LEAGUE," *DAILY TELEGRAPH*; STEP, 198.)

Eamon de Valera (1882–1975). Served Ireland as President and Premier, among other offices, between 1917 and 1973. Determinedly anti-British, in 1938 he was urging recognition of the Italian Conquest of Abyssinia. See also Nations...Ireland.

de Wiart, Carton

... another Italian general [has] arrived, bringing with him as his credentials no less a person than General Carton de Wiart VC, one of our most famous military figures, whom the Italians captured two years ago through a forced landing in the Mediterranean. This second mission, however, did not affect the general course of events, and when General de Wiart realized this he immediately offered to return to captivity. The Italian officer, however, rejected this proposal and General Carton de Wiart is now safe and free in this country.

1943, 21 SEPTEMBER.

Adrian Carton de Wiart (1880–1963), British officer renowned for his bravery and escapades, with black eye-patch and an empty sleeve, exactly the type who appealed to WSC. The Italian general, Zanussi, had brought him to Lisbon as an interpreter, hoping to arrange terms for Italy's surrender. De Wiart insisted he provide English clothes, refusing to wear "one of their bloody gigolo suits".

Disraeli, Benjamin

The Primrose League was founded to keep green the memory of a great and wise nineteenth-century statesman, and to uphold the ideals and principles that he enunciated. Those principles have an abiding validity. They have stood the test of time and of experiences unimaginable in those tranquil Victorian times. The speeches and writings of Disraeli are a mine of political sagacity. He loved his country with a romantic passion. He had a profound faith in the greatness of the English character, and a burning desire to bring about an improvement in the condition of the people.

1944, 31 DECEMBER. LONDON. MESSAGE TO THE PRIMROSE LEAGUE. (DAWN, 326.)

Benjamin Disraeli, First Earl of Beaconsfield (1804–81), Conservative MP, Prime Minister 1868, 1874–80. The Tory support organization, the Primrose League, was named for the primrose he wore in his buttonhole.

Dulles, John Foster

I will have no more to do with Dulles, whose great slab of a face I dislike and distrust.

1953, 7 JANUARY. (COLVILLE, FRINGES II, 320.)

Reconstructed from Colville's third-person rendition in his diaries. John Foster Dulles (1888–1959), US Secretary of State under Eisenhower 1953–59, took a hard line against new approaches to the Russians advocated by Churchill. Colville added to this note:

W. was really worked up and, as he went to bed, said some very harsh things about the Republican Party in general and Dulles in particular, which Christopher [Soames] and I thought both unjust and dangerous.

Dulles is a terrible influence. Ike now wants to postpone the conference for a fortnight to give the French a chance to settle down after the election. And every day it's getting hotter in Bermuda.

1953, 16 JUNE. (MORAN, 433.)

In the event, the Bermuda summit was postponed until December following Churchill's stroke a week later.

This fellow preaches like a Methodist Minister, and his bloody text is always the same: That nothing but evil can come out of meeting with Malenkov. Dulles is a terrible handicap. Ten years ago I could have dealt with him. Even as it is I have not been defeated by this bastard. I have been humiliated by my own decay. Ah, no, Charles, you have done all that could be done to slow things down.

1953, 7 DECEMBER, BERMUDA. (MORAN, 540–41.)

Moran added: "When I turned round he was in tears. That was the last I heard of Moscow [Churchill's desire for a summit with the Russians]." Georgy Maximillianovich Malenkov (1902–88), Soviet politician, Premier of the Soviet Union 1953–55.

He is the only case of a bull I know who carries his china closet with him.

1954, 24 JUNE, WASHINGTON. (HALLE, IRREPRESSIBLE, 325.)

Not positively verified, and misquoted by Manchester I, 34. Represented only as "ear witness" by Kay Halle. WSC last visited Dulles when the latter was dying of cancer in May 1959, as a characteristically generous gesture; but his thoughts on that occasion are unrecorded.

Eden, Anthony

I venture to suggest to my Hon. Friend, in whose career the whole House has a common interest, because we do like to see new figures emerge, to be careful not to be too obliging in his departmental duties and not to be too ready to do what is asked of him on all occasions, because he is very valuable, and we all hope that he will be associated with real success in the domain of foreign affairs.

1934, 14 MARCH.

Robert Anthony Eden (1897–1977), First Earl of Avon, Conservative MP and thrice Foreign Secretary between 1935 and 1955; Prime Minister, 1955–57. Considered WSC's heir-apparent from the mid-1940s. Politically ruined following the 1956 Suez Crisis. See also Chapter 23...Suez.

[He] is the one fresh figure of the first magnitude arising out of a generation which was ravaged by the war.

1938, FEBRUARY. (RHODES JAMES, 289.)

He has to conceal what he would most wish to make public, and make public what he would most wish to conceal.

1941, 6 JUNE. (EDEN, 251.)

Churchill was remarking that his Foreign Minister was not free to be perfectly frank in all matters.

Here is the moment when the House should pay its tribute to the work of my Rt. Hon. Friend the Foreign Secretary. I cannot describe to the House the aid and comfort he has been to me in all our difficulties. His hard life when quite young in the infantry in the last war, his constant self-preparation for the tasks which have fallen to him, his unequalled experience as a minister at the Foreign Office, his knowledge of foreign affairs and their past history, his experience of conferences of all kinds, his breadth of view, his powers of exposition, his moral courage, have gained for him a position second to none among the Foreign Secretaries of the Grand Alliance. It is not only my own personal debt, but even more that of the House to him, which I now acknowledge.

1945, 27 FEBRUARY.

Come in, come in; that is if you can bear to see me in a gold bath when you only have a silver one.

1945, 11 NOVEMBER, PARIS. (EDEN, 494.)

At the French Foreign Office, Churchill was ensconced in a suite whose bathroom had gold fixtures, previously installed by Field Marshal Goering. Eden, bearing a telegram, was greeted at his door with this remark.

I don't believe Anthony can do it.

1955, 4 APRIL. DOWNING STREET. (COLVILLE, CHURCHILLIANS, 171.)

WSC to John Colville over Eden as Prime Minister, following WSC's retirement dinner. This premonition proved correct less than two years later.

Eisenhower, Dwight D.

...General Eisenhower assumed the command of the Expeditionary Force gathered in Britain. No man has ever laboured more skilfully or intensely for the unification and goodwill of the great forces under his command than General Eisenhower. He has a genius for bringing all the Allies together, and is proud to consider himself an allied as well as a United States commander.

1944, 2 AUGUST.

Dwight David Eisenhower (1890–1969), 34th President of the United States (1953–61), Supreme Commander, Allied Expeditionary Force, 1944–45.

In him we have had a man who set the unity of the Allied Armies above all nationalistic thoughts. In his headquarters unity and strategy were the only reigning spirits. The unity reached such a point that British and American troops could be mixed in the line of battle, and that large masses could be transferred from one command to the other without the slightest difficulty. At no time has the principle of alliance between noble races been carried and maintained at so high a pitch. In the name of the British Empire and Commonwealth, I express to you our admiration of the firm, far-sighted, and illuminating character and qualities of General of the Army Eisenhower.

1945, 10 MAY. VICTORY, 173.

WSC to President Truman after Victory in Europe.

For your private ear, I am greatly disturbed. I think this makes war much more probable.

1952, 9 NOVEMBER. (COLVILLE, FRINGES II, 131.)

WSC to John Colville following the election of Eisenhower as President of the United States. Colville added that Churchill thought of Eisenhower as "violently Russophobe".

When I had a chance to speak to the President he told me he did not need converting. We ought not to pay any more attention to McCarthy than they did to Aneurin Bevan. I cannot make it out. I am bewildered. It seems that everything is left to Dulles. It appears that the President is no more than a ventriloquist's doll.

1953, 7 DECEMBER, BERMUDA. (MORAN, 540.)

The most damning thing WSC said about Eisenhower. Like most extreme statements, he soon thought it over, and had more generous ideas. Joseph Raymond McCarthy (1908–57), US Senator from Wisconsin 1947–57, famous for overstated claims about communists in the US Government.

Mr. President, I am most happy once again to set foot in the United States—my mother's country I always think of it and feel it. I have come here on a quiet visit to see some of my old comrades…

1959, 4 May, Washington. (Pildel, 267.)

The change in Churchill since his last visit in 1954 was palpable, Robert Pilpel wrote:

Eisenhower observed sorrowfully to his daughter-in-law, Barbara, "I only wish you had known him in his prime." The President was visibly choked up.

Emperor Franz Josef I

Alone upon his rocky pinnacle from which the tides of time had sunk, this venerable, conscientious functionary continued in harness, pulling faithfully at the collar, mostly in the right direction, to the last gasp.

1931. (Crisis V, 23–4.)

Franz Josef (1830–1916) Emperor of Austria, Apostolic King of Hungary, King of Bohemia from 1848 until his death. Churchill considered him a victim of events.

Everest, Elizabeth

My nurse was my confidante. Mrs. Everest it was who looked after me and tended all my wants. It was to her I poured out my many troubles….Death came very easily to her. She had lived such an innocent and loving life of service to others and held such a simple faith that she had no fears at all and did not seem to mind very much. [She was] my dearest and most intimate friend during the whole of the twenty years I had lived.

1930. (MEL, 19, 87.)

Elizabeth Everest (d. 1895) was the beloved nurse of Winston and his brother Jack; they paid for her tombstone, which is inscribed with their names, at the City of London cemetery. Despite the use of "Mrs.", she never married.

Finucane, Paddy

If ever I feel a bitter feeling rising in me in my heart, about the Irish, the hands of heroes like Finucane seem to stretch out to soothe it away.

1948, 28 October.

Brendan Eamonn [sic] Fergus Finucane (1920–42), known as "Paddy", Irish RAF fighter pilot, the youngest Wing Commander in its history. He destroyed thirty-two enemy aircraft and promised that the Luftwaffe would never get him; sure enough, he died when his plane was shot down by ground fire over France.

Fisher, Admiral Lord

[The more] Lord Fisher's contribution to our naval efficiency is studied and examined, and tested by the passage of time, the more certainly will it be established that there has been within living memory no naval administrator possessed of abilities so rare and so distinguished.

1912, 5 August.

Admiral of the Fleet John Arbuthnot "Jackie" Fisher, First Baron Fisher (1841–1920) was the fiery Admiral known for reforms such as the conversion from coal- to oil-fired ships. His resignation as First Sea Lord precipitated Churchill's removal from the Admiralty in 1915, but WSC remained, in general, his ardent admirer.

I feel that there is in the present Admiralty administration, for all their competence, loyalty, and zeal, a lack of driving force and mental energy which cannot be allowed to continue, which must be rectified while time remains and before evil results, and can only be rectified in one way….I urge the First Lord of the Admiralty without delay to fortify himself, to vitalise and animate his Board of Admiralty by recalling Lord Fisher to his post as First Sea Lord.

1916, 7 March. (CS III, 2411.)

An astonishing reversal, since Fisher's resignation had caused Churchill's ouster only ten months earlier. WSC later explained his reason:

…my apprehension and foreboding of the sudden development of a new German submarine campaign, which actually occurred a year later, and my desire to see the utmost energy used in preparing against it (WSC to George Lambert, 4 December 1928; OB, CV5/1, 1393).

But he was seventy-four years of age. As in a great castle which has long contended with time, the mighty central mass of the donjon towered up intact and seemingly everlasting. But the outworks and the battlements had fallen away, and its imperious ruler dwelt only in the special apartments and corridors with which he had a lifelong familiarity.

1923. (CRISIS I, 403.)

Foch, Marshal Ferdinand

He began his career a little cub brushed aside by the triumphant march of the German armies to Paris and victory; he lived to see all the might of valiant Germany prostrate and suppliant at his pencil tip. In the weakest position he endured the worst with his country; at the summit of power he directed its absolute triumph.... Fortune lighted his crest....In 1914 he had saved the day by refusing to recognise defeat. In 1915 and 1916 he broke his teeth upon the Impossible. But 1918 was created for him.

1929, JULY. "FOCH THE INDOMITABLE," PALL MALL; GC, 117.

Ferdinand Foch (1851–1929), French general and military theorist, who nearly lost the war at Morhange in 1914, conducted the costly battles of the Somme and Picardy, and was supreme commander of the allied armies in 1918.

...at a moment of great disaster, when it seemed that the French and British armies might well be severed from one another by the German advance, the illustrious Marshal took command of the stricken field, and after a critical and even agonizing month, restored the fortunes of the war. General Weygand, who was head of his military family—as the French put it—said: "If Marshal Foch were here now, he would not waste time deploring what has been lost. He would say: 'Do not yield another yard.'"

1939, 19 MAY, CORN EXCHANGE, CAMBRIDGE. (BLOOD, 155.)

On 3 April 1939, WSC had referred to Marshal Foch taking command of the Allied Armies "at a moment when the battle seemed

a stricken field". For origins and usage of the phrase "stricken field", see this subject in Chapter 3, "Churchillisms".

Franco, Francisco

...by subtlety and trickery [he kept] Spain out of the war.... It is fashionable at the present time to dwell on the vices of General Franco, and I am therefore glad to place on record this testimony to the duplicity and ingratitude of his dealing with Hitler and Mussolini. I shall presently record even greater services which these evil qualities in General Franco rendered to the Allied cause.

1949. (WW2 II, 469.)

Generalissimo Francisco Paulino Hermenegildo Teodulo Franco Bahamonde (1882–1975), Caudillo of Spain, 1939–75.

French, Sir John

When you get to the end of your luck, there is a comfortable feeling you have got to the bottom....French brushed all this aside. He treated me as if I were still First Lord of the Admiralty, and had come again to confer with him upon the future of the war.

1930, JANUARY. ("LORD YPRES," PALL MALL; GC, 55.)

Field Marshal John Denton Pinkstone French, First Earl of Ypres (1852–1925), first commander of the British Expeditionary Force in WWI. Churchill is writing of their meeting in the field, 1916.

Gandhi, Mohandas

It is alarming and also nauseating to see Mr. Gandhi, a seditious Middle Temple lawyer, now posing as a fakir of a type well-known in the East, striding half-naked up the steps of the Vice-regal palace, while he is still organising and conducting a defiant campagn of civil disobedience, to parley on equal terms with the representative of the King-Emperor.

1931, 23 FEBRUARY, LONDON. (INDIA, 94.)

Mohandas Karamchand Gandhi (1869–1948), known as "Mahatma" (Great Soul), spiritual leader and father of Indian independence. They parted on higher ground. In 1944

Gandhi wrote WSC (in a letter that alas was not delivered):

> You are reported to have a desire to crush the simple "Naked Fakir", as you are said to have described me. I have been long trying to be a fakir and that (too) naked – a more difficult task. I, therefore, regard the expression as a compliment, though unintended. I approach you then as such, and ask you to trust and use me for the sake of your people and mine and through them those of the world. Your sincere friend, M. K. Gandhi (Kripalini, 155).

Already Mr. Gandhi moves about surrounded by a circle of wealthy men, who see at their finger-tips the acquisition of an Empire on cheaper terms than were ever yet offered in the world. Sir, the Roman senator, Didius Julianus, was dining in a restaurant when they told him that the Praetorian Guard put the Empire up to auction and were selling it in the ditch in their camp; he ran out, and, according to Gibbon, bought it for £200 sterling per soldier. That was fairly cheap; but the terms upon which the Empire is being offered to this group surrounding Mr. Gandhi are cheaper still.

1931, 12 MARCH.

I am against this surrender to Gandhi. I am against these conversations and agreements between Lord Irwin and Mr. Gandhi....Gandhi stands for the permanent exclusion of British trade from India. Gandhi stands for the substitution of Brahmin domination for British rule in India. You will never be able to come to terms with Gandhi.

1931, 18 MARCH, ROYAL ALBERT HALL, LONDON. (INDIA, 120.)

I do not care whether you are more or less loyal to Great Britain. I do not mind about education, but give the masses more butter....Tell Mr. Gandhi to use the powers that are offered and make the thing a success....I am genuinely sympathetic towards India. I have got real fears about the future...But you have got the things now; make a success and if you do I will advocate your getting much more.

1935. (OB V: 618–19.)

Churchill invited G. D. Birla, a leading Gandhi supporter, to lunch at Chartwell after passage of the India Bill, which he had opposed. His words

should be quoted alongside his earlier vivid descriptions of Gandhi. When Birla repeated the conversation Gandhi replied:

> I have got a good recollection of Mr. Churchill when he was in the Colonial Office and somehow or other since then I have held the opinion that I can always rely on his sympathy and goodwill.

Now Pendar, why don't you give us Morocco, and we shall give you India. We shall even give you Gandhi, and he's awfully cheap to keep, now that he's on a hunger strike.

1943, JANUARY, CASABLANCA. (HALLE, IRREPRESSIBLE, 211.)

Kenneth W. Pendar, an American diplomat who served as vice-consul in Marrakech and Casablanca, 1942–43, was hosting Churchill at dinner.

Giraud, Henri

While there are men like General de Gaulle and all those who follow him—and they are legion throughout France—and men like General Giraud, that gallant warrior whom no prison can hold, while there are men like those to stand forward in the name and in the cause of France, my confidence in the future of France is sure.

1942, 19 NOVEMBER.

Henri Honoré Giraud (1879–1949), French general who joined the Free French Forces and was promoted by Roosevelt as a more reliable French leader than de Gaulle.

We all thought General Giraud was the man for the job, and that his arrival would be electrical. In this opinion, General Giraud emphatically agreed....

1942, 10 DECEMBER. (SECRET, 83.)

Gladstone, William

Mr. Gladstone was frequently portrayed as Julius Caesar, an august being crowned with myrtle, entitled to the greatest respect, a sort of glorified headmaster. We knew he was Prime Minister and the cleverest man in the country; a man of virtue, correctitude, and impeccability, the sort of man who was always telling you what you had done wrong, and never had to form up and be told what he had done wrong himself; the sort of man who made the rules and enforced them and never had to break them. He was venerable, majestic, formidable, benevolent.

1931, JUNE. ("CARTOONS AND CARTOONISTS," *STRAND MAGAZINE*; THOUGHTS, 11.)

William Ewart Gladstone (1809–98), Liberal MP, Prime Minister 1867–74, 1880–85, 1886, 1892–94.

Gordon, Charles

...a man careless alike of the frowns of men or the smiles of women, of life or comfort, wealth or fame.

1899. RIVER I, 27.

Charles George "Chinese" Gordon (1833–85), soldier and colonial governor of the Sudan, was probably assassinated by forces of the Mahdi, leading to Kitchener's reconquest of Sudan in 1898.

Guillotin, Joseph-Ignace

We have all heard of how Dr. Guillotin was executed by the instrument that he invented. [Sir Herbert Samuel: "He was not!"] Well, he ought to have been.

1931, 29 APRIL.

Sir Herbert was right. Joseph-Ignace Guillotin (1738–1814) was not guillotined, nor did he invent the guillotine, but it was he who suggested its use during the French Revolution in 1789.

Halifax, Edward

In Edward Halifax we have a man of light and leading, whose company is a treat and whose friendship it is an honour to enjoy. I have often disagreed with him in the twenty years I have known him in the rough and tumble of British politics, but I have always respected him and his actions because I know that courage and fidelity are the essence of his being....As a man of deep but unparaded and unaffected religious convictions, and as for many years an ardent lover of the chase, he has known how to get the best out of both worlds.

1941, 9 JANUARY, LONDON. (PILGRIMS SOCIETY LUNCHEON FOR HALIFAX.)

Edward Frederick Lindley Wood, First Earl of Halifax, Viscount Halifax (1881–1959), Foreign Secretary at the 1938 Munich Agreement; earlier, as Lord Irwin, he was Viceroy of India; on this occasion he was Churchill's ambassador-designate to the United States.

Hamilton, General Sir Ian

He has a most happy gift of expression, a fine taste in words, and an acute perception of the curious which he has preserved from his literary days....His mind is built upon a big scale, being broad and strong, capable of thinking in army corps and if necessary in continents, and working always with serene smoothness undisturbed alike by responsibility or danger.

1900, 10 AUGUST. (HAMILTON'S, 135; BOER, 284.)

Ian Standish Monteith Hamilton, (1851–1947), British general from the Boer War days, first met WSC returning from India in 1897, later commanded the ill-fated Mediterranean Expeditionary Force during the invasion of Gallipoli. Despite his failure there, he and WSC remained lifelong friends. WSC sold Lullenden, his first country home, to Hamilton in 1919.

Hanfstaengl, Ernst "Putzi"

...in the course of conversation with Hanfstaengl I happened to say, "Why is your chief [Hitler] so violent about the Jews? I can quite understand being angry with Jews who have done wrong or are against the country, and I understand resisting them if they try to monopolise power in any walk of life; but what is the sense of being against a man simply because of his birth? How can any man help how he is born?" He must have repeated this to Hitler, because about noon the next day he came round with rather a serious air and said that the appointment he had made for me to meet Hitler could not take place....Thus Hitler lost his only chance of meeting me. Later on when he was all-powerful, I was to receive several invitations from him. But by that time a lot had happened, and I excused myself.

1948. (WW2 I, 65–6.)

Churchill refers to 1932 – as close as he came to meeting Hitler, who balked when these remarks were repeated to him. Ernst Franz Sedgwick Hanfstaengl (1887–1975), known as "Putzi", half-American and a Harvard graduate, was chief of the Nazi Party's Foreign Press Department. Later he fled to America, where he became an adviser to the US Government. See also Maxims...Anti-Semitism.

Hankey, Sir Maurice

He knew everything; he could put his hand on anything; he knew everybody; he said nothing; he gained the confidence of all.

1929. (CRISIS IV, 134.)

Maurice Pascal Alers Hankey, First Baron Hankey (1877–1963), British civil servant, secretary to the War Cabinet in WWI and an adviser to Chamberlain when forming the 1939 War Cabinet. Always diffident towards Churchill, he wrote brash diaries and was very wise after the fact.

The sleuth-hound of the politicians was Sir Maurice Hankey, Secretary of the Committee of Imperial Defence and Secretary to the War Cabinet. He had a lawful foot in every camp—naval, military, professional, political—and while observing every form of official correctitude he sought ruthlessly "the way out."

1931, 16–25 NOVEMBER. (*DAILY TELEGRAPH*; THOUGHTS, 90.)

Harcourt, Sir William

In the year 1895 I had the privilege, as a young officer, of being invited to lunch with Sir William Harcourt. In the course of a conversation in which I took, I fear, none too modest a share, I asked the question "What will happen then?" "My dear Winston," replied the old Victorian statesman, "the experiences of a long life have convinced me that nothing ever happens." Since that moment, as it seems to me, nothing has ever ceased happening.

1923. (CRISIS I, 25–6.)

Sir William George Granville Venables Vernon Harcourt (1827–1904), statesman; Home Secretary, 1880–85; Chancellor of the Exchequer, 1886, 1892–94, 1894–95.

Harding, Warren

I have high hopes of this Washington Conference. It has been called together by President Harding in a spirit of the utmost sincerity and good will.

1921, 24 SEPTEMBER, CAIRD HALL, DUNDEE. (CS, 3139.)

Warren Gamaliel Harding (1865–1923), 29th President of the United States (1921–23), died in office. The Washington Naval Conference (November 1921 to February 1922) fixed limits on the navies of nine nations.

Hearst, William Randolph

...a grave simple child—with no doubt a hasty temper—playing with the most costly toys. A vast income always overspent: Ceaseless building and collecting not very discriminatingly works of art: two magnificent establishments, two charming wives; complete indifference to public opinion, a strong liberal and democratic outlook, a 15 million daily circulation, oriental hospitalities, extreme personal courtesy (to us at any rate) the appearance of a Quaker elder—or perhaps Mormon elder.

1929, 29 SEPTEMBER, BARSTOW, CALIFORNIA. (OB, CV5/2, 96.)

WSC to his wife after Churchill, his brother and two of their sons were the guests of Hearst at his "castle" at San Simeon. William Randolph Hearst (1863–1951), American newspaper publisher. The "two charming wives" were Millicent Hearst and Hearst's mistress, actress Marion Davies.

Hess, Rudolf

[This] is one of those cases where the imagination is sometimes baffled by the facts as they present themselves.

1941, 13 MAY. (OB VI, 1087.)

Walter Richard Rudolf Hess (1894–1987), Hitler's Deputy Fuehrer. Churchill was asked in Parliament about the surprise parachute arrival in Scotland by German Deputy Fuehrer Rudolf Hess, who had taken it upon himself personally to contact "anti-Churchill people". He found none, and was imprisoned. See also Chapter 32...Marx Brothers.

Include reference to health and fall over banisters, etc....Why not say on verge of insanity?

1942, 4 NOVEMBER. (DIARIES OF CABINET SECRETARY SIR NORMAN BROOK, *NEW YORK TIMES*, 22 JANUARY 2006.)

Churchill is here suggesting what to tell Stalin about Hess's mission.

Himmler, Heinrich

Negotiate with, e.g., Himmler and bump him off later.

1945, 3 MAY. (DIARIES OF CABINET SECRETARY SIR NORMAN BROOK, *NEW YORK TIMES*, 22 JANUARY 2006.)

Heinrich Luitpold Himmler (1900–45), Chief of the SS, second in power to Adolf Hitler. He committed suicide when captured in 1945.

Hindenburg, Paul von

Hindenburg had nothing to learn from modern science and civilisation except its weapon; no rule of life but duty....In the last phase we see the aged President, having betrayed all the Germans who had re-elected him to power, joining reluctant and indeed contemptuous hands with the Nazi leader. There is a defence for all this....he had become senile.

1934, 2 AUGUST. ("HINDENBURG," *DAILY MAIL*; GC, 67, 74.)

Paul von Hindenburg (1847–1934), German field marshal in World War I, President of Germany 1925–34. He defeated Hitler in the elections of 1932, but another election forced him to name Hitler Chancellor in January 1933. He died in office, Hitler declaring the presidency vacant and naming himself Head of State.

Hitler, Adolf

There must not be lacking in our leadership something of the spirit of that Austrian corporal who, when all had fallen into ruins about him, and when Germany seemed to have sunk for ever into chaos, did not hesitate to march forth against the vast array of victorious nations, and has already turned the tables so decisively upon them.

1938, 14 OCTOBER. ("FRANCE AFTER MUNICH," *DAILY TELEGRAPH*; STEP, 275.)

Adolf Hitler (1889-1945) German Chancellor 1933–45 and Nazi Party leader. Colin Coote wrote:

This is not merely a case of giving the devil his due. Sir Winston was speaking to an audience many of whom could objectively admire Hitler's resuscitation of German might against great odds, and was tempering the wind to those gambolling and still unshorn lambs.

I have always said that if Great Britain were defeated in war I hoped we should find a Hitler to lead us back to our rightful position among the nations. I am sorry, however, that he has not been mellowed by the great success that has attended him. The whole world would rejoice to see the Hitler of peace and tolerance, and nothing would adorn his name in world history so much as acts of magnanimity and of mercy and of pity to the forlorn and friendless, to the weak and poor....Let this great man search his own heart and conscience before he accuses anyone of being a warmonger.

1938, 6 NOVEMBER.

The film Judgment at Nuremberg *suggests that Churchill "praised Hitler" in this speech, which considerably oversimplifies what Churchill actually said.*

What is Herr Hitler going to do? Is he going to try to blow up the world or not? The world is a very heavy thing to blow up. An extraordinary man at a pinnacle of power may create a great explosion, and yet the civilised world may remain unshaken. The enormous fragments and splinters of the explosion may clatter down upon his own head and destroy him and all who stand around him, but the world will go on. Civilisation will not succumb; the working people in the free countries will not be enslaved again.

1939, 28 JUNE. CARLTON CLUB, LONDON. (BLOOD, 180.)

The gent has taken off his clothes and put on his bathing-suit, but the water is getting colder and there is an autumn nip in the air.

1940, 4 OCTOBER. (WW2 II, 441.)

WSC to Roosevelt relative to Hitler's preparations to invade Britain (which by then had already been put off).

...Herr Hitler is not thinking only of stealing other people's territories, or flinging gobbets of them to his little confederate. I tell you truly what you must believe when I say this evil man, this monstrous abortion of hatred and defeat is resolved on nothing less than the complete wiping out of the French nation, and the disintegration of its whole life and future.

1940, 21 October. Broadcast, London.
(Blood, 464.)

...I certainly deprecate any comparison between Herr Hitler and Napoleon; I do not wish to insult the dead....

1940, 19 December. (CS, 6321.)

I hate nobody except Hitler—and that is professional.

Circa 1940. (Colville, Churchillians, 3.)

Churchill to private secretary John Colville, who wrote,

I thought it remarkable that, disliked by so many in his youth and presumably both snubbed and thwarted, he never spoke ill of his critics in later days.

Some have compared Hitler's conquests with those of Napoleon. It may be that Spain and Russia will shortly furnish new chapters to that theme. It must be remembered, however, that Napoleon's armies carried with them the fierce, liberating and equalitarian winds of the French Revolution, whereas Hitler's empire has nothing behind it but racial self-assertion, espionage, pillage, corruption and the Prussian boot.

1941, 7 May.

There is a winter, you know, in Russia. For a good many months the temperature is apt to fall very low. There is snow, there is frost, and all that. Hitler forgot about this Russian winter. He must have been very loosely educated. We all heard about it at school; but he forgot it. I have never made such a bad mistake as that.

1942, 10 May. Broadcast, London. (End, 126.)

Hitler's "first blunder", Churchill had said earlier in this speech, was invading Russia in

the first place, which broke his hitherto unbeaten army.

If Hitler falls into our hands we shall certainly put him to death. Not a sovereign who could be said to be in the hands of ministers, like Kaiser. This man is the mainspring of evil. Instrument—electric chair, for gangsters no doubt available on Lease-Lend.

1942, 6 July. (Diaries of Cabinet Secretary Sir Norman Brook, *New York Times*, 22 January 2006.)

Negotiation with Hitler was impossible. He was a maniac with supreme power to play his hand out to the end, which he did; and so did we.

1943, 23 January, Casablanca.
(Sherwood II, 693.)

It is, indeed, quite remarkable that the Germans should have shown themselves ready to run the risk and pay the price required of them by their struggle to hold the Tunisian tip. While I always hesitate to say anything which might afterwards look like over-confidence, I cannot resist the remark that one seems to discern in this policy the touch of the master hand, the same master hand that planned the attack on Stalingrad, and that has brought upon German armies the greatest disaster they have ever suffered in all their military history.

1943, 11 February.

Commenting on this at a Churchill Centre/Roosevelt Institute symposium in June 2007, Professor David Reynolds made the point that this "really stupid" decision by Hitler, while extending the war in North Africa, may have eased the pressure on Stalingrad: an illustration of the unexpected turns war takes. See next entry.

...I am free to admit that in North Africa we builded better than we knew. The unexpected came to the aid of the design and multiplied the results. For this we have to thank the military intuition of Corporal Hitler. We may notice, as I predicted in the House of Commons three months ago, the touch of the master hand. The same insensate obstinacy which condemned Field-Marshal von Paulus and his army to destruction at Stalingrad has brought this new catastrophe upon our enemies in Tunisia.

1943, 19 May. Congress, Washington.
(Onwards, 99.)

WSC frequently referred to "Corporal Hitler" (or "Corporal Shicklgruber"; see 28 September). Robert Lewis Taylor wrote:

The contemptuous flinging of the name and rating at the end typifies Churchill's attitude toward his antagonist.

See also Chapter 18...Origins of the war.

I know of no reason to suppose that Hitler is not in full control of his faculties and the resources of his country. I think he probably repents that he brought appetite unbridled and ambition unmeasured to his dealings with other nations. I have very little doubt that if Hitler could have the past back he would play his hand a little differently. He probably regrets having turned down repeated efforts to avoid war, efforts which almost brought the British Government into disrepute. I should think he now repents that he did not curb his passions before he brought the world to misery.

1943, 25 MAY, PRESS CONFERENCE, WASHINGTON. (ONWARDS, 105.)

In view of repeated revisionist claims that Hitler was desperate for peace with Britain, which would have saved millions of lives, one is required to ponder the question of what Hitler meant by peace. He certainly was offered many opportunities for it.

...Russian success has been somewhat aided by the strategy of Herr Hitler—of Corporal Hitler. Even military idiots find it difficult not to see some faults in some of his actions....Altogether, I think it is much better to let officers rise up in the proper way.

1944, 2 AUGUST.

I always hate to compare Napoleon with Hitler, as it seems an insult to the great Emperor and warrior to connect him in any way with a squalid caucus boss and butcher. But there is one respect in which I must draw a parallel. Both these men were temperamentally unable to give up the tiniest scrap of any territory to which the high watermark of their hectic fortunes had carried them. Thus, after Leipzig in 1813, Napoleon left all his garrisons on the Rhine, and 40,000 men in Hamburg...Similarly, Hitler has successfully scattered the German armies all over Europe,

and by obstinating at every point, from Stalingrad and Tunis down to the present moment, he has stripped himself of the power to concentrate in main strength for the final struggle....

When Herr Hitler escaped his bomb on July 20th he described his survival as providential; I think that from a purely military point of view we can all agree with him, for certainly it would be most unfortunate if the Allies were to be deprived, in the closing phases of the struggle, of that form of warlike genius by which Corporal Schicklgruber has so notably contributed to our victory.

1944, 28 SEPTEMBER.

Hitler's father, Alois, changed the family name from "Schicklgruber" to "Hitler" in 1876, thirteen years before Adolf was born. This did not prevent WSC from deploying it with effect.

Well, I must say I think he was perfectly right to die like that.

1945, 1 MAY. (OB VII, 1325.)

When the German radio brought news that Hitler had died "fighting with his last breath against Bolshevism", Churchill did not know the actual details of Hitler's squalid death. This was first announced by the arriving Russians some days later. Some memoirists, but no contemporary accounts, include the explanatory note that Hitler died by suicide.

Hoover, Herbert

Since Mr. Hoover became President of the United States it has seemed to me, at any rate, that a more comprehending and sympathetic spirit has been imparted to the policy of the United States, not only towards this country but towards Europe in general.

1929, 14 JUNE.

Herbert Clark Hoover (1874–1964), 31st President of the United States, 1929–33.

The decision and inspiration, the wisdom and the comprehension which led President Hoover and the United States of America to proclaim a general moratorium for a year in the payment of War Debts and indemnities has, I feel sure, been received by all members of the university with sincere acclaim. The unwholesome accumulation of gold in the only two countries which benefit from those uneconomic and non-commercial payments has largely paralysed world credit, checked the flow of trade, paralysed prices, especially the prices of prime commodities, and has made it impossible for millions of workers on both sides of the Atlantic to earn their daily bread.

1931, 27 JUNE, BRISTOL UNIVERSITY. (CS, 5052.)

Hopkins, Harry

Sancho P. [Sancho Panza = Harry Hopkins] was looking extraordinarily well, and twice as fit as he was before the combined restoratives of blood transfusions and matrimony were administered to him.

1943, 15 JANUARY, CASABLANCA.
(SOAMES, SPEAKING, 473.)

WSC to his wife. Harry Lloyd Hopkins (1890–1946), Roosevelt's personal envoy to Britain and Russia, 1941 and Special Assistant to the President, 1942–45. WSC and CSC nicknamed him after Don Quixote's faithful squire – more out of respect than derision.

Hopkins was of course jealous about his personal influence with his Chief and did not encourage American competitors. He therefore in some ways bore out the poet Gray's line, "A favourite has no friend". But this was not my affair. There he sat, slim, frail, ill, but absolutely glowing with refined comprehension of the Cause. It was to be the defeat, ruin, and slaughter of Hitler, to the exclusion of all other purposes, loyalties, or aims. In the history of the United States few brighter flames have burned.

1950. (WW2 III, 21.)

Hore-Belisha, Leslie

If you attack me I shall strike back and remember, while you have a 3.7-inch gun I have a 12-inch gun.

1941, JUNE. ("HOW CHURCHILL INFLUENCES AND PERSUADES," HORE-BELISHA IN EADE, 274.)

Isaac Leslie Hore-Belisha, First Baron Hore-Belisha (1893–1957), Liberal MP, Chamberlain's War Minister from 1937, who left the Cabinet in 1940, declining the Board of Trade and Ministry of Information.

Inönü, Ismet

Do you know what happened to me today, the Turkish President kissed me. The truth is I'm irresistible. But don't tell Anthony, he's jealous.

1943, 7 DECEMBER, CONSTANTINOPLE. (EDEN, 429.)

WSC to his daughter Sarah. Mustafa Ismet Inönü (1884–1973), Turkish soldier and statesman, second President of Turkey, 1938-50. Churchill had tried unsuccessfully to woo Turkey into the war on the Allies' side.

Inskip, Sir Thomas

I am sure everyone will feel that the Rt. Hon. Gentleman who fills the office of Minister of Coordination of Defence is extraordinarily capable of coordinating the Parliamentary defence of the Government and its policy against whatever criticism may be directed upon it from any quarter of the House.

1936, 29 MAY.

Thomas Walker Hobart Inskip, First Viscount Caldecote (1876–1947), Conservative MP, Lord Chancellor 1939–40, Minister for Coordination of Defence 1936–39. Churchill said this tongue-in-cheek, since he considered Inskip incompetent in his defence role, and thought it should have gone to himself.

Ismay, General Lord

Pug, you should have been in your basket ages ago.

1944, MAY. (ISMAY, MEMOIRS, 347.)

General Hastings Lionel Ismay, First Baron Ismay (1885–1965), known as "Pug", WSC's chief of staff in his capacity as Minister of Defence. He was momentarily caught with no answers when Churchill, before D-Day, asked him when William the Conqueror had landed during the invasion of England in 1066.

Jellicoe, Admiral of the Fleet Sir John

Jellicoe was the only man on either side who could lose the war in an afternoon.

1927. (CRISIS III, PART 1, 112.)

John Rushworth Jellicoe, First Earl Jellicoe (1859–1935), commander in chief, Grand

Fleet, British commander at the inconclusive Battle of Jutland (1916), the greatest encounter between armoured warships in history. Maurice Ashley misquotes this as, "... the only man on either side who could have lost the war in an afternoon".

Joan of Arc

There now appeared upon the ravaged scene an Angel of Deliverance, the noblest patriot of France, the most splendid of her heroes, the most beloved of her saints, the most inspiring of all her memories, the peasant Maid, the ever-shining, ever-glorious Joan of Arc. In the poor, remote hamlet of Domrémy, on the fringe of the Vosges Forest, she served at the inn.

1956. (HESP I, 417.)

Joan of Arc (1412–31), national heroine of France, canonised as a saint in 1920.

Joynson-Hicks, William

The worst that can be said about him is that he runs the risk of being most humorous when he wishes to be most serious.

1931, 9 AUGUST. (SUNDAY PICTORIAL, 8.)

William Joynson-Hicks, First Viscount Brentford, known as "Jix", (1865–1932), Conservative MP and one-time Home Secretary. The official biography (OB II, 114) incorrectly references Churchill's book Thoughts and Adventures *as the source.*

Kaiser Wilhelm II

...the defence which can be made will not be flattering to his self-esteem...."Look at him; he is only a blunderer"....Finally, in his own Memoirs, written from the penitential seclusion of Doorn, he has naïvely revealed to us his true measure....It is shocking to reflect that upon the word or nod of a being so limited there stood attentive and obedient for thirty years the forces which, whenever released, could devastate the world. It was not his fault; it was his fate.

1930, NOVEMBER. ("THE EX-KAISER," STRAND MAGAZINE; GC, 21–4.)

Wilhelm II (1859–1941), last Emperor of Germany, brought that country into the First

World War. After the war he lived in exile in Doorn, Netherlands.

Mr. Lloyd George, himself an actor although a man of action, would, if he had had his way, have deprived us of this invaluable exposure in order to gratify the passions of victorious crowds. He would have redraped this melancholy exile in the sombre robes of more than mortal guilt and of superhuman responsibility and led him forth to a scaffold of vicarious expiation. Upon the brow from which the diadem of Empire had been smitten he would have set a crown of martyrdom; and Death, with an all-effacing gesture, would have refounded the dynasty of the Hohenzollerns upon a victim's tomb.

1930, NOVEMBER. (OP. CIT., 24.)

Kelly, Denis

Denis, you're a disgrace to the British Empire.

1949, 23 AUGUST, CAP D'AIL, FRANCE. (OB VIII, 485.)

Richard Denis Lucien Kelly (1916–90). Very slight and thin, he was one of Churchill's post-war literary assistants.

Kennedy, John F.

Kennedy certainly has tremendous tasks before him. I had a friendly exchange of messages with him after his election.

1960, 2 DECEMBER. (OB VIII, 1318; KENNEDY LIBRARY, BOSTON.)

WSC to Consuelo Balsan. John Fitzgerald Kennedy (1917–63) 35th President of the United States, 1960–63. Churchill first met Kennedy aboard the Onassis yacht Christina *in 1959. The exchanges are routine congratulations.*

Kent, HRH the Duke of

There is something about death on active service which makes it different from common or ordinary death in the normal course of nature. It is accepted without question by the fighting men. Those they leave behind them are also conscious of a light of sacrifice and honour which plays around the grave or the tomb of the warrior....Nothing can fill the awful gap, nothing can assuage or comfort the loneliness and deprivation which fall upon wife and children when the prop and centre of their home is suddenly snatched away. Only faith in a life after death in a brighter world where dear ones will meet again—only that and the measured tramp of time can give consolation.

1942, 8 SEPTEMBER.

George Edward Alexander Edmund, Prince George, Duke of Kent (1902–42), fourth son of George V and brother of George VI, killed in a plane crash in Scotland while on active service in the RAF.

King Alfonso XIII

The Spanish people had a view of their own; and that is the view that must prevail. Alfonso would not wish it otherwise himself.

Men and kings must be judged in the testing moments of their lives.

1931, JULY. ("ALFONSO THE UNLUCKY," STRAND MAGAZINE; GC, 137.)

Alfonso XIII (1886–1947), King of Spain 1886–1931, formally abdicated 1941 after Franco, whom he favoured, declared that the Nationalists would never accept his return. Churchill, who admired him, was surprised at this.

King Canute

He made a point of submitting himself to the laws whereby he ruled.

1956. (HESP I, 140.)

Canute I (995–1035), known as Canute the Great, Viking King of England, Denmark, Norway and Sweden.

King Edward VII

…I am curious to know about the King. Will it entirely revolutionise his way of life? Will he sell his horses and scatter his Jews or will Reuben Sassoon be enshrined among the crown jewels and other regalia? Will he become desperately serious? Will he continue to be friendly to you? Will the Keppel be appointed the 1st Lady of the Bedchamber? Write to tell me all about all this.

1901, 22 JANUARY, WINNIPEG, MANITOBA. (OB, CV1 PART 2, 1231.)

WSC to his mother. Albert Edward (1841–1910), King of Great Britain and Ireland and Emperor of India, 1901–10. Alice Frederica Keppell née Edmonstone (1869–1947), British socialite, most famous mistress of Edward VII.

King Edward VIII

May I ask my Rt. Hon. Friend [Prime Minister Baldwin] whether he could give us an assurance that no irrevocable step… [Hon. Members: "No."] …that no irrevocable step will be taken before the House has received a full statement, not only upon the personal but upon the constitutional issues involved. May I ask him to bear in mind that these issues are not merely personal to the present occupant of the Throne, but that they affect the entire Constitution. [Hon. Members: "Speech," and "Sit down."] If the House resists my claim it will only add the more importance to any words that I might want to use. [Mr. Speaker: "Will the Rt. Hon. Gentleman confine what he has to say to a simple question?"] Mr. Churchill: I am grateful for what the Rt. Hon. Gentleman has said, but I ask that there should be an assurance that no irrevocable decision will be taken until at least a statement has been made to Parliament of the constitutional issues involved, and of the procedure involved in such an event? [Hon. Members: "Order."]

1936, 7 DECEMBER.

Edward Albert Christian George Andrew Patrick David (1894–1972), King of Great Britain 1936. Churchill lost carefully built political capital by rising to defend Edward VIII, who was facing abdication over his insistence on marring Wallis Simpson, a divorced American. In this exchange he was shouted down by MPs and ruled out of order for making a speech during Questions, temporarily destroying his growing stature over the defence question – but not for long.

…I hope the House will bear with me for a minute or two, because it was my duty as Home Secretary, more than a quarter of a century ago, to stand beside his present Majesty and proclaim his style and titles at his investiture as Prince of Wales amid the sunlit battlements of Carnarvon Castle, and ever since then he has honoured me here, and also in war-time, with his personal kindness and, I may even say, friendship. I should have been ashamed if, in my independent and unofficial position, I had not cast about for every lawful means, even the most forlorn, to keep him on the Throne of his fathers....In this Prince there were discerned qualities of courage, of simplicity, of sympathy, and, above all, of sincerity, qualities rare and precious which might have made his reign glorious in the annals of this ancient monarchy. It is the acme of tragedy that these very virtues should, in the private sphere, have led only to this melancholy and bitter conclusion....Danger gathers upon our path. We cannot afford—we have no right—to look back. We must look forward; we must obey the exhortation of the Prime Minister to look forward. The stronger the advocate of monarchical principle a man may be, the more zealously must he now endeavour to fortify the Throne and to give to His Majesty's successor that strength which can only come from the love of a united nation and Empire.

1936, 10 DECEMBER.

Edward VIII had now announced his Abdication in favour of his brother, who became George VI. This was in essence Churchill's apology for his un-Parliamentary behaviour three days before, and did much to repair his reputation among his colleagues; for indeed many of them were beginning to understand that in the face of Hitler, Churchill might well be needed.

The Windsors dine here and we dine back with them. They have a lovely little place next door to La Dragonnière. Everything extremely well done and dignified. Red liveries, and the little man himself dressed up to the nines in the Balmoral tartan with dagger and jabot etc. When you think that you could hardly get him to put on a black coat and short tie when he was Prince of Wales, one sees the change in the point of view. I am to dine with him tomorrow night with only Rothermere. No doubt to talk over his plans for returning home. They do not want him to come, but they have no power to stop him.

1939, 18 JANUARY. CHÂTEAU DE L'HORIZON, GOLFE JUAN, FRANCE. (CV5/3, 1347.)

WSC to his wife. The villas mentioned, in the south of France were Lord Rothermere's La Dragonnière and Château de L'Horizon, home of their long-time friend Maxine Elliott.

I'm glad I was wrong. We could not have had a better King. And now we have this splendid Queen.

1953. (SIR ANTHONY MONTAGUE BROWNE TO THE EDITOR.)

Churchill was referring to his strident support of Edward VIII in the 1936 Abdication crisis.

King George V

His reign has seen enormous perils and a triumph the like of which the annals of war cannot equal. It has seen moral, social, political and scientific changes in the life of all countries and of all classes so decisive that we, borne along upon the still hurrying torrent, cannot even attempt to measure them. The means of locomotion, the art of flying, the position of women, the map of Europe, the aims and ideals of all nations—East and West, white and black, brown and yellow—have undergone a prodigious transformation.

But here at the centre and summit of the British Empire, in what is the freest society yet achieved in human record, a King who has done his duty will be reverenced by the ceremonial of his ancestors and acclaimed by the cheers of his faithful people.

1935, 9 MAY. ("THE KING'S TWENTY-FIVE YEARS," EVENING STANDARD; ESSAYS III, 240.)

George Frederick Ernest Albert (1865–1936), King of Great Britain and Emperor of India, 1910–36.

King George VI

I have seen the King, gay, buoyant, and confident, when the stones and rubble of Buckingham Palace lay newly scattered in heaps upon its lawns.

1942, 12 OCTOBER, USHER HALL, EDINBURGH. (END, 236.)

Albert Frederick Arthur George (1895–1952), King of Great Britain from 1936, last Emperor of India (until 1947) and last King of Ireland (until 1949). Initially holding little confidence in Churchill, he grew to be an ardent admirer.

I do not think that any Prime Minister has ever received so much personal kindness and encouragement from his Sovereign as I have. Every week I have my audience, the greater part of which occurs most agreeably at luncheon, and I have seen the King at close quarters in every phase of our formidable experiences. I remember well how in the first months of this administration the King would come in from practising with his rifle and his tommy-gun in the garden at Buckingham Palace, and if it had come to a last stand in London, a matter which had to be considered at one time, I have no doubt that His Majesty would have come very near departing from his usual constitutional rectitude by disregarding the advice of his Ministers.

1945, 15 MAY.

Anthony, imagine the worst thing that could possibly happen…

1952, 6 FEBRUARY. ("THE QUEEN AND
MR. CHURCHILL," DAVID DILKS, *FINEST HOUR* 135,
SUMMER 2007.)

Churchill on the telephone to Anthony Eden on hearing of the King's death.

The last few months of King George's life, with all the pain and physical stresses that he endured—his life hanging by a thread from day to day—and he all the time cheerful and undaunted—stricken in body but quite undisturbed and even unaffected in spirit—these have made a profound and an enduring impression and should be a help to all. He was sustained not only by his natural buoyancy but by the sincerity of his Christian faith. During these last months the King walked with death, as if death were a companion, an acquaintance, whom he recognized and did not fear. In the end death came as a friend; and after a happy day of sunshine and sport, and after "good night" to those who loved him best, he fell asleep as every man or woman who strives to fear God and nothing else in the world may hope to do.

1952, 7 FEBRUARY. BROADCAST, LONDON.
(STEMMING, 238.)

King George VI and Queen Elizabeth

…your majesties are more beloved by all classes and conditions than any of the princes of the past.

1941, 5 JANUARY. (WW2 II, 554.)

Elizabeth Angela Marguerite Bowes-Lyon (1900–2002), Queen Consort, 1936–52.

King Ibn Saud

I was the host and I said that if it was his religion that made him say such things, my religion prescribed as an absolute sacred ritual smoking cigars and drinking alcohol before, after, and if need be during, all meals and the intervals between them. Complete surrender.

1945, 17 FEBRUARY, LAKE FAYYUM, EGYPT.
(GILBERT, LIFE, 825.)

Abdul Aziz ibn Saud (1876–1953). When told that the King could not allow drinking or smoking in his presence, WSC replied thusly. More seriously, Churchill asked the King's assistance, "to promote a definite and lasting settlement between the Jews and Arabs" in Palestine, through a Middle East Federation headed by Ibn Saud, in which Jewish Palestine would be an integral independent part.

Kinglake, Alexander

…I shall take refuge in Kinglake's celebrated remark, that "a scrutiny so minute as to bring a subject under a false angle of vision is a poorer guide to a man's judgment than the most rapid glance that sees things in their true proportions."

1898, AUGUST. ("THE ETHICS OF FRONTIER
POLICY," UNITED SERVICE MAGAZINE.)

Alexander William Kinglake, historian (1809–91). Churchill highly admired him. When asked how to excel at writing history, Churchill once recommended, "Read Kinglake," and there are lines in Kinglake's The Invasion of the Crimea *(beginning 1863) which prefigure Churchill's style.*

Kitchener, Field Marshal Lord

My relations with Lord Kitchener had been limited. Our first meeting had been on the field of Omdurman.…He had disapproved of me severely in my youth, had endeavoured to prevent me from coming to the Soudan Campaign, and was indignant that I had succeeded in getting there. It was a case of dislike before first sight.

1923. (CRISIS I, 234.)

Horatio Herbert Kitchener, First Earl Kitchener of Khartoum (1850–1916). WSC was describing his first encounter since the Sudan campaign with Kitchener, who in 1914 was Secretary of State for War.

I cannot forget that when I left the Admiralty in May, 1915, the first and, with one exception, the only one of my colleagues who paid me a visit of ceremony was the over-burdened Titan whose disapprobation had been one of the disconcerting experiences of my youth.

1923. (CRISIS I, 234.)

Lord Kitchener was always splendid when things went wrong.

1923. (CRISIS II, 249.)

It was during this interval that I had the honour of receiving a visit of ceremony from Lord Kitchener....he asked me whether it was settled that I should leave the Admiralty. I said it was. He asked what I was going to do. I said I had no idea; nothing was settled. He evidently had no idea how narrowly he had escaped my fate. As he got up to go he turned and said, in the impressive and almost majestic manner which was natural to him, "Well, there is one thing at any rate they cannot take from you. The Fleet was ready." After that he was gone. During the months that we were still to serve together in the new Cabinet I was condemned often to differ from him, to oppose him and to criticize him. But I cannot forget the rugged kindness and warm-hearted courtesy which led him to pay me this visit.

1923. (CRISIS II, 374–5.)

Kruger, Paul

One thought to find the President [Kruger]— stolid old Dutchman—seated on his stoep, reading his Bible and smoking a sullen pipe. But...On the Friday preceding the British occupation [of Pretoria] he left the capital...taking with him a million pounds in gold and leaving behind him a crowd of officials clamouring for pay, and far from

satisfied with the worthless cheques they had received.

1900, 8 JUNE, PRETORIA. (HAMILTON'S, 296–7; BOER, 355–6.)

Stephanus Johannes Paulus Kruger (1825–1902), known as "Oom Paul", President of the Transvaal, 1883–99; fled to Utrecht, Holland, in 1900.

Lauder, Harry

Let me use the words of your famous minstrel—he is here today—words which have given comfort and renewed strength to many a burdened heart: "Keep right on to the end of the road, Keep right on to the end."

1942, 12 OCTOBER, USHER HALL, EDINBURGH. (END, 243.)

Sir Harry Lauder (1870–1950), Scottish entertainer. Churchill is alleged to have described him as "Scotland's greatest ever ambassador", but this quotation cannot be tracked in the canon. Music hall songs were Churchill's favourites.

Laval, Pierre

I am afraid I have rather exhausted the possibilities of the English language.

1942, 29 SEPTEMBER.

Pierre Laval (1883–1945) was Vichy France's Prime Minister, executed for treason after the war. This was Churchill's reply in the House to a request for a "categorical denunciation" of the French Quisling.

Lawrence of Arabia

He was indeed a dweller upon the mountain tops where the air is cold, crisp and rarefied, and where the view on clear days commands all the Kingdoms of the world and the glory of them...one of those beings whose pace of life was faster and more intense than the ordinary. Just as an aeroplane only flies by its speed and pressure against the air, so he flew best and easiest in the hurricane. He was not in complete harmony with the normal. The fury of the Great War raised the pitch of life to the Lawrence standard. The multitudes were swept forward until their pace was the same as his. In this heroic period he found himself in perfect relation both to men and events.

1935, 26 MAY. ("LAWRENCE OF ARABIA'S NAME WILL LIVE!," *NEWS OF THE WORLD*; GC, 104.)

Lieut.-Col. Thomas Edward Lawrence (1888–1935), renowned for helping to lead the Arab revolt from the Turks in World War I; author of the acclaimed book, The Seven Pillars of Wisdom, *and exactly the kind of swashbuckling figure who appealed to WSC.*

Those who knew him best miss him most; but our country misses him most of all; and misses him most of all now. For this is a time when the great problems upon which his thought and work had so long centred, problems of aerial defence, problems of our relations with the Arab peoples, fill an ever larger space in our affairs....

> All is over! Fleet career,
> Dash of greyhound slipping thongs,
> Flight of falcon, bound of deer,
> Mad hoof-thunder in our rear,
> Cold air rushing up our lungs,
> Din of many tongues.

1935, 26 MAY. (OP. CIT., 105.)

Churchill reached into his store of quotations for "The Last Leap", by the Australian poet Adam Lindsay Gordon (1833–70).

He had the art of backing uneasily into the limelight. He was a very remarkable character...and very careful of that fact.

1955. (MONTAGUE BROWNE, 201–2.)

Lawson, John James

The former Secretary of State for War is deservedly popular and respected in all sections of the House. His many good and charming qualities, high patriotism and public spirit, are admired by all. That, however, does not in any way efface the fact that he was not qualified to discharge, or capable of discharging, the extraordinary and complicated tasks with which the War Office is cumbered and pressed in the transition period at the end of a great war.

1946, 12 NOVEMBER.

John James Lawson, Labour MP (1881–1965), Secretary of State for War, 1946–47.

Lenin, Vladimir

Lenin was sent into Russia by the Germans in the same way that you might send a phial containing a culture of typhoid or cholera to be poured into the water supply of a great city, and it worked with amazing accuracy....he gathered together the leading spirits of a formidable sect, the most formidable sect in the world, of which he was the high priest and chief. With these spirits around him he set to work with demoniacal ability to tear to pieces every institution on which the Russian State and nation depended. Russia was laid low. Russia had to be laid low. She was laid low to the dust.

1919, 5 NOVEMBER.

Vladimir Ilyich Ulyanov, alias Lenin (1870–1924), Russian revolutionary, first head of the Russian Soviet Federated Socialist Republic (1917–22). In The Aftermath *ten years later, Churchill would write that the Germans, "transported Lenin in a sealed truck like a plague bacillus from Switzerland into Russia" (Crisis IV, 76).*

Implacable vengeance, rising from a frozen pity in a tranquil, sensible, matter-of-fact, good-humoured integument! His weapon logic; his mood opportunist. His sympathies cold and wide as the Arctic Ocean; his hatreds tight as the hangman's noose. His purpose to save the world: his method to blow it up. Absolute principles, but readiness to change them. Apt at once to kill or learn: dooms and afterthoughts: ruffianism and philanthropy: But a good husband; a gentle guest; happy, his biographers assure us, to wash up the dishes or dandle the baby; as mildly amused to stalk a capercailzie as to butcher an Emperor.

1929. (CRISIS IV, 74.)

Churchill's vocabulary was impressive: an "integument" is a tough outer protective layer, especially in an animal or plant. A "capercailzie" is the Scottish version of capercaillie, a large grouse found only in mature pine forests.

He alone could have led Russia into the enchanted quagmire; he alone could have found the way back to the causeway. He saw; he turned; he perished. The strong illuminant that guided him was cut off at the moment when he had turned resolutely for home. The Russian people were left floundering in the bog. Their worst misfortune was his birth; their next worst—his death.

1929. (CRISIS IV, 76.)

Colin Coote believed that Churchill "had a certain admiration for Lenin's talents", that had he lived, he might have curbed the worst excesses of Stalin. Sir Martin Gilbert stunned a Soviet audience in the 1980s by revealing discovery of Churchill's suggestion that the Allies send an envoy to get Lenin back into World War I, in exchange for which WSC proposed to recognise the Bolshevik revolution. See also Roosevelt, Theodore and Chapter 10...Aiding the Bolsheviks.

Lincoln, Abraham

To those who spoke of hanging Jefferson Davis he replied, "Judge not that ye be not judged." On April 11 [1865] he proclaimed the need of a broad and generous temper and urged the conciliation of the vanquished....But the death of Lincoln deprived the Union of the guiding hand which alone could have solved the problems of reconstruction and added to the triumph of armies those lasting victories which are gained over the hearts of men.

1958. (HESP IV, 262–3.)

Abraham Lincoln (1809–1965), 16th President of the United States; in the American Civil War he freed the slaves and saved the Union.

Litvinov, Maxim

Later on the President had a long talk with [Litvinov] alone about his soul and the dangers of hell-fire. The accounts which Mr. Roosevelt gave us on several occasions of what he said to the Russian were impressive. Indeed, on one occasion I promised Mr. Roosevelt to recommend him for the position of Archbishop of Canterbury if he should lose the next Presidential election.

1943, 3 JANUARY. CASABLANCA. (WW2 III, 604.)

Maxim Litvinov (1876–1951), Soviet Ambassador to the US, 1941–43. Roosevelt had persuaded him to include a clause providing for religious freedom in the United Nations Pact.

Lloyd, George

Lord Lloyd and I have been friends for many years and close political associates during the last twelve years. We championed several causes together which did not command the applause of large majorities; but it is just in that kind of cause, where one is swimming against the stream, that one learns the worth and quality of a comrade and friend....As honorary commodore of an air squadron, he learned to fly a Hurricane aeroplane and obtained a pilot's certificate when almost sixty years of age, thus proving that it is possible for a man to maintain in very high efficiency eye and hand, even after a lifetime of keen intellectual work.

1941, 6 FEBRUARY.

George Ambrose Lloyd, First Baron Lloyd (1879–1941) Conservative MP 1910–25, Colonial Secretary and Leader of the House of Lords under Churchill, died in office.

Lloyd George, David

Personally, I think Lloyd George a vulgar, chattering little cad....

1901, 23 DECEMBER. (OB, CV2 PART 1, 104.)

WSC to J. Moore Bayley. David Lloyd George, First Earl Lloyd-George of Dwyfor (1863–1945), Welsh MP, Liberal Prime Minister 1916–22. WSC's opinion soon changed; Lloyd George welcomed him to the Liberals in 1904 and together they canvassed the country on behalf of Liberal reforms.

He [Mr. Lloyd George] has distinguished himself upon this subject in a manner which deserves the widest public notice. He said on Saturday: "You are blessed, for you will not receive, you will give. Every time the lamp illuminates your cottage, and perfumes it, as it used to do in my own days, you will have the feeling that the wick is oozing wealth for Sir Alfred Mond [Imperial Chemicals] and Mr. Courtauld [silk industry]." That is the contribution to an important public controversy of a man who has been nine years Chancellor of the Exchequer and five years Prime Minister, who, after having held the greatest situation in Europe, looks forward with the utmost gusto to another series of "Limehouse Nights."

1928, 1 MAY.

Churchill is here referring to Lloyd George's 1909 Limehouse speech, attacking vested interests.

The Rt. Hon. Gentleman has always been a man of expedients, never a man of theme and system. The great services which he rendered to the country were rendered by instinct and nimbleness in dealing with point after point as they arose, but they did not take the form of laying out a smooth and ordered scheme either in politics or in strategy

1928, 5 JUNE.

At his best he could almost talk a bird out of a tree. An intense comprehension of the more amiable weaknesses of human nature; a sure gift of getting on the right side of a man from the beginning of a talk; a complete avoidance of anything in the nature of chop-logic reasoning; a deft touch in dealing with realities; the sudden presenting of positions hitherto unexpected but apparently conciliatory and attractive—all these are modes and methods in which he is a natural adept. I have seen him turn a Cabinet round in less than ten minutes, and yet when the process was complete, no one could remember any particular argument to which to attribute their change of view.

1931, FEBRUARY. ("PERSONAL CONTACTS," STRAND MAGAZINE; THOUGHTS, 38.)

...I did not think Mr. Lloyd George's speech...was the sort of speech one would have expected from the great war leader of former days, who was accustomed to brush aside despondency and alarm, and push on irresistibly towards the final goal. It was the sort of speech with which, I imagine, the illustrious and venerable Marshal Pétain might well have enlivened the closing days of M. Reynaud's Cabinet....I am grateful to my Rt. Hon. Friend for the note which he struck, [making] it clearer that we ought to close our Debate by a Vote of Confidence.

1941, 7 MAY.

WSC generally regarded Lloyd George as a mentor, but the Welshman refused to support WSC in World War II, hoping to replace him. The subsequent Vote of Confidence was supported 473 to 3, Lloyd George voting in the negative. Reynaud was the French Prime

Minister who had wished to fight on against the Germans in June 1940 but was ousted by the defeatist Marshal Pétain, who formed the Vichy Government.

His eye ranged ahead of the obvious. He was the champion of the weak and the poor. Those were great days. Nearly two generations have passed. Most people are unconscious of how much their lives have been shaped by the laws for which Lloyd George was responsible. Health Insurance and Old Age Pensions were the first large-scale State-conscious efforts to set a balustrade along the crowded causeway of the people's life, and, without pulling down the structures of society, to fasten a lid over the abyss into which vast numbers used to fall, generation after generation, uncared-for and indeed unnoticed....I was his lieutenant in those bygone days, and shared in a minor way in his work. I have lived to see long strides taken, and being taken, and going to be taken, on this path of insurance by which the vultures of utter ruin are driven from the dwellings of the nation....

When the calm, complacent, self-satisfied tranquillities of the Victorian era had exploded into the world convulsions and wars of the terrible Twentieth Century, Lloyd George had another part to play....Although unacquainted with the military arts, although by public repute a pugnacious pacifist, when the life of our country was in peril he rallied to the war effort and cast aside all other thoughts and aims...

1945, 28 MARCH.

In this tribute following Lloyd George's death, Churchill was careful to avoid reviewing his old friend's performance in the Appeasement years and early years of WWII, when Lloyd George was convinced Hitler would win and built a bomb shelter at his estate, Churt, which reminded a friend of "Piccadilly underground station".

His warm heart was stirred by the many perils which beset the cottage homes: the health of the breadwinner, the fate of his widow, the nourishment and upbringing of his children, the meagre and haphazard provision of medical treatment and sanatoria and the lack of any organized accessible medical service from which the mass of the wage earners and the poor in those days suffered. All this excited his wrath. Pity and compassion lent their powerful wings.

1945, 28 MARCH.

WSC repeated these words in 1955, in his last speech in the House of Commons.

Longmore, Air Chief Marshal Sir Arthur

I must not forget the work which has been done in this battle by Air Chief Marshal Longmore, who at the most critical moment in [the Battle of the Libyan Desert] his preparations had to have a very large portion of his force taken away from him for Greece, but who nevertheless persevered, running additional risks, and whose handling of this situation, in co-operation with the Army, deserves the highest praise. It is, indeed, a pleasure to me personally, because when I was at the Admiralty in 1912, forming the Royal Naval Air Service, he was one of the first few fliers there, and in those days of very dubious machines he several times used to fly me about. We were personal friends as long ago as that.

1940, 19 DECEMBER.

Air Chief Marshal Sir Arthur M. Longmore headed Coastal Command from 1936 to 1940.

Lothian, Lord

He was a man of the very highest character, and of far-ranging intellectual scope....the contacts which he established, the intimate relations which he developed with the high personnel of the United States Administration, the friendship to which the President of the United States has himself testified—all the evidence showed the remarkable efficiency and success with which he discharged his important and extremely delicate and difficult mission....

I cannot help feeling that to die at the height of a man's career, the highest moment of his effort here in this world, universally honoured and admired, to die while great issues are still commanding the whole of his interest, to be taken from us at a moment

when he could already see ultimate success in view—is not the most unenviable of fates.

1940, 19 DECEMBER.

Philip Henry Kerr, Eleventh Marquess of Lothian (1882–1940), politician and diplomat, British Ambassador to the United States 1939–40.

MacArthur, General Douglas

The ingenious use of aircraft to solve the intricate tactical problems, by the transport of reinforcements, supplies, and munitions, including field guns, is a prominent feature of MacArthur's generalship, and should be carefully studied in detail by all concerned in the technical conduct of the war.

1943, 11 FEBRUARY.

Douglas MacArthur (1880–1964), American general, Supreme Allied Commander, South-West Pacific in World War II, supervised occupation of Japan 1945–51, led United Nations forces in Korea 1950–51.

Here I would like to congratulate you upon, and pay a tribute to, the work of General MacArthur in Japan. He has seemed to show a genius in peace equal to the high renown he gained in war.

1949, 25 MARCH, RITZ CARLTON HOTEL, NEW YORK. (BALANCE, 35.)

Macaulay, Lord

It is beyond our hopes to overtake Lord Macaulay. The grandeur and sweep of his story-telling style carries him swiftly along, and with every generation he enters new fields. We can only hope that Truth will follow swiftly enough to fasten the label "Liar" to his genteel coat-tails.

1933. (MARLBOROUGH I, 129.)

Thomas Babbington Macaulay (1800–59), poet, historian and Whig politician. WSC was impelled to write his Life of Marlborough in part to refute Macaulay's charges against the First Duke.

MacDonald, Ramsay

The Government...are defeated by thirty votes and then the Prime Minister rises in his place utterly unabashed, the greatest living master of falling without hurting himself, and airily assures us that nothing has happened.

1931, 21 JANUARY.

James Ramsay MacDonald (1866–1937), first Labour Prime Minister, 1924; formed his second government in 1929; coalition Prime Minister 1931–35. See also Chapter 3, Churchillisms...Boneless Wonder.

We know that he has, more than any other man, the gift of compressing the largest number of words into the smallest amount of thought....

The Prime Minister's interventions in foreign affairs have been—not through any fault or neglect on his part—remarkably unsuccessful. His repeated excursions have not led to any solid, good result. Where anything has been achieved it has nearly always been at British expense and to British disadvantage. On the whole, his four years of control of our foreign relations have brought us nearer to war, and have made us weaker, poorer and more defenceless....

We have got our modern Don Quixote home again, with Sancho Panza [Sir John Simon] at his tail, bearing with them these somewhat dubious trophies which they have collected amid the nervous tittering of Europe. Let us hope that now the Rt. Hon. gentleman is safely back among us he will, first of all, take a good rest, of which I have no doubt he stands in need...

1933, 23 MARCH.

MacDonald had just returned from Rome. Sir John Simon (1873–1954) was Foreign Secretary in the 1931–35 Government; later he served Churchill's coalition Government as Lord Chancellor, 1940–45.

Maclean, Fitzroy

Here is the young man who has made a Public Convenience of the Mother of Parliaments.

1942. MACLEAN, CHURCHILL PROCEEDINGS, 1987.

WSC, with a grin, to Jan Smuts on introducing Fitzroy Maclean, who had got himself out of the Foreign Office and into the Army by standing for Parliament. Fitzroy Hew Royal Maclean of Duncannon KT (1911–96) was a diplomat,

writer and politician, a swashbuckler and favourite of WSC, whom he served in the war as special representative to Tito and the Yugoslav partisans.

Mahdi, The

...whatever is set to the Mahdi's account, it should not be forgotten that he put life and soul into the hearts of his countrymen, and freed his native land of foreigners.

1899. (RIVER I, 55.)

Muhammad ibn Abdullah (1844–85), the Mahdi ("expected one") massacred General Gordon and many of Khartoum's inhabitants in 1885, creating the Dervish Empire, which Britain reconquered in 1899. Colin Coote writes:

> *On this principle of giving the devil his due, Sir Winston sometimes said much the same about Hitler in the latter's early days; but he never mistook the devil for an angel. (Coote, 262).*

Marlborough, First Duke of

[Marlborough and Sarah] loved each other well enough not to worry too much about external things.

1933. (MARLBOROUGH I, 129.)

John Churchill, First Duke of Marlborough (1650–1722), soldier and statesman, the subject of WSC's most masterful biography.

[Marlborough's] toils could only be for England, for that kind of law the English called freedom, for the Protestant religion, and always in the background for that figure, half mystic symbol and the rest cherished friend, the Queen.

1934. (MARLBOROUGH II, 260.)

What a downy bird he was. He will always stoop to conquer. His long apprenticeship as a courtier had taught him to bow and scrape and to put up with the second or third best if he could get no better. He had far less pride than the average man.

1935, 1 JANUARY. (OB, CV5/2, 983.)

WSC to his wife, in the first of his "Chartwell Bulletins", written while she was on a South Seas voyage.

It was said of Marlborough that he could refuse a favour with more grace than others could grant one.

1936. (MARLBOROUGH III, 248.)

He set himself, as usual, to bring about the best results possible with the means at his disposal.

1938. (MARLBOROUGH IV, 55.)

Marsh, Edward

Eddie stripped himself naked and retired to the Bush, from which he could only be lured three times a day by promises of food.

1907, 11 DECEMBER, UGANDA. (HASSALL, 139.)

Sir Edward Howard Marsh (1872–1953), litterateur, arts patron, private secretary to Churchill, 1906–29. Eddie accompanied WSC on his African fact-finding journey in 1907, which resulted in WSC's book, My African Journey.

All his long life was serene, and he left that world I trust without a pang and I am sure without a fear.

1953, 13 JANUARY, JAMAICA. (OB VIII, 794.)

A. L. Rowse, in The Later Churchills, *records:*

Winston, with "a natural desire to have everything handsome about him", wanted to make Eddie a KCMG, which they interpreted to mean, for such was Eddie's function, Kindly Correct My Grammar.... He did not get his KCMG; he got a KCVO instead.

See Chapter 3, Churchillisms...choate, destrigulating.

Marshall, George C.

Perhaps the greatest Roman of them all.

CIRCA 1943–47. (ISMAY, 253.)

General of the Army George Catlett Marshall, Jr. (1880–1959), US Army Chief of Staff 1939–45, US Secretary of State 1947–48. Ismay is not clear whether this refers to the wartime Marshall or the post-war statesman.

Hitherto I had thought of Marshall as a rugged soldier and a magnificent organiser and builder of armies—the American Carnot. But

now I saw that he was a statesman with a penetrating and commanding view of the whole scene.

1950. (WW2 IV, 726–7.)

Marie François Sadi Carnot (1837–94), President of the Third Republic 1887–94, was a unifier and reconciler who, like so many who shared his character (but not Marshall), died by assassination.

Maugham, Somerset

I have just finished your brilliant and delightful book, The Moon and Sixpence, and I thought I would let you know how glad I am to have read it. It has many of the qualities of Gauguin's pictures.

1919. (BOSTON GLOBE, 31 AUGUST 2005.)

William Somerset Maugham (1874–1965), playwright and novelist.

"The rapier of sarcasm was more effective than the bludgeon of invective," [Maugham] was fond of saying, and he employed the former weapon so skillfully that no less nimble a tongue than Churchill struck a pact with his favorite novelist; he would promise to make no sport of Maugham if Maugham would extend him the same protection. – Boston Globe.

McKinley, William

I stayed with Chauncey Depew in Washington and he was very civil; showed me the Capitol, introduced me to a great many Senators of note and also presented me to the President, with whom I was considerably impressed.

1900, 21 DECEMBER, BOSTON. (OB, CV 1/2, 1223.)

WSC to his mother. William McKinley, Jr. (1843–1901), 25th President of the United States, assassinated in 1901. Chauncey Depew was Senator from New York 1899–1911; a railroader, he was much involved with the creation of Grand Central Station – when he was known jokingly as "Chauncey Depot of Grand Central Depew".

Menzies, Sir Robert

Mr. Menzies brings with him the strong assurance of the Australian Commonwealth that they will, with us, go through this long, fierce, dire struggle to the victorious end. It is, indeed, a marvellous fact that Australia and New Zealand, who are separated from us and from Europe, with all its passions and quarrels, by the great ocean spaces, should send their manhood and scatter their wealth upon this world cause. No law, no constitution, no bond or treaty pledges them to spend a shilling or send a man. We welcome Mr. Menzies here. He has sat with us in Cabinet. He has seen every aspect of our life at home. And he is going back presently by the United States to Australia. Much will have happened by the time he returns there. Australian and New Zealand troops may well be in contact with the enemy today. There, to the classic scenes of the ancient lands of Greece, they will bring the valour of the sons of the Southern Cross.

1941, 12 APRIL, BRISTOL UNIVERSITY. (CS, 6377.)

Sir Robert Gordon Menzies (1894–1978), Australian politician, Prime Minister of Australia 1939–41, 1949–66. A frequent critic of the wartime Churchill, after the war Menzies showered him with praises.

Mikolajczyk, Stanislaw

I have fervent hopes that Mr. Mikolajczyk, the worthy successor of General Sikorski, a man firmly desirous of friendly understanding and settlement with Russia, and his colleagues may shortly resume those important conversations in Moscow which were interrupted some months ago.

1944, 28 SEPTEMBER.

Stanislaw Mikolajczyk (1901–66), Polish Prime Minister in exile during WWII, later deputy Prime Minister.

I have the greatest respect for Mr. Mikolajczyk, and for his able colleagues who joined us at Moscow...I am sure they are more qualified to fill the place of the late General Sikorski than any other of the Polish leaders.

1944, 15 DECEMBER.

Wladyslaw Eugeniusz Sikorski (1881–1943), Polish general and statesman, Prime Minister of the Polish government in exile in London, 1940–43, was killed in an aeroplane crash.

Milner, Lord

Lord Milner's position in regard to the native question in South Africa is necessarily a very weak one. Being regarded after [the Boer War] as an inveterate enemy of the Dutch, as prime author of all their miseries, he had to fall back for his support upon the British section of the population, and upon that particular section of the population which is called the mine-owning group. In order to placate the mine-owning group, he had somewhat to ignore the interests of the British population. In order to propitiate the British population he had to sacrifice the interests of the Dutch, and in order to compensate the mine-owners, British and Dutch, for these disadvantages he had to sacrifice the interests of the natives.

1906, 28 FEBRUARY.

Alfred Milner, First Viscount Milner (1854–1925), German-born British colonial administrator, took a hard line towards the Boers before and after the Boer War.

Having been for many years, or at all events for many months, the arbiter of the fortunes of men who are "rich beyond the dreams of avarice," he is today poor, and, I will add, honourably poor. After twenty years of exhausting service under the Crown he is to-day a retired Civil servant, without pension or gratuity of any kind whatsoever.

1906, 21 MARCH.

Milner had been censured for refusing to allow light corporal punishment of coolies in South Africa in accord with the Chinese labour ordinance.

Molotov, Vyacheslav

I have never seen a human being who more perfectly represented the modern conception of a robot....In the conduct of foreign affairs, Mazarin, Talleyrand, Metternich, would welcome him to their company, if there be another world to which Bolsheviks allow themselves to go.

1948. (WW2 I, 288–9.)

Vyacheslav Molotov (1890–1986), Soviet politician and diplomat, Soviet Foreign Minister 1938–49. Jules Cardinal Mazarin (Italian, 1602–61), Charles Maurice de

Talleyrand-Périgord (French, 1754–1838) and Prince Klemens Wenzel von Metternich (Austrian, 1773–1859) were all brilliant diplomatists.

Monro, Gen. Sir Charles

General Monro was an officer of swift decision. He came, he saw, he capitulated.

1923. (CRISIS II, 489.)

Charles Carmichael Monro (1860–1929) replaced Ian Hamilton as Commander of British forces at Gallipoli, October 1915, and supervised the evacuation.

Montgomery, Field Marshal Sir Bernard

If he is disagreeable to those about him he is also disagreeable to the enemy.

1942, 9 AUGUST, CAIRO. (OB VII, 168.)

WSC to his wife.

Let me also pay my tribute to this vehement and formidable General Montgomery, a Cromwellian figure, austere, severe, accomplished, tireless, his life given to the study of war, who has attracted to himself in an extraordinary measure the confidence and the devotion of his Army.

1943, 11 FEBRUARY.

Field Marshal Bernard Law Montgomery, First Viscount Montgomery of Alamein (1887–1976), known as "Monty". British commander at the victory of El Alamein, Commander Eighth Army in North Africa and Italy, C-in-C of 21st Army Group in Europe.

Young, enthusiastic and triphibious.

1943, 9 AUGUST. (OB VII, 467.)

For more on "triphibious" and "triphibian", see People...Mountbatten and Churchillisms... Triphibious.

Field Marshal Montgomery is one of the greatest living masters of the art of war. Like Stonewall Jackson, he was a professor and teacher of the military science before he became an actor on the world stage. It has been my fortune and great pleasure often to be with him

at important moments in the long march from Mersa Matruh to the Rhine. Either on the eve of a great battle, or while the struggle was actually in progress, always I have found the same buoyant, vigorous, efficient personality with every aspect of the vast operation in his mind, and every unit of mighty armies in his grip.

1945, 23 OCTOBER, ALBERT HALL. (SINEWS, 25.)

See also Appendix I...Montgomery.

Monty has become a mellow, lovable exhibitionist; tamed but lonely and pathetic. He is not afraid of saying anything to anybody.

CIRCA 1953. (COLVILLE, FRINGES II, 304.)

Colville added a reference to Monty's famous proclamation that he lacked all vices: "But Maria de Casa Valdes scored (to Monty's great delight) when she asked him: 'But you tell me you don't drink, and you don't smoke: what do you do that is wrong? Bite your nails?'"

Don't use Montgomery in any of your revolutions. He will bankrupt you before you start. He will need thirteen Divisions before he'll ever make a move.

1960. (HALLE, IRREPRESSIBLE, 340.)

WSC in jest to Roberto "Tito" Arias, Panamanian Ambassador to Britain and husband of Margot Fonteyn.

Moran, Lord

...we divide our labours; he instructs me in the art of public speaking, and I teach him how to cure pneumonia.

1944, 2 MARCH, ROYAL COLLEGE OF PHYSICIANS, LONDON. (DAWN, 22.)

Charles McMoran Wilson, First Baron Moran (1882–1977), Churchill's personal physician 1940–65.

Morley, John

Lord Morley's reputation in this house is well known. For many a year he was an ornament of our Debates, and his learning and intellectual elevation, his brilliancy of phrasing, and the range of his experience, constitute assets and qualifications which the Government value in the highest degree.

1914, 25 MARCH.

John Morley, First Viscount Morley of Blackburn (1838–1923) was a Liberal MP, writer and newspaper editor. A confirmed pacifist, he quit the Asquith Cabinet at the outbreak of war in 1914, retaining nevertheless Churchill's admiration.

Such men are not found today. Certainly they are not found in British politics. The tidal wave of democracy and the volcanic explosion of the War have swept the shores bare....The old world of culture and quality...was doomed; but it did not lack its standard-bearer.

1929, NOVEMBER. ("JOHN MORLEY," *PALL MALL*; GC, 61–5.)

Morrison, Herbert

I hope he is not going to lecture us today on bringing party matters and party feelings into discussions of large public issues. There is no man I can think of from whom such rebukes and admonitions come less well. I would not go so far as to describe him in words used by the Minister of Health [Mr. Aneurin Bevan] a year ago when he was in an independent position as, a third class Tammany boss...I thought it was very much to be deprecated using disparaging expressions about important institutions of friendly countries.

1946, 31 MAY.

Herbert Stanley Morrison, Baron Morrison of Lambeth (1888–1965), Labour MP, at various times Foreign and Home Secretary and Deputy Prime Minister. First Minister of Supply in the Churchill coalition Government.

The Rt. Hon. Gentleman has an obvious, unconcealable, well-known relish for petty dictatorship. He has many good qualities, but he should always be on guard against his propensities and love to cat-and-mouse the people from morning until night....

There are, I must admit, moments when I am sorry for the Lord President of the Council, a man outpassed at the moment by his competitors, outdated even by his prejudices, scrambling along trying to regain popularity on an obsolete issue and on an ever-ebbing tide. I hope he will not mind my quoting or adapting some lines, although they are of a martial character, about his position:

"Crippses to the right of him. Daltons to left of him, Bevans behind him, volleyed and thundered....What tho' the soldiers knew. Some one had blunder'd....Then, they came back, but not the four hundred."

1947, 11 NOVEMBER.

WSC was paraphrasing Tennyson's "Charge of the Light Brigade".

The Rt. Hon. Member for Lewisham, South, is a curious mixture of geniality and venom. The geniality, I may say after a great many years of experience, is natural to himself. The venom has to be adopted in order to keep on sides with the forces [Labour MPs] below the Gangway.

1952, 21 MAY.

Moses

He was the greatest of the prophets, who spoke in person to the God of Israel; he was the national hero who led the Chosen People out of the land of bondage, through the perils of the wilderness, and brought them to the very threshold of the Promised Land; he was the supreme law-giver, who received from God that remarkable code upon which the religious, moral, and social life of the nation was so securely founded. Tradition lastly ascribed to him the authorship of the whole Pentateuch, and the mystery that surrounded his death added to his prestige.

1931, 8 NOVEMBER. ("MOSES," *SUNDAY CHRONICLE*; THOUGHTS, 205.)

Late in life, Churchill and David Ben-Gurion once argued about who was the greater prophet: Churchill argued for Moses, Ben-Gurion for Jesus!

Mountbatten, Lord Louis

Have you no sense of glory? What could you do if you returned to sea, except to be sunk in a larger and more expensive vessel?

1941, OCTOBER. (LORD MOUNTBATTEN TO THE CHURCHILL SOCIETY OF EDMONTON, ALBERTA, 11 APRIL 1966.)

Admiral of the Fleet the Earl Mountbatten of Burma (1900–79). WSC to Mountbatten after the latter expressed reluctance to become Chief of Combined operations. Mountbatten's destroyer, HMS Kelly, *had been sunk under him during the evacuation of Crete on 23 May 1941.*

It is not often under modern conditions and in established military professions that a man gets so great a chance so early. But if an officer having devoted his life to the military art does not know about war at 43, he is not likely to learn much more about it later on. As Chief of Combined Operations, Lord Louis has shown rare powers of organisation and resourcefulness. He is what—pedants notwithstanding—I will venture to call "a complete triphibian," that is to say, a creature equally at home in three elements— earth, air and water—and also well accustomed to fire.

1943, 31 AUGUST. BROADCAST, LONDON. (ONWARDS, 179.)

The first appearance of "triphibian" seems to be in the Baltimore Sun *of 26 October 1935: one Constantine Vlachos saw his invention collapse during a demonstration: "the device...called a triphibian, has never been seen off the ground, his wife said". See Chapter 3...Triphibious and Chapter 15... Royal Naval College.*

Moyne, Walter

I have known him almost all his life. For over thirty years, mostly in this House, we were intimate friends. Very young indeed did he succeed in getting out to the South African War, where he proved his courage and shed his blood. The bitter party strife which preceded the last world war made no difference to our relations, or to his relations with many of his opponents.

1944, 7 NOVEMBER.

Walter Edward Guinness, First Baron Moyne (1880–1944), Conservative MP 1906–31. Clementine Churchill's host on her 1935 South Seas voyage. Deputy Minister of State, Cairo, 1942, where he was assassinated by the Zionist group Lehi (Stern Gang).

Mussolini, Benito

Italy is a country which is prepared to face the realities of post-war reconstruction. It possesses a Government under the commanding leadership of Signor Mussolini which does not shrink from the logical consequences of economic facts and which has the courage to

impose the financial remedies required to secure and to stabilize the national recovery.

1926, 27 JANUARY, TREASURY, LONDON. (CS, 3824.)

Benito Amilcare Andrea Mussolini (1883–1945), Prime Minister and dictator of Italy 1922–43. Churchill was speaking on the signing of an agreement settling the Italian war debt to Britain.

The greatest law-giver among living men.

1933, 17 FEBRUARY. (OB V, 457.)

Speech to the anti-Socialist and Anti-Communist Union Meeting, Queen's Hall, London. A favourable early remark about Mussolini not recorded in the Complete Speeches, *which includes only an excerpt of this speech.*

...I must pay my tribute to Signor Mussolini...whose prestige and authority—by the mere terror of his name—quelled the wicked depredations of these marauders.

1937, 21 DECEMBER.

Following the Nyon Conference, which determined to sink submarines attacking merchant ships on the way to Spain; Churchill's irony was that the submarines were Italian.

...we are at war...How has this come about, and what is it all for? Italians, I will tell you the truth. It is all because of one man. One man and one man alone has ranged the Italian people in deadly struggle...That he is a great man I do not deny, but that after eighteen years of unbridled power he has led your country to the horrid verge of ruin can be denied by none. It is one man who...has arrayed the trustees and inheritors of ancient Rome upon the side of the ferocious pagan barbarians.

1940, 23 DECEMBER. BROADCAST TO THE PEOPLE OF ITALY, LONDON. (CS, 6322.)

...the Italian Dictator has congratulated the Italian army in Albania on the glorious laurels they had gained by their victory over the Greeks. Here surely is the world's record in the domain of the ridiculous and the contemptible. This whipped jackal, Mussolini, who to save his own skin has made all Italy a vassal state of Hitler's Empire, comes frisking up at the side of the German tiger with yelpings not only of appetite—that can be understood—but even of triumph....this absurd impostor will be abandoned to public justice and universal scorn.

1941, 27 APRIL. BROADCAST, LONDON.
(UNRELENTING, 95.)

The organ grinder still has hold of the monkey's collar.

1941, 30 DECEMBER. PRESS CONFERENCE, OTTAWA.
(DILKS, 210.)

A frequent reference to Mussolini as Hitler's puppet.

The end of Mussolini's long and severe reign over the Italian people undoubtedly marks the close of an epoch in the life of Italy. The keystone of the Fascist arch has crumbled, and without attempting to prophesy, it does not seem unlikely that the entire Fascist edifice will fall to the ground in ruins, if it has not already so fallen.

1943, 27 JULY.

...the successful campaign in Sicily brought about the fall of Mussolini and the heartfelt repudiation by the Italian people of the Fascist creed. Mussolini indeed escaped, to eat the bread of affliction at Hitler's table, to shoot his son-in-law, and help the Germans wreak vengeance upon the Italian masses whom he had professed to love, and over whom he had ruled for more than twenty years. This fate and judgment, more terrible than death, has overtaken the vainglorious dictator who stabbed France in the back and thought his crime had gained him the empire of the Mediterranean.

1944, 26 MARCH. BROADCAST, LONDON.
(DAWN, 39.)

Napoleon Bonaparte

I certainly deprecate any comparison between Herr Hitler and Napoleon; I do not wish to insult the dead.

1940, 19 DECEMBER. (OB, CV6 PART 2, 1263.)

Napoleon Bonaparte (1769–1821), French general, First Consul of France 1799–1804, Emperor 1804–14, 1815. See also Hitler.

Nehru, Jawaharlal

It was a cardinal mistake to entrust the government of India to the caste Hindu, Mr. Nehru. He has good reason to be the most bitter enemy of any connection between India and the British Commonwealth.

1947, 6 MARCH.

Pandit [Scholar] Jawaharlal Nehru (1889–1964), Indian National Congress leader, first Indian Prime Minister, 1947–64. After Nehru became Prime Minister, he and Churchill, old Harrovians both, became quite chummy. See next entry.

I am so much obliged to you for sending me the fascinating book of paintings taken from the Ajanta Caves. The reproductions are beautifully executed and I am indeed happy to possess such a wonderful book. It also gives me great pleasure that it should have come from you, and that our personal relations, after all that has happened, are so agreeable. I hope you will think of the phrase "The Light of Asia". It seems to me that you might be able to do what no other human being could in giving India the lead, at least in the realm of thought, throughout Asia, with the freedom and dignity of the individual as the ideal rather than the Communist Party drill book.

1955, 21 FEBRUARY. (OB VIII, 1094.)

WSC to Nehru.

Northcliffe, Viscount (Harmsworth, Arthur)

There can be no doubt that Lord Northcliffe was at all times animated by an ardent patriotism and an intense desire to win the war. But he wielded power without official responsibility, enjoyed secret knowledge without the general view, and disturbed the fortunes of national leaders without being willing to bear their burdens.

1927. (CRISIS III PART 1, 245.)

Arthur Harmsworth, First Viscount Northcliffe (1865–1922), the newspaper proprietor who successfully launched or rescued the Daily Mail, Daily Mirror, The Observer *and* The Times.

Onassis, Aristotle

Randolph brought Onassis (the one with the big yacht) to dinner last night. He made a good impression upon me. He is a v[er]y able and masterful man & told me a lot about Whales. He kissed my hand!

1956, 17 JANUARY, LA PAUSA, CAP MARTIN, FRANCE. (SOAMES, CLEMENTINE, 462.)

Aristotle Socrates Onassis (1906–75), Greek shipping magnate. From the evidence he genuinely loved Churchill and respected what WSC had done to save Greece from the communists in 1944. This meeting led to many agreeable voyages on the "big yacht", Christina, which comforted Sir Winston in his old age.

Patton, George S.

I earnestly hope that you are making a good recovery. Your accident has caused pain to your British friends and comrades who have admired your brilliant services in the common cause.

1945, 12 DECEMBER. MARSHMAN. ("CHURCHILL AND PATTON," FINEST HOUR 129, WINTER 2005–06.)

George Smith Patton, Jr. (1885–1945), nick-named "Old Blood and Guts", leading US general in North Africa, Sicily, France and Germany 1943–45. He died of an embolism following a car accident. Churchill had been particularly impressed by Patton's relief of hopelessly outnumbered Americans at Bastogne in December 1944.

Peake, Osbert

Osbert Peake came to dine & sleep last night and Christopher and I had 4 hours' v[er]y informative talk w him about OAP [Old Age Pensions], which is the dominant feature of next year's Cons[ervative] Programme....

Peake hates old people (as such) living too long and cast a critical eye on me....I felt v[er]y guilty. But in rejoinder I took him in to my study and showed him the 4 packets of proofs of the *History of the E.S. Peoples* wh[ich] bring 50,000 dollars a year into the island on my account alone. 'You don't keep me. I keep you.' He was rather taken aback.

1954, 19 AUGUST. (SOAMES, SPEAKING, 586.)

Osbert Peake, later First Viscount Ingleby (1897–1966), Minister of Pensions and National Insurance in the Churchill govern-ment during 1954–55. Arthur Christopher John Soames, Baron Soames (1920–87), married Mary Churchill 1947, Parliamentary Private Secretary to WSC 1951–55, Conservative MP 1955–66, served in numer-ous diplomatic posts including Ambassador to France and Governor of Rhodesia.

Pétain, Marshal

Pétain was of all others fitted to the healing task...He thus restored by the end of the year [1917] that sorely tried, glorious Army upon whose sacrifices the liberties of Europe had through three fearful campaigns mainly depended.

1927. (CRISIS III PART 1, 285–6.)

Henri Philippe Omer Joseph Pétain (1856–1951), French general in WWI (when he was known as the "Victor of Verdun"); head of state of Vichy France, 1940–44; condemned to death for treason, his sentence was commuted to life imprisonment by Charles de Gaulle.

Many Frenchmen who admire General de Gaulle and envy him in his role nevertheless regard him as a man who has rebelled against the authority of the French State, which in their prostration they conceive to be vested in the person of the antique defeatist who to them is the illustrious and venerable Marshal Pétain, the hero of Verdun and the sole hope of France.

1942, 10 DECEMBER. (SECRET, 82.)

Phillips, Vice-Admiral Sir Thomas

He was well known to us at Whitehall, and his long service at the Admiralty in a central posi-tion as Vice-Chief of the Navy Staff made him many friends, who mourn his loss. Personally, I regarded him as one of the ablest brains in the naval Service, and I feel honoured to have established personal friendship with him....It is a very heavy loss that we have suffered.

1941, 11 DECEMBER.

Sir Thomas Spencer Vaughan Phillips (1888–1941), Royal Navy admiral, lost in the South China Sea when his capital ships, HMS

Repulse *and* Prince of Wales, *were sunk by Japanese naval forces.*

Pick, Frank

Shake him by the hand! Shake him by the hand! You can say to St. Peter that you have met the perfect man....if I am stricken down by enemy action, I hope that, when I appear before my Maker, it will serve me in good stead to have been so recently in the company of a man without sin.

1941. (LORD MELCHETT IN HALLE,
IRREPRESSIBLE, 189.)

Frank Pick (1878–1941), Chairman of the London Passenger Transport Board, 1933–40, had rejected publishing a clandestine newspaper to subvert the enemy, on ethical grounds. He said he had never committed a mortal sin and was unwilling to be associated with one. Hearing this, WSC grasped Attlee's hand and uttered this exclamation.

Plimsoll, Samuel

No man could have offended more against the Rules of the House than Mr. Plimsoll, for he used violent language, was disorderly in debate, preferred a serious charge against another Hon. Member which was found afterwards to be baseless, shook his fist in the face of Mr. Disraeli, and left the House stating that he would not withdraw one single word of what he had said....but he made amends for his disorderly conduct, which showed that a respectful apology was not incompatible even with the most strenuous protest. But although Mr. Plimsoll's apology was of a qualified nature, the House was disposed to be generous, and he was allowed to resume his seat, and the mark of his work was set upon every ship that went to sea.

1902, 11 FEBRUARY.

Samuel Plimsoll (1824–98) devised the Plimsoll Line which to this day marks the capacity limit of each ship on her hull. When Prime Minister Disraeli abandoned the pursuit of more stringent inspection of ships, Plimsoll shook his fist and complained of "villains" in the House, for which he was reprimanded. The Plimsoll Line was made compulsory on British ships in 1894.

Pound, Admiral Sir Dudley

Dudley Pound's a funny old boy. People think he's *always* asleep, but you've only got to suggest reducing the naval estimates by a million and he's awake in a flash.

1941. (PAWLE, 29.)

Admiral of the Fleet Sir Alfred Dudley Pickman Rogers Pound (1877–1943), First Sea Lord 1939–43.

Queen Anne

On her throne she was as tough as Marlborough in the field.

1936. (MARLBOROUGH III, 185.)

Queen Anne (1665–1714), Queen of Great Britain and Ireland, 1702–14.

Queen Elizabeth II

...a character...She has an air of authority & reflectiveness astonishing in an infant....

1928, 25 SEPTEMBER, BALMORAL.
(SOAMES, SPEAKING, 328.)

Elizabeth Alexandra Mary (1926–), Queen of Great Britain and Northern Ireland, 1952–. This is Churchill's first known opinion on the future Queen, then aged two and with no expectation of ascending the throne.

"One touch of nature makes the whole world kin," and millions will welcome this joyous event as a flash of colour on the hard road we have to travel.

1947, 22 OCTOBER.

*Churchill's capacious memory brought forth his quotation of Shakespeare (*Troilus and Cressida, *iii. 3) on the marriage of Princess Elizabeth to the Duke of Edinburgh.*

Madam, the whole nation is grateful to you for what you have done for us and to Providence for having endowed you with the gifts and personality which are not only precious to the British Commonwealth and Empire and its island home, but will play their part in cheering and in mellowing the forward march of human society all the world over.

1951, 19 NOVEMBER. GUILDHALL, LONDON.
(STEMMING, 194.)

[She is] heir to all our traditions and glories never greater than in her father's days, and to all our perplexities and dangers never greater in peacetime than now. She is also heir to all our united strength and loyalty.

1952, 11 FEBRUARY.

Lovely, she's a pet. I fear they may ask her to do too much. She's doing so well....Lovely, inspiring. All the film people in the world, if they had scoured the globe, could not have found anyone so suited to the part.

1953, 18 & 24 FEBRUARY. (MORAN, 425, 429.)

Both remarks were made as WSC gazed at a new photograph of the Queen. "She was in white," wrote Lord Moran, "with long white gloves, smiling and radiant." It was his favourite photo of Her Majesty. On the second occasion, Moran recounts, WSC began singing a hymn: "Yet nightly pitch my moving tent a day's march nearer home." (WSC had recited the same words to the Eighth Army at Tripoli ten years earlier; see Chapter 18...1943.)

Our Island no longer holds the same authority or power that it did in the days of Queen Victoria. A vast world towers up around it and after all our victories we could not claim the rank we hold were it not for the respect for our character and good sense and the general admiration not untinged by envy for our institutions and way of life. All this has already grown stronger and more solidly founded during the opening years of the present Reign, and I regard it as the most direct mark of God's favour we have ever received in my long life that the whole structure of our new formed Commonwealth has been linked and illuminated by a sparkling presence at its summit.

1955, 18 APRIL. SICILY. (OB VIII, 1127–8.)

Reply to the Queen's message following his retirement. Elizabeth II had referred to WSC as:

my first Prime Minister, to whom both my husband and I owe so much and for whose wise guidance during the early years of my reign I shall always be so profoundly grateful.

Queen Victoria

So the Queen is dead. The news reached us at Winnipeg and this city far away among the snows—fourteen hundred miles from any British town of importance began to hang its head and hoist half-masted flags. A great and solemn event....

1901, 22 JANUARY, WINNIPEG, MANITOBA.
(OB, CV1 PART 2, 1231.)

WSC to his mother. Alexandrina Victoria (1819–1901), Queen of Great Britain and Ireland 1837–1901, first Empress of India 1876–1901.

It was very different in the days of Queen Victoria. Then the world seemed set in a frame, and the paths of progress were clearly marked before us. Free trade, the gold standard, our Indian Empire, a supreme Navy, universal education, the sweeping away of class privilege, and the gradual but constant extension of the franchise—these seemed to be the well-defined plans of the British people.

1934, 13 JANUARY. ("DEFENCE NOT DEFIANCE,"
PICTORIAL WEEKLY; ESSAYS I, 312.)

Rawlinson, General Sir Henry

I had known him since Omdurman....He had always the same welcome for a friend, be he highly or lowly placed....Now [in WWI] we met at the zenith of his career, when he had largely by his personal contribution gained a battle which we now know ranks among the decisive episodes of war. During these vicissitudes he was always the same. In the best of fortunes or the worst, in the most dangerous and hopeless position or on the crest of the wave, he was always the same tough, cheery gentleman and sportsman.

1927. (CRISIS III PART 2, 507.)

Henry Seymour Rawlinson (1864–1925). Commander, 4th Army at the Somme and Amiens in World War I. In 1919 he became Lord Rawlinson of Trent.

Reves, Wendy

Daisy, Wendy is three things you will never be. She is young, she is beautiful, and she is kind.

CIRCA 1959. LA CAPPONCINA, CAP D'AIL, FRANCE.
(SIR ANTHONY MONTAGUE BROWNE TO THE EDITOR.)

Wendy Russell Reves (1916–2007), wife of Churchill's literary agent Emery Reves and his frequent hostess in the south of France. The socialite Daisy Fellowes was at the Beaverbrook villa with Churchill. Thinking WSC asleep, she remarked about WSC's cruises aboard the Onassis yacht:

> What a tragedy that so great a man must spend his declining years in the company of Onassis and Wendy Reves.

Ribbentrop, Joachim von

There was a large map on the wall, and the Ambassador several times led me to it to illustrate his projects…I thought it right to say to the German Ambassador—in fact I remember the words well, "When you talk of war, which no doubt would be general war, you must not underrate England. She is a curious country, and few foreigners can understand her mind. Do not judge by the attitude of the present Administration. Once a great cause is presented to the people, all kinds of unexpected actions might be taken by this very Government and by the British nation." And I repeated, "Do not underrate England. She is very clever. If you plunge us all into another Great War, she will bring the whole world against you like last time."

1948. (WW2 I, 174–5.)

Joachim von Ribbentrop (1893–1946), German Ambassador to Britain 1936–38 (visits to Lord Londonderry found him dubbed the "Londonderry Herr"). At this 1937 meeting, Churchill added that Ribbentrop angrily retorted, "Ah, England may be very clever, but this time she will not bring the world against Germany." Churchill continued:

> When he was on trial for his life by the conquerors Ribbentrop gave a distorted version of this conversation and claimed that I should be summoned as a witness. What I have set down about it is what I should have said had I been called.

At one moment I came in contact with Frau von Ribbentrop, and in a valedictory vein I said, "I hope England and Germany will preserve their friendship." "Be careful you don't spoil it," was her graceful rejoinder. I am sure they both knew perfectly well what had happened, but thought it was a good manoeuvre to keep the Prime Minister away from his work and the telephone. At length

Mr. Chamberlain said to the Ambassador, "I am sorry I have to go now to attend to urgent business" and without more ado he left the room. The Ribbentrops lingered on, so that most of us made our excuses and our way home. Eventually I suppose they left. This was the last time I saw Herr von Ribbentrop before he was hanged.

1948. (WW2 I, 212.)

Conversation at a reception thrown by Chamberlain for the German Ambassador to Britain Ribbentrop, in March 1936, just as German troops were entering the Rhineland. The final sentence is typical of the master literary stylist that Churchill was.

Roberts, Field Marshal Lord

I have never seen a man before with such extraordinary eyes. I remember to have been struck with them on several occasions. The face remains perfectly motionless, but the eyes convey the strongest emotions. Sometimes they blaze with anger, and you see hot yellow fire behind them. Then it is best to speak up straight and clear, and make an end quickly. At others there is a steel grey glitter—quite cold and uncompromising—which has a most sobering effect on anyone who sees it.

1900, 2 JUNE, JOHANNESBURG. (HAMILTON'S, 281; BOER, 348–9.)

Frederick Sleigh Roberts, First Earl Roberts (1832–1914), known as "Bobs", one of the most distinguished generals of the Victorian era.

Robertson, Sir William

The reader may pass lightly over such incidents as that of General Robertson (who had never himself at any time led even a troop in action, and whose war duties involved him in no more risk than many clerks) speaking of the Cabinet as "poltroons."

1928, NOVEMBER. ("DOUGLAS HAIG," PALL MALL; GC, 145.)

Field Marshal Sir William Robert Robertson, First Baronet of Beaconsfield (1860–1933), Chief of the Imperial General Staff, 1916–18.

Rommel, Erwin

He was a splendid military gambler, dominating the problems of supply and scornful of opposition....His ardour and daring inflicted grievous disasters upon us, but he deserves the salute which I made him—and not without some reproaches from the public—in the House of Commons in January 1942, when I said of him, "We have a very daring and skilful opponent against us, and, may I say across the havoc of war, a great general." He also deserves our respect because, although a loyal German soldier, he came to hate Hitler and all his works, and took part in the conspiracy of 1944 to rescue Germany by displacing the maniac and tyrant. For this he paid the forfeit of his life. In the sombre wars of modern democracy chivalry finds no place....Still, I do not regret or retract the tribute I paid to Rommel, unfashionable though it was judged.

1950. (WW2 III, 176–7.)

Erwin Johannes Eugen Rommel (1891–1944), known as "the Desert Fox", distinguished German Field Marshal and commander of the Afrika Korps. After his opposition to Hitler became known, he was given the choice of suicide or execution; he chose the former, and was given a state funeral by the Fuehrer. Churchill wrote much the same thing later (WW2 IV: 59).

Roosevelt, Franklin

The United States is a land of free speech; nowhere is speech freer, not even here where we sedulously cultivate it even in its most repulsive forms. But when I see some of the accounts of conversations that I am supposed to have had with the President of the United States, I can only recall a Balfourian phrase at which I laughed many years ago, when he said that the accounts which were given bore no more relation to the actual facts than the wildest tales of the Arabian Nights do to the ordinary incidents of domestic life in the East.

1944, 28 SEPTEMBER.

Franklin Delano Roosevelt (1882–1945), 32nd President of the United States (1933–45).

We shall be delighted if you will come to Malta. I shall be waiting on the quay. You will also see the inscription of your noble message to Malta of a year ago, Everything can be arranged to your convenience. No more let us falter! From Malta to Yalta/Let nobody alter....and I elaborated this for private use: No more let us alter or falter or palter. From Malta to Yalta, and Yalta to Malta.

1945, 1 JANUARY. (WW2 VI, 295.)

WSC to Roosevelt en route to the Yalta Conference.

Our friendship is the rock on which I build for the future of the world, so long as I am one of the builders.

1945, 18 MARCH. (WW2 VI, 377.)

Have you heard the awful news, Thompson? President Roosevelt has passed away. No one realises what he has meant to this country and the world. He was a great friend to us. He gave us immeasurable help at a time when we most needed it. I may, I hope, be able to go across tomorrow for the funeral which takes place this week-end. I do not know for certain yet. Moreover it is Friday, the 13th.

1945, 13 APRIL. THOMPSON, SHADOW 153.

When Roosevelt died on 12 April, Churchill's immediate wish was to fly over for the funeral. It has been suggested in a recent book that he did not go out of pique that Roosevelt and he had grown apart since Teheran and Yalta, or that he felt FDR got more credit for winning the war. This would not have been like Churchill. In fact, as this and subsequent quotations show, his sense of duty intervened.

It would have been a solace to me to be present at Franklin's funeral, but everyone here thought my duty next week lay at home, at a time when so many Ministers are out of the country.

1945, 13 APRIL. (OB VII, 1294.)

WSC to Harry Hopkins. In fact, WSC put off his decision not to go to within forty-five minutes of his plane's scheduled departure for Washington. Personal Telegram T.459/5, Churchill Papers, 20/99.

I conceived an admiration for him as a statesman, a man of affairs, and a war leader. I felt the utmost confidence in his upright, inspiring character and outlook, and a personal regard—affection I must say—for him beyond my power to express today. His love of his own country, his respect for its constitution, his power of gauging the tides and currents of its mobile public opinion, were always evident, but added to these were the beatings of that generous heart which was always stirred to anger and to action by spectacles of aggression and oppression by the strong against the weak.

...When I took my leave of him in Alexandria harbour I must confess that I had an indefinable sense of fear that his health and his strength were on the ebb. But nothing altered his inflexible sense of duty. To the end he faced his innumerable tasks unflinching. One of the tasks of the President is to sign maybe a hundred or two State papers with his own hand every day, commissions and so forth. All this he continued to carry out with the utmost strictness. When death came suddenly upon him "he had finished his mail". That portion of his day's work was done. As the saying goes, he died in harness, and we may well say in battle harness, like his soldiers, sailors, and airmen, who side by side with ours are carrying on their task to the end all over the world.

...In the days of peace he had broadened and stabilized the foundations of American life and union. In war he had raised the strength, might and glory of the Great Republic to a height never attained by any nation in history....

But all this was no more than worldly power and grandeur, had it not been that the causes of human freedom and of social justice, to which so much of his life had been given, added a lustre to this power and pomp and warlike might, a lustre which will long be discernible among men....For us, it remains only to say that in Franklin Roosevelt there died the greatest American friend we have ever known, and the greatest champion of freedom who has ever brought help and comfort from the new world to the old.

1945, 17 APRIL.

...to encounter Roosevelt, with all his buoyant sparkle, his iridescent personality, and his sublime confidence, was like opening your first bottle of champagne. That physical effect it had on you was like the effect champagne had.

UNDATED. (HALLE PAPERS, KENNEDY LIBRARY, BOSTON.)

The full remark was quoted without attribution by Doris Kearns Goodwin, 109th Landon Lecture, Kansas State University, 22 April 1997, and would not normally be admissible here. But part of it appears in Jon Meacham's excellent Franklin and Winston *(New York: Random House, 2003, xiv), who cites as his source the papers of Kay Halle, a friend of the Churchills over thirty years.*

Roosevelt, Theodore

[If Theodore Roosevelt] were with Trotsky at the inevitable moment when war is again declared between Germany and Russia, a rallying point might be created sufficiently prominent for all Russians to fix their gaze upon.

1918, 5 APRIL. (GILBERT, LIFE, 389.)

Memo to the War Cabinet. Theodore Roosevelt, Jr. (1858–1919), 26th President of the United States (1901–09). In a remarkable Cabinet memo, Churchill suggested that Theodore Roosevelt might be the right representative to persuade Lenin to re-enter the war against Germany. For more of this quotation see Russia...Aiding the Bolsheviks.

Theodore Roosevelt, on the outbreak of the First [World] War, asked to see Woodrow Wilson. Wilson gave him an appointment, but received him very coolly. Roosevelt wanted to command something in the field. On going out, he met Colonel House and said to him: "Wilson was very rough with me. After all, all I asked was to be allowed to die." House replied (in his silkiest tones): "Did you make that last point clear to the President?"

1944, 21 SEPTEMBER. (MORAN, 198.)

Paraphrased from Moran's third-person account. Edward Mandell House (1858–1938) was foreign policy adviser to Woodrow Wilson through 1918.

Rosebery, the Earl of

It might be said that Lord Rosebery outlived his future by ten years and his past by more than twenty....Rosebery flourished in an age of great men and small events....He was one of those men of affairs who add to the unsure prestige of a minister and the fleeting successes of an orator the more enduring achievements of literature. Some of his most polished work is found in his Rectorial Addresses and in his appreciations of great poets and writers like Burns and Stevenson.

1929, OCTOBER. ("LORD ROSEBERY," PALL MALL; GC, 3, 10, 13.)

Archibald Philip Primrose, Fifth Earl of Rosebery (1847–1929), succeeded Gladstone as Liberal Prime Minister, 1894–95.

Roskill, Stephen

...I have an overwhelming case against the Admiralty historian [Roskill]. He belongs to the type of retired Naval Officers who think that politicians should only be in the Admiralty in time of War to take the blame for naval failures, and provide the Naval Officers with rewards in cases of their successes, if any.

1954, 25 MAY. (SOAMES, SPEAKING, 579.)

WSC to his wife. A rare case where Churchill's judgement of one of his future detractors preceded the critic's book. Roskill published the highly critical Churchill and the Admirals *(London: Collins) in 1977. Stephen Wentworth Roskill (1903–82) was official historian of the Royal Navy.*

Runciman, Walter

Is this the sort of welcome you will give the Lancashire Fusiliers when they come home from Omdurman? Mr. Runciman has not had the experience of the Lancashire Fusiliers—his contests have been more pacific, and while they were fighting at Omdurman for their country he was fighting at Gravesend for himself; while they were gaining a victory, Mr. Runciman at Gravesend was being defeated.

1899. (BROAD, 18.)

Walter Runciman, First Viscount Runciman of Doxford (1870–1949), Liberal MP 1899–1934, defeated Churchill in the Oldham election of 1899. There was a long antipathy. It was Runciman who, years later, threatened to transfer Ralph Wigram to Asia, stranding his wife with their disabled child in London, for passing Churchill details of German rearmament.

Saint Patrick

For six years...he tended swine, and loneliness led him to seek comfort in religion.

(HESP I, 72.)

Saint Patrick (ca. 373–493), Christian Irish missionary, patron saint of Ireland.

Savinkov, Boris

He was that extraordinary product—a Terrorist for moderate aims. A reasonable and enlightened policy—the Parliamentary system of England....freedom, toleration and good will—to be achieved wherever necessary by dynamite at the risk of death....[He] seemed to be the appointed agent of Russian salvation. A little more time, a little more help, a little more confidence, a few more honest men, the blessing of Providence, and a rather better telephone service—all would have been well!

1929, FEBRUARY. ("BORIS SAVINKOV," PALL MALL; GC, 76, 78.)

Boris Victorovich Savinkov (1879–1925), Vice Minister of War in the 1917 Kerensky Government, ousted by Lenin's Bolsheviks in November 1917. He supported the White Russians; ultimately he was lured to Russia, where he received a show trial and was apparently murdered by Soviet authorities. WSC wrote, "He was the essence of good sense expressed in terms of nitroglycerine" (Crisis IV, 78).

Scrymgeour, Edwin

...a quaint and then dim figure in the shape of Mr. Scrymgeour, the Prohibitionist, who pleaded for the kingdom of God upon earth with special reference to the evils of alcohol.

1931, SEPTEMBER. ("ELECTION MEMORIES," STRAND MAGAZINE; THOUGHTS, 151.)

Edwin Scrymgeour (1866–1947), known as "Neddy", the only Prohibitionist MP, 1922–31. He fought six elections against Churchill and finally defeated him in 1922. The unsubstantiated quotation, "he has none of the vices I admire" was allegedly said of Scrymgeour or Cripps. (See Appendix I.)

Shaw, George Bernard

...I possess a lively image of this bright, nimble, fierce, and comprehending being, Jack Frost dancing bespangled in the sunshine, which I should be very sorry to lose....Few people practise what they preach, and no one less so than Mr. Bernard Shaw....He is at once an acquisitive capitalist and a sincere Communist. He makes his characters talk blithely about killing men for the sake of an idea; but would take great trouble not to hurt a fly....

When nations are fighting for life, when the Palace in which the Jester dwells not uncomfortably is itself assailed, and everyone from Prince to groom is fighting on the battlements, the Jester's jokes echo only through deserted halls, and his witticisms and commendations, distributed evenly between friend and foe, jar the ears of hurrying messengers, of mourning women and wounded men. The titter ill accords with the tocsin, or the motley with the bandages.

1929, AUGUST. ("BERNARD SHAW," PALL MALL;
GC, 27, 30, 34.)

George Bernard Shaw (1856–1950), celebrated Irish playwright, literary critic and socialist. See also Chapter 33...Bring a Friend.

Shinwell, Emanuel

I do not challenge the Hon. Gentleman when the truth leaks out of him by accident from time to time.

1944, 8 DECEMBER.

Emanuel Shinwell, Baron Shinwell (1884–1986) Labour MP 1922–67. He often sparred with Churchill across the floor, but beneath it they had considerable affection for each other, as was common in the days when collegiality rather than soundbites guided our politicians.

Phrases which he used have run all over the country. The "tinker's cuss" was a household word, and he has made that homely and necessary instrument of an honoured profession common to the daily usage of all classes in the land.

1948, 1 DECEMBER.

In English vernacular, "I don't give a tinker's cuss" is a euphemism for being unimpressed with something, in this case the orations of Manny Shinwell.

I should, of course, treat with great attention anything he might say upon the subject of contradictory statements by politicians or Ministers. He is a past master of the art himself.

1952, 28 OCTOBER.

I must have been too complimentary to the Rt. Hon. Gentleman. He has explained what harm any compliment from me did to him, I must really rake up a few more compliments.

1953, 17 NOVEMBER.

Smuts, Jan Christian

I cannot say there has never been a kick in our gallop. I was examined by him when I was a prisoner-of-war, and I escaped; but we made an honourable and generous peace on both sides, and for the last forty years we have been comrades working together.

1942, 31 OCTOBER, WESTMINSTER CENTRAL HALL.
(END, 254.)

Jan Christian Smuts (1870–1950), was twice Prime Minister of South Africa (1919–24, 1939–48). One of Churchill's closest friends from the time of the Boer War forward. The formalisation of total apartheid came in after Smuts left office.

Smuts and I are like two old love-birds moulting together on a perch, but still able to peck.

CIRCA 1944–45. (COLVILLE, CHURCHILLIANS, 135.)

No one knew better than he how to "meet with Triumph and Disaster, and treat those two impostors just the same."

1951. WW2 IV, 386.

The quotation is from Rudyard Kipling's poem "If", published 1895.

We believe that the people of Britain may wish to share in a memorial to Smuts by contributing to a fund to preserve Doornkloof in memory of this man who shone among his contemporaries, was a devoted friend of this country, and whose counsels and initiatives in war and peace were on a high plane of statesmanship and humanity.

1964, 18 JANUARY. (THE TIMES.)

This was Churchill's last letter to The Times. *Smuts's home, Doornkloof, ten miles outside Pretoria, was preserved and is today a museum.*

Snowden, Philip

A perverse destiny has seemed to brood over the Rt. Hon. Gentleman's career; all his life has been one long struggle to overcome the natural amiability of his character.

1925, 25 MAY.

Philip Snowden, First Viscount Snowden (1864–1937), Labour MP and first Labour Chancellor of the Exchequer (1924); he returned to the post with Labour's 1929 victory and remained Chancellor in the National Government, until his retirement in 1931. Churchill thought highly of him.

He was really a tender-hearted man, who would not have hurt a gnat unless his party and the Treasury told him to do so, and then only with compunction....We must imagine with what joy Mr. Snowden was welcomed at the Treasury by the permanent officials. All British Chancellors of the Exchequer have yielded themselves, some spontaneously, some unconsciously, some reluctantly to that compulsive intellectual atmosphere. But here was the High Priest entering the sanctuary. The Treasury mind and the Snowden mind embraced each other with the fervour of two long-separated kindred lizards, and the reign of joy began....He was a preaching friar with no Superior to obey but his intellect....

The British democracy should be proud of Philip Snowden. He was a man capable of maintaining the structure of Society while at the same time championing the interests of the masses....

1931, 2 AUGUST. ("PHILIP SNOWDEN," *SUNDAY PICTORIAL*; GC, 185–90.)

Spee, Admiral Maximilian von

To steam at full speed or at high speed for any length of time on any quest was to use up his life rapidly. He was a cut flower in a vase; fair to see, yet bound to die, and to die very soon if the water was not constantly renewed.

1923. (CRISIS I, 295.)

Maximilian Graf von Spee (1861–1914), commanded the German East Asia Squadron from 1912. WSC is describing his actions between sinking two outclassed British cruisers

off Coronel, Chile, in November 1914, and being sunk himself in the Battle of the Falkland Islands a month later.

Stalin, Josef

He is a man of massive outstanding personality, suited to the sombre and stormy times in which his life has been cast; a man of inexhaustible courage and will-power, and a man direct and even blunt in speech, which, having been brought up in the House of Commons, I do not mind at all, especially when I have something to say of my own. Above all, he is a man with that saving sense of humour which is of high importance to all men and all nations, but particularly to great men and great nations. Stalin also left upon me the impression of a deep, cool wisdom and a complete absence of illusions of any kind. I believe I made him feel that we were good and faithful comrades in this war—but that, after all, is a matter which deeds, not words, will prove.

1942, 8 SEPTEMBER.

Josef Vissarionovich Dzhugashvilli, later Stalin (1878–1953), General Secretary of the Soviet Communist Party Central Committee, 1922–53, Soviet leader in WWII.

Large man; great sagacity...never stops smiling.

1942. (DIARIES OF CABINET SECRETARY SIR NORMAN BROOK, *NEW YORK TIMES*, 22 JANUARY 2006.)

Poor Neville Chamberlain believed he could trust Hitler. He was wrong, but I don't think I'm wrong about Stalin.

1945, 23 FEBRUARY. (PIMLOTT, 835.)

Events proved otherwise.

But do not, I beg you, my friend Stalin, underrate the divergences which are opening about matters which you may think are small to us, but which are symbolic of the way the English-speaking democracies look at life.

1945, 25 APRIL. (WW2 VI, 433–4.)

Silly tales have been told of how these Soviet dinners became drinking-bouts. There is no truth whatever in this. The Marshal and his colleagues invariably drank their toasts from tiny glasses, taking only a sip on each

occasion. I had been well brought up....
[Stalin said], "You are leaving at daybreak.
Why should we not go to my house and have
some drinks?" I said that I was in principle
always in favour of such a policy.

1950. (WW2 IV, 442–6.)

Steevens, G. W.

...the most brilliant man in journalism I have
ever met.

1930. (MEL, 227.)

George Warrington Steevens (1869–1900),
leading war correspondent of the 1890s, wrote
With Kitchener to Khartum and Monologues
of the Dead. Like Churchill, he went to South
Africa in 1900; but he died of enteric fever at
Ladysmith.

Stevenson, Adlai

It is as well to build up a personality on a solid
structure of sound argument. In America,
when they elect a President they want more
than a skilful politician. They are seeking a
personality: something that will make the
President a good substitute for a monarch.
Adlai Stevenson will have to build himself up
gradually if he is to do any good.

1955, 19 MAY. (MORAN, 698.)

Adlai Ewing Stevenson II (1900–65),
Democratic candidate for President of the
United States, 1952, 1956. US Ambassador to
the United Nations, 1961–65.

...I envy you your forthcoming visit to Hatfield
with the meeting with Adlai Stevenson. He is
v[er]y well thought of in English political circles
& I hope he will run again for the Presidency;
but that is a long time yet....Darling one do
write again and tell me about Hatfield and Adlai.

1957, 21 MAY, LA PAUSA, CAP MARTIN, FRANCE.
(OB VIII, 1243.)

WSC to his wife. Evidently Churchill was one
of Stevenson's longest-lasting supporters; but
Stevenson did not run again in 1960.

Summerskill, Edith

[Her] authoritarian demeanour would inspire
all, if her agreeable personality did not somewhat discount it.

1947, 12 MARCH.

Edith Summerskill, Deputy Minister of Food
in the post-war Labour Government. See also
Chapter 4...words/man.

Trotsky, Leon

All his scheming, all his daring, all his writing, all his harangues, all his atrocities, all
his achievements, have led only to this—
that another "comrade," his subordinate in
revolutionary rank, his inferior in wit,
though not perhaps in crime [Stalin], rules
in his stead, while he, the once triumphant
Trotsky whose frown meted death to thousands, sits disconsolate—a skin of malice
stranded for a time on the shores of the
Black Sea and now washed up in the Gulf of
Mexico.

He possessed in his nature all the qualities requisite for the art of civic destruction
—the organising command of a Carnot, the
cold detached intelligence of a Machiavelli,
the mob oratory of a Cleon, the ferocity of a
Jack the Ripper, the toughness of Titus
Oates....

1929, DECEMBER. ("LEON *ALIAS* BRONSTEIN,"
PALL MALL; GC, 123–5.)

Leon Trotsky (Lev Davidovich Bronstein,
1877–1940), Communist leader after Lenin's
death; defeated by Stalin, 1924, for control of
the Communist Party, exiled to Mexico and
later killed by Soviet agents. During World War
II, with Russia now an ally, Churchill
expunged the Trotsky chapter from
Great Contemporaries; it was reinserted in
1947. Lazare Carnot (1753–1823), a rebel
known as "le grand Carnot". Titus Oates
(1649–1705), author of the fictitious "Catholic
Plot" to murder Charles II.

Truman, Harry

At any rate, he is a man of immense determination. He takes no notice of delicate ground,
he just plants his foot down firmly upon it.

1945, 16 JULY, POTSDAM. (MCCULLOUGH, 412.)

Harry S Truman (1884–1972), 33rd President
of the United States (1945–53). To make his
point, McCullough told the Churchill Centre
in 1993, Churchill "gave a little hop, smack-
ing his bare feet on the floor".

On this side of the House we hold, in full agreement with the Government, that President Truman's action in South Korea was right and that His Majesty's Government, accompanied as their action has been by the action of other members of the Commonwealth, were also right in acting as they have done under the mandate of the Security Council by giving armed support to the intervention of the United States.

1950, 5 JULY.

The date is interesting. Seven weeks earlier in America, the famous National Security Council memorandum NSC-68 proposed massive spending "to ensure that Munich never happens again", ostensibly in the event of war with the USSR, actually to provide American clout in a protracted Cold War. It was, Professor Warren Kimball wrote, "the closest thing to a declaration of the Cold War".

I was eager to meet a potentate with whom my cordial relations, in spite of differences, had been established by the correspondence included in this volume. I called on him the morning after our arrival, and was impressed with his gay, precise, sparkling manner and obvious power of decision.

1953, POTSDAM. (WW2 VI, 545.)

Venizelos, Eleftherios

That remarkable man, throughout the whole of this great War, has shown the utmost wisdom and courage in all the counsels he has offered to his country, and has shown himself not only a wise statesman in regard to Greece, but has evinced a perfect grasp of those great international and human issues which are at stake.

1917, 5 MARCH.

Eleftherios Kyriakos Venizelos (1864–1936), Prime Minister of Greece, 1917–20, 1928–32.

Venizelos is entitled to plead that in going to Smyrna he acted as mandatory for the four greatest Powers. But he went as readily as a duck will swim.

1929. (CRISIS IV, 366.)

Venizelos had sent an expedition to Ionia that was defeated by the Turks under Atatürk, Turkish President, 1923–38.

Voltaire

When Voltaire was invited to visit the Prussian Court he stipulated that all expenses should be paid, and that the Order of Merit should be thrown in. Both were forthcoming.

1944, 22 MARCH.

François-Marie Arouet (1694–1778), known as Voltaire, French writer and philosopher, Freemason and critic of Christian dogma.

Washington, George

Simply to have kept his army in existence during these years was probably Washington's greatest contribution to the Patriot cause. No other American leaders could have done as much.

1956. (HESP III, 204.)

George Washington (1732–99), first President of the United States, commander of the Continental Army in the American Revolution, 1775–83.

Disinterested and courageous, far-sighted and patient, aloof yet direct in manner, inflexible once his mind was made up, Washington possessed the gifts of character for which the situation called. He was reluctant to accept office. Nothing would have pleased him more than to remain in equable but active retirement at Mount Vernon, improving the husbandry of his estate. But, as always, he answered the summons of duty....the prestige of Washington lent dignity to the new, untried office.

1956. (HESP III, 260.)

Wavell, Field Marshal Sir Archibald

General Wavell, commander-in-chief of all the Armies of the Middle East, has proved himself a master of war, sage, painstaking, daring, and tireless.

1941, 9 FEBRUARY. BROADCAST, LONDON.
(CS VI, 6346.)

Archibald Percival Wavell (1883–1950) commanded British Forces in the Middle East, 1939–41 and British Forces in India, 1941, 1942–43. He was later Viceroy and Governor General of India, 1943–47. See also Chapter 26...Biblical shorthand.

It may not have escaped your attention that I have brought with me to this country and to this conference Field Marshal Wavell and the other two Commanders-in-Chief from India. Now, they have not travelled all this way simply to concern themselves about improving the health and happiness of the Mikado of Japan.

1943, 19 MAY, CONGRESS, WASHINGTON. (ONWARDS, 92–3.)

Webb, Beatrice

I refuse to be shut up in a soup-kitchen with Mrs. Sidney Webb.

1908. (MARSH, 163.)

When WSC turned down the presidency of the Local Government Board. Martha Beatrice Potter Webb (1858–1943), socialist and early ally of the Liberal reformer Churchill, although she soon realised that WSC was no socialist.

You should leave the work of converting the country to us, Mrs. Webb, you ought to convert the Cabinet.

1909, 3 OCTOBER. (MORGAN, 279.)

Weizmann, Chaim

There is the figure of Dr. Weizmann, that dynamic Jew whom I have known so long, the ablest and wisest leader of the cause of Zionism, his whole life devoted to the cause, his son killed in the battle for our common freedom. I ardently hope his authority will be respected by Zionists in this dark hour, and that the Government will keep in touch with him, and make every one of his compatriots feel how much he is respected here.

1946, 1 AUGUST.

Chaim Azriel Weizmann (1874–1952), Zionist leader, first President of Israel, 1949–52.

Those of us who have been Zionists since the days of the Balfour Declaration know what a heavy loss Israel has sustained in the death of its President, Dr. Chaim Weizmann. Here was a man whose fame and fidelity were respected throughout the free world, whose son was killed fighting for us in the late war, and who, it may be rightly claimed, led his people back into their promised land, where we have seen them invincibly established as a free and sovereign State.

1952, 10 NOVEMBER. GUILDHALL, LONDON. (STEMMING, 364.)

Welldon, Bishop

I wrote my name at the top of the page. I wrote down the number of the question "I." After much reflection I put a bracket round it thus "(I)." But thereafter I could not think of anything connected with it that was either relevant or true. Incidentally there arrived from nowhere in particular a blot and several smudges....It was from these slender indications of scholarship that Mr. Welldon drew the conclusion that I was worthy to pass into Harrow. It is very much to his credit. It showed that he was a man capable of looking beneath the surface of things: a man not dependent upon paper manifestations. I have always had the greatest regard for him.

1930. (MEL, 29–30.)

James Edward Cowell Welldon (1854–1937), Head Master of Harrow 1885–88, later Bishop of Calcutta. WSC admired and corresponded with him throughout his life. Harrow archivists have never found the subject examination paper; also, not even Lord Randolph's son could have entered Harrow in those days without some knowledge of Latin.

Wellington, Duke of

Wellington was always at his coolest in the hottest of moments.

1957. (HESP III, 374.)

Arthur Wellesley, First Duke of Wellington (1769–1852), Anglo-Irish Field Marshal, defeated Napoleon at Waterloo, twice Prime Minister 1828–30, 1834.

Wigram, Ralph

I admired always so much his courage, integrity of purpose, high comprehending vision. He was one of those—how few—who guard the life of Britain. Now he is gone—and on the eve of this fateful year. Indeed it is a blow to England and to all the best that England means.

1936, 31 DECEMBER. (OB V, 834.)

WSC's letter of condolence to Ava Wigram. Ralph Follett Wigram (1890–1936) headed up the Central Department in the Foreign Office as from 1934. He was soon supplying Churchill with information on German rearmament, continuing to do so until he died on 31 December 1936.

He was a charming and fearless man, and his convictions, based upon profound knowledge and study, dominated his being. He saw as clearly as I did, but with more certain information, the awful peril which was closing in upon us.

1948. (WW2 I, 63.)

Wilson, Admiral of the Fleet Sir Arthur

Whether he was commanding the British Fleet or repairing an old motor car, he was equally keen, equally interested, equally content.

1923. (CRISIS I, 80.)

Sir Arthur Knyvet Wilson (1842–1921), First Sea Lord 1909–12.

Wilson, Field Marshal Sir Henry Maitland

General Wilson, who actually commands the Army of the Nile, was reputed one of our finest tacticians—and few will now deny that quality.

1941, 9 FEBRUARY. BROADCAST, LONDON.
(CS VI, 6346.)

Wilson, Woodrow

He played a part in the fate of nations incomparably more direct and personal than any other man....In all his strength and in all his weakness, in his nobility and in his foibles, he was, in spite of his long academic record and brief governorship, an unknown, an unmeasured quantity to the mighty people who made him their ruler in 1912.

1927. (CRISIS III PART 1, 229–31.)

Thomas Woodrow Wilson (1856–1924) 28th President of the United States, 1912–20.

[He was] the inscrutable and undecided judge upon whose lips the lives of millions hung....He did not truly divine the instinct of the American people. He underestimated the volume and undervalued the quality of the American feeling in favour of the Allies. Not until he was actually delivering his famous war message to Congress...did he move forward with confidence and conviction; not until then did he restate the cause of the Allies in terms unsurpassed by any of their own statesmen; not until then did he reveal to the American people where in his judgment world-right was founded, and how their own lives and material interests were at stake.

1927. (CRISIS III PART 1, 229–31.)

The spacious philanthropy which he exhaled upon Europe stopped quite sharply at the coasts of his own country.... It is difficult for a man to do great things if he tries to combine a lambent charity embracing the whole world with the sharper forms of populist party strife.

1929. (CRISIS IV, 128–9.)

Winant, John G.

It is a great pleasure to see Mr. Winant among us. He gives us the feeling that all President Roosevelt's men give me, that they would be shot stone dead rather than see this cause let down.

1941, 27 MARCH. EMPLOYER'S ASSOCIATION
AND TRADES UNION CONGRESS, LONDON.
(UNRELENTING, 71.)

John Gilbert Winant (1889–1947), Republican Governor of New Hampshire 1925–27, 1931–35, Roosevelt's Ambassador to Britain 1941–46.

Wingate, Orde

There was a man of genius who might well have become also a man of destiny. He has gone, but his spirit lives on in the long-range penetration groups, and has underlain all these intricate and daring air and military operations based on air transport and on air supply.

1944, 2 AUGUST.

Major General Orde Charles Wingate (1903–44), British general who saw action in Africa, the Middle East and Burma in WWII, killed in a plane crash over Burma.

Winterton, Lord

He [Lord Winterton] is a comparatively young Father of the House; he has many years of life before him. We still hope they may be years of useful life in this House, but unless in the future his sagacity and knowledge of the House are found to be markedly more superior to what he has exhibited today, I must warn him that he will run a very grave risk of falling into senility before he is over-taken by old age.

1945, 7 MARCH.

Edward Turnour, Sixth Earl Winterton (1883–1962), Anglo-Irish politician, Conservative MP 1904–51, given the honorific "Father of the House" 1945–51. Winterton's continuous service of forty-nine years as an MP was longer than Churchill's, whose service was interrupted in 1922–24.

Wodehouse, P. G.

Let him go to hell—as soon as there's a vacant passage.

1944, 6 DECEMBER. (OB VII, 1087.)

Sir Pelham Grenville Wodehouse (1881–1975), English comic writer famed for "Jeeves and Wooster". He made five anti-British broadcasts to America over German radio. Martin Gilbert records that he was "much vilified, but no charges were ever

brought against him". After the war he moved to the United States.

Woolton, Lord

Well, what about meat? Even red meat! Lord Woolton cannot any longer be derided for what he said because it has been made good.

**1953, 10 OCTOBER, PARTY CONFERENCE, MARGATE.
(UNWRITTEN, 60.)**

Frederick James Marquis, First Earl of Woolton (1883–1964), businessman and politician, Minister of Reconstruction 1943–45, chairman of the Conservative Party 1946–55. Credited with turning the Labour tide and helping re-elect Churchill and the Tories in 1951.

...our achievements...would have been impossible without the devotion to national duty which the Conservative and National Liberal Members of Parliament have shown in the discharge of their public duty, and the efficiency of the management of Parliamentary business of our whips department in the House of Commons, and the ever-improving and widening strength of the party organization which Lord Woolton has built up throughout the country.

**1954, 30 APRIL. ROYAL ALBERT HALL, LONDON.
(UNWRITTEN, 142.)**

21

POLITICAL
THEORY AND
PRACTICE

*"I do not believe that there is any way in which, by chanting some
incantation, we shall be able to produce a solution of the difficulties
with which we are confronted."*[69]

"Boldly and earnestly occupied, the platform will always beat the Press."
Campaigning in a 1936 Packard.

Here are Churchill's thoughts on politics and movements from Bolshevism to
Fascism, dictatorship to democracy; his prescriptions for the conduct of govern-
ment; and how he thought politics affected "civilisation", by which he included the
Welfare State he helped organise.

Churchill considered the State necessary to alleviate poverty and provide security
through "discipline, organisation and relief". He held it the "reserve employer" in bad times,
advocating a "minimum standard" beneath which no Briton was allowed to fall. But he

---

69 WSC, House of Commons, 24 July 1928.

resisted the nationalisation of industry and redistribution of wealth advocated by socialists.

The extent to which he thought about political theory may astonish those who visualise him, as so often represented, as a reactionary. Early on, for example, he argued for taxing land rather than production or earnings. (See Land and Taxation of land.) After world wars and depressions, reformers of the Left shifted to massive state intervention and benefits. Here they lost Churchill, who regarded socialism as "the philosophy of failure, the creed of ignorance, and the gospel of envy".

Included is his famous "Gestapo speech", said to have been instrumental in losing the Conservatives the 1945 General Election. Yet, though he said hard things about his Labour opponents, he believed in coalitions (when possible) and courtesy (off the floor). He was deeply grateful for Labour's support in Britain's darkest hour. (See Collegiality.)

Churchill favoured light taxation, allowing money "to fructify in the pockets of the people, as they used to say in my young days". Once the "minimum standard" was guaranteed by the state, he thought citizens should be free to pursue their own interests, according to their lights and talents. He rejected experts, particularly among ministers, and did not think doctrinaire theories of much use because no one theory ever applied to every situation.

The impression he leaves is of a politician occupying the "middle ground", but not a "moderate", for he had firm opinions. He sought however a medium between the extremes of Left and Right, while relying upon the British democracy to ensure equality and a decent life for all. He was a patrician, but not a snob; he enjoyed luxuries, but believed in taxing them; though he found fault with democracy, he always respected the "little man". Justice and equality were prominent among his principles.

Bolshevism

Bolshevism is not a policy; it is a disease. It is not a creed; it is a pestilence. It presents all the characteristics of a pestilence. It breaks out with great suddenness; it is violently contagious; it throws people into a frenzy of excitement; it spreads with extraordinary rapidity; the mortality is terrible; so that after a while, like other pestilences, the disease tends to wear itself out. The population of the regions devastated by its first fury are left in a sort of stupor. Then gradually and painfully they begin to recover their sanity; they are feeble; they are shattered; and the light of human reason once again comes back to their eyes. Those regions which have been most afflicted by the fury of this storm are the first to recover, and once having recovered...they are specially immune from all subsequent attacks.

1919, 29 MAY.

See also Communism.

[My] hatred of Bolshevism and Bolsheviks is not founded on their silly system of economics, or their absurd doctrine of an impossible equality. It arises from the bloody and devastating terrorism which they practise in every land into which they have broken, and by which alone their criminal regime can be maintained.

1920, 8 JULY.

If I had been properly supported in 1919, I think we might have strangled Bolshevism in its cradle, but everybody turned up their hands and said, "How shocking!"

1954, 28 JUNE. NATIONAL PRESS CLUB, WASHINGTON. (OB VII, 1008.)

WSC mentioned "strangling Bolshevism" in his March 1949 speech at M.I.T.; but this version is more poetic.

Bolshevism vs. Fascism

Between the doctrines of Comrade Trotsky and those of Dr. Goebbels, there ought to be room for you and me, and a few others, to cultivate opinions of our own.

1936, 24 OCTOBER. ("I ASK YOU – WHAT PRICE FREEDOM?," *ANSWERS*; ESSAYS I, 363.)

Capitalism vs. Socialism

See Socialism vs. Capitalism.

Centralisation

One of [the Tory Party] principles, whose truth is borne out again and again upon the pages of history is Disraeli's oft-cited maxim, "Centralization is the death-blow of public freedom." The truth of these words was never more apparent than it is today, nor more relevant to the thought and resolve of those who would have men not only live, but live freely.

1950, 8 FEBRUARY. NINIAN PARK, CARDIFF.
(BALANCE, 182.)

Civilisation

The central principle of Civilisation is the subordination of the ruling authority to the settled customs of the people and to their will as expressed through the Constitution....

When civilisation reigns in any country, a wider and less harassed life is afforded to the masses of the people. The traditions of the past are cherished, and the inheritance bequeathed to us by former wise or valiant men becomes a rich estate to be enjoyed and used by all.... Civilisation will not last, freedom will not survive, peace will not be kept, unless a very large majority of mankind unite together to defend them and show themselves possessed of a constabulary power before which barbaric and atavistic forces will stand in awe....

1938, 2 JULY. UNIVERSITY OF BRISTOL.
(BLOOD, 53–4.)

...civilisation implies, in any society, the freedom to criticise the government of the day; free speech; free press; free thought; free religious observance; no racial persecution; fair treatment of minorities; and courts of law and justice which have an authority independent of the executive and untainted by Party bias.

1939, 19 MAY.

The strength and character of a national civilisation is not built up like a scaffolding or fitted together like a machine. Its growth is more like that of a plant or a tree....no one should ever cut one down without planting another. It is very much easier and quicker to cut down trees than to grow them.

1952, 6 SEPTEMBER. ST. BARNABAS SCHOOL,
WOODFORD, ESSEX. (STEMMING, 332–3.)

Class divisions

I sympathize very strongly with the objection against drawing class distinctions based solely on the possession of money. To draw a distinction between a man who could afford a cabin passage and a man who could only afford a steerage passage was absurd. If a man were a lunatic or an idiot he could come in if he could pay for a cabin passage.

1905, 27 JUNE.

[Where] you will find the seeds of Imperial ruin and national decay [is in] the unnatural gap between rich and poor, the divorce of the people from the land, the want of proper discipline and training in our youth...the constant insecurity in the means of subsistence and employment which breaks the heart of many a sober, hard-working man, the absence of any established minimum standard of life and comfort among the workers, and, at the other end, the swift increase of vulgar, joyless luxury—here are the enemies of Britain. Beware lest they shatter the foundations of her power.

1910. (PEOPLE'S, 139–40.)

I am sure that class hatred and class warfare, like national revenge, are the most costly luxuries in which anyone can indulge.

1950, 24 APRIL.

Coalitions

Is [this coalition] to be above party Government or below party Government?

1931, 11 NOVEMBER.

Speaking of the National Government formed by Ramsay MacDonald and Stanley Baldwin in the face of the economic depression.

The only chance for the defenders of liberty and democracy in a world like this is to substitute for the many advantages which despotic authority gains in the field of action a lively comradeship and association which enables them, by the cooperation of all sorts and kinds of citizens, to produce not merely an equally fine but a more flexible and more durable organization.

1937, 16 NOVEMBER.

Even here it is hard enough to keep a Coalition together, even between men who, although divided by party, have a supreme object and so much else in common. But imagine what the difficulties are in countries racked by civil war, past or impending, and where clusters of petty Parties have each their own set of appetites, misdeeds and revenges.

1945, 18 JANUARY.

I am quite sure that a coalition between men and parties as the result of a lot of petty bargains and deals and compromises would be no use at all. There must be some great common bond of union, like we had in 1940, to lead to that melting of hearts where sacrifice seems to be an indulgence and pain becomes a joy, and when life rises to its highest level because death has no terrors.

1950, 4 FEBRUARY. TOWN HALL, LEEDS.
(BALANCE, 180.)

Coercion

...no more force should be used than is necessary to secure compliance with the law.

1920, 8 JULY.

Collectivism vs. individualism

Man is an individualist for some purposes, a collectivist for others, and it is in the harmonious combination of the opposite philosophies that future statecraft is comprised....But no one seems to have yet discovered the principle or code of principles by which these compromises should be governed and limited; and in the absence of any such code, all minds are vexed by inconsistencies and apparent insincerities which render them very unequal in combating the clear-cut arguments of doctrinaire extremists on either hand.

1906, 5 JUNE, BLENHEIM PALACE. (MCMENAMIN
AND ZOLLER, 218.)

WSC to his American friend and mentor, Bourke Cockran.

No man can be a collectivist alone....He must be both an individualist and a collectivist. The nature of man is a dual nature. The character of the organisation of human society is dual.... collectively we light our streets and supply ourselves with water....But we do not make love collectively, and the ladies do not marry us collectively, and we do not die collectively, and it is not collectively that we face the sorrows and the hopes, the winnings and the losings of this world of accident and storm.

1906, 11 OCTOBER. ST. ANDREW'S HALL, GLASGOW.
(LIBERALISM, 163.)

Collegiality

Hon. Members opposite may not agree with the millions of their fellow-countrymen who vote for the Liberal and Radical party, but after all, those millions belong to the same stock as they do.

1910, 31 MARCH.

I should not be at all alarmed for the future of this country if we had to return to party government...[but] things can never be quite the same again. Friendships have been established, ties have been made between the two parties, minglings have taken place, understandings have been established, which, without any prejudice to each man's public duty, will undoubtedly have a mellowing effect on a great deal of our relations in the future; and for my part I must say that I feel I owe a great debt to the Labour Party, who were a most stalwart support to me at the time when I first undertook the burden which I am still being permitted to bear.

1943, 13 OCTOBER.

Here in this country, the forerunner of all the democratic and Parliamentary conceptions of modern times, we in this country, who are very old at the game of party politics hard fought out, have learned how to carry through and debate great fiercely-contested political issues without the severance of personal and private friendships.

1944, 9 NOVEMBER.

Communism

It is a curious fact that the Russian Bolsheviks, in carrying by compulsion mass conceptions to their utmost extreme, seem to have lost not only the guidance of great personalities, but even the economic fertility of the process itself. The Communist theme aims at universal standardization. The individual becomes a function: the community is alone of interest: mass thoughts dictated and propagated by the rulers are the only thoughts deemed respectable....The Beehive? No, for there must be no queen and no honey, or at least no honey for others.

1931, MAY. ("MASS EFFECTS IN MODERN LIFE,"
STRAND MAGAZINE; THOUGHTS, 185.)

See also Bolshevism.

Everyone can see how Communism rots the soul of a nation; how it makes it abject and hungry in peace, and proves it base and abominable in war.

1940, 20 JANUARY. BROADCAST, LONDON. (BLOOD, 251.)

In the Communist sect it is a matter of religion to sacrifice one's native land for the sake of the Communist Utopia. People who, in ordinary life, would behave in a quite honourable manner, if they are infected with the disease of the mind will not hesitate a moment to betray their country or its secrets.

1946, 5 JUNE.

Communism vs. Fascism

[Communism and Fascism remind me] of the North Pole and the South Pole. They are at opposite ends of the earth, but if you woke up at either Pole tomorrow morning you could not tell which one it was. Perhaps there might be more penguins at one, or more Polar bears at the other; but all around would be ice and snow and the blast of a biting wind. I have made up my mind, however far I may travel, whatever countries I may see, I will not go to the Arctic or to the Antarctic Regions. Give me London, give me Paris, give me New York, give me some of the beautiful capitals of the British Dominions. Let us go somewhere where our breath is not frozen on our lips because of the Secret Police. Let us go somewhere where there are green pastures and the shade of venerable trees. Let us not wander away from the broad, fertile fields of freedom into these gaunt, grim, dim, gloomy abstractions of morbid and sterile thought.

1937, OXFORD. (ESSAYS I, XXV.)

Communism vs. Nazism

I will not pretend that, if I had to choose between Communism and Nazism, I would choose Communism. I hope not to be called upon to survive in the world under a government of either of those dispensations.

1937, 27 JUNE. ("THE CREEDS OF THE DEVIL," SUNDAY CHRONICLE; ESSAYS II, 395.)

Conduct in opposition

No one should be deterred in wartime from doing his duty merely by the fact that he will be voting against the Government, and still less because the party Whips are acting as tellers.

1941, 29 JULY.

No one...need be mealy-mouthed in debate, and no one should be chicken-hearted in voting. I have voted against Governments I have been elected to support, and, looking back, I have sometimes felt very glad that I did so. Everyone in these rough times must do what he thinks is his duty.

1942, 27 JANUARY.

No doubt it takes two parties to make a quarrel and we certainly have done our duty....

1951, 2 OCTOBER, LIVERPOOL STADIUM. (STEMMING, 121.)

...we have found a strong measure of responsibility among many of the Leaders of the Opposition and among the strongest—I did not say the loudest—elements in their rank and file.

1954, 9 NOVEMBER. LORD MAYOR'S BANQUET, GUILDHALL, LONDON. (ALLIANCE, 193.)

Democracy

If I had to sum up the immediate future of democratic politics in a single word I should say "insurance." That is the future—insurance against dangers from abroad, insurance against dangers scarcely less grave and much more near and constant which threaten us here at home in our own island.

1909, 23 MAY. FREE TRADE HALL, MANCHESTER. (LIBERALISM, 265.)

Whatever one may think about democratic government, it is just as well to have practical experience of its rough and slatternly foundations.

1929, OCTOBER. ("THE EARL OF ROSEBERY," PALL MALL; GC, 6.)

Democracy as a guide or motive to progress has long been known to be incompetent. None of the legislative assemblies of the great modern states represents in universal suffrage even a fraction of the strength or wisdom of the community. Great nations are no longer led by their ablest men, or by those who know most about their immediate affairs, or even by those who have a coherent doctrine.

Democratic governments drift along the line of least resistance, taking short views, paying their way with sops and doles, and smoothing their path with pleasant-sounding platitudes. Never was there less continuity or design in their affairs, and yet toward them are coming swiftly changes which will revolutionize for good or ill not only the whole economic structure of the world but the social habits and moral outlook of every family....

1931, DECEMBER. ("FIFTY YEARS HENCE," STRAND MAGAZINE; THOUGHTS, 202.)

Churchill's vaunted faith in democracy was not total. In this famous essay he identifies and worries over democracy's inability to make the right decisions every time.

With all their weakness and with all their strength, with all their faults, with all their virtues, with all the criticisms that may be made against them, with their many shortcomings, with lack of foresight, lack of continuity of purpose or pressure only of superficial purpose, they [democracies] nevertheless assert the right of the common people—the broad masses of the people—to take a conscious and effective share in the government of their country.

1942, 15 JANUARY. HOUSE OF ASSEMBLY, HAMILTON, BERMUDA. (END, 7.)

Democracy is no harlot to be picked up in the street by a man with a tommy gun. I trust the people, the mass of the people, in almost any country, but I like to make sure that it is the people and not a gang of bandits from the mountains or from the countryside who think that by violence they can overturn constituted authority, in some cases ancient Parliaments, Governments and States.

1944, 8 DECEMBER.

With all their virtues, democracies are changeable. After a hot fit, comes the cold. Are we to see again, as we saw the last time, the utmost severities inflicted upon the vanquished, to be followed by a period in which we let them arm anew, and in which we then seek to appease their wrath?

1946, 5 JUNE.

Democracy is not a caucus, obtaining a fixed term of office by promises, and then doing what it likes with the people. We hold that there ought to be a constant relationship between the rulers and the people. Government of the people, by the people, for the people, still remains the sovereign definition of democracy.

1947, 11 NOVEMBER.

Devolution

No party in the future would refuse to consider the delegation of administrative and legislative functions to provincial or national boards in the four parts of the Kingdom, and the handing over to them of large slices and blocks of business which could not properly be dealt with at Westminster.

1905, 20 FEBRUARY.

Such arrangements as Churchill then favoured came to pass with the creation of the Welsh and Scottish Parliaments nearly a century later.

The old Radical campaign against exploitation, monopolies, unfair rake-offs and the like, in which I took a part in my young days, was a healthy and necessary corrective to the system of free enterprise. But this grotesque idea of managing vast enterprises by centralized direction from London can only lead to bankruptcy and ruin.

1948, 28 MAY, PERTH. (EUROPE, 344.)

Dictatorship

Dictators and those who immediately sustain them cannot quit their offices with the easy disdain—or more often relief—with which an American President or a British Prime Minister submits himself to an adverse popular verdict. For a dictator the choice may well be the throne or the grave.

1937, 2 OCTOBER. ("CAN AMERICA KEEP OUT OF WAR?," COLLIERS; ESSAYS I, 375.)

A state of society where men may not speak their minds, where children denounce their parents to the police, where a business man or small shopkeeper ruins his competitor by telling tales about his private opinions... cannot long endure if brought into contact with the healthy outside world.

1938, 16 OCTOBER. BROADCAST TO AMERICA, LONDON. (BLOOD, 89.)

It is in this fear of criticism that the Nazi and Bolshevik dictatorships run their greatest risk. They silence all criticism by the concentration camp, the rubber truncheon, or the firing party. Thus the men at the top must very often only be fed with the facts which are palatable to them. Scandals, corruption and shortcomings are not exposed, because there are no independent voices. Instead of being exposed they continue to fester behind the pompous frontage of the State. The men at the top may be very fierce and powerful, but their ears are deaf, their fingers are numb; they cannot feel their feet as they move forward in the fog and darkness of the immeasurable and the unknown.

1940, 27 JANUARY. FREE TRADE HALL, MANCHESTER. (CS VI, 6189.)

One of the disadvantages of dictatorship is that the dictator is often dictated to by others, and what he did to others may often be done back again to him.

1953, 11 MAY.

Election pledges

All these balancings, limitations, and half-pledges, these little devices by which an embarrassed Government, staved off ruin from day to day would, after the next election, be swept as smooth as the sands of the shore after a flood tide.

1904, 10 FEBRUARY. FREE TRADE HALL, MANCHESTER. (CS I, 249.)

...I never remember a General Election which was not followed by a disagreeable, sterile, bickering over election pledges.

1919, 6 MARCH.

Equality

...the only safe rule for doing justice between man and man was to assume—a large assumption in some cases—that all men are equal and that all discriminations between them are unhealthy and undemocratic.

1906, 31 JULY.

Experts

It was a principle of our Constitution not to employ experts, whether business men or military men, in the highest affairs of State.

1902, 21 MARCH.

Expert knowledge, however indispensable, is no substitute for a generous and comprehending outlook upon the human story with all its sadness and with all its unquenchable hope.

1946, 26 FEBRUARY. UNIVERSITY OF MIAMI, FLORIDA. (SINEWS, 92.)

Fascism

Socialism is bad, jingoism is worse, and the two combined in a kind of debased Italian fascism is the worst creed ever designed by man.

1941, 11 JANUARY. DITCHLEY PARK, OXFORDSHIRE. (COLVILLE, FRINGES I, 394.)

Reconstructed in the present tense from Colville's diary ("Winston expressed the opinion...”). See also Bolshevism vs. Fascism.

Free enterprise

Where you find that State enterprise is likely to be ineffective, then utilise private enterprises, and do not grudge them their profits.

1906, 11 OCTOBER. ST. ANDREW'S HALL, GLASGOW. (LIBERALISM, 164.)

At the head of our mainmast we, like the United States, fly the flag of free enterprise. We are determined that the native genius and spirit of adventure, of risk-taking in peace as in war, shall bear our fortunes forward, finding profitable work and profitable trade for our people, and also we are determined that good and thrifty house-keeping, both national and private, shall sustain our economy.

1945, 15 MARCH. CENTRAL HALL, WESTMINSTER. (VICTORY, 80.)

Free speech

One cannot say that the man or the woman in the street can be brought up violently and called to account because of expressing some opinion on something or other which is *sub judice*. They are perfectly entitled to do that. They may say things that are deplorable— many deplorable things are said under free speech.

1951, 18 JUNE.

Free Trade

I humbly submit to Hon. Gentlemen opposite that the essence of protection is protection.

1902, 12 MAY.

Churchill espoused the Free Trade principles that had made Britain great in the nineteenth century; in the twentieth, rival empires, war and depression soon put Free Trade to the test.

[The] corn trade is scarcely less important to the people of the United States than to ourselves. I have always thought that it ought to be the main end of English statecraft over a long period of years to cultivate good relations with the United States, and that we should not allow ourselves to be turned from that purpose by gusts of ill-humour or bad manners...what greater security can we have for our food supply across the Atlantic than that the preservation of an open English market should be a matter of supreme consequence to the farmers of the Western States? [First person paraphrase.]

1903, 22 JUNE.

They [Protectionists] watch the river flowing to the sea, and they wonder how long it will be before the land is parched and drained of all its water. They do not observe the fertilizing showers by which in the marvellous economy of nature the water is restored to the land.

1903, 29 JULY.

To say that Protection means greater development of wealth is unspeakable humbug. The Democratic Party in America and the Socialist Party in Germany are made up of the poorest and least fortunate of the people of those countries; and have they not learned by bitter experience that high protective tariffs, whatever profits they may confer on capital, whatever privileges they may bring to certain of the higher ranks of labour, are to the poor and to the poorest of the poor an accursed engine of robbery and oppression?

1903, 11 NOVEMBER, BIRMINGHAM TOWN HALL. (FFT, 42.)

Will the shutting out of foreign goods increase the total amount of wealth in this country? Can foreign nations grow rich at our expense by selling us goods under cost price? Can a people tax themselves into prosperity? Can a man stand in a bucket and lift himself up by the handle?

1904. FREE TRADE HALL, MANCHESTER. (MACCALLUM SCOTT, 180; PARAPHRASED.)

....under no conceivable circumstances could any duty that the wit or folly of man could impose, stimulate, or increase the growth of cotton. Tariff duties, whether Retaliatory, Preferential, or Protective, would not make the cotton fields larger, would not ensure good harvests, would not promote cheap transit, would not destroy the ravages of cotton insects, American speculators, or other pestiferous vermin.

1904, 19 FEBRUARY. FREE TRADE HALL, MANCHESTER. (FFT, 58.)

They knew that as to Imperial Preference the Rt. Hon. Gentleman [A. J. Balfour] was opposed to it, not because he thought it was not good for the country, but because he thought it would not win many votes at the general election. It was not a noble reason, but it was a practical one, and it was a reason of some sort.

1904, 29 MARCH.

Imperial Preference was the dressy name for a system of preferential tariffs between states of the British Empire. Prime Minister Arthur Balfour seemed to hesitate between it and Free Trade. Scarcely a month after this remark, Churchill quit the Conservatives to join the Liberals.

...all the great nations of the world are Protectionist; they have been for 100 years past....Have they reached Free Trade? On the contrary, their tariffs have risen higher and higher, and at this moment Free-trade England, which does nothing, Free-trade England, with masterly inactivity, occupies in regard to the nations of the world so far as tariffs are concerned, a position of advantage to which few of the Protectionist countries have attained and which none of them have surpassed.

1904, 15 JUNE. MIDLAND HALL, MANCHESTER. (FFT, 89.)

[We will] prove to the country that you [Protectionists] are wrong all along the line— wrong in your logic, wrong in your statecraft, wrong in your arithmetic, wrong even in your demagogy—right only in having at last found the candour and courage to avow your true opinions and, by so doing, [to] warn the public throughout the Empire of the catastrophe from which they have been preserved.

1907, 19 FEBRUARY.

...the real essential fallacy of the protectionist proposal is the idea that taxation is a good thing in itself, that it should be imposed for the fun of the thing, and then, having done it for amusement, we should go round afterwards and look for attractive methods of expenditure in order to win support to the project.

1907, 15 JULY.

The idea that if you murder a man you may subsequently steal his money is a very primitive one.

1908, 2 JUNE.

Churchill was attacking the idea of patents being denied because they might prove deleterious to protected industries.

Free Trade is to be tried by drumhead court-martial and shot at dawn.

1923, 16 NOVEMBER. FREE TRADE HALL, MANCHESTER. (CS IV, 3396.)

I shall stick to you [and Free Trade] with all the loyalty of a leech.

1929, ATLANTIC VOYAGE. (GILBERT, SEARCH, 227.)

WSC to Leo Amery, a Tory Free Trader who suggested that Churchill might break with the Conservatives when they moved back to tariffs and protectionism. In the event, Churchill did accept protectionism a few years later, in the wake of the Depression. See next entry.

...I have always held the view that where tariff protection is given in any effective form to a particular industry, the State should, if it thinks fit, make sure that the interests of the consumer are safeguarded, and also those of the smaller producers.

1948, 16 NOVEMBER.

Freedom

What was the good of an abstract assertion of freedom unless there was an understanding of the use that was to be made of it?

1904, 29 MARCH.

...the cause of freedom has in it a recuperative power and virtue which can draw from misfortune new hope and new strength.

1938, 16 OCTOBER. BROADCAST, LONDON. (BLOOD, 84.)

Establish a basic standard of life and labour and provide the necessary basic foods for all. Once that is done, set the people free, get out of the way, and let them all make the best of themselves, and win whatever prizes they can for their families and for their country....Only in this way will an active, independent, property-owning democracy be established.

1947, 28 OCTOBER.

Human rights

Since the dawn of the Christian era a certain way of life has slowly been shaping itself among the western peoples, and certain standards of conduct and government have come to be esteemed. After many miseries and prolonged confusion, there arose into the broad light of day the conception of the right of the individual; his right to be consulted in the government of his country; his right to invoke the law even against the State itself.

1938, 16 OCTOBER. BROADCAST, LONDON. (BLOOD, 85.)

[...we] must never cease to proclaim in fearless tones the great principles of freedom and the rights of man which are the joint inheritance of the English-speaking world and which through Magna Carta, the Bill of Rights, the Habeas Corpus, trial by jury, and the English Common Law, find their most famous expression in the American Declaration of Independence....

The people of any country have the right, and should have the power by constitutional action, by free unfettered elections, with secret ballot, to choose or change the character or form of government under which they dwell: that freedom of speech and thought should reign; that courts of justice, independent of the executive, unbiased by any party, should administer laws which have received the broad assent of large majorities or are consecrated by time and custom. Here are the title-deeds of freedom which should lie in every cottage home. Here is the message of the British and American peoples to mankind.

1946, 5 MARCH. WESTMINSTER COLLEGE, FULTON, MISSOURI. (SINEWS, 97.)

See Chapter 1 for Churchill's memorable tests of freedom.

Land

The immemorial custom of nearly every modern State, the mature conclusions of many of the greatest thinkers, have placed the tenure, transfer and obligations of land in a wholly different category from other classes of property. The mere obvious physical distinction between land, which is a vital necessity of every human being and which at the same time is strictly limited in extent, and other property is in itself sufficient to justify a clear differentiation in its treatment, and in the view taken by the State of the conditions which should govern the tenure of land from that which should regulate in other forms of property.

1909, 4 MAY. (LIBERALISM, 251.)

WSC was attracted to Progress and Poverty, *by American economist Henry George, who proclaimed the public right to "elements", including air, water, sunshine and land, the private ownership of which produces inevitable exploitation. Many Liberals wished to shift taxation to the value of land, on the basis that land value was created not by the existence and work of the whole community. But the world wars and Depression brought an end to George's notion and ushered in the era of state intervention in almost every area of human activity. For Churchill's explanation of why George's theories proved impractical, see final entry herein.*

It is quite true that the land monopoly is not the only monopoly which exists, but it is by far the greatest of monopolies; it is a perpetual monopoly, and it is the mother of all other forms of monopoly. It is quite true that unearned increments in land are not the only form of unearned or undeserved profit which individuals are able to secure; but it is the principal form of unearned increment, derived from processes which are not merely not beneficial, but which are positively detrimental to the general public. Land, which is a necessity of human existence, which is the original source of all wealth, which is strictly limited in extent, which is fixed in geographical position—land, I say, differs from all other forms of property in these primary and fundamental conditions.

1909, 17 JULY, EDINBURGH. (LIBERALISM, 269–70.)

For related quotations see Taxation of land.

Henry George failed in his single tax proposal...because he had been studying the world as it had been for generations and centuries...and the conclusion he arrived at was that land was practically the sole source of all wealth. But almost before the ink was dry on the book he had written it was apparent that there were hundreds of different ways of creating and possessing and gaining wealth which had either no relation to the ownership of land or an utterly disproportionate or indirect relation [and] that is why radical democracy...has turned unhesitatingly towards the graduated taxation of the profits of wealth rather than to this discrimination in the sources from which it is derived.

1928, 24 MAY. (CS V, 4421.)

Law

It seemed an utterly irrational argument to put forward, that because a law was broken, therefore it should be changed.

1903, 1 MAY.

But see next statement on the inadvisability of unpopular laws.

I cannot think of any greater restraint that could possibly be imposed on reckless or sectional legislation than that it should be hung round the neck of its authors, not merely as something attempted and failed in, but as an actual real living issue when they next present themselves to the electorate.

1910, 31 MARCH.

These sentiments were in a different context from those Churchill expressed in 1940, of magnanimity towards the "Guilty Men" of the 1930s. But more was at stake in 1940 than re-election of politicians.

As always happens when prohibitions are imposed which do not carry public opinion with them, there is both wholesale evasion and occasional connivance, and the law is brought into disrepute.

1926, 26 APRIL.

Law vs. charity

[I object] on principle to doing by legislation what properly belonged to human good feeling and charity.

1902, 31 JULY. (CS I, 155.)

Leisure

...the general march of industrial democracy is not towards inadequate hours of work, but towards sufficient hours of leisure. That is the movement among the working people all over the country. They are not content that their lives should remain mere alternations between the bed and the factory: They demand time to look about them, time to see their homes by daylight, to see their children, time to think and read and cultivate their gardens—time, in short, to live.

1908, 6 JULY.

Liberalism vs. Socialism

Liberalism has its own history and its own tradition. Socialism has its own formulas and aims. Socialism seeks to pull down wealth; Liberalism seeks to raise up poverty. Socialism would destroy private interests; Liberalism would preserve private interests in the only way they can be safely and justly preserved, namely, by reconciling them with public right. Socialism would kill enterprise. Liberalism would rescue enterprise from the trammels of privilege and preference. Socialism assails the pre-eminence of the individual; Liberalism seeks...to build up a minimum standard for the mass. Socialism exalts the rule; Liberalism exalts the man. Socialism attacks capital; Liberalism attacks monopoly.

1908, 14 MAY. KINNAIRD HALL, DUNDEE. (LIBERALISM, 196.)

Martial law

Martial law is no law at all. Martial law is brute force. Of course all martial law is illegal, and an attempt to introduce illegalities into martial law, which is not military law, is like attempting to add salt water to the sea.

1906, 2 APRIL.

Middle ground

It was always found in the past to be a misfortune to a country when it was governed from one particular point of view, or in the interests of any particular class, whether it was the Court, or the Church, or the Army, or the mercantile or labouring classes. Every country ought to be governed from some central point of view, where all classes and all interests are proportionately represented.

1903, 29 JULY.

Minimum standard

We seek to benefit private enterprise with the knowledge and guiding power of modern Governments, without sacrificing the initiative and drive of individual effort under free, competitive conditions. Our policy is based on the two main principles of fair play and adequate opportunity. We seek to establish a minimum standard of life and labour, below which no one who is prepared to meet the obligations of good citizenship should be allowed to fall. Above that minimum standard, we wish to give the fullest possible play for competitive individual enterprise and every chance for the native genius of our Island race, springing perennially from every class, to win its full and fair reward.

1947, 16 MAY, AYR, SCOTLAND. (EUROPE, 100.)

Mistakes in politics

John Bull is a stupid creature, but faithful. My own idea is that it does not matter how many mistakes one makes in politics, so long as one keeps on making them. It is like throwing babies to the wolves; once you stop, the pack overtakes the sleigh.

1901, 15 NOVEMBER. (OB II, 34.)

Letter to his mentor and onetime Prime Minister, Lord Rosebery. For another "pack and sleigh" analogy, see Chapter 2...Resources.

Mob law

One must have some respect for democracy, and not use that word too lightly. The last thing which resembles democracy is mob law, with bands of gangsters, armed with deadly weapons, forcing their way into great cities, seizing the police stations and key points of government, endeavouring to introduce a totalitarian regime....

1944, 8 DECEMBER.

Moderates

They are a class of Rt. Hon. Gentlemen—all good men, all honest men—who are ready to make great sacrifices for their opinions, but they have no opinions. They are ready to die for the truth, if they only knew what the truth was.

1903, 14 AUGUST. (CS I, 215.)

Churchill was referring to Conservative leaders who refused to take a principled stand for or against Free Trade.

Nationalisation

Before they [the Socialists] nationalized our industries they should have nationalized themselves. They should have set country before party, and shown that they were Britons first, and Socialists only second.

1947, 12 MARCH.

Nationalization of industry is the doom of trade unionism.

1950, 14 OCTOBER, BLACKPOOL. BALANCE, 399.

WSC repeated this line several times in the weeks before the 1951 general election.

The complete nationalization of all the means of production, distribution and exchange would make it impossible for this small island to support a large part of its population.

1951, 15 OCTOBER, HUDDERSFIELD. (STEMMING, 149.)

Nationalism

Where Nationalism means the lust for pride and power, the craze for supreme domination by weight or force; where it is the senseless urge to be the biggest in the world, it is a danger and a vice. Where it means love of country and readiness to die for country; where it means love of tradition and culture and the gradual building up across the centuries of a social entity dignified by nationhood, then it is the first of virtues.

1946, 9 MAY. STATES-GENERAL OF THE NETHERLANDS, THE HAGUE. (SINEWS, 131.)

Party splitting

Splitting an infinitive isn't so bad—not nearly so bad—hmph, as splitting a party; that is always regarded as the greatest sin.

1946. (GRAEBNER, 25.)

Planning

There is nothing new in planning....Did not Joseph advise Pharaoh to build granaries and fill them for the lean years when the Nile waters failed?....planning, with all the resources of science at its disposal, should aim at giving the individual citizen as many choices as possible of what to do in all the ups and downs of daily life....This kind of planning differs fundamentally from the collectivist theme of grinding them all up in a vast State mill which must certainly destroy in the process the freedom and independence which are the foundation of our way of life and the famous characteristic of our race.

1949, 14 OCTOBER. EMPRESS HALL, LONDON. (BALANCE, 115.)

Platform vs. Press

Boldly and earnestly occupied, the platform will always beat the Press.

1909, 13 JANUARY, BIRMINGHAM. (LIBERALISM, 222.)

Churchill's version of the American adage about the politician's "bully pulpit", which is thought by some to be more powerful than, or at least a counter to, the media.

Policy reversal

It is always bad for a government to change its mind, yet it ought to do so from time to time, out of respect to the House of Commons and out of the influence made upon its collective mind by the Debates. But what is still worse is to change your mind and then have to change it again. That is a double disadvantage....

1944, 6 OCTOBER.

Political allies

Politics is like waking up in the morning. You never know whose head you will find on the pillow.

1902. (*MORNING POST* INTERVIEW; HALLE, IRREPRESSIBLE, 50.)

Political cause and effect

Militarism degenerates into brutality. Loyalty promotes tyranny and sycophancy. Humanitarianism becomes maudlin and ridiculous. Patriotism shades into cant. Imperialism sinks to jingoism.

1898, 22 MAY. BANGALORE, INDIA. (OB CV1/2, 938.)

WSC to his mother, referring to his opposition to an anti-Russian policy in India, which he thought would play into the hands of the Germans. See Germany...Mercantile advantage.

All great movements, every vigorous impulse that a community may feel, become perverted and distorted as time passes, and the atmosphere of the earth seems fatal to the nobler aspirations of its peoples. A wide humanitarian sympathy in a nation easily degenerates into hysteria. A military spirit tends towards brutality. Liberty leads to licence, restraint to tyranny. The pride of race is distended to blustering arrogance. The fear of God produces bigotry and superstition.

1900. (RIVER I, 57.)

Political office and military experience

It is always dangerous for soldiers, sailors or airmen to play at politics. They enter a sphere in which the values are quite different from those to which they have hitherto been accustomed.

1948. (WW2 I, 107.)

There are lots of people who have been employed in political office who have had a professional military experience. Even I myself was nearly five years a cadet and a lieutenant in the Army and I have frequently interfered in civilian matters.

1952, 20 JANUARY.

Political systems

Political systems can to some extent be appraised by the test of whether their leading representatives are or are not capable of taking decisions on great matters on their merits, in defiance of their own interests and often of their best friends.

1929. (CRISIS IV, 302.)

Politicians

He is asked to stand, he wants to sit and he is expected to lie.

1902. (*MORNING POST* INTERVIEW; HALLE, IRREPRESSIBLE, 49.)

WSC's view, at age twenty-eight, of the responsibilities of a politician, does not sound unfamiliar. Non-English readers may like to know that in Britain one "stands" for office and "sits" for a constituency; but "to lie" has the same definition in all countries.

For my own part I have always felt that a politician is to be judged by the animosities which he excites among his opponents. I have always set myself not merely to relish but to deserve thoroughly their censure.

1906, 17 NOVEMBER. INSTITUTE OF JOURNALISTS DINNER, LONDON. (CS I, 693.)

The world today is ruled by harassed politicians absorbed in getting into office or turning out the other man so that not much room is left for determining great issues on their merits.

1932, 25 JANUARY, NEW YORK. (CS V, 5129.)

Power politics

With that marvellous gift which he [Roosevelt] has of bringing troublesome issues down to earth and reducing them to the calm level of ordinary life, the President declared, in his recent Message to Congress, that power politics were "the misuse of power." I am sure I can say, on behalf of all Parties in the House, that we are absolutely in agreement with the President.

1945, 18 JANUARY.

Private enterprise

Among our Socialist opponents there is great confusion. Some of them regard private enterprise as a predatory tiger to be shot. Others look on it as a cow they can milk. [Here WSC made the motion of milking a cow with his hands.] Only a handful see it for what it really is—the strong and willing horse that pulls the whole cart along.

1959, 29 SEPTEMBER, WOODFORD, ESSEX. (ALLIANCE, 324.)

This is from Churchill's last political speech. Henceforth he was to speak in public only at dedications and memorials, such as at Churchill College and his Woodford statue unveiling.

Private property

We are often assured by sagacious persons that the civilization of modern states is largely based upon respect for the rights of private property. If that be true, it is also true that such respect cannot be secured, and ought not, indeed, to be expected, unless property is associated in the minds of the great mass of the people with ideas of justice and of reason.

1909, 17 JULY, EDINBURGH. (LIBERALISM, 269.)

See also Land and Taxation of land.

The vital processes of civilisation require, and the combined interests of millions guarantee, the security of property. A society in which property was insecure would speedily degenerate into barbarism; a society in which property was absolutely secure, irrespective of all conceptions of justice in regard to the manner of its acquisition, would degenerate, not into barbarism, but death.

> 1909, 7 OCTOBER, ABERNETHY, SCOTLAND.
> (LIBERALISM, 301.)

...private property has a right to be defended. Our civilization is built upon private property, and can only be defended by private property.

> 1947, 11 AUGUST.

Conservatives [support] a property-owning democracy. And the more widely it is distributed and the more millions there are to share in it, the more will the British democracy continue to have the spirit of individual independence, and the more they will turn their backs on the Socialist delusion that one ought to be proud of being totally dependent on the State.

> 1950, 14 FEBRUARY. EDINBURGH. (BALANCE, 202.)

Privatising monopolies

There is a growing feeling, which I entirely share, against allowing those services which are in the nature of monopolies to pass into private hands.

> 1906, 11 OCTOBER. ST. ANDREW'S HALL, GLASGOW.
> (LIBERALISM, 163.)

Proportional representation

It is quite true that I expressed a view many years ago, which I have seen no reason to dismiss from the region of theoretical principle, in favour of proportional representation in great cities. I have not expressed any views in favour of proportional representation as a whole, on account of the proved ill effects it has had on so many Parliaments.

> 1953, 17 FEBRUARY.

Proportional representation matches the percentage of a party's votes to the percentage of its seats in a legislature. While it more accurately reflects the preferences of the electorate, WSC saw it as preventing the

legislative programme of the majority party and leading to a proliferation of parties and unstable coalitions.

Protection

See Free Trade.

Redistribution

You may, by the arbitrary and sterile act of Government—for, remember, Governments create nothing and have nothing to give but what they have first taken away—you may put money in the pocket of one set of Englishmen, but it will be money taken from the pockets of another set of Englishmen, and the greater part will be spilled on the way. Every vote given for Protection is a vote to give Governments the right of robbing Peter to pay Paul, and charging the public a handsome commission on the job.

> 1903, 11 NOVEMBER. BIRMINGHAM TOWN HALL.
> (FFT, 34.)

WSC repeated these words in his 1905 essay, "Why I am a Free Trader" (Essays II, 24).

Representative government

The system of representative government without responsible Ministers, without responsible powers, has led to endless friction and inconvenience wherever and whenever it has been employed. It has failed in Canada, it has failed in Natal and Cape Colony.

> 1906, 17 DECEMBER. (LIBERALISM, 151.)

In representative government, an institution or leader acts on behalf of the people by representing their beliefs. WSC believed it must be accompanied by responsible ministers entrusted with the power to act without constant reference to the electorate.

Resignation etiquette

It is an unwholesome way of conducting public affairs in time of peace that Ministers or Viceroys should be dismissed or should resign, and should not feel it necessary to their self-respect to explain to the nation the reasons for their departure.

> 1947, 6 MARCH.

Revolution

Those who talk of revolution ought to be prepared for the guillotine.

1912, 10 OCTOBER.

Rule of law

His Majesty's Government are bound by the laws which they administer. They are not above the law.

1906, 22 FEBRUARY.

Socialism

Let them [Socialists] abandon the utter fallacy, the grotesque, erroneous, fatal blunder of believing that by limiting the enterprise of man, by riveting the shackles of a false equality...they will increase the well-being of the world.

1926, 21 JANUARY. (CS IV, 3821.)

The follies of Socialism are inexhaustible.... Even among themselves they have twenty discordant factions who hate one another even more than they hate you and me. Their insincerity! Can you not feel a sense of disgust at the arrogant presumption of superiority of these people?....Then when it comes to practice, down they fall with a wallop not only to the level of ordinary human beings but to a level which is even far below the average.

1925, 11 DECEMBER. TOWN HALL, BATTERSEA. (CS IV, 3809.)

When losses are made, under the present system these losses are borne by the individuals who sustained them and took the risk and judged things wrongly, whereas under State management all losses are quartered upon the tax-payers and the community as a whole. The elimination of the profit motive and of self-interest as a practical guide in the myriad transactions of daily life will restrict, paralyse and destroy British ingenuity, thrift, contrivance and good housekeeping at every stage in our life and production, and will reduce all our industries from a profit-making to a loss-making process.

1947. 6 DECEMBER. BELLE VUE, MANCHESTER. (EUROPE, 212.)

Churchill had been reading, and was deeply impressed by, the Austrian economist Friedrich Hayek's seminal book, The Road to Serfdom. This statement could have been made by Hayek himself.

Socialism is the philosophy of failure, the creed of ignorance, and the gospel of envy.

1948, 28 MAY, PERTH, SCOTLAND. (EUROPE, 347.)

I do not at all wonder that British youth is in revolt against the morbid doctrine that nothing matters but the equal sharing of miseries, that what used to be called the "submerged tenth" can only be rescued by bringing the other nine-tenths down to their level....

1948, 13 JUNE.

A variation on Churchill's dictum that capitalism was the unequal sharing of blessings, while Socialism was the equal sharing of miseries. (See Chapter 2.)

I doubt if it gives very much pleasure to the average Socialist when he wakes up in the morning to say to himself, "Oho, I own the Bank of England, I own the railways, I own the coal mines." But if it does give him any actual pleasure, he is certainly paying dearly for it.

1950, 14 FEBRUARY. USHER HALL, EDINBURGH. (BALANCE, 201.)

...never forget that fifty millions have come into being in Great Britain under the impulse and inspiration of former generations; and now if our native genius is cribbed, cabined and confined these fifty millions will be left physically stranded and gasping, like whales which swum upon the high tide into a bay from which the waters have receded.

1951, 21 JULY, WOODFORD, ESSEX. (STEMMING, 93.)

Socialism vs. Capitalism

Will not the daily toil of the actual producing worker have a heavier burden thrust upon it by the enormous hordes of disinterested and largely uninterested officials than would be the case under private management? And will not these officials be less efficient, more costly, and far more dictatorial than the private employers?

1947, 16 MAY, AYR, SCOTLAND. (EUROPE, 97–8.)

For related quotations see Capitalism.

The bureaucrats suffer no penalties for wrong judgments; so long as they attend their offices punctually and do their work honestly and behave in a polite manner towards their political masters they are sure of their jobs and their pensions. They are completely disinterested in the directness of their judgment. But the ordinary private trader, as you know in your own lives, faces impoverishment or perhaps bankruptcy if he cannot measure things right from day to day and those who show themselves unable to do this are replaced by more capable men and organisers.

1948, 28 MAY, PERTH, SCOTLAND. (EUROPE, 344.)

The choice is between two ways of life: between individual liberty and State domination; between concentration of ownership in the hands of the State and the extension of ownership over the widest number of individuals; between the dead hand of monopoly and the stimulus of competition; between a policy of increasing restraint and a policy of liberating energy and ingenuity; between a policy of levelling down and a policy of opportunity for all to rise upwards from a basic standard.

1949, 23 JULY, WOLVERHAMPTON. (CS VII, 7835.)

We [Tories] are for the ladder. Let all try their best to climb. They [Labour] are for the queue. Let each wait in his place till his turn comes. But, we ask: "What happens if anyone slips out of his place in the queue?" "Ah!" say the Socialists, "our officials—and we have plenty of them—come and put him back in it, or perhaps put him lower down to teach the others." And when they come back to us and say: "We have told you what happens if anyone slips out of the queue, but what is your answer to what happens if anyone slips off the ladder?" Our reply is: "We shall have a good net and the finest social ambulance service in the world."

1951, 8 OCTOBER. BROADCAST, LONDON.
(STEMMING, 134.)

Socialism vs. Communism

Of the differences between Socialism and Communism if I may make another quotation from the past, I said a good many years ago: "A strong dose either of Socialism or Communism will kill Britannia stone dead, and at the inquest the only question for the jury will be: Did she fall or was she pushed?"

1948, 16 NOVEMBER.

Socialist "Gestapo"

No Socialist Government conducting the entire life and industry of the country could afford to allow free, sharp, or violently worded expressions of public discontent. They would have to fall back on some form of *Gestapo*, no doubt very humanely directed in the first instance. And this would nip opinion in the bud; it would stop criticism as it reared its head, and it would gather all the power to the supreme party and the party leaders, rising like stately pinnacles above their vast bureaucracies of civil servants, no longer servants and no longer civil.

1945, 4 JUNE. BROADCAST, LONDON.
(VICTORY, 189.)

The "Gestapo" remark in his election campaign speech, which his daughter Sarah suggested he take out, is supposed to have cost Churchill votes in the 1945 election. In fact, Labour's victory had been ensured by events of the past decade.

Socialistic "society"

Translated into concrete terms, Socialistic "society" is a set of disagreeable individuals who obtained a majority for their caucus at some recent election, and whose officials in consequence would look on humanity through innumerable grills and pigeon-holes and across innumerable counters, and say to them, "Tickets, please." Truly this grey old world has never seen so grim a joke.

1908, 4 MAY. KINNAIRD HALL, DUNDEE.
(CS I, 1029.)

State activism

...there were some things which a government must do, not because the government would do them well, but because nobody else would do them at all.

1904, 10 FEBRUARY. FREE TRADE HALL,
MANCHESTER. (CS I, 250.)

State and industry

The functions of Government in relation to industrial life may be divided into three categories—discipline, organisation and relief.

1909, 19 MAY. (LIBERALISM, 240.)

State as reserve employer

I am of the opinion that the State should increasingly assume the position of the reserve employer of labour.

1906, 11 OCTOBER. ST. ANDREW'S HALL, GLASGOW. (LIBERALISM, 163.)

State controls

Control for control's sake is senseless. Controls under the pretext of war or its aftermath which are in fact designed to favour the accomplishment of quasi-totalitarian systems, however innocently designed, whatever guise they assume, whatever liveries they wear, whatever slogans they mouth, are a fraud which should be mercilessly exposed to the British public.

1945, 15 MARCH. (VICTORY, 80.)

Taxation

We have reached the extreme limit of practical and prudent peace-time taxation, and unless effective means were taken to curb and control the growing expenditure of the country, we would be confronted with important social, economic, and political problems, which might be most dangerous to the country and the empire, and very damaging to many causes which the Conservative Party held near and dear to their hearts.

1902, 14 APRIL.

It is a curious thing in our system of taxation how much easier it is to revive an old tax than to impose a new one.

1902, 12 MAY.

Certainly it is not the object of our taxation that any class should derive profit from it.

1903, 22 JUNE. (FFT, 3.)

It makes no difference to the total amount of our accumulated wealth whether it is taxed though one or twenty or even 500 outlets— except this, that every outlet which is made from the reservoir has its own leakages....

...when the tax collector comes to the private citizen and takes from him of his wealth for the service of the public, the whole of that money taken shall go for the purposes for which it is intended, and that no private interests, however powerfully they may be organised and however eloquently advocated,

shall thrust their dirty fingers into the pie and take the profit for themselves....

1908, 2 JUNE.

It is a tremendous question, never previously in this country asked so plainly, a new idea pregnant, formidable, full of life, that taxation should not only have regard to the volume of wealth, but, so far as possible, to the character of the processes of its origin.

1909, 5 SEPTEMBER, LEICESTER. (LIBERALISM, 295.)

Taxation of land

...the taxes on incomes over £3,000 a year, upon estates at death, on motor cars before they cause death, upon tobacco, upon spirits, upon liquor licences, which really belong to the State and ought never to have been filched away; and, above all, taxes upon the unearned increment in land are necessary, legitimate and fair; and that without any evil consequences to the refinement or the richness of our national life, still less any injury to the sources of its economic productivity, they will yield revenue sufficient in this year and in the years to come to meet the growing needs of Imperial defence and of social reform.

1909, 23 MAY. FREE TRADE HALL, MANCHESTER. (LIBERALISM, 264.)

See also Land.

The land taxes always seem to excite the peculiar hostility of Conservative speakers, but you will note this curious fact—no one ever advocates their repeal.

1913, 15 NOVEMBER. ALEXANDRA PALACE, LONDON. (CS II, 2191.)

Taxation of luxuries

I have never had much fiscal sympathy with the consumer of luxuries, and particularly of foreign luxuries.

1929, 15 APRIL. (CS V, 4599.)

His meaning here should not be misconstrued. Churchill loved luxuries; he was referring here to taxing them, which he favoured.

Theories

I myself do not believe that we shall come through our difficulties by reliance on any particular logical or doctrinaire theory. I do not believe that there is any way in which, by chanting some incantation, we shall be able to produce a solution of the difficulties with which we are confronted.

1928, 24 July.

Welfare State

I think it is our duty to use the strength and the resources of the State to arrest the ghastly waste not merely of human happiness but of national health and strength which follows when a working man's home which has taken him years to get together is broken up and scattered through a long spell of unemployment, or when, through the death, the sickness, or the invalidity of the breadwinner, the frail boat in which the fortunes of the family are embarked founders, and the women and children are left to struggle helplessly on the dark waters of a friendless world.

1909, 23 May. Free Trade Hall, Manchester. (Liberalism, 268.)

All the boastings of the welfare State have to be set against the fact that more than what they have given with one hand has been filched back by the other.

1951, 21 July, Woodford, Essex. (Stemming, 94.)

22

POLITICS:
THE HOME
FRONT

"Few Parliaments in our modern experience have been less deserving of respect. A majority elected under the spell of patriotic emotion, upon a national issue, in the stress of an anxious war, has been perverted to crude and paltry purposes of party....Seven more years of dodge and dole and dawdle! Seven years of tinker, tax and trifle! Seven years of shuffle, shout and sham! Do not be taken in again." [70]

"I have always been in favour of extending the franchise."
Post-war electioneering with Clementine and Mary.

The political writer Joe Klein recently reminded us of Churchill without mentioning him.[71] In an interview, Klein was asked how you can measure the worth of political leaders. Listen to what they say, he replied. If there is not a single statement in their

---

70 Colonial Office, 6 January 1906. OB, CV2/1, 423: WSC, at his oratorial heights, and with obvious relish, employing massive alliteration to delight the Liberal electors.
71 Klein, Joe: *Politics Lost : How American Democracy was Trivialized by People Who Think You're Stupid.* New York: Doubleday, 2006.

speech that is not unpleasant to hear, you know they are empty suits relying on polls and focus groups.

Mr. Klein thus defined a chief attribute of Winston Churchill – the willingness to say not what people wanted to hear, but what he thought they *should* hear. His maxims were employed to that end with devastating effectiveness.

Above all Churchill was consistent. Paul Addison called him the "unexpected hero". Michael Mink explained: "Until the Second World War his two changes of party from Conservative to Liberal and back again, his egotism and his independence of spirit at all times led orthodox politicians to mistrust him and his judgment. Not until he was in his mid-60s did a crisis arise in which party politics were irrelevant and his greatest qualities could be demonstrated and recognized."[72]

His approach to domestic politics was consistent with his approach to war: fight with might and main while the battle is engaged; be magnanimous in victory, and try to assuage the causes of the quarrel. Again and again – on Irish Home Rule, curbing the power of the House of Lords, the 1926 General Strike, tax policy – we see this aspect of Winston Churchill in countless examples.

So often defined by "blood, toil, tears and sweat", Churchill's early years as a radical crusader for social change are almost forgotten. Together with Lloyd George, he criss-crossed the country in the years before World War I, arguing for improved workplace conditions, widows' and orphans' benefits, workmen's compensation and labour exchanges, national insurance – comprising what he called "the Minimum Standard", below which no citizen of a great nation should be allowed to fall.

His remarks on the role and status of women may cause raised eyebrows: of approval. Churchill was hardly as negative towards woman's suffrage as is commonly believed, and his views progressed with those of the British electorate, particularly after the performance of women in World War I. His words speak for themselves.

So often depicted as an enemy of labour – through imprecise knowledge of his actions and motivations during the 1910 Welsh coal mines strike and the 1926 General Strike – Churchill was in fact a strong proponent of trade unions. "I have been taught it all my public life, that the employers of this country are deeply thankful there is in existence a strong organised trade union movement with which they can deal, and which keeps its bargains and which moves along a controlled and suitable path of policy."[73] He didn't think unions should be involved in politics, but was resigned that this was inevitable. He even was invited to join a union as a bricklayer; more radical elements within the union saw that his membership was withdrawn.

Many subjects will be startlingly familiar to modern readers: the child tax credit, collective bargaining, elections fought over foreign policy, immigration, legislative cure-alls, media defeatism, minimum wage, national debt, outsourcing, protestors, women's rights. Perhaps they went by different terms in Churchill's day, but they occupied his thoughts, and his opinions are rarely uninteresting.

For clarity and order, I have arranged the first group of quotations, which are date-relevant, in chronological order, and the second group, which are more general observations or remarks, in alphabetical order by subject.

---

72 Mink, Michael, "Winston Churchill's Uphill War," *Investor's Business Daily*, 30 August 2007 (http://xrl.us/bcmae).
73 Broadcast, London, 27 March 1941. Unrelenting, 71.

1894 Anti-Prudes Campaign

[I would like] to see England better and more moral, but whereas the Vigilantes Societies wish to abolish sin by Act of Parliament, and are willing to sacrifice much of the liberty of the subject into the bargain, the "anti-prudes" prefer a less coercive and more moderate procedure.

1894, 18 OCTOBER. (OB, CV1/1, 528.)

Letter to the Westminster Gazette, *when Churchill led the youthful protesters against the "Prudes on the Prowl" who wished to shut down gentlemanly entertainments.*

1901 Retrenchment and economy

I am very glad the House has allowed me, after an interval of fifteen years, to lift again the tattered flag of retrenchment and economy....I stand here to plead the cause of economy. I think it is about time that a voice was heard from this side of the House pleading that unpopular cause....If such a one is to stand forward in such a cause, then I say it humbly, but with I hope becoming pride, no one has a better right than I have, for this is a cause... for which the late Lord Randolph Churchill made the greatest sacrifice of any Minister of modern times.

1901, 13 MAY.

Churchill's belief in filial duty was his earliest motivation as a new Member of Parliament. His father had resigned as Chancellor of the Exchequer in 1886 over a minor point of expense, but in reality the resignation had been a tactic to increase his power. It backfired when the Prime Minister, Lord Salisbury, did not allow Lord Randolph back.

...I would say to the military party, the party whose motto is "Hang the expense!," the party who to strengthen the arm of Empire would impoverish the brain, the belly, and the heart, beware how you burden the trade of Britain, for if it fails through your exactions, not all your armies and all your ironclads, not all your sacrifices and all your skill, will hold the State together.

1901, 1 JUNE. CAMBRIDGE UNIVERSITY CARLTON CLUB. (MBA, 44.)

1906 Election

[I] should advise the Rt. Hon. Gentleman [Mr. Arnold Poster, Secretary of State for War] not to worry too much about details, because, after all, there would be an election some day, and when it came the waters of the boundless ocean would come in and all the castles on the sands would be washed completely away.

1905, 23 FEBRUARY.

There had been, if [one] might say so, almost a conspiracy of silence. One might almost have thought that Hon. gentlemen opposite were mutes celebrating the obsequies, or approaching obsequies, of His Majesty's Government.

1905, 31 JULY.

WSC's prediction was borne out: in the January–February general election, the Liberals gained 216 seats for a total of 399, while the Conservatives lost 246 seats and were reduced to 156. A future portent was the twenty-seven-seat gain of the new Labour Party, which now had twenty-nine MPs.

The Liberal Government of 1906 was built around and upon those great principles of Liberalism which have since passed into the possession of every party except the Communists, and are still spreading with irresistible appeal throughout the world.

1949, 28 SEPTEMBER.

1906 Opposition

Call them not "the Party opposite," but "the Party in that corner!"

1906. PILPEL, 67.

I will only venture to congratulate the great Imperial statesmen [Conservatives] who sit upon that bench upon the ease and celerity with which they have exchanged the responsibilities of office for the irresponsibilities of opposition.

1906, 22 FEBRUARY.

1909 Election

We are going, fearless of the consequences, confident of our faith, to place before the nation a wide, comprehensive, interdependent scheme of social organisation....And I am confident that in the day of battle the victory will be to the earnest and to the persevering;

and then again will be heard the doleful wail of Tory rout and ruin, and the loud and resounding acclamations with which the triumphant armies of democracy will march once again into the central place of power.

1909, 30 January, Nottingham.
(Liberalism, 233.)

In this election speech are portents of the great war speeches, though over domestic battles: Free Trade, House of Lords reform, and the welfare state, all of which Churchill supported with the fervour of the committed Liberal that he was.

1909 Liberal programme

What we propose to do for human labour, for the service which one man has to render to another, which is the only thing the majority of human beings have to sell, is to give it the same facilities and advantages which every other trader and merchant in the world has secured for his less important and less sensitive commodity.

1909, 16 June.

1910 Tonypandy miners' strike

Absolute order has been maintained around all the threatened collieries....The 1,400 Police at the disposal of the Chief Constable will, it is expected, be able not merely to prevent attacks upon the collieries but to control the whole district and to deal promptly with any sign of a disorderly gathering large or small. No need for the employment of the military is likely to occur. They will be kept as far as possible out of touch with the population, while sufficiently near to the scene to be available if necessary.

1910, 10 November. (OB II, 373–4.)

It has become a part of socialist demonology that Churchill sent troops who fired upon the miners of Tonypandy. Socialist propagandists have sought to make martyrs of the miners of Tonypandy comparable to those of Tolpuddle in 1834. Tonypandy in reality is only distinguished from the other Welsh villages involved because of the high degree of looting in which the miners indulged; but a lie once started can seldom be overtaken (OB II, 373).

1924 Labour programme

[What Labour offers is] our bread for the Bolshevik serpent; our aid for the foreigner of every country; our favours for the Socialists all over the world who have no country; but for our own daughter States across the oceans, on whom the future of the British island and nation depends, only the cold stones of indifference, aversion, and neglect.

1924, 25 September, Edinburgh.
(Gilbert, Life, 463.)

1924–29 Conservative programme

There was nothing sensational or controversial to boast about on the platforms, but measured by every test, economic and financial, the mass of the people were definitely better off, and the state of the nation and of the world was easier and more fertile by the end of our term than at its beginning. Here is a modest, but a solid claim.

1949. (WW2 I, 21.)

What are the twin supreme objectives of public policy at the present time? I can give them in a single sentence. Security of the home of the wage-earner against exceptional misfortune and encouragement of enterprise through a relief of the burdens resting upon industry.

1925, 28 April.

1926 General Strike

The General Strike of 3–12 May 1926 was called by the Trades Union Congress in an unsuccessful attempt to force the Government to prevent wage reduction and worsening work conditions for the coalminers. Churchill edited the government newspaper, The British Gazette, building up a huge circulation but being accused of violent partisanship. When the strike ended he immediately sought to redress the miners' grievances.

The State cannot be impartial as between itself and that section of its subjects with whom it is contending.

1926. ("Churchill the Editor,"
Beric Holt in Eade, 126.)

[The Strike] can only end in the overthrow of Parliamentary Government or in its decisive victory. There is no middle course open....We are seeking peace, we are defending ourselves, we are bound to defend ourselves from the terrible menace which is levied upon us from tomorrow morning, but…the Trade Union Congress have only to cancel the general strike and withdraw the challenge they have issued, and we shall immediately begin, with the utmost care and patience with them again, the long, laborious task which has been pursued over these many weeks of endeavouring to rebuild on economic foundations the prosperity of the coal trade.

1926, 3 MAY

For ten days the nation was paralysed. In the thick of it as usual, Churchill fought tenaciously for the Government, and everyone forgot his words of appeal for peace.

But this I must say; make your minds perfectly clear that if ever you let loose upon us again a general strike, we will loose upon you—another *British Gazette!*

1926, 9 JUNE. (OB V, 174.)

As WSC, defying the opposition after the General Strike, reached his punch line, the jeers and catcalls dissolved into laughter. "It was much easier to disagree with Churchill," wrote Robert Pilpel, "than to dislike him" (Pilpel, 77).

I decline utterly to be impartial as between the fire brigade and the fire.

1926, 7 JULY.

We now know with accuracy the injury which has been done, at any rate to our finances. We meet this afternoon under the shadow of last year. It is not time to bewail the past; it is the time to pay the bill. It is not for me to apportion the blame; my task is only to apportion the burden….I am only the public executioner.

1927, 11 APRIL.

1926 General Strike economics

I said that if I could have foreseen the General Strike and the coal stoppage I should not have felt justified in making an addition to taxation.

1930, 15 APRIL.

Taxation was one of the factors Churchill failed to consider when he returned Britain to the Gold Standard. It placed higher value on

British goods, including coal; combined with continued high taxes, this placed stress on the industry. Miners were offered lower wage increases and fewer benefits, which contributed to the General Strike.

1927 Budget

I am not going to follow the Rt. Hon. Member for Ross and Cromarty [Mr. McPherson] in the arguments he has used as to whether the money raised by the Motor Licence Duties was for all time finally assigned to the upkeep of the roads, I went through all that last year. At that time the argument was used that it belonged to the motorists and that it was "Government of the motorists, by the motorists, for the motorists"…I am not fighting that battle this year….I am merely pursuing and collecting some of the baggage which they left behind.

1927, 28 APRIL.

1928 Budget

It would be easy to give an epitome of the financial year which has closed. The road has lain continually uphill, the weather has been wet and cheerless, and the Lords Commissioners of His Majesty's Treasury have been increasingly uncheered by alcoholic stimulants. Death has been their frequent companion and almost their only friend….

1928, 28 APRIL.

Churchill was comparing his 1928 Budget allowance for road building to the £860,000 allocated for that purpose by Lloyd George in 1910: "That was the value of his [Lloyd George's] generosity. My stinginess, what is left over after my rapacity…amounts to £20,000,000."

1929 Spending proposals

…the Rt. Hon. Member for Carnarvon Boroughs [Mr. Lloyd George] is going to borrow £200 million and to spend it upon paying the unemployed to make racing tracks for well-to-do motorists to make the ordinary pedestrian skip….Lord Rothermere, chief author of the anti-waste campaign, has enlisted under the Happy Warrior of Squandermania…. This is the policy which used to be stigmatised by the late Mr. Thomas Gibson Bowles as the policy of buying a biscuit early in the morning and walking about all day looking for a dog to give it to.

1929, 15 APRIL.

1930s Depression

We see our race doubtful of its mission and no longer confident about its principles, infirm of purpose, drifting to and fro with the tides and currents of a deeply disturbed ocean. The compass has been damaged. The charts are out of date. The crew have to take it in turns to be Captain; and every captain before every movement of the helm has to take a ballot not only of the crew, but of an ever-increasing number of passengers.

1930, 19 JUNE, OXFORD. ("PARLIAMENTARY
GOVERNMENT AND THE ECONOMIC PROBLEM";
THOUGHTS, 173.)

In six months' time, it will not be the Socialist Government that will be in the dock; but the Government of the day; and those whom I shall never cease to declare have very largely brought these misfortunes upon us will once again be...boasting of all they could do if only they came back into power.

1931, 8 SEPTEMBER.

1945 Election

This is no time for windy platitudes and glittering advertisements. The Conservative Party had far better go down telling the truth and acting in accordance with the verities of our position than gain a span of shabbily-bought office by easy and fickle froth and chatter.

1945, 15 MARCH. CENTRAL HALL, WESTMINSTER.
(VICTORY, 79.)

To the astonishment of many outsiders, the July 1945 general election would produce a Labour sweep that would end Churchill's premiership.

I shall be glad when this election business is over. It hovers over me like a vulture of uncertainty in the sky.

1945, 20 JULY, POTSDAM. (MORAN, 297.)

For more vulture references see Chapter 18, World War II...1944/D-day weather and Chapter 12, War...Boer War.

I dreamed that life was over. I saw—it was very vivid—my dead body under a white sheet on a table in an empty room. I recognized my bare feet projecting from under the sheet. It was very life-like...Perhaps this is the end.

1945, 25 JULY. (MORAN, 306.)

[Lord Moran: "I spoke of the ingratitude of the people."]
Oh, no, I wouldn't call it that. They have had a very hard time.

1945, 26 JULY. (MORAN, 307.)

WSC and Moran had now heard the election results.

A friend of mine, an officer, was in Zagreb when the results of the late General Election came in. An old lady said to him, "Poor Mr. Churchill! I suppose now he will be shot." My friend was able to reassure her. He said the sentence might be mitigated to one of the various forms of hard labour which are always open to His Majesty's subjects.

1945, 16 AUGUST.

1945 National goals

What noble opportunities have the new Government inherited! Let them be worthy of their fortune, which also is the fortune of us all. To release and liberate the vital springs of British energy and inventiveness, to let the honest earnings of the nation fructify in the pockets of the people, to spread well-being and security against accident and misfortune throughout the whole nation, to plan, wherever State planning is imperative, and to guide into fertile and healthy channels the native British genius for comprehension and good will—all these are open to them, and all these ought to be open to all of us now....

Freedom and abundance—these must be our aims. The production of new wealth is far more beneficial, and on an incomparably larger scale, than class and party fights about the liquidation of old wealth. We must try to share blessings and not miseries.

1945, 16 AUGUST.

WSC was throwing down a gauntlet; he did not expect this from the Labour Government. The last paragraph is a variation of a frequent aphorism. See Chapter 2, Maxims...Capitalism and socialism.

1946 Conservative programme

Our main objectives are: To uphold the Christian religion and resist all attacks upon it. To defend our Monarchical and Parliamentary Constitution. To provide adequate security against external aggression and safety for our seaborne trade. To uphold law and order, and impartial justice administered by courts free from interference or pressure on the part of the executive. To regain a sound finance and strict supervision of national income and expenditure. To defend and develop our Empire trade, without which Great Britain would perish. To promote all measures to improve the health and social conditions of the people. To support as a general rule free enterprise and initiative against State trading and nationalisation of industries.

1946, 5 OCTOBER. CONSERVATIVE PARTY CONFERENCE, BLACKPOOL. (SINEWS, 213–14.)

1947 Budget

But what is this balanced Budget, even when thus produced? It is a balance between three thousand millions of extravagant expenditure on the one hand, and three thousand millions of crushing, paralysing taxation on the other. One set of evils are balanced against another set of evils, and we are invited to admire a perfect equilibrium.

1947, 18 APRIL.

1947 Bureaucracy

There are three times as many people employed by the Government to manage our affairs as were used by the Conservative Governments before the war. A mighty army of 450,000 additional civil servants have been taken from production and added, at a prodigious cost and waste, to the oppressive machinery of Government and control.

1947, 18 APRIL.

1947–49 Labour programme

It is this vital creative impulse that I deeply fear the doctrines and policy of the Socialist Government have destroyed, or are rapidly destroying, in our national life. Nothing that they can plan and order and rush around enforcing will take its place. They have broken the mainspring and until we get a new one the watch will not go.

1947, 28 OCTOBER.

As a free-born Englishman, what I hate is the sense of being at anybody's mercy or in anybody's power, be he Hitler or Attlee. We are approaching very near to dictatorship in this country, dictatorship that is to say—I will be quite candid with the House—without either its criminality or its efficiency.

1947, 11 NOVEMBER.

A repeat of Churchill's 1945 election speech warning that Labour would resort to "a kind of Gestapo" (see Chapter 21 ... Socialism). The Nazi allusion was probably just as unwelcome in 1947; nobody could imagine mild-mannered Clement Attlee as Hitler.

...A continuance of Socialist experiments in theory, and of their ineptitude and incompetence in practice, will bring upon us not only worse privations and restrictions than those we now bear, but economic ruin; and not only economic ruin but the depopulation of the British Isles on a scale which no one has ever imagined or predicted.

1948, 21 APRIL. ROYAL ALBERT HALL, LONDON. (EUROPE, 296.)

...our Socialist spendthrifts and muddlers have...exacted and extracted from our people a higher rate of taxation than was required in the very height of the war, from which we victoriously emerged. It will be incredible to those who come afterwards that so much should have been cast away in so short a time, so many sacrifices demanded, so many restrictions and regulations imposed and obeyed, and that at the end we should be where we are now. Never before in the history of human government has such great havoc been wrought by such small men.

1949, 23 JULY, WOLVERHAMPTON. (CS VII, 7831–2.)

1948 Nationalisation of steel

I say this [steel industry nationalisation plan] is not a Bill, it is a plot; not a plan to increase production, but rather, in effect, at any rate, an operation in restraint of trade. It is not a plan to help our patient struggling people, but a burglar's jemmy to crack the capitalist crib.

1948, 16 NOVEMBER.

1949 Nationalisation

We are now threatened, besides the nationalization of steel, with that of insurance, sugar and cement. All of these thriving industries are to be disturbed, mauled and finally chilled and largely paralysed by the clumsy and costly grip of State bureaucracy....But in all matters of good housekeeping the Socialists have proved themselves an effective substitute for some of the evils we overcame in the war.

1949, 14 OCTOBER. PARTY CONFERENCE, EARL'S COURT, LONDON. (BALANCE, 114–17.)

1950 Election

It is a great advantage in a dairy to have cows with large udders because one gets more milk out of them than from the others. These exceptionally fertile milch cows are greatly valued in any well-conducted dairy, and anyone would be thought very foolish who boasted he had got rid of all the best milkers, just as he would be thought very foolish if he did not milk them to the utmost limit of capacity, compatible with the maintenance of their numbers. I am quite sure that the Minister of Agriculture would look in a very different way upon the reduction of all these thousands of his best milkers from that in which the Chancellor of the Exchequer looks upon the destruction of the most fertile and the most profitable resources of taxation. I must say the cows do not feel the same way about it as do the Socialists. The cows have not got the same equalitarian notions and dairy farmers are so unimaginative that they think mainly of getting as much milk as possible; they want a lot of political education.

1950, 20 APRIL.

1952 Conservative inheritance

It is said reap where you have sown. That is a hard rule, a stern rule and we accept it. But we are not now reaping where *we* have sown, we are reaping where others have sown, where they have sown weeds as well as grain.

1952, 11 OCTOBER, SCARBOROUGH. (STEMMING, 340.)

WSC's Conservative Government had been in office for a year, following six years under Labour.

1953 Conservative programme

Our Conservative principles are well known....We stand for the free and flexible working of the laws of supply and demand. We stand for compassion and aid for those who, whether through age, illness or misfortune, cannot keep pace with the march of society....We are for private enterprise with all its ingenuity, thrift and contrivance, and we believe it can flourish best within a strict, and well-understood system of prevention and correction of abuses....In a complex community like our own no absolute rigid uniformity of practice is possible.

1953, 10 OCTOBER. PARTY CONFERENCE, MARGATE. (ALLIANCE, 63.)

1953 Legislative priorities

The curious fact that the House prefers to give two days to the television White Paper and only one day to foreign affairs may be noted by future historians as an example of a changing sense of proportion in modern thought.

1953, 17 DECEMBER.

1954 Conservative Government

Remember that we can't expect to put the whole world right with a majority of eighteen.

1954, 24 FEBRUARY.

Diaries of Cabinet Secretary Sir Norman Brook, Sunday Telegraph, 5 August 2007.

Politics on the Home Front: General Observations

Abdications

Abdications have taken place in the history of the world, but if you look at the course of history you will see that they have usually been made by masculine rather than by feminine monarchs. Kings have abdicated but never Queens, and it is one of the attractive qualities of Mr. Balfour [the Prime Minister] that his nature displays a certain femininity.

1905, 27 JANUARY.

Arthur James Balfour, first Earl of Balfour (1848–1930) Prime Minister from 1902 to 1906, was thrown out by the Liberals, including Churchill, in the 1906 general election.

"Above Party"

I have noticed that whenever a distinguished politician declares that a particular question is above Party, what he really means is that everybody, without distinction of Party, shall vote for him.

1905, 8 MARCH.

Bureaucracy

There is...no surer method of economising and saving money than in the reduction of the number of officials.

1928, 24 APRIL.

Capital punishment

The only capital decision with wh[ich] I have been dissatisfied during my tenure was about a man I reprieved just before I started on grounds wh[ich] I do not feel wholly convinced were adequate. He has since committed suicide! To most men—including all the best—a life sentence is worse than a death sentence...

1910. (OB II, 418.)

WSC to Sir Edward Grey (n.d.).

All his life Churchill supported capital punishment. Yet when it fell to him to take the decision in a particular case he found it most painful. Conscious of his direct responsibility, he would brood long over each case – Randolph S. Churchill.

...when justice and the law have done their best within their limits, when precedents have been searched and weighed, mercy still roams around the prison seeking for some chink by which she can creep in.

1948, 15 JULY. (EUROPE UNITE, 390.)

As Home Secretary WSC had commuted a death sentence to life imprisonment, only to have the prisoner commit suicide:

I mention this case in order that those who shrink from the horror of inflicting the death penalty may not underrate the gravity and torment of the alternative.

If I was assured that abolishing the death penalty would bring all murders to an end, I would certainly be in favour of that course....A bargain between politicians in

difficulties ought not to be the basis of our criminal law.

1948, 15 JULY. (CZARNOMSKI, 95.)

Labour's 1948 Criminal Justice Bill contained a clause on the death penalty which attempted to bridge the gap between pro- and anti-capital punishment MPs.

Cartoons

Just as eels are supposed to get used to skinning, so politicians get used to being caricatured....If we must confess it, they are quite offended and downcast when the cartoons stop....They fear old age and obsolescence are creeping upon them. They murmur: "We are not mauled and maltreated as we used to be. The great days are ended."

1931, JUNE. "CARTOONS AND CARTOONISTS," STRAND MAGAZINE; THOUGHTS, 15.

"Eels get used to skinning" was also deployed in World War II, when WSC urged people to get used to the bombing.

Child tax credit

This increasing of the children's allowances is another application of our general policy of helping the producer.

1928, 24 APRIL. (CS IV, 4403.)

Churchill was promising a 100 per cent rise in tax remission for families with children.

Child welfare

...there was something rather hypocritical about tactics which tried to parade the claims of the children as an excuse for the acts of the parents....

1903, 1 MAY.

Civil service

If there was one principle which had kept our Civil Service and public service free from corruption it was the test of a competitive examination....

1905, 13 JULY.

Class struggle

[It] goes on tirelessly, with perpetual friction, a struggle between class and class which never sinks into lethargy, and never breaks into violence, but which from year to year makes possible a steady and constant advance. It is on the nature of that class struggle in Britain that the security of life and property is fundamentally reposed. We are always changing; like nature, we change a great deal although we change very slowly. We are always reaching a higher level after each change, but yet with the harmony of our life unbroken and unimpaired.

1908, 14 MAY. KINNAIRD HALL, DUNDEE.
(LIBERALISM, 201.)

See also Chapter 21 ... Socialist "Gestapo".

Class system

The class line must become, if the party system is shattered, the line of demarcation.

1910, 31 MARCH.

...during this war great changes have taken place in the minds of men, and there is no change which is more marked in our country than the continual and rapid effacement of class differences.

1944, 1 DECEMBER, HARROW SCHOOL. (DAWN, 271.)

Coal miners

We must not only regard the financial interests of these prosperous companies, but we must remember the human interest of the miner at the bottom of the mine.

1904, 5 MAY.

A speech made shortly before Churchill "crossed the aisle" from the Conservatives to the Liberals, this statement made clear which party he considered his "natural home". See also 1926 General Strike.

I do not wonder a bit at the miners' demand. I cannot find it in my heart to feel the slightest surprise, or indignation, or mental disturbance. My capacity for wonder is entirely absorbed, not by the miners' demand, but by the gentleman in the silk hat and white waistcoat who has the composure and the complacency to deny that demand and dispute it with him...

What about mining royalties? In all this talk about the importance of cheap coal to our industries and to the poor consumer we have had no mention of mining royalties. No. We never mention that.

1908, 6 JULY.

I am very sorry that we have had to debar so many miners from going to the war in the Armed Forces. I respect their feelings, but we cannot afford it; we cannot allow it. Besides the need for their services in the pits, there is danger in the pits too, and where there is danger there is honour. "Act well thy part, there all the honour lies," and that is the motto I want to give out to all those who in an infinite variety of ways are playing an equally worthy part in the consummation of our high purpose.

1942, 31 OCTOBER. WESTMINSTER CENTRAL HALL.
(END, 254.)

The quotation is from Alexander Pope; the following line reads, "Act well thy part, there all the honour lies."

The only quarrel I have ever had with the miners was in the war when I had to forbid them from pouring out of the mines to join our armies in the field. Let [Socialists] dismiss from their minds these malicious tales that a Conservative Government would be hostile to the mining community. I have always affirmed that those who work in these hard and dangerous conditions far from the light of the sun have the right to receive exceptional benefits from the nation which they serve.

1951, 21 JULY. WOODFORD. (STEMMING, 97.)

Collective bargaining

It is in the interest of the wage-earner to have many other alternatives open to him than service under one all-powerful employer called the State. He will be in a better position to bargain collectively and production will be more abundant; there will be more for all and more freedom for all when the wage-earner is able, in the large majority of cases, to choose and change his work, and to deal with a private employer who, like himself, is subject to the ordinary pressures of life and, like himself, is dependent upon his personal thrift, ingenuity and good housekeeping.

1946, 5 OCTOBER, BLACKPOOL. (SINEWS, 214.)

We support the principle of collective bargaining between recognized and responsible trade unions and employers, and we include in collective bargaining the right to strike. They [the trade unions] have a great part to play in the life of the country and…they should keep clear of Party politics.

1949, 13 OCTOBER. CONSERVATIVE TRADE UNION CONGRESS, LONDON. (BALANCE, 103.)

Conscription

I have regarded compulsion not as the gathering together of men as if they were heaps of shingle, but the fitting of them into their places like the pieces in the pattern of a mosaic. The great principle of equality of sacrifice requires in practice to be applied in accordance with the maxim, "A place for every man and every man in his place."

1916, 23 MAY.

There are many countries where a national Army on a compulsory basis is the main foundation of the State and is regarded as one of the most important safeguards of democratic freedom. It is not so here. On the contrary, the civil character of our Government institutions are one of the most deeply cherished convictions of our island life, a conviction which our island position alone has enabled us to enjoy.

1920, 23 FEBRUARY.

…it is certainly an irony of fate that the Prime Minister and the Minister of Defence should be the men to bring a Conscription Bill before the House now….Why, these were the very politicians who, four months before the outbreak of the war, led their followers into the Lobby against the principle of compulsory military service, and then had the face to accuse the Conservative Party of being "guilty men"…

Compulsory military service is not necessarily a problem for a regular standing army; but the only way of making us a nation of fighting men in time of war is by national service in time of peace. As all our habits in the past have been to live in a peaceable manner, we have entered all our wars unprepared or ill-prepared, and the delay before we are able to place an army in the field at the side of our Allies has been a very serious weakness, not only in the physical but in the moral sphere.

1947, 31 MARCH.

Churchill's argument in favour of the draft may have gone out of fashion, but applied to some broader form of compulsory national service, it still has much to recommend it.

At the age of 18, a year in His Majesty's uniform…may very well fill a part of their continuous education. Also, how good it is that there should be at that time when people's minds are so pliant, a mingling of classes, on terms of equality.

1947, 6 MAY.

…it does not depend on us whether war comes; less than ever in our history does it depend on us; it depends on events largely beyond our control, and on decisions and factors which are inscrutable—but should it come, I say…that a terrible accountancy will be required from those to whom Parliament has accorded, in time of peace, unparalleled resources and unprecedented power.

1948, 1 DECEMBER. (EUROPE, 486.)

In its National Service Bill, Labour, which had voted against conscription before the war, reduced the term of conscription from two years to eighteen months after it.

Conservative Free Traders

Events had gone a long way towards showing that the reasons which had already induced some Hon. Members to separate themselves altogether from the Party opposite [Conservatives] and to take the course of moving over to the other side of the House [Liberals], a course accompanied by every odious circumstance of abuse…

1905, 7 JUNE.

WSC was of course one of these Hon. Members, and his switch to the Liberals had certainly earned him "odious circumstance and abuse".

Conservative Party

Cabinet Ministers abuse, contradict, and disavow each other. Members of the Government and of the Conservative Party fight over the Prime Minister as dogs worry over a bone.

1903. (BROAD, 49.)

We know perfectly well what to expect [from the Tories]—a party of great vested interests, banded together in a formidable confederation; corruption at home, aggression to cover it up abroad; the trickery of tariff juggles, the tyranny of a party machine; sentiment by the bucketful; patriotism and imperialism by the imperial pint; the open hand at the public exchequer; the open door at the public house; dear food for the millions, cheap labour for the millionaire.

1904, 13 MAY. FREE TRADE HALL, MANCHESTER. (FFT, 78.)

This oration was retreaded almost word for word in WSC's final speech to the electors of Dundee on 8 May 1908, just before they elected him as Member of Parliament.

Deep down in the heart of the old-fashioned Tory, however unreflecting, there lurks a wholesome respect for the ancient forms and safeguards of the English Constitution, and a recognition of the fact that some day they may be found of great consequence and use.

1906. (LRC, 766.)

I will never stifle myself in such a moral and intellectual sepulchre.

1922, NOVEMBER, DUNDEE. (BROAD, WC, 201.)

The "moral and intellectual sepulchre" was the "do-nothing" policy of the Bonar Law Conservatives, whom Churchill saw as "unprogressives". In the event, WSC was defeated in the subsequent election, and out of Parliament for nearly two years.

We must not forget that afternoon in May 1940...when the enormous Tory majorities in both Houses of Parliament voted into the hands of the Government, for the sake of our country's survival, practically all the rights of property and, more precious still, of liberty on which what we have called civilisation is built. That ought not to be forgotten when Hon. Members opposite mock at us as exploiters, rack renters and profiteers. It ought not to be forgotten...that Conservative majorities in both Houses of Parliament in one single afternoon, offered all they had and all that they were worth.

1947, 12 MARCH.

We [the Conservative Party] are a party met together on a party occasion and we have to fight as a Party against those who oppose us and assail us. But faction is not our aim. Party triumphs are not our goal. We think it a high

honour to serve the British people and the worldwide Commonwealth and Empire of which they are the centre.

1953, 10 OCTOBER. PARTY CONFERENCE, MARGATE. (ALLIANCE, 58.)

Credit and thrift

I was also taught that it was one of the first duties of Government to promote that confidence on which credit and thrift, and especially foreign credit, can alone stand and grow. I was taught to believe that those processes...would produce a lively and continuous improvement in prosperity. I still hold to those general principles.

1949, 27 OCTOBER.

Four years earlier WSC memorably said: "...let the honest earnings of the nation fructify in the pockets of the people." See Labour Party/1945 herein.

Crime and punishment

The mood and temper of the public in regard to the treatment of crime and criminals is one of the most unfailing tests of the civilisation of any country. A calm and dispassionate recognition of the rights of the accused against the State...a constant heart-searching by all charged with the duty of punishment, a desire and eagerness to rehabilitate in the world of industry all those who have paid their dues in the hard coinage of punishment, tireless efforts towards the discovery of curative and regenerating processes, and an unfaltering faith that there is a treasure, if only you can find it, in the heart of every man—these are the symbols which in the treatment of crime and criminals mark and measure the stored-up strength of a nation, and are the sign and proof of the living virtue in it.

1910, 20 JULY.

Sir Martin Gilbert wrote:

Underlying Churchill's prison reforms was a real understanding of the nature of imprisonment from the perspective of the prisoner (Gilbert, Life, 214).

The approximate net average cost of maintaining a convict is £18 3s per annum or about £690 for thirty-eight years.

1911, 12 APRIL. (CZARNOMSKI, 84)

As Home Secretary, Churchill worked to reduce the prison population by releasing, or not jailing, people convicted of trivial offences, and searching for other means of correction for young offenders.

I could not help feeling impressed with how easy it must be for a very distinguished lawyer to procure the conviction of an innocent man.

1914, 30 MARCH.

I have always felt the keenest pity for prisoners and captives…Each day exactly like the one before, with the barren ashes of wasted life behind, and all the long years of bondage stretching out ahead.

1930. (MEL, 273–4.)

The identical phrase was used in WSC's article, "The Effects of Modern Amusements on Life and Character" (1938).

To create and multiply offences which are not condemned by public opinion, which are difficult to detect and can only be punished in a capricious manner, is impolitic.

1941, 9 AUGUST. (WW2 III, 724.)

Prime Minister to General Ismay. WSC was deploring the notion that motorists receiving supplementary petrol rations should keep a log of their every journey.

Currency

Up to this moment I have been talking only about our buying power abroad. If we lose that we should be like a swimmer who cannot keep his head above water long enough to get a new breath. (No fun at all!)

1952, 3 MAY. BROADCAST, LONDON. (STEMMING, 284.)

The pound was devalued from $4 to $2.80 by the Labour Government in September 1949.

Daylight Saving Time

…the first thing the House of Commons has to do about this Bill is not to laugh at it.

1909, 5 MARCH.

It is one of the paradoxes of history that we should owe the boon of summer time, which gives every year to the people of this country

between 160 and 170 hours more daylight leisure, to a war which plunged Europe into darkness for four years, and shook the foundations of civilization throughout the world. I was one of the earliest supporters of Daylight Saving. I gave it my voice and my vote in Parliament at a time when powerful interests and bitter and tenacious prejudices were leagued against it, and while the mass of the population was either indifferent or scornful.

1934, 28 APRIL. ("A SILENT TOAST TO WILLIAM WILLETT," PICTORIAL WEEKLY; ESSAYS III, 116.)

Willett conceived what is now British Summer Time; WSC supported it in Parliament.

Economic reality

…on questions of economic law it does not matter at all what the electors think or vote or say. The economic laws proceed.

1929, 16 JULY.

Economic strength

…there can be no assurance of lasting military strength without a firm economic foundation, and no defence programme can stand without the economic resources to carry it through.

1952, 30 JULY.

Elections fought over foreign policy

An election fought on ordinary domestic issues is a process with which we are all familiar; but an election turning on the dread issues of defence and foreign policy, might leave us a deeply divided nation, with an evenly balanced, incoherent Parliament, and this at the very moment when the danger on the Continent had reached its height. That is why I plead for national unity, and for a policy upon which alone it is to be achieved.

1938, 9 MAY. FREE TRADE HALL, MANCHESTER. (BLOOD, 25.)

Emigration

I say to the general mass of those who wish to leave this country, "Stay here and fight it out"….Do not desert the old land. We cannot spare you.

1947, 16 AUGUST. PARTY POLITICAL BROADCAST, LONDON. (EUROPE, 132–3.)

WSC was shocked that after two years of Labour Government, more than half a million

Britons had emigrated to the Dominions or the United States.

Under Socialism, with all its malice and class jealousy, with all its hobbling and crippling of diligence, initiative and enterprise, it will not be possible for more than two-thirds of our present population to live in this island. That is why there is all this talk of emigration.

1947, 27 September. Royal Wanstead School. (Europe, 142.)

Employer powers

It might well be in the interest of the factory workers, or indeed of the wage earners generally, not to have too strong an employer over them. I should like to feel that he would be strong in the sense of being capable and efficient as a producer or competitor in the world markets. But it is abhorrent to our idea of freedom that the employer should have undue power over his employees.

1945, 21 June.

Expenditure

Expenditure always is popular; the only unpopular part about it is the raising of the money to pay the expenditure.

1901, 13 May.

Public expenditure divided itself into three aspects. There was the policy of expenditure, the merit of expenditure, and the audit of expenditure.

1905, 26 July.

One may aim at a reduction, as one may aim at a target, but one does not promise to hit it.

1927, 11 April.

Exports

...I do not believe that a successful export trade can be founded upon a starved home market....Exports are only the steam over the boiling water in the kettle. They are only that part of the iceberg that glitters above the surface of the ocean.

1947, 28 October.

Churchill believed the post-war Labour Government was stressing exports at the cost of national prosperity.

Finance, philatelic

Observe that the caprice of the philatelist yields in a normal year sufficient to defray exactly the annual cost of education and religion: and thus Christianity is sustained by variations in the watermark! Such are the unseen foundations of society.

1906, 27 April. (Hyam, 499.)

WSC was observing that the sale of its unique postage stamps by the Seychelles approximately covered its annual budget for education and religion. (Although WSC watched Roosevelt work on his stamp collection with polite interest, this is the only appearance of "philatelist" or "philately" in the entire canon.)

Franchise

It has often been remarked by bewildered foreign observers that every extension of the franchise in Great Britain has left the Conservative Party in a stronger position. But the reason, or one of the main reasons, which they do not see for this undoubted fact is the steady and ceaseless improvement in the education of the people and in the conditions of their life, and in their growing conscious power to govern their country effectively.

1945, 15 March. Central Hall, Westminster. (Victory, 76.)

...I have always been in favour of extending the franchise. I believe in the will of the people. I do not believe in the perversion of the will of the people by actively organised and engineered minorities, who, having seized upon power by force or fraud or chicane, come forward and then use that power in the name of vast masses with whom they have long lost all effective connection.

1946, 12 December.

See also Women's Suffrage.

Gold Standard

I wish [Montagu Norman, Philip Snowden and the monetary experts] were admirals or generals. I can sink them if necessary. But when I am talking to bankers and economists, after awhile they begin to talk Persian, and then they sink me instead.

1924. (Daily Telegraph, 5 August 1965.)

Churchill to Robert Boothby, quoted by Boothby in the House of Lords, 1965. When WSC was Chancellor of the Exchequer, Boothby, his Parliamentary Private Secretary, said that the return of Britain to the Gold Standard was made on the advice of Montagu Norman, Governor of the Bank of England, and Philip Snowden, later Labour's Chancellor of the Exchequer.

We are often told that the gold standard will shackle us to the United States. I will deal with that in a moment. I will tell you what it will shackle us to. It will shackle us to reality. For good or for ill, it will shackle us to reality.

1925, 4 MAY.

Churchill later regretted that as Chancellor of the Exchequer, he had been persuaded by Montagu Norman, head of the Bank of England, to return Britain to the Gold Standard. Monetarist economists insist that he was right to do so on the merits, but the failure to adjust wage and tax policy to the new realities of a gold-backed pound helped bring about the General Strike. See General Strike in this chapter.

In carrying out a great change like the return to the gold standard it has been necessary to move with extreme care. So many objects have to be kept in view at the same moment that delicacy and judgment are required at every step. I think that in the Treasury and in the Bank of England we have the most skilful advisers and financiers that any country can show. At any rate they are respected all over the world, so there is no reason why they should be looked down upon at home.

1925, 3 NOVEMBER. HIPPODROME, SHEFFIELD. (CS IV, 3777.)

Britain suspended the Gold Standard under pressures of the Depression on 20 September 1931.

Government, forming a

The formation of a modern British Administration is a complex affair, involving nearly eighty persons and offices. When I thought of the elaborate processes of personal correspondence or interviews with which in Gladstonian days Governments had been

formed I felt that only extreme emergency could excuse the use I made of the telephone.

1954. (WW2 VI, 517.)

Never a fan of the telephone over the written word, WSC admitted to its use in May 1945, assembling his second Government, this time of his own party, after the break-up of the wartime coalition.

Government and Opposition

The leader of the Liberal Party speaks of the Government and rebels. He seems to think that all Governments must be infallible and all rebels must be vile. It all depends on what is Government, and what are rebels.

1937, 14 APRIL.

Hansard

It is open to any person or organisation to publish an extract from Hansard with what comments they please.

1943, 23 MARCH.

Hansard is the official transcript of Parliamentary debates.

Housing

Houses are built of bricks, mortar and good-will, not of politics, prejudices and spite.

1950, 8 FEBRUARY, CARDIFF. (BALANCE, 186.)

Good housing is the first of the social services. Bad housing makes more disease than the best health service can cure.

1951, 18 MAY, GLASGOW. (STEMMING, 84.)

Idlers

It must not however be forgotten that there are idlers and wastrels at both ends of the social scale.

1911, 10 FEBRUARY. (OB, CV2/2, 1037.)

A cheeky remark by the Liberal Home Secretary in a letter to the King – who considered it "quite superfluous", and Churchill's views "very socialistic".

We cannot afford to have idle people. Idlers at the top make idlers at the bottom. No one must stand aside in his working prime to pursue a life of selfish pleasure. There are wasters in all classes. Happily they are only a small minority in every class. But anyhow we cannot have a band of drones in our midst, whether they come from the ancient aristocracy or the modern plutocracy or the ordinary type of pub crawler.

1943, 21 MARCH, BROADCAST, LONDON. (ONWARDS, 39.)

Immigration

How was the Aliens Bill passed? It was introduced to the House of Commons in a tumbril. They began debating it on the steps of the scaffold, and before two days had passed in Committee they were hurried to the framework of the guillotine.

1905, 31 JULY.

The first Aliens Act since 1836, the 1906 Act set up a new system of immigration control and registration, making the Home Secretary responsible for all matters of immigration and nationality. WSC's opposition to the legislation won him early support from the Jewish community in Manchester, who would help to elect him to office in the general election of January 1906.

In dealing with nationalities, nothing is more fatal than a dodge. Wrongs will be forgiven, sufferings and losses will be forgiven or forgotten, battles will be remembered only as they recall the martial virtues of the combatants; but anything like chicane, anything like a trick, will always rankle.

1906, 5 APRIL.

It is highly important that the workmen should be assigned the noble status of citizenship in all our legislation.

1911, 30 MAY.

A view that has its modern counterpart in the ideas of some that illegal aliens should be placed on a legal track to citizenship.

Problems will arise if many coloured people settle here. Are we to saddle ourselves with colour problems in the UK? Attracted by Welfare State. Public opinion in UK won't tolerate it once it gets beyond certain limits....[We should let] public opinion develop a little more before taking action.

1954, 3 FEBRUARY. (DIARIES OF CABINET SECRETARY SIR NORMAN BROOK, *SUNDAY TELEGRAPH*, 5 AUGUST 2007.)

Churchill's proposal was accepted and no restrictions were imposed. The 1962 Commonwealth Immigrants Act allowed any Commonwealth citizen to enter and stay in Britain. In 1954, the foreign-born in Britain numbered 60,000; in 2007 they numbered 6,000,000.

Income

There is all the difference in the world between the income which a man makes from month to month or from year to year by his continued exertion, which may stop at any moment, and will certainly stop if he is incapacitated, and the income which is derived from the profits of accumulated capital, which is a continuing income irrespective of the exercise of the owner.

1909, 17 JULY, EDINBURGH. (LIBERALISM, 276.)

Industry, management

Management by whom? Is it to be management by business men under all the inducements of profit and all the penalties of bankruptcy, or is it to be management by politicians interested in their careers or prejudiced by their Party doctrines, but otherwise not specially distinguished—or, I should say, who otherwise have their distinction yet to win—who are assisted in their task by officials themselves impartial in the sense that it makes no difference to them whether the industry shows a profit or a loss?

1948, 16 NOVEMBER.

Industry, tests of

...I select four main tests by which to tell what is a depressed industry or an industry which is not flourishing....The first is that unemployment is abnormal; the second, that the ratio of rates to profits is excessive; the third that the profits are subnormal and the fourth that profits have been decreasing in recent years.

1928, 5 JUNE.

Inflation and wages

On the whole, when there is inflation and undue expansion, I believe it to be true that wages follow with somewhat slower footsteps the swiftly rising scale of prices.

1925, 4 MAY.

Insurance, Blitz

...unless the House was prepared to draw the distinction very sharply between war damage by bomb and shell and the other forms of loss which are incurred, we could not attempt to deal with this matter; otherwise we should be opening up a field to which there would be no bounds. If, however, we were able to embark upon such a project as would give complete insurance, at any rate up to a certain minimum figure, for everyone against war damage by shell or bomb, I think it would be a very solid mark of the confidence...about the way in which we are going to come through this war.

1940, 5 SEPTEMBER.

At the beginning of the blitz I pressed upon him [Sir Kingsley Wood, Chancellor of the Exchequer] the vital need of doing something for the poor people whose houses were smashed up and whose businesses were destroyed, and he devised the elaborate insurance scheme, which has come into the fullest possible fruition. At one time, it looked as if the State were taking on a very heavy burden; but trees never grow up to the sky, and...the scheme has ultimately turned out to be highly profitable to the Exchequer.

1943, 22 SEPTEMBER.

Insurance, life

The only anxiety which the Socialists have about nationalizing life insurance is whether it will lose them support among the very large number of insurance agents....What they now seek is the control of the vast sum of money which represents the savings over many years of millions of people to provide by self-denial and forethought, for their widows, their orphans and their own old age or infirmity. The control over this great mass of investments would be another most powerful means of bringing the whole financial, economic and industrial life of Britain into Socialist hands.

1950, 28 JANUARY, WOODFORD, ESSEX.
(BALANCE, 167.)

Insurance, national

If I had my way I would write the word "Insure" over the door of every cottage, and upon the blotting-book of every public man, because I am convinced that by sacrifices

which are inconceivably small, which are all within the power of the very poorest man in regular work, families can be secured against catastrophes which otherwise would smash them up forever.

1909, 23 MAY. FREE TRADE HALL, MANCHESTER.
(LIBERALISM, 267–8.)

When I think of the fate of poor old women, so many of whom have no one to look after them and nothing to live on at the end of their lives, I am glad to have had a hand in all that structure of pensions and insurance which no other country can rival and which is especially a help to them.

1930. (MEL, 87.)

Churchill's interest in social insurance did not end with the pre-World War I Liberal Government; he was also the author of the Widows, Orphans, and Old Age Contributory Pensions Act of 1928.

I have been prominently connected with all these schemes of national compulsory organised thrift from the time when I brought my friend Sir William Beveridge into the public service thirty-five years ago, when I was creating the labour exchanges, on which he was a great authority, and when, with Sir Hubert Llewellyn Smith, I framed the first unemployment insurance scheme. The prime parent of all national insurance schemes is Mr. Lloyd George. I was his lieutenant in those distant days, and afterwards it fell to me as Chancellor of the Exchequer eighteen years ago to lower the pensions age to sixty-five and to bring in the widows and orphans.

1943, 21 MARCH. BROADCAST, LONDON.
(ONWARDS, 38–9.)

I am the oldest living champion of Insurance in the House of Commons....In 1909 I obtained the power to spread a network of [labour] exchanges over the whole of Great Britain and Ireland. For that purpose we [the Liberal Government] brought into the public services Mr. Beveridge....The time is now ripe for another great advance, and anyone can see what large savings there will be in the administration once the whole process of insurance has become unified, compulsory, and national. Here is a real opportunity for what I once called "bringing the magic of averages to the rescue of the millions." Therefore you must rank me and my colleagues as strong partisans of national compulsory insurance for all classes for all purposes from the cradle to the grave.

1945, 13 JUNE. POLITICAL BROADCAST, LONDON.
(VICTORY, 197; CZARNOMSKI, 188–9.)

Labour claimed that the Conservatives never intended to implement the wartime Beveridge Plan for comprehensive social insurance. WSC replied that it was he who gave Beveridge his first opportunity, in 1909. Another evidence of Churchill's realisation of the need for post-war domestic reforms. "Magic of averages" is one of eight appearances of a phrase dating at least to 1911: see Chapter 3, Churchillisms.

Insurance, unemployment

See now how intricate are its details and its perplexities; how foolish it would be to legislate in panic or haste; how vain it would be to trust to formulas and prejudices; how earnest must be the study; how patient and laborious the preparation; how scientific the spirit, how valiant the action, if that great and hideous evil of insecurity by which our industrial population are harassed is to be effectually diminished in our national life.

1908, 10 OCTOBER. KINNAIRD HALL, DUNDEE.
(LIBERALISM, 219.)

It is in the interests of trade unionists, who are long established contributors, as well as of the employers in industries, to make sure that there is not growing up a certain habit of learning how to qualify for the unemployment insurance.

1925, 30 APRIL.

The whole principle of unemployment insurance rests upon largeness of area and variety of industry. It is only by spreading the risks over very great areas of population and over an extensive diversity of trades that the general contributions of the whole body of subscribers, by averaging the risks, are enabled to guard against seasonal and cyclical disturbances of industry.

1926, 22 FEBRUARY.

See also Unemployment.

Keynesian economics

The idea that you can vote yourself into prosperity is one of the most ludicrous that ever was entertained.

1944, 7 SEPTEMBER. RMS *QUEEN MARY*,
EN ROUTE TO SECOND QUEBEC CONFERENCE.
(COLVILLE, FRINGES II, 139.)

Per Colville's diaries, WSC believed Britain's peacetime prospects were grim, that he no longer felt he had a message to deliver, "and that all he could now do was finish the war, to get the soldiers home and to see that they had houses to which to return".

The idea that a nation can tax itself into prosperity is one of the crudest delusions which has ever fuddled the human mind.

1948, 21 APRIL. THE ROYAL ALBERT HALL,
LONDON. (EUROPE, 301.)

Labour, unskilled

...the casual unskilled labourer who is habitually underemployed, who is lucky to get three, or at the outside four, days' work in the week...is not the natural product, he is an article manufactured, called into being, to suit the requirements, in the Prime Minister's telling phrase, of all industries at particular times and of particular industries at all times.

1908, 10 OCTOBER. KINNAIRD HALL, DUNDEE.
(LIBERALISM, 217.)

Labour exchanges

Labour Exchanges are the gateway to industrial security.

1909, 17 FEBRUARY.

Labour influence

When [MPs] considered how vast the Labour interest was, how vital, how human, when they considered the gigantic powers which by the consent of both Parties had been given to the working classes, when, on the other hand, they considered the influence in this House of company directors, the learned professions, the service members, the railway, landed and liquor interests, it would surely be admitted that the influence of labour on the course of legislation was even ludicrously small.

1904, 22 APRIL.

With this remark Churchill faltered, lost his place, and sat down, thanking Hon. members for having listened to him. It was the last time he spoke without a complete text of his speech in hand.

Labour Party

A balloon goes up quite easily for a certain distance, but after a certain distance it refuses to go up any farther because the air is too rarefied to float it and sustain it. And, therefore, I would say, let us examine the concrete facts.

1906, 11 OCTOBER. ST. ANDREW'S HALL, GLASGOW. (LIBERALISM, 162.)

WSC on the rapid rise of the Labour Party, said its mission was to destroy the Liberal Party, because "Liberalism enlists hundreds of thousands upon the side of progress," while "militant Socialism would drive [the same people] into violent Tory reaction". But Churchill refrained from predicting which would survive.

They will be invited to continue in office on sufferance in order that if they are violent they may be defeated, and if they are moderate they may become divided.

1924, 18 JANUARY. (OB, CV5/1, 95.)

Letter to a correspondent on the current minority Socialist Government.

If the Labour Party had their way they would reduce the country to one vast soup kitchen.

1929, 16 DECEMBER, LONDON. (CS V, 4675.)

We have a Socialist Government, with a very large majority. They have been in office for two years…The Socialists are quite in favour of the Monarchy, and make generous provision for it.…The Labour men and the trade unions look upon the Monarchy not only as a national but a nationalised institution. They even go to the parties at Buckingham Palace. Those who have very extreme principles wear sweaters.

1947. ("THE DREAM," OB VIII, 367.)

Churchill's reply to his father's ghost, in "The Dream", who asks which party is in power, Liberal or Conservative.

…government of the duds, by the duds, and for the duds.…

1947. (TAYLOR, 220.)

No government has ever combined so passionate a lust for power with such incurable impotence in its exercise.

1947, 11 NOVEMBER.

They keep the British bulldog running round after his own tail till he is dizzy and then wonder that he cannot keep the wolf from the door.

1948, 14 FEBRUARY. (SUNDAY EXPRESS.)

Criticising the Government Churchill had said, "…our whole life is being handled the wrong way round. The planners have miscalculated and mismanaged everything they have touched."

"All men are created equal," says the American Declaration of Independence. "All men shall be kept equal," say the British Socialist Party.

1951, 15 OCTOBER, HUDDERSFIELD. (STEMMING, 150–51.)

Legislative cure-alls

Once an improper or unjust contract has received the sanction of law it becomes the basis on which all manner of perfectly healthy and unobjectionable agreements are founded. Bargain is added to bargain, plan is built on plan, and a whole economic structure rises, tier above tier, upon the faulty foundation.

1906, 22 FEBRUARY.

I do not believe in looking about for some panacea or cure-all on which we should stake our credit and fortunes trying to sell it like a patent medicine to all and sundry. It is easy to win applause by talking in an airy way about great new departures in policy, especially if all detailed proposals are avoided.

1946, 5 OCTOBER, BLACKPOOL. (SINEWS, 213.)

It is very much easier and quicker to cut down trees than to grow them. In cases where bad, oppressive laws warp the free development of human society, much cutting down may be needed, and sometimes the forest itself has to be cleared. Great work was done by the Liberal and Conservative Parties in the nineteenth century, but the twentieth century with its terrible events has brought us problems of a different order, not many of which can be solved merely by passing Acts of Parliament.

1952, 6 SEPTEMBER, WOODFORD, ESSEX.
(STEMMING, 333.)

Churchill was arguing for retaining the level of defence expenditures.

Liberal Party

In my judgment, a Liberal is a man who ought to stand as a restraining force against an extravagant policy. He is a man who ought to keep cool in the presence of Jingo clamour. He is a man who believes that confidence between nations begets confidence, and that the spirit of peace and good-will makes the safety it seeks. And, above all, I think a Liberal is a man who should keep a sour look for scaremongers of every kind and of every size, however distinguished, however ridiculous—and sometimes the most distinguished are the most ridiculous—a cold, chilling, sour look for all of them, whether their panic comes from the sea or from the air or from the earth or from the waters under the earth.

1909, 23 MAY. FREE TRADE HALL, MANCHESTER.
(LIBERALISM, 262.)

In this world of human error and constant variations, usually of an unexpected character, the Liberal Party can range themselves in party doctrine, few but impeccable. They have no need to recur for safety or vindication to that well-known maxim, or dictum, that "Consistency is the last resort of feeble and narrow minds."

1947, 31 MARCH.

The quote was a paraphrase of "Self-Reliance", Ralph Waldo Emerson's 1841 essay: "Consistency is the hobgoblin of small minds" (Keyes, 35).

Liberalism

Liberalism supplies at once the higher impulse and the practicable path; it appeals to persons by sentiments of generosity and humanity; it proceeds by courses of moderation. By gradual steps, by steady effort from day to day, from year to year, Liberalism enlists hundreds of thousands upon the side of progress and popular democratic reform whom militant Socialism would drive into violent Tory reaction. That is why the Tory Party hate us.

1906, 11 OCTOBER. ST. ANDREW'S HALL, GLASGOW.
(LIBERALISM, 162.)

See also Liberalism and related topics in Chapter 21, Political Theory and Practice.

Liberalism is a quickening spirit—it is immortal. It will live on through all the days, be they good days or be they evil days. No! I believe it will even burn stronger and brighter and more helpful in evil days than in good—just like your harbour-lights, which shine out across the sea, and which on a calm night gleam with soft refulgence, but through the storm flash a message of life to those who toil on the rough waters.

1908, 14 MAY. KINNAIRD HALL, DUNDEE.
(LIBERALISM, 199.)

The great triumphs and successes of Liberalism in the nineteenth century came from the fact that they were consistently, over several generations, advocating the striking off of shackles on enterprise, trade and the social life of the country.

1928, 7 JUNE.

Liberals and Conservatives

Between us and the orthodox Socialists there is a great doctrinal gulf, which yawns and gapes….There is no such gulf between the Conservative and National Governments I have formed and the Liberals. There is scarcely a Liberal sentiment which animated the great Liberal leaders of the past which we [Conservatives] do not inherit and defend.

1945, 4 JUNE. ELECTION BROADCAST, LONDON.
(VICTORY, 187.)

Media defeatism

The Press also should be a prompt and vigilant alarm bell, ringing when things are not going right. But it is a heavy burden added to the others we have to bear if, without a vote being cast, the idea should be spread at home and abroad that it is the opinion of the House of Commons that our affairs are being conducted in an incompetent and futile manner and that the whole gigantic drive of British industry is just one great muddle and flop.

1941, 29 July.

Media reporting

We sneer at the Press, but they give an extremely true picture of a great deal that is going on, a very much fuller and detailed picture than we are able to receive from Ministers of the Crown.

1939, 13 April.

Media twilight

If I might be allowed to revive a half-forgotten episode—it is half-forgotten because it has passed into that period of twilight which intervenes between the bright glare of newspaper controversy and the calm rays of the lamp of history....

1901, 13 May.

The episode WSC recalled was his father's resignation over expenditures in 1886.

Minimum Standard

We want to draw a line below which we will not allow persons to live and labour, yet above which they may compete with all the strength of their manhood. We want to have free competition upwards; we decline to allow free competition to run downwards.

1906, 11 October. St. Andrew's Hall, Glasgow. (Liberalism, 164.)

I look forward to the universal establishment of minimum standards of life and labour, and their progressive elevation as the increasing energies of production may permit. I do not think that Liberalism in any circumstances can cut itself off from this fertile field of social effort, and I would recommend you not to be scared in discussing any of these proposals, just because some old woman comes along and tells you they are Socialistic.

1906, 11 October, Glasgow. (Liberalism, 164; People's, 154.)

See Chapter 3, Churchillisms...Minimum Standard.

We have to face the growing discontent of the immense labouring population of this country with the social and economic conditions under which they dwell. We have somehow or other to create for them decent and fair conditions of living and of labour.

1912, 30 April.

Minimum wage

It is a serious national evil that any class of His Majesty's subjects should receive less than a living wage in return for their utmost exertions.

1909, 28 April.

Money

A Government can usually raise money and can always print it, but the labour and materials represented by the money come in a different category. Labour and the savings of the community are the key.

1945, 6 December.

National Debt

There are two ways in which a gigantic debt may be spread over new decades and future generations. There is the right and healthy way; and there is the wrong and morbid way. The wrong way is to fail to make the utmost provision for amortisation which prudence allows, to aggravate the burden of the debts by fresh borrowings, to live from hand to mouth and from year to year, and to exclaim with Louis XV: "After me, the deluge!"

1927, 11 April.

National unity

What does national unity mean? It surely means that reasonable sacrifices of Party opinions, personal opinion, and Party interest, should be made by all in order to contribute to the national security.

1939, 2 August.

In war we were united, now in peace we find ourselves torn apart by quarrels which bear no relation to our dangers, and, while we brawl along, our thought and action are distracted by a vast superficial process of reciprocal calumniation. We have to live our life from day to day and give back as good as we get, but I warn you that without an intense national realization of our position in all parties and by all classes, we shall find it very hard to reach that security without which all that we have achieved, all that we possess and all our glories may be cast away.

1952, 11 June. Press Association, Savoy, London. (Stemming, 300.)

Oil supply

The kind of oil we prefer is no longer the kind it suits refiners to make....The open market is becoming an open mockery.

1913, 17 July.

WSC was speaking on his conversion of the Royal Navy from coal to oil during the Naval Estimates debate. He went on to argue for establishing a reliable source of oil, even if it required "State enterprise".

Outsourcing

...I can quite understand that a man who works with his brain, however hard he works, cannot...understand how this alliance, this conjunction between cosmopolitan capital and the immense unmeasured reservoirs of Asiatic cheap labour, how this strange conjunction which the improving civilisation of the world has, I think for the first time, rendered possible...strikes the man who has nothing to sell but the sweat of his brow.

1906, 21 March.

The term "outsourcing" was of course unknown by WSC; but principles are timeless.

Parliamentary Privilege

I do not mind confessing to you that I sustained a very evil impression of the treatment I received and some day I hope to nail up this bad behaviour up upon a board, as stoats and weasels are nailed up by gamekeepers.

1934, 8 August. (OB, CV 5/2, 843.)

WSC to Cyril Asquith. Churchill refers to his Breach of Privilege allegations against Sir Samuel Hoare, who had altered the testimony of Lancashire cotton magnates in favour of the pending India Act, which Churchill opposed. Hoare was cleared by a Joint Select Committee which downplayed Churchill's evidence. He never succeeded in convincing his colleagues of Hoare's transgressions. Nor did Hoare ever forgive him for trying. WSC defines Parliamentary Privilege in Chapter 7.

Party credit

It is an error to believe that the world began when any particular party or statesman got into office. It has all been going on quite a long time....

1951, 9 November. Guildhall, London. (Stemming, 187.)

Pensions

Without a hitch, perfectly smoothly, punctual to the minute, regular as clockwork, nearly 600,000 aged persons are being paid their pensions every week. That is a wonderful and beneficent achievement, a good job well worth some risk and sweat to finish. Nearly eight millions of money are being sent circulating through unusual channels, long frozen by poverty, circulating in the homes of the poor, flowing through the little shops which cater for their needs, cementing again family unions which harsh fate was tearing asunder, uniting the wife to the husband, and the parent to the children.

1909, 30 January, Nottingham. (Liberalism, 232.)

There is no inconsistency or contradiction between a non-contributory system of Old Age Pensions and a contributory system of insurance against unemployment, sickness, invalidity, and widowhood. The circumstances and conditions are entirely different. The prospect of attaining extreme old age, of living beyond threescore years and ten, which is the allotted span of human life, seems so doubtful and remote to the ordinary man, when in the full strength of manhood, that it has been found in practice almost impossible to secure from any very great number of people the regular sacrifices which are necessary to guard against old age.

1909, 23 May. Free Trade Hall, Manchester. (Liberalism, 266.)

Everyone knows that he has a prospect of getting five shillings a week when he reaches that age. It is not much, unless you have not got it.

1911, 25 May.

I have always understood that the theory upon which a pension is granted is that it has been earned, and is to be regarded as deferred pay.

1913, 9 April.

Planning

Ah! Yes! I know: town planning—densities, broad vistas, open spaces. Give me the romance of the 18th-century alley, with its dark corners, where footpads lurk.

1942. (ROSE, 319.)

Norman Rose refers to this remark as "a curious dimension to Churchill's thinking, archaic yet attractive in its own way" (Rose, 319).

Politicians in military

I believe that the Army would be better entrusted to men who are not engaged in the most bitter strife of politics, nor should the War Office be regarded as a receptacle for Ministerial failures.

1948, 1 DECEMBER.

Poor of Britain

...to compare the life and lot of the African aboriginal—secure in his abyss of contented degradation, rich in that he lacks everything and wants nothing—with the long nightmare of worry and privation, of dirt and gloom and squalor, lit only by gleams of torturing knowledge and tantalizing hope which constitutes the lives of so many poor people in England and Scotland, is to feel the ground tremble underfoot.

1908. (MAJ, 41.)

I remember in Victorian days anxious talks about "the submerged tenth" (that part of our people who had not shared in the progress of the age) and then later on in the old Liberal period (the grand old Liberal period) we spoke of going back to bring the rearguard in. The main army we said had reached the camping-ground in all its strength and victory, and we should now, in duty and compassion, go back to pick up the stragglers and those who had fallen by the way and bring them in.

1950, 8 FEBRUARY, CARDIFF. (BALANCE, 188.)

Population

[I] had often felt how great was the responsibility devolving upon the rulers of this country when [I] had travelled through Lancashire, and had seen what a vast number of people were gathered together upon a soil so utterly inadequate to sustain them.

1903, 22 JUNE.

Price controls

...to begin to restrict consumption, which it may be necessary to do, merely through the agency of price, through the agency of unregulated, fortuitous rises of price, is the most cruel and the most unfair manner of dealing with a great national and economic problem. In time of war particularly you should have regard for the broad claims of social justice.

1916, 22 AUGUST.

Promises, political

Nothing would be more dangerous than for people to feel cheated because they had been led to expect attractive schemes which turn out to be economically impossible.

1942, 17 DECEMBER. (WW2 IV, 812.)

WSC to Foreign Secretary, Paymaster-General and President of the Board of Trade.

Prosperity

I do not underrate what lies before us, but I must say this: I cannot doubt we have the strength to carry a good cause forward, and to break down the barriers which stand between the wage-earning masses of every land and that free and more abundant daily life which science is ready to afford.

1939, 1 OCTOBER.

A rare reflection on the domestic agenda as war was breaking out in Europe.

In this period of "hell for all except the profiteers" the expectation of life for all babies who had the courage to be born rose by nine years. That was an important fact to be borne in mind not only by the parents but by the baby. When these survivors of five years of hell went to the elementary schools in London it was found that they had gained an average of two inches in height and five pounds in weight compared with the standards before the First World War. How very surprising! The warm climate must have suited them. There was also a steady improvement in the food of the people, and a marked increase in the consumption of milk, cheese, butter and eggs, and of fruit and vegetables. But I do not wish to make your mouths water.

1949, 8 FEBRUARY, CARDIFF, WALES. (BALANCE, 184.)

WSC was referring the pre-war Conservative administration, and alluding to the continued rationing of food by the post-war Labour Government.

Protestors

We will not submit to the bullying tyranny of the featherheads. We will not submit to the roar of the mob, the supporters of the Socialist candidate, who, if they had their way, would reduce this great country to the same bear-garden that they have reduced this meeting to.

1922, 13 NOVEMBER. DRILL HALL, DUNDEE. (CS IV, 3379.)

One of Churchill's last speeches in his vain attempt to hold his Dundee constituency.

There was a custom in ancient China that anyone who wished to criticize the Government had the right to memorialize the Emperor, and, provided he followed that up by committing suicide, very great respect was paid to his words, and no ulterior motive was assigned. That seems to me to have been, from many points of view, a wise custom, but I certainly would be the last to suggest that it should be made retrospective.

1941, 12 NOVEMBER.

Radicals

Radicals, who are never satisfied with Liberals, always liberal with other people's money [laughter], ask why [the Employers Liability Bill] is not applied to all. That is like a Radical—just the slap-dash, wholesale, harum-scarum policy of the Radical. It reminds me of the man who, on being told that ventilation is an excellent thing, went and smashed every window in his house, and died of rheumatic fever.

1897, 26 JULY. CLAVERTON MANOR, BATH. (CS I, 26.)

From WSC's maiden political speech.

Rationing

When the Socialist Government, in their clumsy arrogance, imposed upon us wartime controls for five more long years, they had not got a majority of the electorate behind them....The Socialists have no majority in the

nation; even with all the adventitious aid they got at the last election, they are a minority. They have a right to govern and administer the country but they have no right to ride rough-shod over the majority of their fellow countrymen.

1945, 28 NOVEMBER. FRIENDS HOUSE, LONDON. (SINEWS, 54.)

The editor had to look up "adventitious", which appears nine times in Churchill's canon: "happening or occurring according to chance, rather than by design or inherent nature".

The German U-boats in their worst endeavour never made bread rationing necessary in war. It took a Socialist Government and Socialist planners to fasten it on us in time of peace when the seas are open and the world harvests good. At no time in the two world wars have our people had so little bread, meat, butter, cheese and fruit to eat.

1946, 5 OCTOBER. CONSERVATIVE PARTY CONFERENCE, BLACKPOOL. (SINEWS, 206.)

In war time, rationing is the alternative to famine. In peace it may well become the alternative to abundance.

1950, 9 FEBRUARY, DEVONPORT. (BALANCE, 194.)

Right to work

There is not much use in proclaiming a right apart from its enforcement; and when it is enforced there is no need to proclaim it.

1908, 10 OCTOBER. KINNAIRD HALL, DUNDEE. (LIBERALISM, 215.)

Royal succession

Agree that the Duke of Edinburgh should be the guardian....Regency is another matter. How will Parliament and country regard it, especially if we can't say Princess Margaret doesn't want it. Both Queen and Duke of Edinburgh may die together and then Princess Margaret would have to be regent.

1953, 27 MAY. (DIARIES OF CABINET SECRETARY SIR NORMAN BROOK, SUNDAY TELEGRAPH, 5 AUGUST 2007.)

WSC in Cabinet when the Queen asked him to amend the 1937 Regency Act in favour of her husband. WSC and some Cabinet members questioned the suitability of both the Duke and Princess Margaret, who was romantically linked with the divorced Group Captain Peter Townsend.

Social security

No one is able to forecast the exact moment of his death. That is a mystery which is hidden from all of us. Still, as the years pass by, and as each of us, in our turn, pass the summit of the way and descend slowly and gradually or rapidly as the case may be, the actuarial position of each taxpayer is definitely and effectively altered.

1926, 21 June.

Socialists

How many political flibbertigibbets are there not running up and down the land calling themselves the people of Great Britain, and the social democracy, and the masses of the nation!

1906, 11 October. St. Andrew's Hall, Glasgow.
(Liberalism, 160.)

For quotations on Socialism in general see Chapter 21, Political Theory and Practice.

Speaker, congratulations to

I rise to commit an irregularity, and I will venture to ask the indulgence of the House. The intervention which I make is without precedent, and the reason for that intervention is also without precedent, and the fact that the reason for my intervention is without precedent is the reason why I must ask for a precedent for my intervention.

1941, 19 November.

WSC congratulating the Speaker, the Hon. Edward Fitzroy, on his golden wedding anniversary. WSC said he had searched without success for any Speaker so celebrating back to "Mr. Speaker Rous in 1653, before which time the occupants of the Chair held their tenure for shorter and more precarious periods".

State expansion

The whole tendency of civilisation is, however, towards the multiplication of the collective functions of society. The ever-growing complications of civilisation create for us new services which have to be undertaken by the State, and create for us an expansion of the existing services.

1906, 11 October. St. Andrew's Hall, Glasgow.
(Liberalism, 163.)

The average British workman in good health, in full employment at standard rates of wages, does not regard himself and his family as objects for compassion.

1925, 28 April.

Nothing is so expensive as general elections and new Governments. Every new administration, not excluding ourselves, arrives in power with bright and benevolent ideas of using public money to do good. The more frequent the changes of Government, the more numerous are the bright ideas; and the more frequent the elections, the more benevolent they become.

1927, 11 April.

Sugar Convention Bill

The union between sugar and fruit is natural, pleasant, profitable, and prolific.

1903, 29 July.

Sweated labour

We have seen from the investigations of the last twenty years, that there is no power of self-cure within the area of the evil.

1909, 28 April. (Liberalism, 235.)

Tax, beer

Again, the failure of beer was repaired by the harvest of death.

1929, 15 April. (CS V, 4575.)

Referring to beer taxes and death duties in his final budget speech as Chancellor of the Exchequer.

Tax, betting

Does anyone suppose that a man or woman who now bets with a credit bookmaker, who has only to go to the telephone and make his wager by word of mouth under the full sanction of the law...is going, for the sake of avoiding...a deduction from his winnings of one shilling in the pound...to wander round a particular district in some manufacturing town looking for a mysterious individual into whose hand he may surreptitiously place half a dollar?

1926, 28 April.

Opponents of a betting tax argued that bookmakers and backers had only to transact their business in the street in order to evade the tax. They were proven right, and WSC wrong.

It may be there has been a certain check to betting. If so, my sorrows on the Exchequer account are to some extent assuaged by my satisfaction as a moral reformer.

1927, 5 JULY.

Tax, death

There is no real gain to British democracy when some family leaves a home of its ancestors and hands it over to a transatlantic millionaire or wartime profiteer.

1930, 15 APRIL.

Tax, income

Exemption from income tax is in effect a subsidy.

1926, 21 JUNE.

The foundation of the British Income Tax is deduction at a standard rate at the source from every form of income capable of being so treated.

1927, 11 APRIL.

The long battle that I have waged over this 6d. off the Income Tax is over. For four years I successfully defended that remission. I defended it against the assaults of the General Strike—I beg pardon, the assaults of the difficult events of 1926. But at last I am beaten. [Mr. Snowden, Labour Chancellor of the Exchequer] and his party have had their way....The popularity of the measure is assured by reducing the number of taxpayers involved to limits where the voting powers of those who are left may be considered negligible.

1930, 15 APRIL.

The extension of the Income Tax to the wage-earners was a very remarkable step. That it should have gained the assent of this House, elected on universal suffrage, is also a remarkable fact, showing how extremely closely the wage-earning masses of the country and those who represent them feel associated with the vital issues now being fought out in the field.

1943, 22 SEPTEMBER.

[Lord Randolph's ghost on the Boer War: "What a shocking drain on the Exchequer!"] "It was," I said. "The Income Tax went up to one and threepence." He was visibly disturbed. So I said that they got it down to eightpence afterwards.

1947. ("THE DREAM," OB VIII, 369.)

WSC meant one and threepence or eightpence on the pound, the rate in the early 1900s.

Tax, kerosene

Perhaps the House may remember that only seven or eight years ago I got into some trouble myself about the Kerosene Tax. It was a very good tax. I was quite right about it. My Rt. Hon. Friend [Neville Chamberlain] slipped it through a year or two later without the slightest trouble and it never ruined the homes of the people at all.

1937, 1 JUNE.

Some sources erroneously quote Churchill as saying, "There is no such thing as a good tax." Searches of the canon reveal no such statement; but here at least was proof that he considered at least one tax a good one.

I acted with great promptitude. In the nick of time, just as Mr. Snowden was rising with overwhelming fury, I got up and withdrew [the tax on kerosene.] Was I humiliated? Was I accused of running away? No! Everyone said, "How clever! How quick! How right!" Pardon me referring to it. It was one of my best days.

1937, 1 JUNE. (TAYLOR, 222.)

See also Chapter 20...Snowden.

Tax, luxury

I do not grudge anybody any reason which may lead them to vote for the reimposition of these duties. To some they are a relish, to others a target, and to me a revenue.

1925, 28 APRIL.

Reference was to the McKenna Duties, imposed by Chancellor of the Exchequer Reginald McKenna in 1915, and repealed by Labour Chancellor Snowden in 1924. Now Chancellor himself, WSC declared these duties would bring in up to £3 million a year: "We can't afford to throw away a revenue like that." Free-trader Churchill did not mention the main intent of the duties, which was a measure of protection for British industries.

Tax, spirits

[Taxes on] spirits…hold their own somewhat better under bleak conditions, but they must be expected in normal weather to resume their continuous descent.

1928, 24 APRIL.

Tax, targeted

I am not basing myself on individual promises, but on the work of inexorable laws.

1928, 5 JUNE.

Members had suggested that the Government should pick and choose among industries, exempting the unprosperous from taxes while taxing the prosperous. Churchill said, "It is utterly impossible to do any such thing…relief in the cost of production in a prosperous trade like this will infallibly make its way to the consumer" through the free market.

Taxation

…taxes are an evil—a necessary evil, but still an evil, and the fewer we have of them the better.

1907, 12 FEBRUARY.

Churchill was referring to Protection vs. Free Trade, concluding, "…every arrangement between protectionist States which takes the form of a reduction in the tariff barriers of the world is a distinct advantage."

Tory democracy

…the British workman has more to hope for from the rising tide of Tory democracy than from the dried up drain-pipe of Radicalism.

1897, 26 JULY. CLAVERTON MANOR, BATH.
(CS I, 27.)

Maiden political speech. "Tory democracy" was coined by Lord Randolph Churchill to symbolise bringing more working people into alignment with the Conservative Party.

Tory prosperity

Here is the plain vulgar fact. In the first two years of Tory Government the British nation has actually eaten 400,000 tons more meat, including red meat, than they did in the last two years of Socialist administration. That at any rate is something solid to set off against

the tales we are told of the increasing misery of the people—and the shortage of television sets.

1953, 10 OCTOBER. PARTY CONFERENCE, MARGATE.
(ALLIANCE, 61.)

Trade regulations

I was brought up to believe that trade should be regulated mainly by the laws of supply and demand and that, apart from basic necessaries in great emergencies, the price mechanism should adjust and correct undue spending at home, as it does…control spending abroad.

1949, 27 OCTOBER.

Trade unions

They are the most highly organised part of Labour; they are the most responsible part; they are from day to day in contact with reality. They are not mere visionaries or dreamers weaving airy Utopias out of tobacco smoke. They are not political adventurers who are eager to remodel the world by rule-of-thumb, who are proposing to make the infinite complexities of scientific civilisation and the multitudinous phenomena of great cities conform to a few barbarous formulas which any moderately intelligent parrot could repeat in a fortnight.

1906, 11 OCTOBER. ST. ANDREW'S HALL, GLASGOW.
(LIBERALISM, 160.)

It is quite true that the Socialistic element has imposed a complexion on Labour, rather against its will, and is now supported in its action by funds almost entirely supplied by Trade Unions. But Trade Unions are not Socialistic. They are undoubtedly individualist organisations, more in the character of the old Guilds, and lean much more in the direction of the culture of the individual than in that of the smooth and bloodless uniformity of the mass.

1908, 14 MAY. KINNAIRD HALL, DUNDEE.
(LIBERALISM, 197.)

Although it may be very difficult to define in law what is or what is not a trade union, most people of common sense know a trade union when they see one. It is like trying to define a rhinoceros: it is difficult enough, but if one is seen, everybody can recognize it.

1911, 25 MAY. (CZARNOMSKI, 369.)

...everyone knows, and I have been taught it all my public life, that the employers of this country are deeply thankful there is in existence a strong organised trade union movement with which they can deal, and which keeps its bargains and which moves along a controlled and suitable path of policy.

1941, 27 MARCH. LUNCHEON, LONDON.
(UNRELENTING, 71.)

At the present time they have more influence upon the Government of the country, and less control over their own members, than ever before. But we take our stand by these pillars of our British society...

1947, 4 OCTOBER. PARTY CONFERENCE, BRIGHTON.
(EUROPE, 153.)

I have always been a firm supporter of British Trade Unionism. I believe it be to the only foundation upon which the relations of employers and employed can be harmoniously adjusted. I have always advised Conservatives and Liberals to join the Trade Unions. I tried to join the Bricklayers' Trade Union and it is a complicated legal point whether I have in fact succeeded in doing so.

1948, 10 JULY, WOODFORD, ESSEX. (EUROPE, 371.)

Churchill applied for and joined the Bricklayer's Union in the 1920s, but his unpopularity over the General Strike caused his membership to be revoked.

Trade unions in politics

...I should have no hesitation in saying that it is quite impossible to prevent trade unions from entering the political field. The sphere of industrial and political activity is often indistinguishable, always overlaps, and representation in Parliament is absolutely necessary to trade unions, even if they confine themselves to the most purely industrial forms of action....

1911, 30 MAY.

Unemployment

I think it is our duty to use the strength and the resources of the State to arrest the ghastly waste, not merely of human happiness but of national health and strength, which follows when a working man's home, which has taken him years to get together, is broken up and

scattered through a long spell of unemployment, or when, through the death, the sickness, or the invalidity of the bread-winner, the frail boat in which the fortunes of the family are embarked founders, and the women and children are left to struggle helplessly on the dark waters of a friendless world.

1909, 23 MAY. FREE TRADE HALL, MANCHESTER.
(LIBERALISM, 268.)

I never heard any argument more strange and ill founded than that the return to the Gold Standard is responsible for the condition of affairs in the coal industry. The Gold Standard is no more responsible for the condition of affairs in the coal industry than is the Gulf Stream.

1925, 25 JULY. WEST ESSEX CONSERVATIVE AND
UNIONIST ASSOCIATION. (CS IV, 3734.)

Churchill was responding to Lloyd George, who had blamed conditions in the coal mining industry on the return to Gold, which in fact did influence unemployment, through lack of adjustments in wages and taxes (see Gold Standard above). This remark is remindful of WSC's 1931 declaration that India was no more a nation than the Equator (see Chapter 11, Nations of the World...India).

...the best way to insure against unemployment is to have no unemployment.

1943, 21 MARCH. BROADCAST, LONDON.
(ONWARDS, 39.)

All Parties are agreed that the prevention of unemployment ranks next to food in the duties of any government.

1950, 21 JANUARY. BROADCAST, LONDON.
(BALANCE, 159.)

Wage restraint

In asking for wage restraint, I want to emphasize that we do not in any way wish to limit the earnings of any section of the working population...It is our aim to encourage the highest possible level of earning in every industry, provided these swim upon increased output and efficiency.

1952, 6 SEPTEMBER, WOODFORD, ESSEX.
(STEMMING, 332.)

Wages vs. profits

There is no greater delusion than that low wages mean high profits. No labour is so dear as cheap labour, and the labour which costs nothing is the dearest of all.

1906, 22 FEBRUARY.

Welfare State

But that is not the only spirit which has been awakened in our country; there are others not less powerful, and a greater number, who will never allow that door to be closed; they have got their foot in it, they are resolved that it shall be kept open. Nay, more, they are prepared to descend into the abyss, and grapple with its evils—as sometimes you see after an explosion at a coal mine a rescue party advancing undaunted into the smoke and steam.

1908, 9 OCTOBER.

Witchcraft

Let me have a report on why the Witchcraft Act, 1735, was used in a modern court of justice. What was the cost of this trial to the State?—observing that witnesses were brought from Portsmouth and maintained here in this crowded London for a fortnight, and the Recorder kept busy with all this obsolete tomfoolery, to the detriment of necessary work in the courts.

1944, 3 APRIL. (WW2 V, 618.)

WSC to Home Secretary; vast was the scope of his curiosity.

Women in war

We take the immunity of women from violence so much for granted that we do not perceive what inroads are being made upon it. These inroads come from opposite quarters. The first is the feminist movement, which claims equal rights for women, and in its course prides itself in stripping them of their privileges. Secondly, the mud-rush of barbarism which is breaking out in so many parts of the world owns no principle but that of lethal force. Thus we see both progressive and reactionary forces luring women nearer to danger, and exposing them to the retaliation of the enemy...

The part which our women played in winning the War was enshrined in the grant to them of the vote which for so many years they had vainly sought to wrest from successive Governments by methods too often suggesting that they had not the civic sense to use the privilege rightly. It was the War which solved that problem, as it solved so many others in our internal affairs...

On the other hand, even in the last war there were many things that women could do apart from killing which added to the fighting power of the army. There were innumerable duties of all kinds behind the front which brought them ever nearer to the line and into danger. We must expect that this will continue to develop in a war of the future.

1938, FEBRUARY. ("WOMEN IN WAR," *STRAND MAGAZINE*; ESSAYS I, 380–86.)

It may seem strange that a great advance in the position of women in the world in industry, in controls of all kinds, should be made in time of war and not in time of peace. One would have thought that in the days of peace the progress of women to an ever larger share in the life and work and guidance of the community would have grown, and that, under the violences of war, it would be cast back. The reverse is true. War is the teacher, a hard, stern, efficient teacher. War has taught us to make these vast strides forward towards a far more complete equalisation of the parts to be played by men and women in society.

1943, 29 SEPTEMBER. ROYAL ALBERT HALL, LONDON. (ONWARDS, 224.)

Women's status

[The future role of women should be] the same, I trust, since it has been since the days of Adam and Eve.

1952, 17 JANUARY. PRESS CONFERENCE, WASHINGTON. (FISHMAN, 394.)

An uncharacteristic aside, in that Churchill had written cogently about the changing role of women from the 1930s, and had changed his views in favour of female suffrage in the 1920s, as his daughter Mary remarked, "...when he realised how many women would vote for him."

When I think what women did in the war I feel sure they deserve to be treated equally.

1958. (COLVILLE, CHURCHILLIANS, 123.)

John Colville recalled the "astonishment" when Churchill said he hoped that Churchill

College, founded as a national memorial to him, would admit women on equal terms with men. "No college at Oxford or Cambridge had ever done any such thing," Colville wrote. "I asked him afterwards if this had been Clementine's idea. 'Yes,' he replied, 'and I support it'" (Colville, Churchillians, 123).

Women's suffrage

We are getting into very g[rea]t peril over Female Suffrage. Be quite sure of this—the Franchise Bill will not get through without a dissolution [of Parliament] if it contains a clause adding 8,000,000 women to the electorate. Nor ought it to get through...Votes for women is so unpopular that by-elections will be unfavourable....

What a ridiculous tragedy it will be if this strong Government and party which has made its mark in history were to go down on Petticoat politics!....

The only safe and honest cure is to have a referendum—first to the women to know if they want it; and then to the men to know if they will give it. I am quite willing to abide by the result.

1911, 18 DECEMBER, ADMIRALTY.
(OB, CV2/3, 1473.)

WSC to the Master of Elibank.

23

POLITICS:
THE WORLD
SCENE

"If men ever create a world where peace and human
dignity prevail, they will have created the only monument
worthy of him."

– *Bernard Baruch* [74]

"We must all turn our backs upon the horrors of the past."
University of Zürich, 19 September 1946.

This chapter presents Churchill's general observations on international politics. More
specific entries will be found in Part 2, or the war chapters in Part 3. Readers interested in Churchill's thoughts on specific nations and leaders should consult Chapters
8–11 and 20. General remarks on "summit meetings" are here, but specific summits are
covered by Chapters 18–19, on World War II and the Nuclear Age.

There are many quotations on the League of Nations, mainly because the League and

---

74 *New York Times*, 25 January 1965.

its actions – or lack of actions – greatly exercised Churchill between the two World Wars. His initial hopes for a League that would act together to prevent conflict were quickly doused, and he saw the calls for disarmament, issued in the 1930s by the League or its partisans, as the sheerest folly (see Chapter 17). He turned instead to Collective Security (q.v. below), which found its culmination in the "Grand Alliance" of World War II.

Churchill's experiences with the League made him more cautious than Roosevelt about its successor, the United Nations, though he realised the UN's prospects were better with American involvement. But he thought rather that more could be accomplished by what he described as "meetings at the summit" between government leaders with plenary powers.

Although he became ardent about summit conferences after he himself had taken part in them during World War II, he was talking of "three or four Great Powers shaking hands together" as early as March 1933,[75] two months after Hitler had come to power. Earlier, he had hoped to stave off World War I by a "naval holiday" in battleship construction, which he recommended in 1911.[76]

Modern readers may be drawn to what he had to say about the Middle East and Terrorism. On the former, he sadly concluded that "power politics" might prove the only method of defending one's interests in that area; he observed so many examples of ungovernability that he concluded that "Force, or perhaps force and bribery, are the only things that will be respected."[77]

Churchill's views on terrorism are little quoted, probably because it was not the problem in his time that it later became; but his views are not without relevance. A 1935 remark on the Government of India Act, warning of the danger if terrorists were elected to the Bengal Assembly, puts us in mind of the election of a Hamas government in Palestine in 2006.[78]

No countries are less prepared to deal with terrorism than Western democracies, he said in 1947. He warned that "squalid warfare with terrorists" should be avoided: "and if a warfare with terrorists has broken out, every effort should be made – I exclude no reasonable proposal – to bring it to an end".[79] Above all he emphasised that national politics must stop at the water's edge (see Foreign policy unity). If it does not, he believed, all hopes are lost, all plans squandered: wise words that alas would go mainly unheeded in later times.

Sir Martin Gilbert is frequently quoted for admiring "the truth of Churchill's assertions, the modernity of his thought…and most remarkable of all, his foresight". I admit to being struck by those qualities as I assembled this chapter. At Teheran, Churchill told Stalin that the three Allies were "the trustees for the peace of the world", and if they failed "there would be, perhaps, a hundred years of chaos".[80] The cynical would say that when this book was first published we were entering the sixty-fifth year.

---

75 House of Commons, 23 March 1933. Covenant, 70.
76 See Chapter 3, Churchillisms…Naval holiday.
77 Montague Browne, 167.
78 House of Commons, 12 March 1935. CS V, 5537.
79 House of Commons, 31 January 1947. Europe, 2.
80 OB VII, 575–6.

Aggression

When the designs of wicked men or the aggressive urge of mighty states dissolve over large areas the frame of civilised society, humble folk are confronted with difficulties with which they cannot cope. For them all is distorted, all is broken, even ground to pulp.

1946, 5 MARCH. WESTMINSTER COLLEGE, FULTON, MISSOURI. (SINEWS, 95.)

Balance of power

There is something to be said for isolation; there is something to be said for alliances. But there is nothing to be said for weakening the Power on the Continent with whom you would be in alliance, and then involving yourself further in Continental tangles in order to make it up to them. In that way you have neither one thing nor the other; you have the worst of both worlds.

1934, 14 MARCH.

WSC was continually conscious of Britain's historic role of balancing power in Europe through alliances with the weaker side.

Boundary settlements

...it is vain and idle for any one country to try to lay down the law...or to trace frontiers or describe the intricate instruments by which these frontiers will be maintained without further bloodshed;...The man who sold the hyena's skin while the beast lived was killed in hunting it....

1944, 2 AUGUST.

Collective security

The whole history of the world is summed up in the fact that when nations are strong they are not always just, and when they wish to be just they are often no longer strong. I desire to see the collective forces of the world invested with overwhelming power. If you are going to run this thing on a narrow margin...one way or the other, you are going to have war. But if you get five or ten to one on one side, all bound rigorously by the Covenant and the conventions which they own, then, in my opinion, you have an opportunity of making a settlement which will heal the wounds of the world. Let us have this blessed union of power and justice: "Agree with thine adversary quickly, while thou art in the way with him." Let us free the world from the approach of a

catastrophe carrying with it calamity and tribulation, beyond the tongue of man to tell.

1936, 26 MARCH.

The Biblical quotation is from Matthew V:25.

I hold that the doctrine of collective security must mean that no one is in until enough are in. It seems to me good sense. If other powers and small powers are not going to do their part, they must take their fate. Some of the small countries have vast colonial possessions, empires almost. If there is to be a stampede among them to join the martial dictators, the Western democracies can do nothing to save them, still less to save their possessions.

1936, 5 NOVEMBER.

What is there ridiculous about collective security? The only thing that is ridiculous about it is that we have not got it. Let us see whether we cannot do something to procure a strong element of collective security for ourselves and for others.

1938, 14 MARCH.

President Roosevelt one day asked what this War [World War II] should be called. My answer was, "The Unnecessary War." If the United States had taken an active part in the League of Nations, and if the League of Nations had been prepared to use concerted force, even had it only been European force, to prevent the rearmament of Germany, there was no need for further serious bloodshed. If the Allies had resisted Hitler strongly in his early stages, even up to his seizure of the Rhineland in 1936, he would have been forced to recoil, and a chance would have been given to the sane elements in German life, which were very powerful, especially in the High Command, to free Germany of the maniacal government and system into the grip of which she was falling.

1945, 16 NOVEMBER, BRUSSELS. (SINEWS, 41.)

For us [the free nations] to become divided among ourselves because of divergences of opinion or local interests, or to slacken our combined efforts would be to end forever such new hope as may have broke upon mankind and lead instead to their general ruin and enslavement. Unity, vigilance and fidelity are the only foundations upon which hope can live.

1953, 11 MAY.

Communist conspiracies

It is very easy for foreign observers in a position of perfect detachment to abuse a Government which is struggling against a Communist conspiracy, fomented and supported by outside intrigues. An armed Communist advances upon you, you react against him; therefore you are a reactionary.

1946, 23 OCTOBER.

Communist expansion

The great objective of the Prime Minister's [Mr. Lloyd George's] policy has been Moscow, to make Great Britain the nation in the closest possible relations with the Bolsheviks, and to be their protectors and sponsors before Europe. I have been unable to discern any British interest, however slight, in this....

1922, 26 APRIL. (CRISIS IV, 415.)

WSC to Foreign Secretary Lord Curzon.

Communist negotiations

Trying to maintain good relations with a Communist is like wooing a crocodile. You do not know whether to tickle it under the chin or to beat it over the head. When it opens its mouth you cannot tell whether it is trying to smile or preparing to eat you up.

1944, 24 JANUARY. (BRYANT, TRIUMPH, 114.)

Condominiums, colonial

We should be opposed to the idea of condominiums, which have always been found to bring about very bad results to the regions affected, but we naturally shall be in the closest touch and intercourse with our great Allies, whose interests are closely connected with our own in some parts of the world.

1943, 17 MARCH.

Churchill had declared that British Colonies would continue to be the sole responsibility of Great Britain. He was then asked if he still adhered to the principles of the Atlantic Charter.

Council of Europe

I will not prejudge the word of the committee, but I hope they will remember Napoleon's saying: "A constitution must be short and obscure." Until that committee reports, I think we should be well advised to reserve our judgment....To take a homely and familiar test, we may just as well see what the girl looks like before we marry her.

1949, 17 AUGUST.

The Council of Europe, founded by the Treaty of London in 1949, is the oldest organisation working for European integration, but separate from the European Union, whose flag it shares.

Credit of nations

There can be no other test of the credit of a country than the price at which it can borrow.

1908, 2 JUNE.

There is among us...a small but highly intellectual school of thought which reaches its fullest expression in Russia, but also flourishes among some of our smaller neighbours, and which proclaims openly that it is much better for a nation to go through the bankruptcy court and start business again...and either to repudiate its debts and start again or pay as much in the pound as it finds convenient by writing its currency down to the necessary figure.

1929, 15 APRIL.

Danubian confederation

Bavaria, Austria and Hungary might form a broad, peaceful, cow-like confederation.... Prussia should be dealt with more severely than the other parts of the Reich, so that the latter would not want to go in with Prussia.

1943, 29 NOVEMBER, TEHERAN. (OB VII, 575.)

Conversation at the first Big Three meeting. Stalin replied that this was "very good but insufficient", to which Churchill responded that the three Allies were "the trustees for the peace of the world", and if they failed "there would be, perhaps, a hundred years of chaos".

Declaration of rights

...it is vain to imagine that the mere perception or declaration of right principles, whether in one country or for many countries, will be of any value unless they are supported by those qualities of civic virtue and manly courage—aye, and by those instruments and agencies of force and science which in the last resort must be the defence of right and reason.

1938, 2 JULY. UNIVERSITY OF BRISTOL. (BLOOD, 54.)

Dictatorships

It is this very conflict of spiritual and moral ideas which gives the free countries a great part of their strength. You see these dictators on their pedestals, surrounded by the bayonets of their soldiers and the truncheons of their police....they boast and vaunt themselves before the world, yet in their hearts there is unspoken fear. They are afraid of words and thoughts; words spoken abroad, thoughts stirring at home—all the more powerful because forbidden—terrify them.

1938, 16 OCTOBER. BROADCAST, LONDON.
(BLOOD, 88–9.)

Diplomacy

While one party in a dispute is prepared to go to extremes—and it is firmly believed that under no circumstances will the other party even take the necessary action to defend its right and to discharge its duties—there is no possibility of any effective parley between them.

1914, 28 APRIL.

We must not allow our insular pride to blind us to the fact that some of these foreigners are quite intelligent, that they have an extraordinary knack on occasion of rising fully up to the level of British comprehension.

1933, 14 MARCH.

Referring to disarmament talks occurring at Geneva.

It is always an error in diplomacy to press a matter when it is quite clear that no further progress is to be made. It is also a great error if you ever give the impression abroad that you are using language which is more concerned with your domestic politics than with the actual fortunes and merits of the various great countries upon the Continent to whom you offer advice.

1934, 14 MARCH.

It is hard enough to understand the politics of one's own country; it is almost impossible to understand those of foreign countries.

1944, 22 FEBRUARY.

It is even harder to understand the politics of other countries than those of your own.

1944, 11 OCTOBER. BRITISH EMBASSY, MOSCOW.
(WW2 VI, 200.)

Same expression as above, in different words. Stalin, dining with WSC, had assured

Churchill that the Conservatives would win the next British election.

I have, therefore, not hesitated to travel from court to court like a wandering minstrel, always with the same songs to sing—or the same set of songs.

1944, 27 OCTOBER. (DAWN, 220.)

WSC's love of music hall songs suggests that his "wandering minstrel" was from George M. Cohan's musical comedy The Merry Malones *(1927).*

While we feel acutely our position, we must not lose the faculty of understanding that of other people.

1945, 13 DECEMBER.

Patience and perseverance must never be grudged when the peace of the world is at stake.

1954, 25 FEBRUARY.

Diplomatic precedence

[I insist] that I be host at dinner tomorrow evening. I think I have one or two claims to precedence. To begin with, I came first in seniority and alphabetically. In the second place, I represent the longest established of the three governments. And, in the third place, tomorrow happens to be my birthday.

1943, 29 NOVEMBER. TEHERAN.
(SHERWOOD II, 779.)

WSC to W. Averell Harriman, US Ambassador to Russia, 1943–46. WSC was perhaps too diplomatic to add that Britain had been fighting Germany longer than the others, while Russia had been allied to Hitler and the USA officially neutral.

English-speaking alliance

I care as little as any man in this House for the cant of Empire which plays so large a part in the jargon of modern political discussion, but I should like to see the great English-speaking nations work together in majesty, in freedom, and in peace. The road is open.

1911, 15 FEBRUARY.

With virtually the same words, Churchill ended his first speech to a joint session of the United States Congress, thirty years later.

When one beholds how many currents of extraordinary and terrible events have flowed together to make this harmony, even the most sceptical person must have the feeling that we all have the chance to play our part and do our duty in some great design, the end of which no mortal can foresee.

1941, 24 AUGUST. BROADCAST, LONDON.
(UNRELENTING, 233.)

Here in Britain, and I doubt not throughout the British Empire and Commonwealth... we always follow a very simple rule, which has helped us in maintaining the safety of this country: "the worse things get, the more we stand together". Let it also be seen that the English-speaking world follows the same plan.

1950, 30 NOVEMBER.

Europe, Eastern

At the present time—I trust a very fleeting time—"police governments" rule over a great number of countries....The family is gathered round the fireside to enjoy the scanty fruits of their toil and to recruit their exhausted strength by the little food that they have been able to gather. There they sit. Suddenly there is a knock at the door, and a heavily armed policeman appears. He is not, of course, one who resembles in any way those functionaries whom we honour and obey in the London streets. It may be that the father or son, or a friend sitting in the cottage, is called out and taken off into the dark, and no one knows whether he will ever come back again, or what his fate has been. All they know is that they had better not inquire. There are millions of humble homes in Europe at the moment, in Poland, in Czechoslovakia, in Austria, in Hungary, in Yugoslavia, in Rumania, in Bulgaria—where this fear is the main preoccupation of the family life.

1945, 16 AUGUST.

We see before our eyes hundreds of millions of humble homes in Europe and in lands outside which have been affected by war. Are they never to have a chance to thrive and flourish? Is the honest, faithful, breadwinner never to be able to reap the fruits of his labour? Can he never bring up his children in health and joy and with the hopes of better days?

1947, 14 MAY. UNITED EUROPE MEETING, ROYAL ALBERT HALL. (EUROPE, 84.)

Let there be sunshine on both sides of the Iron Curtain; and if ever the sunshine should be equal on both sides, the Curtain will be no more.

1947, 4 AUGUST, BLENHEIM PALACE. (EUROPE, 118.)

For origins of the famous expression see Writer and Speaker...Iron Curtain.

Ten ancient capitals of Europe are behind the Iron Curtain. A large part of this continent is held in bondage. They have escaped from Nazism only to fall into the other extreme of Communism. It is like making a long and agonizing journey to leave the North Pole only to find out that, as a result, you have woken up in the South Pole. All around are only ice and snow and bitter piercing winds.

1949, 17 AUGUST, STRASBOURG. (BALANCE, 81.)

You remember Fulton. I got into great trouble being a bit in front of the weather that time. But it's all come out since—I won't say right, but it's all come out.

1953. PRESS CONFERENCE, NEW YORK.

Anthony Montague Browne to the editor. For the speech referred to see Chapter 1...Iron Curtain.

Europe, post-war

I do not think it would be wise at this moment, while the battle rages and the war is still perhaps only in its earlier stage, to embark upon elaborate speculations about the future shape which should be given to Europe or the new securities which must be arranged to spare mankind the miseries of a third World War. The ground is not new, it has been frequently traversed and explored, and many ideas are held about it in common by all good men, and all free men.

1940, 20 AUGUST.

Europe, Third Force

I wholeheartedly agree [with] the declaration against Europe becoming a Third Force between America and Russia and creating a "neutral geographical bloc"....I should myself regard the neutralisation of Germany...still more of France and the rest of the six [Western European] Powers...as a disaster second only to actual war. It would simply mean that not only Western Germany but the European States in the neutral zone would be undermined and overcome one by one and bit by bit—exactly as we have seen Czechoslovakia devoured before our eyes.

1950, 27 JUNE.

Europe and Britain

We in these islands, with our heavy burdens and with our wide Imperial responsibilities, ought to be very careful not to meddle improvidently or beyond our station, beyond our proportionate stake, in this tremendous European structure. If we were to derange the existing foundations, based on force though they may be, we might easily bring about the very catastrophe that most of all we desire to avert....

We can press for the redress of grievances by merely threatening, if our counsels are not attended to, to withdraw ourselves at the proper time from our present close entanglement in European affairs.

1932, 23 NOVEMBER.

Our country has a very important part to play in Europe, but it is not so large a part as we have been attempting to play, and I advocate for us in future a more modest role than many of our peace-preservers and peace-lovers have sought to impose upon us.

1933, 13 APRIL.

The best way in which a British Member of Parliament or statesman can be a good European is to make sure that our country is safe and strong in the first instance. The rest may be added to you afterwards, but without that you are no kind of European. All you are is a source of embarrassment and weakness to the whole of the rest of the world.

1934, 30 JULY.

Even an isolationist would, I think, go so far as to say: "If we have to mix ourselves up with the Continent, let us at any rate, get the maximum of safety from our commitments."

1938, 24 MARCH.

We are bound as well by our twenty-year Treaty with Russia, and besides this—I, for my part, hope to deserve to be called a good European—we have the duty of trying to raise the glorious Continent of Europe, the parent of

so many powerful states, from its present miserable condition as a volcano of strife and tumult to its old glory as a family of nations and a vital expression of Christendom.

1944, 24 MAY.

European Community

In my conception of a unified Europe, I never contemplated the diminution of the Commonwealth....I think that the Government are right to apply to join the European Economic Community, not because I am yet convinced that we shall be able to join, but because there appears to be no other way by which we can find out exactly whether the conditions of membership are acceptable.

1961, AUGUST. (MONTAGUE BROWNE, 273–4.)

WSC to his Constituency Chairman Mrs. Moss, after Montgomery had inaccurately said he was "opposed" to British entry in the EC. "This was a fence-sitting letter," wrote his private secretary. "In the conflicting circumstances of WSC's age, the public need for an expression of his views...and WSC's family's (and my own) determination that improper use should not be made of him, such a position was inevitable."

European unity

The safety of the world requires a new unity in Europe, from which no nation should be permanently outcast. It is from the quarrels of the strong parent races in Europe that the world wars we have witnessed, or which occurred in former times, have sprung.

1946, 5 MARCH. WESTMINSTER COLLEGE, FULTON, MISSOURI. (SINEWS, 101.)

We must build a kind of United States of Europe.

1946, 19 SEPTEMBER, ZURICH. (SINEWS, 134.)

Europe can only be united by the heartfelt wish and vehement expression of the great majority of all the peoples in all the parties in all the freedom-loving countries, no matter where they dwell or how they vote....

A high and a solemn responsibility rests upon us here this afternoon in this Congress of a Europe striving to be reborn....if we all pull together and pool the luck and the comradeship...and grimly grasp the larger hopes of humanity, then it may be that we shall move into a happier sunlit age, when all the little children who are now growing up in this tormented world may find themselves not the victors nor the vanquished in the fleeting triumphs of one country over another in the bloody turmoil of destructive war, but the heirs of all the treasures of the past and the masters of all the science, the abundance and the glories of the future.

1948, 7 MAY. CONGRESS OF EUROPE, THE HAGUE.
(EUROPE, 311, 317.)

Foreign policy, 1933

I remember when I was very young, before I came into this House, a denunciation by Dr. Spence Watson of what he called "the filthy Tory rag of a spirited foreign policy". In those days the feelings of the forerunners of those who sit opposite were directed against jingo policies of bombast and Palmerstonian vigour. But you may have another kind of spirited foreign policy...in which, without duly considering the circumstances in which others are placed, you endeavour to press upon them disarmament or to weaken their security, perhaps with a view to gaining a measure of approbation from good people here who are not aware of the dangerous state of affairs in Europe. There you could have a peace which may be too spirited.

1933, 13 APRIL.

Churchill's phenomenal memory again assisted his Parliamentary repartee. Stationed in India in 1896–99, he had read the Parliamentary debates for the past fifty years, considering which side he would have taken on issues great and small.

Foreign policy, 1938

...there must be a moral basis for British foreign policy. People in this country, after all we have gone through, do not mean to be drawn into another terrible war in the name of old-world alliances or diplomatic combinations. If deep causes of division are to be removed from our midst, if all our energies are to be concentrated upon the essential task of increasing our strength and security, it can

only be because of lofty and unselfish ideals which command the allegiance of all classes here at home, which rouse their echoes in the breasts even of the Dictator-ridden peoples themselves, and stir the pulses of the English-speaking race in every quarter of the globe.

1938, 9 MAY. FREE TRADE HALL, MANCHESTER.
(BLOOD, 26.)

Foreign policy, 1945

We seek nothing for ourselves.

1945, 13 MAY. BROADCAST, LONDON.
(VICTORY, 138.)

Foreign policy unity

However we may differ in political opinion, however divergent our Party interests, however diverse our callings and stations, we have this in common. We mean to defend our Island from tyranny and aggression, and so far as we can, we mean to hold out a helping hand to others who may be in an even more immediate danger than at this moment we are ourselves.

1938, 9 MAY, MANCHESTER. (BLOOD, 19.)

I submit to you that these matters of national defence and foreign policy ought to be considered upon a plane above Party, and apart from natural antagonisms which separate a Government and an Opposition. They affect the life of the nation. They influence the fortunes of the world.

1939, 19 MAY. CORN EXCHANGE, CAMBRIDGE.
(BLOOD, 165.)

...we must rise above that weakness of democratic and Parliamentary Governments, in not being able to pursue a steady policy for a long time, so as to get results. It is surely our plain duty to persevere steadfastly, irrespective of party feelings or national diversities, for only in this way have we good chances of securing that lasting world peace under a sovereign world instrument of security on which our hearts are set.

1949, 12 MAY.

On the occasion of the signing of the NATO pact (see North Atlantic Treaty Organization). A theme of Churchill throughout his life that in every country, "politics must stop at the water's edge".

Franco-German rapprochement

I am now going to say something that will astonish you. The first step in the recreation of the European family must be a partnership between France and Germany. In this way only can France recover the moral leadership of Europe. There can be no revival of Europe without a spiritually great France and a spiritually great Germany.

1946, 16 SEPTEMBER, ZÜRICH. (SINEWS, 201.)

To me [in 1925] the aim of ending the thousand-year strife between France and Germany seemed a supreme object. If we could only weave Gaul and Teuton so closely together economically, socially and morally as to prevent the occasion of new quarrels, and make old antagonisms die in the realisation of mutual prosperity and interdependence, Europe would rise again. It seemed to me that the supreme interest of the British people in Europe lay in the assuagement of the Franco-German feud, and that they had no other interests comparable or contrary to that. This is still my view today.

1948. (WW2 I, 23.)

Here is the forward path [European Unity] upon which we must march if the thousand-year feud between Gaul and Teuton is to pass from its fierce destructive life into the fading romance of history.

1950, 28 MARCH.

"Free Trade England"

[...the sugar] bounty-giving Governments are confronted with deficits and financial embarrassment, and sugar is 7d. a pound to the population of the country in which the sugar is grown. And all this time Free Trade England, anchored by irrefragable logic to economic truth, rides out the gale—indolent, prosperous, triumphant.

1903, 29 JULY.

For extensive quotations on this subject see Chapter 21, Political Theory and Practice...Free Trade.

Governments, failures of

It is not nature which has failed mankind. It is Governments, which, misled and steeped in folly or perversity, have rejected and squandered the fruits of nature, endeavouring to prevent the normal working of its processes, even though those fruits are presented by the ever-more efficient servitors of an ever-widening science.

1947, 28 OCTOBER.

Great and small powers

We may deplore, if we choose, the fact that there is a difference between great and small, between the strong and the weak in the world, but there undoubtedly is such a difference, and it would be foolish to upset good arrangements which are proceeding on a broad front for the sake of trying to obtain immediately what is a hopeless ideal.

1946, 15 MARCH.

Grievances

The removal of the just grievances of the vanquished ought to precede the disarmament of the victors. To bring about anything like equality of armaments [between the vanquished and the victor nations] if it were in our power to do so, which it happily is not, while those grievances remain unredressed, would be almost to appoint the day for another European war—to fix it as if it were a prize-fight.

1932, 23 NOVEMBER.

Human destiny

It is not in the power of one nation, however formidably armed, still less is it in the power of a small group of men, violent, ruthless men, who have always to cast their eyes back over their shoulders, to cramp and fetter the forward march of human destiny.

1938, 16 OCTOBER. BROADCAST, LONDON. (BLOOD, 88.)

Ideological preferences

This is no time for ideological preferences for one side or the other, and certainly we, His Majesty's Government, have not indulged ourselves in this way at all. Thus, in Italy we are working for the present through the Government of the King and Badoglio; in Yugoslavia we give our aid to Marshal Tito; in Greece, in spite of the fact that a British officer was murdered by the guerrilla organization called E.L.A.S., we are doing our best to bring about a reconciliation, or at least a working agreement, between the opposing forces.

1944, 22 FEBRUARY.

E.L.A.S. (Ethnikos Laikos Apeleftherotikos Stratos) was the communist National Popular Liberation Army.

Indigenous peoples

I do not admit that the dog in the manger has the final right to the manger, even though he may have lain there for a very long time. I do not admit that right. I do not admit, for instance, that a great wrong has been done to the Red Indians of America, or the black people of Australia. I do not admit that a wrong has been done to those people by the fact that a stronger race, a higher grade race, or, at any rate, a more worldly-wise race, to put it that way, has come in and taken their place.

1937, 12 MARCH. (OB, CV5/3, 616.)

Churchill's evidence in the Palestine Royal Commission, concerning the Arabs in Palestine.

Korean war: invading China

That would be the greatest folly. It would be like flies invading fly-paper.

1951. (MONTAGUE BROWNE, 317.)

League of Nations

I have sympathy with, and respect for, the well-meaning, loyal-hearted people who make up the League of Nations Union in this country, but what impresses me most about them is their long-suffering and inexhaustible gullibility. Any scheme of any kind for disarmament put forward by any country, so long as it is surrounded by suitable phraseology, is hailed by them, and the speeches are cheered, and those who speak gain the meed of their applause....

I hope that the League of Nations is not going to be asked now to do the impossible. Those who believe, as I do sincerely, that the League of Nations is a priceless instrument of international comity, which may play as great a part as the most daring, hopeful founders

ever forecast for it, should be especially careful not to put upon the League strains which in its present stage it is utterly incapable of bearing.

1932, 23 NOVEMBER.

...I could not help feeling that the proposals which were made...would give great gratification to the League of Nations Union, who, poor things, have to content themselves with so little.

1933, 14 MARCH.

I have been trying to seek out for myself what would be the best way of preventing war, and it has seemed to me that the League of Nations should be the great instrument upon which all those resolves to maintain peace should centre, and that we should all make our contribution to the League of Nations....

I must say that I do not see how anyone who wishes to induce Germany to come back to the League, as she has a perfect right to do at any moment, can possibly find reasons for objecting to Russia also joining that body....

1934, 13 JULY.

When I hear extreme pacifists denouncing this act of the League of Nations I am left wondering what foundations these gentlemen offer to countries for abandoning individual national armaments.

1935, 2 MAY.

Churchill was referring to the complaint of the Council of the League of Nations on German rearmament and Hitler's violation of treaties.

In this august association [the League of Nations] for collective security we must build up defense forces of all kinds and combine our action with that of friendly Powers, so that we may be allowed to live in quiet ourselves and retrieve the woeful miscalculations of which we are at present the dupes, and of which, unless we take warning in time, we may some day be the victims.

1935, 2 MAY.

Some people say: "Put your trust in the League of Nations." Others say: "Put your trust in British rearmament." I say we want both.

1935, 24 OCTOBER.

...I think we ought to place our trust in those moral forces which are enshrined in the Covenant of the League of Nations. Do not let us mock at them, for they are surely on our side. Do not mock at them, for this may well be a time when the highest idealism is not divorced from strategic prudence. Do not mock at them, for these may be years, strange as it may seem, when Right may walk hand in hand with Might.

1937, 4 MARCH.

If the League of Nations has been mishandled and broken, we must rebuild it. If a League of peace-seeking peoples is set at naught, we must convert it into a League of armed peoples, too faithful to molest others, too strong to be molested themselves.

1938, 9 MAY, MANCHESTER. (BLOOD, 21–2.)

It is said that the League of Nations failed. If so, that is largely because it was abandoned, and later on betrayed: because those who were its best friends were till a very late period infected with a futile pacifism: because the United States, the originating impulse, fell out of the line: because, while France had been bled white and England was supine and bewildered, a monstrous growth of aggression sprang up in Germany, in Italy and Japan.

1943, 6 SEPTEMBER, HARVARD UNIVERSITY. (ONWARDS, 185.)

Liberation

We have one principle about the liberated countries or the repentant satellite countries which we strive for according to the best of our ability and resources. Here is the principle. I will state it in the broadest and most familiar terms: Government of the people, by the people, for the people, set up on a basis of election by the free and universal suffrage, with secrecy of the ballot and no intimidation....

Trust the people, make sure they have a fair chance to decide their destiny without being terrorized from either quarter or regimented. That is our policy for Italy, for Yugoslavia, and for Greece. What other interest have we than that? For that we shall strive, and for that alone.

1945, 18 JANUARY.

Locarno Treaty

The Treaty of Locarno may be regarded as the Old World counterpart of the Treaty of Washington between the United States, Great Britain and Japan, which in 1921 had regulated and ensured the peace of the Pacific. These two august instruments give assurance to civilization. They are the twin pyramids of peace rising solid and unshakable on either side of the Atlantic....

1929. (CRISIS IV, 459.)

Seven treaties agreed at Locarno, Switzerland, in October 1925 were signed to confirm postwar borders and normalise relations with Germany, then the Weimar Republic. "The Spirit of Locarno" was a phrase often invoked later, to describe well-intentioned approaches to Hitler's Reich. The Treaty of Washington, signed 1922, limited naval armaments (see Chapter 15, Navy...Fleet strength).

I believe that we have a considerable breathing space in which to revive again those lights of goodwill and reconciliation in Europe which shone, so brightly but so briefly, on the morrow of Locarno. We shall never do that merely by haggling about cannons, tanks, aeroplanes and submarines, or measuring swords with one another, among nations already eyeing each other with so much vigilance.

1932, 23 NOVEMBER.

Compare the state of Europe on the morrow of Locarno with its condition today. Fears are greater, rivalries are sharper, military plans are more closely concerted, military organizations are more carefully and efficiently developed, Britain is weaker: And Britain's hour of weakness is Europe's hour of danger.

1932, 23 NOVEMBER.

Middle East

The decline of our influence and power throughout the Middle East is due to several causes. First, the loss of our Oriental Empire and of the well-placed and formidable resources of the Imperial armies in India. Second, it is due to the impression which has become widespread throughout the Middle East that Great Britain has only to be pressed sufficiently by one method or another to

POLITICS: THE WORLD SCENE

abandon her rights or interests in that, or indeed any other, part of the world. A third cause is the mistakes and miscalculations in policy which led to the winding up of our affairs in Palestine in such a way as to earn almost in equal degree the hatred of the Arabs and the Jews.

1951, 30 JULY.

Abadan, Sudan and Bevan are a trio of misfortune.

**1951, 12 OCTOBER. WOODFORD, ESSEX.
(CS VIII, 8262.)**

Abadan was one of the locations where Iran had nationalised its oil operations and broke the Anglo-Persian oil agreements. In the Sudan, Churchill was blaming Labour for having encouraged a revolt by local Egyptians. What WSC thought of Aneurin Bevan will be found in Chapter 20, People.

The Middle East is one of the hardest-hearted areas in the world. It has always been fought over, and peace has only reigned when a major power has established firm influence and shown that it would maintain its will. Your friends must be supported with every vigour and if necessary they must be avenged. Force, or perhaps force and bribery, are the only things that will be respected. It is very sad, but we had all better recognise it. At present our friendship is not valued, and our enmity is not feared.

1958. (MONTAGUE BROWNE, 166–7.)

Middle East vs. Africa

In the Middle East you have arid countries. In East Africa you have dripping countries. There is the greatest difficulty to get anything to grow in the one place, and the greatest difficulty to prevent things smothering and choking you by their hurried growth in the other. In the African Colonies you have a docile, tractable population, who only require to be well and wisely treated to develop great economic capacity and utility; whereas the regions of the Middle East are unduly stocked with peppery, pugnacious, proud politicians and theologians, who happen to be at the same time extremely well armed and extremely hard up.

1921, 14 JULY.

Most-favoured nation

The most-favoured nation principle is one of the great foundations of our fiscal system.

1924, 17 DECEMBER.

The term means that a nation receives all the trade advantages, such as low tariffs, that any nation receives with the trading partner.

Multinational forces

I do not believe you will ever succeed in building up an international force in a vague and general manner, or that it can be created in cold blood. But it might well be that an international force would come into being by an alliance of national forces for a particular emergency or for particular purposes, and, once having been started, it might give the security to the world which would avert the approaching curse of war.

1934, 14 MARCH.

Fifteen years later, these precepts attended the founding of the North Atlantic Treaty Organization (q.v.).

National honour

...no nation endeavouring to maintain civilised government and institutions can allow its plighted word to be brought under insult and calumny, and allow those guilty of cruel and brutal murder to go unpunished.

1922, 12 APRIL.

National interests

The only really sure guide to the actions of mighty nations and powerful Governments is a correct estimate of what are and what they consider to be their own interests.

1953, 3 NOVEMBER.

Churchill can be quoted to prove both sides of many arguments. Here is a rare case of him suggesting that national interests are paramount; more often he held that Britain, at least, marched to higher callings. See also Britain, Empire and Commonwealth... Motivations of.

National sacrifice

No state or nation is worthy to take part in this sacred, august duty of rebuilding the world under the protection of a world instrument whose men and women are not prepared to give their lives if need be, and to make whatever preparations are required to ensure that they and their country are not found impotent and unready in the world cause.

1946, 7 MAY. BROADCAST, LONDON. (SINEWS, 127.)

North Atlantic Treaty Organization (NATO)

[You Americans are] in it because there's no way out, but if we pool our luck and share our fortunes I think you will have no reason to regret it....you have not only to convince the Soviet Government that you have superior force—that they are confronted by superior force—but that you are not restrained by any moral consideration, if the case arose, from using that force with complete material ruthlessness. And that is the greatest chance of peace, the surest road to peace. Then, the Communists will make a bargain.

1949, 25 MARCH, NEW YORK.
(GILBERT, LIFE, 883–4.)

WSC to President Eisenhower. The North Atlantic Treaty Organization, established in 1949, is a system of collective defence by which member states agree to mutual defence if any member is attacked by any other. Initially North American and Western European in make-up, the organisation added ten former Iron Curtain states between 1999 and 2004. There are now many more members. See also Chapter 15, Naval Person...NATO command.

NATO and Canada

Now we have the North Atlantic Treaty which owes much to Canadian statesmanship and to the personal initiative of [Canadian Prime Minister] Mr. St. Laurent. The treaty is the surest guarantee not only of the prevention of war but of victory, should our hopes be blasted. So far this solemn compact has been regarded only in its military aspect, but now we all feel, especially since our visit to Washington, that it is broadening out into the conception of the North Atlantic community of free nations, acting together not only for defence but for the welfare and happiness and progress of all the peoples of the free world.

1952, 14 JANUARY. CHÂTEAU LAURIER, OTTAWA.
(STEMMING, 217.)

Population

The idea that only a limited number of people can live in a country is a profound illusion; it all depends on their cooperative and inventive power....There is no limit to the ingenuity of man if it is properly and vigorously applied under conditions of peace and justice.

1949, 26 JANUARY.

Arguing for larger numbers of employed Arabs to live in the former Palestine.

Racism

[The Boer commando said], "Well, is it right that a dirty Kaffir should walk on the pavement—without a pass too? That's what they do in your British Colonies. Brother! Equal! Ugh! Free! Not a bit. We know how to treat Kaffirs." Probing at random I had touched a very sensitive nerve....

What is the true and original root of Dutch aversion to British rule?...It is the abiding fear and hatred of the movement that seeks to place the native on a level with the white man. British government is associated in the Boer farmer's mind with violent social revolution. Black is to be proclaimed the same as white. The servant is to be raised against the master; the Kaffir is to be declared the brother of the European, to be constituted his legal equal, to be armed with political rights. The dominant race is to be deprived of their superiority; nor is a tigress robbed of her cubs more furious than is the Boer at this prospect.

1899, PRETORIA. (LADYSMITH, 131–2; BOER, 60.)

This reflection by the young Winston, convinced as he was of the civilising role of the British Empire, is a remarkable commentary on Churchill's advanced views of racial equality. Though he retained the paternalistic instincts typical of his countrymen, his comments in his Boer War books raised eyebrows at the turn of the last century, when few Britons entertained such ideas.

Realpolitik

Realpolitik meant that the standards of morality in international affairs could be ignored whenever material advantage might be gained.

1958. (HESP IV, 273.)

Referring to the unification of Germany under Bismarck.

Sanitary cordon

The hatreds between the two races [Germans and Russians] have become a sanitary cordon in themselves.

CIRCA 1940S. (ISMAY, 260.)

Sanitary cordon was a term applied to surrounding potential enemies, like Russia or Germany, with a ring of states likely to defend themselves from expansion.

Summit meetings

I have spoken for years of a pyramid of peace, which might be triangular or quadrangular—three or four Great Powers shaking hands together and endeavouring to procure a rectification of some of the evils arising from the treaties made in the passion of war, which if left unredressed will bring upon us consequences we cannot name....

I had an impression that [Prime Minister Ramsay MacDonald] had always condemned anything in the nature of a four-Power or a three-Power agreement and had considered that that was, as it were, inconsistent with the general authority of the League of Nations, on which so many Powers are represented. However, let that pass. Whether he was converted by the eloquence or by the strong personality of Signor Mussolini, or whether he had it in his mind before he went to Rome, are mysteries which are naturally hidden from us.

1933, 23 MARCH.

...no meeting during this war would carry with it so much significance for the future of the world as a meeting [at Teheran] between the Heads of the three Governments, for, without the close, cordial and lasting association between Soviet Russia and the other great Allies, we might find ourselves at the end of

the war only to have entered upon a period of deepening confusion.

1943, 21 SEPTEMBER.

The future of the whole world, and certainly the future of Europe, perhaps for several generations, depends upon the cordial, trustful and comprehending association of the British Empire, the United States and Soviet Russia, and no pains must be spared and no patience grudged which are necessary to bring that supreme hope to fruition.

1944, 28 SEPTEMBER.

Perhaps on this somewhat delicate topic I may be permitted by the House to take refuge in metaphor. Many anxieties have been expressed recently at the severe character of the course of the Grand National Steeplechase, but I am sure that it could not be improved by asking the horses to try to jump two fences at the same time.

1954, 17 JUNE.

On the need for a summit meeting between Soviet, American and British leaders. Churchill had been arguing with Eisenhower for a "meeting at the summit", as he called it, since at least the Bermuda Conference in 1953, but Eisenhower insisted there was no point in meeting with the Russians. Ironically, he did so almost immediately after Churchill had left office, apparently having believed that WSC might try to "give away the store" (Larres, 371).

Terrorism

...Terrorists are naturally drawn to imitate Lenin and Trotsky; while we sh[oul]d take our stand on the will of the people freely expressed in both cases.

1922, 13 MAY. (OB, CV4/3, 1890.)

WSC to Austen Chamberlain.

...there is real danger of dangerous terrorists, persons engaged in the gravest forms of terrorism, standing for the Legislature of Bengal in particular and being elected for the Bengal Assembly, unless this bar is put in their path....If it is a fact that under this constitution the Provincial Legislature of Bengal may select dangerous terrorists and send them to the Federal Legislature then all I can say is that I hope this will be noticed by people outside these doors.

1935, 12 MARCH.

A remark on a clause in the Government of India Act.

...National leaders have often presented themselves as men of fate and instruments of destiny. The distressful country fastened its soul almost superstitiously upon the career of every chieftain as he advanced. [Leaders] appeared, not in the manner of English political leaders, but rather like the prophets who guided Israel.

1936, OCTOBER. ("CHARLES STEWART PARNELL," *STRAND MAGAZINE*; GC, 222.)

A number of persons suspected of active complicity in terrorist activities have been arrested, and on October 19th, 251 were deported from the country, where their presence, with the possibility of a large-scale attempt at rescue, only led to increased insecurity. Since then, numerous further arrests have been made, including those of some wanted terrorists....In Palestine the executive of the Jewish Agency has called upon the Jewish community—and I quote their actual words: "to cast out the members of this destructive band, to deprive them of all refuge and shelter, to resist their threats, and to render all necessary assistance to the authorities in the prevention of terrorist acts, and in the eradication of the terrorist organization." These are strong words, but we must wait for these words to be translated into deeds. We must wait to see that not only the leaders, but every man, woman and child of the Jewish community, does his or her best to bring this terrorism to a speedy end.

1944, 17 NOVEMBER.

WSC following the murder of Lord Moyne by Zionist terrorists. See also Other Nations... Israel and Palestine.

If our dreams for Zionism are to end in the smoke of assassins' pistols, and our labours for its future to produce only a new set of gangsters worthy of Nazi Germany, many like myself will have to reconsider the position we have maintained so consistently and so long in the past. If there is to be any hope of a peaceful and successful future for Zionism, these wicked activities must cease, and those responsible for them must be destroyed root and branch.

1944, 17 NOVEMBER. (OB VII, 1052.)

Churchill was a friend of Jews, but not an uncritical friend. Outraged when his friend Lord Moyne (Walter Guinness), the Minister Resident in Cairo, was shot with his driver by members of the terrorist Stern Gang on 5 November 1944, Churchill suggested the Colonial Secretary, Oliver Stanley, should impress upon Zionist leader Chaim Weizmann "that it was incumbent on the Jewish Agency to do all in their power to suppress these terrorist activities".

The idea that general reprisals upon the civil population and vicarious examples would be consonant with our whole outlook upon the world and with our name, reputation and principles, is, of course, one which should never be accepted in any way. We have, therefore, very great difficulties in conducting squalid warfare with terrorists. That is why I would venture to submit to the House that every effort should be made to avoid getting into warfare with terrorists; and if a warfare with terrorists has broken out, every effort should be made—I exclude no reasonable proposal—to bring it to an end....

No country in the world is less fit for a conflict with terrorists than Great Britain. That is not because of her weakness or cowardice; it is because of her restraint and virtues, and the way of life which we have lived so long in this sheltered island.

1947, 31 JANUARY.

The impression has got about the world that we have only to be kicked or threatened to clear out of any place. The Persians like the idea of nationalization of other people's property and, under the pressure of the terrorists in Teheran, they now propose to seize the Anglo-Persian oilfields, which have been discovered and developed by fifty years of British brains and capital. Iraq threatens the same policy of spoliation....

All this and much else is happening

within six years of the world war, in which for more than a year we sustained the cause of freedom alone and from which we emerged with complete victory and world-wide respect.

1951, 18 MAY. SCOTTISH UNIONIST ASSOCIATION, GLASGOW. (STEMMING, 88.)

Terrorism, state

What I mean by frightfulness is the inflicting of great slaughter or massacre upon a particular crowd of people, with the intention of terrorising not merely the rest of the crowd, but the whole district or the whole country....Frightfulness is not a remedy known to the British pharmacopoeia....

I have heard the Hon. Member for Hull [Lieut.-Commander Kenworthy] speak on this subject. His doctrine and his policy is to support and palliate every form of terrorism as long as it is the terrorism of revolutionaries against the forces of law, loyalty and order. Governments who have seized upon power by violence and by usurpation have often resorted to terrorism in their desperate efforts to keep what they have stolen, but the august and venerable structure of the British Empire, where lawful authority descends from hand to hand and generation after generation, does not need such aid. Such ideas are absolutely foreign to the British way of doing things.

1920, 8 JULY.

Churchill was speaking following a report of the Army Council on a massacre of Indians at Amritsar. Joseph Montague Kenworthy, 10th Baron Strabolgi (1886-1953), was a Liberal MP (1919–26) and Labour MP (1926–31). See also Religion...Islam.

Third World

Those whose practice it is to regard their own nation as possessing a monopoly of virtue and common-sense, are wont to ascribe every military enterprise of savage peoples to fanaticism. They calmly ignore obvious and legitimate motives. The most rational conduct is considered mad.

1899. (RIVER I, 34.)

Trade

The dangers which threaten the tranquillity of the modern world come not from those Powers that have become interdependent upon others, interwoven by commerce with other states; they come from those Powers which are...more or less aloof from the general intercourse of mankind, and are comparatively independent and self-supporting....We do not mind even if we become dependent on foreign nations, because we know that by that very fact we make foreign nations dependent upon us.

1905, 8 MARCH.

United Nations

There must be room in this new great structure of the world for the happiness and prosperity of all, and in the end it must be capable of bringing happiness and prosperity even to the guilty and vanquished nations. There must be room within the great world organization for organisms like the British Empire and Commonwealth, as we now call it, and I trust that there will be room also for the fraternal association of the British Commonwealth and the United States.

1944, 24 MAY.

I do not see any other way of realizing our hopes about World Organization in five or six days. Even the Almighty took seven.

1945, 10 JANUARY. (OB VII, 1138.)

WSC to Roosevelt, a Personal and Top Secret telegram asking FDR to send Secretary of State Stetinnius to Malta forty-eight hours earlier to be debriefed by Eden. WSC added: "Pray forgive my pertinacity."

...the world organisation cannot be based upon a dictatorship of the Great Powers. It is their duty to serve the world and not to rule it.

1945, 27 FEBRUARY.

...it was never contemplated at any time that the veto should be used in the abrupt, arbitrary and almost continuous manner that we have seen it used, but that it should be reserved as a last assurance to a great power that they would not be voted down on a matter about which they were prepared to fight.

1946, 23 OCTOBER.

But now all these millions of humble humans are hustled and harried this way and that, first by nationalistic or imperialistic ambitions or appetites, now by ideological doctrines and hatreds, and all their small lives may be shattered and convulsed, millions at a time, and they may be only regimented up to suffering wounds and unrewarded toil. We, their representatives in this world-famous assembly, have a great responsibility, and we cannot always discharge it by treading easy paths and saying smooth things.

1948, 23 January.

Warmongering

I resented Mr. Stalin calling [Mr. Attlee] a warmonger. I thought this was quite untrue. It was also unfair because the word "warmonger" was, as you have no doubt heard, the one that many of Mr. Attlee's friends and followers were hoping to fasten on me whenever the election comes....Stalin has therefore been guilty, not only of an untruth, but of infringement of copyright. I think Mr. Stalin had better be careful or else Mr. [Sidney] Silverman will have him up for breach of privilege....

1951, 17 March.

24

EDUCATION

"I frankly confess that I feel somewhat overawed in addressing this vast scientific and learned audience....I have no technical and no university education, and have just had to pick up a few things as I went along. Therefore I speak with a diffidence, which I hope to overcome as I proceed..."[81]

"I am surprised...[to] have become so experienced at taking degrees when, as a school-boy, I was so bad at passing examinations."

hurchill often expressed regret that he had not had a formal education, and stood in confessed awe of those who did. (See "Personal experience" herein.)

It wasn't until he was approaching twenty-two that the "desire for learning", as he wrote, "began to press insistently upon me....So I resolved to read history, philosophy, economics, and things like that; and I wrote to my mother asking for such books as I had heard of on these topics. She responded with alacrity, and every month the mail brought me a substantial package of what I thought were standard works."[82]

Churchill's self-education was remarkable. (Chapter IX of *My Early Life* contains the full story.) "All through the long glistening middle hours of the Indian day, from when we quitted stables till the evening shadows proclaimed the hour of Polo",[83] he read. His

---

81 WSC, Massachusetts Institute of Technology, 31 March 1949. Balance, 41.
82 MEL, 125.
83 Ibid.

sponge-like mind was relentlessly engaged: Macaulay, Gibbon, Chatham, Frederick the Great, Clive, Warren Hastings, Southey, Plato, Aristotle, Malthus, Darwin. In the process he lost the rote religion he had been taught as a youngster, though not the idea that there was reason to the universe, and a supreme Creator behind it.

As a politician he was convinced of the importance of education for all citizens. After World War II he lamented Britain's laggard approach to science and technology, and yearned for a British version of the Massachusetts Institute of Technology. This was the impetus behind Churchill College Cambridge, one of the two British national memorials to him (the other being the Winston Churchill Memorial Trust).

Although in an educational context Churchill often spoke of "men", his meaning encompassed both sexes. Sir John Colville recalled the "astonishment" when WSC said he hoped Churchill College would admit women on equal terms with men: "No college at Oxford or Cambridge had ever done any such thing. I asked him afterwards if this had been Clementine's idea. 'Yes,' he replied, 'and I support it.'"[84] Nor was this the only evidence that he considered education universal: an opportunity for all.

Churchill was Chancellor of Bristol University from 1929 until his death,[85] and his role was more than ceremonial. Sir Martin Gilbert learned WSC once wrote to his Vice-Chancellor, asking Bristol to admit a German Jewish dental student whose parents had appealed to him. His request was refused. Martin Gilbert discovered the story and mentioned it some years later at an American lecture. "…someone in the audience told me that the man lived in that very city. We met and corresponded. He could not believe that if Winston Churchill had written on his behalf, the Vice-Chancellor would not have complied. In my long search for Churchill, I found many occasions when, despite his intervention, his will was not executed."[86]

Churchill considered the "information revolution" before that term had been coined. His information was derived from the newspapers, all of which he devoured. But he considered them, "an education at once universal and superficial".[87]

It is difficult to separate Churchill's views on various branches of education, like Ethics, Mathematics and Latin, from his personal experiences with them. The reader should review entries under "Personal experience" as well as individual headings.

Academic courage

Here we are gathered in academic robes to go through a ceremonial and repeat formulas associated with the giving of university degrees. Many of those here today have been all night at their post, and all have been under the fire of the enemy in heavy and protracted bombardment. That you should gather in this way is a mark of fortitude and phlegm, of a courage and detachment from material affairs, worthy of all that we have learned to believe of ancient Rome or of modern Greece.

**1941, 12 APRIL, BRISTOL UNIVERSITY.
(UNRELENTING, 87.)**

Access to education

If there was any board upon which the working classes ought to be represented it is the education authority.

1902, 13 NOVEMBER. (CZARNOMSKI, 117.)

…under the educational reforms which were devised in the National Coalition Government, of which I was the head, very great extension has been made of access to the universities. They are no longer, as they were in bygone generations, the close preserve of wealth and rank. They are no longer a later stage in a career of public school education. On the contrary, three-quarters of the universities are

---

84 Colville, Churchillians, 123.
85 He was also Rector of Aberdeen and Edinburgh Universities, and received twenty-one honorary degrees from universities around the world.
86 Gilbert, Search, 236.
87 See below…Information revolution.

now filled by young men from the public elementary schools and I rejoice that this is so.

Adult education

There is perhaps no branch of our vast educational system which should more attract within its particular sphere the aid and encouragement of the State than adult education. How many must there be in Britain, after the disturbance of two destructive wars, who thirst in later life to learn about the humanities, the history of their country, the philosophies of the human race, and the arts and letters which sustain and are borne forward by the ever-conquering English language? This ranks in my opinion far above science and technical instruction, which are well sustained and not without their rewards in our present system. The mental and moral outlook of free men studying the past with free minds in order to discern the future demands the highest measures which our hard-pressed finances can sustain. I have no doubt myself that a man or woman earnestly seeking in grown-up life to be guided to wide and suggestive knowledge in its largest and most uplifted sphere will make the best of all the pupils in this age of clatter and buzz, of gape and gloat.

1953, 9 FEBRUARY. (ADDISON, HOME FRONT, 414–15.)

Letter to Minister for Education Florence Horsburgh, who had announced a reduction in government support for adult education.

Basic English

I am very much interested in the question of Basic English. The widespread use of this would be a gain to us far more durable and fruitful than the annexation of great provinces. It would also fit in with my ideas of closer union with the United States by making it even more worth while to belong to the English-speaking club.

1943, 11 JULY. (WW2 V, 571.)

Basic English is a constructed language with fewer than 1,000 words, created by Charles Kay Ogden in 1930. WSC favoured it as a means to make English a universal language; in the event, English managed on its own.

Some months ago I persuaded the British Cabinet to set up a committee of Ministers to study and report upon Basic English. Here you have a plan. There are others, but here you have a very carefully wrought plan for an international language capable of a very wide transaction of practical business and interchange of ideas. The whole of it is comprised in about 650 nouns and 200 verbs or other parts of speech—no more indeed than can be written on one side of a single sheet of paper.

1943, 6 SEPTEMBER. HARVARD UNIVERSITY, CAMBRIDGE, MASSACHUSETTS. (ONWARDS, 184.)

Roosevelt took a dim view of Basic English, writing to WSC in June, 1944,

> I wonder what the course of history would have been, if in May 1940 you had been able to offer the British people only "blood, work, eye water, and face water", which I understand is the best Basic English can do with five famous words (Lowenheim, 10).

Basic English is not intended for use among English-speaking people, but to enable a much larger body of people who do not have the good fortune to know the English language to participate more easily in our society.

1943, 4 NOVEMBER. (ONWARDS, 268.)

This clearly would have been WSC's reply to Roosevelt's barb above. This is a reply to a question in the House of Commons.

Propagate our language all over world is best method…Harmonises with my ideas for future of the world. This will be the English-speaking century. Can be learned in 2–4 weeks.

1945, 12 JULY. (DIARIES OF CABINET SECRETARY SIR NORMAN BROOK, *NEW YORK TIMES*, 22 JANUARY 2006.)

Bilingual education

[I cannot] work myself into a passion because in some part or other of the Cape Colony there were some Dutch people who wished to have Dutch teachers to teach Dutch children Dutch. We should regret intolerant action....we have not so poor an opinion of the English language, with its priceless literary treasures and its worldwide business connections, as not to believe that it can safely be exposed to the open competition of a dialect like the *taal....*[the way to preserve] the *taal* would be to make it a proscribed language, which would be spoken by the people with deliberation and with malice as a protest against what they regarded, and would rightly regard, as an act of intolerance.

1906, 31 JULY.

A notable quotation that might be used today by proponents of bilingual education. Taal (Afrikaans patois spoken on the Cape) was an official language of South Africa.

Classics

There is a good saying to the effect that when a new book appears one should read an old one. As an author I would not recommend too strict an adherence to this saying. But I must admit that I have altered my views about the study of classical literature as I have grown older. At school I never liked it. I entirely failed to respond to the many pressing and sometimes painful exhortations which I received to understand the full charm and precision of the classic languages. But it seems to me that should the classic studies die out in Europe and in the modern world, a unifying influence of importance would disappear.

1948, 12 MAY. UNIVERSITY OF OSLO. (EUROPE, 326.)

Phrases in this speech were reused later; see next entry.

I would like to say that I have changed my mind about the classics. I had very strong views about them when at Harrow; I have changed my mind about them since. Knowledge of the ancient world and of Greek and Roman literature was a great unifying force in Europe which is now I fear rapidly becoming extinct and I should like to say that university education ought not to be too practical.

1948, 18 NOVEMBER. UNIVERSITY OF LONDON. (EUROPE, 468.)

English

...by being so long in the lowest form [at Harrow] I gained an immense advantage over the cleverer boys...I got into my bones the essential structure of the ordinary British

sentence—which is a noble thing....Naturally I am biased in favour of boys learning English....I would let the clever ones learn Latin as an honour, and Greek as a treat. But the only thing I would whip them for is not knowing English. I would whip them hard for that.

1930. (MEL, 31.)

Ethics

One day, before I left England, a friend of mine had said: "Christ's gospel was the last word in Ethics." This sounded good; but what were Ethics? They had never been mentioned to me at Harrow or Sandhurst. Judging from the context I thought they must mean "the public school spirit," "playing the game," "*esprit de corps*," "honourable behaviour," "patriotism," and the like. Then someone told me that Ethics were concerned not merely with the things you ought to do, but with why you ought to do them, and that there were whole books written on the subject. I would have paid some scholar £2 at least to give me a lecture of an hour or an hour and a half about Ethics.

1930. (MEL, 123.)

Describing his sudden thirst for learning in 1896 at the age of nearly twenty-two.

Higher education

I now began for the first time to envy those young cubs at the university who had fine scholars to tell them what was what; professors who had devoted their lives to mastering and focusing ideas in every branch of learning; who were eager to distribute the treasures they had gathered before they were overtaken by the night. But now I pity undergraduates, when I see what frivolous lives many of them lead in the midst of precious fleeting opportunity.

1930. (MEL, 127.)

During his efforts to acquire learning by reading; see Personal experience.

The facilities for advanced education must be evened out and multiplied. No one who can take advantage of a higher education should be denied this chance. You cannot conduct a modern community except with an adequate supply of persons upon whose education, whether humane, technical, or scientific, much time and money have been spent.

1943, 21 MARCH. BROADCAST, LONDON.
(ONWARDS, 41.)

Churchill College Cambridge, a British national memorial to Churchill, founded to promote his idea for a British version of the Massachusetts Institute of Technology, specialises in science and engineering. It also houses the Churchill Archives Centre.

Not only is the saying true, "It is never too late to mend," but university education may be even better appreciated by those in the early twenties than by those in the later teens. The attention which a mature mind can bring to a study of the philosophies, humanities, and the great literary monuments of the past is stronger and more intense than at an earlier age. The power of concentration, the retentiveness of the memory, the earnestness and zeal with which conclusions are sought, should, in most cases, be greater in the older students.

1946, 26 FEBRUARY. UNIVERSITY OF MIAMI.
(SINEWS, 91.)

He who has received a university training possesses a rich choice. He need never be inactive or bored, there is no reason for him to seek refuge in the clack and clatter of our modern life. He need not be dependent on headlines which give him something new every day. He has the wisdom of all time to drink from, to enjoy as long as he lives....Young people study at universities to achieve knowledge, and not to learn a trade. We must learn to support ourselves, but we must also learn how to live.

1948, 12 MAY. UNIVERSITY OF OSLO.
(EUROPE, 326–7.)

The privilege of university education is a great one; the more widely it is extended the better for any country. It should not be looked upon as something to end with youth but as a key to open many doors of thought and knowledge....

The university education is a guide to the reading of a life-time. We should impress upon those who have its advantages the importance of reading the great books of the world and the

literature of one's own country. One who has profited from university education has a wide choice. He need never be idle or bored and have to take refuge in the clack and clatter of the modern age, which requires something new not only every day, but every two or three hours of the day. There is a good saying, which you may have heard before, that when a new book comes out you should read an old one though I perhaps should not recommend too rigid an application.

1948, 18 NOVEMBER. UNIVERSITY OF LONDON.
(EUROPE, 467.)

History

I devoured Gibbon. I rode triumphantly through it from end to end and enjoyed it all. I scribbled all my opinions on the margins of the pages, and very soon found myself a vehement partisan of the author against the disparagements of his pompous-pious editor....

From Gibbon I went to Macaulay. I had learnt [as a boy] *The Lays of Ancient Rome* by heart, and loved them; and of course I knew he had written a history; but I had never read a page of it....I accepted all Macaulay wrote as gospel, and I was grieved to read his harsh judgments upon the Great Duke of Marlborough. There was no one at hand to tell me that this historian with his captivating style and devastating self-confidence was the prince of literary rogues, who always preferred the tale to the truth, and smirched or glorified great men and garbled documents according as they affected his drama.

1930. (MEL, 125–6.)

Importance of education

Those who think that we can become richer or more stable as a country by stinting education and crippling the instruction of our young people are a most benighted class of human beings.

1925, 27 MAY. WOODFORD COUNTY SCHOOL FOR GIRLS. (CS IV, 3649.)

The future of the world is to the highly-educated races who alone can handle the scientific apparatus necessary for preeminence in peace or survival in war.

1943, 21 MARCH. BROADCAST, LONDON.
(ONWARDS, 40.)

Information revolution

The newspapers do an immense amount of thinking for the average man and woman. In fact they supply them with such a continuous stream of standardized opinion, borne along upon an equally inexhaustible flood of news and sensation, collected from every part of the world every hour of the day, that there is neither the need nor the leisure for personal reflection. All this is but a part of a tremendous educating process. But it is an education which passes in at one ear and out at the other. It is an education at once universal and superficial. It produces enormous numbers of standardized citizens, all equipped with regulation opinions, prejudices and sentiments, according to their class or party.

1932. ("MASS EFFECTS IN MODERN LIFE," *STRAND MAGAZINE*; THOUGHTS, 184.)

Substitute "media and the internet" for "newspapers" and you have a very thought-provoking reflection on the superficiality of the modern "information revolution".

Latin

I was often uncertain whether the Ablative Absolute should end in "e" or "i" or "o" or "is" or "ibus"….Mr. Welldon seemed to be physically pained by a mistake being made in any of these letters. I remember that later on Mr. Asquith used to have just the same sort of look on his face when I sometimes adorned a Cabinet discussion by bringing out one of my few but faithful Latin quotations.

1930. (MEL, 36.)

Bishop Welldon was WSC's Harrow Headmaster; H. H. Asquith was the second Prime Minister Churchill served in Cabinet. WSC, although fairly incompetent at Latin, had to know some of it to enter Harrow. See "Personal experience" herein and Chapter 20, People...Asquith, Welldon.

Mathematics

We were arrived in an "Alice-in-Wonderland" world, at the portals of which stood "A Quadratic Equation." This with a strange grimace pointed the way to the Theory of Indices, which again handed on the intruder to the full rigours of the Binomial Theorem. Further dim chambers lighted by sullen, sulphurous fires were reputed to contain a dragon called the "Differential Calculus." But this monster was beyond the bounds appointed by the Civil Service Commissioners who regulated this stage of Pilgrim's heavy journey. We turned aside not indeed to the uplands of the Delectable Mountains, but into a strange corridor of things like anagrams and acrostics called Sines, Cosines and Tangents. Apparently they were very important, especially when multiplied by each other, or by themselves!….I have never met any of these creatures since.

1930. (MEL 40.)

Delectable Mountains (see also Chapter 29: Patience) is from a book Churchill read avidly as a boy, John Bunyan's Pilgrim's Progress *(1678); the phrase lodged in his capacious memory.*

Of course I had progressed far beyond Vulgar Fractions and the Decimal System.

1930. (MEL, 40.)

A vulgar fraction has a numerator and denominator above and below a horizontal line or slashmark, as opposed to a decimal number. The phrase stuck, and he used it several times. See Writer and Speaker... style.

I had a feeling once about Mathematics, that I saw it all—Depth beyond Depth was revealed to me—the Byss and the Abyss. I saw, as one might see the transit of Venus—or even the Lord Mayor's Show, a quantity passing through infinity and changing its sign from plus to minus. I saw exactly how it happened and why the tergiversation was inevitable: and how the one step involved all the others. It was like politics. But it was after dinner and I let it go!

1930. (MEL, 41.)

Metaphysics

The metaphysicians will have the last word and defy you to disprove their absurd propositions. I always rested upon the following argument which I devised for myself many years ago. We look up in the sky and see the sun. Our eyes are dazzled and our senses record the fact. So here is this great sun standing apparently on no better foundation than our physical senses. But happily there is a method, apart altogether from our physical senses, of testing the reality of the sun. It is by mathematics. By means of prolonged processes of mathematics, entirely separate from the senses, astronomers are able to calculate when an eclipse will occur. They predict by pure reason that a black spot will pass across the sun on a certain day. You go and look, and your sense of sight immediately tells you that their calculations are vindicated. So here you have the evidence of the senses reinforced by the entirely separate evidence of a vast independent process of mathematical reasoning….I am also at this point accustomed to reaffirm with emphasis my conviction that the sun is real, and also that it is hot—in fact as hot as Hell, and that if the metaphysicians doubt it they should go there and see.

1930. (MEL 131–2.)

The opposing strands of Metaphysics that fascinated Churchill were Plato's idea that what exists lies beyond experience; and the theories of Hume and Kant, who held that experience constitutes the only reality. Had Churchill had all three of them in a Cabinet, he probably would have formed a coalition.

National literature

A man's education should be the guiding line for the reading of his whole life, and I am certain that those who have made good use of their university studies will be convinced of the importance of reading the world's great books and the literature of their own land. They will know what to read and how to understand it.

1948, 12 MAY. UNIVERSITY OF OSLO.
(EUROPE, 326.)

Personal experience with education

The Hon. and Learned Member for the Launceston Division [John Fletcher Moulton] has given us a most lucid and interesting lecture. As one who had not the advantage of an academic career it filled me with awe and wonder, and must have awakened in the minds of Hon. Members who enjoyed that advantage

many recollections of their early academic days.

1902, 12 MAY.

John Fletcher Moulton, Baron Moulton (1844–1921) was a mathematician, barrister and judge, and an expert on explosions. WSC was commenting on his remarks on the latter. A Liberal MP in the early 1900s, Moulton headed the Explosives Department in World War I.

It was at the "Little Lodge" that I was first menaced with Education. The approach of a sinister figure described as "the Governess" was announced….

We continued to toil every day, not only at letters but at words, and also at what was much worse, figures….But the figures were tied into all sorts of tangles and did things to one another which it was extremely difficult to forecast with complete accuracy. You had to say what they did each time they were tied up together….In some cases these figures got into debt with one another: you had to borrow one or carry one, and afterwards you had to pay back the one you had borrowed.

1930. (MEL, 17.)

The "Little Lodge" was his home in Dublin.

In all the twelve years I was at school no one ever succeeded in making me write a Latin verse or learn any Greek except the alphabet.

1930. (MEL, 27.)

I had scarcely passed my twelfth birthday when I entered the inhospitable regions of examinations, through which for the next seven years I was destined to journey. These examinations were a great trial to me. The subjects which were dearest to the examiners were almost invariably those I fancied least. I would have liked to have been examined in history, poetry and writing essays. The examiners, on the other hand, were partial to Latin and mathematics. And their will prevailed. Moreover, the questions which they asked on both these subjects were almost invariably those to which I was unable to suggest a satisfactory answer. I should have liked to be asked to say what I knew. They always tried to ask what I did not know.

1930. (MEL, 29.)

I wrote my name at the top of the page. I wrote down the number of the question "I." After much reflection I put a bracket round it thus "(I)." But thereafter I could not think of anything connected with it that was either relevant or true. Incidentally there arrived from nowhere in particular a blot and several smudges.

1930. (MEL, 29.)

For more of this quotation see Chapter 20... Welldon. WSC's professed failure in his Latin exam is almost certainly myth.

Dr. Welldon, assured by Winston's teacher that he was capable of good work, and very much in admiration of Lord Randolph, would let very little stand in the way of young Churchill passing into Harrow Public School (Lee, 77).

It was a curious education. First because I approached it with an empty, hungry mind, and with fairly strong jaws; and what I got I bit; secondly because I had no one to tell me: "This is discredited." "You should read the answer to that by so and so; the two together will give you the gist of the argument." "There is a much better book on that subject," and so forth.

1930. (MEL, 126–7.)

On his self-education, obtained by reading books when stationed in Bangalore, India, 1896–99. See the introduction to this chapter.

My knowledge, such as it is, is not mainly derived from books and documents about foreign affairs, but from living through them for a long time.

1953, 11 MAY.

Privilege of education

Owing to the pressure of life and everyone having to earn their living, a university education of the great majority of those who enjoy that high privilege is usually acquired before twenty. These are great years for young people. The world of thought and history and the treasures of learning are laid open to them. They have the chance of broadening their minds, elevating their view and arming their moral convictions to all the resources that free and wealthy communities can bestow.

1946, 26 FEBRUARY. UNIVERSITY OF MIAMI. (SINEWS, 90–91.)

I never had the advantage of a university education. But it is a great privilege and the more widely extended, the better for any country. It should not be looked upon as something to end with youth but as a key to open many doors of thought and knowledge. A university education ought to be a guide to the reading of a lifetime.

1950, 10 OCTOBER, COPENHAGEN UNIVERSITY. (BALANCE, 387.)

Public Schools

I am all for the Public Schools but I do not want to go there again.

1930. (MEL, 53.)

In Britain, public schools are in fact private, and what Americans think of as public schools were grammar schools and secondary modern schools, many of which have recently been merged into comprehensive schools.

Hitler in one of his recent discourses, declared that the fight was between those who have been through the Adolf Hitler Schools and those who have been at Eton. Hitler has forgotten Harrow.

1940. 18 DECEMBER. HARROW SCHOOL. (UNRELENTING, 20.)

Royal Military College

...to those who enter the College direct from Eton or Harrow or any of the public schools, the life at Sandhurst is a pleasing emancipation, profitable to experience, agreeable to recall. It is a time of merriment and sport, a time of high hopes and good friends, of many pleasures and insignificant worries—a period of gratified ambitions and of attained ideals.

1896, DECEMBER. (*PALL MALL*; OB, CV1/1, 552.)

Letter to the editor, signed A Cornet of Horse. The Royal Military College at Sandhurst was later merged with the Royal Military Academy at Woolwich, to become the Royal Military Academy Sandhurst.

Socratic method

Then someone had used the phrase "the Socratic method." What was that? It was apparently a way of giving your friend his head in an argument and progging him into a pit by cunning questions. Who was Socrates, anyhow? A very argumentative Greek who had a nagging wife and was finally compelled to commit suicide because he was a nuisance! Still, he was beyond doubt a considerable person. He counted for a lot in the minds of learned people. I wanted "the Socrates story"....Evidently Socrates had called something into being long ago which was very explosive. Intellectual dynamite! A moral bomb! But there was nothing about it in The Queen's Regulations.

1896. (MEL, 124.)

Webster's College Dictionary defines "prog" as British slang meaning "to prowl about or forage".

Technology training

The first duty of the university is to teach wisdom, not a trade; character, not technicalities. We want a lot of engineers in the modern world, but we do not want a world of engineers. We want some scientists, but we must keep them in their proper place.

1948, 18 NOVEMBER. UNIVERSITY OF LONDON.
(EUROPE, 468.)

Repeated almost word for word at Copenhagen University on 10 October 1950.

25

PAINTING

"If Churchill were a painter by profession, he'd have no trouble making a living."
– Pablo Picasso [88]

"Painting is a companion with whom one may hope to walk a great part of life's journey." At his easel, 1930s.

Although Sir Winston spoke modestly of what he called "my daubs", his friend Sir John Lavery, an official artist in the First World War, said: "Had he chosen painting instead of statesmanship, I believe he would have been a great master with the brush."[89]

WSC himself was not so sure. General Eisenhower was being driven to meet Churchill at Chequers one day when the chauffeur, an amateur painter, asked if he might show one of his oils to the Prime Minister. Eisenhower (who also painted) said he would ask, and after dinner gave the chauffeur permission. Churchill said the chauffeur's work was very good – "but you, unlike myself, will be judged on talent alone".[90]

Churchill gave his paintings to people he admired and wanted to honour with the most personal of gifts. Presidents Roosevelt, Truman and Eisenhower, Viscount Montgomery and General George C. Marshall were among those who received such tokens of friendship and respect. Interestingly, he chose almost the same view of Marrakech for Truman as he had painted for Roosevelt in 1943 (his only painting during World War II).

---

88 Reynolds, Q., 128.
89 Soames, Painter, 24.
90 Kenneth Rendell to the editor, January 2008.

With his gift to Truman, Churchill enclosed a note: "This picture...is about as presentable as anything I can produce. It shows the beautiful panorama of the snow-capped Atlas mountains in Marrakech. This is the view I persuaded your predecessor [Roosevelt] to see before he left North Africa after the Casablanca Conference [in 1943]."[91] Truman replied: "I can't find words adequate to express my appreciation of the beautiful picture...I shall treasure the picture as long as I live and it will be one of the most valued possessions I will be able to leave to Margaret when I pass on."

Joyce C. Hall of Hallmark Cards, intrigued by this gentle aspect of the old lion, published Churchill paintings on Christmas cards in the 1950s and later arranged for an exhibit of WSC's original oils. With the exhibit in Kansas City, Truman came for a look. "Damn good," he said of his old friend's oils. "At least you can tell what they are and that is more than you can say for a lot of these modern painters." Hall asked Truman if he would like to paint. "Hell no," said the former president, "but I could beat these moderns."[92]

For those interested in authoritative accounts of Churchill's oil painting hobby, three books are essential: his own *Painting as a Pastime*, first published in volume form in 1948 and frequently in print since; his daughter Mary Soames's *Winston Churchill: His Life as a Painter* (London: Collins, 1990), a warm account from the family side and beautifully illustrated with his work; and the complete catalogue of his nearly 600 paintings by David Coombs and Minnie Churchill: *Winston Churchill: His Life Through His Paintings* (London: Pegasus, 2003).

Except for *Painting as a Pastime*, Churchill's remarks about the subject are limited; I have added some of his comments on the art of others, including the horrendous eightieth birthday painting by Graham Sutherland, and the Chartwell loggia murals painted by his artist-nephew John Spencer Churchill.

The arts

Ill fares the race which fails to salute the arts with the reverence and delight which are their due.

1938, 30 April, London. (CS VI, 5949.)

[The Director of the National Gallery, Kenneth Clark, suggested that the paintings in the National Gallery should be sent from London to Canada for safekeeping.]

No—bury them in caves and cellars. None must go. We are going to beat them.

1940, 1 June. (OB VI, 449.)

New York's The Village Voice *started a long-running internet thread to the effect that Churchill ordered there should be no diminution in the arts during the war, saying, "After all, that's what we are fighting for." No such* utterance has been found in the canon, although this comes close.

Beauty and art

Art is to beauty what honour is to honesty, an unnatural allotropic form.

1899. (Savrola, 75.)

"Bottlescape"

Fetch me associate and fraternal bottles to form a bodyguard to this majestic container.

Circa 1930s. Peregrine Churchill
to the editor.

Churchill gave the name "Bottlescape" to one of his famous still life paintings. According to his nephew Peregrine, WSC received a huge bottle of brandy one Christmas and sent the children scurrying around Chartwell to find other bottles to paint with it.

---

91 OB VIII, 615. The painting was auctioned by Truman's daughter in November 2007, making £468,700; a July 2007 auction saw a record of £1,000,000 for a Churchill painting, "Chartwell Landscape with Sheep", originally presented to Clare Booth Luce.
92 *Kansas City Times*, 31 January 1958. Larson, Philip and Susan, "'When You Care Enough': Joyce Hall and Hallmark's Churchill Connection," *Finest Hour* 137, Winter 2007–08.

Cézanne

I was shown a picture by Cézanne of a blank wall of a house, which he had made instinct with the most delicate lights and colours.

1922, JANUARY. ("PAINTING AS A PASTIME," *STRAND MAGAZINE*; THOUGHTS, 232.)

Churchill admired and was inspired by the French impressionists.

Colour

I cannot pretend to feel impartial about the colours. I rejoice with the brilliant ones, and am genuinely sorry for the poor browns. When I get to heaven I mean to spend a considerable portion of my first million years in painting, and so get to the bottom of the subject. But then I shall require a still gayer palette than I get here below. I expect orange and vermilion will be the darkest, dullest colours upon it, and beyond them there will be a whole range of wonderful new colours which will delight the celestial eye.

1922, JANUARY. ("PAINTING AS A PASTIME," *STRAND MAGAZINE*; THOUGHTS, 229–30.)

Painting as a Pastime, first published in the Strand Magazine in two parts, December 1921 and January 1922, was republished in Thoughts and Adventures (1932), and in single-volume form in 1948.

Companionship

Painting is a companion with whom one may hope to walk a great part of life's journey.
Age cannot wither her, nor custom stale Her infinite variety.

1921, DECEMBER. ("PAINTING AS A PASTIME," *STRAND MAGAZINE*; THOUGHTS, 220.)

The last two lines are from Shakespeare's Antony and Cleopatra (II:2, 240–41).

Composition

Well, no picture can be painted without due regard to the background.

1948, 16 NOVEMBER. (UNITE, 449.)

Not really said about painting (WSC was speaking on the Iron and Steel Bill), but this is best classified among his artistic utterances.

Joy of

Painting is a friend who makes no undue demands, excites to no exhausting pursuits, keeps faithful pace even with feeble steps, and holds her canvas as a screen between us and the envious eyes of Time or the surly advance of Decrepitude.

Happy are the painters, for they shall not be lonely. Light and colour, peace and hope, will keep them company to the end, or almost to the end, of the day.

1921, DECEMBER. ("PAINTING AS A PASTIME," *STRAND MAGAZINE*; THOUGHTS, 220–21.)

Landscapes

...a tree doesn't complain that I haven't done it justice.

CIRCA 1930S. (SANDYS, 141.)

WSC was sometimes asked why he preferred landscape painting to portrait painting.

...all the greatest landscapes have been painted indoors...In a dim cellar the Dutch or Italian master recreated the gleaming ice of a Netherlands carnival or the lustrous sunshine of Venice or the Campagna.

1922, JANUARY. ("PAINTING AS A PASTIME," *STRAND MAGAZINE*; THOUGHTS, 233.)

Luxury and art

It is important in the legislation of a country to draw a clear distinction between art and luxury, between the work of art— "a thing of beauty and a joy for ever"—and a mere consumable article of indulgence or ostentation.

1926, 26 APRIL.

Quote adapted from Keats's "Endymion".

Modern art

The portrait is a remarkable example of modern art. It certainly combines force and candour.

1954, 9 NOVEMBER. WESTMINSTER HALL, LONDON. (ALLIANCE, 202.)

This drew a laugh, but Churchill actually despised his portrait by Graham Sutherland, presented by both Houses of Parliament on his eightieth birthday. He so hated it that, after his death, his wife had it burned.

Murals

Can't we get rid of this vast white space?…I always survey the whole scene with greater clarity if I attack the white areas first and afterwards concentrate on the pockets of resistance.

1933. (CHURCHILL, J., 100–01.)

WSC's nephew Johnnie was painting the murals celebrating the victories of the First Duke of Marlborough in the garden loggia at Chartwell, and explained to WSC that his method was "to start at the top and work downward, thus avoiding any danger of messing up the bottom part".

Muse of

Like a sea-beast fished up from the depths, or a diver too suddenly hoisted, my veins threatened to burst from the fall in pressure. I had great anxiety and no means of relieving it; I had vehement convictions and small power to give effect to them.…I was forced to remain a spectator of the tragedy, placed cruelly in a front seat. And then it was that the Muse of Painting came to my rescue—out of charity and out of chivalry, because after all she had nothing to do with me—and said, "Are these toys any good to you? They amuse some people."

1921, DECEMBER. ("PAINTING AS A PASTIME," STRAND MAGAZINE; THOUGHTS, 223–4.)

Churchill is referring to his dismissal from the Admiralty in 1915, after which, during a cheerless holiday, he took up painting.

Starting out

Having bought the colours, an easel, and a canvas, the next step was to begin. But what a step to take! The palette gleamed with beads of colour; fair and white rose the canvas; the empty brush hung poised, heavy with destiny, irresolute in the air. My hand seemed arrested by a silent veto. But after all the sky on this occasion was unquestionably blue, and a pale blue at that. There could be no doubt that blue paint mixed with white should be put on the top part of the canvas. One really does not need to have had an artist's training to see that. It is a starting-point open to all. So very gingerly I mixed a little blue paint on the

palette with a very small brush, and then with infinite precaution made a mark about as big as a bean upon the affronted snow-white shield. It was a challenge, a deliberate challenge; but so subdued, so halting, indeed so cataleptic, that it deserved no response. At that moment the loud approaching sound of a motor-car was heard in the drive. From this chariot there stepped swiftly and lightly none other than the gifted wife of Sir John Lavery. "Painting! But what are you hesitating about? Let me have a brush, the big one." Splash into the turpentine, wallop into the blue and the white, frantic flourish on the palette, clean no longer, and then several large, fierce strokes and slashes of blue on the absolutely cowering canvas. Anyone could see that it could not hit back. No evil fate avenged the jaunty violence. The canvas grinned in helplessness before me. The spell was broken. The sickly inhibitions rolled away. I seized the largest brush and fell upon my victim with berserk fury. I have never felt any awe of a canvas since.

1921, DECEMBER. ("PAINTING AS A PASTIME," STRAND MAGAZINE; THOUGHTS, 224–5.)

Churchill had the benefit of expert coaches, among them Sir John and Lady Lavery, who encouraged him after he took up oil painting seriously in 1915. It is worth noting, however, that his mother, herself an accomplished amateur artist, taught him to draw and to paint as a boy (Lee, 36).

Subjects

The whole world is open with all its treasures. The simplest objects have their beauty.

1922, JANUARY. ("PAINTING AS A PASTIME," STRAND MAGAZINE; THOUGHTS, 227.)

Good gracious! what there is to admire and how little time there is to see it in!

1922, JANUARY. ("PAINTING AS A PASTIME," STRAND MAGAZINE; THOUGHTS, 228.)

Technique

…trying to paint a picture is…like trying to fight a battle. It is, if anything, more exciting than fighting it successfully. But the principle is the same. It is the same kind of problem as unfolding a long, sustained, interlocked argument.

1922, JANUARY. ("PAINTING AS A PASTIME," STRAND MAGAZINE; THOUGHTS, 226.)

If the finished product looks like a work of art, then it *is* a work of art!

1946. RONALD GOLDING TO THE EDITOR.

WSC's retort when his detective, observing him projecting a magic lantern image of an unfinished scene on to a canvas to guide to his brushstrokes, said, "Looks a bit like cheating."

Tiepolo

The old palace where we dined tonight is quite worth seeing—beautiful big rooms with ceilings by Tiepolo (so I was told)—do you admire him or not? It appears to me to belong to the whipped cream and sponge cake style of painting.

1909, 15 SEPTEMBER, WÜRZBURG, GERMANY. (OB, CV2/2, 911.)

WSC to his wife.

Tradition vs. innovation

The function of such an institution as the Royal Academy is to hold a middle course between tradition and innovation. Without tradition art is a flock of sheep without a shepherd. Without innovation it is a corpse....It is not the function of the Royal Academy to run wildly after every curious novelty.

1953, 30 APRIL. ROYAL ACADEMY BANQUET, LONDON. (ALLIANCE, 40.)

26
RELIGION

"I expect that the battle of Britain is about to begin. Upon this battle depends the survival of Christian civilisation."[93]

"It is no exaggeration to say that the future of the whole world and the hopes of a broadening civilization founded upon Christian ethics depend upon the relations between the British Empire or Commonwealth of Nations and the USA."[94]

"I accumulated in those years so fine a surplus in the Bank of Observance..."
Daughter Mary's wedding, February 1947.

Although he had some very religious friends, like Lord Hugh Cecil, Churchill was not a religious man. He was introduced to religious diversity early, being brought up as "High Church", but with a Nanny "who enjoyed a very Low Church form of piety". When in rebellious mood he would tell Nanny Everest "the worst thing that he could think of...that he would go out and 'worship idols'".[95]

After his self-education as a young officer in India, when he read all the popular challenges to orthodox religion, like Darwin's *Origin of Species* and Wynwood-Reade's *The*

---

93 WSC, House of Commons, 18 June 1940.
94 WSC, Pilgrims Society, London, 9 January 1941, CS VI, 6326.
95 Rowse, 327.

Martyrdom of Man, Churchill evolved into what we might term an "optimistic agnostic". He spoke jocularly of the Almighty, suggesting that he himself had made so many deposits in the "Bank of Observance" as a boy that he had been "drawing confidently upon it ever since", and that he was not a "pillar of the church but a buttress".[96] He was sure that if and when he met with the final judgment, it would be "in accordance with the principles of English Common Law".[97]

Why then did Churchill refer so frequently to "Christian civilisation"? First because as well as Darwin he had absorbed the King James Bible, impressed by its beautiful phraseology and the ethics it expounded; and second because he believed its principles applied broadly to all of mankind regardless of religion.

Unlike fundamentalists, he did not accept the Bible as rote. He saw no need to resolve its stories with modern science. Why bother? he asked. "If you are the recipient of a message which cheers your heart and fortifies your soul",[98] what need is there to ask whether the imagery of the ancients is exactly, scientifically, feasible?

When Churchill in speeches referred to "Christian civilisation" (a phrase I have actually seen edited out of certain modern renditions) he did not mean to exclude Jews or Buddhists or Muslims. He meant those words in a much broader sense. Just as, to Churchill, the word "man" meant humankind, his allusions to Christianity embodied principles he considered universal: the Ten Commandments, a "judgemental" set of rules now expunged from certain public places; the Sermon on the Mount; the Golden Rule; charity; forgiveness; courage.Times change. If a President or Prime Minister went round discussing "Christian civilisation" today, a thousand Thought Police would descend screeching out of the sky to proclaim his excommunication from the Church of the Politically Correct. It is not my brief to suggest his reactions to modern situations, but surely Churchill would be mystified by this – as indeed would the Jews, Buddhists and Muslims of his time who wholeheartedly endorsed what he said about the war they were in together. And yet we consider these to be more enlightened times....

Afterlife

Only faith in a life after death in a brighter world where dear ones will meet again—only that and the measured tramp of time can give consolation.

1942, 8 SEPTEMBER.

You know, most people are going to be very surprised when they get to Heaven. They are looking forward to meeting fascinating people like Napoleon and Julius Caesar. But they'll probably never even be able to find them, because there will be so many millions of other people there too—Indians and Chinamen and people like that. Everyone will have equal rights in Heaven. That will be the real Welfare State.

And then there will be the cherubs. How strange it will be to have them around. Do you know the story of the French priest who was so holy that one day in his church he saw fluttering above him a throng of cherubs? He was not only holy, but polite, and begged them to sit down. "*Mais*," replied the cherubs, "*nous n'avons pas de quoi*"...

CIRCA 1946. (GRAEBNER, 24–5.)

The French translates as, "but we haven't anything to sit on".

[I do] not believe in another world; only in black velvet—eternal sleep.

1953, 2 JULY. (MORAN, 444.)

Churchill was non-committal on the possibility of an afterlife. To suggest that this was a double-entendre with a popular drink would be a stretch. (Paraphrased in the first person.)

---

96 See below under "Observance".
97 See below under "Final Judgment".
98 See below under "Faith vs. Reason".

He will take my skin with him, a kind of advance guard, into the next world.

1954, 21 JANUARY. (MORAN, 556.)

WSC on the death of Richard Molyneux, a fellow soldier who had been wounded at Omdurman and had received a skin graft from Churchill at that time. See Personal...cuticle.

Biblical shorthand

[WSC to General Wavell after initial successes in North Africa]: St. Matthew, chapter VII, verse 7.

[Wavell replied, "St. James, chapter I, verse 17."]

1940, 18 DECEMBER. (WW2 II, 543.)

The verses, which neither WSC nor Wavell had to quote to each other, were: "Ask, and it shall be given you; seek, and ye shall find; knock, and it shall be opened unto you" and "Every good gift and every perfect gift is from above, and cometh down from the Father of lights, with whom is no variableness, neither shadow of turning." Wavell's "St." is misplaced; his quotation is from "The General Epistle of James".

[I wrote to Roosevelt:] "See St. John chapter XIV verses 1 to 4." On reading this through more carefully after it had gone, I was a little concerned lest, apart from a shadow of unintended profanity, it should be thought I was taking too much upon myself and thus giving offence. However, the President brushed all objections aside and our plans continued unchanged.

1943, 21 NOVEMBER. (LOWENHEIM, 394; WW2 V, 289.)

Roosevelt had cabled that Cairo, their chosen meeting place, was vulnerable to German air attack. Churchill, assured there was strong protection and in a Bible-quoting mood, cabled the reference:

1. Let not your heart be troubled; ye believe in God, believe also in me.
2. In my Father's house are many mansions: if it were not so I would have told you. I go to prepare a place for you.
2. And if I go and prepare a place for you, I will come again, and receive you unto myself; that where I am, there ye may be also.

4. *And whither I go ye know, and the way ye know.*

For origins of this Biblical allusion see Appendix IV. See also Chapter 6, Britain, Empire and Commonwealth....Commonwealth of many mansions.

Bishops

I have made more bishops than anyone since St. Augustine.

1942, 7 AUGUST. (MORAN, 57.)

WSC to General Smuts. St. Augustine arrived from Rome to convert the English to Christianity in 597 AD. In 601 he was made Archbishop of Canterbury.

Christian ethics

We can find nothing better than Christian Ethics on which to build and the more closely we follow the Sermon on the Mount, the more likely we are to succeed in our endeavours.

1941, 25 JANUARY, CHEQUERS. (OB VI, 995.)

Reconstructed in the first person from Sir Martin Gilbert's narrative of WSC's meeting with Harry Hopkins, Roosevelt's special emissary to Britain. WSC was referring to Christian principles, not the Christian religion.

It is baffling to reflect that what men call honour does not correspond always to Christian ethics.

1948. (WW2 I, 251.)

The flame of Christian ethics is still our highest guide. To guard and cherish it is our first interest, both spiritually and materially. The fulfilment of spiritual duty in our daily life is vital to our survival. Only by bringing it into perfect application can we hope to solve for ourselves the problems of this world and not of this world alone.

1949, 31 MARCH. MASSACHUSETTS INSTITUTE OF TECHNOLOGY, BOSTON. (BALANCE, 48.)

Christ's story was unequalled and his death to save sinners unsurpassed; moreover the Sermon on the Mount was the last word in ethics.

CIRCA 1953. (COLVILLE, CHURCHILLIANS, 157.)

WSC to Viscount Montgomery, as described by John Colville, who said that Monty would often visit, firing questions at WSC "as if from a machine gun".

Christianity

...our duty [is] to preserve the structure of humane, enlightened, Christian society. Once the downward steps were taken, once one's moral and intellectual feet slipped upon the slope of plausible indulgence, there would be found no halting-place short of a general Paganism and Hedonism, possibly agreeable from time to time in this world of fleeting trials and choices....

1931, FEBRUARY. ("PERSONAL CONTACTS," *STRAND MAGAZINE*; THOUGHTS, 36.)

Church and State

...the State cannot control the Church in spiritual matters; it can only divorce it.

1928, 14 JUNE.

Faith-healing

There was nothing more remarkable than this doctrine of faith-healing. The principle was very simple; you said a thing was so and it was so; or you said it was not so and it was not so.... With regard to this faith cure, the faith must be absolute, or the cure did not work.

1905, 3 APRIL. (CS I, 459.)

In a speech on Army Estimates, WSC was doubting the "faith" of Prime Minister Balfour, who had declared there was no need for a home Army since invasion of Britain was not possible.

Faith vs. Reason

...I have always been surprised to see some of our Bishops and clergy making such heavy weather about reconciling the Bible story with modern scientific and historical knowledge. Why do they want to reconcile them? If you are the recipient of a message which cheers your heart and fortifies your soul, which promises you reunion with those you have loved in a world of larger opportunity and wider sympathies, why should you worry about the shape or colour of the travel-stained envelope; whether it is duly stamped, whether the date on the postmark is right or wrong?

1930. (MEL, 130–31.)

There was a time when the Age of Faith endeavoured to prevent the Age of Reason, and another time when the Age of Reason endeavoured to destroy the Age of Faith. Tolerance was one of the chief features of the great liberalising movements which were the glory of the latter part of the nineteenth century, by which states of society were reached where the most fervent devotion to religion subsisted side by side with the fullest exercise of free thought. We may well recur to those bygone days, from whose standards of enlightenment, compassion, and hopeful progress the terrible 20th century has fallen so far.

1945, 16 NOVEMBER, BELGIAN SENATE AND CHAMBER, BRUSSELS. (SINEWS, 43.)

Final Judgment

Mr. President, I hope you have your answer ready for that hour when you and I stand before St. Peter and he says, "I understand you two are responsible for putting off those atomic bombs."

[Robert Lovett: Are you sure, Prime Minister, that you are going to be in the same place as the President for that interrogation?]

Lovett, my vast respect for the Creator of this universe and countless others gives me assurance that He would not condemn a man without a hearing.

[Lovett: True, but your hearing would not be likely to start in the Supreme Court, or necessarily in the same court as the President's. It could be in another court far away.]

I don't doubt that, but, wherever it is, it will be in accordance with the principles of English Common Law....I waive a jury, but not *habeas corpus*. You'll not put me in any black hole!

1953. CLARK CLIFFORD TO THE EDITOR.

Before Truman left office in early 1953, Churchill and the British Ambassador, Sir Roger Makins, hosted the President and his colleagues, Robert Lovett, W. Averell Harriman, General Omar Bradley and Secretary of State Dean Acheson.

God

I don't think much of God. He hasn't put enough in the pool.

1907. (DALTON, *NEW STATESMAN*, 1965.)

Musing on the huge disparity of life between Africans and Europeans.

[Evidence that God exists] is the existence of Lenin and Trotsky, for whom a hell [is] needed.

1929. ON THE ATLANTIC. (GILBERT, SEARCH, 227.)

WSC to Leopold Amery.

...we have our faith that the universe is ruled by a Supreme Being and in fulfilment of a sublime moral purpose...

1948, 21 MAY. WESTMINSTER ABBEY, LONDON. (UNITE, 338.)

At the unveiling of the Commando Memorial.

I wonder what God thinks of the things His creatures have invented. Really, it's surprising he has allowed it—but then I suppose He has so many things to think of, not only us, but all His worlds. I wouldn't have His job for anything. Mine is hard enough, but His is much more difficult. And—umph—He can't even resign.

1949. CHARTWELL. (GRAEBNER, 25.)

I am ready to meet my Maker. Whether my Maker is prepared for the great ordeal of meeting me is another matter.

1949, 30 NOVEMBER. (LONGFORD, 206.)

The old man is very good to me. I could not have managed this [Korean] situation had I been in Attlee's place. I should have been called a war-monger.
[David Maxwell Fyfe: "What old man?"] God, Sir Donald.

1950, 28 JUNE. (NICOLSON III, 191.)

David Maxwell Fyfe (1900–67), politician and jurist, knighted 1942, became Viscount Kilmuir in 1954, advanced to an Earldom, 1962. WSC always referred to him as "Sir Donald". A curiosity: he was married to Rex Harrison's sister.

Heaven

...After I've been there awhile, the good Lord will have to form a Government. And He will certainly call upon me.

Undated. (Sir John Colville in "Churchill and the Italian Campaign," by Ward B. Chamberlin, Jr., Proceedings of the International Churchill Societies 1990–1991, 116.)

Hindus vs. Moslems

While the Hindu elaborates his argument, the Moslem sharpens his sword. Between these two races and creeds...the gulf is impassable.

1931, 18 MARCH. ALBERT HALL, LONDON. (BROAD, 231.)

Islam

That religion, which above all others was founded and propagated by the sword—the tenets and principles of which are instinct with incentives to slaughter and which in three continents has produced fighting breeds of men—stimulates a wild and merciless fanaticism. The love of plunder, always a characteristic of hill tribes, is fostered by the spectacle of opulence and luxury which, to their eyes, the cities and plains of the south display. A code of honour not less punctilious than that of old Spain is supported by vendettas as implacable as those of Corsica.

1898. (MALAKAND, 3–4.)

Several generations have elapsed since the nations of the West have drawn the sword in religious controversy, and the evil memories of the gloomy past have soon faded in the strong, clear light of Rationalism and human sympathy. Indeed it is evident that Christianity, however degraded and distorted by cruelty and intolerance, must always exert a modifying influence on men's passions, and protect them from the more violent forms of fanatical fever, as we are protected from smallpox by vaccination. But the Mahommedan religion increases, instead of lessening, the fury of intolerance. It was originally propagated by the sword, and ever since its votaries have been subject, above the people of all other creeds, to this form of madness. In a moment the fruits of patient toil, the prospects of material prosperity, the fear of death itself, are flung aside. The more emotional Pathans are powerless to resist. All rational considerations are forgotten. Seizing their weapons, they become *Ghazis*—as dangerous and as sensible as mad dogs: fit only to be treated as such. While the more generous spirits among the tribesmen become convulsed in an ecstasy of religious bloodthirstiness, poorer and more material souls derive additional impulses from the influence of others, the hopes of plunder and the joy of fighting. Thus whole nations are roused to arms. Thus the Turks repel their enemies, the Arabs of the Soudan break the British squares, and the rising on the Indian frontier spreads far and wide. In each case civilisation is confronted with militant Mahommedanism. The forces of progress clash with those of reaction. The religion of blood and war is face to face with that of peace. Luckily the religion of peace is usually the better armed.

1898. (MALAKAND, 26–7.)

How dreadful are the curses which Mohammedanism lays on its votaries! Besides the fanatical frenzy, which is as dangerous in a man as hydrophobia in a dog, there is this fearful fatalistic apathy. The effects are apparent in many countries. Improvident habits, slovenly systems of agriculture, sluggish methods of commerce, and insecurity of property exist wherever the followers of the Prophet rule or live. A degraded sensualism deprives this life of its grace and refinement; the next of its dignity and sanctity. The fact that in Mohammedan law every woman must *belong* to some man as his absolute property—either as a child, a wife, or a concubine—must delay the final extinction of slavery until the faith of Islam has ceased to be a great power among men. Individual Moslems may show splendid qualities. Thousands become the brave and loyal soldiers of the Queen; all know how to die: but the influence of the religion paralyses the social developement [sic] of those who follow it. No stronger retrograde force exists in the world. Far from being moribund, Mohammedanism is a militant and proselytising faith. It has already spread throughout Central Africa, raising fearless warriors at every step; and were it not that Christianity is sheltered in the strong arms of science—the science against which it had vainly struggled—the civilisation of modern Europe might fall, as fell the civilisation of ancient Rome.

1899. (RIVER II, 248–50.)

...there was nothing *dulce et decorum* about the Dervish dead; nothing of the dignity of unconquerable manhood; all was filthy corruption.

Yet these were as brave men as ever walked the earth. The conviction was borne in on me that their claim beyond the grave in respect of a valiant death was not less good than that which any of our countrymen could make.

1899. (RIVER II, 221.)

The phrase dulce et decorum *comes from the aphorism* "Dulce et decorum est pro patria mori *(It is sweet and honourable to die for one's country),"* Horace, Odes, *Book III: 2, line 13. But it was the World War I poet Wilfred Owen, who died a week before the Armistice in 1918, who returned the quotation to currency in his lines about the horrors of that war:*

> You would not tell with such high zest
> To children ardent for some desperate
>   glory,
> *The old lie:* Dulce et decorum est
> Pro patria mori.

What the horn is to the rhinoceros, what the sting is to the wasp, the Mohammedan faith was to the Arabs of the Soudan—a faculty of offence or defence.

It was all this and no more. It was not the reason of the revolt. It strengthened, it characterised, but it did not cause.

1899. (RIVER I, 33–4.)

Only the Mahdi's wives, if we may credit Slatin, "rejoiced secretly in their hearts at the death of their husband and master," and, since they were henceforth to be doomed to an enforced and inviolable chastity, the cause of their satisfaction is as obscure, as its manifestation was unnatural.

1899. (RIVER I, 116.)

WSC refers to Fire and Sword in the Sudan *(1896) by Sir Rudolf Carl von Slatin (1857–1932), Anglo-Austrian soldier and administrator in the Sudan under General Charles Gordon.*

Judaism

The conflict between good and evil which proceeds unceasingly in the breast of man nowhere reaches such an intensity as in the Jewish race....We owe to the Jews in the Christian revelation a system of ethics which, even if it were entirely separated from the supernatural, would be incomparably the most precious possession of mankind, worth in fact the fruits of all other wisdom and learning put together. On that system and by that faith there has been built out of the wreck of the Roman Empire the whole of our existing civilization.

1920, 8 FEBRUARY. (ZIONISM VS. BOLSHEVISM, *ILLUSTRATED SUNDAY HERALD*; ESSAYS IV, 26.)

Personally, my heart is full of sympathy for Zionism. This sympathy has existed for a long time, since twelve years ago, when I was in contact with the Manchester Jews. I believe that the establishment of a Jewish National Home in Palestine will be a blessing to the whole world....

1921, 29 MARCH. (GILBERT, JEWS, 56.)

WSC before planting a tree on the building site on Mount Scopus of the future Hebrew University.

It has been well said that wherever there are three Jews it will be found that there are two Prime Ministers and one leader of the Opposition. The same is true [of the Greeks] ....No two cities have counted more with mankind than Athens and Jerusalem. Their messages in religion, philosophy, and art have been the main guiding lights of modern faith and culture. Centuries of foreign rule and indescribable, endless oppression leave them still living, active communities and forces in the modern world, quarrelling among themselves with insatiable vivacity. Personally I have always been on the side of both, and believed in their invincible power to survive internal strife and the world tides threatening their extinction.

1952. (WW2 V, 470–71.)

Missionaries

The life of a missionary is one of hazard; he leaves his home and his friends and goes out to dwell among the heathen, living their lives, adopting their customs, sharing their victuals, and hoping that by precept and example he may gradually raise them to a higher outlook of existence and destiny. Certainly, his life must be very exciting, because he is dependent upon the caprice or temper of the natives or their chief.

1929, 3 JULY.

Observance

Hitherto I had dutifully accepted everything I had been told....I always had to go once a week to church....I accumulated in those years so fine a surplus in the Bank of Observance that I have been drawing confidently upon it ever since. Weddings, christenings, and funerals have brought in a steady annual income, and I have never made too close enquiries about the state of my account. It might well even be that I should find an overdraft.

1930. (MEL, 127–8.)

I am not a pillar of the church but a buttress— I support it from the outside.

CIRCA 1954. (OB VIII, 1161.)

Recollection of Sir Winston's private secretary, Sir Anthony Montague Browne.

Pharisees

Their faults were many. Whose faults are few?

1888, 26 MAY. (GILBERT, JEWS, 1.)

From an essay Churchill, aged thirteen, wrote at Harrow entitled, "Palestine in the time of John the Baptist".

Prayer in Russia

I see them guarding their homes, where mothers and wives pray—ah yes, for there are times when all pray—for the safety of their loved ones....

1941, 22 JUNE. BROADCAST, LONDON.
(UNRELENTING, 171.)

Revolution and religion

It is, I believe, an historical fact that the revolt of a great population has never been caused solely or even mainly by religious enthusiasm.

1899. (RIVER I, 34.)

To Professor Clifford Orwin, considering this remark at a Churchill Centre panel on The River War, *the proposition that religion was never the "main" reason for a popular rebellion "seems questionable. Was it not, for example, the 'main' reason for the Sepoy rebellion?" (The Rebellion, in 1857, was when Muslim soldiers from Bengal mutinied at Meerut, near Delhi, and offered their services to the Mughal emperor.) Readers may think of more recent examples.*

27

SCIENCE AND
MEDICINE

*"I have always considered that the substitution of the internal
combustion engine for the horse marked a very gloomy milestone in
the progress of mankind."*[99]

*"The medical profession at least cannot complain of unemployment
through lack of raw material."* Inspecting nurses, World War I.

hurchill and Science had a nodding acquaintance. WSC would nod respectfully to it,
and Science would occasionally nod back. He had of course no scientific training
whatever. On a personal level he tilted towards tradition, joking that man's "trusty
friend the horse" had been replaced with the "infernal combustion engine",[100] decidedly
preferring a public speech to radio, and radio to television. When forced to take science or
medicine into account, he tried to rely on common sense. Having once pronounced the
value of human microbes in warding off disease, he added: "If this is not scientifically
correct, it ought to be."[101]

For really serious business – and of course his career often required scientific expertise of a high order – Churchill relied on capable advisers, most notably his friend

99 WSC, House of Commons, 24 June 1952. Halle, Irrepressible, 312.
100 Harvard University, 6 September 1943. Onwards, 182.
101 WW2 II, 317.

Frederick Lindemann, Professor of Experimental Philosophy and Director of the Clarendon Laboratory at Oxford. "The Prof" had the unique advantage of being able to explain the most complex scientific treatises on Churchill's always-preferred "one sheet of paper".

Churchill well recognised the ability of science to end the world, and at the same time to usher in an unprecedented era of prosperity, if only people – that weak link in the chain of destiny – could determine how to get along with each other and work out their differences short of war.

I have introduced a few modern subject lines to tag certain uncanny pronouncements. "Energy independence" was not widely mooted in Churchill's day; yet he saw the need for it and recommended conversion to oil using England's "immense deposits of Kimmeridge clay". When he said that "ever-increasing dependence upon [foreign sources of oil] ought to arouse serious and timely reflection",[102] he could have been speaking yesterday. What he said about leaded paint and mosquito eradication was remarkably close to what we might say today. His speculations on the progress of science and the possibility of life on other worlds, under a title I could not resist ("Space: the Final Frontier") are perfectly in keeping with modern concepts.

Advances in medicine

…we ought to have saints' days to commemorate the great discoveries which have been made for all mankind, and perhaps for all time—or for whatever time may be left to us. Nature, like many of our modern statesmen, is prodigal of pain. I should like to find a day when we can take a holiday, a day of jubilation when we can fête good Saint Anaesthesia and chaste and pure Saint Antiseptic.

1947, 10 SEPTEMBER. GUILDHALL, LONDON.
(EUROPE, 138.)

Advances in science

At this moment in history the broad, toiling masses in every country have for the first time the opportunity of a fuller and less burdened life. Science is at hand to spread a more bountiful table than has ever been offered to the millions and to the tens of millions. Shorter hours of labour, greater assurances against individual misfortune: a wider if a simpler culture: a more consciously realized sense of social justice, an easier and a more equal society—these are the treasures which after all these generations and centuries of impotence and confusion, are now within the reach of mankind.

1938, 9 MAY. FREE TRADE HALL, MANCHESTER.
(BLOOD, 20.)

We all speak with great respect of science. Indeed, we have to. One of my great friends, Lord Hugh Cecil, has recently defined science as organised curiosity. We must be careful not to discover too much, not to discover things of such wide implication that our immature civilisation is incapable of manipulating and employing them.

1948, 12 MAY. UNIVERSITY OF OSLO.
(EUROPE, 327.)

It is arguable whether the human race have been gainers by the march of science beyond the steam engine. Electricity opens a field of infinite conveniences to ever greater numbers, but they may well have to pay dearly for them. But anyhow in my thought I stop short of the internal combustion engine which has made the world so much smaller. Still more must we fear the consequences of entrusting to a human race so little different from their predecessors of the so-called barbarous ages such awful agencies as the atomic bomb. Give me the horse.

1951, 10 JULY. ROYAL COLLEGE OF PHYSICIANS, LONDON. (STEMMING, 91.)

Air, conquest of

The conquest of the air and the perfection of the art of flying fulfilled the dream which for thousands of years had glittered in human

---

102 House of Commons, 24 April 1928.

imagination. Certainly it was a marvellous and romantic event. Whether the bestowal of this gift upon an immature civilization composed of competing nations whose nationalization grew with every advance of democracy and who were as yet devoid of international organization, whether this gift was a blessing or a curse has yet to be proved.

1949, 31 MARCH. MASSACHUSETTS INSTITUTE OF TECHNOLOGY, BOSTON. (BALANCE, 43.)

Anaesthesia

With me the nitrous-oxide trance usually takes this form: the sanctum is occupied by alien powers. I see the absolute truth and explanation of things, but something is left out which upsets the whole, so by a larger sleep of the mind I have to see a greater truth and a more complete explanation which comprises the erring element. Nevertheless, there is still something left out. So we have to take a still wider sweep. This almost breaks mortal comprehension. It is beyond anything the human mind was ever meant to master. The process continues inexorably. Depth beyond depth of unendurable truth opens. I have, therefore, always regarded the nitrous-oxide trance as a mere substitution of mental for physical pain.

1932, 4–5 JANUARY. ("MY NEW YORK MISADVENTURE," DAILY MAIL; ESSAYS IV, 94.)

This reflection is part of an article describing Churchill's near-death experience when he was knocked down and nearly killed by a car after looking the wrong way while crossing Fifth Avenue in New York City.

Cancer

You cannot cure cancer by a majority. What is wanted is a remedy.

1930, 19 JUNE.

Cholera

To all, the time was one of trial, almost of terror. The violence of the battle may be cheaply braved, but the insidious attacks of disease appal the boldest. Death moved continually about the ranks of the army—not the death they had been trained to meet unflinchingly, the death in high enthusiasm and the pride of life, with all the world to weep or cheer; but a silent, unnoticed, almost ignominious summons, scarcely less sudden and far more painful than the bullet or the sword-cut.

1899. (RIVER I, 243.)

Disease

The discoveries of healing science must be the inheritance of all. That is clear. Disease must be attacked, whether it occurs in the poorest or the richest man or woman, simply on the ground that it is the enemy; and it must be attacked just in the same way as the fire brigade will give its full assistance to the humblest cottage as readily as to the most important mansion.

1944, 2 MARCH. ROYAL COLLEGE OF PHYSICIANS, LONDON. (DAWN, 22.)

Man is a gregarious animal, and apparently the mischievous microbes he exhales fight and neutralise each other. They go out and devour each other, and Man walks off unharmed. If this is not scientifically correct, it ought to be.

1948. (WW2 II, 317.)

Churchill had feared that long periods underground would weaken London's biological resistance and cause epidemics. WSC earlier said, "man is a gregarious animal, liking to live in herds" ("Great Events of Our Time", 1937).

Drugs

Human inventiveness has been fanned by the fierce wings of war. New drugs of a remarkable healing potency are becoming commonplaces of science, and even the latest textbooks on many diseases require to have very considerable annotations and additions made to them. I personally have never failed to pay my tribute of respect and gratitude to M&B; although I am not competent to give you an exact description of how it works, it certainly has in my case always been attended by highly beneficial results. Then there is penicillin, which has broken upon the world just at a moment when human beings are being gashed and torn and poisoned by wounds on the field of war in enormous numbers, and when so many other diseases, hitherto insoluble, cry for treatment.

1944, 2 MARCH. ROYAL COLLEGE OF PHYSICIANS, LONDON. (DAWN, 22.)

Churchill's doctor, Lord Moran, treated him with M&B, a bacteriostatic sulfonamide made by May & Baker. WSC also used the term in reference to Moran and the famous chest specialist, Brigadier Bedford (Nel, 128, 130).

Science, prodded on by the urge of the age, has presented to us in the last decade a wonderful bevy of new and highly attractive medicinal personalities. We have M&B, penicillin, tetramycin, aureomycin and several others that I will not hazard my professional reputation in mentioning, still less in trying to place in order.

1951, 10 JULY. ROYAL COLLEGE OF PHYSICIANS, LONDON. (STEMMING, 91.)

Energy independence

Immense deposits of kimmeridge clay, containing the oil-bearing bands or seams, stretch across England from Dorsetshire to Linconshire.

1913, 17 JULY.

Was WSC considering the possibility of converting resources Britain had to resources she then lacked? The idea should intrigue Americans, who have enough coal to convert to oil to last fifty years.

We used to be a source of fuel; we are increasingly becoming a sink. These supplies of foreign liquid fuel are no doubt vital to our industry, but our ever-increasing dependence upon them ought to arouse serious and timely reflection. The scientific utilisation, by liquefaction, pulverisation other processes, of our vast and magnificent deposits of coal, constitutes a national object of prime importance.

1928, 24 APRIL.

A remarkably instructive remark given the richness of its coal deposits and emerging coal–oil conversion technology.

Enteric fever

...in time of war, soldiers, however sensible, cared a great deal more on some occasions about slaking their thirst than about the danger of enteric fever.

1902, 21 MARCH.

Enteric fever is another term for typhoid, often contracted by drinking contaminated water.

Explosives

It is a very strange thing to reflect that but for the invention of Professor Haber the Germans could not have continued the War after their original stack of nitrates was exhausted. The invention of this single man has enabled them, utilising the interval in which their accumulations were used up, not only to maintain an almost unlimited supply of explosives for all purposes, but to provide amply for the needs of agriculture in chemical manures. It is a remarkable fact, and shows on what obscure and accidental incidents the fortunes possibly of the whole world may turn in these days of scientific discovery.

1918, 25 APRIL.

Fritz Haber (1868–1934) was a German chemist who, with Karl Bosch, created the process for producing synthetic ammonia as a replacement for sodium nitrate in fertilisers and explosives.

This is one of those rare and happy occasions when respectable people like you and me can enjoy pleasures normally reserved to the Irish Republican Army.

1940. ADMIRALTY, LONDON. (HALLE, IRREPRESSIBLE, 171.)

Churchill to Air Marshal Sir John Slessor, while tinkering with a model bomb thought useful in mining the Rhine to stop German river traffic.

Fingerprints

The adoption of the finger-print system in 1894 was due entirely to the labours of Mr. [later Sir Francis] Galton.

1910, 19 APRIL. (CZARNOMSKI, 136.)

Sir Francis Galton (1822–1911) was a scientist, inventor and explorer. Fingerprinting had been introduced by William Hereschel in India in the 1860s; Galton placed the study on a scientific basis.

Firearms

It is remarkable and indeed odd that the more efficient firearms have become, the fewer people are killed by them. The explanation of this apparent paradox is simply that human beings are much more ingenious in getting out of the way of missiles which are fired at them than they are at improving the direction and guidance of these individual missiles. In fact, the semi-automatic and automatic rifles have already, in a certain sense, gained their triumph by largely putting an end to the very mass attacks they were originally devised to destroy.

1954, 1 FEBRUARY.

Guided missiles

Do you understand, my dear? This CONTRAPTION seeks out the enemy. Smells him out. And devoid of human aid encompasses his destruction.

1952, 15 MARCH. (OB VIII, 714.)

Quoted by Sir Steuart Mitchell, who in 1986 remarked to Sir Martin Gilbert: "This to his wife!! In ordinary conversation!! A most astonishing man!" In 1952 Mitchell was Controller, Guided Weapons and Electronics, Ministry of Supply.

Healing arts

But in all this advance of science which we can no more resist or delay than we can stop the tides of destiny, there is one grand outstanding exception, the healing arts. All that cures or banishes disease, all that quenches human pain, and mitigates bodily infirmity, all those splendid names, the new arrivals which I have just mentioned to you, all these are welcome whatever view you may take of religion, philosophy or politics.

1951, 10 JULY. ROYAL COLLEGE OF PHYSICIANS, LONDON. (STEMMING, 91.)

Human factor

While all knowledge continues to expand, as Lord Balfour said today, the human faculty remains stationary, and that has induced an experimental mood in all our studies and sciences, a desire to test matters and not to yield oneself completely to clear-cut and logical definitions.

1928, 24 JULY.

A consistent theme of Churchill's is that while science progresses geometrically, mankind remains the same imperfect entity.

Man in this moment of his history has emerged in greater supremacy over the forces of nature than has ever been dreamed of before. He has it in his power to solve quite easily the problems of material existence. He has conquered the wild beasts, and he has even conquered the insects and the microbes. There lies before him, as he wishes, a golden age of peace and progress. All is in his hand. He has only to conquer his last and worst enemy— himself. With vision, faith and courage, it may be within our power to win a crowning victory for all.

1950, 28 MARCH.

The power of man has grown in every sphere except over himself. Never in the field of action have events seemed so harshly to dwarf personalities. Rarely in history have brutal facts so dominated thought or has such a widespread individual virtue found so dim a collective focus. The fearful question confronts us: Have our problems got beyond our control? Undoubtedly we are passing through a phase where this may be so.

1953, 10 DECEMBER. (CS VIII, 8515.)

Speech on receiving the Nobel Prize for Literature, read by Lady Churchill in Oslo, since WSC was meeting with Eisenhower in Bermuda.

Inoculation

The operations take place forthwith, and the next day sees haggard forms crawling about the deck in extreme discomfort and high fever. The day after, however, all have recovered and rise gloriously immune. Others, like myself, remembering that we still stand only on the threshold of pathology, remain unconvinced, resolved to trust to "health and the laws of health." But if they will invent a system of inoculation against bullet wounds I will hasten to submit myself.

1899. AT SEA, EN ROUTE TO SOUTH AFRICA. (LADYSMITH 10–11; BOER, 5.)

Churchill refused to be inoculated against enteric fever.

…vaccination is undoubtedly a definite recognition of smallpox.

1951, 10 MAY.

Internal combustion

When internal combustion becomes a realised fact—of course, it has lagged on the road in the last two years, but when it becomes a realised fact—all the advantages which have been described with regard to oil will be very greatly increased, and every ton of oil will do three or four times as much work as is now possible.

1914, 17 March.

As First Lord of the Admiralty, Churchill had instigated the conversion of the Royal Navy from coal to oil power.

Our generation has to a great extent parted company with the horse. Instead, we have been blessed with the internal combustion engine. I can say nothing about the future, which is unknown to us, but I wonder whether the generation to which I belong has won or lost by this change.

1948, 12 May. University of Oslo.

Churchill was full of this sentiment in later life. He said almost the same words at the University of London on 18 November 1948. See also Chapter 32/Tastes...Animals/horses and Chapter 34/Churchill at Large...Mobility.

Jumping

A great many men can jump four feet, but very few can jump six feet. After a certain distance the difficulty increases progressively.

1906, 11 October. St. Andrew's Hall, Glasgow. (Liberalism, 162.)

Leaded paint

Be careful not to let her suck the paint off the Noah's Ark animals. I hovered long on the verge of buying plain white wood animals— but decided at last to risk the coloured ones. They are so much more interesting. The shopman expressed himself hopefully about the nourishing qualities of the paint and of the numbers sold—and presumably sucked without misadventure. But do not trust to this.

1911, 11 July. (Gilbert, Life, 230.)

WSC to his wife, concerning his two-year-old daughter Diana. It is amusing to know that Churchill was well ahead of the health authorities in fearing the effects of ingesting paint.

Limits of science

Our inheritance of well-founded, slowly conceived codes of honour, morals and manners, the passionate convictions which so many hundreds of millions share together of the principles of freedom and justice, are far more precious to us than anything which scientific discoveries could bestow.

1949, 31 March. Massachusetts Institute of Technology, Boston. (Balance, 47.)

Mass effect of science

Science in all its forms surpasses itself every year. The body of knowledge ever accumulating is immediately interchanged and the quality and fidelity of the research never flags. But here again the mass effect largely suppresses the individual achievement.

1931, May. ("Mass Effects in Modern Life," Strand Magazine; Thoughts, 183.)

Medical profession

This College, on whose past you, Lord Moran, have descanted, on whose past you have opened some windows which cast a view upon its former glories, was, I am assured, founded by a man of wide experience of human nature—and of both sexes—King Henry VIII, in 1518. It is claimed that he thus created medicine as a profession and cast a stern Tudor frown upon quackery of all kinds.

1944, 2 March. Royal College of Physicians, London. (Dawn, 23.)

See also Physicians, below.

Medicine, experiences with

I do not profess to be very deeply acquainted with the science of medicine. I am a surgeon myself. My experiences in medicine have been vivid and violent, and completely absorbing while they were going on. Nevertheless, I cannot claim that they have given me that broad, detached, general experience which, I believe, is the foundation for all correct scientific action.

1944, 2 March. Royal College of Physicians, London. (Dawn, 22.)

Military science

We should have a greater chance of applying the gifts of science broadly to the whole texture of our defensive arrangements if there were a reception of all these new inventions and discoveries from a common elevated point of view, removed from the prejudice of any one particular uniformed profession.

1934, 21 MARCH.

Everywhere the manufacture of munitions proceeds apace, and science burrows its insulted head in the filth of slaughterous inventions.

1936, 4 SEPTEMBER. ("ENEMIES TO THE LEFT," EVENING STANDARD; STEP, 47.)

I knew nothing about science, but I knew something of scientists, and had had much practice as a Minister in handling things I did not understand. I had, at any rate, an acute military perception of what would help and what would hurt, of what would cure and of what would kill.

1949. (WW2 II, 338.)

Kay Halle wrote:

Four years on the Air Defense Research Committee and searching questions and briefings from his scientific advisor Professor Lindemann (Lord Cherwell) made him almost an expert though he had nothing but honorary college degrees.

Mind over matter

A bullet in the leg will make a brave man a coward. A blow on the head will make a wise man a fool. Indeed I have read that a sufficiency of absinthe can make a good man a knave. The triumph of mind over matter does not seem to be quite complete as yet.

1898. (MALAKAND, 184.)

Mosquito eradication

I have been told of a method of destroying the larvae of a particular mosquito by means of cows. The mosquito lays its eggs in the protecting grasses at the very edge of the water and stretched out into the water, and in this position it is protected from the depredations of a small fish which otherwise devours it with avidity. But on the introduction of the cow into the area the grass is cropped and nibbled close to the water's edge and the fish immediately attacks the larvae. I cannot guarantee the exact scientific accuracy of that narration....

1921, 14 JULY.

Physicians

The medical profession at least cannot complain of unemployment through lack of raw material. The inventive genius of mankind is stirred and spurred by suffering and emergency, and the long succession of noble discoveries in the application of the healing art stand forth with all the greater brilliance against the dark and hideous background of hatred and chaos. The miseries of the population have given opportunities to the medical profession of rendering service to their fellow mortals on an unexampled scale. Science, in many spheres so baleful, offers an ever-broadening and brightening outlook for the toil and devotion of those who follow the practice of medicine. There is no profession or calling whose members can feel a greater or deeper conviction of duty of lasting value to be done. There is no profession in which they can feel a surer confidence in an expanding future in their fight against pain and disease.

1947, 10 SEPTEMBER. GUILDHALL, LONDON. (CS VII, 7522.)

Psychical communication

The President of the Psychical Research Society extracted rather unseasonably a promise from me after dinner to "communicate" with him, should anything unfortunate occur.

1930. (MEL, 182.)

On the eve of joining the 20,000 British and Egyptian forces under Lord Kitchener, fighting in the reconquest of the Sudan, 1898.

Servant or master?

We have antagonisms now as deep as those of the Reformation and its reactions which led to the Thirty Years' War. But now they are spread over the whole world instead of only over a small part of Europe. We have, to some extent, the geographical division of the Mongol invasion in the thirteenth century, only more ruthless and more thorough. We have force and science, hitherto the servants of man, now threatening to become his master.

1955, 1 MARCH.

An allusion to his prediction of the nuclear age thirty-one years earlier:

*[Death] awaits only the word of command.
He awaits it from a frail, bewildered being,
long his victim, now – for one occasion only
– his master.*

See Chapter 19, *Nuclear Age...Atomic bomb.*

Shield of Science

There is no branch of human knowledge in
which we can pierce the mysteries of the future
so clearly as in the trend of population. Here you
have prophecies which rest on certainty; here
the searchlight of statistics ranges with accuracy
for thirty or forty years ahead. The destiny of
our country, which after all has rendered notable
services to mankind in peace and latterly in war,
depends upon an ever-flowing fountain of
healthy children, born into what we trust will be
a broader society and a less distracted world.
Science, now so largely perverted to destruction,
must raise its glittering shield not only over the
children but over the mothers, not only over
the family, but over the home.

1944, 2 MARCH. ROYAL COLLEGE OF PHYSICIANS,
LONDON. (DAWN, 23.)

Shipbuilding

Never in the whole history of Atlantic travel
has so lavish provision been made for those
who travel "tourist."

1936, MAY. ("QUEEN OF THE SEAS,"
STRAND MAGAZINE; ESSAYS IV, 332.)

Referring to RMS Queen Mary. *An interesting
precursor to his far more famous "Never in
the field of human conflict has so much been
owed by so many to so few." See Chapter 1,*
Immortal Words...The Few.

Space: the Final Frontier

It is rash to set limits to the progress of science.
A man who had maintained at Queen Victoria's
Jubilee that within fifty years one would fly the
Atlantic in a matter of hours would have risked
being certified and locked up; yet we have seen
this happen, and in the circumstances I am not
prepared to rule out with any confidence the
possibility one day of journeys through space
in vessels carrying supplies of food and oxygen
to the moon and the nearer planets....

All we can say is that with hundreds of
thousands of nebulae, each containing
thousands of millions of suns, the odds are
enormous that there must be immense
numbers which possess planets whose
circumstances would not render life impossible. If we are sufficiently self-centred and
choose to deny that any of these support life,
no one can prove we are wrong. But I, for one,
am not so immensely impressed by the
success we are making of our civilization here
that I am prepared to think we are the only
spot in this immense universe which contains
living, thinking creatures, or that we are the
highest type of mental and physical development which has ever appeared in the vast
compass of space and time.

1942, 8 MARCH. ("ARE THERE MEN ON THE MOON?,"
SUNDAY DISPATCH; ESSAYS IV, 497–8.)

*This article was written before the war but not
published.*

I am more interested in looking through the
world's most powerful telescope to see that
there is a Milky Way beyond our Milky Way.
 [Bernard Hailstone: "Is it not true that the
more powerful telescopes we make—the
further we push our horizons—the more
presumptuous is our belief that we are the
only planet with life on it?"]
 I give you that—I give you that!
Nevertheless I think we should treat the other
planets with the contempt they deserve!

1955. (HALLE, IRREPRESSIBLE, 334.)

*Quoted by Bernard Hailstone, who painted the
last portrait from life of Churchill, lunching at
Chartwell, where WSC mused on strange
phenomena such as the Loch Ness Monster
and flying saucers.*

What is the point in crying out for the moon
when you have the sun, when you have the
bright orb of day in whose refulgent beams all
the lesser luminaries hide their radiance?

1938, 16 FEBRUARY. (BROAD, 255.)

For the surprising context see Chapter 20,
People...Chamberlain, Neville.

Television

The television has come to take its place in the
world; as a rather old-fashioned person I have
not been one of its principal champions, but I

don't think it needs any champion. I think it can make its own way and I think it's a wonderful thing indeed to think that every expression on my face at this moment may be viewed by millions of people throughout the United States. I hope that the raw material is as good as the methods of distribution.

1952. PRESS CONFERENCE, NEW YORK. (HALLE, IRREPRESSIBLE, 307.)

WSC took a screen test with the BBC, professed himself dissatisfied, and never ventured close to the medium of television.

I remember a saying I heard in my youth: "Every word of Daniel Webster weighs a pound." But that was before the days of television.

1953, 9 NOVEMBER. LORD MAYOR'S BANQUET, GUILDHALL, LONDON. (ALLIANCE, 80.)

Daniel Webster (1782–1852), American statesman and noted orator, part of the Great Triumvirate of the United States Senate, which also included Henry Clay and John C. Calhoun.

Even though we have to sink to this level, we always have to keep pace with modern improvements.

1955, LONDON. EDITOR'S OBSERVATION.

Stated by Churchill when making his television screen test.

Time

Sidereal time is not solar time. Natural time is not solar time, solar time is not Greenwich time. Clock time never corresponds with the sun time, except on the meridian and on particular days of the year.

1909, 5 MARCH.

28

SPORT AND HOBBIES

"Forty winks in the afternoon and then (unexpectedly) bathing at 7 in pouring rain, intensely cold with a grey half-light of approaching night, yet curiously enough very enjoyable in its oddness. Freda Ward, Winston, Duff, Clemmie, Randolph and a child, in fact the whole party, were splashing about with gleeful screams in this sad crepuscule. The secret is that the bath is heated, and it is Winston's delightful toy."

– Lady Diana Cooper [103]

"I was accustomed in those days to play every chukka I could get into..."
Polo at Madrid, 1914.

Although Churchill liked to declaim against exercise, he was quite active until very late in his life, playing polo until his fifties and riding to hounds in his seventies. His perambulations around Chartwell – including swimming escapades such as Diana Cooper delightfully recounts – were as good an aerobic exercise as any doctor would prescribe for a mature man.

---

103 Cooper, Diana, 155. Diary entry for September 1934.

He preferred sports where individuals could shine, polo being paramount. Though he played the game with his weak right shoulder in a retaining strap to prevent it "going out", he was good at it, and was part of several winning teams.

He took up golf because Prime Minister Asquith played it, and dropped it along with Asquith. His weak shoulder prevented him ever from playing tennis, his wife's game, nor did he share her love for skiing.

He shot at game (reflecting that the game was in the right) and occasionally fished, casting for salmon in Scotland, hooking a huge swordfish off California in 1929. He fished with Roosevelt in Canada and Shangri-La (today's Camp David), but without much luck. He did not share FDR's lifelong philatelic interest, though he collected stamps as a boy.

Among his hobbies – other than painting, which is a separate chapter – were bricklaying and landscaping. In sedentary moments he played bezique, gin rummy and backgammon.

Churchill hunted "a great deal", his son wrote, "principally from Blenheim, where his cousin Marlborough mounted him for three winters while he was writing the Life of Lord Randolph; but after his marriage he did not pursue this sport. [He did enjoy] boar hunting in Normandy with his lifelong friend the Duke of Westminster..."[104]

He remained always a crack shot. His son-in-law Christopher Soames remembers driving up to a small stand of wheat into which a rabbit had darted. "I handed WSC a shotgun, the rabbit ran out, and he dropped it with a single shot..."[105]

Angling

[President Roosevelt] sought to entice the nimble and wily fish. I tried for some time myself at other spots. No fish were caught, but he seemed to enjoy it very much, and was in great spirits for the rest of the day. Evidently he had the first quality of an angler, which is not to measure the pleasure by the catch.

1951. (WW2 IV, 713.)

Baseball

I read in the *Daily Worker* some account of this. I was asked whether I would allow my name to be given to a trophy to be presented to the winner of two American Forces' teams that were to play a baseball match at a Conservative fete. I had not, I agree, fully realized the political implications that might attach to the matter, and in so far as I have erred I express my regret. [Were the situation reversed] I hope we should all show an equal spirit of tolerance and good humour.

1952, 21 JULY.

A Conservative Party Association invited an American servicemen's team to participate for a "Winston Churchill trophy", and WSC had sent a note saying he was honoured to have his name on the trophy.

Bezique

No Marlborough, only a little daub and a little bezique.

1935, 30 DECEMBER, MARRAKESH.
(OB, CV5/2, 1367.)

WSC to his wife. Bezique is a trick-taking card game for two players, originating in France in the seventeenth century. WSC was a regular practitioner; he gave up bridge at an early age, but never lost his fondness for bezique.

Big game hunting

One of the best ways of shooting game in this part of the world, and certainly the easiest, is to get a trolly and run up and down the line. The animals are so used to the passage of trains and natives along the one great highway that they do not, as a rule, take much notice, unless the train or trolly stops, when their suspicions are at once aroused....

There is another method, which we tried on the second day in the hopes of finding a

104 OB II, 224.
105 Lord Soames to the editor, 1985.

water-buck, and that is, to prowl about among the trees and undergrowth of the river-bed. In a few minutes one may bury oneself in the wildest and savagest kind of forest. The air becomes still and hot. The sun seems in an instant to assert his just prerogative. The heat glitters over the open spaces of dry sand and pools of water. High grass, huge boulders, tangled vegetation, multitudes of thorn-bushes, obstruct the march, and the ground itself is scarped and guttered by the rains into the strangest formations. Around you, breast-high, shoulder-high, overhead, rises the African jungle.

1908. (MAJ, 12–13.)

The rhinoceros stood in the middle of this plain, about five hundred yards away, in jet-black silhouette; not a twentieth-century animal at all, but an odd, grim straggler from the Stone Age...

Great is the moral effect of a foe who advances. Everybody fired. Still the ponderous brute came on, as if he were invulnerable; as if he were an engine, or some great steam barge impervious to bullets, insensible to pain or fear. Thirty seconds more, and he will close....There is time to reflect with some detachment that, after all, we were the aggressors; we it is who have forced the conflict by an unprovoked assault with murderous intent upon a peaceful herbivore; that if there is such a thing as right and wrong between man and beast— and who shall say there is not?—right is plainly on his side....But here at the end is only a hide, a horn, and a carcase, over which the vultures have already begun to wheel.

1908. (MAJ, 14–16.)

A man of his era, Churchill blasted away at African game with the best of them, but could not in his nature help reflecting that the hunted not the hunter had right on his side.

Butterflies

I have asked Mamma to get me a few butterfly things—as my garden is full of purple Emperors—White Admirals & Swallow tails and many other beautiful and rare insects. I shall be able to make a fine collection—with very little trouble—and much amusement.

1896, 15 OCTOBER. BANGALORE, INDIA.
(OB, CV1/2, 690.)

WSC to his brother Jack from India, where he began his lifelong fascination with butterflies. He did not collect and mount them for long, being content in later life to provide buddleia to attract them, and to watch chrysalises hatch. See Chapter 32, Tastes and Favourites...butterflies.

Cricket

We had a game of Cricket this afternoon, I hit a *twoer*, as the expression goes, my first runs this year.

1887, 3 MAY, BRIGHTON. (OB, CV1/1, 131.)

WSC to his mother. He played cricket only in his youth; "twoer" is slang for a two-run hit.

Fencing

Except in Fencing, in which I had won the Public School Championship, I had achieved no distinction....[With the Malakand Field Force in 1897] I wore my long cavalry sword well sharpened. After all, I had won the Public Schools fencing medal.

1930. (MEL, 53, 157.)

Football

I am sorry that Mr. Attlee did not have more success in his trip abroad, but even our football team came a cropper in Moscow, and they never meant to go to China. They did not, of course, represent the full strength of Britain, and that may apply to Mr. Attlee's team also.

1954. 9 OCTOBER, BLACKPOOL. (ALLIANCE, 184.)

Fox Hunting

Mr. Jorrocks has described fox hunting as providing all the glory of war with only thirty-five percent of its danger.

1911, 7 AUGUST.

WSC was slightly misquoting the fictional character Jorrocks in the novel Handley Cross, *on fox hunting, by sporting writer Robert Smith Surtees (1803–64), who enjoyed a wide following in the nineteenth century: "...the image of war without its guilt and only five-and-twenty percent of its danger." (For another Surtees reference see Chapter 4...War correspondents.)*

Golf

Like chasing a quinine pill around a cow pasture.

CIRCA 1915. (HALLE, IRREPRESSIBLE, 77.)

See Appendix I for a golf remark he didn't utter.

Hobbies

Change is the master key. A man can wear out a particular part of his mind by continually using it and tiring it, just in the same way as he can wear out the elbows of his coat…one cannot mend the frayed elbows of a coat by rubbing the sleeves or shoulders; but the tired parts of the mind can be rested and strengthened not merely by rest, but by using other parts.…

To be really happy and really safe, one ought to have at least two or three hobbies, and they must all be real.

1925, DECEMBER. ("HOBBIES," *PALL MALL*; THOUGHTS, 216–17.)

Churchill went on to recommend such hobbies as "joinery, chemistry, bookbinding, even bricklaying…".

Horse racing

I told him [Colonist II] this is a very big race and if he won it he would never have to run again but spend the rest of his life in agreeable female company. Colonist II did not keep his mind on the race!

1949. (HALLE, IRREPRESSIBLE, 285.)

At the urging of his son-in-law Christopher Soames, Churchill took up horse racing after World War II, and developed a successful stud and several winners. WSC often conversed with his race horse Colonist II before a race. On this occasion the horse finished an unaccustomed fourth.

I wish indeed that we could both have been victorious—but that would be no foundation for the excitements and liveliness of the Turf.

1951, 20 MAY. (OB VIII, 613.)

WSC thanking Princess Elizabeth for inviting him to luncheon at Hurst Park race course the week previous, when his horse, Colonist II, came in first, closely followed by Above Board, wearing the royal colours.

To stud? And have it said that the Prime Minister of Great Britain is living off the immoral earnings of a horse?

CIRCA 1949. (HALLE, IRREPRESSIBLE, 285.)

It had been suggested that WSC put Colonist II out to stud.

Landscaping

I lived mainly at Chartwell, where I had much to amuse me. I built with my own hands a large part of two cottages and extensive kitchen-garden walls, and made all kinds of rockeries and waterworks and a large swimming-pool which was filtered to limpidity and could be heated to supplement our fickle sunshine. Thus I never had a dull or idle moment from morning till midnight, and with my happy family around me dwelt at peace within my habitation.

1948. (WW2 I, 62.)

The phrase "within my habitation" is from Ecclesiasticus 44:6 ("Rich men furnished with ability, living peaceably in their habitations"). WSC deployed it on several occasions.

[To Inches the butler:] Tell Allen to have a lot more coal on. I want the thing full blast.

[Inches returned to say that Allen was out for the day.] Then tell Arthur I want it full blast.

[Lady Diana Cooper: "But it was Arthur's day out as well, so the darling old schoolboy went surreptitiously and stoked himself for half an hour, coming in on the verge of apoplexy."]

1934, 15 SEPTEMBER. (COOPER, DIANA, 155.)

Lady Diana's further comments on this episode are at the beginning of this chapter.

Philately

Will you send me all the stamps you can get as I am in want of some "Bechuanaland."

I suppose you will not go up the Pungwer river on account of these disturbances. Please don't go trying to conquer the Portuguese. I suppose by the time this reaches you you will have slain multitudes of lions and natives.

1891, 27 MAY, HARROW. (OB, CV1/1, 237.)

WSC to his father in Africa, who replied: "The Bechuanaland stamps I think I can obtain." The stamp hobby apparently did not survive his schooldays.

Polo

It may seem strange to speak of polo as an Imperial factor, but it would not be the first time in history that national games have played a part in high politics.

1898. (MALAKAND, 158.)

I was accustomed in those days [1890s] to play every chukka I could get into....I very rarely played less than eight and more often ten or twelve.

1930. (MEL, 122.)

Polo, 1896

In the spring of 1896...We played polo at Hurlingham and Ranelagh. The Roehampton grounds had not then come into existence. I had now five quite good ponies, and was considered to show promise.

1930. (MEL, 103.)

But before you could play polo, you must have ponies. We had formed on the voyage a regimental polo club, which in return for moderate but regular subscriptions from all the officers (polo-players and non-polo-players alike) offered substantial credit facilities for the procuring of these indispensable allies.

1930. (MEL, 120.)

Never in the history of Indian polo had a cavalry regiment from Southern India won the Inter-Regimental cup. We knew it would take two or three years of sacrifice, contrivance and effort. But if all other diversions were put aside, we did not believe that success was beyond our compass.

1930. (MEL, 121.)

Polo, 1897

Apart from other garrison teams, there were two formidable Indian rivals: the Vicar Al Umra, or Prime Minister's team, and the representatives of the famous Golconda Brigade, the bodyguard of the Nizam himself. The Golcondas were considered incomparably the best team in Southern India....[But] we defeated the Golcondas by 9 goals to 3. On succeeding days we made short work of all other opponents, and established the record, never since broken, of winning a first-class tournament within fifty days of landing in India.

1930. (MEL, 133–4.)

Polo, 1899

Rarely have I seen such strained faces on both sides. You would not have thought it was a game at all, but a matter of life and death. Far graver crises cause less keen emotion. I do not remember anything of the last chukka except that as we galloped up and down the ground in desperate attack and counter-attack, I kept on thinking, "Would God that night or Blücher would come"....It was then or never for us; and never since has a cavalry regiment from Southern India gained the prize.

1930, MEERUT, INDIA. (MEL, 224–5.)

Wellington's quote about Blücher would reoccur in different circumstances. See Chapter 18...Invasion of Britain.

Running

Please see *The Times* of February 4. Is it really true that a seven-mile cross-country run is enforced upon all in this division, from generals to privates? Does the Army Council think this a good idea? It looks to me rather excessive. A colonel or general ought not to exhaust himself in trying to compete with young boys running across country seven miles at a time. The duty of officers is no doubt to keep themselves fit, but still more to think for their men, and to take decisions affecting their safety or comfort. Who is the general of this division, and does he run the seven miles himself? If so, he may be more useful for football than war. Could Napoleon have run seven miles across country at Austerlitz? Perhaps it was the other fellow he made run.

1941, 4 FEBRUARY. (WW2 III, 647.)

Minute to Secretary of State for War Capt. H. D. R. Margesson.

29

LEADERSHIP

"He spoke diffidently about his role in the war, saying that the lion was the people of England, that he had served merely to provide the roar. But it is the roar that we hear when we pronounce his name. It is simply mistaken that battles are necessarily more important than the words that summon men to arms....The genius of Churchill was his union of affinities of the heart and of the mind, the total fusion of animal and spiritual energy."

– William F. Buckley, Jr. [106]

"At the top there are great simplifications." Board of Admiralty in session, 17 November 1939. The painting is of William IV.

W hole books have been written about Churchill's leadership and its relevance today. Why is it still evergreen? Charisma has something to do with it: his unique achievement of 1940, defying imminent distinction, achieving victory despite the odds, with humour and gusto. Had he died in 1939, it is often said, Churchill would be regarded as a historical curiosity; yet his life might still be envied as an example of leadership, a quality evident long before World War II.

As a party leader WSC was less masterful. He was never at home with the Tory old guard, those whom Andrew Roberts amusingly dubbed "The Respectable Tendency".[107]

---

106 1995 International Churchill Conference. *Churchill Proceedings 1994–1995.*
107 Roberts, *Eminent*, 9.

His wife often reminded him that he was a Liberal at heart, and would have remained one if that party hadn't collapsed around him in the 1920s.

Churchill's leadership was manifest as a minister – in every major ministry save the Foreign Office. Politically he was most effective in coalitions: Lloyd George's in 1917–22, his own in 1939–45. During the former, he stitched together an Irish Treaty, negotiating with Sinn Fein revolutionaries who were prepared to despise him. Just before his own assassination, the most prominent of them, Michael Collins, exclaimed: "Tell Winston we could have done nothing without him."

The qualities that made Churchill a leader were brilliantly summarised in 1984 by the Harvard historian Simon Schama. The first, Schama wrote, was hard work: "His capacity to absorb, analyse, and act on mountains of material was an immense asset. It meant that he delegated work as sense rather than laziness commanded. It also instilled a healthy respect among subordinates for their chief's omniscience."[108]

Churchill fought World War II aged sixty-four to seventy-one – ages when most individuals, certainly in those days, had retired. His work habits drove many younger colleagues to exhaustion. His endurance waned as the great conflict wore on; yet later he was writing his two-million-word memoirs of the war in his seventies, while simultaneously serving as Leader of the Opposition.

The second factor was Churchill's impressive grasp of military strategy – more so, certainly, than Hitler or Roosevelt or Stalin, which is not to say he didn't commit military blunders. His personal experience of war on four continents[109] ably qualified him for leadership in the war of 1939–45. "He had an unerring nose for fine commanders," Schama wrote, "and he stuck by them even when they were drawing flak from their staff."

Third on Schama's list was "the passion and the dignity of his rhetoric", Churchill's "metaphorical ripeness....The notion of anything so intellectually supine as a speech writer, let alone a bank of them, would have appalled Churchill." A post-war bodyguard, who had served in the RAF, reminded this writer: "After those speeches in 1940, we *wanted* the Germans to come – even though we had pitifully little to fight them with."[110]

The fourth leadership quality Schama noted was Churchill's "unswerving moral decency....He savoured power and authority [and] was not wartless – but his warts were just that, imperfections on the face of virtue."[111] This view is echoed by Churchill's official biographer. In the thousands of documents and transcripts he has examined, Sir Martin Gilbert writes, "I never felt that he was going to spring an unpleasant surprise on me. I might find that he was adopting views with which I disagreed. But I always knew that there would be nothing to cause me to think: 'How shocking, how appalling'."[112]

A fifth characteristic of his leadership which strikes me as most relevant today was Churchill's indifference to political popularity, and his congruent devotion to principle. Modern political discourse begins with the supposition that every action of a politician occurs only with votes in mind. ("X has read the polls, which show that 80 per cent of the voters favour his proposals.") Churchill by contrast was at his best when few agreed with him at all. In one of his most striking remarks, on 20 July 1936, he confessed that he would endure the "exultation" that would occur if he were proved wrong about Nazi Germany:

---

108 Schama, "The Churchillian" (review of the Official Biography, vol. 6), *Finest Hour* 42, Winter 1984–85, 14.
109 Cuba 1895, India 1897, Sudan/South Africa 1899–1900, Europe 1916.
110 Ronald Golding to the editor, 1984.
111 Schama, op. cit., 14.
112 Hastings, Max, "Life, Love and Liberty: Martin Gilbert Has Devoted Half His Life to Winston Churchill." The Churchill Centre: *Finest Hour* 65, 9.

"What does it matter who gets exposed or discomfited? If the country is safe, who cares for individual politicians, in or out of office?"[113]

The belief that politicians are motivated only by opportunism is responsible for the modern climate of doubt and distrust in government – and, more dangerously, in time-proven institutions and nations. A popular lament is that we have no Churchills. Yet we have some leaders who follow Churchill's dictum, saying what they believe regardless of the consequences. There is hope yet…

Of course there were occasions when Churchill acted out of political considerations – more when seeking government office than when seeking re-election. Examples include his abandonment of Free Trade in the early 1930s; his mild response to Hitler's reoccupation of the Rhineland in 1936, and his push for a "summit" (he coined that word to describe it) with Stalin's successors in Russia in 1953. Yet even then he remained indifferent to public opinion.

Forsaking Free Trade for protective tariffs was his most startling reversal, for he had espoused Free Trade since he had entered Parliament in 1901, even switched parties over it. His "dignified retreat" in the early 1930s, Paul Addison wrote, was owed to the Depression. Yet there is no doubt that he firmly believed in the correctness of his position. Speaking in agreement with Neville Chamberlain in April 1931, he said that "…the compulsive need for revenue must bring the tariff [and] will afford occasion for striking those new bargains with foreign countries which are necessary and which, wisely handled, may play an important part in welding together the production and consumption of our Empire, before the present process of dispersal and disintegration has reached its fatal end".[114]

In 1936, when Hitler reoccupied the Rhineland, Churchill was publicly almost mute. Historian Robert Rhodes James said rather cynically, "He was hoping for Cabinet office and so he said nothing – nothing at all."[115] His critics say he had abandoned principle for opportunity.

Churchill himself didn't think so. He did not see the Rhineland as a British responsibility; he thought France could and would act to reclaim it from the Germans (and had received private assurances to that end). But as Maurice Ashley explains:

…the French, who were alone capable of throwing them out again, had no serious intention of doing so. Churchill's account [in The Second World War], which relies on what Flandin, the French Foreign Minister, said to him at the time, is misleading. The French Cabinet was divided and, when Flandin came to London in March 1936, all he proposed was that the League [of Nations] Council should be summoned. The French advocated sanctions by stages and had no thought-out plan for military action.[116]

In the 1950s, Churchill led from the top, urging a "settlement", as he called it, between the West and the Soviets. It was clear that his colleagues, his party, his country and his American ally would have preferred him to concentrate on domestic policy and the unravelling of the British Empire. "If I remain in public life at this juncture," he maintained,

it is because, rightly or wrongly, but sincerely, I believe that I may be able to make an important contribution to the prevention of a Third World War and to bringing nearer that lasting peace settlement which the masses of the people of every race and in every land fervently desire.[117]

---

113 House of Commons, 20 July 1936; Covenant, 354.
114 Addison, Home Front, 300.
115 Sir Robert Rhodes James, Churchill Centre Symposium on "Winston Churchill as Peacemaker," Woodrow Wilson Centre, Washington, 1994.
116 Ashley, 163.
117 WSC at Plymouth, 23 October 1951. Stemming, 170.

Churchill's approaches to problems, his methods of handling government departments, the military, and civilian office holders, combined with his personal qualities to offer insights to his success as a leader. He accepted blame or criticism with equal grace, and was decisive, as any great leader should be, but never impervious to argument. As Lord Normanbrook wrote, he generally kept an open mind, and was ready to follow advice from people whose judgement he trusted. When he had made up his mind, it was difficult to persuade him to change it. But, until that point was reached, he was ready to listen...and modify it...if fresh evidence was brought up or fresh arguments were introduced. Two of his favourite sayings were: "I would sooner be right than consistent" and "In the course of my life I have often had to eat my words, and I must confess that I have always found it a wholesome diet." Such words would not be used by a man who was truly impervious to argument.[118]

Here are words he never had to eat, which proved their worth over time, and which cast light on the leadership of what Arthur M. Schlesinger, Jr. called "that impetuous, imperious, fallible, glorious man, history's impresario".[119]

Acceptance

Let us reconcile ourselves to the mysterious rhythm of our destinies, such as they must be in this world of space and time.

1931, MARCH. ("A SECOND CHOICE," *STRAND MAGAZINE*; THOUGHTS, 10.)

Accountability

At the top there are great simplifications. An accepted leader has only to be sure of what it is best to do, or at least to have made up his mind about it. The loyalties which centre upon number one are enormous. If he trips he must be sustained. If he makes mistakes they must be covered. If he sleeps he must not be wantonly disturbed. If he is no good he must be pole-axed. But this last extreme process cannot be carried out every day; and certainly not in the days just after he has been chosen.

1949. (WW2 II, 15.)

When one writes things on paper to decide or explain large questions affecting action there is mental stress. But all this bites much deeper when you see and feel it on the spot.

1954. (WW2 VI, 96.)

WSC was referring to the winding down of the Italian campaign in 1944. For more of this quotation see Chapter 18...1944/Italian campaign.

Action

Nobody ever launched an attack without having misgivings beforehand. You ought to have misgivings before; but when the moment of action is come, the hour of misgivings is passed. It is often not possible to go backward from a course which has been adopted in war. A man must answer "Aye" or "No" to the great questions which are put, and by that decision he must be bound.

1915, 15 NOVEMBER.

Referring to the failed attempt to force the Dardanelles and to land and occupy the Gallipoli Peninsula. That campaign having been abandoned, Churchill had resigned from the Cabinet, and was about to join British forces in Flanders, where he could command a battalion of the Sixth Royal Scots Fusiliers.

Adequacy

What is adequacy? Adequacy is no standard at all.

1938, 17 NOVEMBER. (CS VI, 6022.)

There is always much to be said for not attempting more than you can do and for making a certainty of what you try. But this principle, like others in life and war, has its exceptions.

1941, 7 JUNE. (WW2 III, 297.)

---

118 Lord Normanbrook in Wheeler-Bennett, 28.
119 Schlesinger, Arthur M., to the 1995 International Churchill Conference, Boston. *Churchill Proceedings 1994–1995*, 91.

Anticipation

It is very much better sometimes to have a panic feeling beforehand, and then be quite calm when things happen, than to be extremely calm beforehand and to get into a panic when things happen.

1935, 22 MAY.

We must be ready, as we always have been ready, to take the rough with the smooth.

1941, 17 MARCH.

One cannot always provide against the worst assumptions, and to try to do so prevents the best disposition of limited resources.

1942, 19 MARCH. (WW2 IV, 155.)

Appointments

It is better that one notability should be turned away expostulating from the doorstep than that nine just deputations should each fume for ten minutes in a stuffy ante-room.

1930. (MEL, 108.)

If you fall behind in your appointments, WSC continued, you should "cut one or two of the appointments altogether and so catch up".

Broadness of view

...how useful it is in great organisations to have a roving eye.

1952. (WW2 V, 464.)

Chance

We have always to be on our guard against being thrown off our true course by chance and circumstance...

1931, FEBRUARY. ("PERSONAL CONTACTS," STRAND MAGAZINE; THOUGHTS, 31.)

The chance of glory and honour comes now here, now there, to each and every one.

1941, 8 NOVEMBER.

Commitment

No one is compelled to serve great causes unless he feels fit for it, but nothing is more certain than that you cannot take the lead in great causes as a half-timer.

1936, 6 MAY.

Communication

Too often the strong, silent man is silent only because he does not know what to say, and he

is reputed strong only because he has remained silent.

1924, 27 JUNE. LONDON SCHOOL OF ECONOMICS. (CS IV, 3462.)

Sometimes misunderstandings arise because one sends a message and waits a long time for an answer.

1944, 27 MAY. (WW2 V, 629.)

Prime Minister to Foreign Secretary.

We must neither underrate nor exaggerate.

1944, 6 JULY. (DAWN, 129.)

Statement on the Flying Bomb (V-2).

I am a strong believer in transacting official business by *the Written Word....*It is always better, except in the hierarchy of military discipline, to express opinions and wishes rather than to give orders. Still, written directives coming personally from the lawfully-constituted Head of the Government and Minister specially charged with defence counted to such an extent that, though not expressed as orders, they very often found their fruition in action.

1949. (WW2 II, 16–17.)

I still believe that vast and fearsome as the human scene has become, personal contacts of the right people in the right place at the right time may yet have a potent and valuable part to play in the cause of peace which is in our hearts.

1955, 14 MARCH.

Confidence

Above all, my dear friend, do not be vexed or discouraged. We are on the stage of history.

1915, 8 JANUARY. (CRISIS II, 68.)

WSC TO SIR JOHN FRENCH, FIRST COMMANDER-IN-CHIEF, BRITISH EXPEDITIONARY FORCE, 1914–15.

Troubles rise to the surface, and at the same time also there often rise forces to control or remedy them.

1936, 18 SEPTEMBER. ("TESTING TIME FOR FRANCE," EVENING STANDARD; STEP, 52.)

Consideration

Consideration for the lives of others and the laws of humanity, even when one is struggling for one's life and in the greatest stress, does not go wholly unrewarded.

1917, 21 FEBRUARY.

When one is in office one has no idea how damnable things can feel to the ordinary rank and file of the public.

1941, 12 FEBRUARY. (WW2 III, 650.)

Prime Minister to Lord President of the Council.

Consistency

The average politician cares very little about consistency. He produces an assortment of wares with which to tempt the public, but as soon as the interest in them has declined, he quietly sets himself to work to dress the window with still later novelties.

1905, APRIL. (INTERVIEW BY "VIVIAN," *PALL MALL*.)

I would sooner be right than consistent.

CIRCA 1940S. (LORD NORMANBROOK, WHEELER-BENNETT, 28.)

There is great danger in trying to have things both ways.

1951, 15 FEBRUARY.

Courage

How few men are strong enough to stand against the prevailing currents of opinion!

1899, 3 DECEMBER, PRETORIA. (LADYSMITH, 172–3; BOER, 77.)

See also Chapter 2, Maxims...Courage.

When you embark on a course of restriction or oppression, caution and hesitancy should rightly impose themselves upon you; but when you are embarked upon a course of relief and liberation, advance with courage.

1928, 7 JUNE.

It is no use once again leading other nations up the garden and then running away when the dog growls.

1937, 8 JANUARY. ("NO INTERVENTION IN SPAIN," *EVENING STANDARD*; STEP, 85.)

If at last this long story is to end, it were better it should end, not through surrender, but only when we are rolling senseless on the ground.

1940, 28 MAY, DOWNING STREET. (DALTON, 335.)

Said at a meeting of the Cabinet; Lord Halifax was still arguing for exploring, via Mussolini, Hitler's ceasefire terms. Another version reads:

If this long island story of ours is to end at last, let it end only when each of us lies choking in his own blood upon the ground (OB VI, 420).

Then I said quite casually, not treating it as a point of special significance:

"Of course, whatever happens at Dunkirk, we shall fight on."

There occurred a demonstration which, considering the character of the gathering—twenty-five experienced politicians and Parliament men, who represented all the different points of view, whether right or wrong, before the war—surprised me. Quite a number seemed to jump up from the table and come running to my chair, shouting and patting me on the back. There is no doubt that had I at this juncture faltered at all in the leading of the nation I should have been hurled out of office. I was sure that every Minister was ready to be killed quite soon, and have all his family and possessions destroyed, rather than give in. In this they represented the House of Commons and almost all the people. It fell to me in these coming days and months to express their sentiments on suitable occasions. This I was able to do because they were mine also. There was a white glow, over-powering, sublime, which ran through our Island from end to end.

1940, 28 MAY, DOWNING STREET. (WW2 II, 88.)

Churchill's recollection of this "demonstration" by ministers not on the War Cabinet has been challenged by critics, but never by anyone present. While some may have favoured considering German terms, none favoured surrender. See Chapter 18, World War II...1940/Options.

Si une bombe tombe sur la maison, nous mourrons ensemble comme deux braves gens! [If a bomb falls on this building, we will die nobly together.]

1940, 21 OCTOBER, DOWNING STREET. (JEAN OBERLÉ, *FINEST HOUR* 138, SPRING 2008.)

WSC to Jacques Duchesne, head of the BBC French section, who had come to help him practise his famous broadcast to France (see "Nations...France/1940". Bombs were falling and Duchesne remarked that there did not seem much security at Number Ten. Churchill

burst out laughing and delivered this reply.
See Chapter 1, "Vive la France", 1940.

There is only one duty, only one safe course, and that is to try to be right and not to fear to do or say what you believe to be right. That is the only way to deserve and to win the confidence of our great people in these days of trouble.

1941, 30 SEPTEMBER.

Never must we lose our faith and our courage, never must we fail in exertion and resolve.

1951, 27 APRIL. PRIMROSE LEAGUE, ALBERT HALL, LONDON. (STEMMING, 65.)

In a scarce example of speech retreading, Churchill used the exact same exhortation in Glasgow three weeks later on 18 May.

Criticism

It is very easy to say that your opponents have been guilty of a breach of faith, but it is a great mistake to splash the paint about so freely that your words cease to have any real meaning and cease to carry any sense of affront even to those to whom they are applied and cease to bear any connection with any genuine feeling of indignation on the part of those on whose behalf they are spoken.

1911, 27 MARCH.

Culpability

In the course of my life I have often had to eat my words, and I must confess that I have always found it a wholesome diet.

CIRCA 1940s. (LORD NORMANBROOK IN WHEELER-BENNETT, 28.)

Sometimes erroneously quoted as "Eating my words has never given me indigestion."

When we reflect upon the magnitude of modern events compared with the men who have to try to control or cope with them, and upon the frightful consequences of these events on hundreds of millions, the importance of not making avoidable mistakes grows impressively upon the mind.

1941, 30 SEPTEMBER.

Danger, proximity of

When danger is at a distance, when there is plenty of time to make the necessary preparations, when you can bend twigs instead of having to break massive boughs—it is right, indeed it is a duty, to sound the alarm. But when danger comes very near, when it is plain that not much more can be done in the time that may be available, it is no service to dwell upon the shortcomings or neglects of those who have been responsible. The time to be frightened is when evils can be remedied; when they cannot be fully remedied they must be faced with courage. When danger is far off we may think of our weakness; when it is near we must not forget our strength.

1939, 28 JUNE.

Scarcely a month later, on 2 August, as Hitler was preparing to make peace with Russia and invade Poland, Chamberlain announced that the House should rise from 4 August through 3 October. Attacked from all parties, he held fast to his plan. Other decisions being made in Berlin would disrupt it.

Daring

We must not lose our faculty to dare, particularly in dark days.

1942, 24 MARCH. (WW2 IV, 202.)

WSC to General Smuts.

Decision-making

Every man should ask himself each day whether he is not too readily accepting negative solutions.

1918, 22 JUNE. (CRISIS III PART 2, 467.)

Note to the Imperial War Cabinet.

There is always a strong case for doing nothing, especially for doing nothing yourself.

1923. (CRISIS I, 340.)

Hasty work and premature decisions may lead to penalties out of all proportion to the issues immediately involved.

1944, 28 SEPTEMBER.

Statesmen are not called upon only to settle easy questions. These often settle themselves. It is where the balance quivers, and the proportions are veiled in mist, that the opportunity for world-saving decisions presents itself.

1948. (WW2 I, 284.)

One must never be afraid or ashamed of ramming home a point.

1948, 30 APRIL. PRIMROSE LEAGUE, ALBERT HALL, LONDON. (EUROPE, 307.)

Named for Disraeli's favourite buttonhole, the Primrose League was formed to promote his conception of Tory Democracy, strongly advocated by WSC's father. Winston's first step into politics was to join the Brighton branch of the Primrose League as a schoolboy in 1887. His first political speech was at a Primrose League rally near Bath (see Chapter 22...1897). WSC was a Grand Master of the Primrose League from 1944 until his death. The League was not disbanded until 2004.

I let the argument rip healthily between the departments. This is a very good way of finding out the truth.

1950. (WW2 III, 35.)

WSC was referring to differences in 1940 estimates of the future strength of German bombing.

Determination and resolve

The right to guide the course of world history is the noblest prize of victory. We are still toiling up the hill; we have not yet reached the crest-line of it; we cannot survey the landscape or even imagine what its condition will be when that longed-for morning comes. The task which lies before us immediately is at once practical, more simple and more stern. I hope—indeed I pray—that we shall not be found unworthy of our victory if after toil and tribulation it is granted to us. For the rest, we have to gain the victory. That is our task.

1940, 20 AUGUST.

One of the keys to Churchill's leadership: he was looking forward to ultimate victory at a time when others were playing defence.

We have but one aim and one single, irrevocable purpose. We are resolved to destroy Hitler and every vestige of the Nazi regime. From this nothing will turn us—nothing. We will never parley, we will never negotiate with Hitler or any of his gang. We shall fight him by land, we shall fight him by sea, we shall fight him in the air, until with God's help we have rid the earth of his shadow and liberated its peoples from his yoke. Any man or state who fights on against Nazidom will have our aid. Any nation or state who marches with Hitler is our foe.

1941, 22 JUNE. BROADCAST, LONDON. (UNRELENTING, 172.)

Following the German invasion of Russia. Historians have criticised Churchill for failing to see that the war left the Empire prostrate and Britain bankrupt, for failing to see the danger of the Soviets, or for failing to plan for the post-war world. At the time other considerations took priority. The sole reason why Churchill was given the premiership was to defeat Hitler. That unswerving purpose, so indispensable in 1940, was what saw him and his country through the nightmare.

We shall go forward together. The road upwards is stony. There are upon our journey dark and dangerous valleys through which we have to make and fight our way. But it is sure and certain that if we persevere—and we shall persevere—we shall come through these dark and dangerous valleys into a sunlight broader and more genial and more lasting than mankind has ever known.

1942, 16 MAY, LEEDS. (END, 138.)

We have to hold and dominate Athens. It would be a great thing for you to succeed in this without bloodshed if possible, but also with bloodshed if necessary.

1944, 5 DECEMBER. (WW2 VI, 252.)

WSC (italics his) to General Scobie in Athens, whom he sent to help Greeks resist a communist revolution.

The Socialists, in their pamphlet at the election, said "Let us face the future." Surely now we have a more immediate task when all is so grim: "Let us face the present." It is the duty of everyone to do their utmost for the country; night and day they should be thinking about it and its anxious problems. It is incredible to me that any patriotic man or woman could be guilty of apathy at a time like this.

1945, 28 NOVEMBER. CONSERVATIVE PARTY CENTRAL COUNCIL, LONDON. (SINEWS, 54.)

If you should be thrown into a quarrel, you should bear yourself so that an opponent may be aware of it....pugnacity and will-power cannot be dispensed with.

1947, 31 January.

It is wonderful what great strides can be made when there is a resolute purpose behind them.

1947, 7 May.

Let us do our utmost—all that is in us—for the good of all.

1948, 9 May. City Square, Amsterdam.
(Europe, 320.)

Difficulties

When we face with a steady eye the difficulties which lie before us, we may derive new confidence from remembering those we have already overcome.

1941, 27 April.

See also Chapter 2, Maxims...Difficulties.

I wish I could persuade you to overcome the difficulties instead of merely entrenching yourself behind them.

1943, 28 February. (WW2 IV, 831.)

Prime Minister to Minister of Agriculture, which began: "I am not satisfied that it would be a costly business to give the country more eggs."

Essentials of leadership

Avoid chops and changes of policy; avoid thimble-riggers and three-card trick men; avoid all needless borrowings; and above all, avoid as you would avoid the smallpox class warfare and violent political strife.

1929, 30 April. (CS V, 4617.)

In a broad view, large principles, a good heart, high aims, a firm faith, we may find some charts and a compass for our voyage. Still, as we lean over the stern of the ship and watch the swirling eddies in our wake, the most rigid and resolute of us must feel how many currents are playing their part in the movements of the vessel that bears us onwards.

1931, February. ("Personal Contacts," Strand Magazine; Thoughts, 31.)

The Minister or President at the head of some immense sphere of business, whose practical decisions from hour to hour settle so many important things, is no longer a figure of mystery and awe. On the contrary he is looked upon and, what is more important for our present purpose, looks upon himself as quite an ordinary fellow, who happens to be charged for the time being with a peculiar kind of large-scale work.... The question is whether the sense of leadership, and the commanding attitude towards men and affairs, are likely to arise from such simple and unpretentious customs and habits of mind...

1931, May. ("Mass Effects in Modern Life," Strand Magazine; Thoughts, 187.)

Since many candidates for office run proudly on the premise of being just ordinary citizens, this is a remarkably apposite and relevant reflection on political leadership.

We must strive to combine the virtues of wisdom and of daring.

1942, 12 October. Usher Hall, Edinburgh.
(End, 243.)

WSC had received the Freedom of Edinburgh.

I hope you will all nurse high thoughts in your minds, and high ambitions.

1943, 5 November, Harrow School.
(Onwards, 262.)

Try to cut out petty annoyances....

1944, 26 May. (WW2 V, 628.)

Prime Minister to Minister of Food.

Vision, courage, self-denial, faith and faithful service must animate us.

1946, 14 July, Metz, France. (Sinews, 173.)

...I did not like having unharnessed Ministers around me. I preferred to deal with chiefs of organisations rather than counsellors. Everyone should do a good day's work and be accountable for some definite task; and then they do not make trouble for trouble's sake or to cut a figure.

1948. (WW2 I, 328.)

Surround yourself with as few people as possible.

Circa 1949. (Graebner, 106.)

In life people have first to be taught, "Concentrate on essentials."

1952. (WW2 V, 377.)

An efficient and a successful administration manifests itself equally in small as in great matters.

1952. (WW2 V, 583.)

Evaluation

"Everybody who knew Townshend loved him." This last must always be considered a dubious qualification.

1938. (MARLBOROUGH IV, 56.)

Possibly a veiled reference to the well-loved Stanley Baldwin, who had recently retired as Prime Minister. See Chapter 20, People... Baldwin.

My object is to preserve the maximum initiative energy. Every night I try myself by court-martial to see if I have done anything effective during the day. I don't mean just pawing the ground—anyone can go through the motions—but something really effective.

1940, AUGUST. (JOHN COLVILLE IN WHEELER-BENNETT, ED., ACTION THIS DAY, 112.)

There are many tests by which we may try to measure the greatness of the men who have served high causes, but I shall select only one of them this morning, namely, the favourable influence exerted upon the fortunes of mankind.

1946, 11 OCTOBER.

Experience

Perseverance is usually described as a great virtue, but it has two aspects. Perseverance with an eye on the future, perseverance towards a definite objective is a great virtue; perseverance with an eye on the past is an equally serious vice.

1917, 5 MARCH.

Let us first take counsel of the past, and draw wisdom and courage from the memory of the great men who have gone before us.

1947, 18 APRIL. PRIMROSE LEAGUE, ALBERT HALL, LONDON. (EUROPE, 60.)

False optimism

[It] is no kindness to this country to stir up and pay all this lip-service in the region of unrealities, and get a cheap cheer because you have said something which has not ruffled anyone, and then meanwhile do the opposite....If we proceed to argue on lines which have no connection with reality, we shall get into trouble.

1933, 14 MARCH.

We must all do our best, and we shall do it much better if we are not hampered by a cloud of pledges and promises which arise out of the hopeful and genial side of man's nature and are not brought into relation with the hard facts of life.

1943, 4 JANUARY. (WW2 IV, 862.)

WSC to the Cabinet on promises about post-war conditions.

There is no worse mistake in public leadership than to hold out false hopes soon to be swept away. The British people can face peril or misfortune with fortitude and buoyancy, but they bitterly resent being deceived or finding that those responsible for their affairs are themselves dwelling in a fool's paradise.

1951. (WW2 IV, 54.)

Flexibility

The best method of acquiring flexibility is to have three or four plans for all the probable contingencies, all worked out with the utmost detail. Then it is much easier to switch from one to the other as and when the cat jumps

1943, 21 SEPTEMBER.

One must remember that a ship may start out in one direction and turn off in another.

1944, 19 MARCH. (WW2 V, 614.)

WSC to President Roosevelt.

Foresight

[A politician needs...] the ability to foretell what is going to happen tomorrow, next week, next month, and next year—and to have the ability afterwards to explain why it didn't happen.

1902. (HALLE, IRREPRESSIBLE, 50.)

Halle quotes an unnamed newspaper interview in 1902. On the basis of her reliability, this seems in character with WSC's persona, though it is not fully attributed.

You cannot tell from appearances how things will go. Sometimes imagination makes things out far worse than they are; yet without imagination not much can be done. Those people who are imaginative see many more dangers than perhaps exist, certainly many more than will happen; but then they must also pray to be given that extra courage to carry this far-reaching imagination.

1941, 29 OCTOBER, HARROW SCHOOL.
(UNRELENTING, 206.)

Sometimes, though not always, people are wise after the event, but it is also possible to be wise before the event and yet not have the power to stop it happening.

1942, 23 APRIL. (SECRET, 49.)

Haste

To build may have to be the slow and laborious task of years. To destroy can be the thoughtless act of a single day.

1959, 29 SEPTEMBER, WOODFORD, ESSEX.
(ALLIANCE, 320.)

Hindsight

Nothing is more easy, nothing is cheaper, nothing is more futile than to criticise the hazardous and incalculable events and tendencies of war after the event has occurred.

1917, 21 FEBRUARY.

I do not admire people who are wise after the event. I would rather be impaled on the other horn of the dilemma and be called one of the "I told you so's."

1935, 22 MAY.

Inertia

When the situation was manageable it was neglected, and now that it is thoroughly out of hand we apply too late the remedies which then might have effected a cure. There is nothing new in the story. It is as old as the Sibylline books. It falls into that long, dismal catalogue of the fruitlessness of experience and the confirmed unteachability of mankind. Want of foresight, unwillingness to act when action would be simple and effective, lack of clear thinking, confusion of counsel until the emergency comes, until self-preservation strikes its jarring gong—these are the features which constitute the endless repetition of history.

1935, 2 MAY.

In a conference at Stresa, Britain, France and Italy had agreed to cooperate to maintain the independence of Austria. His fear was that this had come too late, as indeed it had; Hitler annexed Austria a year later. If only, Churchill was saying, these three powers had worked for peace and collective security earlier.

I confess that words fail me. In the year 1708 Mr. Secretary St. John, by a calculated Ministerial indiscretion, revealed to the House the fact that the battle of Almanza had been lost in the previous summer because only 8,000 English troops were actually in Spain out of the 29,000 that had been voted by the House of Commons for this service. When a month later this revelation was confirmed by the Government, it is recorded that the House sat in silence for half an hour, no Member caring to speak or wishing to make a comment upon so staggering an announcement. And yet how incomparably small that event was to what we have now to face.

1935, 2 MAY.

Prime Minister Baldwin had confessed that Germany had reached air parity with Britain; six months earlier he had assured the House that Britain would maintain a margin of at least 50 per cent.

It is a great characteristic of the people of our race to throw away with one hand the thing they have gathered so painfully with the other.

1951, 15 AUGUST, DOVER. (COOTE, 213.)

Influence

Sometimes [the reader] will find that people who impressed him least influenced him most.

1931, FEBRUARY. ("PERSONAL CONTACTS,"
STRAND MAGAZINE; THOUGHTS, 31.)

No one knows till he tries how much influence one convinced and well-informed person can exert upon those with whom he comes in contact in the ordinary round of daily life.

1947, 27 SEPTEMBER. ROYAL WANSTEAD SCHOOLS.
(EUROPE, 141.)

Intensity

The more Surprise was absent, the more Intensity was vital.

1923. (CRISIS II, 272.)

Said about the Dardanelles operation. See Chapter 16, World War I.

Logic

There is a great deal more sense and deep reason and sagacity in the lack of logical subtlety than might appear upon the surface.

1911, 30 MAY.

Magnanimity

I thought we ought to have conquered the Irish and then given them Home Rule: that we ought to have starved out the Germans, and then revictualled their country; and that after smashing the General Strike, we should have met the grievances of the miners. I always get into trouble because so few people take this line.

1930. (MEL, 346.)

Do not, whatever be the torrent of abuse which may obstruct the necessary action, think too poorly of the greatness of our fellow countrymen. Let the House do its duty. Let the Government give the lead, and the nation will not fail in the hour of need.

1934, 28 NOVEMBER.

There is no use or advantage in wasting strength and time upon hard words and reproaches.

1940, 25 JUNE. (BLOOD, 371.)

Stated after the Fall of France. WSC generally stuck to this maxim throughout the war; he never looked back.

This is the moment to forget many things, to remember great things...

1944, 12 NOVEMBER. LIBERATION COMMITTEE, PARIS. (DAWN, 247.)

We must rise to a level higher than the grievous injuries we have suffered.

1948, 9 MAY, AMSTERDAM. (EUROPE, 320.)

...we must abandon all bitterness and all wish for revenge.

1948, 12 MAY. HOTEL BRISTOL, OSLO. (EUROPE, 330.)

I have always been astonished, having seen the end of these two wars, how difficult it is to make people understand Roman wisdom,

"Spare the conquered and war down the proud." I think I will go so far as to say it in the original: *Parcere subjectis, et debellare superbos.* The modern practice has too often been, punish the defeated and grovel to the strong....

1950, 14 DECEMBER.

Sometimes quoted as "War down the strong and bear up the weak," from Virgil's Aeneid, *VI, 853. A favourite of WSC's: see also Chapter 12, War...Magnanimity.*

Party management

Leaders who lead their party from day to day by doing the popular thing, by staving off difficulties, and by withholding their true counsel until it is too late, cannot complain if, when disaster culminating in catastrophe is reached, some of their followers are reluctant to share in the odium of capitulation, however necessary, however inevitable.

1911, 7 AUGUST. (CS II, 1849.)

It is remarkable that WSC spoke these words thirty years before exactly such leadership almost cost Britain her life.

...anyone leading a Party must have a brain larger than his own, must have numbers of people through whom he can operate.

1936, 10 JULY.

The Conservative Party possessed a very large majority in the House of Commons over all other parties combined. Owing to the war conditions no election appeal to the nation was available in case of disagreement or deadlock. I should have found it impossible to conduct the war if I had had to procure the agreement in the compulsive days of crisis and during long years of adverse and baffling struggle not only of the Leaders of the two minority parties but of the Leader of the Conservative majority....

These arguments do not apply in the same degree in time of peace; but I do not feel I could have borne such a trial successfully in war.

1949. (WW2 II, 439.)

In 1940, not everybody agreed that Churchill should have become Tory leader, including his wife, who thought that he should remain above politics, as head of the wartime Coalition. This is his case for taking on the task.

Patience

Patience, however, and good temper accomplish much...

1912, 14 APRIL. (CRISIS I, 110.)

WSC to his friend and sometime mentor Sir Ernest Cassel.

In my experience of large enterprises, I have found it is often a mistake to try to settle everything at once. Far off, on the skyline, we can see the peaks of the Delectable Mountains. But we cannot tell what lies between us and them. We know where we want to go; but we cannot foresee all the stages of the journey, nor can we plan our marches as in a military operation.

1947, 14 MAY. ROYAL ALBERT HALL, LONDON. (EUROPE, 79.)

Delectable Mountains (see also Chapter 24, Education...Mathematics and Chapter 34, Churchill at Large...Change) is from John Bunyan's Pilgrim's Progress *(1678).*

We must not lose patience, and we must not lose hope.

1952, 17 JANUARY. CONGRESS, WASHINGTON. (STEMMING, 227.)

Planning

Fresh plans for fresh contingencies.

1899, 22 DECEMBER. LOURENÇO MARQUES (NOW MAPUTO, MOZAMBIQUE). (LADYSMITH, 194; BOER, 86.)

...it is much better to set up an objective, even if it be beyond your reach, than it is to give up the struggle at the outset.

1927, 11 APRIL.

We may have taken decisions which will prove to be less good than we hoped, but at any rate anything is better than not having a plan.

1943, 11 FEBRUARY.

We have to consider practical steps, and to consider these coolly and sagely.

1944, 21 APRIL.

It is a mistake to try to write out on little pieces of paper what the vast emotions of an outraged and quivering world will be either immediately after the struggle is over or when the inevitable cold fit follows the hot. These awe-inspiring tides of feeling dominate most people's minds, and independent figures tend to become not only lonely but futile. Guidance in these mundane matters is granted to us only step by step, or at the utmost a step or two ahead. There is therefore wisdom in reserving one's decisions as long as possible and until all the facts and forces that will be potent at the moment are revealed.

1945, 4 JANUARY. (WW2 VI, 306.)

WSC to Foreign Secretary on post-war Germany.

It is one thing to see the forward path and another to be able to take it. But it is better to have an ambitious plan than none at all.

1950. (WW2 III, 480.)

...failing to gain one's way is no escape from the responsibility for an inferior solution.

1954. (WW2 VI, 96.)

Churchill was expressing regret over the failure to exploit Allied gains in Italy.

Polls

Nothing is more dangerous in wartime than to live in the temperamental atmosphere of a Gallup Poll, always feeling one's pulse and taking one's temperature. I see [it] said that leaders should keep their ears to the ground. All I can say is that the British nation will find it very hard to look up to the leaders who are detected in that somewhat ungainly posture.

1941, 30 SEPTEMBER.

We have a deep respect for public opinion but we do not let our course be influenced from day to day by Gallup Polls, favourable though they may be. It is not a good thing always to be feeling your pulse and taking your temperature; although one has to do it sometimes, you do not want to make a habit of it. I have heard it said that a Government should keep its ear to the ground but they should also remember that this is not a very dignified attitude.

1953, 10 OCTOBER. PARTY CONFERENCE, MARGATE. (ALLIANCE, 58.)

Power

When one has reached the summit of power and surmounted so many obstacles, there is a danger of becoming convinced that one can do anything one likes and that any strong personal view is necessarily acceptable to the nation and can be enforced upon one's subordinates.

1920, 4 DECEMBER. (OB, CV4/2, 1261.)

WSC to Prime Minister David Lloyd George, a remark that has been proven repeatedly many times since.

Power, for the sake of lording it over fellow-creatures or adding to personal pomp, is rightly judged base. But power in a national crisis, when a man believes he knows what orders should be given, is a blessing.

1948. (WW2 II, 14.)

Power without responsibility

I was ruined for the time being in 1915 over the Dardanelles, and a supreme enterprise was cast away, through my trying to carry out a major and cardinal operation of war from a subordinate position. Men are ill-advised to try such ventures. This lesson had sunk into my nature.

1948. (WW2 II, 15.)

Principle vs. politics

...there was a difference in a policy when it was put forward on the faith and honour of a public man, and when it was put forward avowedly as a matter of convenient political tactics.

1904, 29 MARCH.

A Statesman should always try to do what he believes is best in the long view for his country, and he should not be dissuaded from so acting by having to divorce himself from a great body of doctrine to which he formerly sincerely adhered. Those, however, who are forced to these gloomy choices must regard their situation in this respect as unlucky.

1927, JULY. ("CONSISTENCY IN POLITICS," PALL MALL; THOUGHTS, 29.)

Nothing would give me greater pleasure than to be absolutely stultified in a secret session by the Government, and proved to be an alarmist. I would endure with patience the roar of exultation that would go up when I was proved wrong, because it would lift a load off my heart and off the hearts of many Members. What does it matter who gets exposed or discomfited? If the country is safe, who cares for individual politicians, in or out of office?

1936, 20 JULY. (COVENANT, 354.)

This ringing declaration goes far in showing how Churchill ranked above the ordinary politician in his devotion to principle regardless of personal cost – a characteristic that distinguished him from the crowd.

What is the use of Parliament if it is not the place where true statements can be brought before the people? What is the use of sending Members to the House of Commons who say just the popular things of the moment, and merely endeavour to give satisfaction to the Government Whips by cheering loudly every Ministerial platitude, and by walking through the Lobbies oblivious of the criticisms they hear? People talk about our Parliamentary institutions and Parliamentary democracy; but if these are to survive, it will not be because the Constituencies return tame, docile, subservient Members, and try to stamp out every form of independent judgment.

1939, 14 MARCH.

If today I am very kindly treated by the mass of the people of this country, it is certainly not because I have followed public opinion in recent years. There is only one duty, only one safe course, and that is to try to be right and not to fear to do or to say what you believe to be right. That is the only way to deserve and to win the confidence of our great people in these days of trouble.

1941, 30 SEPTEMBER.

However tempting it might be to some when much trouble lies ahead to step aside adroitly and put someone else up to take the blows, I do not intend to take that cowardly course, but, on the contrary, to stand to my post and persevere in accordance with my duty as I see it.

1942, 24 FEBRUARY.

...human life is presented to us as a simple choice between right and wrong. If you obey that law you will find that that way is far safer in the long run than all calculation which can ever be made.

1948, 12 MAY. HOTEL BRISTOL, OSLO. (EUROPE, 330.)

Churchill preceded this by saying:

Human judgment may fail. You may act very wisely, you think, but it may turn out a great failure. On the other hand, one may do a foolish thing which may turn out well.

Promises

You must never make a promise which you do not fulfil.

1942, 11 NOVEMBER.

WSC had been asked if he had broken a promise to Stalin to open a Second Front in 1942, which, of course, he had not.

Purpose

A weakening in our purpose and therefore in our unity—that is the mortal crime. Whoever is guilty of that crime, or of bringing it about in others, of him let it be said that it were better for him that a millstone were hanged about his neck and he were cast into the sea.

1942, 15 FEBRUARY. BROADCAST, LONDON. (END, 70.)

Revenge

Revenge is, of all satisfactions, the most costly and long drawn-out; retributive persecution is, of all policies, the most pernicious.

1948, 28 OCTOBER.

Rewards

As long as the job is done, it does not matter much who gets the credit.

1942, 10 DECEMBER. (SECRET, 81.)

In the ordinary day-to-day affairs of life, men and women expect rewards for successful exertion, and this is often right and reasonable. But those who serve causes as majestic and high as ours need no reward; nor are our aims limited by the span of human life. If success come to us soon, we shall be happy. If our purpose is delayed, if we are confronted by obstacles and inertia, we may still be of good cheer, because in a cause, the righteousness of which will be proclaimed by the march of future events and the judgment of happier ages, we shall have done our duty, we shall have done our best.

1947, 14 MAY. ROYAL ALBERT HALL, LONDON. (EUROPE, 86.)

Sincerity

If it is thought that there is nothing behind your words, when you are in fact in a position of greater danger yourself, not much attention is paid to what you say; the march of events takes place regardless of it.

1934, 30 JULY.

Subordinates

I am very well accustomed to weigh expert evidence, and most of the important decisions which have been taken in the last three or four years at the Admiralty have been taken by me on a divergence of expert evidence.

1915, 15 NOVEMBER.

There is no excuse for superior authority not choosing the most suitable agents for particular duties, and not removing unsuitable agents from particular duties.

1920, 8 JULY.

Not only the best, but the second and third best, must be made to play their part.

1940, 26 OCTOBER. (WW2 II, 448.)

WSC to Anthony Eden.

Everyone can help in some way or other.

1947, 27 SEPTEMBER. ROYAL WANSTEAD SCHOOLS, ESSEX. (EUROPE, 141.)

Time

Time is a tremendous lever and a tremendous weapon either in peace or in war. In fact, I think in the government of states a judicious use of time is very often one of the most potent and effective weapons.

1910, 12 APRIL.

...time is a changeable ally. He may be with you in one period and against you in another, and then if you come through that other, he may return again more faithful than before.

1940, 30 MARCH.

Things happen so quickly nowadays and there are such a lot of them going on that one finds it somewhat difficult to measure evenly the march of time. For myself, I can say there are weeks which seem to pass in a flash and then again there are others which are unutterably long and slow. At times it is almost difficult to believe that so much has happened and at another that so little time has passed.

1940, 9 NOVEMBER. MANSION HOUSE, LONDON. (BLOOD, 485.)

I really do not see that I am called upon to draw up such precise regulations for those who may be departing on week-ends. It does not follow that the week-ends are spent in idleness. I have often known them to become more fruitful than the mid-week period.

1951, 29 NOVEMBER.

A proposal to include Saturday in the working week seemed silly to Churchill, who himself never stopped working, in particular during World War II, at the Prime Minister's country residence at Chequers.

The great thing is to get the true picture, whatever it is.

1940, 24 NOVEMBER. (WW2 II, 615.)

Prime Minister to Gen. Sir Alan Brooke.

Unexpected events

Allowance must be made for the intervention of the unexpected.

1923. (CRISIS II, 263.)

30

CHURCHILL
CLAIRVOYANT

*"[A politician needs…] the ability to foretell what is going to
happen tomorrow, next week, next month, and next year – and to
have the ability afterwards to explain why it didn't happen."* [120]

"I can see further ahead than you do. I see into the future."
At the opening of a YMCA youth hostel, Enfield, 1915.

I have searched diligently for Churchill predictions that *did not* come true. They do exist:
strikingly, less than a year before Hitler came to power, he declared, "I do not believe
that we shall see another great war in our time." [121]

But the missed predictions are overwhelmed by the accurate ones. Call this proof of his
prescience, or just a manifestation of being half a century on the scene with fifteen million
words in print – he had to get something right! Nevertheless, Churchill ran up a remarkable string of forecasts.

---

120 Halle, *Irrepressible*, 50. At a 1902 press interview, WSC was asked, "What are the desirable
qualifications for any young man who wishes to become a politician?"
121 New York, 10 March 1932. See World War II below.

He was right on the big questions – about Hitler above all, but also about modern war in Europe, several operations of World War I, and the perils of submarine warfare. In 1936 he predicted Japan would start a war in the Far East if Germany attacked in Europe, a remark largely forgotten by those who quote only his speeches against defence expenditures in the 1920s – when there was no Hitler – to prove his inconsistency.

Cell phones and nuclear-powered warships were fairly easy to predict, given what he, and his scientific adviser Frederick Lindemann, observed of technical progress. But we have not yet arranged to grow only those parts of chickens we wish to eat, as he forecast in 1931.[122]

In World War II he predicted the survival of Russia, the London Blitz, the decline of post-war Britain, the rise of America as a superpower and the renaissance of post-war France and Germany. Shortly after it ended he expressed certainty that Soviet communism would fall, perhaps not in his time, but eventually.

Sadly, but perhaps more significantly, Churchill also foresaw the rise of materialism, which would come to dominate the politics and culture of the English-speaking peoples, at the expense of the old verities of duty, honour, country: "comforts, activities, amenities, pleasures will crowd upon them, but their hearts will ache, their lives will be barren, if they have not a vision above material things".[123]

Churchill was wrong about a peaceful Palestine and the impregnability of Singapore; his hopes for détente between the West and the Soviets were premature, as was his belief that science would usher in a new age of universal prosperity. His ideas on climate change were that mankind could control climate to its benefit; today we are told that man's influence is negative, and we control climate to our detriment.

Kay Halle before she died was at work on a book of quotations entitled *Churchill Clairvoyant: Canny and Uncanny*. This chapter is entitled in her memory and that of the leader who forecast so much of what happened, for better or worse, in the "Century of the Common Man".

1900s

...I can see vast changes coming over a now peaceful world; great upheavals, terrible struggles; wars such as one cannot imagine; and I tell you London will be in danger—London will be attacked and I shall be very prominent in the defence of London. I see further ahead than you do. I see into the future. This country will be subjected somehow, to a tremendous invasion, by what means I do not know, but I tell you I shall be in command of the defences of London and I shall save London and England from disaster....dreams of the future are blurred but the main objective is clear. I repeat—London will be in danger and in the high position I shall occupy, it will fall to me to save the Capital and save the Empire.

1891, JULY. HARROW SCHOOL. (GILBERT, SEARCH, 215.)

WSC to schoolmate Muirland Evans, who recalled their conversation

in one of those dreadful basement rooms in the Headmaster's House, a Sunday evening, to be exact, after chapel evensong....We frankly discussed our futures. After placing me in the Diplomatic Service...or alternatively in finance, following my father's career, we came to his own future.

Is it not a much more splendid dream that this realm of England...should be found bold enough and strong enough to send forth on the wings of honest purpose the message which the Russian Emperor tried vainly to proclaim: that the cruel and clanking struggle of armaments is drawing to a close, and that with the New Century has come a clearer and a calmer sky.

1903, 13 FEBRUARY. WALLSEND. (MBA, 84.)

---

122 "Fifty Years Hence," *Strand Magazine*, December 1931; Thoughts, 200.
123 Ibid., Thoughts, 204.

...strange methods, huge forces, larger combinations—a Titanic world—have sprung up around us. The foundations of our power are changing. To stand still would be to fall; to fall would be to perish. We must go forward. We will go forward. We will go forward into a way of life more earnestly viewed, more scientifically organised, more consciously national than any we have known. Thus alone shall we be able to sustain and to renew, through the generations which are to come, the fame and the power of the British race.

1909, 23 MAY. FREE TRADE HALL, MANCHESTER.
(LIBERALISM, 268.)

1930s

We are faced, not with the prospect of a new war, but with something very like the possibility of a resumption of the War which ended in November, 1918.

1935, 19 MARCH.

In his World War II memoirs, Churchill was to look back on the period 1914–45 as "another Thirty Years' War". The original, between 1618 and 1648, was fought mainly in what was later Germany, and involved most major continental Powers.

It would be folly for us to act as if we were swimming in a halcyon sea, as if nothing but balmy breezes and calm weather were to be expected and everything were working in the most agreeable fashion. By all means follow your lines of hope and your paths of peace, but do not close your eyes to the fact that we are entering a corridor of deepening and darkening danger, and that we shall have to move along it for many months and possibly for years to come.

1935, 31 MAY.

...unless there is a front against potential aggression there will be no settlement. All the nations of Europe will just be driven helter-skelter across the diplomatic chessboard until the limits of retreat are exhausted, and then, out of desperation, perhaps in some most unlikely quarter, the explosion of war will take place, probably under conditions not very favourable to those who have been engaged in this long retreat.

1936, 5 NOVEMBER.

The forces of aggression are actually gathering, have, indeed, already been to a large extent gathered. Many people say that nothing will happen till the [1939] harvest has been garnered, and perhaps they are right, but personally I always distrust dates which are mentioned beforehand, because they may so easily be antedated, and, after all, the harvest itself is not far off. I think we must consider July, August, and September as months in which the tension of Europe will become most severe.

1939, 28 JUNE. CITY CARLTON CLUB, LONDON.
(BLOOD, 175–6.)

Before the harvest is gathered in—we shall be at war.

1939, 23 AUGUST, FRANCE. (OB, CV5/3, 1592.)

Remark to his secretary, Mary Shearburn, while driving between Dreux and Paris. Three days earlier, as they painted together on this holiday, WSC also told his friend the artist Paul Maze "This is the last picture we shall paint in peace for a very long time" (OB V, 1103).

1941

A *busy* Christmas and a *frantic* New Year.

1940, 24 DECEMBER. (GILBERT, LIFE, 686.)

To his staff on Christmas Eve.

1942

Here's to 1942, here's to a year of toil—a year of struggle and peril, and a long step forward towards victory. May we all come through safe and with honour.

1942, 1 JANUARY. EN ROUTE FROM OTTAWA TO
WASHINGTON. (END, 3.)

Churchill called his staff and newspaper reporters to the dining car of his train to welcome the New Year. Then, raising his glass to the company, he made this toast.

1942–43

Provided that every effort is made, that nothing is kept back, that the whole man-power, brain power, virility, valour and civic virtue of the English-speaking world with all its galaxy of loyal, friendly, associated communities and States— provided all that is bent unremittingly to the simple and supreme task, I think it would be reasonable to hope that the end of 1942 will see us quite definitely in a better position than we are now, and that the year 1943 will enable us to assume the initiative upon an ample scale.

1941, 26 DECEMBER. CONGRESS, WASHINGTON. (UNRELENTING, 356.)

1943

The dawn of 1943 will soon loom red before us, and we must brace ourselves to cope with the trials and problems of what must be a stern and terrible year. We do so with the assurance of ever-growing strength, and we do so as a nation with a strong will, a bold heart and a good conscience.

1942, 29 NOVEMBER. BROADCAST, LONDON. (END, 303.)

1944–45

I shall certainly not hazard a guess—it could be no more—as to when the end will come. Many persons of the highest technical attainments, knowledge, and responsibility have good hopes that all will be over by the end of 1944. On the other hand, no one, and certainly not I, can guarantee that several months of 1945 may not be required.

1944, 28 SEPTEMBER.

Biotechnology

We shall escape the absurdity of growing a whole chicken in order to eat the breast or wing, by growing these parts separately under a suitable medium.

1931, DECEMBER. ("FIFTY YEARS HENCE," STRAND MAGAZINE; THOUGHTS, 200.)

Britain, gratitude to

There is much gratitude toward us because we stood alone. It will not last. When we have beaten the "Narzees" we shall have to take our coats off and work for our livings. Never forget, King-Hall! We have to import fifty percent of what we eat! If the scrunch came, I very much doubt whether, notwithstanding our admirable constitutional arrangements, it would be easy to arrange in an amicable manner which half of the population should eat and which should starve.

1942. (KING-HALL NEWSLETTER; HALLE, IRREPRESSIBLE, 202.)

WSC to Sir Stephen King-Hall (1893–1966), British journalist, politician and playwright, Labour MP, 1939–45.

Britain, loss of Empire

Stripped of her Empire in the Orient, deprived of the sovereignty of the seas, loaded with debt and taxation, her commerce and carrying trade shut out by foreign tariffs and quotas, England would sink to the level of a fifth-rate Power, and nothing would remain of all her glories except a population much larger than this island can support.

1933, 24 APRIL. ROYAL SOCIETY OF ST. GEORGE, LONDON. (COVENANT, 93.)

Britain, loss of insularity

We are no longer an island. When once the navigation of the air has been brought to a high degree of perfection, as it must undoubtedly be in the generation which lies in front of us, we have lost to a very considerable extent that distinctive insular position on which our safety and our greatness have hitherto depended.

1922, 21 MARCH.

Nearly a century later, the Channel Tunnel and the European Union have carried on the process Churchill predicted.

Britain, post-World War II

I have two convictions in my heart. One is that, somehow or other, we shall survive, though for a time at a lower level than hitherto. The late Lord Fisher used to say "Britain never succumbs." The second is that things are going to get worse before they get better.

1947, 12 MARCH.

Brotherhood

...when [the war] is won, when the hateful aggressive Nazi and Fascist systems have been laid low, and when every precaution has been taken against their ever rising again, there may be a new brotherhood among men which will not be based upon crude antagonisms of ideology but upon broad, simple, homely ideals of peace, justice and freedom.

1944, 2 AUGUST.

The day may dawn when fair play, love for one's fellow men, respect for justice and freedom, will enable tormented generations to march forth serene and triumphant from the hideous epoch in which we have to dwell. Meanwhile, never flinch, never weary, never despair.

1955, 1 MARCH.

Cell phones and mobiles

Wireless telephones and television, following naturally upon their present path of development, would enable their owner to connect up with any room similarly installed, and hear and take part in the conversation as if he put his head in through the window. The congregation of men in cities would be become superfluous.

1931, DECEMBER. ("FIFTY YEARS HENCE," STRAND MAGAZINE; THOUGHTS, 199.)

Climate change

The discovery and control of such sources of power [as nuclear energy] would cause changes in human affairs incomparably greater than those produced by the steam-engine four generations ago. Schemes of cosmic magnitude would become feasible. Geography and climate would obey our orders....The amount of rain falling yearly upon the Epsom racecourse would be enough to thaw all the ice at the Arctic and Antarctic poles. The changing of one element into another by means of temperatures and pressures would be far beyond our present reach, would transform beyond all description our standards of values.

1931, DECEMBER. ("FIFTY YEARS HENCE," STRAND MAGAZINE; THOUGHTS, 198.)

Communism

[I do not believe that any people can be held in thrall for ever.] The machinery of propaganda may pack their minds with falsehood and deny them truth for many generations of time. But the soul of man thus held in trance or frozen in a long night can be awakened by a spark coming from God knows where and in a moment the whole structure of lies and oppression is on trial for its life.

1949, 31 MARCH. MASSACHUSETTS INSTITUTE OF TECHNOLOGY, BOSTON. (GILBERT, LIFE, 884.)

I won't see its end—but you will.

1953, 1 JANUARY. SIR JOHN COLVILLE TO THE EDITOR.

Colville recorded in his diary for this date: "He said that if I lived my normal span I should assuredly see Eastern Europe free of Communism." Colville died in 1987, just as WSC's prediction was coming true.

[The] complications and palliatives of human life that will render the schemes of Karl Marx more out of date and smaller in relation to world problems than they have ever been before. The natural forces are working with greater freedom and greater opportunity to fertilise and vary the thoughts and the power of individual men and women....in the main human society will grow in many forms not comprehended by a party machine.

1957. (WW2 ABR. ED., 973.)

Czechoslovakia

I venture to think that in future the Czechoslovak State cannot be maintained as an independent entity. I think you will find that in a period of time which may be measured by years, but may be measured only by months, Czechoslovakia will be engulfed in the Nazi régime. Perhaps they may join it in despair or in revenge. At any rate, that story is over and told.

1938, 5 OCTOBER.

True to WSC's prediction, Hitler marched into Prague in early 1939, abrogating the Munich agreement and creating the German protectorate of Bohemia and Moravia. After the war it was put back together again, only to divide into Slovakia and the Czech Republic after the fall of the Soviet Union.

Death

When my time is due, it will come.

1940. (THOMPSON, SHADOW, 62.)

WSC to his bodyguard Inspector Thompson. Churchill was a fatalist about death, and utterly disdainful of personal safety, as he proved on many occasions. Aside from believing he would die on 24 January (see next entry), he refrained from predicting his departure.

Today is the 24th of January. It's the day my father died. It's the day I shall die, too.

1953, 24 JANUARY. (COLVILLE, "HE HAD NO USE FOR SECOND BEST," FINEST HOUR 41, AUTUMN 1983, 7.)

Expressed while shaving one morning. Twelve years later, Churchill lapsed into a coma in early January, and Colville assured the Queen's private secretary, "He won't die until the 24th." Mostly unconscious, Sir Winston survived until the predicted date.

Détente

I hope however that the "fraternal association" of the British Commonwealth and the United States, together with sea- and air-power, may put us on good terms and in a friendly balance with Russia at least for the period of rebuilding. Further than that I cannot see with mortal eye, and I am not as yet fully informed about the celestial telescopes.

1943, 5 SEPTEMBER. (WW2 V, 115.)

WSC to Field Marshal Smuts.

...I for one, being an optimist, do not think peace is going to be so bad as war, and I hope we shall not try to make it as bad.

1943, 13 OCTOBER.

France

Is France finished? Is that long and famous history, adorned by so many manifestations of genius and valour, bearing with it so much that is precious to culture and civilisation, and above all to the liberties of mankind—is all that now to sink for ever into the ocean of the past, or will France rise again and resume her rightful place in the structure of what may one day be again the family of Europe? I declare to you here, on this considerable occasion, even now when misguided or suborned Frenchmen are firing upon their rescuers, I declare to you my faith that France will rise again.

1942, 10 NOVEMBER. MANSION HOUSE, LONDON. (END, 268.)

I feel that de Gaullist France will be a France more hostile to England than any since Fashoda.

1944, 17 AUGUST, NAPLES. (OB VII, 888.)

WSC to his wife: an accurate prediction. De Gaulle blocked Britain's application to the

European Common Market fifteen years later. The Fashoda Incident in 1898 saw sabre-rattling between the UK and France over territorial claims in Africa, but ended in a diplomatic victory for Britain and, ironically, to the Entente Cordiale which allied the two countries for World War I.

Germany

Germany has indeed been partitioned, but only by a hideous division into zones of military occupation. About this tragedy it can only be said IT CANNOT LAST.

1952. (WW2 V, 360.)

Hitler

[I am] convinced that Hitler or his followers [will] seize the first opportunity to resort to armed force.

1930, 18 OCTOBER. (GILBERT, WILDERNESS, 36.)

WSC to Prince Otto von Bismarck. In the light of Churchill's oft-quoted 1935 Hitler article (reprinted in Great Contemporaries*) – which, taken out of context, might seem to praise Hitler and hope for the best – this was a much earlier and more accurate representation of WSC's forebodings. See also Chapter 20, People...Hitler.*

Even if the Nazi legions stood triumphant on the Black Sea, or indeed upon the Caspian, even if Hitler was at the gates of India, it would profit him nothing if at the same time the entire economic and scientific apparatus of German war power lay shattered and pulverized at home.

1940, 20 AUGUST.

*A similar quotation was reported by Sir Martin Gilbert (*Churchill: A Life*, 668):*

> *Even if That Man reached the Caspian, he would return to find a fire in his backyard. It would avail him nothing if he reached the Great Wall of China.*

Japan

...should Germany at any time make war in Europe, we may be sure that Japan will immediately light a second conflagration in the Far East.

1936, 27 NOVEMBER. ("GERMANY AND JAPAN," EVENING STANDARD; STEP, 72.)

Churchill is often accused of underestimating and ignoring the threat of Japan; here, however, he warned of the likely outcome of a Germany–Japan alliance.

Labour Party

The whole tribe of highly intellectual left-wing scribblers assure us that the Socialist Administration will rule for twenty years....They will sing quite a different tune once they realise, and are made to realise, that they have a growing majority of the nation against them.

1946, 5 OCTOBER. PARTY CONFERENCE, BLACKPOOL. (SINEWS, 211–12.)

The Labour Government would last only until 1951.

If there was a General Election tomorrow the Socialist majority would vanish. If they wait another year, they themselves will vanish for a considerable period, "unwept, unhonoured, and unsung—and unhung."

1947, 11 NOVEMBER.

This prediction missed by several years. Labour clung to a small majority in 1950, finally losing to the Conservatives in 1951.

London bombings

This group of well-known, prominent buildings and towers between three major railway stations, with the river as a perfect guide by night and day, is the easiest of all targets, and I have very little doubt that they will need extensive repairs before very long.

1940, 17 SEPTEMBER.

Churchill was right. Buckingham Palace was hit, and on the first anniversary of his becoming PM, 10 May 1941, the House of Commons was destroyed by German bombs.

Materialism

Projects undreamed-of by past generations will absorb our immediate descendants; forces terrific and devastating will be in their hands; comforts, activities, amenities, pleasures will crowd upon them, but their hearts will ache, their lives will be barren, if they have not a vision above material things.

1931, DECEMBER. ("FIFTY YEARS HENCE," STRAND MAGAZINE; THOUGHTS, 204.)

It was of course easy to predict sweeping technological change in the 1930s; it was rarer among thinkers, let alone politicians, to ponder the implications, should materialism become an end in itself.

Norway

In my view, which is shared by my skilled advisers, Herr Hitler has committed a grave strategic error in spreading the war so far to the north and in forcing the Scandinavian people, or peoples, out of their attitude of neutrality....we shall take all we want of this Norwegian coast now, with an enormous increase in the facility and in the efficiency of our blockade.

1940, 11 APRIL.

Things did not work out as WSC predicted, and the Norwegian lodgments were abandoned in June.

Palestine

Jewish immigration into Palestine can only come as it makes a place for itself by legitimate and honourable means....The present form of Government [Palestine Mandate] will continue for many years, and step by step we shall develop representative institutions leading up to full self-government. All of us here today will have passed away from the earth and also our children and our children's children before it is fully achieved.

1921, 27 MARCH, CAIRO. (OB IV, 566.)

The Arabs of Palestine had petitioned Churchill, in Cairo, to settle the borders of the Middle East, to abandon the Balfour Declaration that Britain favoured a Jewish National Home in western Palestine, and to put a stop to Jewish immigration. Churchill refused, and pointed out that Britain, not the Arabs, had ensured the liberation of Palestine from the Turks.

Poland

The heroic defence of Warsaw shows that the soul of Poland is indestructible, and that she will rise again like a rock, which may for a spell be submerged by a tidal wave, but which remains a rock.

1939, 1 OCTOBER. BROADCAST, LONDON. (BLOOD, 205.)

Post-World War II era

...if the dangers of war and tyranny are removed, there is no doubt that science and cooperation can bring in the next few years to the world certainly in the next few decades newly taught in the sharpening school of war, an expansion of material well-being beyond anything that has yet occurred in human experience. Now, at this sad and breathless moment, we are plunged in the hunger and distress which are the aftermath of our stupendous struggle; but this will pass and may pass quickly, and there is no reason except human folly or sub-human crime which should deny to all the nations the inauguration and enjoyment of an age of plenty.

1946, 5 MARCH. WESTMINSTER COLLEGE, FULTON, MISSOURI. (SINEWS, 97.)

Return to office

Thirty years of my life have been passed in this room. I shall never sit in it again. You will but I shall not.

1945, 27 JULY, DOWNING STREET. (EDEN, A., 551.)

Churchill to Eden, in a prediction which was doubly wrong. Not only did Churchill return as Prime Minister (1951), but he did so before Eden, who became Prime Minister in 1955.

Russia

I bet anybody here a Monkey to a Mousetrap that the Russians are still fighting, and fighting victoriously, two years from now.

1941, 22 JUNE. (COLVILLE DIARIES; OB VI, 550.)

Sir Martin Gilbert explains of this quotation that a monkey is horse racing parlance for £500, while a mousetrap is a sovereign. Churchill was therefore offering odds of 500:1 in favour of Russia surviving the German invasion. (Churchill was in the minority. There was widespread feeling in Britain and America that the Soviet Union would be defeated.)

Science

When we have degenerated, as we must eventually degenerate, when we have lost our intrinsic superiority, and other races, according to the

natural law, advance to take our place...Our morals will be gone, but our Maxims will remain. The effete and trembling European will sweep from the earth by scientific machinery the valiant savages who assail him.

1899. (SAVROLA, 79.)

Ship power

We are not very far away—we cannot tell how far—from some form of internal combustion engines for warships of all kinds, and the indirect and wasteful use of oil to generate steam will, in the future, give place to the direct employment of its own explosive force.

1913, 26 MARCH.

As First Lord of the Admiralty Churchill had just completed changing Royal Navy ships from coal to oil firing; he was already predicting a successor form of energy, which sounds very much like a diesel engine, and at the outside, nuclear power.

Singapore

I have never made any predictions, except things like saying Singapore would hold out. What a fool and a knave I should have been to say it would fall!

1942, 2 JULY.

The result of this prediction was already evident, but Churchill was saying it would have been foolhardy to predict defeat.

Submarines

We are increasingly convinced of the power of the submarine and the decisive part which this weapon, aided perhaps in some respects by the seaplane, may play in the naval warfare of the future.

1914, 17 MARCH.

United States

There is one country where a man knows he has an unbounded future: the USA, even though I deplore some of your habits....You stop drinking with your meals.

1946, 4 MARCH. EN ROUTE TO FULTON, MISSOURI. (HALLE, AMERICA AND BRITAIN, 34–5.)

Reported by Clark Clifford, aide to President Truman.

War in Europe

A European war cannot be anything but a cruel, heartrending struggle, which, if we are ever to enjoy the bitter fruits of victory, must demand, perhaps for several years, the whole manhood of the nation, the entire suspension of peaceful industries, and the concentrating to one end of every vital energy in the community....when mighty populations are impelled against each other, each individual severally embittered and inflamed—when the resources of science and civilisation sweep away everything that might mitigate their fury, a European war can only end in the ruin of the vanquished and the scarcely less fatal commercial dislocation and exhaustion of the conquerors. Democracy is more vindictive than Cabinets. The wars of peoples will be more terrible than those of kings.

1901, 13 MAY. (MBA, 22–23.)

Misdated 12 May in Mr. Brodrick's Army.

Let it not be thought for a moment that the danger of another explosion in Europe is passed. For the time being the stupor and the collapse which followed the World War ensure a sullen passivity, and the horror of war, its carnage and its tyrannies, has sunk into the soul, has dominated the mind, of every class in every race. But the causes of war have been in no way removed; indeed they are in some respects aggravated by the so-called Peace Treaties....

1924, SEPTEMBER. ("SHALL WE ALL COMMIT SUICIDE?," PALL MALL; THOUGHTS, 177.)

Wars of great powers

There is an idea against which I want to warn the House, for it is very common, and lies at the back of much that is said. It is that if we by taking thought can add a cubit to our military stature we shall be able to glide by a smooth transition from peace to war, and to fight great civilised Powers easily, comfortably, and cheaply. The battles will be won without casualties, the campaign will progress without misfortune, a swift and glorious triumph will crown the operations, and, in the spirit of the football field, will be hailed by the vanquished with hardly less satisfaction than by the conquerors, while the delighted spectators will hurry home to a General Election.

Sir, let us make no mistake: if by wicked counsels we are drawn into war with a great European State, we shall fight that war - whatever our forethought—with breaking hearts and straitened means, with hunger in our streets and ruin in our market-places; success will be robbed of all its triumph; and when it is over—whatever the issue—we shall turn in poverty and grief, to find all our most formidable commercial rivals entrenched on all our old vantage-grounds.

1903, 23 FEBRUARY. (MBA, 100–01.)

The text quoted is from Mr. Brodrick's Army, *rather than Hansard, from which it differs in some details, and which dates it 23 February. It is possible that WSC edited his speech for his book; in the few instances where I encounter such differences I invariably rely on his own published words as the authoritative version. (A more famous examples is in Chapter 1,* Immortal Words...Stairway to a Dark Gulf.)

World War I

The German armies in advancing through Belgium and onwards into France will be relatively weakened...By the fortieth day Germany should be extended at full strain both internally and on her war fronts, and this strain will become daily more severe and ultimately overwhelming, unless it is relieved by decisive victories in France. If the French army has not been squandered by precipitate or desperate action, the balance of forces should be favourable after the fortieth day, and will improve steadily as time passes.

1911, 13 AUGUST. (CRISIS I, 62.)

From Churchill's Cabinet memo, "Military Aspects of the Continental Problem": a remarkable prediction. General Sir Henry Wilson, director of operations at the War Office, labelled it "ridiculous and fantastic", but it turned out almost exactly right. The French halted the German advance on its forty-second day on the Marne, virtually as Churchill had forecast.

The times are harsh, the need is dire, the agony of Europe is infinite; but the might of Britain hurled united into the conflict will be irresistible.

1915, 5 JUNE, DUNDEE. (GILBERT, LIFE, 321.)

...the carnage grows apace, and the certainty that no result will be reached this year fills my mind with melancholy thoughts. The youth of Europe—almost a whole generation—will be shorn away.

1915, 19 JUNE. (OB, CV3/2, 1042.)

WSC to his brother Jack. He added:

I find it very painful to be deprived [because of his dismissal from the Admiralty the month before] of direct means of action.

We are passing through a bad time now, and it will probably be worse before it is better, but that it will be better, if we only endure and persevere, I have no doubt whatever.

1915, 15 NOVEMBER.

...the old wars were decided by their episodes rather than by their tendencies. In this War the tendencies are far more important than the episodes. Without winning any sensational victories, we may win....Germany may be defeated more fatally in the second or third year of the War than if the Allied Armies had entered Berlin in the first.

1915, 15 NOVEMBER.

Churchill was slightly off: Germany was defeated in the fifth year of World War I. He quoted these same remarks during World War II, on 24 February 1942 – and was off again.

World War I victory

No one can tell how far this great adventure may carry us all. Unless we win, I do not want to live any more. But win we will.

1914, 24 AUGUST, ADMIRALTY. (GILBERT, LIFE, 279.)

WSC to his brother Jack.

World War II

I do not believe that we shall see another great war in our time. War, today, is bare—bare of profit and stripped of all its glamour. The old pomp and circumstance are gone. War now is nothing but toil, blood, death, squalor, and lying propaganda.

1932, 10 MARCH. RADIO INTERVIEW, NEW YORK. (GILBERT, WILDERNESS, 45.)

A year later WSC was to be disabused of this prediction. See Appendix III for the development of Churchill's "Blood, toil, tears and sweat".

[Questioner: "Will there be war?"]
    Certainly, a very terrible war in which London will be bombed and Buckingham Palace will be razed to the ground, and the lions and tigers will escape from the zoo and roam through the streets of London attacking people.

1936, 6 OCTOBER. ALL SOUL'S, OXFORD. (ADDISON, UNEXPECTED, 144.)

Isaiah Berlin to Paul Addison, 30 January 1991.

Carnivores will win this war!

1940. ("CHURCHILL THE CONVERSATIONALIST," COLLIN BROOKS IN EADE, 247.)

Possibly a derisive reference to Hitler being a vegetarian. Remarked when WSC was offered salmon; also recorded when he asked that the Ministry of Food make beef more widely available.

[We shall] draw from the heart of suffering itself the means of inspiration and survival....

1940, 11 SEPTEMBER. BROADCAST. (BLOOD, 430.)

The date is interesting: 11 September.

Do you play poker? Here is the hand that is going to win the war: a Royal Flush—Great Britain, the Sea, the Air, the Middle East, American aid.

1941, 16 FEBRUARY, DITCHLEY PARK. (KENNEDY, BUSINESS, 79.)

Churchill speaking in French to Polish General Sikorski and the Polish Ambassador.

I have never shared the view that this would be a short war, or that it would end in 1942. It is far more likely to be a long war. There is no reason to suppose that the war will stop when the final result has become obvious. The Battle of Gettysburg proclaimed the ultimate victory of the North, but far more blood was shed after the Battle of Gettysburg than before.

1942, 2 JULY.

I have always expected that this war would become worse in severity as the guilty Nazis feel the ring of doom remorselessly closing in upon them.

1942, 12 OCTOBER. USHER HALL, EDINBURGH. (END, 241.)

The long and terrible march which the rescuing Powers are making is being accomplished stage by stage, and we can now say, not only with hope but with reason, that we shall reach the end of our journey in good order, and that the tragedy which threatened the whole world and might have put out all its lights and left our children and descendants in darkness and bondage—perhaps for centuries—that tragedy will not come to pass.

1944, 26 MARCH. BROADCAST, LONDON. (DAWN, 39.)

World War II victory

Let the great cities of Warsaw, of Prague, of Vienna, banish despair even in the midst of their agony. Their liberation is sure. The day will come when the joybells will ring again throughout Europe, and when victorious nations, masters not only of their foes, but of themselves, will plan and build in justice, in tradition, and in freedom, a house of many mansions where there will be room for all.

1940, 20 JANUARY. BROADCAST, LONDON. (BLOOD, 253–4.)

"House of many mansions" (from John 14:2) was actually the title of this famous speech. The phrase was quoted by Churchill on many significant occasions: see Britain, Empire and Commonwealth....Commonwealth of many mansions, and Appendix IV.

We cannot yet see how deliverance will come, or when it will come, but nothing is more certain than that every trace of Hitler's footsteps, every stain of his infected and corroding fingers, will be sponged and purged and, if need be, blasted from the surface of the earth.

1941, 12 JUNE. BROADCAST, LONDON. (UNRELENTING, 163.)

I have never given any assurances of a speedy or easy or cheap victory. On the contrary, as you know, I have never promised anything but the hardest conditions, great disappointments, and many mistakes. But I am sure that at the end all will be well for us in our island home, all will be better for the world and there will be that crown of honour to those who have endured and never failed which history will

accord to them for having set an example to the whole human race.

1941, 7 NOVEMBER. GUILDHALL, HULL. (UNRELENTING, 291.)

Victory is sure, and it will belong to all who have not faltered or flinched or wearied on the long road.

1944, 10 FEBRUARY. (DAWN, 61.)

A message to the Marquess of Hartington, National Government candidate in the West Derbyshire by-election.

So we had won after all!...England would live; Britain would live; the Commonwealth of Nations and the Empire would live....I thought of a remark which Edward Grey had made to me more than thirty years before— that the United States is like "a gigantic boiler. Once the fire is lighted under it there is no limit to the power it can generate."

1950. (WW2 III, 539–40.)

Recalling 7 December 1941, after hearing that the Japanese had attacked Pearl Harbor and that the United States was in the war. For more of this passage see Chapter 8, America...Pearl Harbor.

"World War III"

I am sure that the mistakes of that time [German Reparations after World War I] will not be repeated; we shall make another set of mistakes.

1944, 8 JUNE.

It may well be that an even worse war is drawing near. A war of the East against the West. A war of liberal civilisation against the Mongol hordes. Far gone are the days of Queen Victoria and a settled world order. But, having gone through so much, we do not despair.

1947. ("THE DREAM," OB VIII, 371.)

For the background of this article, see Chapter 5, Anecdotes and Stories...The Dream. WSC alternated between expecting an apocalypse and a lasting peace. See also Brotherhood in this chapter, and, for more of this quotation, Chapter 19, Nuclear Age...1945–49.

31

PERSONAL
MATTERS

"The heights by great men reached and kept
Were not achieved by sudden flight,
But they, while their companions slept,
Were toiling upward in the night."
– Henry Wadsworth Longfellow [124]

"This is the sort of company I should like to find in heaven."
Duncan and Diana Sandys and WSC at baby Celia's christening, 1943.

Here are quotations relating to Churchill personally: his character, habits and family, and his prescriptions for living life to the full, which he certainly did. (His method for squeezing a day and a half out of every day, symbolised by the verse above, will be found under "Sleep".) Personal tastes and favourites will be found in the following chapter.

A variety of quotations speak to his political and personal philosophies, some of them with a high degree of frankness. See for example Ambitions, Conceit, Consistency, Criticism and Disposition. On debates in the Commons, he freely confessed using provocative language, musing that he was surprised "that a great many of my colleagues are on speaking terms with me".

---

124 Both Churchill and his son and biographer frequently repeated these lines, with some variation, from Longfellow's "The Ladder of Saint Augustine," stanza 10.

Reactions to election results, and thoughts about his being variously a Conservative and a Liberal, are pithy and pointed. And there are examples of self-doubt, which he rarely confessed publicly but sometimes wrote about later: see *Déjà vu*, Fate, Fear, Overconfidence and, in particular, Faults.

Churchill's domestic existence, which it is safe to say always came second after politics, was generally a rousing, warm affair, except for an occasionally tempestuous relationship with his son Randolph. Sir Fitzroy Maclean remembered being asked with his wife "now and then to Chequers or Chartwell to join him and his family in their noisy, affectionate, hilarious, often uproarious family life".[125]

WSC's comments to and about his wife, the best of which I trust are here, would make a perfect series of greeting cards for any husband wondering how to express himself. As Sir Fitzroy put it, "Mrs. Churchill was one of the sweetest and most remarkable women I ever met, and all those years a marvellous wife to Winston, soothing him or bullying him as necessary and standing by him through thick and thin."[126] Their own daughter's books about her parents are ample testimony to one of her father's favourite maxims describing his marriage: "Here firm though all be drifting."[127]

What strikes me about these quotations as a group is what one of his secretaries said about Churchill: "…he was so human, so funny – that always saved the day."[128] Humorous allusions to animals are poignant; illnesses are treated like invading armies. Interestingly, a wartime ally drew the same conclusion. Marshal Tito, a perceptive man, was once asked what most struck him about WSC. "His humanity," Tito said immediately. "He is so human."[129]

Action vs. waiting

…I myself find waiting more trying than action.…

1942, 22 SEPTEMBER. (WW2 IV, 501.)

WSC to Sir Stafford Cripps.

Age

Old age is sufficiently ugly and unpleasing without its too frequent accompaniments, capriciousness and malevolence.

1897, 21 JANUARY, MADRAS, INDIA. (OB, CV1/2, 727.)

WSC to his mother.

I am 25 today. It is terrible to think how little time remains.

1899, 30 NOVEMBER, PRETORIA. (PILPEL, 30.)

Postscript in a letter from WSC to Bourke Cockran, while Churchill was imprisoned by the Boers after the Armoured Train ambush. Given his father's early death, WSC long believed that he too would die young.

Curse ruthless time! Curse our mortality! How cruelly short is the allotted span for all we must cram into it!

CIRCA 1906. (BONHAM CARTER, 15.)

WSC to Violet Asquith.

I must be the oldest man ever to have been in the White House.

1942, 14 JANUARY. WHITE HOUSE, WASHINGTON. (WARD, 166.)

Daisy Suckley diaries. Suckley wrote, "The Pres. said there had been someone ninety-five there, so he cheered up."

I notice in the newspapers that the Central Office or Party Chiefs have issued instructions that no one over seventy should be tolerated as a candidate at the forthcoming election. I naturally wish to know at the earliest moment whether this ban applies to me.

1945, 19 MARCH. (WW2 VI, 632.)

---

125 Maclean, Sir Fitzroy, "Humanity: A Churchillian Characteristic," *Proceedings of the International Churchill Societies 1987*, 31.
126 Ibid., 25.
127 Soames, Clementine, 426.
128 Grace Hamblin in Gilbert, Search, 170.
129 Maclean, op. cit., 31.

WSC to the Rt. Hon. Ralph Assheton, Chairman of the Conservative Party Organisation, 1944–46.

Who is that?
[Julian Amery: Morrison, he used to be your Home Secretary.]
Are you sure? He looks very much aged!

1956. (HALLE, IRREPRESSIBLE, 337.)

Julian Amery MP to Kay Halle.

I am so bored with it all.

1965, JANUARY. (SIR JOHN COLVILLE TO THE EDITOR.)

A remark to family and friends at the end of his life.

Ambitions

Of course it is not my intention to become a mere professional soldier. I only wish to gain some experience. Some day I shall be a statesman as my father was before me.

1896. (GILBERT, JEWS, 3.)

WSC to Sir Felix Semon, the throat specialist he consulted about pronouncing the letter "s" – something he never mastered, and turned into a prop of his oratory.

Two years in Egypt my dearest Mamma—with a campaign thrown in—would I think qualify me to be allowed to beat my sword into a paper cutter & my sabretache into an election address.

1896, NOVEMBER, INDIA. (OB I, 300.)

WSC to his mother; an early manifestation of his determined objective: the House of Commons. The Oxford English Dictionary describes "sabretache" as a leather satchel suspended on the left side by long straps from the sword-belt of a cavalry officer. First use 1812. Abolished by King Edward VII in 1901.

It is a pushing age and we must shove with the best.

1898, 10 JANUARY, BANGALORE, INDIA. (OB, CV1/2, 856.)

WSC to his mother.

"I presume" [Lord Curzon] said to me, "it will not be long before we hear you declaim in the House of Commons." Though greatly hampered by inability to compose at the rate necessary for public speaking, I was strongly of the same opinion myself.

1896, CALCUTTA. ("GEORGE CURZON," PALL MALL; GC, 176.)

Dining with the Viceroy of India, Lord Curzon, 1898.

Don't you [Lloyd George] make any mistake. You're not going to get your new world. The old world is a good enough place for me, and there's life in the old dog yet. It's going to sit up and wag its tail….if you are going to include all parties, you will have to have me in your new National Party.

1920, 17 JANUARY. (OB, CV4/2, 1005–6.)

Lloyd George replied, "Oh no! To be a party you must have at least one follower. You have none." From the diaries of Frances Stephenson, secretary, mistress and finally wife of Lloyd George, who commented: "A most amusing meal, at which Winston waxed very eloquent on the subject of the old world and the new, taking arms in defence of the former."

I might have gone into the Church and preached orthodox sermons in a spirit of audacious contradiction to the age. I might have gone into the City and made a fortune….I might even have gravitated to the Bar and persons might have been hanged through my defence….

1930. (MEL, 41.)

Many years later WSC mused of a career in the Church: "What would have become of me then?" he asked his private secretary. Anthony Montague Browne said, "I suggested that he would have crossed the floor and become Pope."

At my time of life I have no personal ambitions, no future to provide for. And I feel I can truthfully say that I only wish to do my duty by the whole mass of the nation and of the British Empire as long as I am thought to be of any use for that.

1943, 21 MARCH. BROADCAST, LONDON. (ONWARDS, 34.)

If I remain in public life at this juncture it is because, rightly or wrongly, but sincerely, I believe that I may be able to make an important contribution to the prevention of a Third World War and to bringing nearer that lasting peace settlement which the masses of the people of every race and in every land fervently desire. I pray indeed that I may have this opportunity. It is the last prize I seek to win. I have been blessed with so much good fortune throughout my long life, and I am treated with so much kindness by my fellow countrymen far outside the ranks of party, and indeed also in the United States and in Europe, that all the daydreams of my youth have been surpassed.

1951, 23 OCTOBER, PLYMOUTH. (STEMMING, 170.)

I have no more ambitions, but a last task I still see in front of me, which possibly nobody can take from me, is to ease world tension, to pave the way for peace and freedom. Powerful political manoeuvres are no longer practicable. One must negotiate.

1953, 16 DECEMBER. (COOTE, 59.)

Reported conversation by the son of German Admiral von Tirpitz in the London Evening News.

Ancestry

Solitary trees, if they grow at all, grow strong; and a boy deprived of a father's care often develops, if he escape the perils of youth, an independence and vigour of thought which may restore in after life the heavy loss of early days.

1902. (RIVER, ABR. ED., 21.)

A quotation which many have observed was a reflection of WSC about himself, although it is by no means established that his father cared as little about him as Churchill implied in My Early Life. *This is Churchill's final (1902) edit. His original 1899 text (River I, 37) uses the older spelling "developes" and carries a freestanding colon, thus: "...strong : and..."*

[Adlai Stevenson: "What message would you like me to bring from you to the English-Speaking Union?"]

My mother was American, my ancestors were officers in Washington's army; so I am myself an English-Speaking Union!

1953, 29 JULY, LONDON. (FISHMAN, 217.)

Adlai Stevenson to the English-Speaking Union, 1965. See also Chapter 20, People...Stevenson.

Going back to 1776, you may have heard that as a lineal descendant on my mother's side from a Captain in Washington's armies, I am a member of the [Society of] Cincinnati. As I told them when admitted to the Society I must have been on both sides then. Certainly in judging that historic quarrel I am on both sides now.

1954, 7 APRIL. (ALLIANCE, 138.)

Accepting in absentia an honorary Doctor of Law degree from the University of New York. For his remark to the Society of Cincinnati see America...American Revolution.

Belief and reason

I...adopted quite early in life a system of believing what I wanted to believe, while at the same time leaving reason to pursue unfettered whatever paths she was capable of treading.

1930. (MEL, 131.)

Birth and marriage

At Blenheim I took two very important decisions: to be born and to marry. I am happily content with the decisions I took on both those occasions.

UNDATED. (COWLES, WINSTON CHURCHILL, 287.)

Remark to a friend, first quoted by Virginia Cowles.

Blood sample

You can use my finger, or my ear and, of course, I have an almost infinite expanse of arse.

1943, DECEMBER, TUNIS. (THE TIMES, 11 APRIL 1990.)

From a biography of Lt. Col. Pulvertaft, deputy chief hygiene officer in Cairo, brought in to take a blood sample when Churchill was ill with pneumonia after the Teheran conference.

Changes of mind

At Stormberg [South Africa] I changed my mind, or, rather—for it comes to the same thing and sounds better—I made it up.

1900, 13 APRIL. BETHANY, SOUTH AFRICA. (HAMILTON'S 17; BOER, 232.)

Childbirth

...we are in the grip of circumstances, and out of pain joy will spring, and from passing weakness new strength will arise.

1909, 30 MAY. (OB, CV2/2, 893.)

WSC to his wife, pregnant with their first child, asking her to avoid any social events.

Mary [his daughter] is a fortnight overdue. It's an extraordinary business this way of bringing babies into the world. I don't know how God thought of it.

1954, 14 JULY. (MORAN, 617.)

[You must have four children.] One for Mother, one for Father, one for Accidents, and one for Increase.

1945. (NEL, 187.)

Winston and Clementine recited this jointly to secretary Elizabeth Layton advising her on the size of her family. He gave the same advice to others. The Churchills followed their own advice, having four children from 1910 to 1918; Mary (1922) followed after Marigold had died in 1921.

Churchill, Clementine

I am not rich nor powerfully established, but your daughter loves me & with that love I feel strong enough to assume this great & sacred responsibility; & I think I can make her happy & give her a station & career worthy of her beauty and her virtues.

1908. (DILKS, 31.)

Letter to Lady Blanche Hozier upon his engagement to Clementine.

Sweet cat—I kiss your vision as it rises before my mind.…God bless you darling and keep you safe and sound. Kiss the P.K. for me all over.

1909, 15 SEPTEMBER, WURZBERG, GERMANY. (OB, CV2/2, 912.)

The "P.K." was their daughter Diana, nick-named the "Puppy Kitten".

Sometimes also I think I wd not mind stopping living vy much—I am so devoured by egoism that I wd like to have another soul in another world & meet you in another setting, & pay you all the love & honour of the gt romances.

1916, 28 MARCH, FLANDERS. (OB, CV3/2, 1467.)

Twelve times now I have seen y[ou]r birthday come, & each time y[ou]r gracious beauty & loving charm have made a deeper impression

on my heart. God bless you my darling in the year that now opens & give you happinesses wh[ich] fill yr life.

1920, 30 MARCH. MIMIZAN, FRANCE. (SOAMES, CLEMENTINE, 192.)

What it has been to me to live all these years in your heart and companionship no phrases can convey. Time passes swiftly, but is it not joyous to see how great and growing is the treasure we have gathered together, amid the storms and stresses of so many eventful and to millions tragic and terrible years?

1935, 23 JANUARY. (OB, CV5/2, 1042.)

[My marriage] was much the most fortunate and joyous event which happened to me in the whole of my life, for what can be more glorious than to be united in one's walk through life with a being incapable of an ignoble thought?

1935, 24 FEBRUARY. ("MY LIFE" PART VII, *NEWS OF THE WORLD*; ESSAYS III, 176.)

Now Clemmie will have to be a lady at last.

1953. (HART-DAVIS, 340.)

Churchill had declined the Garter from George VI in 1945, deeming it inappropriate on the morrow of his rejection at the general election. This time, as Professor Dilks related, "he capitulated without much resistance but with a good deal of emotion".

My ability to persuade my wife to marry me [was] quite my most brilliant achievement.… Of course, it would have been impossible for any ordinary man to have got through what I had to go through in peace and war without the devoted aid of what we call, in England, one's better half.

PASSIM. (DE MENDELSSOHN, LONDON EDN., 352.)

Quoted only by de Mendelssohn and Fishman, but family members agree that he often expressed this sentiment.

Here firm, though all be drifting.

PASSIM. (OB II, 275.)

One of WSC's favourite expressions, quoted in many contexts but highly applicable to Clementine. A famous recycle of this line was in a wartime broadcast, 29 November 1942: "Here we stood, firm though all was drift-ing…" (End, 296).

Clemmie sits behind me on the platform, shaking her beautiful head in disagreement with some new and pregnant point I am developing.

UNDATED. (COOPER, LADY DIANA, "WINSTON & CLEMENTINE," *FINEST HOUR* 83, 11.)

Colleagues

The light of history will shine on all your helmets.

1945, 28 MAY. (GILBERT, LIFE, 846.)

Churchill's tearful farewell to his Coalition Cabinet after forming a caretaker party government until the forthcoming election. To Labour's Ernest Bevin he had written, "We must hope for reunion when passions are less strong."

Collegiality

I was vy glad that my chaff did not vex you. My shafts though necessarily pointed are never intentionally poisoned. If they cut, I pray they do not fester in the wound.

1932, 3 MAY. (OB V, 431.)

WSC to Stanley Baldwin.

I certainly think that Englishmen ought to start fair with one another from the outset in so grievous a struggle, and so far as I am concerned the past is dead.

1940. (THORNTON-KEMSLEY, 114.)

WSC to Colin Thornton-Kemsley, who in early 1939 tried to have Churchill dismissed as MP for Epping and Woodford owing to WSC's stance on Munich. Thornton-Kemsley had written to say he'd been wrong, and to apologise. See Critics.

Of course, I've forgiven you. Indeed, I agree with very much that you are saying about the Germans. Very good. Such hatred as I have left in me—and it isn't much—I would rather reserve for the future than the past. H'mm. A judicious and thrifty disposal of bile.

1948. (A. P. HERBERT, "CHURCHILL'S HUMOUR" IN EADE, 298.)

Labour's Richard Stokes was an ardent critic of WSC's war leadership, especially concerning tanks. Churchill said this to Stokes one night on leaving the Smoking Room of the House of Commons.

Conceit

Bullets—to a philosopher my dear Mamma—are not worth considering. Besides I am so conceited I do not believe the Gods would create so potent a being as myself for so prosaic an ending. Anyway it does not matter.

1897, 22 DECEMBER, BANGALORE.
(OB, CV1/2, 839.)

WSC to his mother.

You must not however suppose I am so conceited as to place myself with the great men of the past. It was only the crisis which stood at an equal or even higher level. Those were the days of great men and small events. We have endured an age in which the reverse proportions apply.

1948. (SIR JOHN COLVILLE TO THE EDITOR.)

Confidence

…I must say I do not think any public man charged with a high mission from this country ever seemed to be barracked from his homeland in his absence—unintentionally I can well believe—to the extent that befell me while on this visit to the United States; and only my unshakeable confidence in the ties which bind me to the mass of the British people upheld me through those days of trial.

1942, 2 JULY.

Conscience

Let each man search his conscience and search his speeches. I frequently search mine.

1940, 18 JUNE.

My conscience is a good girl I can always come to terms with her.

1942, 7 AUGUST, CAIRO. (SARVEPALLI GOPAL IN BLAKE AND LOUIS, 470.)

WSC to de Gaulle. WSC mentioned he was next visiting Stalin, over which he had "great concern". De Gaulle had replied: "...you will doubtless inform [Stalin] that the second front will not be opened this year...you will easily surmount [your concerns] the moment your conscience has nothing to reproach you for."

Conservatism

I am what I have always been—a Tory Democrat. Force of circumstance has compelled me to serve with another party, but my views have never changed, and I should be glad to give effect to them by rejoining the Conservatives.

1923, 30 MAY. (OB V, 8.)

WSC to English newspaper proprietor George Allardice Riddell, First Baron Riddell (1865–1934); WSC was about to become Chancellor of the Exchequer and to rejoin the Tories.

Am I by temperament and conviction able sincerely to identify myself with the main historical conceptions of Toryism, and can I do justice to them and give expression to them spontaneously in speech and action? My life, such as it has been, has been lived for forty years in the public eye, and very varying opinions are entertained about it—and about particular phases in it....I have always faithfully served two public causes which I think stand supreme—the maintenance of the enduring greatness of Britain and her Empire and the historical continuity of our island life.

1940, 9 OCTOBER. CAXTON HALL, LONDON. (BLOOD, 458.)

Upon deciding to become leader of the Conservative Party after the death of Neville Chamberlain.

I was surprised, and the Conservative Party dumbfounded, when [Prime Minister Stanley Baldwin] invited me to become Chancellor of the Exchequer, the office which my father had once held. A year later, with the approval of my constituents, not having been pressed personally in any way, I formally rejoined the Conservative Party and the Carlton Club, which I had left twenty years before.

1948. (WW2 I, 19.)

Consistency

The only way a man can remain consistent amid changing circumstances is to change with them while preserving the same dominating purpose.

1927, JULY. ("CONSISTENCY IN POLITICS," PALL MALL; THOUGHTS, 23.)

I shall not be like that saint to whom I have before referred in this House, but whose name I have unhappily forgotten, who refused to do right because the devil prompted him. Neither shall I be deterred from doing what I am convinced is right by the fact that I have thought differently about it in some distant, or even in some recent, past.

1942, 29 JANUARY.

The Saint was St. Anthony the Hermit. See also People...Chamberlain, Neville.

Nothing would be easier for me than to make any number of promises and to get the immediate response of cheap cheers and glowing leading articles. I am not in any need to go about making promises in order to win political support or to be allowed to continue in office.

1943, 21 MARCH.

It is curious that, while in the days of my youth I was much reproached with inconsistency and being changeable, I am now scolded for adhering to the same views I had in early life and even for repeating passages from speeches which I made long before most of you were born. Of course the world moves on and we dwell in a constantly changing climate of opinion. But the broad principles and truths of wise and sane political actions do not necessarily alter with the changing moods of a democratic electorate. Not everything changes. Two and two still make four, and I could give you many other instances which go to prove that all wisdom is not new wisdom.

1947, 6 DECEMBER. BELLE VUE, MANCHESTER. (EUROPE, 211.)

My views are a harmonious process which keeps them in relation to the current movements of events.

1952, 5 MAY.

Coolness under fire

I never felt the slightest nervousness and felt as cool as I do now.

1898, 4 SEPTEMBER, SUDAN. (OB I, 414.)

Letter to his mother about the charge at Omdurman, Sudan.

Corporate life

In 1930, when I was out of office, I accepted for the first and only time in my life a directorship. It was in one of the subsidiary companies of Lord Inchcape's far-spreading organisation of the Peninsular and Oriental shipping lines. For eight years I regularly attended the monthly board meetings, and discharged my duties with care.

1948. (WW2 III, 131.)

Criticism

I never complain of hard words across the floor of the House, but I claim to be allowed to match them with arguments equal to the attack which has been made.

1911, 4 APRIL.

I have derived continued benefit from criticism at all periods of my life and I do not remember any time when I was ever short of it.

1914, 27 NOVEMBER.

Don't get torpedoed; for if I am left alone your colleagues will eat me.

1916, 22 JULY. (CRISIS III PART 2, 335.)

WSC to Lloyd George who, even before WSC joined his Government, "used to discuss the war situation with me freely". But Churchill knew how unpopular he was with some members of the Lloyd George coalition.

Because half-a-dozen grasshoppers under a fern make the field ring with their importunate chink, whilst thousands of great cattle repose beneath the shadow of the British oak, chew the cud and are silent, pray do not imagine that those who make the noise are the only inhabitants of the field, that of course they are many in number; or that, after all, they are other than the little shrivelled, meagre, hopping, though loud and troublesome insects of the hour.

1939, APRIL. CHIGWELL. (THORNTON-KEMSLEY, 97.)

Colin Thornton-Kemsley, chairman of the Chigwell Conservative Association, was campaigning to dismiss Churchill as an MP. See collegiality. WSC was quoting Edmund Burke. Thornton-Kemsley commented, "This was good knockabout stuff."

...I do not at all resent criticism, even when, for the sake of emphasis, it for a time parts company with reality.

1941, 22 JANUARY.

I do not think...any expression of scorn or severity which I have heard used by our critics has come anywhere near the language I have been myself accustomed to use, not only orally, but in a continued stream of written minutes. In fact, I wonder that a great many of my colleagues are on speaking terms with me.

1941, 25 JUNE. (CS VI, 6437.)

So long as I am acting from duty and conviction, I am indifferent to taunts and jeers. I think they will probably do me more good than harm....I am not at all worried about anything that may be said about me. Nobody would attempt to take part in controversial politics and not expect to be attacked.

1945, 6 DECEMBER.

Every kind of insult was flung out, not that we seasoned politicians mind what was said about us by people for whom we entertain no respect.

1946, 12 NOVEMBER.

I do not in the least mind being called a goose. I have been called worse things than that.

PASSIM. (GRAEBNER, 65.)

Cursing

I scrambled up all right, made a few remarks of a general character, mostly beginning with the earlier letters of the alphabet....

1930. (MEL, 116.)

Disembarking from his ship at Bombay Harbour in 1896, Churchill wrenched his shoulder reaching for a ring on the quay. See also Health in this chapter.

Cuticle

[Silk underwear] is essential to my well-being. I have a very delicate and sensitive cuticle which demands the finest covering. Look at the texture of my cuticle—feel it [uncovering his forearm by rolling up his sleeve]. I have a cuticle without a blemish—except on one small portion of my anatomy where I sacrificed a piece of skin to accommodate a wounded brother-officer on my way back from the Sudan campaign.

CIRCA 1908. (BONHAM CARTER, 230.)

Clementine told Violet Bonham Carter that WSC spent £80 a year on silk underwear, purchased from the Army and Navy Stores. Violet taxed WSC over his extravagance. The brother-officer was Richard Molyneux: see Religion...Afterlife.

Death

Death comes often early to such men, whose spirits are so wrought that they know rest only in action, contentment only in danger, and in confusion find their only peace.

1899. (SAVROLA, 35.)

Savrola was WSC's eponymous hero in his only novel. Here he seems to be contemplating his personal certainty that he would die young, like his father.

Two days ago I was walking up to the trenches & we heard several shells on our left, each shot coming nearer….I felt—20 yards more to the left & no more tangles to unravel, no more anxieties to face, no more hatreds & injustices to encounter: joy of all my foes, relief of that old rogue [Asquith], a good ending to a chequered life, a final gift—unvalued—to an ungrateful country—an impoverishment of the war-making power of Britain wh[ich] no one w[oul]d ever know or measure or mourn.

1916, 28 MARCH, FLANDERS. (OB, CV3/2, 1467.)

WSC to his wife from the trenches. A rare reflection of his inner doubts.

…I am tired out in body, soul and spirit…All is planned and ready, in what better place could I die than here—in the ruins of Carthage.

1943, DECEMBER, CARTHAGE. (THOMPSON, SIXTY MINUTES, 77.)

WSC, suffering from pneumonia, to his body-guard, Inspector Walter H. Thompson.

I am informed from many quarters that a rumour has been put about that I died this morning. This is quite untrue. It is however a good sample of the whispering campaign which has been set on foot. It would have been more artistic to keep this one for Polling Day.

1951, 15 FEBRUARY. (OB VIII, 511.)

A Churchillian twist on Mark Twain's "reports of my death are greatly exaggerated". The general election of February 1950 had returned 315 Labour MPs to 298 Conservatives; WSC's return to Downing Street was put off until another election in October 1951.

I am weary of a task which is done & I hope I shall not shrink when the aftermath ends. My only wish is to live peacefully out the remaining years—if years there be.

1957, 21 MAY. LA PAUSA, ROQUEBRUNE. (OB VIII, 1242.)

I want to die in England.

1962, 28 JUNE, MONTE CARLO. (GILBERT, LIFE, 957.)

After breaking his hip.

Déjà vu, *1939*

My thoughts went back a quarter of a century to that other September when I had last visited Sir John Jellicoe and his Captains in this very bay, and had found them with their long lines of battleships and cruisers drawn out at anchor, a prey to the same uncertainties as now afflicted us. Most of the captains and admirals of those days were dead, or had long passed into retirement. The responsible senior officers who were now presented to me as I visited the various ships had been young lieutenants or even midshipmen in those far-off days….an entirely different generation filled the uniforms and the posts. Only the ships had most of them been laid down in my tenure. None of them was new. It was a strange experience, like suddenly resuming a previous incarnation….

I motored from Loch Ewe to Inverness, where our train awaited us. We had a picnic lunch on the way by a stream, sparkling in hot sunshine. I felt oddly oppressed with my memories.

For God's sake, let us sit upon the ground.
And tell sad stories of the death of kings.

No one had ever been over the same terrible course twice with such an interval between. No one had felt its dangers and responsibilities from the summit as I had or, to descend to a small point, understood how First Lords of the Admiralty are treated when great ships are sunk and things go wrong. If we were in fact going over the same cycle a second time, should I have once again to endure the pangs of dismissal? Fisher, Wilson, Battenberg, Jellicoe, Beatty, Pakenham, Sturdee, all gone!

I feel like one
Who treads alone
Some banquet-hall deserted,
Whose lights are fled,
Whose garlands dead,
And all but he departed!

1948. (WW2 I, 339.)

On 18 September 1939, after inspecting the fleet at Scapa Flow as First Lord of the Admiralty, twenty-five years almost to the day since he last held that post, Churchill's literary mastery did not desert him. "For God's sake" is from Shakespeare's Richard II (III:2, 155–6). "I feel like one" is from Thomas Moore's National Air, "The Light of Other Days" (1815).

Depression

I have got a black dog on my back today.

PASSIM. (GILBERT, SEARCH, 210.)

Dogma has it that Churchill suffered from frequent periods of depression which he described as "Black Dog". His wife said that although WSC "was occasionally depressed—as indeed most normal people are—he was not abnormally subject to long fits of depression". "Black Dog" was well used by Victorian nannies, including Winston's nanny, Mrs. Everest, to describe their charges' dark moods.

Discretion abroad

…when I am abroad I always make it a rule never to criticise or attack the Government of my own country. I make up for lost time when I come home.

1947, 18 APRIL.

Discretion at home

I make it a rule, as far as I possibly can, to say nothing in this House upon matters which I am not sure are already known to the General Staffs of foreign countries.

1936, 12 NOVEMBER.

Dismissal

I owe my advancement entirely to the House of Commons, whose servant I am. In my country, as in yours, public men are proud to be the servants of the State and would be ashamed to be its masters. On any day, if they thought the people wanted it, the House of Commons could by a simple vote remove me from my office. But I am not worrying about it at all.

1941, 26 DECEMBER. CONGRESS, WASHINGTON.

Political dramas are very exciting at the time to those engaged in the clatter and whirlpool of politics, but I can truthfully affirm that I never felt resentment, still less pain, at being

so decisively discarded in a moment of national stress.

1948. (WW2 I, 29.)

Churchill was never troubled for long at being rejected for high office (1915, 1936, 1945). As a politician, he was singularly without malice, free of the towering ego often ascribed to him. His ego was greater in terms of his self-image, however.

Disposition

I am not usually accused, even by my friends, of being of a modest or retiring disposition.

1908. (MANCHESTER I, 35.)

Ego

Of course I am an egotist. Where do you get if you aren't?

1940S, CABINET ROOM, DOWNING STREET.
(LONGFORD, 205.)

Related by Clement Attlee to Elizabeth Longford, who said that Attlee quoted this "with leniency amounting to relish".

Election 1899

Everyone threw the blame on me. I have noticed that they nearly always do.

1930. (MEL, 240.)

After WSC was narrowly defeated in Oldham in 1899.

Election 1922

In a twinkling of an eye I found myself without an office, without a seat, without a party, and without an appendix.

1931, SEPTEMBER. ("ELECTION MEMORIES,"
STRAND MAGAZINE; THOUGHTS, 154.)

Three days before beginning his re-election campaign for Dundee – the seat he had held since 1908 – Churchill had been struck down by appendicitis. As he recovered from the operation, his wife and friends tried to keep the battle going, but he lost the seat to an opponent who had tried repeatedly to defeat him in past elections. (See Chapter 20... Scrymgeour.) The lost office was Secretary of State for the Colonies; the lost party was the Liberals.

Election 1935

Now one can see how lucky I was. Over me beat the invisible wings.

1948. (WW2 I, 141.)

While Churchill was handily returned by Epping, he was not asked to join the new Baldwin Government.

Election 1945

Yes, I won the race—and now they have warned me off the turf.

1945, 1 AUGUST. (NICOLSON II, 479.)

Someone had said, "But at least, sir, while you held the reins, you managed to win the race." See also Ripostes...Election 1945.

I was myself deeply distressed at the prospect of sinking from a national to a party leader. Naturally I hoped that power would be accorded to me to try to make the settlement in Europe, to end the Japanese war, and to bring the soldiers home. This was not because it seemed less pleasant to live a private life than to conduct great affairs. At this time I was very tired and physically so feeble that I had to be carried upstairs in a chair by the Marines from the Cabinet meetings under the Annexe. Still, I had the world position as a whole in my mind....I could not believe this would be denied me.

1954. (WW2 VI, 512–13.)

Election 1951

...this is the first occasion when I have addressed this assembly here as Prime Minister. The explanation is convincing. When I should have come here as Prime Minister the Guildhall was blown up, and before it was repaired I was blown out! I thought at the time they were both disasters.

1951, 9 NOVEMBER. LORD MAYOR'S BANQUET, GUILDHALL, LONDON. (STEMMING, 187.)

Energy

Because I show robust energy, it does not follow that I have a sensitive or injured disposition.

1953, 23 APRIL.

Labour nemesis Emanuel Shinwell (they had a well-hidden respect for each other) had asked

whether WSC was in better temper than he was earlier in the day.

Energy prod

I am certainly not one of those who need to be prodded. In fact, if anything, I am a prod.

1942, 11 NOVEMBER.

Family

There is no doubt that it is around the family and the home that all the greatest virtues, the most dominating virtues of human society, are created, strengthened, and maintained.

1948, 16 NOVEMBER.

On the birth of Prince Charles.

Where does the family start? It starts with a young man falling in love with a girl. No superior alternative has yet been found!

1950, 6 NOVEMBER.

Farming

I am going to make my farm pay, whatever it costs.

1926, CHARTWELL. (BEAVERBROOK, LLOYD GEORGE, 306.)

WSC to Lloyd George, during his first attempt at farming at Chartwell. He had tried beef cattle, sheep, pigs and chickens; all proved disastrous, but in April 1926 he proposed to build a dairy and acquire a milking herd. Clementine wrote him a seven-page letter to dissuade him; apparently it worked.

Fate 1895

I could not help reflecting that the bullet which had struck the chestnut had certainly passed within a foot of my head. So at any rate I had been "under fire." That was something. Nevertheless, I began to take a more thoughtful view of our enterprise than I had hitherto done.

1930. (MEL, 98.)

WSC, observing the Cuban revolution with Spanish forces, was shot at ("without result", as he later put it) for the first time.

Fate 1908

Why have I always been kept safe within a hair's breadth of death except to do something like this? I'm not going to live long.

1908. (DE MENDELSSOHN, 380.)

Quoted by WSC's private secretary Charles Masterman, after he and WSC learned of the terminal illness of Prime Minister Campbell-Bannerman. WSC was referring to his ambition to occupy Downing Street.

Fate 1930

Although always prepared for martyrdom, I preferred that it should be postponed.

1930. (MEL, 72.)

Fate 1941

While I am always prepared for martyrdom, there is no point in tempting Providence.

1941, DITCHLEY PARK. SIR JOHN COLVILLE TO THE EDITOR.

About spending the weekend at Ditchley Park, Oxford, in lieu of Chequers, country house of prime ministers, which during the full moon was deemed too obvious to German bombers. For the original variation of this remark see Martyrdom in this chapter.

Fate 1943

I am the victim of caprice, and travel on the wings of fancy.

1943, 10 DECEMBER, CAIRO. (OB VII, 603.)

Fate 1953

I will get on the plane and take my pill and I will wake up either in Bermuda or in heaven. Unless one of you gentlemen has another fate in mind for me.

1953, 6 OCTOBER, LONDON. (*NEW YORK HERALD TRIBUNE*.)

WSC to the Cabinet before the Bermuda Conference with Presidents Eisenhower and Laniel.

Faults – Chancellor

Everybody said that I was the worst Chancellor of the Exchequer that ever was. And now I'm inclined to agree with them. So now the world's unanimous.

1930. (ROWSE, 439.)

A. L. Rowse commented:

> *There is something endearing about a head of that grim department who could say [that] after dinner one evening...[But]*

the economic historian of the period calls him dramatic, resourceful, ingenious. If the return to the Gold Standard at such a high parity was a mistake...Churchill's instinct was rather against the measure, and in any other realm where he had confidence in his own judgement, he would have insisted on having his way – to the country's advantage.

Faults – contentiousness

You see these microphones? They have been placed on our tables by the British Broadcasting Corporation. Think of the risk these eminent men are running. We can almost see them in our mind's eye, gathered together in that very expensive building, with the questionable statues on its front. We can picture Sir John Reith, with the perspiration mantling on his lofty brow, with his hand on the control switch, wondering, as I utter every word, whether it will not be his duty to protect his innocent subscribers from some irreverent thing I might say about Mr. Gandhi, or about the Bolsheviks, or even about our peripatetic Prime Minister.

1933, 24 APRIL. ROYAL SOCIETY OF ST. GEORGE, LONDON. (COVENANT, 91.)

Sir John Reith, managing director of the BBC and no admirer, had often acted to prevent Churchill from broadcasting on political subjects; Churchill took advantage of the celebration of St. George's Day (on which Reith apparently judged him a safe risk) to fire back at his self-appointed censor.

I am by no means sure I have been right. It is no part of my case that I am always right.

1952, 21 MAY.

Faults – dress

How should I not be out at elbows when my father is out of office?

1894. (CAWTHORNE, 14.)

Response when reproved for returning home from Harrow with a torn jacket.

Faults – interrupting

All the years that I have been in the House I have always said to myself one thing: "Do not interrupt," and I have never been able to keep to that resolution.

1935, 10 JULY.

Randolph, do not interrupt me while *I'm* interrupting!

CIRCA 1930S. (GILBERT, WILDERNESS, 13.)

WSC to his son. Sir Martin Gilbert writes:

Churchill's own impish sense of humour cajoled and won over the disputants. Once, amid a ferocious quarrel over some topic long since forgotten, Churchill reduced the whole family to mirthful convulsions with [this remark].

Faults – rudeness

Good Heavens, you mustn't mind me. We're all toads beneath the harrow you know.

CIRCA 1941. (NEL, 58.)

Churchill to Secretary Elizabeth Layton, after she burst into tears following his rude criticism of her typing errors. WSC's reference to toads is from the preamble to Kipling's poem "Pagett, MP":

The toad beneath the harrow knows
Exactly where each tooth-point goes.
The butterfly upon the road
Preaches contentment to that toad.

See also Chapter 7, British Government... Members of Parliament.

You were very rude to me, you know.
[Nurse Roy Howells: "Yes, but you were rude too." WSC replied "with just a hint of a smile":]
Yes, but I *am* a great man.

CIRCA 1958. (HOWELLS, 61.)

Faults – sententiousness

I suppress with difficulty an impulse to become sententious.

1897, 25 FEBRUARY, BANGALORE.
(OB, CV1/2, 734.)

WSC to his mother. The original sense of sententious (Middle English) was "full of meaning or wisdom", but the word later became deprecatory, meaning "moralising in a pompous or affected manner".

Faults – unpunctuality

I realized that I must be upon my best behaviour: punctual, subdued, reserved, in short display all the qualities with which I am least endowed.

1930. (MEL, 107.)

Before attending an 1896 dinner for HRH the Prince of Wales, later Edward VII. The dinner party was thus thirteen, so the superstitious Prince annoyingly delayed it until WSC showed up.

I do think unpunctuality is a vile habit, and all my life I have tried to break myself of it.

1930. (MEL, 108.)

WSC never quite succeeded, as his wife once remarked when he missed a train. "Winston always likes to give the train a sporting chance to get away."

Faults – volubility

Asking me not to make a speech is like asking a centipede to get along and not put a foot on the ground.

1940, 20 JANUARY. (GILBERT, LIFE, 633; ROBERTS, HALIFAX, 189; GARROWBY ALBUMS 1940.)

The Foreign Minister, Lord Halifax, had passed protests to Churchill over his bellicose speeches from four neutral states: Norway, Holland, Denmark and Switzerland.

Five months ago, on 11 May, I made a speech in the House of Commons. I have not spoken since (the first time in my political life that I have kept quiet for so long).

1953, 10 OCTOBER, MARGATE. (ALLIANCE, 65.)

Churchill did not say that this period of silence had included a stroke and recovery. This speech, at the Conservative Party conference, marked his remarkable comeback.

Fear

Normally I wake up buoyant to face the new day. Then [summer 1940] I awoke with dread in my heart.

1940, 19 DECEMBER. (EDEN, A., 182.)

Churchill in conversation with Anthony Eden: the only confession of apprehension at that time. Eden had told WSC that in summer 1940, he and Air Marshal Portal had confessed to each other "that in our hearts we had both despaired".

Finance

You say I never write for love but always for money. I think you are right but remember that you are my banker and who else have I to write to?

1892, 7 FEBRUARY, HARROW. (OB, CV1/1, 320–21.)

WSC to his mother.

I am v[er]y proud of the fact there is not one person in a million who at my age could have earned £10,000 without any capital in less than two years. But sometimes it is vy unpleasant work. For instance last week, I arrived to lecture in an American town & found Pond had not arranged any public lecture but that I was hired out for £40 to perform at an evening party in a private house—like a conjurer.

1901, 1 JANUARY, TORONTO. (OB, CV1/2, 1225.)

WSC to his mother as he was winding up a Canadian lecture tour, which ended on 22 January.

I sent my ten thousand pounds to my father's old friend, Sir Ernest Cassel, with the instruction, "Feed my sheep." He fed the sheep with great prudence. They did not multiply fast, but they fattened steadily, and none of them ever died. Indeed from year to year they had a few lambs; but these were not numerous enough for me to live upon. I had every year to eat a sheep or two as well, so gradually my flock grew smaller, until in a few years it was almost entirely devoured. Nevertheless, while it lasted, I had no care.

1930. (MEL, 376.)

On the first money he earned from an American lecture tour. The banker Sir Ernest Cassel (1852–1921), a lifelong friend of WSC, was the father of Edwina, Lady Mountbatten.

I earned my livelihood by dictating articles which had a wide circulation not only in Great Britain and the United States....I lived in fact from mouth to hand.

1948. (WW2 I, 62.)

Friends

This is the sort of company I should like to find in heaven. Stained perhaps—stained but positive. Not those flaccid sea anemones of virtue who can hardly woggle an antenna in the turgid waters of negativity.

1930. (BONHAM CARTER, 154.)

Kay Halle wrote:

> At a birthday party given him by Mrs. Edwin Montagu, he revelled in the gathering of worldly divorcées she had seated around him.

Mrs. Montagu, the former Venetia Stanley, was the friend of Prime Minister Herbert Asquith, from whom she heard detailed confidences about inside Cabinet discussions during World War I.

Funeral

What about the Army's horses?

[Montgomery: "Some would remain."]

What about the bands?

[Montgomery: "You know, Winston, you are an extraordinary chap. I come to tell you about your old regiment and you talk about the horses and the bands."]

I want to make sure I get a good funeral.

1958, OCTOBER. (SUNDAY TELEGRAPH, 1967.)

Monty was asked to break the news to Churchill that his old regiment, the 4th Hussars, was being amalgamated with the 8th King's Royal Irish Hussars, the new regiment titled "The Queen's Royal Irish Hussars". WSC had been Colonel of the 4th Hussars since 1941; he continued as Colonel of the new regiment until his death.

Gratitude

I must acknowledge with gratitude the extraordinary kindness with which I have been treated in the House and out-of-doors throughout the land. That is a very great help in these days of continuing crisis and storm.

1943, 8 JUNE.

WSC had just returned from the United States and North Africa.

Happiness

I was happy as a child with my toys in my nursery. I have been happier every year since I became a man.

1930. (MEL, 52.)

Hate

I have never considered myself at all a good hater—though I recognize that from moment to moment it has added stimulus to pugnacity.

1950, 6 NOVEMBER.

Health

I, at present, am blessed with that inestimable treasure, i.e. "Good Health" which I trust will not be withdrawn from me, for a long time.

1887, 3 MAY, BRIGHTON. (OB, CV1/1, 131.)

Not particularly noteworthy, except for the phrasing of the sentence, which seems remarkably expert for a twelve-year-old.

Health – anaesthesia

Whenever I have taken gas or chloroform I always follow this rule. I imagine myself sitting on a chair with my back to a lovely swimming bath into which I am to be tilted, and throw myself backwards; or, again, as if one were throwing one's self back after a tiring day into a vast armchair. This helps the process of anaesthesia wonderfully. A few deep breaths, and one has no longer the power to speak to the world.

1932, 4–5 JANUARY. ("MY NEW YORK MISADVENTURE," *DAILY MAIL*; ESSAYS IV, 94.)

Health – deafness

Why do you stop reading? Don't you know that water is a conductor of sound?

1952. (LEASOR, 31.)

In his bath, listening to secret reports being read by Sir Leslie Hollis, Churchill suddenly submerged, and Hollis stopped reading.

Who's that speaking?
[Julian Amery: "Braine."]
James?
[Amery: "No! Braine."]
Drain. He can't be called Drain. Nobody's called Drain.

[Amery wrote "Braine" on the back of an order paper.]
Ah! I see. Is he well named?

1956. (HALLE, 337.)

Churchill's loss of hearing produced numerous amusing exchanges with colleagues in the House. The speaker, Bernard Braine, was just behind Churchill, in the second bench below the gangway.

Health – diet

Except for our Fighting Services, we have been driven back to a large extent from the carnivore to the herbivore. That may be quite satisfactory to the dietetic scientists who would like to make us all live on nuts, but undoubtedly it has produced, and is producing, a very definite effect upon the energetic output of the heavy worker.

1941, 29 JULY.

See also Predictions...World War II outcome.

Health – dislocated shoulder

[Landing at Bombay] we came alongside of a great stone wall with dripping steps and iron rings for hand-holds. The boat rose and fell four or five feet with the surges. I put out my hand and grasped at a ring; but before I could get my feet on the steps the boat swung away, giving my right shoulder a sharp and peculiar wrench. I scrambled up all right, made a few remarks of a general character, mostly beginning with the earlier letters of the alphabet, hugged my shoulder and soon thought no more about it. Let me counsel my younger readers to beware of dislocated shoulders. In this, as in so many other things, it is the first step that counts. Quite an exceptional strain is required to tear the capsule which holds the shoulder joint together; but once the deed is done, a terrible liability remains. Although my shoulder did not actually go out, I had sustained an injury which was to last me my life, which was to cripple me at polo, to prevent me from ever playing tennis, and to be a grave embarrassment in moments of peril, violence and effort....

This accident was a serious piece of bad luck. However, you never can tell whether bad luck may not after all turn out to be good luck. Perhaps if in the charge of Omdurman I had been able to use a sword, instead of having to adopt a modern weapon like a Mauser pistol, my story might not have got so far as the telling....Life is a whole, and luck is a whole, and no part of them can be separated from the rest.

1930. (MEL, 115–16.)

Health – fitness

[Gen. Montgomery: I neither drink nor smoke and I am 100 percent fit."]

I drink and smoke and I am 200 percent fit.

CIRCA 1940s. (*FINEST HOUR* 86; MEMOIRS OF FIELD MARSHAL MONTGOMERY.)

I get my exercise serving as pall-bearer to my many friends who exercised all their lives.

CIRCA 1950s. EDMUND MURRAY TO THE EDITOR.

Actually Churchill led a vigorous life, played polo into his fifties, rode to hounds in his middle-seventies, and walked daily when at Chartwell.

I'm very feeble. I can only drink and smoke—hardly anything else. I'm tired all the time. I have no physical energy. I suppose it's no good trying to do things unless one wants to?....I don't want to make any more speeches. Why should I? I'm paired all this week, and anyway they are doing what I told them. You see, Charles, it's no good giving up power only to take on more work and worry. I don't want to move from Chartwell, except of course to see Clemmie.

1955, 26 JUNE. (MORAN, 715.)

WSC made good his intent, never speaking in Parliament after his retirement in April 1955. Paired refers to the collegial practice of pairing of one Government and one Opposition MP to allow them both to be absent without affecting House votes.

Health – flu

It was an English bug which I took abroad with me, and no blame rests on the otherwise misguided continent of Europe.

1932, 25 SEPTEMBER. (OB, CV5/2, 477.)

WSC to the Duke of Marlborough.

All my household has been down with this minor scourge, and a certain number of days of complete relief from work of any kind is absolutely necessary for perfect recovery. So far I have survived and if I escape altogether I shall attribute it to a good conscience as well as a good constitution.

1937, 14 JANUARY. (OB, CV5/3, 542.)

WSC to Sir Thomas Inskip.

Health – malaria

In view of your salvo, all surrender unconditionally and hoist the yellow flag.

1944, 6 AUGUST. (MORAN, 176.)

Churchill had refused to take mepacrine against malaria, saying Field Marshal Alexander had refused it. Moran replied:

> *I venture to wonder if General Alexander's views on medical matters have the same value as mine on military affairs.*

WSC gave in.

Health – pedestrian accident

There was one moment...of a world aglare, of a man aghast...I do not understand why I was not broken like an eggshell, or squashed like a gooseberry.

1931, 4–5 JANUARY. ("MY NEW YORK MISADVENTURE," *DAILY MAIL*; ESSAYS IV, 90–91.)

Visiting New York on a lecture tour, Churchill looked the wrong way half-way across Fifth Avenue and was almost killed by a passing car. From his hospital bed he drafted a generously remunerative article on his experience.

Health – pneumonia

Well, surely you can deal with that. Don't you believe in your new drug? Doctor Marshall said he called pneumonia "the old man's friend." "Why?" I asked. "Because it takes them off so quietly." I made a suitable reply.

1943, DECEMBER, CARTHAGE. (WW2 IV, 651.)

Health – ruptured kidney

...for a year, I looked at life round a corner. They made a joke about it in those days at the Carlton Club. "I hear Randolph's son met with a serious accident." "Yes? Playing a game of

'Follow my Leader.'"—"Well, Randolph is not likely to come to grief in that way!"

1930. (MEL, 44–5.)

After WSC nearly died falling from a tree in 1892.

Health – seasickness

I thought the little ship would be overwhelmed amid the enormous waves or else be cast away upon the rocks which showed their black teeth...But all these misgivings were quickly dispelled by the most appalling paroxysms of seasickness....I remembered that Titus Oates lived in good health for many years after his prodigious floggings, and upon this reflection, combined with a firm trust that Providence would do whatever was best, were founded such hopes as I could still retain.

1930. (MEL, 255.)

At sea between East London and Durban, South Africa, in a 150-ton steamer, Churchill referred to Titus Oates and the fictitious Popish Plot to burn London. Oates was imprisoned for life, but was pardoned when William of Orange ascended the throne.

Health – staphylococcus

The bug seems to have caught my truculence. This is its finest hour.

1946, 27 JUNE. (MORAN, 335–6.)

After consulting Sir Alexander Fleming, discoverer of penicillin, on a staphylococcus infection which had resisted penicillin.

Health – ulcers

I am recovering, and recruiting red corpuscles at about 100,000 a day. At present, though increasing in numbers rapidly, they are still rather a raw militia and I do not feel that I could wisely commit my army to any first class operations.

1932, SEPTEMBER. (GILBERT, WILDERNESS, 52.)

Churchill to a friend while recovering from a paratyphoid ulcer, his second serious physical setback in 1932.

Honeymoon

We have only loitered & loved—a good & serious occupation for which the histories furnish respectable precedents.

1908, 20 SEPTEMBER, VENICE. (OB, CV2/2, 820.)

WSC to his mother during his honeymoon with Clementine. He was indeed a straight-arrow and loyal husband. One of only three references to sex I have found in Churchill's canon. (The others are under Sex in this chapter; a fictitious quote is in Appendix I.)

Honours – Churchill College Cambridge

It is very nice of them. And I ought certainly to be pleased. After all, it will put me alongside the Trinity.

1958. (COLVILLE, FOOTPRINTS, 258.)

A pun on Trinity College, Cambridge. Speaking about his work in setting up Churchill College, John Colville had asked Churchill, "What memorial could be more lasting than a great university college?" See Trinity House, below.

Honours – dukedom

Duke of Bardogs would sound well, and Randolph could be Marquess of Chartwell.

1947, FEBRUARY. (OB VIII, 327; DIXON TO GILBERT, 15 MARCH 1982.)

In February 1947, Churchill acquired 120-acre Bardogs Farm, adjacent to Chartwell Farm, for £8,700. About a quarter of it was rented to tenants. From a letter discussing a possible dukedom with his barrister, Leslie Graham-Dixon.

I should have to be the Duke of Chartwell, and Randolph would be the Marquess of Toodledo.

1952. 22 FEBRUARY. (OB VIII, 703; MORAN, 402.)

Quoted by John Colville in a discussion with Lord Salisbury and Moran about WSC going the Lords.

First, what could I be Duke of? Secondly even if I were Duke of Westerham, what would Randolph be? He could only be Marquis of Puddledock Lane, which is the only other possession I have apart from Chartwell. And thirdly, and quite seriously, I wish to die in the House of Commons as Winston Churchill.

1955, 5 APRIL. (OB VIII, 1123–4.)

WSC's reasons for refusing a dukedom. Quoted by Colville to Randolph Churchill, 8 June 1965. Puddledock, where WSC owned a cottage, is a hamlet a mile south-east of Chartwell.

Honours – Lord Warden of the Cinque Ports

No dispute ever arose between the Lord Warden and the Minister of Defence…if any unfortunate division had occurred we should have both gone to the Prime Minister who, I may tell you in confidence, was very much on our side.

1946. GRACE HAMBLIN TO THE EDITOR.

Churchill was Prime Minister and Minister of Defence from 10 May 1940 and became Lord Warden of the Cinque Ports on 30 December 1941. The Lord Warden, whose post dates at least to the twelfth century, was originally responsible for all writs to the crown. The Cinque Ports were Hastings, New Romney, Hythe, Dover and Sandwich, later augmented by Rye and Winchelsea. Most of these ports have long since silted up. See also Ripostes…Callooh! Callay!

Honours – medals

…I care nothing for the glittering baubles of honour *for my own sake*: but I have like others as you know to "think of my constituents" and perhaps I ought also to consider the feelings of my possible wife.

1901, 4 MAY. MOUNT STREET, LONDON. (OB, CV1/2, 1070.)

Interesting private note to Joseph Chamberlain, considering that WSC was thought in those days to be a medal hunter. His "possible wife" at that time was probably Pamela Plowden, later Lady Lytton.

Honours – peerage

[Emrys Hughes: "May we be assured that the Prime Minister is not on the slippery slope to Another Place?"]

Provided the term, "Another Place" is used in its strictly Parliamentary sense, I am glad to give the assurance required.

1953, 1 MAY.

Churchill, who had been made a Knight of the Garter a week earlier, was greeted by Members of both sides of the aisle with the traditional waving of order papers and cries of "Hear Hear!" In citing "Another Place" Hughes, who despite ardent political differences had an affection for WSC, was using the Parliamentary term for the House of Lords.

Honours – surgeon

…I must thank you for according me an Honorary Fellowship of the Royal College of Physicians. I also had the honour to be made a surgeon eight years ago, and now I can practise, in an honorary fashion, the arts of surgery and medicine. Unless there is a very marked shortage of capable men in both these professions, I shall not press myself upon you. No doubt in these difficult times it will be a comfort not only to the profession but to the nation at large that you have me in reserve. I have not yet taken any final decision as to which of these beneficent branches I should give priority to (in case an emergency arises). Being temperamentally inclined to precision and a sharp edge, it might be thought that I should choose the surgeon's role.

1951, 10 JULY. ROYAL COLLEGE OF PHYSICIANS, LONDON.

Honours – Trinity House

Moi, je suis un frère aîné de la Trinité.

1914, 10 SEPTEMBER, ANTWERP. (HALLE, IRREPRESSIBLE, 75.)

In Antwerp to rally the city's defenders, an ambassador on the Foreign Ministry staff asked about WSC's uniform of an Elder Brother of Trinity House (Britain's lighthouse authority), distinguished by a naval cap with badge and a pea jacket. Churchill explained with this wonderful line. The confused Belgian thought Churchill considered himself divine: "Mon dieu! La Trinité?"

Interfering

You mean like a great blue-bottle buzzing over a huge cowpat!

1942. (EDEN, A., 333.)

Churchill had proposed that he visit the commanders in the Middle East; this was his description of what he would be like when Eden suggested he should not go.

Learning

...I am always ready to learn, although I do not always like being taught....

1952, 4 NOVEMBER.

Liberalism

I am an English Liberal. I hate the Tory party, their men, their words and their methods. I feel no sort of sympathy with them—except to my own people at Oldham. I want to take up a clear practical position which masses of people can understand.

1903, 24 OCTOBER. MOUNT STREET, LONDON. (OB, CV2/1, 243.)

Unsent letter to Lord Hugh Cecil. Written six months before he crossed the aisle from the Tories to the Liberals, this was as frank an admission of Churchill's political intentions as anything up to that time. But he decided not to send it to his friend Cecil, who was committed to working for reform within the Tory Party.

Life

Was it worth it? The struggle, the labour, the constant rush of affairs, the sacrifice of so many things that make life easy, or pleasant— for what? A people's good! That, he could not disguise from himself, was rather the direction than the cause of his efforts. Ambition was the motive force, and he was powerless to resist it.

1899. (SAVROLA, 35.)

Most readers agree that in the hero of his novel, WSC saw himself.

Memory, earliest

My earliest memories are Ireland....I remember...the Viceroy, unveiling the Lord Gough statue in 1878. A great black crowd, scarlet soldiers on horseback, strings pulling away a brown shiny sheet, the old Duke, the formidable grandpapa, talking loudly to the crowd....I quite understood that he was speaking about war and fighting and that a "volley" meant what the black-coated soldiers....used

to do with loud bangs so often in the Phoenix Park where I was taken for my morning walks. This, I think, is my first coherent memory.

1930. (MEL, 15.)

Ministerial manner

I hope you admire my Ministerial manner in making colonial pronouncements. Vacuity, obscurity, ambiguity and pomposity are not much less difficult to practise than their opposites.

1905, JANUARY. (MORGAN, 202.)

Letter to the Liberal journalist A. Spender. Churchill was Undersecretary for the Colonies, under Colonial Secretary Lord Elgin, in the new Liberal Government. Since Elgin was in the Lords, WSC had much exposure as a junior minister in the Commons.

I have today to deal with a Motion of censure and therefore I hope I shall be pardoned if I do not confine myself entirely to the uncontroversial methods which I usually practise.

1952, 4 DECEMBER.

Mistakes

If I am accused of this mistake, I can only say with M. Clemenceau on a celebrated occasion: "Perhaps I have made a number of other mistakes of which you have not heard."

1945, 18 JANUARY.

I would rather make mistakes in propaganda than in action. Events are the final rulers and time is needed for them to make their pronouncements clear.

1952, 11 OCTOBER, SCARBOROUGH. (STEMMING, 340.)

Moral

I was once asked to devise an inscription for a monument in France. I wrote, "In war, Resolution. In defeat, Defiance. In victory, Magnanimity. In peace, Goodwill." The inscription was not accepted. It is all the fault of the human brain being made in two lobes, only one of which does any thinking, so that we are all right-handed or left-handed; whereas if we were properly constructed we should use our right and left hands with equal force and skill according to circumstances. As it is, those who can win a war well can rarely make a good peace, and those who could make a good peace would never have won the war. It would perhaps be pressing the argument too far to suggest that I could do both.

1930. (MEL, 346.)

See also Maxims...World War II.

Opinions

His Excellency, after the health of the Queen Empress had been drunk and dinner was over, was good enough to ask my opinion upon several matters, and considering the magnificent character of his hospitality, I thought it would be unbecoming in me not to reply fully...There were indeed moments when he seemed willing to impart his own views; but I thought it would be ungracious to put him to so much trouble; and he very readily subsided.

1930. (MEL, 118.)

An 1895 conversation with Lord Sandhurst, Governor of Bombay; Winston was a subaltern aged twenty-one.

I give my opinion, and I dare say it will weigh as much as a mocking giggle.

1944, 28 SEPTEMBER.

I always try, especially in a new House of Commons, to study the opinions of those to whom I am opposed, their expressions and moods, so far as I can.

1950, 24 APRIL.

Optimism

What is the use of living, if it be not to strive for noble causes and to make this muddled world a better place for those who will live in it after we are gone? How else can we put ourselves in harmonious relation with the great verities and consolations of the infinite and the eternal? And I avow my faith that we are marching towards better days. Humanity will not be cast down. We are going on— swinging bravely forward along the grand high road— and already behind the distant mountains is the promise of the sun.

1908, 10 OCTOBER. KINNAIRD HALL, DUNDEE. (LIBERALISM, 221.)

For myself I am an optimist—it does not seem to be much use being anything else....

1954, 9 NOVEMBER. LORD MAYOR'S BANQUET, GUILDHALL, LONDON. (ALLIANCE, 195.)

Overconfidence

Looking back with after-knowledge and increasing years, I seem to have been too ready to undertake tasks which were hazardous or even forlorn.

1923. (CRISIS I, 322.)

Patriotism

I admire men who stand up for their country in defeat, even though I am on the other side.

1948. (WW2 I, 65.)

On the possibility of meeting Hitler in 1932. WSC added: "I had no national prejudices against Hitler at this time. I knew little of his doctrine or record and nothing of his character." See Chapter 20...Hanfstaengel.

Praise

The Rector has mentioned the trials and tribulations through which we have passed, and he has referred to my contribution to our efforts during that time in a manner which no man should hear until he is dead. I shall long remember the eloquent words which he has used, and I hope that I shall do nothing in the span of life which still remains to me to cause him to alter his opinion.

1948, 12 MAY. UNIVERSITY OF OSLO. (EUROPE, 325.)

In introducing Churchill for the awarding of an honorary degree of Doctor of Philosophy, the Rector of Oslo University called him

a statesman and soldier of pre-eminent powers, an orator whose speeches, though richly laden with substance and replete with extraordinary mental energy and willpower, nevertheless sparkle [and] warm and cheer our hearts.

Premiership

It took Armageddon to make me Prime Minister. But now I am there I am determined that Power shall be in no other hands but mine. There will be no more Kitcheners, Fishers or Haigs.

1940, MAY. (BOOTHBY, 145.)

WSC to Robert Boothby. One could hardly blame Churchill. Kitchener's lack of celerity in sending ground troops had doomed the World

War I Gallipoli expedition; Fisher's abrupt resignation over the Dardanelles (which he had originally supported) had doomed Churchill. WSC admired Haig, but disapproved of the slaughter on the Western Front.

When I was called upon to be Prime Minister, now nearly two years ago, there were not many applicants for the job. Since then, perhaps, the market has improved.

1942, 27 JANUARY.

Thus then, on the night of the tenth of May, at the outset of this mighty battle, I acquired the chief power in the State, which henceforth I wielded in ever-growing measure for five years and three months of world war, at the end of which time, all our enemies having surrendered unconditionally or being about to do so, I was immediately dismissed by the British electorate from all further conduct of their affairs....

I was conscious of a profound sense of relief. At last I had the authority to give directions over the whole scene. I felt as if I were walking with destiny, and that all my past life had been but a preparation for this hour and for this trial....I thought I knew a good deal about it all, and I was sure I should not fail. Therefore, although impatient for the morning, I slept soundly and had no need for cheering dreams. Facts are better than dreams.

1948. (WW2 I, 526–7.)

Following the German landings in Norway, on 9 May 1940, Prime Minister Neville Chamberlain, having lost a great portion of his support in the House of Commons, had resigned and had advised the King appoint WSC in his place.

If I stay on for the time being bearing the burden of my age it is not because of love for power or office. I have had an ample share of both. If I stay it is because I have a feeling that I may, through things that have happened have an influence on what I care about above all else, the building of a sure and lasting peace.

1953, 10 OCTOBER, MARGATE. (ALLIANCE, 67.)

Churchill was ultimately frustrated in his failure to achieve a summit meeting with the Russians, which Eisenhower arranged as soon as he left office.

Principle

...I always prefer to accept the guidance of my heart to calculations of public feeling.

1937, 1 JANUARY. (OB, CV5/3, 521.)

WSC to Bernard Baruch: a sterling example of the philosophy that so distinguished Churchill from run-of-the-mill politicians, then and now.

I have a tendency, against which I should, perhaps, be on my guard, to swim against the stream. At all times, according to my lights and throughout the changing scenes through which we all hurried, I have always faithfully served two public causes which, I think, stand supreme—the maintenance of the enduring greatness of Britain and her Empire, and the historical continuity of our island life.

1940, 9 OCTOBER. (GILBERT, BIOGRAPHY, 39.)

Said after becoming leader of the Conservative Party, the last new office he would hold. By changing parties twice (1904, 1924), Churchill effectively put himself against all of the people, some of the time. See Chapter 3, Churchillisms...Re-rat.

Prominence

Now for a short spell I became "the man on the spot." Instead of sitting at home waiting for the news from the front I could send it myself. This was exhilarating.

1951. (WW2 IV, 412.)

In July 1942, Churchill had flown to Cairo to review and make changes to the Middle East command.

Prophesying

...I always avoid prophesying beforehand, because it is much better policy to prophesy after the event has already taken place.

1943, 1 FEBRUARY. PRESS CONFERENCE, CAIRO. (ONWARDS, 7.)

Purpose

There would be no purpose in living when there is nothing to do.

1954, 16 DECEMBER. (MORAN, 662.)

WSC certainly believed this; he was clearly tired of living after all his books had been published and his last painting completed (1958), and after what he expected was his last campaign for Parliament (1959). The last five years were a sad time for him and his family.

Regrets

I have no intention of passing my remaining years in explaining or withdrawing anything I have said in the past, still less in apologizing for it.

1944, 21 APRIL.

Responsibility

No one knew how many Anarchists there were or what measures were going to be taken. In these circumstances I thought it my duty to see what was going on myself....I must, however, admit that convictions of duty were supported by a strong sense of curiosity which perhaps it would have been well to keep in check.

1924, FEBRUARY. ("THE BATTLE OF SIDNEY STREET," *NASH'S PALL MALL*; THOUGHTS, 44.)

As Home Secretary in 1910, Churchill appeared on the scene of a skirmish with anarchists cornered in a Sidney Street house in the East End, directing the police. When a fire broke out in the house, WSC directed the fire brigade to let it burn. He was much criticised for intervening personally in what was a police matter.

You may imagine how deeply I feel my own responsibility to all these people; my responsibility to bear my part in bringing them safely out of this long, stern, scowling valley through which we are marching, and not to demand from them their sacrifices and exertions in vain.

1941, 27 APRIL. BROADCAST, LONDON.
(UNRELENTING, 93.)

Referring to the civil populace of Britain.

Retirement

[The editor of *The Times* sent Churchill the draft of an editorial suggesting that Churchill campaign in the 1945 general election as a non-partisan world leader.]

Mr. Editor, I fight for my corner.

[The editor added that Churchill should then retire gracefully soon after the election...]

Mr. Editor, I leave when the pub closes.

1945, MAY. (*THE ECONOMIST*, 1965.)

I remember well that my father...called Mr. Gladstone "An old man in a hurry." That was in the year 1886, and sixteen years later Mr. Gladstone was engaged in forming another Administration. I do not want to suggest that such a precedent will be repeated, for that would dishearten Hon. Members opposite.

1951, 21 MARCH.

Churchill became Prime Minister eight months later.

[Reporter: "Do you have any thoughts of retiring?"]

Not until I am a great deal worse and the Empire a great deal better.

1953, 8 FEBRUARY, NEW YORK.
(*SUNDAY TIMES*, LONDON.)

If you wish to play dog in the manger, you cannot leave your manger....I must retire soon. Anthony [Eden] won't live forever.

1952. (*DAILY EXPRESS*; HALLE, IRREPRESSIBLE, 333.)

Kay Halle derived this quotation from a newspaper article. "When Churchill's in his seat, the Opposition breathes fire. When he is not, the Tory front bench has the venom of a bunch of daffodils," wrote the Daily Express. *Asked why he had not retired earlier, he voiced this maxim.*

I am glad to be freed from responsibility which was not in every case accompanied by power, and have not yet made any plans concerning the new freedom. It is very nice to reach a milestone in the journey on which I may sit and rest.

1955, 14 APRIL. SYRACUSE, ITALY. (OB VIII, 1131.)

WSC to Bernard Baruch who, four years older than Churchill, would have understood WSC's need to sit and rest.

Reward poster

I am very much obliged to you for your courtesy and good wishes. I look back with feelings of thankfulness to my share in that long South Africa story. I earnestly hope that all will now be peace. I think you might have gone as high as fifty pounds without an over-estimate of the value of the prize—if living!

1908. (TAYLOR, 186.)

WSC to Mr. de Haas, the police officer who issued the handbill offering £25 reward for the recapture of Churchill dead or alive. In 1908 Churchill had just been married, and to his surprise and delight, he received a letter of congratulation from de Haas.

School

...this interlude of school makes a sombre grey patch upon the chart of my journey. It was an unending spell of worries that did not then seem petty, and of toil uncheered by fruition; a time of discomfort, restriction and purposeless monotony.

1930. (MEL, 52.)

For more specific remarks on his early schooling see Chapter 24: Education.

I am surprised that in my later life I should have become so experienced in taking degrees, when, as a schoolboy I was so bad at passing examinations. In fact one might almost say that no one ever passed so few examinations and received so many degrees. From this a superficial thinker might argue that the way to get the most degrees is to fail in the most examinations. This would, however, Ladies and Gentlemen, be a conclusion unedifying in the academic atmosphere in which I now preen myself, and I therefore hasten to draw another moral with which I am sure we shall be in accord: namely, that no boy or girl should ever be disheartened by lack or success in their youth but should diligently and faithfully continue to persevere and make up for lost time.

1946, 26 FEBRUARY. UNIVERSITY OF MIAMI. (SINEWS, 90.)

Self-expression

I have in my life concentrated more on self-expression than on self-denial.

1953, 8 AUGUST, CHEQUERS. (MORAN, 478.)

Lord Moran noted, "He likes this aphorism and often repeats it in conversation."

There is no such thing as a negative virtue. If I have been of any service to my fellow men, it has never been by self repression, but always by self expression.

1955, FEBRUARY. (SIR JOHN ROTHENSTEIN IN HALLE, IRREPRESSIBLE, 331.)

Rothenstein, art historian and former Director of the Tate Gallery, declined the cigar offered him at Chartwell, saying that every man should have one virtue and his was not smoking.

Self-image

We are all worms. But I do believe that I am a glow-worm.

1906. (BONHAM CARTER, 16.)

Everything trends towards catastrophe & collapse. I am interested, geared up & happy. Is it not horrible to be built like that?

1914, 28 JULY. (SOAMES, SPEAKING, 96.)

WSC to his wife as World War I was about to break out.

I like things to happen, and if they don't happen I like to make them happen.

UNDATED. (HASSALL, 566.)

Quoted in a 1929 letter from Arthur Ponsonby to Eddie Marsh. Ponsonby adds that WSC said this "many years ago".

I am like a bomber pilot. I go out night after night, and I know that one night I shall not return.

1942, 22 APRIL. (NICOLSON II, 223.)

During a lunch with Malcolm Macdonald, WSC said he had no illusions about the decline in his popularity, and then made this remark.

[General Ismay: "But why don't you tell them to go to hell?"]
You should not say those things: I am the servant of the House.

1942, 7 AUGUST. (NICOLSON II, 238.)

Ismay had found WSC in distress at having to prepare a speech to a hostile Commons.

[His father's ghost:] "Winston, you have told me a terrible tale. I would never have believed that such things could happen. I am glad I did not live to see them. As I listened to you unfolding these fearful facts you seemed to know a great deal about them. I never expected that you would develop so far and so fully. Of course you are too old now to think about such things, but when I hear you talk I really wonder you didn't go into politics. You might have done a lot to help. You might even have made a name for yourself."

1947. THE DREAM. (OB VIII, 372.)

In this imaginary conversation, his father never learns what Winston had accomplished. After this remark Lord Randolph's ghost strikes a match to his cigarette, and disappears.

I am ready to meet my Maker. Whether my Maker is prepared for the great ordeal of meeting me is another matter.

1949, 30 NOVEMBER. (LONGFORD, 206.)

I feel like an aeroplane at the end of its flight, in the dusk, with the petrol running out, in search of a safe landing.

1954, 12 MARCH. (OB VIII, 958.)

WSC to R. A. Butler.

I am not the man I was. I could not be Prime Minister now.

1956, 26 NOVEMBER. (MORAN, 755.)

WSC to Lord Moran, when the doctor suggested of the thwarted Anglo-French attempt to take the Suez Canal, "A lot of people are wishing you had been in charge."

Yes, I have worked very hard and achieved a great deal, only to achieve nothing in the end.

CIRCA 1960S. (SIR ANTHONY MONTAGUE BROWNE TO THE EDITOR.)

I speculated with Sir Anthony's agreement that Churchill's ultimate disappointment was his failure to achieve a permanent peace, and to cement a true partnership with the United States.

I'm not a statesman. You aren't a statesman until you're dead—and I'm not dead yet!

NO DATE. SHEFFIELD. (CAWTHORNE, 34.)

Servants

Servants exist to save one trouble, and sh[oul]d never be allowed to disturb one's inner peace.

1928, 4 APRIL. (OB, CV5/1, XIII.)

WSC to his wife. Churchill also wrote her:

Mind you rest and do not worry about household matters. Let them crash if they will. All will be well.

My dear Maxine, do you realise I have come all the way from London without my man?

[Maxine Elliott, for once getting the last word: "Winston, how terribly brave of you."]

CIRCA 1939. CHÂTEAU DE L'HORIZON, GOLFE JUAN, FRANCE. (SIR JOHN COLVILLE TO THE EDITOR.)

Maxine Elliott (1868–1940), the former Jessie Dermott, Maine-born actress, a friend of the Churchills from the early years of the century. During World War I she devoted time and money to the cause of Belgian relief. Before World War II, WSC occasionally holidayed at her villa. There is at least one other version of this exchange (McGowan, 71).

Sex

Tobacco is bad for love; but old age is worse.

1951. (GRAEBNER, 25.)

Sex was not born till protoplasm—or protozoa if you prefer—divided itself. But for this split the sexes would not have had all the fun of coming together again.

1954, 7 APRIL.

Sleep

You must sleep some time between lunch and dinner, and no half-way measures. Take off your clothes and get into bed. That's what I always do. Don't think you will be doing less work because you sleep during the day. That's a foolish notion held by people who have no imagination. You will be able to accomplish more. You get two days in one—well, at least one and a half, I'm sure.

CIRCA 1946. (GRAEBNER, 55.)

In 1895, WSC picked up two lifetime habits in Cuba: cigars and siestas. The editor has tried this and advises that with a valet, cook, gardeners, butler, maids and secretaries, it is quite easily done.

In a long life I have had many ups and downs. During all the war soon to come and in its darkest times I never had any trouble in sleeping....I could always flop into bed and go to sleep after the day's work was done....I slept sound and awoke refreshed, and had no feelings except appetite to grapple with whatever the morning's boxes might bring.

1948. (WW2 I, 201.)

For the exception to this rule, and the rest of this quote, see Chapter 17...1938 – Eden's resignation.

Stomach-time

I adhered to my rule in these long flights that meals should be regulated by stomach-time. When one wakes up after daylight one should breakfast; five hours after that, luncheon. Six hours after luncheon, dinner. Thus one becomes independent of the sun, which otherwise meddles too much in one's affairs and upsets the routine of work.

1951. (WW2 IV, 727–8.)

Sunburn

Here I am in camp at this arid place—bare as a plate and hot as an oven. All the skin is burnt off my face and my complexion has assumed a deep mulberry hue.

1897, 21 JANUARY, MADRAS, INDIA.
(OB, CV1/2, 726.)

WSC to his mother. His pink complexion was susceptible to sun.

Troubles in life

Everyone remembers the remark of the old man at the point of death: that his life had been full of troubles most of which had never happened

1924, MARCH. ("PLUGSTREET," *PALL MALL*;
THOUGHTS, 76; PARAPHRASED IN 1949, WW2 II, 418.)

Often misquoted (See Appendix I) and as Churchill here states, not his creation. Fred Shapiro (editor, Yale Book of Quotations) believes the likely originators were Mark Twain or Thomas Jefferson. Twain said: "I am an old man and have known a great many troubles, but most of them never happened." (Reader's Digest, April 1934.) Jefferson, in an 1816 letter to John Adams, wrote: "To these I say How much pain have cost us the evils which have never happened!"

Will and testament

I am anxious that you should get hold of all my papers, especially those which refer to my Admiralty administration. I have appointed

you my sole literary executor.... There is no hurry; but some day I should like the truth to be known. Randolph will carry on the lamp. Do not grieve for me too much. I am a spirit confident of my rights. Death is only an incident, and not the most important which happens to us in this state of being. On the whole, especially since I met you my darling one I have been happy, and you have taught me how noble a woman's heart can be. If there is anywhere else I shall be on the look out for you. Meanwhile look forward, feel free, rejoice in life, cherish the children, guard my memory. God bless you.

1915, 17 JULY. (CV 3/2, 1097–8.)

WSC to his wife, in a letter to be opened in the event of his death. Lady Soames writes: "The letter shows what deep faith he had in her judgment and resolution..." (Soames, Clementine, 127).

Woe

I never take pleasure in human woe....

1953, 17 APRIL, GLASGOW. (ALLIANCE, 33.)

Worry

I have a remedy for worries that always works. Never let one worry, no matter how great, be in your mind all alone. It will drive you mad. Give it company, preferably something smaller, and write it down on a piece of paper. Then you will spend some time thinking about the second worry, and the first one will gradually diminish.

1951. (GRAEBNER, 25–6.)

Writing, fondness for

...I feel devoutly thankful to have been born fond of writing.

1908, 17 FEBRUARY. AUTHOR'S CLUB, LONDON.
(CS I, 904.)

For extensive remarks on the writing art, see Chapter IV, Writer and Speaker.

All my life, or all the time I have been out of public office—about half my life—I have earned my living by selling words, and, I hope, sometimes thoughts.

1952, 13 JANUARY. PRESS ASSOCIATION, OTTAWA.
(CS VIII, 8319.)

Churchill had just been made an honorary member of the Canadian press.

32

TASTES AND FAVOURITES

"Mr. Churchill is easily satisfied with the best."
– F. E. Smith, Lord Birkenhead [130]

*"[Chartwell's birds] consist of five foolish geese, five furious black swans,
two ruddy sheldrakes, two white swans – Mr. Juno and Mrs. Jupiter, so
called because they got the sexes wrong to begin with, two Canadian geese
('Lord and Lady Beaverbrook') and some miscellaneous ducks."*
– Lady Diana Cooper [131]

"A day away from Chartwell is a day wasted." Churchill's number one
favourite, looking up to the bedroom window, 1930s.

This chapter runs the gamut from food and drink to animals, insects, music, publicity, sea voyages, picnics and photography, simply because they all qualify better as "tastes" than as personal characteristics.

In any Churchill lexicon, "A" is for Alcohol, thanks to WSC's assiduous fanning of his reputation for his capacity – though only once (after a bout of Russian toasts at Teheran)

---

130 This famous remark was apparently by WSC's great friend Lord Birkenhead and not, despite many
     attributions, by Churchill himself. See Appendix I...Simple tastes. Colville, Churchillians, 215.
131 Cooper, Diana, 155. Diary for September 1934.

did anyone testify to seeing him the worse for drink. Despite his reputation for enjoying only "the best", his preferences were quite often ordinary. His musical choices ran to martial marches and the music hall ditties of his youth; in film he liked the Marx Brothers, Disney cartoons and, of course, his all-time favourite, *Lady Hamilton*.

His favourite whisky was Johnnie Walker (Red and Black Label, variously). He enjoyed vintage Hine brandy and Pol Roger champagne, but for the rest his wine tastes were unremarkable. According to a reliable source, Hatch Mansfield, WSC's wine merchants, "bought up all the '28 and '34 Pol Roger champagne in France after the war for his exclusive consumption. In 1954, they investigated Chartwell's cellars and pronounced them a 'shambles'. Ralph Mansfield threw out the dross and instituted a cellar book, but WSC told him not to touch some bottles of white burgundy WSC had personally bottled with Hilaire Belloc, said to be 'awful'. Most of the cellar was filled with Pol Roger, vintage Hine, and Black Label."[132]

His food favourites included clear soup ("it must be limpid"), oysters, caviar, Gruyère cheese, foie gras, trout, shoulder of lamb, lobster, dressed crab, petite marmite, scampi, Dover sole, chocolate eclairs, and, of course, roast beef and Yorkshire pudding. "Winston never eats tripe, crumpets, sausages, cabbage, salami, sauerkraut, corned beef, or rice pudding."[133]

His taste in animals was catholic and indiscriminate. He fancied them people, and conversed with them like Doctor Doolittle. At a certain distance from his black swans (a gift from Australia after the war), "he would give a loud and rather weird 'swan noise' cry and the birds would invariably answer", recalled Ronald Golding. "I found they would call whenever a human came within a certain distance [and one day with WSC] I called out in 'swan-talk' and the birds dutifully replied. Mr. Churchill stopped dead [and] looked me full in the eye…then silence. No comment was ever made that this secret was shared."[134]

Golding added a note on one of WSC's charming livestock collections: "A very successful scheme was put in hand and some of the rarest butterflies and moths of the greatest beauty were hatched out. By careful provision of the right flowers and bushes, the butterflies were kept and well fed."[135] It would seem therefore that "fauna" is a good subject with which to start.

Fauna:
The Churchill Menagerie
Birds

"stoning" should not be misinterpreted; WSC, who would not hurt a fly, was frequently seen feeding small birds who came to his hand.

[We must be] feeding the poor little birds….We must make a policy. You stone them and we will get the five flying fools on their right flank.

1934, 14 SEPTEMBER. (COOPER, 155.)

Lady Diana explained: "The basket of bread on Winston's arm is used first to lure and coax them and then as ammunition." The "five flying fools" were geese. See her further description of the birds at the beginning of this chapter. The

Bulls

Very difficult. Do you think the Russians know the bull belongs to me?….We cannot discriminate against the Russians over a bull…. But they'll have to pay a good price to get it. I'm not going to have that poor fellow sent to Russia for nothing.

CIRCA 1946. (GRAEBNER, 94.)

WSC advertised a prize bull, giving only a box number. The Russians professed interest.

---

132 Dalton Newfield, International Churchill Society president and editor, 1970–75, *Finest Hour* 37, Autumn 1982, 4.
133 Manchester II, 25.
134 Golding, Ronald. "Glimpses: 'Did you fly? Hmph!,'" *Finest Hour* 34, Winter 1981, 5.
135 Ibid., Part 2, *Finest Hour* 35, Spring 1982, 5.

Butterflies

The bright butterfly flutters in the sunshine, the expression of the philosophy of Omar Khayyám, without the potations.

1900, 4 FEBRUARY. (LADYSMITH, 340; BOER, 152.)

Churchill had a lifetime fascination with butterflies, mounting them in his youth, seeking them in Africa, and establishing a butterfly farm at Chartwell. See also Personal...butterflies.

I stopped once in the hope of catching butterflies, but found none of distinction—only a profuse variety of common types, a high level of mediocrity without beauties or commanders...

1908. (MAJ, 107.)

I have always loved butterflies....gleaming, fluttering, settling for an instant with wings fully spread to the sun, then vanishing in the shades of the forest. Whether you believe in Free Will or Predestination, all depends on the slanting glimpse you had of the colour of his wings.

1930. (MEL, 42.)

In Uganda I saw glorious butterflies the colour of whose wings changed from the deepest russet brown to the most brilliant blue, according to the angle from which you saw them. In Brazil as everyone knows there are butterflies of this kind even larger and more vivid. The contrast is extreme. You could not conceive colour effects more violently opposed; but it is the same butterfly. The butterfly is the Fact—gleaming, fluttering, settling for an instant with wings fully spread to the sun, then vanishing in the shades of the forest.

1930. (MEL, 42.)

Camels

I started on a camel and I will finish on a camel.

1921, MARCH, CAIRO. ("GUARDING CHURCHILL," WALTER THOMPSON IN EADE, 164.)

During the Cairo conference, while riding out on camels to see the pyramids, WSC was thrown when his saddle slipped. This remark came when a Bedouin offered Churchill his horse instead.

Cats

...if Cat cares to come home, all is forgiven.

UNDATED, CHARTWELL. (HAMBLIN, *CHURCHILL PROCEEDINGS 1987.*)

Message WSC placed in the window after he had slashed at a "snooty" pet cat who ran away. Grace Hamblin added: "Cat did come home several days later with a wire around his neck. Given cream and the best salmon and so on, he did recover, I'm glad to say."

Take these kittens away—before I fall in love.

UNDATED. (GRACE HAMBLIN TO THE EDITOR.)

A neighbourhood boy brought WSC a basket of white kittens, which Grace Hamblin brought to his bedroom, saying, "You are not to have these, they are just visiting." She was summoned to remove them an hour later, finding them all over his bed, playing with his papers and nibbling his toes.

Nelson's the bravest cat you ever saw. Once chased a big dog right out of the Admiralty.

1941, CHEQUERS. (REYNOLDS Q, 148.)

Cows

One of the heifers has committed an indiscretion before she came to us and is about to have a calf. I propose however to treat it as a daughter.

1935, 10 MARCH. (OB, CV5/2, 1116.)

Chartwell Bulletin No. 9: WSC to his wife in the South Seas.

Dogs

Dog—little did you think when you awoke this morning that you would meet a man called Winston Churchill and enjoy the best meal of your life.

1943, MOROCCO. (CAWTHORNE, 36.)

During a picnic of cold chicken, a lean, starving Alsatian was attracted by the food. Churchill coaxed it with a few pieces and ended giving it his own chicken and everybody else's as well. The dog came to him and lay down in his arms.

Come, Paprika, let us go forward together!

1946. (RONALD GOLDING, "WSC: THE MEMORIES," *FINEST HOUR* 35, SPRING 1982, 11.)

WSC was taking his russet poodle Rufus, whom he occasionally referred to as Paprika, for a walk.

You've stolen my dog's affection!

1950S. (HAMBLIN, *CHURCHILL PROCEEDINGS 1987*.)

Secretary Grace Hamblin took care of WSC's second poodle, Rufus II, who returned her affection. But "...after Sir Winston had been away, Rufus would always welcome him back – which was very decent of him."

Fish

One big goldfish was retrieved from the bottom of the pool at Chartwell. All the rest have been stolen or else eaten by an otter. I have put Scotland Yard on the work of finding the thief. I fear we shall never see our poor fish any more, and nothing is left but unfruitful vengeance, and that about 1,000-1 against a thief & 20,000-1 against an otter.

1945, 6 APRIL. WSC TO HIS WIFE. (BUCZACKI, 206.)

Churchill began stocking his garden pond with ornamental fish, favouring the golden orfe, before the war, and soon re-established the colony after the war ended. It is believed that present specimens are descendants of the original pre-war stock.

[Grace Hamblin: "A neighbourhood boy brought you these black mollies. You can't keep them; they have to be kept in hot water."] Hmpf. Get an expert down to advise us.

1950S. (GRACE HAMBLIN TO THE EDITOR.)

Grace Hamblin admitted, "I was a beast; I was afraid I'd have to take care of them." But WSC duly became a fan of tropical fish, and established some lovely tanks at Chequers, as well as Chartwell. A tank is still maintained at Chartwell as a token of this hobby.

Geese

You carve, Clemmie. He was a friend of mine.

CIRCA 1958. (HOWELLS, 123.)

A goose from Chartwell Farm was placed before WSC to carve. There is, however, no reliable attribution for the oft-quoted variant, "I could not possibly eat a bird I have known socially." Sarah Churchill wrote that Chartwell

"was not a working farm, because my father had very strong views about no animal being slaughtered for food once he had said Good morning to it" (Churchill, Sarah, 26–7).

Horses

And here I say to parents, especially to wealthy parents, "Don't give your son money. As far as you can afford it, give him horses." No one ever came to grief—except honourable grief—through riding horses. No hour of life is lost that is spent in the saddle. Young men have often been ruined through owning horses, or through backing horses, but never through riding them; unless of course they break their necks, which, taken at a gallop, is a very good death to die.

1930. (MEL, 59.)

Lions

You are quite right in your assumption that I don't want the lion at the moment either at Downing Street or Chequers owing to the Ministerial calm which prevails there....I consider you personally bound to receive the lion at Chatsworth should all else fail.

1943. (HALLE, IRREPRESSIBLE, 216.)

WSC to the Duke of Devonshire, President of the London Zoo, whose estate was Chatsworth. An admirer had presented Churchill with a lion, about which there was some consternation. "Rota" was duly kept at the Zoo. See Chapter 18...Rota the lion.

Pigs

Dogs look up to you, cats look down on you. Give me a pig! He looks you in the eye and treats you as an equal.

1952 CA. SIR ANTHONY MONTAGUE BROWNE TO THE EDITOR.

Variously reported in different forms, but this is the most frequent. Often exclaimed by Churchill to a visitor at Chartwell Farm, as he scratched the back of his favourite pig with a stick. A version posted at Chartwell, which doesn't sound like his style, reads:

...Cats look down on human beings, dogs look up to them, but pigs just treat us as human beings.

Swans

All the black swans are mating, not only the father and mother, but both brothers and both sisters have paired off. The Ptolemys always did this and Cleopatra was the result. At any rate I have not thought it my duty to interfere.

1935, 21 JANUARY. (SOAMES, SPEAKING, 376.)

WSC to his wife, who was abroad in the South Seas.

Tastes: Preferred and Unpreferred

Alcohol

Whatever else they may say of me as a soldier, at least nobody can say I have ever failed to display a meet and proper appreciation of the virtues of alcohol.

1916, BELGIUM. (TAYLOR, 291.)

WSC taking leave of the 6th Royal Scots Fusiliers, quoted by a soldier present. See also individual entries for beer, whisky and wine.

It is imperative that I should fortify the revenue, and this I shall now, with the permission of the Committee, proceed to do.

1925, 28 APRIL. (CS IV, 3566.)

Pausing in a speech and lifting a glass beside him; the glass contained water, but the House got the point and laughed.

I had been brought up and trained to have the utmost contempt for people who got drunk— except on very exceptional occasions and a few anniversaries....

1930. (MEL, 141.)

Take my aircraft and a case of Scotch for "Jumbo," a case of arak for Riad el-Sohl, and six cases of champagne for the Frenchman.

1941, 10 JUNE. (HALLE, IRREPRESSIBLE, 229–30.)

Lebanese Prime Minister Riad el-Sohl was deposed and riots broke out in Beirut. Desmond Morton was sent as WSC's representative to the French, el-Sohl, and British General Maitland "Jumbo" Wilson. This was WSC's response to Morton's request for instructions. Kay Halle reported that a reconciliation was promptly arranged.

I need a little more to drink. You see, I have a war to fight and I need fortitude for the battle. And there is one favour I hope you will do for me. I hope you will come to my defence if someday, someone should claim that I am a teetotaller.

1943. WHITE HOUSE, WASHINGTON. (FIELDS.)

WSC to White House butler Alonzo Fields.

When I was younger I made it a rule never to take strong drink before lunch. It is now my rule never to do so before breakfast.

1952, 31 JANUARY. (ISMAY, 457.)

WSC to King George VI.

The people in the stands at Hyde Park corner, by Byron's statue, will be there from seven in the morning till five in the evening [watching Coronation ceremonies]. They were seeing to their sanitary needs, but doing nothing for them in food and drink....Looking after their exports while neglecting their imports. And why? Because alcohol had not been drunk in the royal parks for a hundred years, they were to have nothing to drink. I altered all that.

1953, 24 FEBRUARY. (MORAN, 429.)

I neither want it nor need it but I should think it pretty hazardous to interfere with the ineradicable habit of a lifetime.

1953, 6 JULY. (TIME MAGAZINE.)

Ascribed by the usually reliable Kay Halle to Lord Moran, but not in Moran's diaries.

All I can say is that I have taken more out of alcohol than alcohol has taken out of me.

PASSIM. ("CHURCHILL THE CONVERSATIONALIST," COLLIN BROOKS IN EADE, 248.)

Beer

The object of the duty is to protect the culture of hops, and there is a special element of depravity attaching to this duty. A certain school of thinkers contend that beer is food, and if so, hops are certainly, I am advised, an ingredient of beer—but I am encouraged in the matter by the fact that those who hold that beer is a food are also, on the whole, very favourable to a protective duty on hops and, on the other hand, those who dislike the duty on hops still more dislike the suggestion that beer is food.

1925, 28 APRIL.

Boodles

I do like this Club. Most of your members are decent country gentlemen.

[Anthony Montague Browne: "Well, of the six I can see, I think three are stockbrokers." WSC was indignant:]

You shouldn't say such things about your fellow-members! Really, my dear, you must avoid this penchant for pessimistic judgement.

CIRCA 1950S. (MONTAGUE BROWNE, 120.)

Sir Anthony elaborated on this story from his book:

We were seated in the large curved window looking out on St. James's. It was diverting to see passersby arrested by the sudden vision of Sir Winston Churchill, puffing his cigar and staring benignly down on them. Later WSC realised he was himself a member of Boodles and attempted to settle the account, which I resisted manfully (AMB to the editor, 1985).

Breakfast

My wife and I tried two or three times in the last forty years to have breakfast together, but it didn't work. Breakfast should be had in bed, alone. Not downstairs, after one has dressed. I don't think our married life would have been nearly so happy if we both had dressed and come down for breakfast all these years.

1946. (GRAEBNER, 56.)

According to Walter Graebner, WSC pronounced this with "his eyes twinkling".

Champagne

A single glass of champagne imparts a feeling of exhilaration. The nerves are braced, the imagination is agreeably stirred, the wits become more nimble. A bottle produces a contrary effect. Excess causes a comatose insensibility. So it is with war, and the quality of both is best discovered by sipping.

1898. (MALAKAND, 9.)

Have another glass, my dear boy. I shan't write it down in my diary.

CIRCA 1920S. (HALLE, IRREPRESSIBLE, 267.)

WSC was referring to Earl and Lady Haig's habit, revealed in Haig's diaries, of counting the number of glasses of brandy their guests drank.

First things first. Get the champagne.

1931, NEW YORK. (HALLE, IRREPRESSIBLE, 117.)

WSC was told by his lecture agent, Louis Albers, that Scotland Yard feared that his life was threatened.

As I strolled…along the river bank we were hailed from the gunboats which lay 20 or 30 feet from the shore. The vessel was commanded by a junior naval Lieutenant named Beatty…."How are you off for drinks?….Can you catch?" Almost immediately a large bottle of champagne was thrown from the gunboat to the shore. It fell in the waters of the Nile, but happily where a gracious Providence decreed them to be shallow and the bottom soft. I nipped into the water up to my knees, and reaching down seized the precious gift which we bore in triumph back to our Mess.

1930. (MEL, 194.)

Before the Battle of Omdurman in 1898. The lieutenant was later Admiral of the Fleet and hero of Jutland. See also Chapter 20…Beatty.

I returned to London with those feelings of deflation which a bottle of champagne or even soda-water represents when it is half emptied and left uncorked for a night.

1930. (MEL, 240.)

After his first campaign at Oldham, 1899, which he lost by 1,300 votes.

I could not live without Champagne. In victory I deserve it. In defeat I need it.

1946, EPERNAY. CHRISTIAN POL-ROGER TO THE EDITOR.

WSC to Mme. Odette Pol-Roger in proposing a visit (unrealized) to her home, which he called "the world's most drinkable address".

Chicken

…the American chicken is a very small bird compared with the standard English fowl. Attractively served with rice and auxiliaries of all kinds, he makes an excellent dish. Still, I am on the side of the big chicken as regularly as Providence is on that of the big battalions.

1933, 5 AUGUST. ("LAND OF CORN AND LOBSTERS," COLLIER'S; ESSAYS IV, 262.)

Cigars

Never relight a cigar.

PASSIM. (ASHLEY, 9.)

WSC did not follow this advice, since he liked to keep a candle (rather than matches) burning so he could relight – often, as it happened, because he tended to chew on his cigars more than he drew on them. Although he was presented with many cigars by Havana admirers, his favourite commercial brands were Romeo y Julieta and Camacho.

I remember my father in his most sparkling mood, his eye gleaming through the haze of his cigarette, saying, "Why begin? If you want to have an eye that is true, and a hand that does not quiver, if you want never to ask yourself a question as you ride at a fence, don't smoke."

But consider! How can I tell that the soothing influence of tobacco upon my nervous system may not have enabled me to comport myself with calm and with courtesy in some awkward personal encounter or negotiation, or carried me serenely through some critical hours of anxious waiting? How can I tell that my temper would have been as sweet or my companionship as agreeable if I had abjured from my youth the goddess Nicotine? Now that I think of it, if I had not turned back to get that matchbox which I left behind in my dug-out in Flanders, might I not just have walked into the shell which pitched so harmlessly a hundred yards ahead?

1931, MARCH. ("A SECOND CHOICE," STRAND MAGAZINE; THOUGHTS, 7.)

Not these you damn fool!

1946, HYDE PARK GATE, LONDON. ("WSC: THE MEMORIES," RONALD GOLDING, FINEST HOUR 35, SPRING 1982, 10.)

WSC's butler Greenshields, commanded to "bring the cigars" at a gathering of ardent but not very important dignitaries, had made the mistake of handing round WSC's best cigars. The stage whisper brought all conversation to an embarrassed silence.

I have not for quite a time imported any cigars from hard currency areas. I have nevertheless received some from time to time.

1951, 19 NOVEMBER. WINSTON S. CHURCHILL (GRANDSON) TO THE EDITOR.

...of two cigars, pick the longest and the strongest.

UNDATED. (FINEST HOUR 107, SUMMER 2000, 33.)

WSC to his son Randolph.

Cocktails

...these short, hard, wet drinks may be freely enjoyed without any presumption of illegality. I am no devotee of cocktails, still I must admit that this preliminary festival while the guests are arriving is most agreeable.

1933, 5 AUGUST. ("LAND OF CORN AND LOBSTERS," COLLIER'S; ESSAYS IV, 263.)

Although his mother is incorrectly credited with inventing the Manhattan, WSC was no fan of such drinks. During White House visits, he "apparently became adept at using the nearest bathroom or flower pot as a disposal" for Roosevelt's vermouth-laden martinis (Warren F. Kimball, "The Alcohol Quotient," Finest Hour 134, Spring 2007, 33).

Coffee

The coffee in the United States is admirable, and a welcome contrast to the anaemic or sticky liquid which judicious Americans rightly resent in English provincial towns.

1933, 5 AUGUST. ("LAND OF CORN AND LOBSTERS," COLLIER'S; ESSAYS IV, 263.)

Cooking

I shall go to Chartwell next weekend.

[Clementine Churchill: "Winston, you can't! It's closed and there will be no-one to cook for you."]

I shall cook for myself. I can boil an egg. I've seen it done.

CA. 1950S, DOWNING STREET. (MONTAGUE BROWNE, 118.)

Anthony Montague Browne adds:

Churchill's threat was received in dumbfounded silence on all sides but it was not carried out. His gastronomic priorities clearly prevailed!

Dinner

[My ideal of a good dinner] is to discuss good food, and, after this good food has been discussed, to discuss a good topic—with myself the chief conversationalist.

1925. (EPHESIAN, 196–7.)

Later versions have been embroidered with the words in brackets, although Churchill may well have said them.

Dinner. At the White House (Dry, alas!); with the Sultan. After dinner, recovery from the effects of the above.

1943, 21 JANUARY. CASABLANCA. (SHERWOOD II, 682.)

WSC to Harry Hopkins suggesting a programme for the following day which included this item. (Roosevelt's Casablanca villa was always referred to by Churchill as the White House.)

Eighteenth century

I am happiest in the 18th Century.

1931, 1 FEBRUARY. GLENN HOROWITZ TO THE EDITOR.

Autograph note on typed letter signed to George Harrap regarding WSC's life of Marlborough.

Grinning

First of all grin, or, as they say, "smile." There is nothing like it.

1931, SEPTEMBER. ("ELECTION MEMORIES," STRAND MAGAZINE; THOUGHTS, 145.)

Do you know why I hate the Nazis? I hate them because they frown when they fight. They are grim and sullen. Now, take our magnificent Air Force lads—they grin when they fight. I like a man who grins when he fights…

1941. (REYNOLDS Q., 152.)

A luncheon remark recalled by Quentin Reynolds (1902–65), journalist and World War II war correspondent. From 1933 to 1945 he was associate editor at Collier's, which had published many Churchill articles in the 1930s.

Hats

You should wear a hat in this weather. It is imprudent not to.

[After Anthony Montague Browne had shown him a hat on his lap:] Why don't you put it on your head?

[AMB: "Because we are passing the Cenotaph, Prime Minister."]

1953, NOVEMBER. (MONTAGUE BROWNE, 156.)

AMB adds,

He removed his own, with a glance that said, "Don't do that too often." I felt as though I had teased a bull-dog in its basket.

Hors d'oeuvres

The cocktails are supported by all sorts of dainty, tasty little dishes continually handed round upon trays or displayed upon tables. This custom is nothing more nor less than the old custom of Imperial Russia called "the zakouski."

I remember as a child, nearly fifty years ago, being taken by my mother on a visit to the Duke of Edinburgh, who had married a Russian princess. There I saw exactly the same ritual, with kümmel and vodka instead of the cocktails, and the same attractive, eatable kickshaws to keep them company. It was only after this was over that the regular dinner began. There is much to be said for this arrangement. No doubt it encourages unpunctuality, but on the other hand it protects those who have already arrived from starving helplessly till the late comers make their appearances.

1933, 5 AUGUST. ("LAND OF CORN AND LOBSTERS," COLLIER'S; ESSAYS IV, 263.)

Kippers and pancakes

This hotel is a great trial to me. Yesterday morning I had half-eaten a kipper when a huge maggot crept out & flashed his teeth at me! To-day I could find nothing nourishing for lunch but pancakes. Such are the trials wh[ich] great & good men endure in the service of their country!

1909, 17 OCTOBER. QUEEN'S HOTEL, DUNDEE. (OB, CV2/2, 914.)

WSC to his wife. The Queen's Hotel, which is still there in WSC's old constituency of Dundee, recently asked the Churchill Archives Centre for a facsimile of this letter to frame, showing their good sportsmanship.

Marx Brothers

There was nothing I could do about [the raid on London], so I watched the Marx Brothers in a comic film which my hosts had arranged.

[WSC was then informed that Rudolf Hess had parachuted into Scotland.]

Tell that to the Marx Brothers!

[When assured it was true:]

Hess or no Hess, I'm going to watch the Marx Brothers.

1941, 11 MAY. DITCHLEY PARK. QUOTATIONS FROM: (1) WW2 III, 43; (2) SHERWOOD I, 294 (A BIT UNCERTAINLY); AND (3) ADDISON, CHURCHILL, 185.

WSC would later learn that the 10 May 1941 raid had destroyed the House of Commons. According to Robert Lewis Taylor, WSC

likes films of sprightly tone. He wants to be entertained and not instructed. His favourite theme still is the extolling of England; his favourite actor was the late Leslie Howard, whose death in an airplane [crash] Churchill publicly deplored.

For a Marx Brothers non-quotation, see Appendix I.

Music

In default of a smell the next best mnemonic is a tune. I have got tunes in my head for every war I have been to, and indeed for every critical or exciting phase in my life. Some day when my ship comes home, I am going to have them all collected in gramophone records, and then I will sit in a chair and smoke my cigar, while pictures and faces, moods and sensations long vanished return; and pale but true there gleams the light of other days.

1930. (MEL, 138.)

WSC was referring to an 1897 visit with the Fourth Dragoon Guards in Rawalpindi, India, where he attended a dinner at the Sergeant's mess. By all accounts WSC was atonal, but this did not stop him from outbursts of song from time to time; he was particularly fond of the music hall ballads of his youth, and the songs of the First World War.

Music: Harrow Songs

I like the song "Boy," although when I was at the School I did not advance to that position of authority which entitles one to make that call. The songs and their spirit form a bond between Harrovians all over the world, and they have played a great part in the influence which has been exercised in national affairs by men who have had their education here.

1940, 18 DECEMBER. HARROW SCHOOL. (UNRELENTING, 20.)

Certainly I think the songs are very important. I enjoy them very much. I know many of them by heart. I was telling the Head Master just now that I could pass an examination in some of them. They are a great treasure and possession of Harrow School, and keep the flame burning in a marvellous manner. Many carry them with them all their lives. You have the songs of Bowen and Howson (whom I remember well as House Masters here) with the music of John Farmer and Eaton Faning. They are wonderful; marvellous; more than could be put into bricks and mortar, or treasured in any trophies of silver or gold.

1942, 18 NOVEMBER. HARROW SCHOOL. (END, 292.)

See also Chapter 18...1941/Sterner days.

Mustard

Ten demerits! You should know no gentleman eats ham sandwiches without mustard.

1942, AUGUST. EN ROUTE FROM TEHERAN TO MOSCOW. (PAWLE, 5.)

WSC to naval aide Tommy Thompson. WSC was consistent. In 1929, at the Governor's Mansion, Richmond, Virginia, he was asked if he would like mustard with his Virginia ham. "Yes, English, please," he replied. Mrs. Byrd slowed the dinner to a crawl because she had to send out for some. "Harry," she said to the Governor as WSC left the next day, "don't you ever invite that man here again" (Senator Harry F. Byrd, Jr. to the editor).

Photography

It is the misfortune of a good many Members to encounter in our daily walks an increasing number of persons armed with cameras to take pictures for the illustrated Press which is so rapidly developing.

1911, 26 JUNE.

Picnics: Toast for the Day

To Absent Friends [Sunday].
To Men [Monday].
To Women [Tuesday].
To Religion [Wednesday].
To Our Swords [Thursday].
To Ourselves [Friday].
To Wives and Sweethearts [Saturday].

CIRCA 1950S, MARRAKESH. (GRAEBNER, 78.)

Walter Graebner recalled WSC's delight in picnic customs which he elevated

> *to the rank of formal ceremonies. One was the drinking of old Indian Army toasts... and at the end of every picnic we would solemnly rise and drink the Toast for the Day....*

Graebner said WSC had learned these from his friend and literary assistant General Sir Henry Pownall; in fact, Churchill had quoted them aboard RMS Dunottar Castle *en route to South Africa in 1899 (Ladysmith, 15). Churchill says they originated in the Peninsular Wars.*

Picnics: Verse

"Beside some water's rushy brink
With me the Muse shall sit and think
(At ease reclined in rustic state)
How vain the ardour of the Crowd
How low, how little are the Proud,
How indigent the great."
[One night at dinner Mrs. Walter Graebner asked him to repeat the verse.]
Oh no, I couldn't. I can only say it at picnics.

CIRCA 1950S, MARRAKESH. (GRAEBNER, 78.)

The second "formal ceremony" at picnics, Graebner recalled, was a verse from Thomas Gray's "Ode to Spring", which he "gravely recited at each picnic".

Publicity

Mr. Lionel James, Reuters' correspondent, even proposed to telegraph some account of this noteworthy capture. But I prevailed on

him not to do so, having a detestation of publicity.

1899. (RIVER II, 73.)

Certainly facetious, following WSC's capture of an Arab he thought to be an enemy, who emerged as an agent of British Intelligence.

Pudding (dessert)

Take this pudding away—It has no theme!

1950S. LORD SOAMES. (*FINEST HOUR* 50, 16.)

A remark sometimes heard by his family. Queried as to what gave pudding a theme, Lord Soames thought what WSC wanted was a distinctive flavour or ingredient.

Quail

...these miserable mice should never have been removed from Tutankhamen's tomb!

1942, CHEQUERS. (PAWLE, 172.)

Rebelling at a dish of quail served during a visit by Soviet officials.

Rabbit

Have you done justice to rabbit production? Although rabbits are not by themselves nourishing, they are a pretty good mitigation of vegetarianism. They eat mainly grass and greenstuffs, so what is the harm in encouraging their multiplication in captivity?

1941, 14 JUNE. (WW2 III, 689.)

WSC to Minister of Agriculture.

Salmon

That is indeed a magnificent fish: I must "have some of him"...No! No! I will have meat. Carnivores will win this war!

CIRCA 1940S, DOWNING STREET. ("CHURCHILL THE CONVERSATIONALIST," COLLIN BROOKS IN EADE, 363.)

Widely read with a photographic memory, Churchill put the last four words in quotes, having recalled the words of the Moorish boy Xury, who kills a lion in Charles Dickens's Martin Chuzzlewit, *Chapter 2:*

> *Xury said he would have some of him; so he comes on board, and asked me to give him the hatchet.*

The "carnivores" may refer to the vegetarian Hitler.

Sandwiches

The bread must be wafer-thin. It is nothing more than a vehicle to convey the filling to the stomach.

1942. (Pawle, 190.)

Lunching on his cold beef sandwiches while flying to Cairo in August.

Sea voyages

Yet all earthly evils have their compensations, and even monotony is not without its secret joy.

1899, 26 October. At sea, RMS *Dunottar Castle*. (Ladysmith 5; Boer, 2.)

Steaming for Cape Town and the Boer War.

Ah, the first day you are on the ship you won't be feeling very well. The second day you will be feeling better. The third day you will meet a pretty girl and then you will be nearly there.

1932. (Gilbert, Wilderness Years, 47.)

WSC after Randolph told him he would prepare for an upcoming American lecture tour while crossing the Atlantic. Randolph later admitted that his father had been right in all respects.

It is astonishing how quickly a voyage can pass if one has enough to do to occupy every waking minute.

1943, 7 August. At sea, RMS *Queen Mary*. (WW2 V, 71.)

WSC to Chiefs of Staff, en route to the first Quebec Conference.

Seafood

The American Blue Point [crab] is a serious undertaking. On the other hand, the American lobster is unrivalled anywhere in the world; he has a succulence and a flavour which I have found nowhere else. Shad roe and terrapin I have eaten only in the United States; I find them both entertaining. Soft-shell crabs and corn on the cob are by no means unpalatable, but should not be eaten too often.

1933, 5 August. ("Land of Corn and Lobsters," *Collier's*; Essays IV, 263.)

Smells

Nothing recalls the past so potently as a smell.

1930. (MEL, 138.)

WSC was referring to a visit with the Fourth Dragoon Guards in Rawalpindi, India, in 1897, where he attended a dinner at the Sergeants' mess.

Starters

American meals nearly always start with a large slice of melon or grapefruit accompanied by iced water. This is surely a somewhat austere welcome for a hungry man at the midday or evening meal. Dessert, in my view, should be eaten at the end of the meal, not at the beginning. The influence of American customs is now so all-pervading, that during the last few years I have noticed this habit creeping into England. It should be strongly repulsed.

1933, 5 August. ("Land of Corn and Lobsters," *Collier's*; Essays IV, 262.)

Stilton and port

Stilton and port are like man and wife. They should never be separated. "Whom God has joined together, let no man put asunder." No— nor woman either.

1946. (Graebner, 61.)

Telephones

Hullo! Hullo! Hullo! Christ damn your soul. Why do you keep me waiting?
  [A soft voice answered which he recognized as his housekeeper's: "Is that Mr. Churchill?"]
No!

1907. (Morgan, 223.)

Churchill was impatient with appliances. The special phone to Roosevelt in the Cabinet War Rooms during World War II had often to be replaced because WSC angrily banged the handset during the routine bad connections. (Phil Reed, Cabinet War Rooms, to the editor, 1996.)

I've just asked the Washington operator for a glass of sherry, thinking that I was speaking on the house telephone. I'm afraid I gave her rather a shock.

1932. (Moir, 99.)

WSC to a New York secretary Phyllis Moir.

Traditional form

If people who are dealing with matters of great consequence write their letters in their own hand instead of dictating them, walk to their business instead of riding, and send a message instead of speaking through the telephone, some people think economies will result, but, as a matter of fact, very few suggestions are less helpful than these.

1919, 15 DECEMBER.

Churchill was, of course, defending his own habitual practices.

Trees

...no one should ever cut one down without planting another. It is very much easier to cut down trees than to grow them.

1952, 6 SEPTEMBER. ST. BARNABAS SCHOOL, WOODFORD. (STEMMING, 332.)

Vegetarians

Almost all the food faddists I have ever known, nut-eaters and the like, have died young after a long period of senile decay....The way to lose the war is to try to force the British public into a diet of milk, oatmeal, potatoes, etc., washed down on gala occasions with a little lime-juice.

1940, 14 JULY. (COLVILLE, FOOTPRINTS, 98.)

Letter to the Minister of Food, Lord Woolton, seeking to avoid imposing too severe rationing on the people.

Everyone knows the distinguished talents which the Rt. Hon. Gentleman [Sir Stafford Cripps] brings unstintedly to the services of his fellow countrymen. No one has made more sustained exertions to contribute to the common pot and few take less out of it than he does. I have got my vegetarian too, my honoured friend Lord Cherwell. These ethereal beings certainly do produce a very high level and a very great volume of intellectual output, with the minimum of working costs in fuel.

1945, 6 DECEMBER.

Water

A dangerous, yet almost universal, habit of the American people is the drinking of immense quantities of iced water. This has become a

ritual. If you go into a cafeteria or drug store and order a cup of coffee, a tumbler of iced water is immediately set before you. The bleak beverage is provided on every possible occasion; whatever you order, the man behind the counter will supply this apparently indispensable concomitant.

1933, 5 AUGUST. ("LAND OF CORN AND LOBSTERS," COLLIER'S; ESSAYS IV, 262.)

At this point I will take a little lubrication, if it is permissible. I think it is always a great pleasure to the Noble Lady, the Member for the Sutton Division of Plymouth [Lady Astor] to see me drinking water.

1944, 8 DECEMBER. (DAWN, 281.)

Pausing during a long speech on the crisis in Greece.

Whisky

...have some whisky and soda-water—on the sideboard there. It is a good drink to draw the sword on—the best in fact.

1899. (SAVROLA, 113.)

See also Alcohol above.

Until this time [1899] I had never been able to drink whisky. I disliked the flavour intensely....I now found myself in heat which, though I stood it personally fairly well, was terrific, for five whole days and with absolutely nothing to drink, apart from tea, except either tepid water or tepid water with lime-juice or tepid water with whisky. Faced with these alternatives I "grasped the larger hope."...Wishing to fit myself for active-service conditions I overcame the ordinary weaknesses of the flesh. By the end of those five days I had completely overcome my repugnance to the taste of whisky. Nor was this a momentary acquirement. On the contrary the ground I gained in those days I have firmly entrenched and held throughout my whole life. Once one got the knack of it, the very repulsion from the flavour developed an attraction of its own; and to this day, although I have always practised true temperance, I have never shrunk when occasion warranted it from the main basic standing refreshment of the white officer in the East.

1930. (MEL, 141.)

Churchill's original description of how he became attracted to Scotch, with the Malakand Field Force in 1897, is a classic narrative, not the least through its inversion of the meaning of "weaknesses of the flesh". Yet no one in his family ever saw him the worse for drink. (The oft-quoted remark that in South Africa "the water was unfit to drink. We had to put a bit of whisky into it. By diligent effort I learned to like it" is not traceable in WSC's canon.)

Come here, Desmond, drink this and tell me what you think of it. [Morton protested; it was before lunch.]

Never mind, try this. [Morton did and admitted it was a drinkable but not remarkable scotch.]

It was made from seaweed three weeks ago by that remarkable little man in the corner. The question is, what are we do to with this formula? Flood the market with cheap whisky and make a killing? But what then? Some wretch will discover the formula, and the Scotch whisky trade will be ruined forever.

1942, CHEQUERS. (HALLE, IRREPRESSIBLE, 201.)

Will you have a whisky and soda, Mr. Prime Minister of Pakistan?

[Nazim, horrified: "No, thank you!...I'm a teetotaller, Mr. Prime Minister."]

A teetotaller! Christ! I mean God! I mean ALLAH!

1941. (MENZIES, 93.)

For WSC's reply when another offer of whisky and soda was repulsed, see Chapter 33, Ripostes.

On no account reduce the barley for whisky. This takes years to mature and is an invaluable export and dollar producer...It would be most improvident not to preserve this characteristic British element of ascendancy.

1945, 3 MARCH. (WW2, VI, 638.)

WSC to Minister of Agriculture.

I find alcohol a great support in life. Sir Alexander Walker, who keeps me supplied with your native brew, told me that a friend of his, who died the other day, drank a bottle of whisky a day for the last ten years of his life. He was eighty-five.

1948, AUGUST. SOUTH OF FRANCE. (BOOTHBY, 60.)

Said to Bob Boothby, MP for East Aberdeenshire for many years. Boothby's reply was "If you ever gave it up, you'd die." This was greeted by silence from WSC.

Wine

No, I am going to lunch at Buckingham Palace and it would not look well if I were to slither under the Royal table!

1942, JANUARY. (A. P. HERBERT IN HALLE, 187.)

Declining sherry in the Smoking Room of the House of Commons.

I [have a] profound distaste on the one hand for skim milk and no deep rooted prejudice about wine....[So I have] reconciled the conflict in favour of the latter...

1943, 22 JANUARY, CASABLANCA. (SHERWOOD, II, 685.)

WSC to Harry Hopkins. Rephrased in the first person, from Hopkins's account.

It's *white* port, you know. All the ladies must have some because it's only *white port*.

CIRCA 1950S. MARRAKESH. (GRAEBNER, 77.)

I could have respected the ancient tradition of a dry Navy, but this tantalising business of the empty wine glass—and then this matter of too little and too late—I hope you don't follow such barbarous practices in *your* house, Franks!

1952, 17 JANUARY, WASHINGTON. (HALLE, IRREPRESSIBLE, 268.)

To the British Ambassador Sir Oliver Franks during a visit to the White House.

33
RIPOSTES

"I said to him once, 'Winston, how do you do it – how do you get off these perfect ripostes?' He replied, 'Patience, my dear Dickie, patience – I've been waiting years to get that one off!"

– *Earl Mountbatten* [136]

"Calooh! Callay! Oh frabjous day. And so he chortled in his joy."
Being honoured in Oslo, with King Haakon, May, 1948.

Churchill's reputation for lightning parries and razor-edged responses to critics and opponents is perhaps overblown. His son Randolph was a much better off-the-cuff debater, and his best friend, F. E. Smith (Lord Birkenhead), certainly uttered some of the wonderful barbs which Churchill is often credited as having said (see Appendix I).

Like Groucho Marx, Churchill had his straight men and sparring partners, particularly at Question Time in the House of Commons, which he relished and carefully anticipated. Two of these were the Labour MPs Emmanuel Shinwell and Emrys Hughes, who held him in an odd affection which WSC returned. He gave less quarter to some of his Tory colleagues, particularly the fussy and aptly named Sir Waldron Smithers.

Churchill's *bête noire* was the formidable Socialist Aneurin Bevan, whom Churchill always distinguished from Labour Foreign Secretary Ernest Bevin (a Socialist he admired) by emphasising the second syllable when mentioning the former: "Mr. Be-*van*." (See entries for both in Chapter 20.)

Lord Mountbatten, in his famous 1966 speech to the Winston S. Churchill Society, made the point that Churchill, in his experience, had often to lie in wait for the opportunity to loose a verbal ambuscade, which he had carefully composed and filed in his photographic memory.

---

136 To the Sir Winston S. Churchill Society of Edmonton, Alberta, 1966.

Aborigine missionaries

[Mr. Hughes (Lab.): "Is the Prime Minister aware that the Australian aborigines who are converted to Christianity are now thinking of sending missionaries to this country, because they think that the atom bomb can only have been invented by savages and barbarians?"]

I hope that the Leader of the Opposition [Mr. Attlee] will not feel unduly hurt.

1952, 1 MAY.

Above comprehension

[Mr. Lewis (Lab.): "Is the Prime Minister aware of the deep concern felt by the people of this country at the whole question of the Korean conflict?"]

I am fully aware of the deep concern felt by the Hon. Member in many matters above his comprehension.

1952, 18 NOVEMBER. (WILLANS AND ROETTER, 32.)

[Mr. M. Steward (Lab.): "Will the Prime Minister remember the Greek proverb, 'Much learning does not teach sense'?" Mr. Lewis (Lab.): "May I ask the Prime Minister whether that is above his comprehension?"]

I am sorry to see that I hit so deeply home.

1952, 19 NOVEMBER. (WILLANS AND ROETTER, 32.)

Abstaining

We [Conservatives] thought it better and wiser to abstain as a body, and that is the course we intend to pursue.

[Mr. Bevin: "How can you pursue it when you are sitting still?"]

We are discussing the movements of the mind, and not the much more bulky shiftings of the human body.

1945, 13 DECEMBER.

Abuse

[Mr. Attlee (Lab.): "The Rt. Hon. Gentleman has often heard, 'No case, abuse the other side.'"]

With great respect, I would ask your permission, Mr. Speaker, to correct the misquotation—"When you have no case, abuse the plaintiff's attorney."

1953, 26 FEBRUARY.

WSC had announced the merging of two government departments; Labour doubted this would save money.

Agitated opponents

I was very much surprised that the Hon. Member for Silvertown [Jack Jones, MP] who certainly does not bear the reputation of being mealy-mouthed, should have been brought into such a state of extreme agitation by language which, I should have thought, a man of his moral fibre and physical structure could have afforded to sustain with a fair degree of composure.

1921, 15 DECEMBER.

Alcohol

[A Mormon visitor, when offered a whisky and soda: "May I have water, Sir Winston? Lions drink it."]

Asses drink it too.

[Second Mormon: "Strong drink rageth and stingeth like a serpent."]

I have long been looking for a drink like that.

1950S, CHARTWELL. (MONTAGUE BROWNE, 305.)

Anthony Montague Browne congratulated WSC on this riposte. "None of it was original," he grinned. "They just fed me a music hall-chance."

Prof, pray calculate the amount of Champagne and spirits I have consumed in my life and indicate how much of this room they would fill.

[Lindemann, pretending to calculate with his slide rule: "I'm afraid not more than a few inches, Winston."]

How much to do, how little time remains!

PASSIM.

A favourite riposte about WSC's alcohol intake, usually enacted with the help of "the Prof", his friend Professor Lindemann.

Anglo-American mongrel

[Gen. Slim: "I suppose we shall end up with some mongrel weapon, half British and half American."]

Pray moderate your language, Field Marshal—that's an exact description of me.

1952. (CAWTHORNE, 32.)

Churchill as the new Prime Minister in 1951 inherited the controversy over the relative merits of the new British and American automatic rifles. Field Marshal Sir William Slim, Chief of the Imperial General Staff, voiced his opinion.

Attacking one's party

[Lloyd George: "Judging from your sentiments, you are standing against the Light."]

You take a singularly detached view of the British Empire.

1930. (MEL, 380.)

Churchill in his maiden speech, 18 February 1901, criticised his own party. This exchange may have been the beginning of a relationship which would see Churchill desert the Conservatives for Lloyd George and the Liberals in May 1904.

Baths

[Hugh Gaitskell, MP: "Personally, I have never had a great many baths myself, and I can assure those who are in the habit of having a great many that it does not make a great difference to their health if they have less."]

When Ministers of the Crown speak like this on behalf of His Majesty's Government, the Prime Minister and his friends have no need to wonder why they are getting increasingly into bad odour. I had even asked myself, when meditating upon these points whether you, Mr. Speaker, would admit the word "lousy" as a Parliamentary expression in referring to the Administration, provided, of course, it was not intended in a contemptuous sense but purely as one of factual narration.

1947, 28 OCTOBER.

Gaitskell, Minister of Fuel and Power in the post-war Labour Government, was urging energy conservation; his advice proved too much for Churchill, a renowned bather.

Belgian rifle

I am quite ready that it [the adoption of the Belgian rifle by British forces] should be attributed to me, and whether it is attributed by the Hon. Gentleman to weakness or to wisdom I am entirely indifferent.

1954, 19 JANUARY.

[Mr. Paget MP: "If the Prime Minister will not tell us whether the Americans have accepted the Belgian rifle, will he tell us whether

anybody has accepted it? Have the French? Have even the Belgians? Are we not alone?"]

I am not in the least alarmed by being shouted at. In fact, I rather like it. The descendant of Paget's *Examen* will, I hope, be very careful and precise in his facts, and be careful in not misrepresenting and misquoting and otherwise defaming other people. He was a great defender of my ancestor.

1954, 1 FEBRUARY.

Paget's Examen *was a defence of Churchill's ancestor, John Churchill First Duke of Marlborough. Churchill wrote an introduction to a new edition of Paget's work in the 1930s.*

Black Welsh

I would not use the word "imprudently" if I had not long studied all the economic advantages of the Cardwell system, with a battalion abroad and a battalion at home, and an interflow of reserves and reinforcements between them. These battalions now raised, in one of which the Hon. Member for Ayrshire, South [Mr. Emrys Hughes], took so much interest... the Black—what was it?

[Mr. Hughes: "The Black Watch?"]

I thought it was the "Black Welsh."

1952, 5 MARCH.

The Black Watch is a famous Highland Regiment; there is of course no such thing as the Black Welsh.

Bloody black sheep

[Mr. Maurice Webb: "We are like a lot of sheep, aren't we?"]

Yes, bloody black sheep.

1946, 29 OCTOBER. (WILLANS AND ROETTER, 46.)

Maurice Webb (1904–56), Labour MP 1945–55, recounted WSC's riposte in a speech of this date.

Bring a friend if you have one

[Bernard Shaw: "Am reserving two tickets for you for my premiere. Come and bring a friend—if you have one."]

Impossible to be present for the first performance. Will attend the second—if there is one.

1922, LONDON. (HALLE, IRREPRESSIBLE, 116; DALTON NEWFIELD.)

The play was Saint Joan. *It had a good run. Halle misdates this as 1932.*

Caesar's wife

[Mr. Emanuel Shinwell, Lab.: "In this field of foreign relations the Rt. Hon. Gentleman, like Caesar's wife, must be above suspicion. (Interruption.) I assure Hon. Members that any reference that I am suspecting the Rt. Hon. Gentleman of feminine qualities is quite wrong."]

It was Caesar's wife, not Caesar.

1954, 1 December.

Callooh! Callay!

[Grace Hamblin: "Mr. Churchill, Cinque Ports flag has arrived and Allen has put it up."]

Callooh! Callay! Oh frabjous day! And so he chortled in his joy.

1946, Chartwell. (Hamblin, *Churchill Proceedings* 1987.)

When WSC reopened Chartwell after the war he wanted to fly his flag of Lord Warden of the Cinque Ports. Grace Hamblin (secretary, 1932–65) said he responded in this way because he knew she was fond of Lewis Carroll's Through the Looking Glass. *(The actual quotation is: "O frabjous day! Callooh! Callay! / He chortled in his joy.")*

Combing out

[The War Office was urging the "combing out" of various industries or departments.]

Physician, comb thyself.

1916, 23 May.

Common ground

Personally, I am in full agreement with the noble Lord on this point, and I am glad that we have found a common ground to stand on, though it be only the breadth of a comma.

1910.

Responding to a question about the punctuation used in Prayer Books by his High Church friend Lord Hugh Cecil MP (1869–1956). Debate over revising The Book of Common Prayer was protracted, lasting from 1906 to 1927.

Constipated

Ah, there goes that constipated Britannia.

1948 CA. Lord Carrington. (*Finest Hour*, III, Summer 2001, 19.)

Not as famous as the "you're drunk...you're ugly" exchange (see "Drunk and ugly"), this nevertheless is an accurate description of what Lord Carrington described as "the portly Labour MP", Bessie Braddock.

Cooing dove

Pray remember, Captain, that I come here as a cooing dove of peace, bearing a sprig of mistletoe in my beak—but far be it from me to stand in the way of military necessity.

1944, December. Athens. (Pawle, 338–9.)

Churchill arrived in Greece to mediate between the government and E.L.A.S. (Ethnikos Laikos Apeleftherotikos Stratos or National Popular Liberation Army) communist rebels. The government was backed by British troops. Captain Cuthbert of HMS Ajax, *on which he was quartered, said that he hoped they might not have to open fire, but would have to do so if asked to give supporting fire.*

Crackling of thorns

...our policy is an adequate basic standard—within just laws, let the best man win. [Laughter]

The crackling of thorns under a pot does not deter me.

1947, 28 October.

Churchill, defending Conservative Party policy, replied to Labour ridicule by recalling Ecclesiastes VII:6. "For as the crackling of thorns under a pot, so is the laughter of the fool: this also is vanity."

Craft

[Labour will] make the British people drain their cup to the last dregs....Here I see the hand of the master craftsman, the Lord President...

[Herbert Morrison, Lord President: "The Rt. Hon. Gentleman has promoted me."]

Craft is common both to skill and deceit.

1947, 11 November.

Crooked deal

[Mr. Frederick Pethick-Lawrence: "The Rt. Hon. Gentleman, like a bad bridge player, blames his cards."]

I blame the crooked deal.

CIRCA 1930. (HALLE, 112.)

Damned old fool

[Mr. Snow (Lab.): "Damned old fool." Col. Gomme-Duncan (Cons.): "Is it in order for an Hon. Member to refer to the Rt. Hon. Gentleman as 'a damned old fool'?" Mr. Snow: "I beg to withdraw that statement and to apologize but, of course, the Rt. Hon. Gentleman has been extremely provocative." Hon. Members: "Get out."]

The Hon. Gentleman must accept the position of being subordinate; although let me make it quite clear that this is the first time that I have ever heard the word "subordinate" regarded as un-Parliamentary or even as almost an obscene expression. However, the "damned old fool" has accepted the apology.

1951, 19 APRIL.

de Gaulle, Charles

[Brendan Bracken: "But...remember, Winston...he thinks of himself as the reincarnation of St. Joan."]

Yes, but *my* bishops won't burn him!

1943. (HALLE, IRREPRESSIBLE, 213.)

[Charles de Gaulle: "Do you mean that I am your prisoner? Are you going to send me to the Isle of Man?"]

No. Since you are a distinguished General, I will send you to the Tower of London.

1943, 2 APRIL. (PERUCCA AND MAURE, 109.)

The interchange was in French, of course. This is a secondary source and is not verified, but sounds so much in character that it is included provisionally.

Dead birds

[Aneurin Bevan: "Winston, for heaven's sake, your flies are undone."]

You needn't bother yourself about that. Dead birds never fly from the nest.

1946 CA., BUCKINGHAM PALACE. RONALD GOLDING TO THE EDITOR.

Bevan had arrived at the Palace in a lounge suit. WSC, resplendent in court dress, had started the exchange by saying, "Well! At least you could have come properly dressed."

Dead or Alive

[Michael Collins: "You hunted me night and day. You put a price on my head."]

Wait a minute. You are not the only one. At any rate it was a good price—£5,000. Look at me—£25 dead or alive. How would you like that?

1924, JANUARY. ("THE IRISH TREATY," *PALL MALL*; THOUGHTS, 161–2.)

Michael Collins (see Chapter 20) was the Irish revolutionary Churchill invited to London to negotiate the compromise Irish Treaty which gave Home Rule to the South and left Ulster in the Union. Collins, Churchill remarked, "was in his most difficult mood, full of reproaches and defiances, and it was very easy for everyone to lose his temper". After reading Churchill's wanted poster from the Boer War, Collins "broke into a hearty laugh. All his irritation vanished...we never to the best of my belief lost the basis of a common understanding."

Deadly shaft

[Mr. James Glanville: "The electors did not accept the Rt. Hon. Gentleman's advice."]

I am afraid that that is a shaft too deadly for me to reply to.

1948, 8 MARCH.

Speaking on Naval Estimates, WSC said that the Navy would have been stronger if the Government had done what he had urged in 1945.

Deaf member

Look at that fellow ignoring the advantages which a beneficent Providence has bestowed upon him.

DATE UNKNOWN. (CAWTHORNE, 24–5.)

On seeing an MP striving to catch through an ear-trumpet the speech of a dull backbencher.

Demagogic gestures

[Mr. W. Wyatt (Lab.): "Is it not a fact that when Income Tax has been deducted the saving is relatively negligible, and would it not be more appropriate if at his time of life the Prime Minister abandoned these cheap demagogic gestures?"]

I think the Hon. Gentleman is a judge of cheap demagogic gestures, but they do not often come off when he makes them.

[Mr. Shinwell (Lab.): "In view of the castigations of the Rt. Hon. Gentleman on the members of the former Government, does he not realize that, even at the reduced salary, the members of his Government are not worth it?"]

The Rt. Hon. Gentleman is no doubt trying to live up to the cheap demagogic gestures mentioned by his Hon. Friend.

1952, 29 JULY.

Dirty dogs and palings

[Sir Wilfred Paling (Lab.) violated Parliamentary decorum by shouting at Churchill, "Dirty dog!"]

The Hon. Member should realise what dirty dogs do to palings.

1920S. LORD MOUNTBATTEN TO THE EDMONTON
CHURCHILL SOCIETY, 1966.

Discards

[Sir J. E. Masterton-Smith: "But First Lord— you discarded the knave."]

The cards I throw away are not worthy of observation or I should not discard them. It is the cards I play on which you should concentrate your attention.

1912. (BONHAM CARTER, 279.)

During a bridge game on the Admiralty yacht Enchantress, *when WSC headed the Admiralty.*

Driving on the left

[Richard Miles, from the British Embassy in Washington, suggested Britain might contribute to Anglo-American understanding by switching to driving on the right.]

No! No!—It *won't* do. If a band of ruffians should set upon you, your sword arm wouldn't be free!

1942, JUNE, HYDE PARK. (HALLE, AMERICA AND
BRITAIN, 32.)

Drunk and ugly

[Bessie Braddock MP: "Winston, you are drunk, and what's more you are disgustingly drunk."]

Bessie, my dear, you are ugly, and what's more, you are disgustingly ugly. But tomorrow I shall be sober and you will still be disgustingly ugly.

1946. RONALD GOLDING TO THE EDITOR.

Not original to Churchill, but world famous, and confirmed by Ronald Golding, a body-guard present on the occasion, as WSC was leaving the House of Commons. Lady Soames, who said her father was always gallant to ladies, doubted the story – but Golding explained that WSC was not drunk, just tired and wobbly, which perhaps caused him to fire the full arsenal. However, he was relying on his photographic memory for this riposte: in the 1934 movie It's a Gift *W. C. Fields's character, when told he is drunk, responds, "Yeah, and you're crazy. But I'll be sober tomorrow and you'll be crazy the rest of your life." Verdict: Churchill editing W. C. Fields.*

Election 1945

[Clementine Churchill: "It may well be a blessing in disguise."]

At the moment it seems quite effectively disguised.

1945, 1 AUGUST. (WW2 VI, 583.)

Facts

I like the martial and commanding air with which the Rt. Hon. Gentleman [George Wyndham, MP] treats facts. He stands no nonsense from them.

1909, 9 FEBRUARY.

False arguments

It seems to me—and I have a lengthening experience in the House—that false arguments very rarely pay in debate.

[An Hon. Member: "You are using them now."]

I always try to economise the use of false arguments as much as possible, because a false argument is so often detected, and it always repels any listener who is not already a convinced and enthusiastic partisan.

1926, 28 APRIL.

Fanatical intelligentsia

Conservative and Liberal trade unionists... must not let themselves be discouraged in their national efforts by the political and party manoeuvres of a fanatical intelligentsia—The Home Secretary [James Chuter Ede] is laughing; I did not mean to include him in the intelligentsia. The Rt. Hon. Gentleman could surely find other things in life to laugh at beside those which do not include himself. Otherwise life might be rather gloomy for him.

1950, 19 SEPTEMBER.

Feet on the ground

I am sorry if personal jealousies, or other motives below the level of events, have led the Socialist Party at first to embark upon the unnatural plan of narrowing United Europe down to United Socialist Europe....I hope that their recent publication, "Facing the Facts," or "Face the Facts"...

[Hon. Members: "Feet on the Ground."]

..."Feet on the Ground". If Hon. Gentlemen opposite were to persist very long in facing the facts they would find their feet on the ground. And they might very soon find the rest of their bodies there as well.

1948, 28 OCTOBER.

Food Ministry

[Mr. I. O. Thomas (Lab.): "Will the Prime Minister indicate if he will take the precaution of consulting the consuming public before he decides to abolish the Food Ministry?"]

On the whole, I have always found myself on the side of the consumer.

1953, 27 OCTOBER.

Foot and Mouth Disease

[Mr. Robert Boothby (Cons., Aberdeen): "Is my Rt. Hon. Friend aware that there is a torrent of complaints from Scotland at the present time?"]

I am sure my Hon. Friend would be fully capable of giving full vent to any such torrent, but the difficulty is that we are not sure that Foot and Mouth Disease is as well educated on the subject of borders and questions arising out of them as he is.

[Mr. Boothby: "I beg to give notice that I shall raise this matter on the Adjournment."]

I am afraid I cannot undertake to be present when this new red herring is drawn across the border.

1952, 6 MAY.

Boothby wanted Foot and Mouth Disease in Scotland to be handled in Edinburgh rather than by the Ministry of Agriculture in London.

Force and favour

[An MP in the Division Lobbies, as Churchill forged forward: "It's wonderful to see Winston bulldozing his way through, in spite of his growing deafness and the noisy lobby."]

Partly by force, partly by favour!

1955. (SIR JOHN FOSTER, MP IN HALLE, IRREPRESSIBLE, 331.)

Foreign secretaries unite

Foreign Secretaries of the world unite; you have nothing to lose but your jobs.

1954, 7 MAY. (COLVILLE, FOOTPRINTS, 242–3.)

A paraphrase of Marx's "Workers of the world unite. You have nothing to lose but your chains." Returning from America, Churchill had (without Eisenhower's agreement) cabled Molotov for a meeting with Malenkov in Moscow. But the Russians had invited thirty-two nations to meet for a Soviet European Security Plan, so the bilateral talks Churchill wanted were off.

Foresight

[Mr. Jay (Lab.): "Would we be right in inferring from the Prime Minister's answer that he himself has given no thought to this question?"]

That would be a rather hazardous assumption on the part of the Rt. Hon. Gentleman, who has not, so far as I am aware, at any time in his Parliamentary career distinguished himself for foresight.

1952, 23 JULY.

Frustrated teacher

[Harrow tutor Mr Mayo, circa 1888: "I don't know what to do with you boys!"]

Teach us, Sir!

1954, 1 DECEMBER. (NICOLSON 1907–1963, 394.)

Sir Arthur Bryant to Harold Nicolson:

The voice came from a chubby imp with carrot hair – Winston Churchill. Mayo never forgot it.

German rearmament

[Mr. Harold Davis (Lab.): "May I interrupt the Rt. Hon. Gentleman? This is of vital importance. I put this question in no partisan spirit whatever. [Laughter.] Hon. Members opposite need not smile—this is vital to the destiny and peace of the world. Is the Rt. Hon. Gentleman prepared to take the risk of completely rearming Germany at this juncture, because that is what his proposal ultimately means?" (Hon. Members: "Nonsense.")]

I must leave the House to judge of the total lack of connection between what the Hon. Member has said and any language being used by me, or anything in the immediate circumstances before us in Europe.

1949, 17 November.

Churchill had forcefully argued for reconciliation between France and Germany and the latter's inclusion in a united Europe.

Guillotine

We have all heard of how Dr. Guillotin was executed by the instrument that he invented.

[Sir Herbert Samuel: "He was not!"]

Well, he ought to have been.

1931, 29 April. (Halle, 115.)

Guilty conscience

My Rt. Hon. Friend…has not been long enough in office to grow a guilty conscience.

1938, 17 November. (Blood, 106.)

WSC was referring to Sir Kingsley Wood, Air Minister from May 1938 through April 1940.

Hanging

Hanging, under English law, if properly conducted, is, I believe, an absolutely painless death.

[Mr. A. E. Stubbs: "Try it."]

Well, it may come to that.

1948, 15 July.

Churchill was comparing life imprisonment with what he regarded as the more preferable death sentence.

[A female admirer: "Doesn't it thrill you…to know that every time you make a speech the hall is packed to overflowing?"]

It is quite flattering, but whenever I feel this way I always remember that if instead of making a political speech I was being hanged, the crowd would be twice as big.

1952, 17 January. Press Conference, Washington. (McGowan, 222.)

Head shaking

It is no good the Rt. Hon. Gentleman [Ramsay MacDonald] shaking his head. He cannot shake away the facts.

1926, 27 September.

[Sir William Joynson-Hicks: "I see my Rt. Hon. Friend shaking his head. I wish to remind him that I am only expressing my own opinion."]

And I wish to remind the speaker that I am only shaking my own head.

Circa 1928. (Taylor, 219.)

The Rt. Hon. and Learned Gentleman [Attorney General Sir Hartley Shawcross] may shake his head till he shakes it off, but it does not affect the argument.

1948, 15 July.

The Rt. Hon. Gentleman is shaking his head, but he will have to shake it a great deal to shake off his personal responsibility in this matter.

1951, 6 November.

The argument was over abolishing University seats in the House of Commons, which Churchill opposed, but Labour's Herbert Morrison shook his head in dissent.

Health

[Photographer: "I hope, sir, that I will shoot your picture on your hundredth birthday."]

I don't see why not, young man. You look reasonably fit and healthy.

1949, 30 November. Hyde Park Gate, London. (McGowan; Manchester I, 34.)

WSC was celebrating his seventy-fifth birthday.

Impartial historian

…it is absolutely necessary to invoke the great name of Mr. Gladstone, a name which is received with reverence below the Gangway on the Opposition side, and with a certain amount of respect by some Hon. Members who sit opposite.

[Hon. Members: "What about yourself?"]

I occupy the impartial position of historian.

1927, 26 APRIL.

Indians

[Mrs. Ogden Reid: "What are you going to do about those wretched Indians?"]

Before we proceed further let us get one thing clear. Are we talking about the brown Indians in India, who have multiplied alarmingly under the benevolent British rule? Or are we speaking of the red Indians in America who, I understand, are almost extinct?

1943, 5 SEPTEMBER, WHITE HOUSE, WASHINGTON.
(PAWLE, 250; PILPEL, 199; WARD, 235.)

FDR mischievously invited to lunch the Vice President and de facto publisher of the New York Herald Tribune, a notable campaigner for India's independence. Her query came on the White House verandah. Mrs. Reid was rendered speechless, and Roosevelt was convulsed with laughter. Pilpel, and Lord Mountbatten in two speeches (1966, 1970), produced a more melodious version of WSC's remark, but Pawle's pre-dates both of theirs.

Indignation

My Hon. and Gallant Friend [Capt. Wedgwood Benn] must really not develop more indignation than he can sustain.

1920, 23 FEBRUARY.

Wedgwood Benn had worked himself into what seemed to be apoplexy over a speech Churchill was making.

Ingratitude

[WSC was told that a German bomb had fallen on former Prime Minister Stanley Baldwin's London house.]

What base ingratitude!

1940. (HALLE, IRREPRESSIBLE, 131.)

[Lord Londonderry: "Have you read my book?"]

Not at all. I only read for pleasure or profit.

1940. (MANNING AND BRONNER, 239.)

Insubordinate

[Emanuel Shinwell (Lab.): "I am not prepared to rely exclusively on the views expressed by [WSC]. There are other Members of the House who are subordinate to him, but who, nevertheless, are entitled to express an opinion."]

Or insubordinate.

1951, 19 APRIL.

Interruptions, answering

The Hon. Gentleman [Mr. Logan]...has abrogated to himself a function which did not belong to him, namely, to make my speech instead of letting me make it.

1931, 26 JUNE. (CS V, 5046–7.)

Judgement Day

[Mr. Hughes (Lab.): "Is the Prime Minister aware...that the Dean of Westminster is now wondering whether, on the Day of Judgement, he will appear with the Prime Minister on a charge of accepting stolen property?"]

I should have thought that the Hon. Member would be more concerned with the future of the Dean of Canterbury.

1952, 3 MARCH.

Concerning the decision to return the Coronation Stone to Westminster Abbey. Hewlett Johnson, the "Red Dean" of Canterbury, was a frequent Soviet apologist.

Jujube

I was only looking for a jujube!

1951, 15 FEBRUARY. (CHANNON, 453–4.)

During a speech by Hugh Gaitskell, WSC, on the Opposition front bench, began searching his pockets, then the floor, derailing Gaitskell, who finally stopped speaking and offered to assist in the search. The Scotsman recorded the incident the next day as "The Fall of the Pastille".

Korea vs. Crimea

[Mr. Harold Davies (Lab.): "Does the Rt. Hon. Gentleman realise that the House is getting less information on the Korean situation than his equally great predecessor Mr. Gladstone was giving the House in the time of the Crimean War?"]

I am afraid I have not at my fingers' ends the exact part which Mr. Gladstone took in the Crimean War. It was even before my time.

1952, 28 MAY.

Korean armaments

[Churchill was asked where the North Korean armaments had come from. Sir Waldron Smithers (Cons.) shouted, "Moscow."]

Although there are movements ever being made in aerial locomotion, it would be premature to suppose that they came from the moon.

1952, 28 MAY.

Latin "O table"

What does it mean, sir?

[Form Master: "'O table' is the vocative case....you would use that in addressing a table, in invoking a table."]

But I never do!

1930. (MEL, 25.)

It was 1888. Winston's form master led him to an empty classroom and asked him to learn the first declension of mensa, *the Latin word for table. The master returned and Churchill posed a question.*

Listening

[Mr. Bevan (Lab.): "I wish the Prime Minister would listen, because he will not hear as much good sense from the Chief Whip as I am giving him."]

I apologize to the Rt. Hon. Gentleman. I am afraid I did not hear what he said. I am so sorry to have missed it. Would he mind repeating it?

1952, 26 FEBRUARY.

Loyalty to a colleague

When I am invited, under threats of unpopularity to myself or the Government, to victimise the Chancellor of the Duchy [Alfred Duff Cooper] and throw him to the wolves, I say to those who make this amiable suggestion, I can only say to them, "I much regret that I am unable to gratify your wishes"—or words to that effect. [Laughter]

1942, 27 JANUARY.

Made during debate on a vote of confidence in the coalition Government, which was carried by 464 votes to one.

Making up his mind

[Emanuel Shinwell (Lab.): "Why can he not make up his mind?"]

I long ago made up my mind. The question is to get other people to agree.

1952, 3 DECEMBER.

Marriage

[When someone suggested that his son and his new bride did not have enough money to marry.]

What do they need?—cigars, champagne and a double bed.

1939, 4 OCTOBER. ST JOHN'S CHURCH, SMITH SQUARE, LONDON. (GILBERT, LIFE, 627.)

Randolph Churchill married Pamela Digby; they divorced in 1945, and Pamela later married Leland Hayward, followed by Averell Harriman.

Meeting Stalin

[Mr. Emrys Hughes (Lab.): "Has the Prime Minister forgotten that in at least half a dozen important speeches on the eve of the last Election he pressed for a meeting with Mr. Stalin? Is he aware that earlier in this year Mr. Stalin declared himself favourable towards a meeting? Why does he not unite with Mr. Stalin, and invite President Eisenhower?"]

I think we must try to understand the general position as it moves. We in this country would feel very severe domestic preoccupations, making it difficult to have conversations with heads of Governments, if for instance so many of our best doctors were being charged with poisoning so many of our best politicians.

1954, 17 JUNE.

Soviet doctors had been accused of trying to poison members of the Politburo.

Ministry of Economic Warfare

I only marked the paper "M.E.W." It seems he has mewed.

1940. (EDEN, A., 144.)

Churchill forwarded a secret paper criticising his Minister of Economic Warfare, who replied with affront.

Moustache and politics

[Newly introduced young woman: "There are two things I don't like about you...your new moustache and...your new political party."

Pray do not disturb yourself, *you are not likely to come into contact with either.*

1900. (CAWTHORNE, 17–18.)

Since Churchill cultivated a moustache only briefly, during and after the Boer War, this had to be circa his first campaign for Parliament.

Musketry

[A Bren gun went off nearby.]
Hark! I hear the sound of musketry.

1944. (OBITUARY OF MAJOR ION CALVOCORESSI, *DAILY TELEGRAPH*, 9 AUGUST 2007.)

Naked encounter

The Prime Minister of Great Britain has nothing to hide from the President of the United States.

[Or: You see, Mr. President, I have nothing to hide.]

1941, DECEMBER. WHITE HOUSE, WASHINGTON. (LOWENHEIM 8; THOMPSON, ASSIGNMENT, 248; PILPEL, 142.)

Uncertain but possible: Roosevelt, inspired to call the new world body "United Nations", wheeled himself into Churchill's room, finding the PM, as Harry Hopkins said, "stark naked and gleaming pink from his bath". Later, queried by FDR biographer Robert Sherwood, WSC said: "I could not possibly have made such a statement as that. The President himself would have been well aware that it was not strictly true." Whatever was said, such an encounter apparently did happen: see next entry.

Sir, I believe I am the only man in the world to have received the head of a nation naked.

1942, JANUARY. BUCKINGHAM PALACE. (WARD, 384–5.)

WSC to the King, recounted by WSC to Roosevelt, then by FDR to his confidante Daisy Suckley and the British Ambassador, Lord Halifax, on 17 January 1945. In this version, WSC did not say he had "nothing to hide", which he denied to Robert Sherwood. FDR simply said, "United Nations!" and Churchill responded, "Good!"

Nein demerits

[Schoolmistress: "Nine demerits seems even too much for you, Winston."]
The word I used was nein, German for no.

1882. (MARTIN, BATTLE; TAYLOR, 58.)

At the end of one school day he lined up with other students to report their day's demerits.

Old age ailments

[Tory Member: "They say the old man's getting a bit past it."]
And they say that the old man's getting deaf as well.

1960. (PASSIM.)

Reported by Kay Halle, who also provides a second, similar rejoinder, when Lord Hinchingbrooke whispered to a colleague, "He can't hear you, he's very deaf." WSC allegedly replied, "Yes, and they say the old man is gaga too."

Opinions

If I valued the Hon. Gentleman's [Sir J. Lonsdale, MP] opinion I might get angry.

1913, 1 JANUARY.

Pawn and utensil

The Hon. Member should not get so excited...I was eleven years a fairly solitary figure in this House and pursued my way in patience and so there may be hope for the Hon. Member....

1944, 8 DECEMBER.

Churchill was often interrupted by Willie Gallacher (1881–1965), the only Communist MP from 1935 to 1945, when another one was elected. I cannot verify a WSC reference to Gallacher as a Member "who consents to be used as the pawn and utensil of a foreign power".

Shut up, Moscow!

1947. (HALLE, IRREPRESSIBLE, 244.)

Gallacher responded: "Shut up, voice of Wall Street."

Plastiras

[Aide: "The Greek Prime Minister is Gen. Plastiras, sir."]

Has he feet of clay?

1945. (HALLE, IRREPRESSIBLE, 244.)

As with so many foreign words, WSC's pronunciation of the name was literal: "plaster-ass". General Nikolaos Plastiras (1883–1953) was Greek Prime Minister, in 1945, 1950 and 1951–52.

Power

[Mr. Dobbs (Lab.): "Does the Rt. Hon. Gentleman deny that he himself some years ago made a statement as to what he would do if he got the power? He has had it for eighteen months and he has done nothing in that respect."]

I did not get the power to regulate the way in which the affairs of the world would go. I only got the power to preside over a party which has been able to beat the Opposition in Divisions for eighteen months.

1953, 22 APRIL.

Dobbs was complaining over Churchill's inability to arrange for a summit meeting with Eisenhower and the new Soviet leaders following the death of Stalin.

Practice

I can well understand the Hon. Member speaking for practice, which he badly needs.

1920. (MARSH, 172.)

Said in response to a speech by Sir Oswald Moseley, who was known for his frequent and superfluous speeches.

Prayer

[Someone remarked that the Greek political leader, Archbishop Damaskinos, was in the habit of securing himself from interruption by hanging a notice on his door: "His Beatitude is at prayer."]

I'd like to try that at Downing Street, but I'm afraid no one would believe it.

1944, 27 DECEMBER. ATHENS. (FISHMAN, 97.)

Churchill installed Archbishop Damaskinos, whom he regarded as a "scheming medieval prelate" and "pestilent priest from the Middle

Ages", as a regent in Greece to quell factions warring for power. See Nations...Greece.

President, running for

[Reporter: "Would you become an American citizen if we could make you President of the United States?"]

There are various little difficulties in the way. However, I have been treated so splendidly in the United States that I should be disposed, if you can amend the Constitution, seriously to consider the matter.

1932. PRESS CONFERENCE, NEW YORK. (HALLE, AMERICA AND BRITAIN, 14.)

Prigs, prudes and faddists

[Walter Runciman (WSC's 1899 Liberal opponent): "I have not been a swashbuckler around the world."]

And I do not belong to a Radical Party composed of prigs, prudes and faddists.

1899. (HALLE, IRREPRESSIBLE, 32.)

Primus inter pares

As to the Chairman of the committee, he is not *"facile princeps"*, but *"primus inter pares"*....

[At this Labour members rose at what they saw as a slur on their non-classical education, and some demanded, "Translate!"]

...which, for the benefit of any old Etonians who may be present, I should, if very severely pressed, venture to translate.

1941, 22 JANUARY. (UNRELENTING, 32.)

When offering to translate, Churchill, an old Harrovian, turned to his Labour colleague Hugh Dalton, Minister for Economic Warfare, who was an old Etonian.

Rat swimming

[When informed that a Conservative MP was standing for a by-election as a Liberal.]

The only instance of a rat swimming toward a sinking ship.

1905. (HALLE, IRREPRESSIBLE, 53.)

Readable disagreement

I find [your paper] eminently readable. I entirely disagree with it!

1940. (MENZIES, 71.)

Robert Menzies had gone to Ireland to investigate Irish neutrality, and written a paper for the Cabinet.

Re-creating the world

[Chancellor Adenauer: "If I were re-creating the world, I would suggest that this time we not put a limit on man's intelligence without putting a limit on man's stupidity."]

That would not do at all, because it would deprive me of many of my Cabinet members.

1951, 5 DECEMBER. (HALLE, IRREPRESSIBLE, 306.)

Red Meat

[Mr. Gordon Walker (Lab.): "Does the Rt. Hon. Gentleman's answer mean that the part of 'Britain Strong and Free' which set out Conservative Party policy on the Commonwealth in the Election has now been abandoned?"]

Nothing that we set out in our statement of policy before the Election has now been abandoned, and we all look forward to the moment when we shall be able to ram red meat down the throats of Hon. Members opposite.

1952, 8 JULY.

Labour Members were asking for the beef the Conservatives had promised would follow the end of food rationing. "Britain Strong and Free" was the 1951 Conservative Party Manifesto.

Removing MPs

[Mr. Schurmer (Lab.): "Will the Rt. Hon. Gentleman consider taking the Hon. Member for Orpington (Sir Waldron Smithers) to Bermuda with him, as it would please both sides of the House if he would take him and leave him there?"

Sir Waldron Smithers (Cons.): "On a point of order. May I tell you Mr. Speaker that I take no objection to that, but I wish the Hon. Member for Sparkbrook (Mr. Schurmer) would go away too."]

I will try to answer that question. I earnestly hope that it will be arranged through the usual channels so that equal numbers on both sides of the House have this unfortunate experience offered to them.

1953, 23 JUNE.

Reprisals

[Oswald Lewis (Cons.) asked whether German bombing of England would bring about reprisals.]

If the answer were in the negative, it would remove a deterrent for the enemy. If it were in the affirmative, it might spur him to increase his preparations and add to the difficulties of our airmen. If it were noncommittal, it would not add to the enlightenment of my Hon. Friend.

1940, 23 JULY. (OB, CV6/2, 564.)

Retirement

[Reporter: "Are you going to retire, sir?"]

Not until I am a great deal worse and the Empire a great deal better.

1953, 8 FEBRUARY, NEW YORK.
(SUNDAY TIMES, LONDON.)

Ring a friend

[David Lloyd George at a telephone booth: "Winston, loan me a penny so I may ring a friend." Churchill elaborately searched his pockets…]

Here, David, is sixpence. Now you can ring all your friends.

NO DATE.

Ronald Golding to the editor, who recalled that WSC told him of this exchange, which occurred before World War II.

Roman Christian Communists

[When Churchill asked an Italian group what Party they represented, they replied: "We are the Christian Communists."]

It must be very inspiring to your party having the Catacombs so handy.

1944, AUGUST, ROME. (WW2 VI, 102.)

WSC added:

They did not seem to see the point, and, looking back, I am afraid their minds must have turned to the cruel mass executions which the Germans so recently perpetrated in these ancient sepulchres. One may however be pardoned for making historical references in Rome.

Scottish dilemma

[Mrs. Jean Mann (Lab.): "Is the Prime Minister aware that...the Mint has decided to issue coins with 'Elizabeth II' and Scots who object to this title are placed in an awful dilemma?"]

I hope that theoretical refinements will not stop the normal conduct of business.

1953, 15 APRIL.

Scottish Loyalty Oath

[An Hon. Member: "Is the Prime Minister aware that there is a strong feeling in Scotland about the Oath being taken to a Queen Elizabeth II on the ground of historical inaccuracy? In view of his great claim to historical accuracy himself, will he not do something to meet this very strong resentment in Scotland?"]

I shall be very glad to hear from the Hon. Member if he will put his question in the pillar-box.

1953, 3 APRIL.

Churchill displayed his awareness of current events: Scottish dissidents had been blowing up pillar boxes containing the new Queen's Royal Cipher.

Secret vs. awkward questions

[Mr. De la Bere asked the Prime Minister to define the difference between a secret and an awkward question.]

One is a danger to the country, and the other a nuisance to the Government.

1940, 11 SEPTEMBER. (BOYLE, 273.)

Sidney's perch

[Mr. Sidney Silverman (Lab.): "I wonder what the Rt. Hon. Gentleman would say if he abandoned restraint."]

The Hon. Gentleman is always intervening. On this occasion he did not even hop off his perch.

1949, 21 JULY.

Silverman had very short legs which dangled when he sat. Churchill often referred to his "perch", especially when provoked by Silverman failing to rise to ask a question.

Speaking volume

[A Labour heckler: "Speak up—don't be afraid!"]

I find I speak quite loud enough to silence any of *you* when I like.

1945. (COWLES, 5.)

Special relationship temperature

[Edward Floored, *Washington Post*: "Sir Winston, in your communiqué at Quebec with Mr. Roosevelt you spoke of 'blazing friendship' between our two countries. What is the temperature of that friendship now?"]

Normal!

1952, 17 JANUARY. PRESS CONFERENCE, WASHINGTON. (PILPEL, 261.)

Speechmaking

He spoke without a note, and almost without a point.

1931. (MANCHESTER II, 107.)

WSC had endured a lengthy speech by Labour MP William Graham.

Spiritual resources

[Mr. Gower (Cons.): "Will the Prime Minister assure the House that, while we have quite properly attended to the physical needs of defence and of our other problems, we should not forget these spiritual resources which have inspired this country in the past and without which the noblest civilization would decay?"]

I hardly think that that is my exclusive responsibility.

1952, 25 MARCH.

Springboard not sofa

[Aneurin Bevan remarked that the Allies pondering the invasion of Sicily was "like an old man approaching a young bride: fascinated, sluggish and apprehensive."]

The Army is like a peacock—nearly all tail...I intended North Africa to be a springboard, not a sofa.

1942, NOVEMBER. (KENNEDY, 274.)

Supplementary questions

[Mr. Shinwell (Lab.): "Will the Prime Minister tell us why he has suddenly become so shy? Usually he is very anxious to add a great deal on supplementary questions. Could he not expand a little on this occasion? What is the matter with him?"]

I have to measure the length of the response to any supplementary question by the worth, meaning and significance of that supplementary question.

1952, 18 JUNE.

Tanks

[Richard Stokes (Lab., Liverpool), a strong critic of Churchill's war leadership, twice suggested that a German and British tank might usefully be comparison-tested in the House of Commons yard.]

I think the trouble and expense involved, though not very great, is still more than is justified to satisfy the spiteful curiosity of my Hon. Friend....Since the word "untruthfulness" has been used, no one has been a greater contributor than the Hon. Member.

1944, 30 MARCH, 4 APRIL. (DAWN, 58, 116.)

Toast declined

[An MP suggested the House should toast, "Death to all Dictators and Long Life to all Liberators among whom the Prime Minister is first."]

It is very early in the morning.

1944, 18 JANUARY. (DAWN, 53.)

Two Gentlemen of Verona

[Private secretary John Colville's Italian cook turned up six months pregnant: "I told Winston that I believed the cook's downfall to have been brought about by a man in a street in Verona after dark."]

Obviously not one of the Two Gentlemen.

1954, 6 JULY. SOUTHAMPTON. (FRINGES II, 368.)

WSC referred to The Two Gentlemen of Verona *by William Shakespeare, whose works he adored and largely memorised.*

Unloved sons

Isn't it enough to have this parent volcano continually erupting in our midst? And now we are to have these subsidiary craters spouting forth the same unhealthy fumes!

1930S. ("CHURCHILL'S HUMOUR," A. P. HERBERT IN EADE, 297.)

WSC following the maiden speech of the son of an unpopular Minister.

Unobjectionable sentiments

[Sir Waldron Smithers (Cons.): "Would not the Prime Minister agree that the only way to improve the standards of living of backward races and to avert economic disaster is to allow all peoples to buy in the cheapest and sell in the dearest markets, because if goods cannot cross frontiers, armies will? Will he set the people free?"]

Those seem to me, on the whole, unobjectionable sentiments.

1953, 23 JUNE.

"Set the People Free" was the title of a Conservative Party election manifesto. Smithers was well known for "condensing the largest amount of words into the smallest amount of thought", to use a Churchillism.

Uproar in the Opposition

...the spectacle of a number of middle-aged gentlemen who are my political opponents being in a state of uproar and fury is really quite exhilarating to me.

1952, 21 MAY.

Virtue

[Jack Seely: "No, no, *mea virtute me involvo.*"]

Yes, you get tied up in your own virtue.

CIRCA 1916.

WSC's friend Jack Seely, later Lord Mottistone, had a grievance with the War Office. WSC had asked why he did not bring it to the attention of the authorities.

Welsh sovereign

[Mr. Gower (Cons.): "Can the Prime Minister state what course will be followed if a future British monarch should bear the name Llewellyn?"]

I hope I may ask for a long notice of that question.

1953, 15 APRIL.

Welsh studies

[Mr. Hughes (Lab.): "Is the Rt. Hon. Gentleman aware that the Minister of Defence was absent from the first Home Guard Parade last night? Is he now on open arrest awaiting court martial?"]

I was pursuing my studies into the Welsh language.

1951, 28 NOVEMBER.

After becoming Prime Minister again, Churchill appointed himself Minister of Defence, as he had in 1940, although the job was soon passed on. In a debate on recruitment of the Home Guard personnel, WSC was challenged by Hughes, a frequent but affectionate Welsh critic.

Welsh treats

We have therefore appointed an Under-Secretary under the Home Office who is a Welshman, and whose name is, I believe, quite well known throughout the Principality...

[Mr. George Thomas (Lab., Cardiff, West): "Pronounce his name."]

I will—Lewellyn. *Môr o gân yw Cymru i gyd.*

1951, 6 NOVEMBER.

For the source of Churchill's astonishing outburst of Welsh ("All Wales is a sea of song"), see Chapter 6...Wales.

[Mr. Hughes (Lab.): "Owing to the popularity the Government has gained by the reduction of their salaries, is not the Prime Minister prepared to apply the principle to the big item of more than £500,000 spent on the Civil List?"]

Dim o gwbl.

1951, 12 NOVEMBER.

Stunning the Welshman Emrys Hughes, Churchill had responded with the Welsh words meaning "Nothing at all". Evidently that November, he was in a Welsh mood.

Yelping

[Mr. George Craddock (Lab.), calling out from his seat: "Scandalous."]

We are still allowed to debate and not merely to yelp from below the Gangway.

1954, 14 JULY.

The gangway is the aisle separating the leading members of the Government or Opposition from the other members, or backbenchers.

34

CHURCHILL
AT LARGE

"The Prime Minister was at his most benign, and suddenly, towards the end of dinner, looking across the table at the man who had carried England through her dark years, I felt an upsurge of gratitude that melted into hero worship. This was a profoundly significant moment in the history of our country; the long, long hoped-for victory was so very near, and the fact that we were in the presence of the man who had contributed so much foresight, courage and genius to winning it struck Juliet and Venetia at the same instance that it struck me. Emotion submerged us and without exchanging a word, as simultaneously as though we had carefully rehearsed it, the three of us rose to our feet and drank Mr. Churchill's health."

– *Noël Coward* [137]

"Let us be contented with what has happened to us and thankful for all we have been spared."

---

137 Coward, recalling a dinner with WSC on 2 May 1954. The ladies mentioned were mutual friends of Coward and Churchill, Juliet Duff and Venetia Montagu. Coward, 327–8.

*

A valedictory by an old friend is an appropriate beginning of our final chapter, a cache of quotations that didn't seem to fit any specific categories. They constitute in the main a cornucopia of Churchill's reflections on humanity, manners, mores, life and death. (If you fear death, read Churchill.)

His optimism for humanity was tempered with a conviction that "the *genus homo*" never changes. The same imperfect being, he is presented by the advance of science with increasingly potent and dangerous toys: "This vast expansion was unhappily not accompanied by any noticeable advance in the stature of man, either in his mental facilities, or his moral character. His brain got no better, but it buzzed the more."[138]

His essay "Mass Effects in Modern Life" took up his concern about the levelling of man to a low common denominator: "Are not modern conditions—at any rate throughout the English-speaking communities – hostile to the development of outstanding personalities and to their influence upon events?"[139] Churchill wondered.

Would the "moral philosophy and spiritual conceptions of men and nations" hold their own against "formidable scientific evolutions"?[140] Was it possible that, in abandoning its theocratic principles, mankind would lose the ability to distinguish between right and wrong, that it would substitute instead a kind of vague, utopian concept of wishful thinking? Churchill worried not so much that those who forget the past are condemned to relive it, but that the loss of the past would mean "the most thoughtless of ages. Every day headlines and short views."[141]

In the end Churchill hoped that a merciful Providence would pass "the sponge of oblivion across much that is suffered":[142] a "blessed dispensation", through which pain would be forgotten and glory and honour exalted. Although often pilloried by the Left or Right, Churchill believed in a "middle road" between radicals and reactionaries, jingoes and appeasers. He was proud in that his country's constitution was unwritten, that "the English never draw a line without blurring it".[143]

Sir Martin Gilbert, who, while writing and editing over eight million words about Churchill, has the ability to summarise him in a few paragraphs – with which there is no better way to close these chapters:

> Churchill was indeed a noble spirit, sustained in his long life by a faith in the capacity of man to live in peace, to seek prosperity, and to ward off threats and dangers by his own exertions. His love of country, his sense of fair play, his hopes for the human race, were matched by formidable powers of work and thought, vision and foresight. His path had often been dogged by controversy, disappointment and abuse, but these had never deflected him from his sense of duty and his faith in the British people....
>
> In the last years, when power passed, to be followed by extreme old age with all its infirmity and sadness, Churchill's children expressed to him in private the feelings which many of his fellow countrymen also felt. In August 1955, four months after the end of his second Premiership, his son Randolph wrote to him: "Power must pass and

---

138 Massachusetts Institute of Technology, Boston, 31 March 1949.
139 "Mass Effects in Modern Life," *Strand Magazine*, May 1931; Thoughts, 183.
140 "Fifty Years Hence," *Strand Magazine*, February 1931; Thoughts, 203.
141 OB V, 319.
142 Fourth Alamein Reunion, Empress Hall, London, 21 October 1939. Balance, 119.
143 House of Commons, 16 November 1948.

vanish. Glory, which is achieved through a just exercise of power – which itself is accumulated by genius, toil, courage and self-sacrifice – alone remains"….From his daughter Mary had come words of equal solace nine years later, when at last his life's great impulses were fading. "In addition to all the feelings a daughter has for a loving, generous father," she wrote, "I owe you what every Englishman, woman & child does – Liberty itself."[144]

Alternatives

The questions which have to be settled are not always questions between what is good and bad; very often it is a choice between two very terrible alternatives.

1941, 10 June.

Animals

The world would be better off if it were inhabited only by animals.

Circa 1946. (Graebner, 97.)

WSC to his Life *editor, Walter Graebner: an uncharacteristically pessimistic view.*

Man is a land animal. Even rabbits are allowed to have warrens, and foxes have earths.

1946, 30 July. (OB VIII, 253.)

Chance

When by extraordinary chance one has gained some great advantage or prize and actually had it in one's possession…the idea of losing it becomes almost insupportable.

1930. (MEL, 303.)

Reflections as WSC was about to leave his mineshaft hiding place during his escape from the Boers in 1899.

Change

If in erecting some great building it is found that a girder in the lowest story is defective, the building becomes a cause of peril and danger to the public, but it is not possible immediately to withdraw it. To wrench it away would be to involve the certainty of ruin; but to whom? The jerry-builder might have decamped. The contractor might have made a fortune from the job and retired. It is upon the humble occupants that the miseries of the downfall would descend.

1906, 22 February.

The oldest habit in the world for resisting change is to complain that unless the remedy to the disease can be universally applied it should not be applied at all. But you must begin somewhere.

1911, 25 May.

Changes in personnel are caused from time to time by the march of events and by the duty of continual improvement. Changes in machinery are enjoined by experience, and, naturally, while we live we ought to learn. Change is agreeable to the human mind, and gives satisfaction, sometimes short-lived, to ardent and anxious public opinion.

1941, 29 July.

Changing views

We live in such a febrile and sensational age that even a month or two is enough to make people not merely change their views, but forget the views and feelings they entertained before.

1935, 24 October.

Civilisation

There are few words which are used more loosely than the word "Civilisation." What does it mean? It means a society based upon the opinion of civilians. It means that violence, the rule of warriors and despotic chiefs, the conditions of camps and warfare, of riot and tyranny, give place to parliaments where laws are made, and independent courts of justice in which over long periods those laws are maintained. That is Civilisation—and in its soil grow continually freedom, comfort, and culture.

1938, 2 July. University of Bristol. (Blood, 53.)

Conformity

…it is quite true that in all societies and in all times there is a pressure operative upon individuals to make them conform to the dominant

144 OB VIII, 1365–6.

tendencies. Within reasonable limits it is not an unhealthy pressure.

1911, 30 MAY.

Consultation

...one can always consult a man and ask him "Would you like your head cut off tomorrow?" and after he has said "I would rather not," cut it off. "Consultation" is a vague and elastic term.

1947, 7 MAY.

Death

It often happens that, when men are convinced that they have to die, a desire to bear themselves well and to leave life's stage with dignity conquers all other sensations.

1900. (SAVROLA, 189.)

My darling I grieve for you. An old & failing life going out on the tide, after the allotted span has been spent & after most joys have faded is not a case for human pity. It is only a part of the immense tragedy of our existence here below against wh[ich] both hope & faith have rebelled. It is only what we all expect & await....

1925. (OB V, 107.)

WSC to his wife on the death of her mother, Lady Blanche Hozier (1852–1925).

I saw with grief the approaching departure, and—for all human purposes—extinction, of a being high uplifted above the common run. As I observed him regarding with calm, firm and cheerful gaze the approach of Death, I felt how foolish the Stoics were to make such a fuss about an event so natural and so indispensable to mankind.

1931, APRIL. ("ARTHUR JAMES BALFOUR," *STRAND MAGAZINE*; GC, 163.)

The span of mortals is short, the end universal; and the tinge of melancholy which accompanies decline and retirement is in itself an anodyne. It is foolish to waste lamentations upon the closing phase of human life. Noble spirits yield themselves willingly to the successively falling shades which carry them to a better world or to oblivion.

1938. (MARLBOROUGH IV, 539.)

On the death of John Churchill First Duke of Marlborough (1650–1722).

Old age, by blanching the seat of reason, may cut off the fear of death even in a once imaginative mind, or it may, on the other hand, undermine fortitude, softening the will.

1956, 11 NOVEMBER. (MORAN, 753.)

Destiny

The destiny of mankind is not decided by material computation. When great causes are on the move in the world, stirring all men's souls, drawing them from their firesides, casting aside comfort, wealth, and the pursuit of happiness in response to impulses at once awe-striking and irresistible, we learn that we are spirits, not animals, and that something is going on in space and time...which, whether we like it or not, spells duty.

1941, 16 JUNE. BROADCAST, LONDON. (UNRELENTING, 166.)

Diversity

Human beings are endowed with infinitely varying qualities and dispositions, and each one is different from the others. We cannot make them all the same. It would be a pretty dull world if we did.

1943, 21 MARCH. BROADCAST, LONDON. (ONWARDS, 41.)

Duty

It is not given to the cleverest and the most calculating of mortals to know with certainty what is their interest. Yet it is given to quite a lot of simple folk to know every day what is their duty.

1943, 31 AUGUST. BROADCAST, LONDON. (ONWARDS, 180.)

...victory or defeat are things which happen, but duty is a thing which is compulsory and has to go on irrespective, and carries with it its own rewards whatever the upshot of the struggle may be.

1949, 25 MARCH. RITZ-CARLTON HOTEL, NEW YORK. (BALANCE, 38.)

End of History

How strange it is that the past is so little understood and so quickly forgotten. We live in the most thoughtless of ages. Every day headlines and short views. I have tried to drag history up a little nearer to our own times in case it should be helpful as a guide in present difficulties.

1929, 5 APRIL. (OB V, 319.)

One might add that little has changed since 1929.

Existence

"It is a strange riddle, is it not?"
"We shall learn the answer when we die."

1899. (SAVROLA, 82.)

Failure

The penalties for misfortune and failure are terrible today: they are wholly disproportionate, even when they are brought on by a man's own fault, either through the culpability of the individual or neglect of what is necessary to make him try or to make him take care.

1911, 25 MAY.

Fate and acceptance

Let us be contented with what has happened to us and thankful for all we have been spared.

1931, MARCH. ("A SECOND CHOICE," *STRAND MAGAZINE*; THOUGHTS, 10.)

The human story does not always unfold like an arithmetical calculation on the principle that two and two make four. Sometimes in life they make five or minus three; and sometimes the blackboard topples down in the middle of the sum and leaves the class in disorder and the pedagogue with a black eye.

1946, 7 MAY. (SINEWS, 123.)

Upon receiving the Freedom of the City of Westminster.

Future

Let us see how the course of events develops, and let us not endeavour to pry too closely or speculate too audaciously upon those mysteries of the future which are veiled from our eyes, and which, if they were not veiled from our eyes by the wisdom of Providence, would confront us with a state of existence here below very much less interesting and exciting than that in which we find ourselves.

1943, 1 FEBRUARY. PRESS CONFERENCE, CAIRO. (ONWARDS, 8.)

I have no fear of the future. Let us go forward into its mysteries, let us tear aside the veils which hide it from our eyes, and let us move onward with confidence and courage. All the problems of the post-war world, some of which seem so baffling now, will be easier of solution once decisive victory has been gained, and once it is clear that victory won in arms has not been cast away by folly or by violence when the moment comes to lay the broad foundations of the future world order, and it is time to speak great words of peace and truth to all.

1943, 29 SEPTEMBER. ROYAL ALBERT HALL, LONDON. (ONWARDS, 225.)

Homosexuality

...homosexuals might indeed be a security risk, not so much because they might be subject to blackmail, but because they often feel themselves alien and apart from the mainstream of the country, like a black in a white country, or a white in a black one.

CIRCA 1950S. (MONTAGUE BROWNE, 219–20.)

Churchill's only concern about homosexuals seems clear in this remark. Yet in 2007 a shallow thinker, discovering a 1942 letter to the King in which WSC advised against a knighthood "just now" for Noël Coward, announced that this proved WSC was a homophobe. In fact, Coward had recently been convicted of breaching currency regulations, always a barrier to an honour. WSC, advised by the Treasury, was simply exercising his responsibility to the King. For Coward's own feelings about Churchill, see his recollection at the beginning of this chapter.

Humanity

I believe that, generally speaking, given free institutions on a fair basis, the best side of men's nature will in the end surely come uppermost. But this doctrine has its limits.

1906, 22 FEBRUARY.

A major issue for the Liberals in the 1906 election was importation of "Chinese slaves" to work the Rand mines in South Africa as indentured labourers. See also Chapter 3, Churchillisms...Terminological inexactitude.

Broadly speaking, human beings may be divided into three classes: those who are billed to death, those who are worried to death, and those who are bored to death.

1925, DECEMBER. ("HOBBIES," NASH'S PALL MALL; THOUGHTS, 217.)

Human beings, happily for them, do not have to direct all their bodily functions themselves. They do not have to plan in advance how many heartbeats they are to have in the next twenty-four hours or what relation their temperature or blood pressure should bear to those heartbeats. They do not have to decide, as a part of the daily routine, what secretions are to be made by the liver or kidneys. No official quota is set for lymph or bile. Otherwise I fear the President of the Board of Trade [Sir Stafford Cripps] would find he had overdrawn his account very much. Providence has relegated these problems to the subconscious mind and left the commanding sphere to human reason.

1945, 6 DECEMBER.

The *genus homo*—if I may display my Latin—is a tough creature who has travelled here by a very long road. His nature has been shaped and his virtues ingrained by many millions of years of struggle, fear and pain, and his spirit has, from the earliest dawn of history, shown itself upon occasion capable of mounting to the sublime, far above material conditions or mortal terrors. He still remains man—still remains as Pope described him 200 years ago:

Placed on this Isthmus of a middle State,
A being darkly wise and rudely great...
Created half to rise and half to fall;
Great Lord of all things, yet a prey to all;
Sole judge of truth, in endless error
* hurled;*
The glory, jest and riddle of the world.

1949, 31 MARCH. MASSACHUSETTS INSTITUTE OF TECHNOLOGY, BOSTON. (BALANCE, 46–7.)

Alexander Pope (1688–1744) is stated by the Oxford Dictionary of Quotations to be "the third most frequently quoted writer in the English language". I am not sure they have recently tallied Churchill. WSC was quoting from Pope's "Essay on Man" (1733–34).

Humanity, unchanging nature of

Certain it is that while men are gathering knowledge and power with ever-increasing and measureless speed, their virtues and their wisdom have not shown any notable improvement as the centuries have rolled. The brain of a modern man does not differ in essentials from that of the human beings who fought and loved here millions of years ago. The nature of man has remained hitherto practically unchanged. Under sufficient stress—starvation, terror, warlike passion, or even cold intellectual frenzy—the modern man we know so well will do the most terrible deeds, and his modern woman will back him up.

1931, DECEMBER. ("FIFTY YEARS HENCE," STRAND MAGAZINE; THOUGHTS, 202.)

A theme that resonates consistently through Churchill's prose from his earliest years in Parliament to the nuclear age was the unchanging nature of man, contrasted with the constant metamorphosing in every school of science and technology – a combination of potentially explosive elements.

It is sometimes said that good men are scarce. It is perhaps because the spate of events with which we attempt to cope and which we strive to control have far exceeded, in this modern age, the old bounds, that they have been swollen up to giant proportions, while, all the time, the stature and intellect of man remain unchanged.

1941, 6 FEBRUARY.

[Some believe it would be a disaster] if the particular minor planet which we inhabit blew itself to pieces, or if all human life were extinguished upon its surface, apart, that is to say, from fierce beings, armed with obsolescent firearms, dwelling in the caverns of the Stone Age. There is a general feeling that that would be a regrettable event. Perhaps, however, we flatter ourselves. Perhaps we are biased but everyone realises how far scientific knowledge has outstripped human virtue. We all hope that men are better, wiser, more merciful than they were 10,000 years ago. There is certainly a great atmosphere of comprehension. There is a growing factor which one may call world public opinion, most powerful, most persuasive, most valuable. We understand our happy lot, even if we have no power to control it.

1945, 7 NOVEMBER.

In the nineteenth century Jules Verne wrote *[A]Round the World in Eighty Days*. It seemed a prodigy. Now you can get around it in four; but you do not see much of it on the way. The whole prospect and outlook of mankind grew immeasurably larger, and the multiplication of ideas also proceeded at an incredible rate. This vast expansion was unhappily not accompanied by any noticeable advance in the stature of man, either in his mental faculties, or his moral character. His brain got no better, but it buzzed the more.

1949, 31 MARCH.

Individuality

Is not mankind already escaping from the control of individuals? Are not our affairs increasingly being settled by mass processes? Are not modern conditions—at any rate throughout the English-speaking communities—hostile to the development of outstanding personalities and to their influence upon events; and lastly if this be true, will it be for our greater good and glory? These questions merit some examination from thoughtful people.

1931, MAY. ("MASS EFFECTS IN MODERN LIFE," *STRAND MAGAZINE*; **THOUGHTS, 183.)**

I have always taken the view that the fortunes of mankind in its tremendous journey are principally decided for good or ill—but mainly for good, for the path is upward—by its greatest men and its greatest episodes.

1941, 9 JANUARY.

Life

Such is life with its astonishing twists and turns. You never can tell what is going to happen next, nor can you tell what will be the consequences of any action you may take. The principle of the boomerang, a weapon which we owe to the genius of the Australian aboriginals, is, it would seem, increasingly operative in human affairs.

1946, 7 MAY.

...the life of man does not depend upon the external conditions to which he is subjected, provided, of course, that they are compatible with the maintenance of his existence.

1948, 18 NOVEMBER. UNIVERSITY OF LONDON. (EUROPE, 468; BALANCE, 388.)

This speech is one of the few from which Churchill repeated some sentences almost or entirely word for word in a subsequent speech: when he received an honorary doctorate from the University of Copenhagen, 10 October 1950.

Those whose minds are attracted or compelled to rigid and symmetrical systems of government should remember that logic, like science, must be the servant and not the master of man. Human beings and human societies are not structures that are built or machines that are forged. They are plants that grow and must be tended as such. Life is a test and this world a place of trial. Always the problems, or it may be the same problem, will be presented to every generation in different forms.

1949, 31 MARCH. MASSACHUSETTS INSTITUTE OF TECHNOLOGY, BOSTON. (BALANCE, 47.)

Memory

Providence has ordained that human beings should have short memories, and pain and anxiety are soon forgotten. But are we always to oscillate between panic and torpor?

1911, 25 MAY.

Mistakes

If we look back on our past life we shall see that one of its most usual experiences is that we have been helped by our mistakes...

1931, MARCH. ("A SECOND CHOICE," *STRAND MAGAZINE*; **THOUGHTS, 6.)**

Nature

Nature is merciful and does not try her children, man or beast, beyond their compass. It is only where the cruelty of man intervenes that hellish torments appear.

1932, 4 JANUARY. ("MY NEW YORK MISADVENTURE," *DAILY MAIL.*)**

Optimism

...it is the habit of architects and builders to be more sanguine when putting forward their plans than is subsequently found to be justified by the actual facts.

1943, 28 OCTOBER.

Pain

By a blessed dispensation, human beings forget physical pain much more quickly than they do their joyous emotions and experiences. A merciful Providence passes the sponge of oblivion across much that is suffered and enables us to cherish the great moments of life and honour which come to us in our march through life.

1949, 21 OCTOBER. FOURTH ALAMEIN REUNION, EMPRESS HALL, LONDON. (BALANCE, 119.)

Personal contacts

What an ineffectual method of conveying human thought correspondence is—even when it is telegraphed with all the rapidity and all the facilities of modern intercommunication! They are simply dead blank walls compared to personal contacts.

1944, 16 SEPTEMBER. CITADEL, QUEBEC.

One wonders what Churchill would think about email: a digital blank wall?

Poverty

Fancy living in one of those streets—never seeing anything beautiful—never eating anything savoury—*never saying anything clever!*

1906, 4 JANUARY, MANCHESTER. (MARSH, 150.)

WSC to his private secretary Eddie Marsh, as they walked through a poor section of Manchester, where he was standing for Parliament. His reflections influenced WSC's development as a reforming Liberal in the early 1900s.

Progress

Every day you may make progress. Every step may be fruitful. Yet there will stretch out before you an ever-lengthening, ever-ascending, ever-improving path. You know you will never get to the end of the journey. But this, so far from discouraging, only adds to the joy and glory of the climb.

1922, JANUARY. ("PAINTING AS A PASTIME," *STRAND MAGAZINE*; THOUGHTS, 229.)

Progress and reaction

Progress and reaction are no doubt relative terms. What one man calls progress another will call reaction. If you have been rapidly descending the road to ruin and you suddenly check yourself, stop, turn back and retrace your steps, that is reaction, and no doubt your former guide will have every reason to reproach you with inconsistency.

1906, 11 OCTOBER. ST. ANDREWS HALL, GLASGOW. (LIBERALISM, 206.)

Reason and the infinite

Close reasoning can conduct one to the precise conclusion that miracles are impossible: that "it is much more likely that human testimony should err, than that the laws of nature should be violated"; and at the same time one may rejoice to read how Christ turned the water into wine in Cana of Galilee or walked on the lake or rose from the dead. The human brain cannot comprehend infinity, but the discovery of mathematics enables it to be handled quite easily. The idea that nothing is true except what we comprehend is silly, and that ideas which our minds cannot reconcile are mutually destructive, sillier still...I therefore adopted quite early in life a system of believing whatever I wanted to believe, while at the same time leaving reason to pursue unfettered whatever paths she was capable of treading.

1930. (MEL, 131.)

For further remarks on this theme see Chapter 24, Education...Metaphysics. See also Spiritual conceptions below.

Sensationalism

I am inclined to think that in a free community every evil carries with it its own corrective, and so I believe that sensationalism of all kinds is playing itself out, and, overdoing, is itself undone.

1909, 23 MAY. FREE TRADE HALL, MANCHESTER. (LIBERALISM, 206.)

Spiritual conceptions

It is therefore above all things important that the moral philosophy and spiritual conceptions of men and nations should hold their own amid these formidable scientific evolutions. It would be much better to call a halt in material progress and discovery rather than to be mastered by our own apparatus and the forces which it directs.

1931, FEBRUARY. ("FIFTY YEARS HENCE," *STRAND MAGAZINE*; THOUGHTS, 203.)

Some argue that Western civilisation has abandoned its theocratic and moral precepts, without which there is no distinguishing right and wrong, truth and falsehood. Churchill foresaw this possibility many years ago.

Wisdom and Folly

...it would be a great reform in politics if wisdom could be made to spread as easily and as rapidly as folly.

1947, 10 SEPTEMBER. GUILDHALL, LONDON.
(EUROPE, 138–9.)

Youth

Elderly people and those in authority cannot always be relied upon to take enlightened and comprehending views of what they call the indiscretions of youth.

1930. (MEL, 72.)

All the days were good and each day better than the other. Ups and downs, risks and journeys, but always the sense of motion, and the illusion of hope. Come on now all you young men all over the world. You are needed more than ever now to fill the gap of a generation shorn by the War. You have not an hour to lose. You must take your places in life's fighting line. Twenty to twenty-five! These are the years! Don't be content with things as they are. "The earth is yours and the fulness thereof." Enter upon your inheritance, accept your responsibilities. Raise the glorious flags again, advance them upon the new enemies, who constantly gather upon the front of the human army, and have only

to be assaulted to be overthrown. Don't take No for an answer. Never submit to failure. Do not be fobbed off with mere personal success or acceptance. You will make all kinds of mistakes; but as long as you are generous and true, and also fierce, you cannot hurt the world or even seriously distress her. She was made to be wooed and won by youth. She has lived and thrived only by repeated subjugations.

1930. (MEL, 74.)

Churchill's classic challenge to Youth is still as relevant as ever. Psalms 24:1 (King James version) reads: "The earth is the Lord's, and the fulness thereof; the world, and they that dwell therein." The modification Churchill quoted ("The earth is yours...") was by John Ruskin (1819–1900) in "The Two Paths: Being Lectures on Art, and Its Application to Decoration and Manufacture", first delivered at the Kensington Museum, January 1858.

You young men here may be in the battle, in the fields or in the high air. Others will be the heirs to the victory your elders or your parents have gained, and it will be for you to ensure that what is achieved is not cast away either by violence of passion or by sheer stupidity. But let keen vision, courage, and humanity guide our steps, so that it can be said of us that not only did our country do its duty in the war, but afterwards in the years of peace it showed wisdom, poise, and sincerity, which contributed in no small degree to bind up the frightful wounds caused by the struggle.

1943, 5 NOVEMBER. HARROW SCHOOL.
(ONWARDS, 262.)

APPENDIX I

RED HERRINGS:
FALSE ATTRIBUTIONS

In 1686 the *Oxford English Dictionary* described "red herring", a metaphor to draw pursuers off a track, as "the trailing or dragging of a dead Cat or Fox (and in case of necessity a Red-Herring) three or four miles...and then laying the Dogs on the scent....To attempt to divert attention from the real question..."

Hence this appendix. "You could fill a book with what Winston Churchill *didn't* say," remarked his sometime colleague, "Rab" Butler. "It would be almost as long as one made up of genuine quotes."[145] Well, not quite; but false attributions are a real problem.

Churchill is persistently credited with numerous remarks he never uttered, put in his mouth to make them more interesting. In a few cases (e.g., "rum, buggery and the lash") he was actually asked about them, and denied authorship. In other cases he prefaced a remark by a qualifier like "as has been said..."

Listed below are over eighty common misquotes, some of which (as the notes indicate), sound very much like him. For example, "Dull, Duller, Dulles" is so well established that I was astonished not to find attribution.

Many remarks which Churchill *did* use originated with others (e.g., "Democracy is the worst system, except for all the other systems.") He deployed these favourites with delight, not always with attribution, nor even with quote marks, because he assumed his listeners would recognise them instantly as an old saying or the words of a famous writer. In his time people were simply better read than they are today. Regarding WSC's quoting from Clough's "Say Not the Struggle Nought Availeth", in his broadcast of 27 April 1941 (see Chapter 1), Bernard Darwin (grandson of Charles) wrote in the *Oxford Dictionary of Quotations*:

> Mr. Roosevelt quoted Longfellow to Mr. Churchill; Mr. Churchill passed on the quotation to us and subsequently quoted Clough on his own account. Thousands of listeners to that broadcast speech must have experienced the same series of emotions. When the Prime Minister said that there were some lines that he deemed appropriate we sat up rigid, waiting in mingled pleasure and apprehension. How agreeable it would be if we were acquainted with them and approved the choice! How flat and disappointing should they be unknown to us! A moment later we heard "For while the tired waves, vainly breaking" and sank back in a pleasant agony of relief. We whispered the lines affectionately to ourselves, following the speaker, or even kept a word or two ahead of him in order to show our familiarity with the text. We were if possible more sure than ever that Mr. Churchill was the man for our money. He

---

145 "Hague's baseball cap, Mandelson's mushy peas: True tales or just great political myths?" by Simon Hoggart, *Daily Mail*, London, 7 January 2007 (www.dailymail.co.uk).

had given his ultimate proofs by flattering our vanity. He had chosen what we knew and what, if we had thought of it, we could have quoted for ourselves.[146]

Ribald quotations are also often ascribed to Churchill, but are so far out of character as to be undeserving of notice here. One example will suffice: a curvaceous female admirer who met WSC at the unveiling of his sculpture says: "I got up at dawn and drove a hundred miles for the unveiling of your bust"; WSC supposedly replies, "Madam, I would happily reciprocate the honour." In reality, Churchill simply was not given to salacious remarks, and nearly always treated the opposite sex with Victorian courtesy.

These entries are sorted by key phrases, and secondarily by date. In cases of "old chestnuts" long attributed to WSC, I provide explanatory notes, feeling that devoted Churchillians may demand proof. "No attribution" means that the quote, variations and segments of it are not in the fifty million words by and about Churchill scanned for this book.

America and World War I

America should have minded her own business and stayed out of the World War. If you hadn't entered the war the Allies would have made peace with Germany in the Spring of 1917. Had we made peace then there would have been no collapse in Russia followed by Communism, no breakdown in Italy followed by Fascism, and Germany would not have signed the Versailles Treaty, which has enthroned Nazism in Germany. If America had stayed out of the war, all these "isms" wouldn't today be sweeping the continent of Europe and breaking down parliamentary government—and if England had made peace early in 1917, it would have saved over one million British, French, American, and other lives.

1936, August. (*New York Enquirer*; *New York Times*, 22 October 1942, 13.)

Posted on the Internet in 2002 (http://xrl.us/2s8z), this quotation caused a stir. In 1942 a $1 million lawsuit was brought against WSC (who had denounced the quotation as fiction) by publisher William Griffin of the New York Enquirer. *It was dismissed when WSC admitted to the interview but denied the statement. See Chapter 16...American entry.*

Amusing and serious

You cannot deal with the most serious things in the world unless you also understand the most amusing.

In subsequent entries, no editor's note means that no attribution to Churchill was found in all of Churchill's own published books, articles, speeches and correspondence, or from other reliable quotation sources.

Arboricide

You are guilty of arboricide!

Circa 1935.

Alleged remark to Clementine Churchill when she cut down a favourite tree. Although Churchill once accused his wife of "arboricidal mania"(5 September 1926, OB, CV5/1, 778) he did not originate this word (meaning "wanton destruction of trees"). The Oxford English Dictionary *tracks it to H. G. Graham's* Social Life of Scotland *(1899): "the crime of arboricide was distressingly frequent".*

Attlee, Clement

An empty car drew up and Clement Attlee got out.

Circa 1950.

No attribution.

A sheep in sheep's clothing!

Circa 1950.

Some sources say the wording was "A sheep in wolf's clothing." Allegedly said but unverified: "When asked, Churchill said this was based on a more pointed remark he'd once made about someone else," wrote The Quote Verifier

---

146 Darwin, Bernard, *Oxford Dictionary of Quotations* (Oxford: Oxford University Press, 1941), xiii. Darwin signed his Introduction "May 1941". See Chapter 1..."Westward look...".

editor Ralph Keyes to the editor. "British quote maven Nigel Rees thought the comment might have originated with newspaper columnist J. B. Morton in the 1930s." Morton (1893–1979) wrote a joke-filled column called "By the Way". Credit Churchill as publicist for the words of an unknown aphorist.

Balfour, Arthur

If you wanted nothing done, Arthur Balfour was the best man for the task. There was no one equal to him.

Supposedly WSC made this wry remark when Lloyd George said he heard that Arthur Balfour was "dominating the League of Nations". The quote has been ascribed to Lord Riddell's War Diary, but no such words appear there.

Beer bottles, hit them with

...we shall fight in the fields and in the streets, we shall fight in the hills...And we will hit them over the heads with beer bottles, which is about all we have got to work with....

1940, 4 JUNE. BBC. (TAYLOR, 223–4.)

The only published reference to this offhand remark (with Churchill allegedly covering the BBC microphone during his rebroadcast of the speech), was by Robert Lewis Taylor, who says it was heard by "one of England's highest clergymen, who was present at the studio...." Sir John Colville, who was present, did not hear it. Regrettably, for it is a wonderful line, it must be considered unsubstantiated.

Birth

Although present on that occasion I have no clear recollection of the events leading up to it.

(MANCHESTER I, 107.)

Remarkably, this famous and oft-quoted expression cannot be tracked. In the canon it is not among Churchill's own words, and it appears only in Manchester, whose notes do not lead the reader to its origin.

Botswana

What is Botswana worth?

1960.

Allegedly posed by Churchill in Parliament (£40,000 was the supposed answer). But he

said nothing in Parliament after retiring as Prime Minister in 1955, and Bechuanaland did not adopt the name Botswana until 1966.

Cigars and women

Smoking cigars is like falling in love; first you are attracted to its shape; you stay for its flavour; and you must always remember never, never let the flame go out.

Published without attribution in The American Spectator, July–August 2005.

Common language

Britain and America are two nations divided by a common language.

1940s.

Also credited to Bernard Shaw and Dylan Thomas, but without attribution. Ralph Keyes in The Quote Verifier *suggests it originated in Oscar Wilde's "The Canterville Ghost" (1887): "We have really everything in common with America nowadays, except, of course, language." Verdict: adapted Wilde.*

Courage

Courage is what it takes to stand up and speak; courage is also what it takes to sit down and listen.

No attribution.

Cross of Lorraine

The heaviest cross I have to bear is the Cross of Lorraine.

1943.

In reference to de Gaulle and the Free French, this remark was actually made by General Edward Louis Spears, WSC's military representative to the French in 1939–40.

Defenders of the peace

People sleep peaceably in their beds at night only because rough men stand ready to do violence on their behalf. [Alternative: We sleep safely at night because rough men stand ready to visit violence on those who would harm us.]

Though occasionally attributed to WSC, it is more often assigned to George Orwell. Wikiquotes reports:

There is no evidence that Orwell ever wrote or uttered either of these versions of this idea. They do bear some similarity to comments made in an essay that Orwell wrote on Rudyard Kipling.

Democracy

The best argument against Democracy is a five-minute conversation with the average voter.

Commonly quoted, but without attribution. Though he sometimes despaired of democracy's slowness to act for its own preservation, Churchill had a much more positive attitude towards the average voter. See Chapter 21, Political Theory and Practice...Democracy.

Many forms of Government have been tried, and will be tried in this world of sin and woe. No one pretends that democracy is perfect or all-wise. Indeed it has been said that democracy is the worst form of Government except for all those other forms that have been tried from time to time....

1947, 11 NOVEMBER. (EUROPE, 200.)

Although these are Churchill's words, he clearly did not originate the famous remark about Democracy. William F. Buckley, Jr., commenting on trickery in presidential debates, reminded us of Churchill's remark when he wrote: "We are made to ask what it is that political democracy gives us. The system is utilitarian. But is it a fit object of faith and hope?" (Buckley, "On the Right," June 2007). Credit Churchill as publicist for an unsourced aphorism.

Dignity

I know of no case where a man added to his dignity by standing on it.

(MANCHESTER II, 25.)

Rather than answer Labour attacks, Churchill's colleagues supposedly urged him to "stand on his dignity". Quoted in Manchester's The Last Lion, but unconfirmed in the canon.

Dinner, wine and women

Well, dinner would have been splendid if the wine had been as cold as the soup, the beef as

rare as the service, the brandy as old as the fish, and the maid as willing as the Duchess.

SALTER, 409.

Sometimes there are quotations which one almost knows intuitively to be manufactured. WSC would not have stayed for the second course of such a meal, and his remarks about women were, with rare exceptions, gallant.

Dog days

Every dog has his day

1944, 16 NOVEMBER. 10 DOWNING STREET.
(WW2 VI, 611.)

An old saying not originated by Churchill, used in his memo to chief of staff General Ismay regarding the shipping of World War I-era long-range heavy guns to bolster the invasion of Germany.

Drugs

Dear nurse, pray remember that man cannot live by M&B alone.

1943, CARTHAGE.

Not found in the canon, though it sounds like him. Churchill delighted in the sulfa drug M&B, and referred to his doctors, Lord Moran and Dr. Bedford, as "M&B". For genuine remarks about M&B, see Chapter 27...Drugs.

Dukes

...a fully equipped duke costs as much to keep as two dreadnoughts; and dukes are just as great a terror and they last longer.

1909, 9 OCTOBER, NEWCASTLE.

Sometimes attributed to Churchill, this amusing line was actually uttered by his ally in the campaign to reform the House of Lords, David Lloyd George. Dreadnought was the name given to the new class of fast, powerful battleships developed by the Royal Navy. Credit Lloyd George.

Dulles, John Foster

Dull, Duller, Dulles.

CIRCA 1953. (MANCHESTER I, 34.)

Quoted without attribution by Manchester, this remark is not in the scanned canon. However, Dulles bodyguard Louis Jefferson attributed it to Anthony Eden: see http://xrl.us/bchtc. For Churchill on Dulles, see Chapter 20, People...Dulles.

Enemies

You have enemies? Good. That means you've stood up for something, sometime in your life.

No attribution.

Fanatic

A fanatic is someone who won't change his mind, and won't change the subject.

Often attributed to Churchill or President Truman.

It's a quotation I see often, but without a source. I doubt that it's Truman, or, if he ever said it, that the quotation originated with him – Ralph Keyes, editor, The Quote Verifier.

Feet first

Not feet-first, please!

1962.

Supposedly said to the stretcher-bearer after breaking his leg at Monte Carlo, but no attribution can be tracked.

First thoughts

Distrust first thoughts—they are usually honest.

1948, 15 JULY. (EUROPE, 382.)

Churchill uttered these words, but put quotation marks around them, and preceded them by saying, "As the cynic has said..."

France

The destiny of a great nation has never yet been settled by the temporary condition of its technical apparatus.

1944, 2 AUGUST. (DAWN, 160.)

Not WSC, though quoted by him in the Commons: Churchill himself attributed it to Leon Trotsky.

Free lunch

There ain't no free lunch.

*WSC is alleged to have said only these five words at a university commencement ceremony, and then resumed his seat. Ralph Keyes (*The Quote Verifier*) tracks the phrase to various people from Milton Friedman to Merryle Rukeyser: it can also be found in Rudyard Kipling's* American Notes *(1891), who said it was the custom of San Francisco bars to provide food to customers who ordered at least one drink.*

Free speech

Free speech carries with it the evil of all foolish, unpleasant and venomous things that are said; but on the whole we would rather lump them than do away with it.

1952, 15 JULY.

Quoted by the reliable Colin Coote, and many others since, but not traceable in the canon; moreover, I could find no Churchill speech on this date. For a genuine quote along the same lines see Chapter 21, Political Theory and Practice...Free speech.

Gandhi

[Gandhi] ought to be laid, bound hand and foot, at the gates of Delhi and then trampled on by an enormous elephant with the new Viceroy seated on its back.

1920, 4 NOVEMBER. (COOPER, DUFF, 103.)

An example of how hearsay becomes a quotation. This first recollection is in Duff Cooper's memoirs. Sure enough, it appears as a direct quotation in the highly unreliable The Private Lives of Winston Churchill, *and was repeated by Sarvepalli Gopal in "Churchill and India" (Blake & Louis, 459). For genuine quotations see Chapter 20, People...Gandhi.*

Genius

True genius resides in the capacity for evaluation of uncertain, hazardous, and conflicting information.

No attribution.

German resistance

...in Germany there lived an opposition which was weakened by their losses and an enervating international policy, but which belongs to the noblest and greatest that the political history of any nation has ever produced. These men fought without help from within or from abroad—driven forward only by the restlessness of their conscience. As long as they lived they were invisible and unrecognisable to us, because they had to camouflage themselves. But their death made the resistance visible.

1946. (LAMB, 292, 363.)

The only appearance in English of this quotation, also quoted by Rudolf Pechel (Deutscher Wilderstrand, 1947). In a footnote, Richard Lamb says there is doubt that Churchill said these words, but that he did hold the sentiments, quoting WSC to Walter Hammer of Hamburg, 19 November 1946:

> *...I have had a search made through my speeches...but so far no record can be found of any such pronouncement by me. But I might quite well have used the words you quote as they represent my feelings on this aspect of German affairs.*

Golf

A curious sport whose object is to put a very small ball in a very small hole with implements ill-designed for the purpose.

CIRCA 1915. (MANCHESTER I, 213.)

Manchester carries this quotation, but the footnote is not illuminating. It does not, contrary to the footnote, appear in the Official Biography's Companion Volumes, nor in a work by General Sir Hubert Gough. Verdict: Likely to have been uttered by almost any golfer at one time or another.

Grace of God

There but for the grace of God, goes God.

CIRCA 1940.

Supposedly said of Stafford Cripps. For actual remarks see Chapter 20, People...Cripps.

Harlot's prerogative

Power without responsibility...the prerogative of the harlot through the ages.

Not Churchill but Rudyard Kipling. Subsequently used by Baldwin in 1931 without reference to Kipling (his cousin).

Health

Half the world's work is done by people who don't feel well.

Another recent entry on the internet, lacking any attribution to WSC.

Hell

If you're going through hell, keep going.

No attribution.

Horses

The outside of a horse is good for the inside of a man.

Repeatedly attributed to everyone from Woodrow Wilson's physician to Ronald Reagan.

> *Clergyman Henry Ward Beecher (1813–87) is one person to whom the thought was attributed in his time. Oliver Wendell Holmes is another...Verdict: Long-time male equestrian wisdom. – Ralph Keyes, The Quote Verifier, 91.*

What Churchill did say about horses is an amusing substitute. (See Chapter 32, Tastes and Favourites...Horses.)

Impromptu remarks

I am just preparing my impromptu remarks.

Ingratitude towards great men

Ingratitude towards their great men is the mark of strong peoples.

1949. (WW2 I, 10.)

Although often ascribed to Churchill, WSC himself credited Plutarch with this remark. He was commenting on the discarding of the French war leader Georges Clemenceau after the victory of World War I. See Chapter 20, People...Clemenceau.

Italians

[German Ambassador von Ribbentrop: "Don't forget, Mr. Churchill, if there is a war, we will have the Italians on our side this time."]
My dear Ambassador, it's only fair. We had them last time.

1937.

An alleged aside during WSC's famous meeting with the "Londonderry Herr" (see Chapter 20, People...Ribbentrop). A very droll line, but no attribution exists.

Jaw, jaw and war, war

Jaw, jaw is better than war, war.

1954, WASHINGTON. (*FINEST HOUR* 122, 15.)

Sir Martin Gilbert, speaking of this remark, noted that Churchill actually said, "Meeting jaw to jaw is better than war." Four years later, during a visit to Australia, Harold Macmillan said the words usually – and wrongly – attributed to Churchill: "Jaw, jaw is better than war, war." Credit: Harold Macmillan.

Kiss a girl, climb a wall

The most difficult things for a man to do are to climb a wall leaning towards you, and to kiss a girl leaning away from you.

Sometimes quoted with an addition: "...and to make an after-dinner speech." Commonly ascribed, but nowhere in the canon. Recently claimed by religion columnist Marion deVelder, but probably a much older expression.

Liberal and conservative

If a man is not liberal in youth he has no heart. If he is not conservative when older he has no brain.

All over the internet, but not in the canon. A variation is: "When I was a young liberal I thought with my heart; when I grew wiser and conservative I thought with my brain."

Liberty

They who can give up essential liberty to obtain a little temporary safety deserve neither liberty nor safety.

CIRCA 1940.

Often attributed to Churchill, this remark originated at least as early as 1776 with Benjamin Franklin, though it may date back a decade earlier, to 1755. If Churchill used it, he was quoting Franklin.

Lies

There are a terrible lot of lies going about the world, and the worst of it is that half of them are true.

1906, 22 FEBRUARY.

Churchill did use these words, but quickly explained that they were the remark of a "witty Irishman".

A lie will gallop halfway round the world before the truth has time to pull its breeches on.

1940S. (HULL I, 220.)

Although commonly ascribed to Churchill (who would have said trousers, not breeches), this was actually written by Franklin Roosevelt's Secretary of State, Cordell Hull.

Living and life

You make a living by what you get; you make a life by what you give.

Reiterated in many sources including a 2005 TV ad by Lockheed Martin. An old saw put in Churchill's mouth.

Living dog, dead lion

A living dog is better than a dead lion.

(HESP II, 95.)

Used by Churchill, but he was quoting John Dudley, First Duke of Northumberland, before being executed by Mary Tudor (Mary I) upon her ascent to the throne in 1553.

Looking ahead

It is always wise to look ahead—but difficult to look further than you can see.

(CAWTHORNE, 28.)

Reported by the usually reliable Graham Cawthorne, but not in Hansard; possibly an aside to a colleague, however.

Looking backward

The further backward you look, the further forward you can see. [Or: The farther backward you can look, the farther forward...etc.]

1944.

Commonly ascribed to WSC, even by The Queen (Christmas Message, 1999). What Churchill actually said was "The longer you can look back, the farther you can look forward." See Chapter 2, Maxims.

MacDonald, Ramsay

After the usual compliments, the Prime Minister [MacDonald] said [to Lloyd George]: "We have never been colleagues, we have never been friends—at least, not what you would call holiday friends—but we have both been Prime Minister, and dog doesn't eat dog. Just look at this monstrous Bill the trade unions and our wild fellows have foisted on me. Do me a service, and I will never forget it. Take it upstairs and cut its dirty throat."

1931, 28 JANUARY. (HALLE, IRREPRESSIBLE, 114.)

According to Kay Halle, this was "an imaginary conversation dreamed by WSC between Ramsay MacDonald and David Lloyd George, directed at MacDonald because of the debate on the Trades Disputes Act". Halle's quotation begins with "We have never been colleagues" and substitutes "the monstrous Bill" for "this monstrous Bill". No attribution has been discovered.

Marx Brothers

You are my fifth favourite actor. The first four are the Marx Brothers.

Reported in at least one Churchill quotations book, but no sign of this comment appears in the literature. WSC enjoyed the Marx Brothers; for what he did say about them, see Chapter 32, Tastes and Favourites...Marx Brothers.

Montgomery, Field Marshal Bernard

In defeat, indomitable; in victory, insufferable. [Or:] Indomitable in retreat, invincible in advance, insufferable in victory.

Widely bruited about, but not in the canon. Likely adapted from "Indomitable in victory, insufferable in defeat", by American football coach Woody Hayes. For a number of genuine remarks see Chapter 20, People...Montgomery.

The Field Marshal lived up to the finest tradition of Englishmen. He sold his life dearly.

1958.

WSC allegedly said this when advised that Monty's memoirs were earning more than his History of the English Speaking Peoples. It seems unlike Churchill. "Sold his life dearly" comes up only once in the canon, when Alanbrooke opined that Churchill would have done so if ever backed up against a wall by invading Germans.

Naval tradition

Don't talk to me about naval tradition. It's nothing but rum, buggery [sometimes "sodomy"] and the lash.

CIRCA 1914–15, ADMIRALTY.

In dinner conversation ca. 1955, private secretary Anthony Montague Browne confronted WSC with this quotation. "I never said it. I wish I had," responded Churchill. (AMB to the editor.) "Compare 'Rum, bum, and bacca' and 'Ashore it's wine women and song, aboard it's rum, bum and concertina', naval catchphrases dating from the nineteenth century" – Oxford Dictionary of Quotations.

Never give in

Never give in [or: Never give up].

1941, 29 OCTOBER, HARROW SCHOOL. (UNRELENTING, 286.)

Often represented as a three-word speech which Churchill allegedly made, and then sat down. This is incorrect. The complete quotation is in Chapter 2, Maxims...Perseverance.

Never quit

Never, never, never quit! [Also sometimes quoted as "Never, never, never give up!"]

Misquotations of "Never give in – never, never, never, never, except to convictions of honour and good sense."

Nuisenza

It is a nuisenza to have the fluenza.

1943, 25 OCTOBER. (WW2 V, 279.)

Represented in places as a Churchillism, this was actually Roosevelt writing to Churchill.

Oats and sage

The young sow wild oats, the old grow sage.

Constantly ascribed to Churchill, it is not among his published words. Henry James Byron (1835–84) in "An Adage" wrote:

> The gardener's rule applies to youth and age;
> When young "sow wild oats", but when old, grow sage.

Opportunity

To each there comes in their lifetime a special moment when they are figuratively tapped on the shoulder and offered the chance to do a very special thing, unique to them and fitted to their talents. What a tragedy if that moment finds them unprepared or unqualified for that which could have been their finest hour.

Commonly attributed, but neither the quotation nor parts of it can be found. That it is manufactured is suggested by its use of "finest hour", from WSC's famous speech of 18 June 1940, which he would have been unlikely to repeat in so offhand a context. Verdict: Apocryphal Churchill.

People will put you out

[Lord Shawcross: "We are the masters at the moment, and not only at the moment, but for a very long time to come."]

Oh no you're not. The people put you there and the people will put you out again.

1946. (*FINEST HOUR* 121, WINTER 2003–05, 13.)

The late Lord Shawcross is often misquoted as having said, "We are the masters now." He always maintained that he spoke as quoted above. However, Churchill's supposed retort is not established and is likely apocryphal.

Pessimist and optimist

A pessimist sees the difficulty in every opportunity; an optimist sees the opportunity in every difficulty.

Poison in your coffee

[Nancy Astor: "If I were married to you, I'd put poison in your coffee."]

If I were married to you, I'd drink it.

CIRCA 1912, BLENHEIM PALACE.
(BALSAN, 162; SYKES, 127.)

Official biographer Martin Gilbert (In Search of Churchill, 232) suggested the author was F. E. Smith, Lord Birkenhead, "a much heavier drinker than Churchill, and a notorious acerbic wit". But Fred Shapiro (Yale Book of Quotations) says the riposte dates back even farther, to a joke line in the Chicago Tribune *of 3 January 1900: "'If I had a husband like you,' she said with concentrated scorn, 'I'd give him poison!' 'Mad'm,' he rejoined, looking her over with a feeble sort of smile, 'If I had a wife like you I'd take it.'" Verdict: F. E. Smith, giving new life to an old wisecrack.*

Prepositions

This is the kind of tedious nonsense up with which I will not put.

[Sometimes rendered as "pedantic nonsense" or "tedious nuisance."]

1944, 27 FEBRUARY. (BENJAMIN ZIMMER, HTTP://XRL.US/IZBQ.)

Originally attributed to WSC in cable reports in The New York Times *and* Chicago Tribune, *28 February 1944. "The Times...made one change that seems to undercut Churchill's humour completely: they 'fixed' the quote so that there are no fronted prepositions," writes Fred Shapiro (Yale Book of Quotations). "The Wall Street Journal, 30 September 1942, quotes an undated article in* Strand Magazine. *When a memorandum passed round a certain Government department, one young pedant scribbled a postscript drawing attention to the fact that the sentence ended with a preposition, which caused the original writer to circulate another memorandum complaining that the anonymous postscript was 'offensive impertinence, up with which I will not put'."*

Prisoners of war

A prisoner of war is a man who tries to kill you and fails, and then asks you not to kill him.

No attribution.

Risk, care and dream

Risk more than others think is safe. Care more than others think is wise. Dream more than others think is practical. Expect more than others think is possible.

Another piece of prose ascribed to Churchill to make it more interesting. Quoteworld.org ascribes this remark to Claude Thomas Bissell (1916–2000), Canadian author and educator.

Sex

It gives me great pleasure.

In a supposed after-dinner activity of The Other Club, a member drawn at random would chalk a word on a blackboard, and a second member, also chosen by lot, had to make an impromptu speech about it. Churchill drew the response when a member chalked "sex" on the blackboard. If actually delivered, this would be Churchill's shortest speech. But no attribution is found.

Shy a stone

You will never get to the end of the journey if you stop to shy a stone at every dog that barks.

1923, 3 DECEMBER. SHEPHERD'S BUSH EMPIRE, LONDON. (CS IV, 3426.)

WSC was quoting someone else. He preceded this by stating, "As someone said…" A similar statement urging courage "when the dog growls" is in Chapter 29, Leadership…Courage.

Simple tastes

I am a man of simple tastes—I am quite easily satisfied with the best of everything.

1930s, PASSIM.

According to Sir John Colville, WSC's close friend F. E. Smith, Lord Birkenhead, originated the remark, "Mr Churchill is easily satisfied with the best" (without "man of simple tastes" or "of everything"). Churchill with his great memory could quite easily have repeated and embroidered on Birkenhead's remark when he visited the Plaza Hotel in New York, shortly after Birkenhead's death, in 1931, as is sometimes recorded. Credit: F. E. Smith.

Sitting down

Never stand too long when there is an opportunity to sit down—and never sit down when there is an opportunity to lie down.

No attribution.

Speeches, long vs. short

I am going to make a long speech today; I haven't had time to prepare a short one.

If he said this (there is no evidence), WSC borrowed the idea from Blaise Pascal who, in 1656, wrote to a friend: "I have only made this letter rather long because I have not had time to make it shorter." ("Je n'ai fait celle-ci plus longue que parceque je n'ai pas eu le loisir de la faire plus courte.")

Stalin and Russia

In the course of three decades, however, the face of the Soviet Union has become transformed. The core of Stalin's historic achievements consists in this, that he had found Russia working with wooden ploughs and is leaving her equipped with atomic piles. He has raised Russia to the level of the second industrial Power of the world. This was not a matter of mere material progress and organisation. No such achievement would have been possible without a vast cultural revolution, in the course of which a whole nation was sent to school to undergo a most intensive education.

1953. (DOITCHER, ISAAK, *ESSAYS IN CONTEMPORARY COMMUNISM*, 1953.)

Supposedly a tribute by WSC after Stalin's death or later, this has no relation to any known statement by Churchill. For his actual appraisal of the Soviet leader in 1942, see Chapter 20, People…Stalin.

Strategy

However beautiful the strategy, you should occasionally look at the results.

No attribution.

Success

Success is not final, failure is not fatal: it is the courage to continue that counts.

No attribution.

Success is going from failure to failure without losing your enthusiasm.

Broadly attributed to Churchill, but found nowhere in his canon. An almost equal number of sources credit this saying to Abraham Lincoln; but none of them provides any attribution.

Taking office

"Take office only when it suits you, but put the government in a minority whenever you decently can."

1906. (LRC, 188.)

WSC put this maxim in quotations because he did not claim it, but ascribed it to his father.

Trees and the sky

The trees do not grow up to the sky.

1938, 25 SEPTEMBER. ("THE EFFECT OF MODERN AMUSEMENTS ON LIFE AND CHARACTER," NEWS OF THE WORLD.)

Described by WSC as an "old German saying", following his expressed concerns about dramatic falls in future birth rates. Also deployed with slightly different wording over bombing London. See Chapter 22...Insurance, blitz. Churchill used this phrase on thirteen later occasions

Troubles

Most of the things I have worried about never ended up happening.

Inaccurate version of a phrase Churchill himself quoted. (See Chapter 31, Personal

*Matters...troubles.) Fred Shapiro (*Yale Book of Quotations), *believes the originator was Mark Twain or Thomas Jefferson. Twain:*

> *I am an old man and have known a great many troubles, but most of them never happened.*

*(*Reader's Digest, *April 1934; a similar remark, attributed to an anonymous octogenerian, appeared in* The Washington Post, *11 September 1910.) Jefferson:*

> *How much pain have cost us the evils which have never happened! (to John Adams, 8 April 1816).*

Urinal humour

[Attlee: "A bit stand-offish today, are we, Winston?"]

Every time you socialists see something big, you want to nationalise it.

CIRCA 1948.

Alleged remark when WSC, seeing Attlee approach the trough in the House of Commons toilet, ostentatiously shuffled a few feet away. Recorded by Manchester and others, but not attributed. Verdict: Apocryphal Churchill.

Virtues and vices

He has all the virtues I dislike and none of the vices I admire. [Or: he was possessed of all the virtues I despise and none of the sins I admire.]

(ADLER, 29.)

Often and prominently quoted, with respect to Stafford Cripps and Edwin Scrymgeour; no evidence of this or variations on it in the canon.

While England Slept

1938. (LOCKHART – CONFIRMED BY LADY CHURCHILL – 201.)

The American edition of Arms and the Covenant, *whose title inspired young John Kennedy's subsequent* Why England Slept, *was not Churchill's. WSC's cable, suggesting* The Locust Years *to publisher Putnam, was garbled to read* The Lotus Years. *Baffled, Putnam's staff looked up "lotus", which was described as a plant inducing dreaminess. Then one director said, "I've got it: While England Slept." WSC was delighted.*

White meat

[After asking for a chicken breast at a Virginia buffet, Churchill was informed by his genteel Southern hostess that Southern ladies preferred the term "white meat." The next day he sent her a corsage, with a card:]

I would be much obliged if you would pin this to your white meat.

CIRCA 1946.

No attribution.

Winston is back!

I therefore sent word to the Admiralty that I would take charge forthwith and arrive at 6 o'clock. On this the Board were kind enough to signal the fleet, "Winston is back".

1948. (WW2 I, 320.)

Although quoted by Churchill, and repeated by Lord Mountbatten in his famous speech at Edmonton in 1966, Sir Martin Gilbert and others have never found any record of such a signal being sent when Churchill returned to the Admiralty.

Words

We are the masters of the unsaid words, but slaves of those we let slip out.

No attribution.

It has been said words are the only things which last forever.

1909, 10 JUNE. PRESS CONFERENCE, FOREIGN

OFFICE, LONDON. (CS II, 1262.)

Used by Churchill several times in his writings and speeches, but as this first appearance indicates, he said it did not originate with him.

Yale and MIT

An after-dinner speaker was giving the audience at least 15 minutes for each of the four letters that spell "Yale"… "Y is for Youth…A is for Achievement…L is for Loyalty…E is for enterprise," etc. Halfway through "enterprise" a voice was heard: "Thank God he didn't go to the Massachusetts Institute of Technology."

Occasionally attributed to Churchill but no instance has been found, though members of his family use the joke frequently (not attributing it to him).

Ypres, Belgium

I should like us to acquire the ruins of Ypres….a more sacred place for the British race does not exist in the world.

1918.

Widely attributed but no reliable source can be found, although these were certainly Churchill's sentiments, according to his private secretary Eddie Marsh's diary of 29 October 1918:

> *…there is nothing left but here and there a shapeless mass of bricks.…Winston wants to turn that group of buildings into a cemetery, with lawns and flowers among the ruins, and the names of innumerable dead (Hassall, 455).*

APPENDIX II

TIMELINE

R eaders may find it useful to refer to this appendix for background knowledge of the time at which Churchill's remarks were uttered. All unnamed references ("enters, leaves, elected", etc.) are to Winston Spencer Churchill.

1873
15 August: Jennie Jerome meets Lord Randolph Churchill at Cowes.

1874
15 April: Marriage of Jennie and Randolph, British Embassy, Paris.
30 November: Winston Leonard Spencer Churchill born prematurely at Blenheim Palace.

1880
4 February: John Strange Spencer Churchill born in Ireland.
April: His family sets up house at 29 St. James's Place, London.

1882
November: Enters St. George's School, Ascot.

1884
Summer: Leaves St. George's and is taught by the Misses Thomson in Brighton.

1886
March: Suffers a bad attach of pneumonia.

1888
15 March: Takes entrance examination at Harrow.
17 April: Enters Harrow.

1892
December: Leaves Harrow.

1893
January: Falls from bridge at Bournemouth and is briefly near death.
September: Enters Royal Military College, Sandhurst, as a cavalry cadet.

1895
January: Passes out of Sandhurst twentieth in class of 130.
24 January: Lord Randolph Churchill dies in London.
20 February: Gazetted to the Fourth Queen's Own Hussars.
3 July: Mrs. Everest dies in London.
9 November: First visit to United States, meets Bourke Cockran.
30 November: Observes fighting at Arroyo Blanco during visit to Cuba.

1896
3 October: Arrives at Bangalore, India. Begins self-education by reading.

1897
September: Joins the Malakand Field Force on the North-West Frontier.
October: Begins writing *Savrola* and an account of the Malakand operations.

1898
March: Publishes first book, *The Story of the Malakand Field Force.*
2 September: Charge of the Twenty-First Lancers at Omdurman, Sudan.
December: Returns to India.

1899
April: Resigns from army; returns to London to pursue a political career.
6 July: Defeated in his first attempt at Parliament, running as a Conservative, at the Oldham by-election.
14 October: Sails to South Africa as war correspondent of *The Morning Post.*
November: Publishes *The River War: An*

Historical Account of the Reconquest of the Soudan.

15 November: Captured by the Boers in an ambush of an armoured train near Chively, South Africa.

13 December: Escapes from prison in Pretoria.

1900

1 February: Publishes *Savrola* in New York (the London edition follows on 12 February).

16 May: Publishes *London to Ladysmith via Pretoria.*

5 June: Enters Pretoria with victorious British troops.

July: Returns to England.

1 October: Elected Conservative Member of Parliament for Oldham.

12 October: Publishes *Ian Hamilton's March.*

1 December: Embarks on lecture tour of North America.

10 December: Meets Governor Theodore Roosevelt, the Vice President-elect, in Albany.

11 December: First lecture, Philadelphia.

1901

31 January: Final lecture, Carnegie Hall, New York.

2 February: Embarks for England.

14 February: Takes seat in the House of Commons.

28 February: Maiden Speech, House of Commons.

April: Attacks his Government's Army Estimates.

1903

Circa 20 April: Publishes *Mr. Brodrick's Army,* a collection of speeches against the Army Estimates

1904

31 May: Breaks with the Conservatives, taking his seat with the opposition Liberals.

1905

13 December: Becomes Under-Secretary of State for the Colonies in a Liberal Government formed by Sir Henry Campbell-Bannerman.

1906

2 January: Publishes *Lord Randolph Churchill.*

January: Liberal Party triumphs in the general election.

March: Publishes *For Free Trade.*

1907

October: Begins an official tour of East Africa, returning January, 1908.

1908

12 April: Becomes President of the Board of Trade.

9 May: Elected Member of Parliament for Dundee.

12 September: Marries Clementine Hozier.

December: Publishes *My African Journey.*

1909

11 July: Birth of first child, Diana ("Cream-gold Kitten").

12 September: Meets Kaiser Wilhelm II at German Army manoeuvres.

26 November: Publishes *Liberalism and the Social Problem.*

December (or January 1910): Publishes *The People's Rights.*

1910

14 February: Becomes Secretary of State for the Home Department.

8 November: Halts dispatch of troops to quell the Welsh coal mine strike; two miners are killed at Tonypandy.

1911

3 January: Battle of Sidney Street; WSC observes the police attack on London anarchists.

28 May: Birth of only son, Randolph ("Chumbolly").

July: German gunboat *Panther* anchors off Agadir, provoking possible war with France.

13 August: Writes a Cabinet paper, "Military Aspects of the Continental Problem", accurately predicting the opening phase of the Great War.

25 October: Becomes First Lord of the Admiralty.

1914

17 June: Secures Persian oil supply for Royal Navy.

28 June: Assassination of Archduke Franz Ferdinand at Sarajevo.

1 August: Orders mobilization of the fleet.

4 August: Great Britain declares war on Germany.

3–6 October: Organizes the defence of Antwerp.

7 October: Birth of second daughter, Sarah ("Mule").

29 October: Brings in Lord Fisher as First Sea Lord, replacing Prince Louis of Battenberg.

1 November: British Pacific squadron defeated in the Battle of Coronel, off Chile.

8 December: Royal Navy victorious in the Battle of the Falkland Islands.

1915

3 January: Proposes naval and military attack on the Dardanelles, supported by Fisher and Kitchener.

18 March: Combined Franco-British naval attack on the Dardanelles withdraws after losses to mines.

15 May: Lord Fisher resigns in protest over Dardanelles action. WSC resigns as First Lord of the Admiralty.

27 May: Becomes Chancellor of the Duchy of Lancaster.

11 November: Resigns from Cabinet.

19 November: Attached Second Battalion, Grenadier Guards in France; after training, commands 6th Battalion, The Royal Scots Fusiliers.

1916

7 May: Returns to London and the House of Commons (having remained MP for Dundee while in the field).

1917

8 February: Purchases Lullenden, first country home, East Grinstead, Sussex.

18 July: Becomes Minister of Munitions in Lloyd George's coalition Government.

1918

11 November: Armistice signed ending World War I.

15 November: Birth of third daughter, Marigold ("Duckadilly").

1919

9 January: Becomes Secretary of State for War and Secretary of State for Air.

28 June: Peace Treaty signed at Versailles.

30 September: Sells Lullenden to General Sir Ian Hamilton.

1921

14 February: Becomes Secretary of State for the Colonies.

March: Convenes Cairo Conference to settle the borders of the Middle East; appoints T. E. Lawrence chief adviser on Middle Eastern affairs.

1 April: Hands over Air Ministry.

26 June: Lady Randolph Churchill dies in London.

23 August: Marigold Churchill dies of septicaemia of the throat in Broadstairs, Kent.

6 December: Helps negotiate the Irish Treaty, signed in London by David Lloyd George, Michael Collins and Arthur Griffiths.

1922

15 September: Birth of fourth daughter, Mary.

19 October: Leaves Colonial Office as Lloyd George resigns following the withdrawal of Conservatives from his coalition.

14 November: Defeated at Dundee in the general election; out of Parliament for the first time in twenty-two years (except for a brief spell between defeat at Manchester North-West and election in Dundee in 1908).

November: Buys Chartwell Manor near Westerham, Kent.

1923

6 April: Publishes *The World Crisis*, volume I in New York. The British edition follows on the 10th; volume II follows in October. (In all, five volumes in six parts will be published between 1923 and 1931.)

6 December: Defeated, running as a Liberal Free-Trader, in the West Leicester by-election.

1924

19 March. Defeated, running as an independent, in the Abbey Division of Westminster by-election.

29 October: Elected as a "Constitutionalist" for

Epping in the general election; he would hold this seat, and the derivative seat for Woodford after World War II, to 1964.

7 November: Becomes Chancellor of the Exchequer in Stanley Baldwin's Conservative Government.

1925

28 April: First budget proposes return to the gold standard.

October: Officially rejoins Conservative Party.

1926

3 May: General Strike begins.

13 May: General Strike ends, WSC having edited *The British Gazette* from 5 to 13 May.

1927

January: Visits Mussolini in Rome.

1 March: Publishes *The World Crisis 1916–1918* in two parts.

1928

March: Disputes rating reform with Neville Chamberlain.

July: Successfully proposes extension of the Ten Year Rule (military budget assumes no major war within ten years).

12 August: Neville Chamberlain writes: "There is too deep a difference between our natures for me to feel at home with him or to regard him with affection. He is a brilliant wayward child who compels admiration but who wears out his guardians with the constant strain he puts on them."

10 October: Joins Amalgamated Union of Building Trade Workers as a bricklayer.

1929

7 March: Publishes *The Aftermath*, vol. IV of *The World Crisis*.

4 June: Resigns as Chancellor of the Exchequer following Labour victory in the general election.

3 August: Embarks for North American tour with son Randolph, brother Jack and nephew Johnnie; travels across Canada to Victoria.

7 September: Arrives in the USA and, two days later, tours the Napa Valley wine country.

September: Hosted by William Randolph Hearst at San Simeon. Lands 188-pound marlin off Catalina Island on the Hearst yacht.

20 September: Meets Charlie Chaplin in Hollywood, departing for Yosemite the next day.

29 October: Witnesses Black Tuesday, the New York Stock Market Crash.

6 November: Returns to England.

1930

18 October: Tells Prince Otto von Bismarck that "Hitler and his followers [will] seize the first opportunity to resort to armed force."

20 October: Publishes *My Early Life*.

1931

27 May: Publishes *India*.

10 November: Publishes *The Eastern Front*, fifth and final volume of *The World Crisis*.

December: Embarks for New York on a lecture tour, arriving on the 11th.

13 December: Knocked down and almost killed by car on Fifth Avenue.

31 December: Departs for Nassau to recuperate.

1932

28 January: Resumes lecture tour in Brooklyn, New York.

February–March: Lectures in Hartford, Springfield, St. Louis, Cleveland, Toledo, Detroit, Chicago, New York, Atlanta.

11 March: Embarks for England.

13 May: First speech warning of German rearmament.

10 November: Publishes *Thoughts and Adventures*.

1933

14 March: First speech in the House warning of the need to rebuild Britain's air defences.

6 October: Publishes *Marlborough, His Life and Times*, volume I; four volumes would be published in the years to 1938.

8 October: Tells James Roosevelt: "I wish to be Prime Minister and in close and daily communication by telephone with the President of the United States."

1934

7 February: Argues in Parliament for maintenance of fleet strength and creation of "shadow factories" quickly convertible to war production.
2 August: Following Hindenburg's death Hitler proclaims himself leader and chancellor of Germany.

1935

July: Joins Committee of Imperial Defence.
October: Mussolini invades Abyssinia.

1936

20 January: Death of King George V.
7 March: Hitler reoccupies the Rhineland.
7 December: Shouted down and ruled out of order in the Commons pleading on behalf of Edward VIII; a temporary eclipse in his political comeback.
10 December: Abdication of King Edward VIII.

1937

May: Warns German Ambassador von Ribbentrop, "do not underrate England".
12 May: Coronation of King George VI.
4 October: Publishes *Great Contemporaries.*

1938

20 February: Eden resigns as Foreign Secretary.
2 April: Hitler proclaims *Anschluss*: the union of Germany and Austria.
20 May: With German troops massed on her border, Czechoslovakia mobilises.
30 September: Munich agreement cedes Sudetenland portions of Czechoslovakia to Germany.
9 November: *Reichkristallnacht* pogrom in Germany.

1939

15 March: German troops enter Prague, Hitler proclaims the protectorate of Bohemia and Moravia and the end of Czechoslovakia.
22 March: Lithuania cedes Memel to Germany.
31 March: Britain guarantees Poland's independence.
7 April: Mussolini invades Albania.
15–25 August: Visits Rhine front.

24 August: German–Soviet Non-Aggression Pact signed.
1 September: Hitler invades Poland.
3 September: Becomes First Lord of the Admiralty as Britain and France declare war on Germany.
17 December: *Graf Spee* scuttled off Montevideo.

1940

9 April: Germany invades Denmark and Norway.
10 May: Becomes Prime Minister and Minister of Defence and forms coalition Government. Germany invades France, Luxembourg, Holland and Belgium.
13 May: First speech as Prime Minister: "Blood, toil, tears and sweat".
15 May: Unsuccessfully asks Roosevelt for the loan of fifty destroyers. Guderian's panzers break through at Sedan, France. Holland surrenders.
24 May: Germans reach Calais.
26 May–4 June: Dunkirk evacuation.
28 May: Convinces Cabinet to fight on. Belgium surrenders.
16 June: On fourth visit to France as Prime Minister, offers Anglo-French Union, which is declined.
21 June: Latvia, Estonia and Lithuania are occupied by the Soviet Union.
22 June: France signs armistice.
4 July: Orders bombardment of French fleet at Oran.
10 August: Battle of Britain begins.
17 September: Hitler postpones "Operation Sea Lion".

1941

7 March: Sends British troops to Greece, which is nevertheless overwhelmed by German forces.
10 May: House of Commons bombed in the last major raid of London Blitz.
22 June: Assures aid to Russia after invasion of USSR by Germany.
10 August: Meets with Roosevelt at Argentia Bay, Newfoundland.
12 August: Signs Atlantic Charter communiqué.
7 December: Japan attacks Pearl Harbor, Malaya, Hong Kong and the Dutch East Indies.

10 December: HMS *Prince of Wales* and *Repulse* sunk off Malaya.

22 December: Arrives in Washington.

26 December: First speech to joint session of Congress.

1942

27 January: Wins vote of confidence, 464 to 1.

15 February: Singapore surrenders to the Japanese.

17 June: Flies to Washington to discuss invasion of North Africa.

2 July: Defeats a vote of no confidence, 475 to 25.

2 August: Flies to Cairo to change Middle East command.

12 August: Flies to Moscow; first meeting with Stalin.

1943

14–22 January: Confers with Roosevelt and Anglo-American military commanders at Casablanca.

30 January: Flies to Adana for meeting with Turkish President Inönü.

2 February: Germans surrender at Stalingrad.

5 May: Leaves London for Washington.

30 May: Confers with Eisenhower and other commanders in North Africa.

10 July: Allied invasion of Sicily begins.

14 August: First Quebec Conference begins.

4 September: Allied invasion of South Italy.

22–26 November: Confers with Roosevelt at Cairo.

28 November–1 December: Confers with Roosevelt and Stalin at Teheran.

10 December: Flies to Tunis, contracts pneumonia.

1944

22 January: Anglo-Americans land at Anzio.

5 June: Rome falls to Allied troops.

6 June: D-Day, the Allied invasion of France.

12 June: Visits Normandy beachheads.

13–14 June: First V-1 flying bomb lands on England.

20 June: Visits US sector, Cherbourg.

21–22 July: Visits Montgomery's HQ in near Caen.

11 August: Flies to Naples for talks with Tito; visits Italian front.

24 August: Liberation of Paris.

9 September: First V-2 rocket lands on London.

12 September: Second Quebec Conference begins.

9 October: With Stalin in Moscow, makes "percentages" agreement about spheres of influence in Eastern Europe.

11 November: Celebrates Armistice Day in Paris.

5 December: Orders British troops to Greece.

25 December: Flies to Athens.

1945

4–12 February: Confers with Roosevelt and Stalin at Yalta.

16–17 February: Cairo and Fayoum meetings with King Saud and other Middle East leaders.

25 March: Crosses Rhine two days after Allied Armies.

12 April: President Roosevelt dies in Warm Springs, Georgia.

28 April: Mussolini executed by Italian partisans.

30 April: Hitler commits suicide in Berlin.

8 May: V-E Day. Germany surrenders.

23 May: Forms Conservative caretaker Government following break-up of the wartime coalition.

4 June: Delivers "Gestapo" speech warning of perils of a Labour victory.

16 July: First explosion of atomic bomb, Alamogordo, New Mexico.

17 July: Confers with Truman and Stalin at Potsdam.

26 July: Resigns as Prime Minister following the general election; becomes Leader of the Opposition.

6 August: Atom bomb dropped on Hiroshima.

9 August: Atom bomb dropped on Nagasaki.

14 August: V-J Day. Japan surrenders.

1946

8 January: Awarded the Order of Merit.

5 March: Delivers "Iron Curtain" speech at Fulton, Missouri.

1948

21 June: Publishes *The Gathering Storm*, volume I of *The Second World War*, in Boston; the London edition followed on 4 October. Five more volumes would follow in the years to 1954.

19 August: Publishes *The Sinews of Peace*, the first of five volumes of post-war speeches published in the years to 1961 (see Bibliography).
December: Publishes *Painting as a Pastime*, his 1921–22 essay, for the first time in volume form.

1951

26 October: Becomes Prime Minister and Minister of Defence, following Conservative victory in the general election.

1952

6 February: King George VI dies in London.
1 March: Hands over as Minister of Defence to Field Marshal Alexander.
3 September: Publishes *The War Speeches*, three volumes collecting speeches from six volumes of World War II speeches published from 1941 until 1946 (see Bibliography).

1953

2 June: Attends Coronation of Queen Elizabeth II.
4–8 December: Confers in Bermuda with Eisenhower and Laniel.
10 December: Awarded Nobel Prize for Literature.

1954

14 June: Becomes Knight of the Garter and, therefore, "Sir Winston Churchill".
30 November: Attends celebrations of his eightieth birthday at Westminster Hall.

1955

5 April: Resigns as Prime Minister.

1956

23 April: Publishes the first volume of *A History of the English Speaking Peoples*: *The Birth of Britain*.
29 October: Suez Crisis; British and French troops land in Egypt; lacking support from the United States, a cease-fire is announced on 6 November.
26 November: Publishes *The New World*, vol. 2 of *HESP*.

1957

17 October: Publishes *The Age of Revolution*, vol. 3 of *HESP*.

1958

17 March: Publishes *The Great Democracies*, fourth and final volume of *HESP*.
12 September: Celebrates golden wedding anniversary.

1959

5 February: Publishes an abridged one-volume edition of *The Second World War* with an Epilogue on 1945–57, his last original writing.

1961

27 April: Publishes *The Unwritten Alliance*, his last volume of speeches.

1962

28 June: Falls and breaks a hip in Monte Carlo, flies home to hospital. ("I want to die in England.")

1963

9 April 9: Declared an honorary citizen of the United States by President Kennedy.
19 October: Diana Churchill dies in London.

1964

28 July: Presented with unprecedented Vote of Thanks by House of Commons upon his retirement from Parliament.
30 November: Celebrates ninetieth birthday, London.

1965

24 January: Dies in his London home at Hyde Park Gate.
30 January: Buried in St. Martin's churchyard in Bladon, Oxfordshire.

BLOOD, TOIL, TEARS
AND SWEAT: EVOLUTION
OF A PHRASE

Though he gave them permanent life, Churchill's five best-remembered words did not originate with him, and similar expressions date very far back. Ralph Keyes, editor-author of *The Quote Verifier*, writes:

> Cicero and Livy wrote of "sweat and blood". A 1611 John Donne poem included the lines "That 'tis in vaine to dew, or mollifie / It with thy Teares, or Sweat, or Bloud." More than two centuries later, Byron wrote, "Year after year they voted cent per cent / Blood, sweat, and tear-wrung millions – why? – for rent!" In his 1888 play *Smith*, Scottish poet-playwright John Davidson wrote of "Blood-sweats and tears, and haggard, homeless lives". By 1939, a Lady Tegart reported in a magazine article that Jewish communal colonies in Palestine were "built on a foundation of blood, sweat, and tears"....Since this phrase was obviously familiar when Churchill gave his memorable speech the following year, even though he rearranged the words and added "toil" for good measure, our ears and our memory quickly returned them to the more familiar form.[147]

Blood, Tears and (occasionally) Toil

But Churchill's use of the term started long before World War II, in his Boer War days. In 1899, he had a conversation with Mr. Grobelaar, the Boer Under-Secretary for Foreign Affairs, during his imprisonment in Pretoria the year before, following his capture in the armoured train skirmish:

> "Self. 'My opinion [that Britain will win] is unaltered, except that the necessity for settling the matter has become more apparent. As for the result, that, as I think Mr. Grobelaar knows, is only a question of time and money expressed in terms of blood and tears.'"[148]

A year later Churchill used the phrase again, in an article entitled, "Officers and Gentlemen":

> As we have frequent little local manoeuvres, so there must be greater ones, all carefully supervised, at longer intervals. And the knowledge gained at every manoeuvre must be used remorselessly to control the progress of mediocre men up the military

---

147 Keyes, 15–16.
148 Ladysmith, 166; Boer, 74.

ladder; to cast the bad ones down and help the good ones towards the top. It will all seem very sad and brutal in times of peace, but there will be less blood and tears when the next war comes.[149]

The phrase must have stuck in Churchill's photographic memory, because thirty years later, in his final volume of *The World Crisis*, he regarded with a shudder the demise of the Hohenzollern, Hapsburg and Romanov empires – a precursor, though he could not know it then, of the second world conflagration to come:

In the Parliaments of the Hapsburgs bands of excited deputies sat and howled at each other by the hour in rival languages, accompanying their choruses with the ceaseless slamming of desks which eventually by a sudden crescendo swelled into a cannonade. All gave rein to hatred; and all have paid for its indulgence with blood and tears.[150]

"Toil", a favourite word of Churchill's, was in the mix as early as 1932. Leaving New York after a lecture tour, he was asked by a radio interviewer whether "a war between two or more powers is about to take fire". He responded with one of his few strikingly bad predictions:

I do not believe that we shall see another great war in our time. War, today is bare – bare of profit and stripped of all its glamour. The old pomp and circumstance are gone. War now is nothing now but toil, blood, death, squalor and lying propaganda.[151]

"Blood and tears" (with "toil and sweat" temporarily deleted) next appeared in a 1939 article speculating on the likelihood of war:

Although the sufferings of the assaulted nations will be great in proportion as they have neglected their preparations, there is no reason to suppose that they will not emerge living and controlling from the conflict. With blood and tears they will bear forward faithfully and gloriously the ark which enshrines the title deeds of the good commonwealth of mankind.[152]

"Toil, Waste, Sorrow and Torment"

An allied expression came in an article written during late stages of the Spanish Civil War and reprinted in his 1939 collection of articles, *Step by Step 1936–1939*:

Surely this is the supreme question which should engage the thoughts of mankind. Compared with it all other human interests are petty and other topics trivial. Nearly all the countries and most of the people in every country desire above all things to prevent war. And no wonder, since except for a few handfuls of ferocious romanticists, or sordid would-be profiteers, war spells nothing but toil, waste, sorrow and torment to the vast mass of ordinary folk in every land. Why should this horror,

---

149 *The Saturday Evening Post*, 29 December 1900, reprinted in Essays I, 53.
150 Crisis V, 21.
151 Gilbert, Wilderness, 45. From a radio interview in Boston on 10 March 1932. It is unlikely that he would have made the same prediction a few months later: by May 1932 the Nazi Party had become the largest single party in Germany.
152 "Will there be War in Europe – and When?," *News of the World*, 4 June 1939, also published slightly abridged as "War, Now or Never," *Colliers*, 3 June 1939 and reprinted in full in Essays I, 443.

which they dread and loathe, be forced upon them? How is it that they have not got the sense and the manhood to stop it?[153]

"Blood, Sweat and Tears"

Churchill added "sweat" in 1931, in the last volume of his World War I memoirs, as he described the devastating battles between the Russians and the Central Powers. His pages, he said, "record the toils, perils, sufferings and passions of millions of men. Their sweat, their tears, their blood bedewed the endless plain."[154]

Another piece on war in Spain carried the expanded phrase eight years later:

> But at length regular armies come into the field. Discipline and organisation grip in earnest both sides. They march, manoeuvre, advance, retreat, with all the valour common to the leading races of mankind. But here are new structures of national life erected upon blood, sweat and tears, which are not dissimilar and therefore capable of being united. What milestone of advantage can be gained by going farther? Now is the time to stop.[155]

"Blood, Toil, Tears and Sweat"... "Blood, Tears, Toil and Sweat"

Finally, and when it counted most, on 13 May 1940, all four famous words came together in Churchill's inspiring first speech as Prime Minister: "I have nothing to offer but blood, toil, tears and sweat." Clearly he had considered and arranged the words for maximum impact, and his post-war recording of the speech comes down very hard on the "sweat".[156] The response to those words was electric and gratifying, though Churchill was sorrowful in expressing his thanks to the people: "One would think one had brought some great benefit to them, instead of the blood and tears, the toil and sweat, which is all I have ever promised."[157]

An indefatigable reviser, like most good writers, Churchill created an addendum to his famous phrase a year after he first used it, at a particularly grim time in the war. Rommel was rebounding in North Africa, Nazi submarines were taking a deadly toll on the Atlantic, the Blitz continued, and Britain was still alone. WSC recognised the perils, but ended on a high note:

> I ask you to witness, Mr. Speaker, that I have never promised anything or offered anything but blood, tears, toil and sweat, to which I will now add our fair share of mistakes, shortcomings and disappointments....When I look back on the perils which have been overcome, upon the great mountain waves through which the gallant ship has driven, when I remember all that has gone wrong, and remember also all that has gone right, I feel sure we have no need to fear the tempest. Let it roar, and let it rage. We shall come through.[158]

A more hopeful evaluation of the cost of the war to date was offered just before Pearl Harbor:

---

153 "How to Stop War," *Evening Standard*, 12 June 1936; Step, 25.
154 Crisis V, 17.
155 "Can Franco Restore Unity and Strength to Spain?," *Daily Telegraph*, 23 February 1939; "Hope in Spain," Step, 319.
156 *Winston S. Churchill: His Memoirs and His Speeches 1918–1945*, New York: Decca Records (12 LPs), 1965.
157 House of Commons, 8 October 1940.
158 House of Commons, 7 May 1941.

I promised eighteen months ago "blood, tears, toil and sweat". There has not yet been, thank God, so much blood as was expected. There have not been so many tears. But here we have another instalment of toil and sweat, of inconvenience and self-denial, which I am sure will be accepted with cheerful and proud alacrity by all parties and all classes in the British nation.[159]

Votes of Confidence

Although Russia and America had joined Britain in the battle by the end of 1941, the situation was bleaker than ever when Churchill called for a Vote of Confidence in January 1942 – which he handily won, 464 to one. Winding up for the Government, he reminded the House that nothing had changed: "I stand by my original programme, blood, toil, tears and sweat, which is all I have ever offered, to which I added, five months later, 'many shortcomings, mistakes and disappointments'."[160]

A more contentious Vote of No Confidence was faced down in July. After Tobruk had fallen to Rommel, dissident MPs tabled a motion: "That this House, while paying tribute to the heroism and endurance of the Armed Forces of the Crown in circumstances of exceptional difficulty, has no confidence in the central direction of the war." Churchill defeated that one, too, 475 to 25, falling back on his old prescription and giving it a new twist: "I have not made any arrogant, confident, boasting predictions at all. On the contrary, I have struck hard to my 'blood, toil, tears and sweat', to which I have added muddle and mismanagement, and that, to some extent, I must admit, is what you have got out of it."[161]

Finally in the autumn of 1942, the victory at Alamein turned the tide of the war for Britain. It marked, wrote Churchill, "the turning of 'the Hinge of Fate'. It may almost be said, 'Before Alamein we never had a victory. After Alamein we never had a defeat.'"[162] Doubtless he felt it right to reiterate the original phraseology:

I have never promised anything but blood, tears, toil and sweat. Now, however, we have a new experience. We have victory – a remarkable and definite victory. The bright gleam has caught the helmets of our soldiers, and warmed and cheered all our hearts.[163]

Despite all of Churchill's many iterations and elaborations on it, the best-remembered version remained "Blood, Sweat and Tears". In 1941, when publishing Churchill's first volume of war speeches, both Putnam in New York and McClelland & Stewart in Toronto chose *Blood, Sweat and Tears* instead of the English title *Into Battle*. And when modern politicians voice his words, they usually leave out "toil", too.

---

159 House of Commons, 2 December 1941.
160 House of Commons, 27 January 1942.
161 House of Commons, 2 July 1942.
162 WW2 IV, 541.
163 Lord Mayor's Day luncheon, Mansion House, London, 9 November 1942. End, 265–6.

APPENDIX IV

THE BIBLICAL CHURCHILL

"In my Father's house are many mansions: if it were not so, I would have told you. I go to prepare a place for you."[164]

"Arm yourselves, and be valiant men, and see that ye be in readiness against the morning...For it is better for us to die in battle, than to behold the calamities of our people and our sanctuary. Nevertheless, as the will of God is in heaven, so let him do."[165]

"More than to any other book or group of books, Churchill alludes to the King James Bible," wrote Darrell Holley in *Churchill's Literary Allusions*. "It is for him the primary source of interesting illustrations, descriptive images, and stirring phrases. His knowledge of the Bible manifests itself in direct quotations, in paraphrased retellings of Biblical stories, and in his frequent, perhaps even unconscious, use of Biblical terms and phrases.

"The Tower of Babel, Belshazzar's feast...the millstone around the neck, the 'great gulf fixed' between Paradise and Hell [from Luke 16:26 – Ed.], the last great Battle of Armageddon – these occur often in Churchill's writing."[166]

All this may come as a surprise to casual observers, since it is well known that Churchill was not a religious man. Having read the leading anti-religious tracts of the late nineteenth century, weighing them against the Anglican teachings of his boyhood, he held a pragmatic attitude towards spiritual questions: "I therefore adopted quite early in life a system of believing what I wanted to believe, while at the same time leaving reason to pursue unfettered whatever paths she was capable of treading."[167]

What moved Churchill was the beauty of the King James's English, badly mutilated by "new revised" Bibles ostensibly designed to make them more "relevant". He had an ear for

---

164 St. John 14:2, Holy Bible, King James edition. The same verse in Basic English, which WSC championed as a lingua franca, is: "In my Father's house are rooms enough; if it was not so, would I have said that I am going to make ready a place for you?"

165 I Maccabees 3:58–60, King James Bible. Apocrypha: "1. a group of books not found in Jewish or Protestant versions of the Old Testament included in the Septuagint and in Roman Catholic editions of the Bible. 2. various religious writings of uncertain origin regarded by some as inspired, but rejected by most authorities." – *Random House Webster's College Dictionary* (New York: Random House, 1992).

166 Holley, 7.

167 MEL, 131.

the memorable phrase, and he never hesitated to deploy Biblical allusions both famous and obscure. One of each is sufficient to demonstrate his expertise.

1. "A House of Many Mansions"

The New Testament Gospel according to St. John, Chapter 14, contains an inspiring passage that the young Winston must have read and re-read as a boy:

1. *Let not your heart be troubled: ye believe in God, believe also in me.*
2. *In my Father's house are many mansions; if* it were *not so, I would have told you. I go to prepare a place for you.*
3. *And if I go and prepare a place for you, I will come again, and receive you unto myself; that where I am,* there *ye may be also.*
4. *And whither I go ye know, and the way ye know.*

Churchill particularly liked verse 2, "a house of many mansions", and used it during five important moments in his career. An excellent early instance was in Dundee, Scotland, in May 1908, which he won and would hold for fourteen years. Here he spoke of the broadness and diversity of the British Commonwealth and Empire:

Cologne Cathedral took 600 years to build. Generations of architects and builders lived and died while the work was in progress. Still the work went on. Sometimes a generation built wrongly, and the next generation had to unbuild, and the next generation had to build again. Still the work went on through all the centuries, till at last there stood forth to the world a mighty monument of beauty and of truth to command the admiration and inspire the reverence of mankind. So let it be with the British Commonwealth. Let us build wisely, let us build surely, let us build faithfully, let us build, not for the moment but for future years, seeking to establish here below what we hope to find above – a house of many mansions, where there shall be room for all.[168]

The thought remained with him three years later, when as Home Secretary he said in London:

The British Empire must be a house of many mansions, in which there shall be room for each and all to develop to the fullest his personal or national contribution to the common united welfare and to the strength of the indivisible whole.[169]

The words from St. John lodged comfortably in his commodious memory for almost thirty years before Churchill found need of them again, to assure the peoples under the Nazi boot that liberation was sure:

The day will come when the joybells will ring again throughout Europe, and when victorious nations, masters not only of their foes, but of themselves, will plan and build in justice, in tradition, and in freedom, a house of many mansions where there will be room for all.[170]

---

168 Kinnaird Hall, Dundee, 4 May 1908. Liberalism 202; CS I, 1035.
169 Trocadero Restaurant, London, 11 March 1911. CS II, 1720.
170 Broadcast, London, 20 January 1940. Blood, 254.

He certainly thought this a serviceable line, because he invoked it to President Roosevelt in 1943, quoting only the chapter and verse – for he knew FDR kept a Bible handy. The President had cabled that Cairo, their proposed meeting place before the Teheran Conference with Stalin, was vulnerable to German air attack, and had wondered if they should choose another rendezvous. Churchill replied in nine words: "See St. John, chapter 14, verses 1 to 4."[171]

The text of the verses (see the beginning of this appendix) was typed on the message by his Map Room staff. "On reading this through more carefully after it had gone," Churchill wrote, "I was a little concerned lest, apart from a shadow of unintended profanity, it should be thought I was taking too much upon myself and thus giving offence. However, the President brushed all objections aside and our plans were continued, unchanged."[172]

Again at Fulton in 1946, in perhaps his most crucial speech of the post-war years, Churchill argued for a continuation of the Anglo-American "special relationship". There was nothing in the United Nations Charter, he said, that precluded any special relationships between countries:

> The British have an alliance with Portugal unbroken since 1384, and which produced fruitful results at critical moments in the late war. None of these clash with the general interest of a world agreement, or a world organisation; on the contrary they help it. "In my father's house are many mansions." Special associations between members of the United Nations which have no aggressive point against any other country, which harbour no design incompatible with the Charter of the United Nations, far from being harmful, are beneficial and, as I believe, indispensable.[173]

2. "As the Will of God is in Heaven"

On 19 May 1940, Churchill made his first broadcast as Prime Minister, a speech which lifted the hearts even of his former and current critics. "A tremendous battle is raging in France and Flanders," he said, adding forthrightly that the Germans, "by a remarkable combination of air bombing and heavily armoured tanks, have broken through the French defences". In assuring his listeners that Britain would fight on, Churchill chose a majestic coda, an obscure Biblical allusion for the first and only time in all his writings and speeches. It proved to be exactly right for the occasion:

> Today is Trinity Sunday. Centuries ago words were written to be a call and a spur to the faithful servants of Truth and Justice: "Arm yourselves, and be ye men of valour, and be in readiness for the conflict; for it is better for us to perish in battle than to look upon the Outrage of our nation and our altar. As the Will of God is in Heaven, even so let it be."[174]

Even some Biblical scholars were uncertain about the origins of this phrase, and with good reason. It is from I Maccabees 3:58–60, a text not found in every Bible. Further, Churchill altered the quotation. Evidently the writer in him could not resist an editorial improvement. The original words were:

---

171 WSC to Roosevelt, 21 November 1943. Lowenheim, 394.
172 WW2 V, 289.
173 Westminster College, Fulton, Missouri, 5 March 1946. Sinews, 99.
174 Blood, 334.

58. And Judas said, Arm yourselves, and be valiant men, and see that ye be in readiness against the morning, that ye may fight with these nations, that are assembled together against us to destroy us and our sanctuary:

59. For it is better for us to die in battle, than to behold the calamities of our people and our sanctuary.

60. Nevertheless, as the will of God is in heaven, so let him do.

There are two Books of the Maccabees, also spelled "Machabbes", neither of which is in the Hebrew Bible but both of which appear in some manuscripts of the Septuagint and in the Vulgate, since they are canonical to Roman Catholicism and Eastern Orthodoxy. They are also included in the Protestant Apocrypha, which is doubtless where WSC read them.

Churchill's first broadcast as Prime Minister caught the imagination of millions. Sir Martin Gilbert has collected some of those reactions that very evening, Trinity Sunday, 19 May, in Volume VI of the Official Biography. Anthony Eden wrote: "You have never done anything as good or as great. Thank you, and thank God for you." Lord Halifax, who nine days later would urge approaching the Germans for armistice terms, was momentarily bowled over: "It was worth a lot," he wrote from the Foreign Office, "and we owe you much for that, as for a great deal else, in these dark days." The *Evening Standard* declared the broadcast a speech of "imperishable resolve".[175]

Perhaps the most unexpected, a note that must have encouraged Churchill, came from his old chief Stanley Baldwin, who had done more than any other British leader to put the country in so perilous a state of readiness, but who on 19 June was moved more perhaps than at any other time:

My dear PM,

I listened to your well known voice last night and I should have liked to have shaken your hand for a brief moment and to tell you that from the bottom of my heart I wish you all that is good – health and strength of mind and body – for the intolerable burden that now lies on you.

Yours always sincerely,
SB[176]

---

175 OB VI, 365.
176 Ibid.

APPENDIX V

THE CHURCHILL CENTRE

www.winstonchurchill.org

Headquartered in London and Chicago, the Churchill Centre was founded in 1968 "to inspire leadership, statesmanship, vision, and boldness among democratic and freedom loving peoples through the thoughts, words, works and deeds of Winston Spencer Churchill". In 2008 the Centre merged with the American Friends of the Churchill Museum at the Cabinet War Rooms in London, expanding its programmes to benefit and sustain the Museum, as well as its own programmes of education and publishing. Membership numbers over 4,000, including the affiliated organisations in Great Britain, Canada and Australia.

The Churchill Centre publishes a quarterly magazine, *Finest Hour*; a quarterly newsletter, the *Chartwell Bulletin*; and special publications and monographs, and supports commercial publishing of an educational nature. It sponsors international and national conferences and Churchill tours, which have visited Britain, Australia, France, South Africa, Morocco, and Germany. Its expansive website includes "classroom" components to educate young people on Sir Winston's life and times.

The Churchill Centre has helped bring about republication of over thirty of Winston Churchill's long-out-of-print volumes. In 1992, it launched a campaign for completion of the remaining document volumes to the Official Biography, three of which have now been published. This project is now being completed by the Hillsdale College Press.

More recently, the Centre sponsored academic symposia in America and Britain; seminars where students and scholars discuss Churchill's books; scholarships for Churchill Studies; and important reference works. In 2005 it received a grant to distribute 5,000 Churchill biographies to high school teachers in North America who use Churchill in their curricula, and began a series of seminars for teachers conducted by college professors. Thanks to grants from the United States National Endowment for the Humanities, it conducts two-week summer institutes for teachers at the secondary school level.

The overall aim of the Centre is to impress Churchill's leadership, wisdom and experience firmly on future generations. Membership is available worldwide. For further information please visit the Cabinet War Rooms and Churchill Museum in London, or contact:

The Churchill Centre
200 West Madison Street
Suite 1700
Chicago IL 60606 USA
Toll free in USA telephone: (888) WSC-1874
UK dial (00-1-888) WSC-1874.

email: info@winstonchurchill.org

BIBLIOGRAPHY

Any quotation not annotated as to source is from the Parliamentary Debates (Hansard) as transcribed in *Winston S. Churchill: His Complete Speeches 1897–1963*, edited by Sir Robert Rhodes James (8 vols., New York: Bowker, 1974). All other quotations are identified by source. Works by Churchill himself are conveyed by key words, e.g. "Liberalism" for *Liberalism and the Social Problem*. Works by other authors are identified by the author's name and, if more than one work by an author is cited, part of the title, e.g. "Gilbert, Life, 89".

Books by Winston S. Churchill

Alliance. *The Unwritten Alliance: Speeches 1953-1959.* London: Cassell, 1961.

Balance. *In the Balance: Speeches 1949 & 1950.* London: Cassell, 1951.

Blood. *Blood, Sweat and Tears.* Toronto: McClelland & Stewart, 1941. Published in London as *Into Battle*, 1941.

Boer. *The Boer War.* London: Leo Cooper, 1989. Combining *London to Ladysmith via Pretoria* and *Ian Hamilton's March.*

Correspondent. *Winston S. Churchill War Correspondent 1895–1900.* London: Brassey's, 1992. Extended edition of *Young Winston's Wars*, first published 1972.

Covenant. *Arms and the Covenant.* London: George G. Harrap & Co., 1938.

Crisis (I–V). *The World Crisis.* 5 vols. in 6 parts. London: Thornton Butterworth, 1923–31.

CS (I–VIII). *Winston S. Churchill: His Complete Speeches, 1897–1963.* 8 vols. New York: Chelsea House/Bowker, 1974.

Dawn. *The Dawn of Liberation.* London: Cassell, 1945.

Dream. *The Dream.* Text is from the official biography (OB), vol. VIII. First published in *Daily Telegraph*, 1966. First published in volume form by the Churchill Literary Foundation (International Churchill Society), 1987.

End. *The End of the Beginning.* Boston: Little, Brown & Co., 1943.

Essay (I–IV). *The Collected Essays of Sir Winston Churchill.* 4 vols. London: Library of Imperial History, 1975.

Europe. *Europe Unite: Speeches 1947 & 1948.* London: Cassell, 1950.

FFT. *For Free Trade.* Sacramento: The Churchilliana Co., 1977. Facsimile edition. First published 1906.

GC. *Great Contemporaries.* Revised and extended edition. London: Leo Cooper, 1990. First published 1937.

Hamilton's. *Ian Hamilton's March.* London: Longmans Green, 1900.

HESP (I–IV). *A History of the English Speaking Peoples.* 4 vols. New York: Dodd, Mead & Co., 1956–58.

India. *India.* Hopkinton, N.H.: Dragonwyck Publishing Inc., 1990. First published 1931.

Ladysmith. *London to Ladysmith via Pretoria.* London: Longmans Green, 1900.

Liberalism. *Liberalism and the Social Problem.* Reprinted in *The Collected Works of Sir Winston Churchill.* Vol. VII, *Early Speeches.* London: Library of Imperial History, 1974. First published 1909.

LRC. *Lord Randolph Churchill.* 1 vol. Edition. London: Macmillan, 1907. First published in 2 vols., 1906.

MAJ. *My African Journey.* London: Leo Cooper, 1989. First published 1908.

Malakand. *The Story of the Malakand Field Force 1897.* London: Leo Cooper, 1991. First published 1898.

Malakand 1899 ed. *The Story of the Malakand Field Force 1897.* Silver Library edition. London: Longmans Green, 1899.

Marlborough (I–IV). *Marlborough: His Life and Times.* 4 vols. London: Sphere Books, 1967. First published 1933–38.

MBA. *Mr. Brodrick's Army.* Sacramento: The Churchilliana Co., 1977. Reset edition. First published 1903.

MEL. *My Early Life: A Roving Commission.* London: Thornton Butterworth, 1930.

Onwards. *Onwards to Victory.* London: Cassell, 1944.

People's. *The People's Rights.* London: Jonathan Cape, 1970. First published 1910.

River (I–II). *The River War: An Historical Account of the Reconquest of the Soudan.* 2 vols. London: Longmans Green, 1899.

River abr. ed. *The River War*, abridged one-volume edition. London: Eyre & Spottiswoode, 1933.

Savrola. *Savrola: A Tale of the Revolution in Laurania.* London: Leo Cooper, 1990.

Savrola 1956 ed. *Savrola.* New York: Random House, 1956.

Secret. *Secret Session Speeches.* London: Cassell, 1946.

Sinews. *The Sinews of Peace: Post-War Speeches.* London: Cassell, 1948.

Stemming. *Stemming the Tide: Speeches 1951 & 1952.* London: Cassell, 1953.

Step. *Step by Step 1936–1939.* London: Odhams, 1947. First published 1939.

Thoughts. *Thoughts and Adventures.* London: Leo Cooper, 1990. First published 1932.

Unrelenting. *The Unrelenting Struggle.* Boston: Little, Brown & Co., 1942.

Victory. *Victory.* London: Cassell, 1946.

WW2 (I–VI). *The Second World War.* 6 vols. London: Cassell, 1948–54.

WW2 abr. ed. *The Second World War.* Abridged 1 vol. edition with an Epilogue on 1945–57. London: Cassell, 1959.

The Official Biography

Winston S. Churchill, by Randolph S. Churchill (vols. I–II) and Sir Martin Gilbert (vols. III–VIII), together with the accompanying Companion (Document) Volumes was published between 1967 and 1982 by Heinemann, London, and Houghton Mifflin, Boston. Three additional Companion Volumes (*The Churchill War Papers*) were published between 1993 and 2000 by Heinemann and W. W. Norton (New York). In 2006, the complete work began to be reprinted, and seven additional Companion Volumes added by Gilbert, by the Hillsdale College Press, Hillsdale, Michigan. Page references are to the Heinemann editions.

Biographic Volumes

OB I. *Youth 1874–1900.* Published 1966.

OB II. *Young Statesman 1901–1911.* Published 1967.

OB III. *The Challenge of War 1914–1916.* Published 1971.

OB IV. *The Stricken World 1917–1922.* Published 1975.

OB V. *The Prophet of Truth 1922–1939.* Published 1976.

OB VI. *Finest Hour 1939–1941.* Published 1983.

OB VII. *Road to Victory 1941–1945.* Published 1986.

OB VIII. *"Never Despair" 1945–1965.* Published 1988.

Companion (Document) Volumes

OB, CV1/1: *Companion Volume I, Part 1 1874–1896.* Published 1967.

OB, CV1/2: *Companion Volume I, Part 2 1896–1900.* Published 1967.

OB, CV2/1: *Companion Volume II, Part 1 1901–1907.* Published 1969.

OB, CV2/2: *Companion Volume II, Part 2 1907–1911.* Published 1969.

OB, CV2/3: *Companion Volume II, Part 3 1911–1914.* Published 1969.

OB, CV3/1: *Companion Volume III, Part 1: Documents, July 1914–April 1915.* Published 1972.

OB, CV3/2: *Companion Volume III, Part 2: Documents, May 1915–December 1916.* Published 1972.

OB, CV4/1: *Companion Volume IV, Part 1: Documents, January 1917–June 1919.* Published 1977.

OB, CV4/2: *Companion Volume IV, Part 2: Documents, July 1919–March 1921.* Published 1977.

OB, CV4/3: *Companion Volume IV, Part 3: Documents, April 1921–November 1922.* Published 1977.

OB, CV5/1: *Companion Volume V, Part 1: Documents, The Exchequer Years 1922–1929.* Published 1979.

OB, CV5/2: *Companion Volume V, Part 2: Documents, The Wilderness Years 1929–1935.* Published 1981.

OB, CV5/3: *Companion Volume V, Part 3: Documents: The Coming of War 1936–1939.* Published 1982.

OB, CV6/1: *The Churchill War Papers, Volume I: At the Admiralty, September 1939–May 1940.* Published 1993.

OB, CV6/2: *The Churchill War Papers, Volume II: Never Surrender, May 1940–December 1940.* Published 1994.

OB, CV6/3: *The Churchill War Papers, Volume III: The Ever-Widening War, 1941.* Published 2000.

Works by Other Authors

No secondary sources are referenced where primary sources can be found; however, some of these works are referenced in the editor's notes. For authors with multiple titles, works are stated in chronological order of publication.

Acheson, Dean, *Present at the Creation.* New York: W. W. Norton & Co., 1969.

Addison, Paul, *Churchill on the Home Front 1900–1955.* London: Jonathan Cape, 1992.

___, ___, *Churchill: The Unexpected Hero.* Oxford: Oxford University Press, 2005.

Adler, Bill, ed., *The Churchill Wit.* New York: Coward-McCann, 1965.

Amery, Leopold, *Diaries,* 2 vols. London: Hutchinson, 1980.

Ashley, Maurice, *Churchill as Historian.* London: Secker & Warburg, 1968.

Balsan, Consuelo, *The Glitter and the Gold.* London: Heinemann, 1953.

Beaverbrook, Max, *Politicians and the War 1914–1916.* London: Thornton Butterworth, 1928.

___, ___, *The Decline and Fall of Lloyd George.* London: Collins, 1963.

Ben-Moshe, Tuvla, *Churchill: Strategy and History.* Boulder, Colorado: Lynne Rienner Publishers, 1992.

Birkenhead, Earl of, *The Life of Lord Halifax.* Boston: Houghton Mifflin, 1966.

Blake, Robert, and Louis, William Roger, eds., *Churchill: A Major New Assessment of His Life in Peace and War.* Oxford: Oxford University Press, 1993.

Blunt, Wilfrid Scawen, *My Diaries: Being a Personal Narrative of Events 1888–1914.* New York: Alfred Knopf, 1932.

Bonham Carter, Violet, *Winston Churchill: An Intimate Portrait.* New York: Harcourt Brace & World, 1965.

Boothby, Robert, *Recollections of Rebel.* London: Hutchinson, 1978.

Boyle, Andrew, *Poor, Dear Brendan: The Quest for Brendan Bracken.* London: Hutchinson, 1974.

Boyle, Peter, *The Churchill–Eisenhower Correspondence 1953–1955.* Chapel Hill, N.C.: University of North Carolina Press, 1990.

Broad, Lewis, *Winston Churchill.* Revised and extended edition. London: Hutchinson, 1945.

Bryant, Arthur, *The Turn of the Tide 1939–1943.* New York: Doubleday & Co., 1957.

___, ___, *Triumph in the West 1943–1946.* London: Collins, 1959.

Buczacki, Stefan, *Churchill & Chartwell: The Untold Story of Churchill's Houses and Gardens.* London: Frances Lincoln, 2007.

Cappelens, pub., *Churchill's Visit to Norway.* Oslo: J. W. Cappelens Forlag, 1949.

Cawthorne, Graham, *The Churchill Legend: An Anthology.* London: Cleaver-Hume Press, n.d. [1965].

Channon, Henry, *The Diaries of Sir Henry Channon.* London: Weidenfeld & Nicolson, 1993.

Chaplin, E. D. W., *Winston Churchill at Harrow.* Harrow, Middlesex: The Harrow Bookshop, n.d. [1941].

Charmley, John, *Churchill: The End of Glory.* London: Hodder & Stoughton, 1993.

Chisholme, Anne, and Davie, Michael, *Beaverbrook: A Life.* London: Hutchinson, 1992.

Churchill, John Spencer, *Crowded Canvas.* London: Odhams, 1961.

Churchill, Sarah, *A Thread in the Tapestry.* London: Deutsch, 1967.

Cohen, Ronald, *Bibliography of the Writings of Sir Winston Churchill.* 3 vols. London: Continuum, 2006.

Colville, John, *Footprints in Time: Memories.* London: Collins, 1976.

___, ___, *The Churchillians.* London, Weidenfeld and Nicolson, 1981.

___ , ___, *The Fringes of Power: Downing Street Diaries 1940–1955.* 2 vols. Sevenoaks, Kent: Sceptre Publishing, 1986–87.

Coombs, David, and Churchill, Minnie, *Winston Churchill: His Life Through His Paintings.* London: Pegasus, 2003.

Cooper, Alfred Duff. *Old Men Forget: The Autobiography of Duff Cooper.* London: Rupert Hart-Davis, 1953.

Cooper, Diana, *The Light of Common Day.* London: Rupert Hart-Davis, 1959.

Coote, Colin R., *Sir Winston Churchill: A Self-Portrait.* London: Eyre & Spottiswoode, 1954.

Coward, Noël, *Future Indefinite.* London: Heinemann, 1954.

Cowles, Virginia, *Winston Churchill: The Era and the Man.* London: Hamish Hamilton, 1953.

Czarnomski, F. B., *The Wisdom of Winston Churchill.* London: George Allen & Unwin, 1956.

Dalton, Hugh, *The Fateful Years: Memoirs 1931–1945.* London: Frederick Muller, 1957.

Deakin, F. W., *Churchill the Historian.* Zurich: Foundation Suisse Winston Churchill, 1970.

de Mendelssohn, Peter, *The Age of Churchill: Heritage and Adventure 1874–1914.* New York: Knopf, London: Thames and Hudson, 1961.

Dilks, David, *The Great Dominion; Winston Churchill in Canada 1900–1954.* Toronto: Thomas Allen, 2005.

Donaldson, Frances, *Edward VIII: A Biography of the Duke of Windsor.* Philadelphia: Lippincott, 1974.

Eade, Charles, ed., *Churchill by His Contemporaries.* London: Reprint Society, 1955.

Eden, Sir Anthony, *The Eden Memoirs: The Reckoning.* London: Cassell, 1965.

Eden, Guy, *Winston Churchill.* London: Hutchinson, 1945

"Ephesian" [Roberts, C. Bechhofer], *Winston Churchill.* London: Mills & Boon, 1927.

___, ___, Third Edition. London: George Newnes, 1936.

Fields, Alonzo, *My 21 Years in the White House.* New York: Coward McCann, 1960.

Fishman, Jack, *My Darling Clementine.* London: W. H. Allen, 1963.

Gardner, Brian, *Churchill in His Time: A Study in a Reputation 1939–1945.* London: Methuen, 1968.

Gilbert, Martin, *Churchill: A Biography.* London: Park Lane Press, 1979.

___, ___, *Churchill's Political Philosophy.* Oxford: Oxford University Press, 1981.

___, ___, *Churchill: The Wilderness Years.* Boston: Houghton Mifflin, 1982

___, ___, *Churchill: A Life.* London: Heinemann, 1991.

___, ___, *In Search of Churchill.* London: HarperCollins, 1994.

___, ___, *Churchill and America.* London: Free Press, 2005.

___, ___, *Churchill and the Jews.* London: Simon & Schuster, 2007.

Graebner, Walter, *My Dear Mr. Churchill.* London: Michael Joseph, 1965.

Gretton, Peter, *Former Naval Person.* London: Cassell, 1968.

Grunwald, Henry Anatole, ed., *Churchill: The Life Triumphant.* New York: American Heritage Press, 1965.

Guedalla, Philip, *Mr. Churchill: A Portrait.* London: Hodder & Stoughton, 1941.

Halifax, Edward, *Garrowby Album 1940.* (Lord Halifax's personal photo albums, held by the present Earl Halifax at Garrowby, Yorkshire. Information by courtesy of Andrew Roberts.)

Halle, Kay, *Irrepressible Churchill.* Cleveland: World, 1966.

___, ___, *Winston Churchill on America and Britain: A Selection of His Thoughts on Anglo-American Relations.* New York: Walker, 1970.

Harris, Leon, *The Fine Art of Political Wit.* New York: Bell, 1964.

Hart-Davis, D., ed., *King's Counsellor.* London: Weidenfeld & Nicolson, 2006.

Hassall, Christopher, *Edward Marsh.* London: Longmans Green & Co., 1959.

Herbert, A. P., *Independent Member.* London: Methuen, 1950.

Holley, Darrell, *Churchill's Literary Allusions.* Chapel Hill, N.C.: MacFarland, 1987.

Howells, Roy, *Simply Churchill.* London: Robert Hale, 1965.

Hull, Cordell, *Memoirs of Cordell Hull.* 2 vols. New York: Macmillan, 1948.

Hyam, Ronald, *Elgin and Churchill at the Colonial Office 1905–1908.* London: Macmillan, 1968.

Ingrams, Harold, *Uganda: A Crisis of Nationhood.* Corona Library. London: HMSO, 1960.

Ismay, Hastings, *Memoirs of General the Lord Ismay.* London: Heinemann, 1960.

Kennedy, John, *The Business of War: The War Narrative of Major-General Sir John Kennedy.* London: Hutchinson, 1957.

Kersaudy, François, *Churchill and de Gaulle.* New York: Athenaeum, 1982.

Kershaw, Ian, *Fateful Choices: Ten Decisions that Changed the World, 1940–1941.* London: Allen Lane/Penguin Books, 2007.

Keyes, Ralph, *The Quote Verifier.* New York: St. Martins Griffin, 2006.

Kimball, Warren F., ed., *Roosevelt and Churchill: The Complete Correspondence.* 3 vols. Princeton: Princeton University Press, 1984.

King, Cecil, *With Malice Toward None.* London: Sidgwick & Jackson, 1970.

Kripalini, Krishna, *Gandhi: A Life.* Delhi: National Book Trust India, 1982.

Lamb, Richard, *Churchill as War Leader: Right or Wrong?* London: Bloomsbury, 1991.

Langer, William L., and Gleason, S. Everett, *The Challenge to Isolation, 1937–1940.* New York: Harper, 1952.

Larres, Klaus, *Churchill's Cold War.* New Haven, Ct.: Yale University Press, 2002.

Leasor, James, *War at the Top*. London: Michael Joseph, 1959.

Lee, Celia and John, *Winston & Jack: The Churchill Brothers*. London: Privately published, 2007.

Lockhart, Robert Bruce, *Comes the Reckoning*. New York: Putnam, 1947.

___, ___, *Your England*. London: Putnam, 1955.

Longford, Elizabeth. *Winston Churchill*. London: Sidgwick & Jackson, 1974.

Lowenheim, Francis, Langley, Harold, Jonas, Manfred, *Roosevelt and Churchill: Their Secret Wartime Correspondence*. New York: Saturday Review Press/E. P. Dutton & Co., 1975.

Lysaght, Charles Edward, *Brendan Bracken: A Biography*. London: Allen Lane, 1979.

MacCallum Scott, A., *Winston Churchill*. London, Methuen: 1905.

McCullough, David, *Truman*. New York: Simon & Schuster, 1992.

McGowan, Norman, *My Years with Churchill*. London: Pan Books, 1959.

McMenamin, Michael, and Zoller, Curt, *Becoming Winston Churchill*. Westport, Ct., Greenwood Press: 2007.

Macmillan, Harold, *The Blast of War*. New York: Harper & Row, 1968.

___, ___, *Riding the Storm 1956–1959*. New York: Harper & Row, 1971.

Manchester, William, *The Last Lion: Winston Spencer Churchill*. Vol. 1 *Visions of Glory 1874–1932*. Boston: Little, Brown, 1983. Vol. 2. *Alone 1932–1940*. Boston: Little, Brown, 1988.

Manning, Paul, and Bronner, Milton, *Mr. England: The Life Story of Winston Churchill*. Philadelphia: John C. Winston, 1941.

Marchant, James, ed., *Winston Spencer Churchill: Servant of Crown and Commonwealth*. London: Cassell, 1954.

Marsh, Edward. *A Number of People*. London: Heinemann, 1939.

Mee, Charles L., Jr., *Meeting at Potsdam*. New York: Evans, 1975.

Menzies, Robert, *Afternoon Light: Some Memories of Men and Events*. London: Cassell, 1967.

Moir, Phyllis, *I was Winston Churchill's Private Secretary*. New York: Funk, 1941.

Montague Browne, Anthony, *Long Sunset: Memoirs of Winston Churchill's Last Private Secretary*. London: Cassell, 1995.

Moran, Charles, *Churchill: Taken from the*

Diaries of Lord Moran. The Struggle for Survival 1940–1965. Boston: Houghton Mifflin, 1966.

Morgan, Ted, *Churchill: The Rise to Failure 1874–1915*. London: Jonathan Cape, 1983.

Murray, Edmund, *I was Churchill's Bodyguard*. London: W. H. Allen, 1987.

Nel, Elizabeth, *Mr. Churchill's Secretary*. London: Hodder & Stoughton, 1958.

Nemon, Oscar, Unpublished memoirs, by courtesy of Lady Young and James R. Lancaster, 2007.

Nicolson, Nigel, ed., *Harold Nicolson: Diaries and Letters*. 3 vols. London: Collins, 1966–68. ("Nicolson I, II, III.")

___, ___, *Harold Nicolson Diaries and Letters 1907–1963*. London: Weidenfeld & Nicolson. 2004. ("Nicolson 1907–1963.")

Olson, Lynne, *Troublesome Young Men: The Rebels Who Brought Churchill to Power in 1940 and Helped Save Britain*. London: Bloomsbury, 2007.

Pawle, Gerald, *The War and Colonel Warden*. London: George G. Harrap & Co., 1963.

Pearson, John, *The Private Lives of Winston Churchill*. New York: Simon & Schuster, 1991.

Pelling, Henry, *Winston Churchill*. Revised and extended softbound edition. Ware, Herts.: Wordsworth Editions, 1999.

Perucca, Fabien and Maure, Huguette, *Le Meilleur de Sir Winston*. Paris: Michel Lafon, 2005.

Pilpel, Robert, *Churchill in America 1895–1961*. New York: Harcourt, Brace, Jovanovich, 1976.

Pimlott, Ben, ed., *The Second World War Diary of Hugh Dalton 1940–45*. London: Jonathan Cape, 1986.

Reynolds, David, *In Command of History: Churchill Writing and Fighting the Second World War*. London: Allen Lane, 2004.

Reynolds, Quentin, *All About Winston Churchill*. London: W. H. Allen, 1964.

Rhodes James, Sir Robert, *Churchill: A Study in Failure 1900–1939*. London: Weidenfeld & Nicolson, 1970.

Riddell, George Allardice, *Lord Riddell's War Diary*. London: Ivor Nicholson and Watson Ltd., 1933.

Roberts, Andrew. *Eminent Churhcillians*. London: Weidenfeld & Nicolson, 1994.

___, ___, *The Holy Fox* [Lord Halifax]. London: Phoenix, 1997.

Roskill, Stephen, *Churchill and the Admirals*. London: Collins, 1977.

Rowse, A. L., *The Later Churchills*. London: Macmillan, 1958.

Salter, Kay and Jim, *Life is Meals: A Food Lover's Book of Days*. New York: Knopf, 2006.

Sandys, Celia, *From Winston with Love and Kisses*. London: Sinclair Stevenson, 1994.

Shapiro, Fred, *Yale Book of Quotations*. New Haven, Ct.: Yale University Press, 2007.

Sherwood, Robert, *The White House Papers of Harry L. Hopkins*. 2 vols. London: Eyre & Spottiswoode, 1948–49.

Soames, Mary, *Clementine Churchill*. London: Cassell, 1979.

___, ___, *Winston Churchill: His Life as a Painter*. London: Collins, 1990.

___, ___, ed. *Speaking for Themselves: The Personal Letters of Winston and Clementine Churchill*. London: Doubleday, 1998.

Spears, Edward Louis, *Assignment to Catastrophe*. 2 vols. London: Heinemann, 1954.

Stevenson, Frances, *Lloyd George: A Diary*. London: Hutchinson, 1971.

Stimson, Henry L., and Bundy, McGeorge, *On Active Service in Peace and War*. London: Hutchinson, 1949.

Stuart, James, *Within the Fringe*. London: Bodley Head, 1967.

Sykes, Christopher, *Nancy Astor*. New York: Harper & Row, 1972.

Taylor, Robert Lewis, *Winston Churchill: An Informal Study of Greatness*. Garden City, N.Y.: Doubleday, 1952.

Thompson, R. W., *The Yankee Marlborough*. London: George Allen & Unwin, 1963.

Thompson, Walter H., *I was Churchill's Shadow*. London: Christopher Johnson, 1951.

___, ___, *Sixty Minutes with Winston Churchill*. London: Christopher Johnson, 1953.

___, ___, *Assignment Churchill*. New York: Farrar, Strauss & Young, 1955.

Thornton-Kemsley, Colin, *Through Winds and Tides*. Monrose: Standard Press, 1974.

Ward, Geoffrey C., ed., *Closest Companion: The Unknown Story of the Intimate Friendship Between Franklin Roosevelt and Margaret Suckley*. New York: Houghton Mifflin, 1995.

"Watchman", *Right Honourable Gentlemen*. London: Hamish Hamilton, 1939.

Weidhorn, Manfred, *Sword and Pen: A Survey of the Writings of Winston S. Churchill*. Albuquerque: University of New Mexico Press, 1974.

Wheeler-Bennett, John, ed., *Action This Day: Working with Churchill*. London: Macmillan, 1968.

Willans, Geoffey and Roetter, Charles, *The Wit of Winston Churchill*. London: Max Parrish, 1954.

Young, Kenneth, *Churchill and Beaverbrook*. London: Eyre & Spottiswoode, 1966.

Periodicals and Articles

Passim: *Chicago Tribune, The New Statesman, The New York Times, The Times* (London), *The Washington Post*.

Churchill Centre publications: *Finest Hour, The Journal of Winston Churchill*, 1968– date; *Proceedings of the International Churchill Societies, 1987, 1988–1989, 1990–91; Churchill Proceedings, 1992–1993, 1994–1995, 1995–1996, 1996–1997, 1998–2000, 2001–2003*.

Colville, Sir John, "He Had No Use for Second Best." *Finest Hour* 41, Autumn 1983.

Cooper, Lady Diana, "Winston and Clementine." *Finest Hour* 83, Summer 1994.

Dalton, Hugh, "Winston: A Memoir." *New Statesman*, April 1965.

Hamblin, Grace, "Chartwell Memories." Remarks at the 1987 Churchill conference, Dallas. *Proceedings of the International Churchill Society, 1987*. Hopkinton, N.H.: International Churchill Society, 1989.

Harmon, Christopher, "'Are We Beasts?': Churchill and the Moral Question of World War II 'Area Bombing.'" *Finest Hour* 76, Third Quarter, 1992.

Marshman, John, "Churchill and Patton." *Finest Hour* 129, Winter 2005–06.

Mink, Michael, "Churchill's Uphill War," *Investor's Business Daily*, 30 August 2007 (http://xrl.us/bcmae).

Vivian, Herbert "Winston Churchill." *Pall Mall*, April, 1905.

Interviews

Peregrine Spencer Churchill, WSC's nephew; Clark Clifford, aide to President Truman; Denis Kelly, literary assistant to WSC; Ronald Golding, bodyguard 1946–47; Grace Hamblin, secretary 1932–35; Sir John Colville, personal private secretary 1940–55; Sir Fitzroy Maclean, personal representative to Tito, 1943–45; Sir Anthony Montague Browne, personal private secretary 1952–65; Edmund Murray, bodyguard 1950–65; Christian Pol-Roger; Lord and Lady Soames.

INDEX

Winston Spencer Churchill (1874–1965), one of the most famous political figures of the twentieth century, was the son of an American mother and a British father. He served as a British army officer and a war correspondent before becoming a member of Parliament, and was the only major statesman to hold high office in both World Wars. Forming a coalition government in 1940, he led Britain through the Second World War, and was again Prime Minister from 1951–1955. Churchill was a prolific writer, a prodigious correspondent and commentator, a noted orator, and a distinguished historian and biographer. His works include *My Early Life, Marlborough, The World Crisis, The Second World War,* and *A History of the English-Speaking Peoples.* His speeches have been collected into a number of volumes, including most recently by his grandson Winston S. Churchill as *Never Give In!* Sir Winston was both knighted and awarded the Nobel Prize for Literature in 1953.

Richard M. Langworth is the author of *A Connoisseur's Guide to the Books of Winston Churchill* and the editor of *Finest Hour,* the journal of Winston Churchill. He served as president of The Churchill Centre from 1990 to 1999 and has since served on its board of trustees.

For more information, visit www.winstonchurchill.org

Churchill By Himself is fully authorized by
the Estate of Sir Winston Churchill